Inside Adobe Photoshop 3

Gary David Bouton

Barbara Bouton

NEW RIDERS PUBLISHING

New Riders Publishing, Indianapolis, Indiana

Inside Adobe Photoshop 3

By Gary David Bouton and Barbara Bouton

Published by:
New Riders Publishing
201 West 103rd Street
Indianapolis, IN 46290 USA

Printed in the United States of America 2 3 4 5 6 7 8 9 0

Library of Congress Cataloging-in-Publication Data

Bouton, Gary David, 1953-
      Inside Adobe Photoshop 3 for Windows/Gary Bouton, Barbara Mancuso Bouton.
         p.   cm.
      Includes index.
      ISBN 1-56205-356-6
      1. Computer graphics. 2. Adobe Photoshop for Windows.
I. Bouton, Barbara Mancuso, 1955-   . II. Title.
T385.B682 1995   94-48224
006.6'869--dc20   CIP

Warning and Disclaimer

Publisher	*Don Fowley*
Associate Publisher	*Tim Huddleston*
Product Development Manager	*Rob Tidrow*
Marketing Manager	*Ray Robinson*
Director of Special Projects	*Cheri Robinson*
Managing Editor	*Tad Ringo*

About the Authors

Gary David Bouton has been an illustrator, designer, and art director for almost 20 years, and presently uses computer technology to shape and expose complex visual ideas in the real world. As an author for New Riders Publishing, Gary hopes to help others, who have similar backgrounds in the traditional communications arts, to make the emotional and artistic connection between conventional, physical tools and their digital equivalents. "The recipe for creating solid design work doesn't change when you port your craft to the personal computer," says Gary, "the approach and techniques to digital imaging might be an initial challange, but the rewards are immense and a finished digital design can have many qualities that are impossible to express through the use of traditional art materials."

He and his wife are owners of Exclamat!ons, a company "that polishes rough ideas" for clients, whose needs vary from electronic presentations to desktop publishing. Gary is more than a believer in the personal computer's capability to magnify productivity and to lend incredible precision to a trade—the work, the exercises, and the techniques developed through practice all prove it throughout this book.

Inside Adobe Photoshop 3 is Gary's fifth New Riders book, and his second collaboration with his wife, Barbara. In addition to *Photoshop NOW!* and *Inside Adobe Photoshop 2.5*, Gary has written *CorelDRAW! for Beginners*, and is a contributing author to *CorelDRAW!:The Professional Reference*, and *Inside CorelDRAW!5*. Gary is a two-time winner in the CorelDRAW World Design Contest, and as editor of *NewsBytes*, a publication of the Central New York PC Users Group, he has received two international awards.

Barbara Bouton is a computer consultant and author, whose technical and artistic contributions to *Inside Adobe Photoshop 3* stem from a rich background in operating systems and authoring tools. She is also a contributing author to NRP's *Inside WordPerfect 6 for Windows,* and has compiled online references for *NetWare: The Professional Reference,* and *Inside Adobe Photoshop.* Barbara's personal commitments to education and communication are only equaled by her desire to learn about cutting-edge technology.

"Photoshop 3 is almost identical in functionality and appearance on both the Macintosh and Windows platforms, as was the previous version," says Barbara. "However, Adobe Systems obviously didn't rest for one moment after the release of 2.5, and it has been a pleasure and a challenge to explore the new features and design new assignments in this book for readers of all skill levels to use as guides."

Trying something new and approaching the conventional with a sense of freshness is a challenge for any author, and is especially demanding in the computer publication field. It is the wish of the authors that the reader have as much fun trying and doing the exercises prepared for *Inside Photoshop 3* as the authors have had.

The Boutons can be reached on CompuServe at 74512,230.

Trademark Acknowledgments

All terms mentioned in this book that are known to be trademarks or service marks have been appropriately capitalized. New Riders Publishing cannot attest to the accuracy of this information. Use of a term in this book should not be regarded as affecting the validity of any trademark or service mark.

Dedication

To Eileen, Jack, Wilma, and John: our parents. Our families understand why we go into hibernation with every book we write, and it's this understanding that allows us to continue reaching our readers. Whatever medium is used for communication—a book, a broadcast, or digital highway—it does strange things to inter-personal relationships. We're very close with our readers, although some of you might be a thousand miles away. Conversely, we're only about half hour from any of our parents, but we never see them because we're busy writing! We love you all dearly, and recognize that your hearts are large enough to hold both your children's caring and their careers.

Acknowledgments

They say that in a well-written book, you can gain a sense of the author—that the emotions, feelings, thoughts, and spirit of the author all travel with the words to create a special relationship with the reader. If our voice speaks clearly to you in this book, however, we must acknowledge that it's due to a combination of skills, and a blend of talents from many different sources. No single person could possibly present you with the sort of documentation you have before you on the world's most popular professional imaging tool. For this reason, we need to give special thanks, right here, to those who contributed to making this book a reality.

We want to thank:

- Cheri Robinson, Director of Special Projects at New Riders Publishing, for giving us the creative and artistic leeway to present *Inside Adobe Photoshop 3*'s information in a way that's accessible, informal, and as human as a discussion between artistic peers. Through Cheri's support and guidance, we have a book that travels in many directions to address the needs of many types of users, yet retains a focus on the information you really need to know to make working in Photoshop a satisfying experience. Cheri tied all this together, and it's nothing short of a privilege to continue to work with her.

- Production Editor Suzanne Snyder, who was also an editor on the *Inside Photoshop 2.5* book. Suzanne was faced with the challenge of making this book

bigger, better, and more complete than the previous book, yet she was only provided with the same authors as last year! Suzanne, your encouragement was deeply felt by us. You helped assemble a fine cast and crew for our second outing. We thank you for riding with us and guiding us on a trip that seemed to span continents and decades on occasion!

- Gail Burlakoff, editor on the Inside Photoshop 2.5 book, who agreed to come back for a second helping of our free-association and occasional (?) silliness. Gail is in tune with the way we communicate, displays a remarkable ability to sort the meanderings from the meat of our writing, and generally tweaks a phrase so it still retains the authors' voices. Gail, we want to thank you for making the editorial process a smooth-sailing one, and yes, that is an "Inside" line!

- Peter Kuhns, editor extrordinaire, who helped with a great deal of the exercise portions of this book. A Photoshop user himself, Peter questioned us for information along the way about things we sometimes took for granted. Peter, it was a learning process for all of us, we've known you for almost three years, and we're thankful for the chance to finally work with you professionally.

- Technical Editor Gary Kubicek, a friend of ours with whom we never anticipated we'd get the chance to professionally collaborate. Gary is a fine professional photographer who's also wise to the ways of the digital darkroom, and provided us with technical accuracy in the exercise chapters. Gary also provided us with valuable artistic insights along the way, and we're not sure we returned the favor by asking him to pose as the "MegaGuy" in Chapter 16.

- Editors Amy Bezek, Lillian Yates, Laura Frey, Fran Blauw, Geneil Breeze, and Cliff Shubs, who magically transformed American into English, and made sense of exercise steps that seemed to have none on occasion. You made us think a little deeper, and made this a richer book through your efforts. Welcome to the club, and thank you for your assistance.

- Acquisitions Editor Alicia Krakovitz, for allowing us to assemble a hand-picked crew of experts and friends to work on this book. When all the cogs and wheels are in the right place at the right time, the machinery works a lot more smoothly, and Alicia recognizes this. Thanks for letting us produce the fine piece of documentation the reader now holds, Alicia!

- Rob Lawson, for diving in at the ninth inning, and becoming an invaluable player on the team that's responsible for this book. Rob was Lead Editor on the 2.5 book, and helped Suzanne this year in the last-minute organization of chapters as they went into Production. Rob, like all the editors we get to work with only once a year or so, your friendship and professional sensitivity means more than words can say in an acknowledgement section of a book. So simply know it—and thanks!

- Stacy Beheler, Aquisitions Editor at NRP, who authors don't thank enough. Stacy was responsible for contacting the various software manufacturers so we could offer the fantastic special versions of many of the programs you'll see how to use in this book. They're on the Bonus CD, but you'd only be hearing about them instead of using them if it weren't for Stacey's determination and talents.

- Macmillan Production Department, for their valuable efforts in making this book look handsome and easy to read. Production was accomodating to a fault with last-minute changes, and should be especially acknowledged for the after-hour and weekend work most authors don't get the privelege of tapping into. You're a talented and thoughtful organization, and we thank MPD.

- Patricia Pane and Sonya Schaefer at Adobe Systems, who kept us up to date with Photoshop versions through the testing cycle of the program in late summer of 1994. We quite literally couldn't have written this book in a timely fashion without your help. You're the sort of professionals that make authoring a pleasure. We believe that the success that Adobe Systems has had with applications on both the Windows and Macintosh platforms is due to the knowledge, professionalism, and positive attitude of individuals like you.

- Matt Brown and Eric Thomas at Adobe Systems: the Macintosh and Windows experts on Photoshop 3, who shared with us some of the undocumented inner workings of the program throughout the writing of this book. You helped us organize our thoughts to allow us to present exercises that clearly demonstrate incredible Photoshop imaging possibilities. We hope we did you proud, and we appreciate your time and insight.

- Rick Brown at Adobe Systems, for the latest version of Adobe Acrobat Pro, the suite of applications that was used to create the *Inside Photoshop 3* OnLine Glossary you'll find on the Bonus CD that comes with this book. Rick, you gave us the tools to create both a Windows and Macintosh electronic version of the printed glossary in this book, that can be read by anyone who has Acrobat Reader (it's on the *Adobe Photoshop Deluxe CD-ROM*). Portable electronic documents are the wave of the future, and we feel Adobe is riding the crest of this one. Thank you, Rick!

- Caroline De Bie, Media Relations Representative at Matrox Graphics, Inc., for the gracious donation of the Ultima II video adaptor card. For a program as demanding on a system as Photoshop is, you need the right card and video drivers. Caroline's gesture made it possible for us to design the execise images almost as quickly as we could conceive them. A user couldn't ask for a faster card that delivers accurate screen colors, and actually comes with video driver software that is as well designed as the hardware.

- Jan Sanford at PIXAR, who provided us with software used to create a lot of the wonderful figures in this book. Additionally, Jan gave us permission to offer our

readers an exclusive working copy of PIXAR One Twenty-Eight and two tiling textures, and the demo version of Typestry 1.1 you'll find on the Bonus CD that came with this book. Jan, you people are tops, and we hope the full-length animation Pixar is releasing in cooperation with Disney studios in 1995 is a huge success. We definitely will attend!

- Rix Kamlich and Mary Leong for MacroModel v1.1, the modeling program used throughout this book to illustrate concepts and images that simply can't be photographed in real life!

- John and Susan Niestemski of Graphic Masters, friends and imaging profession-als, who have offered our readers a substantial discount on imaging services through the coupon in this book. We've use your services, and we know readers will be absolutely thrilled to take you up on your offer. Film recorders can turn your digital creations into physical transparencies, and our friends are the best in the business at this art.

- Corel Corporation's Bill Cullen, Mike Bellefeuille, and Kelley Grieg for CorelDRAW! 5, and other support items we needed for this book. You folks were just as gracious and responsive to our requests concerning this book, as you were when we wrote *CorelDRAW! 5 for Beginners*.

- Douglas Richard, and Nick Josephs at Visual software for giving us a chance to show our readers Renderize Live! Many of the images in this book were created with this modeling program, which is part of a suite of 3D tools for Windows. Thank you both, and we appreciate the support that generous contributors like yourselves make to creating a book.

- Mike Plunkett, our live lifeguard in Chapter 13. Mike took his acting assign-ment in the spirit of good humor that we intended, and as far as this book's exercises go, Mike's cooperation proved to be a virtual livesaver. Thanks, Mike!

- Harry Magnan at HSC Software, for some of the secret tips you'll learn about Kai's Power Tools in Chapter 19. Harry's understanding of pre-press image enhancement is invaluable for the Inside Photoshop reader who wants beautiful hard copy made from their digital creations.

- Carol DiSalvo at CM DiSalvo Photography, for allowing us to use the photo-graph of Lauriellen in one of our chapter exercises.

- Lauriellen Murphy, for permitting us to use Carol's picture of her in our book. Laur, remember what I said back at Ted Bates about the alternative to going for "the big laughs"? You can find it throughout this book! Thanks for letting us convert you to other image modes, and we know you were smiling at the time this picture was taken for a special reason.

- Lou Misenti, for allowing us to poke a Logitech FotoMan digital camera in his face all too early on a Sunday morning.

- David Bouton, for your modeling contribution in this book. In various books, we've cloned Dave, blown him up, and put an assortment of ridiculous props in his hands. You never complaining once about the circumstances we put you through, the hours, or the pay. Dave, you're everything a brother should be about. Thank you.

- Barbara at Federal Express, who unlocks the door after closing at 9:45 pm, because she understands we need to get hard copy to Indy by next morning, and because she likes us.

- Chuck, who replaced Harry at Pizza Hut, and who gave us a dollar off our last order because we mentioned his franchise in our last book.

Product Director
CHERI ROBINSON

Acquisitions Editor
ALICIA KRAKOVITZ

Production Editor
SUZANNE SNYDER

Copy Editors
AMY BEZEK
FRAN BLAUW
GENEIL BREEZE
GAIL BURLAKOFF
LAURA FREY
PETER KUHNS
ROB LAWSON
CLIFF SHUBS
JOHN SLEEVA
LILLIAN YATES

Technical Editor
GARY KUBICEK

Editorial Assistant
KAREN OPAL

Cover Designer
GARY BOUTON

Book Designer
KIM SCOTT

Production Team Supervisor
KATY BODENMILLER

Graphics Image Specialists
DENNIS SHEEHAN
CLINT LAHNEN
CRAIG SMALL

Production Analyst
DENNIS CLAY HAGER

Production Team
DON BROWN
MONA BROWN
MICHAEL BRUMITT
ELAINE BRUSH
CHARLOTTE CLAPP
JUDY EVERLY
ROB FALCO
ALEATA HOWARD
AYANNA LACEY
SHAWN MACDONALD
BRIAN-KENT PROFFITT
SA SPRINGER
MARVIN VANTIEM
JEFF WEISSENBERGER
DENNIS WESNER

Indexer
BRONT DAVIS

Contents at a Glance

Introduction,   *1*

Preface   *17*

Part One: From the Source to the Sample   25

   1   *Understanding Image Types, Formats, and Resolutions*   *27*

   2   *Acquiring a Digital Image*   *63*

   3   *Color Theory and the PhotoCD*   *107*

   4   *Photoshop Defaults and Options*   *149*

   5   *It's All Done with Palettes*   *195*

   6   *The Photoshop Test Drive*   *237*

Part Two: Steak and Potatoes Assignments   287

   7   *Restoring an Heirloom Photograph*   *289*

   8   *Retouching an Heirloom Photograph*   *323*

   9   *Using Type in Photoshop*   *363*

   10   *Stamping Out Photo Errors*   *411*

   11   *Using Paths, Selections, and Layers*   *457*

Part Three: Gourmet Assignments   511

   12   *Correcting an Image*   *513*

   13   *Combining Photographs*   *589*

   14   *Enhancing Images*   *635*

   15   *Special Effects with Ordinary Photographs*   *687*

   16   *Creating a Digital Collage*   *743*

   17   *The Wonderful World of Black and White*   *801*

   18   *Photoshop's Native Filters*   *841*

Part Four: Fantastic Assignments in Photoshop   907

   19   *3rd-Party Plug-In Filters*   *909*

   20   *Mixed Media and Photoshop*   *957*

   21   *Advanced Type Usage and Presentations*   *1025*

   22   *Virtual Reality: The Ingredients of Dreamwork*   *1069*

Part Five: Inking Up and Doing Yourself a Service 1131

23   *Personal Printing Basics* *1133*

24   *The Service Bureau* *1173*

25   *The Film Recorder* *1221*

26   *How Good is Good?* *1247*

Part Six: Back o' the Book 1263

Appendix A: What's on the Bonus CD? *1265*

Appendix B: How to Install the Online Glossary: PC and Macintosh Versions *1275*

Index *1281*

Table of Contents

Introduction 1

The Tool for Expressing a Graphical Idea 2
What Is Digital Imaging? 2
    The All-Encompassing "Imaging" 3
Where *Inside Photoshop* Fits In 3
Syntax: How To Read the "Shorthands" in Our Exercises 4
    A Note to Southpaws 5
Other Conventions Used in This Book 7
    Special Text 7
    Mouse Notes 8
The Six Parts to Inside Photoshop 9
    Part I: From the Source to the Sample 9
    Part II: Steak and Potatoes Assignments 10
    Part III: Gourmet Assignments 10
    Part IV: Fantastic Assignments 11
    Part V: Inking Up and Doing Yourself a Service 12
    Part VI: Appendixes, Back O' the Book 13
Preparing for Photoshop 14
    System Configurations 14
    Additional Equipment 15
Folks Just Like You 15

Preface: The Photoshop Resource for PC and Macintosh Users 17

Different Keys for Different Versions 19
    Function Keys and Their Assignments 20
    Accelerator Keys 22
Online Help 22
Miscellaneous Terminology and Interface Differences 22
Putting It All Together 23

Part One: From the Source to the Sample 25

1   Understanding Image Types, Formats, and Resolutions 27

Comparing Traditional Photography to Digital Imaging 28
What You Get Is What You See 28

Phases of Digital Imaging 29

Types of Computer Images 29

Exploring the PC Graphics Tree **30**

The Vector Branch 30

The Bitmap Branch 31

Acquiring Various Image Types **33**

Picking the Line Art Graphic **33**

The Half-Breed Halftone 35

Acquiring the Grayscale Image **36**

Blossoming into Color Images **38**

Creating Indexed Color **39**

Photoshop's Preference of Color Modes 40

Understanding Color Capability Relationships 41

Defining a Lookup Table 43

Where Do the Extra Colors Go? 45

The Color Reduction Experiment 46

The Adaptive Palette 48

Should You Index an RGB Image? 49

The RGB Image **50**

TrueColor and RGB Color 50

Using Channels 51

Using Photoshop Tools and Filters with RGB Color Images 52

Spotting the Differences between Pixels, Dots, and Samples **54**

Samples versus Dots 54

Pixels and Resolution 55

Understanding File Formats **57**

Formats for RGB Images 58

PCX Images 59

BMP 59

PICT 59

GIFs 60

Less Frequently Used File Formats 60

The Long and Short of the Data Byte Stream 61

2   Acquiring a Digital Image   63

Viewing an Acquired Image Accurately **64**

Understanding Video Display Modes 64

Installing a Video Driver 66

Matching Video Display to Image Type 68

Examining Scanner Hardware **70**

The Sheet-Fed Scanner 71

Hand-Held Scanners 71
Flatbed Scanners 71
Which Scanner Is Right for You? 73
Developing Scanner Standards **73**
Color Scanning Recommendations 74
How Does TWAIN Work? 75
Preparing To Scan **78**
Resolution Versus Image Dimensions 78
Controlling File Size 81
Getting the Information Straight 84
Scanning the Image 85
A Histogram of the Scan 86
Saving Your Scanned Image **90**
Squeezing the Most Out of an Image 91
Seeing Is Disbelieving 100
The Digital Camera **101**
Downloading a Captured Image 101
The Proper Tool for the Right Occasion 104

3 Color Theory and The PhotoCD 107

Understanding Models **108**
Defining Key Terms **108**
Light and Hue 109
Saturation 109
Brightness 109
Chromacity and Lightness 110
Tints, Shades, and Tones 110
Using Different Color Models in Photoshop **110**
The RGB Color Model 110
LAB Color 111
Understanding the Interrelationship of Color Models **112**
How Hue, Saturation, and Brightness Affect an Image **113**
Understanding Oversaturation and Video Clipping 113
Using Brightness To Control Hue and Saturation 114
Manipulating a Range of Digital Information **114**
Managing an Image's Brightness through Mapping **115**
Remapping a Histogram 117
Controlling Midpoints and Midtones 117
Adjusting an Image's Gamma 118
Photo CDs—Optimized for TV, Not PC **118**
Adjusting a PhotoCD's Tonal Levels **119**
Viewing Current Brightness Distribution 125
Looking Back on Brightness 129

Understanding the Basis of Resolutions 130
   Choosing an Appropriate Resolution 131
   Putting Resolutions to Work 132
   Resizing a PhotoCD Selection 136
Understanding PhotoCD Technology 139
   The PCD Format 140
   A CD-ROM Player Isn't a *Photo*CD-ROM Player 140
   Types of PhotoCDs 141
   Working Smarter with PhotoCD Technology 142
   The PhotoCD Drive 146
Evaluating the Importance of PhotoCDs 148

4   Photoshop Defaults and Options   149

Fine-Tuning Your Monitor 150
   Methods of Calibration 150
   Setting Up the Monitor 151
Expressing Your General Preferences 158
   Using Photoshop's Color Picker 158
   Interpolation 159
   Setting Display Preferences 159
   Use Diffusion Dither 163
   Video LUT Animation 163
   Choosing Different Screen Cursors 163
   More Preferences 166
Specifying Photoshop's Memory Settings 172
   Scratch Disks 173
   Secondary Considerations 174
   Maximizing Windows' Physical Memory 174
   Macintosh Memory Usage 175
Specifying Units of Measurement 176
Gamut Warning Preferences 178
Plug-Ins Preferences 179
From the Preference Menu to Workspace Options 182
   Brushes Palette Options 182
   Creating a Brush Tip 183
   Stroking Foreground Color into a Selection Area 188
   Loading and Resetting the Brushes Palette 190

5   It's All Done with Palettes   195

Why Palettes? 196
   The Commands Palette 196
   Your Wish—Photoshop's Commands 198
   Exploring the Channels Palette 203

How Image Channels Relate to Selection Areas 205
Using and Saving Selections 207
Masking and Selecting 210
Editing in Quick Mask Mode 212
Converting Quick Mask to Selection Information 214
Converting a Saved Selection to a Path 217
Working with Paths and Selections Together 220
Choosing Thumbnail Sizes 224
Screen Real Estate and the Detachable Palettes 226
Transparency Options and the Layers Palette 228
Layer Views and Options 229
Coloring behind Transparent Pixels 229
Applying a Pattern Fill to a Layer 231

6 The Photoshop Test Drive   237
Families of Tools 238
Adjusting Your View 239
Understanding Viewing Resolution 241
Using the Marquee Selection Tools 242
Adding to a Selection 246
Enhanced Functions of the Selection Tools 248
Masking an Area and Cloning 250
Completing the Image Retouching 252
Changing the Visual Content of an Image 255
Exploring Selections on Layers 257
Isolating and Applying an Effect to a Layer Object 260
Using a Combination of Selection Features 262
Linking and Merging Layers 267
Merging Layers 269
Painting, Layers, and Compositing Modes 272
Painting in Color Mode 275
Modes and Layers 276
Loading a Selection from a Different Image 279
Displaying Your Finished Work in Photoshop 283
Protecting Your Artwork 283

Part Two: Steak and Potatoes Assignments   287

7 Restoring an Heirloom Photograph   289
Acquiring Photo Images: From an Old Shoe Box to the Monitor 290
Improving Image Detail 291
The Relationship between Hue and Tonal Values 292
Evaluating Color Changes 293

Redistributing Tonal Relationships 294
Understanding Contrast 296
Using the Variations Command 300
Clipping is Obvious in a Photo 302
Using Curves and Quartertones 303
Understanding the Relativity of Changes 308
Color-Balancing the Color-Corrected Image 308
Isolated Area Color Correction 311
Manually Editing a Color Range Selection 315
Using Color Balance and Color Range 318
Reviewing Your Work 320

8   Retouching an Heirloom Photograph   323

Removing Stains from a Photograph 324
Assessing the Damage 324
Fixing Edgework with the Smudge and Blur Tools 328
Fixing Chipped Emulsion with the Rubber Stamp Tool 331
Burning In Lens Flare 334
Smoothing Out Saturated Pixels 336
Reducing Random Saturation 338
Cloning with a Pattern Sample 338
Restoring Organic Patterns 342
Using Source Material from Another Image 344
Setting the Image Up for a Sky Replacement 345
Scaling a Floating Selection 348
Digital Pruning and the Layer Mask Option 351
Editing the Layers as One Image 355
Adding a Border to Your Retouched Piece 357
Retouching Essentials 360

9   Using Type in Photoshop   363

How Does Photoshop Treat Type? 364
Installing a Type 1 Font 364
Creating a Really Hip Postcard 365
Using a Path To Define an Image Area 366
Removing Lettering with the Paint Brush Tool 368
Retouching a Damaged Image Area 370
Measuring the Image Area for Type 373
Setting Type Specifications 375
Creating Perspective with Type 379
Finalizing an Image Effect Command 381

Adding Text and Graphics to a Photograph 383
   Refining a Scan 383
   Creating a Selection Mask for Painting 385
   Adding Attention-Getting Colors 387
   Airbrushing a Van 389
   Manually Editing a Saved Selection 392
   Measuring the Logo To Fit the Truck 395
   Resizing the Logo for the Truck 397
   Dynamic Copying 399
   Putting Fred's Business in Perspective 401
Adding Photoshop Type to the Truck 402
   Weathering the Selection 405
   Taking a Sponge to the Truck 407
   Viewing the Final Image 410

10   Stamping Out Photo Errors   411
This Chapter's Assignment 412
   Cloning a Sample 412
   Don't Make Cloning Obvious 416
   Cloning in the Right Direction 416
   Using the Lighten Rubber Stamp Mode 418
   Bigger Brush, Looser Strokes 419
Using the Color Cloning Mode 421
Using Toning Tools To Finish the Retouching 423
The Human Element in Retouching Work 425
Taking Photoshop Outdoors 426
   Pick Your Tools before Digging In 426
   Cloning To Build Up an Image Layer 430
   Putting a Pattern in Its Place 432
   Other Techniques for Different Image Areas 435
   Touch-Up Work with the Paint Bucket 439
   Selecting a Range within a Selection 441
   Using the New Window Command 445
   Using Broads Strokes and Layers To Finish the Yard 447
   Flattening an Image 451
   Color-Correcting the Retouched Image 452

11   Using Paths, Selections, and Layers   457
Integrating Tools and Effects 458
   Selecting the Sky, Using the Color Range 459
   Semiautomatically Measuring a Working Canvas 461
   Cloud-Making, Photoshop Style 464

Creating Paths **468**
The Anatomy of a Path 468
Path Tools 469
Defining the Outline of an Image Element 472
Using the Convert Direction Point Tool 476
Creating a Saved Selection 477
Encore Performance for the Paths Palette 481
Copying without the Clipboard 482
Creating Realistic Shadows 487
Defining a Selection Area for Shadow-Making 488
The Paint Bucket Tool 492
Designing on Layers **494**
Preplanning Image Elements 494
Adding Tonal Detail to the Gumball 495
Duplicating and Modifying the Gumball 500
Adding and Moving Gumballs 503
Adding Shadows to the Background Image 504
Turning Off Photoshop's Magic 505
File Management and Saved Images **508**
Moving to a Higher "Layer" of Photoshop Skills **510**

Part Three: Gourmet Assignments   511

12   Correcting an Image   513

Surveying the Layout **514**
Evalutating the Image 514
Working with Layers **515**
Trimming Image Areas with a Layer Mask 519
Creating an Asphalt Texture **528**
Changing Stone into Asphalt 528
Separating an Image from Its Background **532**
Using the Color Range Command 533
Using Color Range Fuzziness To Define a Selection 536
Refining the Selection 541
Thoughts on Creating Your Own Bitmap ClipArt Collection 547
Transferring an Image **547**
Selecting an Image on a Transparent Background 547
Adding Realism with Shadows **553**
Using Photoshop's Image Commands 553
Image Resolution and Image Detail 558
Clapboard Cloning with the Rubber Stamp Tool 572

A Sports Car for the Drive **575**
Creating a Dimensional Shadow 578

13   Combining Photographs   589

This Chapter's Assignment **590**
Using a Stock Photography Resource 590
Scaling a JPEG Image **591**
Using the Crop Tool's Fixed Target Size Feature 594
The Paths Palette and Sampled-Down Images 598
Using Shortcuts 601
Converting Paths to Selections 603
Enhancing Lighting Conditions **605**
Copying Layer Images 608
Making Waves 611
Editing the Duck's Reflection in Layer Mask Mode 615
Adding Realistic Touches to the Duck's Reflection 617
Playing with a Second Property of Image Reflections 623
Integrating the Reflection with the Duck 626
Adding the Finishing Touches **628**
Using a Layer Mode for Merging Layers 631

14   Enhancing Images   635

This Chapter's Assignment **636**
The Action Plan 636
Evaluating Stock Images **637**
Changing the Color Scheme in an Image **639**
Using Your Own Aesthetic Judgment 639
Doing a Balancing Act with Photoshop 639
Fine-Tuning with the Variations Command 642
Adjusting Saturation 646
Matching Lighting Conditions 647
Adding Layers to a Target Image **649**
Using Color Range: First Step toward a Magical Sky 652
Refining a Selection with the Layer Mask 655
Copying the Sky into the Target Image **658**
Harmonizing Colors Within an Image **662**
Warming Up the Colors in the Landscape 662
Using One of Photoshop's Premade Selections **664**
The Background Copy Mask 664
Painting on a Layer Mask 666
Applying the Layer Mask 668
Filling in the Trees **670**

Doing Mother Nature One Better 670
Fixing Background Areas within Trees 670
A Soft Touch for Invisible Retouching 671
Picking a Few Pixels and Darkening Them 672
Making a Beeline for the Tree Line 675
Adding Reflections of New Sky in the Lake **678**
Selecting a Place for the Reflection 678
Using a New Layer for the Reflection 680
Using a Gradient Fill in a Layer Mask 682
Cleaning Up 685

15   Special Effects with Ordinary Photographs   687

Creating the Source Images for an Identical Twin Picture **688**
Creating a Perfect Tonal Landscape in an Image **689**
Applying an Auto Level Setting to an Image **695**
Resizing an Image Selection **696**
Understanding the Secrets of Trick Photography **701**
Copying and Positioning a Floating Selection **704**
Blending Natural Texture Using the Rubber Stamp Tool **709**
Using the Layer Mask To Remove Superfluous Areas **713**
Quick Masking an Area for Retouching **718**
Retouching with the Paint Brush Tool **723**
Using the Blur Tool in Lighten Mode **727**
Restoring and Editing Between Image Layers **729**
A Potpourri of Detail Work **735**
Using Creative Cropping as Another Magic Trick **740**

16   Creating a Digital Collage   743

This Chapter's Assignment **744**
Using the Color Range Command **744**
Editing Alpha Channel Information **746**
Using Layers to Create a Composite Image **749**
Masking Layers 753
Layer Mask Options 756
Applying a Layer Mask 757
Replacing Image Areas with Copies from the Original **759**
Reusing a Copied Selection 763
Creating a Shadow **765**
Cloning in a Realistic Shadow 765
Creating Shadows with Multiply Painting Mode 767
Blurring Image Edges **769**
Shading an Area with a Sampled Value **771**

Assembling the Collage Pieces 772
The Magic Wand Versus the Color Range Command 773
Creating a Color Logo Pattern 776
Creating a Splashy Poster Background 780
Using a Saved Selection as a Shadow 781
Displacing Text 784
Creating Special Effects with Type 784
Making an Arc out of Lettering 787
Displacing Text in a Negative Direction 790
Using Text as Its Own Selection Mask............................ 792
Assembling the Digital Collage 793
Adding the Actor to the Poster 796
Advanced Type Enhancements 798

17 The Wonderful World of Black and White   801

From 24-bit Color to 8-bit Grayscale 802
Sampling Original Colors in an Image 802
The Scratch Palette... 803
The Type Tool and Scratch Palette Labels 806
Working with LAB Color 811
Translating RGB Values to LAB Values............................ 812
Using a Single LAB Color Component 814
Creative Uses of Filters and Grayscale Images 817
Adding Noise to a Grayscale Image 818
Creating a Crystallized Image 820
The Zoom Blur Effect 825
Using Filters with Grayscale Still Life Images 829
Setting Up Texture Channel Information 829
Creating a Relief Picture 833
Using Black-and-White Imaging in Your Profession 836
Converting Grayscale to RGB 837

18 Photoshop's Native Filters   841

Using Filters in the File Menu 842
Using the Place Command 842
Anti-Aliasing and the Color Range Command 846
Building a Bitmap from a Vector Design 849
Embossing and Tinting Foreground Pixels 852
Using Hue/Saturation on an Embossed Texture............... 855
Using Other File Menu Filters 858
The Filter Menu 859
Photoshop's Blur Filters 860

The Distort Filters 864
Noise Filters 872
Photoshop's Sharpen Filters 874
The Other Photoshop Filters 875
The Pixelate Filters 880
The Stylize Filters 883
Additional Photoshop Filters 884
The Filter Factory **885**
Removing the Attributes of the FFACTORY.8BF File 886
Making a Filter Factory Filter 887
Using Filters, Tools, and Features Together **890**
The Clouds Filter and Saving Selections from Channels 893
Using the Subtract From Selection Shortcut 895
Adding a Texture Fill 896
The Physics of the Lighting Effects Filter 900
Adding Lighting and Texture to the Continents 902

Part Four: Fantastic Assignments in Photoshop   907

19   3rd-Party Plug-In Filters   909

Adding Only the Plug-Ins You Really Want **910**
Kai's Power Tools **910**
Using the KPT Gradient Designer 911
Copying a Gradient Fill to the Gradient Designer 911
Touring the Rest of the Gradient Designer Interface 916
Using the Other Gradient Designer Buttons 920
Using the KPT Gradient Bar 921
Accessing Extended Functions of the Gradient Designer 928
Using the KPT Filters 929
Creating Effects Worthy of an Art Gallery **930**
Using the Watercolor Filter 931
Using the Note Paper Filter 934
Using the Plastic Wrap Filter 937
Exploring Alien Skin Software's Drop Shadow Filter 940
Creating a "Punch Out" Graphic 941
Using PIXAR's One Twenty-Eight Filter 945
Creating an Instant Background 945
Using the Andromeda Software Sampler **949**
Using the cMulti Filter 949
Using the Andromeda 3D Filter 952
Looking At the Changing Shape of Photoshop Plug-Ins 955

20 Mixed Media and Photoshop   957

This Chapter's Assignment... 958
Creating, Modifying, and Filtering Source Artwork 958
  Removing Imperfections 958
  Enhancing the Image 960
  Exporting an EPS Vector Image to Photoshop 962
Setting Up the Digital Design 962
  Converting to CMYK Color 963
Creating an Airbrush Effect 967
  Using the Picker Palettes 968
Using Gradient Fills 971
  Shading and Refining Your Coloring Work 973
Using a Minimalist Approach to Suggest Lighting 975
Fleshing out the Design 978
  The Suggestion of Color 981
Putting a Glass Lens on a Wristwatch 985
  Installing the Filters...985
  Using the Glass Lens Filter..985
  Patterned Textures and the Layered Cartoon 988
  Using PIXAR Filters 988
Using the Toning Tools on Texture Fills 991
  Creating a Plausible Hammer 994
Subtracting from a Selection, and the Picker Palette 997
The Behind Mode Color "Wash" 1002
The KPT Gradient Designer "Jump Start" Instructions 1004
Kai's Ties 1006
  Coloring and Drop-Shadowing the Lettering 1009
  Using Digital Correction Fluid on Digital Acetate 1014
  Creating a Photographic Wash 1017
  Addressing the "Colored Outside the Lines" Syndrome...............1021
  The KPT Sharpen Intensity Filter 1022
  Mixing Other Media with Your New Skills 1023

21 Advanced Type Usage and Presentations   1025

This Chapter's Assignment... 1026
Acquiring the Image... 1026
Using an Exported Path as Vector Information 1028
Using Typestry to Create Presentation Elements............................ 1030
  Defining the Dimension and Resolution of An Image 1031
  Creating Realistic Text 1032
  Organizing the Presentation Elements 1036
  Giving a 3D Image a 3D Background 1041

Moving From Slide 1 to Slides 2 and 3 1044

Measuring Type with the Info Palette 1049

Duplicating Layers and Switching Layer Contents 1054

Creating Multiple Slides from a Layered Image 1058

Creating the Splashy Exit Slide 1062

    Curtain Call for Slide Presentations 1067

22   Virtual Reality: The Ingredient of Dreamwork   1069

This Chapter's Assignment 1070

Creating a Texture Map 1070

    Understanding Mapping 1071

    Creating an EPS Design for an Image Map 1071

    Adding Dimension to a Texture 1073

Selective Color Adjustment 1075

Filtering and Editing Details in An Image 1078

Blurring an Image Channel 1081

Using the Dodge Tool 1083

Instant Robots: Rendering a 3D Image 1085

    Putting the Pieces Together 1086

Creating A Surrealistic Background 1088

    Colorizing the Stones 1090

Texture Fills and the Lighting Effects 1094

    Texture Mapping, Photoshop-Style 1096

    The Omni Light and Texture Mapping 1099

    Reinforcing Original Design Elements 1102

    Defining a Glowing Area 1104

    Creating the "Neon Glow" Effect 1106

Adding a Second Virtual Reality Element 1111

    The "From Behind" Neon Glow Effect 1113

Completing the Detail Work on the Image 1117

Adding Some Text Appeal 1120

    Adding Some Drama to Text 1121

    Embellishing the Text 1125

    Shifting Compositional Elements 1127

Part Five: Inking Up and Doing Yourself a Service   1131

23   Personal Printing Basics   1133

From the Source to the Sample to the Printer 1134

    Personal Color Printers 1134

Converting a Color Image for Grayscale Printing 1135

Choosing RGB or CMYK 1136

Choosing Grayscale 1136

Saving as Grayscale 1137

Deciding on Your Final Output **1137**

Using a Printer Command Language (PCL) Printer **1138**

Resolution Enhancement.. 1140

Disadvantages of PCL Printers 1140

Error Diffusion Printing **1141**

Using an Effects Screen with Your Images **1143**

PostScript Printers **1145**

Examining a Digital Halftone Image 1146

Understanding the Halftone Cell, Resolution, and Other Factors ... **1148**

Line Angles 1149

Line Frequency 1151

Math for Determining Lines per Inch 1152

The Number of Grays in a Grayscale Image 1156

Using Calculations To Determine Image Quality 1156

Higher-Resolution Printers 1157

Setting Up Images for Commercial Printing **1157**

Optimizing the Quality of Home-Brew Camera-Ready Imaging ... 1158

How Many Shades of Gray Should You Render? 1158

Ink Is Different from Toner 1162

The Math Behind Optimizing an Image for Press 1163

Adding a Style to Your Camera-Ready Print **1165**

Shaping the Dots in a Laser Copy 1165

How a Squashed Dot Fits in a Screen 1166

A Word on Corruption **1168**

Increasing Print Quality, Decreasing Artist Involvement **1171**

24 The Service Bureau **1173**

From Source, to Sample, to the Printed Page **1174**

What Is a Service Bureau? 1174

Why Do You Need Service Bureaus? 1175

How Pre-Press Savvy Do You Need to Be? 1175

Two Ways To Get Your Image to Press **1176**

Glorious Color from Digital Printers **1176**

Printing a Color Image from Photoshop **1178**

Common Considerations When Printing **1179**

Using the Page Setup Dialog Box 1180

Using Printer Specific Options 1184

Using the Print Command from the File Menu 1189

Creating Duotones **1191**

Creating Duotones from Grayscale Images 1191
Specifying a Type of Duotone 1191
Taking a Duotone to Another Application 1195
Placing a Duotone in a Desktop Publishing Document 1196
Printing Duotone Separations 1197
Producing Spot Color **1198**
Working with CMYK images **1199**
Using the Gamut Warning Feature 1200
Converting RGB Images to CMYK 1204
Printing Color Separations 1206
Deciding Whether To Do Your Own Color Separations 1207
Knowing When Not To Create Color Separations **1208**
Schemes for Getting an Image out the Door **1209**
JPEG Compression 1210
File-Compression Programs 1213
Large-Format Removable Media 1218
Questions (and Answers) for the Commercial Printer **1218**
Do They Have the Right Drive? 1219
Does Your Printer Own Photoshop? 1219

25 The Film Recorder   **1221**

What Film Recorder Output Is Used For **1222**
Examining the Components of a Film Recorder **1222**
The Purpose of a RIP 1223
The Light Source—a CRT 1223
Developing the Film 1223
Transferring a Photoshop Image to Film **1224**
Your Monitor's Setup 1224
Using the Proper Aspect Ratio? 1225
Achieving the Proper Aspect Ratio 1226
File Formats and Data Types 1233
Converting a Portrait Design to a Landscape Slide 1233
Rotating Extremely Large Images 1234
Sending the Right Size File 1241
How Large Is Large Enough? 1241
What To Do if Your File Is Too Small 1243
Having a Negative Made **1244**
File Sizes for Making 35mm Negatives 1244
Aspect Ratios for 35mm Negatives 1244
Choosing a Service Bureau **1245**
Shop Around for the Best Capabilities 1245

26   How Good Is Good?   **1247**

   The Uniqueness of the Photoshop Professional **1248**
     Color-Correcting Is a Breeze 1248
     Treating Visual Information as Data 1249
     The Infinite Malleability of a Digital Image 1250
     An Integrated Workspace 1250
     Putting Your Skills to Work 1251
   Can I Make a Career out of Photoshop? **1252**
     The Private Road to an Imaging Career 1253
     The Picture of Your Profession 1253
     Private Partnerships 1253
     Taking Your Skills to a Business... 1254
     Careers and Applications Are Personal Decisions 1254
   Expanding Your Artist's Toolbox beyond Photoshop's **1255**
     Plug-Ins... 1255
     The Drawing Application 1256
     Utilities 1257
     Image Cataloguing 1257
     The Shareware Video Slide Show Utilities 1258
     Commercial Slide Show and MultiMedia Programs.................... 1258
     Full-Featured MultiMedia Applications as "Utilities" 1259
     The Fully Equipped Windows Shell 1259
   How Good Can You Get? **1260**

Part Six: Back O' the Book   1263

A   What's on the Bonus CD?   **1265**

   Bonus CD Operating Requirements and Directories **1266**
     The EXERCISE Directory 1266
     The ARIS Directory 1267
     The GLOSSARY Directory 1267
     The MATERIAL Directory 1267
     The IMAGECEL Directory 1268
     The ZECH Directory 1268
   Identical Programs for Different Operating Systems **1269**
     The PIXAR128 Directory/Folder 1269
     The TYPESTRY Directory/Folder 1269
     The ALIENS Directory /Folder 1270
     The KPT Directory/Folder 1270
   Modeling and Rendering Programs **1270**
     The 3DPRO Folder (Macintosh) 1270

The TRUSPACE Directory (Windows) 1271
The Shareware on the Bonus CD **1271**
The BOOLEANS Directory (Windows) 1271
The COMPACT Folder (Macintosh) 1272
The FONTS Directory/Folder (PC and Macintosh) 1272
The Bouton's Directory/Folder (PC and Macintosh) 1273
The Haber Directory/Folder (PC and Macintosh) 1273
The Sansone Directory/Folder (PC and Macintosh) 1273
The PAINTSHP Directory (Windows) 1273
The PKZIP Directory (Windows/DOS) 1274
The WINZIP Directory (Windows) 1274
The ZIPIT Folder (Macintosh) 1274

B   How to Install the Online Glossary: PC and Macintosh Versions 1275
Installing the Acrobat Reader for Windows **1276**
Installing the Acrobat Reader for Macintosh **1277**
Using the Inside Adobe Photoshop 3 OnLine Glossary **1277**
Navigating Within the Document 1277
Index **1281**

Introduction

Adobe Systems has once again reinvented the way you manipulate computer images with Photoshop 3 and for the Macintosh. If you're new to the image-editing game, you're in for the time of your life; Photoshop can assist you in creating positively spectacular, photo-realistic images. The quality of your work increases exponentially as you experiment and understand the principles of bitmap image editing.

If you've recently upgraded to version 3 from Photoshop 2.5, the good news is that Adobe has made virtually every "wish list" feature you might have hoped for come true. Image areas can now be placed and edited on layers; layers are composed of transparent pixels and offer see-through preview editing of composite images—it's the closest thing to vector design in a bitmap editing program! Additionally, palettes are now grouped, and can be user-configured to make the workspace a personalized designer's environment. There are more filters, and drag and drop support for many command menu items; and you can now open partial areas of images. Working with large files is easier than ever.

The Tool for Expressing a Graphical Idea

In its various versions, Photoshop has been used for years to edit and create images as diverse as cosmetic ads, news photos, motion picture footage, animation cells, and fine artwork. Yet when John Warnock, Adobe's CEO, was asked in an interview about where his company stood technologically, he replied with a laugh, "Oh, we're always at the beginning!" And this is where we'll begin our adventures with Adobe Photoshop.

By using Photoshop, you become a player in the big leagues. Photoshop is the image editing software of choice for photographers, retouchers, graphic artists, and designers. Hollywood and Madison Avenue use Photoshop to make images come alive and to add magic to images that lack that certain "something."

Photoshop is a professional tool, to be sure. But you *don't* have to own a Fortune 500 company or have a pair of hands like DaVinci to use it. *Inside Adobe Photoshop 3* shows you how to make the best use of the program, and the best use of your skills, regardless of whether you use Windows or System 7. Starting something new can be a challenge, but where we begin exploring Photoshop is on the ground floor, with the most basic element people have to work with—the graphic *image*.

What Is Digital Imaging?

There are 1,001 ways a picture can become flawed on its way from the designer's eye to the finished product. It is rare to find a picture or image that couldn't use help, specifically, Photoshop's help. Photoshop contains all the tools for retouching, compensating, correcting, enhancing, and manipulating images at all stages of their creation.

Although most people use Photoshop to retouch photographs, Photoshop is more than a retouching program. It is a *digital imaging* program. It works with a wide range of source material—still photos, video and film frames, paintings that have been digitized, and even computer graphics that have no roots in the physical world!

All of this is possible because computers handle visual material as *digital data*—lots of little ones and zeros. Our adventure in the "digital darkroom" with Photoshop, and the manipulation of what we see, is called *imaging*, not "photography," and not "painting."

The All-Encompassing "Imaging"

To a computer, the information that makes up a photograph, drawing, or a spread-sheet is the same—it's a lot of mathematics that can be *manipulated*. You recognize a digitized photo on your monitor as a photo, a cartoon as a cartoon, and so on, and the two kinds of graphics will never meet or be mistaken for one another. The computer from the other side of the cathode tube, however, sees it all the same way— as data. This data describes an image that can be changed by the user.

Our computer's ignorance about the subject matter within images, then, is our gain. The possibilities for spectacular melding and modifying of images are endless! You can put drawings in your photos and photos in your drawings because the computer sees both the same way.

Retouching a physical photograph is hard work and expensive to have done. Adding type to a drawing is not easy and requires a separate discipline. Creating photo or multimedia collages is painstaking, exacting work that often requires razor-sharp tools and noxious fumes. But *imaging* with Photoshop is done in a common workspace. You're freed from the conventions of the real world because the world of computer graphics is a *virtual* one, and anything visual can be worked on with an integrated set of tools.

In this book we'll show you how to take images and make the most of them, regard-less of their physical origin. Even if you have an idea in your head that *cannot be physically photographed*, we'll show you how Photoshop, and some programs that work with Photoshop, can make your ideas a reality.

So, is our adventure in Photoshop about drawing, painting, photography, typography, or pure imagination? The answer is "yes." Imaging encompasses all these things, and it's all because you're simply doing one thing with your computer; you're handling data.

Where *Inside Photoshop* Fits In

We've mentioned a little about imaging and Photoshop here, but not very much about this book. *Inside Adobe Photoshop 3* is *not* a rehash of Adobe's Owner's Manual or the other literature and tutorials that came with the program. *Inside Adobe Photoshop 3* is a hands-on book full of exercises that directly relate to your work. But more importantly, it tells you *why* things work as they do, so you can apply what you learn to any project that comes your way no matter how different it is from the examples we show. You can use this book as a reference guide, as a book on advanced techniques; and you can also learn while participating in exercises geared toward solving real design problems. If it's about Photoshop 3 and digital imaging, it's between these covers. You might find that some of the chapters contain larger-than-life assignments, but you also will find that the concepts and techniques developed by doing the exercises in the chapters help you express and execute ideas you already have, and perhaps generate a few new ones.

Inside Adobe Photoshop 3 exercises, along with the images on the Bonus CD, show you methods to overcome many of the most common obstacles separating you from an excellent, finished, commercially viable image. Through the course of this book, you'll learn that previously insurmountable tasks are actually the "easy stuff" when Photoshop is used. Later, we'll take you beyond to a plateau of the seemingly impossible, where your imagination can breathe and express itself freely and unencumbered by chemical photography and framed canvas. Imaging begins with imagination, and this book and Photoshop will be your guides.

David Oglivy, owner of one of New York's most prestigious advertising agencies, once commented about the creative role of people in his trade: "It's a lot easier to take a great idea and tone it down, than to try to make a dull idea great." If this strikes a chord in you, if you feel a profound need for that "I-don't-know-what" to get your work off the pavement and give it wings, you're starting in the right place! Let's talk about the approach to this book before you approach Adobe Photoshop.

Syntax: How To Read the "Shorthands" in Our Exercises

In this book we presume that you are familiar with your operating system's interface. This includes knowing how to copy, save, and delete files, make directories, and back up your work. And that you are fairly comfortable navigating an extended keyboard and using a mouse. But you also need to get comfortable with how to follow the exercises, and how to execute many of the keyboard actions and mouse moves you make in Photoshop.

Each *Inside Adobe Photoshop 3* exercise is laid out step-by-step. If you follow along, your screen should look exactly like this book's figures, except yours will be in color! Each exercise is set up in a two-column format—in the left column is what you should do, and in the right column is what will happen when you do the step, or an explanation of why we asked you to do a particular step.

Most of Photoshop's tools have different or enhanced functions when you hold down the Shift, Alt, or Ctrl keys (Shift, Option, or ⌘Command key for Macintosh users) while you mouse click or press other keyboard keys. These commands appear in exercises as Ctrl(Cmd)+, Alt(Option)+click, Ctrl(Cmd)+D, and so on. The keys Macintosh users should substitute for the Alt and Ctrl keys appear within the parentheses. Function keys appear as F1, F2, F3, and so on.

A Note to Southpaws

This book was written a little chauvinistically, in that we assume you are right-handed and haven't reset the mouse in Windows Control Panel to be a "right-click" mouse. If you have, use the right button instead of the left one in the following situations. *Dragging* in this book refers to holding down the *left* mouse button and moving the mouse. *Click* means to press and release the left mouse button once; *double-click* means to press quickly the left mouse button twice; and directions like *Shift+Click* mean that you should hold down the Shift key while you click with the left mouse button.

Photoshop does not support the use of more than one mouse button because the Macintosh platform uses a single-button mouse. There are no special features to be accessed within Photoshop for Windows by alternate mouse button clicking.

Here's a short exercise to help you get familiar with our exercise format.

Creating a Minimalist Painting

Select **F**ile, **N**ew (or press Ctrl(Cmd)+N)	Calls up Photoshop's New options box.
Type **ART** in the **N**ame: field	Gives a working name to your new image that appears on the title bar of the new image window.
Type **640** in the Image Size **W**idth box, and choose pixels from the drop-down list	This is the width of the image window you are creating.
Type **480** in the Image Size H**ei**ght box, and choose pixels from the drop-down list	This is the height of the image window you are creating.
Type **72** in the **R**esolution box, and choose pixels/inch from the drop-down list	Specifies how many pixels per inch your new image will be.
Choose RGB Color from the Mode drop-down list	Tells Photoshop you want to work in 16.7 million colors.
Click on the **W**hite radio button in the Contents field	Tells Photoshop you want the "canvas" for your new creation to be white.

continues

continued

Click on OK	Confirms your selections, and you are returned to Photoshop's workspace, with a new image window entitled "ART."
Double-click on the Paint Brush tool	Activates the Paint Brush tool, and displays the Brushes palette, which by default displays the Paintbrush Options tabbed menu.
Click on the Brushes tab on the Brushes Palette	Displays the Brushes tips.
Click on the Brushes tip on the Brushes palette with the "45" on it	Sets the characteristics of the Paint Brush to 45 pixels in diameter with a soft edge.
Click and drag the cursor diagonally across the ART image window	Applies foreground color to the new image, as shown in figure I.1.

Figure I.1

Photoshop palettes have tabbed menus that are used to choose additional options relating to the active tool.

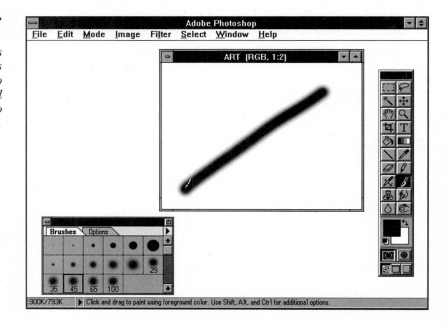

There are more Photoshop commands in store, for sure, and we reference "key" operations with figures along the way, but the steps shown here illustrate the setup for all the exercises.

Other Conventions Used in This Book

Throughout this book, conventions are used to help you distinguish various elements of Windows, DOS, their system files, and sample data. These conventions include the following:

Special Text

◆ **Shortcut Keys.** Accelerator keys sometimes appear in the text, but normally appear in the exercises to indicate a keyboard technique for achieving several steps with a couple of key strokes. For example, (Ctrl(Cmd)+N) is the shortcut key for calling up Photoshop's **N**ew options dialog box. When in Photoshop, these shortcut key commands apply to Windows. Macintosh users should always press the ⌘ Command key (noted in parentheses) along with the letter key.

◆ **Key1+Key2.** When you see a plus sign (+) between key names, hold down the first key while you press the second key. Then release both keys. If, for example, you see "Press Ctrl(Cmd)+Shift," hold down the Ctrl key and press the Shift key, then release both keys.

◆ **Hot Keys.** Onscreen, Windows underlines the letters on some menu names, file names, and option names. The File menu name, for example, is displayed on-screen as File. This underlined letter is the letter you type to choose that menu, command, or option. In this book, such letters are displayed in bold, underlined type: **F**ile.

◆ Information you type is in **boldface**. This rule applies to individual letters, numbers, and text strings. The convention, however, does not apply to special keys, such as Enter, Tab, Esc, or Ctrl.

◆ New terms appear in *italic*.

◆ Text that is displayed onscreen but is not part of Windows or a Windows application—such as DOS prompts and messages—appears in a `special monospace typeface`.

◆ In the text, function keys are identified as F1, F2, F3, and so on.

Mouse Notes

This book repeatedly uses terms that refer to mouse techniques: *click, double-click, Shift-click, drag,* and *marquee-select.* These terms are explained here:

◆ **Clicking.** You click on an object or menu item to select the object or item.

◆ **Double-clicking.** Usually you double-click to perform a function without the need to click an OK button in a dialog box. In addition, when you double-click on a tool in Photoshop's toolbox, a menu, palette, or dialog box appears.

◆ **Shift+clicking.** With Photoshop's selection tools (identified in upcoming chapters), you use *Shift+clicking* to select more than one object. By holding down Shift, you add objects to the already selected objects.

◆ **Alt+clicking (Option-clicking for Mac users).** You use Alt(Option)+clicking to change the function of the tools in the toolbox. You will use this technique in future chapter assignments.

◆ **Dragging.** The term dragging means to hold the mouse button and move the mouse and onscreen cursor to a new location, usually taking a selected area to the new position.

◆ **Marquee-dragging.** To marquee drag, you click, then diagonally drag, which produces different results depending on which Photoshop tool you have chosen. You *Marquee-zoom* into a view of an image when you click and diagonally drag using the Zoom tool, whereas you *Marquee-select* an image area when you have the Rectangular marquee tool chosen. In the latter instance, using the mouse cursor, you click and drag a rectangle around the objects to be selected.

The Shift, Alt(Option), and Ctrl(Cmd) keys, when used in combination with clicking, offer variations on a tool's function. Specific features are mentioned throughout this book.

Note The programs Adobe Photoshop for Windows and Adobe Photoshop for the Macintosh are both commonly referred to in this book as simply *Photoshop.*

The Six Parts to Inside Photoshop

Inside Adobe Photoshop 3 is divided into six parts, and five of these are broken into chapters. The exercises are goal-oriented and have a clear beginning and end, so that you can put this book down once in a while without losing where you left off! Each part addresses a different element of imaging with Photoshop.

Part I: From the Source to the Sample

Part I starts with some information that makes using Photoshop with digital images more meaningful. If you've had experience in a traditional, chemical darkroom, you'll want to check out Chapter 1, "Understanding Image Types, Formats, and Resolutions," where we define image types and how each one is equivalent to physical images you may have worked with in the past.

Chapter 2, "Acquiring a Digital Image," is all about *acquisition techniques*, and the best way to use a scanner to copy a physical image to your computer. It also discusses the formats you can use to save the scanned image and how to optimize your video display.

Chapter 3, "Color Theory and the PhotoCD," teaches you the language and uses of color theory and color models, and how they affect your work. Theory is put to practice by exploring one of the hottest new technologies—Kodak's PhotoCD.

Chapter 4, "Photoshop Defaults and Options," is devoted to setting up Photoshop's workspace so that you can feel more at home while working in it. You even have your choice of what sort of cursor is displayed when using a tool. Preferences for how Photoshop uses memory, calibrating your monitor to ensure your image reads the same on a service bureau's system, and tuning Photoshop for optimized performance are all covered in detail.

Chapter 5, "It's All Done with Palettes," shows you how Photoshop performs some of its magic. You'll work with and learn how to configure Photoshop's new floating grouped palettes. Your productivity in Photoshop will soar when you use some of the tips and techniques you find in this chapter.

Chapter 6, "The Photoshop Test Drive," will give you a hands-on, trial-size run through Photoshop's workspace, where you'll get a feel for the power and integration of Photoshop's tools. You'll also discover the power of working with selections and Photoshop's new layers feature. This chapter is where the information you've read in Chapters 1–5 is put to real use, as you perform some "basic magic" in Photoshop 3!

Part II: Steak and Potatoes Assignments

This is where we put some of Photoshop's tools, filters, and effects to the test in everyday situations. You'll quickly learn how to overcome workaday photo errors, and learn simple methods for making a common photograph sparkle.

Chapters 7, "Restoring an Heirloom Photograph," and 8, "Retouching an Heirloom Photograph," are an in-depth two-parter on the fine points of restoring a photograph that's aged and been damaged. You'll discover how to change the tonal qualities of the image to reveal original image detail, and how to color-correct and restore lost image areas.

Chapter 9, "Using Type in Photoshop," teaches you how to handle text in a graphical image. Adobe's other claim to fame is Adobe Type Manager, so you'd better believe that Photoshop can do some pretty sophisticated stuff when it comes to integrating type within a digital image. And because Photoshop treats text as a graphic, we'll explore wonderful things you can do with scanned text and text as an *Encapsulated PostScript* (EPS) graphic.

Chapter 10, "Stamping Out Photo Errors," reveals all the wonderful retouching work you can do with a single tool—Photoshop's Rubber Stamp. It's only part of Photoshop's complete set of tools, but its robustness and retouching capability deserve exclusive and complete coverage.

Chapter 11, "Paths, Selections, and Layers," is all about using effects and tools together. Coverage of Photoshop's Paths palette is emphasized. Paths are a Photoshop feature that gives the designer vector tools within a bitmap editing program. Paths are important for accurately selecting irregular, geometric image areas because they can be used as the basis for creating selection areas. The Paths palette offers a whole subset of Photoshop tools, and your mastery of the program should include a working knowledge of how paths can be used to select, define, and apply special effects to your images.

Part III: Gourmet Assignments

As you quickly grow comfortable with imaging Photoshop-style, you'll become hungry for more sophisticated imaging challenges. We move from the everyday to very special assignments in this part. These chapters contain exercises that take your skill level and work from great, to heights that will gain you recognition in professional business circles.

In Chapter 12, "Correcting an Image," you'll get into the construction business when you take a photo of an unfinished house and pick up where the carpenters and landscapers left off. In the process you'll discover how to choose, adapt, and integrate material from a variety of sources to complete your assignment. If you do industrial or commercial photography for a living, this chapter is for you.

Chapter 13, "Combining Photographs," is where you'll discover the ins and outs of transplanting an image area to a different background. Combining photographic images has been the sport of all classes of designers, but with Photoshop 3, composite imaging becomes a professional craft that offers eye-catching, realistic results. Learn the secrets for seamless photographic combinations right here.

Chapter 14, "Enhancing Images," includes an exercise demonstrating how to create a dream scene out of two lifeless images. You'll learn how to create reflections in an image that weren't originally photographed, and how to color-balance a cold, harsh landscape into a warm, breathtaking landscape.

Chapter 15, "Special Effects with Ordinary Photographs," shows you how to accomplish the impossible once again: how do you create a convincing photo from two images of the same person so that the person appears to be identical twins? Television shows in the '60s used split-screen photography to accomplish this feat, but using Photoshop 3 and 1990s technology, you'll learn how to compose the scene so that the two subjects interact and create a reality that formerly required hiring two identical actors. Learn how to manipulate people in this chapter. *Digitally*, of course!

Chapter 16, "Creating a Digital Collage," demonstrates how to bring text, graphics, photographic images, and a corporate logo together to create an eye-catching, mind-boggling advertisement. You'll distort text within Photoshop and create complex selection borders using Photoshop's new Color Range command.

Chapter 17, "The Wonderful World of Black and White," is devoted to the black and white, or Grayscale, image. The world still publishes in black and white, and this chapter shows you how to create powerful, striking photographs in this Photoshop mode.

Chapter 18, "Photoshop's Native Filters," explores the creative uses of Photoshop's filters, for both image enhancement and the creation of original computer graphics. Why you'd want to filter an image, when you wouldn't want to, and artistic suggestions and ideas are explored in this chapter.

Part IV: Fantastic Assignments in Photoshop

This is the part of imaging that many graphics people get very excited about. The power that used to be reserved for graphics workstations is now at your disposal on the Windows and Macintosh platforms. Creating Virtual Reality via Photoshop is our destination in Part IV's chapters.

Chapter 19, "3rd-Party Plug-In Filters," is an extension of Chapter 18's adventures with filters. Because Photoshop's filters are built around the openly published Plug-Ins architecture, third-party manufacturers have served up tools that extend Photoshop's powers from the exceptional to the extraordinary. Kai's Power Tools,

Pixar One-Twenty-Eight texture filters, Alien Skin's The Black Box filters, Andromeda's 3D Filters, and Aldus Gallery Effects are shown in this chapter, with instructions for their use and some hands-on experiments. Limited versions of Kai's Power Tools, Pixar One-Twenty-Eight texture filters, and Alien Skin's The Black Box filters are included on the Bonus CD that came with this book.

Chapter 20, "Mixed Media and Photoshop," demonstrates how to enhance draw-ings—physical pen and ink sketches. You'll see how to bring a piece of physical line art into the Photoshop workspace and use filters, photographic elements, and lighting effects to add substance, warmth, and a bit of whimsy to an illustration.

Chapter 21, "Advanced Type Usage and Presentations," shows how PIXAR Typestry can be used with Photoshop to produce Hollywood-quality slides for presentations. Like Photoshop, Typestry "speaks" Alpha channels, so your composite work with real images and Typestry's photo-realistic designs can be integrated in Photoshop to produce show-stopping results. A limted version of Typestry (for Windows and the Macintosh) is on the Bonus CD that came with this book!

Chapter 22, "Virtual Reality: The Ingredients of Dreamwork," goes one step beyond photo-realism, as we show you how to build an image for a science-fiction book cover. It's not hyper- or even ultra-reality. Virtual Reality and Photoshop go hand in hand as we explore the how-tos of fantastic imagery.

Part V: Inking Up and Doing Yourself a Service

Becoming a master at imaging through Photoshop doesn't do you much good unless you can show your work to the world on hard copy. This section helps you get a handle on the fine points of mapping digital images to a physical medium instead of to your monitor.

Chapter 23, "Personal Printing Basics," is all about questions, answers, and little-known math that play a very direct role in your printed images quality. How many shades of gray can your laser printer produce? What's a halftone cel? Even if you've never asked yourself these, or dozens more questions, you will eventually. Chapter 23 is where some of the answers lie.

Chapter 24, "The Service Bureau," is a guide to possibly the best resource an imaging-type person could have. The Imaging Center, or *Service Bureau*, has lots of expensive hardware and trained professionals who are responsible for making prints out of your image files or getting your files ready for high-quality reproduction at the commercial printer. No, it's not too good to be true, but the Service Bureau and the commercial print shop are definite stops on your road to wonderful computer graphics, and we knock on their doors for you right here.

Chapter 25, "The Film Recorder," opens the possibilities of the film recorder's role in bringing your finished image to life as a glorious color transparency. Unlike printing, a digital film recorder renders an image to slide format, containing all the rich values you'd normally expect from film passed through a physical camera. How large an image file you need to record on film, what's the proper aspect ratio, and suggestions for optimizing an image before sending it to a service bureau are covered in this chapter.

By the time you've done all the exercises and waded through this entire book, you'll have more questions than answers about your new imaging skills and Photoshop. A good one that all successful artists ask themselves is, "How good am I?" It's all relative. We figure, "hey, we don't know each and every one of our readers, so we can assist objectively with the pressing questions you may have about the whole process of creating images out of light." Chapter 26, "How Good Is Good?," is a peer-to-peer reflection on your new skills, ambitions, and the possibilities that are out in the real world once you shut off the computer.

Part VI: Back O' the Book

Don't you hate reaching the end of a good book, and then finding out the authors skimped on the research work they put into it?! Everyone who works with a computer has a natural curiosity about where they can learn more, where the best sources are for more tools, and what stuff means when they read it out of context.

"Appendix A: What's on the Bonus CD?" You might have noticed when you picked up this book that there's a little bonus tucked in the back. The *Inside Adobe Photoshop 3* Bonus CD contains all the exercise images and materials shown in this book so that you can actually produce the images shown by following the steps in each chapter. How Windows and Macintosh users access the CD to load the exercise images is covered in this section.

 Note *Inside Adobe Photoshop 3 refers to two different CDs. The Bonus CD accompanies this book and supplies images and shareware that help you complete most of the exercises. The Deluxe CD is packaged with Photoshop 3. Occasionally, you are asked to use images from this CD. Just note the difference in name before you look for a particular image or program.*

In addition, we've gathered and placed trial versions of knockout commercial software, invaluable shareware, freeware, and sample images for your perusal and use on the CD. Descriptions of these are also found here.

"Appendix B: How to install the Online Glossary: PC and Macintosh Versions." This section contains instructions on how to use the Adobe Acrobat versions of the Photoshop Online Glossary.

"The Online Glossary" is an electronic Super-Glossary, written in Adobe Acrobat format. Both Windows and Macintosh users can use our Online Glossary as a resource for terms and tips while running Photoshop. Instructions for installing and operating the Online Glossary can be found in this section.

And don't overlook the special discount offers from service bureaus and third-party software companies you'll find in the back of the book. These offers can save you hundreds of dollars!

Finally, New Riders feels that a good judge of a book's quality is its index. Inside Adobe Photoshop has been diligently indexed.

Preparing for Photoshop

Photoshop lives up to its reputation and yields better and more sophisticated results than the average computer program. But to do so, it requires a computer setup with higher than average capabilities. The hardware requirements that Adobe puts on the outside of the box—386, 486, or Pentium processor, DOS 5, Win 3.1, 8 MB RAM, and 20 MB free hard disk space—are the *bare* minimums. The adage, "You get what you pay for" holds true here. Getting results with the minimum hardware/software recommendations will be tedious, and you will be limited in what you achieve. Trust us. You will *not* be happy with the minimum configuration.

System Configurations

For Windows Photoshop users, we recommend at *least* a 486 running at least 33 MHz, or Pentium processor (Photoshop program code is optimized for the Pentium), 16 to 20 MB of RAM, DOS version 6.*x*, a display adapter and monitor capable of displaying 24-bit, 16.7 million colors, and 60 MB of free hard disk space on a 340 MB drive.

Macintosh users will need *at least* a 68040 or Power Macintosh system with 16 MB of application RAM and 60 MB of free hard disk space. Apple System 7 supports Photoshop, but System 7.1.2 supports it better. In addition, Macintosh users can improve Photoshop performance by purchasing *Data Signal Processor* (DSP) adapter cards for their computer that are specifically designed to speed up processor-intensive tasks, such as Photoshop's Gaussian Blur filter.

These setups are only to learn Photoshop through this book, with no extra-curricular activities. If you're serious about imaging as a profession or even as a hobby, a PhotoCD-capable XA standard CD-ROM drive, and a color scanner should be additions to your base system configuration as soon as your wallet heals! PhotoCDs and scanners are vital links to your computer that bring image samples from the physical world to your Photoshop workspace.

The exercises in this book were created by using systems that are not all that exotic when compared to industry preferences and budgets for imaging. We don't believe them to be out of the reach of a serious creative type. Both the authors used 486DX2 66 MHz processors, 20-32 MB of RAM, a 24-bit display adapter (Matrox Ultima Plus with 2MB VRAM), and compatible monitors. For the Macintosh research, the authors used a Quadra 950 with 32 MB RAM, and 2 MB of video RAM.

Additional Equipment

At the time of this writing, Windows 95 (Chicago) is still half a year away from general distribution, and until the IBM/PC platform can take advantage of Windows 95's advanced memory-handling, third-party products that circumvent the DOS 640 K barrier are a must. We strongly recommend that Windows 3.1*x* users get an upper memory manager like Helix's *Netroom 3* or Quarterdeck's *QEMM*. You also should have a disk compression program such as Stac's *Stacker*, to expand your hard drive's storage capacity further because high-quality digital images are typically more than 1 or 2 MB *each*.

A hard disk optimizing program, such as Symantecs *Norton Speed Disk*, can also speed up your work by defragmenting files stored on your hard disk so that your PC can read them more quickly. You'll want to use a backup program regularly, too, because the only way to completely insure your imaging work is to keep a copy separate from your hard disk.

Note For more information on optimizing your system to work better with Photoshop, both Mac and PC users should look to Chapter 4, "Photoshop Defaults and Options," where we give detailed instructions on setting up scratch disks and memory allocations for working quicker in Photoshop.

Folks Just Like You

Our equipment and resources for getting the images we've included on the Bonus CD and used in this book are middle of the road. For the live images, we used available lighting most of the time, a 35mm SLR camera, and the patience of a lot of family and friends as subjects. We believe that the business professional will see where these examples can lead with their own work, and the novice isn't put off by the loftiness of an image outside of their grasp.

We kept in mind while designing *Inside Adobe Photoshop 3*'s exercises that techniques you'll learn can be tailored and patterned toward *your own* work. And because understanding a technique or process is an important part of mastering it, we've explained the concepts, the why's and wherefore's behind each task. For the artist in us all, we've devoted some space to Art for Art's sake. We've also tried to be as commercial as possible because we understand the appeal of Photoshop to commerce, and we'd like you to enjoy both the personal and business rewards of using Photoshop.

Electronic imaging is such a wonderful, magical thing that it's impossible to keep the child in us quiet, and for that reason, some of our exercises are a little played up—they stretch reality a tad in the same way you'll learn to stretch a pixel or two using Photoshop. We want to show you some of the fun we've had with a very serious product, and perhaps that will kindle or fan the flame of the creative spark in you, as well.

From both ends of the spectrum, Photoshop and this book are within easy reach. But the proof is in the learning.

So let's get started!

The Photoshop Resource for PC and Macintosh Users

*I*nside Adobe Photoshop 3 was written by authors who use IBM/PCs, but this book is also a great guide to Adobe Photoshop 3 for the Macintosh. Adobe Systems has worked very hard to make the functionality, the look, the layout, and the feel of the Windows and the Macintosh versions of Photoshop identical. Feature for feature, menu for menu, the programs are as similar as the respective operating systems allow. (See figures P.1 and P.2.) When you learn to use the Windows version of Photoshop 3, you also are learning how to use the Macintosh version and vice-versa.

Figure P.1

The Windows version of Adobe Photoshop 3 with all the palettes open.

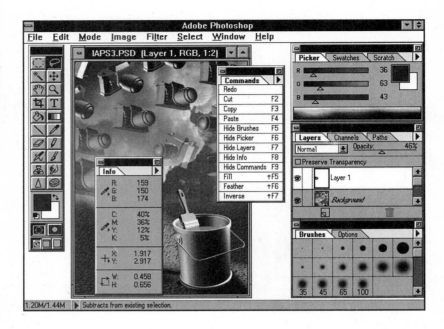

Figure P.2

The Macintosh version of Adobe Photoshop 3 with all the palettes open.

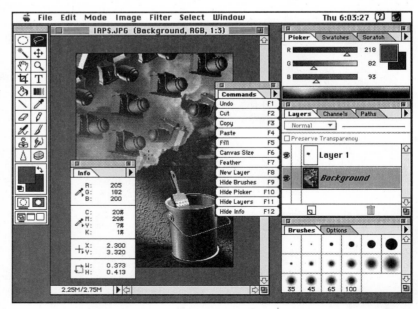

It only is natural that this book also should address the needs of both Windows and Macintosh users. Inside this book you find hands-on, assignment-oriented chapters that fully explore the power that Photoshop 3 can bring to your graphics work. The *Inside Adobe Photoshop 3* Bonus CD at the back of the book contains all of the images and support material needed to do the exercises. The CD also contains a handsome stockpile of textures, fonts, stock photography, shareware, and commercial software samples that you can use in your own exploration of the digital graphics world that Photoshop opens to you. The material on the Bonus CD can be read and used by both Windows and Macintosh computer users.

Note that 99 percent of this book was written using the Windows version of Photoshop 3. Adobe Systems accomplished quite a feat in offering near-identical feature sets within both versions of Photoshop, but each operating system has its own conventions that necessitated minor, but consistent differences between the two versions.

Different Keys for Different Versions

Although there are one or two minor variations in each platform's feature set, the primary difference between the Windows and Macintosh versions of Photoshop 3 is due to the different keyboards used by each system. Many Photoshop users only use the keyboard occasionally, and if you're comfortable designing and accessing commands using a mouse, the differences in the two versions won't create any confusion as you follow this book's exercises. But do take a look at the following section that outlines the different key combinations that are used, because using the keyboard is faster than using the mouse at times, and you want to be sure you're pressing the right keys.

In the exercises, when the steps say to use the *Ctrl (Cmd)* key, Windows users should press the *Ctrl* key and Macintosh users should use the ⌘ *Command* key. Similarly, when the steps say to use the *Alt (Option)* key, Windows users should press the *Alt* key while Macintosh users should use the *Option* key. Both the Macintosh and the Windows keyboards support *Shift* key use and its function is the same on both platforms—to create uppercase letters and to modify a tool's function.

Stop The Macintosh keyboard does have a key that says Ctrl on it, but *don't* use it. It won't produce the results you expect—the Mac Ctrl key switches whatever tool you have active to the Magic Wand tool.

The first column in Table P.1 shows a typical exercise instruction, and the second and third columns show what keys Windows and Macintosh users press to achieve the intended results. See Chapter 5, "It's All Done With Palettes," for information on how to customize the Command palette, and assign function keys to menu shortcuts.

TABLE P.1
Keyboard Substitutions for Macintosh Users

Exercise Instructions	Windows Keyboard	Macintosh Keyboard
Press Ctrl(Cmd)+Z to Undo	Ctrl+Z	⌘Command+Z
Alt(Option)+click to set the sampling point	Alt+click	Option+click
Press the Shift key while dragging the Elliptical Marquee tool to add to the selection	Both Windows and Macintosh users use the Shift key.	

Function Keys and Their Assignments

One area where Adobe has not maintained total continuity between the Windows and Macintosh versions of Photoshop is the new Command Palette. The two versions have different features associated with different F key (Function key) keystrokes. Users can add new commands to the palette, or reassign existing key combinations to other features.

Both Windows and Macintosh users have the option of assigning commands to any F key from F2 to F12 (F1 is reserved for Windows Online Help) and you can double your fun by assigning commands to Shift+F key combinations as well. Macintosh users who have keyboards without F keys aren't able to edit or add any commands to the Command Palette, but still can use the default palette by clicking on any of the predefined buttons to access the associated command.

In this book, when we refer to F key shortcuts, the shortcut key for Windows is given first and the Macintosh equivalent is listed second and is within parentheses. In both cases, the shortcuts listed will produce the intended results only if you are using the default Command palette that shipped with your version of Photoshop. Tables P.2 and P.3 show the default Command Palette F key assignments for both Windows and Macintosh versions of Photoshop.

Choose **W**indow, **P**alettes, Show Co**mm**ands if the Command Palette is not visible in your workspace. If your Command palette doesn't have buttons that are assigned to the same actions and key combinations as listed in Tables P.2 or P.3, you'll want to reset the Command Palette to accurately follow along with the instructions in this book. To restore the default assignments to the default palette, click on the pop-up menu button on the Command palette (the black arrowhead) and choose Reset Commands. Click on OK when asked if you want to replace the current commands with the default commands. Chapter 5 has the scoop on working with the Command and other palettes that can be completely customized.

TABLE P.2
The Windows Default Command Palette

Command	Key
Undo	None
Cut	F2
Copy	F3
Paste	F4
Show/Hide Brushes	F5
Show/Hide Picker	F6
Show/Hide Layers	F7
Show/Hide Info	F8
Show/Hide Commands	F9
Fill	Shift+F5
Feather	Shift+F6
Inverse	Shift+F7

TABLE P.3
The Macintosh Default Command Palette

Command	Key
Undo	F1
Cut	F2
Copy	F3
Paste	F4
Fill	F5
Canvas Size	F6
Feather	F7
New Layer	F8
Show/Hide Brushes	F9
Show/Hide Picker	F10
Show/Hide Layers	F11
Show/Hide Info	F12

Accelerator Keys

Another area where the Macintosh and Windows versions of Photoshop differ is in the use of *accelerator keys*. The Windows interface standard enables programmers to underline letters in menus and dialog boxes to signify letters that can be typed to select an option. These keys are noted in this book as bold, colored, underlined letters. The Macintosh system does not support accelerator keys, and Macintosh users can ignore these notations.

Online Help

On occasion in this book, we suggest that you check the status line for help prompts. Status line help prompts are not supported on the Macintosh platform. However, limited Macintosh Balloon Help is available and can be toggled on and off by clicking on the Help icon on the right side of the menu bar, and then choosing Show/Hide Balloons.

Windows users can access context-sensitive online help by pressing F1, or by choosing **H**elp from the Help menu on the menu bar. Windows Help is not supported by the Macintosh operating system.

Another form of useful online information is available to both Windows and Macintosh users if they install the Adobe Acrobat software found on the *Adobe Photoshop 3 Deluxe CD-ROM*. With the Acrobat Reader, the documentation that Adobe put on the *Deluxe CD-ROM* (that shipped with Photoshop) can be read. Additionally, the *Inside Adobe Photoshop 3 Online Glossary* is in Acrobat format and is found on the *Inside Adobe Photoshop 3* Bonus CD. You must install the Adobe Acrobat reader and have the latest version Adobe Type Manager installed on your system to use these extra documentation files. See Part Six of this book for more information on the Acrobat Reader files.

Miscellaneous Terminology and Interface Differences

Throughout the book, you see references to directories and subdirectories. These are places where Windows users store files. IBM/PC platform directories are roughly equivalent to Macintosh Folders.

Windows 3.1x does not support the use of long file names and usually requires the use of file-format-specific filename extensions. Macintosh users do not have to limit themselves to naming their work with names such as PARKBLAH.TIF. It is, however, recommended that Macintosh Photoshop people adopt the 8.3-character file-naming convention when working with this book. Using the short names makes it easier to follow the examples, and getting used to the file extensions used by Windows programs makes working with DOS/Windows users and service bureaus easier.

Putting It All Together

As you can see, the differences between the Windows and Macintosh versions of Photoshop 3 are minimal. The commonality Adobe provides across both platforms is refreshing in the world of personal computers where incompatibility and division tends to rule, and many computer users define (and limit) themselves in part by the type of operating system they use.

When you purchased Adobe Photoshop 3 and this book, you took important steps toward professional imaging ability, and made a decision about the platform-independence of your future work with digital imaging. What you learn as you master Photoshop is not tied to the kind of hardware that sits in front of you. After spending some quality time with the program and the exercises to follow, when someone asks you "Do you know how to use Photoshop?" your response will be an unqualified "Yes."

You'll begin your cross-platform learning experience in the next chapter where you'll explore different kinds of image formats, what they are good for, and when to use a particular file format when working with folks who use different types of computers than you do.

Get ready to explore Adobe Photoshop 3 for *everyone*.

Part I

From the Source to the Sample

1 Understanding Image Types, Formats,
   and Resolutions 27

2 Acquiring a Digital Image 63

3 Color Theory and the PhotoCD 107

4 Photoshop Defaults and Options 149

5 It's All Done with Palettes 195

6 The Photoshop Test Drive 237

Understanding Image Types, Formats, and Resolutions

As an artist or a photographer, understanding the technical workings and characteristics of your tools—cameras, brushes, paint, and pens—leads you to gain more control over a finished piece. Whenever you add a new tool (such as the personal computer and Adobe Photoshop) to your trade, you are able to broaden your scope as an artist. Photoshop, like any serious, professional-level computer application, does not feature "push button" or "instant artist" tools; instead, it offers some equivalents to the traditional tools you're familiar with, as well as quite a few tools *no one* has had experience with!

To master the powerful new tools that Adobe Photoshop provides, you must develop an understanding not only of the tools themselves but also of what you produce with them. When you have this understanding, you'll find that the results that you can achieve with Photoshop's digital image creation and manipulation processes are nothing short of extraordinary.

Comparing Traditional Photography to Digital Imaging

As you might expect, the correlation between a traditional chemical photograph and a digital image is not a direct one. Each has its own peculiarities, advantages, and stumbling blocks. Although conventional photography has produced beautiful keepsakes for almost two centuries, traditional chemical photography has its limitations. Time fades even the best of photographic emulsions, and depending on the format of a film negative, a photo may appear smooth or extremely grainy when enlarged.

Conversely, a digital image can be created or sampled so that it can be printed as large as the side of a house—but the size of the computer file that could hold such an image would be preposterously large. Additionally, today's art purists sometimes dismiss digital images in the same way that painters, 40 years ago, balked at the medium of photography. *Digital imaging* has become such a blanket term for artwork produced with the assistance of a computer that the distinction between representative art and photo-realistic creations is often blurred. So-called "real" art, then, becomes an entirely subjective phrase. Once again in art history, a new medium of artistic expression becomes secondary to artistic *content*, and digital imaging is embraced by artists and art viewers as an exciting technological advancement. Quite simply, if you understand its limitations and capabilities, imaging with the personal computer holds more potential for *any* individual to make their creative statement, than with any other medium to date.

The main difference between a photographic image and a digital image is the means by which an image is produced. The grains in photographic film and the pixels in a data stream are simply two paths to a common goal: to communicate an image to the viewer.

What You Get Is What You See

Digital imaging and traditional chemical photography share a closeness because they both are mediums used to express ideas. Don't think of electronic images as a compartmentalized technology set apart from the chemical photo, because both media depend on one another at this time in history and can actually benefit from their "alter ego's" strong points. Chemical photography is a static medium in which an image is fixed on a coated surface; from that moment on, editing options are limited. An experienced Photoshop user, however, can work with that same image and take it in a multitude of creative directions because making one perfect digital copy is as easy as creating a thousand perfect copies, and this invites experimentation

with variations on a graphical idea. Nevertheless, digital imaging would be an impoverished medium without a camera lens to capture the original image that is then digitized, filtered, corrected, and enhanced in Photoshop.

Microsoft Windows' *WYSIWYG* (what you see is what you get) capability ensures that the files you acquire, view, and build are *mapped* (displayed) the same way to the monitor as they are output to the printer. Usually, with spreadsheets and word processing programs, you can trust WYSIWYG and perform your work without considering *how* WYSIWYG works.

And from its inception, the Macintosh operating system has provided accurate output when compared to an onscreen view of an image, chart, or other graphical item. Photoshop, on both operating platforms, is designed to take advantage of the graphical interface and keep you visually updated on the editing changes you make to an image.

However, if you're going to do extraordinary things with images, you need to understand *why* the images behave as they do in various circumstances.

Phases of Digital Imaging

From the time you capture a digital image until it is converted to the binary soup that resides on your hard drive, an image goes through three phases in which it is examined:

◆ The *acquisition phase*, during which a scanner looks at a physical source image. If you're *creating* an image, however, the design program you're using examines your input about the image's size and color capability.

◆ The *viewing phase*, during which the image is displayed onscreen as the image is loaded in system RAM.

◆ The *saving phase*, during which the computer looks at the image while saving it to your hard drive in the format of your choice.

Because each image can have different data properties, you must learn to evaluate each digital image and make different determinations during each phase—for example, how faithfully the image is reproduced or how closely the digital data matches the original image. To make these determinations, you need a basic understanding of different types of computer images.

Types of Computer Images

Vector-based images, for example, are strongly suited for technical illustrations but don't usually provide the features used to produce photo-realistic images. The qualities of focus and lighting are hard to achieve in a vector image. On the other hand, certain types of bitmap images—such as 1 bit/pixel line art—cannot successfully be scaled to different dimensions the way vector art can. Line art (a.k.a. 1 bit/pixel, and black-and-white art) is discussed in the section entitled "The Line Art Graphic," later in this chapter.

A good way to see the similarities and differences is in a tree-shaped diagram that illustrates the relationships between different computer images. To examine these relationships, let's start at the root of the tree and work our way up toward the branches.

Exploring the PC Graphics Tree

At the root or ground level of the computer graphics tree is a single image or collection of images. Computer animation, for example, consists of a series of still digital images. Although Photoshop can provide an animator with valuable tools for refining individual *cels* (from the traditional, physical *cel*luloid sheets) within a computer animation, you need a separate application to compile and orchestrate the collection of images.

The Vector Branch

At the first branch in the graphics tree, the still digital image can either exist as a vector or bitmap (raster) image. *Vector* images are not scanned or acquired from a PhotoCD. They are created with design software such as CorelDRAW! and Adobe Illustrator. Vector drawing programs define (as mathematical calculations) angles, circles, squares, and their spatial orientations relative to the page. Vector images consist of wireframes to which fill and outline properties have been assigned.

A vector graphic also is called an *object-oriented* drawing because an image file of this type contains discrete, separate image elements that are free to be rearranged ad infinitum. Vector graphics also are *resolution-independent*—you can scale a peanut as large as a Winnebago, and the image still has the same amount of visual detail, clarity, and smooth edges when printed. This resolution independence is achieved because no actual rendering (or rasterizing) is involved when the vector graphic is saved to a file format. A vector graphic exists as *mathematical equations* that are only rasterized to the screen each time you draw or edit the image, and only rasterized to a printer after you've specified the image dimensions and resolution.

Figure 1.1 is an example of a vector graphic created in a vector drawing program. Geometric precision and perfect focus in a computer design often point toward a vector-based application as the artist's tool.

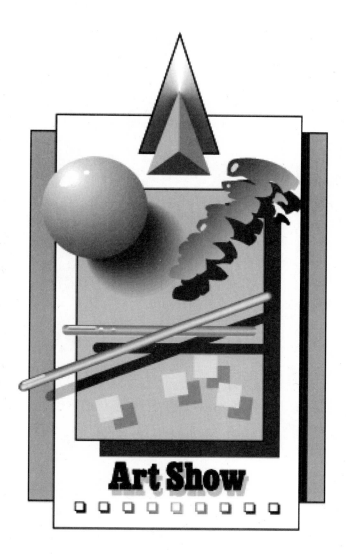

Figure 1.1

Vector art consists of fills and outlines applied to a precise geometric description of a wireframe design.

The Bitmap Branch

Figure 1.2 was designed in a bitmap design program. In contrast to figure 1.1, the bitmapped image evokes a more photographic feeling because qualities of lighting, transparency, and depth of field can be represented successfully.

Bitmapped images are not created or saved as pure mathematical equations. You must specify the resolution and image dimensions the moment you decide to create this type of graphic. The most common way imaging-type people can create a bitmapped image is by scanning a photograph. You also can create a bitmapped image by filling an imaginary grid with colored dots, or *pixels*, using a paint-type program rather than a vector drawing program. (Later in this chapter, you learn more about pixels.) A bitmapped image can convey wonderful nuances and subtleties about the image it represents, mostly because it doesn't depend on any outline and fill math equations as vector art does.

Figure 1.2

Bitmapped images can simulate photographs and paintings. Bitmaps can display image focus; vector images cannot.

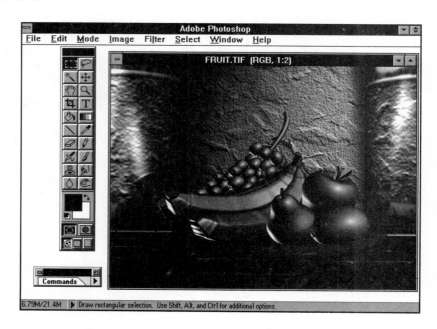

Figure 1.3 shows the graphics tree in full bloom. As you can see, it branches out into four distinct categories of bitmapped images. These categories refer to the color

Figure 1.3

Four distinct "fruits" grow on the bitmap branch of the graphics tree.

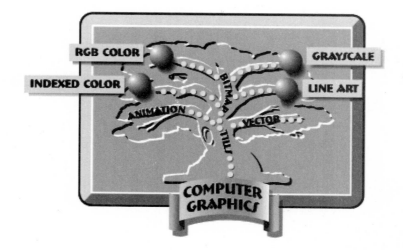

capability of the image types and the way bitmapped information is organized to compose a graphic.

Acquiring Various Image Types

During the acquisition phase of digital imaging, most color scanners have settings that enable you to control how the scanner *samples*, or looks at, a physical image. Note that specifying an inappropriate setting during the acquisition phase can result in a digital image that doesn't contain enough information. Without enough information about the physical, *source* image, it's hard to do satisfying work in Photoshop. Additionally, when you use Photoshop's File, **N**ew command to create a new background to paint on, the mode (Bitmap, RGB Color, Grayscale, and so on) of the new image you specify determines how much visual information you'll be able to create in the background image.

After an image has been digitally acquired with a scanner, Photoshop sees the image as having a mode of color-capability. Bitmap, RGB, and grayscale are all examples of modes, and each refers to how thoroughly the scanner sampled visual information about the original, physical image. Scanners can sample a full-color image as a grayscale mode, but doing this deprives the acquired image of important visual content. A color image scanned at a grayscale setting can't spring back to color in Photoshop because the scanner sampled inadequate visual information.

Picking the Line Art Graphic

Of the four "fruits" of the graphics tree, the most basic one is line art. Let's take a look at how meaningful line art is to your work in Photoshop.

When a pen-and-ink drawing is scanned into your computer, you can specify a scanner setting that usually is called *line art*. Software developers and artists also call this setting black-and-white art, bitmap art, and art that has a one-bit depth. A *bit*, or *b*inary dig*it*, is the smallest amount of information people deal with on their PCs.

When set to line art, the scanner looks at your source image with a one-bit color capability. The scanner sees a zero, a turned-off pixel if the sample is of a black area, and a turned-on pixel if the sample is a white portion of a source image. Original image areas that fall somewhere between black and white values are assigned black or white pixels—other values simply don't exist in line art acquiring mode. This is why a color image scanned at a line art setting results in a digital image that appears to have been photocopied several times. Pixels, fortunately, can handle more than one bit of digital sampling information. Otherwise, color images would not be possible.

When you have an image that consists of black and white only (with no shades of gray), the line art scanner setting is proper and prudent. The scanning goes quickly and results in a small, manageable file. This scanned image is a faithful representation of the source image because you have perfectly captured the very limited amount of information contained in the original.

During your imaging adventures with Photoshop, line art acquisitions can be useful when you have a pen-and-ink sketch you want to build on. Because the density of pencil marks tends to be lighter than the density a pixel must have for the scanner to assign a black pixel to the image, you can make the pencil marks on pen-and-ink drawings (mostly) disappear by sampling them at one bit of information per pixel. By scanning black and white designs at a line art setting, you can "clean up" a sketch you want to use or modify as a digital image. See Chapter 20, "Mixed Media and Photoshop," for some advice on modes to choose for acquiring a digital sample of physical pen and ink drawings.

 Stop   Don't scan a color photo or illustration while your scanner is set to line art. This setting assigns all the glorious color information to either a black register or a white one, performed with none of the judgment or aesthetics a designer typically exercises. This is called letting a machine run your life and decide things for you!

A line art scan, when acquired from a source image composed of lines, produces a digital image similar to figure 1.4.

Figure 1.4

One-bit graphical images contain information about black and white only.

The Half-Breed Halftone

Photoshop and many scanners support a type of image called a halftone. *Halftone* images, like line art, have a color capability of one bit of information per pixel, but the way the scanner sees the image during the acquisition phase is a little different.

Halftones are the representation of *continuous-tone* images through the arrangement of different sized dots, each dot representing (by its relative size) a shade of gray found in the original image. Because halftone dots are arranged in a pattern (usually in lines), the human eye perceives the larger dots as corresponding to a darker shade, with the smaller dots representing lighter shades. Halftone images are used by commercial printers. See Chapter 23, "Personal Printing Basics," for information about how halftone dots should be arranged to produce the best looking printed designs.

Although a halftone setting might be available on your scanner, it is not the recommended mode of color capability to acquire an image you want to modify by using Photoshop's features. A halftone digital image gets its tonal qualities from simulated tones expressed as dots having a 1 bit/pixel color capability. Figure 1.5 shows an image of a ball acquired in grayscale mode, and the same image acquired as a halftone. If you hold the book about three feet away from you and squint, you might recognize the halftone image as being a ball, but clearly, with the visual information organized as black and white dots, future editing options for the image are severely limited.

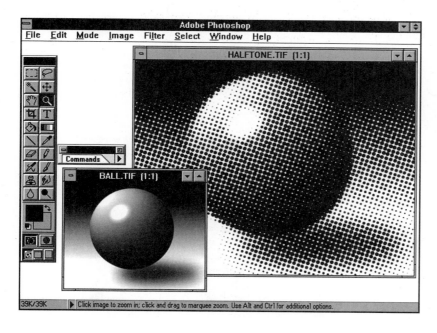

Figure 1.5

Halftones are the representation of continuous-tone images by dots of different sizes.

Because print presses and laser printers cannot accurately produce a continuous-tone image, you must use an image with a halftone color capability (black *or* white image areas) when you want to represent many shades with only the color of the toner (or ink) and of the paper. Whenever an image is printed commercially (as in a newspaper, magazine, or an FBI Wanted poster), it must be screened to create a halftone.

If you run a commercial printing press for a living, you might want to scan a continuous-tone image with a halftone setting that's optimal to print from to create press plates. You'd know what line frequency and screen angle works best with your printing press and the types of ink you use. But you'd also have to forgo any of Photoshop's wonderful image-enhancement powers because a scan that converts a continuous-tone image to camera-ready halftone art removes and distorts information necessary for performing photo-realistic editing in Photoshop.

Think of halftones as a "post-production" type of image rather than a true digital image color mode. Halftone conversion is the final step to getting a digital image in a physical format, not the first step of creative image manipulation. Even though your scanner may support a halftone option, *don't* use it. Part 5 of this book discusses halftones in more detail.

Acquiring the Grayscale Image

When you acquire an image in grayscale mode, you enter a realm in which the scanner views an image with greater color capability. Grayscale images are represented as eight bits of information per pixel, in contrast to line art's one bit per pixel, and a grayscale image's information is organized in a different fashion to accommodate the enhanced color capability.

Line art can be considered "simple math"—a pixel is either turned on or turned off to represent image areas. In contrast, think of the grayscale image mode as "advanced math," offering 256 brightness values with which image detail can be expressed. The information in a grayscale image is organized into a single-color *channel*, which Photoshop calls a Black channel. Channels play an important role in Photoshop image editing, and we'll get into color channels more extensively in Chapter 5, "It's All Done with Palettes."

Binary machines express everything as two to a certain power. For the on/off pixel quality, when eight bits are assigned to each pixel, two to the eighth power results in 256 distinct combinations. The number 256 is an important one to remember because that's the number of shades of gray that can be rendered when grayscale is specified as your scanner mode. Photoshop recognizes a grayscale digital image as having a one-color (*monochrome*) channel of information consisting of 256 different levels of densities. When you save a grayscale image in a proper format, the resulting file contains a 256-shade, eight-bit digital image.

As well-adjusted, normal people, we usually refer to the snapshots taken with black and white film as being "black and white." However, they actually should be called "black and white, and a whole lotta shades in between" photos. Technically, these are monochrome images whose values run a 256-density gamut from black to white. *Gamut* is a fancy term for the range of available values within a setting on your scanner, monitor, or stored image file. To capture a monochrome photo properly, use the grayscale setting on your scanner.

Tip   You may want to scan an aged monochrome photo in the scanner's color mode. Even though the photo was taken with black and white film years ago, some of the grayscale information has turned to brown (as with sepia tones). To capture all the available information in this photo, you must scan not only for the grayscale information, but also include information about the brown, that once was part of the rest of the shades in the continuous-tone, black and white photo.

To accurately capture *all* the tonal information in an aging photo, you need a capture setting on your scanner of 256 *and then* a few shades of brown. This puts the potential number of colors in the image at greater than 256, which an 8-bit grayscale scan can't faithfully acquire. An image such as this should be saved in RGB color mode, then restored using Photoshop's tools. *Chapter 17, "The Wonderful World of Black and White," has details about working between color and black and white imaging; Chapters 7 ("Restoring an Heirloom Photograph") and 8 ("Retouching an Heirloom Photograph") have the how-to's on image restoration.*

Grayscale imaging has long been considered a "pure" art by photographers because the viewer's eye is not attracted to splashy colors within a poor image composition. Indeed, the success or failure of a grayscale image depends on composition and the lighting represented by contrasting tonal values. Many beautiful color images translate poorly to grayscale because color areas are similar in the amount of tonal density each color exhibits. Generally, you get the best grayscale digital image if you begin with a monochrome source image with image areas well defined by contrasting shades.

Figure 1.6 shows a grayscale mode, eight-bit-per-pixel image. Note the difference between this type of image and the line art image shown in figure 1.4. Although both figures are scans of artwork, figure 1.6 has much more warmth and realism than one-bit scanning can capture.

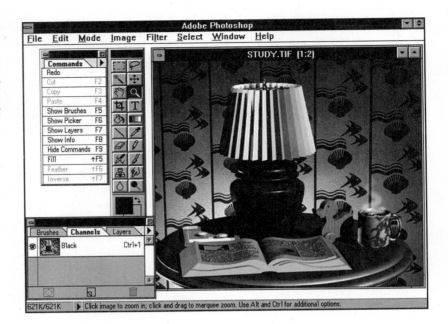

Figure 1.6

Grayscale mode images can express visual information with a gamut of 256 unique shades.

Blossoming into Color Images

As you've ascended the graphics tree so far, you've focused on the wonderful world of black and white for so long that you're probably beginning to feel like a character trapped in a Humphrey Bogart, black-and-white, eight-bit, grayscale movie! But as you climb still farther up the graphics tree, you find that color is blossoming from the next branches.

Color information, as gathered by a scanner, seen by Photoshop, and then rendered to a file format, is fairly complex. Chapter 2, "Acquiring a Digital Image," discusses the best way to view a color digital file. But before going out on a limb with color graphics types, you need to understand how Photoshop and your PC handle color.

The vast majority of color scanners currently on the market sample a color source image in a 24-bit, *RGB* (red, green, and blue) mode. This gives you the ability to sample 16.7 million different colors in a scan of a source image. Although a source image might consist of only a handful of colors, a color scanner nevertheless acquires data and presents it in a mode *capable* of showing 16.7 million colors.

Photoshop, and many technical folks at service bureaus, call this *RGB color.* Red, green, and blue are the building blocks of color for your system (your monitor uses RGB as a color model).

Creating Indexed Color

Color information in an image needs to be described and organized in a way that computer programs can understand. When you scan a color image in RGB mode, for instance, Photoshop looks at the resulting pixels as having the color capability of 24 bits per pixel. The colors in an RGB image are usually arranged as three separate channels—Red, Green, and Blue—each having a gamut of 256 levels of brightness with which to express the presence of red, green, and blue color components.

Pioneers in computer graphics, however, didn't begin designing with RGB mode images, and instead invented the *indexed color* image type. Indexed color is not arranged in three different color channels; rather, it consists of one channel of color where the red, green, and blue components for each pixel are written to a *color table* as a fixed value. Each indexed color image file contains a unique header that tells the host application what the color table is for the image and where each color is mapped to pixels. It is by "shorthanding" explicit RGB color values that indexed color images can be saved to disk as compact files.

Although indexed color images provide the computer with a speedy, convenient system for color management, indexed color images—because of their limited *color table*—fail to represent truly photographic images. Photoshop, in fact, stops reading color images as indexed mode and considers a color bitmap to be an RGB image when the color capability of the image file exceeds 256 unique values. Indexed color images typically are written to one, four, and eight bits per pixel. For instance, Windows 3.1*x* supports an eight-bits-per-pixel color table (or *system palette*, described later), but Windows Program Manager and some applications only support four-bits-per-pixel icons and menus.

Figure 1.7 is an example of how a four-bits-per-pixel indexed color image (a picture of a Windows icon) gets its colors. At four bits of information per pixel, 16 unique colors can be displayed. When the Windows Icon is read from a hard disk, the header of the image file tells the system to place a pixel with an index register of, for example, 7, at a certain location. The system then looks at the color table, sees the "recipe" for the value 7 as being R: 0, G: 128, and B: 0 (a dark green), and displays this color value onscreen.

Indexed color is often called *mapped* color. Indexed color images aren't acquired. They are created—either in a program such as Windows PC Paintbrush, or by *converting* an image that was scanned with an RGB, 24-bit-per-pixel setting. In indexed color mode, colors are predefined, like color crayons, and you are provided only a limited set of them to do your coloring. The reason for this restriction is that color palettes for images become ungainly and inefficient when they are used to describe more than 256 unique values. Did you see how large the color (or *lookup*) table was for the four-bits-per-pixel indexed image in figure 1.7?

Figure 1.7

Color values for indexed color images are read from a color table, then assigned a predetermined RGB value.

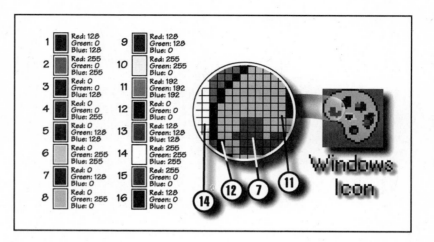

Photoshop's Preference of Color Modes

As color capability is increased for the digital image, color channels (as found in RGB, CMYK, and L*A*B Mode images) organize pixel colors more efficiently than color tables do. Although all color images have a color table, RGB images have no "map;" colors are written as explicit RGB values instead of offering a corresponding value the application must look up. After all, unless you own a paint store, why would you want to index 16.7 million colors? Both mapped and unmapped color image types serve their purposes in business today, and for that reason, indexed color is still used.

However, because of the reduced color capability and the organization of the colors in indexed color images, indexed color mode is inadequate for serious image editing in Photoshop. Photoshop cannot *interpolate* image areas, a process necessary for adjusting global color values, such as color cast, and make the calculations needed to smoothly resize a bitmap image when the image is in an indexed format. Interpolation is the heart of Photoshop's power when it comes to twisting, recoloring, and modifying a digital image.

Interpolation is the averaging of two neighboring pixels color values, to come up with a pixel that appears to fit smoothly between the two. Interpolation occurs whenever you command Photoshop to stretch or recolor a bitmapped image. Anti-aliasing, soft-tip brushes, and effects filters in Photoshop need to avail themselves of a full, 16.7 million color range of expression to do the sophisticated sort of bitmap manipulation they do. You can't take full advantage of these sophisticated features when you're using indexed color images, whose range of expression is limited to displaying only 256 unique colors. In fact, some Photoshop options are unavailable in an indexed color mode.

In this chapter, you'll see how to switch color modes in Photoshop. First, though, you need to understand how a mode gets to be a mode. This depends largely on the bit-depth of image types.

Understanding Color Capability Relationships

Earlier you learned that a grayscale image contains eight-bits per pixel to provide 256 shades in which an image can be rendered. The eight-bits-per-pixel indexed color image is quite common, and it has the same capability to express unique values as a grayscale image. The difference between the two image types has to do with the way color values are organized in their respective bitmap image structures.

A grayscale image is an image *type* recognized as being different than indexed color in Photoshop. This is because pixels in a grayscale image are modeled (represented) as having only a brightness value, ranging from 0 to 255. The color components that pixels use to display grayscale tonal values are equal—for example R=200, G=200, B=200—in order to come up with a very light shade of gray in an image area. For this reason, software developers decided not to reference equal amount of colors used to represent each of the 256 possible tonal values in grayscale images, but to adopt a single channel, a noncolor channel, if you will, for grayscale mode, where brightness values ranging from 0 (black) to 255 (white) are expressed.

To express color, which requires *un*equal RGB values to create different colors in a single channel, the colors have to be indexed in order to keep track of the 256 possible single-channel shades. There *are* no other brightness values or shades of gray a Photoshop user can add to a grayscale image because the mode expresses all the tones the software engineers believe the human eye can see in this format. In reality, the human eye can distinguish simultaneously only 10 or 11 different gray shades in an image. But our eyes move around as we view an image, and 256 shades of gray express quite faithfully the tonal range of a monochrome original image.

The indexed color mode can create reasonable approximations of real-life photo-graphic images. Indexed color is commonly used in word processors and slide presentation programs, but Photoshop balks at the indexed image mode when you attempt to perform any sophisticated image editing. The moment you want to paint a new color into an indexed image, you need to expand the images color capability to be greater than its predefined color palette. Photoshop can switch color modes for an image so that the designer can add color to both a grayscale and an indexed color image. In both cases, the way to do this is to change the grayscale or indexed color image to RGB mode. You gain color capability in a specific image this way. Photoshop won't make your grayscale spring to living color, and it won't make an indexed color image look more refined than the way it was saved to file, but you're changing the image mode, the *type* of the image, to accept more colors than were originally specified in its native type.

Indexed color depends totally on the saved image's bit-depth. This is unlike grayscale, which represents in eight bits all the information about a black and white image type. For example, when an eight-bit indexed color image is forced to portray a 24-bit color image, you know it looks somewhat like a caricature of the original; there are simply too many intermediate-level shades to produce faithfully.

The bits-per-pixel unit of measurement indicates how many colors the image type can contain. A simple way to determine how many colors can exist in a color image by image type, or mode, is to calculate two to the power of the bit-depth. An even *simpler* method is to refer to table 1.1.

TABLE 1.1
Color Counts

Bit-Depth (Bits/Pixel)	Maximum Number of Different Colors	Underlying Math	Common Mode Name
1	2	2 to the 1st	Bitmap, Line Art
4	16	2 to the 4th	VGA, Indexed
8	256	2 to the 8th	SVGA, Indexed
15	32,768	2 to the 15th	HiColor
16	65,536	2 to the 16th	HiColor
24	1,667,216	2 to the 24th	TrueColor, RGB

Photoshop handles an indexed color image up to eight bits per pixel. Grayscale and line art images always are mapped to an eight-bits-per-pixel index because they fit comfortably within a larger index scheme that many other indexed images use.

When an image expresses more colors than can be saved at eight bits per pixel, Photoshop, by default, uses straight, unmapped RGB color values when writing the image to a file format capable of holding the information. Photoshop does this because otherwise there are too many different color possibilities to index, and the indexed color information must be written to the same file as the format, header, and other information.

You have some control over how an indexed color image turns out, even if the image uses only a few different colors. Keep in mind that many scanned color photographs contain only a few thousand unique colors in their RGB color mode, even though 16.7 million are possible in this mode. In the next section, you'll see how to fine-tune an indexed color image made from an RGB file. But first, let's take a look at how you build the palette for indexing.

Defining a Lookup Table

A *lookup table* is the part of a graphics image file that contains the information about how color is supposed to be mapped. In Photoshop, the lookup table is called an *indexed color palette*. A lookup table's task is to map the colors to an indexed image according to how the user specifies the mapping. Photoshop plays a very active role in the indexing process. After you select how many color "opportunities" can exist in an indexed image by specifying a bit-depth, Photoshop then identifies for the lookup table the closest matches to the original image. Then the lookup table fills the indexed color image's registers with the colors that you and Photoshop select.

Here's an example of the decisions and processing that goes on when you want to do some color mapping of an RGB image to create an indexed color image out of it.

Suppose you want to design some Windows wallpaper. You have a 24-bit, RGB, TrueColor (a popular slang among computer manufacturers for super-realistic, 24-bit, "true color") image that looks promising for this wallpaper. You decide to make it four bits deep because that's the color resolution (bit-depth) of most of the wallpaper shipped with Microsoft Windows 3.1.

In figure 1.8, you can see the Indexed Color dialog box that pops into Photoshop when you select **I**ndexed Color from the **M**ode menu to change an RGB image to one of lesser color capability.

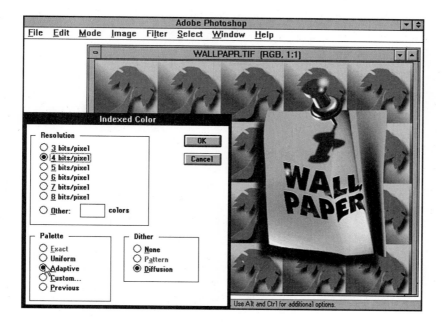

Figure 1.8

The Indexed Color dialog box is used to set specifications for reducing an RGB image to an Indexed one.

By clicking on the **4** bits/pixel radio button in the Resolution field of the Indexed Color dialog box, you specify that Photoshop has a maximum of 16 different colors to portray your RGB original. The term *resolution* has many applications in digital imaging; in this instance, resolution refers to the pixel "depth" of the indexed color image—how many bits per pixel you want as color information.

Beneath the Resolution field is the Palette field. A color palette for an indexed image contains all the values used in the image. Photoshop offers four options for the construction of the palette, or color table, when you reduce an RGB image to an indexed one. You can't use an Exact palette in this example because your RGB image consists of thousands of unique colors, and Photoshop obviously cannot fit this many colors into 16, so the Exact palette radio button is dimmed. Instead, you have Uniform, Adaptive, and Custom palette options (the **P**revious radio button is always dimmed unless you're converting a previous color mode).

In a *Uniform palette,* all the visible colors in the spectrum are represented in 16 colors, each segment of the spectrum being represented by a proportionate amount of the 16 unique colors.

A *Custom palette* is user-defined; you can hand-pick each value. This option can produce absolutely awful RGB conversions to indexed color, however, since you have the responsibility of estimating which 16 indexed colors can best represent the thousands of colors in an RGB original. This is one of those situations in which the computer can evaluate color approximations far better than the human eye. Unless you're trying to create a stylized image from an original, defining a Custom palette has a limited appeal.

If you wanted to convert an RGB to eight bits per pixel, the Uniform radio button in the Indexed Color box would be replaced by the **S**ystem palette option because Photoshop can read the maximum 256-color capacity that Windows supports. However, the System palette contains no user-definable colors, and a Uniform palette is a pretty pathetic method of approximating thousands of unique RGB colors. Some shades in the WALLPAPR image are *weighted* more heavily toward the orange part of the spectrum, and therefore not distributed evenly across the visible spectrum in the image.

Using either palette, Photoshop chooses from the 16.7 million possible shades found in the format of the RGB original image to pick its 16 best ones to create this wallpaper. For tough assignments such as this one, Photoshop's default is the Adaptive palette.

The *Adaptive palette* enables Photoshop to calculate the mean difference between certain ranges of the same hues and then do *averaging*—estimating how these calculations portray the overall image scheme. Photoshop then can determine which 16 colors convey the original RGB image with the least degree of error. If fidelity is your prime goal in reducing an RGB image to indexed color, the Adaptive palette option is accurate and automatic.

Where Do the Extra Colors Go?

Although Photoshop can be used to produce attractive, compact indexed image files, the color reduction from thousands to only 16 in this example goes beyond the averaging of all values to represent the same image with a limited palette. *Dithering* is a process by which Photoshop "fakes" colors from the original image, using colors found in the indexed color palette created for an image. Dithering requires the intelligent placement of neighboring pixels in a bitmap image to create an arrangement of values the human eye integrates and perceives as a color that may not actually exist in an indexed image. Dithering is accomplished in two ways in Photoshop, and your selection of Dither type in the Indexed Color dialog box depends largely on your personal aesthetics.

Diffusion Dithering

Diffusion dithering attempts to "soften the blow" when important color information gets knocked out of an image during indexing. Diffusion dithering bumps a color pixel into an adjacent pixel's place when Photoshop determines that the pixel falls out of the range of available colors you established in the index. The bumped pixel in turn bumps another adjacent one, and this musical chairs routine continues until the last pixel is deemed close enough to a color in the Index to hold a place.

Diffusion dithering creates subtle currents and eddies in an image, as though you were viewing the image through ground glass. When you reduce the available color of an RGB image to Indexed, diffusion dithering is one possible way to reduce harshness and image areas displayed as flat colors. The next section describes another solution.

Pattern Dithering

Unlike diffusion dithering, *pattern dithering* uses two adjacent pixels of available indexed colors to approximate a third, unavailable color. Consider, for example, an Adaptive color table that includes deep red and mustard, but no brown. If you specify a pattern dither when you index, Photoshop "weaves" red and mustard pixels together to create brown.

Whether or not Pattern is your dithering preference is mostly a question of your own taste or an assignment requirement. If you stand far enough away from your monitor, your eyes meld the two colors together and the image appears more full-bodied. If you sit in front of a 21-inch monitor all day while imaging, however, this sort of dithering can be distracting, and your mind may wander off to thoughts of knitting a sweater.

Chapter 2 covers dithering as it applies to your monitor. Dithering on your monitor is an attempt by your video card to display more colors than it is set to—like viewing a 24-bit RGB image with a 16-color video driver. It doesn't affect the RGB *image*, it just causes the *display* to look a little funky. Index color dithering differs from monitor dithering in only one way, but the difference is important: index color dithering *is permanent* and actually *changes* the file.

The Color Reduction Experiment

There will be occasions, professionally, when you want to convert an RGB image to indexed color. In the next example, however, the step-by-step procedures are simply for the fun of creating something. In addition to your choice of color palettes when you perform color mode changes, you can specify the region of an image that contains color values you want emphasized in the indexed color image. For instance, if you want to preserve most of the tonal variations in a photo of a person, and don't care all that much whether a background of a forest is expressed with only five or six shades of green, you use the Rectangular Marquee tool to marquee select a part of the person's face in the image. In this way, you tell Photoshop to fill most of the indexed palette for this image with shades of skin tones.

Now that you understand what indexing accomplishes and how it accomplishes it, you're ready for your first exercise:

Creating a Decent Indexed Color Image from an RGB Image

Open SOFTCONE.TIF from the companion CD.

Click on the Rectangular Marquee tool	Selects a rectangular portion of an active image.

If you've done some independent exploring in Photoshop before reading this, the Elliptical Marquee tool might be displayed on the toolbox instead of the Rectangular Marquee. No problem. Press and hold the Alt key while you click on the Elliptical Marquee to toggle its function to Rectangular. Additionally, feel free to move or close some of the palettes to better see the SOFTCONE.TIF image. For this exercise, all you need is the toolbox.

Click and drag the area in SOFTCONE.TIF where you can pick up some blue, white, brown, and pink all in one selection	Tells Photoshop to refer to this area when indexing, as shown in figure 1.9.

Choose **M**ode	Displays menu of modes.

In the **M**ode menu, Photoshop places a check mark to the left of the **R**GB Color option, indicating that it has identified this image type as the active image.

Choose **I**ndexed Color	Displays the Indexed Color dialog box, in which you specify the color resolution and color palette of the indexed image.

Click on **8**-bits per pixel	Specifies 256 as the maximum number of different colors that can be displayed.
Click on **A**daptive Palette	Tells Photoshop to build a lookup table with a weighted consideration for the colors in the area you selected with the Rectangular Marquee tool.
Click on **D**iffusion in Dither field	Causes pixels in the image with the highest degree of error, compared to the original, to "fan out," so that an obvious color error is thinned and spread over a greater area.
Click on OK	Confirms your choices and returns you to Photoshop's workspace.
Choose **F**ile, **S**ave, name the image, and save it to a directory (folder) on your hard disk	Saves your work to hard disk. You may not *care* to save this work, though; you may ignore this step (our feelings won't be hurt).

Figure 1.9

Marquee-selecting an area in an active image lets Photoshop concentrate on optimizing an Adaptive lookup table.

Figure 1.10 shows a close-up view of the results of your indexing. As you can see, you didn't fare too badly. Some values are missing, certainly, but most of the visual detail from the RGB original remains. By marquee-selecting the area shown in figure 1.9, you gave fewer registers in the indexed color palette to the blues in the SOFTCONE.TIF image, even though blue accounts for more than half of the image's total content. When a foreground element of an image has delicate shading like that found in the ice cream cone, it's worth sacrificing image background quality to create more color values to represent the "star" of the image.

Figure 1.10

*Smaller file sizes
and more
common file
formats are the
advantages of
indexed color
images.*

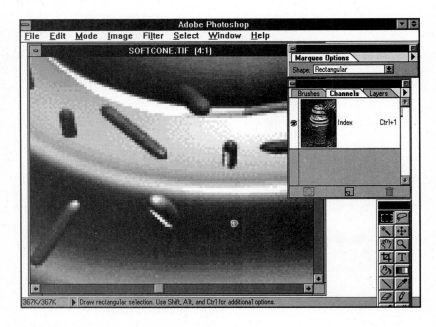

The whole point of learning about the best settings for converting images is so that your designs can be used for a variety of purposes. Presentation packages and desktop-publishing applications sometimes insist on using a BMP or PCX indexed color image as import criteria. After rendering SOFTCONE.TIF as an eight-bit image, you now can conserve disk space by saving the file in BMP or PCX format. A TIF image is inherently burdened with substantial data overhead because it can hold up to 16.7 million colors. Some currently available presentation packages don't even accept TIF images.

Before moving on to the ripest images available from the graphics tree, let's examine a few of the finer points of indexing images.

The Adaptive Palette

Although the Adaptive palette would be the option of preference in *most* cases in which you want to perform color reduction, you should use an Adaptive lookup table on a case-by-case basis. Different photos have different areas that need Photoshop's attention most during the indexing process. With the SOFTCONE image, selecting an area that represented the prime color values was easy because there weren't that

many of them. Photoshop gave preference to the pinks and whites that you selected and didn't give much consideration to the murky blue shadows in the background of the image. If you have an image of a sunset over the ocean at dusk, the Adaptive lookup table weights the palette toward warm reds and golden shades, and places no emphasis on displaying purple or green.

But consider a photo of a peacock holding a PANTONE swatch book and throwing confetti against a rainbow background. In addition to being weird, such an image might well include hundreds of thousands of unique colors, with each unique color requiring Photoshop's attention as much as the next. For fair indexing, you would not choose the Adaptive palette, but rather the Uniform palette from the Indexed Color dialog box. A Uniform palette is an *unweighted* palette; that is, the visible spectrum of colors is segmented with each segment equally represented in the lookup table.

 Tip

Photoshop 3 doesn't offer a feature for counting the number of unique colors found in an image type. If you're ever curious about how many unique colors are present in an RGB image, load the Windows shareware utility PaintShop Pro from the SHAREWAR subdirectory on the companion CD. PaintShop Pro is used in combination with Photoshop in Chapter 23, "Personal Printing Basics."

After you install PaintShop Pro, load an image by selecting the **O**pen command from the **F**ile menu. When your image is displayed, select the **C**ount Colors Used command from the **C**olors menu. PaintShop Pro then tells you how many unique colors an image has. The number may surprise you!

PaintShop Pro can help you determine the best bit-depth (bits per pixel) to use when converting an RGB image to an indexed image. It's a handy little sidekick to Photoshop, and registering the product costs about as much as a piano lesson—and piano lessons usually aren't as much fun.

Should You Index an RGB Image?

For all the methods, techniques, and rationale behind indexed color images, a cursory evaluation of this color mode would suggest that it's inferior to the RGB color mode and presents more creative limitations than advantages. Why, then, have you just spent so much time learning so much about indexed color?

The personal computer enables you, for the first time in the history of art, to make exact duplicates of your work. Because you can generate digital copies, you can experiment with an effect and still keep the original somewhere on disk. More importantly, you can make an image and then specify different modes for the copies, creating each image file for a different application or use. When you send an RGB image directly to a laser printer, the printed image looks lousy. Not only does too much color information slow you down, but before printing a color image expressed as black and white, you'd want to do a little "tweaking" to it. (See Chapter 17, "The Wonderful World of Black and White," for more info on the black and white image.) But you'd definitely want to create a grayscale copy of an RGB image that you knew was destined to become an image for the front page of a black-and-white newsletter.

The same holds true on occasions when you need an indexed color copy of your original RGB masterpiece. Wallpaper is only one instance in which using the right Index commands gives you pleasing results from a less color-capable file type. Video screen shows, word processing programs, and other applications need a graphical helping hand on occasion, and they don't always have the capability to display or import an RGB-mode image saved in a TIF file format.

When you installed Photoshop, you took a big step toward professional imaging. But the level of perfection you can achieve won't matter much if your client runs a presentation package in DOS on an XT that can display only 16 colors. For such an assignment, you gain more control by decreasing the image's resolution and the number of colors available for the image. You still have the 24-bit original, and you will overwhelm the client with the clarity and graphical sumptuousness in your art that you bring to the client's system.

Try using 256-color wallpaper in Windows. Before you boot into the Windows session, though, specify Windows' default VGA video driver. You'll be appalled by how awful the image looks. This reaction is analogous to how your client would respond to your work if you failed to fine-tune it with indexed color that suits its modest monitor capabilities.

You broaden your knowledge, and then your abilities, by knowing how to swing from limb to limb on the graphics tree.

The RGB Image

Earlier, when you learned about indexed color, you also learned something about 24-bit RGB images. The RGB image is the pinnacle of pixel-rendering capability—and also eats up hard drive space as though megabytes are equivalent to so many salted peanuts. When you want to edit a superb color picture into an award-winner, this is definitely the image type you want to use. RGB should also be your preferred image mode for working in Photoshop, and you'll soon see why.

TrueColor and RGB Color

TrueColor is the popular name for what color experts in the computer field have called RGB color since its inception. Technically, *TrueColor* is a description of color capability as it applies to both RGB images and a video display running 16.7 million colors. RGB images are unmapped and freely draw from the "color well" of your system because the file type's capacity matches the technological capability to display color on a PC. This lack of mapping constraints leads to another quality of the RGB file—its organization of color into channels.

Using Channels

Photoshop sees a 24-bit RGB image as having three channels of color information: one for red, one for green, and one for blue. Each channel works with eight bits of color information—a gamut of brightness values from 0 and 255. The three channels, when combined, can hold 256 by 256 by 256, or 16.7 million, possible colors.

Grayscale and indexed color, on the other hand, have a maximum of 256 values, and Photoshop sees them as having only one channel. The three channels of 24-bit RGB image files give you a lot of room for experimentation. Figure 1.11 shows the channels of a 24-bit scanned image as displayed on Photoshop's Channels palette. If you'd like to see how the three component channels display brightness to make up an RGB image, choose **W**indow, **P**alettes, Show **C**hannels (or simply press F7; Macintosh users press F11). Next, click on the Channels tab, click on the pop-up menu button (to the right of the Channels tab) to choose Palette Options, and then click on the large thumbnail-size radio button.

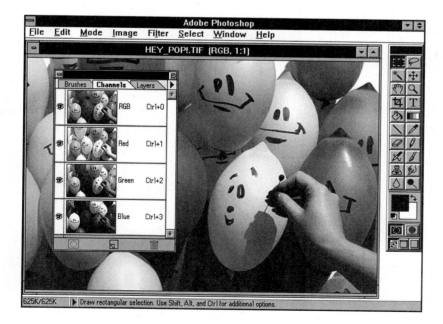

Figure 1.11

An RGB image has three separate channels that you can work with in Photoshop.

Notice the different densities in each component image. The "fourth channel" on the Channels palette, the RGB composite, is actually the normal view of an image, as you'd see it in Photoshop. The default view of an image is always the RGB composite "channel," and the individual color-component channels can be seen by clicking on the title bar of the Channels palette, or by pressing Ctrl+1, 2, 3, and so on. Channels that users create are called Alpha channels.

In Photoshop, an RGB image can have a total of 24 channels of information within it, as later chapters explain. The important thing to note here is that because you can work with RGB components in different channel views, you have ample opportunity to fine-tune parts of an image to enhance it overall.

In addition to channels, RGB image mode also supports layers: a way of isolating bitmap image areas, refining them, then merging different image areas back into the background image. Indexed color mode does not support layers.

Vector images are called *object-oriented images* because each piece you build in this sort of design program always remains a separate object that you can change later. By using channels and layers in an RGB-type bitmap image, you can achieve close to the same advantage. TrueColor, 24-bit, RGB image quality, combined with the flexibility of saving selections in user-defined channels (Alpha channels) and on discreet layers, provide the Photoshop user with advantages found on both the bitmap and vector branches of the computer graphics tree.

Using Photoshop Tools and Filters with RGB Color Images

As mentioned earlier, some of Photoshop's tools and filters don't really work with an indexed, line art, or grayscale image unless you convert the image to RGB color, using the **M**odes menu. This action doesn't improve the quality of the image; it simply provides higher color capability in which your designs can grow. The reason you'd want to convert these images to RGB color is to apply color to a grayscale image, to color in line art, or to refine an indexed color image.

You can define Photoshop's Brush tips as having a certain degree of hardness, or amount of "spread." You do this by double-clicking on a Brush tip on the Brushes palette, or by creating a new brush by double-clicking on a blank space on the palette. Additionally, the Brushes palette's Paintbrush Options tab provides a mode in which to paint, degrees of opacity, options for fading a stroke to transparent or background color, and a Wet **E**dges option that creates paint strokes similar to watercoloring.

All the Brush tip options are available for use with grayscale and RGB mode images. They enable you to create a very soft edge wherever you paint and can be useful when you retouch photographic images. For example, you can make the SOFTCONE

image look a little more drippy by painting an area at the bottom of the ice cream. In figure 1.12, the left side of the screen shows the ice cream cone as an RGB image; the right side, as an indexed color image. As you can see, the RGB image has greater color capability and Photoshop offers greater control over how foreground color is applied. In contrast, an indexed color image provides Photoshop with a very narrow range of color capability; while you edit the image, the options for the brush tip are practically nonexistent.

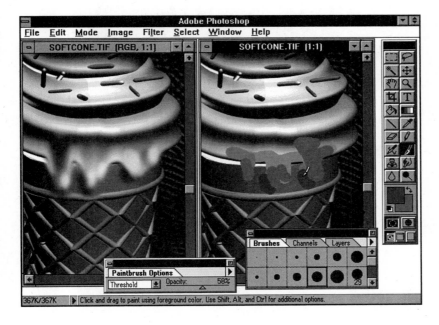

Figure 1.12

You cannot use all of Photoshop's powers with an indexed color image.

Many other Photoshop features—including gradient fills, soft edges for the editing and painting tools, and stretching or skewing an image—cannot be used with an indexed color image. Other Photoshop techniques simply do not work as well with indexed color images because they cannot use the gamut of 16.7 million colors available to RGB images. For example, with an RGB image, Photoshop can use the gamut of 16.7 million colors to simulate ink or paint "bleed" left on a canvas by a physical brush, by lightening adjacent pixels ever so slightly. Figure 1.13 zooms in on an RGB image (shown on the left side) and an indexed color image (shown on the right) to demonstrate Photoshop's soft-edge capability.

High color capability is the secret to soft and smooth edges in Photoshop. Even when you use the Type tool to caption an image, the Type tool's Anti-Aliasing feature requires that you use an RGB image mode to create clean type.

Figure 1.13

Soft edges are produced by using several different shades of the same value with an RGB mode image.

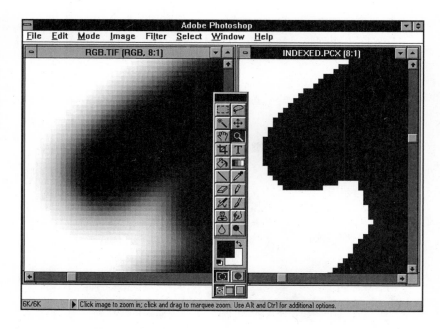

Spotting the Differences between Pixels, Dots, and Samples

Although these digital image types differ substantially, they also have much in common. The common heritage all bitmap image types share is in their fabrication from pixels. *Pixels* are a unit of measurement, like inches or gallons, but refer to a quantity specific to computer graphics.

Occasionally you also see and hear references to *dots* and *samples*. Pixels, dots, and samples are used to measure work at various stages of its completion on a PC. A common misconception is that they are the same thing, especially because professionals tend to use the terms interchangeably. In this section you learn the difference between pixels, dots, and samples.

Samples versus Dots

When scanning an image, you set the scanner to a certain *sampling resolution*. This resolution determines how many digital *samples per inch* the scanner creates from a source image. At the acquisition phase, the scanner views the image through an imaginary grid and then assigns each space in this grid a color value based on an equal area of original, physical image.

However, most documentation that accompanies scanner hardware refers to samples per inch as *dpi*, or *dots per inch*. Therefore, you can call your scanner settings 150 dpi, 75 dpi, and so on. Don't confuse different kinds of dots per inch, however. A laser printer's dpi is not the same as the dots (samples) per inch that a scanner produces. In fact, a scanned image at 150 dpi (*samples* per inch) is actually best represented by a laser print generated at 1200 dpi.

Throughout this book, resolutions for scanned images are measured in dpi to follow convention. In chapter 23, "Personal Printing Basics," we redefine the term "dot" as it's used to describe a basic component of printing.

Pixels and Resolution

For acquired (sampled) images in Photoshop, different measurements are used. A *pixel* is a unit of light as displayed on your monitor, which is usually where you view your actual imaging work. *Pixels per inch* is called a measurement of *resolution* also when you work on an acquired image.

Figure 1.14 shows two images in Photoshop that are exactly the same height and width, but are expressed in different pixels per inch. The left side shows a 25-pixel-per-inch image, and the right side shows the same image at 150 pixels per inch. When you acquire an image at a low sampling rate, such as 25 dpi, Photoshop is forced to display the image information using fewer pixels per inch. To do that, Photoshop makes the pixels larger. A pixel's dimensions aren't fixed the way a centimeter or an inch is.

To do precision work on an image, you depend on pixel resolution. Chapter 2, "Acquiring a Digital Image," explains the relationship between resolution and image dimensions, but your basic working knowledge starts here: Sample your work at a resolution and image size that's a comfortable fit for your work. Later if you want to enlarge a saved image, you must lower the pixel-per-inch ratio. The image then tends to get fuzzy and "computery" looking. This effect is similar to what happens when you blow up a film negative too much and begin to see the film's grain. Pixels are the digital image's equivalent to film grain. Bitmap images are resolution-dependent; as with film photography, a finite amount of visual detail is captured during the acquisition phase. The only way to add more original information to the digital image is to scan the source image again.

If you need to produce wallpaper or a computer slide show, using pixels per inch as the standard of measurement in Photoshop is very helpful. To switch to pixels, first select Image Size from the Image menu. This displays the Image Size dialog box. Then, in the box's New Size window, click on the buttons adjacent to the scroll boxes to the right of the Width, Height, and Resolution text boxes until the scroll boxes display pixels as the new unit of measurement. Photoshop then tells you that the drippy ice cream cone measures 514 by 730, at 250 pixels per inch.

Figure 1.14

*Examples of a
low-resolution
and high-
resolution image.*

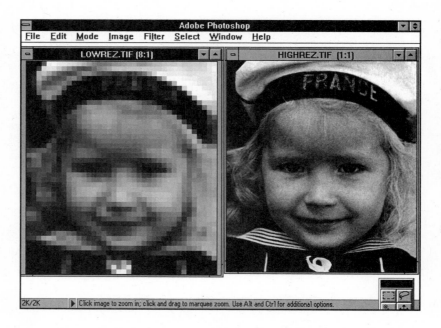

If you want to fill the screen from border to border, the image size would have to be 640 by 480 pixels, 600 by 800, or 1024 by 768 pixels, depending on the monitor mode you are using with your video card.

Regardless of monitor mode, 72 to 96 pixels per inch is the maximum a monitor displays, so if your slide show consists of the drippy ice cream cone, it contains more than three times the number of pixels per inch necessary to display it. By unchecking the File Size box in the Image Size dialog box, you can respecify the number of pixels per inch for the image, and decrease the number of pixels so that the long dimension of the image fits comfortably onscreen, as shown in figure 1.15. When a pixel-per-inch value for an image is greater than your display resolution, your system simply ignores the excess information when displaying it, it takes longer to read the image into system RAM, and the file size is needlessly large for the purposes of viewing at a 1:1 size.

To better see the relationship between image dimension and resolution, try leaving the File Size box checked, then increase or decrease the dimensions of an image. You'll see that as image size increases, resolution decreases. This is the way Photoshop maintains original image information when you resize a bitmap image.

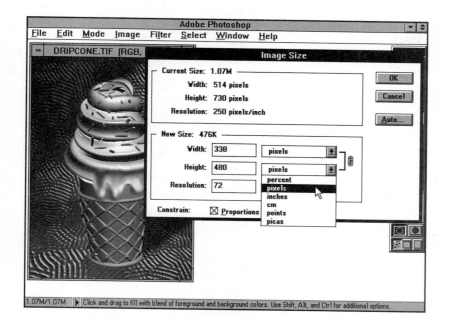

Understanding File Formats

No chapter on digital images would be complete if it didn't make some recommendations as to how to store your acquired image in an ideal file format, so the next few sections focus on the different types of file formats in which different types of images are best saved.

Digital images are like ideas; they literally live as information stored from one nanosecond to the next as electrical impulses stored in RAM as the "thought is being held." These digital ideas eventually have to be given a shape, a format written to disk. Before you choose File, Save, consider which file format is proper for holding your digital image/idea. The image may not look the same the next time it's read into RAM if the form—the file format you give it—isn't capable of holding the visual information you want it to hold.

The right format for a specific image type sustains the quality of the image you toiled over in Photoshop, but the wrong one can turn the image into a cartoon. The following sections cover the most popular file formats in which you can save your image. If you have a special application you use with your imaging, it may require a special file format, in which case it's best to check the application's documentation for file-format preferences. In any case, this chapter briefly covers some of the more exotic formats in addition to the most common ones.

Formats for RGB Images

The TIF (Tagged Image File) format was created as the most versatile format for color channel images. One of the advantages of saving images in this format is *portability*. A TIF image saved on a PC can be read by a Macintosh, a host of UNIX platforms, and other, proprietary platforms. An image saved in the TIF format, unlike formats associated only with indexed color, can have special information (Alpha) channels within it. The TIF format has an open-ended architecture. The bitmap image is tagged with a header that tells applications what sort of image it is; this header can be written to include information software engineers haven't even thought of yet, to ensure future compatibility with whatever innovations are dreamed up in later versions of Photoshop and other programs.

You can save line art and indexed images in the TIF format. Before you do, however, you should consider whether a larger file size is okay because the construction of a TIF header is larger and more complex than that of other formats. Because the TIF format enables you to access all of Photoshop's sophisticated tools and filters, you should save your grayscale scanning in the *.TIF format.

The TrueVision Company developed the Targa file format (which uses the file extension TGA) to work with its proprietary video boards. Since the format's inception, many other companies have adopted it, and Photoshop currently supports the TGA format. A Targa image ports nicely to the Macintosh and vice versa. Like the TIF format, TGA handles high-quality images organized into color channels. However, because Photoshop 3.0 recognizes only a total bit-depth of 32 in images saved to this format, a TGA image file can retain only one extra information channel in addition to the Red, Green, and Blue ones. Additionally, the gamma of Targa format images is higher than that of images saved to the TIF format. Targa images are tuned to take advantage of broadcast television standards; if you're ever handed this format file, the colors may appear washed out when viewed in Photoshop. For information on gamma adjustment, see Chapter 3, "Color Theory and the PhotoCD."

PSD is Photoshop's default file format. It supports all image types, from line art to camera-ready CMYK color. The only problem with saving a file to the PSD format is that few other graphics programs can read this proprietary format. You should save an image in PSD format only if you haven't decided the final format you want for the image, have left user-defined Alpha channels in the image, or have unmerged layers you need to work on later within the image.

PSD and TIF files both support multiple image channels, as well as vector-based paths you can create in Photoshop. *Un*like a TIF image, Photoshop's PSD format can hold a theoretically unlimited number of user-defined channels. The Background layer of a PSD image file can hold 24 channels (including the color component channels), and every layer you assign to the image can hold 24 channels; there is no mathematical limit to the number of layers you can add to a PSD image. So you'll probably run out

of system RAM before you run out of channel space! Later in this book you'll become familiar with the virtues and dangers associated with saving an image with extra channels, layers, and paths.

TIF, TGA, and PSD are the most common file formats for saving RGB images as data that includes channel information. Some of the formats in the next section retain color values but cannot save data organized in channels.

PCX Images

The ZSoft Corporation created the PCX file format quite some time ago as a proprietary format that many software companies have since adopted. The PCX format is excellent for indexed and line art images because its file format is not as complex as the TIF format. The downside of PCX images, besides featuring only one channel of color information, is that so many versions of the format exist. Because the PCX standard was openly published so that independent developers could tinker with it, this format is continually being upgraded.

Photoshop supports version 5 of PCX, but you may encounter an image saved in an earlier version. If so, the image might not look very good. You're safe in saving an indexed, grayscale, or line art image as a PCX file as long as you remember that you must convert it to RGB mode in Photoshop to take advantage of soft brushes, gradient fills, and other useful features.

BMP

The BMP file extension indicates that Microsoft technology was used to create the file's image. Like PCX, the BMP file format uses indexed color. BMP is also a platform-independent format, so you can view it on a PC running DOS, Windows on DOS, Windows NT, or OS/2. However, you cannot use BMP files with Macintosh programs, so if you, your service bureau, boss, or friends use a Macintosh, save your images as TIFs rather than BMPs. Although Photoshop encodes a color image to BMP format in 1-, 4-, 8-, or 24-bit color, the color space of the BMP format does not support channels. You may wind up with a single-channel BMP image as large as the same image saved as a TIF, because the lookup table for a 24-bit BMP is positively overwhelming!

PICT

Many Macintosh applications, including the Macintosh System software, use PICT format graphics. This is the format that the Macintosh Clipboard uses to transfer graphic information between programs. The PICT file format can save images with either a 16- or 32-bit color capability, but not 24 bits/pixel. Although this format is the most basic and common format used on Macintosh computers, PICT files can't be used by programs that run other operating systems. If you need to share images with non-Macintosh users, or if you intend to send the image to a service bureau (imagesetters have a very hard time processing PICT files), use another format such as TIF or TGA.

GIFs

H&R Block's CompuServe information service created the file format *GIF* (Graphics Interchange Format) to shorten downloading time for its subscribers. GIF files are small and support indexed color image types, as well as line art and grayscale images. Different types of computers can read this format, but only if your software reads the GIF format. Photoshop reads GIF files just fine, whereas other, less capable programs may display a less-than-perfect GIF image on their workspace. Photoshop also writes to the GIF format, but only if an image is in indexed color mode.

Beware of different versions of GIF. GIF files can be read in a DOS environment, and they're created as both *interlaced* and *noninterlaced* varieties so that someone reading a GIF image on-line on a BBS can get a low-resolution preview to help him or her decide whether to download the image. Interlaced versions of GIF files cannot be read by some programs. Use a GIF file format for an indexed image only after you know what the specific programs GIF format requirements are.

Less Frequently Used File Formats

The following formats are not used as frequently as those you'll be using in this book's Photoshop exercises. However, Photoshop is a very complete imaging program designed to accommodate every need and file format. The following sections cover some of the lesser-known Photoshop Save As capabilities you may want to use for special situations.

JPEG

JPEG is both a file format and compression scheme that Photoshop supports. Chapter 2 discusses this scheme in detail. File compression is always a useful capability to have when dealing with images whose file size is more than a megabyte, but don't save your original as a JPG file until you've read about JPEG in Chapter 2.

IFF for the Amiga

If you're sending an image to an Amiga Commodore computer system, use an IFF file format on a copy of your work.

RAW

If you need to work on an image for a different application on a platform with which you're not familiar, you might try using the RAW file format. Photoshop takes an image saved in RAW format and creates several channels of color information, each having levels of color in a gamut from 0 (black) to 255 (white). RAW saves unmapped images, writing the color information as a stream of bytes rather than using the lookup table method of indexed color images.

Still *Other* File Formats!

You can also write Scitex CT, MacPaint, PIXAR, EPS, and a few other really exotic file formats from Photoshop. However, if you are new to computer graphics, you are unlikely to encounter the need. Chapter 20, "Mixed Media and Photoshop," covers encapsulated PostScript images (EPS) and explains how this vector-type image file is converted to bitmap format for use in Photoshop. For further information, check the Photoshop documentation, Photoshop Help, or the service bureau that does your imaging work.

The Long and Short of the Data Byte Stream

Usually you want to acquire an image in 24 bits, view it as an RGB image, and save it as a TIF file. This chapter has provided ample examples to justify this preference. Photoshop can make the most out of an image sampled at high resolution rates, one that has the color capability to allow the full complement of Photoshop tools to be at your disposal.

Photoshop takes into account the physical dimensions and the resolution of an acquired image when it presents you with a view of the image on your monitor; the larger the image file size, the more completely the image fills the workspace. You must decide at what viewing resolution you're comfortable with editing an image—someplace between an image file so large it slows down your system when loaded, and one so small it requires a 3:1 or 4:1 viewing resolution to fill the screen.

Although you can always elect to zoom out of an image that is larger than one megabyte to see it in its totality, reduced viewing resolutions are less of a problem than images you must enlarge to view. If a small image has been inadequately sampled, the more you zoom in, the more conspicuous the pixels—the image's color building blocks—become. When you don't have sufficient acquired information about an image, editing becomes a chore and causes eyestrain.

PCX, BMP, and MacPaint are the most common file formats for storing line art and indexed images. To work with such formats with Photoshop's full complement of features, you must convert them to RGB mode. To see the wonderful ways you can enhance grayscale images in Photoshop, you should store them in TIF format, not as indexed images. Any conversion from a higher color capability to a lesser color mode involves the reduction of colors. With bitmap images, colors are everything; you necessarily destroy image information when you switch color modes. The solution is to always save an image to a file format that retains an acquired image's native color characteristics.

Acquiring a Digital Image

In addition to creating a digital painting in Photoshop or in another bitmap graphics application, there are two main methods for making a digital copy of a source image to bring into Photoshop. One way is to let Kodak digitize your camera film onto a PhotoCD. Another method involves scanning your source image. PhotoCDs are explored in the next chapter, but for now let's devote some time to the most versatile tool for acquiring digitized images—the scanner.

Scanning is almost an art in itself. A well-executed scan can be used immediately as a digital image that you can enhance or edit in Photoshop. On the other hand, a hastily done scan can delay your creative endeavors, requiring time and effort just to get the image into a workable state. Whether it's artwork, a photo, or a simple cartoon, different scanner options are available for bringing different image types into Photoshop.

Your monitor's settings and capabilities also play a substantial role in the scheme of scanning, because it's difficult to work with a wonderful RGB image if you can't see it! If your work deals more with acquired images than original computer graphics, this chapter shows you how to get the best information from the source material, so that you can refine and work with it in Photoshop.

Viewing an Acquired Image Accurately

Before you *capture* (scan) an image, it's vital that your monitor can display the same bit-depth or bits-per-pixel ratio as your capture. Have you ever looked at a high-quality image in Windows while you were using a standard VGA video driver? The image looks posterized, hard on the eyes, and generally crummy, right?

The posterization happened because many files in the TIFF and Targa image file format contain 24 bits per pixel. This 24-bit-per-pixel color is RGB mode, which contains much more information than the 4-bit-per-pixel standard VGA mode can handle.

Understanding Video Display Modes

When you use a standard VGA video driver, you can display only 16 unique colors. A VGA display mode is good enough for working on most spreadsheets, but it's a display mode with an inadequate number of colors if you want to realistically view or work with high-quality digital images. Before you begin to scan (and certainly before you begin to edit!) a high-quality color image, make sure that your video card supports at least 16-bit (32,768 colors, or *HiColor*). Better yet is a 24-bit, TrueColor, RGB (16.7 million colors) video mode.

An important practice to adopt before scanning is to make sure you are running a video mode that's in synch with the bit-depth of the scanner setting. For example, if you're scanning an original image with a 24-bit scanner setting, your monitor should be capable of displaying 24 bits per pixel. When Photoshop is forced to display a 24-bit image with an inadequate number of display colors, it performs something called "dithering."

Dithering is a method of arranging adjacent colored pixels on the screen to "fake" a color that's in your work, but not available in the current video mode. Monitor display dithering is something that happens only on your screen; it doesn't change the information in your image file. If you're viewing a 24-bit, 16.7 million color digital image with an 8-bit video driver loaded, you'll see a dithered display of the image on your monitor. Yet when you then switch to the appropriate 24-bit video driver, you'll then see the true image colors without any dithering.

In figure 2.1, an RGB, 24-bit depth image is displayed in Photoshop's workspace while using an 8-bit depth video mode. By default, Photoshop represents the 16.7 million possible colors by dithering all of the image's color information into patterns, using only 256 colors to crudely represent the image. This look is similar to the patterns Windows uses to simulate different colors in its Paintbrush program while working with a 4-bit video driver.

Figure 2.1

Dithered patterns are an attempt to approximate colors in an image that a particular video mode won't handle.

Diffusion dithering is another way Photoshop displays an image's colors when a limited number of display colors are available (see fig. 2.2). Although it's not as obvious or as visually distracting as pattern dithering, it is still an inaccurate view of the image and not an acceptable one for proofing captured images. TrueColor, RGB images that are displayed by using diffusion dithering look the same on-screen as image files to which diffusion dithering has actually been applied.

As you learned in Chapter 1, "Understanding Image Types, Formats, and Resolutions," when an RGB image is dithered down to an indexed color image type, the image file displays and prints with patterns instead of unique, solid color areas. Diffusion dithering is also called *error diffusion*, because it's an imprecise view of the color data in an image file.

Stop Unlike its predecessor, Photoshop 3 does not run with less than a 256-color video driver loaded.

Figure 2.2

Diffusion dithering approximates the full range of colors, using a limited palette.

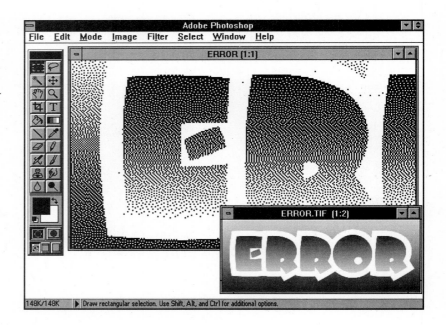

If you are a Macintosh user, you can set the color capability of the video display by choosing the System folder, then the Control Panel folder, and finally the Monitors control panel. With the Monitors control displayed, click on the Color radio button, then choose Millions. If Millions (or Thousands) is not available, this means either the VRAM on the video card or the VRAM in the Macintosh computer is not sufficient to run HiColor (Thousands) or TrueColor (Millions) with your monitor and model of Macintosh.

Windows users have a choice between Microsoft generic video drivers and special drivers that came with their computer system's video card. If you're running Windows with Microsoft's VGA driver (16 colors) loaded, you'll get the message shown in figure 2.3 when you double-click on the Photoshop icon in Program Manager. Your only option is to Quit.

Installing a Video Driver

Installing a video driver of sufficient color capability to run Photoshop isn't hard; it's simply procedural. The following steps lead you through the process of loading a new video driver into Windows. After the process is complete, you'll need to restart Windows to complete the changes.

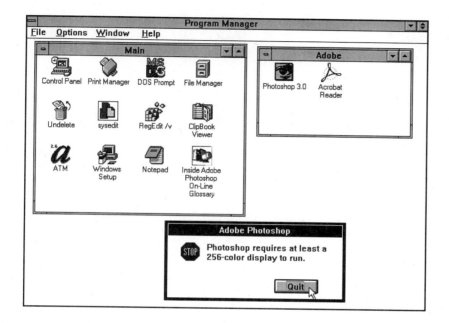

Figure 2.3

Photoshop 3 does not load if your video driver can't display 8 bit-per-pixel color.

Changing Video Drivers

Close any active Windows applications you may have open	Changing system settings with an application running is not a good idea.
Double-click on the Windows Manager	Displays the Windows Setup icon in Program Setup dialog box.

If Windows Setup is not visible in any of the program groups in Program Manager, choose **F**ile, **N**ew. Click on the Program Item radio button, click on OK, and type **SETUP.EXE** in the Command Line: field. Type **Windows Setup** in the **D**escription field, and click on OK.

Click on **O**ptions, then choose **C**hange System Settings	Displays the Change System Settings dialog box.
Click on the down arrow next to the **D**isplay drop-down list, then choose OEM display (requires disk from OEM)	Displays the Windows Setup dialog box.

Depending on who manufactured your video card, the disks that came with your card might require a separate installation routine to decompress the video driver files onto your hard disk. Additionally, some manufacturers insert a program in the Windows Control Panel and recommend that you use their utility program to change video drivers instead of using

continues

continued

Windows Setup. Check your video card's documentation to find out the correct procedure for decompressing their video drivers from floppy disk.

If an MIS director or a store sets up your computer for you, you might already have video drivers of high color capability installed. Check the Drivers drop-down list as you scroll down to the OEM option. The driver you need might already be on the list (it's already installed on your system).

Type the path where the video drivers are located on floppy or on your hard disk in the field in the Windows Setup dialog box; click on a video driver of at least 256 colors (more is better); click on OK, then click on OK again	Windows displays the Change System Settings dialog box.
Click on **N**ew	Windows loads the new video driver from floppy or other location on your hard disk, then displays the Exit Windows Setup dialog box.
Choose **R**estart Windows	Closes Windows and restarts it with your new video driver loaded.

Figure 2.4 is a visual synopsis of the video driver swapping procedure. It's not as complicated as it looks, but it's necessary for Photoshop to run.

Figure 2.5 is a screen capture of a monitor that uses a 24-bit color video display driver, displaying an RGB image. You can find the NONE!.TIF image in the CHAP02 subdirectory of the *Inside Adobe Photoshop 3* Bonus CD. Open the file if you'd like to see, on your own system, an example of an RGB image when you have the appropriate video driver installed.

Matching Video Display to Image Type

You don't need an expensive SVGA video board to use Photoshop. The important thing is to have a video display that matches the type of digital images you acquire, so that you can view them accurately. Most 1 MB video cards today support 16.7 million colors at a 640 × 480 pixel screen resolution. This is the resolution (24-bit, TrueColor) at which you can do your most satisfying and accurate color-image editing. However, if most of your work involves grayscale art and photos, an 8-bit video card and driver can display a grayscale scan of a source image with perfect fidelity.

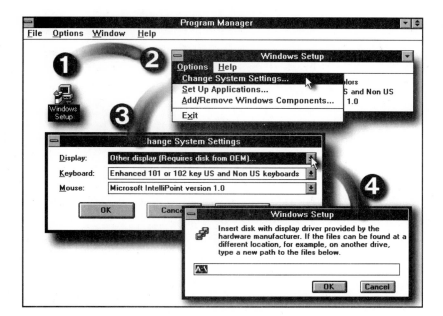

Figure 2.4

Choose a video driver that's capable of displaying at least 256 colors.

Figure 2.5

An image captured at 16.7 million colors, displayed with a 16.7 million color video driver.

Even though you can accurately display a grayscale image that you scanned and saved using a 256-color video driver, editing a grayscale image in Photoshop is a frustrating experience unless you first switch to a driver capable of supporting 16 or 24 bits. Although an 8-bit, 256-color-capable video driver can display all the possible 256 shades of gray in a grayscale image, Photoshop has special features that require more information than 256 shades to be displayed.

For instance, Photoshop's Quick Mask feature makes easy work of defining a selection area in an image by displaying a selected or masked image area in a tinted color. This additional color needs to be mapped to the display *in addition to* the other 256 shades, and a 256-color video driver then becomes inadequate for showing you 257 colors! In this instance, Photoshop dithers your display when Quick Mask mode is active, then returns you to the accurate representation of a grayscale image when Quick Mask is turned off.

Having Photoshop re-map your display back and forth between dithered and nondithered is a confusing way to edit an image, and it taxes your computer's video subsystem needlessly. When acquiring or viewing a grayscale image, an 8-bit, 256-color video display capability is fine, but when it comes time to edit a digital image, use at least a 16-bit, 32,768-color video display mode.

Accuracy is a prime element in the successful manipulation of delicate digitized images in the PC world. Your image goes through many twists and turns in the acquiring, modifying, enhancing, and reproducing phases. It is best, then, to get an honest look at an acquired image from the very beginning. And this means not bothering with dithering.

A trip through the scanning process is next, starting from a pre-purchase point of view. Many different kinds of scanners can sample 24-bit color that you can display on your monitor in 24-bit, RGB, nondithered color. We'll narrow the field as we take a look at each type of scanning hardware.

Examining Scanner Hardware

Scanning hardware can be classified into three basic types: sheet-fed scanners, hand-held scanners, and flatbed scanners. Each type has advantages and disadvantages. The type of scanner you choose depends on the type of work you want to do.

All scanning devices bounce light off a physical sample source onto a photo-sensitive grid. The grid is composed of lots of cells; each cell passes along the unit of light information it receives. A single light information unit (a pixel) becomes a part of a collective tapestry that winds up on your computer as a digital image.

Where this photo-sensitive grid is located in the scanner, how well the hardware is designed, and the method of transporting the source image across the photo-sensitive grid are what distinguishes the different types of scanners.

The Sheet-Fed Scanner

The sheet-fed scanner is an economical approach to scanning. You can get one for under $300 if you shop smart. The reason a sheet-fed scanner is so inexpensive is that it uses rollers to pass the source image across the scanner's photo-sensitive cells. Rollers are a very economical transport mechanism used in every sort of electronic and household device, from photocopiers to fax machines.

Many sheet-fed scanners support color, but before you're sold on this scanner type, consider how they work—you are required to affix a 4×6 color photo to a sheet of copier paper to feed it through! This sometimes jams the scanner, and the photo is going to look the worse for wear after it is fed through a scanner of this type. Sheet-fed scanners are inexpensive and ideal for capturing the printed word on paper, but definitely are not suited for serious image acquisition.

Hand-Held Scanners

The hand scanner is inexpensive, fast, small, and currently comes in grayscale as well as 24-bit color versions. Hand-held scanners are compact because there's no transport mechanism to pass source material across the photo-sensitive cells. Instead, the transport mechanism is your hand! Figure 2.6 shows the Logitech Color ScanMan used to digitize some of the exercise images you'll find on the companion CD.

The downside to all hand-scanners is that they work best with source material that is less than four inches wide. You also need a very steady hand to evenly guide the scanner across your source material. A cough or a wiggle on your part produces a noticeable defect in the digital image that's almost impossible to correct later. But all things considered, hand scanners are good entry-level hardware for the budding imagist.

Flatbed Scanners

Although flatbed scanners are more expensive, are physically the size of a photo-copier, and take longer to digitize sources than hand-held scanners, they produce more professional results. They handle larger and bulkier source material, and you don't need a steady hand to operate them because the scanner controls the speed and motion of the sampling pass.

Figure 2.6

The Logitech Color ScanMan.

Flatbed scanners also offer an array of options. The flatbed scanner shown in figure 2.7 offers a wide range of resolutions, can produce halftones, and handles up to 8 1/2-by-14 inch source material.

Figure 2.7

A flatbed scanner.

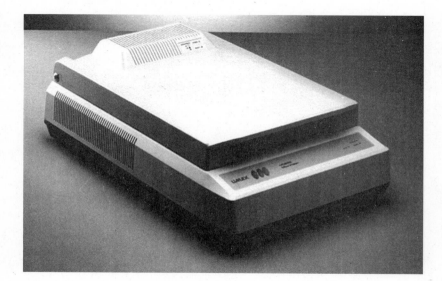

Which Scanner Is Right for You?

Flatbed and hand-held scanners are good choices for Photoshop work. A color flatbed was used to scan source images for figures in this book and to acquire sample images for the companion CD. If you plan to use Photoshop professionally, purchase a flatbed scanner that gives you the features described and explained next. The imaging hobbyist can get terrific results with a color hand-held or even a grayscale scanner, but professional work demands professional tools, from the source image straight through to Photoshop.

The digital camera is yet another method for acquiring digital images. A digital camera comprises a technology somewhere between scanners and camcorders. It captures images in much the same way as a scanner, but you use them under different circumstances. Digital cameras are currently a young technology, offering varying degrees of quality and a typically steep price, but they are becoming more capable, affordable, and important in the digital imaging world. Digital cameras are covered later in this chapter.

Developing Scanner Standards

Scanning on the IBM/PC platform was not the easiest thing to do before the development of a standard in late 1990. You usually had to scan with the proprietary software supplied by your scanner manufacturer, save your file, start your imaging application, and then view the image. Every scanner's software worked differently. Sometimes you couldn't even see the resulting image as you scanned! This process worked for many professionals, but it was primitive, clumsy, and limited.

The development and popularity of Windows 3.0 encouraged a consortium of companies to create a standard that worked in Windows, making scanning easier and more flexible for the user. The consortium, made up of representatives from Aldus, Logitech, Hewlett-Packard, Caere, and Eastman Kodak, developed and promoted the TWAIN standard. Any scanner that supports TWAIN works with any software that supports the TWAIN standard. Installing and using a TWAIN-compliant scanner is a breeze.

The lion's share of scanners manufactured in 1994 are TWAIN-compliant and offer TWAIN interfaces for both IBM/PC and the Macintosh. Programs such as Photoshop that speak TWAIN can recognize a TWAIN driver and host a scanning session from directly within the application's interface.

Note　Aldus Corporation dubbed TWAIN the *Toolkit **W**ithout **A**n Interesting **N**ame.
However, Logitech's explanation is a tad less whimsical and more descriptive: "We
selected this name to describe this unique interface that brings together two
entities—applications and input devices—in a meeting of the 'twain.'"*

If you bought a scanner recently, it probably supports TWAIN. If you are not sure,
check your documentation or call your scanner manufacturer. Additionally, you may
be able to get a TWAIN upgrade for an existing, non-TWAIN scanner. Because
Photoshop is TWAIN compliant, you can scan an image directly into the Photoshop
workspace and have it immediately available for use—if your scanner is also TWAIN
compliant.

Photoshop also supports some common scanners that do not use TWAIN. When you
install Photoshop, pick your scanner from the list that the installation program offers
(or one that your scanner can emulate), and you should be in business in terms of
Photoshop imaging. The procedures for starting a scanner and operating its controls
vary from manufacturer to manufacturer, but from within an imaging application, the
TWAIN interface is almost always found under the Acquire command, usually under
the File menu. Check your scanner documentation for more details.

Color Scanning Recommendations

Inevitably, monetary considerations go hand-in-hand with investing in a digital
darkroom. If you're coming from a chemical photography background, you already
appreciate the magnitude of difference between outfitting your darkroom with color
versus black-and-white developing and printing goods. New hardware and software
add-ons to your equipment, as well as to your wish list, crop up almost daily. For this
reason, it's difficult to recommend a specific scanner that suits your individual taste
and budget.

But we, the authors, do have a personal preference we can share as to the type (not
brand) of scanning device that, through experience, has proved to be of the most
worth for digitally capturing images. Buy either a 24-bit color scanner, or buy a 256
grayscale model. Don't try to hedge with one of the 16-bit (also called HiColor)
models available for less money, because if you do this, you'll be cheating your own
vision. Grayscale and 24-bit color are the standards most high-end image editing
programs prefer to work with, and they're also the color modes that correspond to
real-world photography.

An 8-bit grayscale scanner captures all the available tonal information in a black-and-
white photo. Computer images of the grayscale type are built around 256 possible
shades, and an 8-bit-capable scanner captures them all. A TrueColor, 24-bit sampling
accurately captures all the color information contained in an RGB-type image; 8 bits

for the red channel, 8 for green, and 8 for blue. A 16-bit scanner simply can't fill the maximum 8-bits-per-color channel an RGB image format is capable of handling. An RGB, 24-bit scanner is the closest you can afford to capture color the way the human eye sees it.

24-bits is not the upper threshold of scanning capability, just a sampling rate nonmillionaires use to produce fine work. 32-bit scanning is commonly used when original color photographs are destined for direct output to commercial process color printing presses that produce high-quality magazine work. Photoshop 3 supports 32-bit TWAIN acquisition, but only if your scanner supports 32-bit color.

In 32-bit scanning, the scanner records the Cyan, Magenta, Yellow, and Black (CMYK) color values in the original image. Information about each of the four CMYK color values is stored in a channel that has an 8-bit color depth. By basing the scan of the original color photo around the CMYK color model instead of the RGB color model, the scanned image produces results that are more faithful to the original when transferred to the four process plates used to create an image on the printed page. See Chapter 20, "Mixed Media and Photoshop," for a good example of working with the CMYK color model.

Stop Be aware, though, that 32-bit scanning is not necessarily better than 24-bit RGB acquisition of an image, and that the increase of bit-depth with CMYK scanning is "special purpose" scanning. The CMYK color gamut is different than RGB values— CMYK represents color inks used by commercial presses, and CMYK color images look a little "flat" compared to RGB, 24-bit scans. 32-bit scanning fits the bill only if your intended final output is to process color printing.

In your Photoshop adventures, however, 24-bit sampling captures original image information with perfect fidelity for practically all professional output needs.

How Does TWAIN Work?

For all of its intricacies, TWAIN is simple to understand and easy to use. The application software (Photoshop, for example) calls the source interface supplied by the scanner manufacturer. A *source interface* is an option/dialog box that appears on your screen and offers the controls for the scanner. The exact arrangement of options and the extent of options available to you depend on how many features your scanner has and how the scanner manufacturer decided to arrange the items on the screen.

The following example shows how the Microtek version of the TWAIN source interface is called from Photoshop. If you have a different scanner, your source interface looks a little different, but works in a similar fashion.

Connecting a Scanner to Photoshop through TWAIN

Turn on your scanner and place an image in it to scan. Then from within Photoshop, do the following:

Choose File, Acquire	This command makes selecting a scanning source possible.
Choose Select TWAIN Source	Lists the available source interfaces to connect Photoshop with the desired TWAIN device (see fig. 2.8).

If you own a 32-bit scanner, you can choose Select TWAIN32 Source from the Acquire menu.

Choose your scanner from the list	The Microtek Image Scanner was selected in this example. You'll see other selections, depending on your own scanner.
Click on the OK button	Selects the source interface.

You shouldn't have to set this option again unless you install a different TWAIN-compliant scanner.

Choose File, Acquire, TWAIN	Calls the source interface (see fig. 2.9).
Click on the Prescan button	This tells the Microtek scanner to run a low-resolution pass over the entire sampling area so that the photo's position and orientation can be checked.

Figure 2.9 shows you what the layout of the Microtek interface looks like with a photo in place.

Because a fair amount of time is involved when a flatbed scanner digitizes a photo, many scanners of this type offer a preview (called *Prescan* on the Microtek model of scanner). It's important to be certain about the image you'll be acquiring *before* you press the Scan button. Otherwise you'll waste valuable time waiting for the flatbed scanner to make its pass(es) over an unwanted, poor, or crooked image. Hand-held scanner owners don't have this preview luxury, or need it, because they have immediate feedback as to whether an image is crooked or upside-down—all they have to do is look down at the scanner as they guide it across the source image.

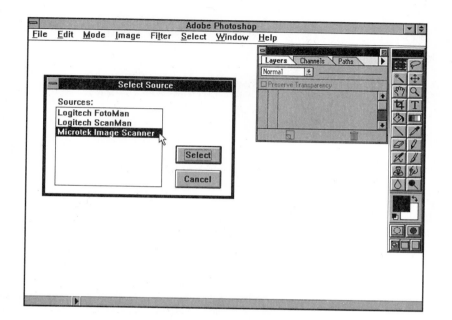

Figure 2.8

Different TWAIN devices require different source interfaces.

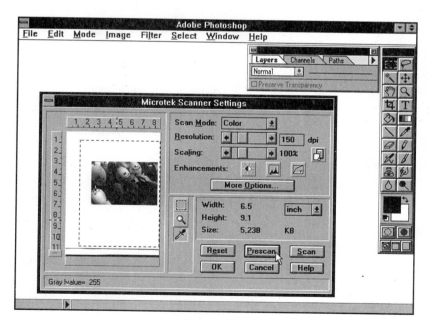

Figure 2.9

The source interface for a TWAIN-compliant scanner appears on top of the Photoshop workspace.

Preparing to Scan

Before you press the Scan button, consider the *type* of image you want to acquire. Color-capable scanners also have settings for grayscale and line art images. Is your source image a black-and-white photo? Is it a line art drawing? Through the TWAIN interface, set your scanner to a mode that matches the type of color information in the source image.

We are using a color photo in this example. The mode choices the Microtek source interface offers are Line Art, Halftone, Grayscale, and Color. We chose Color to capture the full-color image as a 24-bit, 16.7 million possible color, RGB color datastream. This is also the *only* color option the scanner offers, so it wasn't a tough decision to capture the color photo in a color mode!

Tip   If you want to turn a color photo into a grayscale digitized image, let Photoshop do the converting. In the real world, *luminosity*—the brightness found in colors, is not evenly distributed within the RGB channels that make up an RGB digital image. To get a natural-looking grayscale image from a color picture, the relationship of the relative luminosities must be preserved when the color is removed from the original. Most scanners don't automatically compensate for the weighted average of Red, Green, and Blue luminosities when you capture a full-color image using a grayscale setting. But *Photoshop* does when it makes a conversion.

Because Photoshop has the right tools for transforming a color image to grayscale, you scan a color image as a color image when acquiring it digitally. You'll learn all about how Photoshop sees and transforms colors to grayscale in Chapter 17, "The Wonderful World of Black and White."

Resolution Versus Image Dimensions

Before you scan, you should consider what image resolution you want to wind up with. *Resolution* is the frequency of digital samples per inch the scanner creates from a source image. *Image dimensions* (the height and width) are dependent on your scanner's resolution. Both play a role in determining the size and quality of an image you edit and then send to a printer.

If your scanner can change the size, as well as the resolution of a scanned image, let it do the math for you. Otherwise, you'll have to use the relationship between image dimension and resolution to calculate the ideal scan for a specific assignment.

Digital images are made up of pixels, which in turn have a relative size depending on how many per inch you decide to scan from an original image. Without altering the

structure of a digital image file, you can take advantage of a digital truth: Image dimensions increase as image resolution decreases.

Try scanning a 1" × 1" image at a 300 dpi setting, then use the **I**mage, Image **S**ize command within Photoshop to decrease the image's resolution. If you check the Constrain: **F**ile Size box item and then enter **150** in the pixels/inch box, the image's dimensions increase to 2" × 2". By constraining the file size, you change the size of the pixels, not the number or placement of the pixels. Because this process doesn't require any interpolation on Photoshop's part, you don't lose any image quality. What you end up with is a good image size and resolution for printing to a medium-quality publication. When you're given a photo to work with that is destined to appear in print at a size *other* than its original width and height, the benefit of understanding the interrelationship of file size, image dimensions, and image resolution becomes immediately apparent.

On the other hand, you may want to underscan an 8" × 10" photo at 75 dpi, if you know it's going to press as a 4" × 5" image at 150 dpi. It's also important that a scanned image is easy to see when you use Photoshop's tools to modify it. The smaller the pixel-per-inch sample, the larger the pixels appear onscreen, each pixel representing a coarser view of the corresponding area in the original that was scanned. You can retouch an image area more easily if the pixels that make up the image aren't visible at your chosen viewing resolution. It's the same as traditional chemical retouching; restoring a photo that has fine film grain is much easier than muddling through a mass of grain the size of a coffee can lid.

Before you scan an image, ask yourself the following questions:

◆ What dimensions are you comfortable working with when editing a particular image?

A 6" × 4" snapshot sampled at more than 100 dpi, for example, fills your Photoshop workspace at a 100-percent view. When you scan a larger photograph that will be used at a smaller size, you can set your scanner sampling rate anywhere from 100–150 dpi. You'll get a fair-to-average image that you can zoom in on to do your work, and a small image file so that your system's RAM isn't deluged with surplus digital information.

◆ How big is the final print from your Photoshop work going to be?

In this example, a 4" × 6" photo would make a good accompanying graphic for an article in a newsletter. If you're targeting a publication for your work and you want your digital image to be the same size as your original photo, the question then becomes one of resolution.

Chapter 23, "Personal Printing Basics," explains the formulas used to create the best resolution image for hard copy output, but as a simple rule of thumb, use table 2.1 to approximate the resolution of the digitized image for the best printing type.

TABLE 2.1
Sampling Resolutions (Approximate)

Type of Printer	Printer Lines/Inch	Ideal Scanning
2540 dpi imagesetter	133–150 lpi	300 dpi
1200 dpi laser printer or imagesetter	85 lpi	150 dpi
300 dpi laser printer	43–50 dpi	75–100 dpi

Remember that these figures are approximations—a mixture of math combined with experience. Commercial printers' line screens vary, but you can estimate the ideal sampling rate for your scanner by multiplying a printer's lines-per-inch value by two.

Tip   Ask your commercial printer how many lines per inch are the best for his or her presses. The printer can tell you what line screen will be used on your piece to produce the best printed results, and this in turn should be a deciding factor before you scan any image destined for publication.

The hard and fast rule for computer screen presentations, however, is entirely different. A monitor displays graphical images at 72 to 96 pixels per inch. A commercial printers' ink dots are not the same size as a monitor's pixels. If you're scanning an image at a 100-percent, one-to-one ratio, and the image will end up in a computer slide show (such as Lotus Freelance Graphics or Microsoft PowerPoint, for example), you don't need to *sample* (scan) an original image any higher than 96 dpi.

Determining the Best Sampling Rate

Determining the best sampling rate for an image can be a little tricky. If you specify too low a sampling rate, you'll have a coarser image, containing fewer pixels per inch and much less information to work with than you'd have with a higher-resolution scan. The size of the file you get is nice and small, but you can't refine the image or do detail work on the image in Photoshop because "the dots are too big."

More is not necessarily better, though. If you over-sample an image, you end up with a large file that contains more information than you need for editing and/or printing purposes. Large files are a burden on your system's memory resources and hard drive space. Printing a file that has more information in it than a printer can handle takes an eternity, and will most likely irritate any commercial printer or service bureau you engage. Time is money to an imaging service, just as it is to you. Even if you're not professionally printing an image, an image file whose resolution exceeds a laser printer's capability to reproduce is bound to bottleneck the printer queue in an office environment and will not win you a lot of thanks from your coworkers!

One of a Linotronic imagesetter's output resolutions, for example, is 2,540 dots per inch on film. It typically uses a line screen value of 133 lines per inch at this resolution. If you send the Linotronic an image file that was scanned at 600 dpi (twice the ideal scanning resolution for the imagesetter, as shown in table 2.1), the data in the image file is read into memory, spooled to the imagesetter, and then half of it is discarded in the printing process as unnecessary and unusable information.

Always keep an image's final printed dimensions and resolution in mind before you scan an image. It's very easy to get carried away with ambitious scanning without a clue as to the consequences or what the resulting file sizes for these digital captures will be.

Use the information in table 2.2 as a guide to the file size you can expect when scanning 24-bit color images.

TABLE 2.2
Typical Graphic File Sizes

At a sample of	A photo that's (in inches)	Becomes
75 dpi	4 × 6	400 KB
150 dpi	4 × 6	1.5 MB
300 dpi	4 × 6	6.2 MB
75 dpi	5 × 7	578 KB
150 dpi	5 × 7	2.2 MB
300 dpi	5 × 7	9 MB
75 dpi	8 × 10	1.3 MB
150 dpi	8 × 10	5.1 MB
300 dpi	8 × 10	20.6 MB

Controlling File Size

As you can see from the preceding table, you need to select an ideal resolution for your digital samples. You also need extra RAM, hard drive space, and a file-compression utility if you're going to be working with even a handful of high-quality images.

But if you have an assignment that's due tomorrow, you don't have the luxury of mulling over the numbers. We have, therefore, provided some ballpark guesstimates as to the dpi settings for scanning different kinds of output:

◆ If you're printing an image at a 1:1 size for an in-house newsletter, using a 300 to 600 dpi PostScript laser printer, scan black-and-white photos at a grayscale setting of no more than 125 dpi.

◆ If you're scanning a 1-to-1 image that will be shown only on a monitor, scan no higher (in color or black-and-white) than 96 dpi.

◆ If you're going to the cover of Vogue magazine, scan at 300 dpi, color, 1-to-1, and we'd like to talk with you about future business collaborations!

A good first step in economizing file sizes is to watch out for white space. *White space* is the empty, uncropped area surrounding an image. It contributes nothing and creates needlessly large digital-image files. In figure 2.9, notice the dotted-line cropping box in the active window of the Microtek source interface. Most of the content of the box is the white of the scanner's cover, not the photo. If the white space isn't cropped out before scanning, it will be captured along with the balloons.

With the scanner set at 100 percent at 150 dpi, the file size is a whopping 5.24 MB file! In figure 2.10, the cropping box was dragged to fit the photo. With most of the white space cropped from the active window, the file size decreased to a comfortable 1.6 MB. If you have a scanner with a similar interface, pay attention to what is inside the cropping box.

Figure 2.10

Decreasing white space around an image creates smaller files.

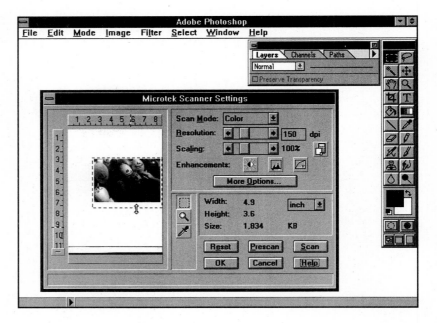

Many scanner models provide, directly through the TWAIN interface, controls you can use for Brightness/Contrast and Gamma correction, as well as tone controls for specific density regions (highlights, midtones, and shadows). Some source images might lack contrast, might appear too dark to register good detail in certain areas, or might be faded and not contain enough visual information to produce a good scan using the scanner's default settings.

You can compensate for poor exposure and contrast to a certain degree with an automatic feature found in several scanning software packages or by using the physical on-board adjustments many scanners have. On some less expensive scanners, the density adjustment controls bear a plain, straightforward name: the *Brightness and Contrast control*. Is adjusting density ranges the same thing as adjusting the brightness and contrast? Not quite. It's analogous to having a graphic equalizer on your stereo, or simple bass and treble controls.

Tip   If the scanner you're thinking of buying doesn't have any sort of prescanning adjustments, keep shopping. It's important to be able to compensate for source deficiencies at the earliest possible stage of the digitizing process. Otherwise, having to use Photoshop to make these corrections (when they are so easy to make before scanning) is a time-consuming pain.

Many scanners, such as the Microtek, also offer a tool that serves as a virtual densitometer, with which you can click over areas to see what the darkest and lightest values are within the image. Out of a possible 256 density values, the balloons image in figure 2.10 has a density range from 13, the darkest value, to 221, the "whitest white." These figures (and experienced eyes) indicate that this is a pretty good photo and will make a good scan. There won't be any areas blocking in or blowing out because we have a wide range of values, with lots of in-between values expressed.

When an image has most of its density values toward the center (the midtones), the image (information-wise) is low in contrast, muddy-looking, and *blocked in*. Conversely, an image with no gray values near the center of the density range, and with only absolute blacks and whites, is high in contrast and is said to be *blown out*.

Note   When any one particular density range from 0 to 255 is packed—absolutely saturated—with image information, the scanner's photosensitive cells *clip* that range, and your scan will feature an ugly spot in that image area. Clipping in an image area can be *corrected* in Photoshop (as well as *created* in Photoshop). For more information about saturating and clipping, see Chapter 7, "Restoring an Heirloom Photograph," which describes the process of color-correcting an heirloom image.

Getting the Information Straight

Make sure your image is parallel to the scanner's edge when you scan. In English—don't scan crookedly, unless you're trying to achieve this effect. Many people take things for granted when they scan, figuring that imaging software can compensate for careless scanning practices.

After taking a taxi driver's tour of Photoshop's (or another imaging program's) feature set, new users sometimes discover that it's possible to rotate a sloppy scan to get the telephone poles vertical in an image. *Rotating* is the spinning of the image around an imaginary center spoke, and Photoshop does this very well. But Photoshop's ability to rotate an image isn't the point.

Stop The rotate effect in Photoshop is intended for creating artistic effects, not to compensate for poor scanning procedures. The **R**otate command requires processing power (RAM) proportional to the file size of the image. It is conceivable, and even possible, to rotate an image to straighten it out, but if the image exceeds 3 MB or so, you force your computer's processor to gnash and churn for minutes on end. Then your system might crash because you ran out of memory or scratch disk space on your drive.

There's another disadvantage to correcting an image's angle with software. To rotate an image, Photoshop has to perform *interpolation*, which involves reassigning each pixel in the image a new color and tonal value. Sometimes this comes out looking fine, sometimes not. When you skew, rotate, or otherwise distort an image, you're actually creating an effect, and this requires "translating" the data that makes up the image. Something is always lost in the translation. Save translations for creating a new effect, not to compensate for a bad scan.

There's one exception to the rule. You *do* want to scan an image crooked if you're scanning a screened photo from a magazine or other printed source. The trick is to scan it at precisely the exact amount of crookedness necessary to eliminate *moiré* patterns (those zigzags patterns that disrupt an image's visual content. *Moiré* patterns occur when the angle of a pattern is laid on top of another pattern whose angle is neither complementary, nor exactly opposing). Photos that have been printed on a press are made up of ink dots that were produced using the line screens and frequencies mentioned in table 2.1. For black-and-white printing, the screen is usually applied at a 45-degree angle. Screens used in process color printing are set at varying angles to each other.

Experiment with scanning a printed image at various angles until you get the results you want. Don't scan at a rate of more than 100 dpi. Unlike a continuous-tone photographic print, an image printed using dots of ink has only a limited, fixed amount of information you can capture.

Stop Before you dive into scanning printed material, check out the copyright on the source material. Many budding desktop publishers have been nipped because they used another professional's work without permission or paying royalties. Scanning your own original art yields better quality, is more rewarding, and costs less than getting hauled into court for appropriating someone else's craft.

Scanning the Image

Now, having covered important considerations about the way image placement, resolution, image dimensions, and tonal balance fit into optimizing the scan of an image, it's time to resume the actual process. In the following exercise, you can put all the theory and explanations into practice.

Scanning the Right Image at the Right Settings

Choose an appropriate image type (Color/24-bit was chosen in this example)	Determines the type of image created.
Change your image dimensions or percentage if necessary	In the balloon example, nothing was changed. It was set to 100% or 1:1 ratio.
Set your sampling rate (resolution) to 150 dpi	Produces a digital image that's easy to edit, moderate in file size, and will print well to a high-resolution output device.
Position your cropping box loosely around the preview image	Sets the area the scanner will scan and turn into a file.
Use your scanner hardware or software controls to adjust the lightness/darkness of the scan	The Microtek Automatic Contrast Control Option was used, and the results were double-checked by eye. In this case the setting was okay.
Click on the Scan button	The image is scanned.
Exit the scanner source interface by clicking on OK (or press Alt+F4)	You are returned to the Photoshop workspace with your newly acquired image in a window, ready for editing, naming, and saving.

 Tip Try to leave a *little* bit of white space or room around your photo when scanning. *Rough* cropping should be done in the scanning process, with final cropping performed in Photoshop, where you get a better view of the image than in a source interface preview.

Transferring all of the information generated from a 4" × 6" photo captured at 24-bits-per-pixel and 150 samples per inch into your PC's memory is a time-consuming task. (The authors calculated it to be 0.7 coffee breaks.) But it was worth the wait. Figure 2.11 shows the image we scanned, as it appears in Photoshop's workspace.

Figure 2.11

Photoshop displays the scanned image that's in your computer's RAM.

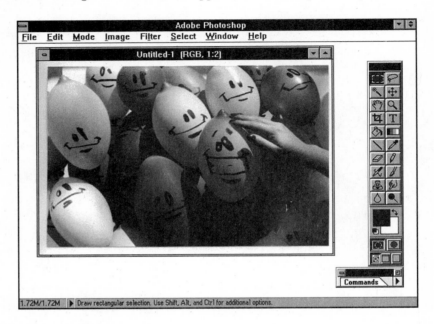

A Histogram of the Scan

Now that the scanned image is displayed in Photoshop, think about the density-level setting that was used for the scan. The scanner evaluated the photo's white point as being 221 and the black point as 13. It then based all the other in-between values' densities on this initial information about absolute white and black points.

You might never have total control over how color densities are arranged in a digital image to create the "perfect" picture. But Photoshop's powerful mapping options can go a long way toward making a dull picture sparkle and a good picture great. One such mapping function has to do with seeing (and changing!) the actual levels of densities from where the scanner originally mapped them. You can snap up a dull picture, or retrieve parts of an image you thought had faded away through time, by redistributing the amount of pixels in a given area in the density range.

Redistributing the tonal densities in an image is accomplished by using one of the Adjust commands in Photoshop's Image menu. Several of Photoshop's commands have the capability to redistribute densities, and they vary in their level of sophistication and ease of use. Photoshop's Levels command is the second most robust command and the easiest to use. With an image open and active in the Photoshop

workspace, choosing **I**mage, **A**djust, then Levels (or pressing Ctrl+L) brings the Levels command dialog box to the screen.

The Levels dialog box sports a graph, called a *histogram*, of the active image. As you'll see in Chapter 3, "Color Theory and the PhotoCD," a histogram is a map that represents graphical data plotted against a set of parameters. The Levels histogram initially presents a map that shows the location of all the pixels in the active image. The histogram's X axis tells you how bright a pixel is, and the Y axis shows how many pixels in the image occupy a specific brightness value. Color and grayscale images alike are portrayed in the Levels histogram according to one set of criteria—tonal density, or brightness, measured between absolute white (255) and the darkest point (0).

A histogram of a digital image is unique to that image; you rarely find identical brightness maps for different pictures. One picture may have wild fluctuations in neighboring brightness values between 0 and 255, whereas another might have a flat curve, as you'd find in a dim, low-contrast picture.

You'll be using the image of the balloons in this chapter's exercises. The file, named THEBUNCH.TIF, is on the companion CD. Now's a good time to open this file, so that you can see for yourself how the Levels command maps brightness ranges for an image, and how this information can be modified to produce a clearer, more dynamic digital photograph. In figure 2.12, the Levels histogram displays the "landscape" of brightness values in the image just scanned.

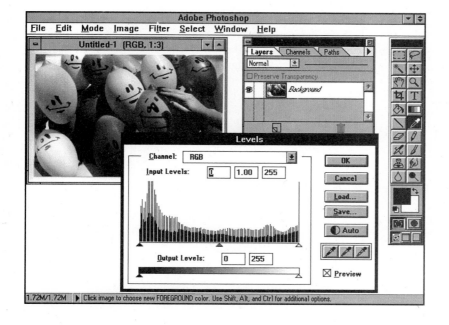

Figure 2.12

Graduations from dark to light are uneven; there are missing components to an even tonal transition from light to dark.

As you can see, the scanner did a good job of separating neighboring pixel brightness values to create a digital image with a lot of detail and contrast. Note that numerous spikes in the histogram are followed by "dropouts"—tonal points on the brightness scale that contain no pixels. The extreme, narrow differences in the tonal, brightness scheme of this image are visually represented in the picture as slightly harsh contrasts in areas across the balloons.

What we'd expect to see should be an even gradation of tones on the main subjects, the balloons, as sunlight gently cascades across their surfaces from light to shadow. The picture might be a technically accurate representation of the source image, but it's presently aesthetically wrong, partially due to the sun's extreme highlight effect on the balloons' surfaces, and partially because the auto contrast controls on the scanner artificially "pumped up" the digital image through filtering.

Using the Auto Range Option

Fortunately, post-processing work can be performed on a captured image in Photoshop before an image is saved to hard disk. The Auto range button in the Levels dialog box enables you to automatically clip five percent off the bottom- and topmost ranges of the image's brightness scale. In effect, the Auto range option redefines the Black Point and White Point in an image, allowing Photoshop to recalculate and redistribute tonal values proportionately along the image's brightness scale. Typically, this creates vacancies in the midtone range of an image, where pixels may "fill in" and smooth the flow of the image's tones from light to dark.

 Tip

If you want to increase or decrease the Auto options' range, Alt(Option)+click on the Auto button in the Levels dialog box. The Auto Range Options dialog box appears; here you can set the **B**lack Clip and **W**hite Clip points used by the Auto option.

To understand more about the effects of increasing or decreasing the Auto clip percentages, however, read Chapter 3, "Color Theory and the PhotoCD," first!

With the Auto range option selected, the histogram in the Levels dialog box reflects the proposed changes Photoshop will execute if you click on OK (see fig. 2.13). After you click on the Auto button, or make any other changes to an active image with the Levels command, the resulting histogram does not represent the future distribution of pixels on the brightness scale, but rather represents the *delta*, the change from the original histogram of the image. If Photoshop could speak, it would say, "these are the changes I propose to make when you allow me to Auto-adjust the range of tonal densities in this image."

But Photoshop doesn't speak (at least the authors' copy doesn't), and the changes Photoshop proposes as reflected in the histogram aren't easily understood at a casual

glance. That's why you should look at the digital image with your own eyes, with the Preview box in the Levels dialog box checked, so that you can see the visual effect of the proposed changes before you click on OK.

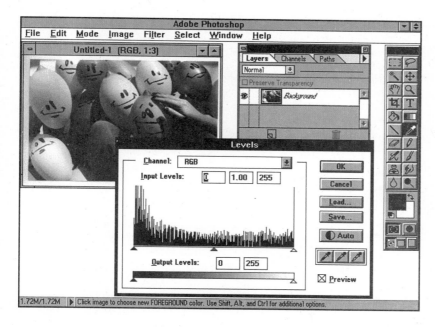

Figure 2.13

In general, the Auto Levels adjustment enhances the scanner's capture of an original photograph.

Our observation was that Photoshop's Auto range option did indeed smooth out the distribution of pixels in the image, creating a more eye-pleasing digital capture from the scan of the original. In your own experiences with particular images, though, you may not want to do any adjusting before saving an image to your hard disk.

The important observation here is that although you have several means available for precisely viewing and adjusting an image according to detailed information Photoshop can provide, never forfeit the years of experience of your own trained eyes. There are several artificial means for whipping an image into mathematical perfection, but your vision and judgment are the best tools you have when scanning.

Tip

You can move the Photoshop Levels dialog box around your workspace, but you can't move your photo if the Levels box covers it up. Before you issue the Levels command, tuck your photo up into a corner of Photoshop's workspace so that you can preview any changes you may decide on. This also holds true for any number of Photoshop dialog boxes; keeping images positioned away from the center of Photoshop's workspace is always a prudent move.

How a histogram should be "read" and how manual changes should be made based on these readings is discussed in detail in Chapter 3, "Color Theory and the PhotoCD."

Now that the image has been acquired and adjusted, it's time to save the data that makes up this digital image to your hard drive. It's a good idea to save a scanned image to hard disk as soon as you are happy with the tonal balance and basic look of the scan. Scanned images continue to reside in system RAM after acquisition; naming the image and saving it to disk ensures that a sudden power outage or other unscheduled event doesn't wipe out your work!

A scanned image, regardless of color content, can be saved in any number of graphical file formats—and this is the topic covered in the next section.

Saving Your Scanned Image

Now, this balloon picture is a good one but not a great one. The bottom-left corner of the Photoshop status bar (the image window on the Macintosh version) tells you that saving the picture as is, in an uncompressed format, will cost you 1.72 MB of hard disk space. What the authors usually do with example or experiment images is JPEG (jay-peg) them. It sounds violent, but for the most part, it simply reduces the stored file size of an image to about a 10:1 ratio. When you open a JPEGged file (when Photoshop loads the file into system RAM), the file expands in size once more. JPEG compression is pretty useful, but it's also "lossy compression," a scheme that discards almost undetectable color information within the image in the process.

JPEG file compression is covered in the next section. But one or two things need to be done with this image first, and audience participation is required now so that you can actually evaluate the JPEG format. If you don't already have the THEBUNCH.TIF image from the companion CD active in Photoshop, now's an ideal time to open it.

Saving an Image, JPEG-Style

If you have not already done so, click on the Auto button in the Levels dialog box

Choose OK to accept the changes and return to the workspace

Changes the distribution of intermediate density levels, as previously discussed.

From the toolbox, press Alt and click on the Marquee tool (upper-left icon) until it toggles to the Rectangular marquee, then click and drag the cursor from the upper-left corner to the lower-right corner of the live image area	You want to select only the photo and none of the surrounding white space.
From the **E**dit menu, choose C**r**op	You have cropped the picture so that no white border shows, and you have reduced the image's file size.
Choose **F**ile, Save **A**s	Displays the Save As dialog box, where you can choose the file name, location, and file format.
From the Save File as Format **T**ype drop-down box, in the lower-left corner, choose JPEG (*.JPG)	Chooses the JPEG compressed file format.

Windows Photoshop users should type a name (eight characters or less) in the File **N**ame: field, type a period, then type **JPG** (or use the JPG extension that Photoshop automatically places in the File **N**ame field). Macintosh users don't need to enter an extension to save the copy as a JPG.

Click on OK to save the file	The JPEG Options box appears.
Click on the Medium Image Quality radio button, then click on OK (see fig. 12.14)	Saves the scan to your hard disk as THEBUNCH.JPG.

An image ultimately has to become a saved file. It can't stay in your system's RAM indefinitely unless you have a weird arrangement with your local power company. The preceding discussion has outlined a solid working path from source image to Photoshop. Now it's time to talk about file compression for digital images.

Squeezing the Most Out of an Image

If you're really into image enhancing, you'll quickly amass an entire hard disk full of images. At the tune of 1 to 12 MB each, you'll have no elbowroom for other programs, files, or games! But you can *compress* images so that they take less disk space. The two compression scheme categories are called *lossless* and *lossy* compression—terms that mean exactly what you think they mean. With one method, you don't lose any information; with the other, you lose some image information when you compress, as when you use JPEG.

Figure 2.14

Stored as a JPEG compression format, this image is 52 KB. When loaded into memory, it expands to almost original size!

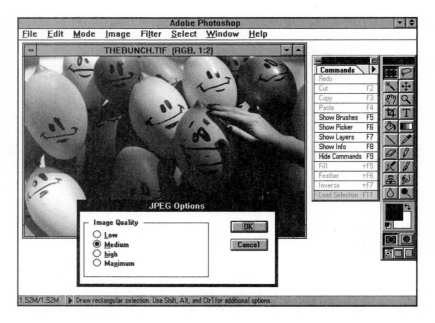

Lossless Compression

Photoshop supports LZW lossless compression of files saved as *Tagged Image File Format* (TIFF) images. Figure 2.15 shows an uncompressed file on the right (taken from HANDBAG.TIF on the companion CD) and an LZW-compressed file on the left. When the file on the left was saved with a different name—HANDBAGZ.TIF—IBM PC Byte Order and LZW Compression were checked in the TIFF Options box; Macintosh users have the same LZW Compression option. This dialog box pops up whenever you save a TIFF format image.

A side-by-side comparison of the two files shows no difference between the two. That's because the image on the left, the LZW *losslessly* compressed file, and the image on the right contain identical information. HANDBAGZ.TIF expands back to its original size of 1.13 MB when it's called up in Photoshop and loaded into system RAM.

Note Lempel and Ziv, two mathematicians who wrote a treatise in the late 1960s on algorithmic compression, are responsible for the many types of lossless compression available today in programs such as Photoshop. They understood the eventual need for condensing, or compressing, mathematical data in a secure way that didn't lose any of the data's information.

The LZW compression scheme recognizes repetitive streams of data within a file and "shorthands" them. Imagine a file that contained a 1, followed by a hundred zeros, then another 1 on the end. Then try writing it! It's much simpler to write "1," then "100 zeros," then "1," isn't it? This is the basic theory of lossless compression based on Lempel and Ziv's postulate. Photoshop's particular flavor of Lempel-Ziv's lossless compression is called *LZW* (for Lempel, Ziv, and Welch, a third contributor), and it's available for the TIF file format type.

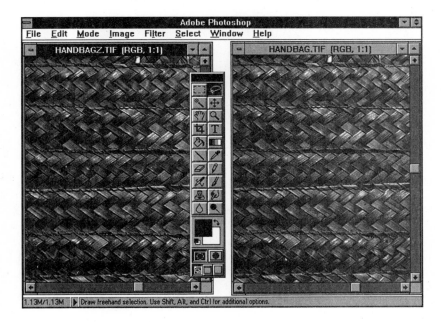

Figure 2.15

Lossless compression only shrinks the image's file size while it's inactive, stored on hard or floppy media.

Before anyone goes running off saying, "Oh, yes, lossless compression is for me! The handbags are identical! Total integrity and fidelity using LZW compression!," take a look at how well (how much) you compressed the handbag. Windows File Manager shows where the two handbags are stored and what their file sizes are. Check out HANDBAG.TIF and then HANBAGZ.TIF highlighted at the bottom of the directory tree (see fig. 2.16). It's apparent that the handbag would be better stored in your *closet* than on your hard disk using LZW compression.

Don't get the idea that LZW lossless compression always squashes an image file three percent. This number varies on a case-by-case incidence. The handbag has a repeating pattern in it, but the weave does not repeat exactly from border to border, and this slight variation may be the reason that LZW compression couldn't condense the information very well.

For example, if you took a picture of a Japanese flag, a red circle on a field of white, LZW compression would compress the image substantially because of the flag's simple design and repeated information about the white background.

Figure 2.16

Compared to HANDBAG.TIF, HANDBAGZ.TIF shows only about a 3.5-percent overall compression.

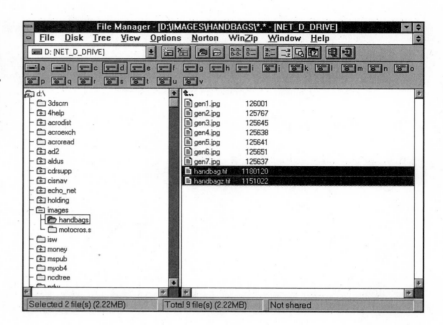

The role LZW compression can play in the struggle to keep file sizes small is a minor one, yet it offers absolute visual integrity. If you deal with a lot of images in your work, there's a clear need for a more substantial compression scheme, though, and this is where JPEG enters the scene.

Taking a Hint from the Experts

JPEG, which stands for the Joint Photographer's Experts Group, is both a file format and a compression technology. It's a special sort of compression that's intended to be used with photographic images that are color-channel capable, such as RGB and grayscale mode images. During JPEG compression, some information about the image is discarded, or lost.

Is a JPEG image a flagrantly inaccurate one, then? Not at all. A group of professional photographers took great care in deciding exactly which component of visual information in an image can be discarded without the human eye really perceiving it.

Note   The HSB *color model* (covered in Chapter 3) that can be used to describe color's components has Hue, Saturation, and Brightness (sometimes also called Intensity or Value). *Saturation* is the purity of a hue in a specific color; when all hues in a photo are present in equal amounts, the resulting image is a monochrome photo (often called a black-and-white photo). When a particular color is made up of only one hue, the color exhibits much saturation; when several hues are present in equal

amounts, the resulting color is a shade of gray. Saturation expresses the relationship, the measure of the difference, between a pure hue and tonal density (gray) in an image. Although hue is an important component in an image, it is the neutral component of saturation that is responsible for setting the tone in an image—whether the image displays a little or a lot of contrast. The human eye is very sensitive to changes in contrast. Contrast is affected when grayscale values are altered.

JPEG doesn't touch the grayscale components, but instead does some averaging of the *hues* in a photo. This is a fairly safe thing to do because, in reality, the human eye sees only a limited amount of different hue information at a glimpse. By reducing the overall number of unique hues, JPEG compression can create a file similar to the original, but with greater economy.

Because the grayscale screen captures in this book don't reflect the subtleties and nuances in color photography, you may want to follow along with both the HAND-BAG and the MOTOCROS files (they're on the companion CD) as you examine the lossey, JPEG method of compression.

In figure 2.17, the HANDBAG.TIF file was saved as GEN1.JPG. Medium Image Quality, as offered in Photoshop's JPEG Options, was chosen for the quality of the JPEG image. If you look at both images side by side on your own screen, you probably won't notice any difference in photographic quality.

Figure 2.17

A picture that's been JPEGged once, compared to the original.

The Medium Image Quality (which is Photoshop's default setting) yielded about a 10:1 compression ratio. The range of compression that may be set is from Low to Maximum Image Quality. The faithfulness with which JPEG compression renders a file is based on the compression ratio (the higher the quality, the less compression) and the nature of the photo.

The handbag photo may be described as a *low-frequency* picture. It has only a few different hues in it. It has large areas of similar color, with only slight overall variation in the brown hue of the handbag. The actual number of colors used in this 16.7 million color, 24-bit file is 9,111.

Surprising, isn't it? The human eye finds more visual information in the weave of the handbag (the variations in contrast, the grayscale components) than the 9,111 different shades of color. It's simple for JPEG to average out the hue differences with little perceivable alteration to the overall image quality.

By using JPEG compression to store this image, you now have a lot more hard drive space. Look back at the file sizes shown in figure 2.16. If you delete the original TIF file and keep only the GEN1.JPG, you'll recover more than a megabyte of precious drive space!

 Stop   If you have a once-in-a-lifetime, you're-never-going-to-see-it-again photo you've digitized, you may not want to use a lossy compression scheme like JPEG on it at all. In the examples that follow, you'll learn exactly what part of the original image JPEG discards. You are the best judge of how to treat your images.

It would be unfair to suggest that all your valuable images should be compressed in a lossy format. Most of the time you'll be satisfied with a JPEG, and you can delete the original, uncompressed file, but there may be exceptional circumstances and times you won't want to do this.

It was mentioned earlier that the handbag image is a low-frequency image with a small "palette" of colors. What happens when you JPEG a *high-frequency* image, with a wider color range? To perform a little experiment in Photoshop with an image, to see what is actually lost when you do lossey compression, open the MOTOCROS.TIF file from the companion CD, and follow these steps.

Putting the Squeeze on Some Bikers

Open the MOTOCROS.TIF file

Choose File, Save As   You are about to rename the file.

Choose *.JPG from the Save File as Format Type drop-down list	Specifies the JPEG compression scheme as your new file format.
Type **MOTOGEN1.JPG** in the File **N**ame box; click on OK to save the file	Indicates that this file is the first generation of lossey compression done on the image.
Click on the Medium radio button on the JPEG Options dialog box	Saves the image with moderate compression and moderate loss of image information.
Open the MOTOCROS.TIF file from the companion CD once again	This is the original image that will be used for comparison.
Choose **I**mage, **C**alculations	The command for creative mapping between two different images or channels that have the same size and resolution.
Choose MOTOGEN1.JPG and Red Channel as the Source **1** selections, choose MOTOCROS.TIF and Red Channel as the Source **2** selections, choose Difference from the Blending drop-down list, choose New for both Result and Channel, then click on OK	You are creating a new image made up of the differences between the Red color Channels in the JPEG and original TIF images, as shown in figure 2.18.
Choose **I**mage, **M**ap, and then Threshold (or press Ctrl+T)	The new Untitled-1 image contains information too subtle to see clearly. The Threshold command casts all visual data into a white category or a black one, super-contrasting any and all visual data.
Enter **9** in the Threshold Level box	This is an arbitrary value, which revealed file discrepancies in this instance. Other levels of Thresholding might work better, depending on the image.
Click on OK	Returns you to Photoshop's workspace, with an Untitled-1 image similar to that shown in figure 2.19.

The preceding exercise was not a perfect, "man-in-white-lab-smock" experiment in testing the differences JPEG compression creates in original image information; Photoshop 3 has no feature for comparing differences found in the RGB composite channels of two images. The Red channel (and the Blue and Green) have had color information altered through JPEGging, and if you were to try the last exercise using the other color channels as the Sources, you'd find similar differences. The Gray channel Photoshop offers as a Source option would display no difference, because the Gray channel is a view of the tonal density of an individual RGB image; no color values are displayed. As mentioned earlier, JPEG compression reduces the number of unique hues, but not the tonal relationships found within images.

Figure 2.18

The Difference dialog box displays the difference between any two channels in images of the same color mode.

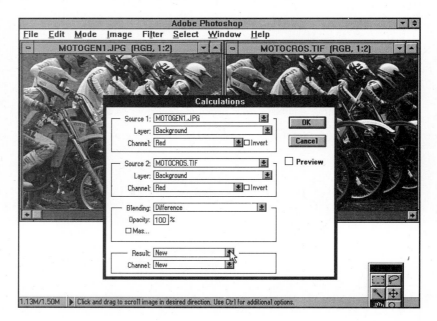

Figure 2.19

Use the Difference menu option to see the differences between two images of the same subject.

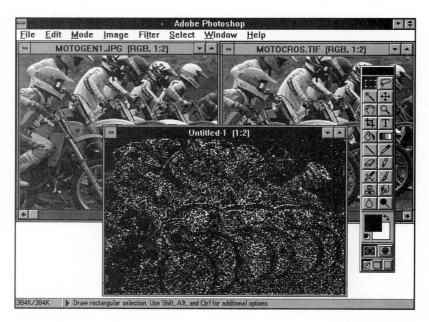

The motocross bikers and their bikes create a high-frequency scheme within the image because the colors vary drastically from neighboring pixel to pixel. The way JPEG handled the averaging of these color differences is obvious in Untitled-1. There's practically no difference in the bike wheels, but when red graduates quickly to white, the dirt shifts sharply in color value, and so on. JPEG had to perform some averaging of unique color values to reduce the file size.

How Far Can You Go Before I Notice?

A very natural question people ask about JPEG compression is whether you lose some of the original material with every *successive* opening and closing of the file. This is a fair question; in theory it's analogous to what a fifth-generation photocopy looks like compared to the original.

You are not going to be asked to perform compression four more times on the motocross image in order to witness the net effect. After all, this book is supposed to make your work easier! The authors' own curiosity was piqued, however, and the following examples may shed some light.

Whatever discernible loss performed on MOTOCROSS.TIF occurred on the *first* instance of JPEGging it. Figure 2.20 demonstrates the difference between the first JPEG and one done five times later. As you can see, the difference is nominal.

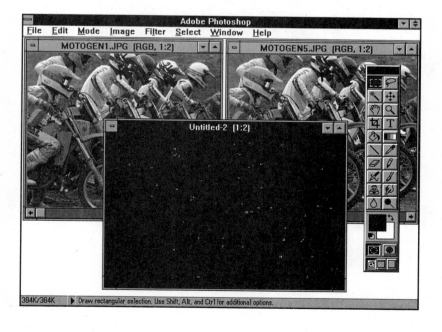

Figure 2.20

The difference between the two images has been exaggerated, using the Threshold command, so that you can see if there is a difference.

Figure 2.20 bears out the observation that once you've used lossey compression on an image, no more significant compression takes place, whether you've re-squashed the file once or a half a dozen times. The difference in file size between a first-generation JPEG and a fifth is in the bytes range, which is very small. Part of the reason for this is that certain pixels that were questionable candidates for averaging in the first generation may have been sitting exactly on the "halfway point" of JPEG's compression criteria. Successive generations of JPEGging simply "tipped the scales" in favor of including these pixels in the lossey process.

Most of the reason for the nominal discrepancies between generation one through five is caused by the authors' use of Stacker, and not by JPEG or Photoshop. Stacker is a hard drive compression utility, similar to the Macintosh StuffIt, that actively optimizes a computer's available hard disk space.

Therefore, our numbers for the JPEG files are not hard-and-fast data, but rather reflect Stacker's reportage of the file sizes at the time of compression. Use JPEG with the same image on different days, and a hard disk outfitted with "on-the-fly" compression like Stacker reports different, yet similar numbers.

So Should I Use JPEG or Not?

Sorry, the ball's in your court on this one. The authors' personal practice is to JPEG images on their hard disks, but also to archive an uncompressed original on floppy and tape backups.

The Joint Photographer's Experts Group gave a lot of mathematical and aesthetic consideration to imaging when they cooked up JPEG. It was designed to accommodate the professional photographers' need to relieve their hard disks of an overwhelming sea of visual information. JPEG is more subtle than you imagine when it comes to lossey compression, and the authors suggest that the real-world difference between a JPEG image and an uncompressed image is very close to *none*.

Toss the hard-core, empirical data you've been shown out the window for a moment. Skip the Difference Calculation and look at the two images side by side with your own eyes.

Seeing Is Disbelieving

Perceived differences are not always *actual* differences. Perceived differences are skewed by other information we are given that doesn't relate to the absolute evaluation we have before us. Remember the coffee commercials where people are asked to taste the difference between fresh-brewed and freeze-dried? They were blindfolded to remove the extra visual information about the two coffees, so they could concentrate on true differences. We all know that Coffee #2 tastes just fine with the blindfold on, but the moment you see the freeze-dry jar, this coffee doesn't taste as good! That's a false perceived difference that had nothing to do with the *actual* difference in coffees.

The same holds true when you compare a JPEGged file to the original. There is a difference between the two, but it's virtually imperceptible. Any perceived difference is really in your head because we've shown you the Difference Experiment. The bottom line is that you can save lots of hard disk space by JPEGging your work. Period. Use your eyes to honestly evaluate the images when you choose a storage method. And understand, too, that the way you store a digital image is as important as the effort you put into creating it.

Computer hardware and software enhance your productivity as an imaging-type of person. But computers take instructions from you; they can't evaluate your specific needs on a particular assignment. Simply know your tools and have confidence in your eyes and your own judgment. The next section has a perfect example of how to select the right tool and decide the best use for it in your work.

The Digital Camera

As mentioned earlier, a digital image can be generated in several ways. Aside from generating an image within a PC design program, this chapter has dealt mostly with using a scanner to bring a real-world photo or piece of art into the Land of Binary Files. A recent invention, however, the digital camera, needs to be discussed. Instead of using film, the digital camera uses a photo-sensitive grid consisting of thousands of cells that respond to reflected light as it's passed though the lens. Its importance to the field of imaging will become more prevalent in the coming years.

The advantages a digital camera presents are ones of convenience, ecology, and timeliness. Since the data a digital camera captures is piped directly into the computer, there is no developing time, no intermediate film negative, no running to the store for film, and no chemical waste that calls for proper environmental disposal methods.

Digital cameras currently range in price from $600 to $10,000. The wide variation in price reflects both the newness of the technology and the wide range in capability that these cameras have. Logitech's FotoMan, a modestly priced digital camera, was used for the following experiment.

Downloading a Captured Image

Like a modem, a digital camera downloads the captured information to the computer through an umbilical cable. The FotoMan camera needs to be attached to the cable during a download only, so a PC wasn't needed on site during our field excursion.

FotoMan is a monochrome (black-and-white) camera, capable of capturing a 3×4.133 image at 8 bits-per-pixel, and 120 digital samples (dots) per inch. Depending on the complexity of the subject, this averages out to about 150 KB per image. When you consider that you can take 32 images before downloading the visual information, it's a well-designed little camera. FotoMan is also TWAIN-compliant, so you're able to do your downloading directly from Photoshop's workspace. In figure 2.21, **F**ile, Acq**u**ire, Select TWAIN Source was chosen from the Photoshop menu; you can see the FotoMan TWAIN interface.

Figure 2.21

The source interface for the TWAIN-compliant FotoMan digital camera.

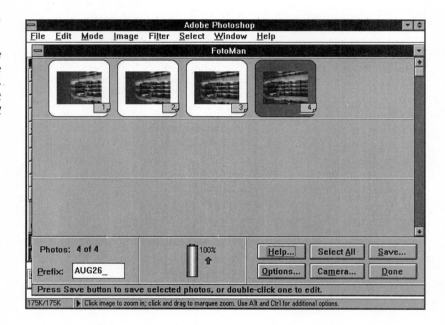

All you do is double-click on the thumbnail picture of the image you want from FotoMan, then click on **D**one in its source interface, and you'll have the selected image in Photoshop in seconds. In figure 2.22, notice that the image is sideways! (The camera was turned sideways to produce a portrait view of the building.) You can remedy this by choosing **I**mage, **R**otate, and then selecting 90CW from the submenu list. The image is then turned in a 90-degree clockwise direction.

A digital camera is very much like a video camcorder in that *hot spots*—intense highlights, like the reflections from chrome—cause undesired effects in the captured image, often seen as streaking. Although this image was taken on a brilliant day, the highlights on the building aren't really noticeable. So what *is* noticeable?

The intention in photographing the building was to do a study in geometry. We wanted the art-deco figure that graces the building's fourth floor to be the central point of the composition. So the artist's eye and judgment were correct in selecting and framing the subject, *but the selection of the best tool was wrong.*

FotoMan's standard 64mm lens was used, which permitted a fixed view of the building. The problem was with FotoMan's fixed resolution of 120 samples per inch. After blowing the image up to twice its original size, both the fixed resolution and the camera's lens design became obvious.

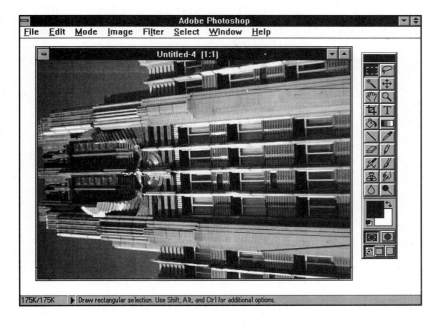

Figure 2.22

Employees at the Niagara Mohawk building complain about vertigo and papers falling off their desks.

For comparison's sake, figure 2.23 shows a conventional chemical print on the left, captured on film with a Minolta 35mm, Single Lens Reflex camera, and the digital camera's capture of the building on the right. A similar length lens (53mm) was used, and the print was scanned at 150 dpi, a little better than FotoMan's 120 dpi fixed rate.

Any sort of digital imaging equipment—be it scanner or digital camera—reveals its "building blocks" to the naked eye when an image is enlarged. A *pixelated* image is similar to the undesired effect of film grain when a small film negative is used to reproduce a wall-sized poster. If you go back to the observation that the correct tool is part of the key to successful imaging, you learn that in this instance, a scanned chemical photograph is better suited than the inexpensive digital camera to capture the art-deco winged figure four stories away.

Resolution was the problem, and the right tools for this situation were a regular photo print and a scanner whose resolution could be increased and decreased. The lessons here are to use the right tool for the assignment and to sample stuff with a resolution that will hold up if you intend to enlarge it.

Figure 2.23

The digital camera's fixed resolution "pixelated" the image when it was enlarged.

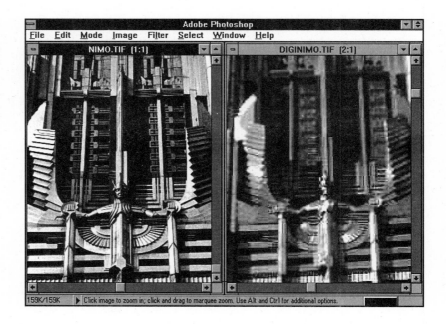

The Proper Tool for the Right Occasion

But don't dismiss the digital camera by any means (see fig. 2.24). First, you can purchase separate lenses for digital cameras; you can buy more expensive, full-featured models; and you can even equip a lot of conventional cameras with a digital film replacement part. If we had performed the same experiment with one of the $10,000 digital cameras, the results would have been dramatically different. The digital camera would have produced an image equivalent to that of the 35mm camera. Digital cameras are also quick, candid, and unobtrusive. And if people do by chance catch you using a digital camera to take their picture, they're usually fascinated with its design and the technological wonder of it. Both qualities made it an excellent tool for capturing Lou—a friend who hates having his picture taken.

Lou agreed to pose for the picture in figure 2.25 basically because he wanted to see this gizmo work. The authors impressed upon him the immediate gratification of seeing himself onscreen in Photoshop, and his camera-shyness abated. So, quick as a Polaroid, his picture was snapped, the information downloaded to Photoshop's workspace, and the Levels command was called for a fast Auto range adjustment. In about four mouse clicks, here's a before and an after photo suitable for placing in a 1200 dpi publication at its original size.

Digital photography, like the digital image enhancing covered later in this book, is an exciting medium. In fact, the two go hand-in-hand. You can compensate for an affordable digital camera's lack of maturity at this time with the techniques covered in this book.

Figure 2.24

The FotoMan digital camera.

Scanning, the digital camera, and original PC artwork all can be combined to create original imaging work. Photoshop accepts them all, and enables you to take advantage of the wonderful plastic quality of working with images that your computer sees as electronic data.

Figure 2.25

It's not the cover of Time, *but it's a solid, workable, everyday image.*

Color Theory and the PhotoCD

The Kodak PhotoCD is an important new technology and tool invaluable to any Photoshop user. PhotoCDs contain photographic images that have been scanned at very high resolutions and then stored in a compressed format on a special type of CD. This process provides the imaging professional and novice alike with an inexpensive way to acquire and store very high-quality source images. Using this technology, which is becoming the digital photographic standard within the graphics, publishing, and photographic worlds, is simple. But using PhotoCD images so that the resulting work is tonally balanced, crisp, and clear is only possible if you understand a few things about the unique properties of PhotoCD.

The concepts and techniques you learn in this chapter are geared specifically toward optimizing and working with PhotoCD images. However, many non-PhotoCD images also need the same enhancement and adjustment techniques applied to them because all digital images' color properties revolve around the same types of color models.

The chapter begins with a look at the underlying concepts behind light and color theory and then moves on to using Photoshop tools with an actual PhotoCD file. You learn how to put the theories into practice when you learn the best methods for acquiring and gamma-correcting a PhotoCD image. Your tour of PhotoCD imaging ends with hardware and software utilities that make working with PhotoCDs easier, and you see how to get *your* photographs transferred to a PhotoCD.

Understanding Models

A *model* is an analogy, a description; a model is a way of representing or simulating something. Through the use of models, you can manipulate, control, and predict the behavior of something that you can't easily touch or physically control. A child playing with a model train, chugging the model around a dining room table, experiences what it feels like to drive a train and can predict what will happen if the train falls off the tracks. This experience of a real process—driving a train—can only be easily (and legally) made available to a child through the use of a model.

As an imaging person, it is important to understand the models that have been designed to describe color. The phenomenon of light and its color properties surround us everywhere, yet they are elusive concepts that are difficult to describe and work with without a model. Paul Newman, an actor famous for his blue eyes, is color blind. How would you describe his eyes to him when he has never seen and *will* never see the blue? You can't point to another blue object because he has no basis for comparison, no frame of reference, no structure within which he can compare dissimilar qualities. Use a model, and you can describe exactly what blue is to Paul Newman. He still will never see the color or personally know its emotional appeal, but if he understood the model he would understand blue's place within the model, and its relationship to other colors. With the knowledge provided by the model he could, if he wanted to, order clothing or decorate his home by specifiying colors that complement blue.

And when you understand a number of *different* color models, you can describe, modify, and manipulate color with precision. Photoshop provides a number of color models to work with, so when one model doesn't fit your need, another can.

Defining Key Terms

Before you could describe blue to Mr. Newman, or effectively use the color models that Photoshop puts at your disposal, you need to understand the terms—the "language" of color—the first of which is light. Other terms that need defining are hue, saturation, brightness, lightness, chromacity, tints, and shades.

Light and Hue

Light is energy emitted from things as diverse as the sun, a light bulb, or a phosphor on a computer monitor. Visible light occupies a tiny portion of the electromagnetic spectrum. Other portions of the spectrum contain radio waves, microwaves, x-rays, and infrared waves. Each of these energy waves, along with visible light, occupies and is described by the different range of frequencies it occupies within an energy spectrum. The part of the spectrum you are interested in is the visible spectrum of light.

Every source of light emits a *mixture* of waves that has different frequencies. High frequency light has short wavelengths, and low frequency light has long wavelengths. When the light emitted from a source is made up of a fairly even mixture of wavelengths, the light is perceived as white. When a particular wavelength is predominant, however, that light is perceived as having a particular *hue*. For example, light whose predominant wavelength is about 450 nanometers is perceived by non color-blind people as the hue commonly called blue.

But which blue? Navy blue, sky blue, periwinkle blue, powder blue, electric blue, or royal blue? All these common colors share a predominant hue, but our perception of these hues tells us they are different. What makes them different is how much or how little they contain of the other components that our eyes and minds interpret as being part of color. These other components of perceived color are described in the following sections.

Saturation

Hue is not the only aspect of color that humans perceive. *Saturation* is another component. Saturation is the purity of a color; it's the difference between a particular, predominant wavelength and the other wavelengths that make up a color. The stronger and more clearly we perceive the sensation of hue, the more highly saturated the color is. Pastel blue is a "washed-out" blue and has very little pure hue in it. When colors are desaturated, they become neutral, displaying no single, strong hue characteristic. Gray is neutral, but so are white and black. When a color is totally desaturated, the factor that determines if you perceive the color as a shade of gray or as white or black is determined by the third component of color—brightness.

Brightness

Brightness is how intensely you perceive the energy of light to be. Brightness is also sometimes called *luminance*. A spotlight is intense (bright); the light from a dying ember is not. When we speak of brightness in terms of color, white is total brightness, and black is a total lack of brightness. Gray is somewhere in between.

Chromacity and Lightness

Chromacity, or *chroma*, refers to the combination of two components of color—hue and saturation. *Lightness* is a term that refers to the components of saturation and brightness. Chroma is often referred to as hue, and brightness and lightness are used interchangeably as color component descriptions. These are inaccurate uses of the terms, in the same way that the term *dot* is used to describe a digital sampling unit taken from a source image with a scanner.

Tints, Shades, and Tones

When black is added to a pure hue (a hue that is 100-percent saturated), a *shade* is produced. A *tint* of a color is produced when white is added to a pure hue. *Tones* are produced when a mixture of black and white is added to a pure hue.

Using Different Color Models in Photoshop

The preceding section broke down the color components of the *Hue/Saturation/Brightness* (HSB) color model so that you could understand what each component contributes to the HSB color model. HSB is only one of three color models in Photoshop that can be used to describe the *color gamut*, the range of expression within a color model, that most closely matches the color space the human eye can see.

On Photoshop's Mode menu, you see several different organizations of color components, called *modes*, that might be thought of as an abbreviation for models. Not all of the available color models are on the Modes menu; some are found on the Picker, Color Picker, and Info palettes. When you specify a foreground color in Photoshop, it's usually easiest to use the HSB color model because HSB color was designed to give designers "user-friendly" control over color definition. The following sections describe the other two color organizations that are modeled after the way humans see color and light.

The RGB Color Model

Unlike the HSB color model, RGB color expresses colors through a combination of the relative strengths of the brightnesses of Red, Green, and Blue. Like HSB color, the RGB color model is based on additive color; when the three primary colors that make up RGB color are present at full brightness value, the resulting color is white.

RGB color is the mode in which color images are scanned, and RGB color is a technical specification used to describe the amount of energy emitted from the red, green, and blue phosphor of your monitor.

RGB color was constructed as a model after the way the human eye's cones receive light; the eye's cones have red, green, and blue receptors that respond to each wavelength's stimuli, and it's up to our minds to integrate the information into a value of color.

The RGB color model can be used on the Info, Color Picker, Scratch, and Picker palettes to specify a foreground or background color you might want to use for painting. However, as a designer, you might have problems defining the right shade or the strength of the color you want to use through the RGB color model. This is because the model expresses the colors within the visible gamut as three unique primary values whose combination in unequal parts, coincidentally, defines the hue, saturation, and brightness of a color.

The RGB color model is terrific for technicians who want to calibrate a monitor. And because RGB color is an additive color model, it accurately quantifies the components of the colors on your screen. RGB color fails, however, to give the user a real grasp of color components that can be used to quickly specify a shade or tint of color for retouching, painting, or editing.

LAB Color

The LAB color model (also called CIELAB) was created as an international color specification standard by the *Commission Internationale d'Eclairage* (CIE). The advantage the LAB model has is that it is device independent; the same values of LAB's color components can be used to describe printed color, as well as colored light emanating from a monitor. A need has always existed in the world to be able to specify color in a way that can be used by devices of all different kinds. The LAB color model is a way to accurately specify color to anyone in the world, for use with any kind of output, display device, or material. Its use is similar to the widely accepted use of PANTONE swatches to specify exactly the color of ink you want a printer to use.

LAB performs this feat of international legerdemain by describing color using three values. Instead of using Red, Green, and Blue like the RGB color model or the HSB models of Hue, Saturation, and Brightness, LAB color is built around the models of lightness and chroma. The L channel in a LAB image contains all the information about the luminance in an image. The A channel stores information about hues from green to magenta, and hues from blue to yellow fall within the B channel.

As a Photoshop user, you choose to use the LAB color model under the following circumstances:

◆ When printing to a PostScript Level 2 printer.

◆ When opening a PhotoCD image.

◆ When converting a color image to grayscale. (See Chapter 17, "The Wonderful World of Black and White," for information on using LAB to produce the best grayscale images from color photos).

◆ Whenever you want to change the brightness or lightness values in an image without disturbing the hues in the image.

Photoshop uses LAB as an intermediate step when converting RGB images to CMYK. For more information on the CMYK color model, see Chapter 20, "Mixed Media and Photoshop" and Chapter 24, "The Service Bureau."

LAB color is great to use when you are working between devices—monitors, printers, PhotoCD, print presses. LAB strengths lie in the breadth of its color gamut and in the way it separates luminance information from hue. But when your editing involves choosing or modifying colors, the LAB color model is almost impossible to use. Virtually no one intuitively understands or can describe color in the way LAB does. HSB, on the other hand, is a very accessible way to work with color. HSB color is by far the most natural way for humans to define a digital color. In this book, you will almost always use the HSB model when choosing a color.

Understanding the Interrelationship of Color Models

Because LAB, RGB, and HSB color models are all additive color models and are based on the way humans see and recognize color, they have overlapping color spaces. For example, there are some colors that you can define in terms of the LAB color model, or the RGB color model or the HSB color model, while other colors might not be found within all three color models. This is because the methods each color model uses to describe color produce a different range or gamut of colors. The range or gamut of color a model can describe is often called a *color space*. LAB color has the widest color space, therefore the RGB and HSB color models fit inside; they are a *subset* of LAB color.

You have a certain flexibility, then, when defining and editing colors for use in Photoshop. If you can't create a pleasant-looking grayscale image from a component of an RGB mode image, you can convert the RGB image to LAB color and use only the lightness component to achieve a grayscale image. And when you're trying to fine-tune a LAB color image, you'll have an easier time using HSB color sliders on the Picker palette than the L, A, and B sliders that define LAB components.

You can use all of Photoshop's color models for color definition. As an imaging person, you need to understand the types of control you have over a digital image; then examine an image for color characteristic defects. After isolating the problem with an image, use the commands and features Photoshop presents within a specific color mode to correct the problem.

Understanding the components of a color model will lead you to a working methodology when correcting and enhancing digital images, especially those found on a PhotoCD. You have the means to isolate a color image's color components in the same way we've taken apart several color models in this chapter. You can create changes to an aspect of a color image without altering the other aspect because the digitized color images you work with in Photoshop are all built around a color model.

How Hue, Saturation, and Brightness Affect an Image

The next sections show you practical examples of how an image is evaluated according to its color properties. Color theory is the key to understanding why light behaves the way it does, but there's a difference between *specifying* color for painting and *evaluating* the color an image already has. The next section presents some examples of images that display strong color characteristics that can be isolated and manipulated using Photoshop's features.

Understanding Oversaturation and Video Clipping

Saturation, as modeled (represented) digitally, is the amount of predominance a particular hue has when other color hues are present in a specific color. Gray (also called *neutral density*) is an equal amount of all hues. When this equal amount is combined in an increasing percentage to the predominant hue, the predominant hue is no longer unique, and gray steals from the saturation of the color. An object with highly saturated color (such as a bright, colorful detergent package or bubble gum wrapper) includes almost no gray component. Conversely, color with *no* saturation, no particularly strong hue, is a combination of fairly equal percentages of all hues and displays as a monochrome part of a picture.

For example, an image consisting of rocks, such as that shown in figure 3.1, does not feature highly saturated colors. As figure 3.1 shows, Photoshop's Info palette provides a direct reading of saturation on the spot over which you place the cursor. A reading of three-percent saturation indicates that the rocks have more gray component than color. Oversaturation, on the other hand, causes clipping in a video image. You learn how to recognize and correct oversaturation in Chapter 8, "Retouching an Heirloom Photograph."

Figure 3.1

*This photograph
lacks color
saturation.*

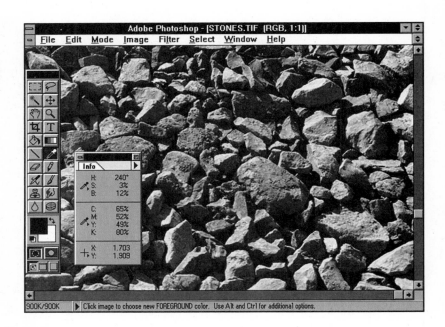

Using Brightness To Control Hue and Saturation

The brightness component of the HSB model shapes, bends, and drags the most out
of a picture, using the *color content* of the pixels in the digital image to control the
image's *visual content*.

Brightness is the only component in the color model that has nothing to do with a
color value (referring instead to the *tonal* quality of an image), and yet destroys a
picture when it is featured too little or too much in image areas. When mismanaged,
this component can wipe out a subject's facial features, turn a sunset into a "blobset,"
and generally make a photo look like an artist's overused palette.

Manipulating a Range of Digital Information

A *pixel* is the smallest unit of light displayed on a monitor and the smallest element in
a digital image. Everything that happens in the digital world—the things that you
create, modify, and work with—aren't physical in the sense that they are things you
can touch. Pixels are light when you see them on your monitor, but the *qualities* of

that light are based on information about color *associated* with the pixel. How light behaves, and how color is defined and expressed, is done through *models*: virtual representations of a phenomenon.

Models are concepts that are plotted out in wheels, circles, or other types of *maps*. A color wheel is a *model* of the various hues found in visible light, and a color wheel is an inadequate description of all visible colors because color wheels also don't describe saturation and brightness of colors.

Photoshop offers the "handles," the controls you click and drag, to change the components of color based on color models. You'll usually find that a Photoshop dialog box associated with a Photoshop command, such as Levels, offers independent control over a single component of color. In the case of the Levels command dialog box, you can change the brightness assigned to the hues and saturations of an image, the *tonal* relationships within an image, without affecting the colors of each pixel.

The relationship of color values between pixels in an image is the essence of a digital image; you would find little reason to change a single pixel's color in a digitized photo, but by changing the tonal and color relationships of a *range* of pixels, you can achieve sophisticated retouching. The HSB model can be used instead to rearrange color components in part, or in all, of a digital image's pixels.

You are indirectly affecting changes to pixels when you edit an image's tonal ranges. The two most common ranges that cause the most dramatic enhancement of an image's realistic qualities are brightness and gamma. *Brightness*—the degree of intensity that you perceive as a color—is reflected by (or passed through) an object. *Gamma* is a measurement of contrast—how much different pixels vary in their brightness values—in a specific brightness range: the image's *midtones*. Gamma is a very important quality to be able to adjust in an image because the midtones represent much of the visual content in most images.

Photoshop enables you to isolate and modify the components of color as expressed in a number of different color models.

Managing an Image's Brightness through Mapping

You can express an image's overall brightness as a map. A computer map is just like a physical map; it has an axis and things are plotted on it. However, computers display mapping of different image aspects in a very simplified format. Massive number-crunching is performed behind the scenes when you make what seems to be the simplest adjustment to a map.

Most computer programs and tools can map one object to another, which means that you can use your PC's innate capability to make swift calculations to help with your imaging work, if you have *coordinates* to plot on a brightness map.

Photoshop provides several types of maps, including one for the brightness component. Before you begin experimenting with the PhotoCD images on the companion CD, you need to understand a brightness mapping feature, which is the **L**evels command from the **I**mage, **A**djust menu. When you understand the principle behind this option, you can use it to make educated evaluations of what you need to modify in both PhotoCD format and regular digital images.

Figure 3.2 is a highly stylized illustration of the Levels histogram you find when you open an image in Photoshop, select **A**djust from the **I**mage menu, and then choose the **L**evels option. A *histogram* is a graph that represents the range of brightness in an image measured against the number of pixels in a particular value in the range. Each pixel contains color information, which is used with that of the other pixels to weave an image. Unless you change an image's size or resolution, the number of pixels is a constant within an image.

Figure 3.2

A Photoshop histogram plots brightness against pixel population at each brightness value in an image.

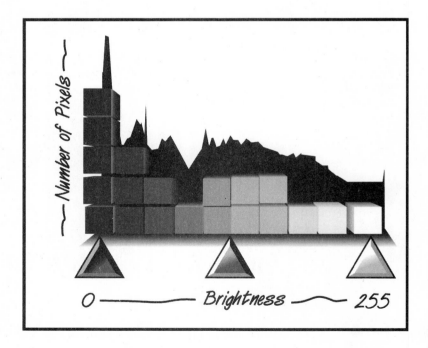

Although the histogram shown in figure 3.2 represents an incredibly small, 19-pixel digital image, you can make some observations from the graph. The Levels command lets you define a black point, white point, and midpoint value other than that which was used to create the original histogram of the image. This histogram was created on the scale of 0 (no brightness) to 255 (absolute brilliance). The result of changing an image's original histogram is the *redistribution* or *reassignment* of the image's color pixels.

Using the Levels dialog box, you can specify an input and output range. When you open the Levels dialog box, the figures and the histogram report the current condition of the image. Changing the input black-and-white point level values invariably increases the contrast in the image. Conversely, the output values decrease the contrast in the image. You change the output by typing in new numbers or moving the sliders on the bar at the bottom of the Levels dialog box.

Tip

A difference exists between *points* and *ranges*. Although the Levels command enables you to adjust points along the ranges (and enhance an image significantly by doing so), the command doesn't give you full control over ranges of tonal values. See Chapter 7, "Restoring an Heirloom Photograph," for a discussion of how to use the Curves command. The Curves command offers the user more control over the adjustment of tonal ranges.

Remapping a Histogram

To remap a histogram, begin by specifying the ideal darkest and lightest shades in the brightness range. By moving the black point up within an image, you eliminate some shades of brightness, thereby *increasing* the contrast in part of the image. You don't destroy pixels by increasing the black point, you simply reassign a higher brightness value to the pixels existing at that point.

The same holds true when you decrease the white point in an image; you don't change the hue or saturation of any pixels, but simply squeeze out part of the brightness range. This forces a sharper shift in brightness values between neighboring pixels to create more contrast.

Controlling Midpoints and Midtones

Photoshop goes a step beyond the simple brightness and contrast controls that you find on even the least-expensive television set. Within the range of brightness on the histogram is a slider that controls where an image's midtones lie. In the center of the midtones is a *midpoint*, represented by the middle slider on the Levels histogram.

As mentioned before, the middle of the brightness scale is a vital information range for many snapshots. Fleshtones, nature colors, and even the texture of clouds require much visual information in the pixels that sit in the middle of the histogram. These midtones must express enough contrast within this range so that you can clearly see, for example, the ridges in a piece of wood. To correct the midtones of your image's brightness range, you should move the middle Input Levels slider to the right or left while the Preview check box is marked so that you can see how these changes affect the midtones in your image.

Adjusting an Image's Gamma

If the shadows in the midtones are mottled rather than crisp, and the highlights are faded and provide little contrast between brightness values, the gamma of the image is too high for your PC. Image *gamma* is a measurement of contrast in the midtones of an image. If you calibrate this midtone part of an image too high, you get a dull, yet brilliant, overall image. The "perfect" picture has sharp blacks, crisp whites, and much *variation* (contrast) between the midtones. If the whites in your image seem whiter than possible and the darkest shadows have too much visual information, you can't fix these gamma problems by adjusting brightness and contrast. Photoshop can adjust the levels in the midtones right down to the quartertones to reduce the brilliance overkill in specific ranges of the image.

Photoshop offers three tiers of sophistication in adjusting the brightness map this way: the Curves command provides the most complex map; the Levels command is the next most complex; and the Brightness/Contrast command results in the roughest tuning. The next exercise, which introduces the PhotoCD image with all its superluminescent virtues, uses the Levels command to adjust tonal values in the image.

Photo CDs—Optimized for TV, Not PC

PhotoCDs were developed to hold high-quality photographic images in a digital format. Although the images look and behave like your average RGB TrueColor file, Kodak has given the PhotoCD (*.PCD) file format some extraordinary qualities.

A PhotoCD image is created by scanning a photographic negative using a very expensive, high resolution scanner. The information from the scanner is sent to a graphic workstation that takes the information and stores the image in a single file that contains five different copies of the image, each at a different resolution. This master file, called an *Image Pac*, then is written in a highly compressed proprietary format and stored on a CD. When you want to use a PhotoCD image, you must use software that can read and extract the file that has the resolution you've specified from Kodak's proprietary format. Photoshop is fully Kodak PhotoCD-aware and you can open any PhotoCD image you want by using the <u>F</u>ile, <u>O</u>pen commands.

Originally, Kodak thought that the average consumer would be the most excited about this technology. So they developed and marketed playback equipment that can display PhotoCD images on a household television set. Kodak, believing that there would be strong consumer demand for PhotoCDs, matched the gamma of all PhotoCD images to that of an analog television receiver, and not that of the digitally-fed PC monitor. As a result, when PhotoCD images are opened on a computer, they look overly brilliant, washed out, and rather unappealing. Before PhotoCD images can be used as elements in your Photoshop work, they must be adjusted to bring the image gamma in line with that of your computer.

Although Kodak discovered that the computer graphic and publishing industries are more interested in the technology (and provide more of the research and development moneys) than Uncle Bob at the family get-together, PhotoCDs are still produced in 1994 with gammas that are too high. Kodak modified and improved the software that they license to software companies, and reduced the problem of miscalibrated gamma somewhat, but until the images are created expressly for computer imaging use, you will have to adjust PhotoCD images before you begin to use them in Photoshop.

It is quite easy to adjust a PhotoCD image in Photoshop and this is where the color theory that you've learned becomes *color practice* when you follow the steps in the next exercise.

Adjusting a PhotoCD's Tonal Levels

If the gamma is off on PhotoCDs, why bother with PhotoCD images at all? Why not scan all your Photoshop work? The answers become clear in the following exercise.

The *Bonus CD* that accompanies this book contains a number of images in Kodak's compressed, proprietary PCD image format. They are exactly as you would get the image back from Kodak on a PhotoCD disk. Soon you'll see exactly how to open this image, and then how to perform a little gamma correction that results in the image blossoming into unbelievable color. You simply cannot acquire better color and resolution for a photographic image by scanning a color print with a desktop flatbed scanner.

Bear in mind two things in this first exercise:

◆ You can't save any changes you make to a PhotoCD image back to a PhotoCD (PCD) file format. The PCD format is proprietary, and only Kodak knows how to write a PCD file. Additionally, as you run through the exercises in this book, you are asked to save your editing work. This can't be done to a PhotoCD, or any *other* sort of **C**D-**R**ead-**O**nly **M**emory medium. If you want to save changes made to a PhotoCD image or any image you open from our Bonus CD (and others you come across), you must do so to a floppy disk, hard drive, Bernoulli cartridge, or other rewritable media.

◆ Changes that you make to the brightness, contrast, and gamma of an image are *relative* changes, not absolute ones that are based on the original image's values. Therefore, every time you use any one of Photoshop's **I**mage, **A**djust menu commands, the changes you make are *in addition* to any previous changes you've made. For example, when you use the Levels command to modify the image (as you do in the next exercise), you change the *distribution* of pixels along the Levels graph, not the graph itself, or the number of pixels in an image. For example, the histogram always represents the brightness scale from 0 to 255, so the second time that you display the Levels command dialog box to make additional changes, a black point that you reset to 10 is still shown as set to 0.

You're now ready to begin the exercise, which provides a unique visual demonstration of how you can use tonal controls to bring out an image's visual information.

Opening a PhotoCD Image

Choose **F**ile, **O**pen, and choose IMG0003.PCD from the CHAP03 subdirectory (folder) on the Bonus CD	The Kodak Precision CMS PhotoCD dialog box appears.
Click on the Source button. Make sure that the PhotoCD Color Negative is the highlighted entry in the Choose Source Precision Transformation dialog box; click on OK	Ensures that the software opens the image with the best settings for images that are on a PhotoCD.
Click on the Destination button. From the Destination drop-down list on the Destination Precision Transform dialog box choose Adobe Photoshop CIELAB; click on OK	Sets the software to open the PhotoCD image as a LAB color mode image. This preserves all the colors and Lightness information in the image.
Choose 512×768 from the Resolution drop-down list	Selects the BASE image size whose dimensions are measured in pixels. This setting will open a 1.13 MB file.
Uncheck the Landscape (faster) check box (see fig. 3.3)	Opens the image in portrait mode.

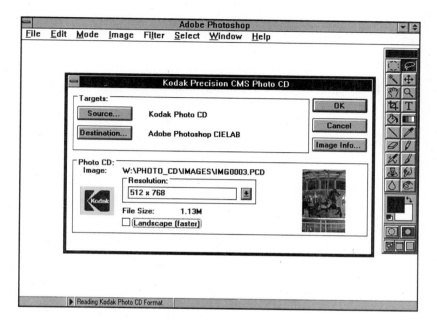

Figure 3.3

The Kodak Precision CMS PhotoCD dialog box appears whenever you open a PhotoCD file.

This image will open faster if you leave the check box checked, but the image will be sideways. You would have to rotate it in Photoshop after the image has opened to avoid working with your head cocked to one side. Unless you are reading the file over a very slow network, it's faster to let Kodak rotate the image, and it saves you a step.

Click on OK	The 1.13 MB image opens in Photoshop.

This will take a little longer than opening a similarly sized file from your hard disk because the file needs to be extracted from the master file and decompressed.

Press Ctrl (Cmd) + −	Changes the viewing resolution to 1:2; providing you with a better view of the image.
Drag the image by its title bar into the extreme upper left-hand corner of the workspace, then drag all open palettes and the toolbar to the extreme right of the workspace	Makes space so that you can see the image and the Levels command dialog box you'll use in the next exercise.

The image is pretty, but washed out. Television, the medium for which Kodak developed PCD files, has a gamma display setting of 2.2, but the monitor on which you're viewing this image has a gamma of about 1.8. Before you can take full advantage of a PhotoCD's quality in Photoshop, you have to adjust the image to bring out the detail lost due to the high gamma of the image.

Typically, PhotoCDs do not have a true black point and extend the white point beyond 100-percent white to include the whiter-than-white information commonly found in natural highlights, such as direct reflections over water. The combination of high gamma and the extension of the white point produces a low-contrast image, with midtones that are higher than an ideal image's midpoint. In plain English, the image doesn't look so hot.

Fortunately, you and Photoshop can bring the heightened brightness values back to a range that results in spectacular color. You've already started the process by choosing to open the image in the Adobe Photoshop CIELAB mode. Opening the image in the CIELAB format preserves all the whiter-than-white information typical of PhotoCD images so that when you make your adjustments, you have all the information contained in the original file to work with. If instead you had opened the file in the Adobe Photoshop RGB mode, some of this information would have been lost before you started. This is because the color model Kodak uses (YCC) is a variant of the LAB color model that Photoshop uses, and both models can express the same information; they have the same gamut. As discussed earlier in this chapter, all the colors that the RGB color model can express are contained *within* the LAB color gamut, but the LAB and Kodak's YCC color models are capable of defining more colors than RGB.

In the following exercise, you use Photoshop's Levels command to create a dramatic change in the PhotoCD image's quality.

Finding the Right Levels

Press Ctrl(Cmd)+L or choose **I**mage, **A**djust, and then choose **L**evels. Drag the dialog box down into the lower-right corner so that you can see the dialog box and the image	Displays the Levels dialog box.
Check the **P**review box in the Levels dialog box if it is not already checked	Activates the Preview feature.

With Preview set, Photoshop displays changes in the image so that you can see what changes the settings you make will have on the image. The changes displayed by the preview don't actually occur in the image file until you choose OK and implement the changes.

Enter the following values in the Input Levels boxes: **31**, **.73**, and **214** as shown in figure 3.4	Sets new values for the black point, midpoint a, and the white point.

The corresponding black point, gray midpoint, and white point sliders move in. Notice how the photo changes as you enter each value.

The correct values were determined by moving the sliders until the results look good. You have to trust your eye to find the right values, so feel free to enter other values or to drag on the sliders until the image looks perfect to you.

Click on OK	Applies the corrections and closes the Levels dialog box.
Press Ctrl(Cmd)+L (**I**mage, **A**djust, **L**evels)	Displays the Levels dialog box again, histogram looks like figure 3.5.

The histogram in the Levels dialog box has changed dramatically to reflect the changes you made in the preceding steps.

Click on the Cancel button	Closes the Levels dialog box without making any changes.
Choose **M**ode, then choose **R**GB	Converts the image from the LAB color format to the RGB format.

RGB mode is typically used when editing images. It is also the mode that should be used when saving a color image to file formats other than Photoshop's PSD format. Many programs, other than Photoshop, do not understand LAB color mode and will not be able to work with the file if you save it when it is in LAB color mode.

If you think you may want to work with this file in the future, save the file to your hard disk now using the steps that follow; otherwise press Ctrl(Cmd)+W and don't save changes.

Choose **F**ile, Sa**v**e As; enter a new name for the file in the File **N**ame field and choose Photoshop 3.0 (*.PSD) from the Save File as Format **T**ype drop-down list; use the Directories and Drives fields to choose a place to store the file on your hard disk; choose OK	Saves the file to your hard disk in Photoshop's file format.
Double-click on the control menu button the upper right-hand corner of the image window or press Ctrl(Cmd)+ W	Closes the file; you're done with it now.

Figure 3.4

*The Levels dialog
box with user
settings entered.*

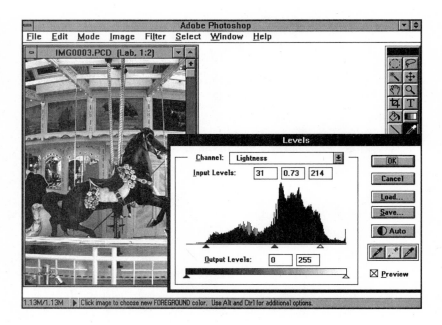

Figure 3.5

*As you input
values in the
Levels dialog box,
the image changes
to reflect the new
values.*

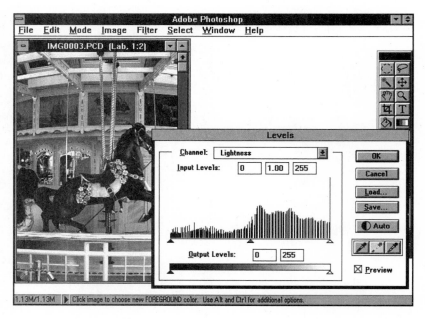

The PhotoCD image has much more punch, and its detail is restored by adjusting the image's gamma. As you can see in figure 3.5, altering the histogram can result in a better tonal distribution of pixels. Although your own eyes are your best tool in this process, learn to rely on them *in addition* to all the visual information that Photoshop can map for you.

The first level's histogram that you saw (see fig. 3.4) for this image showed no pixels at the black point and almost none in the upper white range. Everything was bunched together in a small range of tonal values that displayed little contrast; the number of pixels that displayed a brightness value of, say 127, weren't prominent because a near-equal amount of pixels with a brightness of 128 were within the image.

The second level's histogram (see fig. 3.5) shows color values across the entire range; you've established a definite cluster of values near the black point that corresponds to the dark horse and chair, and broadened the range of values in the mid to upper ranges than in the first histogram. The clearly defined spaces you see between values (the *spikes*) indicate that much more contrast is within the image. All these changes produce an image that shows much more visual detail in the midranges. The midrange values in an image are where most of the details that define an image are found. This concentration of well-separated and distributed values in the mid and upper ranges is particularly good for this image because with the exception of the horse and the loveseat upholstery, the image consists of whites and pastels.

Viewing Current Brightness Distribution

Earlier you learned that the brightness curve on the Levels histogram has no effect on the hue and saturation components in an image, just the brightness, which is the intensity with which light appears to be cast from a color object. The **H**istogram command in the **I**mage menu (not the one in the Levels command dialog box) keeps you updated as to the *current* status of the tonal distribution and by default presents a Gray channel view that shows how the brightness of the pixels affects their position in the histogram.

 Note As you continue with this book's Photoshop exercises, the concept of a Gray channel may seem odd because an RGB image does not include a Gray channel. Remember that a histogram is a view of properties in a color model, and this is simply a different view. Photoshop's Histogram command represents pixel frequency on a scale that represents the weighted average of the brightness found in the Red, Green, and Blue color channels of an image. You can't change it directly, but the Levels command, which corresponds to the **H**istogram command, can.

When a graph shows only tonal differences, Photoshop offers a Gray channel that's a tonal composite of the color information channels.

Telling a Good Histogram from a Bad One

Histograms are like fingerprints: no two are identical. Therefore, no such thing as "the best histogram for all pictures" exists. But like fingerprints, tell-tale signs at the scene of the crime always reveal where a histogram may have gone amiss.

Take a look at the FALL.TIF image, shown in figure 3.6 and included on the companion CD. The gamma for this PhotoCD image has been corrected, so it looks pretty good.

Figure 3.6

A gamma-corrected PhotoCD image.

Now let's walk through the areas in this image as they correspond to the Gray channel view—the view that shows how bright each pixel is and where each is located within this image.

From the Bottom Up

FALL.TIF shows a sunny, cloudless view over a cornfield into some trees that are changing their seasonal colors. Although some dark areas emerge from shadows cast between the trees and the corn stalks, absolute black rarely occurs in this picture. Therefore, a histogram view of the overall brightness in this image should indicate some density near the low end of the midtones and even some toward the black point, but not much.

The Midtones of Fall

For this image, you shouldn't expect a high frequency of color pixels on the high end of the midtones. Earth colors, like leaves and the dried, sandy-colored cornstalks, should occupy the lower end of the midtones and contribute little brightness to the high end of the midtone map. This makes sense if you consider that a grouping of leaves creates a texture that consists of great variation in brightness between neighboring values, all within a moderate range of tones.

The Sky's the Limit

You see the greatest contrast in this image where the treeline reaches the blue sky. The sky in FALL.TIF accounts for about a quarter of the visual information in this image, and therefore many of its pixels. You should expect, then, to find a high occurrence of color pixels in an upper range on the histogram map. Whatever highlights this image contains will be represented in the same brightness range as the sky because the histogram plots brightness, not color.

Because the image content doesn't include any physical objects that are highly reflective, you shouldn't expect an appreciable amount of white points in FALL.TIF. Still, there should be some, if not many, 255-value pixels because some of the hues in this image are almost pure colors (a hue plus 100-percent saturation).

Figure 3.7 shows a histogram of FALL.TIF after undergoing some gamma- and contrast-correcting of the image, using the same steps in the last Levels exercise. The figure includes some notes along the Brightness map, and you should see the points described in the last section as Photoshop plotted them.

Figure 3.8 shows what can happen in a histogram if some of the visual information in FALL.TIF is *destroyed*. In this case, deliberate misuse of Photoshop's tools incorrectly changed the image's gamma. (Trust us; you don't want to see the image.) Compare this histogram to that in figure 3.7, noting which areas lack brightness, and which are filled in.

Figure 3.7

A histogram of FALL.TIF after some intelligent tonal adjustments.

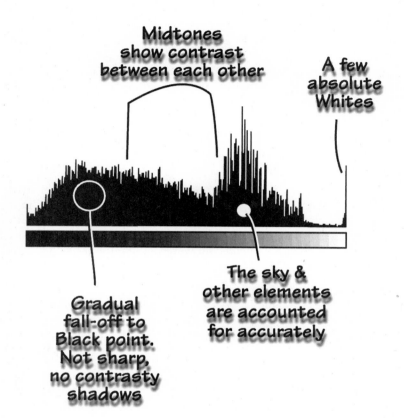

Midtones show contrast between each other

A few absolute Whites

Gradual fall-off to Black point. Not sharp, no contrasty shadows

The sky & other elements are accounted for accurately

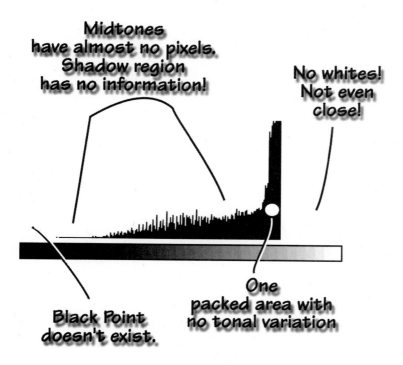

Midtones
have almost no pixels.
Shadow region
has no information!

No whites!
Not even
close!

One
packed area with
no tonal variation

Black Point
doesn't exist.

Figure 3.8

A FALL.TIF histogram after the image was tonally maladjusted.

Looking Back on Brightness

In this chapter, you have spent quite a bit of time learning about how brightness affects pixels in an image, particularly those in PhotoCD images. This time is well spent, though, because any image scanned either by you or by the Kodak PhotoCD process usually needs this kind of correction.

Note   The Kodak Precision CMS system that Photoshop installed on your system was designed to automatically correct many of the contrast and gamma problems computer users have with PhotoCD images. You use this system each time you open a PhotoCD image. Although this is a vast improvement over the way PhotoCD images were handled in version 2.5, images still need to be corrected.

The module is "automatic," which means that it is calibrated to address the gamma problems of an the average image. The only problem with taking that approach is that no such thing as an "average" image exists; every image is unique. The automatic part of the system does get you most of the way to a tonality-balanced image, but you must always use your eyes and Photoshop's tools to fine-tune the image so that it meets your needs. The adjustments you make are somewhat idiosyncratic in that everyone sees images differently and has different preferences. This is only one example of how your personal sense of aesthetics and your judgment must be your final guide in your imaging work. Take the time to make your images reflect your aesthetics and don't let convenient, automated controls make design decisions for you.

Call it a challenge or a hurdle, but brightness is one of the first components that you should adjust before you retouch an image. But brightness is only one component of the overall information that the digital image contains. You'll use the Levels and Curves commands and several other global modifying features in the exercises, and you should learn how to use a combination of Photoshop features to enhance digital images.

Note   Whenever you make an important change to an image in Photoshop, remember to use your own judgment to evaluate how the work is going. Although Photoshop helps you plot an image's contrast and gamma, your eyes will always tell you far more about eye-pleasing qualities. When something is drastically wrong with the display of visual content in an image, remember to use the tone controls that you have learned about as a resource or guide to remapping. Then, after these controls have improved the image's overall quality, rely on your own judgment as you apply the finishing touches.

Understanding the Basis of Resolutions

Before you even begin adjusting the gamma of a PhotoCD image, consider how large a file you want to load in your system RAM while you work with the image in Photoshop. The file extension PSD indicates that not one but five different resolutions of the same image are tucked away in that Kodak box. This section explores what the PSD format is, what it does, and how it affects your imaging work.

When you open a PhotoCD image in Photoshop, you are immediately presented with the Kodak Precision CMS PhotoCD dialog box (refer back to fig. 3.4). In the dialog box, you choose one of the five resolutions (measured in pixel height and width) with which to open the image. For the color-correcting exercise, you used the 512×768 resolution that produced a 1.13 MB file, but that's not always the best choice. This section and the next series of exercises helps you make the right choice from a not-so-intuitive dialog box.

Choosing an Appropriate Resolution

Which resolution you should use when loading an image into Photoshop is a good question, and the dialog box is pretty oblique on the subject. Images are stored in PhotoCD format as one highly compressed file that ranges from about 2.5 MB to 6 MB. This file contains five different versions of the image with each file differing only in its resolution. These files were created from the original, physical negative scan.

The PhotoCD Options dialog box essentially asks, "If you had scanned this image, how much information would you have captured?" The five different sizes (sometimes called BASES) correspond to five different (and arbitrary) scanner settings that you could have chosen. They range from a very low-resolution scan to a very high one.

When you choose a file resolution from the Kodak Precision CMS PhotoCD dialog box, the image file component that has the resolution you requested is opened and expanded to its original size in your computer's RAM (memory).

PhotoCDs are always set at a 72-pixel-per-inch setting because that is the optimal setting for viewing an image at 1:1 resolution on a television set or a monitor. This resolution is far too low to produce good results from a commercial printing press. Fortunately, you can change this setting using Photoshop's Image Size dialog box (Image, Image Size). In the Image Size dialog box, you reduce the size of a large-dimensioned, low-resolution image so that it has a higher pixel-per-inch value. As you'll recall from Chapter 2, "Acquiring a Digital Image," image resolution has an inverse relationship to image dimension: the smaller the dimension, the higher the pixel-per-inch value. As long as the file size (as measured in megabytes) remains the same, changing either an image's dimensions or its resolution doesn't change an image's quality. It's only when the changes you make are allowed to change the size of the file as measured in megabytes that image quality changes.

When choosing a resolution at which to open a file, you must consider if the file you are opening will provide enough information to create a finished image that has the proper dimensions and resolution for printing:

◆ The image size you want to create should be the same height and width as you intend to print.

◆ The resolution (dpi) should be approximately twice that of a commercial printer's line screen frequency. For example, if the printer uses a 133 lpi line screen, your file should have a resolution somewhere between 270–300 dpi. (More on how to determine this is covered in Chapter 23, "Personal Printing Basics.")

The 512×768 PhotoCD resolution is the most common and convenient size for general usage in Photoshop. A PhotoCD with this resolution loads into Photoshop as a file that is 512 pixels wide (7.11 inches) and 768 pixels high (10.66 inches) and has a pixel-per-inch resolution of 72. The file will occupy 1.13 MB of memory, and if you save it to disk as a TIF file, it will occupy 1.18 MB of hard disk space. The extra space is taken up by the header information when the TIF file is created. *Headers* are information stored at the beginning of a file that tells other programs how the information within the file is organized.

Using an image of this size, 512×768, you can print a high-quality image using a 133-lpi line screen (magazine quality) at a maximum size of 2.56-inches wide by 3.84-inches high. A medium-quality image printed with a 85-lpi line screen (newsletter quality) has a maximum size of 4-inches wide by 6-inches tall using the same 512×768 image.

If you need a larger image, you can choose either the 1024×1536 resolution (also called BASE*4) or the 2048×3072 resolution (BASE*16) and then increase the pixel-per-inch resolution (and thus decrease the image dimensions) to get a correctly sized image for a specific printer's line screen. Conversely, if you need your finished image to be smaller, you can choose either the 256×384(BASE/4) or the 128×192 (BASE/16) size images.

Putting Resolutions to Work

Although all the different size images that Kodak offers for the PhotoCD are a wonder of modern technology, using them in different situations requires that you plan carefully before choosing an image size to open. In the next section, you get an opportunity to experiment with an image that's "larger than life," in more ways than one.

Like traditional photography, digital imaging often involves cropping. In many of the assignments for which you use Photoshop, you need to use only part of a photographic image, and a cropped section often winds up with a resolution lower than you want. In chemical photography, an excessively enlarged image displays grain, marring the quality of the image, but there isn't much you can do about it.

However, if you're using Photoshop, and especially if you're using a PhotoCD image, you *can* do something about this problem: open a *higher resolution* version of the image. The higher the resolution of the image (and consequently the larger the *file dimensions*), the more information you have to work with. If you have enough information to work with after you crop and resize the image, you can achieve a final image that looks good when printed. The only limitations of PhotoCD technology lie in the grain of the film from which the PhotoCD image is scanned.

A new feature to Photoshop 3 is the Quick Edit feature found on the File, Acquire menu. This feature enables you to open and work on a portion of a file. This means that if you have a very large TIFF or Scitex CT format file, you can open only the part of the file you need. You don't have to tax your system's memory resources with the entire file; instead, you can open only the section you need to edit. The portion of the file that you opened can be saved back to the original file, and the edits you made will be incorporated into the large file. You can also save the portion you opened from a large file as a separate file. This means that you can crop a small area out of a large image without opening the large file.

Unfortunately, this feature only works on image files that are in the TIFF and Scitex CT format. If you need only a small portion of a PhotoCD image, you have two courses of action:

◆ Ask someone who has sufficient RAM and hard disk space to open and save the PCD image as a TIFF image, get the image backed up on tape of large format removable media to transport to your own system, and then use Photoshop's Quick Edit command, or...

◆ Open the entire image yourself, and crop what you need of the image.

The following exercise uses Photoshop's Cropping tool to select only the day lily flower in the PhotoCD format image shown in figure 3.9. In this exercise, your imaginary assignment is to come up with a flower for the cover of a threefold brochure. The layout calls for the flower photo to be about 2-inches square, and the printer wants the image at a resolution of 150 ppi.

To meet the assignment's specifications, you need a high-resolution version of the image, the 1024×1536 resolution (BASE*4), so that the small, cropped portion of the image ends up the right size and resolution. Part of the convenience of using the Kodak PCD format is that it eliminates the need to rescan an image each time you use it for a different purpose. Recall that PhotoCDs present you with five different sizes of the image scanned at different resolutions, and not one megabyte of image information has to reside on your hard drive.

Figure 3.9

You need to select this flower, but it's not very big in this photo.

Stop   Before you start this exercise, be aware of the processing demands in opening a 1024 ×1536 image. On a fast 486 IBM/PC or Quadra 850/900 with 20 MB of RAM, this action may take as long as 15 minutes.

Now that you know the downside of the following exercise, you can choose to pass it up and still not suffer from the lack of experience. Be aware, however, that the problems of cropping and maintaining resolution in an image may come up in your own imaging assignments, and that this exercise shows the only way that you can handle such problems with a PhotoCD image.

So, while your PC loads this image, you may want to take a coffee break or read ahead for an overview of the next steps in this exercise. Rest assured that the purpose of this exercise is *not* to tie up your machine as a mean-spirited practical joke played on you by the authors.

Picking a Flower

Choose **F**ile, **O**pen, then choose IMG0005.PCD from the CHAP03 subdirectory (folder) on the Bonus CD

Opens the PhotoCD and displays the Kodak Precision CMS PhotoCD dialog box.

Choose 1024×1536 from the Resolution drop-down list (the other settings should be as you set them in the preceding exercise); click on OK

Specifies the image resolution of the file that you're opening. Settings you make in one session remain the same (stick) in other sessions unless you change them.

Don't panic if the results aren't immediate; you're opening a 4.5 MB file.

Click on the up-arrow box in the upper-right corner of the screen

This maximizes your view in the active image window.

Press **Z** (**Z**oom tool). Click the Zoom tool twice over the flower

Displays a full-screen, 1:2 viewing resolution of the area you need to crop out of the image.

Press **C** (**C**rop tool) or click on the Crop button on the toolbox

Chooses the Crop tool.

The Crop tool is used to eliminate image areas outside the marquee border that you define with the tool.

Place the cursor to the upper left of the flower; then, while holding down the Shift key, click and drag down and to the right to create a square around the flower; then release the mouse button and the Shift key

Creates a special selection border around the flower as shown in figure 3.10.

If you're dissatisfied with the marquee cropping border, click outside the border area. Your cursor turns into a small international "no" symbol, and the marquee border disappears. Then retry the last few steps.

Click inside the marquee when you're satisfied with the Crop tool selection

Turns your cursor into a small pair of scissors, and removes the portions of the image that lie outside the marquee selection.

Notice that on Photoshop's status bar the file size has decreased significantly, from 4.5 to 200 or 300 KB, depending on where you made the Cropping selection.

Choose **F**ile, Sa**v**e As; enter a new name for the file in the File **N**ame field and choose Photoshop 3.0 (*.PSD) from the Save File as Format **T**ype drop-down list; use the

Saves the file to your hard disk in Photoshop's file format.

continues

continued

Directories and Drives fields to
choose a place to store the file on
your hard disk; choose OK

Don't close the file, you'll need it in the next exercise.

Figure 3.10

*The area that you
want to select is
inside the
cropping border.*

The trick to the technique demonstrated in the last exercise is to be patient while
loading the oversized files and then to crop to the dimensions that you want as
quickly as you can.

Resizing a PhotoCD Selection

PhotoCD images are always brought into your computer at a 72-ppi resolution, which
is too low for high-quality commercial printing. So now that you have cropped your
flower, you need to adjust the size and resolution by using the Image Size dialog box.

Keeping Things in Proportion

You want your final image to maintain its aspect ratio—the proportional ratio of width to height—and the file size in bytes. If you Uncheck the **P**roportion and the **F**ile Size check boxes and then increase the resolution, the file size increases as Photoshop adds information, but the height and width remain the same. In this instance, Photoshop *interpolates* pixels in the image to create "in-between" pixels that are calculated on an average of the neighboring pixels' color values. The result is a loss of image fidelity because Photoshop *changes the image information*. You might not be able to see the degradation of image quality on your screen, but it becomes evident when you print the image. A non-proportionately resized image becomes *pixellated*—that is, it looks like a chemical photograph that was enlarged excessively and became grainy.

You can solve this problem by using a higher resolution scan (as you did in the last exercise by cropping from a 1024×1536 image) so that more native information is used. In the next exercise, when you change the resolution from 72 to 150, the height and width change but the file size does not. The resulting image then has enough information to print correctly. Let's see how this is done.

Sizing Up an Image

With the cropped image of the lily from the last exercise open and in the active window in Photoshop's workspace...

Choose **I**mage, **I**mage Sizes as shown in figure 3.11	Displays the Image Size dialog figure box.

Your file dimensions and file size may differ slightly from those shown in figure 3.11.

Make sure that the **P**roportion and **F**ile Size check boxes are checked and change the **R**esolution setting to **150**	Changes the **W**idth and H**ei**ght from about 4 inches to about 2 inches; the file size remains the same.
Choose **F**ile, Sa**v**e; type **LILY.TIF** in the File **N**ame box, and then click on OK	Saves the adjusted image with the file name LILY.TIF, as shown in figure 3.12.

Choosing the right resolution when you start a project is an intelligent, informed move. Table 3.1, which shows the relationship between the PhotoCD sizes as measured in pixels and the image and file sizes, can help you choose the right BASE for your project.

Figure 3.11

Use the Image Size dialog box to adjust the resolution of an image.

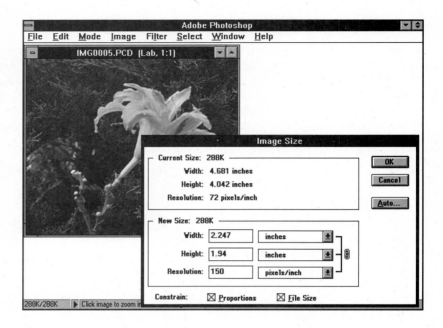

Figure 3.12

The cropped image of the lily with the correct size and resolution.

Table 3.1
PhotoCD Files Sizes in Real Terms

Dimensions (Width×Height) in Pixels	Dimensions (Width×Height) in Inches	Size in Memory W×H	Size When Saved to Disk as a TIF
128×192	1.8×2.7	72 KB	74.2 KB
256×384	3.6×5.3	288 KB	295 KB
512×768	7.11×10.7	1.13 MB	1.2 MB
1024×1536	14.2×21.3	4.5 MB	4.7 MB
2048×3072	28.4×42.7	18 MB	18.8 MB

 Tip
Here's a quick rule of thumb for picking the right image size when working with PhotoCDs. This rule works if you are going to use the whole image and your printer uses an 85-lpi screen (a common screen size for medium-quality brochures, reports, and newsletters).

Double the width and height at which you will print the finished image, and then open a PhotoCD file whose width and height is greater than or equal to the doubled dimensions.

For example, if you want to print a 1.5-inch by 2-inch image, double those dimensions to get 3-inches by 4 inches. As table 3.1 shows, the 256×384 size image has a dimension of 3.6×5.3, so for this job you would choose this size from the Kodak Precision CMS PhotoCD dialog box's Resolution drop-down list.

Understanding PhotoCD Technology

These PhotoCD images as well as a number of others are included on the Bonus CD to give you a taste of the technology in action (check Appendix A, "What's On the Bonus CD?" for what's where). But it would be unfair to give you this taste without explaining how the technology works and the equipment that you need to take full advantage of it while you work in Photoshop.

Probably the most exciting thing about PhotoCDs is that they can contain *your own photos.* You can take your undeveloped 35mm film, negatives, or slides to just about any photofinisher and tell them "PhotoCD it!" You can also take existing 35mm negatives you may already own and have a PhotoCD copy made from them. In about a week or two you'll get a PhotoCD back with your pictures in the same PCD format that you've been working with throughout this chapter. The cost for developing 24

PhotoCD images is only about $20. In contrast, to transfer your images to a conventional CD would cost at least $250.

Unlike a conventional CD-ROM disk, a PhotoCD disk is *multisession.* This means that you can return your PhotoCD to the photofinisher and have them put more images on the same PhotoCD. You can do this as many times as you want until you fill the 550 MB PhotoCD (which takes about 100 images). You can't add more photos to a conventional CD; instead, you would have to have a new CD made, which would again cost you over $250.

The PCD Format

The Kodak PhotoCD process scans a 35mm film negative or slide and produces five different resolutions, or sizes of the image. If stored as TIF images on your hard disk, the five versions of your image would occupy over 25 MB of hard drive space. However, the PhotoCD process uses a proprietary image format, PCD, to store these five versions in one large, highly compressed file called an *Image Pac.* This file typically is about 4.5 MB, but file sizes for color images can range from about 3.5 MB to 8 MB.

If you scanned the images without using the PCD format, it would take 2 gigabytes of hard disk space to store the uncompressed images that one PhotoCD can hold!

The Image Pacs are then written to a special kind of compact disk, the Photographic Quality Kodak PhotoCD Master, which can hold up to 100 24-bit TrueColor images. These CDs are designed to take the years and usage with exceptional grace. Kodak estimates the life cycle of a PhotoCD to be 100 years; supporting data to confirm this estimate obviously hasn't been reached. You can also put black-and-white images on the same PhotoCD as color images.

A CD-ROM Player Isn't a *Photo*CD-ROM Player

All this may sound too good to be true, and—you're right—there is a catch. Not all computer CD-ROM drives can read a PhotoCD disk from a photo finisher. If you want to use PhotoCDs to archive your own photographs, you need a CD-ROM drive that is PhotoCD-compatible. A PhotoCD-compatible drive (which includes most drives manufactured after 1992) can also read conventional CD-ROMs, so you can use it with any conventional CDs you already have.

Any CD-ROM drive can read the PhotoCD images on the companion CD because the PCD image files were copied from a PhotoCD disk to a conventional, single-session CD-ROM disk. Companies that sell stock photos in PhotoCD file format also transfer the PhotoCD images to conventional CD-ROM disks so that everyone can use the photos, regardless of the kind of CD-ROM drive he or she has. But whenever you send a roll of film to the photofinisher to get your images back on PhotoCD, you can read the disk only on a PhotoCD-capable CD-ROM drive.

This is the key to taking advantage of PhotoCD technology: you can buy PhotoCD stock photography from a vendor who sells images in the Kodak PSD format. Commercial photographers have spent many years taking exquisite shots of scenes you could never travel to. Furthermore, many companies now include volumes of work (categorized by topic at very low fees) a Photoshop user can purchase. Or you can have your own photos transferred to a Kodak PhotoCD—the choice is yours.

You can also copy from a PhotoCD Image Pac (file) to a hard drive, tape, or other removable media. Third-party stock photo companies often do this as an intermediate step between writing the images to regular CD-ROM standards. A copied PCD file can be opened and used just as if it were still on the original CD. This is useful if you need to transfer the file to someone who wants to be able to use any of the five files stored in PhotoCD Image Pac but lacks a PhotoCD player.

So the catch is, if you want to transfer your photos to a PhotoCD, you need a PhotoCD-compatible CD-ROM drive to read them. The drive you are using for the companion CD may be PhotoCD-compatible if it is a newer drive. Later in this chapter you learn how to determine whether your drive is PhotoCD-compatible and what to look for in a CD-ROM drive if you need to buy a new one.

Note PhotoCDs can also be read by CD-I and 3DO players, which are designed for CD-based interactive books and games. However, these players don't hook up to a PC properly. So, although you cannot do any Photoshop work with a CD-I player, you can preview your PhotoCD images on your television set with these Nintendo-like units.

Types of PhotoCDs

More than one kind of PhotoCD exists. The type of PhotoCD discussed in this chapter is the simplest, least expensive, most universal format that Kodak has introduced. This is the consumer version, the Photographic Quality Kodak PhotoCD Master. For most Photoshop work, this format will suit your needs quite nicely.

The Professional Photographic Quality format, called the *Kodak Pro PhotoCD Master*, can hold film formats other than 35mm. You can transfer 35mm, 70mm, 120mm, and 4-inch by 5-inch negatives and chromes to this PhotoCD format. With the Pro PhotoCD Master format, you can request that the Image Pac contains an additional higher resolution scan, (which yields a whopping 72 MB file). With this format you have a copyright notice embedded within the PhotoCD image file.

These Pro PhotoCDs can be quite expensive, but are still a bargain compared to buying an expensive ($10,000 and up) drum scanner and then scanning negatives yourself. A service bureau charges as much as $150 to do a high-resolution scan of a 4-inch by 5-inch negative or positive. You can have the same image transferred to a Pro PhotoCD for about $50.

Working Smarter with PhotoCD Technology

After you start using PhotoCDs and Photoshop, you start to collect images and need a convenient way to view them. Photoshop opens PhotoCD image files the same as other file formats that it supports, but you still must open image files one at a time. This is definitely a handicap when working with a collection of PhotoCD images. According to the PhotoCD file-naming convention, every PhotoCD starts with IMG0001.PCD, then IMG002.PCD, and so on—and such titles aren't very helpful when you're scrambling to find an image. When you have 24 images on a PhotoCD, searching for the one that you want is a tedious process; with a hundred images, you *definitely* will want an overview of the PhotoCD's contents.

However, inexpensive image display and management programs are available that catalog the entire contents of a PhotoCD. Some even let you enter keyword descriptions of each image so that you can quickly find the image you're looking for. Let's take a look at how these programs work.

Interfaces for Viewing a PhotoCD

You can get an overview of what is on a PhotoCD in two ways. One way is to use the paper index sheet attached to the PhotoCD's plastic cover. The other is to use a computer-image browsing program, like Kodak Access or Corel Corporation's CD-ROM Utilities.

Index Sheet

Your PhotoCD images return to you with a small piece of photographic paper that has 5/8-inch by 3/4-inch miniature thumbnails (or reproductions) of all the images contained on the disk. This index sheet is like a traditional contact sheet, with each thumbnail sequentially numbered starting with number 1.

Because all PhotoCDs look alike and use the same file names, the index sheet is the only physical directory to the files on the PhotoCD, so it's important not to misplace it. Number 1 on the index sheet corresponds to the file IMG0001.PCD on the PhotoCD.

The index sheet is helpful for figuring out which PhotoCD you need to insert in your drive. The thumbnails on the index sheet are tiny reproductions (about the size of a gnat), so using them to evaluate the quality of the images can be frustrating—after much squinting, you usually find that you've wasted time loading the wrong, huge, resource-intensive image. You can avoid this frustration, however, by using a software browsing program.

Image-Browsing Software

Many companies offer software for viewing and managing images, including PhotoCD images. These programs come in two basic types: those that work only with PhotoCDs, and those that work with PhotoCDs in addition to file formats like TIF, PCX, and BMP.

When working with PhotoCDs, both types of overview software read and display OVERVIEW.PCD, which is the contact sheet file written on each PhotoCD. Some browsing software also lets you load and display a single image.

Programs that provide overviews of *any* graphical file type typically build a catalog of images that you select and display in groups. An overview of a group of files is extremely helpful for Photoshop work. As you continue using Photoshop, you save to your hard drive copies of the same image that you've enhanced in several different ways. Viewing thumbnails of files side-by-side onscreen beats trying to figure out which file name corresponds to which variation.

Image-browsing programs usually provide simple editing tools and file-conversion capabilities. As a Photoshop user, you have no need for such utilities; a good cataloging feature is all you need. While writing this book, we found Corel Corporation's Corel CD-ROM Utilities, and Kodak's PhotoCD Access to be the two most helpful. (Macintosh users will want to check out the trial version of Fetch, and Windows users will want to look at the trial version of Kudo, both of which are found on the *Adobe Photoshop 3.0 Deluxe CD-ROM*.)

Kodak's PhotoCD Access software shows you a contact sheet of all the photos on the PhotoCD, or you can choose a single photo to view, as shown in figures 3.13 and 3.14. You can specify how large to display the images and how many colors to display. Included on Access package's CD is an assortment of 24 full-color photographs that you can use royalty-free. Access offers a basic suite of editing tools—cut, copy, paste, rotate, flip, and crop—and lets you save a PhotoCD format image to a variety of more common formats, such as TIF.

Currently, Access does not work across a network or with Windows for Workgroups. You can access Access only by using a PhotoCD drive attached directly to the PC on which you're working. The Access program file takes up about 1 MB on your hard disk.

Corel doesn't sell you utilities that come with sample images; instead, you can purchase sample images, and the utilities are included for free as part of the bundle! The Corel Professional Photos CD-ROM series disks contain over 100 photos that you can use royalty-free, and the Corel CD-ROM Utilities are free with each collection. Thus you can choose a collection of photos and get some useful software to boot, taking advantage of a marketing approach that is the opposite of that used by Kodak.

Figure 3.13

A PhotoCD contact sheet displayed by the Kodak Photo CD Access program.

Figure 3.14

A single PhotoCD image displayed by the Kodak Photo CD Access program.

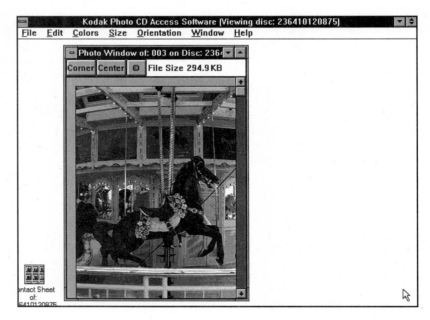

The utilities included with the Corel Professional Photos are CorelMOSAIC! Visual File Manager, Corel PhotoCD Lab, Corel Screen Saver, Corel Wallpaper Flipper, and Corel CD-Audio. Two of these utilities—CorelMOSAIC! and Corel PhotoCDLab—are of special interest to the Photoshop user.

With CorelMOSAIC!, you can display a PhotoCD "contact sheet" or build an equivalent to this contact sheet (also called a *catalog*) of the images as shown in figure 3.15. CorelMOSAIC! also can build catalogs from images belonging to other graphics formats. If you build a catalog consisting of other types of images, or consisting of both PhotoCD images and other types of images, you can assign keywords to each image. This speeds up your image-hunting process later.

Figure 3.15

A PhotoCD contact sheet shown in CorelMOSAIC!.

Corel PhotoCDLab works only with PhotoCD images. This utility quickly loads and displays your PhotoCD images in either an automatic or manual slide show on your screen, as shown in figure 3.16. PhotoLab also contains all the editing and conversion features of Access, except you can't use PhotoLab to crop an image.

Corel CD-ROM Utilities work with Windows for Workgroups and with networked PhotoCD drives. If you install all the utilities, they take approximately 4.5 MB of hard disk space.

No matter which browsing software you eventually decide to use, such a program is necessary to make cataloging your Photoshop-bound images a breeze.

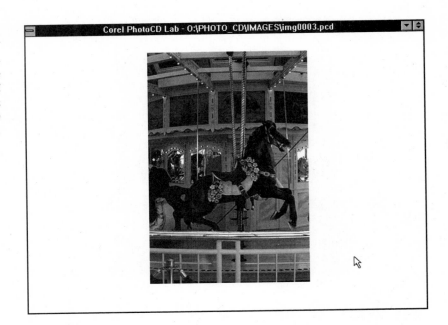

Figure 3.16

A Corel Photo-CDLab slide show is good for viewing a PhotoCD quickly at a large size.

The PhotoCD Drive

Making PhotoCD technology part of your Photoshop tools is not a decision to make overnight. Adding a PhotoCD drive *complements* your current hardware, but doesn't replace your need for a scanner or a large hard disk. However, with it you can bring your photos into Photoshop in a higher-quality digital format than is privately affordable. Also, it's one way of keeping a mountain of source images off your hard drive.

If you already own a CD-ROM drive that isn't PhotoCD-compatible and want to take advantage of all the power the PhotoCD format brings to your work, you must invest in a PhotoCD drive. This section helps you thread your way through technical specifications a little more easily.

Choosing the Right CD-ROM Drive

If you currently own a CD-ROM drive manufactured before 1992, you probably cannot use it to play a PhotoCD. A PhotoCD drive and a regular, older CD-ROM drive look identical. Only the technology inside is new, and just like everything else in the PC world, you have to reinvest regularly to keep up with better, faster technology.

The keywords that you should look for in a PhotoCD drive's documentation are the following: *PhotoCD-ready* or *-compatible*, *XA* or *XA Mode 2*, or *multisession*. When purchasing a CD-ROM drive, be sure to look for one that is a *multisession*, *PhotoCD-compatible*

drive. Some drive manufacturers also certify their drives with Kodak and display a PhotoCD logo on their packaging and literature.

 Stop When shopping for a PhotoCD drive, beware of CD-ROM drives that advertise that they are PhotoCD-compatible but seem much less expensive than their competitors. Some early drives could read PhotoCDs, but only if they were recorded in a single session. You don't want one of these drives because they have already fallen behind in the technology—buying one would be like buying a 286-class computer at a really good price. Insist on a multisession drive to protect the investment you'll be making as you accumulate PhotoCD disks.

Choosing a Fast Drive

In addition to demanding a multisession drive, you also want to buy as fast a PhotoCD-compatible drive as you can afford. Fast drives are more expensive, but the amount of visual information held on a PhotoCD is immense. You'll come to appreciate a fast drive, particularly if you have several Photoshop image assignments going on at once.

The speed of a CD-ROM drive is primarily measured by its sustained data-transfer rate, its average access time, and the size of its onboard cache. You should look for these three technical specifications when comparing the speed of one drive to another:

◆ **Data Transfer Rate.** This specification measures how much data the drive can read from the disk in one second. This measurement is important when reading large image files. The higher the number, the better.

◆ **Average Access Time.** This figure refers to how long it takes on average to find the part of the CD that contains the information you or your application requested. The lower the access time, the better. To a PhotoCD user working with images, this specification is not as critical as the transfer rate. However, it is an important consideration when you use the drive for other types of CDs, like encyclopedias or multimedia hypertext.

◆ **Onboard Cache.** Caches usually range in size from 64 KB to 1 MB, and the larger the cache the better. Onboard cache is the amount of memory in the drive itself that's dedicated to storing data it "thinks" you may want to use next. If it guesses right, it can send it to you quicker than reading it from the CD.

Drives get faster and cheaper all the time. The rates that define a fast PhotoCD drive will certainly change. But a high data-transfer rate, a low average access time, and a large cache will always define a fast drive.

Evaluating the Importance of PhotoCDs

Besides explaining the technical aspects of the PhotoCD, this chapter has shown you how useful the PCD file format can be in your Photoshop imaging. A digital image file is just like any computer file, except that it's usually much, much larger. Imaging people collect image files the same way that spreadsheet people collect spreadsheets, and both types of files do the same thing to your hard drive—they fill it up!

But if storage were the only perk of owning a PhotoCD player and a collection of PhotoCD disks, you would be as well served buying a removable media player, like a Bernoulli or a SyQuest. Of course, PhotoCD technology offers many other advantages.

Quite simply, you can't beat PhotoCD technology for the cost-efficient negative scanning it provides. Without PhotoCD technology, we couldn't have brought you the high-quality original images found on the Bonus CD. The technology gives us the freedom to crop images and maintain a high resolution for each TIF file. And yes, we had to open a very large image or two in the process! You'll have to do this too, from time to time, when you work with high-quality images—the kind you can do the most with in Photoshop.

Photoshop Defaults and Options

When designing Photoshop for the personal computer, Adobe Systems had no idea who you, the person in personal, might be—your preferences, the way you'd like to see cursors and non-printing colors in an image display on-screen, how the free space you have on your hard disk is used, and so on. But Adobe Systems made Photoshop version 3's workspace a very open-ended place, one in which you can create a personalized environment that fits your needs.

Optimizing Photoshop to offer the features that are the best for you, and for your computer, is no more difficult than choosing a different color scheme for your personal computer's workspace. The secret to designing Frank's or Susan's Photoshop, then, lies in knowing where the controls for the customizable features are, and what they do.

Fine-Tuning Your Monitor

Calibrating (adjusting) your monitor's settings may sound like a funny, nit-picky thing to most users, an action reserved for hi-tech nerds who wear white lab smocks while they work. But calibrating your monitor helps ensure that the images you see will look the same on other computers, and print with the same color values. The right calibration is critical to creating work in Photoshop that can be accurately repro-duced as hard copy. But even if you calibrate your monitor perfectly, your finished image may not look so great when it's processed by a service bureau or viewed on another monitor. Essentially, although system calibration does not guarantee accurate image editing and output, Photoshop's calibration features are much better than using no system calibration at all.

Every computer monitor, printer, scanner, and film recorder has its own inherent range of colors it can express (its *gamut*), and its own calibration settings. And in this sense, monitor calibration is relative. If you find through experience that when you send your file to a specific output source (printer, film recorder) everything prints too dark or too light, or that blues turn into purples, you might want to calibrate your monitor to match that particular output more closely. Fortunately, Adobe has made calibrating your monitor easy, and you can save and recall different sets of custom calibration information that match different situations. When calibrating your monitor, you will want to make relative adjustments that fit your own needs while maintaining consistency with the world of clients and suppliers you send your files to.

Methods of Calibration

The method Photoshop provides to calibrate your monitor is not the most scientifi-cally precise method available. Photoshop's method relies on the user trying to match things by eye. The most precise and objective way to calibrate a monitor or other output device requires expensive special equipment that actually reads the wave-lengths of light produced, or measures the density and color values of printed output. These physical calibration systems are often used with color management software, which helps ensure that the settings for all devices—your scanner, your monitor and your output device—are tuned to match each other.

If you have a physical color-calibration system, you should use it instead of Photoshop's eyeball method. If you don't, then use Photoshop's features to calibrate your monitor. If your clients also use Photoshop, you can adjust their monitors' settings, if necessary, so that they can view your work accurately. Chapter 25, "The Film Recorder," contains some additional tips on how to compare the colors on your monitor to different custom color-matching systems—such as PANTONE or TRUEMATCH—for specifying color.

Setting Up the Monitor

The first step in calibrating your monitor for use with Photoshop is to load a video driver for your system that displays the maximum color capability offered by your video adapter card. See the Understanding Video Display Modes section in Chapter 2, "Acquiring a Digital Image", for video driver installation instructions. Next, you need a little patience: you should warm up your monitor for at least one hour before performing any sort of calibration.

After the monitor has been on for a while, and you have the correct video driver installed, you need to refer to your monitor's documentation, which should include important information you need for Photoshop's Monitor Setup command. In particular, you need to know the brand of your monitor and the type of phosphors used in its screen. If your monitor is an OEM (Original Equipment Manufacturer) unit that you bought as part of a system package, you may not have access to these details. However, there is a work-around you can use to get the right settings. The next exercise shows you how to tell Photoshop what kind of monitor you have, and make only those changes that apply to your monitor.

Photoshop's Monitor Setup

Launch Photoshop | Monitor settings you'll specify are made in Photoshop.

Windows users, double-click on the Photoshop icon in the Adobe group in Program Manager; Macintosh users, click on the Photoshop icon in the program's folder.

Choose File, Preferences, then choose Monitor Setup | Displays Monitor Setup dialog box (see fig. 4.1).

Choose Monitor | Displays drop-down list of 45 monitors, plus NTSC and Barco Calibrator.

The NTSC is a television broadcast standard. You can calibrate your monitor to match the NTSC standard if you're doing designs for television. Additionally, if you have a Barco system, choose the Barco Calibrator from the Monitor drop-down list.

Choose the monitor you are using, or choose Default, or Other | Sets parameters listed in Monitor Parameters window so that they match your monitor.

Figure 4.1

The Monitor Setup dialog box.

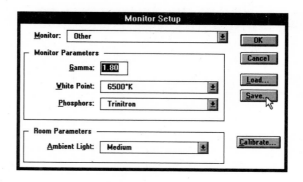

If you choose Default, the monitor parameters don't change. If you choose Other, you must set the parameters manually by choosing one of the options from the drop-down boxes next to each parameter. Be sure to read the following tip and section on Monitor Parameters before you make these changes.

Tip

You don't harm your PC, your monitor, or Photoshop by selecting from the Monitor drop-down list a monitor other than the one you use. Monitor Setup and the following calibrations simply specify the range within which Photoshop displays contrast, colors, and values.

For example, the specification sheet for my own Philips 17-inch monitor, which is not listed in the **M**onitor drop-down list, is almost identical to a Nanao monitor, which is listed. Including the Nanao as part of the setup that follows resulted in a dramatic difference in my personal viewing and editing of images in Photoshop.

The gamma of the display was lowered, and the colors on the monitor more closely matched the original source material I worked with. In addition, the Photoshop work imported into other programs (like PageMaker) looked closer in tone and color values to the images as I saw them during a Photoshop session.

None of the changes you make with your monitor settings in Photoshop affect other applications or your system's workspace. Although you can save indefinitely any changes to the Photoshop environment, you also can reset them at any time.

Monitor Parameters

If your monitor isn't listed in the **M**onitor drop-down list, you can adjust the Monitor Parameter settings by choosing Other. In such cases, Adobe recommends that you choose a **W**hite Point of 6500 degrees Kelvin. This setting complies with most newer displays.

If your whites don't look as white as you think they should with this setting, try the following before you change it:

◆ Wipe your monitor's screen with a damp cloth. Your screen attracts dust and other airborne matter, which accumulates and dims your view faster than you realize.

◆ Adjust your monitor's brightness and contrast. These dials are usually located on the monitor in a place where it's easy to nudge them out of position accidentally. Sometimes a little tweak can restore brighter whites. Taping the dials in position when you have them properly adjusted is a good idea.

When you select different setup settings, you actually change how Photoshop responds to your image editing, so make certain a less-than-ideal monitor view is due to the wrong <u>W</u>hite Point color temperature, and not dust or a misadjusted knob on your set before you change the setting.

Click on the <u>P</u>hosphors drop-down list. If your monitor is one of the six listed, choose it. Otherwise, leave the setting at its default of Trinitron. Many modern monitor tubes are Trinitrons. However, if your monitor uses red, green, and blue phosphors not manufactured according to Sony's Trinitron standards, this setting enables Photoshop to compensate. And you *do* have to be a rocket scientist to give Photoshop custom phosphor information.

Room Parameters

Adobe included the Room Parameters window in this dialog box with the most finicky folks in mind. In theory, the high, medium, and low options can compensate for bright, dim, or average lighting in your work environment. These definitely are not precise settings, and you should pick the Ambient Light setting that seems to describe your situation the best.

But instead of pondering over Photoshop's Room Parameters, it's better to ask yourself a question at this point: why would a serious imaging person want bright lights bouncing off their monitor? Or lighting conditions that change dramatically throughout the day? Unless your boss is a tyrant, you can do something yourself about harsh, dim, or inconsistent lighting conditions that will make a much greater difference than choosing one of the Ambient Light settings.

Target Gamma

In the Target Gamma window you specify the setting that may make the most difference for viewing your Photoshop work. *Gamma* is the measure of the breadth of neutral midtone values as an image is displayed. But what does this rather complex definition actually mean?

When your monitor displays an image with a narrow midtone range, the image's contrast seems excessive because little image information is retained for showing variations in skin tones, a view of the sky, and other features that require this range of values to adequately describe detail in an image. In the **G**amma setting, a lack of midtone ranges is expressed as a low number. To display images consisting of dramatic black and brilliant white, many imaging software products set this point low, to 1.0. Conversely, television gamma is around 2.2. Although such images appear light and color-filled, they lack a neutral midrange color component and sometimes appear washed-out.

If you're using an IBM/PC, try setting your Photoshop gamma to 1.8, the default, and then refine it as necessary. Macintosh monitors have a slightly higher gamma display, about 2.0, although both of these figures are approximations, and even one-tenth of a percent difference in the gamma of your monitor will show a discernible on-screen difference. You can honestly evaluate the best gamma for your monitor display only after you spend some time working with different images. The perfect gamma is not realized with one image in five minutes.

Stop   The gamma on your display will affect your finished work in two situations.

First, if you're working in Photoshop for Windows on a file that originated from a Macintosh machine, you must match the gamma of that particular Mac to get consistent results in your imaging.

Second, if you're editing a file to be used on an imagesetter, film recorder, or video output device, you must also set your monitor's gamma to match the gamma of that particular device.

Saving Your Settings

Even before you're certain that the settings you entered in the Monitor Setup dialog box are final, you can save them to an AMS file. AMS is the file extension Photoshop gives to files that contain monitor settings. You cannot load an AMS setting saved in Photoshop 2.5 or earlier versions into Photoshop 3. The next exercise shows you how to save your monitor settings.

Saving a Photoshop Setting

Click on **S**ave button of Monitor Setup dialog box	Displays Save As dialog box for monitor settings.
Find PHOTOSHOP directory and then CALIBRAT subdirectory	Use Drive and Directory fields in dialog box to locate CALIBRAT subdirectory.

The CALIBRAT subdirectory, which Photoshop installed when you ran the installation program, is a good place to store all your Photoshop calibrations.

In File **N**ame text box, enter a   Specifies name of the file
name for your custom calibration   (see fig. 4.2).

Choose a name that's easy to remember. In figure 4.2, the name MY_OWN.AMS makes the file easy to identify; one of the other files in this figure contain pre-press settings, and the third is used for viewing the monitor to reflect different working conditions. Macintosh users need not enter the three character file extension at the end of your monitor settings name; Windows users should type AMS after the name in the File **N**ame field.

Click on OK   Displays Monitor Settings dialog box.

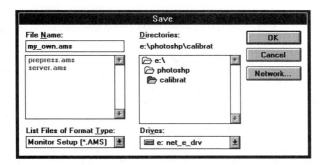

Figure 4.2

Save Photoshop Monitor settings to a file that you can load later for special viewing purposes.

Now every time you experiment with your monitor settings, you can return to any setting you previously made and saved by clicking on **L**oad from the Monitor Setup dialog box and then clicking on the AMS file of your choice.

Tip

The Save and Load options are available in several Photoshop's dialog boxes, not just the Monitor Setup dialog box. As you'll see throughout this book, you can save Calibration, Levels adjustment, Variations, and other global changes to Photoshop and your images, and then load them at any time.

Saved settings are very useful in Photoshop work, and the saved file sizes are very small, typically 50 to 200 bytes. You should take advantage of this Photoshop feature when it's offered in a dialog box because it often enables you to backtrack when you make a mistake.

Monitor Calibration

Your monitor's color temperature, its make, and the phosphor characteristics are only part of setting up the monitor to provide accurate, consistent viewing conditions.

Calibrating your monitor is another important step in setting up your monitor so that it faithfully represents your image. You need to set it up so that its display capability is optimized when you edit images.

From the Monitor Setup dialog box, click on the **C**alibrate button to display the Calibrate dialog box. This section explains how the settings in this dialog box affect your imaging.

At the top of the dialog box is the Gamma Adjustment window, which consists of a pattern of stripes with a slider beneath it. This setting enables you to manually adjust the gamma value in the Gamma window of the Monitor Setup dialog box. If you fine-tune the gamma for your monitor, people who view your images from other workstations will see color values that are closer to those you intended. Although this isn't the perfect solution, it is the best available, short of buying a monitor-calibration package. So, let's learn how to use this feature of the Calibrate dialog box.

The stripes above the slider are something like an eye test. In this eye test, you try to blend the stripes together by moving the slider in either direction. First, click on the Balance radio button (see fig. 4.3), which controls the balance between the black point and white point. In figure 4.3, the stripes are pretty well blended together, with a value of 28 showing beneath the stripes in the Gamma Adjustment window. The value 28 is an arbitrary point on the scale; it doesn't correspond to the absolute value of the gamma. The scale setting you see when the bands blend together may be different than ours, since you may not own the same monitor as we do.

Figure 4.3

To set the best gamma balance for your monitor, click on the Balance radio button and adjust the slider until the stripes go away.

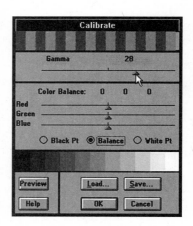

Do the same for the black point and the white point. First, click on their radio buttons, and then adjust the slider so that the stripes at the top invisibly blend. Finally, click on the Balance radio button again and readjust the balance, if necessary, to blend the bands together.

ote Your settings in the Calibrate dialog box affect Photoshop differently than your settings in the Monitor Setup dialog box. Whereas the Monitor Setup settings— Monitor type, Phosphors, and the like—change your view of the image, the Calibrate settings change an image file's color properties.

Monitor calibration has a direct impact on how Photoshop translates the RGB color model (the model your monitor uses to display color) into the CMYK color model (used when creating color separations for four-color process printing). The CMYK color model has four channels (Cyan, Magenta, Yellow, and Black) compared to RGB's three channels. Accurate CMYK imaging depends on having accurate RGB information to start with. Calibration is designed to help ensure that the RGB information is correctly displayed.

Calibration is not critical for displaying an RGB image in its native RGB monitor mode, but a badly calibrated monitor will affect the color information generated and written to a file for an image that has been translated into CMYK.

Whenever image data is translated, it adheres to the old computer adage GIGO, or garbage in, garbage out; don't expect to get great results if you don't feed your computer great information.

Additionally, if your monitor setup is not optimized, the result will be less than perfect when you try to blend a selection area into a background image. The brightness of the overall image is affected as well.

Keep all these concerns in mind if you ever doubt that fine-tuning your monitor is worth the hassle.

On Color Balance

Some monitors have a bluish color cast to them. This is obviously a problem if you try to do precise retouching to a color image. To compensate for a color cast from your monitor, Photoshop offers a color correction feature. This feature enables you to achieve color balance in the same way you correct gamma, except that you use Red, Green, and Blue sliders instead of the Gamma slider to make the stripes match.

Most monitors manufactured in the last two years don't display a noticeable color cast, however, and you won't need to reset the color balance for Photoshop. But you should check to make sure. Try sliding the little triangles from the zero point; if this causes the stripes at the top of the dialog box to blend better, your monitor needs calibration. If the stripes' contrast increases, you should leave the settings alone.

Ideally, the test strip near the bottom of the dialog box should have nice, sharp, even graduations of black. This provides another visual clue as to how you can get the best display in Photoshop. When you move a calibration slider, this strip's shades of black change. This, in addition to matching the stripes at the top of the dialog box, optimizes your monitor calibration for working in Photoshop. For additional details about calibration, see Photoshop's documentation.

Again, when you have the best settings for gamma calibration, click on the **S**ave button to save them; then you can always recall them, as you can the monitor settings. Windows users need to specify the AGP extension at the end of the saved gamma settings file.

Expressing Your General Preferences

After the preferences for your monitor's gamma and other parameters have been defined, it's time to take a tour of Photoshop's General Preferences. This category of Pre**f**erences has to do with the way you see Photoshop's element; palettes, cursors, your selection of a color model from which to choose colors, and many other things that indirectly relate to the quality of the finished image.

The following sections describe the options in General Preferences. You should press Ctrl+K (or choose **F**ile, Pre**f**erences, then **G**eneral) in Photoshop now, and choose the options that'll be the most worthwhile in your own work. The General Preferences can be respecified at any time, so if you find that a Preference simply isn't working out, General Preferences is the place to change something.

Using Photoshop's Color Picker

Photoshop supports the Macintosh Color Picker, the Windows Color Picker, and comes with an incredibly full-featured Color Picker of its own. By default, when you first launch Photoshop after installation, Photoshop's Color Picker is loaded. The **C**olor Picker drop-down list is at the top of the General Preferences dialog box.

Unless you've grown really attached to the Macintosh or Windows Color Picker, you should leave the Color Picker preference set to its default—Photoshop Color Picker. Most imaging folks find the Photoshop Color Picker to be more robust and easier to use than the other two. It is the Color Picker shown in figures throughout this book. You access the Color Picker by clicking on the foreground/background colors on Photoshop's toolbox; to display the Color Picker dialog box, double-click on the foreground/background colors on the Picker palette.

Why is Photoshop's Color Picker a better general preference than your operating system's? Photoshop's Color Picker displays HSB, RGB, CMYK, and LAB color models from which you can specify a color. These color models are described in detail in Chapter 3, "Color Theory and The PhotoCD." Additionally, you can choose from

Custom color palettes, which represent the digital equivalents of the PANTONE, FOCOLTONE, TOYO, TRUEMATCH, and other physical color sample systems. We'll show you how to pick a Custom color palette later in this chapter, but you can select a Custom color matching system only if you have chosen the Photoshop Color Picker in General Preferences.

Photoshop's Color Picker is also aware of illegal video colors—colors that might display onscreen but can't be created with process colors on a commercial printing press. If you specify in the Color Picker a color that can't be printed, an exclamation button appears in the Color Picker's dialog box, indicating that a color is out of CMYK gamut. If you work at a commercial printer, or frequently send your work to a commercial printer, Photoshop's Color Picker is a must, to ensure that CMYK colors are faithfully represented in your work and onscreen.

Interpolation

As Chapters 1 and 2 discussed, Photoshop uses interpolation rather than diffusion to make the changes you specify for an image's new dimensions, resolution, or other edits you specify in images while you work with RGB, TrueColor images. Interpolation may seem to rearrange color pixels in an image, but it actually adds and deletes pixels to complete an action or edit, then reassigns different colors to existing pixels to execute a particular command. The quality of Photoshop's interpolation calculations depends on the speed with which you choose to accomplish them. Speed is the trade-off for accuracy, and you have three choices as to how Photoshop interpolates your editing work:

◆ The *Bicubic* option is the most accurate method of rearranging pixels. It takes the longest for Photoshop to calculate, but on a Pentium or PowerMac the wait is nominal, and the result is the highest quality image. Usually this is the option you should choose.

◆ The *Bilinear* option is the middle ground between quality and speed of interpolation. If you have deadlines to meet, and you own a Quadra or a 386 class IBM/PC compatible, the results are good, and your work will go quickly.

◆ The *Nearest Neighbor* method of interpolation is Photoshop's on-the-fly estimate of what an altered pixel in your image should look like. It's fast, but not terribly precise. You should reserve this option for the night you need to retouch 100 images by morning for a client with no taste in art.

Setting Display Preferences

In the Display area of the General Preferences dialog box is a series of check boxes that determine how you see the images you work with in Photoshop. Figure 4.4 shows the General Preferences box onscreen when you pick this File menu item. As discussed in Chapter 2, display options don't directly affect an image file, because a saved image and the way it displays on-screen are two different things. However, if your monitor is miscalibrated, or you choose a Display option in General Preferences that alters the way an image should actually display in Photoshop, you can do a world of harm while editing the picture.

CMYK Composites

If you're new to commercial printing or electronic imaging, CMYK may be a buzz word that means nothing to you. So before you learn how to use the CMYK Composites radio buttons of the General Preferences dialog box, you need to understand what CMYK (pronounced see-mac) is.

Color models serve a very real purpose in the imaging world, and different models were invented for different reasons. Many artists like to describe color by using the Hue, Saturation, and Brightness (HSB) model, as was classically taught before the advent of computer technology. The Red, Green, Blue (RGB) color model serves a very useful purpose, enabling artists to communicate clearly with electronics folks by describing color output to a monitor's red, green, and blue phosphors.

The Cyan, Magenta, Yellow, and Black (CMYK) model is used for color-separation printing. The mixture of these colors as ink, not light, makes up the color images you see in magazines and books. Also known as process color, CMYK is a subtractive color-building process. As you'll recall from school, pigments are subtractive colors and light is additive.

To make an RGB image printable on a commercial print press that uses the standard four process colors for printing, the image must be converted to the CMYK standard. This is the reason you must calibrate your monitor. Photoshop does the conversions very adeptly. A CMYK color file has four channels, as opposed to an RGB image's three, and they can be stored as TIF images. TIF images get to be CMYK mode images either by acquiring a color image with a 32-bit scanner, or by having a program like Photoshop convert the image from RGB.

You probably won't often encounter a CMYK TIF file unless it's been converted from an RGB image as part of the pre-press process. *Pre-press* is the work and the procedures a commercial printer or service bureau goes through to take the elements (digital or otherwise) that make up a finished piece and create printing plates from them.

Tip

The color mode change from RGB to CMYK, which is part of the pre-press process, should take place after you've finished creating and enhancing your image in Photoshop. Each time you change the mode, Photoshop must interpolate the information to change from a three-channel color model (RGB) to a four-channel model (CMYK). Interpolation always causes some reduction in the quality of the image.

Do all your work in RGB mode, and when you finish your editing and enhancing, save the RGB mode file. Then save a copy of the RGB file to a new name. Use the Mode menu command to change the image type from RGB to CMYK mode.

If you need to, make any minor corrections in the CMYK mode file and then print your separations, or save the file for your service bureau. If you must make major adjustments, discard the CMYK file, and make your changes in the original RGB copy. Repeat the previous procedure for saving the RGB file to a new name and converting the copy to CMYK.

The reason Photoshop offers a choice of CMYK display is that Photoshop has to simulate CMYK values on-screen, because your monitor isn't truly capable of displaying colors based on the CMYK color model (it's an RGB monitor). You have your choice of Smoother or Faster display simulations of an image based on commercial press colors. Like Interpolation, CMYK Composite display is another speed/accuracy trade-off. When you select **F**aster, Photoshop uses interpolation and a lookup table to assign CMYK color values to any color image you convert to the CMYK color mode, or choose to view in CMYK **P**review (also in the Modes command, which is covered later in this chapter). This method is quick, but not very accurate. When you select **S**moother, Photoshop then takes its time to translate and assign the CMYK color values to the RGB image onscreen. This latter method is slower but more accurate.

If you work in the production department of a magazine or other publication, you want to render CMYK files to the screen using the Smoother option. The Smoother option will show you potential problems that may occur when you use Photoshop to generate color separations from a digital image. Also, if you want to view a CMYK file that you intend to convert to RGB image mode with the **M**ode menu command, select the Faster display option in the General Preferences dialog box; CMYK has a smaller range of colors visible to the human eye, and you don't get a better view of changes when you go from a less capable color mode to a more capable one. The CMYK Composites option determines the methodology Photoshop uses to generate the display of the image, not how it converts the image type when you change image modes from RGB to CMYK using the **M**ode menu commands.

Show Channels in Color

As previously noted, Photoshop can display the color channels that your image contains. You can edit the channels, copy them, and treat them as parts of a composite image. You can also choose to display them in color as you view the component channels. To do this, you check the Color Channels in Color option in the General Preferences dialog box. Toward the end of this chapter you'll see how color channels display in grayscale; when the Channels palette is displayed, it displays thumbnail views of color channels.

All channels are actually based on an eight-bit grayscale color model, and as such, don't actually contain any color information to display. By default, each channel, except the RGB composite channel, appears the same (grayscale) when you view it. Checking this option tells Photoshop to fake it and show you the channel in shades of the color that corresponds to the channel being viewed. Although it's easier to tell exactly which channel of an image you're viewing in Photoshop when the channel views are displayed in color, this option is bound to cause errors in advanced image editing, because you're not truly seeing what the color channel information looks like. Try placing a colored gel in front of a grayscale image, then consider how accurately you'd be able to edit the grayscale image. This is exactly the same effect you get when you check the Color Channels in Color check box; the option is candy-coating that contributes nothing to your imaging techniques.

Use System Palette

A *system palette*, as the name implies, is a palette of colors that is directly supported by your operating system and video card. In Chapter 2, "Acquiring a Digital Image," we described lookup tables (or *color palettes*), and how colors are stored in an index in the image file. When you choose Use System Palette in the General Preferences dialog box, you're telling Photoshop to use your computer's color support mechanism instead of a custom lookup table to display inactive image windows (images you have open, but aren't editing). The Use System Palette option can be helpful if you're running only a 256-color video driver, because Photoshop then can optimize the active image window, and let system colors represent the inactive document. (Photoshop doesn't read the lookup table for the inactive image windows.)

When you're running HiColor or TrueColor video drivers, you won't see a difference in display quality of images when this option is checked. Additionally, the Use Diffusion Dither option (covered next), works hand in hand with the Use System Palette option to better approximate display colors when you don't have a video driver capable of handling more than 256 colors.

Use Diffusion Dither

The first two chapters discussed dithering. Now here's your big chance to have a say in how you prefer images to be displayed when you're running less than a 16.7-million-color video driver. You should check the Use **D**iffusion Dither option. If you do, the next time you run a 256-color driver while viewing an RGB image, the resulting color-depth mismatch will be diffused across the image. Although it's a tedious way to work with an image, it beats using a patterned dither, which is Photoshop's default when you leave this option unchecked. Chapter 1, "Understanding Image Types, Formats, and Resolutions," provides good examples of patterned and diffusion dithers.

Video LUT Animation

This option speeds up Photoshop screen redraws when you make editing changes. Because the screen colors in an image constantly change as you perform color corrections and other editing, the LUT (or Look Up Table) Animation option keeps the image you're working on updated on-screen (and in preview windows of dialog boxes) to reflect changes you make or propose to make. LUT Animation is a dynamic updating of the color table used to display an image, and only works in a 16-bit or higher display mode. Leave **V**ideo LUT Animation checked. It asks more of your processor but will speed up your work.

Choosing Different Screen Cursors

A new feature of Photoshop 3 gives you control over the way your tool cursors look on-screen. Uniquely shaped cursors can be a blessing when you have as many tools to work with as you do in Photoshop, but they sometimes can be a hindrance to precision editing. You can have it any of three ways in Photoshop, and the next section describes why you should have a strong preference as to what your cursor looks like.

Standard Tool Cursors

You can see Photoshop's Standard cursors in the figures in this book—partially as a quick indicator of which tool is being used in an exercise, but mostly because this is Photoshop's default. As you'll see on-screen, and throughout this book, Photoshop cursors are icons, shaped like the tool they represent. Photoshop's tools generally fit into three categories: selection tools, painting tools, and editing tools, all covered in Chapter 6, "The Photoshop Test Drive." The Tool cursor settings, shown in figure 4.4, are divided into two of these three categories; you can specify the appearance of painting tools and of all the other toolbox tools.

Figure 4.4

You can choose Standard, Precise, or Brush Size for the painting tool cursors; Photoshop's other cursors can be Standard or Precise.

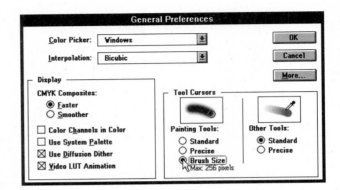

When you want the utmost precision, right down to the pixel, in selecting or painting an image area during a Photoshop session, you can switch between standard and precise cursors by pressing Ctrl+K. You don't have to restart Photoshop to put any of the changes you make in General Preferences into effect.

Although Standard tool cursors appear to be handsomely crafted, overstated representations of the tools you choose, there is a hot spot you can identify onscreen for Standard tool cursors if you want to know exactly where a brush stroke begins, or where the Lasso tool begins its selection. Look carefully at a Standard cursor. One single pixel in the cursor shape is an inverted color; for example, when the Paint brush tool is represented in black, a white pixel on its tip indicates the center of the Paint brush's stroke. This is not an obvious feature of the Standard tool cursors, and we can't recommend that you depend upon the dot at the edge of the Standard cursors if you require precision in your editing work. Nevertheless, the Standard tool cursors provide an instant reference as to which tool is currently active. If you're just beginning to learn Photoshop, you'll benefit from the default settings for the tool cursors.

Precise Tool Cursors

When you choose the Precise tool cursors option in the General Preferences dialog box, whether for the Painting or the Other tools, the cursor remains the same shape—a small crosshair, its center marked with a reverse-video color pixel. With this option checked, pinpoint accuracy, as it were, is ensured in your editing, painting, and selection work; you must constantly reference the toolbox, however, to see which tool is currently chosen. An additional piece of helpful information about each tool is displayed on the Photoshop for Windows' status line, although each tool's function is described on the status line, not the name of the tool itself.

Precision tool cursors also can be accessed immediately in the workspace without paying a trip to General Preferences; press the Caps Lock key to toggle from a

Standard tool cursor to the Precise option (and vice versa). Additionally, when the Brush Size tool cursor is chosen, you can toggle between Precise and Brush Size by pressing the Caps Lock key.

Brush Size Tool Cursors

When you choose Brush Size as the tool cursor for Painting tools, an empty circle appears over an active image window that signifies the approximate dimensions of the painting tool's tip. We must stress the word approximate here; most tips on the Brushes palette have soft edges, and the Brush Size tool cursor doesn't accurately reflect the spread that foreground color with a soft tip creates in an image.

In figure 4.5, you can see the Rubber stamp tool being used to remove a basketball pole from an otherwise pretty image of a tree. The crosshair you see in this figure is the sampling point for the Rubber stamp, and the circle is the location and relative size of the Rubber stamp tip. For detailed information about working with the Rubber stamp tool, see Chapter 10, "Stamping Out Photo Errors."

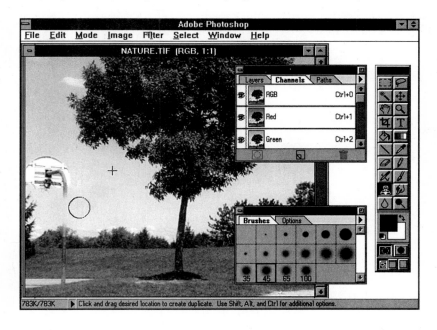

Figure 4.5

The Brush Size tool cursor uses a circle to represent the size of the tip of any painting tool on an active image.

One of the more subtle disadvantages of working with the Brush Size tool cursor has to do with a drag you might feel when using a painting tool. Because Photoshop must redraw and constantly update the display of the Brush Size cursor, the circle (or other custom brush-tip shape) with which you paint can feel sticky and unresponsive. Some users don't mind the touch of a tool in an application, but more experienced users depend on the feedback of the mouse or digitizing tablet to guide brush strokes. If you're sensitive as a user to the responsiveness of a tool cursor, you might want to skip Photoshop's Brush Size tool cursor option.

More Preferences

Beyond the General Preferences dialog box are still more preferences—how you want to type to render to an image file, whether you'd like to be alerted to an on-screen event—all very useful, handy stuff. The next section describes the options in the More Preferences dialog box (yes, that's its name—see fig. 4.6), and situations in which one of these options might be useful.

Figure 4.6

*More Preferences can be found in General Preferences by clicking on the **M**ore button.*

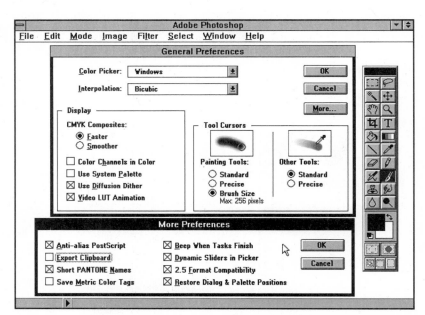

Anti-alias PostScript

EPS, or *Encapsulated PostScript*, is a vector image format designers frequently use as an intermediate step for bringing vector design information into Photoshop as bitmap, or *raster* image data. The problem with vector design data is that when it becomes bitmap information it displays jagged, or *aliased*, edges characteristic of the primitive bitmap imaging of a decade ago. In an effort to defeat (or at least disguise) the telltale, stair-steppy edges of bitmap-converted vector graphics, Photoshop performs

Anti-aliasing, the placing of semitransparent pixels around the edges of a design detail. You'll definitely want to check the Anti-alias feature if you're importing an Adobe Illustrator file (by using either the **O**pen or **P**lace **F**ile commands). Many drawing and other graphics applications besides Illustrator can export a design in either EPS or AI format, so you should check the documentation of such a program, then check the Anti-Alias option in the More Preferences dialog box, for smooth, beautiful conversions of vector-to-bitmap file types in Photoshop.

Note   Photoshop cannot import a vector graphic, through either the Windows or Macintosh Clipboard, to make it rasterize in an image window with Anti-aliased edges. The Macintosh Clipboard automatically converts clipboard information to PICT format, so if you export an AI file through the Clipboard, it's a bitmap type image before it even reaches Photoshop. Windows users can be similarly disappointed when copying, say, a CorelDRAW vector image into Photoshop through the Windows Clipboard.

If you want anti-aliased edges around a vector design, you must use the Place or Open commands, and your file must be of the AI or EPS data types.

Export Clipboard

You probably should leave the **E**xport Clipboard option turned off, because Clipboard exports from Photoshop yield often disappointing and sometimes bizarre results in the application into which you paste the exported bitmap.

Photoshop is a very special bitmap editing application, and the tweaks it performs to bitmap images can't always be successfully translated through the Clipboard to other applications. For example, bitmap images in most programs have to be rectangular; bits of information mapped to an imaginary grid (bit-map) are always rectangular. However, you can select and copy an elliptical or irregularly shaped portion of a bitmap image to the Clipboard from Photoshop.

The irregularly shaped bitmap image pastes into another application as an irregular shape surrounded by a white background rectangle whose dimensions touch the irregular shape on each side. The same phenomenon happens when you copy an image area from a Photoshop image layer. You'll learn all about Photoshop's layer feature (beginning with Chapter 5, "It's All Done with Palettes"), but for now, you should understand that the transparent pixels on a Photoshop layer aren't read as transparent by other applications.

Photoshop simplifies image information for use by the Clipboard, and you'll almost never get the results you need by copying an image from Photoshop to another application. If you want to export an image for use in another program, save the image as a TIF, BMP, or other bitmap format the target application can handle.

Additionally, Photoshop images, like all nonvector images, can get quite large, and the Macintosh and Windows Clipboards work best when they doesn't have to hold massive amounts of information. The result of copying (and holding) a Photoshop image on the Clipboard is slower system performance. Copied items are held in system RAM, along with all the other changes you make to an image. So let your system run as fast as it can, and don't check **E**xport Clipboard.

Short PANTONE Names

You can paint with colors that approximate PANTONE colors in Photoshop. PANTONE colors (like those you find in the fanning swatch books) are color specifications for paints and inks. If your assignment calls for using a specific PANTONE color for corporate colors, for example, Photoshop is very good at approximating paint and ink values to the screen.

When you use a genuine PANTONE color in a design, it is reproduced at press time as a combination of ink colors mixed to exacting standards. The purpose of the PANTONE color-matching system is to ensure that a design is faithfully reproduced from a printing press that may be a thousand miles away from the designer. Or when someone another thousand miles away wants you to design a graphic and has an exact shade of color in mind. If you check the Sh**o**rt PANTONE Names option in the More Preferences dialog box, the PANTONE colors you then select can be matched when you export an image to other programs.

For example, figure 4.7 features a TropicAir logo that uses two PANTONE colors. To access PANTONE colors (or other matching standards) to use in your work, you can do either of the following:

◆ Click on the foreground or background color on the toolbox. This displays the Color Picker. Click on Custom, to display the Custom Colors dialog box, and then select a color-matching standard from the **B**ook drop-down list (see fig. 4.7).

◆ To select several colors from a color-matching standard without multiple trips to the Color Picker, use the Picker palette (**W**indow, **P**alettes, Show **P**icker). Then, click on the Swatches tab of the Picker/Swatches/Scratch palette group. Click on the pop-up menu button (to the right of the Picker tab on the palette), and choose Load Swatches. In the Photoshop directory, find the subdirectory (folder) labeled palettes. From this subdirectory, you'll find *.ACO files that contain the same color specifications as those in the Color Picker dialog box.

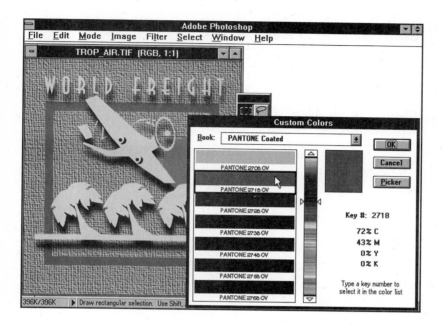

Figure 4.7

A design incorporating PANTONE spot colors.

Photoshop represents the physical matching standards by using colors that closely approximate those that will be reproduced on coated stock paper.

If you've selected your system color picker over Photoshop's in General Preferences, you'll have to use the Swatches palette to choose a color from the PANTONE (or other) collection. The system color pickers do not offer the capability of specifying computer-matching sample colors.

After finishing a graphic in Photoshop where you've used specific PANTONE colors, you can export it to a desktop publishing program, such as PageMaker 5.0, that also enables you to use PANTONE spot colors in your work. Figure 4.8 shows the finishing touches being put on a small announcement incorporating the logo created in Photoshop, highlighted text, and a headline that uses the same PANTONE color specifications. The match in PANTONE colors between PageMaker text and Photoshop paint colors is as close as is possible for a computer image, and the Photoshop Short PANTONE Names option makes it easy to choose PageMaker color matches. If the advertisement in this example is printed from PageMaker, both the highlighted, PANTONE-colored type and the colors in the TIF image design will print with approximately the same CMYK values.

Figure 4.8

Photoshop enables you to select short PANTONE names, which other applications use in CMYK color specifications.

Beep When Tasks Finish

Photoshop may take a while to complete a task, such as opening a large TIF file or applying an effect. Sometimes you ask Photoshop to do something barely perceptible, like subtly sharpening an image. By checking the **B**eep When Tasks Finish option of the More Preferences dialog box, you tell Photoshop to beep whenever you can safely proceed with the next step. When Photoshop is thinking, you can't continue working on an image; leave this option checked so that you can get some feedback on Photoshop's progress.

Tip

If you leave the **B**eep When Tasks Finish box checked and have a sound card or the PC Speaker for Windows file installed on your machine, you can define the beep that Photoshop uses. For example, you can have Photoshop play a loud siren after completing a task. Macintosh personal computers have always been sound-capable, but this is a relatively new option to Windows users.

You select Default Sound from the Windows Control Panel, Sound dialog box, then assign it a sound from a directory in which you have sound files stored. Then, if you scoot down the hall for coffee while waiting for Photoshop to think, you can hear the alert—and so can your coworkers!

Dynamic Sliders in Picker

Leave this box checked. This option is similar to Photoshop's LUT Animation; the sliders on the Color Picker and Picker palette change to reflect a change in one or more color components as you define a color. If you don't check this option, colors on the sliders in both Photoshop color-definition areas remain constant, and you'll have to guess a little more often at a result color when you blend the components (such as Hue and Brightness) of a color.

Restore Dialog and Palette Positions

You should leave the **R**estore Dialog and Palette Positions option checked if you want to return to the same customized setup for palettes and features in future sessions of Photoshop. You will soon learn about the Photoshop palettes—you use them in combination with tools and effects, and often must work in more than one Photoshop session. When you check this option, Photoshop notes the settings, location, and position of palettes whenever you exit the program, and puts them back in place when you next open the program. This option has nothing to do with the last image you worked on, unfortunately; Photoshop always begins a session with an empty workspace (unless you launch Photoshop by clicking on an associated image file). If you leave **R**estore Dialog and Palette Positions checked, you will find that the exercises in this book are easier to follow if you take a break from them.

2.5 Format Compatibility

Photoshop 3.0 gives you the opportunity to work with a bitmap image in extraordinary ways with image layers, and with the capability to store a total of 24 channels in a PSD format image. However, if you are working with other people (a production house or a service bureau, for example) who still have Photoshop 2.5 (or 2.51), they can't read a 3.0 image with these special features unless the 2.5 compatibility option is checked. This option stores a flattened version of your 3.0 document in the 3.0 file, to be used with applications that don't understand the special 3.0 format. When the file is opened in a program that can only read a 2.5 image file, the image displays all the characteristics (such as Alpha channels) it would have had it been created in Photoshop 2.5. This welcome, and fairly invisible, downward compatibility with Photoshop 2.5 comes with only one penalty—the amount of disk space your files take is greater than if 2.5 compatibility is turned off.

There is one exception to this rule, however. If your 3.0 file has more than 16 channels, the file will not open in programs capable of handling only version 2.5 files. If you work with Photoshop 3.0 only, everyone you share files with has upgraded to 3.0, and you don't need the capability to create 2.5-compatible files, you will save a lot of disk space by turning off this feature.

Specifying Photoshop's Memory Settings

The settings you specify in Photoshop's Monitor Setup and General Preferences dialog boxes become invaluable when you use Photoshop extensively in imaging work. Now that you are familiar with these settings, it's time to see how you can optimize system resources while you're in Photoshop so that Photoshop practices its magic more quickly and smoothly.

Macintosh and IBM/PCs have different operating systems and handle RAM differently. The following sections contain special instructions that pertain to the way Photoshop taps into system RAM on both the Macintosh and Windows sides of Photoshop.

First, choose Preferences from the File menu, and then choose Memory. Although the options for Scratch Disks in the Memory Preferences dialog box are identical on both operating platforms, the following sections provide examples that show you how to give Photoshop the necessary hard disk temporary space and system RAM to operate properly.

As you can see in figure 4.9, the Memory Preferences dialog box offers a choice of location for scratch disk, and the amount of physical RAM you want to allocate to Photoshop when the application is running.

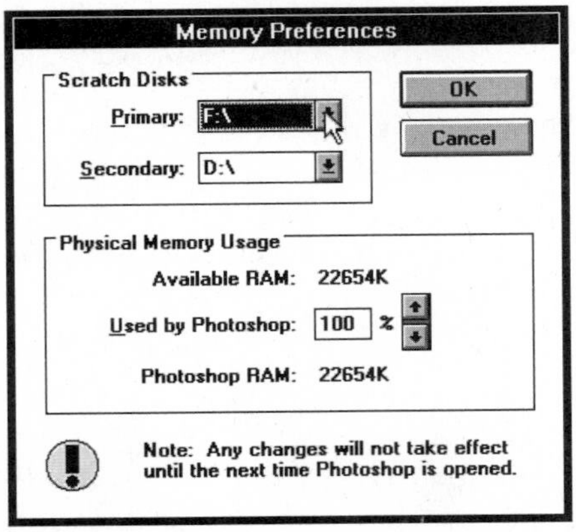

Figure 4.9

The Memory Preferences dialog box for Photoshop for Windows.

Memory Preferences

Scratch Disks
Primary: F:\
Secondary: D:\

OK
Cancel

Physical Memory Usage
Available RAM: 22654K
Used by Photoshop: 100 %
Photoshop RAM: 22654K

Note: Any changes will not take effect until the next time Photoshop is opened.

Scratch Disks

When you work on an image, Photoshop needs to store multiple copies of the image in your system RAM. To reside in RAM, a 1 MB image may require only 1 MB of RAM, but to do fancy stuff like performing an Undo, Photoshop needs memory more than two to three times that of the file size, depending on the effects or tools you're using. Additionally, having several images open simultaneously on the Photoshop workspace is a serious drain on system RAM. Photoshop's memory requirements can easily exceed the amount of RAM in your machine.

Even though Windows users may have set up a permanent *swap file*—a buffer most programs use to swap segments of program code and current file information into and out of when you have insufficient RAM—Photoshop won't use the Windows swap file. Instead, Photoshop offers both Mac and Windows users proprietary Scratch Disks on which it keeps pieces of images while you're working with Photoshop.

Photoshop can locate the Scratch Disk(s) on any drive, and you can specify two different drives to use if you don't have much space on one drive. When you end your Photoshop session, all the temporary files in the scratch disk are deleted. The next time you start Photoshop, it creates a new scratch disk on the drive or drives that you specify in the Primary and Secondary field boxes of this dialog box. This is a particularly nice way to handle the need for temporary storage because it doesn't lock you out of precious hard drive space when you're not running Photoshop.

It is important to note, however, that in Photoshop 3 there is a definite link between the scratch disk and memory usage. You must have enough free hard disk space to hold an entire image (file size times 5). For example, if you work on a 3 MB file and have 32 MB of RAM installed on your system, the entire file, even when multiplied by 5 (to 15 MB), fits comfortably in RAM. But if you don't have at least 15 MB of open disk space, Photoshop will send you an out of memory message. In version 3 of Photoshop, you need tons of open disk space for scratch disk use. Also, regularly defragmenting the hard disk location where you set up the scratch disk usually helps give speedier access to Photoshop.

Note   Photoshop (like many other programs) prefers a scratch disk location on an uncompressed disk drive. Users of on-the-fly compression utilities such as Stacker, or DriveSpace (the compression scheme that comes with MS-DOS v6.2x), may experience a performance hit when a compressed drive is assigned as a Primary or Secondary scratch disk in the Memory Preferences dialog box.

The reason for the performance penalty is that Photoshop writes very quickly to scratch disk, and compressed disk drives can't be written to as quickly. However, you *can* make a compressed drive a scratch disk location, and that's the truly important point for users who would otherwise have to back up and unmount their hard drive to work with Photoshop 3.

> Under no circumstances should you assign a removable media disk, such as a Bernoulli or SyQuest cartridge, as your Photoshop scratch disk. Many Macintosh users run Photoshop 2.5 from removable media. The Adobe Systems documentation contains a specific warning to discourage the use of removable media as a scratch disk location.

Refer back to figure 4.9 to see how the authors set up the memory preferences for a 486 IBM-compatible machine used to write this book. As this section continues, we'll explain why these choices were made for our particular setup. Your settings may vary, and you should apply the settings in the Memory Preferences dialog box based on the specifications of your system.

The **P**rimary drop-down list specifies the location at which Photoshop sets up a scratch disk (a *virtual* memory file) in which to store data if the program runs out of available system RAM. By default, Photoshop specifies your startup drive. On Windows systems, Adobe defines the startup drive as the drive on which Windows, not Photoshop, is installed. For Macintosh systems, the startup drive is the drive that holds the System software, not the drive where the Photoshop folder is found.

Secondary Considerations

In the **S**econdary selection box, you can specify a secondary scratch disk location or simply select None from the drop-down list. Usually, because you should give Photoshop everything it needs to do its work, you should specify both a primary and secondary place to swap data into and out of when Photoshop has used all available system RAM.

Try to free as much space as possible on your hard drives for your Photoshop work. If you have multiple hard disks and one is faster or has more open space than the other, you should click on the down arrow next to the **P**rimary selection box, choose that drive from the list of drive options, and let the slower or smaller drive become a secondary location for the scratch disk. Keep images on a PhotoCD, and save them on floppy disks (or other removable media) when you aren't using them. Use your own judgment to balance hard drive space for use as both storage and virtual memory.

Maximizing Windows' Physical Memory

The bottom part of the Memory Preferences dialog box is the Physical Memory Usage window. This memory refers, not to the scratch disk virtual memory, but rather to the collective talents of the little SIMM chips you have installed that provide system RAM.

Notice, in figure 4.9, that in the **U**sed by Photoshop option 100 percent of all system RAM has been specified—that is, 100 percent of what Windows allows an application

to use for its session is devoted to Photoshop work. Actually, this machine has 32 MB of RAM installed, but Windows has earmarked 8 MB for environment housekeeping, and the screen-capture utility used to create the figure ate into the total; Photoshop can hook into only 22 MB while it operates.

Again, you should give Photoshop everything it needs to work its magic, so don't run other applications while you're working in Photoshop. Until Windows 95 is available, Windows 3.1*x* is a *co-operative multitasking environment;* only one application can truly operate in the foreground, and background applications that might be running steal from Windows' overall resources. If you try downloading a modem file, or recalculating a spreadsheet in the background while Photoshop is running, your system will crash, or at the very least your performance will bog down.

If you have 12 MB of RAM or more installed on your system, dedicate 100 percent in the Used by Photoshop box. If you have only 8 MB of RAM, or less, seriously consider buying more. Photoshop is a power application in every sense of the word, virtual and physical.

When you change a Memory Preferences option, remember to restart Photoshop so that the changes take effect.

Tip   Because Photoshop for Windows is Windows-compliant, 100 percent of available RAM is never really allocated to Photoshop. Windows does not allow any application that's written to spec to take control of system resources this way.

When the Memory Preferences dialog box's **U**sed by Photoshop spin box reads 100%, about 75–80 percent of available RAM is actually being used. This is close to 100 percent, but not quite.

Macintosh Memory Usage

Macintosh users are faced with a different set of options for optimizing Photoshop 3's memory usage, but it's the same game on both platforms—give Photoshop the resources it needs, and your imaging work will go smoothly and quickly.

By default, Photoshop takes 6 MB of RAM for 68 KB Macintosh computers, and 11 MB for PowerMacs. If you have more than 6 MB available, increasing the allocation size for Photoshop enables you to work faster. To change the memory allocation size, start any application you think you'll use during your session in Photoshop, except Photoshop. Make it a small application, because—ideally—you should have no other program except Photoshop running at one time. Click on Finder, then choose About This Mac from the Apple menu. In the dialog box, refer to the Largest Unused Block. Subtract 500 KB from whatever number you see in the dialog box; the resulting figure is the amount of RAM you can afford to allocate to Photoshop.

Select the Photoshop icon, then choose Get Info from the File menu. The Photoshop Info window appears (this is a Mac system thing that has nothing to do with Photoshop). Set the Preferred Size option to the figure you calculated by subtracting 500 KB from the Largest Unused Block. Close the Info window, and you're done.

Macintosh users should never use System 7's Virtual Memory when working in Photoshop; Adobe Systems explicitly warns against this practice in Photoshop's documentation for the Mac. You'll crash or halt your system if you use System 7's Virtual Memory while attempting to run Photoshop. And make sure that you have 32-bit addressing turned on in the Memory control panel. Restart your system after making these changes, and start Photoshop with everything the program needs to run.

Our advice for users of Photoshop 3, on both operating systems, is to practice prudent system conservation, leave as much uncompressed hard disk space for Photoshop's scratch disks as you can afford, and buy as much RAM as your budget can bear. Photoshop is one of the world's most elegant handlers of system memory—you can open impossibly large images in the program, where other applications would groan and crash. But you must let Photoshop do its own thing with memory. Don't tinker with the plumbing while the water's running!

Specifying Units of Measurement

As you'll see in the exercises throughout this book, Photoshop can express measurements in different kinds of units to help you size up your work. In two instances you want to specify the unit of your choice: when you check the Image Size and Canvas Size settings (both under the Image menu), and when you select the Show Rulers option (by pressing Ctrl+R) around an active image window.

Figure 4.10 shows the Unit Preferences dialog box, which you access by selecting Preference from the File menu and then choosing Units.

The Rulers window at the top of the Unit Preferences dialog box controls the unit of measurement the rulers use in an active image. You probably should keep Inches as the default. Occasionally, however, you'll need to measure an area for placing text, in which case you might want to specify Points as the unit of measurement for rulers. Additionally, you may be assigned work that is measured in picas or centimeters; Photoshop enables you to rule an image according to these specifications as well.

Note In Chapter 21, "Advanced Type Usage and Presentations," you'll see how to use the Info palette to measure a small amount of type without resetting the Units Preferences in Photoshop. For most of your measuring needs, you need to go to the Units Preferences dialog box to set units for measurements such as inches, pixels, and so on, but in Photoshop 3, there are one or two exceptions to the rule.

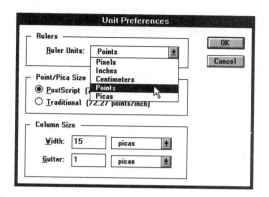

Figure 4.10

You can set Photoshop's Rulers and other measurements to your specifications in the Unit Preferences dialog box.

When measuring how well conventional type sets into an image, click on the Traditional radio button in the Point/Pica Size area of the Units Preferences dialog box. As you can see in figure 14.11, the image window is bordered by rulers set to points of measure; by setting points as the **R**uler Units, you can tell how large you should set the **S**ize of type entered in the Type tool dialog box (see Chapter 9, "Using Type in Photoshop").

In the Column Size window of the dialog box, the **W**idth and **G**utter options show you how an image fits into a page layout of another application, such as a desktop publishing application. When set to inches, this unit of measurement is also used in the **I**mage Size and **C**anvas Size options of the **I**mage menu. You should set this option to inches, unless your work calls for European or typographic standards.

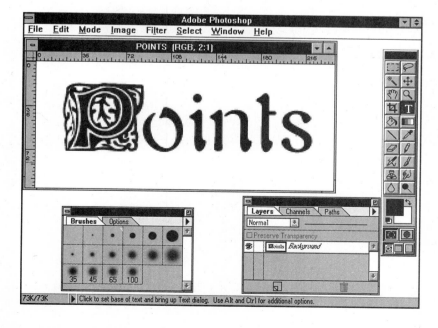

Figure 4.11

To make an image window display rulers set to point sizes, choose points in the Ruler Units box in the Units Preferences dialog box.

Gamut Warning Preferences

If you're using Photoshop to create or retouch images for a slide presentation, or simply for viewing on your monitor, you probably won't have much call for the Gamut **W**arning Preference. *Gamut* is a term used to describe the color space of different color models; *Gamut Warning* refers to the limitations of the CMYK, the commercial printing color space. You can set the Gamut Warning preference to display a colored overlay on any image you intend to use for CMYK output. This is a handy visual reminder that your image will not print as it's displayed, and showing the Gamut Warning above an image is as simple as clicking on a command.

Choose **F**ile, **P**references to display the Gamut Warning dialog box shown in figure 4.12. As you can see, you have an option as to the Color and Opacity of the overlay that indicates out-of-gamut zones in an active image in Photoshop's workspace.

Figure 4.12

Gamut Warning refers to the colors in an image that cannot be reproduced with CMYK (commercial printing) colors.

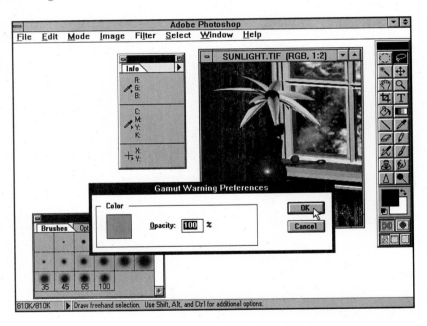

In figure 4.13, **M**ode, Gamut **W**arning has been chosen from the menu. As a result of specifying a tint and opacity for the warning area in Gamut Warning Preferences, areas of color overlay appear on the SUNLIGHT.TIF image where colors in the image exceed the printable range of commercial inks.

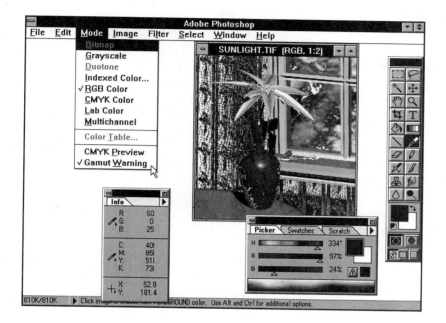

Figure 4.13

Gamut Warning tints image areas that contain color commercial inks can't faithfully reproduce.

Notice also in this figure that both the Picker palette and the Info palette display exclamation warnings when a particular color is sampled or created that cannot be expressed by using a combination of cyan, magenta, yellow, and black pigments. Photoshop is a very capable pre-press tool. In its workspace, you'll find many seemingly oblique features that printing production experts have come to respect and trust. See Part 5, "Inking Up and Doing Yourself a Service," for more information about Photoshop's output capabilities.

Plug-Ins Preferences

Adobe Systems has openly published the specifications for *plug-ins,* a name used to describe wonderful filters that third-party manufacturers have developed independently for use with Photoshop and other programs that have adopted the plug-in architecture. If you've been using Photoshop 2.5 or another imaging program before coming to Photoshop 3, you might have collected some plug-in filters from a number of vendors. And now you're probably trying to figure out how to make them work in Photoshop 3!

The good news is that it couldn't be simpler, but you need to give a little thought to the location on your hard disk that will hold your plug-in filters. Plug-ins can be located in the PHOTOSHP\PLUGINS directory (folder) on your system; genuine plug-ins, ones that follow Adobe's standard to the letter, should have a unique location not associated with another program. This means that if you own BrandXWare's imaging program, and have plug-ins located in BrandXWare's plug-ins directory, it's probably not such a good idea to specify this directory in Photoshop's plug-ins Preferences dialog box. Why? Because Photoshop's own, proprietary filters (the ones that come with Photoshop) would have to be copied into BrandXWare's plug-ins directory for Photoshop to find them—leading to massive confusion for both applications. You can only specify one plug-in directory per Photoshop session.

Save yourself the grief, and put third-party Adobe-standard plug-in filters in the PHOTOSHP\PLUGINS directory created when you installed Photoshop.

After you have your plug-in filters organized in one place, choose **F**ile, Pre**f**erences, then **P**lug-ins to display a dialog box like the one shown in figure 4.14. Choose the subdirectory (folder) that contains the filters, then click on OK.

Figure 4.14

Choose the hard disk location where plug-ins are located.

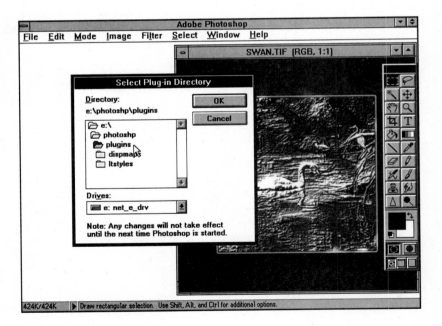

The Bonus CD has several trial-size and working versions of some stupendous Photoshop plug-in filters. When you're asked to load a filter file from the CD in chapters to come (most notably Chapter 19, "3rd-Party Plug-in Filters"), you'll want to keep all these plug-ins in one place on your hard disk. If you read the fine print at the bottom of the Select Plug-in Directory dialog box in figure 4.14, you'll see that you have to restart Photoshop after you select a Plug-In directory. This is true for both Macintosh and Windows users. If you change directories for Plug-ins, you must change the preference, as described earlier. Photoshop reads the current status of your Plug-ins directory each time you launch the program; new filters added to the same directory appear on the Filter menu with each new Photoshop session. In figure 4.15, several non-Adobe Filters have been added to the menu. Andromeda, Alien Skin, Pixar, and KPT are all third-party manufacturers of Plug-in filters. What is a plug-in? Keep reading this book!

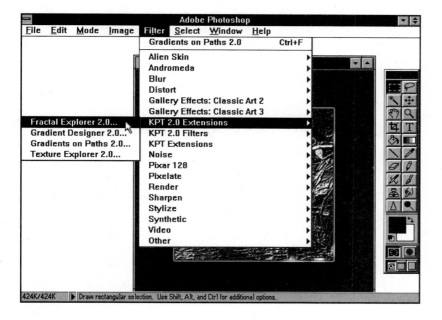

Figure 4.15

Third-party plug-in filters appear on Photoshop's Filters menu every time you start Photoshop.

The SWAN.TIF image in figures 4.14 and 4.15 was created with an ordinary image and third-party plug-in filters. Plug-ins can make special effects come easily to imaging people of all skill levels. Their use (and overuse) is the topic of Chapter 19, "3rd-Party Plug-In Filters."

From the Preference Menu to Workspace Options

We've shown you how to ensure consistent viewing of an image, how to set the appearance of tools used to edit an image, and a lot of prudent preparation work for the imaging experiences that lie ahead in this book and with Photoshop. So how about an image to work on at this point?

We have some actual exercises here to give you a small jump start on the things that lie ahead in Chapter 5, "It's All Done with Palettes." Because practically all of Photoshop can be configured to suit the way you work, its palettes offer customizable features similar to the monitor, tool cursor, memory, and environment preferences you've learned to set. In the next section, we open the curtain for some of the fascinating, original (and productive!) new features found on Photoshop's customizable palettes, beginning with the Brushes/Options group of palettes.

Regardless of what painting tool you use in Photoshop, the Brushes/Options palette is one of the two palette groups (the other is the Layers/Channels/Paths group) you'll want on the workspace at all times. As you get acquainted with the Brushes palette, you'll gain an understanding of how the other eight palettes work.

Brushes Palette Options

Call this section a pre-test drive—we're going to give the directions, you're going to steer, and in the process you'll discover that magic is nothing more than a secret or two that's not yet been shared. Because Photoshop's workspace is a tightly integrated bundle of features, it's important to understand two things before we begin this chapter's assignment:

1. You learn about seemingly unrelated things by performing what you think is an isolated action in Photoshop. You're going to play with the Paint Brush tool and the Brushes palette in the following exercises, but you'll also see how to configure the palette for future use. Additionally, you'll learn how to load a saved selection. A *selection* is an outline shape that defines an underlying image area, created through the use of a selection tool. You don't have to know how to use a selection tool yet to take advantage of a saved selection's capabilities. But you're going to want to know how to use one after you finish these exercises—and you'll learn how in subsequent chapters.

2. You aren't going to break anything, or mess up any of the settings you've done so far, by doing a little image editing at this stage of the game. If you followed the tour earlier in this chapter, the Restore Dialog and Palette Positions check box is

checked in the More Preferences dialog box. Therefore, Photoshop's workspace will retain all of your options when you move on to other chapters and assignments of your own. Additionally, because you'll work with an image from the companion Bonus CD, nothing can be erased, smudged, warped, or filtered in the original image. CDs are Read-Only Memory digital media (as in CD-ROMs), and about the only way to permanently damage LOOK.TIF, the image used in the next exercise, is to use the CD as a coffee coaster.

In addition to the default Brushes palette with which you'll probably perform most of your imaging work, Photoshop ships with three other palettes: Assorted, (Drop)Shadows, and Square. The files for these palettes are all located in the BRUSHES subdirectory of Photoshop. The DOS names for these palette files are ASSORTED.ABR, SHADOWS.ABR, and SQUARE.ABR, respectively; Macintosh users can load the custom palettes by selecting the long file names. Photoshop's default palette of round, soft tips cannot be deleted accidentally because, unlike version 2.5, the default palette of Brushes tips is stored in one of Photoshop's program files (users can't access it).

Although the additional Brushes palettes are not loaded by default, they can be very useful in special situations if you know how to load them. Additionally, you can *create* a brush, or several of them as an entire palette you can work with in Photoshop. The last two exercises in this chapter show you how to make the Brushes palette work the way you want it to while you do your imaging work.

Creating a Brush Tip

As mentioned in the last section, Photoshop's Brushes palette is an Anything Reservoir—it's a palette that contains tips of varying sizes that you use with any tool on the toolbox that can apply foreground material to a background. This is a rather open-ended definition, but the Brushes palette is open-ended—you can modify one of Photoshop's default Brushes tips, create a new one, or define part of an image as a Brushes tip that you paint on other parts of an image!

In the next exercise, you'll see how to go about creating a special Paint brush tip for a special assignment: creating a gentle area of shading in the LOOK!.TIF image. You'll need to use a virtual dropcloth in this assignment to prevent the brush stroke you make with the custom brush tip from straying into areas of the LOOK.TIF image that don't need shading. For an assignment like this, now's a good time to get a feel for the power of *selection marquees*, areas that mark a boundary in an image between *masked* (protected) image areas, and *selected* areas—areas that are available for editing.

The selection you'll load is a saved selection; selection marquees are saved in Alpha channels in an image. You'll see how to create a selection in Chapter 5, "It's All Done with Palettes," but for now, you'll get the chance to work with one, and see what it looks like from a view of the Channels palette. Now you're going to customize and use the first of many palettes you'll use on a daily basis in your imaging experiences with Photoshop.

Making a Large, Angled Brush Tip

Load LOOK.TIF image from CHAP04 subdirectory of Bonus CD	Image you'll edit in this exercise.

If you've experimented with Photoshop before reading this chapter, there's a good chance you already have the Brushes/Options group of palettes onscreen. The Show/Hide Brushes command is a toggling function, so if you already have the palettes onscreen, ignore the following step, or you'll hide the palettes.

Choose **W**indow, **P**alette, Show **B**rushes (or with Windows, press F5; with Macintosh, press F9)	Displays Brushes/Options grouped palette on workspace.
Double-click on Zoom tool (magnifying glass) on toolbox	Double-clicking on Zoom tool zooms view of image to 1:1 viewing resolution, and doing this makes LOOK.TIF image fill workspace.
Choose **W**indow, **P**alette, Show **C**hannels	Displays Layers/Channels/Paths group of palettes.
Arrange palettes and ZOOM.TIF image so that you have a clear view of all workspace elements	Performs sort of optimizing that enables you to work more efficiently in Photoshop.

The saved selection which you'll load can be performed in either of two ways. **S**elect, **L**oad Selection is the menu route to accomplishing what you'll do next, but not nearly as interesting! Your screen should look like the one in figure 4.16.

Scroll to bottom of Channels palette, then press Alt (Option) while clicking on picture icon to left of #4 label	Loads selection information that's in Alpha channel #4, and displays marquee around LOOK lettering (see fig. 4.17). Cool, huh?

The marquee describes the area inside the lettering as a selection; these parts of the image are available for editing. However, the areas outside the marquee—the bricks, the sides of the letters, the polished floor—are protected, or *masked* from paint strokes.

Double-click on an empty space on Brushes palette, next to tip marked 100	Displays New Brush dialog box.
Type **200** in pixels field of **D**iameter setting, leave **H**ardness slider at 0%, and leave **S**pacing at 25%, with check box checked	Specifies that new brush is twice the diameter of Photoshop's largest default brush tip, that the tip has very soft edge characteristics, and that there is a gap of 50 pixels (25% of 200) between individual strokes you make with the new brush.

You might want to play with Spacing options in your future brush tip creations. The setting you just made will create a continuous stroke wherever you click and drag with a painting tool, because the 50-pixel Spacing is less than the diameter of the tip. If you create a 25-pixel diameter brush tip with 100% Spacing, for example, then click and drag quickly with a painting tool, you create an effect of a traditional skip brush stroke—a gap appears in one continuous brush stroke on the canvas.

Click and drag on a dot on the ellipse in proxy tip box in lower-left corner of New Brush dialog box	Sets Roundness of new brush tip. Stop clicking and dragging when **R**oundness field reads about **50%**.
Click and drag arrow of proxy brush tip until it points to northeast	Sets Angle of new brush to about 45° (see fig. 4.18).

You can set values in most of the Photoshop dialog boxes by using proxy boxes (as you did here), text entry fields, or sliders. Photoshop is an imaging application, so it stands to reason that parameters for tools and effects are visually oriented, too!

You've created a new brush tip but haven't put it to any use yet. Stay tuned while we shift into high gear and put the new, angled tip to some practical use in the LOOK image.

Figure 4.16

Conserve screen real estate by arranging images and palettes so that you can access and see everything that's displayed.

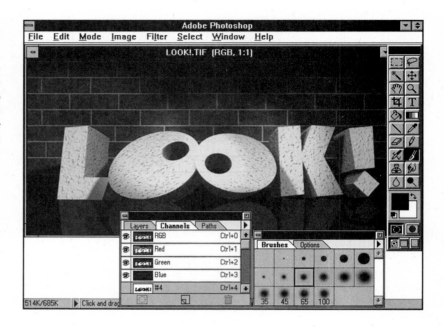

Figure 4.17

Press Alt while clicking on a picture icon of an Alpha channel on the Channels palette to load the information as a selection marquee.

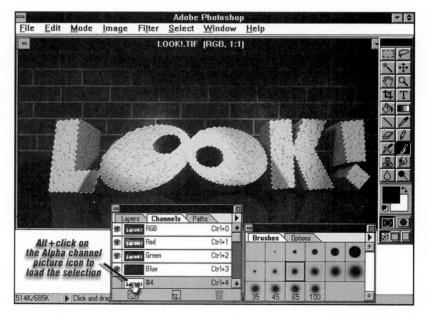

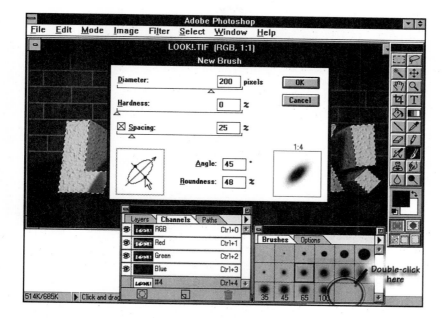

Figure 4.18

Use the controls in a Photoshop proxy box as an alternative to manually entering values for the new brush tip.

Before you click on OK in the New Brush dialog box and continue with your first image-retouching assignment, let's take a moment to reflect on one or two of the object-oriented shortcuts you've performed so far.

Earlier in this chapter (and in Chapter 2, "Acquiring a Digital Image"), we described RGB type images as having a color organization expressed in color channels. You saw in the last exercise that the Channels palette presently has five channel titles—the RGB composite channel (the default channel view for images), three color channels representing the color components of LOOK!.TIF, and an Alpha channel, entitled #4. Pressing Alt while clicking on the picture icon of an Alpha channel loads the selection information contained in the channel, and if you look closely at the picture icon, you'll see that the information we refer to is *graphical* information.

In the next chapter, you'll see how to work with the graphical information stored in an Alpha channel, but for now, understand that you've just learned a shortcut for loading a selection, which you'll use next to confine your painting with this new brush tip to only the areas on the face of the LOOK! lettering. An alternative (longer) way to load the information stored in an Alpha channel is to choose **S**elect, **L**oad Selection, then choose from a dialog box the selection you want loaded. Because Photoshop can store up to 21 Alpha channels in an RGB, single-layer image, the process of retrieving a saved selection is often expedited by pressing Alt while clicking on the pictorial representation of the channel you need on the Channels palette. Unlike Alpha channels, however, the color component channels will not produce a marquee selection if you press Alt while clicking on their icons on the Channels palette—they represent information about the image, not about a selection area.

As you grow more familiar with Photoshop, you'll discover that the two groups of palettes presently on your workspace will be the ones you'll use most in imaging assignments. Let's get back to the new, huge brush tip you're going to add to the Brushes palette in the next exercise.

Stroking Foreground Color into a Selection Area

Now that you've created a new brush tip, it's time to use it. In the next exercise, you'll use the Paint brush tool, one of the eight painting tools on the toolbox (counting the Type tool), to apply a little shading. This is where the other palette in the Brushes/Options group of palettes comes into play. You've defined the characteristics of a new Brush tip, but Photoshop offers more options as to how foreground color (or sampled image areas, in the case of the Rubber stamp tool) is applied with a Brush tip to an image.

The Options palette is *context-sensitive;* it provides options for the specific tool you are currently using. In the next exercise, you'll use a partial opacity of foreground color to add some shading to the areas inside the marquee selection. To do this, you'll use a Paintbrush option on the Options palette.

Here's how to add the new brush tip to the Brushes palette, and use it to create shading in the LOOK!.TIF image:

Applying Partially Transparent Foreground Color

In New Brush dialog box, click on OK	Displays workspace; 200-pixel, angled brush is now selected (highlighted with a box) on Brushes palette (see fig. 4.19).
Press **B** (for Paint **B**rush tool), or click on tool on toolbox	Chooses Paint Brush tool.

Many choices in Photoshop can be executed with a single keystroke. We'll use these shortcuts throughout this book to get you into the practice of taking the shortest route to a command, a selection, and other Photoshop techniques, as in the next step…

Press **D** (for **d**efault colors icon) (or click on tiny icon at lower left of colors on toolbox)	Sets default Photoshop paint colors to black foreground and white background.
Click on Options tab on Brushes/Options palette	Displays Paintbrush Options palette, because Paint Brush tool is currently active.

When you choose other toolbox tools, the Options palette display options that relate to specific properties of the tool, properties that you can adjust.

Click and drag Opacity slider on Options palette to about **70%**	Reduces opacity of black foreground color you'll apply to selection area.
Click and drag Paint brush cursor across selection area in image (see fig. 4.20)	Creates shadow effect in selected area only; areas outside selection marquee are unaffected by your Paint brush stroke.
Press Ctrl(Cmd)+D (or choose **S**elect, **N**one)	Deactivates selection marquee. Because it is a saved selection, you can recall it at any time by pressing Alt while clicking on Alpha channel picture icon again.

Because this is a pre-test drive exercise, you may or may not want to save your masterpiece. However, you do want to keep LOOK!.TIF on-screen because we have a second experiment with the Brushes palette to perform next. If you need to get up and go someplace now, follow the next step:

Choose **F**ile, Sa**v**e As, then save image to your hard disk as LOOK.TIF (choose TIFF format from Save File as Format **T**ype drop-down list)	Saves your work to this point.

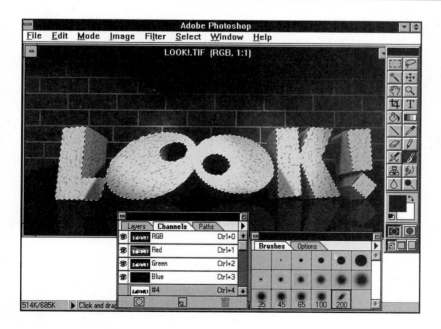

Figure 4.19

Your new addition to the Brushes palette appears in the place where you double-clicked to display the New Brush dialog box.

Figure 4.20

If you decrease opacity in the Paintbrush Option dialog box, your paint strokes will not completely cover up a selected image area.

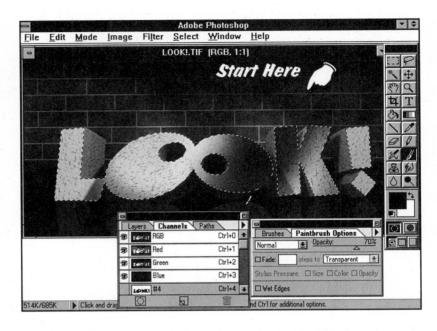

 Tip   You can also modify an existing Brushes palette tip by double-clicking on an existing brush tip space on the Brushes palette.

Adobe Systems did some extensive woodshedding with Photoshop in the past year. If you're coming from an earlier version of the program, things might seem totally rearranged and perhaps a little confusing. However, the good news is that everything has been organized with a definite purpose in mind, and in the next section, new and experienced users alike will benefit from our little tour of the pop-up menu on the Brushes palette. The pop-up menu is where you can save, append, and load an entirely new collection of Brushes tips.

Loading and Resetting the Brushes Palette

As we promised at the beginning of this section, we're going to conclude this chapter with all the settings you defined in the Preferences dialog box intact. The excursion to show you some of the functionality of Photoshop's workspace is intended to be educational, not traumatizing!

In the next exercise, you'll see how to Load a custom set of Brushes tips, the Assorted pack of tips. Brushes tips can be defined as anything you like—Adobe created the Assorted Brushes collection by sampling image areas of typographic characters and other image areas. You can sample a foreground painting by selecting it using a selection tool, then use the Define Brush command (on the pop-up menu) to make it part of an existing collection (use the Append Brushes command), or begin a collection of custom Brushes tips of your own (with the Save Brushes command). See the Tip at the end of this chapter for exact instructions for creating a picture Brushes tip.

If you're just beginning to use Photoshop, you're not likely to outdo the strange, wonderful Assorted collection Adobe Systems has prepared as a palette. In the next exercise, we defend this statement by showing you how to load and use the Assorted collection of Brushes tips. Additionally, we'll show you how to perform some clean up work to restore the Brushes palette to its default setting. Most of the exercises in this book use the default palette, and as you'll see next, you'll have a hard time following along with the rest of this book's exercises when your Paint brush tip is an eyeball.

When you change Brushes palettes in the next exercise, you will lose the 200-pixel custom brush you built and used in the previous exercise, but that's okay. You know how to build a new tip, and in the next exercise you'll see how to use the pop-up menu's commands to save and restore the Brushes palette's collection of tips.

Here's how to create some visual gestalt in the LOOK!.TIF image by using the Assorted tips collection on the Brushes palette:

Using Photoshop's Assorted Brushes

Click on Brushes tab on grouped palette, then click on pop-up menu button (triangle to right of tab), and choose **L**oad Brushes	Displays Load Dialog box.
Click on ASSORTED.ABR in BRUSHES subdirectory (folder) of PHOTOSHP directory, then click on OK	Selects Assorted Brushes collection you need for this exercise; exits Load dialog box.
Say "Oh, wow!" two or three times	Expresses your awe at all the strange Assorted Brushes tips, which look more like little icons than brush tips.

Even experienced users who've read Adobe's documentation for the program might miss this bundle of goodies that are installed with Photoshop!

Press Alt while clicking on Channel #4 picture icon on Channels palette	Loads selection marquee.
Click on eye brush tip in Brushes palette	Selects a tip design that makes painting strokes look like eyes.

continues

continued

Click repeatedly inside selection border	Stamps an eye image wherever you click, leaving area outside border unaffected (see fig. 4.21).

When using the Assorted Brushes, the technique you're likely to prefer isn't to stroke the image canvas, but rather to click on an area, much as you would stamp a check CANCELED.

Now that we've had our fun, we need to show you the way out of being saddled with Assorted brushes tips for the rest of your imaging adventures!

Click on pop-up menu on Brushes and choose Reset Brushes	Displays an exclamation dialog box palette with three options.

Append means to *add to* the default collection of Brushes tips. This creates a tad of a mess on the Brushes palette, because an Appended default palette includes all the Assorted and default brushes tips. You'd have to scroll on the Brushes palette to find the default tips if you clicked on the Append button in the dialog box, so…

Click on OK	Displays Brushes palette with default tips.

Your 200-pixel angled brush is not on the palette, because you didn't save the tip to a collection, and you didn't use the Append command to add it to an existing collection of tips.

Press Ctrl+D (or choose **S**elect, **N**one), then choose **F**ile, Sa**v**e As, and save LOOK.TIF image to your hard disk	Deselects marquee selection, and saves your work.

The last step is not mandatory; you now have a pretty goofy-looking image, but if you work for a cartoon studio, your boss will be impressed when he or she (or it) sees what you've learned so far!

Tip

To create a Custom Brushes tip, you can use the Elliptical, Rectangular or Lasso (selection) tools to select an area on an image that contains a design element you want. You can select as large a size as you like, and the sample area can be in color, but you'll work more quickly with the tip (and it will have more practical use) if you define a small image area consisting of grayscale image information. Try a character from a typeface symbol set, for example. Although you can choose any color area you want, you define the tip only as an eight-bit, grayscale-type image. Then you can paint the image with any color defined with the Color Picker or the Picker group of palettes.

New Riders Publishing
INSIDE
SERIES

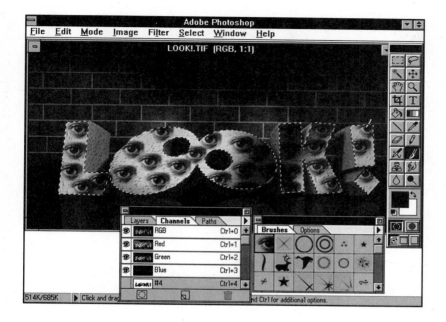

After defining the image area with the selection tool, click on the pop-up menu triangle on the Brushes palette, then select Define Brush—the area is defined as a Brushes tip. It's added after the last tip of the currently loaded collection of tips. If you want to save the tip for future use, use the Append Brushes command on the pop-up menu, then give your appended palette a unique name. Maurice has always been our personal favorite.

Chapter 5, "It's All Done with Palettes," continues our exploration of Photoshop's defaults and options, but in it we move to the workspace, where tools, palettes, and image properties can be defined and refined to best fit your personal imaging needs. If you think the Brushes palette is robust, you haven't seen anything yet!

It's All Done with Palettes

If you've ever heard two people talking as they walked away from a stupendous illusion created at a carnival magic show, you might have heard one person putting a wet blanket on the feat, as follows, "Aw, there's nothin' to it. It's all done with mirrors!" The statement is simultaneously a catch-all and a put-down; the observer is discrediting the magic stunt, because deep down, he or she really did appreciate the illusion, but doesn't know exactly how it was accomplished. It's human nature to play down a remarkable sight when we're not privileged to know the "secrets," the moves with which a sleight-of-hand event is presented.

Similarly, Adobe Photoshop has achieved such a level of recognition for its own brand of digital imaging magic, business professionals often look at an absolutely incredible picture and say, "Oh, they probably used Photoshop." Hopefully, you're now reading this because you want to increase your potential as an imaging-type person, and you want to learn the tricks so that you, too, can perform the magic. If this is the case, come on into this chapter. Your apprenticeship to Wizardhood continues from Chapter 4, "Photoshop Defaults and Options," with a survey of Photoshop's workspace, where all the "really good" stuff is located, configured, and used. It's all done with palettes!

Why Palettes?

This chapter is intended to familiarize you with the editing, viewing, and selecting features found on Photoshop palettes, so when you get to Chapter 6, "The Photoshop Test Drive," you'll feel more at home in your test vehicle (an image we've prepared on the Bonus CD) because you know how to access commands and functions, and you understand how to configure the amazing Photoshop 3 palettes. Floating palettes have been a convention of many graphics programs. Common commands and tools are located on floating palettes so they can be accessed easily, then pushed out of the way when you need a better view of the graphic you're working on.

With the advent of Photoshop 3, the convention of a floating palette in a workspace may never seem the same. You'll understand what we mean after you've worked on an image for a little while with Photoshop's *grouped* floating palettes. We're going to take you through each of the four grouped palettes, explain how you can manipulate the palette itself in Photoshop, and describe how the functions work.

To begin with, every Photoshop palette can be displayed by choosing **W**indow, **P**alette, then choosing any palette (of the ten palettes in the four groups) that isn't presently displayed on-screen. The **W**indow, **P**alette command is a *toggling* function— it alternates between showing and hiding a palette group. The first palette you'll examine in this chapter is the one that can very well replace the menu bar in Photoshop: the completely user-definable Commands palette.

The Commands Palette

Adobe Systems listened to their users and, in version 3.0, designed a palette that cannot be criticized for any functionality shortcomings, because the options displayed are completely up to *you*! The Commands palette is a list of menu commands (see fig. 5.1). The default Commands palette features different commands for the Macintosh and Windows version of Photoshop. You can change any of the Commands palette's settings, but because the *default* keyboard shortcuts associated with commands are frequently referred to in the exercises in this book, you should leave the Commands palette at its default settings (except for in this chapter). In this chapter, we'll show you how to reset the Commands palette to its default commands.

In figure 5.1, the top of the default Commands palettes should be fairly familiar— Edit, Cut, and Copy can be accomplished with a click on the title of the command. It's the esoteric items— such as Lighting Effects, Show Layers, and commands that are nested deeply in menus— that make the Commands palette a welcome feature in a program that's so packed with options!

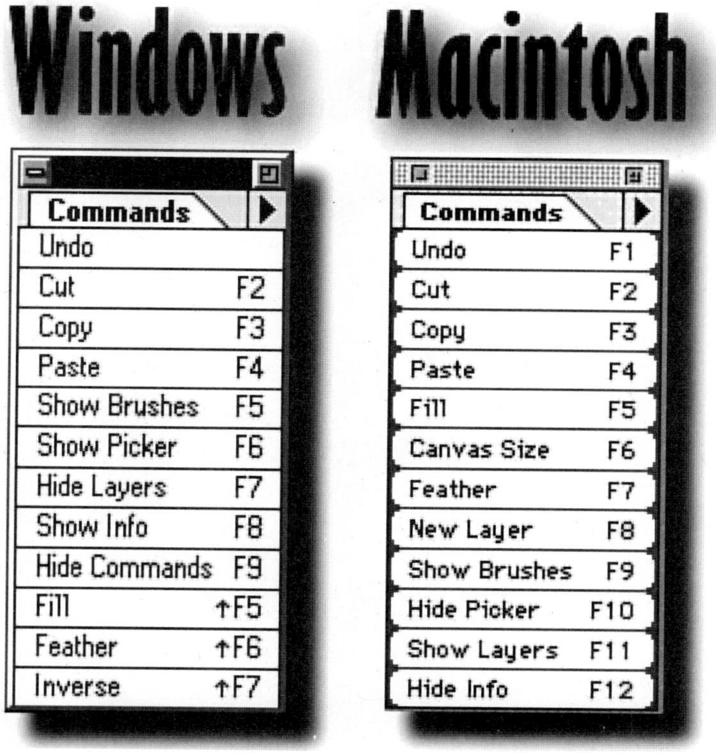

Windows   Macintosh

Commands	▶
Undo	
Cut	F2
Copy	F3
Paste	F4
Show Brushes	F5
Show Picker	F6
Hide Layers	F7
Show Info	F8
Hide Commands	F9
Fill	⇧F5
Feather	⇧F6
Inverse	⇧F7

Commands	▶
Undo	F1
Cut	F2
Copy	F3
Paste	F4
Fill	F5
Canvas Size	F6
Feather	F7
New Layer	F8
Show Brushes	F9
Hide Picker	F10
Show Layers	F11
Hide Info	F12

Figure 5.1

The Windows and Macintosh Commands palettes work identically; the default commands are different, however.

You can add to, reconfigure, and delete commands in the default Commands palette. This palette—like the Brushes palette you explored in Chapter 4, "Photoshop Defaults and Options"—is not stored in a user-accessible program file, so you can't accidentally delete the configuration that's standard in Photoshop 3.

As you become more comfortable and familiar with Photoshop's features, you may find a need or a preference for a specific set of "working" tools and commands. Unlike the Photoshop palettes, the toolbox does not sport a Close button; therefore, tools are always within reach while you design or retouch. However, to make functions just as readily available, and anticipating a need from a specific occupational design niche, Adobe has created five additional Commands palettes (see fig. 5.2). These "specialty" Commands palettes can be loaded from the CMDSETS (Command Sets) subdirectory of Photoshop on your hard disk. Like all Photoshop palettes, the Commands palette has a button (in the top left corner) for closing the palette. Additionally, a Minimize/Maximize button in the top right corner is for conserving screen space when you want a palette available but aren't using it at the moment.

Figure 5.2

*Five preset
Commands
palettes are
located in the
CMDSETS
directory of
Photoshop.*

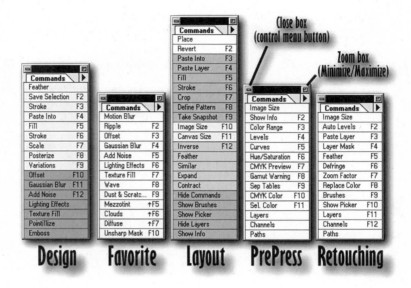

Although the titles of the palette files suggest a specific applicability to a chosen
imaging profession, the custom palettes are more of a convenience for new users than
a perfect collection of "must have" commands for their respective imaging fields. The
Favorite palette, for example, is packed with commands from the Filter menu.
Although filters provide a valuable source of image enhancement, the Favorite
Commands palette features many of the "cool effects" users are eager to experiment
with before they learn and understand some of Photoshop's less obvious power
features.

Your Wish—Photoshop's Commands

As you'll notice throughout this book, Photoshop's integrated environment creates
overlapping areas of functionality. You'll usually find at least two ways to accomplish a
single task; and on occasion, you'll find the same Photoshop command in different
dialog boxes. This chapter is a perfect reflection of Photoshop's polymorphous
parameters. In the first exercise, you customize the Commands palette; then, at the
end of the chapter, you use the customized palette for a small experiment in using
tools and features together in Photoshop. And in between lies an explanation of the
palettes that'll help you take the best advantage of their features.

People who are fond of using hot keys to speed up their work will have a ball with the
Commands palette, because you can associate function keys with a command. Any
function key (F2 through F12) can be assigned, with an overall total of 22 unique key
combinations. (In Photoshop, you can assign the Shift key to work in combination
with a function-key command). The hot keys you define operate independently of the
Commands palette; although you have to set up the function keys in the Edit Com-

mands dialog box, you *don't* have to have the Commands palette displayed to use the keys you've assigned to a command.

The goal in the next exercise is to copy the Define Pattern command to the default Commands palette. Define Pattern is a sampling command (similar to the Define Brush command seen in Chapter 4, "Photoshop Defaults and Options") that can be used in a variety of design situations. Its multipurpose capability is demonstrated in several chapters of this book. Although it's located under Photoshop's **E**dit command, let's suppose it would be much more convenient on the workspace. Your wish is Photoshop's command when you know where the customizing options are located.

Customizing the Commands Palette

Start Photoshop, then choose **W**indow, **P**alettes, Show Co**m**mands (if Commands palette isn't already on-screen)

Displays Commands palette on workspace.

In the Windows version of Photoshop, F9 is the default command for displaying the Commands palette; if you're running a Macintosh and you'd like to add the Show Commands command to the Commands palette (is this like those Chinese boxes, or what?), you'll soon see how to do it.

Click on pop-up menu triangle below Minimize/Maximize box on Commands palette, then choose Edit Commands...

Displays Edit Commands dialog box (see fig. 5.3).

You'll return to this dialog box before you finish customizing the Commands palette, but here's a note in passing: to reorganize the position of the default commands, click and drag—either up or down—on a title in the Edit Commands dialog box. (Clicking and dragging sideways doesn't do anything.)

Click on New

Displays New Command dialog box.

Click on **E**dit, then click on **D**efine Pattern on menu bar

Adds Define Pattern menu item to Menu Item field.

If you can't remember a menu command you'd like to add, or the Edit Commands dialog box is blocking the menu bar from behind the New Command box, you can type the few letters you're sure of in the Menu Name box, then click on **F**ind. Photoshop performs a text string search and automatically enters the proposed menu name. You do *not* have to enter the first letters of the command you want. For example, typing **LA**, then clicking on **F**ind will produce Show Layers in the Menu Name box (or Hide Layers, if the Layers palette is already on the workspace).

continues

continued

Choose F2 from Function Key drop-down list, then click on Shift check box	Assigns Define Pattern command to Shift+F2 key combination.

Some commands, such as Cut (F2 for both Windows and Macintosh) are reserved function keys; their names are dimmed in the drop-down list. You can use them, but you first have to remove their association. To disassociate Cut with F2, for example, you'd click on Cut in the Edit Command dialog box, then click on Change. Next, from the Function key drop-down list, you'd assign the None function (or a different function key) to Cut.

Click on Color drop-down box and choose Violet (see fig. 5.4)	Define Pattern command now appears in violet on Commands palette list.
Click on OK	Displays Edit Command dialog box.
Click on OK	Displays workspace, with a Commands palette that sports a new command at the bottom (see fig. 5.5).

Figure 5.3

In the Edit Commands dialog box, you can rearrange command order and set the number of columns displayed on the Commands palette.

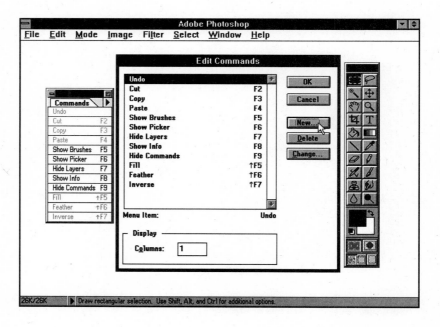

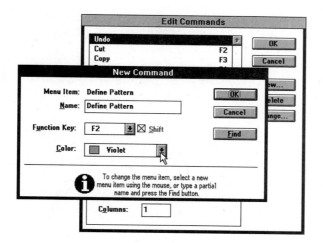

Figure 5.4

Assign a unique function key combination to a command you add to the Commands palette.

Figure 5.5

The Commands palette can hold several of the menu commands you use the most in your Photoshop work.

Tip

If you want to minimize overlapping commands in Photoshop, the first four that can be removed from the Commands palette are Undo, Cut, Copy, and Paste. All these commands are supported by other key combinations you're probably already familiar with. Photoshop supports the following key combinations, in compliance with the conventions of both the Windows and Macintosh operating systems:

	Windows	Macintosh
Undo	Ctrl+Z	Cmd⌘+Z
Cut	Ctrl+X	Cmd⌘+X
Copy	Ctrl+C	Cmd⌘+C
Paste	Ctrl+V	Cmd⌘+V

We refer to these commands several times in this book's exercises, and recommend that you add them to your bag of tricks for working more efficiently in Photoshop (and other applications that support these shortcuts).

A very natural question you might ask at this point is, "How many commands can the Commands palette hold?" The question is best answered by figure 5.6, which shows what happened when the authors decided to use the Append Command option and add every command available in Photoshop's five custom collections that came with Photoshop. Because only about 28 commands can be displayed vertically on the palette, we increased the number of Display Columns in the Edit Commands dialog box to 5 (6 is the maximum).

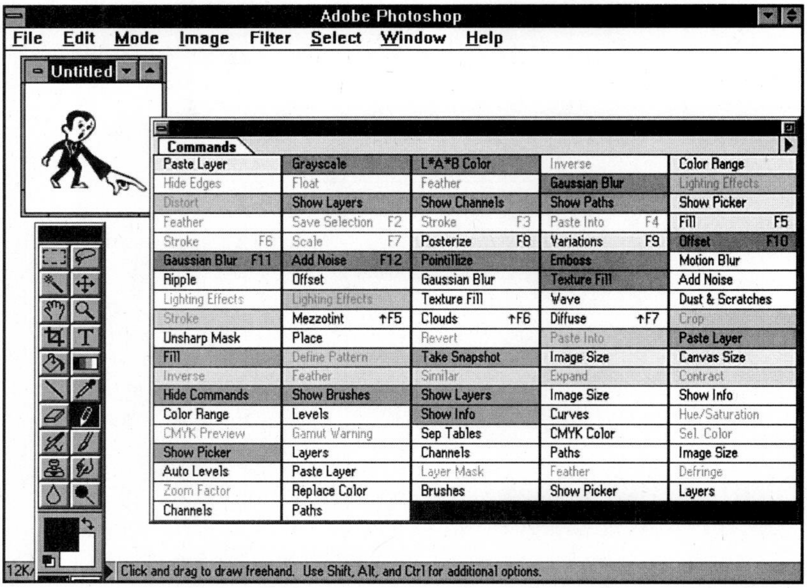

Figure 5.6

The Commands palette is virtually unlimited in its capability to display commands, but you'd need a good reason to do so!

In a few places in the book, we provide bad examples of Photoshop techniques, so that you can avoid similar pitfalls. Making the Commands palette so large that it owns the screen is a perfect example of a Photoshop "don't." If you've played with the pop-up menu commands before reading this section, and have an excess of commands, choose Reset Commands from the pop-up menu, then answer OK to the prompt in the attention box. This restores the Commands palette to its default settings.

Stop   The **R**estore Dialog and Palette Positions option in the General Preferences dialog box (refer to fig. 4.6) does not perform the same function as the Reset commands on all of the Photoshop palette's pop-up menus. The two commands perform entirely different services. The Reset command on the palettes returns each palette to its original default set of options, colors, or settings specific to the palette.

The **R**estore Dialog and Palettes Positions command (which should be checked) returns palettes to the same geographic position on the workspace as when you

leave a Photoshop session. Customized palette display is undone only by clicking on each palette's Reset command; the palette's appearance does not change if you check (or uncheck) the **R**estore Dialog and Palettes Positions check box.

If you're new to Photoshop, you'll do well to keep the Commands palette on-screen to help you understand what commands do, and to provide a visual reinforcement of the shortcut key commands that display other palette and filter dialog boxes. We can't stress enough that you should click on the Size (Minimize/Maximize) button to display only the title bar and tabs for a palette that's not constantly in use. Screen real estate is at a premium in Photoshop, especially if you're running a 640×480 screen resolution.

Exploring the Channels Palette

Although many people will flock to the Favorite Command palette as a source of image enhancement, a single palette depends very much on the others you'll want to work with in Photoshop. A perfect example of this is the Layers/Channels/Paths group of palettes. Adobe Systems has grouped these three palettes into one so that you can switch between palettes quickly, by clicking on a title tab. These three palettes share a common "theme"—each offers an aspect of image editing. They provide the views and tools for creating multichannel, multilayer images that can contain selection information that describes a physical portion of an image.

The Channels palette is of particular interest to anyone who wants to edit parts of two different images together; to apply a special effect or a color to a portion of an image; or to modify a red, green, or blue color component of an image without affecting the other components.

Seeing a View of an Image's Color Channels

As described in Chapters 1 and 2, RGB images are capable of expressing a possible 16.7 million unique color values through the use of red, green, and blue color channels. Each channel of an RGB image is displayed as a grayscale, eight-bit/pixel image, whose areas of black, white, and all the shades in between correspond to the amount of the respective channel's contribution to the overall image. Photoshop can display a view of the red, green, or blue color components' contribution to an overall image—you just click on the color channel's title on the Channels palette. If you'd like to try this one out, load the PRESENT.TIF image from the CHAP05 subdirectory of the Bonus CD into Photoshop, choose Show Layers (it's on both the Win and Mac Commands palette), then click on the Channels tab on the palette group.

We'll use PRESENT.TIF in an exercise or two in this section on Channels, but first you need to understand how and why an *Alpha channel* (a user-defined area in an image, that contains selection information) does what it does. And to understand an Alpha channel, you need to know why Photoshop displays things as it does.

If you look at the Channels palette with the PRESENT.TIF image open, you'll notice thumbnail images, with a title to the right of them indicating the Red, Green, and Blue channel view of the whole RGB composite image. A composite view is the most common way people look at images; after all, no one has come up to you lately and said, "Hey, you want to see the Green color channel of my kids?" Still, being able to dissect an image according to its component colors can come in handy in your digital imaging adventures, and Photoshop provides both the thumbnail and full-image window view of every channel contained in a digital image's file structure.

Click on the wide bar where you see the thumbnail image and the title "Blue" on the Channels palette's list of channels. Doing this changes your view of the color composite image to the view of the Blue channel, so you can see its contribution to the total PRESENT image. It might look like a poorly exposed grayscale photo of the same image, but it's not—the lighter areas of the image correspond to high amounts of blue in the image, and darker areas indicate blue's absence from the RGB composite image. Now, click on the Green channel's title bar. It looks darker overall, right? That's because green's contribution is slight; the gift-wrapped present is made up primarily of blue shades. You'll be similarly disappointed if you click on the Red channel title.

This is the way Photoshop presents color information; we use the term "information" a lot in this book, and not simply "color," because you're handling data when you edit an image. To make color information more palpable and easier to grasp intellectually than if you had to calculate all the ones and zeros necessary for editing an image, Photoshop presents the data graphically.

When you move your view through the channels in an image by clicking anywhere on the channel title, as you just did, you're also indicating to Photoshop that this is the active channel you want to view. An *active*, or *target, channel* is the one you are editing; no other channels can be affected by brushes or selection tools while the channel is displayed in the image window and the title bar is highlighted.

If you prefer to see a graphical representation of what two channels of color look like in the image, without viewing the third, click on the eye icon next to the channel you want to hide from view. If you do this now, you'll see that the channel is still highlighted, although some color content appears to be missing from the RGB view of the picture. The eye icon, which represents visibility, is a toggle. By clicking on a channel's eye icon, you hide the view of that channel in the overall picture. To make the channel visible again, click on the empty space where the icon used to be.

The important thing to remember when viewing color channels is that a highlighted channel is active, even after you hide it from view by clicking on the eye icon. Photoshop gives you ultimate flexibility in viewing and editing aspects of images, but you need to keep *your* eye on the Channels palette while you're working with channels. It's possible to be painting on a channel that's hidden, and not realize it until you've returned to the view of the RGB color composite.

How Image Channels Relate to Selection Areas

The power you'll probably tap into most with the Channels palette is its capability to save (in the form of graphical information) the selections you've created. When you build a border around an image area, the selection information can be displayed in several ways. A *selection* is an actual element of an image that describes either an image area that can be edited (one that is *selected*) or an image area that's protected from editing work (or *masked*). Additionally, you can work with the shape of a selection without altering the underlying image—this is great for modifying a selection border you've already defined. The following sections are explanations of the visual characteristics of an image selection, and the circumstances under which you'll see them.

Selection Marquees

A *selection marquee* is an area above an image that describes an area in which you can work with painting and editing tools, and in which effects can be applied within the marquee. A selection marquee is most commonly created with a selection tool from the toolbox. (Saved selections, described in the next section, also display a selection marquee when they're active, but saved selections are often the result of using a combination of editing tools to describe the marquee's outline.) A selection marquee represents the "live" area in an image, but the marquee itself can be repositioned and edited without disturbing the underlying image information. Unless you save a selection area, the marquee you've created will disappear when you deselect the area—and you've lost the selection marquee for good.

Saved Selections

A *saved selection* is the essence of a selection marquee; whether it is active or inactive in an image file, it, too, describes a shape you can apply to an image to make an area either selected or masked. If you've been laboring over an elegant selection marquee that describes an irregular shape in an image (such as a flower), you'll want to save the selection. After saving a selection, you can move its location, make it inactive while you modify an entire image, or change the saved selection's shape. A saved selection can be modified while it's displayed as a selection marquee, or you can edit a saved selection from a full-image window view of the selection as Alpha channel information. Additionally, you can edit a saved selection when you view an image in Quick Mask mode (described soon).

Alpha Channel Information

Unlike the color channels in an RGB image, an *Alpha channel* is an additional channel you can define in an image file to hold information about a selection, a texture fill (see Chapters 17, "The Wonderful World of Black and White," and 18, "Photoshop's Native Filters"), or another image! Photoshop stores saved selections in an Alpha channel, but you can edit Alpha channel information (thus modifying a saved selection) as easily as you would edit an RGB composite image. Alpha channels are created when you save a selection marquee, but you can also create a "blank" Alpha channel, one that contains no selection information. Alpha channel information is not limited to "on" or "off"; gray represents areas that are *partially* selected. Image areas upon which a partial selection is loaded are partially affected by painting and other Photoshop effects. A *partial selection*, represented as areas of gray in an Alpha channel, is a powerful imaging feature—you can achieve wonderfully photorealistic effects when selection areas are partially transparent and their edges are defined as soft transitions into masked areas over an image.

Alpha channels, like color channels, can contain grayscale pixels that tell Photoshop the degree to which corresponding locations in the composite image are selected or masked when the selection information is activated. But in an Alpha channel—unlike color channels—the brightness of a pixel can represent either the strength of a selected area or the strength of a masked (protected) area in an image. A good example of what selection information stored in an Alpha channel looks like and how you can specify whether the information is selection or masking information is coming up in the next section.

Quick Mask Mode

Photoshop's Quick Mask mode is used expressly for editing a selection, not the underlying image. In Quick Mask mode, as in an Alpha channel selection, you can view a selection area not as a marquee outline, but as a solid representation of a shape that describes a selection area. Quick Mask mode displays a selection as a tinted overlay on a picture, similar to the amberliths traditional designers have used for decades to mask part of a photo or drawing for pre-press separation. You can use painting, editing, and selection tools to modify Quick Mask information. While you're working in Quick Mask mode, you cannot affect the image on which the Quick Mask is displayed, and Photoshop's tools and filters affect only the tinted overlay. Therefore, a Quick Mask isn't a functional selection of an image area until you switch to Standard editing mode for the current image, at which point the Quick Mask becomes a selection marquee. Like selection marquees, Quick Masks aren't permanent—unless you save the editing you've done in Quick Mask mode, the changes made in this mode will disappear as selections when you deselect them.

Clearly, all the different ways a selection can exist in an image file are closely related. Photoshop provides these different appearances of selection information as a means to successfully describe a certain detail in a photo or other bitmap image to isolate it for editing purposes. One of Photoshop's great strengths is its capability to save a selection indefinitely in an image file. You'll use this capability in several of the exercises in this book to help you grow comfortable with an admittedly difficult concept. The next section runs through everything discussed in this section, in a graphical way, and includes an exercise on selecting an image area.

Using and Saving Selections

Chapter 6, "The Photoshop Test Drive," explains in detail how to use the tools in Photoshop's toolbox. Right now, however, you're going to get a little hands-on experience with the most versatile of Photoshop's selection tools, the Lasso tool. The Lasso tool can operate in either of two modes:

◆ *Freehand selection mode*, in which your cursor is free to roam all over an image to define a closed shape that becomes a selection marquee the instant you release the mouse button. In freehand selection mode, you design a selection with the Lasso tool in much the same way you draw an outline with a physical pen or pencil. You can create a self-intersecting shape (such as a figure 8) with the Lasso tool, but any areas inside the outermost edge of a selection made with the Lasso tool are discarded in the resulting selection: that is, you can't draw the letter "o" by making one pass over an image with the Lasso tool.

◆ *Straight line mode*, in which you must hold down the Alt (Option) key while clicking anchor points around an image area. Photoshop automatically creates straight selection lines between the points over which you press Alt while clicking. In this mode, you can develop a technique for quickly defining areas composed of straight edges.

The technique of pressing Alt while clicking produces irregular polygons in an image and is best used with images that feature geometric detail. You can accurately define buildings, packages, and patterns by pressing Alt while clicking with the Lasso tool.

In the next exercise, you use the Lasso tool to outline an image element; then you save the selection for future modification. The Channels palette will be run through its paces as you learn more about how to view and modify your work, using the Channels palette's display of Alpha channel information. In figure 5.7, the PRESENT.TIF image is active in Photoshop's workspace, and we've clicked on the pop-up menu on the Channels palette to display the options for the palette. The options on the Channel palette are context-sensitive; you'll see different options, depending on which channel is currently active, or which channel is currently visible in the image window. The icons at the bottom of the Channels palette offer some of the options on the pop-up menu. We'll use them to show you different graphical shortcuts you can take to execute a command while working with an image.

Here's how to create straight-edge selections in an image:

Picking out a Present

Open PRESENT.TIF image from CHAP05 subdirectory of Bonus CD	This is the image you'll use for editing experimentation.

continues

continued

Press **L**, or click on **Lasso** tool on toolbox	Chooses Lasso tool; shortcut keys are available for every tool on toolbox.
Press and hold Alt (Option) key while clicking on bottom corner of gift in PRESENT.TIF (corner located at about 5 o'clock position)	Sets an anchor point for the straight-edge selection marquee you're going to build.

In the next step, don't worry that the bow intrudes on the straight edges of the gift in the image. In a later exercise, using a different technique, you'll add the bow to the selection marquee you're creating

Press Alt while clicking, in a clockwise direction, on each corner of the gift in PRESENT.TIF image, releasing Alt when you reach the sixth and final corner	Defines outline of gift with a marquee selection (see fig. 5.8).

You can edit inside the selection marquee, but areas outside the selection marquee are protected from editing. Because the selection area will disappear if you click anywhere on the image, this is a good time to save the selection to an Alpha channel.

Click on Save to Selection icon at bottom-left of Channels palette	Creates new Alpha channel (labeled #4, by default), and displays thumbnail image icon on list of channels (see fig. 5.9).
Press Ctrl+D (or choose **S**elect, **N**one)	Deselects marquee selection. Selection is saved, and can be recalled at any time.
Choose **F**ile, Sa**v**e As, then save image to your hard disk as PRESENT.TIF (choose TIFF format from Save File as Format **T**ype drop-down list)	Saves your work to this point.

Figure 5.9 also shows another icon on the Channels palette—the New Alpha Channel icon. Clicking on this icon produces a new, blank Alpha channel in the document. In later chapters you learn how a *blank* channel (one that contains no selection information) can be used as a clean slate upon which you can design a shape Photoshop can load and use as a selection marquee.

By default, the thumbnail image icons on the Channels palette are small (although this chapter shows you how to change this). Nevertheless, you should be able to see a miniature representation of the saved selection in the thumbnail at this point. The black area describes selection information, and the white areas in the thumbnail represent nonselected, or masked, areas in the image window. In the next section, you see how to change the Alpha channel options for the color of selection informa-

tion, and how Quick Mask information is created from the saved selection.

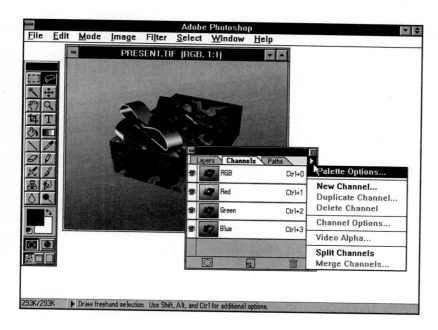

Figure 5.7

Use the Channels palette pop-up menu or icons to access common functions you perform on an image Channel.

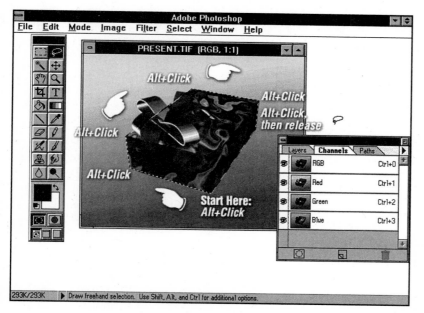

Figure 5.8

When you press Alt (Option) while clicking on an image, Photoshop creates straight selection edges between the points you click.

Figure 5.9

*Icons on the
Channels palette
perform many of
the commands
and functions
found on the
menu bar and on
the pop-up menu.*

Masking and Selecting

Masking and Selecting are opposite functions in Photoshop imaging, but the two imaging properties are interchangeable. Right now, if you were to load the selection you saved for the PRESENT image, the area inside the selection marquee (the gift) could be moved around the image window; and if you were to paste something that's loaded on the Clipboard into this image, only the areas inside the marquee would display the copy of the Clipboard's contents. But suppose that you wanted to slip, say, a different background *behind* the gift in the PRESENT image? If this were your intent, you'd want the gift inside the marquee to be *masked* (protected), and all other areas to be selected so that you could replace them with a background image.

Here's an important point you'll want to consider when you build selections with images of your own: *the black and white areas of an Alpha channel can be inverted to change the way Photoshop makes a selection marquee based on this information.* Pressing Ctrl+I (or choosing **I**mage, **M**ap, **I**nvert) creates a chromatic inversion of a view of any image channel; it's best used when you want to invert a saved selection in an Alpha channel so that selected areas become mask information, and vice versa.

Changing the display of colors in a channel view of a *saved* selection *does not* affect Photoshop's evaluation of the color information contained in an Alpha channel. Photoshop automatically inverts color information in a channel when you select a Color Indicates option in the Channel Options dialog box—you're more or less back where you started if you change Color Indicates: Selected Areas to Masked Areas. It's

only when you begin with a new selection, not a saved one, that you can decide what the color in an Alpha channel indicates. Because this assignment's concept is to accurately define the gift in the image, not the background, you won't be changing the Color Indicates option in the Channel Options dialog box. You need to know where it is, however, for imaging assignments of your own. Usually, editing an image selection by applying black foreground color is easier (and more intuitive) than editing it by applying white to refine *nonselected* area information. For this reason, when you're trying to select (rather than mask) something from your view in an Alpha channel, we recommend that you make it a practice to use the Color indicates: Selected Areas option. Graphically, the difference between this option and the Masked Areas option is similar to the difference between drawing with black ink on a piece of white paper, and drawing with white chalk on a blackboard.

The Alpha channel color corresponds to the tinted areas of a Quick Mask overlay you display on an image. This is the subject of the next exercise, in which you display the saved gift selection in Quick Mask mode and then edit the selection information as a colored overlay on the RGB composite view of the PRESENT.TIF image. In this exercise, we'll look at more of the Channels palette's functionality, and see how saved selections are displayed as Quick Mask overlays.

Setting Up a Saved Selection as a Quick Mask

Double-click on Channel #4 title bar on Channels palette	Displays set of channel options you have for channel #4 and moves active view of PRESENT image to channel #4.
In **N**ame field, type Present	Gives saved selection channel a unique name (see fig. 5.10).

An RGB-type image can contain up to 29 Alpha channels. Alpha channels in an image saved to hard disk can really plump up file size, but if you need more than three or four Alpha channels to store selections, it's best to give them unique names for easy future reference. You can type as many as 30 characters (upper- and lowercase) in the Name field, and you can use spaces (as in "Mike's coffee cup," for example).

Leave Color Indicates: Selected Areas as is	This option indicates that black represents Alpha channel selection information, and white represents unselected (masked) image areas.

The color field is your route to Photoshop's Color Picker. You can set the color of the tint of Quick Mask here by clicking on the color swatch, then choosing a shade for the Quick Mask color. By default, the Quick Mask is red, with a 50 percent opacity. This bright color is usually easy to see and work with as it's displayed over an image. However, if you're trying to create an accurate selection around a fire truck, red is a poor choice of Quick Mask tints. Also, the

continues

continued

authors found that red doesn't "read" in the grayscale figures in this book, so we selected an off-white in this options field. Now that we've surveyed the options for an Alpha channel...

Click on OK	Displays workspace, with Present as title for Alpha channel selection.
Press Alt while clicking on Present thumbnail icon	Loads selection area as a selection marquee.

Now you can see the correlation between the selection information and the selection marquee Photoshop creates when the selection becomes activated. You want to edit the selection based on visual information in the RGB channel, however, since you can't see the bow from this view! So...

Click on RGB title on Channels palette	Displays color composite view of present image.
Click on Quick Mask mode button (filled circle button toward bottom right of toolbox)	Turns selection marquee into a Quick Mask tinted overlay. Now you can edit selection area (colored with Quick Mask), but not image.
Press Ctrl++	Increases your viewing resolution of PRESENT image to 2:1, so you can edit Quick Mask areas with more precision.

Saving the image at this point isn't necessary, because you haven't changed the physical areas of the PRESENT image, or changed selection information.

Editing in Quick Mask Mode

Now that the selection area you defined earlier is displayed in the PRESENT image as a Quick Mask overlay, you can edit it to include the box area (by applying black foreground color). This is where graphical representations of Photoshop data get a little funky; in Quick mask mode, the black you paint into an image appears as the tint shade of the Quick Mask. Conversely, when you paint with white in Quick Mask mode, you remove the tint from areas that have Quick Mask. So in the next exercise, remember—no matter what the color icons on the toolbox tell you, when black is the chosen foreground color, you'll add Quick Mask tint to the bow area to include it in the saved selection; and when white is the chosen foreground color, the Paint Brush tool removes, or erases, Quick Mask from the image.

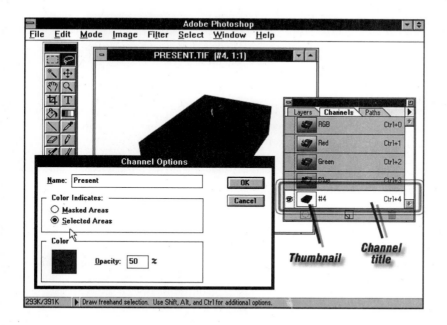

Figure 5.10

In the Channel Options dialog box, you can choose the way saved selections are displayed in an Alpha channel, and name the channel.

In this exercise, you use the Paint Brush tool as an editing tool in Quick Mask mode.

Editing a Quick Mask

Double-click on Paint Brush tool on toolbox	Chooses Paint Brush tool, and automatically displays Brushes/Options palette.
On Brushes palette, click on third tip from left tip in top row	Chooses a small, hard-edged tip for applying Quick Mask to bow.
On Options palette, make sure mode is Normal, Opacity is **100%**, and neither Fade nor Wet Edges is checked	Sets characteristics of Paint Brush to apply foreground color in a regular fashion.
Press **D** (default colors icon)	Resets colors on toolbox to black foreground and white background.

If you had any colors selected on the toolbox other than the defaults, the Paint Brush would apply partial mask; it would use the density (the brightness component) of the current foreground color, and the areas you paint over wouldn't be 100% Quick Masked.

continues

continued

Click and drag a single stroke over box area of PRESENT image	Adds Quick Mask above image area (see fig. 5.11).
Click and drag a single stroke over the ribbon area of the PRESENT image	Adds Quick Mask to the ribbon area (see fig. 5.11).

It's often a wise move to begin with a single brush stroke so that you can check out the relative size of the Paint Brush tip to ensure that this is the best tip size with which to accomplish a task. Additionally, you get a "feel" for the characteristics of the cursor's movement when a specific tool is chosen (the resistance and the speed at which the cursor moves). Now you need to color in the bow area, using Quick Mask to cover it completely.

Click and drag inside edge of bow	Outermost area of Paint Brush stroke should meet edge of bow; covers area you paint over with Quick Mask.
If you go outside the bow, press **X** (switch colors icon), then click and drag Paint Brush tool over these areas	Switches toolbox colors to white foreground, black background. White foreground color removes Quick Mask overlay areas above image.
Press **D** (**D**efault Colors icon), then finish coloring in bow area	Applies Quick Mask to bow area, which now matches Quick Masked gift (see fig. 5.12).

No need to choose **F**ile, **S**ave yet, because you haven't saved the editing changes to the Quick Mask as selection information yet.

The Quick Mask overlay you've edited is not a saved selection. To save your editing changes, you must switch modes. We explain how to do this next.

After you've added the last stroke of Quick Mask to the bow area, double-click on the Hand tool on the toolbox. Doing this takes you to a full-image window view of the PRESENT.TIF image, so you can see the entire picture at a glance.

Converting Quick Mask to Selection Information

As mentioned in the last section, Quick Mask mode is sort of a transitional state for a selection marquee. The selection is inactive, and you can't edit the image itself while you work in Quick Mask mode. In the next exercise, you'll convert the Quick Mask visual information to an active selection marquee, then save the resulting selection outline by overwriting the saved selection in the Present Alpha channel.

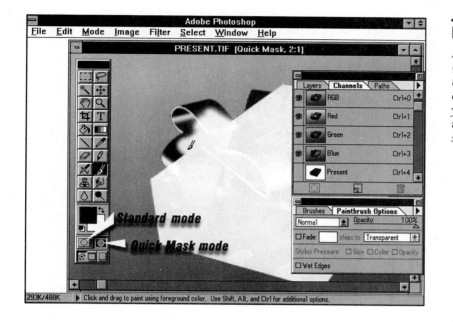

Figure 5.11

Apply a color Quick Mask tint to the areas of the image that you want included in a selection marquee.

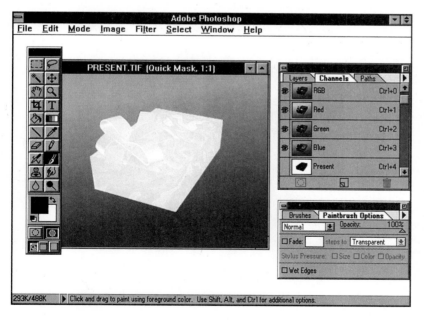

Figure 5.12

Your finished Quick Mask editing work should look like this.

Here's how to save the editing work you've done on the selection that's presently a Quick Mask:

Converting and Saving a Refined Selection Area

Click on Standard mode button toolbox, to left of Quick Mask button (refer to fig. 5.11)	Quick Mask becomes an active selection marquee.
Click and drag (Save to) Selection into thumbnail image of Present channel on Channels palette list (see fig. 5.13)	Replaces saved selection with updated one that includes bow areas.
Press Ctrl+D (or choose **S**elect, **N**one)	Deselects active marquee, now that it's been saved.

Active selection marquees can be a hazard to your image editing; if a selection tool is currently active, you can accidentally move the contents of a selection marquee (the underlying image) out of place and ruin the image. Make it a practice to press Ctrl+D after you've saved a selection marquee.

Press Ctrl+S (or choose **F**ile, **S**ave)	Saves image to your hard disk, with saved selection updated to reflect your editing.

Figure 5.13

The Save to Selection icon is an operational element of the Channels palette; drag it into a thumbnail to replace a saved selection.

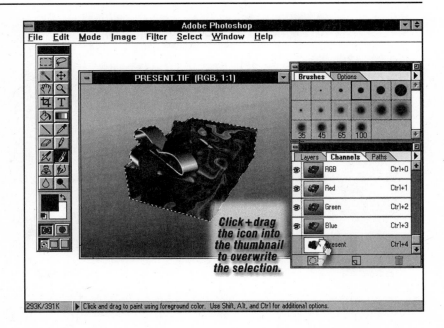

Tip You can also use a selection or other editing tool to refine a Quick Mask overlay. Try using the Lasso tool on a Quick Mask you've created from a saved selection, in the following manner:

Click and drag a selection marquee around an area that displays Quick Mask, then press **D** to make the default colors foreground black and background white. (You can do the same thing by clicking on the default colors icon on the toolbox.) Press the Delete key. The marquee-selected portion of the Quick Mask will be deleted, because both Quick Masks and images are replaced with background color when foreground image pixels are deleted. In this scenario, because white represents lack of Quick Mask (removal, erasure of Quick Mask), by deleting the selection marquee, you've removed the Quick Mask area defined by the marquee. Similarly, if you press Alt(Option)+Delete—the shortcut for filling a selection marquee—you'll flood the selected area with Quick Mask overlay while in Quick Mask mode.

In Chapter 6, "The Photoshop Test Drive," we describe variations on dragging the Selection icon into a channel thumbnail, and the results of doing so.

Although the saved selection is pretty accurate now, the next section shows you another way to define a selection area as visual information. If you have experience with a drawing application, you're going to love working with the Paths palette and paths!

Converting a Saved Selection to a Path

Painting, blurring, smudging, and cloning are the easier parts of image editing in Photoshop. The difficult part, again, is accurately defining an image area through the use of a selection marquee, so you can confine the painting, smudging, and so on, to only a specific part of an image. We've shown you how to use a selection tool and a painting tool in different Photoshop modes to define and refine a saved selection; now it's time to convert the saved selection to still another graphical format so that you can manipulate it.

Using the Paths palette, you create a path either by drawing the path with the Paths palette tools, or by making a path based on a marquee selection. When the information about a selection's shape becomes a path, you can click and drag on direction points to bend and mold the path so that it outlines the desired image area perfectly. After a path has been fine-tuned, its shape can be used to define a selection marquee again. In the next exercise, you'll make a path based on the current saved selection in the PRESENT image, and you'll learn how easy it is to modify a "wireframe" of the graphical data the selection comprises.

Here's how to convert a saved selection to a path:

Working with the Paths Palette

Press Alt while clicking on Present channel's thumbnail icon

Loads saved selection that describes outline of gift and bow.

Click on Paths palette tab at top of grouped palettes

Displays Paths palette tools.

Click on Make Path/Make Selection icon at bottom of palette (see fig. 5.14)

Creates path based on selection marquee and automatically deselects marquee.

To help you distinguish a path from an actual image detail and from selection marquees: A path consists of a solid outline, one screen pixel wide, that reverses video colors of the underlying image areas. Like selection marquees, the path is visible as screen information; it will not print, nor will it become part of an image's visual detail when you save the image.

Press Ctrl++

Zooms to a 2:1 viewing resolution of PRESENT image so that you can better see the path.

Click on Arrow tool at left end of row on Paths palette, then click on path in image

Path reveals anchor points, which control position of path segments between anchor points.

Click on an anchor point

Displays direction handles and direction points (at ends of handles) used to steer slope of curved path segments.

There is much more functionality available in the Paths palette than we describe here, because the intent of this chapter is to help you understand the features of the selecting and viewing palettes, as well as the close relationship Photoshop's elements have to one another. In other words, feel free to experiment—the only mistake you can make here is to fail to follow along! See Chapter 11, "Using Paths, Selections, and Layers," for the complete story of how to get the best results from the Paths palette.

Click and drag on a direction point (see fig. 5.15)

Changes shape of path segment it controls.

If you think you can make the path fit more snugly against the edge of the gift and bow by clicking and dragging on the anchor points or direction points, go for it. Again, we're simply playing here. Because the path now surrounding the gift hasn't been saved, it (like a marquee selection and a Quick Mask) can be deleted accidentally. If you need to take a break now, double-click on the Work Path title, and give the path a name. This saves the path for future recall. If you want to continue…

Press Ctrl+S (or choose **F**ile, **S**ave)

Saves your work at this intermediate stage of completion.

New Riders Publishing
INSIDE SERIES

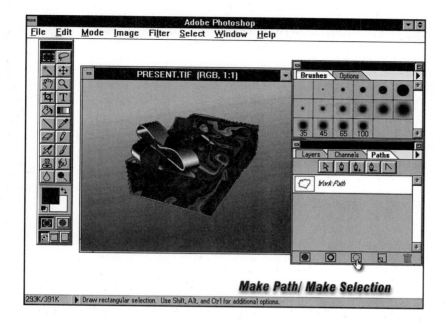

Figure 5.14

You can create a path based on a selection marquee, and vice versa, by using the Make Path/Make Selection icon.

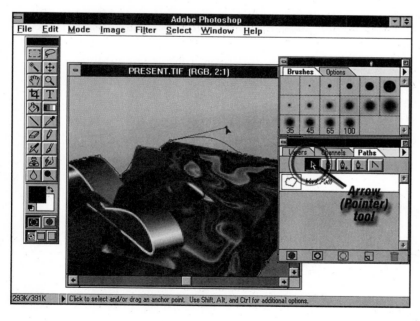

Figure 5.15

Use the Arrow tool to select a path, and to move anchor points and direction points.

Paths can be created to outline intricate shapes that would be time consuming or impossible to create by using only selection tools and painting tools in Quick Mask mode. The functions available on the Paths palette are covered in another chapter—Chapter 11, "Using Paths, Selections, and Layers"—but the concept of anchor points, direction points, and path segments as design elements will seem very familiar if you've used CorelDRAW, Adobe Illustrator, Freehand, or MicroGrafx Designer. Paths belong to the vector family of computer graphics and are a mathematical description of an area: its relative position in a document, the paths' corners and curves. Photoshop displays a path on-screen, but this information isn't saved to a file as a bitmap graphic; it's simply instructions about an outline that you can see and modify. A path is relatively inert on top of an image—only when you apply a foreground color to a path's outline or to its interior, or when you make a selection based on a path's shape, can a path be used as a tool for altering a bitmap graphic.

Tip   The tools on the Paths palette operate independently of the toolbox tools. None of the toolbox editing, painting, or selecting tools is active when the Arrow or another Paths palette tool is chosen.

Pasting an image from the Clipboard into an active document can lead to trouble; you can't click and drag inside the selection to position it, because a selection tool isn't active!

To remedy this situation, always click on the Layers or Channels palette when you need to perform a quick edit with a toolbox tool. Doing this restores the toolbox to the last tool you chose, and paths are hidden (but not deleted) when the Paths palette isn't in view.

Working with Paths and Selections Together

Because a path and a selection marquee are not the same graphical data, both can be displayed simultaneously. This is a Photoshop "perk" that can lead you to some extraordinary image-editing maneuvers. To wind up the assignment in this section about selections and paths, you'll stroke a path while a selection marquee is active. The marquee selection will protect image areas of PRESENT.TIF while foreground color is applied along the path. If you read Chapter 22, "Virtual Reality: The Ingredients of Dreamwork," you'll learn how to create the classic "neon glow" effect, using layers and Photoshop filters. But you don't have to wait until the end of this book to create your first special effect. In the next exercise, you'll make the gift in PRESENT.TIF look as though something special is indeed inside.

To accomplish this effect, you need to create an inverse selection; the Present (saved selection) you designed earlier is set to select the gift and mask the background. You want the neon glow to occur in the background (not in the gift), however, so we'll

show you how to perform this maneuver next. In this exercise you use the Paths and Channels palettes to make a simple present an outstanding one.

Using Paths and Selections To Create an Effect

Click on Make Path/Make Selection icon on Paths palette (refer to figure 5.14 for its location)	Creates a selection based on current shape of path.

Because you "tweaked" the path in the last exercise, the path no longer describes the Present saved selection. The path descriptor of the gift's outline should be more accurate than the saved selection, so you need to update the Present saved selection next.

Click on Channels tab on grouped palettes, then click and drag (Save to) Selection icon into Present thumbnail on Channels list	Overwrites saved selection in Present channel; updates selection to reflect changes you made to path.

The saved selection is the present selection marquee in the image. Paths aren't displayed when you're in the Channels palette view of an image, but selection marquees are displayed in the Paths palette view of an image, so…

Click on Paths palette tab on grouped palettes	Restores view of Work Path; selection marquee is still visible (see fig. 5.16).
Choose **S**elect, **I**nverse	Inverts marquee selection so that background is selected and gift is masked.

Shift+F7 is the default shortcut to the **S**elect, **I**nverse command in Photoshop for Windows, but Macintosh users don't have the command on the Commands palette. This is a handy shortcut if you frequently work with selections. You can add or reassign the command, using the methods described earlier. Actually, selections can be manipulated from the menu bar's Select command, as well as by the shortcuts you've taken on the Channels palette, but it takes longer, and you have to sift through dialog boxes—an inconvenience when you're pressed for time.

Double-click on the Hand tool	Moves you to a 1:1 viewing resolution of the PRESENT image.
Press **B** (for Paint Brush tool), then press **X** (switch colors icon)	Chooses Paint Brush tool and makes current foreground color white.
On Paintbrush Options palette, click and drag Opacity slider to **50%**, and choose Screen from modes drop-down list	Screen painting mode "bleaches" image colors to current foreground color; 50% opacity of foreground color creates subtle neon glow along path.

continues

continued

On Brushes palette, choose last tip (on right) in middle row	Chooses fairly large tip with which Stroke path command will apply foreground color.
Click on Stroke Path icon on Paths palette (see fig. 5.17)	Creates soft haze around gift in PRESENT image.
Press Ctrl+D	Deselects marquee selection.
Click on Work Path title on Paths palette, then drag it into Trash icon	Deletes path. You're done with it.
Press Ctrl+S (or choose **F**ile, **S**ave)	Saves your work to hard disk.
Press Ctrl+W (**F**ile, **C**lose)	Closes the image window.

If your image now looks like figure 5.18, congratulations! You've mastered some of the parlor tricks in this magic show called Photoshop!

Figure 5.16

You can create a selection marquee from a path, and have both displayed and active simultaneously.

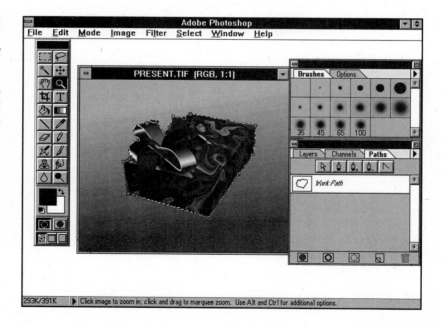

If you don't have a paint application tool currently selected when you click on the Stroke Path icon, Photoshop will use the default settings and tip for the Pencil tool with which to stroke the path. This can lead to some unaesthetic results, so have your tool of preference active before making the Stroke Path command either by using the icon or by choosing Stroke (sub)Path command on the Paths palette's pop-up menu.

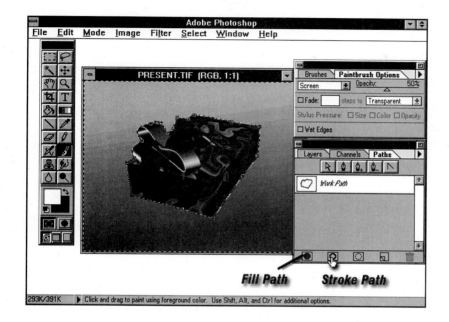

Figure 5.17

Use the Stroke Path icon on the Paths palette and stroke the path's edge with the current painting tool.

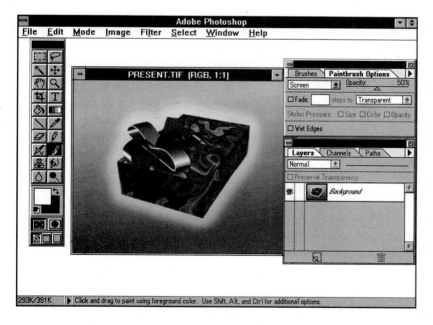

Figure 5.18

This is one of Photoshop's simpler feats. Understand the power of selections, and you'll accomplish wonderful imaging!

As you may recall from earlier in this chapter, you could have inverted the saved selection, Present, by pressing Ctrl+I, instead of by choosing **S**elect, **I**nverse in the last exercise. However, the point of these exercises is to reinforce the idea that creating effects is a procedural matter in Photoshop; if you do things out of sequence, you'll arrive at the wrong effect. For instance, pressing Ctrl+I (or choosing Image, Map, Invert) in the last exercise would have produced disastrous results, because you were in the RGB composite view of PRESENT.TIF, and had an active selection marquee in the image. You would have produced a solarized-looking gift, and nothing would have changed in the areas outside the marquee selection. The Select, Inverse command takes a look at the active selection marquee and turns it inside out. The Map, Invert command, on the other hand, doesn't affect selection marquees; rather, it creates the color opposites of anything it finds inside a selection marquee.

If you're feeling a little overwhelmed at this point, you've learned a lot, but don't feel you have to store *all* of this information in your head! You're not supposed to ingest this book in one gulp. Instead, use it periodically for quick answers you might not have memorized yet. Treat Part One of the book as a reference you can come back to later. As we move on to the assignments in more advanced chapters, you might want to refer back to this and other chapters for explanations of why things work the way they do.

Choosing Thumbnail Sizes

In addition to the grouped Layers/Channels/Paths palettes' capabilities, their configuration can also provide you with more information and a more flexible workspace in Photoshop. Before moving on to exploring the Layers palette, let's take a look at how you can modify this group of palettes to better meet your individual needs.

In figure 5.19, you can see the Layers Palette Options dialog box. This dialog box is almost identical to the Channels Palette's dialog box and that of the Paths palette; you click on the pop-up menu on each palette, then choose Palette Options.

Options is a misnomer; there's really only one option, which relates to the size of the thumbnail preview icon displayed next to the Channels/Layers/Paths titles. We recommend against choosing None as the thumbnail size, for a very good reason. You need a quick visual reference, at times, as to which layer or channel you're currently editing on, and these thumbnails provide the reference. On the other hand, Photoshop must redraw every thumbnail icon to reflect the contents of the current layer or channel, and if you have a small amount of RAM or free hard disk space on your computer (or if your computer is more than a year old), you may experience slowdowns in your work if you set the Thumbnail Size to the largest. Figure 5.20 shows the Layers view of an active image window.

Although a single-layer image doesn't present Photoshop with many screen-redrawing chores, think about a large thumbnail setting, and five or six layers, multiple saved selections, or several paths! Photoshop must redraw every thumbnail to reflect the editing changes you perform, and you must scroll the palette to reach the view you

want of image layers and channels. You can expand a palette to display multiple layers, channels and paths, but again, you'll be faced with a crowded workspace. Remember the gigantic Commands palette in figure 5.6?

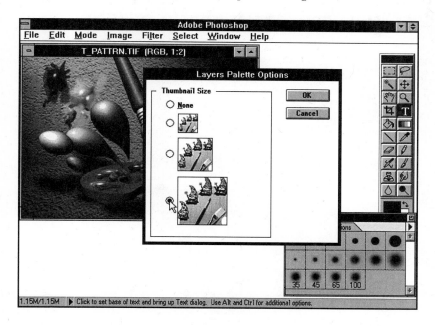

Figure 5.19

The features of the Layers Palette Options dialog box are identical to those of the Channel Palette Options dialog box.

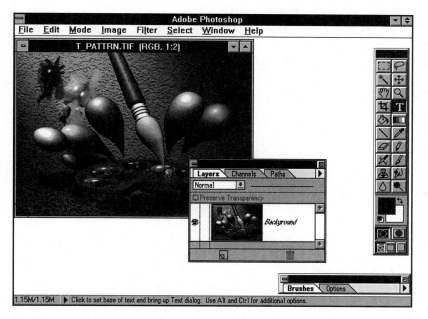

Figure 5.20

A large thumbnail not only presents a clear view of an aspect of an image, but also requires more processing power from your system.

We recommend that unless you suffer from eyestrain or own a 12-inch monitor, you leave the thumbnail sizes to their default of small for all the palettes in this group.

Screen Real Estate and the Detachable Palettes

No one ever said that just because Photoshop comes with grouped palettes, you can't pull them apart and reconfigure them. One of the big thrusts behind this new version is user-customization.

If you haven't discovered yet, through experimentation—all the grouped palettes come apart. You separate them by clicking and dragging the tab of a palette away from the group, as shown in figure 5.21.

Figure 5.21

Click and hold on a palette's tab, then drag it off the group to make it an individual palette.

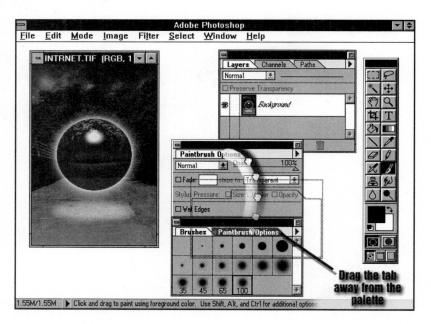

To put a palette in a different group or to regroup a palette you've detached, click on the tab, then drag and drop the palette on the group you want it to be a member of.

Palettes provide several visual clues when you've accomplished something. For instance, when you separate a grouped palette, a dotted outline of the palette's silhouette appears on the workspace. Make certain that the outline clears the outside dimension of the grouped palette, or it won't separate. Additionally, you'll want to make decisive, deliberate moves when you click and drag the Selection icon into a thumbnail; when you reorder layers and Alpha channels; and when you want to trash a path, Alpha channel, or layer. Quick clicking and dragging on a palette element doesn't give Photoshop enough time to process your request. To restructure palettes,

Photoshop has to do a great deal of processing; perform an action in one confident, slower-than-average click and drag, and you'll see the effect almost immediately.

You can see in several figures in this book that the tool palette has been separated from the Options palette. This was done to provide you with a simultaneous view of, for instance, the Paint Brush size, and the opacity and mode used to create an effect. In reality, the more you use Photoshop 3, the less you'll need to detach the palettes. As with larger-than-life thumbnail icons, separate palettes begin to eat up screen space, until your screen is as cluttered as the one shown in figure 5.22.

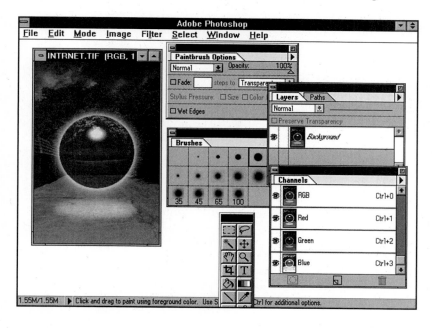

Figure 5.22

Separating Photoshop's grouped palettes provides flexibility, but the trade-off is in available screen space for editing.

Ask yourself what you need in an assignment, and arrange your palettes accordingly. The options that Photoshop 3 offers can help you to work better and smarter, but they also can become toys that clutter the workspace and hinder your work, if you let them.

Tip

The authors have found that a good arrangement of palettes is to group the Picker palette with the Layers and Channels, and to separate the Paths palette from this group. By doing this, you have easy access to image layers and channels, as well as to color specification.

Ultimately, you have to decide which floating palettes should be constantly open on-screen because you use them the most.

continues

The Tool/Options grouped palette doesn't necessarily always have to be on-screen. By double-clicking on a tool in the toolbox, you automatically display the Tool/Options group. The only group of palettes you absolutely need to have on-screen most of the time while editing an image is the Layers/Channels/Paths group. The Layers and Channels palettes provide immediate access to selections and image layers.

Transparency Options and the Layers Palette

If you read Chapter 4, "Photoshop Defaults and Options," you might have noticed that Transparency Preferences is not included in the discussion of optimizing Photoshop. The reason for this is simple—Transparency options go hand in hand with the Layers palette, the means by which you access transparency layers in an image.

Everyone, both experienced users and first-timers, will see Photoshop 3's Layers palette as a wondrous thing, an enabling feature that can provide a new dimension of image editing. At first glance, you might believe that the Layers palette replaces the more familiar Channels palette, but in reality, the more you work in this program, the more you come to depend on the unique advantages both palettes offer. The Channels palette can be thought of as a permanent home for the selections you define, whereas the Layers palette can store the discrete image objects that often are the outcome of creating a selection around something.

Layers are not a new feature in computer graphics; in recent years, software authors have created icon-editing utilities that can make areas of an icon "drop out" to reveal the background (your desk top). Additionally, programs such as Microsoft PowerPoint offer an annotation cursor, with which you can make notes on slides as they appear onscreen—and the annotations are never written to the image layer. The cursor you see onscreen is written by an application to a display layer that's not really part of the image you're viewing. That's why the cursor isn't part of the copy of the display sent to the Clipboard when Windows users press the Print Screen key. Adobe Systems has finally brought part of your system's display technology to Photoshop's workspace, in the form of image layers. Now, in much the same way that you can apply paint in a Normal, Screen, or other mode, you can create, in a bitmap file, discrete image objects whose elements can be repositioned, assigned a different hierarchical order, and assigned a mode.

How to visually indicate pixels that have a transparent quality in a layer, then, becomes problematic. When the eye icon is displayed next to a layer title on the Layers palette, you know that the Background layer of an image is visible, and that the transparent pixels on layers above the Background let the Background areas show through. This is great, because the transparency areas on a layer can help you see how

the opaque pixels fit, compositionally, into the entire image before you merge the layers and make your image one that can be exported to other file formats.

Layer Views and Options

The Transparency Options dialog box, shown in figure 5.23, is accessed by choosing <u>F</u>ile, Pre<u>f</u>erences, then <u>T</u>ransparency. In this dialog box you can choose from several preset color combinations of a checkerboard grid. Photoshop uses the grid to display transparent regions in an image. If you prefer not to display a checkerboard pattern as an indicator of transparent pixels on a layer, choose <u>N</u>one in the Transparency Options box.

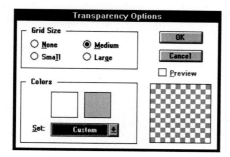

Figure 5.23

In the Transparency Options dialog box, you can select the color and size of a pattern to indicate transparent pixels on layers.

Once in a while you might want to change the color of the Grid, or turn off the display of transparent pixels. One such occasion would be if you were editing a scene that contains the same pattern. Don't laugh. The authors had to retouch a tablecloth in an image, and—you guessed it—it was a lightly colored, checkerboard patterned tablecloth!

The default value of light gray and white might also be too subtle for people who suffer from eyestrain. It is in the Transparency Options box that you can strengthen the contrasting color of the grid by selecting two values that are easily identified as "proxy colors" for the pixels that have no opacity on a layer.

Coloring behind Transparent Pixels

In the next exercise, you learn how to solve a potential problem in a design. In the process, you'll better understand the need for some sort of visible signal that there are transparent pixels in an image layer. Le Café Prétentieux, where the money and spirits both flow like tap water, needs an elegant place mat for the sidewalk tables. We've already done the hard work—creating the cafe's logo on an image layer. Your assignment is to provide the background for the logo.

However, a problem exists in the CAFE_P.PSD image; because the logo design is on a transparent layer, the image's Background layer shows through areas that don't have foreground opaque pixels. This is fine if you want a dark green and white logo, but this piece is for an establishment that's well know for its haute cuisine (French for "expensive food"). Café Prétentieux's owner, Chuck, wants a subtle fleur de lis pattern outside the logo. The task would be simple if the interior of the logo were opaque, but it's not. And if you add a pattern to the Background layer, the pattern will show through in areas of the logo that will make the design elements illegible. The solution is to display the transparent regions of Layer 1 without having the Background visible, then use Behind mode to paint in the logo's interior section only. The Behind painting mode prevents accidentally painting over pre-existing opaque pixels; in effect, the Behind mode of painting is like a selection marquee around the transparent pixels in a layer.

Now that the problem's been qualified, why not follow these steps to arrive at a solution you can use in your own assignments? It's hard not to have fun when you work on image layers—and in this exercise you learn an invaluable lesson while having fun.

Painting behind an Image Layer

Open FLEUR.TIF image from CHAP05 subdirectory (folder) of the Bonus CD	Pattern you'll add to Background of CAFE_P.PSD after you've edited Layer 1.
Open CAFE_P.PSD image from CHAP05 subdirectory (folder) of the Bonus CD	Layered image you'll edit to complete Chuck's place setting. CAFE_P is now active image window (see fig. 5.24).

You'll want the following palettes displayed on the workspace: the Commands palette, the Channels/Layers/Paths palette, and the Brushes/Options palette. Use the **W**indow, **P**alettes, Show Co**m**mands command if the Commands palette isn't already onscreen; the Layers group of palettes should be there already, because you used it in the last exercise. (If not, choose **W**indow, **P**alettes, Show **L**ayers.) The Options palette can wait, because you can display it at any time by double-clicking on any tool.

Arrange palettes and image windows so that everything is in clear view, then press **Z** (for **Z**oom tool)	Arranges elements you'll use in this assignment; chooses tool for zooming without resizing image windows.
Click once over the CAFE_P.PSD image, then use window scroll bars to center one little chef in image window	First area that needs editing.
Click on eye icon next to Background layer on Layers palette, then click on title marked Layer 1	Hides Background from view, and chooses Layer 1 as current editing layer.

Quite often in this book, we refer to the active image layer or channels as the *target* layer or channels. A target layer is available for editing, while the other layers are inactive (cannot be changed). As you can see, some checkerboard is peeking through the little chef. This indicates that any fill you add to the Background layer would peek through also, thus ruining the design. Here's what to do...

Press **B** (for Paint brush tool), then choose third tip from left in top row on Brushes palette	Chooses tool and tip size for filling in little chef.
On Options palette, choose Behind from drop-down list, and make sure the setting is at **100%**	When you work on a layer, Behind mode protects (masks) opaque pixels Opacity and and allows transparent pixels to receive foreground color.
Press **D** (default colors icon), then **X** (switch colors icon)	Makes current foreground color white.
Click and drag inside little chef	Adds white foreground color to interior of chef (see fig. 5.25).

If you accidentally paint outside the logo in the following steps, press Ctrl+Z (or choose **E**dit, Undo) to remove the last paint stroke, then try again. You might need to decrease the size of the Paint brush tip to get in the really tiny interior areas.

Continue clicking and dragging inside chef and other areas (like the other chef) where you want white background color rather than a background pattern	Completely fills areas that will not show Background pattern you add to image.
Choose **F**ile, Sa**v**e As, then save image as CAFE_P.PSD to your hard disk	Saves your work in only image format that can retain layer information in a saved file format.

If you have more patience than precision, you can also use the Lasso tool to trace the outline of image areas, then use the Paint bucket tool to flood the selection area in Behind mode. You'll be working with the tools in various painting modes in Chapter 6, "The Photoshop Test Drive." Thanks to your efforts in this chapter, the more advanced Photoshop imaging techniques will make more sense when you come to them.

Applying a Pattern Fill to a Layer

Here's the payoff—now that the chefs and other areas (like the wisps of steam emanating from the coffee cup) have been painted behind, you can restore the visibility of the Background layer, then use the new Define Pattern command on the Commands palette to pattern-fill the Background.

Figure 5.24

Assemble and organize the elements you need displayed to accomplish a task.

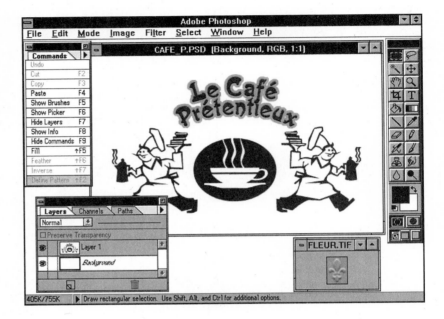

Figure 5.25

Hide the Background layer, and then use paint Behind mode to fill in areas that should not display a Background layer pattern.

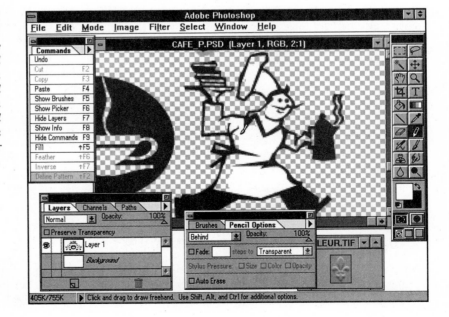

Define Pattern can take a sample of an image that has any color capability, and tile the sample to fill a selection area or the entire image. The only qualifier here is that you must use either the Rectangular marquee tool or the **S**elect, **A**ll command to take the sample from an image. In other words, your sample area has to be perfectly rectangular; ellipses and freehand selections can't be used as patterns.

Now to give the CAFE_P design a little more color. And texture...

Sampling and Using a Pattern Fill

Click on title bar of FLEUR.TIF	Makes FLEUR image the active image window.
Press Ctrl+A (or choose **S**elect, **A**ll)	Selects entire contents of image.
Click on Define Pattern on Commands palette (or press Shift+F2) (see fig. 5.26)	Launches command you added earlier to Commands palette.
Click on the title bar of CAFE_P.PSD	Makes the CAFE_P image the active image window.
Double-click on Zoom tool	Returns viewing resolution of CAFE_P.PSD image to 1:1. Now you can see entire image.
Click to left of Background title on Layers palette, where eye icon used to be	Restores view of white background layer.
Click on title of Background layer	Makes Background the active layer; Layer 1 cannot be edited now.
Press Ctrl+A (or choose **S**elect, **A**ll)	Creates selection marquee around entire Background image.
Choose **E**dit, **F**ill, then choose Pattern from **U**se field (see fig. 5.27)	Displays Fill dialog box; chooses sampled pattern of FLEUR image as contents for fill.
Click on OK	Floods Background selection with repeat pattern of FLEUR sample.
Press Ctrl+D (or choose **S**elect, **N**one), then Ctrl+S (or choose **F**ile, **S**ave)	Deselects selection and saves your work to this point.

Figure 5.26

When you begin an assignment, you can put commonly used commands within easy reach on the Commands palette.

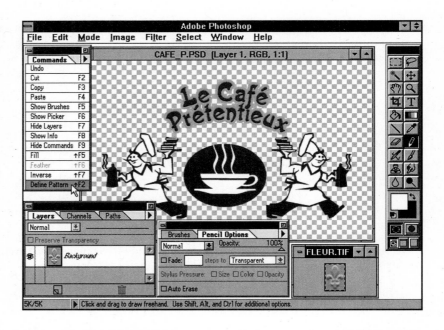

Figure 5.27

Use the Fill command to fill a selected image area with Pattern and other user-defined fills.

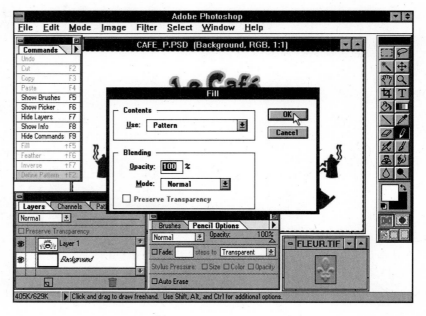

Tip You can use the Define Pattern command on a transparent layer to create a repeat pattern that consists of transparent and opaque areas. The only trick is that you must use the Define Pattern command on a selection of a Layer while the Background is hidden. If the Background layer isn't hidden, the repeating pattern will consist of layer information, plus background areas filling in the transparent areas.

The Windows default Commands palette includes the Fill command, and both Windows and Macintosh Commands palettes can be set up exactly as you want, to make short work of commands you use often. For instance, if you design patterns for a living, putting the Fill and Define Pattern commands on the Commands palette is a must. Think of the hours you'll save by clicking on these commands instead of making your way to them through Photoshop's menus!

We will say good-bye to a successfully completed image-editing assignment and Le Café Prétentieux. Chuck should be pleased with his new place mat, and if the bistro actually existed, he'd probably offer you an imported beer—*aux frais de la princesse* (on the house). It's onward and upward from here, to more complex assignments and outrageous image editing. Some of the assignments in this book are meant to be a little on the lighter side, but we also provide you with the facts, features, and techniques to perform absolutely beautiful, very serious pieces. You'll find qualities from the abstract to the photorealistic in the next chapter, "The Photoshop Test Drive," as we take all the features you've read about in Part One and put them to work, together, in Photoshop imaging.

The Photoshop Test Drive

You've taken it out for a few laps in the past two chapters; you've checked the meters, dials, and options. It's time now to put Photoshop 3 on the road for a test drive. The "course" for this chapter's test drive has some twists and bends, and you learn how Photoshop handles curves through hands-on experience. The examples you find along the route in this chapter are nothing more than glamorized examples of design problems that have one or more solutions using Photoshop's tools and features. Therefore, let this book be your "back seat driver," and you'll be up and running with advanced imaging techniques and a truckload of valuable tips before hitting the high road in the upcoming chapter assignments.

One of the wonders of electronic imaging is that mistakes are never irrevocable. If you get into the practice of always working on a copy of an image, an exact duplicate of its source is always available to go back to; therefore, this unique quality found in digital imaging practically invites experimentation. One reason the GAMES.PSD image is perfect for use in this chapter is because it's stored on read-only media (the Bonus CD that comes with this book). Lesson one is that there's no right or wrong way to enhance an image. You might mistakenly use the "wrong" tool to create an effect, but if the result proves to be pleasing to the eye, then you've just added an effect to Photoshop's and your own repertoire!

Although you use this image in several of this chapter's exercises, there's no proper or improper way to handle it. In fact, you should play with the file and discover ways to modify the image in addition to the ones suggested in this chapter. Playtime is learning time, and experimenting on your own is definitely the order of the day.

Families of Tools

Life in Photoshop's digital darkroom is much easier to understand if you remember that Photoshop provides three different function sets and that you can combine these sets to enjoy fantastic imaging capabilities:

◆ The *selection* functions consist of the toolbox's selection tools, the options on the Options palette, the menus, the Channels palette, and dialog boxes for refining the selections. Selection tools are arranged at the top of Photoshop's toolbox, and automated selection features such as Color Range, Select All, and Select Inverse are located under the **S**elect command.

◆ The *paint application* functions consist of tools and commands that offer still greater control over how you apply "digital paint" to an image. The painting tools are located toward the center of Photoshop's toolbox, and Fill and Stroke are automated painting commands you access through the **E**dit menu when a marquee selection is active within an image. Additionally, you can fill or stroke a path by clicking on the command shortcut icons on the Paths palette.

◆ The *editing* functions are the filters, menu options, and tools that change image areas without the use of paint. Editing tools include the Toning, Focus, and Smudge tools and are located toward the bottom of the toolbox. Photoshop offers digital equivalents to the techniques that photographers use when they retouch their film images in the **I**mage and Fi**l**ter menu commands: color-correction, brightness and contrast, and sharpening and blurring. Throughout this book, sound, working examples of modifying functions are highlighted, and you see a small sample of them shortly.

As varied as each of these sets of functions may seem, their interrelationship in Photoshop is vital to enable you to make passable images look outstanding. Although there is a logic to the layout of Photoshop features, it might not be your own *personal* logic. For this reason, this chapter continues with the "let's get acquainted" methodology of Chapters 4 and 5, but in a much more task-oriented fashion.

The first thing you want to do in any test drive is adjust your mirror. That's why this chapter first takes a look at your "view" of images in Photoshop and the tools used for changing views of an image.

New Riders Publishing
INSIDE
SERIES

Adjusting Your View

Navigating Photoshop's workspace is an important skill to develop early in the game. You'll want to be able to zoom in and out effortlessly and scroll around an image to retouch different areas. Photoshop provides several ways that you can get to different viewing resolutions and areas of an image.

The first exercise in this chapter gives you some experience finding the controls you need to access to view an image. After you finish this brief exercise, you'll be able to move around the digital image easily. You'll be able to concentrate on discovering how to use and apply Photoshop's painting, selecting, and editing tools.

The following exercise gives you the keyboard shortcuts and the moves you can perform with the Zoom and Hand tools.

Just Looking

Open the GAMES.PSD image from the CHAP06 subdirectory (folder) on the Bonus CD that comes with this book	This is one of the images you use for the Photoshop test drive.
Double-click on the Zoom tool on the toolbox	Makes the GAMES.PSD image 1:1 viewing resolution on-screen.

Images frequently fill your workspace view in Photoshop when the image's resolution and dimensions are greater than your monitor's resolution. For example, the GAMES image is 150 pixels/inch resolution, while most monitors have a maximum display capability of 96 pixels/inch. Therefore, Photoshop must display the image with scroll bars on the image window to accommodate a pixel-to-pixel, 1:1 viewing resolution.

Double-click on the Hand tool on the toolbox (see fig. 6.1)	Zooms image window to display entire image with no scroll bars around the active image.

Depending on the image size and resolution, double-clicking on the Hand tool can either zoom you in or out of your current view. Because GAMES.PSD is larger than 640×480 pixels/inch (the standard monitor resolution), the GAMES image is now displayed at 1:2 size to show the entire image.

continues

continued

Click on the Zoom tool

Selects the tool, but does not enlarge
the view of the image.

Click and drag the Zoom tool
diagonally in the image area

Draws a small marquee as you
drag the tool diagonally and
zooms into the area within
the marquee box.

This technique is called *marquee-zooming*. The smaller the area you marquee-zoom, the closer
you get.

Press Alt(Option) while clicking
Zoom tool

Zooms you out of a picture, to a
view that's half the current
image size.

Press Ctrl++key

Increases the image window to full size on the
workspace and zooms into a view one power
greater than the previous one (for example,
2:1, then 3:1, and then 4:1).

Press Ctrl+–key

Performs the opposite action of Ctrl+ + key
combination—you zoom *out* one viewing
resolution increment.

If the Zoom tool is currently chosen, the Options palette has a Never Resize Windows check
box. By default, when you use the Ctrl+ + or – key shortcut for zooming, the image window
resizes to accommodate smaller-than-workspace-sized image windows (that is, the image
window background never shows around an image). With the Never Resize Windows check
box checked, the Ctrl key shortcut for zooming doesn't affect the size of the image window.
This means that you can resize a window by clicking and dragging on the window border, and
it will stay this way when you zoom in and out.

Choose the Hand tool and then click and
drag this tool in the image area

Moves your view within the active
image window.

The Hand tool, which works only when an image is greater than its window size, is an alternative to using window scroll bars. You can shortcut your way to this tool by holding the spacebar
while any tool is currently selected.

Double-click on the Hand tool

Returns you to a full-frame view of
GAMES.PSD that doesn't include scroll bars.

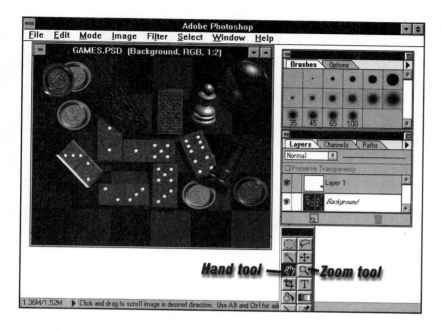

Figure 6.1

Double-clicking on the Hand tool and Zoom tool moves you to different viewing resolutions of an image.

Photoshop offers you so many different ways to zoom in and out from an image because you need each of them at one time or another to work on specific areas in your assignments. The Hand tool is, well, *handy*, because it always returns you to a full-frame view of a piece when you double-click it. If you get caught up on working in a specific area of an image, you should double-click the Hand tool periodically to gain a perspective on how the whole image is coming together.

Understanding Viewing Resolution

The preceding exercise used the term resolution to refer to the various fields of view as a result of zooming. *Resolution*, as described in Chapters 1 and 2, relates to how many pixels per inch are used in the digital information of a saved image file. The same unit of measurement is used when you display an image on your monitor, particularly if you zoom in or out. Photoshop must interpolate pixel size when you zoom in to an image.

Interpolation, when used in this context, means that Photoshop is placing color pixels in between adjacent pixels to convey a smooth tonal transition when the image is viewed as a whole. Therefore, when you zoom in to an image, a single pixel can be *displayed* as 4, 16, 256, and more pixels. This is where the term *pixel* gets a little confusing. When you zoom in to an image, although you may be viewing a single pixel in a file, Photoshop gives you this view by interpolating the image and using several *screen pixels* on your display to represent it.

This effect is called *pixelation* when taken to its extreme. The square sample areas (the pixels) become obvious, and the eye can't integrate them as part of a whole image. You can see the same effect by viewing a chemical photograph under a magnifying glass; you'll see more film grain than actual image.

This is why zooming to a 1:1 viewing resolution is so important in your work. This viewing resolution presents the image as it will print. If the image is too small for a layout, for example, increasing the file dimensions degrades (lessens) the image resolution. In other words, enlarging a picture results in the same effect as zooming in on an image: pixelation.

None of this makes zooming in to an image "bad." In fact, to do retouching work that the observer will not perceive at a 1:1 resolution, you *need* to zoom in to a pixelated view of an image. Understand that the image information sent to a printer is a 1:1, 100-percent view of the image.

Using the Marquee Selection Tools

The GAMES.PSD image was designed to be edited at a comfortable 1:1 viewing resolution most of the time. This means that much of the editing work—the selecting, painting, and rearranging of image elements—can be performed at the same view as the piece would be printed and viewed by others. In the next exercise, you get familiar with the options the Marquee selection tools offer. The Rectangular and Elliptical tools work identically and have the same extended options, except one produces box-shaped selection marquees within an image, and the other produces oval-shaped selections.

Because Adobe systems placed two more tools in the toolbox than in version 2.5, without increasing the size of the toolbox, we now have *toggling* tools. If you press the Alt(Option) key and click over the Toning, Focus, or Marquee tools, different faces, representing different tools, appear. This is noteworthy because you'll be using the Rectangular marquee tool in the next exercise, and the Elliptical Marquee tool might be the current face on the Marquee tool!

GAMES.PSD is a collection of different game pieces, and as the theme of the image suggests, it's intended use is for play. If you look at the dominos in the center of the image, you'll notice that whoever was arranging the dominos wasn't a "neat freak"; the edges of the dominos don't perfectly line up. This is a wonderful opportunity to perform a little image retouching and learn a trick about replacing background color. When you work with the Background layer of a Photoshop image, the following three standard rules of "bitmap physics" (a term the authors coined) apply:

◆ If you move a selection, the area it used to occupy is replaced with the current background color you see on the toolbox.

◆ As long as a moved or pasted selection remains selected, the bitmap information within the selection marquee is floating above the Background layer of the image.

◆ When you deselect the floating selection, the area of the background image that the selection floats over is replaced with the selection's bitmap contents.

Photoshop has some variations on these rules and breaks them regularly, but this topic is discussed shortly—these dominos need tidying up first!

Now that you know the rules for standard bitmap selecting and editing, you can see a problem with moving the dominos. The playing pieces in question, when moved, will expose a default white background because Photoshop's default colors, as you can see on the toolbox, are foreground black and background white. There's a way to minimize the damage done by selecting and repositioning the offending dominos, however, and in the next exercise, you see how to perform a little auto-retouching, how to add to a selection marquee that's already active within an image, and how to hide those blessed "marching ants" (the marquee lines) so that you can precisely reposition a floating selection.

The following exercise shows how to perform a little retouching in the GAMES.PSD image so that the dominos show some use by precision gamesters:

Using the Rectangular Marquee Tool

Double-click on the Zoom tool	Zooms your viewing resolution to 1:1 of the GAMES.PSD image.
Click on the Eyedropper tool (or press **I**); then press Alt(Option) and click on a hot pink square on the checkerboard	Sets the current *background* color to hot pink. You can see this change on the toolbox color selectors (see fig. 6.2).
If the Layers/Channels/Paths group of palettes isn't on the workspace, press F7 (Macintosh: F11)	Displays the Layers palette.
Click on the Background title on the Layers palette	Makes the Background layer the current editing layer. This is where the game board and most of the playing pieces are located.
Press Alt(Option) and click on the Marquee tool (top left of the toolbox) until the Rectangular Marquee tool displays	Choose the tool that produces rectangular marquees where you click and drag diagonally.

continues

continued

Alternatively, you can press **M** (for **M**arquee tool) a number of times until the Rectangular Marquee tool appears. (A keyboard shortcut exists for selecting every tool on the toolbox, and this book references them in every chapter exercise so that you learn to use them instinctively to speed up your work.)

Use the Zoom tool to zoom into a 2:1 viewing resolution of the dominos area	Provides you with a view for accurate image editing.
Click and drag diagonally from the upper-left to the bottom-right of the domino that has two on the left and three on the right side	Creates a selection marquee around the domino.

The marquee selection isn't a floating selection yet because you haven't moved it. The pixels within the selection presently can be edited, and areas outside the marquee are protected, or *masked,* from painting or other modifications. You change this in the following steps.

Press the right-arrow key three or four times	Nudges the contents of the rectangular selection marquee over by one pixel per keystroke. The selection becomes a floating selection, indicated on the Layers palette.
Press Ctrl+H	Hides the edges of the selection marquee, but its contents are still floating above the background image.

Ctrl+H is the shortcut to **S**elect, Hide **E**dges. It's one of the most important Photoshop keyboard shortcuts when you get into serious image editing. You can now clearly see the effect your arrow keystrokes are having on the floating domino. Because the authors want you to see where image elements are moved to in this book's figures, we've left the marquee selections visible, but it's far easier for you to precisely align things with the marquee line hidden.

Press the down-arrow key once or twice	Moves the domino down by one pixel per keystroke.

Stop when the domino is aligned and touching the vertical domino to the right of it, as shown in figure 6.3. This is the end of the exercise, but don't click anywhere on the image with the Rectangular marquee tool, and don't save the image to hard disk yet. You need to straighten out both dominos relative to the one-and-five horizontal one above them and learn a new secret of the selection tool next!

New Riders Publishing
INSIDE
SERIES

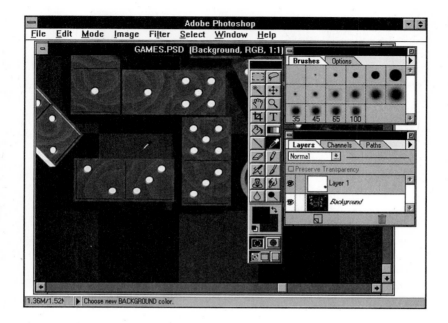

Figure 6.2

Press Alt(Option) and click with the Eyedropper tool to select a new background color.

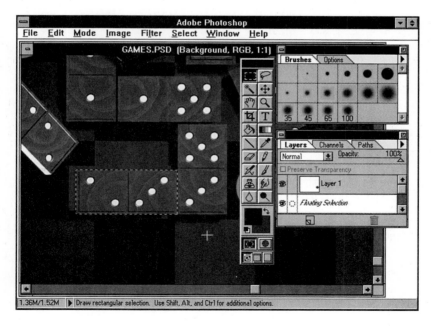

Figure 6.3

Press the keyboard arrow keys to turn a selection into a floating selection, then nudge the area one pixel per arrow keystroke.

Practically everything that moves in Photoshop has extended functions, called *options*, that are accessed by the Alt, Ctrl, and Shift keys in Windows and the Option, Command, and Shift keys on the Macintosh. You saw in the preceding exercise that pressing Alt while clicking with the Eyedropper tool selected a new background color; by clicking without pressing Alt, you select a new foreground color. Additionally, when you want to nudge a floating selection by more than one pixel per keystroke, hold down the Shift key as you press an arrow key. Doing this moves a floating selection by ten pixels per arrow keystroke.

Adding to a Selection

As you saw in the last exercise, by moving the domino to the right and down, you exposed the currently defined background color within the image. Images don't have unique background colors; you can open a dozen different images, and if green is the current background color on the toolbox, green appears everywhere you move a selected image area. By setting the background color in the last exercise to the hot pink you sampled from a checker square, only the black squares in GAMES.PSD are currently messed up. You retouch this area to photorealistic perfection shortly, but right now you're going to see how to move two dominos at once and make them line up with the one-and-five horizontal domino above them.

Adding to an active selection can be performed with any of the selection tools: the Elliptical marquee tool, the Lasso tool, and the Magic Wand tool are legitimate to use to add to a current selection. When you add a second domino to the selection in the next exercise, the floating selection becomes a regular selection marquee once more (the area underneath the floating selection is replaced by the marquee's contents). This is okay, though, because you now know how to convert a selection marquee into a floating selection.

Here's how to add the five-and-three vertical domino to the existing selection marquee and move both pieces to create a neater playing field:

Adding to and Moving a Selection

Use the Zoom tool to zoom into a 2:1 viewing resolution of the dominos area	Provides you with a view for accurate image editing.
With the domino still selected, press Shift while clicking and dragging diagonally, beginning at the five-and-three vertical domino and ending at the bottom-left corner	Adds the five-and-three domino to the existing selection of two-and-three domino (see fig. 6.4).

Press **X** on the keyboard (or click on the bent, two-headed arrow icon to the upper-right of the toolbox colors)	Switches foreground/background colors. Black is the current background color.

If you notice in the GAMES image, the five-and-three domino is mostly covering a black square. Therefore, before you move the selection of both dominos, you want to make the background image area that will be exposed turn to black. This helps to minimize your retouching efforts later. And definitely use the Ctrl(Cmd)+H shortcut here for hiding the edges of the selection marquee, for a good, clear view of your editing work.

Press the keyboard arrow keys to move the two dominos so that the five-and-three domino's five touches and is aligned with the one-and-five horizontal domino above	Repositions the selected image area and exposes black background color in the image (see fig. 6.5).
Click on the Channels palette tab on the group of palettes; then click on the (Save to) Selection icon on the bottom left of the palette	Saves the selection to Alpha Channel #4 for recall and reuse.
Press Ctrl+D (**S**elect, **N**one); then choose **F**ile, Sa**v**e As; then save the image as GAMES.PSD to your hard disk	Saves your work up to this point.

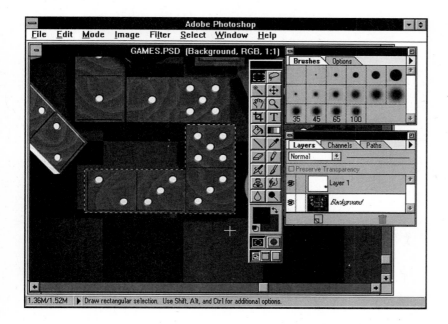

Figure 6.4

Use the Shift key in combination with any selection tool to add to an existing selection.

Figure 6.5

Set the current background color before you make a selection into a floating selection.

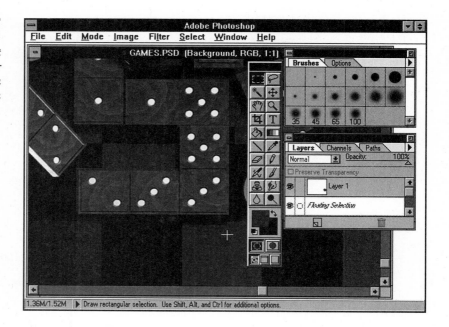

Even more functionality is available from a single selection tool when you use a combination of other keyboard keys. The following section offers a list of alternative possibilities for selecting things.

Enhanced Functions of the Selection Tools

As mentioned earlier, any selection tool on the toolbox can be used interchangeably to modify an existing selection. Photoshop for Windows has a status line that indicates what the current selection tool's function is when the various key combinations are used with it. A status line report is a fleeting thing, however, and the following list makes the options for the selection tools a little clearer for users on both platforms:

◆ **Ctrl (Command) key.** When a selection tool is used with the Ctrl key pressed, the marquee you create with the tool subtracts from an existing selection. This presumes that you have an active selection going at the moment and that your marquee action with the selection tool encompasses part of the current selection. Nothing at all happens to the current selection if the existing selection and the selection you create don't overlap. This is a very useful option to eliminate part of a marquee selection you don't want to reposition.

◆ **Shift key.** As shown in the preceding exercise, holding down the Shift key adds to an existing selection. What's not so obvious here is that the selection you add to an existing one doesn't have to intersect the existing selection.

Therefore, you can select an image area, and then add another area that's inches away from your original selection, to make a compound selection.

◆ **Alt (Option) key.** Pressing the Alt key doesn't do anything to the existing selection. Instead, pressing the Alt key creates a marquee selection starting from the center when the Rectangular or Elliptical marquee tools are chosen. And when used with the Lasso tool, you can create polygonal shapes when you press Alt and click anchor points that represent the corners of a polygonal selection. The exception to this extended option for the Alt key is the Magic Wand tool (described later in this chapter); it doesn't do anything out of the ordinary when the Alt key is pressed in combination with clicking over an image area.

◆ **Ctrl+Alt (Mac: Cmd+Option).** Holding down both keys while clicking and dragging inside a selection marquee does something exceptionally strange and wonderful—it repositions the selection marquee itself without moving the background image area inside the marquee. The use for this option might not be immediately apparent. So here's an example: Suppose that you created an ellipse and wanted to make a polka-dot pattern at irregular intervals all over the background image. You wouldn't use the Define Pattern command (see Chapter 5, "It's All Done with Palettes"), because this command only creates *regular* patterns. Instead, you'd define the polka-dot foreground color, press Alt+Delete to fill the selection, then press Ctrl+Alt while clicking and dragging inside the selection (using a selection tool) to reposition the marquee and fill the next background area.

◆ **Ctrl+Shift+Alt.** Unless performed carefully, this key combination will give your fingers cramps. When you hold down all three keys and then click and drag (or simply click with the Magic Wand tool), this creates a marquee that describes the intersection of an existing marquee and the one you're creating. Like the Ctrl option, you must create the new marquee in such a way that it overlaps the existing selection, or you wind up deselecting everything on the image (the intersection of two non-intersecting areas=nada). You can create a convex lens shape from two ellipses and create other exotic shapes by switching selection tools (for example, create an ellipse that overlaps part of a rectangular marquee), but this option is mostly reserved for creating designs, not precisely selecting photographic image areas.

Additionally, when you have no current marquee within an image, pressing the Shift key constrains the Rectangular Marquee tool's selections to a perfect square, and you can create perfect circles by pressing Shift in combination with the Elliptical Marquee tool's use.

These options are not limited to currently active editing selections. You can use each key combination listed here with the (Save to) selection icon on the lower-left of the Channels palette. The technique is simple to use, but it's not clearly in front of you when you use Photoshop. If you have a saved selection, use any selection tool to create an active selection marquee within the image. Then, if you want to add to the saved selection, press Shift and click and drag the *selection icon* into the thumbnail of the Alpha channel to which you want to perform this operation. Similarly, press Ctrl and drag the selection icon into the thumbnail of the saved selection (in the Alpha channel) to subtract the active selection marquee from a saved selection. Make this click and drag action slowly and deliberately—it takes a moment or two for Photoshop to perform the calculation.

Because this is a test drive and a task-oriented book, this chapter leaves selection tools for a while to concentrate on the mismatching color edges around the dominos. In the next section, you meet the Rubber Stamp tool, and you see how to clone away the mistakes in the GAMES image. You do this by using the saved selection as a mask to protect the areas that are already perfect.

Masking an Area and Cloning

Unless you're Clayton Moore, the reasons for putting on a mask while you work aren't immediately apparent. You saw one use of a selection marquee in Photoshop—to move the contents of the background it encompasses—but you're going to get into a second, perhaps more important usage next. The area inside a selection, whether it's floating or simply describes a shape in an image, is available for editing—you can paint or apply effects within the area the selection marquee encompasses. Conversely, the area outside the marquee is masked; you can't edit this area while the marquee is active. At present, you have a saved selection that describes the geometry and position of the two dominos. The dominos look great, but the area just outside their edges can use a little cleaning up.

Therefore, you want the inverse of the saved selection; and oddly enough, Inverse is the name of the command you use in the next exercise to turn the tables and mask the dominos. All image areas outside the dominos then become selected (available for editing), and the Rubber Stamp tool is used to clone existing image areas into the areas where the background color doesn't quite make the domino repositioning invisible.

The Rubber Stamp tool is covered in detail in Chapter 10, "Stamping Out Photo Errors," but as long as you're cruising along in this test drive of Photoshop's workspace, there's no problem with checking out the tool in its default settings. The Rubber Stamp tool is technically a member of the painting tools in Photoshop, but you don't load foreground or background colors to use this tool. Instead, you define a *sample point* on an image—a location where the Rubber Stamp tool can read image information—and then you duplicate image areas with the Rubber Stamp cursor. In the next exercise, you sample a pristine area of the checkerboard and then "paint" a

pixel-perfect copy into the messed-up areas just around the edge of the repositioned dominos. Like the selection tools, you use the Ctrl, Alt, and Shift keys to add to the Rubber Stamp tool's functionality.

The following exercise shows how to repair the miscolored areas of the checkerboard.

Using a Virtual Dropcloth for Cloning Work

On the Channels palette, press Alt(Option) and click on the thumbnail icon next to the #4 title on the list	Loads the selection you saved in the last exercise.

There's a long way around performing this command, which we get into a little later in this chapter. You took the short route to **S**elect, **L**oad Selection. However, the selection is presently the inverse of what you need to mask the dominos, so…

Choose **S**elect, **I**nverse	Changes the masked areas to selected within the image, and selected areas are now masked.
Double-click on the Rubber Stamp tool	Chooses the Rubber Stamp tool and displays the Options palette.
On the Options palette, make sure the mode is set to Normal, Opacity: **100%**, and Option is Clone (aligned)	These are the default settings for the Rubber Stamp tool and the ones you need to retouch the checker squares.
On the Brushes palette, choose the second from the left, middle-row tip	Chooses the size of the tip for the Rubber Stamp tool.
Press Ctrl++; then scroll the image window so the edges of the repositioned dominos are in clear sight	You have a good, close view of the problem areas within the image at 2:1 viewing resolution.
Press Alt(Option) and click at the top-left corner of the two-and-three domino; then press Shift and click and drag down the left side of the domino	Replaces the hot pink edge on the black square with image samples from where the black square was unaffected by the repositioned dominos (see fig. 6.6).

The Shift key constrains the Rubber Stamp movement to a straight line. It doesn't matter that *the cursor* can be moved all over the place; while the Shift key is held, *the result* is a straight line of cloned image area that restores the black square. The domino's left edge is unaffected by your Rubber Stamp work because it's presently outside the selection marquee. The selection marquee border is "turned on" in figure 6.6, but you should not. Press Ctrl+H to **S**elect, Hide **E**dges, and make your image editing work much easier to see.

continues

continued

Click and drag the (Save to) Selection icon on the Channels palette into the #4 thumbnail icon	Overwrites the selection you saved earlier to inverse selection information.

Hang onto the inverse selection—the selection that masks the dominos, not the background—for the next exercise. Dragging the (Save to) Selection icon into an Alpha channel (Channel #4) replaces saved information with information that describes the active marquee selection.

Press Ctrl+S (**F**ile, **S**ave)	Saves your work at this intermediate stage of completion.

Figure 6.6

Holding down the Shift key as you click and drag with the Rubber Stamp tool constrains the cloning activity to a straight line.

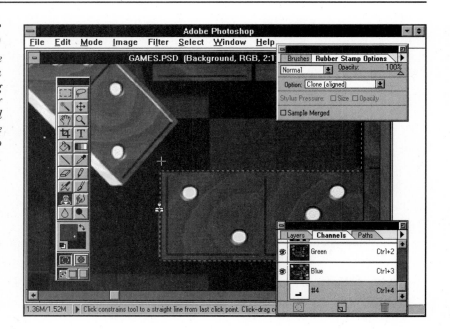

Completing the Image Retouching

You performed quite a few fancy moves in the preceding exercise and saw how Photoshop's tools work in concert to help accomplish a retouching effect. However, the retouching work isn't finished yet—three or four areas of the checkerboard are still scarred with inappropriate background colors left by moving the floating selections of the dominos. Changing resolution was mentioned frequently at the beginning of this chapter for a very good reason—designers do lose perspective of an image while working intently on an isolated area. In fact, the authors missed a spot or two around the checkerboard while creating this exercise!

So, in the next set of steps, you load the modified selection you saved last, use your newfound talents as a Rubber Stamp artist, and correct any of the remaining miscolored areas on the checkerboard. You need to keep an eye on the traveling crosshair cursor that indicates the point from which the Rubber Stamp tool gets its raw materials. Ideally, you should reset the sampling point every time you notice you're cloning into a noticeably different color area within an image.

Here's how to keep your perspective on image retouching and remove all traces from the image that you've been tinkering with someone else's dominos game:

Sampling from Other Image Areas

Press Alt(Option) and click on the #4 title on the Channel palettes list	Loads the selection you modified earlier to include the background and exclude the dominos.
Carefully click and drag to the right, beginning where the shadow beneath the two-and-three domino has been removed to background pink	Copies the shadow area sampled from beneath the two dots into the damaged area (see fig. 6.7).

If you approach this rather silly assignment with an artist's sensitivity, you can get accurate results without using the Shift key to constrain the Rubber Stamp tool to a straight line. As long as you're within a pixel or two of the horizontal location of the sampling point with the Rubber Stamp tool, you don't need to hold down the Shift key. The Clone (aligned) setting for the Rubber Stamp tool keeps the sampling point the same relative distance from the Rubber Stamp tool no matter where you click and drag. When you're finished with the bottom edge…

Press Alt(Option) and click in the center of the black square to the right of the five dots in the five-and-three domino	Samples black from the square.
Click and drag over the right edge of the domino	Fills the hot pink background color with black.

If you made the selection marquee slightly smaller or larger than you intended, you might not be able to clone replacement image areas. To correct this, you should choose **S**elect, **M**odify, then choose **E**xpand or **C**ontract. These commands will grow or shrink a selection marquee anywhere from 1 to 16 pixels in radius.

Double-click on the Zoom tool	Zooms you to a 1:1 viewing resolution of the image (see fig.6.8).

At a 2:1 resolution, you might not see areas where the dominos' repositioning left other miscolored colored squares. If you have a spot or two left to fix, do this now. If not…

continues

continued

Press Ctrl(Cmd)+D (**S**elect, **N**one)	Deselects the selection marquee.
Click and drag the #4 title into the trash icon on the Channels palette	You're done with this saved selection and by trashing it, you conserve on the saved image's file size, by about 25-35%.
Press Ctrl(Cmd)+S (**F**ile, **S**ave)	Saves your work at this intermediate stage of completion.

Figure 6.7

Select an identical image area as your sampling point for the Rubber Stamp tool.

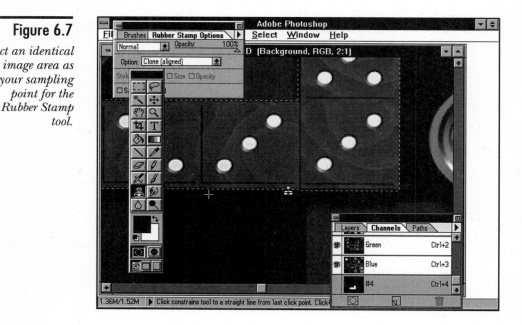

In the last assignment, the task of restoring the checkerboard squares doesn't display the full power of the Rubber Stamp tool, primarily because you cloned a fairly flat color area into another. The Rubber Stamp tool does more than this, though—it takes the visual content of an image area and uses the information to replace other areas. Future chapters show you how to perform feats as complex as retouching the textures and shades of skintones and how to restore the visual content of an image that's been damaged. In the next section, you use the Rubber Stamp tool to change the arrangement of the dominos in a way that's completely undetectable.

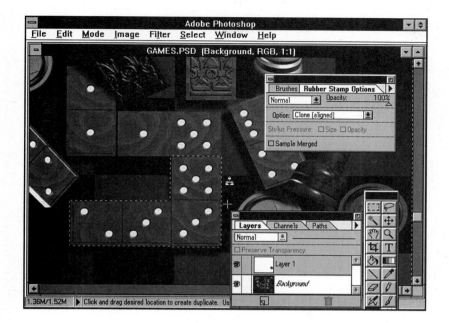

Figure 6.8

Zoom in and out of an image at regular intervals to gain a perspective on your retouching work.

Changing the Visual Content of an Image

One of the unique qualities of the bitmap format of computer graphics is that both image color and the visual content—what makes a bitmap image recognizable as a table, a person, and so on—is accomplished all by the arrangement of pixels. As you've seen so far, the arrangement of pixels to form an image can be reshaped in a seamless, invisible fashion through the use of Photoshop's tools. In the next exercise, you get a chance to change the outcome of the dominos game in GAMES.PSD, by retouching one side of a domino to give it a different number of dots. The retouching is, again, accomplished through the use of the Rubber Stamp tool, but the task is a little more demanding because you need to align the sampling point to exactly the same relative position as the face of the domino you are going to retouch.

This is not a simple trick; the precision required to effectively replace an image area with another one depends more upon your eye and your native talent than any automated feature Photoshop can provide. Succeed at this one, and you're well on the way to accomplishing more advanced editing moves and developing a technique with which you can solve graphical problems.

Here's how to create an effect that would make Messrs. Milton and Bradley gasp in awe:

Changing an Image Area with the Rubber Stamp Tool

Press Ctrl(Cmd)+plus	Zooms you back into a 2:1 viewing resolution of GAMES.PSD.
Scroll the image window until the one-and-five domino is in the center of the window	This is the domino you'll edit with the Rubber Stamp tool.
Press **S** (for Rubber **S**tamp tool), then Press Alt(Option) and click in the center dot of the five dots on the right of the domino	Sets the sampling point for the Rubber Stamp tool.
Click and drag, beginning at the center dot of the dots on the left side of the domino; then click and drag around the face of the left side	Clones in areas sampled from the right side of the domino; adds dots; ruins the game (see fig. 6.9).
When all five dots have been cloned into the left side, press Ctrl(Cmd)+S (**F**ile, Save)	Saves your changes in the file to hard disk.

Figure 6.9

Change the face of reality, or only the face of a domino, by aligning the sample point to a similar cloning area.

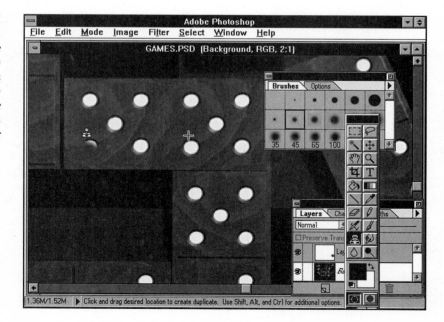

This last exercise was intended as an example of how the Rubber Stamp tool can be used to retain the photorealistic qualities of images you retouch. You start with small accomplishments and before long you have working methodology for larger-than-life assignments. The Rubber Stamp tool is featured in Chapter 15, "Special Effects with Ordinary Photographs," where it's used to create a realistic scene of identical twins from two poses of the same person. You simply have to know a tool's capability and start with a concept to push pixels in the right direction!

Exploring Selections on Layers

In the same sense that the keyboard keys offer more options for working with Photoshop tools, the Layers palette extends the functionality of this concept we've come to know as a *saved selection*. A selection you place on a layer can be repositioned, painted, deleted, and have effects applied to it in the same way the area inside a selection marquee can. However, when you copy a selection to a layer, you get immediate feedback about how a design's composition is coming together. You can hide a layer's contents to preview only the image elements you're presently working with, and layers provide a bitmap imaging program with features similar to those found in a vector design program such as Illustrator or CorelDRAW!.

Repositioning a layer's opaque pixels is the assignment ahead of you in the next exercise. We've placed a blue checker on Layer 1 of the GAMES.PSD image. It's impossible to pick it out from the rest of the image, but if you look at the thumbnail icons on the Layers palette, you see one lone blue dot hanging out on Layer 1. Selecting and repositioning a layer object (the opaque collection of pixels sur-rounded by transparent pixels), can be accomplished in two ways. When you have only one discrete object on a layer, the Move tool is the handiest way to relocate the object. When faced with multiple opaque areas on a layer, however, you might choose to "float" the selection, and in this case, you can use a number of approaches, all equally effective, in repositioning the layer object. In the next exercise, you try it both ways and in the process, you learn about a special key combination that can be used on a selection marquee's contents, not the marquee itself.

The next exercise shows how to move and edit the blue checker through the use of Photoshop's tools and image layers:

Manipulating the Contents of a Layer

Double-click on the Hand tool	Moves your viewing resolution out to 1:2.
On the Layers palette, click on the Layer 1 title	This chooses Layer 1 for editing; the background is now protected from editing.

continues

continued

Press **V** (Move tool)	Makes the Move tool the current tool.
Click and drag on the checker to move it to another black square (see fig. 6.10)	Moves the position of the blue checker relative to the layer.
Click and drag anywhere within the image window	*Also* moves the blue checker piece.

Layer objects don't behave like floating selections because they are surrounded by *placeholders*, transparent pixels that complete the image layer. So what you're actually doing is repositioning the entire Layer 1 relative to the image window. But it sure looks like you can move a layer object without clicking and dragging directly upon it!

Press **L** (Lasso tool); then click and drag around the blue checker	Chooses the Lasso tool and creates a marquee selection around the checker (see fig. 6.11).

An incredible thing happens next. The selection marquee looks, in figure 6.11, as though it encompasses a fairly broad area around the blue checker. At the moment it does, but this is only because you haven't really performed an editing action upon the checker. Photoshop sort of sits back when you've defined a selection marquee on a layer and waits to see whether you want to paint in the area, or move the contents (the opaque pixels). If you were to press Alt(Option)+Delete right now, the marquee selection would retain its shape, and the area would fill with foreground color. However, when you move a selection marquee on a layer, the following happens:

Press the down-arrow key	The selection marquee conforms to the shape of the opaque pixels within the selection.

Transparent pixels can be selected, but they cannot be moved using a selection tool. If you look at the Layers palette now, the checker is a Floating selection. Next, you see what happens when you press Alt(Option) and click and drag within a floating selection's marquee.

Press Alt(Option) and click and drag the selection over to the square to the right of it (see fig. 6.12)	This is an illegal move in checkers, but you've just duplicated the contents of the floating selection.
Press Ctrl(Cmd)+D (**S**elect, **N**one), "Ctrl" your excitement, and then press Ctrl(Cmd)+S (**F**ile, **S**ave)	Deselects the floating selection; you respond to the new discovery; and saves your image to hard disk.

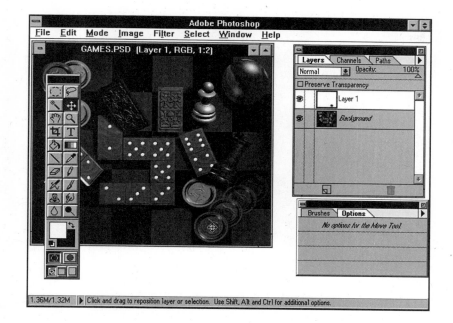

Figure 6.10

Use the Move tool to reposition the opaque contents of a layer relative to the image window.

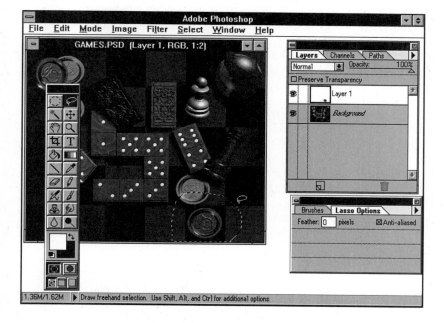

Figure 6.11

You can create a selection marquee on a layer, but only the opaque pixels on the layer can be repositioned.

Figure 6.12

Pressing Alt(Option) while clicking and dragging on a floating selection duplicates the contents within the marquee.

It's really hard not to dump many new features in one location in this book because Adobe has dumped many wonderful, extraordinary features on everyone who's interested in imaging. Users of version 2.5 will applaud the new flexibility of working with selections on layers, and new users should know that the last trick can be performed with floating selections on an image Background layer, too. Pressing Alt(Option) while clicking and dragging deselects the currently selected area and creates a duplicate, which becomes the current selection.

One of the other special properties of floating selections is that if you press Ctrl(Cmd) and click and drag an area within a floating selection with any selection tool, the area is cut from the image. For example, if you pressed Ctrl(Cmd) and clicked and dragged the Rectangular marquee tool so that two sides of the rectangle intruded on the checker in the preceding exercise, a "pie slice" of the checker would disappear—it's deleted from the floating selection. You can also press Ctrl(Cmd) and click and drag beginning your selection on the inside of a floating selection; this produces a floating selection with a hole carved in it. Floating selections have properties different from selection marquees that haven't been moved.

Isolating and Applying an Effect to a Layer Object

You have an interesting situation going on with the two checkers on Layer 1 right now. They might look like two individual pieces, but if you try moving them with the

Move tool, they travel as a set. This is because a whole layer moves as one when using the Move tool; everything, including the transparent placeholders, are repositioned with the Move tool. The layer effect is actually a unique deployment of a transparency mask; pixels on the layer "drop out." Photoshop treats transparent and opaque pixels on a layer as one unit when the Move tool is used.

In the next exercise, you see how to isolate one of the checkers and then apply Photoshop's Rotate Image command to it. Cloning and duplicating image areas is all fine and well, but if you want to make the viewer believe that these are two checkers— not simply a copy of an original—rotating one of them will create a more random, believable composition.

Here's how to edit a selected image by applying an effect to it:

Selecting and Rotating a Layer Element

Double-click on the Zoom tool, then scroll the window so you have a good view of the blue checkers	Zooms you in to the image, and repositions your view within the window frame.
With the Lasso tool, click and drag around the left checker on Layer 1	Selects the left checker.
Choose Image, **R**otate, and then **F**ree	A boundary box appears around the selection.
Place your cursor on one of the corners; then click and drag up or down (see fig. 6.13)	Rotates the selection. Do not click outside the box.

Photoshop pauses for a moment when you freely rotate a selection because Photoshop doesn't know whether you're done moving the Rotate box. Sometimes, a quick, unrelated cursor move causes Photoshop to redraw the selection inside the Rotate box to reflect the changes you specified.

Click inside the Rotate box	Cursor turns into a hammer and "nails" the selection to the specified degree of rotation.
Press Ctrl(Cmd)+D (**S**elect, **N**one), then press Ctrl(Cmd)+S (**F**ile, **S**ave)	Deselects the floating selection and saves your work up to this point.

Figure 6.13

Click and drag on a corner of the Rotate box to specify the amount of rotation for the selected image element.

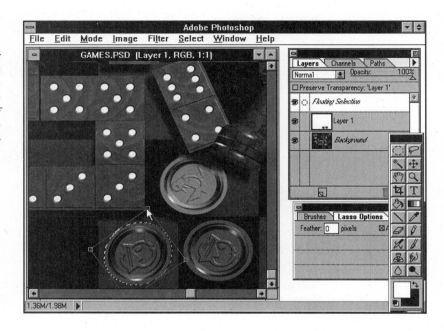

If you click outside the Rotate box before clicking inside it, the Rotate command is canceled. Additionally, you'll notice that the checker inside the Rotate box might not have looked very refined before finalizing the effect. This is because Photoshop must reassign pixel colors within the selection to create the change. Again, image detail in a bitmap image is entirely supported by pixel color, and Photoshop performs *interpolation,* the redistribution of pixel values, as a last step after you confirm the command by clicking inside the Rotate box. While you're rotating the image, Photoshop creates a low-resolution image for the screen, which is not what the final rotated checker will look like. Small preview windows and low-resolution displays of effects help Photoshop perform calculations more quickly.

Using a Combination of Selection Features

It's only fair to concentrate on the gold sparrow checkers for a while now, seeing as the blue sailor checkers have been through some fairly extensive editing. In the next exercise, you select a gold checker from the Background layer using both the Magic Wand tool and the Lasso tool to accurately define the checker.

The Magic Wand tool doesn't select a geometric image area, but instead defines a selection marquee based around adjacent pixels whose color values are similar. You can see that with the exception of minor shading, the gold checkers are mostly of one color, so here is your approach: use the Magic Wand tool to select most of a gold checker; switch selection editing mode to Quick Mask (see Chapter 5 for the

complete story on Quick Mask); then fill in the areas the Magic Wand tool misses by Lassoing the areas and using the Alt(Option)+Delete keystroke combination to fill the selection area. Marquee selections and Quick Mask overlays are two different representations of selected image areas, and a marquee can be used to modify a Quick Mask.

To create an accurate selection marquee around the gold checker in the upper-left corner of GAMES.PSD, follow these steps:

The Magic Wand and Quick Mask Mode

Scroll to the upper-left corner of the GAMES.PSD image, then press Ctrl(Cmd)+ + once

The gold checker that isn't eclipsed by the blue checker is the one you'll select with the Magic Wand; zooms you in to a 2:1 viewing resolution of the area.

Click on the Background title on the Layers palette's list

Chooses the Background layer for your selection work.

Press **W** (Magic **W**and tool), then click on the Options tab on the Options/Brushes grouped palettes

Chooses the Magic Wand; displays options specific to the tool.

Type **120** in the Tolerance field and check the Anti-Aliased box on the Options palette

Makes the Magic Wand select pixels that are within 120 shades of the first pixel you click over.

The Magic Wand's Tolerance range is from 1 to 255. Setting it to 120 ensures that most of the color pixels within the gold checker are selected with one click.

Click over a lighter area of the gold checker (see fig. 6.14)

Encompasses almost the entire gold checker with a selection marquee.

Notice that you now have marquee lines running inside the gold checker. These are unselected, or masked, areas of the checker that aren't close enough in color value to be included in the selection. Setting the Magic Wand tool to a higher tolerance is not the answer; if you set the tolerance too high, *every* pixel in the image will be selected. The best strategy here is to convert the selection marquee to Quick Mask and then refine the Quick Mask to include the non-selected areas. See Chapter 5, "It's All Done with Palettes," for more information on Quick Mask mode and check out figure 6.14 for the location of the Quick Mask button on the toolbox.

Click on the Quick Mask mode button

Creates a tinted overlay where the marquee selection was displayed.

continues

continued

Press **L** (**L**asso tool); then click and drag around the areas within the Quick Mask overlay that aren't tinted	This selects the unmasked areas within the gold checker.
Press **D** (**d**efault colors icon)	Makes the foreground color black and the background color white on the toolbox.
Press Alt(Option)+Delete	Fills the selected area with foreground color; completes the Quick Mask (see fig. 6.15).

When in Quick Mask mode, Photoshop's foreground color corresponds to the opacity of the Quick Mask selection, so that you're not really applying a foreground color, as such. You're applying the maximum amount of opacity a Quick Mask can have, which in turn corresponds to how completely a selection area selects the underlying image. If you chose, say, medium gray for the foreground color, you'd apply a faint Quick Mask; when the Quick Mask is then converted to a selection marquee again, the underlying image area would be *partially* selected. You can create wonderful, transparent image areas when you copy a partial selection to a new image area or layer. Now convert the Quick Mask back to an active selection and find a new layer home for the gold checker.

Click on the Standard mode button on the toolbox; then choose **S**elect, **F**loat	Makes the Quick Mask a selection marquee; floats the selected image area and creates a copy without moving the area.
Click on the pop-up menu on the Layers palette and choose Make Layer (see fig. 6.16)	Displays the Make Layer dialog box.
Type **Sparrow** in the **N**ame field, leave the rest of the options to their defaults, and then click on OK	Moves the selection to its own layer between Background and Layer 1; selection becomes deselected.
Press Ctrl(Cmd)+S (**F**ile, **S**ave)	Saves your work at this intermediate stage of completion.

Figure 6.14

*Use the Magic
Wand tool to
select pixels
adjacent to one
another and that
share a similar
shade of color.*

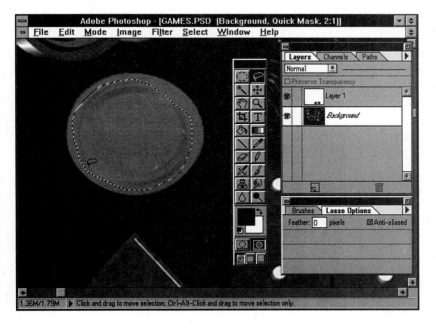

Figure 6.15

*Fill the selection
area with Quick
Mask overlay by
pressing
Alt(Option)+Delete
while in Quick
Mask mode.*

Figure 6.16

Float a selected image area using the Select, Float command; then assign it a uniquely named image layer.

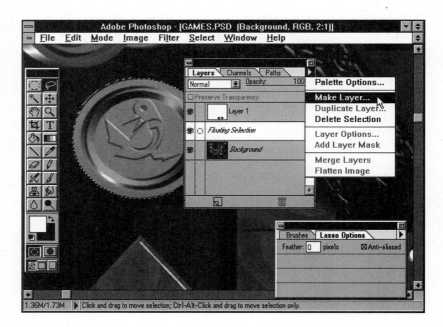

Quick Mask is used extensively in this book's exercises to refine a selection marquee. Read Chapter 5, "It's All Done with Palettes," for an example of a painting tool's use with a Quick Mask.

Because the copy of the gold checker is precisely above the original, you can't really see that you've made a copy. But in the next exercise, you move the checker that's now on the Sparrow Layer and learn how to group the Sparrow Layer with Layer 1 so that all three checkers can be moved at the same time.

Tip

At some point in your imaging adventures with Photoshop 3, you'll create an image that has several layers. This is why it's a good practice to give each layer a unique name. The Make Layer dialog box only appears when you have a floating selection, and therefore, when you use the Paste Layer command (under **E**dit), you don't get the opportunity to name a new image layer.

No problem. You can always change the name of a layer by double-clicking on the layer title on the Layers palette list. This displays the Layer Options dialog box in which you can assign the chosen layer a new name. Layer Options is also a command you can access through the pop-up menu on the Layers palette.

Layers are a wonderful editing feature, however you can at times lose track of what image element is on which layer. To make a layer active that contains an element you want to edit, choose the Move tool, then press Ctrl(Cmd) and click on the image element within the active document. Your cursor turns into a pointed finger, and then the Layers palette highlights the layer that contains the element you pressed Ctrl(Cmd) and clicked over.

Linking and Merging Layers

New layers are created in a sequence; a new layer appears within an image directly on top of the currently active layer. A new layer also becomes the currently active layer, so that you now have the Sparrow layer on top of the background of the GAMES.PSD image, with the two blue checkers at the top of the heap on Layer 1.

In the next exercise, you move the gold checker object on the Sparrow layer so that it fits within a checker square next to the two blue checkers. Because the checkers you've worked with so far are saved on separate layers, moving the gold one doesn't affect the position of the blue checkers. But you also learn how to move all the checkers as a group, by using the linking layers option on the Layers palette.

Here's how to use the Move tool and the arrow keys to quickly reposition the gold checker on the Sparrow layer:

Moving Elements/Linking Layers

Press **V** (Move tool); then press Shift+down-arrow key	Moves the gold checker downwards by ten pixels. You can see the original gold checker on the Background layer now.
Press Shift+down-arrow key; then press Shift+right-arrow key once or twice (see fig. 6.17)	Moves the gold checker down and to the right by ten pixels.
Continue pressing Shift+arrow key until the gold checker is almost at the bottom of the image window	Repositions the gold checker so that it's closer to the blue checkers on Layer 1 toward the bottom-right of the GAMES image.
Scroll the image window down until you can see the blue checkers and the gold checker on the Sparrow layer	Gets both layers' contents in view so you can finalize positioning of the gold checker.

continues

continued

Click and drag (anywhere on the Sparrow layer) down and to the right	Shifts the gold checker so that it's closer to the two blue checkers.

Stop when the gold checker is on the black square to the left of the two blue checkers.

Click in the column between the eye and the Layer 1 title on the Layers palette	Displays an icon next to both the active (Sparrow) Layer and Layer 1. The layers are linked now.
Click and drag on the image with the Move tool	Moves all three checkers.
Move the checkers back, then click on either of the icons next to the layer titles on the Layers palette	Removes the icon; breaks the link (see fig. 6.18).
Press Ctrl(Cmd)+S (**F**ile, **S**ave)	Saves your work at this intermediate stage of completion.

Figure 6.17

A layer object can be moved independently of areas on other layers.

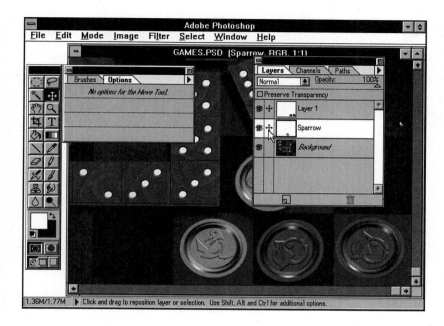

Figure 6.18

*Click to the left of
a layer title to
create a link
between the layer
and the active
(highlighted title)
layer.*

Layer links can be established between two or more layers to offer synchronous
repositioning of the elements you've placed on them. Clicking on the column to the
left of a layer title, as you did in the last exercise, automatically creates a link between
the layer you've clicked next to and the base layer—the currently active layer. To
break this link, you either click again on the linked layer, or click next to the base
layer to break all links with layers in the image.

There's yet another way to get these checkers moving together, and that is to merge
the Sparrow and Layer 1 layers together. You see how this is done in the next section.

Merging Layers

Layers, like saved selections in Alpha channels, can plump up the overall file size of
an image. You can expect anywhere from a 10-percent to a 33-percent increase in a
file's size when you save an image that contains an extra, user-defined Alpha channel,
or a layer. If you take a look at the document size box (on the image window on the
Macintosh and on the left of Photoshop's status line in Windows), you can see the
proposed flattened image size on the left and the file size the document presently has
on the right. When an image is flattened, layers blend, or composite, into the Background layer to create an image format that's less proprietary and can be read by
other applications in a saved format such as TIFF. Generally, you'll want to save a
working copy of an image as a PSD file and then flatten the image for use with other
programs, or to send to a service bureau that might not own Photoshop 3. If you save

an image as a PSD file, you can always delete a flattened copy of the image later and create another one for any special purpose in the future.

However, the next task at hand concerns merging two image layers together, and this is not the same as flattening an image. Merging layers can be performed using any visible layers in an image. This means that you can now merge the Sparrow and Layer 1 layers together and still have a layer containing these objects on top of the Background layer. In its present state, GAMES.PSD should be a little less than 1.8 MB as reported by the right figure on the Document Size box. When you merge the Sparrow and Layer 1 layers together, the figure drops down to about 1.5 MB. Quite differently, the Flatten Image command takes all visible layers and merges them to the background to produce a substantially smaller saved file size. This is an important distinction, and the next exercise has to do with only condensing the collection of checkers you now have on both layers. After you do this, you use the Rotate effect again, but this time you rotate all the checkers you've merged to a single layer.

Here's how to gather the checkers and apply an effect to them as one, grouped unit:

Merging the Contents of Layers

Click on the eye icon next to the Background thumbnail icon on the Layers palette list	Hides the Background layer from view and from editing.

You'll see the grid (checkerboard gray and white) pattern in areas surrounding the three checkers now because this is Photoshop's default display of transparent pixels in an image file when no opaque pixels are behind them.

Click on the pop-up menu triangle to the right of the Layers tab; then choose Merge Layers (see fig. 6.19)	Merges all visible layers into a single layer. Single layer takes on the bottom-most layer's title.

Now see if the checkers act like a group...

Click on the area where the eye icon was on the Background layer title on the Layers palette	Restores the eye icon and the Background layer to view.
Double-click on the Hand tool	Zooms you out to a 1:2 viewing resolution.
Click on the Sparrow layer title, then choose **I**mage, **R**otate, **F**ree...	Displays the Rotate box around all three opaque elements on the Sparrow layer.

Click and drag a corner handle of the rotate box so that the checkers are at a diagonal to the checkerboard squares (see fig. 6.20)	Rotates the group of checkers. The Rotate command, when applied to a layer, auto-selects the opaque pixels.
Click inside the rotate box	Finalizes the Rotate command, and you now have diagonal checkers.

You probably have one checker outside the image window right now because the rotate command uses the center of a selection as its center of rotation, and this is not an option you can change in Photoshop. It's okay to leave a checker outside the window; this is a test drive, and as mentioned earlier, there is no "right" or "wrong" way to go about the exercises in this chapter. In later chapters, you are advised to do things in a specific way to produce a specific effect, but in this chapter, you're experimenting more than creating.

Press Ctrl(Cmd)+S (File, Save)	Saves your work at this intermediate stage of completion.

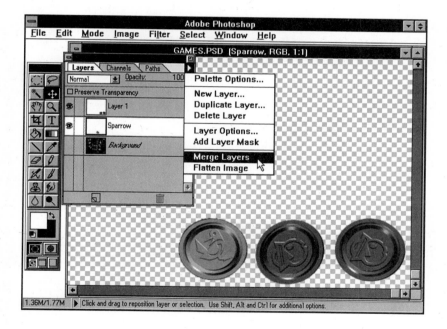

Figure 6.19

Hide the layers you don't want merged before you choose the Merge Layers command.

Figure 6.20

Effects and filters only apply to the opaque contents of an image layer.

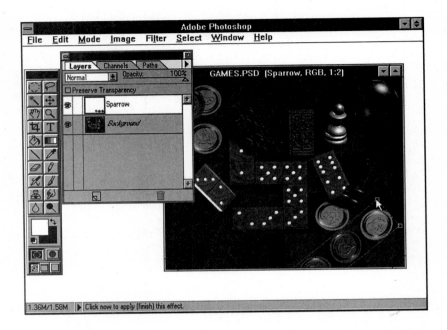

As you travel further into future chapter assignments, you see that opacity plays a big part in professional image retouching. Photoshop "sees" 100-percent transparent pixels as ones that no editing changes can be applied to; but pixels that have even one-percent opacity can be modified, repositioned, and otherwise edited. Because the Sparrow layer only has 100-percent opaque pixels that represent the checkers, the Rotate command could easily calculate and reposition only those pixels that display a 100-percent opacity. In short, you need no selection marquee to apply **I**mage menu effects to a layer's contents.

Painting, Layers, and Compositing Modes

You'll see many different options used throughout this book for the way a floating selection is composited into a background image, as well as special modes that you can paint with and also assign to a layer's opaque pixels. Modes, as defined on the Brushes and Layers palette, are variations on how a foreground color or floating selection is composited into the background. For example, if you chose Dissolve from the Modes drop-down list on the Layers palette while a floating selection is above an image background, the selection would then be composited (blended) into the background image in Dissolve mode. No title on either the Brushes/Options palette or the Layers palette indicates what these modes are (or even that they are modes!). The following list explains what each mode does when you're deselecting an image into a background, assigning a mode to a layer, or painting:

◆ **Normal mode.** This is the default mode for painting and compositing and is the standard mode for a layer. When a color or selected image area is composited into the background, Normal mode replaces the underlying pixels with the pixels you added to the image. It's a straightforward replacement of background pixels. You can change the opacity of the paint or selection before finalizing an edit by clicking and dragging the Opacity slider—found on the Layers palette for compositing and merging layers and on the Brushes palette when you're painting in Normal mode.

◆ **Dissolve mode.** This mode corrupts a selection or paint stroke by randomly distributing foreground pixels throughout the selected area. Dissolve mode is useful for painting; it can create instant "texture" to which you can apply other effects and create complex designs. Dissolve mode can also produce some fairly unaesthetic blends of a selection into a background image, and blending layers together in Dissolve mode can be equally unphotogenic.

◆ **Behind and Clear modes.** These modes can only be used on layers; background images can't be painted clear or behind. Behind mode treats opaque pixels as masked, and only the transparent pixels on a layer can receive color. This creates a simulation of painting on the back side of a sheet of acetate, where a design has already been painted on the front. Clear mode changes opaque pixels to transparent and can only be used with the Line and Paint bucket tools. Additionally, you can use the Edit menu's Fill and Stroke commands to apply Clear to the edges or interior of a selection. The Eraser tool, when clicked and dragged through opaque pixels on a layer, performs the same effect as Clear mode, so erasing is perhaps a more straightforward way of removing a pixel's opacity.

◆ **Multiply and Screen modes.** These are perhaps two of the most useful modes for painting and compositing that a designer could ask for. Multiply is the opposite function of Screen. When painting in Multiply mode, the foreground color (indicated on the toolbox) combines with an image's colors to decrease brightness on the area you're painting. A darker color is always the product of painting in Multiply mode, and the effect can look like soft charcoals or designer markers that have saturated the paper. When used as a mode for compositing floating selections, Multiply mode emphasizes the darker values of the selection as it's blended into the background image, and lighter colors in the selection disappear when you deselect (thus blend) the selection. Multiply is great for creating shadows. See Chapter 22, "Virtual Reality: The Ingredients of Dreamwork," for an example of creating an effect with Multiply mode.

Screening "bleaches" a lighter foreground color out of an image when painting, and a lighter color is always the result of Screen mode. Stay tuned for an example of using Screen mode in an exercise to follow.

◆ **Overlay mode.** This mode intensifies the highlight and shadow areas of the image you paint over; it also creates intense highlight and shadow areas to the background image when you assign Overlay mode to a floating selection. The *midtones* of an image—the areas that have neither highlights nor shadows—are tinted with the current foreground color when you use Overlay mode for painting, and floating selections assigned Overlay mode blend most of their color values into the background image. This is a great mode for creating ghost-like objects in an image and for superimposing titles.

◆ **Soft and Hard Light modes.** These are combination effect modes; both Soft and Hard Light modes react to the base color (the color found in the background image you paint or composite a selection into). If a background area has a brightness of greater than 50-percent, Soft Light mode lightens the paint or composite selection, and Hard Light screens the paint or composite selection. If the underlying background has pixels that fall below a 50-percent brightness value, Soft Light darkens the area, and Hard Light multiplies the color values. So you can achieve a selective Screen and Multiply effect at once when you choose Hard Light as the painting or compositing mode. Use these modes with partial Opacity settings to achieve different effects.

◆ **Darken and Lighten modes.** Darken mode affects only the pixels in the image lighter than the foreground color. Equal or darker pixels are not affected. Conversely, Lighten affects only the pixels in the image darker than the foreground color you selected. Darken and Lighten modes produce painting and compositing effects that are much more subtle than Screen and Multiply modes, but they are closely related. You may decide to use Lighten or Darken modes for painting when Screen or Multiply produces results that are too intense.

◆ **Difference mode.** This mode evaluates the color of both the image area you paint over and the current foreground color. If the foreground color is brighter, the background color is changed to the color opposite its original value. Painting over an image with white produces the most dramatic results; therefore few background images contain a value brighter than absolute white!

◆ **Hue mode.** Hue mode paints with the foreground shade of color only. The luminosity and saturation of the image area you paint over is unaffected. This mode is terrific when you want to tint areas.

◆ **Saturation mode.** If your foreground color is black, this mode converts color areas to grayscale. If your foreground color is a color value, this mode, with each brush stroke, amplifies the underlying pixels' basic color value by reducing the gray component. The non-black foreground color you selected doesn't affect what happens. You have to play with Saturation mode to understand its possibilities in your own work.

◆ **Color mode.** This mode changes both the hue and saturation of a selected image without altering the background image's tonal composition—the quality that comprises visual detail in most photographic images. You use it in the following exercise to change the color of the chess piece in GAMES.PSD.

◆ **Luminosity.** This increases the lightness qualities in the image. This powerful mode doesn't change color values. Use it sparingly when lightening, say, an over-saturated color area in an image. When using Luminosity mode with a brush, set the Opacity on the Brushes palette down to about 30-percent.

Use the preceding list as a reference whenever you decide to change the mode of a painting tool, a floating selection, or a layer. You'll find some of the modes more useful than others in your work, but try out different modes if you can't achieve an effect in the default Normal mode.

Painting in Color Mode

As mentioned in the preceding section, Color mode can be used to apply a tint to an image area—it replaces original color with the foreground you specify, but doesn't affect the neutral tones—the brightness values within a pixel's color. In the following exercise, you tint the pawn in GAMES.PSD to a cheerier color than its present off-white. When you paint in Color mode, the marble texture of the pawn remains, but it becomes blue marble!

Here's how to use the Color mode of painting to hand-tint an image area:

Recoloring an Image Area

Press **Z** (**Z**oom tool); then marquee-zoom to a 2:1 viewing resolution over the pawn in GAMES.PSD	Provides a good view of the area to be edited.
Click on the Background title on the Layers palette list	Chooses the layer that contains the pawn as the current editing, or *target* layer.
Press F6 (Macintosh: Press F10); then click and drag in the Color Bar at the bottom of the Picker palette until you get a rich blue foreground color	Specifies a rich blue for the foreground color with which you'll paint.
Press **B** (Paint **B**rush), then choose Color from the drop-down list on the Options palette	Chooses a painting mode for the Paint Brush.

continues

continued

On the Brushes palette, choose the second, middle-row tip	Defines the size and characteristics of the Paint Brush tip.
Click and drag inside the pawn (see fig. 6.21)	Tints the pawn with foreground blue, but the pawn's detail remains the same.
Click and drag inside the rest of the pawn	Recolors the pawn.

Figure 6.21

Color painting mode doesn't affect the grayscale component—the brightness values of the image areas you paint over.

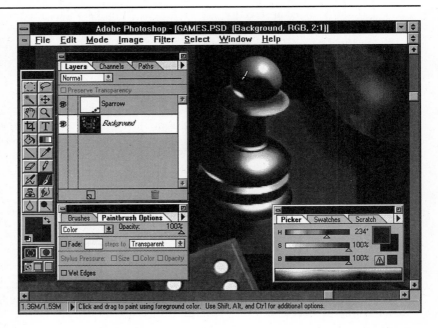

You see more advanced uses for the Color mode of painting in Chapter 17, "The Wonderful World of Black and White," in which Color mode is used to hand-tint a portrait photograph.

Modes and Layers

A very close relationship exists between layers and image selections; practically everything you can do to a floating selection can also be performed to the same selection when it's part of a layer. For this reason, layers need to be included in the discussion of modes. Think of layers for a moment as the precomposited view of a floating selection that can be manipulated indefinitely without fear of deselecting it

and thus compositing (blending) it into the image. You can change and respecify a layer's mode anytime before you merge or flatten the layer into the background of an image. In fact, this is the way most designers prefer to work in Photoshop 3—you arrange the image elements on a layer, and then work with the objects and assign different modes to them as a preview for how a flattened, more standard bitmap image format will look.

The next exercise can be as brief or as long as you like. It simply shows you how Layers modes affect the opaque pixels. The three checkers on the Sparrow layer are there in Normal layer mode. However, you can change this and respecify how the checkers will be blended into the background when you flatten the image at this chapter's end. The whole operation in the following exercise also can be accomplished if the three checkers were a floating selection on the background. The disadvantage would be that you can't respecify a mode or opacity for a floating selection, blend it into the background, and then change your mind. As long as an element is on a layer, you can preview the effect that the final compositing of the image elements will create.

The following exercise shows how to make the checkers look like they're made of a semitransparent plastic:

Changing Layers Modes

Double-click on the Zoom tool; then scroll to the bottom right of GAMES.PSD	Zooms you to a 1:1 viewing resolution; positions the image in the image window for a view of the checkers on Sparrow layer.
Click on the Sparrow layer title on the Layers palette list	Makes the Sparrow layer the current editing (target) layer.
Click on Screen from the Layers palette's Modes drop-down list	Affects the layer's opaque pixels (the checkers) so that darker checker areas become transparent, and only lighter areas retain color and detail values (see fig. 6.22).
Click on all the other modes on the Modes drop-down list	Creates changes to the checkers in manners similar to if you painted using the respective modes.

Because layer modes can be respecified indefinitely before flattening layers into the background, you can specify any mode now and then change your mind without affecting the finished image.

continues

continued

Press Ctrl(Cmd)+S (**F**ile, **S**ave)   Saves the settings for the Layers to
                                                 hard disk.

When you change a layer's mode and then save the image and close it, the next time you
reopen it, the active layer will have the same mode. So you haven't really saved image edits so
much as you've saved settings to hard disk.

Figure 6.22

*You can change
the mode of a
layer and then
respecify the mode
before blending
(merging) the
layer to the
background
image.*

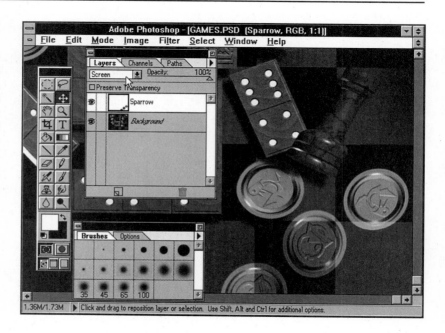

Stop   You should not move any opaque pixels outside the image window before or after
you change Layer modes, and you shouldn't change the Opacity for the layer if you
have a layer element partially outside the image window. Photoshop considers
changing of modes and Opacity to be a layer editing move, and any opaque pixels
outside the image window are then discarded (deleted) from the layer.

See Chapter 15, "Special Effects with Ordinary Photographs," for the inside story
on the perils of moving a layer image element outside the image window.

Loading a Selection from a Different Image

Although saved selections are saved within an image's file format, Photoshop 3 gives you the capability to load a selection from an entirely different image. This can come in very handy when an image is ponderously large; you needn't burden the image with an additional Alpha channel to load a selection on the Background or image layer. This capability can also help designers who use drawing applications—you can design a black and white piece; export it as a TIF, AI, or EPS image; then tell Photoshop to load the image as a selection for the other image. This trick only works if the TIF or EPS image is in Grayscale mode and of equal dimensions and resolution as the target image (the image that receives the selection marquee).

We did a little pre-planning, and the TITLE.TIF image is all prepared for the next exercise. The authors prepared TITLE.TIF by measuring the size and resolution of GAMES.PSD. Then an illustration software was used to create the lettering. Finally, the design was imported into Photoshop as an EPS image converted to bitmap format. For more information on different graphical formats Photoshop can use, refer to Chapter 20, "Mixed Media and Photoshop."

The final effect you create in the GAMES.PSD image is a splashy title toward the bottom of the image. You're going to see how to manually emboss the "GAMES" lettering found in the TITLE.TIF image onto the Background layer of GAMES.PSD. But that's not the splashy part; you'll also use the Brightness/Contrast controls in Photoshop to lighten the selection based on the lettering, so that it appears the "GAMES" lettering is made of frosted glass laid on top of the image.

Here's how to load a selection from a different image and edit the selection area using tonal adjustments:

Cross-Image Selection

Open the TITLE.TIF image from the CHAP06 subdirectory (folder) of the Bonus CD that comes with this book	This is the grayscale image you'll use to base a selection on in the GAMES.PSD image (see fig. 6.23).
Click on the title bar of GAMES.PSD; then click on the Background title on the Layers palette	Makes the GAMES image the active image window; makes the Background the target layer.
Choose **S**elect, **L**oad Selection	Displays the Load Selection dialog box.

continues

continued

This dialog box offers the longer route to commands you've learned the shortcuts to on the Channels palette. However, loading a selection from a different image cannot be accomplished through the use of the icons on the Channels palette—it has to be performed in the Load Selection dialog box.

In the **D**ocument drop-down box, choose TITLE.TIF, then click on OK (see fig. 6.24)	Loads a selection marquee in the GAMES.PSD image based on grayscale brightness values found in the Black channel of TITLE.TIF.

In figure 6.24, the **C**hannel drop-down box has been clicked on to show that no alternative options are available. TITLE.TIF's Black channel is the only one that exists within the document, so it's the only selection. However, if TITLE.TIF had channels, these, too, could be selected in the Load Selection dialog box, and so could channels in an RGB mode image. You must have the document open that contains the potential selection information, but having loaded the selection, TITLE.TIF serves no further purpose.

Close the TITLE.TIF image	Makes GAMES.PSD the active image window, with the selection marquee still loaded.
Press **D** (**d**efault colors icon), then press the down-arrow key once	Makes white the current background color and nudges the selection down by one pixel to expose background color at the top of the selection marquee (see fig. 6.25).
Press Ctrl(Cmd)+H (**S**elect, Hide **E**dges)	Gives you an uncluttered view of how the changes are affecting the image by hiding the marquee lines.
Press Ctrl(Cmd)+B (**I**mage, **A**djust, **B**rightness/Contrast)	Displays the Brightness/Contrast dialog box.
Click and drag the Brightness slider to about **+80**	Lightens the colors of the image areas within the selection on the Background layer (see fig. 6.26).
Click on OK	Returns you to GAMES.PSD.
Press Ctrl(Cmd)+D (**S**elect, **N**one), then Ctrl(Cmd)+S (**F**ile, **S**ave)	Deselects the floating selection and saves your work up to this point.

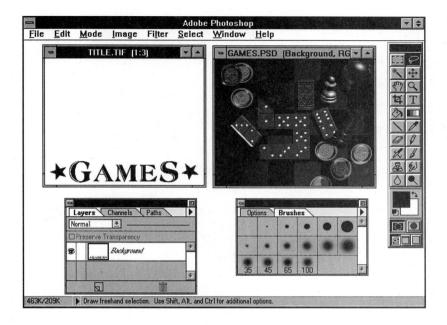

Figure 6.23

The TITLE.TIF image is the same dimensions and resolution as the GAMES image. Grayscale mode images can serve as a selection.

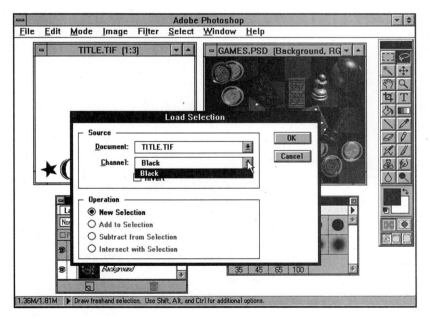

Figure 6.24

Choose TITLE.TIF, not GAMES.PSD, as the Source of Selection information.

Figure 6.25

Nudging an active selection exposes white background and creates an embossed effect.

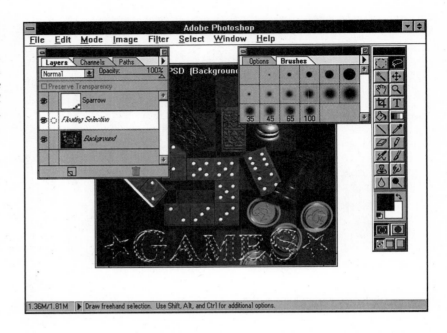

Figure 6.26

Use the Brightness/ Contrast dialog box to lighten the area inside a selection marquee.

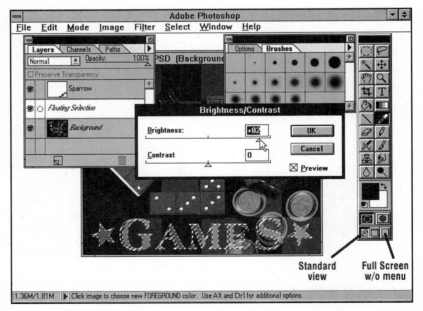

Displaying Your Finished Work in Photoshop

If you look at figure 6.27, you'll see that we've marked the display modes Photoshop offers for viewing an active image. By clicking on the Full Screen without Menu Bar button, you remove the workspace and the menu bar. And if you press the Tab key, you hide all the palettes and the toolbox. In this view, you can still use the current paint tool, but that's not the point.

You've done some remarkable image editing in this test drive, and you and everyone within ten feet of your office should now take a gander at your creation without the distraction of Photoshop's tools and palettes. Click on the Full Screen without Menu Bar button now; then press Tab. A second Tab keystroke makes the toolbox reappear, and from there, you can click on the Standard viewing mode and return Photoshop to functionality. Does your screen look like figure 6.27 now? Hopefully, it's in color!

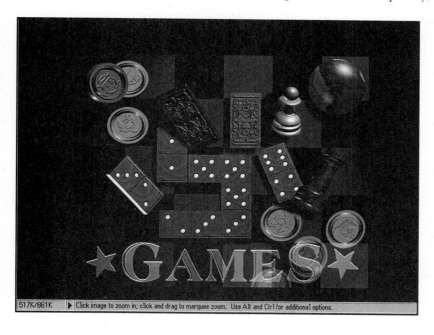

Figure 6.27

A full-screen view of your finished test drive.

Protecting Your Artwork

Before you get much further into your own assignments using Photoshop 3, you should know about a new feature if you're a professional photographer, or you simply want to invisibly "brand" an image to identify it as your own work.

An information standard has been developed for electronic transmission of images; the Newspaper Association of America (NAA) and International Press Telecommunications Council (IPTC) both take advantage of encapsulated information in images sent to newspapers by wire that states what the image is, who took it, and to whom the image belongs. The **F**ile, File **I**nfo command displays a dialog box as shown in figure 6.28. When you're done with an image, you can use the File **I**nfo command to enter information, such as your name and the image's name, if you know you're going to put a file on an online service, or simply give it to a coworker.

Figure 6.28

Enter the credits that you want to travel along with a saved image file.

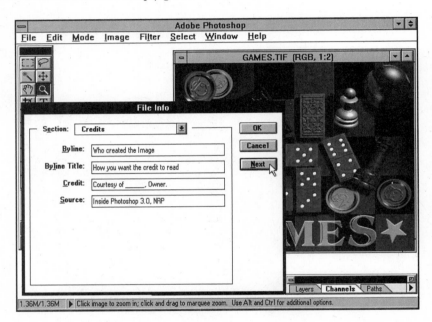

You have the option to fill out parts, or the entire Credits Se**c**tion, and then move on to the other Sections such as Caption, Keywords, Categories, and Origin. By default, File Info always opens to Caption, but you can move through these section fields by clicking on the **N**ext button to find an appropriate section that relates to your image.

Images with the Info embedded text can be saved in TIF, EPS, and PCD formats only. TIF is probably the best format for your images because the Tagged Image File Format can be read by different applications on both the Macintosh and Windows operating platforms.

The information you send along with your file is not iron-clad protection against piracy; you take this risk whenever you post or distribute your work, and another user who owns Photoshop 3 can indeed change the File Info. It's impossible to completely ensure computer data—software manufacturers lose millions of dollars a year of potential revenue from people who make illegal copies of software applications. The best use of Photoshop's File Info is for identifying your work if you upload it to a newspaper, and it's a good space within a file to write notes to yourself about how you created an image. The Caption field can contain 2,000 characters. And if you really want to protect your images, don't tell anyone that you've entered information into the file that you share!

As you approach Part 2, "Steak and Potatoes Assignments," it's time to switch into a higher gear—from learning about Photoshop's theoretical underpinnings, to gaining the practical experience and acquiring the working skills that can be immediately put to good use in your everyday imaging work. It's time to show you how to build an imaging portfolio of your own by way of example.

Part II

Steak and Potatoes Assignments

7   *Restoring an Heirloom Photograph* 289

8   *Retouching an Heirloom Photograph* 323

9   *Using Type in Photoshop* 363

10   *Stamping Out Photo Errors* 411

11   *Using Paths, Selections, and Layers* 457

Restoring an Heirloom Photograph

Photographic restoration is probably the most difficult task you'll
face when working with digital images. A photo that's faded
and has surface nicks, creases, and abrasions leaves you very
little information to work with when retouching. Whenever you add
anything to the picture, you must be careful to keep a watchful eye for
any *cosmetic* effect caused by the addition to keep the picture from
looking hand-tinted. To restore a photo, you must adopt skills similar
to those of a detective *and* a plastic surgeon. Fortunately, Photoshop's
features make this task much simpler.

Digital photo restoration has many advantages over the chemical
photography darkroom. In a darkroom, a professional retoucher
makes a photographic copy of the original image. The copying process
involves applying filters and using many different darkroom techniques to produce a workable base image. The retoucher then applies
transparent dyes to the copy of the photo. If a mistake is made, the
retoucher must make another copy of the photo, use colorful language, and start over from the beginning.

In Photoshop's digital world, Reset and Undo commands are available all along the way so that you can correct a mistake without losing every step you've made. If you use the Save a Copy command at regular intervals (and give unique names to the copies), you can return to an intermediate step of image restoration and try a new strategy if one version of your work isn't producing the intended results. Take advantage of the wonderful, plastic qualities of the electronic pixel to apply *adjustments*, not dyes, to an image to *reveal* the truth behind the layers of Time, instead of further covering up original image information.

Acquiring Photo Images: From an Old Shoe Box to the Monitor

The photo you use in this chapter's assignment was dug out of my family's "virtual archive"—a shoe box in the basement. MY_MOM.TIF, shown in figure 7.1, is a scan of a photo of my mother when she was 11. My Uncle Alan took her picture while doing research work with some of AGFA's first color film. AGFA didn't know then that this photo would actually survive until the 1990s—sort of.

Figure 7.1

Almost no color is displayed in this aged color photo.

Open MY_MOM.TIF from the *Inside Adobe Photoshop 3* Bonus CD now, and see the state of disrepair this photo has fallen into before you begin the exercises.

Note When restoring an heirloom photo, you have to break some rules. Normally, an image is scanned at the resolution that is best matched for your final, printed output. When restoring a faded, discolored, and damaged image like MY_MOM.TIF, you need to scan at *as high a resolution as possible,* regardless of final output considerations. You need all the information that you can possibly wring out of the image. Working with huge files is an art in and of itself—it requires patience and installed system RAM that totals at least three to five times the size of the scanned image.

The image of MY_MOM.TIF was originally scanned at 400 dpi, which yielded an 8.3 MB file. If this was an assignment of your own, you'd want to scan a faded photo to a file size this large, or perhaps even larger, to achieve a high enough resolution so that you can edit with precision and finesse. Your final goal, usually, is to make a print of the image you restore. For this reason, you always need as much digital data from the source image as possible for retouching and for rendering a high-resolution copy.

Working with huge image files is slow and imposes a noticeable burden on a system. When you finish retouching such an image, you can use Photoshop's Image Size command to decrease the resolution and file size to match your final output.

Because this chapter's assignment is a *practice* exercise, you can learn the concepts and methods, and achieve good on-screen results without the burden of a huge file. You won't be giving a print of this image to your mom or anything, so MY_MOM.TIF on the *Inside Photoshop 3* Bonus CD is a conservatively-sized 1.3 MB file.

In your *own* work, remember that when you restore a photo in poor condition, you need to acquire as much original image information as possible. Go ahead and break the rules and work with an image that has been scanned at a very high resolution.

Improving Image Detail

When working with properly exposed (brightness, contrast, and gamma-corrected) scanned photos, you should first color-correct the image. Starting with Photoshop's Variations command is *usually* a wise first step. However, MY_MOM.TIF is *not* a regular image. It looks like a sepia tone but is actually a color photo with the color information hidden beneath a layer of age. Although it may seem like common sense to adjust the *color* to remove the sepia color, the problem actually is related to the image's *brightness* values.

It's also a bad idea to color-correct first for a very basic reason: Photoshop's commands for tonal and color adjustments are all *relative*. Your first change is made to the *original* image, but each subsequent change is made to the image's current (changed) state. You can't go back to your starting point (the original image) without starting over again with a copy of the original.

For MY_MOM.TIF, you need to reassign proportionate values to brightness ranges *before* you adjust the color values. That is, you must get the brown out of view so that you can see the colors that you're correcting.

You can virtually eliminate the predominant sepia browns in MY_MOM.TIF by using the Levels command to respecify the amount of neutral, grayscale component each color pixel contains.

The Relationship between Hue and Tonal Values

Before getting too far into this chapter's assignment—which depends on an under-standing of both tonal and color relationships in a digital image—let's recap a little from Chapter 3 on color models. The HSB, or Hue, Saturation, and Brightness color model, was designed to describe color in a way that is closer to the way people recognize color. Humans perceive color as having qualities, and we typically describe a color with names like bright blue or red-violet, rather than describing them as relative amounts of Red, Green, and Blue light.

Computer monitors and television screens don't perceive color; instead, they display color electronically using red, green, and blue phosphors, which not surprisingly, are easiest to describe using the RGB color model. A color can be defined using either model, so it stands to reason that when you respecify the amounts of Red, Green and Blue assigned to a pixel, you are also changing the corresponding value in the HSB model, and vice versa.

The Levels command gives you control over the tonal (the neutral, grayscale) component of a color image, but when you reassign color pixels a relative brightness value, you're also changing the amount of Saturation (the balance between pure Hue and grayscale component), and to a certain extent, the Hue in areas of the image. Why? Although Photoshop gives you control over the H, S, and B qualities of digital color, the HSB model is synchronous with relative changes in the RGB values, which are the proportions of component color that are actually changing on your monitor and in your file. Pixels are attributed red, green, and blue values—the HSB color model is a convenient, accurate equivalency that simply describes color in a more manageable way.

Therefore, the real trick in the next assignment is to use the Levels command to create dissimilarity in the relationship between the tonal densities in the pixels'

neutral tones of the MY_MOM image (thus creating contrast and adding visual detail) without disturbing the overall *color* values too much. Photoshop has rich tools for correcting only the color values in an image, which is covered later in this chapter.

Evaluating Color Changes

The best way to evaluate proposed color and tone changes before you make them in an image is by using the Info palette (pressing F8 displays it in the Windows version; F12 is the Macintosh Photoshop shortcut). The Info palette can be set up to show RGB and HSB values simultaneously, so that you can see both values of an area underneath the the cursor. When you're in the Levels dialog box, the Info palette displays the current color values for the single pixel which is directly under your cursor, and the values the area will take on should you make a change with the Levels command. If you can create a change in the Brightness values (as displayed on the Info palette) *without* changing the other color components too much, you'll retain many of the original color values in the image, even if you can't *see* the colors in the original image!

The Info palette displays HSB color as a percentage of Brightness and a percentage of Saturation, but reports the Hue of the area you have the cursor over in degrees. If you change the Brightness in an image, but accidentally change the Hue in the process, you create *color-casting* in the image, which is something you *don't* want. Figure 7.2 is a color wheel (based on the Munsell color wheel) that shows the primary and secondary colors, and the degrees that they are assigned around the wheel. Photoshop uses the same measurements on the Info palette. So, for example, when the Info palette reads H: 120°, your cursor is over a green pixel.

Tip

You have the option of changing the pixel sampling rate of the Info palette to a larger 3 × 3 sample average, or a 5 × 5 average. You set the sample area from the Options palette when the Eyedropper tool is the chosen tool.

Regardless of which tool you have active, your cursor still reports single pixel, 3 × 3, or 5 × 5 averages as numerical data on the Info palette. You need the Eyedropper tool to be the current tool to set the option for sampling from the palette because the Options palette is *context-sensitive*; it changes to reflect the options for the current tool.

See Chapter 4, "Photoshop Defaults and Options," for more information on setting and changing defaults in Photoshop.

Although Orange and Violet aren't primary or secondary colors (they're a combination of a primary *and* a secondary color), they are noted on this color wheel to give you an idea of their relative position. Additionally, the frequency of Hues is displayed as a band beneath the color wheel in figure 7.2 because this is also the way color is displayed in other areas of Photoshop, such as in the Hue/Saturation dialog box.

Figure 7.2

*Hue is specified
as degrees around
a color wheel.*

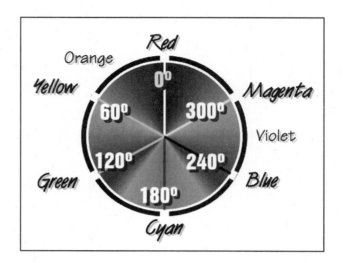

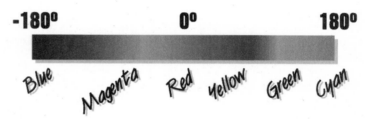

Redistributing Tonal Relationships

In the next exercise, you'll use the Info palette in combination with the Levels command to redistribute the grayscale component of the MY_MOM image. Lack of variation between relative brightness values is the basic cause of the image's muddiness. Additionally, the White Point in the picture is way beneath the point it was when the image was originally photographed.

Note *The White Point is the brightest part of an image area, which should usually be assigned the highest value in the histogram.*

Photoshop's Auto feature is a good starting place for tonally adjusting an image. However, you should always use your artist's eye to evaluate the Auto feature's results and make manual modifications to the values the Auto adjustment proposes, if necessary. Re-establishing the relationship between original color values and the tonal values helps remove much of the brown in MY_MOM.TIF. With the brown

diminished from the image you'll be able to see what other *global* adjustments are needed for subsequent corrections.

Here's how to free the color values in MY_MOM.TIF from the sands of time.

Respecifying Tonal Ranges in an Image

Open the MY_MOM.TIF image from the CHAP07 subdirectory of the *Inside Photoshop 3* Bonus CD	This is the heirloom photo you'll rescue in this chapter.
Double-click on the Hand tool on the toolbox	Zooms the image to fit within the active window.
Click and drag the title bar of MY_MOM.TIF to the top left corner of Photoshop workspace	Positions the image where you can see it and still have room for a palette and a dialog box in the workspace.
Choose **W**indow, Show **I**nfo (or press F8)	Displays the Info palette.
Click on the Eyedropper icon to the left of the CMYK area on the Info palette, then choose HSB color	By default, the Info palette is set to RGB and CMYK color values. You reset the color models that the Info palette displays by clicking on the Eyedropper icons on the palette.
Click and drag the Info palette to the right of MY_MOM.TIF, and to the bottom of the workspace	Helps organize your workspace so that there's enough room for another screen element to pop up.
Press Ctrl+L (or choose **I**mage, **A**djust, then Levels)	Displays the Levels dialog box.
Drag the Levels dialog box to a position where you can see both it and the image, as shown in figure 7.3	Now you can see both the image and Info palette, and use the Levels command to make tonal adjustments.

As you can see, the image displays poor contrast, and most of the color pixels in the image are bunched toward the lower end of the brightness scale.

Click on the Auto button	Ignores the highest .5% and lowest .5% values for tones in the image, and automatically redistributes tonal values for pixels across a narrower brightness range, increasing contrast, and dramatically improving the image detail in MY_MOM.TIF.
Take a break for a moment, and *don't* touch anything!	This ends the first part of the exercise.

This is a break in the steps, but don't think of it as a break in this exercise! You're not done yet, so don't click on OK or leave the Levels command because you need to set a new White Point and adjust the gamma (the midrange contrast) for MY_MOM.TIF. Remember that all changes in the Levels command are relative, and that's why you need to change White *and* Black Points in the same Levels command session. You want to create more tonal balance in the image, and balance is achieved by editing the *entire* tonal range in one Levels session.

Figure 7.3

The Auto option adds contrast to an image by reassigning tonal values to a new, narrower range of brightness values.

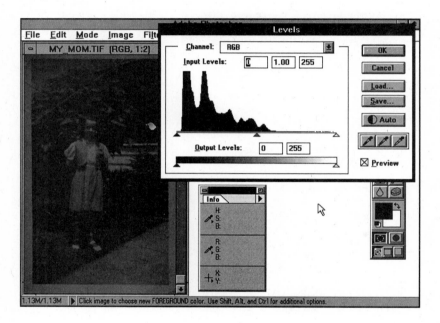

Understanding Contrast

The *histogram,* the graph that shows the color pixel location in the image according to brightness in the Levels command, is now completely different from the original histogram. Areas of upper midrange are now populated with color pixels, and the "comb" effect you see between brightness values indicates that pixels of neighboring brightness values have much better overall contrast.

The Levels command's Auto feature doesn't provide results this dramatic or good on all images, and you might choose to forego the Auto option when an image only needs a little tonal redistribution.

The next step in this assignment is to set a new *White Point,* the point at which the brightest image area should be assigned the highest value in the histogram. Our eyes

tell us that the white clapboard on the house in MY_MOM reflects light with a high intensity, so this should be the target area you use to define the image's White Point.

Here's how to refine the Auto distribution of tonal pixels in the image:

Setting a New White Point

Click on the far right Eyedropper button on the Levels command	This is the tool you use to set the White Point in the image.
Run the cursor over the white clapboard area in the MY_MOM image (see fig. 7.4)	The Info palette displays RGB and HSB information about the pixels beneath your cursor.

You need to find a position for the Eyedropper over the image that creates the least change in the value in the H: (Hue) field on the Info palette, while creating the most difference between the present and proposed changes in the B: (**B**rightness) field, expressed as a fractional amount.

Click over the image when the change in Hue is the least and the change in Brightness is the greatest on the Info palette	Sets a new White Point while creating the least amount of color-casting in the image.

Color-casting is the visible shift in overall Hue in the image. Generally, it's not a good idea to change the Hue this way; instead, you use the color controls explained later in this chapter. The image is a little "cold" (blue color-cast), but the Levels command is for precise *tonal* adjustment, not color adjustment.

Because Photoshop reassigns every pixel in an image a brightness value that's relative to your new White Point setting, it's apparent that a new Black Point doesn't need to be defined. The darker areas in the image support the lighter areas, and compositionally, the tonal "landscape" of the image is well-represented. However, the midrange, where most of the visual detail lies in an image, is a little darker than it should be. To perform *gamma* adjustment—the altering of the contrast in the midtones—let's continue.

Type **1.13** in the middle box of the Input Levels options (see fig. 7.5)	Increases the gamma of the midranges by setting the midpoint slightly lower on the Levels histogram.

The value 1.13 is a midtone setting that looks good when viewed in Preview, although you may prefer another setting. A different value might be better because every change made is relative to the previous change you made, and you may have chosen a slightly different value for the new White Point. You also can click and drag the center slider to make gamma adjustments instead of directly entering a value in the Input box.

continues

continued

Click on OK	Confirms your changes and returns you to Photoshop's workspace.
Choose File, Sa<u>v</u>e As, then save the image as MY_MOM.TIF (in the TIFF format from Save File as Format <u>T</u>ype drop-down list) to your hard disk	Saves your work up to this point.

Figure 7.4

Set a White Point that changes the Brightness without affecting the Hue by too much.

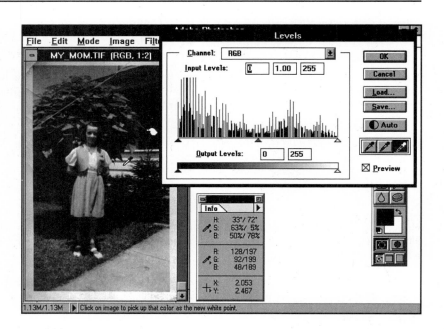

The Levels adjustment that you just performed resulted in extensive changes to this image–very positive ones–that merit a little explanation.

This image, as scanned, contained color pixels that were buried beneath years of chemical deterioration. Setting new values for midtones and the White Point redistributed the brightness values of *all* the pixels across the tonal range. Values that were whiter or blacker than the white or black point the image originally had were automatically *clipped* when you clicked on the Auto button—tonal information in these regions was ignored and discarded by Photoshop. The pixels that occupied these off-the-scale values were reassigned values within the new brightness range, which is always represented as values between 0 and 255. The change you made resulted in a broader midrange of values, which you further

modified with the midrange control. By increasing the gamma–the midrange gray values–slightly to 1.13, still more detail shows in the darker registers in the midrange. Setting a higher gamma reduced the contrast only within the midrange, but didn't affect the top and bottom brightness ranges.

The Info palette is an invaluable assistant in determining the value of changes you create in the Levels dialog box before you click on OK.

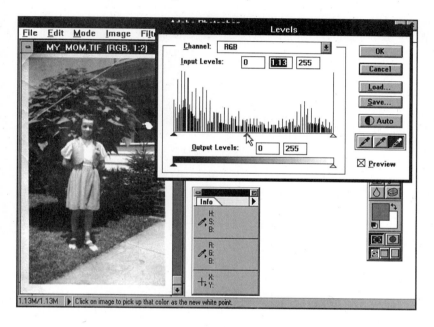

Figure 7.5

Use the Input fields or click and drag the midrange slider to increase brightness (gamma) in the image.

Tip   Most faded photographic images need their brightness values remapped to create more contrast in certain areas of the image. This can be accomplished by adjusting the Input Levels setting of the Levels dialog box. If, however, you need to create *less* contrast in an image area, you can adjust the Output Levels setting to *decrease* the contrast. When you move the Output Levels sliders, you're, in effect, telling Photoshop that the image has values that are darker than the current black point shown on-screen, and values far lighter than the current white point.

Be aware, though, that in both cases, when you decrease or increase image contrast, you *redistribute* brightness values for color pixels, which results in some loss of quality to the image's visual content. By using the Levels dialog box to increase the image's contrast, you are actually *destroying* the brown sepia quality (an *unwanted* piece of visual content) found in MY_MOM.TIF.

Using the Variations Command

You aren't finished "shaping" the brightness map of MY_MOM.TIF yet. You used the Levels command first so you could see something in the image besides brown. Now you can remove some of the awful bluish color-cast you see in the image.

The Variations command is about the only straightforward command in Photoshop. If you want to see what the image would look like with a little more red or yellow, for example, this command displays thumbnail previews (called *Picks*) of an active image window (or selected area) with the proposed changes. Variations gives you hands-on control over an image's hue and saturation components in addition to minor contrast (tonal) changes.

The Variations command uses a color wheel as its *model*. Thumbnail images with contrasting color tints applied to them are arranged directly opposite each other, just as they are displayed in figure 7.2's Hue wheel. The Current Pick thumbnail (the way the image will look if you press OK) is in the center of the wheel.

MY_MOM.TIF has a noticeable, unwanted blue color-cast. Here's how to pick blue's opposite on the color wheel and remove some of MY_MOM's color-casting:

Color-Casting Call

Choose **A**djust from the **I**mage menu, and then choose Variations	Displays the Variations dialog box, which shows different, miniature views of the image.
Click and drag the Fine/Coarse slider to the left two notches	Shifts the amount of color correction from average to subtle, causing the miniature selection photos to vary less.
Check the Show **C**lipping box	Displays a brilliant neon color in areas of the image where the pixels would become saturated and display as pure black or white as a result of your changes.
Click on the **M**idtones radio button	Constrains the effects of changes to only the midtones of the active image.
Click on the More Yellow Pick icon	Changes the center image, Current Pick, to show how adding yellow changes the image's appearance, as shown in figure 7.6.
Click on the Sh**a**dows radio button	Constrains color corrections to affect only the darker regions of the image.

Notice that some of the Pick selections display clipping (neon-colored areas).

Click and drag the Fine/Coarse slider all the way to Fine	Sets the finest degree of change that you can make to an image's saturation, shade, or color-cast.

Notice that the clipping areas disappear in some of the Picks.

Click on the More Red Pick	Changes the tint of the shadows, mostly in the area of the leaves, and removes some of the cyan.
Click on OK	Confirms your selections and returns you to the workspace.
Press Ctrl+S (File, Save)	Saves your work up to this point.

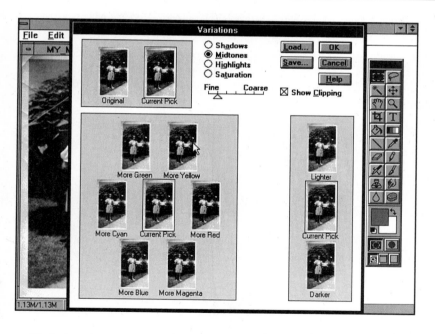

Figure 7.6

The Variations dialog box gives you control over the color-cast in a selected area, or for the entire image.

Variations is a very subjective command because everyone sees an image's color-casting differently. Some users prefer to be a little stingy in using Variations color-correcting because there is a definite limit to what you can do with the command. If you pick a Pick with More Saturation a few times, for example, the picture begins to look like you applied transparent dyes to an image instead of a sophisticated color-correction technique.

And there's a very good reason to limit your use of the Variations dialog box's Fine/ Coarse adjustment. Although these thumbnail images can give you a good idea of the global scheme of an image's colors, their postage-stamp size makes them inadequate for doing precision work. If you have a photo that just needs a little enhancing in one section, however, select the section with any selection tool on the toolbox. Only the selected area appears in the Variations thumbnail, which makes the section a little easier to see.

 Tip

If you make a mistake with any of your Variations selections, you don't have to press Cancel and then return to the Variations command. Instead, you can press the Alt key (on the Macintosh it's the Options key), which toggles the Cancel button to a Reset button, and then click on Reset. Your image reverts to the color properties it originally had before you entered the Variations command.

If you don't like the changes you made in the Variations dialog box, and have already clicked on OK and returned to the full-sized image, press Ctrl+Z or select **U**ndo from the **E**dit menu to undo the Variations changes. This works only if you did no other editing between selecting OK and pressing Ctrl+Z or Edit, **U**ndo.

To use the most processor- and time-intensive "undo command," which applies to Variations as well as every other series of steps performed in Photoshop, select **R**evert from the **F**ile menu. This command returns you to the last version of the image you saved.

Clipping is Obvious in a Photo

The Show **C**lipping check box activates a visual "flag" indicating when you reach a point of complete tonal and color density in areas of an image. In the last exercise, when you wanted to add more red to the overall image, the Fine/Coarse adjustment was too far to the right, resulting in brilliant green-cyan highlights peppering the Current Pick. If you selected the More Red image without adjusting the Fine/Coarse slider to the left, you would reach more than the maximum amount of information possible for the highlighted pixels—either 0 for all three RGB values, or 255.

Photoshop limits, or *clips*, color and tone specifications that fall out of the mathematical possibility for color and presents you with a black or white region in an image. When you use the Variations dialog box, the trick is to add enough color to enhance the image without reaching a clipping point by adjusting the Fine/Coarse slider.

You usually don't want clipped areas in an image, and certainly not when restoring a delicate, faded photo. When you try to go lower than RGB values of zero, areas in the image fill in with flat black and seem to become a separate element from the rest of

the image. Conversely, a clipped white point creates "hot spots"—undetailed high-lights where the visual content is wiped out by "whiter than whites."

When you clip a color image area, you force pixels that formerly had varying bright-ness values into the same percentile. You also force an unrealistic contrast between specific areas and their neighboring pixels. Computer images are a digital display of samples from continuous-tone sources, such as chemical photographs. Inducing a harsh contrast within the *representation* of a continuous tone results in a posterized, phony-looking image.

Using Curves and Quartertones

You make the final adjustment to the color balance of MY_MOM.TIF after you make some additional changes to the color brightness map. With a typical image, you usually want to correct color in one fell swoop and then move on to tonal balance. The unique nature of this heirloom image, however, obliges you to toggle back and forth between Photoshop features.

Unlike the Levels command, Photoshop's Curves command gives you *complete* control over an image's brightness mapping. The Curves command offers fine-tuning for not only the midrange, but the quartertones and any other specific degree of brightness in an image. *Quartertones* are regions at either end of the midtone range. Photoshop's capability to display these tonal regions in a visual, editable fashion is a feature that's necessary for isolating and adjusting tonal areas that need the most help. The star of this chapter's image, my mom, has harsh shadows cast on her face. To correct this, you'll shape the Curve of the tones in the specific area of the image that is affected by the shadows.

You can lighten any area of an image in Photoshop without disturbing the rest of the image by first selecting an area to work on and then using the Curves command to pinpoint a brightness range that needs adjusting. Let's check out the Curves com-mand and its usefulness in restoring this image.

Reshaping an Image's Brightness Curve

Double-click on the Zoom tool	Zooms your view of MY_MOM.TIF to a 1:1 viewing resolution.
Press **L** (or click on the **Lasso** tool on the toolbox), then click and drag a rough outline around mom, from the top of her head to mid-torso	Defines the selection area that you'll change using the Curves command.

continues

continued

Choose <u>S</u>elect, Fea<u>t</u>her, type **2** in the Feather <u>R</u>adius field, and click on OK	Feathers the selection edge.

Feathering isn't displayed as a unique shape for the selection marquee, but the marquee now has a soft edge. The edge makes a two pixel transition between selection and protected image areas. Now, the changes you make in the curves command won't reveal a hard edge between the selection and the unselected image areas.

Choose <u>I</u>mage, <u>A</u>djust, and then choose Curves (or press Ctrl+M)	Displays the Curves dialog box.

If necessary, reposition the box so that you can see the highlighted selection area in the image as well as the Curves dialog box.

Click on the upper right of the Curves graph line so that the Input is about **190**, then pull straight down until the Output value is about **180**, making sure that the Input value remains at 190 as you perform the move	Reduces the contrast in the upper region–the quartertone–of the selection area, as shown in figure 7.7.

Figure 7.7

Lowering a quartertone's value diminishes contrast in the upper regions of an image's brightness.

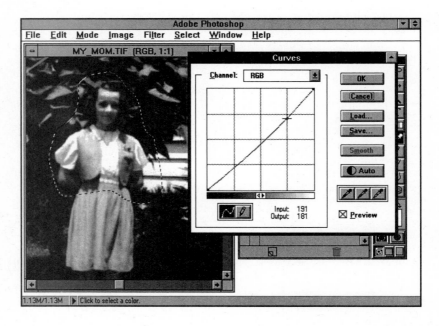

Click on the lower left of the Curves graph line–the lower quartertone –so that the Input value reads **64**, and then pull straight up until the Output value is **74**, making sure that the Input value remains 64 as you do so	Increases the contrast slightly at the bottom end of the midrange.

At this stage, you should have created a shallow, inverted "S" pattern with the graph line, as shown in figure 7.8.

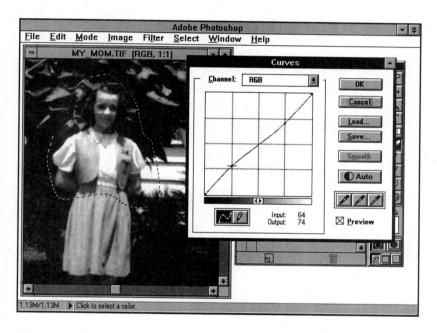

Figure 7.8

Increasing the tonal value in the bottom Quartertone increases contrast and improves image detail.

Click and hold mouse button while moving the cursor over the highlighted area on Mom's forehead in the image	Turns the cursor into an Eyedropper and marks the range of brightness in the forehead area with a little circle on the Curves graph, as shown in figure 7.9.

You may want to write down the Input and Output values at this highlight point because you need to use this figure later. In figure 7.9 the value is 245, but yours may vary depending on the exact position over which you clicked.

Move your cursor over the Curves graph line and stop when the Input and Output values are **245**	Positions your cursor to create a change in this specific brightness point.

continues

continued

Figure 7.9

Choose a specific point of brightness value in an image to adjust using the Curve command's Eyedropper tool.

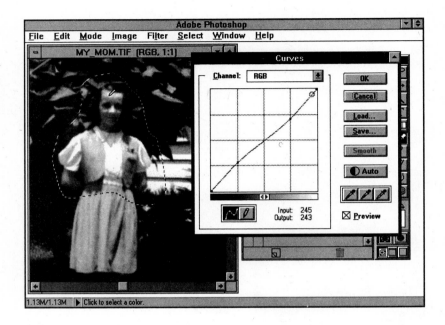

Click on the **255** (White Point dot on the graph), then drag it over to the position of **245** on the graph	Limits the selection area to 245 as the brightest area.

The brightest value possible in the selection area is now the same for the blouse and the forehead highlights. This lessens the contrast and improves the detail in the flesh tones and blouse image areas, as shown in figure 7.10.

Click on OK	Confirms your changes in the Curves dialog box and returns to the Photoshop workspace.
Press Ctrl+D (**S**elect, **N**one)	Deselects the feathered marquee selection in the image.
Press Ctrl+S (**F**ile, **S**ave)	Saves your work up to this point.

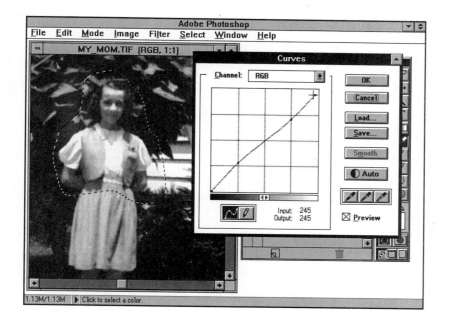

Figure 7.10

Lowering the white point to match a visual highlight in an image adds visual information to lighter areas in the selection.

A "contrary" image, such as the heirloom photo in these exercises, requires that you use a contrary procedure in Photoshop's Curves command. Imaging professionals often speak of an "S" curve in the midrange. An "S" curve is the exact *opposite* of the shape that you defined in the last exercise.

By shaping the Curves graph line like an "S," you add contrast to an image's midrange, and the overall picture gets a little snappier. You add some details in the image's upper shadow areas while losing some in the highlights. By using an *inverted* "S" pattern for the MY_MOM.TIF image in the Curves dialog box, you allocate more of a tonal range to the highlights and lose some detail in the upper shadow, quartertone range.

Fine-tuning selected areas of an image is an important part of your photo-restoration work; we'll get into more of this when modifying color balance. You identify certain aspects of an image's flaws and use Photoshop's precision adjustments to compensate for the flaws. This is the next step in a good work methodology—to go from the general to the specific.

By selecting only the focal point of the image—the subject—then adjusting it to display less harsh contrast, you leave the rest of the image unaffected. The Feather command, when used on a floating selection, destroys image information around the selection edge, but when used on a selection marquee of an area that's already part of the image Background, Feathering turns a hard-edge selection into a soft one.

Tip   If you experience a problem with a specific area in the Curves dialog box, you can achieve more precise control over the image's tonal curve by using the Pencil icon than by clicking and dragging the graph line.

With the Pencil, you draw a new curve in the graph and then click the **S**mooth button several times until you have the Curves mapping that you want.

Understanding the Relativity of Changes

So far, you've made a lot of tonal and color adjustments to MY_MOM.TIF. If you've followed the steps, you can see that the image is coming back to life. But remember, the changes you make are all *relative*—that is, you can't click on an "Absolute" button to return the image to the state it was three or four steps ago.

The "relative" nature of Photoshop also means that you currently might not have the ideal image onscreen, even if you believe you've followed each step in the exercises precisely. For example, if you click on a different white point in the Levels command than what was suggested, all the subsequent changes in the different commands lead you further away from the "ideal" images shown in this chapter's figures.

So how do you know whether you're on track or off-line at this point? It's simple—use your eyes and make your own evaluation. The tonal and color controls aren't automatically predetermined. These exercises are meant to give you an understanding of why and how the controls work, and when you should use them on an image.

Think about the information *behind* the various steps in these exercises. If the exercise tells you to enter a value of 120 when you think 128 looks better, go for it! As long as you understand the *principles* of Photoshop's tonal and color commands, there is no "right" or "wrong" evaluation. It's up to you. Eye-pleasing work is all relative.

Color-Balancing the Color-Corrected Image

While you were using the Variations command, you probably noticed that a good *overall* change in the image's color cast had been made, but that some areas were skewing heavily toward the wrong tint. This tendency is particularly evident in the

New Riders Publishing
INSIDE SERIES

darker areas of the background trees; the More Red option has left them looking parched.

As any good art teacher would gladly tell you, the art to creating a good image (or retouching one) is to work from the general to the specific. You apply broad strokes to a canvas, as you did with the Levels command, then begin to fine-tune specific areas that need more work. The Variations command offers good color control, and the Color Balance command gives you more precise tools for tweaking how each color component of an image "leans" toward its neighboring color values.

Photoshop's Color Balance command lets you separate the various colors in their respective ranges, and refine your initial Variations changes to shift *regions* of color values back in line with what looks most natural.

In the next exercise, you see some dramatic changes in the MY_MOM.TIF image because each primary and secondary additive color on the color wheel model can turn toward its nearest neighboring color, which is its *complementary color*.

The next exercise shows you how to turn the colors *back*.

Balancing the Colors within a Range

Press Ctrl+Y (Image, Adjust, Color Balance)	Displays the Color Balance dialog box, as shown in figure 7.11.
Click on the Midtones radio button	Adjusts the color balance of the midtone range of color pixels; each slider has controls for primary colors and their opposing, complementary color.

Look at the Hue wheel in figure 7.2 again to help understand visually the relationship between the colors you're changing in this exercise.

Enter +15, –5, and –13, in the Color Levels fields, or click and drag the sliders to get these values	Casts the midtone color pixels more toward red than cyan, more toward magenta than green, and more toward yellow than blue.
Click on the Shadows radio button	Applies Color Balance changes to only the darker pixels in the image.
Type –19, +4, and –5 in the Color Levels boxes	Casts the dark, shadow region pixels more toward cyan than red, more toward green than magenta, and more toward yellow than blue.

continues

continued

Click the **H**ighlights radio button	Applies Color Balance changes to only the color pixels that lie in the image's brightest areas.
Type **+6**, **0**, and **–3** in the Color Levels boxes	Creates highlights in the image that are slightly more toward red than cyan, strikes a neutral balance between magenta and green, and is a little more toward yellow than blue.
Click on OK	Confirms your changes and returns you to the Photoshop workspace.
Press Ctrl+S (**F**ile, **S**ave)	Saves your work up to this point.

Figure 7.11

Use the Color Balance command to move primary image colors toward their complement in three specific tonal regions.

Because the color Balance command offers three ranges of brightness—shadows, midtones, and highlights—for color correction, you can color-correct mom's face, which lies mostly in midtone values, and simultaneously "green up" the tree and shrubs a little, with each operation independent of the other. For this reason, you must learn how to evaluate an image with your own eyes, in terms of the flow of the tones and colors in it. It's the only way can you take full advantage of Photoshop's commands.

Isolated Area Color Correction

You'll often find that after global color and tonal correction of an image, further refinements and enhancements require selecting an image area, then modifying the isolated region. This is the point you now come to with the MY_MOM.TIF image. You want to correct the color of the trees while leaving mom's skin tones alone, but "can't get there from here" when the entire image is available for editing.

You've crossed the high hurdles so far in this assignment—the skin tones are accurate, and this means that the rest of your color-correcting is far less critical in restoring the scene. People tend to evaluate an image first on composition, then on the accuracy of skin tones. The background sort of supports the whole image rather than dominating the composition.

Nevertheless, something can be done about the color of the tree and the grass, which has suffered more than the rest of the image because of a traditional, chemical reason. The first photographic emulsions were designed with compounds that didn't age at the same speed; sepia tone photos get this way through the years because the red emulsion retained more of its color property than the other colors. My mom's face and arm areas look like they've retained a lot of their original color, but then again, early photographic film was balanced to record and retain flesh tone colors better than other colors. Uneven aging of color components in a physical medium requires that you separate and isolate the areas, then apply Photoshop's features to a single color area.

Here's the game plan: to hone in on only the leafy and grassy areas of MY_MOM.TIF, you first isolate my mom from the target area. Then you refine the remaining selection areas using the Color Range command. The Color Range command is a "Super Magic Wand" that smoothly selects all image areas based on similar color values. The selected areas lack the hard edge or imprecision around selection areas the Magic Wand sometimes produces.

Here's how to pick the grass and tree and wake them up, color-wise.

Color Balancing a Selection Area

Press **L** on the keyboard (or click on the **Lasso** tool on the toolbox), then click and drag a selection marquee around mom in the MY_MOM.TIF image

Try to leave about 10–15 pixels in diameter around the selection, as shown in figure 7.12.

continues

continued

Choose **S**elect, Fea**t**her, enter **6** in the Feather **R**adius field, then click on OK	Creates a transition between selected areas and masked (protected) image areas, that starts 3 pixels inside the selection edge and ends 3 pixels outside the selection edge.
Choose **S**elect, **I**nverse (Windows: Press Shift+F7) *(There is no Mac equivalent)*	Inverts the selection area; mom is masked, and the background is available for editing.
Choose **S**elect, **C**olor Range	Displays the Color Range dialog box.
Click on the Selection radio button and choose Quick Mask from the **S**election Preview drop-down list	Areas you select in the image will now be displayed on the image as Quick Mask overlay.
Click on the grass with the Eyedropper cursor	Selects the grass in the image and other areas that have the same color value, such as the leaves.
Click on the Eyedropper+ button, then click over grassy areas that aren't selected	Adds the grassy areas to the Color Range selection (see fig. 7.13).
Click and drag the Fuzziness slider until the roof area doesn't display Quick Mask	Fuzziness describes the broadness of colors selected in a range.

Although the best **F**uzziness setting for this step depends entirely upon where you click over in the image, we found that a value of about 20 neatly selected the flora in the image, while leaving the roof out of the Color Range selection.

A lower Fuzziness value excludes similar colors that have different tonal values from the Color Range selection areas.

Click on OK	Returns you to the image on the workspace, and the Quick Mask becomes selection marquees.
Press Ctrl+H (**S**elect, Hide **E**dges)	Hides the marquee *border*; the *selection* is still active however.

The Hide **E**dges command is particularly useful when you have a lot of non-contiguous image areas selected. The marquee is pretty distracting sometimes, isn't it?

Press Ctrl+Y (**I**mage, **A**djust, C**o**lor Balance)	Displays the Color Balance dialog box (see fig. 7.14).

Click on the **M**idtones radio button, then Type **13** in the middle **C**olor Levels field, or click and drag the slider	Casts the midtone color pixels in the selection more toward green than magenta.
Click on the **S**hadows radio button, then enter **−4**, **+4**, and **−12** in the **C**olor Levels boxes (or click and drag the sliders)	Casts the dark, shadow region pixels more toward cyan than red, more toward green than magenta, and much more toward yellow than blue.
Click on the **H**ighlights radio button then enter **−5**, **13**, and **−33** in the Color Levels boxes (the sliders are actually better to use)	Creates highlights in the Type image that are slightly more toward cyan than red, more green than magenta, and much more toward yellow than blue.

These are the *author's* perceptions of the right color balance for the foliage; please feel free to adjust the color balance for the three ranges according to what you now see on your own monitor!

Click on OK	Applies the changes.
Press Ctrl+D (Select, None)	Deselects the marquee selection in the image.
Press Ctrl+S (**F**ile, **S**ave)	Saves your work up to this point.

Figure 7.12

Use a Feathered selection to isolate the subject from the background when making color corrections.

Figure 7.13

Use the Color Range command to select the green foliage in the image.

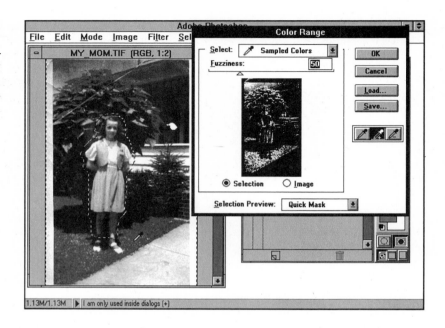

Figure 7.14

Remove the color-casting of a complementary color by clicking and dragging on the sliders.

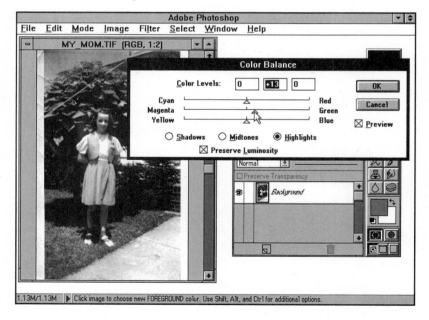

Like the Levels and Curves commands, the color balance command creates a relative change to current image values. However, the Color Balance command does not redistribute pixel values; instead, it moves the colors toward their complementary opposites. Because the Color Balance command changes selected image areas in this way, you can use it on an image twice or more without worrying about clipping.

Manually Editing a Color Range Selection

There's one more area in MY_MOM.TIF that needs color balancing before you're done restoring the scanned image. The dress my mom was wearing was powder blue, yet it presently looks like its been through several thousand machine washes. Although you've come a long way in suppressing the neutral shades of this image to expose original color values, the dress area still has a fair amount of neutral gray in it. Because you've left the color balance alone in this image area, mom's dress still shares a lot of the same tonal and color similarities as the rest of the areas you haven't enhanced.

To clean up the dress, you need to use the Color Range command again to isolate most of the dress area from other areas, then save the selection to an Alpha channel. You'll then be able to remove unwanted selection areas from the saved selection using the Eraser tool.

Here's how to manually edit a saved selection.

Creating a Selection for the Dress

Choose **S**elect, **C**olor Range, then click on the skirt area of the dress	Selects the color range of the dress in the image.
Click and drag the Fuzziness slider to about **50**	Includes more of the dress in the selection, but also includes facial and background areas (see fig. 7.15).

You're doing fine; the extraneous areas selected by the Color Range eyedropper are okay to include in the selection. They're too close to the color range in mom's dress, but you'll manually edit them out of the selection before applying color balance. Your goal is to select parts of the dress area. You'll add a hint of color here and there to the selections—you don't need to select all of the dress perfectly.

Click on OK, then click on the Channels tab on the Layers palette, and click on the Selection icon (far left, bottom on the palette)	Creates a saved selection from the marquee selections.

continues

continued

Press Ctrl+D (**S**elect, **N**one), then click on the Channel #4 title on the Channels palette	Deselects the marquee to the saved selection, and displays the selection as grayscale data in the Channel #4 view.

See Chapter 6, "The Photoshop Test Drive," for a more detailed explanation of how saved selection information becomes grayscale information in Alpha channels.

Press **E** on the keyboard, then press Enter	Chooses the Eraser tool, and displays the Options for the tool.
Press **D** on the keyboard (or click on the **d**efault colors icon on the toolbox)	Makes white the current background color. You'll now remove foreground color to expose white background color with the Eraser tool.
Choose Paintbrush from the Eraser Options drop-down list, set the Opacity to **100%**, then click on the Brushes tab and click on a small tip from the middle row	Sets the characteristics of the Eraser tool to 100% with a medium, soft edge.
Press Ctrl++key, then scroll the image window so that you can see the dress selection	Zooms you into a good viewing resolution for editing the selection information in the Alpha channel.
Click and drag over areas that clearly don't describe the dress	You're removing selection information about the sidewalk, mom's face, and other areas whose color balance doesn't need to be changed (see fig. 7.16).

Alternatively, you can load the selection information as a Quick Mask (see Chapter 6), then edit the Quick Mask with the Eraser tool. The disadvantage to doing this is that the dark pixels (representing selection areas) are easier to see, hence easier to remove, when displayed as black against white.

Press Ctrl+S (**F**ile, **S**ave)	Saves your work up to this point.

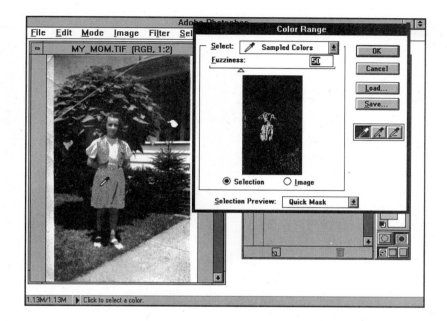

Figure 7.15

The Color Range command's inaccuracy can be corrected by editing the saved selection areas.

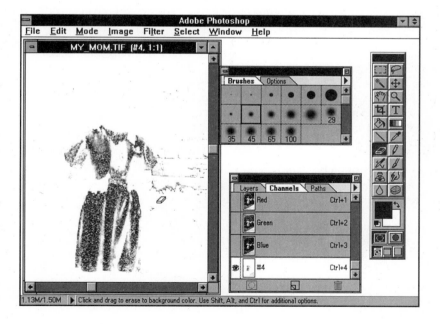

Figure 7.16

Selection areas can be removed before Photoshop loads them again by erasing the black selection areas to white background color.

Stop   Most of the exercises in this book begin with the presumption that you have saved selections defined in the Channel Options command as Color Indicates: Color Areas. You can set this option by double-clicking on the Quick Mask button on the toolbox, and also by clicking on the pop-up menu on the Channels palette in the view of a user-defined Alpha channel. The authors find that it's a lot more visually straightforward to represent a saved selection as black, while masked (protected) areas are represented in white.

You have the option to define either selections or masks in either color; however, you won't get the intended results of the last exercise, or many to follow, if you have masks defined as black and selections defined as white. See Chapters 4 and 5 for more detailed information on how to view an Alpha channel and for setting up your own Photoshop options.

Using Color Balance and Color Range

If you explored Photoshop 3 on your own before picking up this book, you may have come across some incredible-sounding commands under the Image, Adjust menu. If so, you're probably wondering why the Selective Color or Replace Color commands haven't been used to alter the heirloom image.

The Selective Color and Replace Color commands on the Image menu are inappropriate for this assignment because you want to modify colors, not substitute values. As a digital designer (and retoucher, and artist, and...) you have a unique opportunity with Photoshop to break with the tradition of using subtractive color, in the form of physical pigments and dyes, to bring an image back from sepia-land. Selective Color and Replace Color are demonstrated in other chapters in this book, but for this chapter they are inappropriate because both commands alter original image information.

Notice also that we haven't picked up the Paint Brush, or any other painting tool in this entire chapter. Instead, we have pushed and moved existing color material to *restore* image information to a balance that reveals image detail.

The Color Range command gives you the opportunity to select a color range, add to it or subtract from it, then use the selection area it creates to *adjust* the component colors found in the underlying image. In the next exercise, you'll conclude the restoration phase of this assignment by color-balancing the edited selection area of Mom's dress.

Here's how to bring out the color in the dress, without the environmental concerns of phosphor waste.

Revealing the Original Color in the Dress

Press Alt and click on the Channel #4 icon, then click on the RGB channel title	Loads the edited selection area, and displays it as a marquee in the color composite view of MY_MOM.TIF.
Press Ctrl+Y (**I**mage, **A**djust, C**o**lor Balance)	Displays the Color Balance dialog box.
Click on the **M**idtones radio button, then enter **–7**, **–17**, and **23** in the **C**olor Levels boxes (see fig 7.17)	Creates midtones in the dress that are slightly more toward cyan than red, more magenta than green, and much more blue than toward yellow.

At this point, you have the option of moving colors to their complementary opposites for the Shadow and Highlight areas, but it's not really necessary. Sometimes, moving the Color Balance in one tonal range is enough to bring out the original values, and too much Color Balance creates a hand-tinted effect, which is very artificial. Besides, there are no true highlights in the selection area, so the Highlights Color Balance wouldn't produce a noticeable effect.

Click on OK	Applies the Color Balance.
Choose Save a Cop**y** from the **F**ile menu, save the image as MY_MOM2.TIF, and don't check mark the Include **A**lpha Channels check box	Creates a copy of your work to the new file name, and deletes Channel #4, which you no longer need.

The Save a Cop**y** command differs from the Sa**v**e As command. When you choose Save As from the File menu, the copy of an image you Save As becomes the present document in the workspace. However, Save a Copy creates a copy of the active image on the workspace to hard disk, and you're still working with the unsaved image. The Save a Cop**y** command is intended primarily as an option to save a copy as a "standard" bitmap image (no Alpha channels, no proprietary layers), but you now have an image that can be compared to the original without worrying about identical name and file format conflicts.

Figure 7.17

*Use the Color
Balance
command
sparingly to bring
out original color
values in the
selection area.*

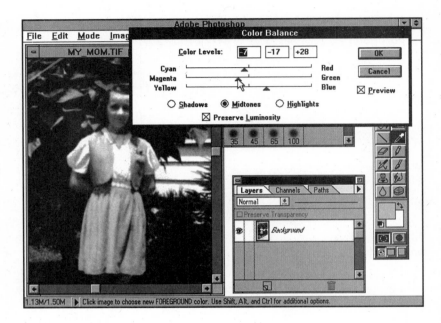

Reviewing Your Work

If you've performed the steps without a break in this chapter, you have a commendable persistence, a healthy eagerness to advance your imaging skills, and probably are suffering from retinal fatigue! This is too bad (the retinal fatigue part) because you've advanced this heirloom image so far from its original state of repair, my own mother wouldn't recognize it.

If you open the MY_MOM2.TIF image from your hard disk, and then re-open the MY_MOM.TIF image from the *Inside Photoshop 3* Bonus CD, then scale the images so that the windows are of equal resolution and dimensions, you'll see the difference a little pixel-pushing can offer when an image has poor contrast and color balance.

For just a moment, look *beyond* the technical details and simply admire the results of your photo-restoration work. It's awe-inspiring what you can do for an image after you have been introduced to Photoshop's restoration features and understand the principles behind them. Figure 7.18 is a before and after comparison.

Tip   Photoshop for Windows supports tiled document windows. Choose **W**indow, **T**ile as a shortcut for creating equally proportioned image windows on Photoshop's workspace.

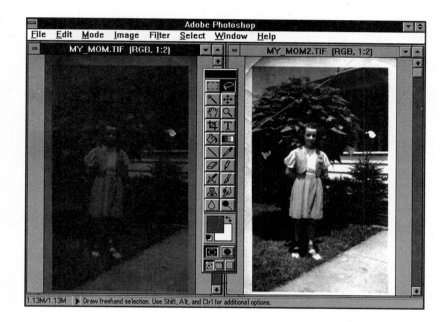

Figure 7.18

A digital copy of a physical original, restored to readability by filtering out unwanted data.

The MY_MOM photo is by no means a complete work of art: the surface has abrasions, a lens flare, and a chemical stain that need expert attention with the aid of Photoshop. Restoring the color to an aged photo is only half the trick to bringing it back to life.

Chapter 8 focuses on Photoshop's tools more than its menu commands. Although the commands in the **A**djust submenu contribute heavily to restoring faded colors, they can't do much to correct the damage a photo suffers from being passed from hand to hand. Nicks, dents, and a camera lens flare are all spoiling the picture of my mom at age 11. If you or a client has an image as valuable and as tarnished as MY_MOM.TIF, you'll definitely want to explore the tricks revealed in Chapter 8, "Retouching an Heirloom Photograph," for removing these defects.

Retouching an Heirloom Photograph

In Chapter 7 you used commands from Photoshop's **A**djust menu to remove a layer of sepia dullness from an heirloom photograph. These commands restored enough visual content in the image so that you could evaluate the color information, then color-correct and balance it.

Enhancing an image that has weathered over a few years brings out both desired and *un*desired visual elements in the digital sample. By the end of your retouching work in Chapter 7, the MY_MOM2.TIF image now has color and balance, but also a few cracks and other flaws that make the picture less than presentable. Fortunately, you can use Photoshop's selection and painting tools to re-create the damaged areas. These problems require a special use of Photoshop features, which is where the second phase of fixing an heirloom photo begins.

Your best tool in Photoshop is your own resourcefulness. Even with Photoshop's many features, the program still requires your input, and this means you often must use your eyes and judgment.

Removing Stains from a Photograph

In this chapter, as you retouch different areas of the MY_MOM2 image, each step requires that you identify a problem and then choose the best set of tools for the task. Let's begin with an assessment of the stain to the right of my mom's head, as shown in figure 8.1. When this area was buried in sepia tones along with the rest of the image's visual content, the part it played in the overall image was unclear. Now you clearly see that this stain has obliterated all visual information about an area that was part of the house's shutters.

Assessing the Damage

The image area of the shutters *directly beneath* the stained area has survived, and it can approximate, if not totally replace, the damaged area. Consider this area as source material you can copy to replace the damaged section.

Figure 8.1

Visual information about the shutters on the house has been completely destroyed by a stain in one area.

Second, consider the resolution of the obliterated area. Although you can clearly see a pattern in the shutters, the number of pixels that represents the shutters, when compared to the whole image, is relatively small. If you set the Info palette to measure inches (on the pop-up menu: Palette Options, Mouse Coordinates), then click and

drag a rectangular marquee selection around the missing shutter area, the stain on the image is only about 40 pixels wide! That's not much information to work with, but it's also not a lot to retouch. In such instances, adopt the credo "less is more;" it's the key to disguising the blemish in this image. If you try to get fancy or overwork the area, the retouching will be obvious.

The best approach is to copy an area of *un*damaged shutter image in the next exercise, then paste the copied selection directly over the photo's stained area. This won't be a perfect "fix" for several reasons, all of which will be discussed shortly. Copying and pasting is only the beginning of several steps you'll perform to complete the image retouching, and through the steps, you'll learn a little more about how Photoshop's integrated feature set makes work easy!

Copying and Pasting To Correct an Image

Open the MY_MOM2.TIF image you saved in the last chapter if it is not already open in your workspace.

If you skipped Chapter 7 and only want to learn the techniques for retouching a damaged image, MY_MOM2.TIF is in the CHAP08 subdirectory of the Bonus CD that came with this book. This image was retouched by the authors using the techniques covered in Chapter 7.

Press **Z** (or click on the **Z**oom tool on the toolbox), then click and diagonal drag around the window in the image	Displays a closer view of the area.

A good viewing resolution to start with is 2:1.

Press **M** once or twice (or press Alt(Option) and click on the **M**arquee tool to choose the Rectangular marquee tool)	Selects a rectangular area within the photo.
Click and drag a marquee around the stain area in the image	Defines a selection border you'll move to encompass an undamaged image area to use as a replacement.
Press Ctrl+Alt(Cmd+Option) inside the marquee, then click and drag the marquee down until it encompasses an undamaged shutter area	Ctrl+Alt moves *only* the marquee, not the image area underneath when you click and drag (see fig. 8.2).

continues

continued

Choose <u>S</u>elect, <u>F</u>loat (Ctrl(Cmd)+J), Ctrl(Cmd)+H (<u>S</u>elect, Hide <u>E</u>dges)	Creates a copy of the image then press area the marquee is over, and becomes a floating selection. Ctrl+H hides the marquee so that you can see the work area better.
Click and drag the floating selection up until the selection covers the stained area	Roughly positions the copy of the shutters.
Press the arrow keys until the wooden shutter pattern in the selection matches the surrounding shutter pattern (see fig. 8.3)	Arrow keys are used to nudge a selection by one pixel in any direction.

The alignment can't be perfect, so accept an eye-pleasing, if somewhat imperfect, match. At a 1:1 view, this dark background area won't be noticed.

Press Ctrl(Cmd)+D (<u>S</u>elect, <u>N</u>one)	Deselects the floating selection, and composites the selection into the background image.
Choose <u>F</u>ile, Sa<u>v</u>e As, then save the image in the PSD format (from Save File as Format <u>T</u>ype drop-down list) to your hard disk	Saves your work up to this point. You want Photoshop's format for this assignment, because you'll be defining Layers for the image later.

The Ctrl+Alt (on the Macintosh: Cmd+Option) key combination in Photoshop lets you move a selection marquee without moving the image area it describes, which is a nice time saver when you need to measure replacement areas without depending on Rulers or the Info palette. After you've marquee selected a damaged image area, the marquee can be moved to an area that has suitable content for copying and covering the exact dimensions of the damaged area. You can't move a selection marquee to a different image window, however, without copying the image area the marquee describes.

When you retouch a photo, maintaining its credibility is of prime concern. By copying the undamaged shutter area to cover the stain, you maintained credibility and aesthetically helped the image in a number of ways. First, the shuttered window is in the background, which is not where most people will focus when viewing a picture with a person in it. Second, the area is dark and low in contrast, which makes it easier to retouch without drawing suspicion.

Finally, because the resolution of the area is small, it's not made up of many pixels. This means that a relatively small effort is required to touch up the selection area because there aren't that many pixels to paint (which is what you'll do next).

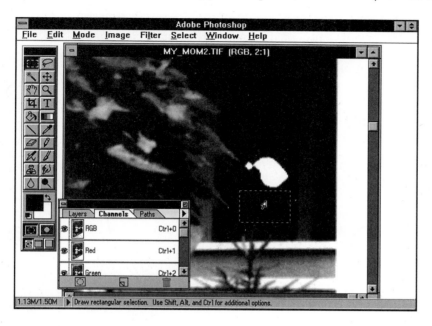

Figure 8.2

Copy an area that's of the same dimensions as the area you need to replace.

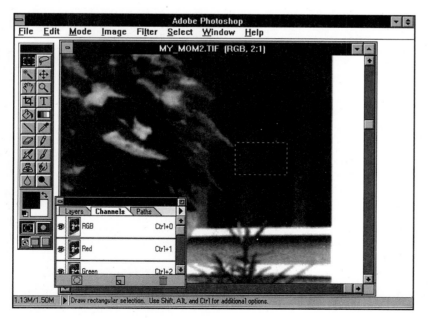

Figure 8.3

Use the keyboard arrow keys to nudge a selection one pixel per keystroke.

Fixing Edgework with the Smudge and Blur Tools

Although the copied selection has visual content that should be identical to the damaged area, its position relative to the camera at the time it was taken was slightly different. Perspective and the natural distortion of a camera lens portray patterns that are slightly different from those perceived by the human eye.

In the next exercise you'll visually integrate the copied area with its surroundings by using the Smudge and Blur tools. Both tools reduce original image detail in different ways, but help accomplish a common goal.

Here's how to add a few Photoshop strokes to the edges of the copied area to make it blend in seamlessly when MY_MOM2.PSD is viewed at a 1:1 resolution.

Blending with the Blur and Smudge Tools

Press Ctrl(Cmd)++ twice	Zooms you into a 4:1 viewing resolution of the area you're working on and expands the image window.

Use the window scroll bars to position the shutter area so that you can see the area you composited in the last exercise.

Press **U** (or click on the Smudge tool on the toolbox), then press Enter	Chooses the Smudge tool and displays the Options for the tool.
Set the Pressure at about 40%, then click on the Brushes tab on the palette and choose the leftmost tip in the second row	Sets the characteristics of the Smudge tool.
Click and drag a short stroke upwards on the frame of the shutter	Eliminates the hard edge between original image and the selection you patched in earlier (see fig. 8.4).
Make short strokes over any other area that displays the edge of the selection that was composited into the background image	Reduces image detail, but also gets rid of any tell-tale edges.

Use the Smudge tool sparingly in your own retouching assignments. A short stroke can perfectly blend a few pixels together; "painting" with the Smudge tool can ruin the focus and detail in an image.

Press **R** (or press Alt(Option) and click on the Blur tool) until the Blur tool is chosen	Pressing Alt and clicking on the tool toggles the tool options from Sharpen to Blur.
Use the same brush tip you currently have selected, but set the mode to Normal and the Pressure to 50% on the Focus Tools Options palette	Sets the characteristics for the Blur tool.
Click and drag in short strokes over any area that displays harsh contrast along the image edge where you composited	The Blur tool reduces contrast between pixels in the area you click and drag over (see fig. 8.5).
Press Ctrl(Cmd)+S (**F**ile, **S**ave)	Saves your work up to this point.

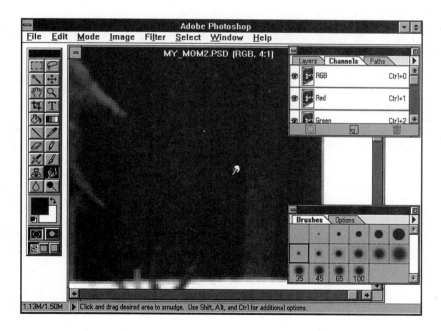

Figure 8.4

The Smudge tool moves pixel colors to neighboring areas, blending colors together and destroying image detail.

Because the selected area is small and composed of only a few pixels, you don't have to use the Blur and Smudge tools extensively to fix the edges and smoothly blend the copy of the shutters into the background image of MY_MOM2. Often, you'll need to spend a little time on a seemingly unimportant image element, such as the shutters, to restore the focus of attention in an image. The shutters now play the proper role in MY_MOM.PSD—background detail that will be ignored by the viewer. As you can see in figure 8.6, there's nothing of particular interest going on behind my mom, but if the chemical stain wasn't addressed, a viewer would immediately be drawn to this area, spoiling the intended composition and focal point of the original image.

Figure 8.5

The Blur tool decreases contrast between neighboring image pixels.

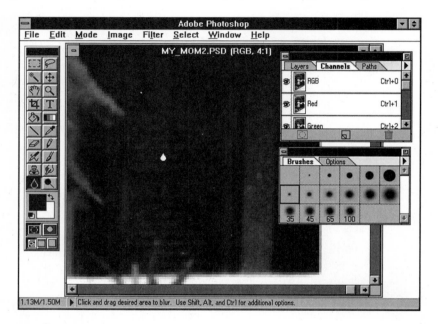

The Smudge tool, as you've just experienced, is the artistic equivalent of mumbling. When you have an area that can compositionally live without great visual detail, "fake it" with the Smudge tool. Try using the Smudge tool in your own assignments in different Paintbrush modes. The Smudge tool doesn't add color to an image. Instead, it "pushes" existing color around to blend areas together. If you want to begin a Smudge stroke with a sample color, click on the Finger Painting check box on the Smudge Options palette.

Always remember that the best use of the Smudge tool is when you have a *direction* for the "wet paint" in the image to flow. In other words, use the Smudge tool *from* an area *to* another area. Never drag the Smudge tool back and forth in one area, unless you want to create an abstract painting within a photo.

Tip   We'll go out of our way on occasion in these exercises to describe a particular Brushes tip for use with a painting or editing tool, and these are suggestions based on personal experience. However, don't take these recommendations as descriptions of all-purpose brush tips. When working on your own assignments, you'll have to experiment to see what brush tips meet the needs of the assignment. Recommending a "general purpose" tip in this book, therefore, becomes similar to recommending a general purpose car. Unless someone is made aware of the specifics of an assignment, it's difficult to make meaningful recommendations. We can, however, give you some guidance on where to start with your experimentation.

You'll get the best results in Photoshop if you scale the tip you use in proportion to the resolution of the image area you're working on. The last exercise, for example, recommended you use the 5-pixel-diameter soft brush. The reason why this is an optimal tip for our assignment is because the image area requiring retouching was less than 200 square pixels total. As a rule, if you can clearly see the pixels in an image at a 2: or 4:1 viewing resolution, use a tip that's only 1-5 pixels in diameter for retouching small image details. By specifying a very small tip, you ensure that your retouching tool is in proportion to the image area that's being retouched.

Figure 8.6

Keep image elements in perspective when you retouch; background elements shouldn't call attention to themselves.

Fixing Chipped Emulsion with the Rubber Stamp Tool

The next area you need to fix is the upper right corner of the image. Some of the emulsion on the original photographic print chipped off, and the flatbed scanner used to acquire the image compounded the flaw by bouncing a highlight off the image.

Tip
You shouldn't press a photo tightly against the glass plate of a flatbed scanner when trying to avoid reflections. Many people place heavy books on the top of the scanner's image window to make sure the source image is flat. This is a mistake because it distorts the surface of the photographic emulsion. Your acquired digital image can end up with blobs like those you see when someone presses their face against a plate glass window.

Strive to get the best scan of an image without exerting unreasonable force to hold a photo in place beneath a flatbed scanner's platen. Then use Photoshop to correct whatever surface detail needs fixing.

Your first move in fixing the upper right corner is to find an undamaged area next to the damaged rain gutter and eaves. You use the Rubber Stamp tool to take samples from the undamaged area and clone the sampled areas over the damaged areas. Precision around the photo's edge is not of prime concern in the next exercise. Don't worry about running into the white photo border; you'll replace the border later. You can delete any errant cloning strokes into the top edge when you define the new border.

Before using the Rubber Stamp tool, notice the diagonal lines that make up the eaves. You'll get the best results with your cloning work if you take your sample directly on an edge of the eaves in the image and then start cloning along the same edge in the damaged image area.

Here's how to align your sample point with the Rubber Stamp tool, so that you can repair the rain gutter and preserve the geometric flow of this image area.

Fixing a Defective Edge with Cloning

Press Ctrl(Cmd)+− twice	Zooms you out two fields of view from your current (4:1) viewing resolution so that you can see the area that needs work.
Scroll or use the Hand tool to reposition the image in the window to show the image's upper-right corner	This is the area you'll work on next.

New Riders Publishing
INSIDE SERIES

Press **S** (or click on the Rubber Stamp tool), then on the Options palette, choose Normal Mode, Clone (aligned) from the drop-down list, and 100% Opacity	Sets the Rubber Stamp tool to move the sampling point synchronously with your cloning brush tip.
Click on the Brushes tab on the palette, then choose the second, middle row tip	Sets the size and hardness of the Rubber Stamp tip.
Hold the Alt(Option) key, then click on a point on the border of the eaves to the left of the damaged area	Sets the traveling sampling point for the Rubber Stamp tool.
Release the Alt(Option) key, then click and drag on the edge of the eaves in the damaged area, moving the cursor diagonally (following the edge) to the right	Replaces the image area beneath the cursor with image samples to the left in the image.

You are creating the border of the eaves by clicking and dragging in an area similar to that of the sample point, as shown in figure 8.7.

Click and drag a diagonal stroke above the first stroke, moving from left to right	The Rubber Stamp samples and clones the eaves in the same diagonal direction as the eaves in the photo.
Continue clicking and dragging single strokes until you've retouched the damaged area	Use diagonal strokes that match the angle of the house as it was photographed.
Press Ctrl(Cmd)+S (**F**ile, **S**ave)	Saves your work up to this point.

Setting a sample point that's on a diagonal line and then setting your initial cloning strokes on the same line helps you clone an entire area that was at an angle from the camera's point of view.

Figure 8.7

Set an initial sample point, then clone an area that's on the same diagonal plane and contains the same image details.

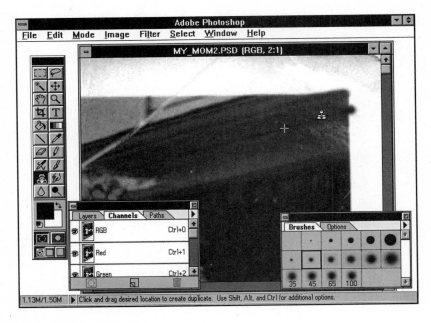

Burning In Lens Flare

The MY_MOM2 image is also marred by a circular lens flare, which wasn't revealed until the sepia tones were removed from the image in the last chapter. Besides photographic film being in its infancy and my mother in her childhood, the lens on Uncle Alan's camera wasn't the most precise contributor to this photograph.

You can correct the lens flare by using a handy digital equivalent to the dodging and burning templates that a chemical photographer uses. In the chemical photography darkroom, underexposed areas are burned in using a cardboard cut-out that is moved under the condenser head as the light shines through the negative onto photographic paper. The result is an area with soft edges that has received more light and becomes darker.

In the *digital* darkroom, the Toning tool, when set to Burn mode, increases Saturation, decreases Brightness, and leaves the Hue component of pixels alone. The nontechnical, photographic effect, however, is remarkably close to that achieved in the chemical darkroom.

Here's how to eliminate the lens flare without altering the color quality of the image.

Eliminating Lens Flare

Press **H** (or click on the **H**and tool on the toolbox), and then click and drag the image up and to the right	Moves the image in the window. Stop when you can see the area to the left of my mom. The leaves on the tree require some burning in.
Press **O** ("oh," not zero) until the Burn tool is displayed on the toolbox (or press Alt(Option) and click on the Toning tool on the toolbox)	Chooses the Burn tool.

This sets the Toning tool to Burn mode, which is the only mode in which you need to use the Toning tool in this exercise; no dodging is required. You can also choose Burn mode from the Options drop-down list when the Toning tool is selected.

Set the Options: mode to Midtones, click and drag the Exposure slider to 50%, and then choose the middle tip, second row on the Brushes palette	Assigns to the Burn tool characteristics that primarily affect the midtones in the image and applies burning at a mild, 50% intensity.
Click and drag over the lens flare once or twice until you remove it	Burns in the area to match the surrounding, unselected areas, as shown in figure 8.8.
Scroll over to other image areas that require burning in, then click and drag with the Burn tool	Only click and drag over areas that display too much brightness.
Press Ctrl(Cmd))+S (**F**ile, **S**ave)	Saves your work up to this point.

The Toning tool is best used to correct an underexposed or overexposed area by choosing a Brushes tip that will cover the area with a minimum of strokes. The effect is very concentrated, and for that reason, you shouldn't use repeated strokes. You can easily over-burn an area.

The Toning tool has two other modes: the Dodge tool mode (see Chapter 11, "Using Paths, Selections, and Layers"), which performs the inverse function of the Burn tool (it increases brightness); and the Sponge tool mode, which changes the saturation of areas.

Figure 8.8

*Use a soft tip and
low Exposure
setting to burn in
areas evenly with
one or two strokes.*

Smoothing Out Saturated Pixels

If you've looked at other areas of this image while retouching, you may have noticed that mom's right forearm is a little funky. Certain areas have become oversaturated with color while neighboring pixels still contain a fair amount of gray component. The contrast within the area gives the appearance of video *noise*—the random distribution of color pixels in an image.

The best tool for correcting this kind of noise is the Focus tool in Blur mode. This mode decreases the contrast in an image area by increasing the similarity of the grayscale components in color pixels, as you did to integrate the shutter area with the rest of the image earlier. The next exercise provides a quick example of how the Blur tool smoothes out the noise in an image area without affecting original color values.

Blurring an Oversaturated Detail

Press **H** (or click on the **H**and tool), then click and drag the image up until you see my mom's right forearm

Positions the image for editing.

New Riders Publishing
INSIDE
SERIES

Press **Z** (for **Z**oom tool), then click once over the forearm area	Zooms you into a 4:1 viewing resolution. The Zoom tool moves you in and out of an image by a factor of 2.
Click on the Blur (Focus) tool, choose Normal mode on the Focus Tool Options palette, click and drag the Pressure to about 80%, then click on the third smallest Brushes palette tip	Sets the characteristics for the Blur tool.
Click and drag a maximum of three separate strokes in the forearm area	Gives the "noise" (random pixels) brightness values closer to the normal, neighboring pixels (see fig. 8.9)
Press Ctrl(Cmd)+S (**F**ile, **S**ave)	Saves your work up to this point.

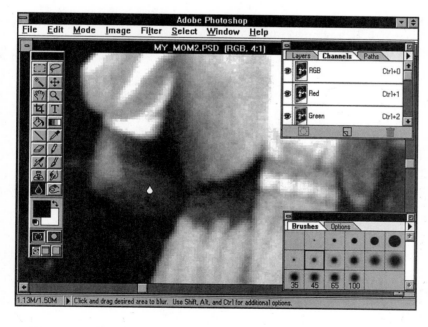

Figure 8.9

The Blur tool averages out the grayscale values of pixels in the selection area.

The Blur setting of the Blur/Sharpen tool operates on a principle similar to that of Photoshop's Blur filters. As you saw in this exercise, the tool is quite useful in diminishing the contrast between pixel brightness in an area without disturbing color information. If a 4:1 viewing resolution of an area looks okay, you can be certain that the image will look and print fine at 1:1.

Reducing Random Saturation

Because Photoshop provides you with separate views of the channels in an RGB image, you can perform editing work in a single color channel. If you have an image in a condition similar to MY_MOM.TIF, try the following steps to reduce random saturation in an area:

◆ Select the area with the Lasso tool, and use <u>S</u>elect, Fea<u>t</u>her to soften the edge where the selection meets the masked areas.

◆ Click on each color channel title on the Channels palette until you find the channel that displays the most random pixelation.

◆ Choose Gaussian Blur, and set the <u>R</u>adius anywhere from **0.5** to **1** pixel, and click on OK.

Return to the RGB composite view of the image, check the results, and press Ctrl+Z (<u>E</u>dit, <u>U</u>ndo) if you're not satisfied. Color channel editing causes some color shifting because you're reassigning brightness values for a single RGB component of a pixel. This trick is worth remembering as an alternate to blurring an area in the RGB view of an image.

Cloning with a Pattern Sample

In addition to messing up my mom's forearm, a combination of aging chemicals and the color correction you performed in the last chapter has introduced a random pattern of saturated pixels in my mom's legs. The random effect is so pronounced, in fact, that it would be a futile effort to use the Blur tool to reduce pixel contrast. The Blur tool is terrific for small areas, but it shouldn't be used as a painting tool over noticeable image detail areas.

The solution for the pixel problem is to replace the leg areas with a sample pattern of a leg area that *isn't* ruined. You'll be painting with the Rubber Stamp tool in the next exercise. This is where the fine artist in you will be much more useful than your photographic skills. You're actually going to be editing the visual content of the image using a painting technique.

Here's how to restore an image area with a pattern sample and a lot of intuitive guesswork!

Image Restoration through Pattern Sampling

Press **M** (**M**arquee tool)	The Rectangular tool should still be displayed from the preceding exercise.
Use the window scroll bars to move the view to my mom's legs area	Moves to the next area to be edited.
Marquee-select an area of the leg that shows the best original image detail and displays the most even shading	You're selecting a pattern area you'll use to clone in areas of the legs that are damaged (see fig. 8.10).

When defining an area you want Photoshop to read as pattern information, make sure you pick an area that displays little or no shading. When the area filled with a pattern is larger than the area the pattern was created from, the pattern *repeats*. A repeating pattern can display hard, visible edges if it doesn't have consistent color and detail qualities.

Choose **E**dit, **D**efine Pattern	Tells Photoshop to hold the selected image area in memory for use with the Fill command, the Paint Bucket tool, and the Rubber Stamp tool.
Press Ctrl(Cmd)+D (**S**elect, **N**one)	Deselects the area you defined as a pattern.
Press **S** (Rubber **S**tamp), then choose Pattern (non-aligned) from the Options palette drop-down list, set Opacity to about 90%, and choose Normal mode	Sets the characteristics for the Rubber Stamp tool. At partial Opacity, some original image area will show through when you stroke over the image.
Choose a small, soft tip from the middle row on the Brushes palette, then click and drag over a leg area that contains random pixels	Replaces the area with the pattern you defined earlier (see fig. 8.11).
Very carefully, click and drag around the edges of the legs where they meet the dark background	If you're not confident about your eye/hand stuff here, you might want to use the Lasso tool to encompass only the leg areas, so the Rubber Stamp can't affect the image background areas.

continues

continued

Stop clicking and dragging when the legs area is restored	Completes the restoration of this image area.
Press Ctrl(Cmd)+S (**F**ile, **S**ave)	Saves your work up to this point.

Tip   The Rubber Stamp's non-aligned pattern option changes each stroke (each click and drag) so that the stamp begins at the center of the sampled pattern and repeats the entire pattern as you lengthen the Rubber Stamp stroke. Conversely, *aligned* pattern cloning starts a stroke in the center of the sampled pattern, and continues to repeat the pattern wherever you click and drag relative to the point where you first start stroking.

Non-aligned pattern cloning is the best method to use in this part of the assignment because, if you use short strokes, you can clone in large image areas without creating a visible tiling effect.

The overall image might not be out of the woods yet, but Mom now looks as though she's out of the poison ivy.

You don't press Alt and click over a sample point in an image when the Rubber Stamp is set to the Pattern option. The sampling point is read from the pattern you defined with the Rectangular marquee tool. A pattern is held in memory until you define a different one. The Pattern (aligned) option was not an appropriate choice in the last example because an aligned pattern tends to display repeating, tiling image information. However, the aligned Pattern option is a very useful one when you're trying to restore a lawn, a tapestry, or similar image elements that clearly *should* display a pattern or texture.

In either case, it's important to define patterns that have as little tonal variation as possible because the moment Photoshop hits the edge of a sample, the pattern is repeated, and tonal variations around the edge of the sample make the repeat pattern obvious. A pattern in Photoshop can only be defined by the Rectangular marquee tool because pixels are rectangular, and patterns should be seamless, with one pixel beginning at the edge of the neighboring pixel.

It's time now to turn our sights to a few of the more noticeable defects in this scanned image, such as the crack in the emulsion running through the tree. Again, you'll use the Rubber Stamp tool in a different option setting to correct this image area.

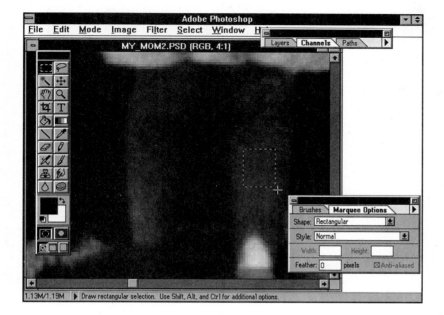

Figure 8.10

Use the Rectangular marquee tool to sample an image area for a pattern.

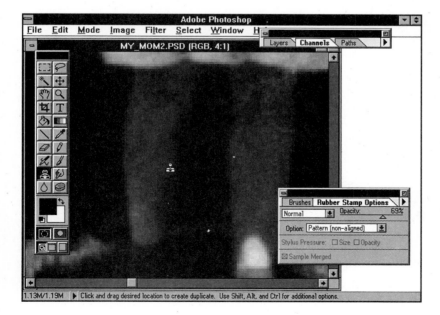

Figure 8.11

Use the Rubber Stamp tool in Pattern (non-aligned) option to "paint" with a sampled image area.

Restoring Organic Patterns

The Rubber Stamp tool in its Clone aligned option setting is great for adding leaves, sand, and other organic material to an area. Masses of material with random patterns are perceived by the human eye as clumps of a single type of material, which people then dismiss without examining closely. When you fix the crack that runs through MY_MOM2.TIF, you can take advantage of the way people perceive background patterns. Even though the image's leaves have clearly defined edges, you can success-fully clone over the crack with samples of other leaf areas, without spending much time trying to match precisely what's missing in adjacent leaves. The viewer's eye won't linger on anything in the background if the overall pattern looks correct at a glance.

Here's how to restore the image area of the tree that's been destroyed by cracked emulsion in the original.

Restoring Foliage

Press Ctrl(Cmd)+– three times, then use the window scroll bars to move your view to the tree area

Ctrl+– moves you out by one field of viewing resolution; you should be at a 1:1 resolution now.

Choose Clone (aligned) from the Option drop-down list, click and drag the Opacity slider to 100%; click on the Brushes tab, and click on a medium sized, soft tip

Sets the characteristics of the Rubber Stamp tool to sample image areas a fixed amount away from the cloning point.

Press Alt(Option) and click near the top of the tree, below the crack in the photo

Sets the sample point for the Rubber Stamp tool.

Be careful not to click too close to the crack, or you'll be using part of the photo's damaged area for the cloning source.

Place your cursor directly on the crack, above and to the right of the sample point, and then click and drag down along the edge of the crack

Replaces the crack with samples of the tree's leaves, as shown in figure 8.12.

Stop clicking and dragging when the sample crosshair reaches the edge of the photo. You don't want to clone an area of the photo's border into the crack area.

Press Alt(Option) and click the middle of the tree	Resets the sample point for the Rubber Stamp tool.
Click and drag the remaining edges of the crack near the border of the tree	Eliminates the damaged part of the image over the tree.
Press Ctrl(Cmd)++ once, then scroll over to area where the tree touches the house gutter	The emulsion crack runs through this too, and needs attention.
Press Alt(Option) and click directly on the bottom edge of the gutter to the right of the emulsion crack	Sets a new sampling point for the Rubber Stamp tool.
Place the cursor over the emulsion crack, then click and drag	Replaces the cracked area with image area to the right of it (see fig. 8.13).

Your cloning work should be synchronous with similar image detail to the right of your cloning cursor. This is the same technique you used on the upper right of the image earlier in this chapter.

Press Ctrl(Cmd)+S (File, Save)	Saves your work up to this point.

Figure 8.12

To avoid creating patterns in cloned-in areas of an image, reset the sampling point of the Rubber Stamp tool regularly.

The secret to convincing clones in an image with random, organic patterns is to resample the Rubber Stamp's source point constantly. You may also want to vary the size of the Rubber Stamp tool to create a more random effect in the cloned-in areas. The sample point for the Rubber Stamp is always the same pixel diameter as the cloning brush point. When you have a small area of suitable sample material, don't set the brush diameter of the Rubber Stamp tool too large, or your sample will include unwanted fringe areas.

Figure 8.13

Align the area you're replacing (cloning into) with the sampling point you defined in the image.

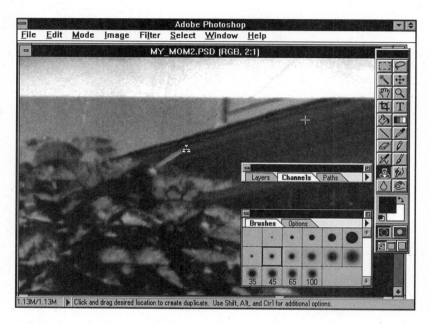

Using Source Material from Another Image

The last sore spot in this picture is the portion of sky in the upper left, which has specks of emulsion imperfections in it—it's the wrong color for a sunny sky. When compared to the rest of the work you've performed to enhance and restore the image, the sky is a wreck!

It's time to bring out the heavy artillery on this image and actually use a different image of a sky to replace the original sky area. This is an exceptional, drastic measure that you should only consider doing in your own work if you have a suitable stock sky image as a replacement part. Let's ponder this one for a moment.

The MY_MOM2.PSD image, for all the color correction and cloning you've performed, still has the focus of a camera lens that's primitive compared to today's photographic equipment. In addition, the colors you've corrected are balanced within the MY_MOM2 image but won't necessarily "play" well against an added image element whose color balance is not the same. These may seem like insurmountable obstacles, but they are actually factors you need to consider when searching for a suitable sky image to add to the MY_MOM2 photo.

The authors found that the ideal candidate for sky-grafting actually proved to be an image of an overcast sky. GOOD_SKY.TIF is far from being a good photograph—it's hazy, and the clouds are fairly uninteresting looking. However, GOOD_SKY.TIF is an ideal image to replace the sky in MY_MOM2 *because* it is bland and lacks character.

The lesson before the lesson here is don't throw away images you think aren't prize-winners; poor images can be integrated into poor areas of other images to subtly enhance the overall image quality. For example, you'd never want to paste a breathtaking sunset into a photo such as MY_MOM2 because the contrasting image elements would destroy any photographic believability. However, when you replace a sky with one that's a *little* better, you have used your artist's eye, practiced moderation, used your aesthetic judgment wisely, and accomplished a masterstroke of professional image editing.

Setting the Image Up for a Sky Replacement

The strategy here is to define the area that needs replacing in the MY_MOM2.PSD image, then use Photoshop's Paste Into command to replace the image area. However, you'll notice that the tree in the image climbs into the sky. If you were to save the area as a selection, this delicate latticework of leaves and sky would require the creation of an accurate, painstakingly created border. Part of the secret to professional image editing, however, is to see how *alternative* methods can accomplish an effect, then weigh the effectiveness of a technique against how much time it takes.

You may find that selecting irregular image areas is more easily accomplished with a painting tool while an image is in mask mode, rather than using the Lasso tool. If this strikes a chord in you (as it does the authors), the best approach to defining the areas where the sky meets the tree is not to accurately define the tree area while it is in place. Instead, create a rough outline around the tree top, and copy it to a Layer where the Layer Mask can be used to refine the edgework. When you've replaced the sky (obliterating some of the original leaves in the image), the tree leaf Layer can be merged on top of the new sky.

Here's how to "prep" the photograph to preserve image areas before copying the new sky into the image.

Saving a Rough Image Selection

Press Ctrl++, then use the image window scroll bars to center the upper left of the image in the window	Zooms you into a 2:1 viewing resolution of the image and gives you a good view of the area you need to copy.
Press **L** (**L**asso tool), and click and drag around the area where the tree extends into the sky	Creates a marquee selection around the tree's leaves.

You don't have to be incredibly precise with the marquee you're creating. Make sure, however, that all the leaf areas that a new sky selection would cover are within the marquee selection. Peek ahead at figure 8.14 for a more graphical description of the optimal marquee selection.

Choose **S**elect, **F**loat (Ctrl+J)	Creates a floating copy of the selected image area of the leaves.
Click on the pop-up menu triangle on the Layers palette, and choose Make Layer (see fig. 8.14)	Choosing Make Layer displays the Make Layer dialog box.
Accept the default options by clicking on OK	Layer 1 contains a copy of the leaves you marquee selected.
Click on the eye icon next to the Layer 1 title on the Layers palette	Hides the layer from view, but it can be edited by accident because Layer 1 is still the target (active) layer.
Click on the Background title on the Layers palette	Makes the Background image the target layer for editing.
With the Lasso tool, press Alt(Option) and click a rough selection border around the area of sky you intend to replace	See fig. 8.15. All you need to do is accurately define the edge of the house's roof.

Because a copy of the leaves is safely hidden on Layer 1, you don't have to perform any fancy selection work at this point. The new sky selection will cover the leaves on the Background, but these areas won't be used in the finished image.

Click on the Channels tab on the Layers palette, then click on the (convert to) Selection icon (the left, bottom icon)	Automatically saves the selection marquee to a new Channel #4 in the image.

Press Ctrl(Cmd)+S (**F**ile, **S**ave)	Saves your work up to this point.

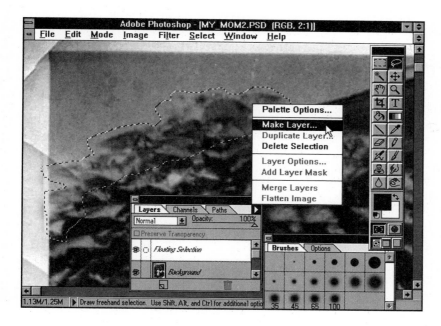

Figure 8.14

Click and drag around the area using the Lasso tool to create a rough selection marquee.

Figure 8.15

Create a selection area that borders the side of the house and roof; the leaves should be included.

Naturally, you'll need to do a little refining work on the hidden leaves on Layer 1 at some point, but you're now free to copy a new sky into the area without worrying about precise image element selection. Your new sky will help clean up the edge of the roof in areas the leaves don't cover, and by hiding a copy of the leaves, you can get a better perspective on the overall image when you add the new sky.

Scaling a Floating Selection

Our perception of color is relative; images appear to have a color-cast based on a different image you might have been looking at a moment ago. You've spent some serious time working on my mom's image through two chapters, and you might be in for a shock when you add the GOOD_SKY image to the MY_MOM2 image in the next exercise.

If you followed the steps since Chapter 7, the overall color balance in the image is good, but the sky isn't sky blue. The sky's color is more like turquoise, but it's *perceived* as the sky because it has more blue than the grass, and its location within the image is appropriate for a sky.

Your perception of the overall image might change soon because the addition of a sky element that's really blue and not turquoise seems to make the rest of the colors in the image take on a different relative hue. Will it be a pleasant change? Will adding a true blue sky drastically change the perception of the color balancing work you've done so far? Let's see!

In the next exercise, you'll copy an area of GOOD_SKY.TIF to the MY_MOM image and use the Scale command to "smush" the image into the relatively narrow selection area you defined for the sky. Like lawn, leaves, sand, and other organic stuff, clouds can be distorted without the viewer taking exception. What you'll gain by dispropor-tionately scaling the sky selection is some soft detail work where the clouds meet the sky. It's a nice touch for the MY_MOM2 image, and adding the background detail doesn't detract from the foreground subject.

Here's how to add an element to MY_MOM2.TIF, and enhance the overall quality of the photo.

Copying/Scaling a New Image Element

Press Alt(Option) and click on the Channel #4 icon on the Channels palette	Loads the Selection area you saved earlier.
Open the GOOD_SKY.TIF image from the CHAP08 subdirectory on the Bonus CD	This is the image that contains the sky you'll use to replace the sky in MY_MOM2.PSD.

With the Rectangular marquee tool, marquee select the sky in the image	You only need the top half of the image (see fig. 8.16).

You'll need to use the Clipboard to move a copy of the selection to the MY_MOM2 image. The smaller a selection you copy, the less stress you place on your system.

Press Ctrl(Cmd)+C (**E**dit, **C**opy), then close the GOOD_SKY.TIF image	Copies the selection to the Clipboard. You don't need the original any more.

MY_MOM2.PSD is now the active image in Photoshop, and the selection you loaded should be visible as a marquee right now.

Choose **E**dit, Paste **I**nto	Pastes the copy of the GOOD_SKY selection into the selection marquee in MY_MOM2.PSD.
Click and drag inside the marquee border so that the pasted into selection is flush with the left side of the MY_MOM2 image	Repositions the floating selection so that much more of the overall selection is to the right of the selection border.

When you issue an Effects command, such as Scale, Photoshop truncates a floating selection (like the one in front of you right now) at the image window edge because a boundary box for Distort effects has to start within the image window. This is why you need to move the selection—if you don't, much more of the image, and a lot of the nice cloud areas, will be lost.

Choose **I**mage, **E**ffects, then **S**cale	A boundary box (the Scale box) appears around the active selection, limited to the image window edge in width.
Click and drag the bottom right corner handle upward and toward the left	Disproportionately scales the selection. You'll see more cloud detail in the area you pasted into (see fig. 8.17).

Stop clicking and dragging the corner handle when you see shrubs from the bottom of the GOOD_SKY copy peeking though the area you pasted into.

Click inside the Scale box	Your cursor turns into a small hammer, and "nails" the selection to the degree of scaling you've specified.

continues

continued

Press Ctrl(Cmd)+D (**S**elect, **N**one), then Ctrl(Cmd)+S (**F**ile, **S**ave)	Deselects the floating selection, and it replaces the original sky in the Background Layer; saves your work up to this point.
With any selection tool, click and drag to define a small image area on MY_MOM2.PSD, then press Ctrl(Cmd)+C (**E**dit, **C**opy)	Copies 2 to 3 KB of image information to the clipboard, replacing the 500 KB or so image currently on it.

"Flushing the Clipboard" is a good practice to reduce demands made on your system when a large image selection is stored in RAM.

Figure 8.16

Select the sky area you want to use as a replacement area for MY_MOM2.PSD.

It's a weird visual phenomenon to have a selection floating behind a Background image, but you can perform any operation, or choose any filter you like to apply to only the selection as long as it hasn't been composited into the background image. By the way, the floating selection has no interaction with the leaves you stashed away on Layer 1. They are safe and secure on their own layer, and will be brought back into the picture in the next section.

If you're wondering why you didn't simply click and drag the sky selection into the MY_MOM2 image in the last exercise, it's because Photoshop 3 does not support drag and drop copying *into* an active marquee selection. Paste **I**nto is sort of a reserved command. You can only click and drag a selection across image windows to copy a selection to a position *in front of* the current image layer.

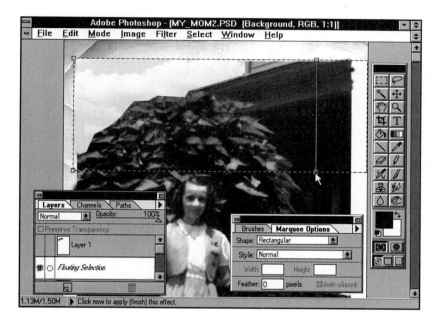

Figure 8.17

Click and drag on a Scale boundary box handle to adjust the width and height of the floating selection.

Digital Pruning and the Layer Mask Option

It's time to make Layer 1 and all the foliage you left behind reappear in this image—rough selection border and all. However, you only need to refine one of the four sides of the leaves; the bottom edge blends into the rest of the tree, so no work is needed here. The left and right side of the leaves sort of trail off from the top of the roof area, so you basically need to trim around five or six leaves to make the Layer 1 selection look as though it's in front of the new sky.

The Layer Mask option is an easy way to preview an image on a layer with areas removed. You can use any painting or selection tool for Layer Mask editing work. Instead of seeing a tinted overlay in areas to which you apply foreground color, Photoshop hides image areas you paint over in Layer Mask mode. However, you don't actually delete the areas that are hidden in Layer Mask mode until you use the Remove Layer Mask command.

Let's walk through this next set of steps for editing out the original sky areas from the leaves on Layer 1. For more information on the Layer Mask mode, check out Chapter 12, "Correcting an Image," and also Chapter 14, "Enhancing Images," which uses the Layer Mask option extensively.

Here's how to take a little off the top and make a perfectly defined selection of only the leaves on Layer 1.

Using the Layer Mask on the Leaves

Click on the Layer 1 title on the Layers palette	Makes Layer 1 visible again and makes it the current (target) layer for editing.
Press **B** (Paint **B**rush tool), then press **D** (or click on the **d**efault colors icon on the toolbox)	Makes the Paint Brush the current tool and specifies black as the foreground color.
Choose Normal mode and 100% Opacity from the Paint Brush Options palette, then click on the Brushes tab on the palette, and click on the far left, middle row tip	Sets the characteristics for the Paint Brush tool.

You'll notice again that the areas you'll remove from around the leaves are quite small in size and resolution. As with the shutters you retouched earlier with the Smudge tool, you need a Brushes tip that's proportional to the image area you're working on—small!

Click on the pop-up menu triangle to the right of the Layers palette tabs, and choose Add Layer Mask (see fig. 8.18)	A blank icon appears to the right of the Layer 1 icon, with a black border around it. This indicates that you're no longer working on Layer 1, but on the Layer Mask corresponding to Layer 1 instead.
Click and drag the Paint Brush over an image area of original sky between the leaves on Layer 1	The area you click and drag over becomes hidden, as shown in figure 8.19.

The following steps are actually variations on the techniques you can use with a Layer Mask in place. These are different ways you can add or remove areas of Layer Mask. Use them to hide or restore areas on the Layer Mask. Remember, when black is the color that is applied, image areas are hidden, and when white is applied, hidden areas are exposed again.

Press **X** (or click on the switch colors icon on the toolbox), then click and drag the Paint Brush over areas you've hidden by mistake	Restores your view of these areas. When white is the current foreground color, applying the color to the Layer Mask restores your view of image areas.

Press **D** (**d**efault colors icon), then press **L** (**L**asso tool); click and drag around an area, then press Delete	Hides the selection area from view, as shown in figure 8.20.
Click and drag around an area with the Lasso tool, then press Alt+Delete	Fills the selection area with hidden areas on Layer 1.

Windows users should exercise caution with the Alt+Delete maneuver. It's one keystroke away from Ctrl+Alt+Delete, which is *not* a Photoshop command—it's a *system* command that warm-boots your PC and ruins your day, at the very least!

When you're sure you have the leaves pruned to perfection, choose Remove Layer Mask from the Layers palette's pop-up menu	Displays a dialog box with Discard, Cancel, and Apply as the options.
Choose Apply	The Layer Mask icon disappears from the palette, as do the image areas you hidden from view on Layer 1. You've made a permanent edit to the leaves on Layer 1.
Press Ctrl(Cmd)+S (**F**ile, **S**ave)	Saves your work up to this point.

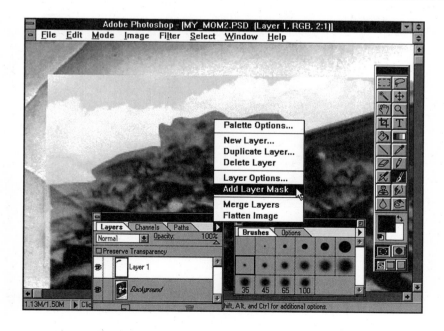

Figure 8.18

The Layers palette pop-up menu.

Figure 8.19

In Layer Mask mode, applying black foreground color hides image areas you click and drag over with a painting tool.

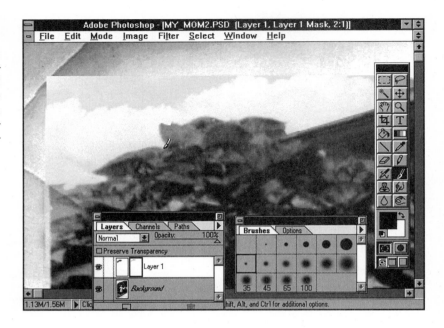

Figure 8.20

In Layer mode, deleting a marquee selection when white is defined for background color hides the area on Layer 1.

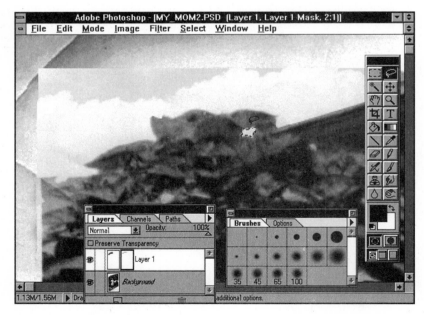

Whether you use a Quick Mask or a Layer Mask as part of your editing work, none of the changes you make to the image file are actually applied to the image. Masks represent proposed changes to an image or Layer; you can't accidentally delete image areas when a Mask is in place.

Hopefully, you found editing away superfluous original sky areas easier to accomplish in the last exercise than the alternative of selecting and trimming with the Lasso tool or Eraser tool. Another benefit with Masks is it's a little easier to see and separate the leaves from a similarly-colored sky when you have an image area of contrasting value, such as the new sky area, on the Background.

Tip   If you want to see exactly where on a Layer Mask you've edited, press Alt(Option) and click on the Layer Mask icon. You'll then see a grayscale representation of your editing work in the image window. You can edit in this view, but you'd be editing without the benefit of seeing the corresponding RGB image areas you want to delete. To return to the normal mode, press Alt(Option) and click again to toggle back.

To get a Quick Mask of your editing work displayed on top of the RGB view of the image, press Shift and click on the Layer Mask icon. Press Shift and click a second time on the icon to remove the Quick Mask view.

Editing the Layers as One Image

You're through refining and editing the edgework on Layer 1, and there's presently no reason not to merge Layer 1 and the Background image together. Although you can use the Blur tool (and Smudge and Toning tools) between image layers by checking the Sample Merged check box on the Options palette, you can conserve system resources *and* perform the same effect when the leaves become part of the Background layer.

If you zoom out of the image now, you'll see that the sky color is harmonious with the original image areas; in fact, the cold blue helps warm up the skin tones of my mom a little. The only quality that identifies your retouching work is the edge, where the leaves meet the sky. This part is too perfect because the focus is apparently too sharp in this one area.

Here's how to soften the edge and make the focus in MY_MOM2.PSD photo graphically consistent:

Merging Layers and Correcting Image Focus

Choose Merge Layers from the Layers palette's pop-up menu	Layer 1 is composited on top of the Background Layer in the mode (Normal) you specified for Layer 1 at the moment you issue the command.
Click on the Blur tool on the toolbox, then click and drag the Pressure slider on the Options palette to about 50%	Chooses the Blur tool and sets the strength to one-half.
Choose a small, soft-edge tip from the second row on the Brushes palette	Defines the size of the tip for Blurring an image area.
Click and drag around the edge where Layer 1's leaves meet the new sky area	Use short strokes; click on a sky area, then drag into the leaves area (see fig. 8.21).

The Blur tool doesn't use foreground or background colors, but it does blur from a color to another color within an image. In Normal mode, you're "moving" the Blur from the sky into the leaves, slightly decreasing the dark edge of the leaves.

Continue clicking and dragging short strokes until the border between the leaves and the sky is as diffuse as other, original image areas	Press Ctrl+Z (**E**dit, **U**ndo) if you've blurred a section of the border too much.
Press Ctrl(Cmd)+S (**F**ile, **S**ave)	Saves your work up to this point.

Partial Opacity, partial Pressure, and partial Intensity all pretty much result in the same thing when you specify a less-than-100-percent value for a painting or editing tool. If you specify 100-percent for the Blur tool's Pressure, for example, you give yourself no option to stroke through an area with the tool a second time, which creates a subtle transition between edited and non-edited areas. You should always consider the "strength" of a color or an effect and give yourself some leeway when using a tool on an image area.

Unless you're trying to cover an area with flat color, experiment with different Options palette settings for a mode, a color, or an effect. The results you'll achieve with, for example, a 50-percent or 70-percent Options palette setting can often produce more photographic results than "pouring on" a tool.

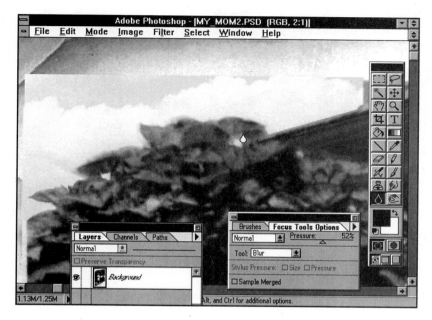

Figure 8.21

Use the Blur tool to create an edge around the leaves that has the same focus as original image areas.

Adding a Border to Your Retouched Piece

The hard work is behind you now, and except for one or two picky details, you've accomplished the near-impossible. If you followed the steps in Chapter 7 and in this chapter, you see that it's a long trail from a damaged, aging photo to a professionally restored one. Photoshop alleviates the tedium and frustration you'd have experienced if you had used traditional chemical photo-retouching methods. MY_MOM2.PSD has many fewer miles on it than before, and the only thing left to retouch is the off-white, dented border of the photo.

You can eliminate the rest of the dents around the border of the photo and clean it up simultaneously by simply deleting the border. As the following exercise demonstrates, the procedure is a quick one.

Creating a Fresh Border

Press **M** (or click on the Rectangular **m**arquee tool)	Creates a rectangular selection area that you can use to replace the original image's border.
Press **D** (or click on the **d**efault colors icon)	Sets the color of the foreground to black and the background to white.
Press Ctrl(Cmd)+S (**F**ile, **S**ave)	Saves your work up to this point.

You should save the file now because if you miss a step in the following process, you'll have to restore the previously saved version.

Double-click the Hand tool	Moves you to a better view of the image.
Marquee-select an area that contains the main elements of the photo, but not the "white" border around it, as shown in figure 8.22	Press Ctrl+Alt to reposition the marquee only (not the image) if you're not happy with the selection.
Choose **S**elect, **I**nverse	Selects everything *except* the image area, so that the photo's border is selected and the retouched work is masked (protected from editing).
Press the Delete key	Removes the selection of the photo's border, which is replaced by a white background color (see fig 8.23).
Press Ctrl(Cmd)+D (**S**elect, **N**one)	Deselects the marquee.
Click on the Channels tab on the Layers palette, press Ctrl+4 (or click on the Channel #4 title), then click and drag the Channel title into the Trash icon	Deletes the Alpha channel you created earlier. It's no longer necessary.
Choose File, Sa**v**e As, then save the image in the TIFF format (from Save File as Format **T**ype drop-down list) to your hard disk	Saves your work in a format that can be read by other applications and operating systems.

Name your work GIRL.TIF or something, though, because it's *my* mom, and probably not yours.

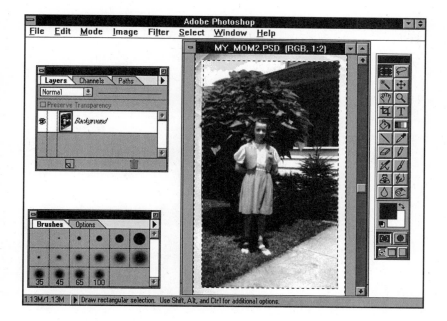

Figure 8.22

Select an area, then choose the Select menu's Invert command to select everything except *the original selection area.*

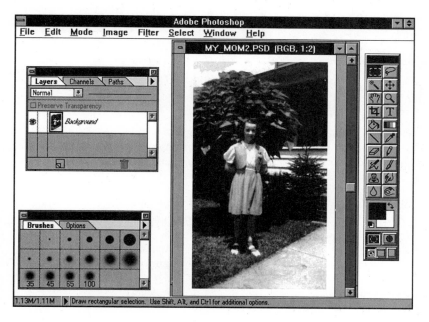

Figure 8.23

Deleting an area exposes background color, the perfect solution to restoring the edge around this photograph.

Figure 8.24 is a triptych of the digital restoration you've done to the image through these past two chapters. All the images you see are also color image files in the GALLERY subdirectory of CHAP08 on the Bonus CD, if you'd like to see the progression in color.

Figure 8.24

MY_MOM—three global adjustments, five tools, a sky graft, and a Layer Mask later.

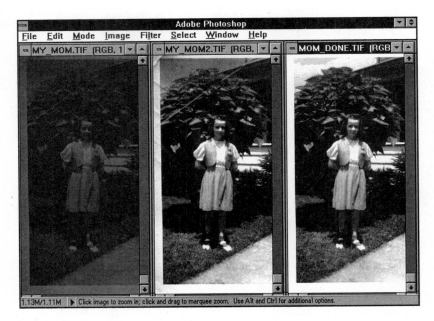

Retouching Essentials

In the last two chapters, you've corrected image flaws specific to MY_MOM.TIF. You should apply the same techniques and rules, perhaps in different areas, to your own faded photographs or to your clients'. The following are some key points to keep in mind when you apply these techniques:

◆ Remember that you always need to see enough detail in an image to accurately assess its color-correction and balance. This means that you may have to make a couple of trips to the **A**djust menu for commands that affect brightness and color balance. Try to *limit* the number of changes you make to the image, with respect to both color and tonal qualities, because changes of this type *are relative to previous changes.*

◆ Try to scan an heirloom photo at the highest resolution your scanner offers, and limit the resulting file size to whatever system RAM you have divided by 5. Photoshop work requires about five times the megabytes in RAM as an image's file size. Check the Status line frequently to see how much RAM Photoshop

needs to hold multiple copies of the image, the extra layers, and image Alpha channels. Gather as much original information about an aging photo as possible, but leave yourself enough system resources to let you actually *work* on the scan!

◆ You can enhance a photo's visual detail through combinations of filters and tonal and color corrections, but you are always losing original image information in the process. Try to limit the scope of these changes wherever possible, while still improving the resolution of the image.

◆ Don't try to add detail in an image area that consists of only a few pixels. The Smudge tool worked well in blending the copy of the shutters back into the original because there was little visual detail. The shutters were an important image area when they were missing, but the actual image area itself contained little information.

◆ Use patterns for your Rubber Stamp tool when you don't have a lot of source material for clones.

The next time you have to work with a cracked, aged photo, think twice about whipping out the transparent dyes and mending tape. Photoshop has the electronic tools you need, and now you have a guide.

Using Type in Photoshop

There will be many instances in professional assignments when you need to label an area on an image, or replace text that the camera lens didn't capture in focus. A picture might indeed communicate the equivalent of a thousands words—in fact, the author of this now-classic line was conservative in his estimate, and probably never used Photoshop. However, on occasion, a picture's focal attraction is the text, and this chapter is devoted to working with digital fonts in the graphically sumptuous enviroment of Photoshop 3. We'll show you how to bend type, how to replace the original type in an image, and how to handle both image detail and typography in an integrated fashion to produce textual elements that look as natural as if you'd taken a class in outdoor sign painting.

How Does Photoshop Treat Type?

Part of Photoshop's capability to deliver clean, smooth text has to do with its Anti-aliasing feature. The effect might appear subtle when you view an image at a 100-percent zoom, but when you select Anti-aliasing from the Type Tool dialog box, Photoshop places semitransparent foreground color around the edges to reduce the appearance of stair-stepping curves in diagonal outlines. Because of anti-aliased type, whatever text you add to a picture takes on a photographic quality that blends into an image.

Photoshop treats type as a graphic. Consequently, editing text in Photoshop is a little trickier than in a word processing program (although this chapter demonstrates a special technique for working around the difficulty that text as graphics poses). But the good news is that, because Photoshop sees type as a graphic element, all of Photoshop's tools and filters can be applied to type in the same manner as any other part of an image. You can even mix type produced using Photoshop's Type tool with scans of lettering and graphics, and blend them into one seamless piece.

You'll find this chapter's adventures with anti-aliasing and the Type tool more rewarding if you first choose a 16.7-million-color driver for your monitor. So if you aren't already running 24-bit color, now's a good time to change video drivers. In this chapter you work with color images from the Bonus CD, but you can also use the Type tool and anti-aliasing with grayscale images.

Installing a Type 1 Font

Before you begin this chapter's assignments, close Photoshop if it's running, check out the fridge, and load this chapter's guest font from the CHAP09 subdirectory on the companion CD. You use Chapter 9 Condensed to create new lettering for the exercise images. Chapter 9 Condensed is a Type 1 font especially created for use with Adobe Photoshop and this book. It's similar to the Helvetica Bold Condensed font family, which is frequently used for outdoor signage, including the lettering on trucks and traffic signs.

You need to install Type 1 fonts on your system using Adobe Type Manager, the font utility that comes with Adobe Photoshop. If you're unfamiliar with installing a program or loading a Type 1 font with Adobe Type Manager, check the README file on the Adobe Photoshop Deluxe CD-ROM, or the documentation that came with Photoshop. Macintosh users should drag the font into the Font folder found in the System folder.

The Chapter 9 Condensed font was cobbled together for the express purpose of giving you a font with the right "look" for this assignment; for this reason, it doesn't contain all the characters you normally get with a commercial typeface. Nevertheless, you have lower- and uppercase characters, decent pair kerning, numbers 0 through 9,

and a few punctuation marks to get you where you need to go in your explorations with Photoshop's Type tool. Again, it's not a good idea to have Photoshop or other programs running when you install a Type 1 font—your system has to be updated so that the applications that use Type 1 type can recognize the new addition.

Creating a Really Hip Postcard

Everyone gets a kick out of a postcard that's been retouched to skew an original image toward the whimsical, like one a friend sent us from Mt. Rushmore, where Lincoln is wearing sunglasses and Washington is honking on a saxophone. But usually these postcards are done rather amateurishly, as though the perpetrators were still using their grade school art kit to retouch images.

For the first type-handling assignment in this chapter, you'll create a novelty postcard while you pick up some new Photoshop techniques. The idea behind the postcard might be sophomoric, but the results will be nothing short of professional.

This assignment uses the file DEADEND.TIF from the CHAP09 subdirectory on the Bonus CD. As shown in figure 9.1, the file's image is a pretty common sight: a dead end sign. You'll be altering the text on this sign to suggest something a little more cheery. Except for a minor defect (which you'll retouch), the image is perfect for your first experiment with Photoshop's Type tool.

Figure 9.1

Road signs are perfect targets for retouching work using Photoshop's Type tool.

Notice that the angle at which this scene was photographed didn't catch the dead end sign dead-on; that is, the left edge of the sign is closer to the camera its right edge. This makes your task a bigger challenge, but also presents an opportunity: if you can match new lettering to the exact angle of the original lettering, you can enhance the illusion that the Department of Transportation actually posts signs with messages as silly as the one you'll create!

Using a Path To Define an Image Area

In Chapter 11, "Using Paths, Selections, and Layers," you'll explore some of the finer points, specifically Anchor Points, for creating a path using Photoshop's Paths palette. Basically, a path is vector information that lies above an image, but cannot interact with the pixels of the underlying image because vector graphics and bitmap graphics typically mix like oil and water. Paths are a useful Photoshop feature for creating a shape that can be stroked with foreground color, used as information that Photoshop can create a selection marquee from, or exported to a drawing program such as Adobe Illustrator.

You don't need to know every detail about the Paths palette and how to create a path for this section's assignment, however. Your use of the path you'll create is a unique one; it will be a "position marker" for the original type on the traffic sign. You can display the path, and hide it, and the path will never become part of the background image because it's a screen display of geometric information, not image file information. Think of a path like you do your cursor—your cursor never gets rendered into an image, and neither does a path you create with the tools on the Paths palette. Your mission in the next exercise is to create four straight lines that describe the outer boundary of the "Dead End" type on the sign. If you have used a drawing application, the tools will feel very familiar.

Your first step to creative sign-making, then, involves using the Pen tool on the Paths palette to outline the border of the original text on the sign. You'll use this path as a guideline to shape the new type to follow the angle and slope of the original lettering.

The Path to a Dead End

Open DEADEND.TIF from the companion CD, then press Ctrl+ plus

This is the image to be retouched; a 2:1 viewing resolution provides a comfortable view within which to edit the type.

Press **t**

Displays the Paths palette, and automatically activates the Pen tool.

Click once on the upper left corner of the sign lettering	Creates the beginning anchor point for your path.
Click once on the upper right corner of the sign lettering	Makes a path segment from first to second anchor point.
Click once on the lower right and then the lower left corners of the sign lettering	Makes the second and third sides of the path box around the lettering area
Click on the upper left corner, the first anchor point you created	A tiny circle appears next to the Pen tool cursor, indicating that clicking will close the Path, with the fourth line segment connecting the anchor points, as shown in figure 9.2.
Hold down the Ctrl key while you click and drag an anchor point	Ctrl key toggles the Pen tool to the Arrow Pointer tool, which is used to reposition anchor points.
Click and drag the anchor points with the Arrow Pointer tool as necessary to precisely define the path box around the type	You can adjust a path segment between two anchor points by dragging one of the anchors with the Arrow Pointer tool.

Notice that the path defined in figure 9.2 is not a parallelogram or a rectangle. Instead, the box angles ever so slightly in perspective—which contributes a quality of realism to this assignment.

Double-click on the Path title (Work Path)	Displays the Save Path dialog box with a default path name suggested in the Name field.
Click on OK in the Save Path dialog box	Accepts the default path name and displays the saved path name on the Paths palette. You can't accidentally delete the path now.
Choose File, Save As, name the image, and save it to a directory on your hard disk	Saves your work to hard disk.

Figure 9.2

You use the path you draw as a template for the new type.

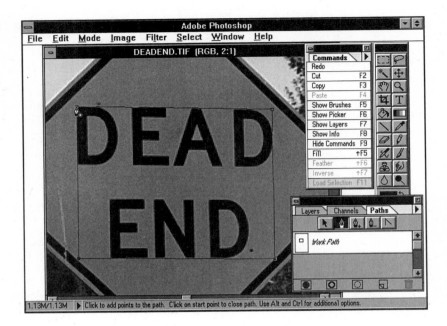

Removing Lettering with the Paint Brush Tool

The Rubber Stamp tool might seem to be the painting tool for removing the black lettering. If you read Chapter 6, "The Photoshop Test Drive," you already know that the Rubber Stamp tool can be used to sample an image area, then the sample can be applied to other image areas by using a paint brush stroke technique with the rubber Stamp. However, if you were to use this tool, the results would be awful. In this image, you have very little orange sign area to clone from; if you constantly resample the limited source area for the Rubber Stamp tool, an undesired texture effect is created and the overall image looks phony.

The sign has subtle variations in shade because the sunlight was striking it at an oblique angle when the picture was taken. The best course of action in this assignment is to create a new layer, sample original color values from the Background image, and simply paint over the lettering. By using separate Layers for your editing work, you can preserve original image areas and modify your retouching work at any phase of the assignment.

Painting over the Sign

Click on the Layers tab on the Layers palette, click on the New icon, then click on OK	Creates new, active Layer for DEADEND image; you've accepted default name of Layer 1 in the New Layer dialog box.
Double-click on Paint brush tool on the toolbox	Selects Paint brush tool, and displays Brushes Options palette.
Press Alt, then click over an orange area of the sign very close to the black lettering	Toggles Paint brush tool to Eyedropper tool, and samples a foreground color to paint with.
Release Alt	Toggles Eyedropper tool back to a Paint Brush.
Click over an orange portion of the sign toward the top of the sign	Selects the new foreground color.
Click on the Brushes tab on the Brushes/Options palette, then click on the number 35 tip	Selects a fairly large brush tip with spread and a 35-pixel diameter.
Click on the Options tab on the Brushes/Options palette, then choose the following: Normal mode, **100%** Opacity; check the Fade box; enter **25** in the Steps box; then choose Transparent	Sets characteristics for Paint Brush tool.

Here's the technique for painting over the lettering area of the sign: you want your brush strokes to blend into the original orange image areas, even though you're working on a separate layer. By setting 25 as the Fade to Transparent for the Paint brush, your strokes fade to transparent within ten diameters of the brush's tip. The Steps value is one that needs to be experimented with on an image-to-image basis to create a successful blending effect. Here, the authors arrived at the Steps value of 25 by experimentation.

Click and drag the Paint brush cursor over the black lettering (see fig. 9.3)	Paints over the black lettering, using a shade of orange identical to the part of the sign you selected with the Eyedropper.
Choose File, Save (or press Ctrl+S)	Saves your work to hard disk.

Figure 9.3

Paint an identical foreground color on the new Layer to cover the original sign lettering.

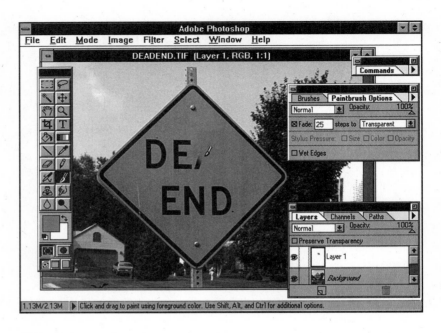

If you look carefully at the sign, you'll notice a slightly darker orange on the lower right. To finish painting over the lettering, press Alt and click on areas of the background image that clearly display a different shade of orange, then release Alt and continue stoking over the letters. The variation in overall orange shades is so slight that the Paint brush tool, with the Fade option checked, should blend together the different values as you paint over the areas.

Tip   To achieve the smooth blending of slightly different shades of orange in this assignment, the amount of Hardness set for the 35-pixel-diameter brush tip plays an important role. You can adjust the amount of spread for any brush tip by double-clicking on the tip to display the Brush Options dialog box, then entering a percentage in the **H**ardness field. The preset brush tips on the Brushes palette are soft-edged (0% Hardness) from the second row down, whereas the tips in top row have a 100% Hardness attribute.

Retouching a Damaged Image Area

After you paint over all the lettering, click on the Zoom tool and marquee-zoom in on the flawed area of the sign. Although the dent in the sign is part of the image's photographic detail, there's no reason why you can't make the retouched sign look like a *perfect* retouched sign. In the next exercise, you'll see a quick technique for sharpening an edge in a digital photograph. If you create a straight-edge, polygonal

marquee, one of whose sides lies directly on an edge in the image, you can paint on one side of the marquee to make one side of an image edge sharper. You then choose the inverse of the same selection marquee, which then *masks* the area you painted, and selects the other side of the edge. This trick removes the need to create two separate selection marquees to sharpen or straighten the edge of a visual element in an image.

The next exercise shows you how to handle some quick, minor retouching.

Reinforcing the Border

Zoom into a 4:1 or 8:1 viewing resolution with the Zoom tool, so that the dent in the traffic sign fills the workspace	Gives you the viewing resolution you need to create an accurate selection marquee.
Press **L** (for **L**asso tool), then press Alt and click a diagonal, rectangular boundary around the damaged black area	Creates polygonal area, so that Paint brush tool can affect only the area within the marquee selection.
Press **B** (Paint **B**rush tool), then Press Alt(Option) and click over a black area of the sign's border, then release the Alt key	Samples a foreground color you can apply to the Layer.
Uncheck the Fade check box on the Options palettes, then click and drag cursor over marquee selection	Applies foreground color to marquee selection area, as shown in figure 9.4.
Choose **S**elect, **I**nverse	Protects area you painted over, and exposes all other image areas for editing.
Press Alt(Option) and click over an orange area next to damaged part of sign, then release the Alt key	Samples foreground color.
Click on the second brush (from the left), middle row on the Brushes palette	Chooses a smaller tip for the Paint brush tool; you need to proceed with precision in the next step.
Click and drag above black border until damaged orange area disappears	Creates nice edge between restored orange and black areas.
Press Ctrl+D (**S**elect, **N**one), then Ctrl+S (File, Save)	Deselects the selection and saves your work up to this point.

Figure 9.4

Apply a similar foreground color to only the area inside the marquee selection.

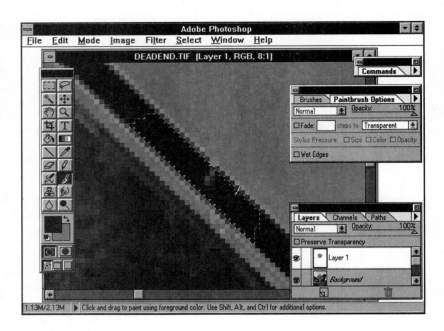

Creating a selection border whose edge lies on the edge of an image area, as does the polygonal selection border you created, is a good trick for perfectly retouching a damaged image area that consists of different colors. You retouch one area, then choose **S**elect, **I**nverse to select "the other side" of the image area, and continue retouching.

Tip   While retouching a detail like the one shown in the last exercise, you should zoom out occasionally, not just to check the overall progress of your retouching work, but also to help relieve visual fatigue. You can saturate your eye's cones and rods while working in a close-up view, particularly if one area is a mass of one color, as is the case with this sign. Although the long-range effects aren't harmful to your eyesight, you can hinder your ability to evaluate a color accurately if you don't keep the picture moving a little. Take breaks, look out the window, change *After Dark* screen savers regularly.

You're now halfway through your assignment. The sign should now look as blank as the expression of someone you loaned money to last week.

As in many of the assignments in this book, you're using the proprietary feature of Layers, which can't be saved to the TIF image file format. If you'd like to save the blank sign at this point, so that you can create other variations in the future, choose **F**ile, **S**ave, then name the file something other than DEADEND. Photoshop only offers the PSD format for a saved image that has layers. A *.PSD copy of the image retains separate layers (giving you the option of removing Layer 1 or doing something else creative with your work later). You're going to be adding text to this image shortly; if you want to retain a pristine copy of the sign, now is a good time to save it as a PSD format image.

Measuring the Image Area for Type

Before you start fitting type into an image, it's important to measure the image area correctly. Photoshop treats type differently than word processors do—type is entered as a graphical element, not an editable one—a *floating* selection (a selection that is not part of the image background) above the background image. If you choose the wrong point size, you're stuck with it; you can't highlight and type over the typeface, change its style, or precisely adjust its size.

The next exercise shows you how to ensure that your type fits the image area.

Measuring with Photoshops Rulers

Choose **F**ile, Pre**f**erences, then choose **U**nits	Displays Units Preferences dialog box.
Click on the **R**ulers Units drop-down box	Offers a selection of units that measure distance.
Choose Points from **R**ulers Units drop-down box	Sets Photoshop's rulers to measure typeface heights (traditionally measured in points).

Photoshop offers two options for Point/Pica Size: the **P**ostScript measurement, and the **T**raditional, nominally larger, increment. Because you'll be using a Type 1, PostScript font in this assignment, leave the PostScript radio button checked.

Click on OK	Applies changes and closes dialog box.

continues

continued

Choose **W**indow, Show **R**ulers (or press Ctrl+R)	Displays rulers on edge of image, with a Zero Origin box in the upper left corner, where the two rulers join.
Click and drag the Zero Origin box, as shown in figure 9.5, to the position at which you want the new type to begin	Moves rulers next to what you want to measure, which makes measuring accurately a much easier task.

Figure 9.5

Use the vertical ruler to determine the height of the lettering; type is measured in point height.

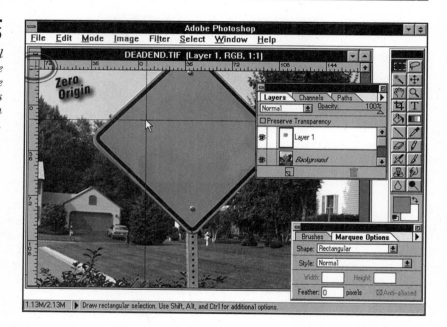

With the point rulers in place, you can get a good idea that 32-point type on two lines fits comfortably inside the sign area.

Now that you have measured the image area to fit your type, you need to select an appropriate foreground color for the new type. You always need to consider what color the type should be *before* you click on the Type tool. When you click a type insertion point in an image, Photoshop sets the type's color attribute to the current foreground color. Again, the Eyedropper tool is ideal for selecting a natural color found in the image for the types color.

Selecting the Color for the Type

Choose the Type tool	You can toggle the Type tool to the Eyedropper tool by pressing Alt (Option); again, you can use the cursor for two different functions.
Click on the Eye icon next to Layer 1 title on Layers palette	Removes view of corresponding Layer. In this case, orange painting disappears to reveal original image.

Don't be alarmed when your retouching work vanishes. The Eye icon simply toggles your *view* of a selected Layer on and off. The active Layer is still Layer 1; you just can't view it—it's hidden.

Press Alt and click on original DEAD END text on the sign	Sets type color to black—not the same black as Photoshop's default black foreground swatch, but black nonetheless.
Click on Eye icon next to Layer 1 title bar	Restores your view of Layer 1 sitting on top of the Background Layer.
Release Alt key	Changes cursor to an I-beam, which you use to place text into an image.
Click the Type tool cursor in top center portion of sign	Sets text insertion point (which specifies where text will start) and displays Type tool dialog box.

Now you see why you have to measure beforehand the available space in which you want to place type—you don't enter type directly on the image.

Setting Type Specifications

The typeface *family*—the weight, leading, and other typographic characteristics you normally assign to lettering—are all chosen from the Type tool dialog box.

Tip   Unlike word processors and other text-handling applications, Photoshop requires type to be set in the Type tool's dialog box, and not directly entered on an image. Type is rendered to an image as a graphic. You can take your time in the Type tool dialog box and preview your type, its alignment, and choice of fonts before adding "type as a graphic" to the image as a floating selection you can then reposition.

Here's how to specify type for the sign:

Selecting the Right Type

Click on the <u>F</u>ont drop-down box in Type tool dialog box	Displays drop-down list of typefaces installed on your computer.
Choose Chapter 9 Condensed	This font appears on the list only after you've installed it, using Adobe Type Manager.
Type **32** in the <u>S</u>ize box, then type **30** in the Lea<u>d</u>ing box	Makes each line of type 32 points tall (a tad under a half inch) and specifies the space between two lines of type, measured in points.

When you use large typeface, as in this exercise, brief lines of type have maximum impact and good readability at a leading of 95 to 100 percent of their point size.

Click on the Anti-aliased check box if it doesn't have an "x" in it already	Ensures that your typeface looks clean rather than pixelated.
Click on the top left radio button in Alignment field	Centers the two lines of type relative to each other, just like the original type you painted over earlier.
Place cursor in type entry field at bottom of dialog box	Cursor changes to an I-beam, just like some word processing type tools.
Click, and then type **PARTY ZONE**, pressing Enter between the two words	Enters the text on two lines.

Because all characters are uppercase in Chapter 9 Condensed, you don't have to press Shift or Caps Lock when you enter text. However, because commercial fonts usually offer genuine lowercase characters, always treat the Type tool as though it belonged to a word processing program.

Click to place an "x" in the Fo<u>n</u>t and Si<u>z</u>e Show boxes	Displays type in font style and approximate size it will have in image (see fig. 9.6).
Click on OK	Applies settings and closes dialog box.

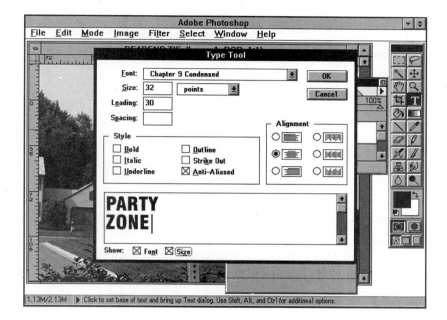

Figure 9.6

*Set the
specifications
for your type in
the Type Tool
dialog box.*

Note The vertical alignment options for type are different on the Macintosh and Windows versions, and this might have been an unexpected enhancement when the program was written for different operating systems. The Macintosh vertical alignment options will create single characters that are aligned downward, vertically, while the Windows vertical alignment options produce type that is rotated clockwise by 90°.

On both platforms, the left, center, and right alignments for vertical type will make two or more lines of text line up flush according to the radio button you click on.

In either case, the vertical alignment option is a convenience, and the effect can be achieved manually. Windows users can type one character per line of type to create "column" type, and Macintosh users can rotate type using the **I**mage, **R**otate command.

On both platforms, you can enter up to 32,000 characters of type in a single session with the Type Tool dialog box.

Figure 9.7 shows the image after you've clicked on OK in the Type Tool dialog box. The black type magically appears very close to the insertion point, with a marquee around every letter. The marquee indicates that Photoshop is treating the type entries as floating selections. You can reposition the text phrase as long as it is a floating selection. When you click outside the selection area you deselect the type, which composites with the orange foreground color on Layer 1 and can no longer be repositioned.

Figure 9.7

Type that is on a layer with other image elements should not *be deselected if you need to reposition it.*

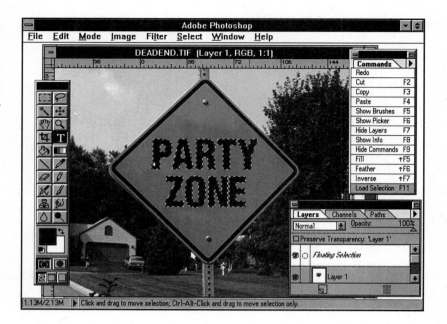

It wasn't really necessary for the purposes of this exercise to give the PARTY ZONE text its own layer. If you had created a new layer before entering the type, an active selection marquee would not be necessary to reposition and modify the type; when image elements have their own layer, they can be edited independently of other layers, and the opaque pixels on a layer, the layer elements, can be repositioned by clicking and dragging with the Move tool.

The perk that layers offer is not relevant to our experiments with the Type tool here, however; and layers, like selections saved in Alpha channels, do contribute to larger overall file sizes.

When you move your I-beam Type tool inside a selection area, it becomes a tiny arrow cursor. Use it to click and drag the type around as necessary until you've positioned it in the center of the sign. Do *not* click outside the selection border yet. For now, leave it as a floating selection.

Click on the Paths tab on the Layers palette now (see fig. 9.8). Note that the path of the original image's lettering (Path 1) falls inside your new type. This discrepancy doesn't invalidate what you've done. You simply need to add an angle to the new type, specifically the angle described by the saved path you traced around the original image lettering.

By using the path as a guideline, you no longer need to refer to the original lettering on the sign on the Background layer, and you can see more easily how this piece is integrating visually.

Creating Perspective with Type

Because the word "PARTY" has one more letter than the word "DEAD," you should condense the new type a bit. Although viewers tend to recognize a condensed typeface, they usually fail to notice *the degree* to which type is condensed.

The Distort command is a wonderful choice of tools to both condense the lettering and add the needed angle to match that of the sign. Like the other Photoshop **E**ffects commands, Distort offers a boundary box around a selection, with four corner handles you can tug on to reshape both the box and the underlying selection.

The next exercise is as simple as aligning the four sides of the Distort boundary to the saved path now displayed on your image. The result is a wonderfully realistic, angled effect that closely matches that of the original sign lettering in the photograph.

Here's how to shape the type you entered so that it conforms to the perspective of the original lettering.

Using the Distort Command on Type

Choose **E**ffects from **I**mage menu, and then choose **D**istort (see fig. 9.9)

Displays, in image area, a box that encloses selection area.

continues

continued

Click on a corner of the Distort box and then drag the corner toward the path	Moves the two lines surrounding the corner outline closer to the path lines (see fig.9.10).
Repeat the preceding step with each corner until the Distort box aligns with all four sides of the Paths outline	Creates an envelope for the type that matches the angling of the original lettering.

Don't click anywhere on the image yet! This is the end of the exercise, but not the end of the process of making the Distort changes permanent. Read on!

Figure 9.9

The Distort command creates a boundary you manipulate to reshape an underlying selection area.

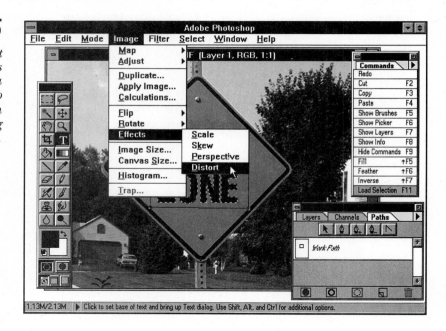

Figure 9.10

Align the Distort box's border with the Paths outline that you drew earlier.

Finalizing an Image Effect Command

There's one more move you have to make with the Distort box to make the changes to the lettering inside the box permanent. You need to click inside the box to finalize the effect. Photoshop gives you plenty of time to finesse the corner handles on the box, but won't actually execute the command until you send the program a signal that you want the contents of the distort box shaped the way you see on-screen.

The sign might say "PARTY ZONE," but it's not party time yet. When you're satisfied with your changes, you need to make them permanent.

Locking Down the Party Zone

Click the center of the Distort box when it matches the Paths outline	Cursor changes into small hammer and "nails" angles of distortion into place.
Click outside the marquee-selection borders around the type	Composites the floating type into the orange painting on Layer 1.

continues

continued

Click on flyout menu to right of tabs on Layers palette, then choose Merge Layers (see fig 9.11)	Merges Layer 1 onto the Background.
Click on Paths tab, then click and drag the Path 1 title into the Trash icon	Removes the path from the image file. You no longer need it.
Choose **F**ile, Sa**v**e As, and then name the file DEADDONE.TIF	Saves your work to hard disk.

The TIF format can't retain Photoshop layers information, but that's okay because you've merged the layer to the background. You now have a finished piece of retouching work that can be read by a number of computer applications on both the Mac and PC platforms.

Figure 9.11

A really nice novelty postcard. Try the college market first.

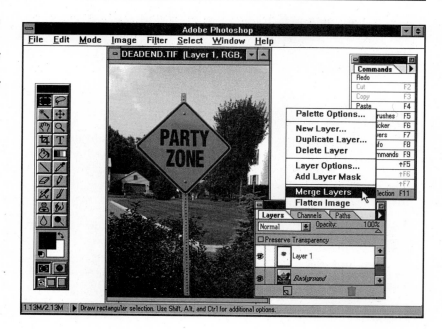

From an ordinary scene, you've created a wonderful "hyper-reality" that has commercial possibilities. The type on the sign looks completely authentic. The finished image will turn a lot of heads, especially if you use something more colorful than the phrase I've suggested here! People will ask "How did you do that? Did you paint over a real traffic sign? How long was your sentence for doing that?"

Adding Text and Graphics to a Photograph

You can use a scanner to bring a client's logo into an imaging program so that you can touch it up and use it for a variety of purposes. In the next assignment, you have an imaginary customer, Fred Glough, who carts and hauls nuclear waste. Fred is considering having a painter reproduce his company letterhead on the side of one of his trucks. But before he hires the sign painter, he wants you to show him what the truck would look like. This assignment provides an opportunity to build upon the skills you acquired by completing the last exercise, and demonstrates some of the flexibility of type that's rendered as a graphic. In this assignment, you'll combine Photoshop type with textual elements acquired from outside sources—scanned lettering and artwork—to create an image that you probably would prefer to see on a monitor than on a truck driving down one of your neighborhood streets.

Refining a Scan

First, you need to clean up the scan of Fred's letterhead a little so that you can use parts of it in the image you'll build. The letter spacing (kerning) in his letterhead is lousy. Besides, Photoshop can generate better type than the scan provides, so you'll want to replace some of the scan's type.

Cleaning Up a Scanned Image

Open the image FREDLOGO.TIF from the CHAP09 subdirectory (folder) of the Bonus CD	Loads the scanned letterhead that you need to clean up (see fig. 9.12).
Press **D** (**d**efault colors icon)	Sets foreground color to black, and background color to white.
Press Alt(Option) and click on Marquee tool until Rectangular Marquee tool displays (or press **M** until the tool is active)	This selection tool is used to perform kerning in this example.
Click and drag a rectangle that surrounds only the "E" and "S"	Selects characters to be moved.

Don't leave a lot of white space to the left of the "E"; one or two rows of pixels space is good. You'll be moving the selection toward the "L," and superfluous white space will prevent you from tightly kerning the characters.

continues

continued

Press left-arrow key several times	Each keystroke moves selection one pixel to the left (see fig. 9.13).
Press Ctrl+D when the selection is in place	Deselects selected areas—the E and the S—at their new positions.
Click on Eraser tool on toolbox (or press E until tool is activated)	Removes foreground image areas, and exposes background color, which is now set to white.
Click on Options tab on Brushes palette, then choose Block from drop-down list	Replaces image foreground with flat, 100-percent opaque background color.
Click and drag over address and telephone number areas	Erases address and telephone number from image.

You don't need the address element of the scanned logo; you'll add your own better, cleaner text later, using Photoshop's Type tool.

Choose File, Save As, and save image as FREDLOGO. PSD to your hard disk	Saves your work in a format that can retain Layer information.

Figure 9.12

Scans of business cards frequently require "cleaning up"; poor character kerning can be adjusted in Photoshop.

Figure 9.13

By pressing an arrow key, you nudge a selection by one pixel.

Tip   Adobe manufactures a handy utility, *Adobe Streamline,* that can make quicker, simpler work of scanning business cards and logos. A demonstration version of Streamline is on the Bonus CD for both the Macintosh and Windows. *Streamline* is a bitmap-to-vector conversion utility that auto-traces a TIF, PCX, or Macintosh PNT image file, and saves a copy of it to an image format that can be edited with a vector design program such as Adobe Illustrator (or you can perform a little editing directly within Streamline).

Vector tracing eliminates the "stairsteppy" jaggedness of type and graphic designs in a bitmap image. Streamline saves the auto-trace of a bitmap to your choice of AI, DXF, or EPS file formats. Because these are vector, resolution-independent image formats, you can import the vector art into Photoshop and rasterize it to the dimensions you need.

Creating a Selection Mask for Painting

Because the logo was scanned at a Grayscale mode setting, it is arranged in an 8-bit per pixel, 256-possible-shades-of-black image format. The maximum amount of color information Photoshop can read in an Alpha channel as selection information is *also* 8-bit per pixel, grayscale. Want to jump to a conclusion as to how you can accurately color in areas of Fred's logo?

By copying the Black channel information to a user-created Alpha channel, and converting the image format to RGB, you can select only the black (or only the white) areas at one time in the RGB composite view of the FREDLOGO image. Once selected, the areas can be filled with any color you choose. This trick can be used in a number of professional situations when you want to quickly and accurately define a selection area in a piece of art that consists of black and white areas: *Let Photoshop create selection marquees based on the brightness values in the Alpha channel!*

The following exercise shows you how to create a selection area that allows editing of only the white areas in Fred's logo.

Using Image Detail as Selection Information

Press Ctrl+A, then Ctrl+C (**S**elect, **A**ll, then **E**dit, **C**opy)	Selects entire logo image area and copies it to clipboard.
Choose **M**ode, then **R**GB Color	Converts logo image to a mode that supports color channels and a color capability of 16.7 million unique values.
Click on Channels tab on Layers palette, then click on New channel icon (see fig. 9.14)	Displays Channel Options box.
Click on the Color Indicates: **M**askedAreas radio button, then click on OK	Darker areas you create or copy to new channel #4 (the default channel name) will be *masked* (protected from change); light areas will be available for editing.

You're moved to a view of new channels; the RGB view of Fred's logo apparently vanishes, and you're looking at a black image window. Because color indicates *masked* areas, any addition now of white or lighter-value grayscale pixels will be "seen" as *selection* information, information that Photoshop will use to create a selection marquee.

Press Ctrl+V (**E**dit, **P**aste)	Pastes the copy of Fred's logo into channel #4.
Press Ctrl+D, then Ctrl+0 (zero) (or choose **S**elect, **N**one, then click on the RGB title bar on the Channels palette)	Deselects copy of logo, displays the color composite view of the logo.

You now have a "template" for coloring in specific areas of Fred's logo in the RGB, composite view of the FREDLOGO image. Your first stop is to make the logo's symbol areas a little more attention-getting.

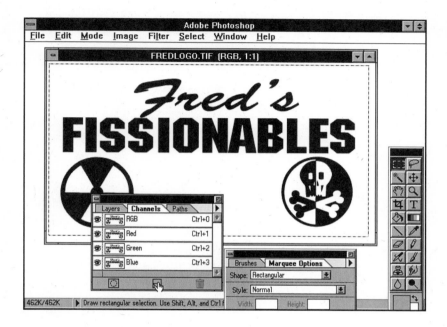

Figure 9.14

Add a new channel to an image by clicking on the New channel icon on the Channels palette.

Adding Attention-Getting Colors

There are five ways to define a color for use with any of Photoshop's painting tools, and you're going to get your hands on two of them in the next exercises. To begin with, Fred's logo would get the recognition it merits if the plain black-and-white symbols were black-and-*mustard* colored. The highly visible combination of black and mustard is commonly used on fallout shelters, high-voltage electric generators, and New York City taxi cabs.

The Swatches palette has a predefined mustard color that will serve beautifully for coloring the logo. By clicking on the mustard-colored swatch you make mustard the current foreground color. And with a little care and the right size tip for the Paint brush tool (you already have your masking work done), none of the mustard color will accidentally intrude on the black areas in the image.

Here's how to create effective truck signage through the use of masked image areas and inspired use of color:

Using a Selection Marquee as a Coloring Template

Click on the Zoom tool, then click and drag around the nuclear energy symbol (the one on the left)	The first area that gets the mustard color. A 2:1 viewing resolution is fine for the level of detail you'll work with.
Click on the Paint brush tool (or press **B**)	Applies foreground color in this exercise.

A paint tool must be active to define paint application characteristics on the Options palette because the palette is context-sensitive.

Choose **W**indow, **P**alettes, Show **P**icker (or press **F6**, Mac: press **F10**)	Displays Picker palette.
Click on Swatches tab on Picker palette, then click on the swatch five rows down and three columns from the left	Selects a mustard color as current foreground color. Background color should still be white.
From Brushes palette, choose a medium tip from the second row, then click on Options tab	Chooses size of Paint brush tip, and displays options for applying color.
Choose Normal (mode), Opacity: **100%**, and leave the Fade box unchecked	You're going to apply straight, flat foreground color to selected logo areas.
Choose **S**elect, **L**oad Selection, then click on OK	Photoshop's Load Selection dialog box offers you no options because you have only one channel defined in the FREDLOGO image.

You now have a marquee border running around image areas that are available for editing. Because you chose color in the Alpha channel (channel #4) to be masked information, only the corresponding white areas in the RGB view of the image can be painted over.

Click and drag the cursor over the white areas in the nuclear energy logo, starting from the center and working your way outward	Get a "feel" for the diameter of the brush and how far it spreads color (see fig. 9.15).

If you go outside the symbol and onto the white background, don't worry. You'll modify the selection information later to encompass only the black and color areas of the logo. The white background, colored on or not, will be left behind when you copy the logo onto the truck.

Repeat the last step, working this time on the skull and crossbones symbol on the right of the logo	Fills white areas of symbol with mustard color.

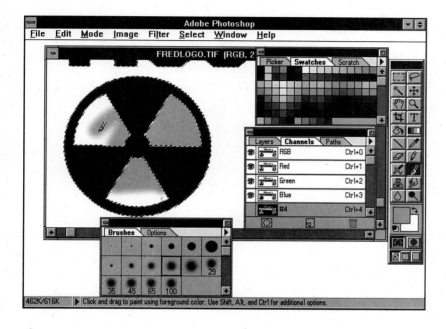

Figure 9.15

Color the white, selected image areas. The background, black areas are masked.

Airbrushing a Van

The symbol portion of Fred's logo looks appropriate now, but the signature portion of it could use some attention. By using the Gradient tool and selecting the right foreground and background colors, you can create an effect similar to those outrageous van murals you see on interstate highways.

Here's how to reuse the selection border defined in the Alpha channel, and add some pizzazz to Fred's pickup:

Gradient Filling the Logo

Choose **S**elect, **I**nverse	Selects all the black image areas, and masks the white areas.

continues

continued

Click on the Rectangular marquee tool, then press Ctrl (Cmd) while you click and drag to encompass the two symbols you colored in last	The Ctrl key subtracts from a marquee selection. Only the FRED's FISSIONABLES lettering should be marquee-selected now (see fig. 9.16).
Click on Picker tab on Picker palette, then click on menu flyout button if HSB color sliders aren't displayed	Although you can pick colors from a number of color models, use the HSB color model here because the values listed in these steps define HSB foreground and background colors.
Click on HSB Sliders and release the cursor	Controls offered by HSB sliders are more "user-friendly" for defining colors than those offered by the RGB, additive color model.

By default, the picker swatch with the box around it (on the right of the Picker palette) is the color you're changing by clicking and dragging the sliders. Make sure that the foreground swatch is highlighted with a black outline; if it isn't, click on it now. Foreground/background color order is important when you use the Gradient tool.

Click and drag the sliders to read H: **8°**, S: **88%**, and B: **93%**	Defines an interesting Cadmium Red for the foreground color.
Click on the background Picker swatch, then set the sliders to H: **240°**, S: **62%**, and B: **42%**	Defines a blue-violet for the background color.
Double-click on the Gradient tool	Displays Gradient Tool Options box on Brushes palette.
Choose Normal (mode), Style: Foreground to Background, Midpoint: **50%**, and Type: **Linear**, and put a check mark in the Dither check box	Sets Gradient tool to an even, linear fill that progresses from foreground to background color.

Note   The Dither option on the Gradient Tool Options palette is offered for ultra-refined blends of foreground and background color. PostScript language limits a Gradient blend to 256 unique colors, and *banding*, the obvious display of the edges of colors used in the 256 transitional steps, is sometimes apparent.

To reduce banding, use the Dither option. Photoshop then uses an advanced form of mathematical dithering to reduce visible banding. A word of caution, however: if you intend to Threshold, Posterize, or perform color reduction on an RGB image that contains a Gradient blend, do *not* choose the Dither option. If you do, your Gradient will look harsh and unappealing.

Click above selection area and drag straight down to a point below selection marquee	Floods selection area with a gradient fill from red to blue, as shown in figure 9.17.
Choose File, Save (or press Ctrl+S)	Saves your work to hard disk.

Figure 9.16

Subtract from the existing selection marquee, by pressing Ctrl (Cmd) and clicking and dragging with the Rectangular Marquee tool.

Figure 9.17

The Gradient tool fills only the selection area.

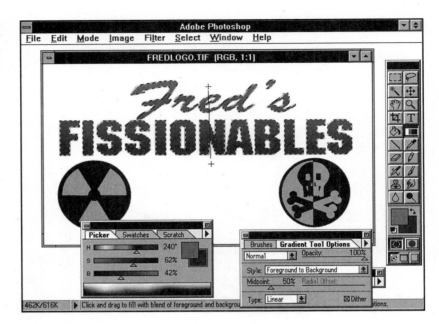

Manually Editing a Saved Selection

Fred's logo looks great. It will look even better when you place it on the truck image. However, there is a hitch in the plans: the saved selection area in Channel #4 can be displayed again for selecting the logo to copy, but the selection area *does not* include the black areas, and the white areas include the background, an unwanted image area.

The easiest way to solve this problem is to manually edit the grayscale information in channel #4. You can use any painting or selection tool to alter the visual contents of an Alpha channel, and by doing this you can quickly add the unselected areas that comprise the interiors of both of the symbols in the FREDFISH.TIF image. The Pencil tool is the best choice of editing tools for a situation like this because the Pencil tool has no soft-edge characteristics like the Paint Brush tool. By "coloring in" the masked areas of the design in the Alpha channel, you'll include these areas in the selection when it's loaded a little later.

Here's how to edit the saved selection to create a marquee only around Fred's logo:

Editing a Quick Mask Selection

Click on the Channel #4 icon, double-click on the Channel #4 title, then click on the Color Indicates: **S**elected Areas radio button in the Channel Options dialog box, then click on OK	Makes Channel #4 the active view of the FREDFISH image, specifies that black areas should represent selected areas in the channel, and Photoshop then inverts the image to reflect the change of color specifications for the Alpha channel.

Photoshop automatically inverts (changes) channel colors when *you* change what you want the channel colors to indicate. So the black areas of the Alpha channel now represent selection areas, and the white areas, those you want selected, presently represent masked areas. But you, too, can invert Alpha channel colors to change the selection information Photoshop uses to make marquee selections. The command you'll use next is not the same as **S**elect, **I**nverse, and you should use it to invert colors in an image. It does *not* create an Inverse selection marquee.

Choose Image, Map, **I**nvert (or press Ctrl+I)	Changes the "negative" of Fred's logo to a positive image, and the selection marquee Photoshop loads from this channel information is represented as black.
Press **D** (**d**efault colors icon), press **P** (for **P**encil tool), choose the second selection from the left tip, middle row on the Brushes palette, then click and drag in the interior of the nuclear symbol to cover the white areas	Adds the interior to the present information in the Alpha channel (see fig. 9.18).
Scroll over to the skull and crossbones area in the Alpha channel, and color the interior wherever it's white	Adds the interior of the symbol to the selection information.

When you manually edit Alpha channel information, there is no need to save the selection; in its state as visual data in the Alpha channel, the black color you add by clicking and dragging in white areas is automatically read as areas to be selected by Photoshop the next time you load the Alpha channel information as a marquee. However, you do need to save the image now because the Alpha channel is a subset of the other channels in FREDFISH.TIF, and you haven't saved the file recently!

Click on the RGB title on the Channels palette	Returns your view of the FREDFISH image to the color composite view.

continues

continued

Press Ctrl+S (**F**ile, **S**ave)   Saves your work at this intermediate
                                                 stage of completion.

Figure 9.18

*You can edit the
graphical
information
Photoshop uses to
create a selection
marquee by
adding color to
an Alpha
channel.*

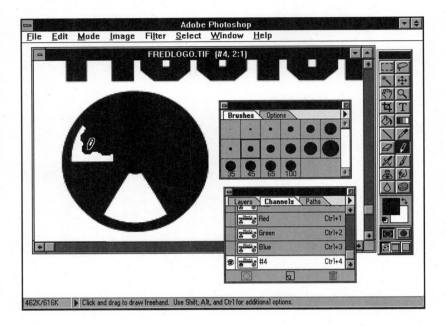

There is a very direct visual correlation to the color areas in an Alpha channel, and what Photoshop displays on an image when you load the Alpha channel information as a marquee. However, the proof is in the pixel, and if you'd like to test your Alpha channel editing work, press Alt (option) and click on the Channel #4 thumbnail icon on the Channels palette to load it as a selection marquee now. If your screen looks like figure 9.19, you're in great shape to proceed with copying the color logo to the truck.

Figure 9.19

You can edit the color information Photoshop uses to load a selection marquee by adding or deleting Alpha channel colors.

Measuring the Logo To Fit the Truck

Somewhere along the way, you'll need to address the difference in size of the truck image and the logo. Business cards are generally 3 1/2 by 2 inches, and this one was scanned at 150 pixels per inch, as was the FREDFISH.TIF image.

Knowing that the two images have compatible resolutions, the problem becomes a question of physical dimensions. Can the logo in its entirety, as is, fit within the border of the truck's box, and still leave room for a snappy slogan?

The next exercise shows you how to find out how much you need to resize the logo before you copy it to the FREDFISH image:

Sizing Up the Images

Open FREDFISH.TIF from the CHAP09 subdirectory (folder) on the Bonus CD

This image is the truck that will "host" the logo selection.

Choose **F**ile, Pre**f**erences, and then choose **U**nits

Displays Units Preferences dialog box.

continues

continued

You need to reset the unit of measurement because inches, not points (which you set in the last assignment) are the required Rulers increments for this assignment.

Click on **R**ulers Units box, select Inches from Rulers drop-down list, then click on OK	Sets Photoshop's rulers to measure in inches.
Press Ctrl+R	Displays Photoshop rulers around active image—the logo.
Press Ctrl+Tab and then Ctrl+R	Toggles to FREDLOGO.TIF as the active selection and adds rulers to it.

Ctrl+Tab is a "Windows-only" shortcut for toggling between images on the Photoshop workspace. Macintosh users should click on the title bar of the FREDFISH image to make it the active image window. In the Macintosh version of Photoshop, pressing Ctrl+Tab causes the toolbox to disappear from the screen and pressing ⌘ Command+Tab removes all of the palettes and the toolbox from the screen. Pressing Tab restores the elements to the screen.

Measure the window of the FREDLOGO.TIF image	Make a note on a piece of paper. You should get 3 and 1/2 inches.
Measure the "live space" on the truck's side in FREDFISH.TIF by clicking and dragging the ruler Zero Origin into the upper left of the truck's box	Make a note of this, also. You should get about 1 3/4 inches (see fig. 9.20).
Click on minimize button on window displaying image of truck	Minimizes FREDFISH.TIF. This is a Photoshop for Windows feature; Macintosh users should use the image's Grow box to reduce the window size, and then drag the window, by the title bar, off to an unused corner of the screen.

Take a moment now to rearrange the image windows and palettes on your screen so that your workspace is comfortable. Unless you manage this stuff prudently, your screen can get pretty cluttered!

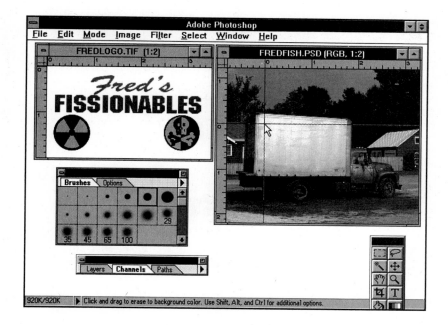

Figure 9.20

Photoshop's rulers provide an accurate measurement for sizing images.

Resizing the Logo for the Truck

Now that you have Fred's logo in color, you need to resize it so that it fits in the clear space on the truck image. Once again, Photoshop's Anti-Aliasing feature for color-channel images can provide valuable assistance in resizing the logo without producing right-angle, harsh pixel edges.

An RGB image uses all 16.7 million available colors to perform anti-aliasing. At the heart of this "intelligent" reassignment of color pixel values to achieve anti-aliasing is something called *interpolation*. Interpolation lets Photoshop make its best guess as to which neighboring color pixels should be shaded to form smooth transitions when you reduce or enlarge RGB image areas.

Whether you sample up or sample down an image through the Image Size command or the Cropping tool, some visual information has to be changed, and this inevitably means the loss of some image focus or quality. Fortunately, the FREDLOGO image has to be sampled down (made smaller), so the loss in image detail will seem quite natural for a logo "painted" on the side of a truck. Truly photographic images of type on an object do not display the crisp edges typically found in vector illustrations; totally sharp type, in fact, indicates that a photo has been retouched, which is *not* our goal here.

Remember those measurements that you jotted down in the "Sizing Up the Images" exercise? Have them handy, because the following exercise requires some intricate math:

Fitting the Logo for the Truck

Windows users: click on the Maximize button (on the right of the title bar); Mac users: click on the Zoom box or click and drag the Resize (Grow) box, both on the image window frame	Resizes FREDLOGO image window so that image window background can be seen.
Double-click on the Cropping tool	Chooses Cropping tool and displays Cropping Tool Options on Brushes/Options palette.
Click on Fixed to Target Size checkbox, then type **1.75** in the Width field, choose Inches from drop-down to the right of the Width field, leave Height field blank, type 150 in Resolution, and choose pixels/inch from drop-down to the right	Resizes image to 1.75 inches in width. New height will be in proportion to dimensions of original image because you did not enter a value.
Click and drag Cropping tool from upper left to lower right corner of FREDLOGO image	Creates cropping marquee that includes entire image (see fig. 9.21).
Click inside marquee area	Cursor changes to scissors icon, and cropping is executed.
Restore FREDLOGO image window to normal size	Restores view of your workspace so that you can see FREDFISH image.

 Stop   Typing a zero in the Cropping tool dimension fields on the Options palette is not the same as leaving it blank. Photoshop gets cranky if you try to specify no (0) width or height for something. It will automatically enter 0.001 if you do this, then move on to another field. If you want to let one image dimension depend on the outcome of cropping the other, leave a space in the field by placing the cursor in the field in question and then backspacing until the field is clear, or choose Reset Tool from the Cropping Tool Options menu flyout.

If you leave the Resolution field empty, the new image resolution is adjusted according to the new Height and Width you specify, to reflect no change in image file size. Resolution is inversely proportional to image dimensions—if you want to make an image smaller, keep the Fixed Target Size box checked.

New Riders Publishing
INSIDE SERIES

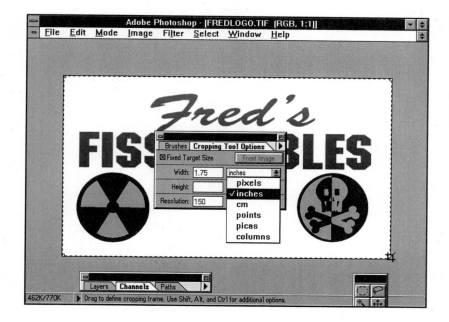

Figure 9.21

Use the Cropping tool to precisely resize an entire image, or only a portion of the image.

Dynamic Copying

Now that you've fitted the logo for the side of the truck, you still have some work to do before you paste the selection to the truck image. You'll click and drag between image windows and sidestep the clipboard, but you need to have target and source images in view before you perform the copy. Additionally, if you want to move and distort the logo as a separate image element, you must store it on a separate layer.

Here's how to get a copy of your resized logo onto Fred's truck:

Pasting the Logo to the Truck

With FREDLOGO.TIF as active image window, press Ctrl+− (minus)	Reduces image to 1:2 viewing resolution. You don't need a clear view of this image—the "host" image is the one you need a good view of.

continues

continued

Double-click on FREDFISH thumbnail at bottom left of Photoshop's workspace, then double-click on Zoom tool	Restores image and zooms you to 1:1 viewing resolution on Windows version. Mac users should resize image with Zoom box, then use Photoshop's Zoom tool to adjust viewing resolution.
Click on New layer icon on Layers Roll-Up, then click on OK	Accepts default name for new Layer 1. Layer 1 is now the target Layer for FREDFISH image.
Adjust both image windows so that you can see all of FREDLOGO image, and only the side of FREDFISH truck image	You don't need to see the whole FREDFISH image; you can drag and drop a selection into any part of an image window.
Click on title bar of FREDLOGO image, then choose **S**elect, **L**oad Selection, and click on OK	Displays marquee selection around logo areas of the image.
With any selection tool (the Lasso tool is good) chosen, click and drag selection onto FREDFISH image window	Copies selection to FREDFISH image Layer 1, as shown in figure 9.22.
Choose **F**ile, **S**ave (or press Ctrl+S),then close FREDLOGO.TIF image	Saves your work up to this point.

Now you can click outside the borders of the logo selection whenever you want; whether the logo is selected or not, it can be modified independently of the Background image because it is on a transparent layer.

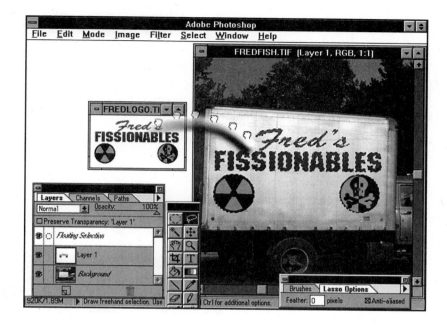

Figure 9.22

Drag and drop selections into different image windows. Skip using the clipboard and conserve system resources!

Putting Fred's Business in Perspective

Although Fred performs a valuable community service, that's not the "perspective" addressed in this section. Rather, Fred's logo on Layer 1 needs to be distorted a little (remember the PARTY ZONE sign in the last assignment?) so that it follows the lines of the truck's side. The truck shows dimension, and so should the logo—you want it to look as though it's painted on the truck, not simply pasted on.

The next exercise shows you how to use the Distort Effect again to tilt this logo ever so slightly. For this job, unlike the traffic sign assignment, you don't need to create a path to follow; simply use the metal edges of the truck's box as visual guides as to how the logo should be adjusted:

Using the Distort Effect To Tilt a Logo

Choose Move tool (press **V**), then press the appropriate arrow keys a few times to position the logo

Gets logo into better position relative to side of truck. The logo needs to be toward the top of the truck's box to allow room for more type, added in the next step.

continues

continued

With the Move tool chosen, the arrow keys serve as nudge tools (similar to nudging an active selection when a selection tool is the current chosen tool).

Choose **I**mage, **E**ffects, and then choose **D**istort	Creates a boundary box around the selection.
Click on corners of Distort box (the small squares) and drag them until they're parallel to edges of truck's side	Skews selection so that it appears to be at same angle as surface of truck's side, (see fig. 9.23).
Click inside Distort box	Cursor changes to a hammer, and "nails" selection to desired degree of distortion.

Figure 9.23

You make the image look more believable by angling the selection to conform to the angle of the truck's side.

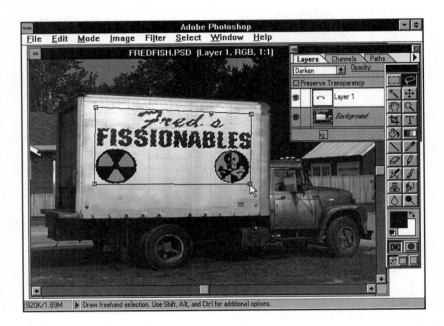

Adding Photoshop Type to the Truck

Every good trucking company that hauls dangerous materials should advertise its line. Accordingly, you now want to use the Type tool to embellish the mock-up of the side of Fred's truck. As you add this text to the image in the upcoming exercises, you discover more of Photoshop's powers.

In the next exercises, you size up Fred's truck for the additional text and choose the color of that text. Keep in mind that you'll be entering the text directly, so you have to choose a good, "photogenic" color before you enter the text. Take the time to choose the right color; to change the color of text after it has been entered, you have to delete the type selection and start over again.

Measuring the Target Image for the Type Tool

Choose **F**ile, Pre**f**erences, and then choose **U**nits	Displays Units Preferences dialog box.
Click on **R**ulers Units drop-down list	Offers a selection of units that measure distance.
Choose Points in **R**ulers Units drop-down list, then click on OK	Sets Photoshop's rulers to use points to measure typeface heights, and returns to your workspace.

Evaluate how large four lines of type can be to fit under Fred's logo. About 50 points of space are blank, so to include some leading, 10-point type seems ideal.

Click on Eyedropper tool, then click over top part of the FRED'S FISSIONABLES lettering	Samples a reddish color from gradient color you used earlier as transitional foreground color.

Directly sampling from an image is an easy technique to use to reacquire a specific color that you've used but didn't save on the Swatches or Picker palette.

Click on New icon on Layers palette, then click on OK	Creates Layer 2 in FREDFISH image.

You want to keep the two text image elements separate because you'll need to distort the Photoshop type without further changing the distorted logo.

Having sized up the space available on the side of Fred's truck and selected your color, it's time for you to enter the type:

TruckType

Click on Type tool, then click an insertion point on the truck image	Displays Type Tool dialog box.

continues

continued

Enter **10** points in the <u>S</u>ize field, **10** points for the Lea<u>d</u>ing, and click on the center horizontal Alignment radio button	Specifies a size of type that will fit nicely on the truck's side.

Because Photoshop "remembers" the last font you used, and the <u>A</u>nti-aliased setting within a session, you don't need to reset them.

Uncheck the Show: Si<u>z</u>e check box	10 points will display too small; with the box unchecked, Photoshop displays the text at 12 points.
Place your cursor in text field at the bottom of the dialog box and type the following, pressing Enter at the end of each line:	Specifies the text to enter into the FREDFISH image, as shown in figure 9.24.

```
ISOTOPES

REACTORS

SHIELDING

CALL 1-800-MELTDOWN
```

Click on OK.	Redisplays the image, with designated text in foreground color as a floating selection.
Click on floating text and drag it into position under the logo	Moves new text into position.
Choose <u>E</u>ffects from <u>I</u>mage menu, and then choose Distort	Creates a Distort boundary box around the floating text.
Click on Distort box's corners and drag them to match box's angle to truck's side	Skews selection so that it appears to be at the same angle in the image as the side of the truck (see fig. 9.25).
Click inside Distort box	Cursor changes to a hammer, and "nails" text into its distorted angle.
Press Ctrl+S (<u>F</u>ile, <u>S</u>ave)	Saves your work at this intermediate stage of completion.

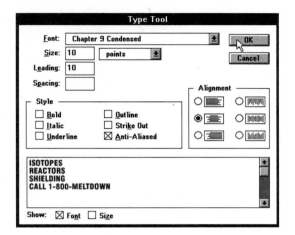

Figure 9.24

The Type Tool Options box "remembers" the last font you used in a single Photoshop session.

Figure 9.25

Use the edges of the top and sides of the truck's back as guidelines for the Distort command's boundary box.

Weathering the Selection

Before you merge the layers that hold the type and logo, let's think about *how* the layers should be merged. Layers are similar to marquee selections in the sense that you can composite layers to a background image, using different modes. You can choose from the Layers palette's 14 modes; their effects are actively displayed on-screen and can add a special effect when you merge a layer to the background. Each layer you click on can be assigned a different mode and opacity before you merge it. For a complete rundown of what each painting or editing mode does, see Chapter 6, "The Photoshop Test Drive."

A common problem occurs when you simply drop type or another graphic element into a scene. Instead of looking like an actual part of the scene, the element usually looks as though you neatly pasted it over the image. For example, if you composite the type layer into the background at 100-percent opacity, normal mode, the lettering covers up the faint weathering on the side of the truck. To make this image convincing, you need to expose some of the mottling and weathering qualities of the metal truck and still maintain the legibility of the type on Layer 2.

Here's how to make the type on Layer 2 look as though it were painted right on the truck:

Weathering the Logo

Click on Layer 1 Eye icon on palette	Hides Layer 1 from editing and from view.
Click on Layer 2 title on Layers palette	Selects Layer 2, containing the type. Layer 2 is the only Layer that can be edited now.
Choose the Move tool, then press 9	Changes opacity of the layer to 90 percent. Alternatively, you can click and drag the Opacity slider to a specific value.

Using the numeric values on the keyboard is a quick way to define any Opacity value in increments of 10, but you must have the Move tool chosen to do this. (The number 0 is equal to 100-percent opacity.)

Choose Darken mode from Layers palette's drop-down list	Specifies that each pixel in Layer 2 will replace corresponding pixels in the background layer, when merged, only if a Layer 2 pixel is darker (see fig. 9.26).

The combination of 90% Opacity and Darken mode lets the truck's texture to show through a little.

Choose Merge Layers from Layers menu flyout	Merges only the Layers that aren't hidden; Layer 2 of the type becomes part of the Background image, and its title disappears from the Layers palette.
Select File, Save (or press Ctrl+S)	Saves your work up to this point.

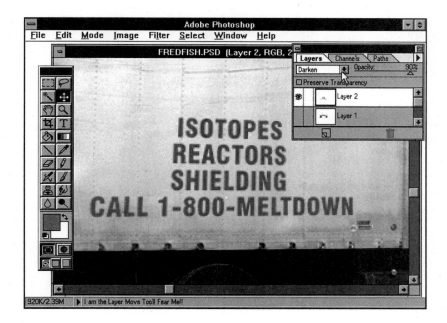

Figure 9.26

Mode and Opacity controls are used to define the way a layer is merged to the background image.

As you can see, you're well on the way toward creating an image that will give Fred a good idea of what his logo will look like on the side of his truck.

Taking a Sponge to the Truck

One of the wonders of working with independent Layers is that you can fine-tune an image element without messing up areas you've already perfected. To conclude designing the mock-up signage for Fred Glough's truck, Layer 1, containing the color logo, needs to go through changes similar to those you performed on Layer 2.

You might notice that although the logo looks great against the original white background of the FREDLOGO.TIF file, it's a little "intense" now that it's in position above the background image of the truck. Photoshop 3 now sports a local Desaturation tool—the *Sponge* tool—that is used like any other painting tool. The Sponge tool is used to reduce hue values and to reveal more grayscale components from areas you paint over. After setting up the right mode and opacity for Layer 1, you use the Sponge tool to finish creating Fred's signage.

Here's how to edit the logo layer, and get this truck into gear:

Merging the Logo Layer

Click on Layer 1 column where Eye icon used to be	Restores Eye icon, and makes the logo Layer visible.
Click on title area of Layer 1 on the Layers palette	Makes Layer 1 the active Layer in the image, for editing purposes.
Choose **90%** Opacity and Darken mode from the Layers palette	Applies qualities identical to those you chose for merging Layer 2 with the type.
Press Alt (Option) and click on Toning tool on the toolbox until you see the Sponge tool (or repeatedly press the letter O)	By default, the last Toning tool used is displayed on the toolbox, and pressing Alt and clicing over the tool cycles through the tools.
Click on Options tab on Brushes palette, then drag Toning Tools Options tab off the palette (see fig. 9.27)	Creates a separate palette for Options; now you can see simultaneously the Brushes setting and the Options for the Sponge Tool.
Click on 45-pixel tip on Brushes palette, then choose Desaturate and **50%** Pressure on the Toning Tools Options palette	Sets size and characteristics for Sponge tool.
Click and drag over the nuclear energy symbol	Removes a little of the mustard color from the area, making it more photo-realistic.
Click and drag over the skull and crossbones symbol	Removes saturation from mustard color (see fig. 9.28).
Choose Merge Layers from Layers menu flyout	Merges logo Layer 1 to Background image.
Choose <u>F</u>ile, Sa<u>v</u>e As, then choose *.TIF from the Save File As Format <u>T</u>ype drop-down list	Saves image in a format other operating platforms and applications can read and use.

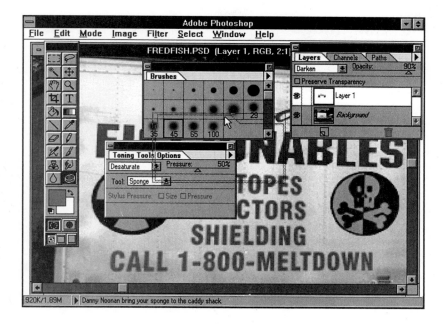

Figure 9.27

Dragging Toning Tools Options tab off the palette.

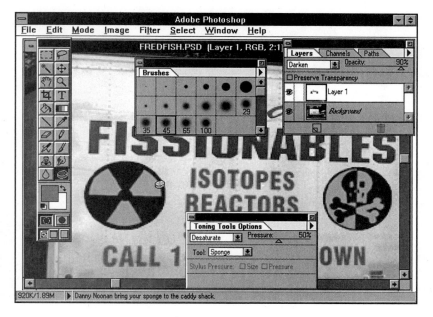

Figure 9.28

Decrease the the amount of predominant hue in an image area with the Sponge Toning tool.

You can click and drag the Toning Tools Options palette by the tab, and drop it over the Brushes palette to regroup the Brushes and Options palette now.

Viewing the Final Image

You're done! To look at the final image, click on the window mode button (which displays a full-screen image view) at the bottom right of the toolbox, or press the F key until your image is displayed full-screen.

You can now choose to close the palettes manually, as the author did, or simply press the Tab key to clear the toolbox and palettes from view. Your screen should now look like figure 9.29. You can get the toolbox back (it has the controls for the window modes!) by pressing Tab again. Think of the Tab key as another of Photoshops toggling functions. The only screen element that cannot be closed manually is the toolbox—because it's a toolbox, and not a palette.

Figure 9.29

The finished piece in Full-Screen Display Mode.

You're now finished with Fred's truck. He likes what he sees, so now he's looking for a sign painter who can't read English.

You can use text generated with the Type tool as you would any other graphical selection in Photoshop because the text you type *is a graphic*. Although you can't edit this text the way you edit text typed with a word processor, you can alter it. You can use Photoshop's Distort command, as well as filters, effects, and any of the other tools on the type you create in a color channel or Grayscale mode image.

Stamping Out Photo Errors

Many of the exercises in this book use the Rubber Stamp tool to retouch little bits and pieces of an image that are flawed or damaged. But sometimes in your imaging work the Rubber Stamp tool moves out of the wings and into the footlights as the star feature in Photoshop that helps you complete an image.

If you've glanced at other chapters or experimented with Photoshop on your own before reading this, you know that the Rubber Stamp tool copies image information from one place and applies it to another. But the tool also has some *special* properties that make it much more versatile than you may have come to think. This chapter shows you two occasions where an understanding of the tool's properties and a technique that takes advantage of the special properties let you accomplish something that no other effect or filter can. *Cloning*, the duplication of image areas, can be accomplished through the use of the many modes of the Rubber Stamp tool, and the various means of sampling and applying photographic detail to restore an image is the highlight of this chapter. We take a look in this chapter at the people, places, and things (also known as *nouns*) that populate your images, and how the Rubber Stamp tool can be best used to correct these elements in pictures that need some help.

This Chapter's Assignment

Portrait photography is big business. Every department store and photo-portrait gallery offers special deals on packages for the family. They make a marginal profit by assembly-line photofinishing the film, which leaves little or no opportunity for retouching a blemish or other flaw in an image. And places that *do* offer retouching usually do so through traditional, chemical methods, not the digital enhancements that Photoshop offers.

As you realize by now, no image is etched in stone when it's a digital sample. A larger-than-life mistake has been made in a portrait photo you'll be working with to serve as an assignment on how to go about correcting a specific type of image. My brother Dave agreed to put a bandage on his forehead, as an example of something unwanted on the skin of the subject in a portrait. The bandage is a metaphor for blemishes, unwanted hair, or any number of a subject's imperfections in a picture.

Cloning a Sample

In the next exercises, you concentrate on developing a technique to use with the Rubber Stamp tool. OUCH.TIF, as shown in figure 10.1, is the image on the Bonus CD that came with this book. Yes, the bandage is oversized, but because this assignment is larger than life, you'll master some techniques that will make your own assignments a breeze by comparison.

Figure 10.1

The bandage represents a skin flaw that you might find in a portrait image.

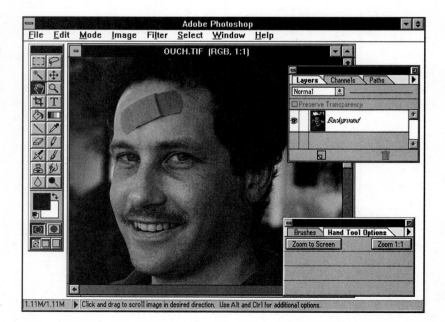

Before beginning the reconstruction of OUCH.TIF, however, you'll create a new layer upon which you'll perform the Rubber Stamp cloning work. Because Photoshop offers a transparent layer for editing, copying, and painting upon, you save original image information when you clone onto a layer and not the background image. If you make a mistake, you can't correct while working on a layer, only the elements on the layer are affected. At the conclusion of the assignment, we'll show you how to flatten the image and make both OUCH layers a single image.

The big bandage on Dave's forehead doesn't leave much unblemished source material for you to use as a replacement for the bandaged area. Therefore, the prudent approach is to first build a small, unblemished area using the Rubber Stamp tool and then use that area to build a larger area from which you can continue to sample. The trick is to work on this area with care and an observant artist's eye to make sure that every area you clone over contains the right shading; Dave's forehead is lit from the left and displays a graduation in skin tones from left to right. To produce good results, don't tackle this problem area dead-on. Working with the Rubber Stamp tool from the outside edge of the bandage inward helps you preserve the continuity between the original forehead areas and the cloned areas that will cover the bandage.

Here's how to begin the assignment by setting up the document and cloning sample areas over the edge of the bandage:

Cloning to Build Up the Source Area

Open the OUCH.TIF image from the CHAP10 subdirectory (folder) of the Bonus CD that came with this book	Opens the image of Dave that requires retouching.
If Layers palette is not showing, press **F7** (Macintosh: F11), or choose **W**indow, **P**alettes, Show **L**ayers	Displays the Layers palette.
Click on the New Layer icon, type **Retouching** in the Name field in the dialog box, and then click on OK	Displays the New Layer dialog box; assigns a name to the layer that you'll use for retouching work; and **Retouching** becomes the current layer.
Hold down the Ctrl key, then press the + key three times; use the scroll bars to center the bandage in the window	Zooms the image to a comfortable viewing resolution of the problem area.

continues

continued

Double-click on the Rubber Stamp tool	Makes the Rubber Stamp tool the active tool and displays the Options palette for the tool.
Set Option to Clone(aligned), Normal mode, and **100%** Opacity on the Options palette	Sets the Rubber Stamp tool to default properties in case you didn't reset them from other usage.
Click on the Sample Merged check box on the Options palette	You can now sample image areas from the Background layer, and apply them to the Retouching layer.

If you don't check the Sample Merged option in a situation like the one presented in this exercise, you can't clone with the Rubber Stamp tool in Clone (aligned) mode. The Retouching layer contains only transparent pixels at the moment, and sampling, then cloning from them wouldn't produce any effect!

Choose the third (from the left) tip, center row on the Brushes palette	Sets the characteristics of the Rubber Stamp tip for your first cloning maneuvers with this image.

You'll see in screen figures to come that the Brushes palette has been detached from the grouped palette that also contains tool Options. We've done this so that you can quickly reference which tool is used for a step, but you'll also see that separating palettes causes "screen congestion," allowing very little workspace room for the image! Therefore, you don't and shouldn't have to separate the grouped palettes to accomplish this assignment.

Press Alt (Option) and click on an area in the center of Dave's forehead between the bandage and his eyebrows	Sets the point at which the traveling cross-hair cursor starts sampling source image.
Click and drag straight up with the Rubber Stamp tool, starting at the bottom edge of the bandage and stopping before the cloning-source (traveling) cross-hair cursor reaches the point where you first started cloning	Removes a small area of the bandage and replaces it with a clone of Dave's unbandaged forehead area, as shown in figure 10.2.
Press Alt (Option) while clicking to the left of your first cloning work, again halfway between the bandage's bottom edge and Dave's eyebrow	Sets a new sample source for the Rubber Stamp tool.

Click and drag from the bottom edge of the bandage straight up, stopping before the sampling cross-hair cursor reaches the point where you started clicking and dragging	Removes still more bandage area and replaces it with the sampled skin area.
Choose File, Save As; then save the image as OUCH.PSD to your hard disk	Saves your work up to this point, with the Retouching layer intact. Photoshop only allows a layered image to be saved in its own, proprietary format.

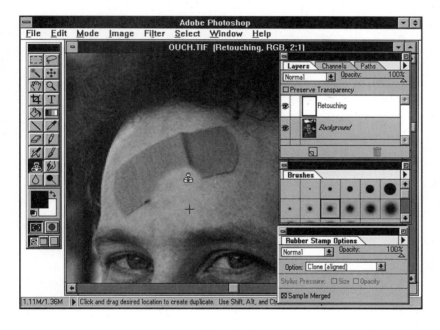

Figure 10.2

Don't let the cross-hair cursor move into the bandage area, or you'll be using it as source material with the Rubber Stamp tool.

Chemical photo retouchers often make a fundamental mistake when handling an assignment like this one. They usually use an airbrush with a semitransparent dye to brush in an area like the one that you're retouching. Besides the fact that photo retouchers must "guesstimate" the exact shade of the skin tone, this process usually airbrushes out *desired* visual information such as freckles and pores.

When you use the Rubber Stamp tool, you paint not only the exact fleshtone but also the subtleties of the skin itself. Texture *and* visual content are cloned into this area, so that it looks as though the bandage is vanishing rather than being covered up. And because all your work on the OUCH assignment is performed on a layer, mistakes can be corrected without having to start from the beginning.

Don't Make Cloning Obvious

The hardest part of this retouching assignment is to avoid creating *patterns* within cloned-in areas. When you lack a decent-sized, clear area to sample source material from, keep the following three tips in mind:

◆ Keep resampling from different areas that have the same tonal value when you use the Rubber Stamp tool. Frequent resampling helps you avoid creating obvious, repetitious patterns that tend to develop when you repeatedly use the same small sample.

◆ For most dimensional surfaces, the brightness and color varies. Use your eye to match the source and the cloning area for changing values.

◆ Reset your brush size as necessary. The Rubber Stamp sampling source point and the tip of the Rubber Stamp tool are both set to the same relative size. When working from a small sample area, using a small brush tip makes the traveling sample cursor take its samples from a smaller area. Use short strokes and change the tip sizes frequently—this helps randomize a cloned-in area, which in turn keeps patterning out of the picture.

Cloning in the Right Direction

In the preceding exercise, you moved your Rubber Stamp strokes upward in a vertical direction for a very good reason: Dave's forehead is lit from the left, so the gradual shading of his forehead is vertical. If you made a horizontal stroke, you would clone a different shade of fleshtone into an area, and then the portrait would be better off with the bandage still in it!

Be patient when working with the Rubber Stamp tool. Many artists use it as though it's an instant remedy for bad photography, but it's not. It's a tool, like any other one in Photoshop, and you need to build experience using it in order to master it.

The objective of the preceding exercise was to work up from the bandage's bottom edge with the Rubber Stamp tool. After you have a fair amount completed on the left of the bottom edge, it's time for you to start over from the *top* edge.

Here's how to increase the cloned areas on the Retouching layer, so that you can begin to sample a combination of original and cloned image areas more freely:

Cloning toward the Center of the Bandage

Press Alt (Option) and click as close as possible to the top of Dave's hairline above the far left of the bandage	Sets a sample point for the Rubber Stamp tool.

Be careful not to sample too close to any hair, or you'll clone in hair where there definitely shouldn't be any!

Click just above the top edge of the bandage and then drag down, stopping before the sampling cross-hair cursor reaches your initial cloning point	Fills in the left part of the top of the bandage with samples of skin tone, as shown in figure 10.3.
Press Alt (Option) while clicking just below Dave's hairline to the right of your last sampling point	Samples a different shade of skin tone, to use to fill in another portion of the bandage area.
Click and drag down into the bandage portion, stopping when the sampling cross-hair cursor reaches the first point in your stroke	Restores more forehead area.
Press Ctrl+S (<u>F</u>ile, <u>S</u>ave)	Saves your work at this intermediate stage of completion.

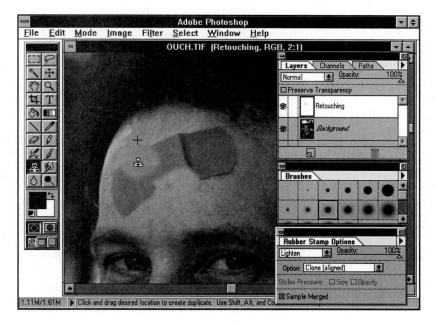

Figure 10.3

Resample the Rubber Stamp source area each time you move into a different shade of skin tone.

If you feel like you're getting into an artist's role with this exercise, it's because you are! It takes skill to mask the bandage area with the right shade and texture on the Retouching layer! But if you think the resampling isn't shaping up flawlessly at this point, don't worry; you haven't gotten to the finishing touches on the piece yet. Proceed with patience.

Using the Lighten Rubber Stamp Mode

As mentioned earlier, the Rubber Stamp tool can be set to a number of different modes, exactly like the Paint Brush tool, to give the sample areas that you clone special properties. In the next exercise, you'll use Lighten mode (found on the Options palette), which makes it easier to match Dave's forehead skin tones. When the Rubber Stamp tool is set to Lighten mode and you have Sample Merged checked for the layer on which you're cloning, only the strokes you make that are lighter than the areas on the layers directly below will appear on the layer on which you are working. The Lighten Mode effectively protects the areas you clone over from displaying image samples that are too dark to look natural upon the gently shaded areas of Dave's forehead.

Here's how to add a little lightness to a potentially painful situation:

Lighten Mode and the Rubber Stamp

Click on the Option drop-down list on the Rubber Stamp Options palette, then click on Lighten

Sets the Rubber Stamp tool to only apply sampled image areas at a tonal density equal to or lighter than the areas you clone over.

In effect, Lighten mode changes the property of the samples you clone in to only reflect a tonal value that's in synch with the areas you clone over. This is a very good way to prevent accidentally darkening an image as you retouch with the Rubber Stamp tool.

Press Alt and click beneath the remains of the the bandage on the left of Dave's forehead; then click and drag on the bottom of the bandage toward the right of the image

Adds cloned samples to cover bandage on the Background layer; keeps the area the same tone (see fig. 10.4).

If you begin to see a tonal variation in skin color where you shouldn't, press Ctrl+Z (**E**dit, **U**ndo)

Removes your last cloning stroke.

Continue sampling original and cloned strokes from the left of the image, and apply them where you see the bottom of the bandage

Covers the bandage with lighter colored skin tones on the Retouching layer.

Press Ctrl+S (<u>F</u>ile, <u>S</u>ave)

Saves your work at this intermediate stage of completion.

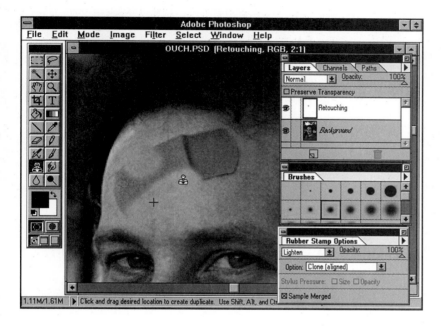

Figure 10.4

Lighten mode will not add a darker sampled area to the area you clone over; instead, the Rubber Stamp tool lightens the sample.

Keep in mind here that the retouching work you've performed so far has been applied to the Retouching layer; there's still a bandage on Dave's noggin on the Background layer. You're adding sampled image areas to the Retouching layer to cover the bandage area, and the samples are quickly becoming a mixture of original and cloned image areas. By editing on a transparent layer, you always have the original source information to go back to in case something goes wrong on the editing layer.

Bigger Brush, Looser Strokes

You've gained more forehead area to sample from now, and you can put it to good use. You'll notice that after all the vertical cloning strokes, there's more skin tone in the overall area on the Retouching layer. This means that you can now increase the size of the Brushes tip for the Rubber Stamp tool and polish off what remains of the bandage more quickly.

If you made the small, vertical strokes with the Rubber Stamp tool recommended in the preceding exercises, you'll notice that the shading on Dave's forehead is nice and even, with no cloned-in areas clashing with the original image areas. At this point, you can relax a little with these vertical strokes and combine a little lateral action with these last, large strokes. Use your eye to determine how best to clone in different shades of sampled skin tones. Dave's forehead isn't perfectly lit from left to right, so just follow the general flow of the lighting in the remainder of the bandage that needs covering up. In the next exercise, you'll remove the rest of the bandage from Dave's face.

Here's how to completely hide the "ouch" on the Background layer:

Tearing Off the Last of the Bandage

Click on the second-to-last tip from the middle row of the default Brushes tip settings	Specifies a new size for sampling and cloning with the Rubber Stamp tool.
Choose Normal mode on the Options palette's drop-down list	Returns the mode of painting with the Rubber Stamp tool to its default.
Press Alt (Option) and click just about anywhere between Dave's eyebrows and what's left of your view of the bandage	Samples an area that is a blend of the original and cloned image areas.

The size of the area on the Retouching layer has been expanded; you can see this on the Layers palette. The image icon for the Retouching layer constantly updates to show the opaque areas on the layer. Therefore, you can sample from both the Retouching layer and the background now with a larger Brushes tip.

Click and drag up and around into the remaining bandage area	Removes large portions of the bandage as shown in figure 10.5.
Press Alt (Option) and click above the bandage's remains on the upper left of Dave's forehead	Sets a new sample point for the Rubber Stamp tool.
Click and drag down and around the remains of the bandage to the left of Dave's forehead	Covers the left portion of the bandage.
Continue resampling in different tonal ranges, clicking and dragging into areas of the remaining bandage where the bordering skin tones match your sample point	Covers the remaining bandage areas with a combination of original and previously cloned-in areas.
Press Ctrl+S (File, Save)	Saves your work at this intermediate stage of completion.

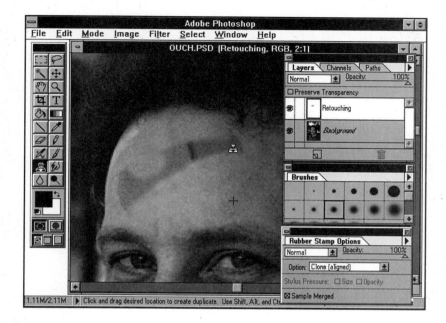

Figure 10.5

Now you can sample areas according to their tonal value instead of sampling only the original image area.

Pretty amazing, isn't it? You've used only one of Photoshop's tools to convincingly remove an oversized bandage from a portrait photo, and Dave didn't complain once.

Using the Color Cloning Mode

If you take a look at the skin on your palm and then on your wrist, you'll notice that human skin is composed of many different textures and colors. Light strikes callused areas and reflects a different shade from smooth areas, and people's skin is represented by a combination of different color values.

In the OUCH.PSD image, you performed a small miracle—you successfully disguised an oversized photographic flaw in a portrait image—but the colors, plural, of the skin aren't quite right. The transition of colors can be successfully blended without changing tonal texture in the OUCH image by using another of Photoshop's painting/editing modes—Color. Color mode only changes the hue and saturation of areas you clone over with the Rubber Stamp tool; you retain the tonal, the luminosity, values in an area when you clone over the image in Color mode. For more information about color and the way you work with color characteristics in Photoshop, check out Chapter 3, "Color Theory and the PhotoCD."

Here's how to make the color transitions within the area you retouched blend seamlessly together:

Blending with the Color Mode of Cloning

Click on the third (from the left) tip on the middle row on the Brushes palette	Sets the size of the tip you'll use with the Rubber Stamp tool in this exercise.
Press **5** on the keyboard (or click and drag the Opacity slider to about **50%**); then click on the Option drop-down list on the Options palette, and click on Color	Sets the cloning mode to Color and decreases opacity for a more subtle Color cloning effect.
Press Alt (Option) and click about 1/4 screen inch above and to the left of Dave's eyebrow; then release the Alt (Option) key and click and drag over the edge of the area on the Retouching layer	Blends a semitransparent tint of sampled color around the edge of your retouching work on the layer (see fig. 10.6).
Press Alt (Option) and click on the same area; then move on to a different area of the retouched edge on the Retouching layer	Blends the color, not the image detail, into the edge of the pixels on the Retouching layer.
Press Ctrl+S (**F**ile, **S**ave)	Saves your work at this intermediate stage of completion.

Figure 10.6

Use the Color mode on the Options palette to only change the hue and saturation of areas you click and drag over.

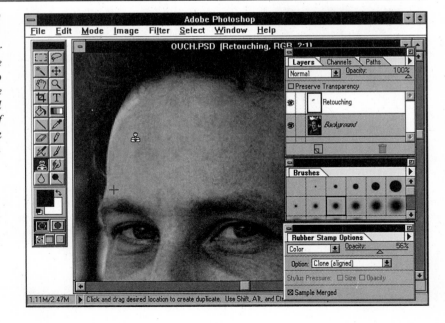

Using Toning Tools to Finish the Retouching

When you're retouching an image as extensively as this chapter's assignment, a little distracting element added to the overall image is sometimes useful to keep the viewer's eye from examining the area you've retouched too closely. After all, you've cloned a sizable area of skin tone into the center of OUCH.PSD; even the most masterfully performed editing work can use a little help from other supporting image elements.

To finish the OUCH.PSD image, use Photoshop's Dodge tool to slightly accentuate the area on the left edge of Dave's temple, where the sun catches a highlight on the smooth skin. The bandage is one of the soft fabric kind, and because it has a diffuse quality, it absorbed some of the reflected light you would naturally see on Dave's forehead. So in the next exercise, you do not actually "fake" an image element within the picture, but instead enhance it and portray the image in a very naturalistic way. Optimizing a photograph is part of any image retoucher's trade; making the best picture possible from the OUCH image is easy when you understand both the aesthetics of your craft and what Photoshop's tools can do.

Here's how to use the Dodge tool to accentuate the highlight on Dave's temple:

Dodging Highlights in an Image

Press **O** until the Dodge Toning tool is displayed on the toolbox (or press Alt (Option) and click on the tool until the Dodge tool is displayed)	Toggles the tool to the Dodge tool; this tool lightens specific tonal ranges within an image.
Choose Highlights from the drop-down list; then click and drag the Exposure slider on the Options palette to about **20%**	Sets the Dodge tool to affect the highlight areas in the image to the greatest degree; specifies a very weak amount of the effect (Exposure).
On the Brushes palette, click on the 65-pixel tip	Sets the tip for the Dodge tool to a soft edge, with a 65-pixel diameter.
Click on the Background layer title on the Layers palette	Specifies the Background layer as current editing layer.

continues

continued

Unlike the Rubber Stamp (and other Photoshop tools), the Toning tools do not use the Sample Merged option; you specify the target layer you want to change with the Dodge tool by clicking on the layer's title on the Layers palette.

Click and drag once, beginning at Dave's hairline on his right temple (your left), and ending at his right eyebrow	Lightens the highlight on Dave's temple (see fig. 10.7).
Press Ctrl+S (**F**ile, **S**ave)	Saves your work at this intermediate stage of completion.

Figure 10.7

Use the Dodge tool at a large size, but weak Exposure setting, to gently lighten an image area's tonal quality.

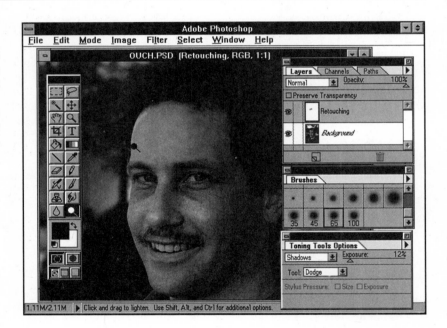

The Dodge tool is very powerful for creating and enhancing image highlights. For this reason, use a low Exposure setting when you want to apply a subtle enhancement to photographs of people.

In general, it's a good working practice to use partial Opacity, Exposure, and Pressure settings when they're offered on the Options palette for editing and painting tools. An edit that's performed at a "partial intensity" leaves an image area that can always be returned to for a second coat. If you use 100 percent as the setting on the Options palette for any tool, you deny yourself some control over the effect you create.

Now that you've finished the assignment, you may elect to choose Flatten Image or Merge Layers from the pop-up menu on the Layers palette to blend your editing work into the Background layer. We'll frequently recommend throughout this book that you save a spare copy of your PSD image in the TIFF format; TIF images don't support Photoshop layers, but they are a common file format that Macintosh and Windows users alike can read and write. Now that your work is done and you have a PSD format OUCH image completely edited, you can now choose Flatten Image; then use the File, Save As command to name your piece AAAH.TIF.

Figure 10.8 shows the original OUCH image compared to AAAH.TIF, which shows the completed retouching work. You have now taken an obviously flawed area and corrected it! If you can successfully remove an object this large from a critical area in a portrait, imagine how easily you can erase a minor skin blemish in an otherwise perfect image!

Figure 10.8

Hey, aren't these the twins from chapter 15?

The Human Element in Retouching Work

Correcting a problem area in an image's composition is no different from fixing a problem that's the result of damaged photographic emulsion, or even a bad scan: you still must use patience and your own judgment. No Photoshop tool estimates and replaces what *would have been* in a damaged or missing area. However, with the Rubber Stamp tool, you can replace damaged areas by using samples from pixels that neighbor the area or from other complementary areas.

But there *is* a difference between filling an area arbitrarily and using Rubber Stamp strokes judiciously. It's called *technique*. Technique marks the difference between someone who simply works with a computer, and one who uses the technology as a part of his or her craft. If you're serious about imaging, you'll get out of it what you put into it. Photoshop makes it easy, but you alone make it an art.

Taking Photoshop Outdoors

If you thought removing a large bandage from a forehead was a big assignment, how do you feel about re-seeding a lawn now? The image KIDSYARD.TIF on the Bonus CD is of a wonderful children's playground. It's a scene with bright, primary-colored toys—a red slide, a lush forest background—and the lawn looks as though some four-year-olds used it for motorcross practice.

If you need a picture of a house that's up for sale and the season's spoiled the yard, this next assignment's for you. In fact, it's for anyone who wants to enhance an outdoor image that's been marred by nature or man.

Pick Your Tools before Digging In

The KIDSYARD.TIF image on the Bonus CD (see fig. 10.9) looks a little rough around the edges; after all, kids play on grass, and this *is* a playground. Because of the many scattered, exposed areas of earth, a cursory assessment of this photo would give a big thumbs down on its retouchability.

Fortunately, random, natural, organic textures, like grass, lend themselves to cloning with the Rubber Stamp tool quite well. As long as an area has a grassy texture, no one would ever spend the time picking out which one, or two, or a thousand blades of grass have been cloned in.

To do the retouching for this assignment, you depend quite heavily on the Rubber Stamp tool. But you also learn how using the Pattern option with the Rubber Stamp and Paint Bucket tools, along with the special digital image properties of layers, makes renovating this chewed-up lawn much simpler. Just as with Dave's forehead, you first need to build up a decent-sized source area to do the initial cloning from, and then work on other cloning sources as the assignment progresses.

But before you begin the yard work, the first exercise shows how to set up the KIDSYARD document so that it becomes an image on a transparency layer. Usually, when you erase or delete a Background image area, you expose the current background color (usually white). But when the photo of the kids' yard is on a Photoshop layer, you can access both "sides" of the transparency—you can paint on both sides of the transparency layer with the Rubber Stamp (or other tools)—and this makes the task ahead go much more quickly. In the next exercise, you add a new layer; call it the

Working Surface; then remove the original background so that you can perform some extraordinary image editing in front of *and* behind the scenes.

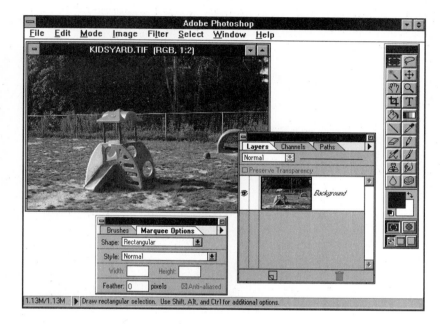

Figure 10.9

Pristine areas of grass are hard to fined in a single section of the KIDSYARD image.

Here's how to set up the KIDSYARD.TIF image for some digital restoration work:

Creating an Image Transparency Layer

Open KIDSYARD.TIF from the CHAP10 subdirectory of the Bonus CD that came with this book

Opens the image of the children's playground you'll restore.

Click on the Layers palette's pop-up menu button (the little triangle to the right of the Tab on the palette), and choose Duplicate Layer

Displays the Duplicate Layer dialog box (see fig. 10.10).

Type **Kid's Playground** in the Name field; then click on OK.

Creates a duplicate of the Background image on a layer on top of the Background, and entitles it "Kid's Playground" on the Layers palette.

continues

continued

Double-click on the Background icon on the Layers palette	Displays the Make Layer dialog box.
Type **Working Surface** in the **N**ame field, then click on OK.	Turns the background into a transparency layer.

Now you have a digital image in a very proprietary format. KIDSYARD is composed of two identical layers, with opaque pixels that don't really have a background to erase to! In the next step, you see that deleting the image information on the Working Surface layer does not fill the layer with background color, but instead replaces the opaque pixels with transparent pixels.

Click on the Working Surface title on the Layers palette; then press Ctrl+A (**S**elect, **A**ll)	Selects the entire area on the Working Surface Layer; the Working Surface layer is the current editing layer.
Press the Delete key; then press Ctrl+D (**S**elect, **N**one)	Deletes the opaque pixels on the Working Surface layer; deselects the selection marquee.
Click on the Kid's Playground layer title on the Layers palette.	Makes the Kid's Playground layer the current editing layer (see fig. 10.11).
Choose File, Sa**v**e As; then save the image as KIDSYARD.PSD to your hard disk	Saves your work up to this point. Images with layers can only be saved in the PSD format.

There is a difference between an image's Background, its native layer, and the layers you create upon the Background in Photoshop. KIDSYARD.PSD doesn't really have a Background to it now. Because the layers presently in the image are transparent and contain opaque pixels that make up the image, you now can do some very interesting (and sophisticated) things with the picture.

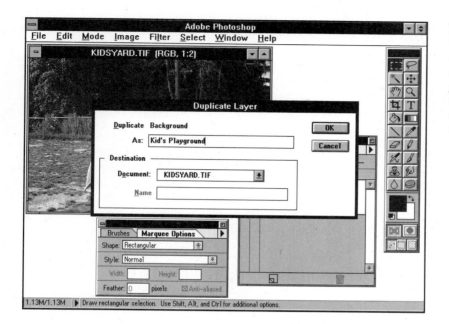

Figure 10.10

Create a duplicate of the Background's image to work with as opaque pixels on a transparent layer.

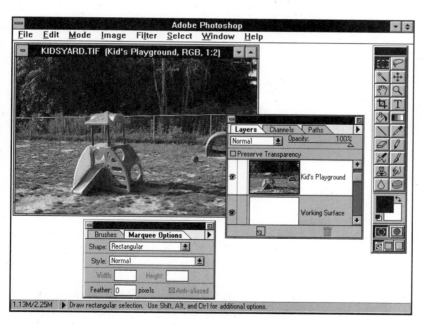

Figure 10.11

Deleting a layer's contents makes the layer consist of only "placeholders"— transparent pixels.

Cloning to Build Up an Image Layer

As with the image of Dave in the preceding exercise, KIDSYARD.PSD now needs to be restored by building up a small area of grass that can be used in successive edits to create larger areas of restoration. What makes this assignment a little easier than OUCH.PSD is that the subject matter is not human; grass displays more texture to the viewer than detail, and if you get an area "wrong," the audience isn't quite as critical.

Throughout this assignment, pay careful attention to the shading in the areas that you clone over with the Rubber Stamp tool. In the next exercise, you begin with a shaded area in the image on the Kid's Playground layer. You need to create a small area that you can use as a cloning source for the first part of your assignment.

Here's how to gradually increase a piece of lawn so that it becomes a contiguous area you can sample from later:

Finding a Little Shade

Press Ctrl++ once, then press **Z** (for **Z**oom tool) and click once over the shadow of the children's slide	This is the first area to be worked on in the image.
Press **S** (Rubber **S**tamp tool)	In its default setting of Clone (aligned), the tool will be used for straight cloning from image areas.
Click on the second tip from the left in the middle row on the Brushes palette; then select Normal mode on the drop-down list of the Options palette and set the opacity to **100%**	Sets the characteristics for the Rubber Stamp tool to sample and clone small, soft-edged areas.

Uncheck the Sample Merged box on the Options palette and drag the opacity slider to 100% if you completed the OUCH assignment earlier. Nothing is on the other layer (Working Surface) to sample visual data from, so the Rubber Stamp tool cannot apply a merged combination sampled from both layers.

Press Alt (Option) and click on a shaded area of grass just above a section of barren ground	Sets the source point for the Rubber Stamp tool.
Click and drag over the barren ground area	Replaces the barren ground area with the shaded grass source.

Continue clicking and dragging until you have an even area of shaded grass that's about 1 inch by 1/2 inch, as shown in figure 10.12	Builds up a sample area to be used by the Rubber Stamp tool.
Press **M** (**M**arquee tool) until the marquee appears on the toolbox	In addition to its regular selection Rectangular properties, you can use this tool to define a pattern.
Marquee-select the 1-inch by 1/2-inch perfectly shaded grass area that you cloned in the last step, as shown in figure 10.13	Specifies the area to be used as a pattern fill.
Choose **E**dit, **D**efine Pattern	Sets a repeating source area that can be used with the Rubber Stamp tool.

Additionally, a defined pattern can be used by the **E**dit, **F**ill command and the Paint Bucket tool for flooding an area with foreground color or, in this case, image contents.

Press Ctrl+S (**F**ile, **S**ave)	Saves your work at this intermediate stage of completion.

Figure 10.12

Use the Rubber Stamp tool to build up a sizable portion of perfect image area that you can sample again.

Figure 10.13

Use the Rectangular Marquee tool to select an area that you want to define as a pattern source.

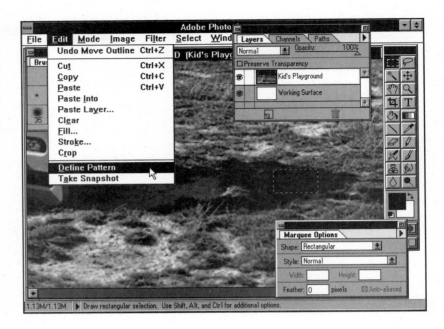

Tip

When setting up a pattern, avoid sampling areas that display "character." For instance, if you marquee-select an area that includes a rock, you'll wind up with a pattern of the repeating, tell-tale rock everywhere you fill in a selection area.

Keep both pattern source areas and areas you use for the other Rubber Stamp options free from distinctive visual content. Instead, try to capture texture that you can weave into the image without drawing much attention.

Putting a Pattern in Its Place

Now that you've defined a pattern of grass, you can apply the pattern to the barren image areas within the KIDSYARD image. Instead of using a selection tool to mark the barren areas in the next exercise for the pattern fill, you'll take advantage of the special property of the Kid's Playground transparency layer upon which you're currently editing.

Photoshop's Eraser tool is used in the next exercise to first remove the barren, shaded areas from the Kid's Playground layer. You will notice something bizarre as you do this; because the Working Surface Layer is empty, Photoshop will display a checkerboard indicator in areas you erase. The checkerboard appears in areas of a transparency layer that contain transparent pixels; the phenomenon is only visible

New Riders Publishing
INSIDE
SERIES

when the Background of an image is hidden, or in this instance, when the image has no background!

The Behind mode of the Rubber Stamp tool is the perfect choice for applying the pattern of the grass because Behind mode paints "behind" the transparent layer. Behind mode is only available when working on a transparency layer, and by using Behind mode, you're assured that not one precious pixel of grassy area on the Kid's Playground layer is replaced with fill. Part of the key to using the Rubber Stamp tool effectively is to integrate cloned with original image areas. A kid's playground covered with a repeating pattern, with no imperfections such as those found in original areas you now have in the image would make the picture look like the playground was covered with Astroturf.

Remember that a pattern consisting of shaded grass is loaded now. This means that you want to erase only the shaded areas of exposed earth.

Here's how to use Photoshop's Layers properties in combination with a defined pattern to seed the shaded portion of the image:

Masking a Selection Area

Press **E** (Eraser tool); then choose Paintbrush (mode) from the drop-down list on the Options palette and set the Opacity to **100%**	The Eraser tool exhibits the characteristics of the Paint Brush tool.

Additionally, the Eraser can be set to erase image areas with the characteristics of the Pencil and Airbrush tools. Photoshop 2.5's default (Block) Eraser tool shape is also available on the Options drop-down list.

On the Brushes palette, click on the second tip from the left on the top row	Sets the characteristics of the Paintbrush tip you'll use to erase the barren image areas.
Click and drag over the shaded areas of barren ground on the Kid's Playground layer (see fig. 10.14)	Erases the opaque pixels on the Kid's Playground layer, exposing the transparency checkerboard Photoshop displays by default when no colored pixels are in an area.

Now that the area is "prepped," it's time to explore one of the wonderful modern conveniences of electronic retouching: the pattern fill.

continues

continued

Press **S** (Rubber **S**tamp tool) and choose Pattern (Non-Aligned) from the Option drop-down list on the Options palette; then choose Behind painting mode	Sets the Rubber Stamp tool to take its samples from the pattern you defined earlier and to only apply the pattern to transparent areas—the areas "behind" the opaque pixels on the Kid's Playground layer.
Click and drag in one of the checkerboard areas with a stroke less than 1 inch long	Paints the pattern into the transparent areas (see fig. 10.15).

It's important in the next steps to keep your Rubber Stamp strokes shorter than the width and height of the pattern sample presently loaded in system memory. Non-aligned patterning mode means that you begin each stroke at the center of the pattern that's in memory. If you move farther than the height or width within the transparent areas, the pattern will repeat, and will surely display a hard edge where it begins/ends.

Continue clicking and dragging until you cover all the selection areas	Fills in the barren ground spots with a pattern fill of shaded grass.
Press Ctrl+S (**F**ile, **S**ave)	Saves your work at this intermediate stage of completion.

Figure 10.14

Use the Eraser tool to remove the barren ground from the image on the layer and expose transparent pixels.

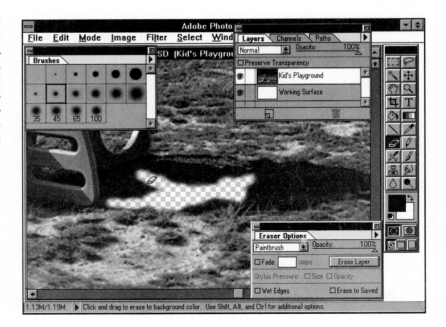

Figure 10.15

The Behind mode of painting doesn't affect foreground pixels on a transparency layer.

The Pattern Fill option for the Rubber Stamp tool makes quick work of filling in selection areas with the same patterned texture. You can use different areas as the target for the pattern, but you should make sure that the sample you define is of the same shade as the area you clone into with the Rubber Stamp tool.

You may want to set the Rubber stamp tool to Clone (aligned) and Normal (painting mode) for a moment now and use the default settings for the tool to blend over areas on the Kid's Playground layer that show a hard edge where the sampled pattern repeats.

Other Techniques for Different Image Areas

The pattern fill that you defined in the last exercise is now worthless because there aren't any more areas in the shaded portion of the layer in which to use it. So, it's time to resample a different part of the image—this time, the brightly lit parts.

It's time to look for a different patch of green that hasn't been trodden upon to address some of the scorched earth near the playset. In this chapter, learning how to define an area for replacement is as important as your selection of tools, so you'll use the Quick Mask mode to define the areas that need replacement. Quick Mask is an editing mode for a selection, rather than an image; you can refine an area you want selected in an image indefinitely until you click on the Standard mode button to make Quick Mask tinted overlay areas into a selection marquee. *See Chapter 6, "The Photoshop Test Drive," for more on the Quick Mask capabilities in Photoshop.*

Here's how to Quick Mask and then pattern fill the brighter shades of grass in the image's foreground:

Pattern Filling and Masking

Double-click on the Zoom tool	Zooms out to a 1:1 viewing resolution of the KIDSYARD.PSD image.
Click on the Hand tool; then drag the cursor in the image all the way up and to the left	Scrolls your view in the active image window to reveal the bottom-right corner of the KIDSYARD.PSD image.
Press **M** (**M**arquee tool; Rectangular should still be on the toolbox); then in the bottom right corner of the layer, marquee-select as large a grass-covered area as you can, as shown in figure 10.16	Samples the pattern to be used next.
Choose **E**dit, **D**efine Pattern	Stores the pattern in memory.
Press Ctrl+D or choose **S**elect, **N**one	Deselects the marquee area.
Double-click on the Quick Mask tool; then make sure that Color Indicates: **S**elected Areas is chosen; then click on OK.	Makes the application of black foreground color in Quick Mask mode represent future selected areas, not masked (protected) areas.
Press **D** (**d**efault colors icon)	Makes current foreground color black.
Press **Z** (**Z**oom tool), then marquee-zoom into the area beneath the first one that you pattern-filled	This brightly lit area of grass and dirt you'll retouch. A is where 2:1 viewing resolution is good.
Press **B** (Paint **B**rush tool), then select Normal mode from the Options palette; choose the third tip on the top row of the Brushes palette	This is the tool and settings you use to create and edit a Quick Mask.
Click and drag in the exposed areas	Fills these earth areas with Quick Mask, as shown in figure 10.17.
Click on the Standard mode button on the toolbox	Creates selection marquee areas out of the areas you previously masked.

Press **S** (Rubber **S**tamp tool); then choose Pattern (aligned) and Normal mode on the Options palette

Sets the Rubber Stamp tool to apply the defined pattern in default, regular cloning mode.

Click and drag over the selection areas

Paints only the selected areas with the pattern that you defined earlier, as shown in figure 10.18.

While you're cloning, you'll find it useful on occasion to press Ctrl+H (**S**elect, Hide **E**dges). This command toggles the selection marquee (or *marching ants*, as software engineers affectionately call them) to invisible. The selection areas *are still active* when you press Ctrl+H, but the marquee no longer obscures your view of the underlying image.

Choose **S**elect, **N**one (or press Ctrl+D)

Deselects the selection borders in the image.

Press Ctrl+S (**F**ile, **S**ave)

Saves your work at this intermediate stage of completion.

Figure 10.16

Sample a new area of grass to define it as a pattern to be used in brightly lit image areas.

Figure 10.17

Cover all the barren parts of an area with the Paint Brush tool in Quick Mask mode.

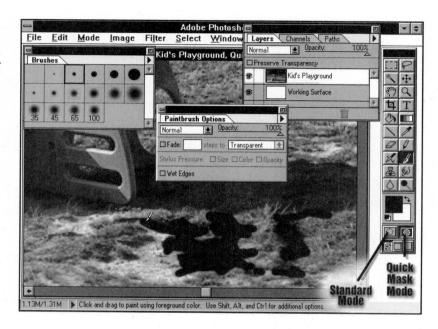

Figure 10.18

The Rubber Stamp fills in only the areas that you've selected.

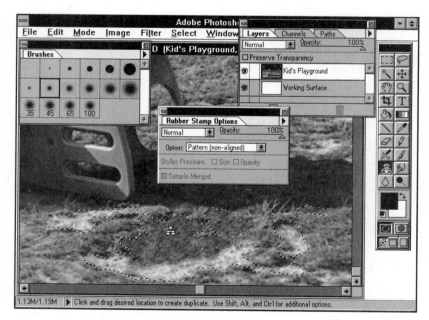

The advantage of using this pattern-fill technique is that it's quick and it lets you accomplish your assignment without requiring a high degree of accuracy. As soon as you have enough pattern-filled and original image areas woven into the retouched area, you can begin sampling areas of it with the Rubber Stamp tool with its Clone (aligned) option and use larger patterns to cover bigger problem areas on the layer more quickly.

Touch-Up Work with the Paint Bucket

Now that you have restored some of the grass in a brightly lit area, you can use this restored area to create another pattern. However, you won't have to use the Rubber Stamp tool to apply the pattern. The area that you restored in the last exercise is large enough to create an excellent pattern that you can use the Paint Bucket tool with to fill other areas.

In the next exercise, you'll use this technique to restore the image's lower-right corner.

Paint Bucket Filling with a Pattern Sample

Click on the Rectangular marquee tool on the toolbox	This is the selection tool that allows you to define patterns in an image area.
Marquee-select a grass-covered area where you applied a pattern fill in the last exercise	Determines the content of the pattern fill.

Try to include both the original image area and the area you Rubber Stamped in.

Choose **E**dit, **D**efine Pattern	Defines the area as a source when you apply the pattern fill.
Press Ctrl+D or choose **S**elect, **N**one	Deselects the current marquee selection.
Press **B** (Paint **B**rush tool); then click on the Quick Mask mode button	Applies Quick Mask with the Paint Brush tool.
Click and drag over the exposed earth in the lower right corner of the image	Defines areas as selection areas wherever you apply Quick Mask.
Click on the Standard mode button on the toolbox	Turns the masked areas that you've painted over into active selection areas.

continues

continued

Press **K** (Paint Bucket tool); then, on the Options palette, set the Tolerance option to **255**, check the **A**nti-Aliased check box, and choose Pattern from the Contents drop-down list.	Allows the Paint Bucket tool to flood-fill non-contiguous areas with a defined pattern.
Click inside a selection area with the Paint Bucket cursor	Flood-fills the opaque foreground pixels within the selection marquee (see fig. 10.19).

At a Tolerance of 255 (the tool's maximum value), the Paint Bucket tool's target is every pixel having every brightness value. The only limitation to the Paint bucket's pattern filling is the marquee selection border you set up by Quick Masking areas.

Choose **S**elect, **N**one (or press Ctrl+D)	Deselects all the selection areas in the image.
Press Ctrl+S (**F**ile, **S**ave)	Saves your work at this intermediate stage of completion.

Figure 10.19

The Paint Bucket tool can flood-fill a selection area with a color or pattern that you define.

Tip   If you have many assignments that require pattern fills like you've seen in these exercises, you may want to leave the Rubber Stamp tool set to Clone (aligned) and set the Paint Bucket tool to apply flood-fill patterns. That way you get the best of both worlds without having to toggle back and forth on the Options palette for the Rubber Stamp tool. However, if you want more control over the application of a pattern, then you'll want to constantly toggle between Rubber Stamp options.

Because you defined such a large sample area for your pattern in the preceding exercise, you won't see a pattern edge in your flood fills.

You should always create a good, opaque mask in an area that you want to flood-fill with a pattern or even a color. If your mask isn't 100-percent opaque in certain areas, the Paint Bucket tool can't apply a 100-percent dense pattern to the selection area, which results in a washed-out fill.

Selecting a Range within a Selection

The next area of KIDSYARD.PSD that requires some retouching is next to the ball in the upper right corner. The grass near the base of the children's bridge is showing some wear, so the area needs the same sort of attention that you gave to the foreground grass in this image.

The Color Range command will be called into action in the next exercise to define areas of barren ground that you'll clone over using the Rubber Stamp tool's default Clone (aligned) setting. The Color Range command creates selection marquees in an image based on the range of color similarity the image exhibits in an area, or in the entire image. You're always better off editing image areas that are in plain view, so in the next exercise you first create a selection area with the Rectangular marquee tool, and then allow the color Range command to pick out similarly-colored areas from within the selection. This way, you can be assured that the color Range's selection marquees fall within the rectangular area you defined, and that you don't have any areas selected outside your view within the image window.

Here's how to get the northeast corner of this playground looking a little greener:

Cloning in Some Background Grass

Press **Z** (**Z**oom tool) and click once over the children's bridge area of the image

This is the area that needs to be isolated in preparation for the the Color Range command.

continues

continued

With the Rectangular marquee tool, click and drag around the area beneath the children's bridge, including the bottom of the bridge	This is the target area on the Kid's Playground layer that will be retouched next.
Hold down Ctrl while clicking and dragging around the nameplate on the bottom of the bridge	This oval nameplate is about the same color as the brown areas you need to retouch. Holding down Ctrl while you select the nameplate subtracts this area from the marquee selection. See figure 10.20 for how the marquee should look before proceeding.
Choose **S**elect, **C**olor Range	Displays the Color Range dialog box.
Choose Sampled Colors on the Sele**c**t drop-down list, click on the **S**election radio button, and then choose None from the Sele**c**tion Preview drop-down list	Displays colors you choose from the image as white in the preview window of the dialog box.
Click the eyedropper cursor on an area of dirt in on the Kid's Playground layer	Preview window in the Color Range dialog box displays a high-contrast view of the selected areas.
Click on the eyedropper+ icon in the dialog box; then click over another area of dirt in the image	Adds another color of dirt to the Color Range's selection.
Click and drag the Fuzziness slider so that only dirt areas are seen as white in the preview window	Fuzziness adjusts the tolerance of the selection marquee the Color Range command creates. A good value is 62 (see fig. 10.21).

If you accidentally click over some green within the Kid's Playground layer of the image, the Preview window will turn mostly white, indicating that you've selected the entire area within the rectangular area you originally defined; this is no problem. Press Alt (Option) to toggle the Cancel button in the Color Range dialog box to Reset; then click on it. This restores the values to the Color Range command to what they were before you chose the command. Perform the following steps when your dialog box looks like the one shown in figure 10.21:

Click on OK	Accepts the Color Range settings, and several marquee borders appear in the area you defined with the Rectangular marquee tool.

Press **S** (Rubber **S**tamp tool); then press Alt and click on a stretch of green on the layer

Samples a mixture of original and cloned grass in the image.

Click and drag over the marquee areas

Clones green grass into the areas the Color Range command defined (see fig. 10.22).

Press Ctrl+D (**S**elect, **N**one)

Deselects the selection marquee.

Press Ctrl+S (**F**ile, **S**ave)

Saves your work at this intermediate stage of completion.

Figure 10.20

Subtract the nameplate area from the marquee selection before using the Color Range command.

Figure 10.21

The Color Range command automatically selects the color or colors you choose in an image.

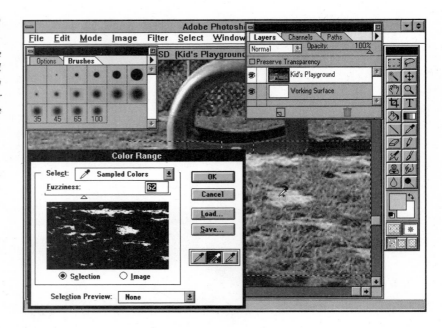

Figure 10.22

Clone in grass that you've sampled from image areas that are a blend of original clone dand cloned image areas.

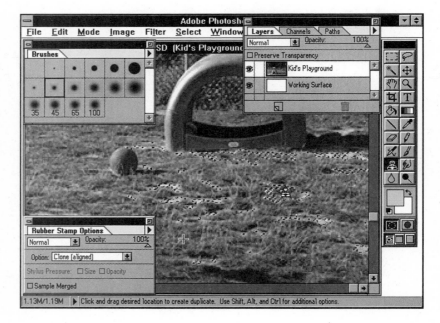

Think of the Color Range command as sort of a "universal Magic Wand tool." It's a terrific command for selecting all the similar colors within an image, and you add to or subtract from color ranges until you isolate the image area that needs attention.

You should now have the right side of KIDSYARD.PSD completely manicured. If you start building perfect little areas with the Rubber Stamp tool, you can use increasingly broad strokes, and your sampling becomes less constrained by the available source area for the tool.

Tip   If an area looks like it has a pattern of brownish grass, sample a greener area with the Rubber Stamp tool and clone one or two strokes of green into the area. If an area looks too flat and green, clone a weed or two into it. The point is to break up any obvious patterns in this image's grass and to create a random, textured surface that won't alert the viewer to your retouching work.

Using the New Window Command

As you progress in your retouching work, you'll notice that it's somewhat of a hassle to set a sampling point that's four or five virtual yards away from the point you want to clone using the Rubber Stamp tool. This is where the **N**ew Window command comes in handy.

The **N**ew Window command creates an identical copy of the active image that updates your editing changes as you make them. A new image window can be zoomed in or out so that you can have two different views of the active document. The most useful feature of opening a new image window, however, is that you can set a sampling point for the Rubber Stamp in one image window and perform cloning in the other!

Here's how to tackle the bottom left corner of the Kid's Playground layer in split-screen view:

Cloning from a New Image Window

Choose **W**indow, and then **N**ew Window	Creates a duplicate of the KIDSYARD.PSD image on the workspace.
Press Ctrl+– twice	Reduces the viewing resolution of the duplicate image window to 1:2.
Click on the title bar of the KIDSYARD.PSD image you've been editing; then double-click on the Zoom tool	Makes the original image the current editing document; scales the viewing resolution to 1:1.

continues

continued

Resize the original KIDSYARD image window, and scroll it so that the bottom left corner is visible	This is the area you'll fix next.
Click on the new image window's title bar; then with the Rubber Stamp tool, press Alt and click in the bottom right corner	This is the sampling point for the Rubber Stamp tool. This area should be mostly green by now.
Click on the title bar of the original image window; then click and drag over dirt areas	Samples grass from a different location within the layer and applies grass to the dirt areas (see fig. 10.23).
When you've retouched this area, press Ctrl+S (**F**ile, **S**ave)	Saves your work up to this point.
Click on the new image window; then press Ctrl+W (**F**ile, **C**lose)	Closes the copy view of the image.

Figure 10.23

A New Window of an image operates like a clone of a whole image file.

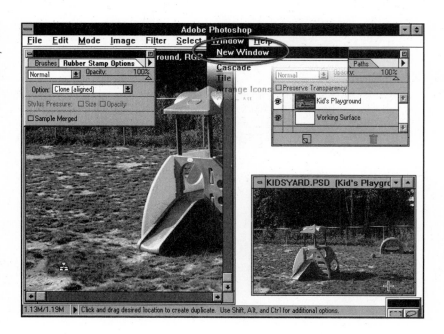

Photoshop didn't present you with a dialog box in the preceding exercise when you closed the new image window, because the new window was actually an alternative view of the same image you've been working on. Use new image windows when you

need to sample from one location, but need to get a close-up view of an entirely different area.

The only limitation a New Window presents is that if you edit on one layer, the duplicate view is of the same layer. This also is true of opening different channel views of a document window.

Using Broad Strokes and Layers to Finish the Yard

You've seen how several selection and cloning techniques can be used to work around virtually any problem in an image. You don't need an additional exercise in this chapter to address the little details—a bare spot here and there—in KIDSYARD.PSD to make the lawn every inch as pretty as when it was first planted. Use the Quick Mask mode to isolate image areas close to regions you want to protect and use the Behind painting mode with the Rubber Stamp tool in areas you want to simply erase and then fill in. Additionally, the Color Range command is a must for getting the bare ground areas close to the slide; click on the bright orange areas in the Color Range command's dialog box to select the color; then use the Select, Inverse command to mask the playset and expose the foreground grass and dirt for retouching. Do not, however, click on the green or blue areas of the playset while in the Color Range command if you want to select these areas. The greens and blues are much too close in color value to the grass, and you'll waste your time trying to narrow the tolerance with the Fuzziness slider.

The big finale to playground restoration happens next, and you discover the secrets of the Layer Mask mode in the next exercise. Because you have a large amount of lawn restored now, it can be defined as a pattern fill, but on the Working Surface layer rather than the Kid's Playground layer. After doing this, you apply a Layer Mask to the Kid's Playground layer, and then "hide" the remaining brown areas from your view of the Kid's Playground layer. Because the two layers that make up this image have transparent layer pixels, areas you hide with the Layer Mask will allow the green pattern fill on the Working Surface layer to show through. When you're happy with your editing on the Kid's Playground layer, make the Layer Mask changes permanent.

Here's how the Layer Mask feature in Photoshop works, and how you can put it to its best use in finishing the lawn:

Pattern Restoration and Layer Masks

With the Rectangular marquee tool, click and drag an area of grass about 2"×2" toward the right background of the Kid's Playground layer (see fig. 10.24)

Defines area as a pattern. Make sure that the kids' ball is *not* in your selection!

continues

continued

Choose **E**dit, **D**efine Pattern	Defines the area within the rectangular marquee selection as a pattern.
Click and drag a selection area that defines the left, background image area on Kid's Playground layer that needs "spot retouching"	Make the select as all-encompassing as you need, but don't select any fence or playset areas.
Click on the eye icon on the Kid's Playground layer on the Layers palette; then click on the Working Surface title	Hides the Kid's Playground layer from view and from editing.

The marquee should still be active at this point.

Choose **E**dit, **F**ill; choose Pattern from the Contents **U**se drop-down box; then click on OK	Applies the pattern you defined earlier to the selection marquee (see fig. 10.25).
Press Ctrl+D (**S**elect, **N**one), click on the space where the eye icon was to the left of the Kid's Playground icon on the Layers palette; then click on the Kid's Playground title on the Layers palette	Deselects the selection, returns the view of the Kid's Playground layer, and then makes the Kid's Playground layer the current editing layer.
Choose Add Layer Mask from the pop-up menu on the Layers palette (see fig. 10.26)	Creates an editing mode on the Kid's Playground layer.

When you're in Layer Mask mode on a layer, by default, adding black foreground color hides the image area. Conversely, adding white reveals areas that are hidden in Layer Mask mode. None of the changes are permanent until you remove the Layer Mask. Hidden areas on the Kid's Playground layer reveal the pattern fill on the Working Surface layer. Here's how to hide the unwanted image areas to expose the grass on the layer beneath:

Press **B** (for Paint **B**rush tool); then with black as the current foreground color, click and drag over a dirt area in the image (see fig. 10.27)	Areas of dirt are hidden, to expose the large pattern on the layer beneath.
Continue clicking and dragging over other areas of dirt, until you see no more dirt	These areas on the Kid's Playground layer become transparent; they are hidden to reveal the grass on the Working Surface layer.

If you reveal a checkerboard instead of grass, press **X** (switch colors icon) then click and drag over the checkerboard area

Applying white foreground color and restores layer areas you've hidden.

The gray-and-white checkerboard can come in handy when editing on a layer. This is Photoshop's signal that only transparent pixels exist in an area.

When you have yourself a grassy playground with no barren ground patches, perform the following steps:

Choose Remove Layer Mask from the pop-up menu on the Layers palette

Displays a dialog box.

Click on **A**pply

Removes the Layer Mask, and areas of the image on the Kid's Playground layer are discarded permanently.

Press Ctrl+S (**F**ile, **S**ave)

Saves your work at this intermediate stage of completion.

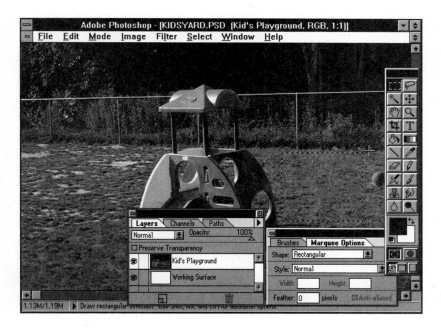

Figure 10.24

Sample a large area of clear grass to define as a pattern.

Figure 10.25

Apply the sampled pattern to the marquee selection on the Working Surface layer.

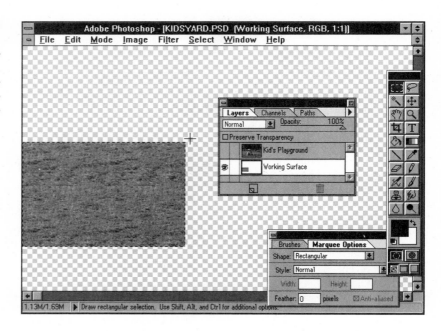

Figure 10.26

A Layer Mask hides the area to which you apply black foreground color, to reveal the underlying layers.

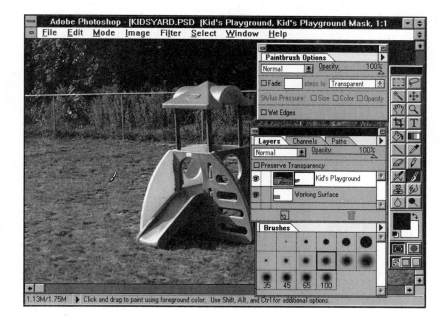

Figure 10.27

Black foreground color on a Layer Mask makes the areas on Kid's Playground transparent; the grass of Working Surface shows through.

Like the Quick Mask mode, Layer Masks are editable previews of selection work—nothing changes in the image until you choose Apply. Unlike the Quick Mask mode, the Layer Mask only works on layers, and by default, you don't see anything on a layer that indicates that a mask is in place. Use the image icon to the right of a Layer icon on the Layers palette for reference when you're in Layer Mask mode. The image icon continually updates and displays black wherever you've hidden an area on the layer.

If you're unhappy with your editing work on a Layer Mask, choose Remove Layer Mask from the pop-up menu on the Layers palette, but choose **D**iscard instead of **A**pply. Discarding a Layer Mask makes the areas you've hidden with foreground color reappear, and everything on the layer reverts to its state before you added the Layer Mask. Chapter 12, "Correcting an Image," features extensive use of the Layer Mask, and you'll find that this new feature of Photoshop 3 comes in handy in a variety of tough image editing concepts.

Flattening an Image

Photoshop has two ways to organize image layers into a single layer, and only one of them is the right choice for organizing KIDSYARD into a conventional bitmapped image that can be imaged, read, and used by other applications. The Merge Layers command is generally a good choice for putting all the different layers you may have in an image on a single layer. However, because KIDSYARD is an exceptional image in that it has no background, choosing to merge layers would not yield a normal bitmap. Instead, it would produce an image that consists of one transparency layer and could only be saved as a Photoshop PSD file. This is the principle difference between the Merge Layers and Flatten Image commands on the Layers palette's pop-up menu. The Merge Layers command is great for merging all the visible layers in an image into a single layer; Flatten Image, however, produces a digital image that has a background layer with pixels that are all opaque.

To restore the KIDSYARD.PSD image to a single-layered image that can be saved to TIF, TGA, or a number of other bitmap formats, follow these steps:

1. Choose Flatten Image from the Layers palette's pop-up menu.

2. Choose **F**ile, **S**ave.

Color-Correcting the Retouched Image

If the exercises so far result in the same effects on your screen as you see in this chapter's figures, your work has come along wonderfully, and you've created some exciting enhancements to an image that needed enhancing!

But in addition to the turf of this playground being a little overrun, it was also a little under-watered this season. The grass isn't exactly a rich color that compositionally supports the brilliant colors of the children's toys. Some spot enhancement is in order here.

If you followed the exercises in the preceding chapters, you already know that you can use the Magic Wand tool to select areas based on a range of color similarity. Unlike the Color Range command, the Magic Wand is a local tool that only selects within a specified tolerance and only selects pixels that touch each other (*contiguous* selection areas).The yard that you retouched in the preceding exercises consists of several shades of green, but they should all fall within a fairly narrow *tolerance* of color—green! Because of this narrow tolerance, the Magic Wand is the tool of choice to select the general area.

Don't concern yourself with precision-selecting in the next exercise. If you accidentally select part of the trees in the background, it's okay. Your objective in this exercise is to enhance the green *quality* in the picture, and the enhancement requires as random an application as that of the natural material in the image. Trees, weeds, and especially the grass, are all good candidates for a quick color boost. However, the brightly colored children's toys are *not*, which is why you'll need to begin the exercise by fine-tuning the Magic Wand's tolerance setting.

Adding Color to the Yard

Press **W** (Magic **W**and tool)	Chooses the tool for selecting only the areas you've retouched in the image.
On the Options palette, set the **T**olerance option to **40** pixels and check the **A**nti-Aliased option	Sets the Magic Wand tool to select pixels similar in color that are adjacent to the image area overwhich you click the Magic Wand cursor.
Click on the center of KIDSYARD.PSD with the Magic Wand tool	Selects all the pixels in the image that share a moderate range of similar color.
Press Shift while clicking inside the areas of the children's slide	Selects these grassy areas as well.

The Magic Wand tool can't initially select these areas because the bright plastic slide borders separate them from the initial area you clicked over.

Choose **I**mage, **A**djust, then **V**ariations	Displays the Variations dialog box, as shown in figure 10.28.
Click and drag the Fine/Coarse slider one tick toward the right	Makes the Picks offered by the Variations dialog box a bit more diverse.
Click on the More Green Pick and then click on OK	Color-casts the selection areas to a more greenish tint than the Current Pick—the image presently in the center of the Variations Picks field.
Choose **S**elect, **N**one (or press Ctrl+D)	Deselects the Magic Wand selection in the image.
Choose **F**ile, Sa**v**e As and save the file to a directory on your hard drive with a new name like YARDWORK.TIF	Saves your finished work to your hard disk.

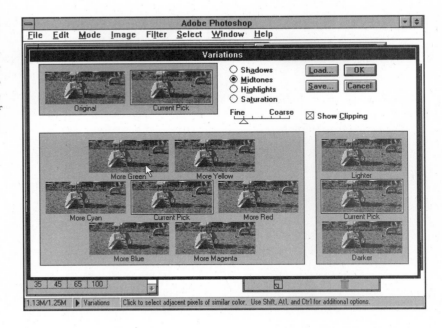

Figure 10.29 shows the finished playground image, saved as YARDWORK.TIF, alongside the original image so that you can compare them.

Figure 10.29

*The original and
the reseeded
image.*

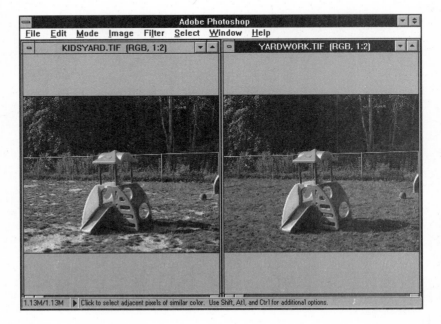

Although in this chapter you used the Rubber Stamp tool to do some miraculous retouching work, it still remains only one of many tools and filters that you can use to retouch an assignment. Painting with photographic samples is one of the best ways to ensure that your finished product looks truly photographic.

Get to know what your tools can do and master a technique or two to use with them. Experiment and pay attention to what works and what doesn't in different situations. This will develop your ability to quickly evaluate a project and select the right tools and techniques for each assignment.

C H A P T E R

11

Using Paths, Selections, and Layers

Correcting image elements or the overall condition of a photograph can be the steak and potatoes of a computer graphics designer's work, as several examples in earlier chapters demonstrate. However, personal expression and creativity also are qualities that a professional graphics-type person cannot ignore, especially when tools as capable as Photoshop's are on the scene. These tools were built for fun and experimentation, *in addition to* image restoration.

Before getting into Part III, "Gourmet Assignments," take a bend in the imaging-experience path and create a free-form, surrealistic image. The ingredients for this assignment include two average photographs and a little Photoshop magic. The real purpose of this chapter is to acquaint you with the interrelationship between Photoshop paths, layers, and selection areas, but we call it "edutainment." This term, popularized by PBS/public television, means, "You're going to simultaneously have fun and understand the principle behind something." With an application like Photoshop, the blend is easy to achieve—so even your boss believes what you're accomplishing here is important!

Integrating Tools and Effects

Suppose that your assignment today is to design an original cover for a children's toy or clothing catalog, and that you have roughly a day to finish the assignment. Getting actors in on such short notice is out of the question, as are exotic locations, and most likely, an arsenal of props.

Fortunately, concepts can blossom much faster than production elements. With Photoshop on your computer, and an understanding of how its integrated feature set brings image elements together, you can create a cover that looks as though it were expensive and time-consuming to produce. To acquire the raw materials for the catalog cover, I took some pictures of a mock-antique gumball machine (available at virtually any gift store) and of a landscape. Then I dropped off the film at a one-hour photo lab and scanned the prints (see fig. 11.1). If this sounds somewhat less than inspired prop-shopping, you have to tip a good concept into the recipe.

Figure 11.1

Source images don't have to be outstanding; you can create outstanding images by using Photoshop and your imagination.

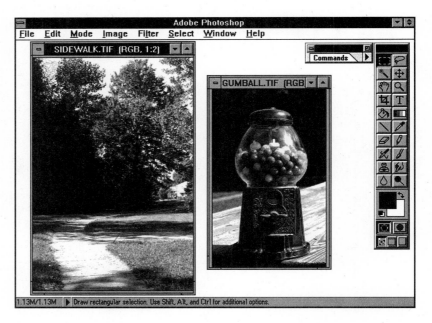

How about a 20-foot-tall gumball machine, hovering over a grassy path, dispensing gigantic, lighter-than-air gumballs? This scene, whose appeal is not restricted to any age group, can serve as a catalog cover, outdoor poster, or any other highly visible medium of communication. It also calls for very precise selection work to isolate the separate image elements, and creative uses of several Photoshop features and filters. When you put the whole picture together, you've made something eye-catching from items that people pass daily without giving them a second glance.

Selecting the Sky, Using the Color Range

In this assignment there's a quality of enchantment to the huge gumball machine floating above the ground, and the background should reflect a magical quality similar to that of the main element (the gum machine). When you have a rush assignment, however, you can't always order up an enchanted sky. In fact, in many photographs the sky can ruin the overall atmosphere of an image (no pun intended). This problem is covered in depth in Chapter 14, "Enhancing Images."

There's no reason to settle for a muddy sky in your final image when you can create your own sky, using Photoshop's Clouds filter. You'll be using this filter soon to replace the bland sky in the SIDEWALK image, but first you need to define the area the synthetic clouds will replace. The Magic Wand tool is quite useful in selecting similar color values in an image, but when you're faced with a uniformly colored sky that pokes through a thousand and one leaves in an image background, your choice of selection tools should be the Color Range command. Unlike the Magic Wand tool, Color Range automatically selects in an image a breadth of color value that is not confined to image areas surrounded by other colors. Color Range can be set to degrees of Fuzziness, to include different tonal densities of the color range you select. You also can preview the color range you're selecting in several preview modes.

The following exercise shows you how to select the boring sky in the SIDEWALK image so that you can replace it with a sky you create.

Selecting Image Areas by Color Range

Open SIDEWALK.TIF image from CHAP11 subdirectory of Bonus CD	This is the background image used to create the catalog cover.
Double-click on the Quick Mask button on the toolbox	Displays the Quick Mask Options dialog box.
Click on the Color Indicates: Selected areas radio button if it is not the current selection, then click on OK	You'll need to display a selection, not a mask over the image in a later step as a Quick Mask. Setting this option now makes the assignment go more smoothly later.
Press Ctrl+plus, then click and drag image window border so that you can see entire image without scroll bars	Increases viewing resolution of SIDEWALK image to a comfortable 1:2, so you can see entire image without scrolling.
Reposition SIDEWALK image so that it is flush left in Photoshop's workspace	Dialog boxes frequently obscure your view of an active image window. Because you need to see both the dialog box and the image

continues

continued

	next, repositioning it before you issue a command is a wise move.
Choose <u>S</u>elect, <u>C</u>olor Range	Displays Color Range dialog box.
Choose Sampled Colors from <u>S</u>elect drop-down box	Tells Photoshop that you want to use Eyedropper tool to sample a color range from active image window.

From the Select drop-down list, you have the option of picking from the primary and complementary colors, and from the grayscale color ranges. These are great options when you want to select values within a specific range of colors in an illustration. But photographic images, such as this one, don't usually display the pure colors encompassed by the preset color ranges. The breadth of color values offered by the preset color ranges cannot be changed, and preset Color Ranges don't offer the Fuzziness option, a valuable feature discussed later in the chapter.

Click on sky in SIDEWALK image (either on the image on the workspace or the image in the preview window)	Selects range of color found in sky of SIDEWALK image.
Choose Quick Mask from <u>S</u>election Preview drop-down list	Displays a tinted Quick Mask above presently selected areas (available for editing) in SIDEWALK image.

Notice that you have the option to preview the active image with selection areas displayed or hidden. Click on the S<u>e</u>lection radio button in the Color Range dialog box to see a visual result of your selection with the Eyedropper tool (the white areas), then click on the <u>I</u>mage radio button. With the active image window in clear view, you can compare the selected areas shown in Quick Mask with the original Image preview.

Click on Fuzziness slider and drag it to the right, stopping when numerical entry field reads **111** or so	Fuzziness option broadens or narrows tonal variations of color range you select.

A value of 111 creates a selection area that encompasses all the sky areas, but keeps the delicate latticework of the trees and leaves from being selected. Some areas—nowhere near the sky—in the SIDEWALK image also are included in the Color Range selection. This is okay; you remove them in the next steps. Smooth surfaces in real life often pick up, or cast, color values from the sky; thus, some of the color range found in the sky is present also in the sidewalk and in a small house in the image background.

Click on Selection radio button, then choose Black Matte from <u>S</u>election Preview drop-down list	Gives an alternative view of the color range selection work (see fig. 11.2). Areas to be protected from change appear in black.
Click on OK when you are happy with your selection	Confirms your Color Range selection and displays active image with a marquee selec-

	tion border running around the chosen areas.
Click on Quick Mask button on toolbox	Displays selection areas as tinted color overlay on active image.
Click on default colors icon on toolbox	Makes foreground color black and background color white.
Choose Lasso tool, then click and drag a selection area to surround Quick Masked sidewalk and house areas of image	Selects Quick Masked areas, not actual underlying image areas.
Press Delete key	Deletes selected Quick Mask areas.

When white is selected as background color in Quick Mask mode, deleting a selection area removes Quick Mask, as shown in figure 11.3.

Click on Standard Mode button on toolbox	Changes Quick Mask back to selection areas defined by marquee lines.
Choose Select, Save Selection	Displays Save Selection dialog box.
Accept the defaults and click on OK	Saves selection area of sky to an Alpha channel, which can be recalled later.
Choose File, Save As, and save image to your hard disk	Saves your editing work to hard disk.

You will find that one of the nicest qualities about the Color Range method of selecting an area is that anti-aliasing is used around the selection borders. This ensures that the selection area contains none of the harsh, jaggy edges that typically brand an image as a computer graphic. Although the scene you're creating is somewhat of a fantasy, the detail must be absolutely photographic to carry off the illusion of charm, wonder, and implausibility.

Semiautomatically Measuring a Working Canvas

To create the new sky—the next phase of building the catalog cover—you need a fresh sheet of virtual canvas. And to create the new canvas, you'll tap into a property of Photoshop that is quite unlike most other applications. In addition to being practically a universe unto itself on your system, Photoshop also reads information about other background processes, such as what's on the Clipboard at any given moment. This Photoshop capability gives the user the opportunity to create new image windows that have precisely the same dimensions, color capability, and resolution of whatever's on the Clipboard.

Figure 11.2

*Protected areas
and selected areas
are represented by
different color
overlays in the
Color Range
preview window.*

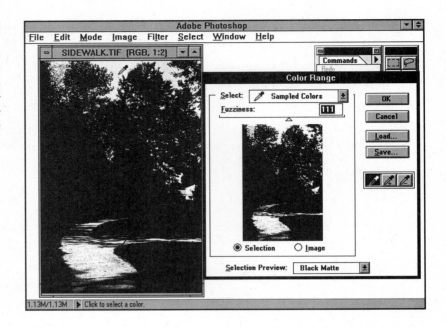

Figure 11.3

*Selection areas in
Quick Mask
mode are deleted
when the
background color
is white and
added to when the
background color
is black.*

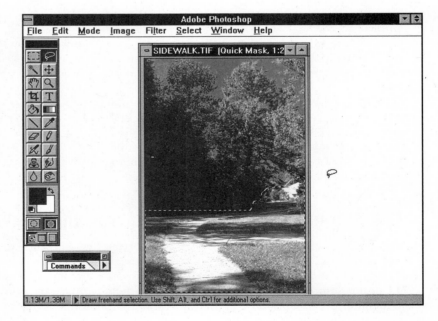

You don't need to use Photoshop's rulers or Image Size command to measure the area occupied by the sky in SIDEWALK.TIF. Instead, select the approximate area the new sky covers in the original image, copy the selection to the Clipboard, and let Photoshop do the measuring for you.

The following exercise shows how to set up a new image window for cloud creation.

Setting Up a New Image Window

Click on Marquee tool on toolbox	Makes Marquee the active tool.
Press Alt and click on Marquee tool if Rectangular marquee tool is not current setting for Marquee tool	Pressing Alt and clicking toggles Marquee tool's setting between Elliptical and Rectangular.

Alternatively, you can select Rectangular from the Marquee Options tabbed menu on the Brushes palette.

Click and drag an area around top half of the SIDEWALK image, then press Ctrl+C (or choose <u>E</u>dit, <u>C</u>opy), or press F3 (click on Copy in the Commands palette), as shown in figure 11.4	Copies selected image area to Clipboard.

Although you won't be using the copy of the SIDEWALK selection, Photoshop reads image areas you've copied to the Clipboard and offers a New file with the same image dimensions and resolution as the current contents of the Clipboard. This is the easiest way to measure a new image canvas for your cloud design.

Choose <u>F</u>ile, <u>N</u>ew (Ctrl+N)	Displays Photoshop's New dialog box, and offers dimensions and resolution of current contents of Clipboard.
Click on Inches increments in both <u>W</u>idth and <u>H</u>eight drop-down boxes	Changes units of measurement of Untitled-1 file so that they are easier to understand.

Depending on the size of your marquee selection, the suggested size for the New image is about 3-and-a-fraction inches wide by 2-and-a-fraction inches tall. Because you're creating the new sky image to fit behind the selection of the sky you defined earlier, it would be nice if you added a little play to the New image size, so you can reposition it when that time comes.

Enter **4** in Width field, and **3** in Height field	Specifies a New image size slightly larger than the area you'll be replacing.
Click on <u>W</u>hite Contents radio button, then click on OK	Specifies a white background for New image.

continues

continued

You don't need to adjust the Resolution or Mode; by default, they are the same as those of the SIDEWALK image. (Photoshop evaluates the Clipboard contents for these settings, also.)

In this exercise, it's all right to leave Untitled-1 untitled. Soon, you are going to copy the sky you create to the SIDEWALK image; in this design, Untitled-1's role is to be a temporary canvas to hold your design element.

Click on Rectangular marquee tool and drag it above Untitled-1 image to create a selection whose sides are about 1/8-inch long, then press Ctrl+C	Replaces contents of Clipboard (currently about 600 KB in memory) with about 3 KB of image. This reduces strain on system resources, and is sometimes called "flushing the Clipboard."
Press Ctrl+D (**S**elect, **N**one)	Deselects the rectangular selection.

Figure 11.4

Select the area of the image that needs replacing.

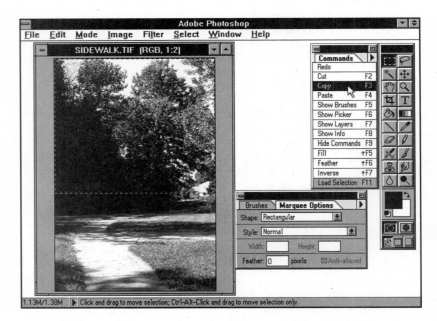

Cloud-Making, Photoshop Style

The Clouds filter is a new feature in version 3 of Photoshop. With the Render command you can create two types of clouds, depending on whether you use the Clouds filter or the Difference Clouds command. So what's the difference between them?

The Clouds filter uses the foreground and background colors selected at the time you issue the command to create fairly realistic patterns from the two colors. If you have blue selected on the toolbox as the foreground color, and white as the background color, the Clouds command creates a cloudy mixture of the two colors in an active image area. The effect is random, and you can be fairly confident that no two clouds patterns look identical. Photoshop gets its color information from the defined foreground and background colors only—color information from the selection area or active image window is not used in cloud-making—and you have no say as to what *percentage* of foreground and background colors comprise a Clouds effect.

In contrast, the Difference Clouds command takes the chromatic opposite of the selected foreground and background colors, in addition to any image areas that are selected, and creates a synthetic texture that can look like anything from an abstract watercolor to marble. A red foreground and white background, for example, produce cyan and black texture on blank white canvas. If you repeat the Difference Clouds command on the same image area, the colors once again reverse themselves chromatically, and further randomizing occurs.

In Photoshop, Ctrl+F (the shortcut key command for the Last Filter command) can provide you with some automated cloud-browsing in the next exercise. When you press Ctrl+F *after* you've chosen the Clouds command for the first time, Photoshop presents you with a different, unique permutation of the foreground/background color combination.

Your next step is to give the SIDEWALK image a better sky. Creating it is entirely up to you and Photoshop. The following exercise shows you how to liven up the SIDE-WALK image and gives you a chance to practice making clouds.

Adding Synthetic Clouds to an Image

Press F6 (Mac: press F10), or choose **W**indow, **P**alettes, Show **P**icker	Displays Photoshop's Color Picker palette.
Click on the menu pop-up on the Picker palette, and choose HSB sliders	Displays the hue, saturation, and brightness color model on the Picker palette, a much more intuitive model for specifying colors in the RGB model.
Click and drag the H slider to **220°**, the S slider to **100%**, and the B slider to **100%**	Specifies a blue foreground color. Background color still should be white.

Alternatively, you can click on the Swatches or Scratch tabbed menu on the Picker palette to specify a foreground color by clicking on color areas.

continues

continued

Choose Filter, Render, then choose Clouds	Executes Clouds command, building clouds from foreground and background colors you defined (see fig. 11.5).
If the random arrangement of clouds doesn't please you, press Ctrl+F	Activates Photoshop's Last Filter command, repeating Clouds command (in this case).

If you press Ctrl+F to get a different sky, and you like the result less than the previous sky, press Ctrl+Z (or choose Edit, Undo) to undo the command. Otherwise, you can continue pressing Ctrl+F until you find the clouds of your dreams for this assignment.

Additionally, you might want to play with the foreground/background colors to make the sky a slightly different shade. To set a new background color, press and hold the Alt key while you select a color from any of the color models on the Picker palette, or click on the foreground/background swatch that doesn't have the box around it, to select it so that you can change it.

Press Ctrl+A (or choose Select, All), then press Ctrl+C (or choose Edit, Copy)	Sends copy of clouds to Clipboard.
Click on down arrow to the right of Untitled-1's title bar	Minimizes Untitled-1 window to a thumbnail on workspace, for easy reference. SIDEWALK.TIF becomes active image window.
Choose Select, Load Selection	Activates selection area you defined earlier.
Choose Edit, Paste Into	Pastes clouds selection into SIDEWALK selection, replacing original sky.
Click on a selection tool	You can use the Marquee, Magic Wand, or Lasso tools to reposition the floating selection.

Stop To reposition selections pasted into, or upon, image backgrounds, you must use a tool that features Photoshop's pointer cursor. Users frequently get into trouble when they reposition a pasted selection because the Hand tool and Layer Move tool look as though they are designed for moving things. These tools are designed to move areas on layers, and your active view, but not to move selections. Selection tools move floating selection areas, and most of the editing and painting tools toggle to a pointer cursor when you hold down the Ctrl key.

Click on the floating selection and drag it until it's in a position you like	As long you don't click on any image area, you can reposition the clouds selection indefinitely, anywhere you choose, as shown in figure 11.6.

Click once (or choose **S**elect, **N**one, then press Ctrl+D)	Permanently composites clouds selection to background image. Areas outside image window are gone now, as are the original sky image areas.
Delete the Channel #5 title from the list	Deletes the saved selection from the image and clears the screen so that you do not get confused as the exercise progresses.
Press Ctrl+S (or choose **F**ile, **S**ave)	Saves your work up to this point.

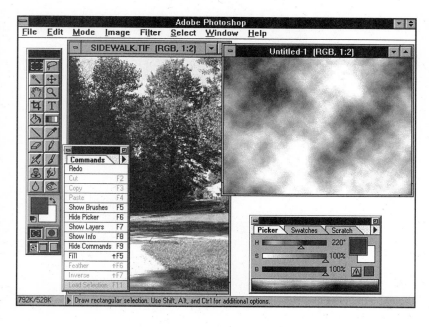

Figure 11.5

The Clouds filter creates clouds from a combination of foreground and background colors.

Tip If you're familiar with Photoshop 2.5, you notice that Photoshop 3 no longer features the Paste Behind command. Instead, use Photoshop 3's Layers feature—you reorder layers of image areas, then use the Merge Layers command to achieve the same effect as pasting behind. To achieve the same results as those that came from using the Paste Behind command, select the area you want to paste behind, choose **S**elect, **I**nverse, then use the Paste **I**nto command.

If you zoom into the image now, you see that the Color Range command made neat work of pasting the clouds into the SIDEWALK image. The spindly areas of branches and leaves are still in perfect shape, and the anti-aliased edges surrounding the selection helped blend the new image area into the original image.

Figure 11.6

Using the pointer cursor, you can move a selected area, even when it's behind the image background.

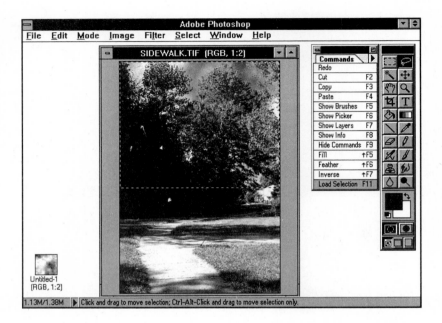

Selecting image areas by color values is a fairly automated process in Photoshop. The real challenge is in selecting hard-edged, irregular geometric elements. The next section covers the use of a tool set within a tool set, the Paths palette, a robust utility that should be very familiar to readers who have used a drawing program.

Creating Paths

In Chapter 9, "Using Type in Photoshop," you used the Paths palette as a simple means for defining an area you needed to distort. Although Photoshop paths are ideal for creating virtual guidelines above an image, their use for defining geometric areas is unsurpassed. Paths are vector shapes that exist within a bitmap image as sort of "spirit guides"; you can change them, add to them, and paths never get involved with your image editing until you create a paint stroke or selection area based upon them.

The Anatomy of a Path

In those high school math classes many of us slept through, the term *vector* was used extensively to describe the plotting of points along a graph. A *path*, which is a vector computer graphic, is defined by Photoshop as a series of anchor points connected by path *segments,* each of which has a *length* and a *direction.* The most useful paths to design, using the Paths palette tools, are closed ones; any path that doesn't end where

it begins is open, and filling and stroking an open path can lead to some unexpected (and unwanted) results.

In addition to length and direction, path segments can be bent to create arcs, and the anchor point at which two path segments meet can be set to a sharp corner angle, or a smooth one. Anchor points can be manipulated by *direction points* at the end of *directions lines*. Direction points and direction lines are the handles running through an anchor point; they are used to steer the direction and slope of curved path segments that are connected together by an anchor point. Before you begin designing a path, take a look at figure 11.7, which illustrates the components that make up a path. A number of the Path tools display the arrowhead cursor to indicate that you're editing a path—moving or modifying segments and anchor points, not drawing them.

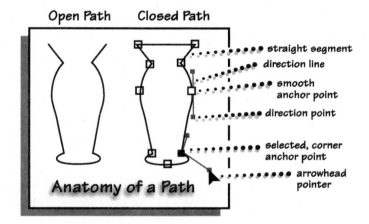

Figure 11.7

Paths are guidelines you design to define a geometric area above an image.

Path Tools

Virtually any geometric shape—a machine part, an airplane, a hand—can be described by a path. Paths can be used to create effects such as stroking, but paths become invaluable when they are used as the blueprints for *selections*. The most powerful and common use for a path is to create a precise, smooth outline around an image element, then to tell Photoshop to base a selection area on your path design. The experience you gain by learning how to define a path around the outline of the gumball machine is important in your own work. Master the Paths palette tools, and you gain the expertise to create perfect selection areas that are essential to image-editing work of professional quality.

The following sections describe the tools on the Paths palette. To display these tools, press T to automatically display the Paths palette, and to have the Pen tools automatically chosen. Read on to learn what each tool does (from left to right).

The Arrow Tool

The Arrow tool is used to move anchor points and direction points. By pressing the Alt key while you click and drag an anchor point, you duplicate an entire path and move it. By pressing the Shift key, you limit anchor point and direction point movement with the Arrow tool to 45° angles.

The Pen Tool

The Pen tool (currently selected if you pressed T earlier) is used to draw paths. By clicking once with this tool you set an anchor point; subsequent clicks create additional anchor points, with straight path segments automatically created between them. If you want to create *curved* path segments between anchor points, you have two options: you can draw straight segments by simply clicking anchor points, then later convert the straight segments to curves with the Corner tool; or you can click and drag when using the Pen tool to produce Bézier curves.

A *Bézier curve* (named after French engineer Pierre Bézier) is an equation that describes the slope of an arc by control points, which Photoshop calls *direction points*. Determining a curved path segment by clicking and dragging with the Pen tool is a two-step process: the click sets the anchor point, and the drag produces the direction point, which changes the slope of the preceding path segment until you click or click and drag the *next* anchor point.

Holding down the Shift key constrains the Pen tool movement to 45° angles. Pressing and holding the Alt key toggles the Pen tool to the Arrow tool, so you might not even need to use the Arrow tool very often.

The click-and-drag method of producing Bézier curves along a path is not the easiest way to define an accurate path around an image area, however. If you're experienced with an illustration application such as CorelDRAW! or Adobe Illustrator, designing paths using the Bézier method might be familiar. If you're new to vector designing, you might want simply to click anchor points to create a path, without dragging to produce curves, then use the Convert Direction Point tool later to modify and perfect the path.

The Pen+ Tool

The Pen+ tool is used to add an anchor point to a path segment. This is a useful tool when you've defined a path with fewer anchor points than you need to accurately describe a shape. You can change a straight path segment to two curved segments when you add an anchor along a segment with the Pen+ tool.

Holding the Alt key while you click with the Pen+ tool toggles its function to the Pen– tool, which removes the anchor point you click over along a path. The Ctrl key toggles the Pen+ tool to the Arrow tool; you also are presented with the Arrow tool if

you click and drag on an anchor point with the Pen+ tool. The Shift key also toggles the Pen + tool to the Arrow tool, but constrains movement of anchor points you click over to 45° angles.

The Pen– Tool

When you click on an anchor point in a path with the Pen– tool, you remove that anchor point. The Pen– tool also functions as the Arrow tool if you have any direction points revealed and want to edit along a path. If you hold down the Alt key and click on an anchor point, all the anchor points along the path are selected, and dragging the selection duplicates the path. Holding down the Ctrl key toggles the Pen– tool to the Arrow tool, so that you can move anchor points and direction points without duplicating a path. Holding down the Shift key while you click and drag on a direction point constrains movement of anchor points you click over to 45° angles.

The Convert Direction Point Tool

The Convert Direction Point tool isn't used for creating paths or moving anchor points. Rather, the Convert Direction Point tool is used to change the property of an anchor point. Clicking and dragging with the Convert Direction Point tool on an anchor point that connects two straight path segments produces a smooth anchor point property, with curved path segments and direction points sprouting at opposing 180° angles, as you saw in figure 11.7. After you've created direction points, a second click and drag with the Convert Direction Point tool on either direction point breaks the symmetrical property of the direction lines.

Once the symmetrical (smooth) property is broken, the anchor takes on corner properties, which means that you then can freely manipulate either direction point independently of the other. In most cases, you should press the Ctrl key immediately after creating a corner anchor point. Pressing the Ctrl key toggles the Convert Direction Point tool's function to the Arrow tool, which can be used to further adjust the curves of the path segments and reposition anchor points. Why switch from Convert Direction Point tool function to Arrow tool right after breaking the direction points' symmetrical quality? Because a third click on a corner anchor point with the Convert Direction Point tool changes the curved path segments connected by the anchor back into straight segments, something you usually don't want.

The function of the Convert Direction Point tool toggles to a different tool depending on what part of a path you click over. If you press Alt and click over a path segment, the Corner tool changes to the Pen+ tool. If you press Alt and click over an anchor point, the Convert Direction Point tool becomes the Pen– tool. If you make the Convert Direction Point tool hover over a direction point while you hold down the Alt key, the Convert Direction Point tool becomes the Arrow tool, and you can click and drag the direction point to edit a curved path segment.

Pressing Shift while you click and drag with the Convert Direction Point tool constrains direction point movement to 45° angles.

The Directions Paths Take

Although Adobe clearly has built a great deal of functionality into the Paths tools, the exact function each tool toggles to when you press the Alt, Ctrl, and Shift keys is not particularly straightforward or intuitive. The best way to develop a methodology for creating paths is to play with the tool set a little—and that is the purpose of the next exercise. You come to appreciate the important role paths play in your work when you use a path as a template for creating selections.

Before beginning the exercise in the next section, keep in mind that paths have a direction—either clockwise or counterclockwise, depending on the direction you took when you clicked to create a second anchor point. You should consistently maintain the path's original direction when you use the Paths palette's editing tools, such as the Corner tool. In other words, if you created a path by clicking in a clockwise direction, and you want to change the path's straight segments to curved ones, click on an anchor point with the Convert Direction Point tool and drag it in a clockwise direction. Going against the flow when you edit a path produces strange, unwanted twists and bends in a path.

Defining the Outline of an Image Element

As mentioned earlier, a path is best used to define the geometry of an image element that has curves and straight lines. Paths can be designed with precision, they can be modified *ad infinitum*, and Photoshop can use path information to create accurate selection marquees. In contrast, it's difficult to create a precise, irregular selection marquee by using the Lasso tool, because every area you define immediately becomes a selection. While working with a selection tool, you're limited to adding and subtracting selection areas as the technique for editing the amount of image area contained within the selection marquee.

In the GUMBALL.TIF image, you must create a tight and accurate selection marquee around the gum machine to isolate it from its background. An accurate selection ensures that only the gumball machine is copied to the SIDEWALK image. Before beginning your experiment with paths, you might want to save and close the SIDEWALK image to help conserve your system resources. You need the image later, but right now it serves no purpose on Photoshop's workspace.

You'll approach path design as a two-part process: outlining with a path first the top of the machine, then the bottom; as your experience using the Paths tools grows, you may want to take on an assignment like this in one fell swoop. Because the two paths are used to create a single selection area, you can overlap the paths, and Photoshop eventually reads the results as one contiguous selection area.

Here's how to use the Paths palette tools to create an outline around the gumball machine:

Defining the Top of an Image Element

Open GUMBALL.TIF image from CHAP11 subdirectory of companion CD; choose File, Save As, and save copy of image to your hard disk	Image around which you'll design paths; you can only save changes to a file located on read/write media, like your hard disk.
Press the up triangle on right of GUMBALL.TIF title bar	Maximizes image window to occupy all of Photoshop's workspace.
Press Ctrl++ twice	Shortcut for zooming in on an image.

Image should be at a 2:1 viewing resolution, good for clearly viewing outline of gum machine.

Choose Hand tool, then click on image and drag down	Scrolls your view upward. Stop when you can see the very top of gumball machine.
Choose Window, Palettes, Show Paths	Displays Paths palette. Alternatively, you can press F7 to Show Layers, then click on Paths tabbed menu.
Click on Pen tool, then click on top of gumball machine	Sets an anchor point.
Click a second point on outline of gum machine, to right of first anchor point	Creates a second anchor point, and creates a straight path segment between first and second anchor points.

You'll notice that the outline of the gum machine includes some straight sides and some curved sides. Your first two or three clicks along the top of the machine produce straight lines that follow the gum machine's straight line architecture. When you clicked to the right of the first anchor point, you defined a clockwise direction for the path, a direction you must continue to follow. You're coming up on a curve in the top piece of the gumball machine, however, and here's your big chance to draw a Bézier curve. Go for it…

Click and drag on edge of gumball machine glass	Produces a curved path segment between second and third anchor points. Cursor is now hanging on to a direction point. *Don't* let go of the direction point yet; you're not done editing the Bézier curve!
Click and drag direction point away from anchor point	Makes slope of last curved path segment steeper.

continues

continued

Click and drag direction point up and down	Changes angle of curved path segment (see fig. 11.8).

The last two steps—more fun than productive—are intended to illustrate one of the ways you fit a curved path to the outline of an image element. Release the mouse button when the curved segment fairly accurately describes the curve of the glass on the gumball machine.

Continue clicking and dragging along curved parts of gumball machine's outline, and single-click where machine has a straight outline	Creates curved and straight path segments around outline of gumball machine.
Hold the space bar	Toggles Pen tool to Hand tool. Scrolls your view of image window up, so you can continue building the path.
Click on Pen tool, and continue building the path in a clockwise direction	Bottom of gum machine's glass globe should be the bottom of your path. When you reach this point, proceed back to top of gum machine, along edge of glass.

Precision in matching the outline of the glass top of the machine is not critical here; you edit the path in the next exercise to tighten up the design of the path.

Tip   The best place to put an anchor point is on a point of inflection of the image you're tracing over. A *point of inflection* is a sharp change in the direction of a line or outline. The gumball machine has points of inflection where each part of the machine meets another; you should click anchor points on these areas. Additionally, curved segments should be built with an anchor point about every 90°, so the direction points used to steer the curve don't have to be three feet away from the anchor point. Think of the way you'd draw a circle using a path; if you click a north, south, east, and west anchor, the arcs used to describe the circle have anchor points every 90°.

When you've come full circle, and you're back at the first anchor point, click on it	A tiny loop appears next to the Pen tool cursor, signifying that you are closing a path.
Double-click on Working Path thumbnail on Paths palette	Displays Save Path dialog box.
Type **Gumball Top** in <u>N</u>ame: field, then click on OK	Saves path and identifies it for easy reference later (see fig. 11.9).
Press Ctrl+S (<u>F</u>ile, <u>S</u>ave)	Saves your work up to this point.

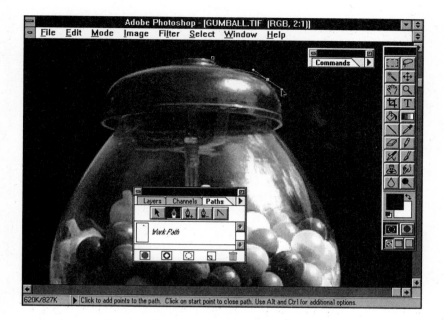

Figure 11.8

Clicking and dragging with the Pen tool produces anchor points and curved path segments you can edit immediately.

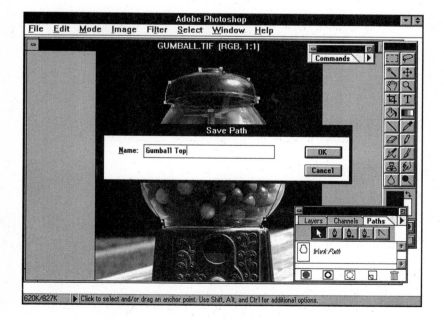

Figure 11.9

You can save a path with any name you choose.

Tip   If you want to preview a path segment before you draw it, double-click on the Pen tool to display the Pen tool options, then check the Rubber Band box. By default, segments are created immediately after you click an anchor point. With the Rubber Band option checked, path segments are displayed before you click an anchor point.

If you didn't match the outline of the gumball machine top perfectly in the last exercise, it's to your benefit—the next section tells you how to edit the path you've created.

Using the Convert Direction Point Tool

If you followed the last exercise, it's pretty evident now that designing a path requires a technique and a rhythm that make the process quick. But getting a path to accurately describe the outline of an underlying bitmap image doesn't always happen during the creation of the closed path. You use the Convert Direction Point tool to edit the path; and by using the Alt key in combination with the Convert Direction Point tool, you can change anchor point properties and move anchor points without changing tools.

The next exercise shows you how to clean up your Gumball Top path. In your own work, you may not have the same problem areas as the ones described in the exercise, but patterning your own clean-up procedure after these steps is useful.

Refining a Path

Press Ctrl++ until Photoshop's title bar says 4:1 after the image name	Zooms in to a 4:1 viewing resolution of image, to provide accurate view of path.
Click on Corner tool, then click and drag on an anchor point connecting straight segment you want curved	Converts anchor point to a smooth anchor point; now you're holding a direction point, not the anchor point you originally clicked on. *Don't* release cursor yet!
If outline has a smooth part, continue dragging the direction point	Repositioning a direction point belonging to a smooth anchor point changes both connecting path segments to create shallow or steep arcs, and controls slope of arcs (see fig. 11.10).
If path area you're editing needs to make a sharp turn, release Corner tool, then click and drag on a direction point	Changes property of anchor point to a corner Anchor; direction point you're now holding manipulates path segment closest to it without altering neighboring path segment.

New Riders Publishing
INSIDE SERIES

Hold Alt (Option) key, then click and drag opposing direction point	Toggles Corner tool to Arrow tool, and controls opposing curve segment independent of anchor point's other direction line and corresponding path segment.
Hold Alt (Option) key, and click and drag an anchor point	Toggles Corner tool to Arrow tool, and repositions anchor point without adjusting direction points.
Hold Alt (Option) key and click over a path segment where you want to add an anchor point	Toggles Corner tool to Pen+ tool, and creates a smooth anchor point (see fig. 11.11).
Repeat any or all of the previous steps to fit Gumball Top path to outline of top of gumball machine	Creates an accurate path that surrounds top of gum machine.

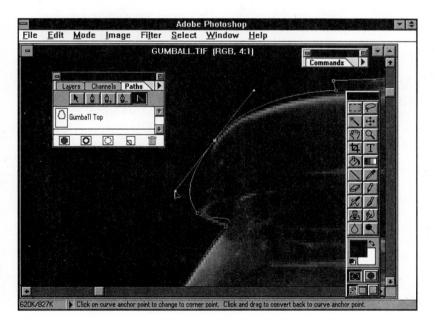

Figure 11.10

The Corner tool changes an Anchor to a smooth Anchor, and changes the connecting straight path segments to curved ones.

Creating a Saved Selection

As you saw in Chapter 6, "The Photoshop Test Drive," selection areas can be saved in an Alpha channel in the image file, and a saved selection can then be called into use at any time. Alpha channels contain grayscale, 8-bit/pixel visual information.

Photoshop evaluates the grayscale information in a channel and builds selection areas based upon the shades of black it finds in the channel. What is contained within the selection that Photoshop produces depends on whether you've specified that colored areas (shades of black) represent the mapping for *selected* areas or for *masked* (protected) areas.

Figure 11.11

The Corner tool toggles to different functions when you press Alt (Option) and click over different parts of a path.

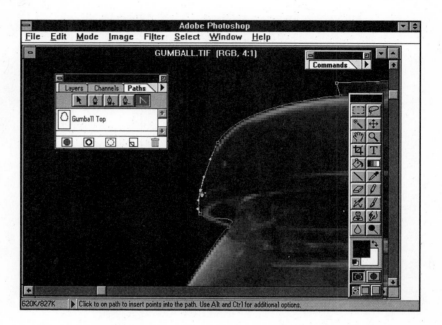

In the next exercise, you create Alpha channel information from the path you drew—information that tells Photoshop, "Hey, the top of the gumball machine is a saved, selected area." On other occasions, you might want to convert a path to a selection by using the Make Selection command on the Paths palette fly-out menu, then choose **S**elect, **S**ave Selection—but this is not the shortest distance between two points. The **S**elect, **S**ave Selection command paints a colored area in a new channel, but you can accomplish the same thing faster if you have a path defined.

This exercise shows you how, by using the geometric design defined by the Gumball Top path, you can create a saved selection that can be activated at any future time.

Creating a Saved Selection from a Path

Double-click on Zoom tool, then scroll the window until top half of image is clearly in view

Takes you to a 1:1 viewing resolution of GUMBALL image, so you can see entire Gumball Top path.

Click on Channels tab on Layers palette	Displays controls for GUMBALL.TIF's channels.
Click on New Channel icon at bottom center of Channels palette	Displays Channel Options dialog box for new channel.
Stick with default **N**ame: of #4 and the default Color option, but click on **S**elected Areas radio button in Color Indicates field, then click on OK (see fig. 11.12)	Creates new channel with white background; now channel #4 is your active image view.

Now any color you add to channel #4 will be seen by Photoshop as part of a saved selection area.

Click on default colors icon on toolbox	Sets foreground color—the color you apply to foreground areas—to black, and sets the background color to white.
Click on Paths tab on Layers palette	Displays Paths tools, and Gumball Top path becomes visible again.
Click on Fill Path icon at bottom left of Paths palette (see fig. 11.13)	Fills path with foreground color, indicating to Photoshop that this area should be loaded as a selection when you choose **L**oad Selection command.
Press Ctrl+S	Saves your work up to this point.

Tip

Although paths are not displayed when you're in the Channels and Layers view of the Layers palette, they are still a part of the image. You must have the Paths palette visible to see the paths you've created.

There are two other ways to hide a path from view. The first is to click on a blank title area on the Paths palette. (The title of a visible path is always highlighted in white on the palette, so you need to click on a gray area beneath the title.) Alternatively, you can choose the Turn Off Path command from the palette's fly-out menu.

To make a path you've turned off visible again, click on its title in the Paths palette.

By default, the Fill Path command uses anti-aliasing to create smooth edges around the filled selection area, and uses no Feathering. If, on an assignment, you have a special need to change the default settings for the icon, choose Fill Path from the Path's flyout menu; additional options for filling a path can be set here. The Fill Path icon is a shortcut when you don't want a fancy fill, but simply want to create a saved selection area from a path.

Figure 11.12

Selected areas can be edited, whereas masked areas are protected from editing.

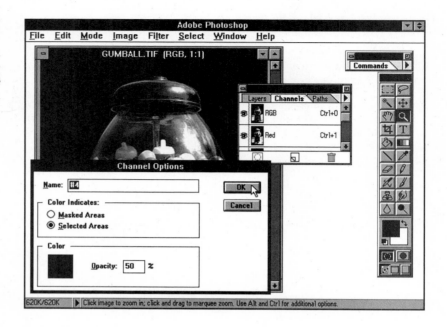

Figure 11.13

Fill the path with foreground color by clicking on the Fill Path icon.

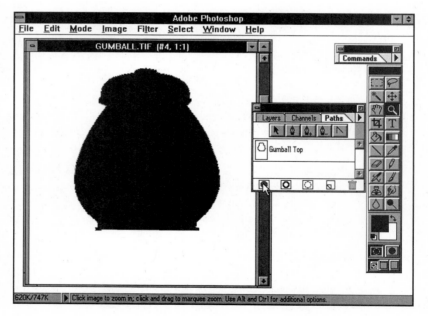

Encore Performance for the Paths Palette

Now you need to define the bottom of the gumball machine, using a path. The bottom path should be filled in, using the same Alpha channel view you used in the last exercise, when you filled in the Gumball Top path.

The steps are essentially the same as those used to save a selection of the gumball machine's top. This section quickly walks through the steps so that you can finish defining a selection for the gum machine and get on with the creative, fun part of the assignment!

Here's how to create the path for the bottom of the gumball machine:

The Paths Palette Revisited

Press Ctrl+0, or click on RGB title on Channels palette	Switches view to color composite view of GUMBALL image.
Click on Paths tab on Layers palette	Switches to Paths palette tool set.
Click on New Path icon at bottom of Paths palette, type Gumball bottom in **N**ame: field, then click on OK	Displays New Path dialog box, and clears active view of Gumball Top path (see fig. 11.14).
Click on Pen tool, then click a clockwise path around bottom of gumball machine. Close path by clicking on beginning anchor point	Creates closed path composed of straight path segments (see fig. 11.15).
Click on Convert Direction Point tool, then click and drag on anchor points that should connect curved path segments	Corner tool changes path segments to curves and gives anchor points a smooth property.
With Convert Direction Point tool, click and drag on direction points where there are sharp angles in gumball machine image	Changes smooth anchor points to corner anchor points (see fig. 11.16).
Press Ctrl while clicking and dragging on anchor points, then press Ctrl while clicking and dragging on direction points	Repositions anchor points and shapes curved path segments.
When Gumball Bottom path fits corresponding outline of gumball image, press Ctrl+4	Moves view to Alpha channel you defined, without hiding newly created Gumball Bottom Path.

continues

continued

Click on Fill Path icon at bottom left of Paths palette	Fills path and adds to saved selection area in channel #4 (see fig. 11.17).
Click on the Channels tab on the grouped palettes	Returns you to the color composite view of the image.

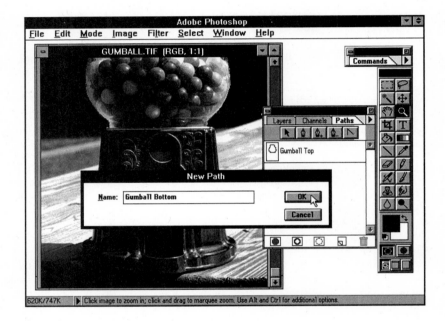

Figure 11.14

The New Path dialog box.

Because you're adding information to an Alpha channel by filling in foreground color, there's no need to use the **S**elect, **S**ave Selection command. Photoshop saves marquee selections as color areas in Alpha channels, but you've completed the same steps directly, manually, and precisely!

Copying without the Clipboard

The Microsoft Windows and Macintosh Clipboards are multiformat import/export filters—Clipboard information can be copied into any application that understands the header information for the file's contents. But because the Clipboard is part of the computer's operating system, holding a large amount of information on it places a strain on system resources. If you're working with a large digital image, you could even crash your system while attempting to copy an equally large selection to the Clipboard.

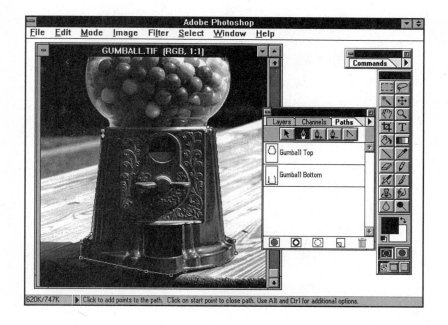

Figure 11.15

Single-click on the points of inflection you find around the outline of the gumball machine's bottom.

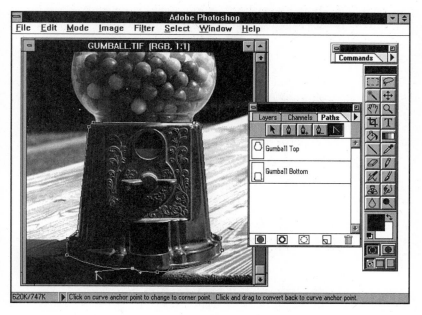

Figure 11.16

Use the Convert Direction Point tool and the Ctrl, Alt, and Shift keys to change functions, and edit the path to fit the image outline.

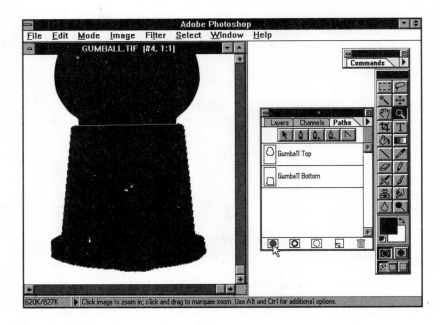

Fortunately, Photoshop 3 offers an internal program scheme for copying selections
that bypasses the Clipboard—it's called dragging and dropping a selection to a
different image window. Dragging and dropping selections is quick, and it's as easy as
it sounds.

You're all set to add the gumball machine to the SIDEWALK image. The next
exercise shows you how to integrate the foreground image, around which you've
defined a selection area, into a new background.

Dropping a Gumball Machine

From your hard disk, open SIDEWALK.TIF
image you edited and saved

This is the background image that hosts the
gumball machine.

Click and drag both image windows so
that you have a clear view of images

Repositions image windows so that you can
copy selection of gum machine to
SIDEWALK image.

Click on title bar on GUMBALL image,
then double-click on Hand tool

Reduces viewing resolution of GUMBALL
image so that you see it full-frame.

Choose **S**elect, **L**oad Selection, then click on OK	Loads selection area around gumball machine you defined by filling paths with foreground color in Alpha channel.
Click on Rectangular marquee tool, then click and drag gumball machine into SIDEWALK image	Moves copy of gumball machine into SIDEWALK image as a floating selection (see fig. 11.18).

To copy selections, you must have a selection tool or a pointer cursor active.

Close GUMBALL image (double-click on its window control menu button), then zoom to a 2:1 viewing resolution of right edge of gumball machine, as it appears in SIDEWALK.TIF	You're done with GUMBALL.TIF image, and you need to check out the edgework on gum machine as it floats atop SIDEWALK image background.

When you make a selection based on a path, the edges of the path, by default, are anti-aliased. This usually provides your selection with smooth edges composed of semitransparent pixels created from pixel color outside the selection area. With the gumball machine, the areas outside the path are light-colored wood. Even though the anti-alias pixels aren't completely opaque, they still clash with the dark background trees in the SIDEWALK image, making the floating selection and background seem somewhat less than integrated. The key here is to defringe the floating selection. Defringing removes edge pixel colors and replaces them with pure color values found only in the selection, not in the background image.

Choose **S**elect, **M**atting, **D**efringe	Displays Defringe dialog box (see fig. 11.19).
Type **2** in **W**idth field, then click on OK	Replaces lighter, anti-alias edge pixels with gumball machine color (see fig. 11.20).
Double-click on Hand tool, then choose Rectangular marquee tool, and click and drag selection to about 1/2 screen inch from top of SIDEWALK image	Zooms out to full-window viewing resolution of image, and repositions gumball machine so that it seems to float above sidewalk.
Choose **S**elect, **S**ave Selection, then click on OK	Accepts default name of #4 for New channel, which now contains selection information about gum machine.
Press Ctrl+D (**S**elect, **N**one)	Deselects the selection marquee.
Press Ctrl+S	Saves your work at this stage.

Figure 11.18

You can move image selections by clicking and dragging them between image windows.

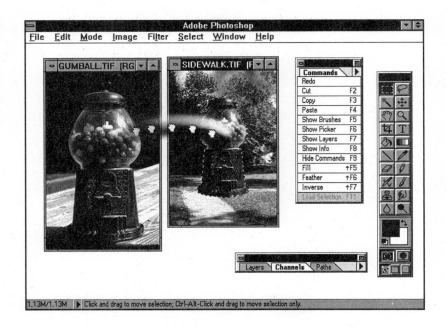

Figure 11.19

When anti-alias pixels along a selection's edge clash with the new image background, they must be removed.

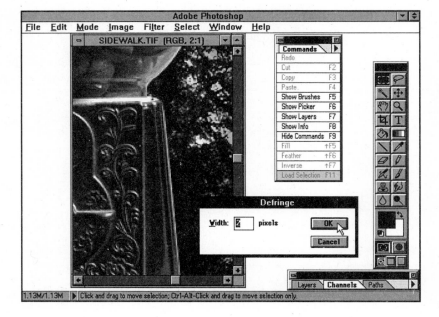

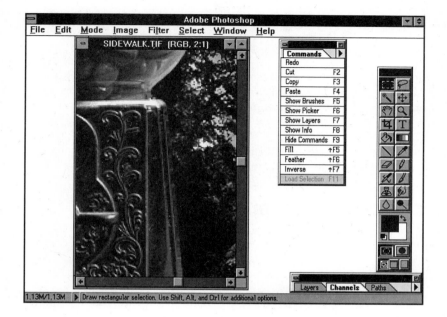

Figure 11.20

The Defringe command replaces edge pixels with selection area colors; no image background colors are added.

Creating Realistic Shadows

A number of visual elements can add to both the fantasy and photorealism of this catalog cover. If you want to pick your own props and create an image similar to this giant gum machine for an assignment of your own, you should keep the following in mind:

◆ *If you're playing tricks with the relative sizes of things, make sure that the element you're going to pose as being huge fills the frame when you photograph it.* The gum machine was photographed at a closer camera range than the sidewalk scene, to give it the appearance of being 20 feet tall when composited into the sidewalk image. You can't really achieve the same effect by taking a small picture and increasing its resolution in Photoshop, because you have a fixed amount of image information that Photoshop can only interpolate, not add to. The result is an image that looks pixelated, not realistic. See Chapter 1, "Understanding Image Types, Formats, and Resolution," and 2, "Acquiring a Digital Image," for more information on image resolution.

◆ *Both background and foreground images should be lit the same way, and should be photographed at the appropriate altitudes.* For example, both the gum machine and the sidewalk background are lit from the sun at about 2 o'clock on a summer afternoon. Additionally, the gum machine was photographed at a low altitude (the photographer got on his knees), suggesting now that it's too high for the camera to look over. Use a low camera angle on a miniature image element that you want to make larger-than-life.

◆ Finally, *everything in the real world that is on or above a surface, and is struck by light, casts a shadow.* Although you have a handsome piece of photo-trickery on your workspace, because the gumball machine fails to cast a shadow on the landscape, it looks pasted *onto* the picture rather than fitting *into* the landscape.

The next exercise shows how to create realistic shadows in the composition, using selection tools and Photoshop's Feather feature.

Defining a Selection Area for Shadow-Making

Ultimate care and precision aren't required to create a convincing shadow in this composition; if you look at the natural shadows in the SIDEWALK image, they're indistinct and basically reflect a little of the surrounding trees' geometry, skewed at a sharp angle.

Armed with nothing more than two selection tools, you can create the basic geometry of the gumball machine's shadow on the sidewalk and the grass. After saving the selection to a channel, you can achieve a soft look by feathering the selection. And you can edit it so that the final shadow appears to be touching the gumball machine. Making the shadow meet the gumball machine adds another touch of realism to the image.

Now you are going to create a selection area for the gumball machine shadow.

Defining a Selection with the Selection Tools

Double-click on Zoom tool, then use scroll bars to move to bottom of SIDEWALK image	Changes viewing resolution of image to 1:1, and hones in on area where you'll design a shadow outline.
Press Alt while clicking on Rectangular marquee tool	Changes marquee tool to Elliptical.
Click and drag an ellipse beneath base of gum machine, so part of ellipse intrudes on gum machine's base (see fig. 11.21)	This is the first part of shadow shape. Shadow will go behind gum machine's base, suggesting that machine is only 2-3 feet off the ground.

Admittedly, it's hard to draw an ellipse and have it perfectly positioned above an image. If your ellipse isn't where you want it right now, press Ctrl+Alt, place the cursor inside the elliptical

marquee, and drag it. The Alt+Ctrl key combination enables you to move only the marquee selection, and not the image area it defines.

Tip

As you can see in figures 11.21 and 11.22, the Brushes/Options palette is displayed, and the Options palette indicates that a 0 value for Feather is active. This is correct; you do not want to feather a selection as you design it in this assignment. You create the gum machine's shadow by combining two selection areas, using two selection tools. Adding Feathering to the combined selection areas is much easier than adding the Feather when you create each selection.

Choose Lasso tool, then press Shift and Alt while clicking a four-sided shape (see fig. 11.22)	The Alt key creates straight lines between points you click with the Lasso tool; the Shift key adds to an existing selection marquee. You're creating a shadow representing the bottom part of the gum machine.
Choose Select, Save Selection, then click on OK	By default, selection is saved to a new Alpha channel, channel #5.
Press Ctrl+5 (or click on Channel #5 title bar on Channels palette)	Displays view of saved selection. Don't deselect marquee yet!
Choose Select, Feather..., then enter 5 in Feather Radius field, and click on OK	Photoshop creates a soft transition between selected and masked areas, five pixels inside the marquee, and five pixels outside.
Choose Select, Save Selection, then choose #5 from Channel drop-down list	Overwrites hard-edged selection you saved earlier, and replaces it with a soft, shadow-like selection (see fig. 11.23).

This fuzzy selection makes a terrific template for a shadow, but it overlaps the base of the gum machine. You want to precisely subtract the base of the machine from the Feathered selection. The easiest way to do this is to load the selection of the gum machine while a view of the fuzzy shadow is displayed, then delete the overlapping gum machine area to background white color.

Choose Select, Load Selection, then choose #4 from Channel drop-down list	Displays marquee outline of channel #4 selection area.
Press Delete key	Removes the part of the fuzzy shadow that overlaps bottom of gum machine (see fig. 11.24).
Press Ctrl+D (Select, None)	Deselects the selection marquee.

Figure 11.21

Create an elliptical marquee that suggests a shadow of the base of the gum machine.

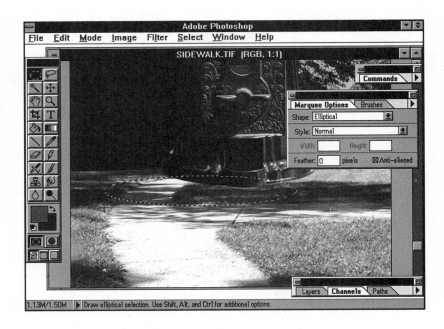

Figure 11.22

Add to an existing marquee selection by holding the Alt key in combination with a selection tool.

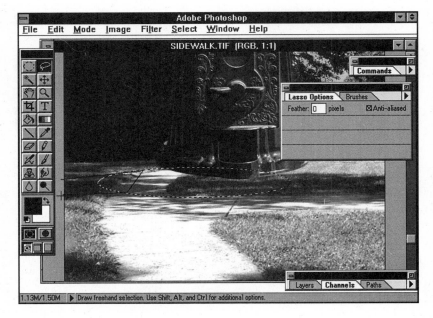

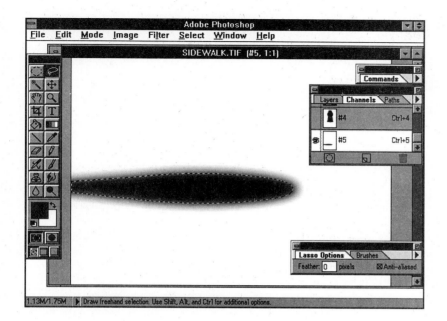

Figure 11.23

Feathering creates a transition between colors on the edge of an active selection.

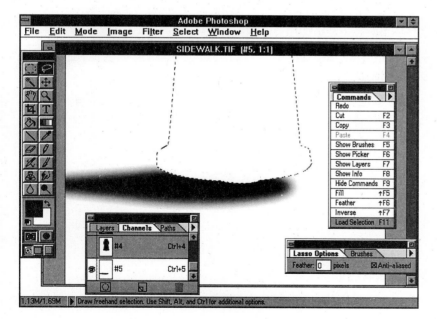

Figure 11.24

When white is the current background color on the toolbox, deleting an active selection turns the image area white.

Now that you have an exellent, lifelike selection area defined for the gum machine shadow, it's time to color it!

The Paint Bucket Tool

The Paint Bucket tool can be set to a tolerance of between 0 and 255 to cover a range of tonal values in a selected area. At a setting of 0, the Paint bucket appears to be empty, but at 255, the Paint bucket covers every pixel in a selected area with foreground color.

Because the selection area for the gum machine shadow is feathered, using the Paint Bucket tool to apply foreground color to the selection results in a soft, indistinct shadow edge, similar to shadows we see in real life. However, you want some image detail to show through in the shadow area, so you won't use the Paint bucket full strength. The Multiply mode and partial Opacity are ideal settings for flooding an area with foreground color you can see through. Accordingly, the next exercise involves some pretty sophisticated editing that incorporates these two paint settings. Fortunately, when you understand the principles behind Photoshop's painting mode, you have at your disposal plenty of options for creating realistic effects. For more information on painting modes in Photoshop, check out Chapter 6, "The Photoshop Test Drive."

Here's how to pour a shadow into the SIDEWALK image:

Using Multiply Mode on a Feathered Selection

Press Ctrl+0 (or click on RGB title on Channels palette)	Switches to color composite view of SIDEWALK image.
Double-click on Paint Bucket tool	Chooses Paint Bucket tool, and displays Paint Bucket Options on Brushes palette.
Press Alt while clicking over a shadowed area in SIDEWALK image	Toggles Paint Bucket tool to Eyedropper tool, and samples color of photographic shadow, which becomes foreground color that Paint Bucket tool applies. (Neat trick, huh?)
Release Alt key	Toggles back to Paint Bucket tool.
Click and drag Opacity slider to **44%**, choose Multiply from drop-down list, then place cursor in Tolerance field and type **255**	Chooses semitransparent quality for foreground color, causes repeated clicks over area to multiply in color density, and 255 tolerance ensures that Paint bucket covers every area in active selection.

With marquee selection still active, click in marquee with Paint Bucket tool	Covers selection area with semitransparent layer of foreground color (see fig. 11.25).
Click again if you think shadow is too faint	Darkens shadow slightly, a function of Multiply mode when applying foreground color.
Press Ctrl+D, then Ctrl+S (**S**elect, **N**one, and **F**ile, **S**ave)	Deselects active marquee, and saves your work at this point.

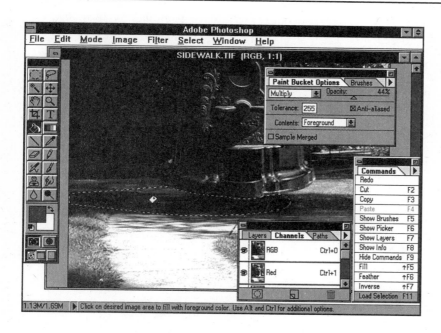

Figure 11.25

Apply semitransparent foreground color to a feathered selection to create realistic shadows.

You should remember three key concepts from the last exercise. First, Multiply mode, when used for applying foreground color, saturates a selected area with repeated applications. This creates a lifelike, dense area of color in an image, because the shadow cast by real-life objects is denser at the center than at the edges. Second, the Feather command, when applied to a saved selection, assists in softening sharp edges. Finally, the Opacity slider is extremely useful when you want to make more than one pass with a painting tool to partially cover an area. If Opacity is set at 100%, you generally saturate a selection area the first time you apply color.

All of these Photoshop features help blend painted creations with photographic source images to create fantastic images.

Designing on Layers

The giant gumball machine is in all its glory now, majestically surveying its surroundings—but where are the goodies? Unless you hurry up and paint some gumballs floating out of the machine, somebody will think the machine is broken!

In the next sections, you'll use Photoshop's layers capability, a feature new to this version of Photoshop. Layers are transparency masks that behave like a stack of acetate sheets over an image. You can add opaque foreground pixels to layers by copying a selection to them, or create image elements by painting directly upon a layer. Layers keep image areas discrete, and layers can be reordered. By using layers for the gumballs, you'll be able to reposition and reorder their "back-to-front" hierarchy, all without disturbing the fine work you did with the gigantic gumball machine.

Preplanning Image Elements

You need to plan ahead and orchestrate this gumball scene. The gumballs will be in front of the machine, and they, too, should cast shadows. By using layers, you're spared much of the guesswork that typically accompanies defining and moving image areas.

First, you need to define a new layer for the SIDEWALK image. Because layers have no background, you are able to define an elliptical shape for a gumball, then apply color to the layer without disturbing the image background layer (the original SIDEWALK image). The gumball can then be copied and pasted to the same layer, and you can move several gumballs around until the overall composition is an exciting, if somewhat strange, one. With the Gradient tool—the tool of choice in the next exercise—you'll make the gumballs you create appear spherical, and can simulate real-life shading and lighting by using Photoshop's Toning tools.

Here's how to create a gumball that looks like a real jawbreaker:

Painting on a Layer

On Layers palette, click on Layers tab	Displays current Layer image (the SIDEWALK background layer). Notice icons at bottom of palette.
Click on New icon at lower-left of Layers palette, then click on OK	Displays New Layer dialog box, as shown in figure 11.26.

Click on Elliptical marquee tool, then press Shift while clicking and dragging an area about 3/4 screen inches in diameter	Pressing Shift key constrains marquee to a perfect circle (see fig.11.27).
Double-click on Gradient tool	Chooses Gradient tool and displays Gradient Tool Options on Brushes palette.
Press Alt while clicking on a dark area of a blue gumball in SIDEWALK image	Pressing Alt toggles Gradient tool to Eyedropper, and sets current foreground color to dark blue.
Click on Inverse Color icon on toolbox	Changes foreground color to white, and background color to dark blue.
Press Alt while clicking on a blue gumball highlight in SIDEWALK image, then release Alt key	Changes current foreground color to very light blue.
On the Options palette, choose Normal as mode, Opacity: 100%, Style: Foreground to Background, Type: Radial; leave other settings at their default	Specifies a Gradient fill that makes the transition from foreground to background colors in a smooth, circular pattern.
Click and drag about 1/16 screen inches inside selection, starting at 2 o'clock position and ending at 7 o'clock	Produces a realistic ball (see fig. 11.28).
Choose File, Save As, and save your work as SIDEWALK.PSD, the Photoshop native file format	Saves your work in the only format that supports Layers. You cannot save a work in progress that has Layers in any other file format.

Because the SIDEWALK.TIF (not SIDEWALK.PSD) image has outlived its purposefulness in this assignment, you might want to delete it from your hard disk. But when you save multiple copies of an image, you can go back to an image at different stages of completion and perhaps take the design in a different direction. You might choose to save the TIF format image with the gumball machine positioned and composited.

Adding Tonal Detail to the Gumball

You'll use the Dodge and Burn tools shortly to enhance the dimensional qualities of the blue gumball, but first we need to examine a thing or two about how the gumball is sitting on the new layer.

Figure 11.26

Create a new layer by clicking on the New Layers icon on the Layers palette.

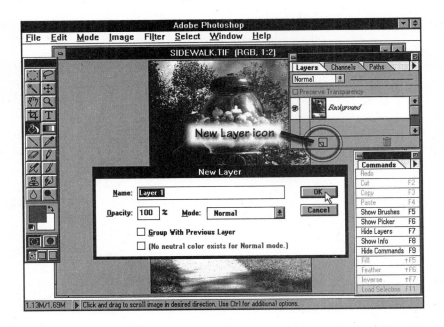

Figure 11.27

Create selections on layers exactly as you would on background.

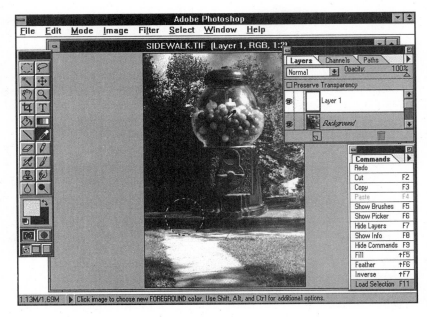

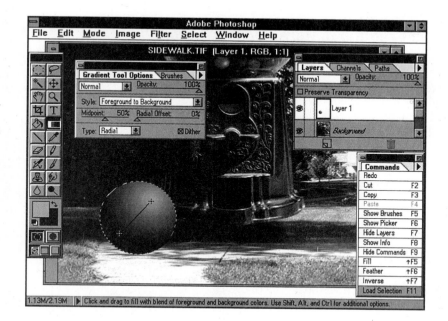

Figure 11.28

The Gradient tool fills selection areas with a transition between foreground and background color.

Elements pasted or painted on layers can be repositioned, because a layer consists of 100% transparent pixels and the opaque (or semi-opaque) pixels you add to it, and Photoshop understands the difference between the two different pixel properties. The only element on a layer that you can reposition is one you create there; the rest of the image space is like a clear sheet of acetate over the background image. Therefore, you don't need the selection border active around the gumball after you create the Gradient fill—you can reposition the gumball by clicking and dragging it with the Move tool.

The only caveat here is that if you decide to do some independent experimenting with the gumball, and decide to use the Gradient or other painting tool on it again, you can indeed go outside the lines and paint over more of the layer itself, spoiling the nice, clean edge around it when the selection border is removed. Transparent pixels *can* be reassigned an opaque quality with painting (and selection) tools. The way to continue to refine the gumball, using editing, painting, or selection tools, is to check the Preserve Transparency box on the Layers palette. Doing this prevents any other editing (such as paint spills!) from occurring on the clear space of the layer.

This exercise shows you how to intensify the highlights and shadows of the gumball by using the Dodge/Burn tools.

Creating a More Realistic Gumball

Press Ctrl+D (or choose **S**elect, **N**one)	Removes marquee border from gumball.
Click on Preserve Transparency check box on Layers palette	Protects areas outside gumball shape from painting.

If you'd like to, on a whim, test the property of the Protect Transparency feature, click and drag the Gradient tool over the gumball, using the same 2-o'clock-to-7-o'clock stroke you used earlier. You might be surprised to find that the maneuver doesn't change anything! The reason is that the Gradient tool can only apply the blend of foreground and background color to the gumball itself; the layer's transparent areas cannot be painted, and selection areas cannot be created on the clear areas now.

Click on Dodge tool	This tool is for lightening various tonal ranges in an image. When Dodge tool is chosen, Options for this tool replace Gradient Tool Options on Brushes palette.
Choose Midtones from drop-down list on the Options palette, then click and drag Intensity slider to **58%**	Dodge tool now affects pixels having a medium brightness in gradient-filled gumball. Tool does not lighten shadows or highlights, and partial Intensity setting enables you to make several passes over the area you're editing.
Click on Brushes tab, then click on 35-diameter brush tip	Specifies brush tip with spread at a fairly large size.
Click and drag Dodge tool over highlight area (at 2 o'clock) on gumball	Intensifies lighter areas in Gradient fill, as shown in figure 11.29.
Release cursor, then click and drag again over lighter areas	Because Photoshop considers each mouse click to be a new session with an editing tool, such as the Dodge tool, clicking and dragging, then clicking and dragging a second time is similar to applying an effect twice.
When highlight on gumball is more intense, choose Burn from drop-down list on the Options palette	This tool is used for darkening selected image areas.
Click and drag through midsection of gumball, going in an 11 o'clock-to-5 o'clock direction, as shown in figure 11.30	Darkens tone of area you click and drag over, without changing color values.

Play with Dodge and Burn tools on gradient gumball until you think it looks photographic in quality	Because you use this single gumball to create additional gumballs, the time you spend perfecting it is worthwhile!
Press Ctrl+S	Saves your work up to this point.

Tip   Brush characteristics and options you can set for tools are a matter of artistic preference. The specific choices described here and in other chapters are a starting place for the tools with which you work. Think of these choices as suggestions that happen to work in these exercises but aren't necessarily the ideal settings for different situations in your own work. Use tool settings as guidelines, but don't be afraid to experiment—this is what Photoshop is all about!

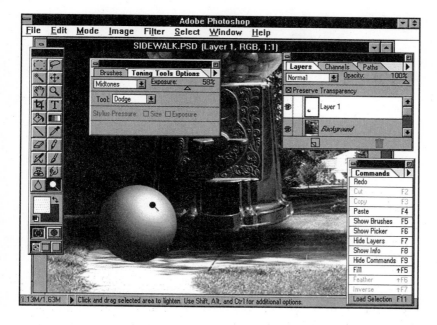

Figure 11.29

The Dodge tool lightens specific tonal regions without affecting a selection's color values.

Images you create with paint programs, modeling programs, and other computer graphics software tend to look a little too clean in photographic surroundings, as seen in the last example. This happens because photographic images tend to display digital *grit*, a random pattern of color values similar to the grain in photographic film. In contrast, digital images, such as the gumball, contain pure, even colors. Sometimes, adding an imperfection or two, or making a gradient less smooth in its transition of colors, as you did in the last exercise, heightens the believability of your work.

Figure 11.30

*The Burn
tool decreases
brightness values
in image areas
without affecting
the original
color values.*

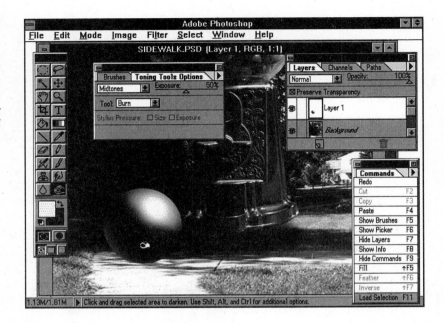

Duplicating and Modifying the Gumball

With Photoshop's tools and effects, you now can resize and recolor a copy of the perfect blue gumball to create a second, third, or as many other gumballs you choose, to populate the catalog image.

The Preserve Transparency option applies to specfic layers; although Layer 1's transparent part is presently protected from change, a New Layer can be added to the SIDEWALK image, and by default, that layer's transparency is not protected.

As you continue with your own adventures in image editing and layers in Photoshop, it's important that you keep the Layers palette open, particularly when you edit or paste in a selection. Layers aren't like color channels—you have a view of image areas on all the layers in a multilayer image, and the possibility exists that you might edit on a layer you don't intend to edit on, unless you're certain which layer is active. The Layers palette is your visual guide to locating selections.

In the next exercise, you create a second gumball and assign it to its own layer so that it can be positioned independently of the first.

Creating a Smaller, Greener Gumball

Press Ctrl+A (or choose <u>S</u>elect, <u>A</u>ll)   A marquee appears around entire image window, but not to worry. Photoshop reads the entire image window, but selects only foreground color, not transparent areas.

Press Ctrl+C (or choose <u>E</u>dit, <u>C</u>opy)   Copies only the gumball image to Clipboard.

Choose <u>E</u>dit, Paste La<u>y</u>er   Displays the Paste Layer dialog box.

Click on OK   Accepts default for New Layer's name (Layer 2), and the mode and opacity for the layer's contents (the gumball copy).

When a layer element, such as the gumball copy, is changed using any of the Effects commands, the effects box that normally surrounds a selection area displays around only the opaque pixels on a layer. Although you can paint a transparent pixel, you can't distort one.

Choose <u>I</u>mage, <u>E</u>ffects, <u>S</u>cale   Displays a boundary box around gumball.

Press Shift while clicking and dragging on upper-left corner of boundary box, and move it toward center of gumball selection (see fig. 11.31)   Resizes boundary box and its contents. Shift key preserves proportion of original image's width-to-height relationship.

When gumball copy is about 3/4 the size of the original, click inside boundary box   Cursor turns into a gavel, and finalizes Scale effect.

Press Ctrl+U (or choose <u>I</u>mage, <u>A</u>djust, <u>H</u>ue/Saturation)   Displays Hue/Saturation dialog box.

Enter **–110** in <u>H</u>ue field, **+22** in Saturation field, leave Lightness field alone, and click on OK   Changes Hue and Saturation properties of gumball copy, turning it green (see fig. 11.32).

Press Ctrl+S   Saves your work up to this stage.

Figure 11.31

The Scale effect can be used to proportionately, or disproportionately, shrink and grow a layer element.

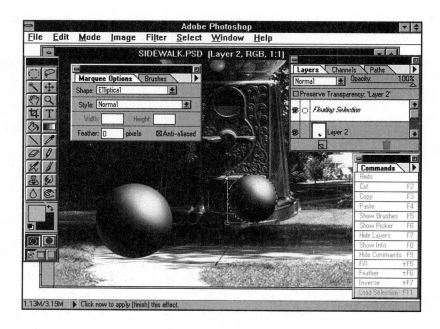

Figure 11.32

You can respecify the basic color components of a selection using the Hue/Saturation command.

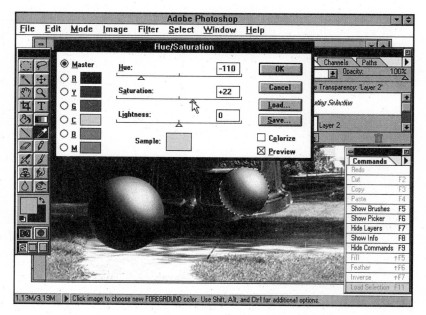

Tip

Although the Hue/Saturation dialog box can be used to shift the overall color cast of a selection area, sometimes you find that "you can't get there from here"; for instance, you may not be able to create the right shade of orange for the blue gumball. The reason is that the Hue/Saturation adjustment shifts color values, it doesn't replace them in normal mode.

You might want to try clicking on the C**o**lorize check box on the Hue/Saturation dialog box when you want to replace all the color components in a selection with a single Hue. C**o**lorize can make a sepiatone from a color image, and you might not want to choose this option if you want to retain several different color areas in a selection. The C**o**lorize trick works with a gumball selection, however, because the gumball basically consists of one Hue. C**o**lorize enables you to define a Hue, then operate the Saturation and Brightness components independently in a selection.

Adding and Moving Gumballs

Now you know the necessary steps for creating additional gumballs, based on a copy of the original blue one you designed. Create as many additional layers as you like for more gumballs, then use the Scale effect and the Hue/Saturation Adjust command to make all the gumballs look different. Compared to saved selections in channels, the Layers feature helps keep down the total image size, so that you can work more quickly without worrying about straining your computer's resources. The reason Photoshop can create layers with an economy of stored data is that the transparency area on a layer doesn't take up a lot of your memory resources. Transparent pixels are assigned a different bit per pixel color capability (8 bits per pixel) than RGB layer elements, whose color capability is 24 bits per pixels.

With, say, four gumballs on top of your image, you want to choreograph their arrangement. To do this, follow the steps in the next exercise.

Choreographing Gumballs

Click on Layer 1 title on Layers palette	Selects Layer 1 and its contents (the original blue gumball). All other Layers are inactive now.
Choose Layer Move tool from toolbox (to the right of Magic Wand tool)	This tool is used for moving foreground images on transparent Layers.

continues

continued

Click and drag anywhere on image	Because blue gumball is the only element on Layer 1, it makes no difference where you click and drag; blue gumball moves along in the direction you drag.
Click on Layer 2 title on Layers palette	Makes Layer 2 the active layer. You can move green gumball now, but not the blue one.
Click and drag anywhere on image	Moves green gumball.
Click on the other layers titles, then click and drag with Layer Move tool	Repositions other gumballs.

There are one or two variations that you can perform on your gumball choreography now. If you want to move two gumballs simultaneously on different layers—Layer 1's blue gumball and Layer 2's green one, for instance—click on the Layer 2 title to select it, then click to the right of the Eye icon on Layer 1. The Layer Move icon appears next to the titles of both layers, which means they're linked. Now you can move the contents of Layer 2 and Layer 1 simultaneously. To break the link, click on either Layer Move icon to remove it.

Additionally, you can reorder the stack of layers to position one gumball behind another. To do this, click on the active title on the Layers palette, and drag down or up. The cursor changes to a fist. Release the mouse button when the selected layer is over the layer you want the selected layer to occupy. The layer over which you drop the selected layer is then forced down in the stack, and the selected layer is above the other one.

Adding Shadows to the Background Image

One of the advantages to working with a multilayer image is that you can go back and adjust any element independently of the others, even when an element apparently overlaps another. Image information is held on discreet layers, and nothing is carved in stone until you merge the layers together to complete an image.

Like the gumball machine, the gumballs now need corresponding shadows to make them appear to float above the sidewalk. Because no additional layers were defined for the gum machine, you had to create a selection area for its shadow, but now that the gumballs are on different layers (and not on the same layer as the sidewalk background), shadow creation is a breeze; all you need to do is create an elliptical selection on the background image—a shadow appears to be behind and below a gumball.

The next exercise shows you how to finish the catalog cover, giving it the wonder and appeal that are possible only when you understand selections and layers.

Adding Background Shadows

Click on Background title on Layers palette	Makes SIDEWALK image active layer; no other layers can be edited now.
Choose Marquee tool, then choose Elliptical from drop-down list on Marquee Options palette	Creates elliptical marquee selections.
Enter **5** in Feather: field on Marquee Options palette	Ellipses you now create with Marquee tool automatically have a Feathered edge.
Click and drag Elliptical marquee tool beneath a gumball in SIDEWALK image	Creates a Feathered selection area.
If your ellipse is not precisely where you want it, press Ctrl+Alt while clicking and dragging inside the marquee	Moves selection marquee, not image area it defines.
Click on Paint Bucket tool, then press Alt while clicking over a shaded area of SIDEWALK image, then release Alt key	Toggles to Eyedropper tool, and samples color of shadow.
Click over ellipse selection	Adds foreground color to ellipse (see fig. 11.33). Photoshop remembers your last use of Paint Bucket tool, and retains Opacity and mode settings.
Repeat last steps with Elliptical marquee tool and Paint Bucket tool	Adds realistic shadows to rest of gumballs.
Press Ctrl+S	Assignment completed!

Next, you want to take one or two digital housecleaning steps to make the SIDEWALK more of a generic bitmap image that other people can read and use—but essentially, you've got your catalog cover now.

Turning Off Photoshop's Magic

You've seen the extraordinary things you can accomplish with a couple of simple images, and should have a pretty good feel for the way selections, paths, and layers interrelate to help bring together an assignment. You'll use one or more of the selection techniques shown in this chapter to solve design problems in your own assignments. You simply have to decide when the appropriate technique and tool is called for.

Figure 11.33

Add foreground color to a selection area only on the Background layer of the SIDEWALK image.

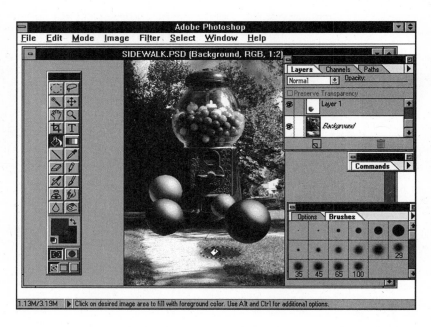

If the image on your screen looks like the one in figure 11.33, you've graduated from steak-and-potatoes assignments to the more exotic, complex gourmet projects that await you in the next part of the book. You're also entitled to take a break for a moment, because if you reflect on what you've accomplished recently, it's quite a feat—you're no longer a beginner in this image-editing game!

The SIDEWALK image has been edited to perfection, but you need to do one or two things now so that you can hand it over to a potential client. Layers, Alpha channels, and paths are all technologies proprietary to Photoshop 3; you can open and edit layers in a *.PSD format, but only Photoshop can read the Photoshop file format.

Part of the terrific quality of RGB bitmap images lies in their portability; the Macintosh, UNIX workstations, and Windows applications other than Photoshop can import bitmaps, but only when they conform to certain file-format conventions. Once you have an image finished, as you do the SIDEWALK image, an important last step is to save the image as a more common, generic file format, such as TIF. Because the Tagged Image File format can support Alpha channels and paths, but not layers, you now need to merge the layers in this design so that it can be saved as a TIF image. Photoshop will offer only the PSD format for a file you want to save if it contains layers. Additionally, you need to clean out the paths and Alpha channels, because they no longer serve a design purpose.

It also is a good idea to delete superfluous paths and channels because some, but not all, applications understand this extra information saved in the TIF format. For instance, PageMaker 5 ignores Alpha channels and happily imports a TIF image containing Alpha channels. On the other hand, Norton Desktop Viewer triggers a system halt when you attempt to view a TIF image that contains an Alpha channel, because the application doesn't understand the file information within the format.

Macintosh users should exercise a little more caution in saving to specific file formats, because the Mac operating system doesn't use or list file extensions. If you're running Photoshop for the Macintosh and you're saving this catalog cover to the TIF format to be shared with a Windows system, save the file in the TIF format, but include TIF as part of the file name.

Here's how to save your image in a bitmap format that other applications and other operating systems can import:

Making a Photoshop Image Generic

On Layers palette, click on fly-out menu, and choose Flatten Image, as shown in figure 11.34	Takes all layers and composites them with background image, in the order (from top to bottom) they appear on the Layers palette.
Choose File, Save As, then choose TIFF(*.TIF) from drop-down list under Save File as Format Type	Chooses a file format for the image so it can be imported by different applications and different computer platforms.
Name the file **FLAVORS.TIF** in File Name: field, then click on OK	You now have a TIF image and a working copy of the SIDEWALK.PSD image saved to your hard disk; you can go back to them later and further modify the layers.
Click on Channels tab on Layers palette	Displays color and Alpha channels in FLAVORS.TIF image.
Click on Channel #5 title, then drag it into Trash icon (see fig. 11.35)	Deletes channel from image.

Stop Because Photoshop does not flash you a confirmation dialog box when you delete channels, layers, or paths, be absolutely certain that you have the correct title selected before dragging it into the Trash icon!

continues

continued

Click on Channel #4 title, then drag it into Trash icon, as shown in figure 11.35	Deletes channel from image.
Click on Paths tab on Layers palette, then click and drag path titles into Trash icon	Deletes paths from FLAVORS.TIF image.
Press Ctrl+S	Saves your image.

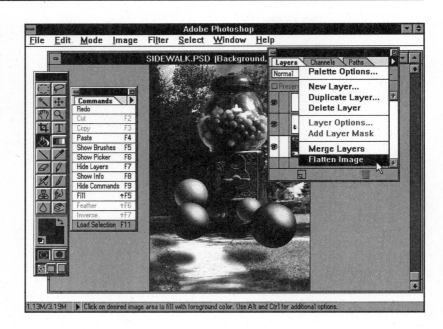

File Management and Saved Images

If this were a paying assignment, you might want to practice some file management now that the finished FLAVORS.TIF image has been saved to hard disk. This involves asking yourself whether you really want or need the SIDEWALK.TIF and SIDEWALK.PSD files anymore. The theme of this image can be changed now that you have two other files saved at various stages of completion; you might want to delete the layers in the SIDEWALK.PSD file, and create toys or clothing, floating out of the gumball machine instead of gumballs. Never underestimate the ability of a client to change their mind is an important lesson in addition to your Photoshop discoveries! You might get a request to create a different colored gumball machine, or reposition

the gumballs, and this can only be accomplished now by going back to previously saved versions of the image.

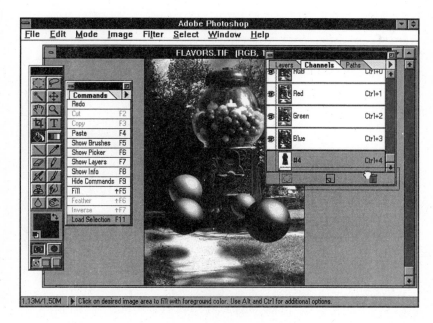

Figure 11.35

Delete paths, layers, and channels by dragging their titles into the Trash icon.

But since this catalog assignment is a hypothetical one, let's hypothesize for a moment that you succeeded; the client is in love with a cover you pulled off in less than a day; and it's time to frame your work, in a manner of speaking, without all the palettes and tools cluttering your view.

The following simple exercise is optional. It's handy for displaying your Photoshop work for a client.

Putting Away Your Imaging Tools

Double-click on Hand tool	Changes viewing resolution of **FLAVORS.TIF** image to full-frame.
Click on right button at very bottom of toolbox	Displays a view of active image without menu or window scroll bars.
Press Tab key	Toggles off all palettes and tools (see fig. 11.36).
Press Tab key again	Displays tools in workspace.

continues

continued

Click on left button on image window   Displays menu and toolbox.

Figure 11.36

Pressing the Tab key toggles off all palettes and tools.

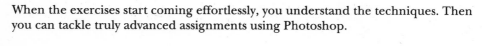

Moving to a Higher "Layer" of Photoshop Skills

This is the final chapter of Part II, "Steak and Potatoes Assignments." And it's only upward from here. Part III, "Gourmet Assignments," covers tougher assignments with richer rewards. Now that you have a good working knowledge of Photoshop's interface, and a grasp of techniques you can use for simple problem-solving, you can concentrate on more advanced image enhancement. In Part III's assignments, none of the images you correct has glaringly obvious mistakes—in fact, the images are quite serviceable. The objective of this book is to familiarize you with Photoshop's tools, and show you how to use them in combination with other tools and effects, so you can create your own Photoshop techniques for getting the results you expect and the ones you've always hoped to achieve.

When the exercises start coming effortlessly, you understand the techniques. Then you can tackle truly advanced assignments using Photoshop.

Part III

Gourmet Assignments

12 Correcting an Image 513

13 Combining Photographs 589

14 Enhancing Images 635

15 Special Effects with Ordinary Photographs 687

16 Creating a Digital Collage 743

17 The Wonderful World of Black and White 801

18 Photoshop's Native Filters 841

Correcting an Image

Photographs usually portray scenes as we see them in real life, but they can go one step beyond and display images of life the way we'd like to see them. Many times a project that's half-finished—a car, a highway, even a house—needs to be shown to an anxious client who needs your skills to help them visualize the finished project.

The subject of this chapter's assignment is "virtually" completing a new home construction project. The house is built, but Mother Nature and the landscapers have lagged behind somewhat. It's a nice house, but if it's going to sell, prospective buyers need a little help picturing themselves in the house of their dreams. And this is where you and Photoshop step in.

You'll landscape, pave, nail up a few clapboards, and even put a car in the driveway—all without leaving your desktop or getting mud under your fingernails. Although you won't receive any aerobic benefits from this assignment, you will exercise a wide range of Photoshop skills, and develop and create variations on a number of techniques.

So get out your digital work gloves, put on your pixel-based hard-hat, and let's get into the construction business.

Surveying the Layout

The first task at any construction site is an accurate survey of the landscape, to see how the lay of the land affects your plans and the list of materials needed for your project. In Photoshop's workspace, you also need to do some survey work. You need to take a look at the house, figure out what you need to do to improve it, then assemble the materials you'll need.

Evalutating the Image

Open NHOUSE.TIF from the Chap12 subdirectory (folder) on the *Inside Photoshop 3* Bonus CD. As you can see in figure 12.1, NHOUSE.TIF is a photo of a typical new house construction project. To make this an image that will look good on the cover of the Realtor's brochure and also appeal to what buyers envision their home will look like, you'll need to do some fancy work.

Figure 12.1

The house might take another three months to complete in the physical world, or only a few hours using Photoshop's tools.

The most obvious "flaw" in this image is the lack of grass and other landscaping. A photo containing the missing elements needs to be found for replacement parts. The ideal grass photo should have a landscape (horizontal) orientation to minimize the need to reuse portions of the grass, which in turn reduces the possibility of creating an unwanted tiling effect. Another consideration when looking for a suitable grass image is the angle at which the photo was taken and if the lighting compares to the angle and lighting in the NHOUSE.TIF image. Fortunately, grass tends to

photograph as a random, organic texture rather than as a series of discrete objects; if the perfect photo can't be found, the problem is not an overwhelming one. If you had to replace a section of embroidery, an area with a distinct pattern, or other visual content, shopping around for a suitable image would be much more difficult.

The house also needs bushes and a tree to look complete. When searching for images of bushes and trees, it's good to select ones with elements that can be separated easily from their backgrounds. Lighting on these elements is important, and images that display matching light sources to those of the target image are the best ones to use. If you are photographing these items yourself, keep an eye on the shadows in the target image and plan your photographic session for a time of day when you can match the lighting conditions and produce similar shadows in your images.

Finally, to make this house a value-added piece of real estate, and to make it a dream house, it would be nice to put a fancy sports car in the driveway. As fate would have it, there wasn't a fancy sports car parked on the gravel of the half-finished home when the NHOUSE image was taken. When you can't dress up your set before you photograph it, you can always add an element later that you've photographed separately. Again, when choosing a photo of a car, look for one that will separate easy, is photographed at an angle that would be believable when placed in the driveway of NHOUSE.TIF, and has similar lighting conditions. If you're photographing a car other than the one you own, it doesn't hurt to buy the owner a drink beforehand— sports car owners are a little apprehensive when they see a stranger's camera pointed at their pride and joy!

Your materials list for this assignment includes a photo of grass, a photo of a tree, one or more photos of bushes, and a picture of a red convertible sports car. You won't need to search far for these images: they're all in the CHAP12 subdirectory (folder) on the *Inside Photoshop 3* Bonus CD.

Let's get started so that this new house will be ready for an *open* house.

Working with Layers

The "foundation" for your Photoshop retouching work will be the lawn for the NHOUSE image. The source for the new lawn grass is an image of a local golf club fairway. You can't find better grass than this, right? LAKSHORE.TIF is a perfect source image for the lawn transplant project because LAKSHORE has the same size, orientation, resolution and lighting as the NHOUSE target image. The apparent size of the blades of grass in LAKSHORE is also important; they won't look too big or too small when placed in the target image.

Three methods can be used to transplant the grass from the fairway into the new lawn. You'll use the last method in the list, but one of the other methods might be used under different circumstances.

◆ A pattern is defined with the Rectangular marquee tool that is then applied to the lawn of NHOUSE with the Fill tool or the Rubber Stamp in their From Pattern painting modes. Pattern filling or cloning is a good technique when you don't have a very large area as the sample source for the pattern (see Chapter 10, "Stamping Out Photo Errors"). But, filling a large area with a pattern sampled from a small area usually creates a visible tiling effect that is difficult to correct.

◆ The LAKSHORE grass could be the sample site for the Rubber Stamp tool in its Clone Aligned mode. This method works best when you have large areas from which to sample, but it takes some diligence and visual dexterity to ensure that the sampling point for the Rubber Stamp doesn't run off the edge of the image and that you don't create patterns by Rubber Stamping over previously cloned-in areas.

◆ Copying the grass to a Photoshop layer and then using the Layer Mask is the third method and the one that fits this assignment best. The Layer Mask is a quick and easy way to tailor the shape of the grass to fit the photo by hiding the portions of the grass that aren't needed. Any of the familiar paint or editing tools can be used to create the mask.

Layer Masks are unique in that areas the mask covers will be removed from the layer image when the Mask is applied to the layer. Editing a Layer Mask is a little like "painting" with the Eraser tool, but much easier because you can see what you are doing. In addition, a Layer Mask is infinitely redefinable because changes aren't definite until you apply the mask.

The Layer Mask method is ideal for this assignment because the LAKSHORE photo is the same resolution and image size, and its lighting matches NHOUSE's size and lighting almost perfectly. Because the grass can be moved into the target image as one piece, there is no chance of creating a tell tale repeat pattern. The grass will look as if it has always grown in front of the new house.

Lets put on a mask and plant some grass. In the process, you'll explore one of Photoshop's new and powerful productivity features.

Transferring Images between Windows

Open NHOUSE.TIF from the Chap12 subdirectory on the Bonus CD if it is not already open

This is the target image you are retouching.

Click on the Standard windows screen mode on the toolbox (leftmost, bottom one), thenpress Ctrl(Cmd)+−

Makes the image fit full size within a small window.

Open LAKSHORE.TIF from the Chap12 subdirectory of the Bonus CD, then press Ctrl (Cmd)+– (minus)	This is the source image for the grass.
Choose **W**indow, **T**ile; drag any palettes and the toolbox out of the way; make sure the Layers Palette is open (F7 [Macintosh:F11] or **W**indow, **P**alettes, Show **L**ayers)	Places the two images side by side in the workspace so that you can work with both.

You need a clear view of the entire LAKSHORE image, but NHOUSE can have tools covering portions of it.

Click on the Rectangular **M**arquee tool or press **M** until it appears on the toolbox. Click and diagonally drag a rectangular selection on the LAKSHORE image. Start the selection on the left side of the image at the point the grass shifts color from dark green to light green, and end it in the lower right-hand corner (see fig. 12.2)	Selects a good looking, large piece of grass suitable for transplant.
Click and drag the selection from LAKSHORE's image window and drop the selection on top of the NHOUSE.TIF image window	The cursor turns into a fist, and the selection turns into a rectangle with a dotted outline. Dropping the selection onto NHOUSE.TIF transfers a copy of the floating selection to NOUSE.TIF and makes it the active image.
Click on the New Layer icon on the left side of the Layers palette, then choose OK	Converts the floating selection into an object on a new Layer that uses the default Layers settings.

NHOUSE.TIF has become the active image, complete with a new Layer that contains the grass selection made in LAKSHORE. Layer 1 is on top of the background and now overlays the bottom fifth of the NHOUSE image as seen in figure 12.3.

Choose **F**ile, Sa**v**e As; in the File **N**ame text box, change the name of the file to NHOUSE.PSD; use the Dri**v**es and **D**irectories list boxes to choose a place on your hard disk to store the file; click on OK	Saves the file to your hard disk in Photoshop's PSD format —the only format that preserves the Layer structure of the file.

continues

continued

Click on the LAKSHORE image, then press Ctrl (Cmd)+W	Closes the file without saving changes.

Figure 12.2

Use the Rectangular Marquee tool to select the greenest grass.

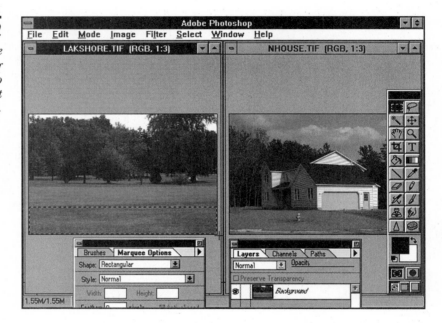

Figure 12.3

The grass in Layer 1 covers the bottom of the image.

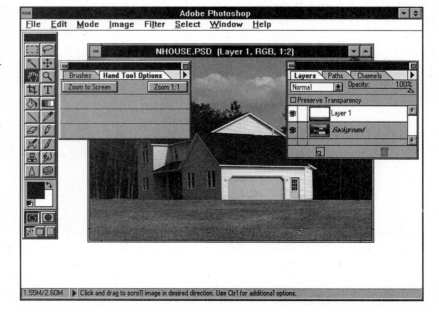

Trimming Image Areas with a Layer Mask

With the grass safely on a layer, it can be edited to fit into place. Just exactly where you need to trim is unclear because the layer that the grass rests on has an opacity of 100% which totally obscures the underlying background image. This is not a problem because the Opacity property of the layer can be changed at any time. The level of opacity a layer exhibits only produces a permanent result in your image when the layer is merged to the Background. You'll need to reduce the opacity of the layer temporarily so that you can peek through the grass and use the underlying Background image as a guide to editing the grass image. After you have finished editing, you then restore the opacity of the layer to 100%.

Directly editing the image on the layer is not the best way to go about this assignment. When you carve away the grass with the standard editing tools (Lasso and Eraser), you permanently remove pixels with each editing move you make. Photoshop only has one level of undo (**E**dit, **U**ndo) available; if you must decide whether a selection area should be deleted, you can't undo your decision several steps later. To be able to modify selection areas until you're happy with them, and only commit to all the edits you've made *after* you're certain everything is okay, you need a *mask*. Specifically, you need a Layer Mask.

Editing the grass image on the layer indirectly by using the Layer Mask feature is a much better and more forgiving choice than directly editing. Instead of permanently carving away at the pixels themselves in a series of irrevocable steps, you create a mask—the Layer Mask—that is designed to *hide* image areas temporarily on the layer from your view. As you add masked areas, more of the image on the Layer disappears from view. If you eliminate the mask overlay that covers an image area, that image area becomes visible.

When you edit using a Layer Mask, you are never prematurely locked into a permanent change to the image on the Layer. Because you can use *any* of Photoshop's paint or editing tools to define precisely the areas that are masked (hidden), you can come back days and many hundreds of Photoshop actions later and change the mask. Only when you are certain that the image on the Layer has been edited to your satisfaction do you choose to Apply the Layer Mask to the image. When the Layer mask is applied to the image, Photoshop uses the mask as a guide for *removing* image areas instead of simply hiding them.

In the following exercise you'll trim the grass down to size *and* get first hand experience at editing image areas with the Layer Mask.

Hiding Image Areas with the Layer Mask

Double-click on the Zoom Tool on the toolbox; use the Hand tool or the scroll bars to move to the bottom, left-hand corner of the image; move any open palettes that cover the grass	Zooms the image to a 1:1 viewing resolution and moves you to a position where you will be able to see the driveway.
Click on the triangle to the right of the tabs on the Layers palette to display the pop-up menu, then choose Add Layer Mask	The Layer Mask icon appears next to the Layer 1 icon. The Layer Mask icon has a thicker border around it to indicate that it is selected.
Double-click on the Layer Mask icon. Click on the Color Indicates: **H**idden Areas radio button, and the Position Relative To: **L**ayer radio buttons if they are not already selected; leave Color Opacity set at 50% and be sure the Do not **A**pply to Layer check box is unchecked (see fig. 12.4); click on OK	Displays the Layer Mask Options dialog box. Sets black as the color that hides pixels and determines how the mask can be moved.
Click and drag the Opacity slider on the Layers palette to the left; stop when you can still see some of the grass but mostly you see the Background image: **45%** is a good setting; make sure the Layer mode drop-down box to the left of the Opacity slider is set to Normal	Reduces the opacity of the layer so that you can see the Background image. Opacity levels can be changed at any time.
Press **D** or click on the **d**efault colors icon on the toolbox, then press **X** or click on the Switch colors icon on the toolbox	Resets Foreground/Background colors to default settings, then inverts them so that white is the Foreground and black is the Background color.

When selection areas on the Layer Mask are removed using the Delete key, they are filled with the background color. Switching the default colors made black the current background color, which is the right color to hide the grass that covers the driveway.

Press **L** or click once on the **L**asso tool on the toolbox; press Enter; set Feather to **1** pixel and make sure anti-aliased is checked	Chooses the Lasso tool. Feather and anti-aliased keep it from making a hard-edged selection.

In the next step you must press the Alt (Option) key and continue to hold it down. You will be creating a selection that removes the grass from the driveway, the trees to the right, and the front of the garage. See figure 12.5 for the shape of the final selection.

Moving counter-clockwise, press and hold down the Alt (Option) key and click the Lasso on the left corner of the garage above the grass line; then click where the garage meets the ground; click your way along the left edge of the driveway, click outside the image window on the right, move up and click outside the window at a point adjacent to the trees and above the grass line, then click back at your starting point on the left corner of the garage	Creates the selection as seen in figure 12.5. Clicking outside the image window causes the selection to snap perfectly to the edge of the image.
Press the Delete key	Fills the selection area in the Layer Mask channel with black. Any area of black in the Layer Mask channel will hide the corresponding area in your view of the image. The grass within the selection disappears from your view.
Press Ctrl (Cmd)+D (**S**elect, **N**one)	Deselects the selection.

Don't worry if your selection is not quite as precise as you would like it at this point. You can always hide more pixels by selecting them and deleting them using the Lasso tool, or by painting black over the area to be removed using a painting tool. If you hide more of the image than you want to, paint white over the area that needs grass and the area comes out of hiding!

One of the Layer Mask's other virtues is that it can continue to be refined. Consequentially, you can continue to work within the same mask as you select other areas of the image where the grass should be trimmed, such as the curb and street, and along the foundation of the house. For this exercise, you need to restore a small sliver of grass to the right of the driveway that you removed.

In the next exercise, you continue to work with the Layer Mask to trim back more grass, and add the grass to areas you need.

Figure 12.4

Set the Layer Mask Options by double-clicking on the Layer Mask icon.

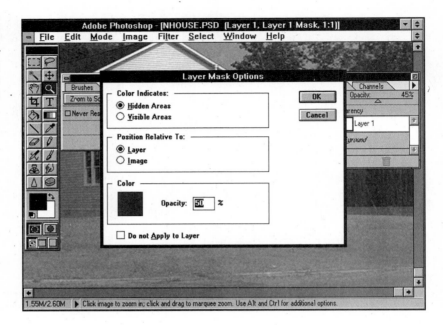

Figure 12.5

Create a selection around the grass you need to remove.

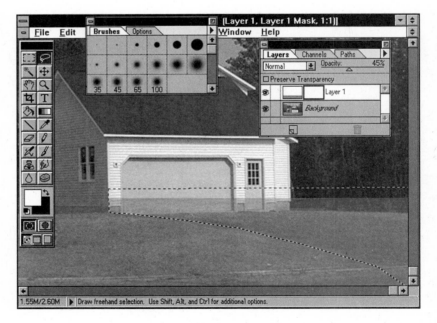

Hiding and Revealing Image Areas

Press and hold down the Alt (Option) key and click the Lasso on top of the curb on the left hand side of the image; continue to hold down Alt (Option) and click along the top of the curb moving toward the driveway, click outside the image window to the right, click in the lower right hand corner, then click in the lower left hand corner of the screen and back up to your starting point (see fig.12.6)	Creates a selection that includes the curb and the street.
Press the Delete key	Adds solid Layer Mask that hides the grass within the selection.
Click on the image window's left scroll bar arrow to move to the image's lower-left corner, then use the Lasso tool to define a curb and road selection then delete the contents of the selection as you did in the preceding steps for the right side of the curb	Moves you into position so that you can finish hiding the grass that currently covers the balance of the curb and street.
With the Zoom tool click once over the lower right-hand corner of the front porch; move palettes as necessary so that you have a clear view of the foundation of the house	Gets you into position for the area you'll work on next. A 2:1 viewing resolution is good.
With the Lasso tool, press Alt (Option) and click on a selection that encompasses the grass where it overlaps onto the house and its foundation; when you've defined the area, press the Delete key	Defines and hides the part of the grass that overlaps the house.

You've removed all of the areas where the grass shouldn't be. Your next move is to put some back.

Press Ctrl (Cmd)++ (plus) and use the Hand tool or the scroll bars to move to the right hand corner of the image	Moves you into position for the area you need to work on next.

continues

continued

Press **X** on the keyboard or click on the to Switch colors icon on the toolbox	Changes the foreground color black, and the background color to white. When white is applied to the Layer Mask, previously hidden grass reappears.
Use the Lasso tool to define a selection around the narrow sliver of dirt between the trees and the driveway. When the selection is defined, (see fig. 12.7) press the Delete key	This time grass is restored to your view of the layer. When you delete areas, they change to the background color, which is white. White in a Layer Mask unhides image areas.
Press Ctrl (Cmd)+D (**S**elect, **N**one)	Deselects the selection marquee.
Press Ctrl (Cmd)+S (**F**ile, **S**ave)	Saves your work to hard disk.

Figure 12.6

Select the area to include the top of the curb and the street.

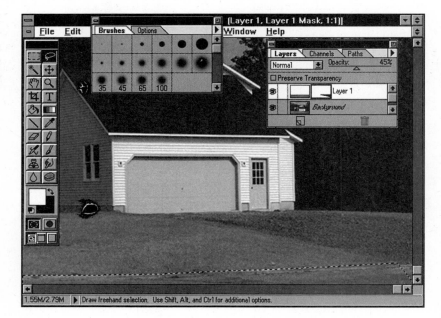

New Riders Publishing
INSIDE
SERIES

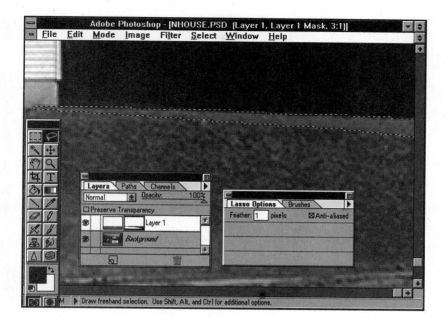

Figure 12.7

Carefully select the narrow sliver of dirt to the left of the drive and fill it with grass.

At least two other areas might need your attention with the use of the Layer Mask. First, the fire plug has been grassed over. If this photo were part of an actual sales prospectus, you would be ethically (and probably legally) required to restore the fire plug to its position of prominence on the lawn. You can use a small brush to remove the Layer Mask that covers the fire plug. However, the plans for this image include planting a virtual tree on the lawn. Poking a hole in the lawn to expose the fire plug on the background layer will interfere with the placement of the tree because the tree trunk can't be easily placed behind a background element.

To give yourself maximum flexibility in placing the tree (and its shadow), it is best to "turf over" the fire plug. You'll find a copy of the fire plug in the CHAP12 subdirectory of the Bonus CD should you want to restore the fire plug to the scene when you've finished working on the image.

The second area that may need attention is the tree line to the left of the image. If you look closely at the image, it looks like hummocks of dirt and fallen branches have been pushed to the edge of the lawn. Depending on how large a piece of grass you transplanted into this image from LAKSHORE.TIF, you may need to cut the grass back from the dips between the hummocks. You also may need to hide or unhide more grass.

In all these edits, the Paint Brush tool with a small soft tip is the best tool for the job. In the next exercise, you'll trim your lawn work and put the finishing touches on the lawn.

Final Touches—Applying the Layer Mask

Double-click on the Hand tool	Zooms you out to a full view of the image.
With Layer 1 still the active layer, click and drag the Opacity slider on the Layers palette to **100%**	The grass is displayed "full strength." Only the grass that does not have any Layer Mask overlay on it shows; the rest is hidden.

Take a good look at your image and check all the borders between grass and other substances. Now is the time to decide if any area needs grass or needs to have grass removed. If you find areas that need correcting follow the next three steps. If everything looks great (see fig. 12.8), skip over the next three steps.

With the Zoom tool click once or twice over the area that needs touching up	Zoom in on the area that needs work.
Double-click on the Paint Brush tool; make sure the mode on the Paintbrush Options palette is Normal and the Opacity is **100%**; click on the Brushes palette and choose either the first or the second Brush tip from the left on the second row	Selects a small, soft brush tip that applies paint in a full strength mode. The size of the brush tip should be slightly smaller than the area you need to fix.
Click and drag the brush over the area(s) to be fixed	Change the foreground color if necessary; use black to hide grass and white to restore grass to the image.

When you finish editing the grass, you then need to Apply the Layer Mask to the image. When the Layer Mask is applied, the mask acts like a cookie cutter: it trims away all the areas on the layer currently hidden from view. This is a permanent action—the removed pixels cannot be recovered. You can, however, create a new Layer Mask to hide and then cut away any of the image areas that are left on the layer. You should only Apply a Layer Mask to a layer when you know you won't want to "unhide" any more of the image areas.

Click on the triangle next to the Tabs on the Layers palette	Displays the options pop-up menu.
Choose Remove Layer Mask from the menu, then click on the Apply button when the Attention box (see fig. 12.9) asks, "Apply mask to layer before removing?"	Applies the mask to the Layer and removes all the hidden image areas. This action also deletes the Layer Mask and its associated Layer Mask Channel.

The Attention box choices are somewhat confusing. If you had chosen Discard, the Mask and all your mask creating\editing work would have been lost instead of the image areas you intended to trim.

Press Ctrl (Cmd)+S (**F**ile, **S**ave)   Saves your work up to this point.

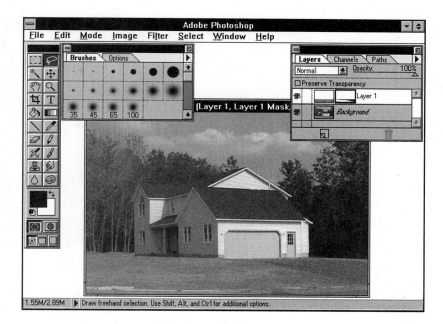

Figure 12.8

Increase the Layer Opacity to 100% to see how the grass will look when it is merged to the Background Layer.

Tip   When the Layer Mask icon is the selected icon for a layer, any painting or other editing work you do is applied to the Layer Mask. If you want to paint or edit on the layer itself and not on its associated mask you must click on the Layer Icon (the thumbnail of the layer's contents) to the left of the Layer Mask icon.

Deselecting the Layer Mask icon shifts the focus of the program back to the layer itself, but it does not affect the work you did in the Layer Mask, and you won't lose any of your work by deselecting the Layer Mask icon. You can return to editing the Layer Mask at any time by clicking on the Layer Mask icon to make it active.

With the lawn trimmed to size and safely stored on its own layer, it's time to put on a hard hat and get into the paving business.

Figure 12.9

*Click Apply
in the Remove
Layer Mask
attention box to
remove the image
areas the Layer
Mask hides.*

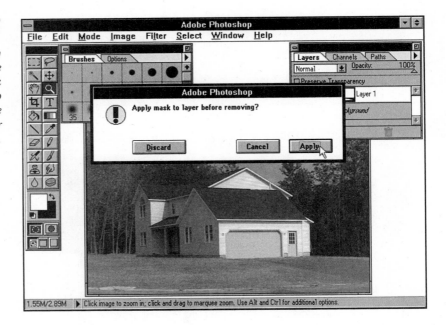

Creating an Asphalt Texture

The crushed stone driveway is the next area that needs your attention. Although crushed stone is an economical and serviceable material for a driveway, the goal here is to make this a *dream* house; sports car, manicured lawn, paved driveway, the whole nine yards. Very few people who own expensive sports cars dream of crushed stone drives. Your "heavy machinery" for paving the driveway in the next section are an unlikely combination of the Lasso tool, tone adjustment commands, and the Blur command. Occasionally, you'll find that the most dramatic results can be achieved using fairly standard features found in Photoshop's workspace.

Changing Stone into Asphalt

Although changing stone into asphalt is not as lucrative as changing lead into gold, it is a useful skill to have. The technique is quite simple and is composed of three basic actions—selecting the driveway, adjusting the brightness and contrast of the driveway to make it darker and less contrasty, and motion blurring the selection to make the "grain" smaller and more uniform.

Here's how to perform a minor process of alchemy.

Creating an Effect with Standard Features

Click on the New Layer icon on the bottom of the Layers palette then click on OK	Creates a new layer and accepts the default settings and name (Layer 2) for the layer.
Zoom into a 1:1 viewing resolution of the lower right hand corner of the image; move palettes out of the way	You need to see the entire driveway and the dirt on both sides of it.
Press the L key (**Lasso** tool) or click on the Lasso tool on the toolbox	The Lasso tool becomes the active tool.
Click on the eye icon on Layer 1, then click on the Background title on the Layers palette	Turns off your view of the grass and the Background becomes the active layer.
Press and hold down the Alt (Option) key and use the Lasso to create a selection around the driveway that looks like figure 12.10. Be precise in your selection work when working by the garage door, and avoid getting any of the street within the selection. Along the sides of the drive stay well within the dirt; you can work quickly here	Creates a selection around the driveway.
Press Ctrl (Cmd)+C (**E**dit, **C**opy), then choose **E**dit, Paste La**y**er; click on OK	Copies the contents of the driveway selection and pastes it on a new Layer (Layer 2) that uses the default settings and name. Layer 2 is now the active layer.
Press Ctrl (Cmd)+B (**I**mage, **A**djust, Brightness/Contrast) enter **-20** in the **B**rightness text entry box and enter **-30** in the **C**ontrast text entry box, or use the sliders; click on OK	The entries made in the Brightness/Contrast command dialog box make the selected area less bright and reduce the contrast.

Fresh pavement should be darker than the dusty street in front, but it shouldn't be black—that would be too harsh in this photo. Layer 2 should still be the active layer.

Choose Fi**l**ter, Blur, Motion Blur; make sure the **P**review check box is checked	The Motion Blur dialog box appears. Preview is enabled.

continues

continued

Leave the Angle set to 0° and enter **25** in the Distance text entry box (see fig. 12.11), then click on OK	Sets the Motion Blur filter to blur the pixels a moderate distance. OK confirms the action and returns you to the image.

The **D**istance value was determined by trial and error. Different values were chosen and the one that looked best in the image window preview was chosen. Motion Blur is a powerful effect; use your eye and judgment to determine the best value for the results you need.

Click on the eye icon on Layer 1	Restores the view of all the image elements.

The driveway now looks neatly and convincingly paved, the grass lines up nicely, and the garage door meets the pavement without overlap (see fig. 12.12). If you like what you see, you are ready to merge the layers. If not, delete Layer 2 by dragging it into the trash can and start over from the beginning of this exercise. The steps that follow merge the layers.

Click on the triangle next to the tab on the Layers palette and choose Merge Layers	The Merge Layers commands sequentially combines all the visible layers into the Background layer. The layer closest to the Background layer is merged first, and so on.
Press Ctrl (Cmd)+S (**F**ile, **S**ave), Ctrl (Cmd)+W (**F**ile, **C**lose)	Saves your work to this point and closes the file; you're done with it for now.

 Stop Neither the Merge Layers nor Flatten Image command ask you to confirm the action. The *only* way to recover from a slip of the mouse that leads to an unintentional merging or flattening of the image is to immediately press Ctrl+Z (**E**dit, **U**ndo). The lack of a confirmation for these potentially devastating actions is another reason to always leave the Layers palette out on the workspace where you can keep a vigilant eye on the palette's display of layer information. If you've spent a lot of time building and refining information on layers, you should save copies of the file to different names as you go along.

Files with layers should always be saved to the Photoshop 3 *.PSD format; no other format offered from the Save File as Format Type box support Photoshop Layers.

With intermediate versions of the file saved, you've given yourself the option to return to an intermediate stage in your work instead of having to start over from the beginning if a disaster strikes.

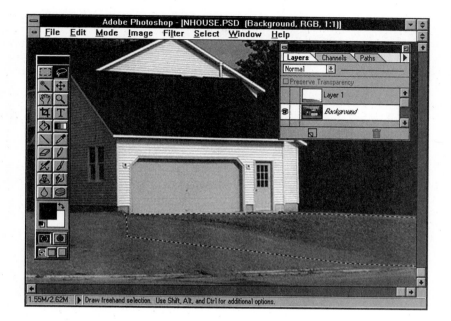

Figure 12.10

Make sure the driveway selection includes part of the dirt on each side of the drive.

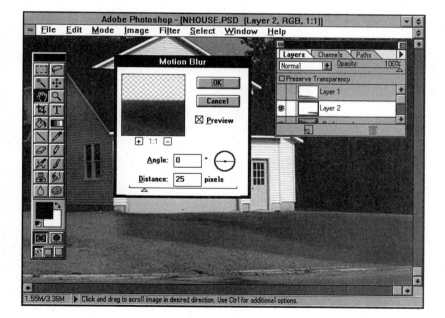

Figure 12.11

Motion Blur settings determine the direction and the intensity of the effect.

Figure 12.12

The grass and the pavement are in place.

Layers add to the size of the file that Photoshop must store in your system's RAM. The more RAM you have installed, the more layers you can have in a document before you feel the burden of their memory requirements. We're not simply harping on memory throughout this book—you need to install as much RAM in your system as your computer and your budget will allow. Even with more than 20 MB of RAM, working with large files can become cumbersome. For this reason, it is a good habit to merge layers when you are certain you are through with them instead of letting them accumulate to the end of the project. For this strategy to work successfully, you should plan the sequence of elements in your composition so that you work from the background up. If you have merged layers and later decide that you need to tuck something behind an element that you've merged to the Background Layer, your work has become harder than necessary.

Separating an Image from Its Background

With the lawn and the driveway done, the new house scene could use a tree to give the scene a sense of scale and permanence. After browsing through a collection of stock photography we'd taken, we found a young tree that was photographed with lighting that matched the lighting in NHOUSE.TIF. All elements in a composite image should have identical lighting, camera angle, and dimensions and resolution.

However, other factors also contributed to the selection of this tree image for use in the NHOUSE image. The tree was photographed at approximately the same point in the season as the house and its surroundings. This means much less color correcting is needed for this tree to match the other trees in the photo. This tree is also "in the clear," with only blue sky around the periphery of most of the tree. The openness of the scene makes creating a tight and accurate selection around the tree easy to accomplish.

Using the Color Range Command

Because the blue sky contrasts with the late summer greens of the tree, the Color Range command is a good one to use for the tree surgery that lies ahead. The Color Range command makes selections based on ranges of color value, which is similar to the method the Magic Wand employs. The Color Range command can also be set to make a selection based on the brightness values of the pixels, which is similar to the way Photoshop makes selections based on the grayscale information of Alpha Channels. You can specify which method of selection the Color Range command uses in the Replace Color dialog box. In the next series of exercises, you'll use the Color Range command in both selection modes.

Here's how to use the Color Range command to select image areas according to brightness values.

Isolating an Image Element

Open NTREE.TIF from the CHAP12 subdirectory (folder) on the *Inside Photoshop 3* Bonus CD; drag the window into the upper left-hand corner of the workspace	The file opens and is positioned so that it can be viewed when dialog boxes are open.
Double-click on the Quick Mask button on the toolbox, click on the Color Indicates: **S**elected Areas radio button if it is not already active, then click on OK	Areas that are overlaid with Quick Mask correspond to areas that are selected.
Click on the Standard Mode button on the toolbox	Returns you to normal editing mode.
Choose **S**elect, **C**olor Range from the menu	The Color Range dialog box appears.

continues

continued

Choose Highlights from the **S**elect drop-down box; choose Quick Mask from the **S**election Preview drop-down box and click on the **S**election radio button (see fig. 12.13)	These settings apply a Quick Mask to high brightness value pixels and display them in the preview box as white or gray pixels.
Click on OK	You are returned to the image with a complex selection marquee in place containing most of the sky.
Choose **S**elect, **I**nverse	Reverses the selection so that everything except the sky is selected.
Press Ctrl (Cmd)+C (**E**dit, **C**opy), then press Ctrl (Cmd)+N (**F**ile, **N**ew)	Copies the image to the Clipboard and opens the New dialog box.
Click on the Transparent radio button in the Contents field of the New dialog box. Leave the other settings as they are. Click on OK	Opens a new file, Untitled-1, with a transparent background.

The entries in the New dialog box that pertain to the size, resolution, and Mode of the new file are automatically set by Photoshop to match the information on the Clipboard. This is a quick way to open a properly sized New file without measuring an image or making entries in the dialog box.

Press Ctrl (Cmd)+V (**E**dit, **P**aste)	Pastes the tree, *sans* most of the sky, into a new image window with a transparent background (gray checkerboard-patterned areas).
Click on the NTREE.TIF window, then double-click on the Control Menu button in the upper left-hand corner of the image window; Macintosh users: click once on NTREE.TIF's Close button; then click on **N**o when prompted	Makes NTREE the active image windows and closes it. You are finished with this image. Closing NTREE conserves system resources. Untitled-1 becomes the active image.
Press Ctrl+D to deselect the copied image, as seen in figure 12.14	The image "lands" on the layer and becomes a layer object.

Press **L** (or click on the **L**asso tool) and make a very small circle at the bottom of the image; press Ctrl (Cmd)+C to copy the small selection to the Clipboard; press Ctrl (Cmd)+D to deselect the area you copied	Replaces the large image on the Clipboard with a small one, freeing up system resources.

Replacing the Windows Clipboard contents with a few copied pixels is a good step when working with large images and layers. It frees up system RAM so that you can work faster. Only replace the contents of the Windows Clipboard when you know you won't need the large image again; the Clipboard only stores one image at a time.

Choose **F**ile, Sa**v**e As; the Save File as Format **T**ype drop-down box only displays Photoshop 3 (*.PSD) as the image format type	Only Photoshop's file format (PSD) can preserve layer and transparency information.
In the File **N**ame text box, change the file name from Untitled to TREE.PSD; use the **D**irectories and Dri**v**es fields to choose a subdirectory (folder) on your hard disk for the image; click on OK	Saves the file to a subdirectory (folder) on your hard disk.

Figure 12.13

Use the Color Range command to select areas that have similar brightness values.

Figure 12.14

*The copied image
lies on top of a
transparent layer.*

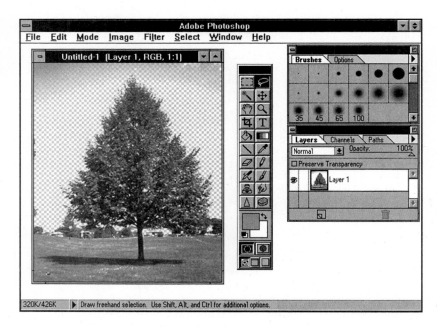

Using Color Range Fuzziness To Define a Selection

TREE.PSD still shows some blue sky, but a still greater problem is that the edges of
the tree are tinged with blue. In the next series of steps, you'll remove the blue from
the picture by using the Color Range command in its user-defined color selection
mode. When used in this mode, the Color Range command offers more user controls, the most useful of which are the Fuzziness controls.

Fuzziness is a new term in Photoshop, which for all practical purposes is synonymous
with Tolerance. *Tolerance* is the user-defined range of color values that a pixel must
fall within to become selected. When Fuzziness values are reduced, only pixels that
are closely related in color and tonal value to the sampled color(s) are chosen. As
Fuzziness is increased, more and more pixels similar in color value are selected.
When choosing Tolerance values for selection tools such as the Magic Wand, you
have to guess if the value you set will encompass all the color pixels you want to select.
With the Color Range command, the preview image in the dialog box and the active
image on the workspace change to reflect new values as you move the Fuzziness
slider. This is a much more interactive and accurate way to select a range of pixels.

The color value that Fuzziness uses as its starting point is defined by you. The Color
Range command's Eyedropper tool is used to select an initial color value; the
Eyedropper+ and Eyedropper– tools are used to add and subtract color ranges in the
image beyond your initial selection. The Eyedropper+ and Eyedropper– tools give you

a great deal of control over which image areas will be selected. For example, if you've selected a blue area by clicking the Eyedropper over blue in the target image, you'd then click on the Eyedropper+ tool to add a different range of blue to the Color Range Selection. If you change your mind about the second blue color range, click on the Eyedropper– tool, then click over the area in the image to remove this range as a selection. You can also add an entirely different hue to a selection by clicking the Eyedropper+ tool over a different colored image area. This is the approach you'd take if you wanted to select both blue and yellow values in an image.

Let's put the Color Range command through its paces in the next exercise. The steps demonstrate how to remove the rest of the sky and the blue fringe pixels around the edge of the tree and the open areas within the tree.

Using Fuzziness To Fine-Tune a Selection

Choose **S**elect, **C**olor Range from the menu

The Color Range dialog box appears.

Choose Sampled Colors from the **S**elect drop-down box, choose Quick Mask from the **S**election Preview drop-down box, and click on the **S**election radio button if it is not already selected

These settings apply a Quick Mask to the pixels within the range of color you select, and display them in the dialog preview box as white or gray pixels.

Click on the Eyedropper tool in the Color Range dialog box, then click over the blue in the upper-left corner of the TREE.PSD image in Photoshop's workspace

The Color Range command uses the blue picked up by the Eyedropper as the basis of the range it covers with Quick Mask.

Notice that the Quick Mask in the image covers most of the sky, but hasn't adequately masked the tree edges. The Eyedropper+ tool will be used to add a color range that includes the edges in the selection.

Press the Ctrl (Cmd) key and the spacebar and click over the top of the tree

Your cursor temporarily turns into the Zoom tool.

Click on the Eyedropper+ on the Color Range dialog box, then Click over the blue fringe around the top of the tree

Adds this range to the selection. Quick Mask now covers the fringe areas as well as a large portion of the foliage (see fig. 12.15).

continues

continued

Click and drag the Fuzziness slider to the left. Somewhere in the range of 35–50 you'll find that the fringe areas are selected, but the foliage is not. Exactly where in the Fuzziness range this occurs depends on which pixels you clicked over with the Eyedroppers.	You are reducing the range of pixels within the defined color range that is selected. The preview window in the dialog box should look similar to figure 12.16 when you've reached a good value for Fuzziness.
Click on OK	You are returned to the image window with a complex marquee selection in place.
Press Ctrl (Cmd)+–	Zooms you back out to a full view of the image.
Press the Delete Key	Deletes the blue, sky, and fringe pixels from the image and replaces them with transparent ones.
Press Ctrl (Cmd)+H	Hides the marquee lines so that you can see the results.

If too much was removed, immediately press Ctrl (Cmd)+Z (**E**dit, **U**ndo), then start over again with the Color Range command, but reduce the Fuzziness.

Press Ctrl (Cmd)+S (**F**ile, **S**ave)	Saves your work to hard disk.

The Fuzziness slider is a remarkable new feature in Photoshop 3, and Color Range can be used in selection situations where the Magic Wand doesn't provide the results you need. So why didn't you slide the Fuzziness up to 200 and select all the blue pixels in one step?

If you had set Fuzziness at 200, you would have selected far too many pixels. Foliage naturally has some blue in it, and foliage also contains reflections of the blue sky. If you deleted all the blue pixels, the tree would have wound up looking like blurry Swiss cheese instead of a nice nursery specimen.

To see the difference between sampling several times using a low Fuzziness setting, and sampling once and using a high Fuzziness value, the selections were copied to separate Alpha Channels. The black areas in the Alpha channel represent image areas that are totally selected, and the gray areas represent partially selected image areas. In figure 12.17, you can see that sampling several times at low Fuzziness creates a much more refined and limited selection. In figure 12.18, one color sample was taken and a Fuzziness setting of 200 was used. Much of the image detail shows up as

partially selected pixels. Deleting pixels from the selection defined in figure 12.18 would destroy the tree's visual detail.

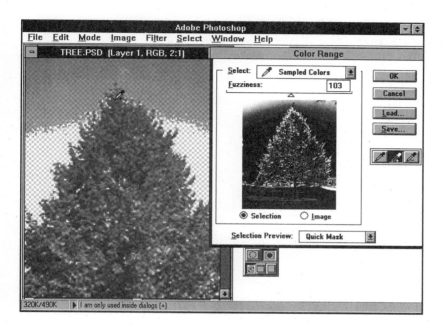

Figure 12.15

Sampling with the Eyedropper+ tool adds colors to the range of colors that are selected.

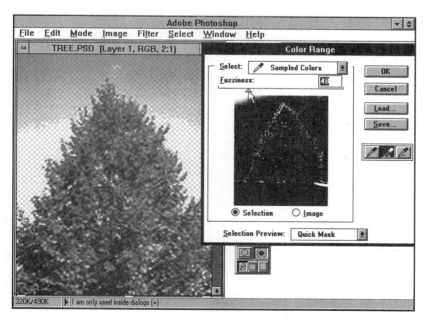

Figure 12.16

Decrease the Fuzziness amount to reduce the number of pixels that lie within the color range you've selected.

Figure 12.17

A selection made by sampling multiple color values and using a low Fuzziness value.

Figure 12.18

A selection made using a single color sample and the maximum Fuzziness value.

Keep these two examples in mind when you need to expand the range of colors you're selecting with Color Range. Add to the selection with the Eyedropper+ tool instead of using a brute force method by cranking up the Fuzziness. The accuracy of your selection eventually adds to an edited image's believability. As you work in the Color Range dialog box, keep an eye on the preview window—the bright areas correspond to a lot of selected pixels. Make sure you don't select more than you need.

Tip   Like most of Photoshop's commands, the Color Range command can be used on selected image areas as well as an entire image (see Chapter 7, "Restoring an Heirloom Photograph"). Select a portion of the image using any of Photoshop's selection tools, and then choose the Color Range command.

Refining the Selection

When you add this tree to the NHOUSE image, you don't want to transplant the grass, the shadow, or the buildings and trees still on the horizon of the TREE.PSD image. Getting rid of the rest of this unwanted image area calls for the use of two other selection tools—the Lasso tool and the Eraser. The Eraser tool has new capabilities in Photoshop 3. It can be configured to use characteristics of the Paint Brush tool, the Airbrush tool, or the Pencil Tool. You can also use it in the classic version 2.5 Block eraser mode.

In the next series of exercises you'll use the Lasso tool and the Eraser tool to remove unwanted image areas from the image. Before you begin, you need to organize the workspace.

Eliminating Workspace Clutter

With the Zoom tool, click once on the trunk of the tree, then click on the Minimize/Maximize button in the upper-right corner of the image window; Macintosh users should use the size box to make the image window fill the screen

Zooms to a 2:1 viewing resolution so that you can see what you're doing.

Press **L** (or click on the Lasso tool), then click on the Lasso Options tab on the Brushes Palette and make sure Feather is set to **1** pixel and Anti-aliased is checked

Sets the characteristics for the Lasso tool.

Roll up the palettes by clicking on the Minimize/Maximize button (Zoom button for Macintosh users) on each palette

Conserves screen space.

continues

continued

Drag the toolbox to the top center of the screen so it covers part of the tree trunk, or press Tab to hide all the palettes and the toolbox	You need to have a clear view of the entire bottom of the image. The toolbox will be in your way no matter where you put it. Macintosh users can press Option+Tab to hide only the toolbox.

The toolbox and the palettes can be hidden from view or restored by pressing the Tab key. Hidden does *not* mean disabled; when the toolbox is hidden, you can still use all the tools and perform keyboard actions like Copy and Delete. Hiding tools and marquee selections (Ctrl (Cmd)+H) is different from hiding views of layers and channels: when a layer is hidden by clicking on its Eye icon, the layer is inert and cannot be affected.

When the toolbox is not displayed, you can use the currently selected tool, and even switch to another tool by pressing the keyboard shortcut for the tool. However, if the Tool Options palette isn't open, you're "flying blind." Without the Options palette on-screen, you can't see what the tool settings are, nor can you change them.

Fortunately, all you need to do is press the Tab key to restore the toolbox and the palettes to view. Macintosh users can choose to hide the tools and the toolbox by pressing Tab or to hide only the toolbox by pressing Option+Tab. Windows users, don't do this: Alt+Tab will "cool switch" you into Program Manager or any other active application!

In the next exercise you'll use the Lasso tool to select most of the unwanted stuff at the bottom of the image. Don't create a precise border around the tree and tree trunk; instead, give these areas some "breathing space" in your Lasso selection. When you reach the edge of the image, don't try to trace a perfect vertical line. Go outside the window, circle around the bottom of the image window, then back to your starting point. This is a quick, easy way to get rid of most of the unwanted image area without having to be precise. The final clean up work will follow after you're unencumbered by distracting extra image areas.

Making a Loose Lasso Selection

Starting in the upper left-hand corner of the image...

Drag down and around the bottom of the tree, around the tree trunk, across to the right side image border,	Selects most of the extraneous material and deletes it.

go outside the image, across the bottom and back up to your starting point; when the marquee becomes active (see fig. 12.19), press the Delete key

Press Ctrl (Cmd)+D, or click on the image with the Lasso tool	Deselects the selection.
Press Tab to restore on-screen any hidden palettes or the toolbox	Tab displays all palettes and turns on and off the toolbox.

Figure 12.19

Make a rough selection with the Lasso tool to delete a large portion of unwanted image area.

The next exercise uses the Lasso tool to make a precise selection around the tree and its trunk. Press and continue to hold down the Alt (Option) key throughout this step. By pressing the Alt (Option) key and clicking with the Lasso tool, a straight line is created between the points where you click. If you release the Alt (Option) key, the selection marquee will close. See figure 12.20 to see how the completed selection should look. ,

Figure 12.20

Hold the Alt (Option) key when using the Lasso to define a precise, straight-line selection.

Trimming with the Lasso Tool

Press and hold down the Alt (Option) key and click on the top right-hand side of the tree trunk with the Lasso tool	Sets the anchor for the marquee selection.
Click at the base of the tree	A line formed by the two points falls on the outline of the tree trunk.
Click on the bottom left edge of the tree trunk	Extends the Lasso selection to include more background area.
Click at the top left-hand side of the trunk; click to the left, then click down and around to your starting point	Creates a tight selection that includes the unwanted image areas that are adjacent to the tree trunk.
Press the Delete key, then press Ctrl (Cmd)+D	Removes the area within the selection border.

Press **Z** (or click on the **Z**oom tool on the toolbox), then click twice over the tree trunk	Takes you in to an 8:1 viewing resolution of the bottom edge of the tree so that you can see your work.

The image before you is well on its way to being liberated from its background. All it needs now is some touch up work with the Eraser tool. When the Eraser tool is used in paintbrush, pencil, or airbrush mode, the size and the characteristics (shape, amount of hardness) of the Eraser tool are defined by the tip you pick in the Brushes palette.

If you look carefully at the Eraser tool icon (you will have to position it over a dark area in the image) you'll see a single white pixel on the lower left corner of the Eraser. This is the "hot spot," or the point on the cursor where the tool becomes active. The white pixel marks the center of the brush tip. If you use a large brush tip, keep in mind that it radiates out from the white pixel on the corner of the eraser. Judge your distances accordingly or you may erase unintended areas.

Pick a brush tip and start "painting" with an eraser in the following exercise.

Using the Eraser's Paintbursh Mode

Click on the Eraser tool, then press Enter (Macintosh users press Return)	Chooses the Eraser tool and displays the Eraser Tool Options palette.
From the Eraser Tool Options palette, choose Paintbrush mode from the drop-down list, keep Opacity at **100%**	When set to Paintbrush mode, the Eraser handles like a paintbrush, but removes pixels instead of adding them.
Click on the Brushes Tab on the Brushes Palette, then choose the third brush tip from the left in the top row	Sets the Eraser to use a small hard brush tip with a 5-pixel diameter.
Click and slowly drag the Eraser from the transparent areas below the area you want to remove up into the area to be removed	Gently erases the unwanted image elements and exposes the tree's natural foliage line (see fig. 12.21).

Try not to knock out the tree's foliage and avoid creating a horizontal line of tree foliage across the bottom of the tree. Be prepared to press Ctrl (Cmd)+Z (**E**dit, **U**ndo), if you erase too much.

continues

continued

Continue using the Eraser tool around the perimeter of the tree; use the Hand tool (release the mouse button and press the spacebar to toggle to the Hand tool) to move the image in the window when necessary	You are done when the tree stands alone on a transparent background.
Double-click on the Hand tool on the toolbox, then check for any remaining areas	Zooms you out to a full view to check your work.
Press Ctrl (Cmd)+S (**F**ile, **S**ave).	Saves the image to your hard disk.

Figure 12.21

*Carefully remove
unwanted
areas with the
Eraser tool in
Paintbrush mode.*

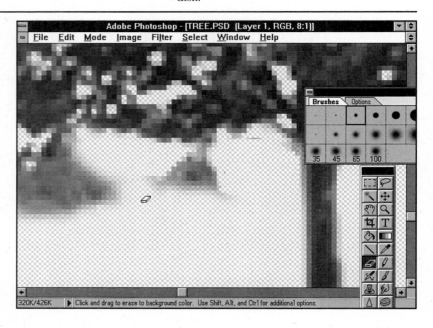

You've done some fancy selecting work in this series of exercises to separate the tree from its natural setting. Isolating a tree's intricate outline as part of a selection would be extremely expensive and time consuming were you to have used traditional methods and physical media. When you invest time and skill to remove a subject from its background without any tell-tale signs, as you did in this assignment, you've created a piece of photographic clip art.

Thoughts on Creating Your Own Bitmap ClipArt Collection

The TREE.PSD image is destined for the NHOUSE image, but you may want to keep a copy of the tree to use in your own imaging assignments. You never know when you may need a good tree, and with Photoshop's set of filters and other tools, you can modify this tree so that no one would ever know you'd used it before.

One of the great advantages of digital imaging is the ability to re-use elements you've saved, which can save you enormous amounts of time on a rush assignment. Whenever you work on an assignment, always take a look at the elements you've created and see if they also deserve a place in your personal clipart/clipobject collection.

Digital clip art isn't a new concept; the images supplied by CMCD on the *Adobe Photoshop 3 Deluxe CD-ROM* are useful commercial examples of clip objects. However, what makes TREE.PSD and other images you create special is that they are yours and yours alone. You'll never see them crop up in a competitor's work.

Transferring an Image

It's time to plant TREE.PSD in the NHOUSE.PSD image. Both these images are of the same resolution (150 dpi), and if you view them side-by-side you'll see that the tree image will be too large for placement on the lawn. Photoshop's Scale feature can be used to take care of this problem. In the next exercise, you'll copy the tree to a Layer in the NHOUSE image and then use the Scale command to resize the tree so that it's in proportion to the house.

Selecting an Image on a Transparent Background

If you were to open the Info palette and run the Eyedropper over some of the transparent background areas in TREE.PSD, you may be surprised to find that some of the pixels have a 2% or 3% Opacity value. This is because they were partially selected when you used the Color Range commands. You don't want to move these areas into the NHOUSE image along with the tree, even though it is unlikely they would show because of the their low amount of Opacity. Fortunately, there is an easy way to avoid selecting them and to select only the tree.

By following these steps, you'll learn a valuable tip that will make selecting objects on a layer a snap.

Selecting the Image from the "Transparent" Background

Press **L** or click on the **Lasso** tool on the toolbox; click and drag a loose selection around the tree as seen in figure 12.22

Creates a selection marquee that loosely follows the outline of the tree.

Press the up arrow key on the keyboard

Moves the selection and its contents one pixel. The selection turns into a floating selection with a tight marquee selection border around the tree (see fig. 12.23).

This is a good trick to use when you need to select an element quickly that is on a transparent background. Any movement of the selection will produce the same results, but pressing the up arrow key once is a good habit to adopt because the image only moves by one pixel. The image element can then be easily returned to its original position by pressing the down arrow key once.

Choose **S**elect, **I**nverse, then press the Delete key

Chooses everything except the tree, then deletes extraneous pixels to reveal the total transparency Layer.

Choose **S**elect, **I**nverse, then press Ctrl (Cmd)+S (**F**ile, **S**ave)

Reverses the selection to include only the tree. Saves the file to disk.

Don't deselect the tree yet!

You'll need the active marquee selection defined around the tree for the next exercise.

Reversing the selection, deleting, and saving so that only the tree is contained within the image file gives you a flawless piece of object art without any stray, almost invisible pixels lurking in the background. Whenever you need to use this tree in another image, as you will in the next exercise, all you'll have to do is select the entire tree image (Ctrl (Cmd)+A) and drag the selection into the other image's window. Let's see how to copy the tree to the house image by dragging it in the next exercise.

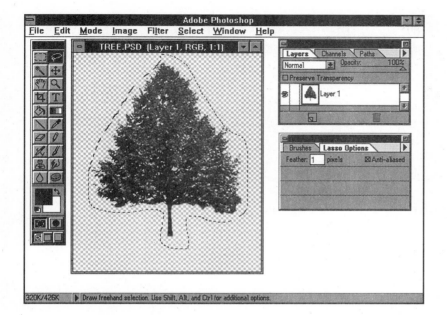

Figure 12.22

Make a loose selection around an object on a layer prior to copying the object.

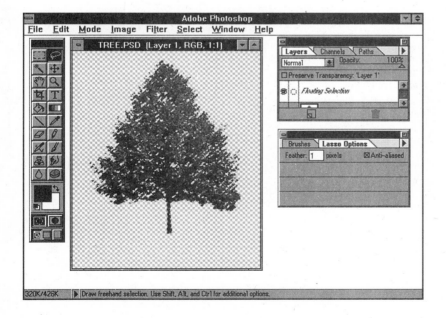

Figure 12.23

Moving a selection on a transparent background brings the selection border in tight around the image element.

Dragging an Image into Another Image Window

Open NHOUSE.PSD from your hard disk	This is the file you saved earlier and is the target image for the tree.
Choose **W**indow, **T**ile. Click in the TREE.PSD title bar; Macintosh users should drag the images by their title bars so they are side-by-side	Arranges the two images so you can see both. Clicking on the title bar makes TREE.PSD the active image window.
Click and drag the tree selection into the NHOUSE.PSD window and let go, then click on the New Layer icon on the bottom of the Layers palette, then choose OK	NHOUSE becomes the active window. The floating selection of the tree is placed on a new Layer in NHOUSE that has default Layer settings.

Floating selections become part of a New Layer you define, and selections are automatically deselected (and the marquee disappears) after the New Layer is created.

Click on the TREE.PSD title bar and press Ctrl (Cmd)+W (**F**ile, **C**lose)	Makes Tree.PSD the active window and then closes the file. You are finished with it.
Press **V** on the keyboard or click on the Mover tool on the toolbox	Chooses the layer Move tool.
With Layer 1 the active layer, click on the image window and drag the tree into position as shown in figure 12.24	Repositions the tree on Layer 1.
Choose **S**elect, **M**atting, **D**efringe, then Enter **1** in the Width text entry box and click on OK	Sets Defringe to replace edge pixels that have traces of the old background color in them with colors found in the tree image.

No matter how carefully you separate an object from its background you are bound to have some semi-opaque pixels that formed the color transition between the object and its surrounding background along the edge of your object. These pixels form a fringe around the element. When the object is placed against a new background that has different colors than the old background the fringe pixels show and look bad. The Defringe command recolors the fringe pixels not with new background color but with colors that match the nearby pixels in the object that *don't* contain any of the old background color.

The tree is too large for the purposes of this assignment; it covers up too much of the house. Next you'll use the Scale command to shrink the tree down to a believable size.

Choose **I**mage, **E**ffects, **S**cale	A bounding box appears around the tree (see fig. 12.25).
Hold the Shift key and click and drag the upper left-hand corner boundary box down and to the right; stop when the top of the boundary box is about even with the crosspiece on the second story window	Shift constrains Scaling to proportional resizing of the height and width of the selection. The tree becomes smaller and more of the house detail is visible.

The tree is the right height now but is too wide. Scaling disproportionately can make the tree narrower.

Without holding the Shift key, click and drag the top right-hand boundary handle to the left; stop when the boundary box is the same width as the depth of the garage as seen in figure 12.26	Makes the tree narrower, changing its height.
When the tree is the proper size, click the cursor within the boundary box	The cursor turns into a gavel and "nails" the effect (change in size) into place on Layer 1.
Press Ctrl (Cmd)+S (**F**ile, **S**ave)	Saves your work up to this point to disk.

Figure 12.24

Drag the tree into position on the layer with the Mover tool.

Figure 12.25

The Scale effects boundary box appears only around the element on a layer, not around the entire layer.

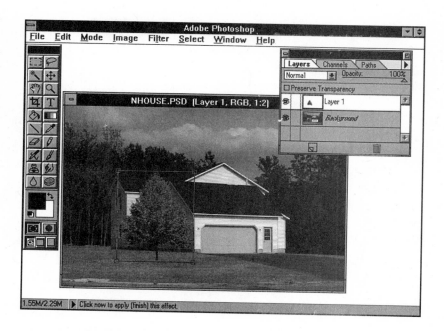

Figure 12.26

When the Scale boundary box looks like this it's time to "nail" down the tree.

Disproportionate, or *"free scaling,"* can usually be performed without making an image element look artificial when you have a selection that contains little distinctive visual detail. The tree in the last exercise has a trunk, and a lot of leaves that the viewer perceives as a mass of texture. When you make a tree look squat or lean by free scaling only one dimension, the tree still retains its tree-like properties.

Don't try this trick on people, cars, or other well-defined geometric image elements, unless you're trying to create a fun-house mirror version of an image. We have a pre-conceived image of many things that won't support distorting without changing the viewer's perception of them. Fortunately, trees don't have definitive geometry, and they can be reshaped quite a lot without calling attention to the editing you've performed.

Adding Realism with Shadows

It is not enough to plant a tree; you also need a corresponding shadow for the tree to make it visually integrate with the NHOUSE scene. No self-respecting tree or any other object goes about in the daylight without its shadow companion. If your work is to be convincing, don't forget the shadows.

Using Photoshop's Image Commands

Shadows can be created in a number of different ways. You've seen in other chapters how to use Gaussian Blur in combination with Alpha channel information to create dramatic drop shadows, and how to paint in shadows using different painting modes. On occasion, you'll have all the elements right on hand in an assignment for instant shadow creation. The next few exercises show you how to create a realistic effect with minimum effort.

You'll make a copy of the tree, put it on its own layer and then use Photoshop's Image commands—Rotate, Scale, and Skew—to create a shadow shape for the tree. The Layers palette's Multiply mode will be used to integrate the shape of the shadow into the grass. The purpose of Multiply mode in this exercise is analogous to painting a single stroke in Multiply mode with a custom brush that is the shape and size of the elements on the layer.

To get started in the next exercise set up the source for the shadowmaking and position it on its own layer.

Creating Shadow Source Material

Press **L** (or click on the **Lasso** tool on the toolbox); click and drag loosely around the tree to select the	Chooses the Lasso tool; creates a selection around the tree; copies the selection to

continues

continued

tree; press Ctrl(Cmd)+C (**E**dit, **C**opy), press Ctrl(Cmd)+D (**S**elect, **N**one)	the Clipboard; deselects the selection.
Click on the New Layer icon on the bottom of the Layers palette and choose OK	Creates a new Layer that uses default settings.
Press Ctrl (Cmd)+V (**E**dit, **P**aste); Do *not* deselect the floating selection	The copy of the tree appears above the New Layer as a floating selection.
Choose **I**mage, **R**otate, then choose 9**0**° CCW	Rotates the image 90° counter-clockwise.
Press **V** (or click on the Move tool on the toolbox); click and drag the rotated tree selection down so that the bottoms of the tree trunks meet at a right angle (see fig. 12.27)	Moves the copy of the tree into place.

Do not click to deselect the floating selection yet!

Figure 12.27

Rotate the copy of the tree 90° counter-clockwise.

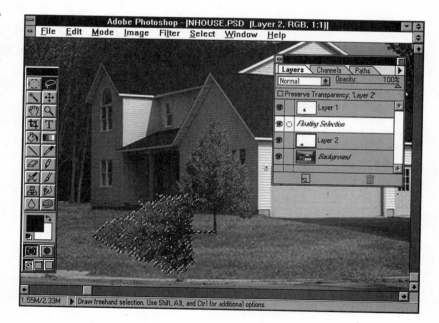

Stop The Rotate and Flip commands can produce unexpected results. If you choose Image, **F**lip or any of the Image, **R**otate commands (except Image, **R**otate, **F**ree) without an active selection area defined, Photoshop will flip or rotate the entire image—the Background and all the layers, not just the active layer.

If you want to flip or rotate an element on a layer or the contents of a layer while leaving the Background and other layers in their present orientation, you must create a selection that includes what you want to flip or rotate. You can use any selection tool, or you can press Ctrl (Cmd)+A (**S**elect, **A**ll) to make the selection. The **S**elect, **A**ll command will not select the entire image (Background and layers); it only selects what is on the current, active layer.

Rotating or flipping an entire image can be time consuming and very annoying when you only meant to change an element on a layer. To cancel a Photoshop action while its processing the calculations, press Ctrl and the period (.) key.

In the next exercise, you'll complete the shadow by using Image commands to shape the copy of the tree, then using the Layers Multiply mode to "paint" the image into the grass.

Scaling and Skewing a Floating Selection

With the copy of the tree still as a floating selection...

Choose **I**mage, **E**ffects, **S**cale; click and drag one of the top boundary box handles straight down; then click and drag straight up on one of the bottom boundary box handles; click inside the boundary box when you selection looks like figure 12.28	Dragging a corner without holding the Shift key disproportionately scales a selection, in this case making the tree very thin. Clicking within the box confirms the scaling action.

The tree should be extremely narrow, but the same length as before. Don't worry if the Scale command moves the tree away from its intended position within the image; it will be repositioned later.

Choose **I**mage, **E**ffects , S**k**ew; click and drag the upper-right boundary box handle to the right about half a screen inch until the boundary box looks like figure 12.29; then click the selection to become wider.	Skews the selection so that it looks like it is lying on the grass and it is slightly distorted. Notice this causes the cursor within the boundary box to become a gavel. Clicking inside the boundary box "nails" the effect into place.

continues

continued

Press Ctrl (Cmd) +D	Deselects the floating selection and the altered copy of the tree becomes a part of Layer 2.
Click and drag the Layer 2 title on the Layers palette on top of the Layer 1 title, then release the mouse button	Reorders the layers so that the shadow will fall behind the tree. Layer 2 remains the active layer.
Choose Multiply from the Layers palette drop-down list, then drag the Opacity slider to the left until it reads about **50%**	Multiply mode darkens the grass pixels under the tree selection and 50% Opacity allows the grass to show through.
With the Move tool, drag the tree into position if necessary; let part of the tree foliage shadow overlap the trunk and don't worry if the shadow trunk runs past the tree trunk	Moves the shadow into position as shown in figure 12.30.
Press **Z** (for **Z**oom tool) and click twice over the tree trunk	Produces a good view of the work area.
Double-click on the Eraser tool; choose Block from the drop-down list on the Options palette; click and drag over the part of the trunk shadow that extends to the right of the actual trunk	Displays the Eraser tool Options and sets the tool to Block mode.

Don't worry about accidentally erasing the tree— it's on a different layer!

Double-click the Hand tool on the toolbox and check your work; press Ctrl (Cmd)+Z if you erased too much and then zoom back in and try again	Zooms you back to a 1:1 viewing resolution where you can check your work.
Press Ctrl (Cmd)+S (**F**ile, **S**ave)	Saves your work up to this point.

New Riders Publishing
INSIDE SERIES

Figure 12.28

Disproportionately scale the copy of the tree to make it very thin.

Figure 12.29

Skewing the copy of the tree makes it look like it is lying in the grass.

Figure 12.30

The transplanted tree with a proper shadow.

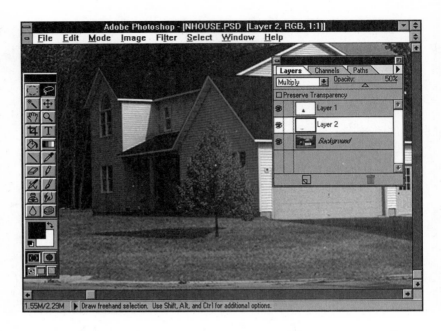

This image is really beginning to shape up, but it still needs some work to make the house a home. In the next section, you'll move from landscaping to gardening, as you learn how to graft some bushes and flowers to trim the new house.

Image Resolution and Image Detail

Now that the larger elements in the image are in place, it's time for some detail work around the house to enhance the realism of the scene. In the next series of exercises, you will add bushes and flowers to the front of the house. Some of the ground-breaking work has already been done for you: BUSH1S.PSD and BUSH2S.PSD are ready for you to use on the *Inside Photoshop 3* Bonus CD. Both images were taken from the photo PLANTING.TIF, which is also on the Bonus CD. Each bush was marquee selected and copied from PLANTING.TIF and then copied into a new image with a transparent background. The same techniques and tools as you used earlier to separate the tree from its background were used to separate the bushes from their backgrounds.

PLANTING.TIF and NHOUSE share the same 150 dpi resolution, but the bushes and flowers in PLANTING.TIF were photographed from a much closer distance, and are disproportionately large when compared to the house image. The bushes in the BUSH1S and BUSH2S files were scaled down to their present dimensions from the PLANTING image using the **I**mage, **I**mage Size command. To accomplish this massive size reduction (often called *sampling down* an image), Photoshop had to discard a lot of pixels, which reduced the image quality of the bushes. In an assign-

ment where the foliage was the main compositional element, sampling down would not be acceptable. The reason is the qualities of image detail and focus are portrayed as pixels in bitmap images, and you lose original image quality when you respecify image dimensions and resolution.

However, the bushes in this assignment are deep background elements where razor sharp image detail and focus is not wanted or required. As a rule, try to photograph image elements you want to re-use later at a field size that's similar to the target image, and make the resolution of both target and selections the same.

In the next exercise, you'll use the Perspective command to wrap the bush images around the side of the new house. Perspective is similar to the skew and scale Distort commands in that there is a bounding box around the selection whose corner handles are manipulated to re-shape a selection area. As with the tree you distorted earlier, the subject for the exercise, the bushes, are "texture" type images, whose visual detail is not compromised very much when pixels are interpolated to create the Perspective effect. Viewers tend to see trees, bushes, flowers, and other collections of random shapes as texture, regardless of a little pixel-bending.

Here's how to add some bushes to the house that will show your prospective client a "lived-in" look.

Using Perspective

Open BUSH2S.PSD from the Bonus CD; arrange your windows so that you can see BUSH2S and NHOUSE.PSD; click the Zoom tool twice over the windows to the left of the entrance in NHOUSE	BUSH2S is the image you'll bring into NHOUSE. NHOUSE should be at a 3:1 viewing resolution.
Click on the BUSH2S title bar and then press Ctrl (Cmd)+A (**S**elect, **A**ll)	BUSH2S becomes active and the entire image is selected.
With any selection tool active, click and drag the BUSH2S selection into the NHOUSE image window; click on the New Layer Icon and choose OK	The bush is placed on a New Layer that uses default settings.
Press **V** or click on the Move tool on the toolbox; drag the bush down and into position under the windows, as seen in figure 12.31	Positions the bush using the Move tool.
Click on the BUSH2S title bar, then press Ctrl (Cmd)+W	Makes BUSH2S the active image and closes it without saving. You are finished with it.

continues

continued

Choose **I**mage, **E**ffects, **P**erspective	A boundary box appears around the bush.
Click and drag the top left handle down and then to the right until it lines up with the end of the house and the tops of the bushes overlap the window sill; click and drag the top right boundary box handle down slightly and then to the left until the right side of the bush extends slightly into the entrance way (see fig 12.32)	Gives the bush a visual perspective that follows the lines of the house.
Click inside the boundary box	Applies the perspective effect.
Choose **I**mage, **E**ffects, **S**kew	A boundary box appears around the bush.
Click and drag the top left handle about one third of a screen inch to the left.(see fig. 12.33), then click inside the boundary box	Adds further dimensionally to the bush. Clicking inside the box applies the effect.
Press Ctrl (Cmd)+S (**F**ile, **S**ave)	Saves your work up to this point.

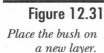

Figure 12.31

Place the bush on a new layer.

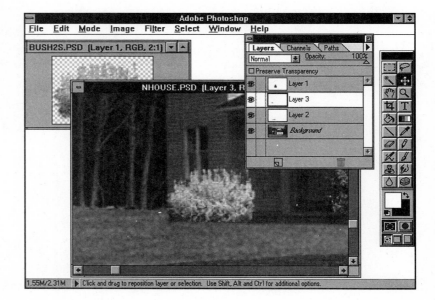

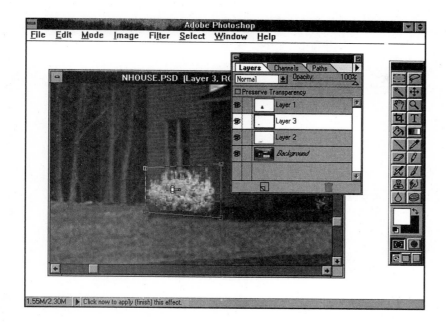

Figure 12.32

Use the Perspective command to make disparate elements share a point of view.

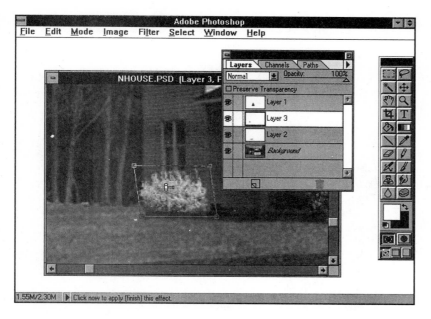

Figure 12.33

Skew can add a sense of liveliness and heighten the dimensional feeling of an element.

The new shape of the bush looks pretty realistic in the setting, but the colors of the bush are too bright. The bush also has a sharper focus than the house. Both of these flaws are easily corrected.

Here's how to make the bushes less prominent so that the focus of the image is on the house.

Using Focus Tools

With Layer 3 (the layer containing the bush) the active layer...

Use the Move tool to click and drag the bush back down to ground level	Repositions the bush.
Press Ctrl (Cmd)+B (**A**djust, **B**rightness/Contrasts)	The Brightness/Contrast dialog box appears. Adjustments made here will only affect the active layer.
Drag the Brightness slider to the left until the box reads about **-44;** drag the Contrast slider to the left until the box reads about **-22**; alternatively you can enter the numbers directly into the input boxes; choose OK	Both the Brightness and the Contrast of the bush have been reduced to match the surrounding values in the image.

The values were determined by what looked best to the author. Always use your own eye to evaluate an image and use the Brightness/Contrast values that look best to you.

Press Ctrl (Cmd)+– until you are at a 2:1 viewing resolution	You need to see the entire image for the next step.
Double-click on the Blur/Sharpen tool on the toolbox; from the Focus Tools Options palette, pick Blur from the Tool: drop-down box if it is not already selected; choose Normal from the mode drop-down box; drag the Pressure slider to 15%; click on the Brushes tab and choose the soft brush tip that has 100 on it	The Focus Tool Options palette appears. The settings choose the Blur tool and set it to blur slightly in Normal mode. The large brush tip will make only one quick pass over the bush necessary.
Click and drag with the Blur tool from right to left across the center of the bush	Slightly reduces the focus of the bush to match the surrounding image focus.

Press Ctrl (Cmd)+– until you are
at a 1:1 viewing resolution or use
the Zoom tool

You need to see more of the
image.

If you think the bush looks good, continue with the next step. If it's too sharp or too blurry, press Ctrl (Cmd)+Z (**E**dit, **U**ndo), and try a different Pressure setting for the Blur tool.

With more of the image elements in place, it becomes evident that the tree shadow is too sharp. With the Blur tool all set up, a quick repair job can defocus the tree shadow.

Click on Layer 2, which holds the
tree shadow

Makes Layer 2 active.

Click on the Focus Tools Options
palette tab and drag the Pressure
slider to about **50%**, then click and
drag from right to left over the
length of the shadow in one quick
stroke (see fig. 12.34)

The 50% setting for Blur was
chosen after trial and error.

Press Ctrl (Cmd)+S (**F**ile, **S**ave)

Saves your work up to this
point.

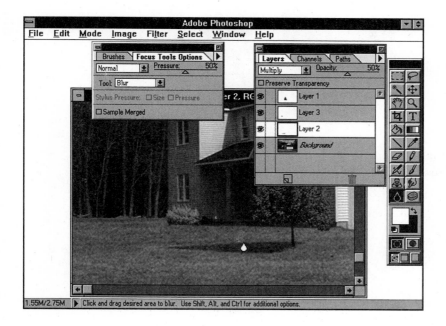

Figure 12.34

*Soften the focus of
the tree with a
single stroke of the
Blur tool.*

You've planted half the bushes very nicely. Now it's time to add bushes and flowers to the rest of the house. A good location for additional greenery in the image, and a logical one for landscaping is along the house foundation to the right of the entry way. As far as image order should go, the bushes and flowers are behind the tree. This will be easy to accomplish because the tree is still on its own layer, and layers can be reordered by click+dragging the layer title to a different position in the "stack" of layers displayed on the Layers palette.

Planting these bushes and flowers will require basically the same steps as you used previously on the first bush. You won't need to use the Skew command in the next exercise though because this side of the house is visually closer to the front of the image and appears flatter. The Perspective command provides the necessary effect for adding a touch of dimension to a copy of the next selection.

The BUSH1S.PSD image that you'll use is not wide enough to cover the area from the entrance way to the edge of the house, so you'll use the image twice. Landscaping often uses symmetrical planting arrangements; you'll accomplish the same gardening work digitally by pasting the image in twice. Making copies of the bushes and flowers for the target image also works well because these elements are not focal points in the image; rather, they are details that give the overall image a finished look. The viewer's eye will not scrutinize these elements, but will register their presence or absence in the image on a subconscious level.

Begin the final planting stage in the image by adding some flowers to the front of the house in the next exercise.

Working with Added Material

Click on the Eye icon on Layer 1; press Z or click on the Zoom tool on the tool box; click and drag diagonally with the Zoom tool under the pair of windows to the right of the entrance way	Turns off your view of the tree. Zooms you into a 3:1 viewing resolution of the area you work on next.
Open BUSH1S.PSD from the CHAP12 subdirectory (folder) on the *Inside Photoshop 3* Bonus CD	This is the image you'll move into NHOUSE next. It is the currently active image.
Press Ctrl (Cmd)+A (**S**elect, **A**ll), then Ctrl (Cmd)+C (**E**dit, **C**opy), then Ctrl (Cmd)+W (**F**ile, **C**lose)	Selects the entire BUSH1S image, copies it to the Clipboard and then closes the image. NHOUSE becomes the active image.
Click on the New Layer icon and then choose OK	Creates Layer 4 and places it above Layer 2 which was the

	last active layer. Layer 4 uses default settings.
Press Ctrl (Cmd)+V (**E**dit, **P**aste)	The copied bush image becomes a floating selection above Layer 4 in NHOUSE.PSD.
Press **L** or click on the **Lasso** tool on the toolbox; click and drag the bush down to ground level and position it on the left side of the window area	Chooses a selection tool to use to move the floating selection.
Press Ctrl+V (**E**dit, **P**aste); with the Lasso tool drag the second copy to the right of the first position it slightly lower; overlap it so that it does not extend beyond the corner of the house	Another copy of the bush becomes a floating selection above Layer 4 in NHOUSE.PSD and is moved into place.
Press Ctrl (Cmd)+D (**S**elect, **N**one), then choose **I**mage, **E**ffects, **P**erspective	Deselects the second paste. A single boundary box for the Skew effect appears around both pasted in copies of the bush.
Click and drag the upper-left boundary box handle down about one or two boards on the house, then drag the handle to the right or left so that several of the flowers overlap the front step; drag the upper-right hand corner handle so the right side of the boundary box aligns with the corner of the house	Defines the shape of the Perspective boundary box as seen in figure 12.35.
Click inside the boundary box	Applies the Perspective effect.
Press Ctrl (Cmd)+B (**I**mage, **A**djust, **B**rightness/Contrast); enter **-6** in the Brightness text entry box and enter **-25** in the Contrast text entry box; press OK	Reduces the Brightness and the Contrast of the Layer 4 bushes to blend them into the scene.
Double-click on the Hand tool. Then click on the Layer 1 eye icon	Zooms you out to a full screen view of the image. Turns on the view of the tree.

Oops, the tree covers up the new flowers (see fig. 12.36)!

continues

continued

Click on the Layer 1 title, then click in the empty box next to the Layer 2 eye icon	Layer 1 becomes the active layer. The Link icon appears next to the eye icons for both Layer 1 and 2.
Press **V** or click on the Move tool on the toolbox and drag the tree and its shadow up and over so that the flowers show and not too much of the entrance way is covered, as seen in figure 12.37	The Move tool moves the tree and the shadow as one when Layers are linked.
Press Ctrl (Cmd)+S (**F**ile, **S**ave)	Saves your work up to this point.

It looks nice, doesn't it?

Figure 12.35

Shape the selection with the Perspective command.

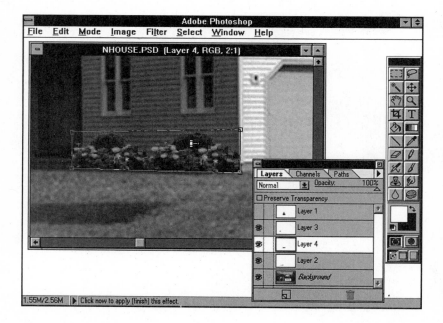

Tip   When two or more layers are linked, they can be moved together and each layer's elements retain their relative spatial relationship to the elements in the other linked layers. Clicking on the Link icon will remove the icon and break the link between the layers.

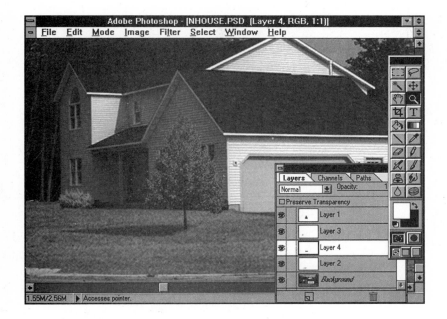

Figure 12.36

The tree covers up the new flowers and bushes!

Figure 12.37

Link layers to move the tree and the tree shadow as one piece.

At this point, take a break from all the exercises and steps and examine your handi-work. Perhaps you need a little inspiration for further embellishing the piece. The image is beginning to look postcard perfect, but perfection lies in the details, and there are a few you need to take care of before NHOUSE becomes a dream house.

The edge where the new bushes meet the grass needs a shadow painted in with a few strokes of the Paint Brush in Multiply mode. The house itself had a shadow that was covered up by the lawn. This shadow also will need to be replaced by using a painting tool in Multiply mode. The tree looks a little too bright; a trip to the Brightness/Contrast controls will take care of that very nicely. One detail you haven't worked on is in an area the *carpenters* didn't finish. A few clapboards are missing in the entrance way next to the first bush you placed. The Rubber Stamp tool will fix that.

All of these details might sound like they amount to a lot of work, but you've learned techniques in this chapter that use Photoshop's tools in a multiplicity of retouching situations. Fortunately, the work gets faster through practice. When you identify a problem area in an image, choose the appropriate tool and the best selection of stock images, and you'll sail through the "hard part" of an assignment.

In simpler terms, if you do the yard work right now, we have a shiny red sports car for you right after this exercise.

Adding Shadows and Other Details

Click on the Layer 1 title on the Layers palette, then click on the Link icon next to the Layer 1 eye icon	Makes Layer 1 (Tree layer) the active layer. Breaks the link between Layer 1 and Layer 2.
Press Ctrl (Cmd)+B (**I**mage, **A**djust, **B**rightness/Contrast); enter **-20** in the Brightness text entry box and enter **-20** in the Contrast text entry box; press OK	Reduces the Brightness and the Contrast of the Layer 1 tree to blend it into the scene.
Click on the Layer 4 title on the Layers palette, then double-click on the Paint Brush tool on the toolbox; press **D** (for **d**efault colors icon)	Makes Layer 4 the active . layer and the Paint Brush tool the active tool. Displays the Paintbrush Options. Ensures that black is the foreground color.
Choose Multiply mode from the Paintbrush Options palette drop-down list; slide the Opacity down to about	Chooses a small soft brush that applies paint in Multiply mode at a low Opacity setting.

36%; click on the Brushes tab and choose the first brush on the left second row of tips

Painting in Multiply mode will darken the area without destroying the image detail. Multiply mode always darkens image areas unless the foreground color you paint with is white.

Zoom in on the area under the flowers in Layer 4; click and drag the Paint Brush along the bottom edge of the bushes; extend the stroke just past the end of the bushes on the left; repeat the stroke	Paints in a shadow (see fig. 12.38).
Double click on the Hand tool	Zooms out to a full view of the image.

If you like what you see move on. If not, press Ctrl (Cmd)+Z (**E**dit, **U**ndo) or carefully erase the shadow with the Eraser tool in Paintbrush mode and paint in the shadow again.

Press Ctrl (Cmd)++ until you reach a 4:1 viewing ratio and then use the Hand tool or the scroll bars to move the image so that the first bush you placed is in the upper right of your screen	Provides a good view of the area you'll work on next.

Figure 12.39 shows the house before all your improvements took place. The house casts a long narrow shadow on the dirt on the left hand side of the image. Take a good look at the shadow; you need to draw one like it using the Lasso tool.

Click on the Layer 3 title to make it active	You could place the shadow you're going to create on a new layer, but reusing layers, (when possible) saves system RAM.
Double-click on the Lasso tool on the toolbox; make sure that Feather is set to **1** and that Anti-aliased is checked on Lasso Options palette	The Lasso tool becomes the the active tool with default settings in place.
Hold down the Alt (Option) key while using the Lasso tool; starting at the corner of the house click a very narrow, tapering selection that resembles the selection in figure 12.40	Creates a long narrow selection.

continues

continued

Double-click on the Paint Bucket tool, then choose Multiply from the modes drop-down list and set the Opacity to about **72%**	Chooses the Paint Bucket tool as the active tool and sets its painting characteristics.
Press the Alt (Option) key and click the Eyedropper tool over the dark greenish shadow on the foundation of the house	Chooses a color from the image that will be good for a shadow.

When you paint the shadow in Multiply mode with a color other than black, the shadow is tinted with the color you choose as the foreground color, making the shadow a little more realistic.

Click the Paint Bucket tool within the marquee selection; press Ctrl (Cmd)+H and then double-click the Hand tool	Paints in a shadow within the selection. With the marquee hidden and zoomed out you can see if the shadow looks good.

If you like the shape and color of the shadow, continue with the steps. If you want to try a different color or opacity, press Delete, then create and fill a new selection or just refill this selection with a different color or opacity.

If you are happy with all the detail work you've performed so far, it's time to merge the layers together. If there is any layer you are uncertain about, work on that layer now before the layers are merged. Click on the layer's title on the Layers palette to make the layer available for editing (you can only edit one layer at a time). If a foreground object on a different layer obstructs your view, click on its eye icon to hide it.

Click on the triangle to the left of the tabs on the Layers palette, then choose Merge Layers	All of the visible layers are combined in their present order into the background.
Press Ctrl (Cmd)+S (**F**ile, **S**ave)	Saves your work up to this point.

Figure 12.38

Paint in a small shadow with the Paint Brush set to Multiply mode.

Figure 12.39

Notice the size, shape, and placement of the shadow in the original image.

Figure 12.40

Create a narrow, tapering selection with the Lasso tool that resembles the shadow in the original image.

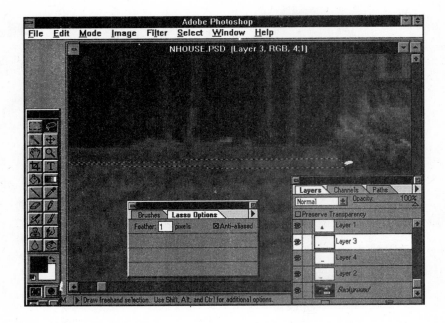

With the yard work done, it's on to some fast carpentry work. Grab your virtual tool belt and clone some siding.

Clapboard Cloning with the Rubber Stamp Tool

The carpenters who worked on this house left the job site without completing a small corner of the entrance way. To finish the siding, the carpenters would need a ruler, a saw, a couple small pieces of clapboard, and a handful of nails. As a Photoshop "carpenter," your materials list is shorter. All you need is a new layer and a Rubber Stamp tool to create and apply the clapboard.

In the next exercise, you'll use the Rubber Stamp tool to copy and add the siding. The source material for the Rubber Stamp is the existing siding on the Background Layer, but you'll apply the sampled material to the layer using the Sample Merged option. The Sample Merged option enables you to use materials that lie on layers below the one you are working on. You can use other layers' materials as source material for cloning or other Photoshop operations such as Smudging and Blurring.

The area you have to fill with the clone tool is not large, but what makes this job slightly tricky is that you don't have a lot of well-lit siding to sample from, and you must maintain the linear pattern that defines each board. If you don't, the board areas you clone will look warped or crooked.

Cloning between Layers

Repeatedly click the Zoom tool over the missing clapboard area in the entrance way until your viewing resolution is 16:1, then double-click on the image's title bar to maximize the window	Zooms you to maximum viewing resolution.
Double-click on the Rubber Stamp tool; make sure the mode is set to Normal, Opacity is set to **100%**, Option: is set to Clone (aligned), and Sample Merged is checked in the Rubber Stamp Options palette; click on the Brushes tab and choose the leftmost brush tip on the second row	Displays the Rubber Stamp Options palette, where you set the characteristics for Rubber Stamp.
Click on the New Layer icon on the bottom left of the Layers palette, then choose OK	Creates Layer 1 with default settings.
Press the Alt (Option) key and click about 1 screen inch to the right of the top of the area that needs cloning; release the Alt (Option) key and position the cursor to the left, just before the area to be replaced; be sure that you place your cursor in the same row of pixels that you sampled in; hold the Shift key and click and drag the cursor to the left	Sets the sample point; holding the Shift key when dragging constrains the Rubber Stamp tool movement to a straight line, which preserves the clapboard's pattern (see fig. 12.41).
Repeat the above step 3 or 4 times, except make the sample point and the area you clone into one row of pixels lower each time	You are done when your image looks like figure 12.42.

Double-click on the Hand tool on the toolbox. If the repair work is unnoticeable, go on to the next step. If your cursor strayed off course and the boards look crooked, drag the layer onto the trash can at the bottom of the Layers palette, click on the New Layer icon and start again.

Click on the triangle next to the tabs on the Layers Palette and choose Merge Layers	The pixels cloned on Layer 1 replace the underlying pixels on the Background Layer.
Press Ctrl (Cmd)+S (<u>F</u>ile, <u>S</u>ave)	Saves your work up to this point.

Figure 12.41

Hold the Shift key to constrain the Rubber Stamp to a straight line and preserve the clapboard pattern.

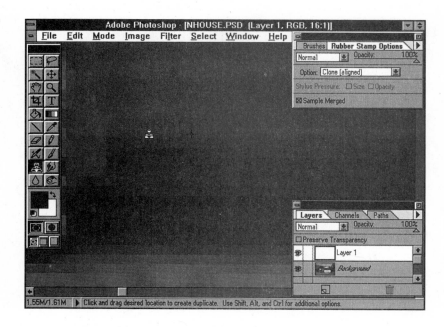

Figure 12.42

Clone from right to left to fill the missing clapboards.

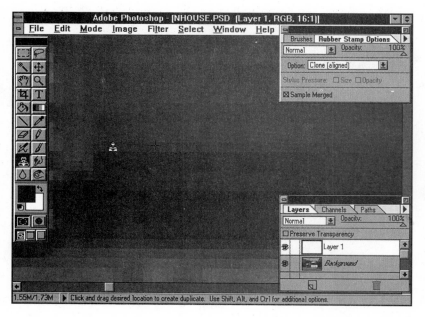

The yard work is done, and this house looks like it's ready to greet an anxious buyer.

A Sports Car for the Drive

Few things in life grab your attention and captivate the imagination more than a shiny red sports car. The car that you'll add to the scene, REDSPORT.PSD, is a perfect choice for an empty driveway of a dream house.

The REDSPORT image has been separated from its original background for you so that you can concentrate on the assignment at hand. The methods used to separate the car from its background were a little different from those that were used for the trees and bushes. Like the gumball machine in Chapter 11, "Using Paths, Selections, and Layers," the clean geometry and clearly defined outline of the car made using Paths the preferred method for separating the car from its background. See Chapter 11 for a discussion and examples on using Paths to create selections.

In the next exercise, you'll park the car in the NHOUSE image and clean up a few rough edges using the Paint Brush and the Smudge tools.

Placing and Integrating a New Image Element

Press Ctrl(Cmd)++, scroll over so that you have a good view of the driveway	You will work on this area next.
Open REDSPORT.PSD from the Chap12 subdirectory (folder) on the Bonus CD	REDSPORT becomes the active image. You'll bring this car into the NHOUSE image.
Press **L** (or click on the **L**asso tool on the toolbox) and click and drag a rough selection around the sports car	The Lasso tool is used to select the sports car.

Selection borders don't have to be accurate when you want to select pixels from a transparent background, as you are here with the REDSPORT.PSD image. Because a transparent background contains no pixels, selection borders automatically conform to the pixels found within a marquee you define, and the sports car in this example, automatically becomes a floating selection.

Press Ctrl (Cmd)+C (**E**dit, **C**opy)	Copies the car to the Clipboard.
Click on the New Layer icon on the bottom of the Layers palette, choose OK, and then press Ctrl (Cmd)+V (**E**dit, **C**opy)	Creates Layer 1 with default settings and then pastes in the car as a floating selection over Layer 1.

continues

continued

Click and drag the car so that it rests on the driveway and the right side of the windshield lines up with the bottom windows to the right of the garage door; when the car is in position, press Ctrl (Cmd)+D (**S**elect, None)	Positions the car in the drive and deselects the floating selection so that it becomes a Layer object (see fig. 12.43).
Double-click on REDSPORT.PSD's control menu button to close the image; Macintosh users should click the close button once	Closes the image; you have no further use for it.
Press **D** (or click on the **d**efault colors icon on the toolbox)	Changes the foreground color to black and the background color to white.
Double-click on the Paint Brush tool on the toolbox; choose Darken from the drop-down mode list, and set the Opacity to about **75%** on the Paintbrush Options palette; click on the Brushes tab and choose the leftmost brush tip on the second row	Chooses a small, soft tipped tip for the Paint Brush that will apply 75% opacity foreground paint to any areas that are lighter than the current black foreground color.
Click the Preserve Transparency check box on the Layers palette or press the forward slash (/)	Any pixels that are currently transparent will remain transparent, even if you paint over them. This enables you to paint only on the car image.
Press Ctrl (Cmd)++ until you can see the area that needs work	A 3:1 or 4:1 viewing comfortably resolution is good.
Click and drag the Paint Brush over the white fringe areas on the shadow under the car and around the front tires	Replaces the white fringe pixels with 75% Opacity black.
Uncheck the Preserve Transparency check box on the Layers palette	You need to be able to change transparent pixels on this Layer in the rest of the steps.
Press Ctrl (Cmd)+– until you are back to a 2:1 viewing resolution	You need to see more of the overall look.

Double-click on the Smudge tool; on the Smudge Tool Options palette drag the Pressure slider to **42%**; make sure the mode is set to Normal, Finger Painting is *un*checked, and Sample Merged is *checked*; click on the Brushes tab and choose the far left tip on the second row	Selects the Smudge tool and configures it to use pixels from both layers when the tool is used.
Click and drag the Smudge tool along the edges, moving from the drive into the shadow under the car; use short strokes and don't overdo it; one stroke of the tool over an area is enough	Gently softens the edge of the shadow, as shown in figure 12.44.
Press Ctrl (Cmd)+S (**F**ile, **S**ave)	Saves your work up to this point.

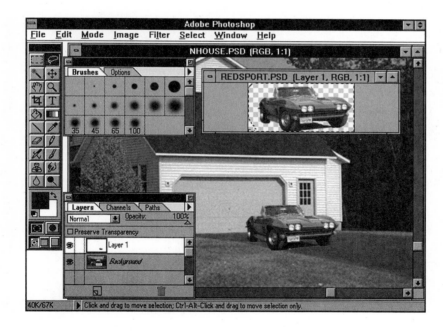

Figure 12.43

Drag the floating selection of the car into place with a selection tool.

Figure 12.44

*Gently soften the
edges of the
shadow with the
Smudge tool.*

Just as all the other elements you've placed into the image need shadows, the sports
car needs one too. The shadow that came with the car is good, but it lacks a certain
something. In the next section, you'll learn some of the secrets of creating realistic
shadows using Photoshop.

Creating a Dimensional Shadow

All the other image elements you've added to the NHOUSE image cast shadows; even
though most of the shadows were manufactured, they are an accurate representation
of the way lighting affects an object within the scene.

You already have a head start creating a realistic shadow for the sports car in the
NHOUSE image; you copied the car in the REDSPORT.PSD image and its original,
natural shadow. However, the shadow is incomplete right now, and it looks photo-
graphically incorrect. Here's the reason why, and what you can do to mend it:

The sports car was photographed at a different time of day than the NHOUSE
image—the sun was at a steep angle, to the right of the car; the NHOUSE image was
photographed with sun coming from the right, far later in the afternoon. The
NHOUSE image's natural shadows are cast from a light source (the sun) that is above
and to the right of the objects planted here. In contrast, the shadow in the
REDSPORT image is only apparent beneath the car; it lacks shading that would be
caused by NHOUSE's light source striking the top *and* the side of the car.

Figure 12.45 is a diagram of the light source in NHOUSE; a three-dimensional cube represents the sports car's top, bottom, front, back, and sides. When the sun strikes the top and left side of the cube, a shadow appears beneath and on the right side of the cube, opposite the location of the sun.

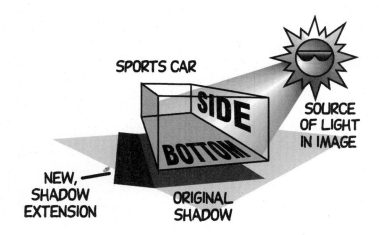

Figure 12.45

Shadows cast on a plane in the opposite direction from the light source.

The solution to adding a realistic shadow to the car as it sits in the driveway, then, is to extend the original shadow area that's presently beneath the car. The *shape* of the border of the shadow as it falls on the grass to the left of the car should look like the profile of the side of the car.

Here's how to apply the theory behind light and shadow properties to something a little more substantial, such as making a really sexy sports car look as though it's actually parked in the driveway!

Extending a Shadow

Double click on the Quick Mask mode button on the toolbox; make sure the Color Indicates: option radio button is set to **S**elected Areas; click on OK

Areas that you cover with Quick Mask will be selected.

Double-click on the Paint Brush tool on the keyboard; click and drag the Opacity slider up to **100%** and choose Normal from the modes drop-down list on the Paintbrush options palette

The Paint Brush becomes the active tool and will apply paint (Quick Mask) at a 100% Opacity in Normal mode.

continues

continued

Click and drag the Paint Brush on Layer 1 to create a shape similar to that in figure 12.46; it's OK to get Quick Mask on the tires but don't get any on the rest of the car be sure to fill in the entire shadow area with Quick Mask	Make the area you fill in with Quick Mask the shape you want the shadow to be.

The shadow should suggest the profile of the car and should skew towards the back of the car. This will produce a shadow consistent with the angle of the sun's illumination in the NHOUSE image and also matching the lighting conditions under which the car was photographed.

Press **Q** on the keyboard or click on the Standard mode button on the toolbox	You are returned to Standard editing mode with a marquee selection border around the area defined by the Quick Mask. Q toggles between Quick Mask mode and Standard Mode.
Choose **S**elect, **S**ave **S**election, then choose OK; press Ctrl (Cmd)+D (**S**elect, **N**one)	Saves the selection to a New selection (# 4), then deselects the selection in the image. Selections are saved in an Alpha Channel.
Click on the Channels tab; press Ctrl (Cmd)+4 or click on the #4 title on the Channels palette	Moves you to a view of channel #4 where the selection is stored. The selection area is filled with black in the channel view.
Choose Fi**l**ter, Blur, Gaussian Blur; enter **0.5** in the **R**adius: entry box; choose OK	The Gaussian Blur dialog box appears. 0.5 specifies a small amount of blur.
Press **L** (or click on the Lasso tool on the toolbox); click and drag a rough circle around the colored selection area in the channel	Selects the Gaussian Blurred image in channel #4 (see fig. 12.47).
Press Ctrl+C (**E**dit, **C**opy), Ctrl (Cmd)+0 (zero), or click on the RGB title on the Channel's palette	Copies the selection to the Clipboard. Restores the RGB composite view of the image.
Click on the Layers tab, press Crtl (Cmd)+V (**E**dit, **P**aste), then choose Multiply from the Layers	Pastes the shadow in as a floating selection over Layer 1. Multiply mode and the

palette drop-down list and drag the Opacity slider to about **54%** (see fig. 12.48)

partial Opacity allow the drive and the grass to show through. The white areas in the selection disappear.

Press Ctrl (Cmd)+D (**S**elect, **N**one)

Deselects the selection.

Press Ctrl (Cmd)+S (**F**ile, **S**ave)

Saves your work up to this point.

Figure 12.46

Paint a shadow shape with Quick Mask.

There is one last area that needs some sprucing up before you blow the whistle on the virtual construction site and show your client an astounding piece of photographic magic. The windshield of the car displays very strong reflections of trees. This is alright to a certain degree; trees are in the NHOUSE image that could reflect into the windshield. In addition to its reflective property, however, light also passes *through* glass, and when you see some of the house through the windshield glass the car becomes more concrete and a more integrated element of your fantasy creation. The Layer Mask is the perfect tool for making both your editing work and the windshield transparent.

Here's how to use the Layer Mask feature to make the windshield area of the car partially opaque.

Figure 12.47

*Use the Lasso tool
to make a rough
selection around
the Gaussian
Blurred shadow.*

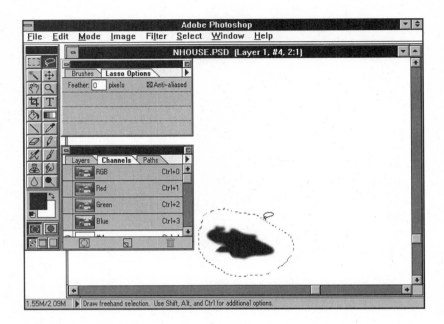

Figure 12.48

*Use the
Layers palette's
Multiply mode to
add the shadow
to the image.*

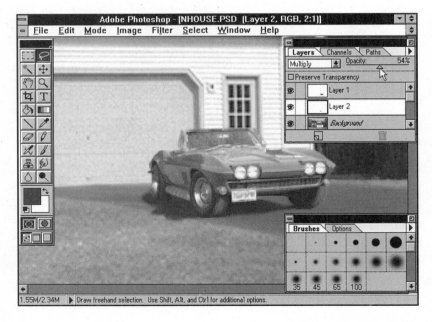

Making an Image Area Partially Opaque

Press **Z** (for **Z**oom tool) and click once over the car	Moves you in a 4:1 viewing resolution so you can see the work area.
Click on the Layer 1 title, then click on the triangle to the right of the tabs and choose Add Layer Mask from the menu	Layer 1 becomes active and a Layer Mask is created for the layer.
Press **L** (or click on the **L**asso tool on the toolbox); press and hold down the Alt (Option) key and click a selection around the inside perimeter of the windshield; leave the rear view mirror out of the selection area	Create a selection similar to the one shown in figure 12.49.
Choose **S**elect, **S**ave Selection, then click on OK	Saves the windshield selection as Channel #5 so that it can be loaded again if you accidentally deselect this selection.
Double-click on the Paint Brush on the toolbox; choose Normal mode and slide the Opacity slider to about **37%** on the Paintbrush Options palette	The Paint Brush becomes the active tool. It is set to apply the Layer mask in Normal mode and at a low Opacity.
Click and drag the Paint Brush over the windshield; try not to go over any area more than once (see fig. 12.50)	"Paints" foreground color (black) at a reduced Opacity, which partially hides the image on the layer allowing the image areas on the Background Layer to show through.
Click on the triangle to the right of the tabs on the Layers palette and choose Remove Layer Mask from the menu; click on the Apply button	Applies the Layer Mask to the image area on Layer 1, which removes the partially hidden pixels to permanently reveal some Background Layer areas.

The windshield looks wonderfully reflective, yet transparent at the same time. The only thing it lacks is a strong reflective highlight. You'll paint one in using Screen mode in the next few steps.

continues

continued

Press **X** (or click on the Switch colors icon on the toolbox)	Reverses the Foreground/Background colors so that white is the Foreground color.
Choose Screen mode and drag the Opacity to about **85%** on the Paint Brush Options palette	Sets the Paint Brush to "bleach" areas it passes over toward the foreground color of white.
With the windshield selection still active...	
Click and drag the Paint Brush over the windshield; make one or two strokes on the far right side of the windshield, and follow the angle of the windshield	Creates a highlight, as seen in figure 12.51.

Figure 12.49

Create a selection around the windshield that excludes the rear view mirror.

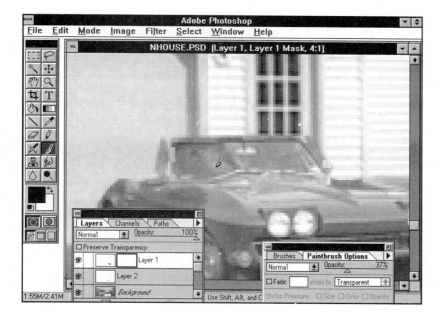

Figure 12.50

Use the Paint Brush set at a reduced opacity setting to partially reveal the Background Layer.

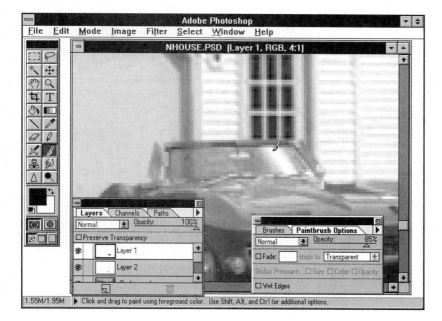

Figure 12.51

Paint a highlight on the semi-transparent image area using Screen mode.

The car looks right at home parked in the driveway. If you feel like this could be *your* home after your extensive retouching work, you've obviously put the care into this assignment that will help sell your skills on an assignment of your own. All that remains to be done to this image is to merge the layers and save the file in a more common file format that other applications can use.

Here's how to make sure that any printer, or almost any other application will be able to work with the finished image.

Merging Layers

Click on the Channels tab; one-by-one drag channels 4 and 5 into the Trash icon at the bottom of the palette	Removes the now unneeded selection channels and reduces the size of the file.

Many other applications do not understand channel information and may crash when asked to open a file that contains extra Alpha channels. Photoshop won't let you drag the Red, Green or Blue channels into the trash; you would destroy your image if you did.

Click on the Layers tab then click on the triangle next to the tabs on the Layers palette; choose Merge Layers from the menu	Combines all the layers into a single Background Layer.
Choose <u>F</u>ile, Sa<u>v</u>e As. Name the file OPENHOUS.TIF; choose TIFF (*.TIF) from the Save File as Format Type drop-down; click on OK; click on OK in the TIFF Options box	Saves the image to the TIF format using the defaults of IBM format and no LZW compression.

Take a look at figures 12.52 and 12.53 and see how far you've come with a rather ordinary image.

If you didn't think you had the "artist's eye" to succeed at the type of professional retouching you did in this chapter, look at what you just did! Image editing is part science, part intuition, and part invention born from personal motivation. Regardless of your point of origin when you begin using Photoshop—photographer, rocket scientist, or sales representative—your ideas begin at the same place: Photoshop's workspace. Where you *take* your idea is down the road to completion: toward reality, and sometimes beyond.

Chapter 13, "Combining Photographs," is a variation on this chapter's theme. Instead of integrating appropriate elements from other sources to make a scene appear absolutely authentic, you'll add absolutely *inappropriate* elements to an image, and intrigue your viewer with an image that looks authentic but obviously can't be real.

Figure 12.52
Before...

Figure 12.53
Postcard perfect!

Combining Photographs

Although cutting and pasting photos into *other* photos has been the practice of grade school students and amateur publishers for fun and humorous effects for a long time, electronic imaging has increased the accuracy, power, and capability of cutting, copying, and pasting. It's no longer kid stuff. You can transport images to entirely different locales, and do it convincingly with Photoshop. And still have fun!

This chapter takes you through creating your own reality, using images taken from sources that bear absolutely no relationship to one another. By creating accurate shading, seamless edge work, and by knowing the ins and outs of integrating digital images, you can make your designs sit precariously on the near side of plausible, and attract viewers from the far side of the room.

The tools you use are in Photoshop, and the materials are on the Bonus CD and Adobe's Deluxe CD-ROM. Set your sights for some serious fun as you learn how to paste into images, Photoshop-style.

This Chapter's Assignment

At one time or another, everyone on earth has had to post a sign. For example, you're having a garage sale, you want to sell your stereo, or someone took the last two spots in front of your apartment by parking diagonally; all of these occasions demand an attention-getting printed message.

Our friend Mike, who's a lifeguard at a private pool, isn't exempt from the pressing need to publish. Despite his neatly hand-lettered signs indicating that inflatable pool paraphernalia are off-limits, every season brings a fresh litter of tub toys that poor Mike has to shepherd out of the drink.

Perhaps Mike's wish can be better expressed graphically, through an art form known as *exaggeration*. We posed Mike in front of the pool with his toy retrieval gear (an insect skimmer), and asked him to adopt a stance that suggested 50-percent vigilance and 50-percent exasperation. The pool was empty at the time the photograph was taken, but that's okay—in this chapter's assignment, you'll add just the right visual element to complete the scene, make a powerful statement, and create a sign that gets Mike's point across to even the most stubborn three-year-old.

Using a Stock Photography Resource

On the Adobe Photoshop Deluxe CD-ROM is a sampler from CMCD, a company that's a valuable resource for high-quality images for use in illustration, design, advertising, desktop publishing, and presentations. Thematically, CMCD's collection can be thought of as iconic symbols that quickly indicate a thought. Because an image of a telephone connotes communication, for example, CMCD's image of a telephone can be used in a variety of design situations to indicate communication. Visual gestalt, if you will.

It so happens that CMCD offers RUBRDUCK.JPG (Rubber Ducky, saved in JPEG format) on Adobe's Deluxe CD; the image is exactly what the file name sounds like, and it's an ideal stock image for this chapter's assignment. You'll use this image of a tub toy to complete the POOLSIDE.TIF image of Mike, which is in the CHAP13 subdirectory of this book's Bonus CD.

Figure 13.1 shows both images, opened in Photoshop's workspace. Mike doesn't looked thrilled, but can you blame him?

The first step in combining these images is to assess the relative scale of the images. If you look at the image dimensions and file size of CMCD's duck, you'll see that it is positively huge compared to POOLSIDE.TIF. To successfully bring together these two images, you need to do some disk shuffling to load the images from the two CDs, and you have to come up with a strategy for handling the gigantic duck.

Figure 13.1
You'll combine these images in Photoshop to create an Anti-Pool-Toy sign.

Scaling a JPEG Image

Because personal computers don't have infinite resources, it's usually a good idea not to have too many megabytes of visual information loaded in Photoshop at one time. POOLSIDE.TIF (at 1.18 MB) is the image you should load first into Photoshop. You need to determine just how large the RUBRDUCK.JPG image should be to fit into the POOLSIDE.TIF image.

JPEG image file sizes can be misleading; the Joint Photographer Expert Group's file format (covered in detail in Chapter 2, "Acquiring a Digital Image") is a *compressed* image format; when JPG files are stored on disk they occupy anywhere from one-fifth to one-one hundredth of their actual uncompressed size. Macintosh Photoshop users aren't tipped off to the JPEG nature of an image because the List View indicates the creator of an image file, but not the file format, so they are unaware of the compressed nature of the file.

Windows Photoshop users can be in for a different, but similar, shock when exploring the file size of a JPEG image from Windows File Manager (or a third-party Windows shell). RUBRDUCK.JPG is 173 KB in its stored, compressed state, but when you open the file in Photoshop, this latex duckling plumps up to 9.47 MB, 1825 pixels in width, 1813 pixels in height, at 288 pixels per inch. CMCD's collection was designed for high-end output; the duck—or any of the other images—could easily fill half a page after being sent to an imagesetter capable of about 2540 dpi output (high-quality magazine or book).

For the purposes of the exercises in this chapter, you need a fraction of the resolution found in the RUBRDUCK.JPG image. In the next exercise, you'll use the Info palette to get the best duck dimensions to use in the POOLSIDE.TIF image. Then you'll set the Crop tool to make quick work of scaling (sampling down) the RUBRDUCK.JPG image. You'll need to perform the next steps in precise order, and we recommend you have as much hard disk space cleared as possible on your scratch disk drives before performing this feat. Photoshop uses temp space in a very sophisticated fashion, but before opening a large image you must point the application to areas on your hard disk where Photoshop can find the space. See Chapter 4, "Photoshop Defaults and Options," for information on setting up scratch disks if you haven't already optimized Photoshop's memory usage.

Measuring an Image Area

Load the Adobe Photoshop Deluxe CD-ROM into your CD-ROM drive, then copy RUBRDUCK.JPG image from STOCKART\PHOTOS\CMCD subdirectory to a location on your hard disk	Copies image so that you can change CDs and load the Bonus CD into your CD-ROM drive.

Macintosh users will find the Rubber Ducky file in the Third Party Products\Stock Photography\ CMCD\Images folder.

Put Bonus CD into your CD-ROM drive	Loads CD with exercise images used with this book.
Start Photoshop, then open POOLSIDE.TIF image from CHAP13 subdirectory (folder) of Bonus CD	Opens image so that you can measure size of area the duck should occupy. These are dimensions you use to crop and size the duck.
Press F8 (Macintosh: F12) or choose **W**indow, **P**alettes, Show **I**nfo	Displays Info Palette.
Press **M** (for **M**arquee tool) until Rectangular marquee tool is displayed on toolbox	Tool used for creating a selection area. Info palette displays outside dimensions of a selection.
On left side of POOLSIDE.TIF image, click and drag a rectangle that reaches slightly above umbrella and extends down into white concrete poolside	Creates a rectangular marquee that defines height the duck should be in finished image.

The duck should appear unusually large in the finished sign because we're making an exaggerated statement. However, the current size of RUBRDUCK.JPG is ten times the file size of POOLSIDE.TIF, *way* too large to be of use. The area inside the rectangular marquee, five and a fraction inches high, is a good height for an exaggerated duck. Because image dimension has

an inverse relationship to image resolution, you need to know the resolution of the POOLSIDE.TIF image. If the resolution of the duck image is the same as that of POOLSIDE.TIF, the duck will have the correct dimensions when it is pasted into POOLSIDE.TIF. When you know the height and resolution you need, you can set the Crop tool to automatically produce an image that has the specified height, width, *and* resolution.

Press Alt (Option) while clicking on Document Sizes box. For Mac users, this box is at bottom left of each image window; Windows users see Document Sizes box at lower left of Photoshop's status bar	Displays file statistics for POOLSIDE.TIF image in Document Sizes pop-up box (see fig. 13.2).

Today's winning numbers for cropping the RUBRDUCK.JPG image are 5 and a fraction height, and 72 pixels/inch. For cropping purposes, you don't need to know what the width of the RUBRDUCK image should be; the width of the duck scales proportionately to the height you set in the Cropping tool's options.

Choose File, Save As, name image DUCKPOND, save image in PSD format, then close it	Saves copy of image in a format that can retain layers, a Photoshop feature you use in this chapter's assignment.

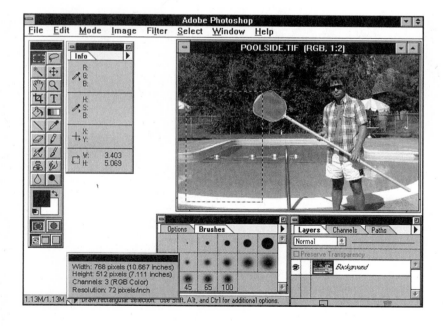

Figure 13.2

Use the Info palette and the Document Sizes box to get cropping information from an image.

In the last exercise, you determined the size and resolution at which the RUBRDUCK.JPG image should be cropped to make a good-sized duck for the pool. You are going to need all the "umph" your system can muster to open and crop the duck image. If you haven't properly set up your memory allocations and scratch disks, as discussed at the beginning of this chapter (and as outlined in Chapter 4, "Photoshop Defaults and Options"), you should do so now.

Tip All the Selection tools can be used to define an area about which the Info palette will report dimensional information. But when you create selection areas with the Elliptical marquee tool or the Lasso tool, the Info palette can provide only the height and width of the outside extremes of such selections. Generally, therefore, the dimensional readings the Info palette provides are more helpful to users if selection areas are created with the Rectangular marquee tool.

Using the Crop Tool's Fixed Target Size Feature

The Crop tool's basic function is to discard image areas you don't want displayed in a final image. In the next exercise, however, you'll be using its capability to resize and discard unwanted image areas as you pare down the RUBRDUCK.JPG image to a size that's appropriate for the DUCKPOND.PSD image.

Photoshop's Crop tool can operate in the same way as the **I**mage, **I**mage Size command. The dimensions and the resolution information you enter in the Cropping Tool Options palette determine whether the cropped area is *sampled up* (adding pixels to the image, which make it bigger) or *sampled down* (discarding pixels from the image, which makes it smaller). The mathematical interpolation method Photoshop uses to sample up or sample down the image is determined by the kind of interpolation method chosen in the **I**nterpolation drop-down box under **F**ile, Pre**f**erences, **G**eneral (or Ctrl (Cmd)+K). See Chapter 4, "Photoshop Defaults and Options," for more information on the methods of interpolation that are available and how to choose one. By default, Photoshop uses Bicubic interpolation, the slowest, yet most accurate, of the three methods of interpolation, whenever you resize, rotate, or create other special effects in an image. Bicubic is the method you should use for this exercise, because it produces results that are more faithful to the original image than the other methods outlined in Chapter 4.

In this exercise, you create a much smaller copy of the duck image by using the Crop tool.

Cropping the Size and Live Area of an Image

Open RUBRDUCK.JPG image from your hard disk	This is the large duck file you copied from the Adobe CD in the last exercise.

This step might take a few minutes—Photoshop decompresses the JPEG format image and reads it into system RAM and on to your hard disk scratch-disk space. Photoshop always offers the option to undo an edit; for this reason, multiple copies of an image are tucked away on your system for Photoshop to read, in the event you change your mind about something, and storing the information can take a few minutes for Photoshop to accomplish.

Double-click on Crop tool on toolbox	Chooses Crop tool, and displays Options palette for the tool.
Click on Fixed Target Size check box on Options palette if it is not already checked	Tells Photoshop to use image Height, Width, and Resolution you enter in the number fields on the Options palette.
Type **5.07** in Height field, and choose inches from drop-down list to right of Height field	Cropping tool will make height of cropped image 5.07 inches.

The Height field entry, 5.07, represents the reading you took from the Info palette in the last exercise. If you created a rectangular marquee whose height was 5.1 or 4.9 in the DUCKPOND.PSD image, then you should substitute the value you arrived at here.

If the Width field is not blank, place cursor inside Width field on Options palette, then press Backspace key until the entry has been removed	Leaves this field blank. Photoshop will determine width of cropped image; original image proportions are maintained when you leave one dimension field blank.

It's important to note that a value of zero is *not* the same as a blank entry in any of the Crop tool Options fields. If you put a zero in an Option field, Photoshop automatically replaces the zero with 0.001 when you click the Crop tool over the image. You definitely don't want that value; it's almost non-existent! But if the field is blank, Photoshop will produce a resulting crop that makes the unspecified dimension of the cropped image one that *doesn't* produce image distortion, *and* matches the length or width you encompassed with the Crop tool.

Type **72** in Resolution field, then choose pixels/inch from drop-down list to right of Resolution field	Sets Cropping tool to create a cropped image with same resolution as that of DUCKPOND.PSD image.

continues

continued

Click and drag a marquee crop from above left to below right of duck image in RUBRDUCK.JPG file	Make it a tight crop, but make sure that all of the duck is inside crop border (see fig. 13.3).

If your marquee crop doesn't include all of the duck, you can click on a corner handle (your cursor turns into an arrow when over a handle) and drag until all the duck is inside the marquee. You might have to adjust the border using one or more selection handles. If your crop marquee is of the correct size, but its position is a little off, press Ctrl (Cmd) while you click and drag on one of the crop marquee's corner handles to move the defined area.

Click inside crop marquee	Cursor changes to shears icon, and clicking inside executes the crop.

Massive amounts of calculations are going on behind the scenes now; Photoshop must delete pixels from the image, and reassign color values to the pixels inside the marquee to represent original image information based on a new image size. So be patient.

After crop is completed, double-click on Zoom tool, then choose **F**ile, Sa**v**e As, and name cropped image DUCK_TOY.TIF	Saves cropped image to your hard disk under a different name (see fig. 13.4).

Figure 13.3

On the Cropping Tool Options palette, specify the image dimensions and resolution you want for the cropped image.

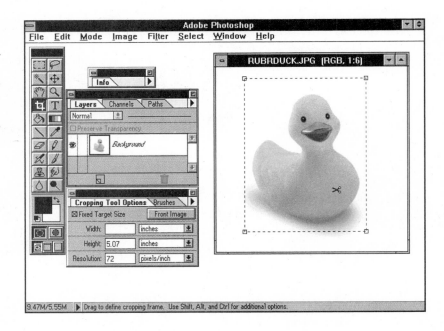

Figure 13.4

Save the cropped image to a different file name and format than the original RUBRDUCK.JPG.

You were asked to save the cropped duck image to the TIFF file format, an uncompressed format, in the last exercise, because JPEG format images are compressed with a lossy compression scheme. JPEG compression averages the unique color values in an image to achieve compression; the smaller the number of unique colors, the better JPEG compression is able to store the image. If you repeatedly open, save to the JPEG format, and reopen a JPEG image, each time you do so the image loses some color information and shifts in color value occur, which progressively degrades the image's quality. That's why opening a JPEG image and saving it to a format that offers no compression is usually a good idea.

If you really need to recompress an image stored in JPEG format, it's best to use a lossless compression scheme for your own archiving purposes. LZH compression is offered for the TIFF format directly through Photoshop's Save As command. Additionally, both Windows and Macintosh users have proprietary compression programs for archiving files, such as PKZIP and StuffIt (both included on the Bonus CD). Archiving programs are separate from, and operate outside of, Photoshop. They are not plug-ins.

It's not a mandatory step here, but you might consider closing Photoshop and restarting your system if you have less than 12 MB of RAM, to refresh system resources after Photoshop has tapped into them to interpolate the cropped-image information.

You were asked to double-click on the Zoom tool in the last exercise because the Crop tool doesn't change your viewing resolution of the active image window after it performs its work. Photoshop opens the RUBRDUCK.JPG image full-window, at 1:6 resolution, and the cropped copy made from the original still displays at a 1:6 viewing resolution, which makes it hard to view and analyze. It's time now to take a qualitative look at Photoshop's quantitative transformation of duck data.

Note   You can delete the POOLSIDE.TIF and RUBRDUCK.JPG images from your hard disk and free some space, now that you have working copies of the files you need on your hard disk. Both POOLSIDE.TIF and RUBRDUCK.JPG are safe in their original state on the Adobe and Bonus CDs. CDs are read-only media, which means that you can only save and edit *copies* of files made from these disks.

The Paths Palette and Sampled-Down Images

Sampling down the RUBRDUCK.JPG image to create the DUCK_TOY copy is really the only way to get the duck and the DUCKPOND.PSD images scaled to compatible dimensions. However, as good as Bicubic interpolation is in Photoshop, incredible amounts of visual data—pixels—had to be averaged to perform the crop, and loss of image quality is the inevitable result. The duck's image detail is in good shape within the interior of the image, but the edge between the duck and the white background displays a harsh, pixelated outline. It's not unusual for a sampled-down image to have stairsteppy edges, because the edge of something in a bitmap image is composed of very few pixels, compared to the rest of the image's visual detail.

The duck needs to be separated from the background and its shadow before it can become a foreground element in the DUCKPOND image. The tools used in other chapters to separate foreground images from their background (the Color Range and the Magic Wand tool, for example) aren't the best choice in this situation, because you need to trim ever so slightly inside the edge around the duck. Trimming inside the edge will create smooth, anti-aliased pixels that will eliminate the harsh transition between the duck and the white background. The Color Range and the Magic Wand can't produce a selection that is as clean or precise as needed in this situation. Therefore, in the next exercise, you'll use the Paths palette's Pen tool to define a border around the duck so that Photoshop can convert it into a selection that has an anti-aliased border. The anti-aliased border will make the duck's edges fade to transparency, and will integrate the duck selection into the DUCKPOND.PSD image seamlessly.

You'll be designing the path outline around the duck using the Bézier method of drawing, covered in detail in Chapter 11, "Using Paths, Selections, and Layers." Basically, you shape the slope of the curved segment by moving around the Pen tool cursor before releasing the mouse button. In this way, you move the slope of the curve that precedes the Anchor point you create by releasing the mouse button. Here's how to define a border:

Selecting Inside a Harsh Image Outline

Click on Paths tab on Layers/Channels/ Paths group of palettes (press **T** if Layers palette isn't currently displayed)

Displays Paths palette tools.

Press **Z** (for **Z**oom tool), then click twice over right side of the duck's mouth

Zooms to clear (4:1) view of area where duck pixels blend into white background pixels; this is where you'll begin the path.

Click on Pen tool (second from left), then click and drag, beginning one pixel inside edge of duck's head (see fig. 13.5), to a point below your initial click point, remaining slightly inside curve of the edge; release mouse button

Creates a path segment inside duck's edge: Releasing mouse button ends the segment, and you're ready to continue the path.

If you get "off course" with the path, press the Ctrl (Cmd) key after you've created an Anchor point to toggle the Pen tool to the Arrow pointer tool. The Arrow pointer tool doesn't create segments; instead, it is used to reposition Anchor points, and to drag the direction points that govern a path segment. Direction points sprout from Anchor points (anchors connect path segments); and by clicking and dragging on direction points, you can shape the direction and slope of a curved path segment.

Continue clicking new Anchor points, and dragging path segments to conform to shape of duck's outline; when you reach the edge of the image window, release mouse button and use scroll bars on image window to move view of duck

Creates a path just inside duck's edge (see fig. 13.6). Use as many Anchor points as you need to accurately define the curves.

In the path, don't include the shadow cast by the duck. If you have trouble seeing where the duck's bottom ends and the shadow begins, you can use the Ctrl (Cmd) key in combination with the + and – keys to zoom in and out of the image area without deselecting the Pen tool to choose the Zoom tool.

After you finish tracing the circumference of the duck, and reach the first Anchor point, click on the first Anchor point

Tiny circle next to Pen tool's cursor indicates that you're about to close the path. Clicking on first Anchor point closes path.

Scroll around image to ensure that path is one (or two) pixels inside duck's edge

Ensures that selection based on this path will contain no white background.

If part of your path is clearly outside the duck's edge, either press the Ctrl (Cmd) key to access the Arrow tool, or click on the Arrow tool on the Paths palette. Then, with the Arrow tool, click and drag an Anchor point and/or the associated direction point to modify the path and get it inside the duck.

continues

continued

Double-click on Work Path icon on Paths palette, then click on OK in Save Path dialog box	Displays Save Path dialog box, and saves path as Path 1 (a default name).
Press Ctrl(Cmd)+S (or choose **F**ile, **S**ave)	Saves your work up to this point.

Figure 13.5

Use the Paths palette to create a smooth outline slightly inside the edge of the duck image.

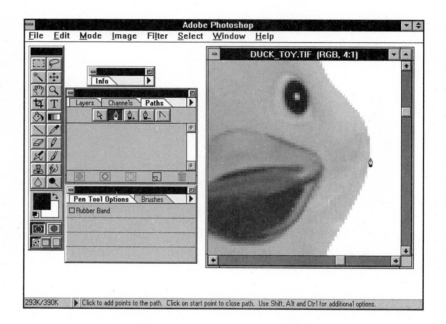

Bézier drawing is a little counter-intuitive, and not an easy way to produce a tight outline around the underlying duck image. By investing a little time tuning and tweaking the path you created in the last exercise, however, you can quickly arrive at a selection border (made from the path) that eliminates the pixelated edge and any white pixels that presently surround the duck edge.

As an alternative to Bézier drawing, you can click (without dragging) around the curves of the duck shape to produce straight path segments between anchor points. If you use this method, you must then use the Convert direction point tool (AKA the Corner tool in version 2.5) to click and drag on every anchor point to produce curved path segments and direction points with which you "steer" the curved segments. Chapter 11, "Using Paths, Selections, and Layers," walks you through the intricacies of the Paths palette and paths.

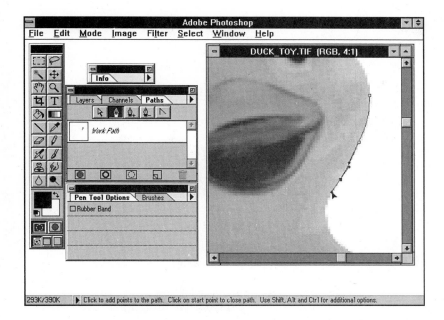

Figure 13.6

A Pen tool click defines an Anchor point; dragging after clicking sets the direction and shape of the path segment to follow.

Tip   To work with more than one tool on the Paths palette, you don't have to move your cursor from where you are working. If you want to use the Arrow tool and Convert direction point tool in alternate editing steps, click on the Arrow tool, then press the Ctrl (Cmd) key to toggle the Arrow to the Convert direction point tool.

The Convert direction point tool appears on-screen only when the cursor is located next to an Anchor point or direction point, however. Positioned over a path segment, the cursor remains the Arrow tool cursor.

Using Shortcuts

Unlike earlier versions of Photoshop, version 3.0 offers a graphical shortcut for creating a marquee selection from the geometric design of a path. The icons at the bottom of the Paths palette are shortcut alternatives to the commands listed on the pop-up menu on the Paths palette. Descriptions of these icons (from left to right) follow:

◆ **Fill Path**—Automatically fills a path with foreground color. If you don't have a closed path (one whose beginning anchor point is connected by two path segments), Photoshop chooses the shortest distance between the beginning and ending Anchor points, and ends the unenclosed fill with a straight edge.

Holding down the Alt (Option) key while you click on the Fill Path icon displays a dialog box, where you can select the mode (Normal, Multiply, and so on), contents (foreground or background color, pattern), how much the selection should be feathered (if at all), and the all-important anti-alias feature.

◆ **Stroke Path**—Strokes foreground color along a path, which is quite useful for creating a "neon" effect along a defined path. The Paths palette can use any of the 11 painting editing tools listed in the Stroke Subpath dialog box, accessed by pressing Alt (Option) while clicking on the Stroke Path icon.

◆ **Make Selection**—Takes the geometric information of the path and bases a selection marquee around it. This is the icon you'll use in the next exercise to make an accurate selection border around the duck. By default, the Make selection command creates an anti-aliased border around a new selection based on a path. You should make it a practice *never* to uncheck this option if you want smooth selection areas in bitmap images.

◆ **New Path**—Clicking on this icon creates a new "workspace" above the active image, within which you can design a path that has no relationship to a previous one you've designed. Clicking on this icon automatically hides a previously made path. You should always check the Paths palette's list of Path titles to see where a path is located in an image. Paths can be hidden, and there is very little visual difference between a hidden path and a path you've accidentally deleted.

Stop The Backspace key deletes paths. To ensure that you don't accidentally delete a path you need, click on the Layers or Channels tab on the grouped palette when you need to use the Backspace key. This hides paths and protects them from unintentional editing.

◆ **Trash**—Although Photoshop 3's functions and the location of its features are virtually the same in Windows and on the Macintosh, the Trash icon will seem more familiar to Macintosh users. (The Macintosh interface sports a trash icon as a graphical alternative to the IBM PC's Delete command.) Quite simply, any time you click and drag a palette title into the trash icon, you discard it. When you perform this action, saved paths, Alpha channels, and layers all go to the binary wastebucket. If you have second thoughts and want to retrieve the design element, press Ctrl (Cmd)+Z (or choose **E**dit, Undo) immediately after you mistakenly drag something to the trash.

Now that you have the low-down on the Paths palette's shortcuts, let's get this show on the road and the duck in the water.

Converting Paths to Selections

You now have at your disposal the necessary elements for transporting the duck to the DUCKPOND image; the pool's open and it's time to give our lifeguard friend something to grouse about.

Creating a Selection

Press Alt (Option) while clicking on Make Selection icon on Paths palette	Displays Make Selection dialog box.
Set **F**eather Radius to **0**, make sure that **A**nti-Aliased box is checked, then click on OK (see fig. 13.7)	Creates most precise selection marquee around duck, based on vector path information; marquee uses partially selected edge pixels to smooth marquee selection.

In subsequent uses of the Make Selection icon, you won't need to hold down the Alt (Option) key before clicking unless you want to change these settings. Because you created the path for the express purpose of removing stairsteppy pixels around the edge of the duck, it would be counter-productive to leave the **A**nti-Aliased check box unchecked. Additionally, you can use the Make Selection dialog box to perform combining functions (Add to selection, Remove from selection), but only when a current selection marquee is active in the image. Because there isn't one now, options are dimmed in the Operation field. And you don't need any Feather attributes for the selection you create from the Path, because you need a definitive border (not a soft one) around the duck. Besides, the duck seems to have enough feathers already.

Copying a Selection to a New Image

Open DUCKPOND.PSD image from your hard disk; it's now the active image window	Target image for duck and subsequent editing work.
Click on Layers tab on palette, then click on New Layer icon, and click on OK in dialog box	Creates Layer 1 on DUCKPOND.PSD image. This layer is now the current (target) layer.
Press **M** (for **M**arquee tool), click on DUCKTOY.TIF image's title bar, then click and drag selection into DUCKPOND.PSD image	Chooses a selection tool, and copies duck selection into Layer 1 on DUCKPOND image (see fig. 13.8).

You can use any tool on the toolbox, except the Hand and Zoom tools, to drag a copy of a selection into a different image window. However, if a painting or editing tool is the currently

continues

continued

chosen tool, you must hold the Ctrl (Cmd) key to toggle the cursor to the arrow cursor to perform the drag-and-drop maneuver. When the selection crosses into the target window, the cursor changes into the small fist cursor you see in figure 13.8.

Press **Ctrl** (Cmd)+**D** (or choose **S**elect, **N**one), then press Ctrl (Cmd)+S (or choose **F**ile, **S**ave)	Deselects floating selection and saves your work to this point.
Close DUCK_TOY.TIF image	You no longer need it on the workspace.

Figure 13.7

Create a precise selection border around the duck image, based on the path you created.

Feathered Versus Anti-Aliased Edges

Before continuing, we should address the subtle difference between the Feather command and the anti-aliased function. On the surface, the two functions seem identical, but they actually serve two distinct design purposes. When you add feathering to a selection, you are creating a gradual transition along the edge of the selection, from selected to masked areas. Depending on the radius of the feather you define for a selection, the feathered selection can appear fairly sharp, or blur to nothingness along the edges, creating around a selection area an appearance similar to a soft spotlight, or photographic vignette, around the target area. Feathering is performed in a radius that encompasses both the inside and outside of a selection; a feather radius of 10 pixels, for example, makes the transition between selected and

masked image areas beginning five pixels inside the selection edge, and ending five pixels outside the image selection edge.

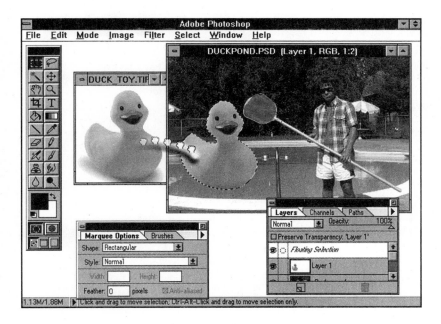

Figure 13.8

Drag and drop the selection of the duck onto Layer 1 in the DUCKPOND.PSD image.

On the other hand, the purpose of Photoshop's anti-aliased function is to maintain a consistent selection edge through the use of semitransparent pixels along the selection edge. The smoothness or lack of smoothness is most noticeable where a selection curves or points in a diagonal direction. Because pixels are rectangular in shape, diagonal and curved lines cannot be expressed smoothly with a series of solid color values. Anti-aliasing "fills in" edge details with pixel color of similar value to the pixels that sit on the edge of a selection border, and helps "fake" a smooth-edged effect very nicely. Theoretically, when anti-aliasing is used on a selection, there should be little or no edge detail lost when the image selection is copied to a different background, as in the last exercise. In contrast, feathering a selection destroys visual detail around the edge of the selection; feathering is useful for creating an effect, but plays a fairly reserved role in photorealistic image editing.

Enhancing Lighting Conditions

CMCD photographed all the stock images on Adobe's Deluxe CD with a sort of "universal light," somewhat like the Lighting Effects Filter's Omni light you'll work with in Chapter 18, "Photoshop's Native Filters." The lighting conditions in the

RUBRDUCK.JPG image were set to maximize image detail while minimizing shadows, except for the very soft shadow you eliminated from the selection in the copy of DUCK_TOY.TIF.

CMCD's use of flat, universal light on the duck presents a seldom-found opportunity for a designer to emphasize a particular lighting characteristic in an image. Imaging software can't really change strong lighting aspects found in an image; you can't make a photo taken at noon look as though it were lit by a brilliant 4 o'clock sun, any more than you can reach up and reposition the sun! Image details such as shadows and highlights are an integral part of a bitmap image.

However, because the duck's source of illumination is indeterminate, you can influence the viewer's perception of this four-foot duck in the DUCKPOND image by using Photoshop's Toning tools to bring out some highlights on the duck's surface.

In some of the following figures (13.9, 13.25–13.29), you'll see the Options and Brushes palettes as two separate screen elements, rather than in their default, grouped state. To show you the settings on both palettes, we clicked on the Options tab and dragged it away from the grouped palette. As a group, you can see one palette or the other, but not both palettes simultaneously. We don't recommend that you do the same thing as you work in the next exercise, because screen "real estate" is at a premium in Photoshop—especially when you're running a 640×480 video driver.

This exercise shows you how to add highlight areas to the duck to make it seem to reflect the lighting source in the DUCKPOND image.

Using the Dodge Tool To Create Highlights

Press **V** (for Move tool), then click and drag duck to reposition it on the left of DUCKPOND.PSD image	Duck should be "in the clear" as a foreground element; lifeguard's skimmer shouldn't touch duck's head.
Press **Z** (for Zoom tool) and click once over the duck's head	Zooms you in to a 1:1 viewing resolution so you can see the work area better.
Press **O** (for Toning tools) until Dodge tool appears (or press Alt (Option) and click on Dodge tool on toolbox)	Chooses Toning tool that increases brightness in three separate tonal ranges of an image.
Choose Highlights from drop-down list on Options palette, click and drag Exposure slider to about **15-20%**, then click on 35 (pixel diameter) tip on Brushes palette	Sets characteristics of Dodge tool to work broadly, with very weak exposure, concentrating tool's effect on the highlights tonal region of an image.
Click and drag a single stroke over upper left edge of duck's head	Gently heightens brightness of duck; creating a small highlight.

The larger the diameter of an editing (or painting) tool, the longer Photoshop takes to process a stroke. The effect of the Dodge tool, therefore, might not be immediately apparent. Resist the urge to make a second stroke until you see how effectively the area's been brightened.

Click and drag a stroke along duck's back, wait, then click and drag a smaller stroke in same area	Creates a more brilliant highlight than you created on duck's head (see fig. 13.9).
Click and drag a stroke along edge of duck, from tail feather to duck's bottom	Completes creation of a light source on duck.
Press Ctrl (Cmd)+S (or choose **F**ile, **S**ave)	Saves your work up to this point.

Figure 13.9

Use the Dodge tool to make highlight areas on the duck's left side slightly lighter.

You'll be looking at the DUCKPOND image frequently in this chapter for visual clues as to what editing steps must be performed to integrate the duck into the image in a convincing fashion. Even though the duck is out of scale with the rest of the image, by adding accurate lighting, shading, and reflections you force the reality of the image upon the viewer, and the implausible qualities form a dynamic tension with the realistic lighting characteristics of the transplanted selection.

As you saw in the last exercise, it didn't take much exposure to brighten the lightly colored duck's left side. When colors are of high saturation and brightness, decrease the Exposure setting for both Dodge and Burn tools. If you're unsure of a pixel's color components, use the Info palette to get more information about the target area.

Copying Layer Images

In the last exercise, you were asked to brighten the left side of the duck for two good reasons: to create lighting conditions in the duck that matched its host image (DUCKPOND.PSD), and because you need to make a copy of the duck with the changes you've made, to create the duck's reflection in the pool.

Now is a good time to start scouting the image for actual pool reflections. You'll use Photoshop's tools and some inspired guesswork to make a photorealistic reflection of the duck. But first, you need to copy and flip the duck.

In this exercise you begin the process of creating a reflection of the duck in the water.

Using the Duplicate Layer Command

Click on Layer palette's pop-up menu button (at upper right of palette)	Displays a list of options and commands for image layers.
Choose Duplicate Layer from menu	Displays Duplicate Layer dialog box (see fig. 13.10).
Click on OK	Creates duplicate of duck on Layer 1 as Layer 1 copy, now on top of original Layer 1.

In the Duplicate Layer dialog box, you have the option to give a copy of a Layer a unique name. This isn't always necessary; but you might want to custom-name image layers when you have four or five layers above an image. If you'd like to now, you can double-click on the layer title to display the Layer Options dialog box, where you can name the layer something else. You'll use the Layer 1 copy as the main duck; Layer 1 (the original pasted-in image) will serve as the raw image material with which you create the duck's reflection.

Click on Layer 1 title on Layers palette	Chooses Layer 1 as target layer beneath Layer 1 copy.
With Rectangular marquee tool, click and drag around duck	Selects duck on Layer 1, the current or target layer, as shown in figure 13.11.

You've actually selected all the duck pixels on the transparent layer *beneath* the one you're viewing. The duck copy is directly on top of the original duck (if you doubt this, click on the eye icon to the left of the Layer 1 copy title on the Layers palette). Clicking on the eye icon toggles your view of the layer, from visible to hidden. If you see no apparent difference on-screen, it's a clear indication that the Duplicate Layer command works, and you now have two ducks.

Choose **I**mage, **F**lip, then choose **V**ertical	Mirrors selection of duck on Layer 1.
While flipped duck is still a floating selection, click inside selection marquee and drag it to right of duck on Layer 1 copy	Moves flipped duck so that you have a clear view of both ducks, in preparation for editing work on it in the next section (see fig. 13.12).
Press Ctrl (Cmd)+D (**S**elect, **N**one), then press Ctrl (Cmd)+S (or choose **F**ile, **S**ave)	Saves your work up to this point.

Figure 13.10

Copying the contents of a layer to a new layer.

Naturally, you can also see the duck on Layer 1 by hiding the Layer 1 copy, instead of moving the duck on Layer 1 as a floating selection. You hide the Layer 1 duck by clicking on the eye icon next to the Layer 1 copy title on the Layers palette. The way you manage your screen element and images is a personal decision, born out of the working methodology you develop through practice and experience. For the authors, keeping Layer 1 displayed and moving the floating duck selection into view from behind the copy was easier and safer than hiding the Layer 1 copy. Occasionally, you might hide a layer from view and then, several steps later, discover that you'd been working on the wrong layer.

In any event, it's important to keep that Layers palette in easy view at all times, and to refer to it before copying, pasting, or editing. Photoshop's layers bring an incredible power to your work with images, but the price you pay for this capability is that you must keep a watchful eye on the icons on the Layers list.

Figure 13.11

*Creating the
duck's reflection.*

Figure 13.12

*Move the floating
selection of the
Layer 1 duck so
that you can see it
(and edit it!).*

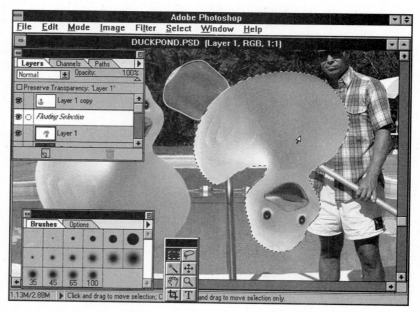

Making Waves

In figure 13.13, we've zoomed in to the pool to get a better look at one of the many reflections. It's apparent that there is some distortion in the reflection of the umbrellas, making this a perfect area to examine before creating similar distortions in the reflection of the duck.

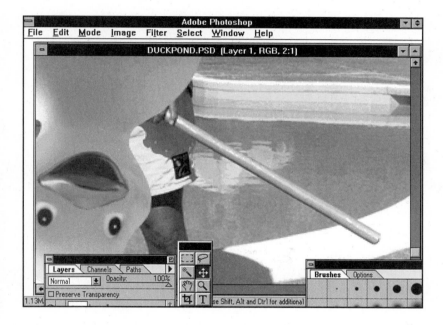

Figure 13.13

Waves are evident in the reflections of trees and the poolside umbrellas.

For the finished image to embody the same image details around the duck as those found in the original image, you must distort the duck on Layer 1 to simulate the rippling effect found in the reflections of the trees, the floating depth markers, and the umbrellas. To accomplish this, Photoshop's Wave filter can be set to generate mild, horizontal-only distortions of the duck image, similar to the natural distortions in the DUCKPOND image display.

Photoshop's filters provide either preview windows or proxy boxes, so you can see a miniature of an image with an effect applied before you issue the Filter command. For all intents and purposes, a *proxy box* is the same as a preview window, except that a proxy box can't provide a zoomed view of the target image—unless you know the trick shown in the next exercise.

In this exercise you use the Wave filter to create a watery reflection of the duck.

Using the Wave Filter

With Rectangular marquee tool, click and drag a loose rectangle around duck on Layer 1	Selects duck. None of the transparent pixels are included in the selection.
Make certain that Preserve Transparency Layer check box is *not* checked for Layer 1	See explanation at the end of this exercise. Preserve Transparency can ruin an effect applied to a Layer.
Choose Filter, Distort, then choose Wave	Displays Wave dialog box.

Because you selected the duck with the Marquee tool, the proxy box in the Wave dialog box shows an enlarged view of the duck. If you had not marquee-selected the duck, the proxy window would have displayed the entire dimensions of the layer, with the duck occupying only a fraction of the available proxy box space. Neat trick, huh?

Choose the following settings for Wave options: Number of **G**enerators: **5**; **W**avelength Min.:**1**, and Max.: **22**; **A**mplitude Min.: **3**, and Max.:**11**; **S**cale Horiz.: **100**%, and Vert.:**0**%; Repeat **e**dge pixels; and Type: S**i**ne	Creates a wave in selection area on Layer 1 that looks similar to the natural reflection distortions in background image.
Click on Randomi**z**e button a few times (see fig. 13.14)	Creates Wave variations, using values between the minimum and maximum you've specified for Wavelength and Amplitude.
When you're happy with image in proxy box; click on OK	Applies wave effect to selection of the duck.
Press Ctrl (Cmd)+D (or choose **S**elect, **N**one), then press **V** (for Move tool)	Deselects floating selection and chooses Move tool.
Press Ctrl (Cmd)+minus	Zooms you out to a 1:2 viewing resolution.
Click and drag distorted duck beneath copy on Layer 1 copy	Move tool moves image areas on a layer, in much the same way a selection tool moves selection marquees.
Position distorted duck so that its bottom falls beneath bottom of duck on copy layer, and what's left of its head falls outside window frame	Positions distorted duck to look like a reflection (see fig. 13.15).
Press Ctrl (Cmd)+S (or choose **F**ile, **S**ave)	Saves your work up to this point.

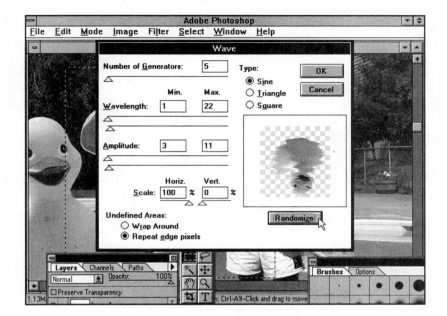

Figure 13.14

Configure the Wave filter to produce a distortion similar to those in the reflections in the DUCKPOND image.

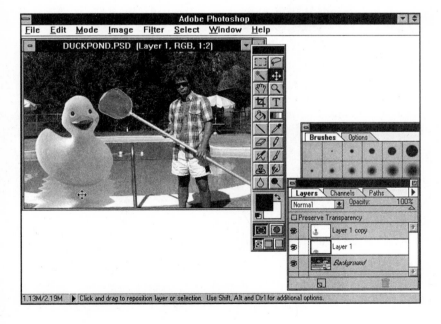

Figure 13.15

Use the Move tool to reposition the image on Layer 1.

Understanding the Preserve Transparency Option

We need to expand upon some of the phenomena that took place in the last exercise, starting with the Preserve Transparency option. In other chapters, you've seen how the Preserve Transparency option on the Layers palette allows editing of colored pixels, but masks transparent regions on a layer. Although this is great for keeping your editing work confined to partially and totally opaque layer areas, it also hinders Photoshop filter effects. Had the Preserve Transparency option been checked in the last exercise, the Wave effect would have proved to be a dud; the displacement of image information would have occurred only within the outline of the duck, and no waves would have been produced outside the original duck's silhouette. Let Photoshop's filters scatter pixels wherever they choose on a layer, and don't use the Preserve Transparency option unless you're trying to achieve an effect even stranger than the one you've learned here.

As to the list of settings recommended for the Wave filter in the last exercise, there is a definite rhyme and reason for the specific values. To qualify these settings:

◆ A *Sine wave* is the rounded, oscillating pattern you've probably seen on the controls of alien spacecraft in bad science fiction movies from the 1950s. This particular waveform creates smooth displacement of image information, most visible on the rounded edges of the waves the duck on Layer 1 now has. Triangle and Square waves also can be generated in the Wave filter. They produce spiked and angular displacements, which look artificial and inappropriate for the effect you need in this assignment.

◆ The Number of Generators field enables you to define how many independent, imaginary sources in the selected image area are "hit" by displacement. The number of generators does not directly correspond to the number of waves the filtered selection will have; rather, it's a fair indicator of how pronounced the Wave effect appears.

◆ The Wavelength minimum and maximum fields specify the "play" in regularity between one wave's *paragee* (the wave's crest) and the next in the overall effect. By setting a minimum of 1 and a maximum of 22, you achieved a fair amount of variation between wave crests, and the distorted duck now looks a lot like the natural reflections in the water.

◆ *Amplitude* is the height of each wave. You set a moderate amount of variation in wave heights in the last exercise. Greater differences in the minimum and maximum amplitude values can simulate reflections in a choppy ocean, so keeping the values small and within a relatively narrow distance of one another helped make the distorted duck a more plausible, serviceable image for the purposes of this assignment.

◆ The Scale controls set the distance across each plane of the image the Wave effect displaces pixels. We recommended that you specify only horizontal displacement for the Wave effect, because horizontal displacement of image reflections in DUCKPOND.PSD are the only ones we can see.

Photoshop truncates (deletes) floating selection image information that falls outside the image window the moment you deselect it if you do any editing after deselecting the image. A layer object (such as the distorted duck) also ceases to be a floating selection the moment you deselect it. With the Move tool, however, you can reposition layer objects to your heart's content, and you can position image areas *outside* the image window, then move them back in without truncating the image. But this works only if you *don't* add or subtract any other object information between repositioning moves. You can move image areas outside the window, then pull them back later, but only by using the Move tool, and only if you *don't* edit the layer between repositioning moves.

Editing the Duck's Reflection in Layer Mask Mode

Because the image elements needed to design the lifeguard's sign are on separate layers, you have at your disposal a very useful feature for removing portions of the distorted duck: the Layer Mask option. A Layer Mask is not visually equivalent to Photoshop's Quick Mask, but it serves an equivalent function. You use painting and selection tools on Layer Masks, and the Layer Mask responds by hiding image details on the target layer or revealing hidden image areas, depending on what you do on the Layer Mask. For a more complete description of Layer Mask properties, see Chapter 5, "It's All Done with Palettes," and Chapter 12, "Correcting an Image."

Basically, a Layer Mask works like this: Adding black foreground color to a layer in Layer Mask mode hides image areas, and lets you peek through to the layers beneath the current layer. Adding white to areas on a Layer Mask while in Layer Mask mode exposes areas that have been hidden with black foreground color. When you create a selection marquee on a Layer Mask, then press the Delete key, the image area inside the marquee is hidden if black is the current background color; if white is the background color, hidden image areas inside the marquee are again displayed.

You have two options as to how a Layer Mask is removed. Discarding the mask returns everything on a layer to its previous condition—not a single pixel on the layer is edited. However, when you choose Apply after choosing Remove Layer Mask, hidden image areas on the layer are deleted.

The areas of the distorted duck that fall outside the pool in the DUCKPOND image are now unnecessary (and someone could slip on them and sue the lifeguard). You can remove them easily by applying a Layer Mask to Layer 1 and "painting" them out. In the next exercise, you'll use the Paths palette to define the edge of the pool, make a selection based on the path, then remove most of the distorted duck areas. You'll also use the Pencil tool as a Layer Mask editing tool, so you'll get a good feel for working with Layer Masks with different types of Photoshop tools.

In this exercise, you use a combination of Photoshop tools to make the reflection of the duck look as though it's in the water, not spilling out of the pool.

Working in Layer Mask Mode

Double-click on Zoom tool, then resize and scroll DUCKPOND image window until you have a good view of edge of pool and duck reflection on Layer 1	Sizes window, and moves viewing resolution to 1:1.
Click on eye icon next to Layer 1 on Layers palette	Hides Layer 1 from view, and displays side of pool around which you need to create a path.
Click on Paths tab on Layers/Channels/Paths group of palettes, then click on Pen tool	Chooses tool with which you'll create a path around edge of pool.
Click and drag Pen tool so that path segment created follows shallow curve of pool's edge	Clicking creates an Anchor point, and dragging "shapes" path segment that follows Anchor point.
Click again when path segment can't be adjusted to fit curve of pool's edge	Creates another Anchor point.

When path segments that Anchor points connect get longer than a few screen inches, they are hard to fit to a path within an image. The best way to create a path along a long curve is to create new Anchor points and path segments every two screen inches or so. Later, you can always delete Anchor points that you don't want or need, by using the Pen– tool.

When you've reached right side of duck on Layer 1 copy, click (don't drag) straight down about one screen inch, then click left to beneath first Anchor point; now complete path by clicking on first Anchor point	Creates closed path that can be used as a model for a selection marquee (see fig. 13.16). Three sides of path are straight path segments because only the top side needs to fit accurately around pool's edge.

In figure 13.16, the Paths palette is detached from the grouped palettes so that you can see the Paths palette as well as the Layers status. As you can also see, the screen is quite cluttered—use this figure as a reference, not necessarily as an example of a well-arranged Photoshop workspace!

Click on Make Selection icon on Paths palette, click on eye icon on Layer 1 title on Layers palette, then click on pop-up	Creates a selection marquee from the path; Layer 1 is visible and is still the target layer. Layer Mask is in position on Layer 1 now.

menu button on Layers palette, and
choose Add Layer Mask

Press **D** (for **d**efault colors icon), then press Alt (Option)+Delete	Fills selection marquee with foreground color; because Layer Mask is active, foreground color in selection hides image areas on Layer 1 within marquee (see fig. 13.17).
Press Ctrl (Cmd)+D	Deselects the selection.
Press **P** (for **P**encil tool), then choose fourth tip in middle row of Brushes palette	Chooses tool for cleaning up rest of duck image that's outside pool.
Set mode to Normal, and Opacity to **100%** on Options palette	Defines characteristics of foreground color that Pencil tool will apply.
Click and drag over image areas outside pool that still have distorted duck image on them	Hides these areas from view (see fig. 13.18).
Choose Remove Layer Mask from pop-up menu on Layers palette	Displays an exclamation dialog box with options to **D**iscard, Cancel, or **A**pply (changes) to layer.
Click on **A**pply	Permanently removes from Layer 1 the image area that was hidden.
Click on the Paths tab on the Layers/Channels/Paths palette, then click and drag the path you created into the Trash icon on the bottom of the Paths palette	You don't need this path anymore.
Press Ctrl (Cmd)+S (or choose **F**ile, **S**ave)	Saves your work up to this point.

You've created the reflection effect, and you've refined the image on Layer 1 so that the reflection seems to be sitting in the pool. Now it's time to concentrate on the "look" of the reflection, and to enhance its realistic qualities.

Adding Realistic Touches to the Duck's Reflection

It's time to pay a little attention to how reflections are cast on the surface of a body of water. The duck reflection is pretty accurate with respect to the way gently moving water reflects an object above it; the reflection contains tiny ripples, which the Wave filter nicely approximated. The Wave filter is an automated routine, however; with a few hand-crafted creative enhancements in the reflection area, you can heighten the effect. In figure 13.19, you can see the Elliptical marquee tool being used to make extremely thin, horizontal marquee selections. The selected areas are then removed (by pressing the Delete or backspace key) to expose water in the background layer image. Pick four or five areas of differing sizes with the Elliptical marquee tool, then delete the selection on Layer 1 to get the same effect.

Figure 13.16

Make an accurate definition of the edge of the pool by creating a path whose outline traces this area.

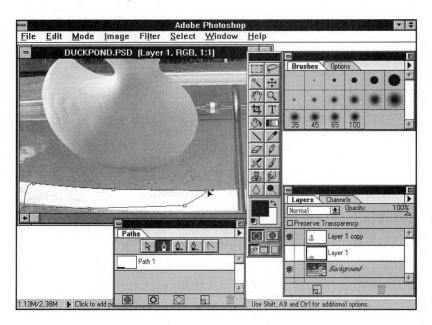

Figure 13.17

Press Alt (Option)+Delete to fill the selection with foreground color, hiding it from view in Layer Mask mode.

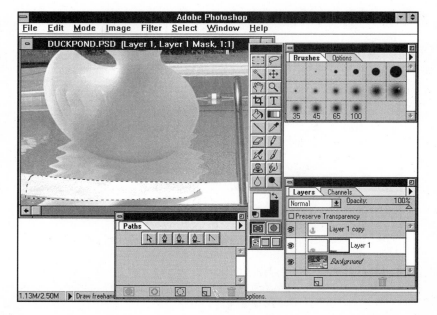

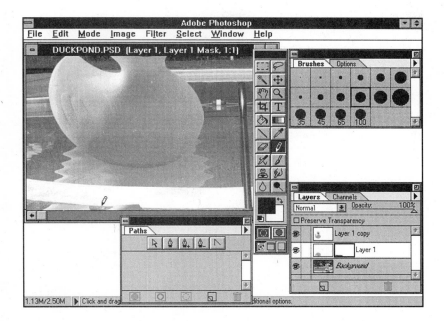

Figure 13.18

Use black foreground color and the Pencil tool to hide image areas when a layer is in Layer Mask mode.

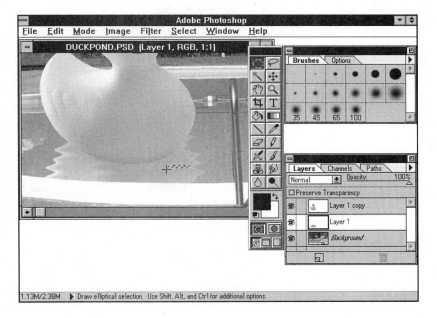

Figure 13.19

Using the Elliptical Marquee tool to remove tiny parts of the reflection on Layer 1 that break up the reflection.

In figure 13.20, you can see a close up of a buoy line that marks the deep end of the pool. Notice what the reflections of the line and the buoys look like. They'll serve as a guide for further modifying the reflection and its relationship to the duck on the Layer 1 copy.

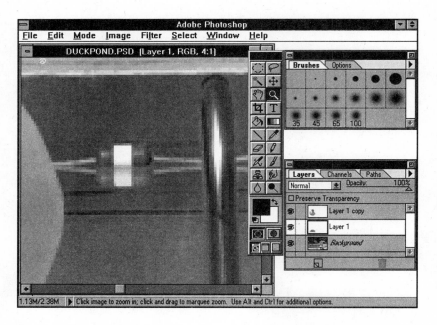

The most prominent quality of everything that's reflected in the pool is that the reflections take on some of the color of the bottom of the pool. This isn't so obvious with the buoys, but the line that ties them together is a light sand color, and its reflective counterpart is a combination of sand color and light turquoise. In the next exercise, you'll copy an area of the turquoise pool into Layer 1 to combine it with the reflection area. You'll use a special compositing mode—Color—to tint the reflection of the duck ever so slightly.

Stop   Compositing modes have to be applied to a floating selection *before* the floating selection is deselected into a layer. Unlike a Layer mode, a mode assigned to a floating selection is permanent and cannot be changed after the selection is deselected.

In the next exercise, you'll see the effect of blending a section of the pool into the distorted duck image on Layer 1. You'll blend the two together, using partial opacity and the Color composite mode.

Using Color Mode to Tint an Area

Click on both the Layer 1 copy and the Layer 1 eye icons	Hides view of both layers so that you can select an area from the background.
Click on Background Layer title on Layers palette	Makes Background the current (target) layer.
With Rectangular marquee tool, click and drag from just above third buoy marker to bottom-left corner of image window	Selects an area large enough to cover the duck reflection on Layer 1 (see fig. 13.21).
Press Ctrl (Cmd)+C (or choose **E**dit, **C**opy)	Copies selection of pool to Clipboard. *Don't* deselect marquee!
Click on eye icons to left of Layer 1 and Layer 1 copy titles on Layers palette's list	Restores view of two layers.

You can click and drag up or down through the eye icon column to restore several views of layers at once.

Click on Layer 1 title on Layers palette, then press Ctrl (Cmd)+V (or choose **E**dit, **P**aste)	Pastes copy of turquoise pool on top of Layer 1 as a floating selection (see fig. 13.22), perfectly aligned with original selection area on Background layer.

Pasted selections are "attracted to" active marquee borders in an image. In this example, the pasted copy happens to be exactly the same size as the marquee, so the copy pastes into Layer 1 in exactly the same position as where you copied it from, right down to the pixel.

Notice that although Layer 1 now has a thumbnail icon of the pasted selection, Floating Selection is a new title above Layer 1, and the title is highlighted, indicating that this is the active image element. This means that the pasted selection doesn't actually *belong* to Layer 1 yet, and that the mode controls on the Layers palette apply to the *compositing mode* of the floating selection, and not to the mode you can assign to an overall Layer.

Choose Color from modes drop-down list on Layers palette, then click and drag Opacity slider to about **30%**	Pasted-in area takes on some of the color of turquoise pool, but duck reflection retains most of its color, and all of its visual detail.

Color mode tints the area on which you place a floating selection with the hue and amount of saturation the floating selection has, but preserves the brightness values of the image area the floating selection is composited into. See Chapter 17, "The Wonderful World of Black and White," for more information on the Color painting and editing mode.

Press Ctrl (Cmd)+D (or choose **S**elect, **N**one), then press Ctrl (Cmd)+S (or choose **F**ile, **S**ave)	Deselects floating selection and saves your work up to this point.

Figure 13.21

*Copy an area of
the pool to use as
a color tint for the
duck reflection on
Layer 1 (presently
hidden).*

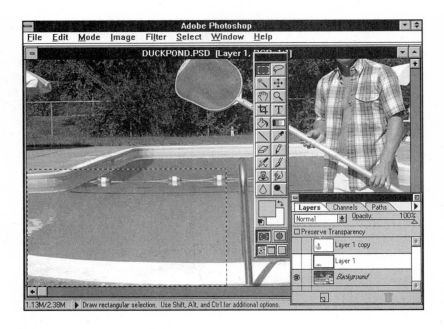

Figure 13.22

*Use Color mode to
composite the
floating selection
into the duck
reflection image
on Layer 1.*

The duck reflection is now tinted with image information copied from the Background layer, and because the floating selection was *composited* (blended) into the existing color pixels on Layer 1, the fusion of image areas is permanent. You'll notice that after you deselected the pool area, the mode on the drop-down list and the opacity reverted to those properties assigned to Layer 1.

Playing with a Second Property of Image Reflections

The duck's reflection on Layer 1 appears to have the correct color cast now, but something is amiss with the duck, and needs to be addressed. An examination of the buoy marker in the pool revealed that the buoy's reflection is tinted with color from beneath the water. But the reflection also *obscures any portion of the buoy that's submerged*. When the sun hits a transparent, reflective surface at an angle that displays strong reflections to the viewer, the reflection destroys the transparent property of the water, and you see more of what's reflected into it than what's beneath the water.

At present, such is not the case with the lifeguard's unwanted companion. The duck looks lighter than water, because CMCD photographed the duck perched on seamless white paper, not sinking into it, as it would were it floating on water. The solution is to remove a portion of the duck's bottom to suggest that part of the duck is submerged and hidden by its own reflection.

The area you'll remove from the duck image on Layer 1 copy needs to be arcing downward, to suggest the following:

◆ That the viewer is at a superior angle to the duck.

◆ That surface tension and the cohesion factor of water exist in this manufactured situation, and that the water is offering slight resistance around the surface to its displacement by the volume of the duck.

Water does this. Trust us.

In the next exercise, you learn the easy way to further integrate the duck into the pool scene. You'll use the Paths palette to define a smooth, accurate selection area that needs to be deleted on Layer 1 copy.

Creating a Sitting Duck

Click on Layer 1 Copy title on Layers palette	Makes layer with duck on it the current (target) layer.
With Pen tool on Paths palette, click an anchor point to left of duck, about 1/2 screen inch above very bottom of duck	Sets first anchor point for path you'll create around duck's bottom.

continues

continued

Press Shift while clicking a second anchor point to right of duck	Creates a straight path segment between first and second anchor points.

Holding the Shift key while you click anchor points constrains the resulting path segment to an angle of 45° (and multiples of 45°) along the width and height axes of the bitmap plane of an image. In the last step, this created a path segment parallel to the horizon of the image.

Click straight down and beneath duck's bottom, click left to beneath first anchor point, then close path by clicking on first anchor point	Creates a four-sided polygon whose interior encompasses bottom of duck.
Click on Pen+ tool, then click an Anchor point in middle of arc created by duck on first path segment you created	Places an anchor point in middle of horizontal path segment.
Press down-arrow key several times	Moves middle, selected anchor point down by one pixel for every keystroke.

When you add an anchor point to a straight path segment, you change the property of the path segment, and both new segments become curved. When you have a shallow arc as the top side of the path, as shown in figure 13.23, stop pressing the down-arrow key.

Click on Make Selection icon, then click on a nonhighlighted area of Paths palette list	Makes a selection based on path, and hides path from view.
Press Delete key	Removes bottom of duck so that it appears to be partially submerged (see fig. 13.24).
Click and drag Work Path title into Trash icon, then click on Layers palette	Deletes superfluous path, and displays view of layers in DUCKPOND image.
Press Ctrl (Cmd)+D (or choose **S**elect, **N**one), then press Ctrl (Cmd)+S (or choose **F**ile, **S**ave)	Deselects floating selection and saves your work up to this point.

You can reposition anchor points on paths as precisely as you can marquee selections, by using the keyboard's arrow keys to nudge an anchor by one pixel per keystroke. Also, as with marquee selections, by holding down the Ctrl (Cmd) key while you press an arrow key, you can make a selected anchor point travel in the direction of the arrow key by 10 pixels.

To move more than one anchor point at a time, press Shift while clicking on the anchors you want to move, then press the arrow keys.

New Riders Publishing
INSIDE
SERIES

Figure 13.23

Pressing Shift while clicking anchor points with the Pen tool ensures that the path segments you create are at multiples of 45°.

Figure 13.24

Remove the marquee area on Layer 1 copy by pressing the Delete key.

Tip

When you want to add an anchor point to an existing, closed path, make certain that you have the Pen+ tool chosen. Clicking on a closed path with the Pen tool does not add an Anchor point, although it may appear this way on-screen.

Clicking an Anchor point on a closed path using the Pen tool begins a new path.

Integrating the Reflection with the Duck

The buoy is the only object in the original image that's actually submerged in the pool, but it provides valuable image information about how the area where object and reflection meet should look. Light is not reflected as much where the buoy meets its reflection; consequently, there's a darkish band at the water's horizon where buoy and reflection meet.

It's not necessary yet to merge the layers in this image to slightly darken the area where duck meets reflection. In fact, we've been holding off on merging layers, because the last step to editing the reflection is to decrease the opacity of the layer it's on. Accurately performing all the editing you've done in this chapter to the reflection on Layer 1 would have been difficult if you'd assigned the layer a blending mode and opacity earlier in the assignment. Because layers that have special modes react to editing and painting according to the mode's properties, and often produce unexpected results, it's usually a good idea to keep a layer in normal mode until all the elements on the layer have been edited—then you can experiment with a particular blending mode.

In the next exercise, you'll see how to create the right amount of shading at the edges of the duck and its reflection, to bring this area together.

Creating an Interlayer Effect

Click on Layer 1 title in Layers list	Makes Layer 1 the current layer for editing. This is where duck's reflection is.
Press **O** (for Toning Tool), then choose Burn from Options palette's drop-down list	An alternative way to select Burn tool from Toning tools.
Choose Midtones from drop-down list on Options palette, and click and drag Opacity slider to about **30%** Exposure	Chooses tonal region in image that will be most affected by Burn tool.

The current Brush tip should still be the 35-pixel one. If it isn't, click on this tip on the Brushes palette.

Click and drag a single stroke across area where duck appears to meet its reflection	Slightly darkens area on Layer 1. Layer 1 copy isn't affected by Burn tool stroke.
Click and drag a second stroke across same area	Darkens image area on Layer 1 so it's more noticeable.
Click on Layer 1 Copy title on Layers palette	Chooses layer with duck on it as target layer for editing.
Click and drag once across bottom edge of duck	Saturates and decreases brightness along bottom of duck (see fig. 13.25).

The greater an area is saturated with color, the more noticeable the effect of the Burn tool. For this reason, the reflection image area could take two strokes with the Burn tool, whereas only a single stroke darkened the edge of the more saturated image of the duck on the Layer 1 copy.

Press Ctrl (Cmd)+S (or choose **F**ile, **S**ave)	Saves your work up to this point.

Figure 13.25

Use the Burn tool on different layers to bring different images together in brightness values.

Adding the Finishing Touches

There is a point in any assignment when you need to stop for a moment, evaluate your work, and seriously consider when you think a piece is finished. We're almost at this point in the lifeguard assignment, but there are a few adjustments you can make, little touches that can help take the viewer's mind off the artificial qualities of the design. For instance, brighter areas in water tend to display shimmering highlights, and we have none of those yet. Also, the duck on the Layer 1 copy is a little too sharp around the image edges to fit perfectly into the DUCKPOND image; the focus of the rest of the image is a teensy bit softer than the duck's edges. This, too, can be corrected in a few steps. And because the reflection is nothing more than a distorted copy of the original duck, the reflection, too, has edges that smack of photo foolery.

In the next exercise, you'll address these problem areas and prepare the image for merging the layers together, a good last step to make the image file one that's compatible with other applications and to send to service bureaus that might not have Photoshop 3.

In this exercise, you use a mixed bag of editing steps to remove some of the telltale signs of image retouching in the DUCKPOND.PSD image, and make folks wonder who owns such a large tub toy.

Softening the Look of Composite Work

Click on Layer 1 title on Layers palette, then choose Dodge from Tool drop-down list on Options palette	Chooses duck's reflection layer and the tool for lightening image areas' tonal values.
Click and drag short strokes in duck reflection below area you burned in earlier (see fig. 13.26)	Adds a luminous, shimmering quality to duck reflection, similar to highlights in water.

Treat the Dodge tool like a physical paintbrush that has a little too much paint on it. A quick flip here and there in the duck reflection area creates tiny pools of lightened areas. Don't click and drag as though you were trying to remove a stain!

With Rectangular marquee tool, click and diagonal-drag a marquee that goes completely around duck's reflection	Selects all color pixels on transparent layer.
Choose Filter, Blur, then choose Blur	Averages difference between neighboring pixels of different color values, and creates semitransparent pixels along edge of reflection image, softening it.

Because the Blur filter averages the difference between neighboring pixel values, this filter creates semitransparent pixels along the border between opaque and transparent pixels, as shown in figure 13.27.

Press Ctrl (Cmd)+D (or choose **S**elect, **N**one)	Deselects marquee selection on Layer 1.
Click on Layer 1 copy title on Layers palette	Makes duck image the current editing layer.
With Zoom tool, marquee zoom into a 2:1 viewing resolution around duck's head	This area needs some edge softening.
Press **R** (for Blu**r** tool), then set Options palette to Normal mode, and about 20% Pressure	Chooses Blur tool, and specifies mode and strength at which you apply the effect.
Click on Sample Merged check box on Options palette, then choose Brushes tip at far left of middle row on Brushes palette	Enables Blur tool to sample from all exposed image Layers to blur Layer 1 copy image, and sets tip of Blur tool to a size that creates subtle changes in image.

You don't actually want to blur the entire edge of the duck—you only want to soften the focus of perhaps one or two pixels along the outline. The tip you'll use is five pixels in diameter; if you run it across the edge of the duck image, the Blur tool will reach only about two or three pixels into the duck's edge.

Click and drag along areas of duck's outline that display sharpest contrast against Background layer	Softens contrast between pixels in Background layer pixels and those in Layer 1 copy (see fig. 13.28).

Notice the focus of the edge pixels of the insect skimmer against the foliage. The skimmer's in perfect focus, yet the pixels that make up its edge are a little diffuse at this viewing resolution. Create the same sort of focus along the duck's edge, using the Blur tool, and don't use more than one or two strokes to do so.

Click and drag over other areas that display too much edge contrast between duck and background	Blur tool softens contrast of pixels that make up edge.

Don't feel compelled to trace around the entire duck outline. Only certain areas require a little blurring. If you blur all the way around the duck, it will look as artificial as if the entire duck periphery displayed sharp edges and harsh contrast.

Press Ctrl (Cmd)+S (or choose **F**ile, **S**ave)	Saves your work up to this point.

Figure 13.26

Add some luminance to the duck's reflection with one or two brief strokes of the Dodge tool.

Figure 13.27

Use the Blur filter to remove a minor amount of focus from the duck's reflection.

Figure 13.28

Use the Blur tool on a few edge areas that display strong contrast against the background image.

When you add an element from another image to a composition, there is a fine line to walk between too much image detail and too little. How much image information you blur, or remove, is a matter of trusting your artist's eye, but a scan or a PhotoCD image generally contains less actual image detail per pixel than one would guess. The eye pieces together image information as part of the mind's recognition process, and the viewer's eye is an inquisitive one. Sharp image edges within a composite photograph call attention to their artificial placement, and avoiding them is a must. By learning some of the techniques in this chapter, you can achieve the right blend of image focus and image integration to make a selection appear as though it *belongs* to an image, and is not simply pasted on top of a background.

Using a Layer Mode for Merging Layers

Before you choose the Flatten Image command for the DUCKPOND.PSD image, Layer 1 should be assigned an opacity and a mode in which it's composited into the background layer. Layers are like floating selections in that each layer on an image can be assigned qualities before it's blended into a background. The main difference between compositing layers and compositing floating selections is that you can preview a layer's mode and opacity now, the next time you open the PSD image, or the Tuesday after Father's Day, and change your mind and respecify the layer's settings. Changes made to an image are permanent only after you've used the Flatten Image or Merge Layers command. Floating selections take advantage of Photoshop's modes, too, as you saw earlier with the selection of the turquoise pool, but the moment you deselect a floating selection, it becomes part of an image layer, the compositing mode and opacity are a permanent change, and you cannot refloat the selection in a different Photoshop session to respecify a mode or undo your work.

Therefore, it's a good idea now to evaluate how you want the duck's reflection to be composited into the Background layer. The authors experimented with several modes, and found that while Overlay and Hard Light posed interesting design effects for the blend, Normal mode gave the most realistic results. The reason Normal might be your best choice for Layer 1 is that Normal mode doesn't blend together the layer colors and the background colors. In Normal mode, layers that are merged retain their original color qualities. You've seen in this chapter that a mode such as Color influences the target layer by tinting it with predominant color values found in a selection you paste into the layer. The same holds true when a layer is merged to the background image—Overlay mode mixes layer color with background color to arrive at a different color. See Chapter 5, "It's All Done with Palettes," for a detailed explanation of what each blending and painting mode does in Photoshop.

You can definitely achieve some interesting effects by assigning a layer a particular mode, but this chapter's assignment requires a modicum of realism in the reflection you've synthesized. Therefore, you'll use Normal mode in the next exercise, along with a partial opacity for Layer 1, to keep color values on both the background image and Layer 1 basically the same while allowing some of the original pool detail to show through in the final image.

Merging Layers in Unique Modes

Layer 1 copy should still be current (target) layer	Layer to which you'll assign an opacity.
Click and drag Opacity slider on Layers palette to about **75%** (see fig. 13.29)	Decreases opacity of duck's reflection, allowing some of background layer's image detail and color to show through.
Click on Layers palette's pop-up menu button, then choose Flatten Image	Merges all layers that are visible (that have an eye icon next to their title).
Choose File, Save As, then name file **SIGN.TIF**, choose TIFF (*.TIF) from Save File as Format **T**ype field, find a good hard disk location for the file, then click on OK	Saves merged image in TIFF format, which can be used in different applications on both Macintosh and IBM/PC computers.

You still have the DUCKPOND.PSD image on your hard drive, with layers intact. If you want to further edit the image, you have the separate elements in the image as a PSD file.

Figure 13.29

Before merging layers, assign Layer 1 a partial opacity to allow some of the background layer detail to show through.

If you look ahead to Chapter 22, "Virtual Reality: The Ingredients of Dreamwork," (or look back to Chapter 9, "Using Type in Photoshop"), you'll get an idea of the steps used to add a headline to the lifeguard's sign (see fig. 13.30). We increased the Canvas size (by choosing **I**mage, Canvas **S**ize) by about 1/2", added a flat color fill, then created drop-shadow lettering using the techniques covered in Chapter 22.

Mike the lifeguard was thrilled to receive the finished sign. He posted it posthaste, and it took care of his pool problems. For a while.

As fate would have it, an ichthyologist became a member of the pool, and decided to bring *his* pool "toys" along. With a little research, we found an appropriate stock image (it's in the CHAP13 subdirectory of the Bonus CD), and created the sign in figure 13.31 for Mike.

Have fun with the SHARK.TIF image on the Bonus CD, and use the techniques in this chapter to create the sign in figure 13.31. You might want to work quickly, though—Mike is understandably anxious.

Figure 13.30

The finished sign for the lifeguard— realistic, overstated, and to the point!

Figure 13.31

An ichthyologist studies sharks.

Enhancing Images

Many things in life cannot be controlled—the weather, deadlines, or when opportunity strikes. In the field of photography, you're often forced to take an image under less than ideal circumstances.

For example, we wanted a photograph of a lakeside gazebo to use as a stock image, but had only one opportunity to take the picture—on a day it had rained. Although the sun was out, the sky and light were gray and hazy. This dreary, overcast element ruins the composition in what could have been an enchanting picture. The bright side of this story (and this image) is that it's an ideal example to be used as an assignment in this book! If this "nice landscape/crummy weather" scenario sounds familiar, you're reading the right chapter—it holds the remedy for this all-too-common situation.

You may not be able to change the deadline or the weather, but with Photoshop, you can enhance a lackluster picture to compensate for prevailing conditions at the time of the photo session. With a little ingenuity and Photoshop's features, you can add life and drama to *any* boring photo and still meet a deadline.

This Chapter's Assignment

The photo that needs a bit of lift is PARKBLAH.PSD. As you can see from figure 14.1 (or by opening the image from the Bonus CD), the sky is a uniform, dull gray. Although the water has some interesting movement and tree reflection, its overall color is also too monotonous to be inviting. The image has many charming elements, but the lighting makes you want to put on a sweater.

Figure 14.1

PARKBLAH.PSD is an example of good composition, but poor color and lighting in an image.

The source of this image is a PhotoCD opened in the CIELAB color mode in Photoshop. The image was cropped, and the Levels command used to adjust the tonal levels in the image. All PhotoCD images (and most images acquired by more conventional scanning) need to have Levels adjustments made to their white and black points and to the image gamma. Adjusting the tonal levels in PARKBLAH.PSD vastly improved the contrast and detail in the image, but did little for the sky. When no image detail exists in an area, no amount of tonal adjustment can *create* detail. Although the tonal adjustments made in PARKBLAH.PSD were important (the better an image is to start with, the better your finished piece will be), these corrections are only a small part in the process of adding visual interest to the image. See Chapter 3, "Color Theory and the PhotoCD," for the scoop on how to work with PhotoCD images and the tonal corrections they require. See Chapter 7, "Restoring an Heirloom Photograph," for more information on making tonal adjustments in scanned images.

The Action Plan

To change the PhotoCD image used in this chapter's assignment from blah to wow, you need to enhance each area of the image—the sky, the land, and the water. You will work on each of these elements separately. The plan for this image is to add drama to the sky, warmth to the scene, and reflections to the water. To add both

drama to the sky and warmth to the image, you must replace the original sky with a more dramatic one from a different photo.

The stock photograph, SKYDARK.PSD, has a very dramatic sky. The problem with this photo is that the sky image is dramatic, but was taken near sunset on a cold fall day. For this sky to integrate successfully with PARKBLAH.PSD, the predominant colors need to change as well as the perceived time of day. Globally changing the colors in the sky poses much less of a problem than in images that contain people or other objects that the viewer expects to look a certain way. Additionally, by lightening the overall color scheme and brightness in a sky, you can to some degree change the apparent time of day. This trick is almost impossible to do with land-based images because of the complexity of shadows and reflections.

After the SKYDARK image is transformed into a dramatic afternoon sky, you bring it into the PARKBLAH.PSD image. To do this convincingly, you must make an accurate selection border around the original sky in PARKBLAH.PSD and remove it. Photoshop 3's Layers and Layer Mask features make this a much easier and forgiving process than in previous versions of the program.

A warm sky casts colored light on everything, so your next step is to raise the "temperature" of the land areas within the PARKBLAH.PSD image so that they display the warmth they should. As with the sky, Photoshop's Color Balance command is ideal to gently shift the color scheme of the land to warmer colors.

The water gets a treatment all its own. Water should reflect both the surrounding land and the sky. Warming up the water and providing reflections that make the image plausible is easy when you use the Layers Opacity feature and the Layer Mask to create a partial selection.

For the plan to work smoothly, you must create accurate selection borders that define the three areas: sky, land, and water. You also must balance the colors in the images that make up the components of the image.

Evaluating Stock Images

You can take a number of approaches to enhance the sky in PARKBLAH. One is to accept the image area "as is" and change its color to a nicer, more vibrant blue. The color might look better, but it would still lack any interesting detail. Another approach is to use Photoshop's new Clouds or Difference Clouds filters to generate a new sky. You can see how these filters work in Chapter 11, "Using Paths, Selections, and Layers." The Clouds and Difference Clouds filters can produce good effects, but they don't work well with the PARKBLAH.PSD image (we tried). The sky is a large focal point in this image, and the synthetic nature of Photoshop's Clouds becomes too obvious when contrasted by actual photographic source material. The third approach, the one taken in this chapter, is to replace the blah sky with a dynamic, natural sky from a different photo.

Tip

Having a collection of photos available, whether they are stock photos you have purchased or photos you have taken, is invaluable in Photoshop imaging work. Often, you need to replace an element in your current composition—a sky, a tree, a pair of hands—and a stock image is the best place to find these replacement parts. With a varied collection of source material, and Photoshop's capability to edit this material, your tool kit for any imaging assignment is pretty complete.

Figure 14.2. is the "private stock" sunset photo that you will use in the upcoming exercises. The predominant colors in it are dark blues and cold yellows. This picture will work beautifully with the park photo because its *visual content* is good. When you sift through source material, you have to use your eye and your judgment to evaluate the composition and the details in a photo. Don't be put off by a photo because it's too dark or light, or because it has the "wrong" colors. All this can be changed in Photoshop.

Figure 14.2

Color correction will make this image better fit into PARKBLAH.PSD.

SKYDARK.PSD (RGB, 1:2)

Note

A trip to the **I**mage, **I**mage Size command would show that SKYDARK.PSD's height and width dimensions are larger than PARKBLAH.PSD's. The difference in dimensions gives you room to move the sky after it's placed on a layer in the PARKBLAH image. It is better to bring the sky into PARKBLAH uncropped. It is often difficult to tell what the most interesting sections of an image are before you see it in place within the target image.

New Riders Publishing
INSIDE
SERIES

Having the image you are transplanting a different height and width from the image you are pasting into is usually a good idea, but the two images should never have different resolutions. SKYDARK.PSD and PARKBLAH.PSD both have a resolution of 150 dpi. Photoshop automatically changes the resolution of the floating selection image to match the resolution of the background image. This throws any image dimension-measuring you've performed down the drain because image resolution has an inverse relationship to image dimensions. You may think that a 72 pixels per inch selection fits wonderfully into a 3 1/2-inch space, only to find the selection much smaller because the image you measured from and pasted to has a resolution of 150 pixels per inch.

Whenever you assemble an image from different sources, always make sure that all the sources have the same resolution.

Changing the Color Scheme in an Image

The first step in park restoration is to get a new sky ready for transplant. On the agenda is color-correcting and flipping the image.

Using Your Own Aesthetic Judgment

Keep two things in mind before you begin: All Photoshop settings suggested in the exercise are arbitrary, in that they were determined by the authors' artistic eyes and judgment. When you do this kind of work in your own assignments, trust your *own* eye. The second point to keep in mind is that the trees and the very bright spots above the tree line in SKYDARK.PSD will not be visible in the final composite image. These areas won't be cropped out of the SKYDARK.PSD image, but rather, they will be concealed behind the park scene on a Photoshop layer above the scene. Focus on what happens to the image above these areas.

Doing a Balancing Act with Photoshop

Your first stop on the Image, Adjust menu is Color Balance. You want to shift SKYDARK's cold colors to warmer colors so that you can see better the image detail you have to work with! When you use the Color Balance command, you are shifting the Red, Green, and Blue components of an RGB image toward or away from their color complements—*complementary colors* are those defined by a combination of two primary values. The Color Balance feature is very useful for changing an entire color scheme without changing the *tonality*—the relationship of the brightness values of pixels in an image. With the Color Balance command, you can remove an undesired color cast in an image or change the whole lighting scheme, producing a new version of an image. Creating different color schemes from the same image produces results not unlike a print dress or a wallpaper pattern available in the same design but in different color combinations. You have quite a bit of control with this command because the three brightness ranges of the image are addressed individually: the shadows, midtones, and highlights. In the next exercise, you make changes in all three areas.

Warming up the Sky

Choose **F**ile, **O**pen SKYDARK.PSD from the Bonus CD. Drag it by its title bar into the bottom left corner of the workspace	Positions the image so that you can see the image and open dialog boxes.
Press Ctrl(Cmd)+Y (**I**mage, **A**djust, C**o**lor Balance)	Displays Color Balance dialog box.
Check the **P**review and the Preserve **L**uminosity check boxes if they're not already checked	Displays changes as you make them and protects the current tonal values.
Click on the **S**hadows radio button; then enter the following values in the **C**olor Levels: input boxes, from left to right: **–20**, **+2**, **+22** (see fig. 14.3) (or use the sliders to perform the same actions)	Increases amount of cyan and blue; touch of green lightens the new mix; blue in shadow regions of image; produces much bluer, more day-like color scheme in the shadows.
Click on the **H**ighlights radio button	Sliders and input boxes move to zero because you haven't made any changes in this region yet. Previous settings to other regions are *not* lost and are still in effect.
Enter the following values in the **C**olor boxes, from left to right: **–17**, **–38**, **+32** (or move the sliders)	Settings increase the amount of Levels: input cyan, magenta, and blue to the highlight areas of the image.
Click on the **M**idtones radio button	Sliders and input boxes move to zero.
Enter the following values in the **C**olor input boxes, from left to right: **–25**, **–5**, **+13** (or you can move the sliders) (see fig. 14.4)	Increases the amount of cyan, and Levels: adds magenta and blue in midtones of the image.

The image is much bluer now, and the highlight clouds have a warm glow. If you like what you see, go on to the next step. If not, feel free to make your own settings to produce the sky of your dreams.

Click on OK	Displays image with the new color scheme.
Choose **F**ile, Sa**v**e As; choose a place on your hard disk for the file; leave the format of the file in Photoshop's PSD format; click on OK	Saves the changed image to hard disk.

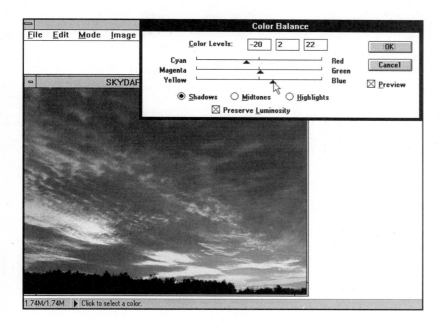

Figure 14.3

Color Balance values are adjusted to alter the color scheme or correct a color cast in an image.

In the preceding exercise, you shifted the color values to produce a much lighter, warmer color balance. The wispy cloud highlights—the predominant element of this sky—changed from a cold yellow to a warm pink-yellow.

Although you made positive alterations to the color scheme, the scene still needs some fine-tuning. In the next exercise, you use the Variations command to fine-tune the adjustments you just made.

Figure 14.4

*Color Balance
can be adjusted
in any one or all
of the tonal
ranges—
Shadows,
Midtones, and
Highlights.*

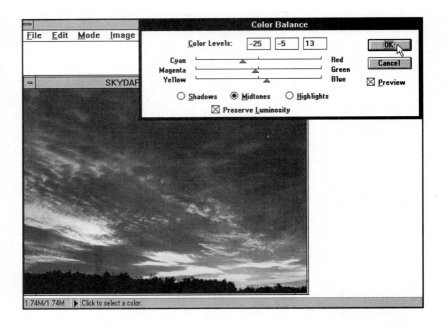

Fine-Tuning with the Variations Command

The Variations command doesn't offer the same level of precision that the Color Balance command does, but it has an important advantage—it simultaneously previews all the possible changes you can make. These previews, called *picks,* are displayed as thumbnails arranged in a fashion that corresponds to the relative positions of colors found on a color wheel. At the hub of the "wheel" is a thumbnail of the *Current Pick*. The Current Pick displays how the image will look if you click on OK and accept any changes you made while in the Variations dialog box. At the top of the screen, the Current Pick is again displayed next to a thumbnail of how the image looked before you entered the Variations dialog box. It's a good thing that it offers this comparison because this dialog box almost entirely fills the screen. You can't really see the current image without moving the Variations dialog box to the side of the screen (by clicking and dragging on the title bar) when using this Photoshop feature.

In addition to controls that affect color balance, Variations also offers similar controls to change brightness. Off to the right of the dialog box are three views; Lighter, Current Pick, and Darker. Saturation in the image can be changed with Variations. Clicking on the Saturation radio button displays picks you can choose to increase or decrease the level of saturation in the image.

Changes are made in this unusual dialog box by clicking on the view that represents the change you want to make. How much change occurs depends on which of the six tick marks on the Fine–Coarse scale the indicator triangle is set. The closer the slider is to Coarse, the more intense the change. This lack of precision makes Variations unsuitable for performing the bulk of your color balance work, but it is useful for performing finishing touches because it gives you a view of alternative choices that you may not have thought of.

If the Show Clipping box is checked, you can tell if the change represented in a pick box produces unwanted clipping in the image. *Clipping* is when too much of something is added to an image, producing ugly flat areas of pure color that wipe out image detail in a photographic image. Photoshop warns if selecting a pick produces clipping in an image by displaying the image area affected in the pick as a hot neon color. You see the clipping warning in some of the choices that we suggest you make, but because the area that is subject to clipping is within the trees at the bottom of SKYDARK.PSD, image clipping in this region of the image will not be noticeable in the finished image. The trees will not show in the PARKBLAH.PSD image.

In the next exercise, you see what alternatives are available to make this image picture perfect by using the Variations command. Remember, feel free to make your own decisions while in this dialog box—the selections the authors thought looked good may not be what your own artistic sense dictates.

Fine-Tuning with Variations

Choose Image, Adjust, Variations; check the Clipping check box (if it is not already checked)	Displays Variations dialog box and then Show sets it to display Clipping (see fig. 14.5).
Click on the Shadows radio button and move the indicator triangle to the center of the Fine–Coarse scale	Picks display what medium amount of change will occur in the shadows of the current image.
Click on the More Blue pick	Adds medium amount of blue to the shadows. Current Pick image changes to reflect the addition of blue; Original Pick remains the same.

Wait a moment while all the picks update their displays.

Click on the More Magenta pick	Adds more magenta to the shadows of Current Pick; all views except Original update.

continues

continued

Click on the **M**idtones radio button and move the indicator triangle to one tick mark to the right of Fine on the Fine–Coarse scale	Picks display what small amount of change would look like if applied to the midtones of the Current Pick. Changes are cumulative; the Current Pick displays changes proposed up to that point.
Click on the More Magenta pick	Adds more magenta to the midtones of Current Pick.
Click on the H**i**ghlights radio button and move the indicator triangle to the Fine tick mark on the left of the Fine–Coarse scale	Picks display what smallest amount of change looks like in the Highlights regions if applied to the Current Pick.

If you think you might reuse these settings on another, similar image, or if you think you may want to use them again with a fresh copy of this image at a later date, you can save settings to your hard disk. You do so in the following step.

Click on the **S**ave button; enter **SKY.AVA** in the File Name text box. Windows users must be sure to use the AVA extension, otherwise Photoshop cannot recognize the file; choose a drive and directory for the file. Click on OK (see fig. 14.6)	Names and saves the settings to your hard disk. The PHOTOSHOP\CALIBRAT subdirectory (folder) is a good place to store the file.

Choose a name you will associate with this image. Macintosh users can use long file names and don't need to include the AVA, but you should include a reference to yourself that this is a Variations setting file.

Click on OK	Applies the changes to your image and returns you to Photoshop's workspace.

Now that you can see the changes you made on a full-screen version of the image, you may not be as happy as you thought. If that's the case, immediately press Ctrl(Cmd)+Z (**E**dit, **U**ndo), go back to the Variations dialog box, and make different choices.

Choose **F**ile, Sa**v**e As SKYDARK.PSD to your hard disk	Saves all changes made up to this point to your hard disk.

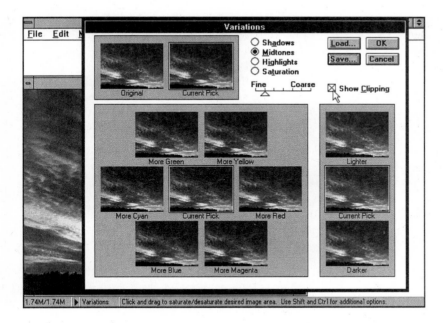

Figure 14.5

The Variations dialog box shows previews (picks) of possible changes you can make; click on a pick to choose it.

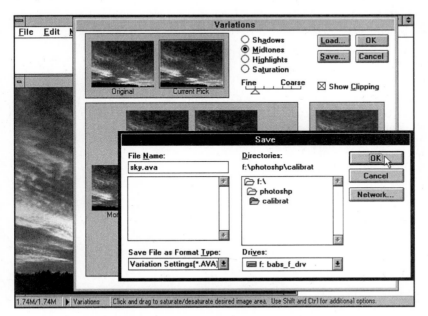

Figure 14.6

Unlike Color Balance settings, Variations settings can be saved and reused in the same or a different image.

Adjusting Saturation

Now that you can see the changes made by the Variations command on a full-screen version of the image, it appears that the image as a whole could use a touch more saturation. These qualities are often difficult to evaluate when looking at the Variations command's thumbnail-sized picks. Increasing the saturation of the entire image makes the colors in the image more intense, and in this case darker. The darkness caused by the increase in saturation can be offset by increasing the lightness of the image.

Photoshop's Hue/Saturation command is just the tool needed for this job. Unlike the other image adjustment commands you've worked with in this chapter, the Hue/Saturation command creates changes to all the tonal regions of the image. This differs from the Color Balance command where you can make entries that affect specific tonal regions. The name of the Hue/Saturation command is somewhat misleading because it also is used to control another image characteristic—*lightness*.

Use the Hue/Saturation command in the next exercise to make the final adjustments to the SKYDARK image:

Intensifying and Lightening an Image

With SKYDARK.PSD open and the active window…

Press Ctrl(Cmd)+U (**I**mage, **A**djust, then **H**ue/Saturation)	The Hue/Saturation dialog box appears.
Place a check mark in the Preview check box and *uncheck* the Colorize check box if they are not already set that way	Enables you to see the effects of the settings you choose in the image before committing to them.

The Colorize mode of the Hue/Saturation command replaces all the different hues in an image with a single hue, which is *not* what you want to do in this exercise. Colorize is usually used to tint a monochrome image. To see an example of when you would want to use this special feature refer to Chapter 22, "Virtual Reality: The Ingredients of Dreamwork."

Enter the following values in the Hue/Saturation dialog box: Hue: **0**, Saturation: **+12**, click Lightness: **+4;** on OK (see fig. 14.7)	Increases both the saturation and the lightness in the image while leaving the hue values in the image untouched.
Press Ctrl(Cmd)+S (**F**ile, **S**ave)	Saves your work up to this point.

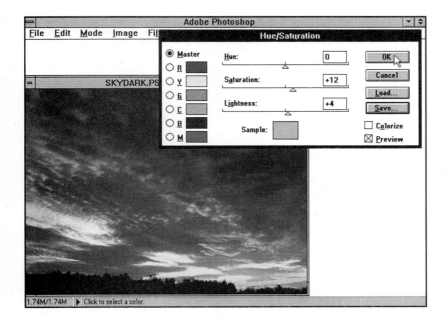

Figure 14.7

The Hue/ Saturation command affects the entire image not just specific tonal regions.

Matching Lighting Conditions

If you look back at figure 14.1, you'll notice that although the lighting is quite flat in the PARKBLAH.PSD image, the light is coming from left to right. The lighting in SKYDARK.PSD, however, transverses from right to left. Matching the direction of the light in both images is necessary to achieve realism. The easiest and least obvious way to match the directions is to flip the sky. Skies have no obvious left–right orientation like man-made landmarks do.

Changing the orientation of an image is a processor-intensive operation. The SKYDARK.PSD image is 1.7 MB, and it may take a moment or two to perform the operation. The next exercise shows you a trick you can use to speed up the operation.

Note In your own assignments, if you need to change the orientation or perform any of Photoshop's many intensive actions, such as applying the Radial Blur filter, on a large image, you may run out of memory resources. Without enough system resources, you cannot perform the desired effect. If this happens to you, you can use an alternative method to perform the action. Instead of asking Photoshop to process the whole image in one gulp, you can apply the effect or filter to one channel of the image at a time. See Chapter 25, "The Film Recorder," for step-by-step instructions on how to do this.

When you have a file open and displayed across your screen, any actions you take usually cause the screen to redraw. Unless you have an ultra-fast system that includes an accelerated video display card, the time it takes to redraw large image files can be stultifying. When you have minimized a file in Photoshop's workspace, it can be selected and acted upon as if it were displayed at a larger size on your screen.

If you make the minimized file the active file in the workspace by clicking on it once, you can perform any Photoshop command that doesn't involve the use of a mouse within the image area. Commands such as **S**elect, **A**ll; **E**dit, **C**opy; and **I**mage, **F**lip work just fine while the file is displayed as an icon. When you issue one of these commands, Photoshop processes the command you requested but doesn't have to redraw the image to the screen, which can save you substantial time if you don't need to immediately see the effects of the command, or when there really isn't anything to see. Copying a selection from an image is a good example of when you can live with a miniature of an image displayed onscreen. Whenever you do maximize an image, you can see the effect of any actions you made while the image was minimized. The representation of the image on the Layers and Channels palette (the image icons on the palette list) are, however, redrawn so that you can be assured that an intended effect took place.

In the next exercise, you flip the image while it is icon-sized, and then save and close the image. When it comes time later in the assignment to bring the file into the PARKBLAH.PSD image, the file will open and display the change in orientation you made.

Flipping an Image

Click on the Minimize/Maximize button in the upper-right hand corner of the image; Macintosh users should click and drag the Resize box to reduce size of the image window as far as possible	Reduces the file down to an icon in the lower left hand corner of Photoshop's workspace.

Because SKYDARK.PSD is the only image in your workspace, it is still the active image.

Choose **I**mage, **F**lip, then choose **H**orizontal and vice versa	Mirrors the image so that what was on the right is now on the left

This may take a moment or so. You'll know when the process has been completed when the hour glass (or stopwatch) turns back into an arrow. Notice that the image icon on the Channels palette changes to reflect the change in orientation.

Press Ctrl(Cmd)+S (**F**ile, **S**ave); press Ctrl(Cmd)+W (**F**ile, **C**lose)	Saves your work up to this point and closes the file. You're done with it for now.

With the sky all set, it's time to move on to the PARKBLAH.PSD target image and make a place for the wonderful, warm sky you created.

Adding Layers to a Target Image

PARKBLAH.PSD is a one-layer image; the only layer it has is the background. If you were to delete any area of the image in its current state, the area you removed would be filled by opaque pixels. To tap into the power of layers and their transparent properties, you need to transfer the PARKBLAH.PSD image to a layer. When the image is on a layer, the sky can be removed. Doing this cuts a "hole" in the image, which means that you can slip the sky (which is on another layer) behind the park scene. When the sky is on a layer that is below the layer the park is on, the new sky shows through the opening you made in the park image. Collectively, the two layers appear as one image.

In the next exercise, you create the new layers in the PARKBLAH.PSD image that are needed to accomplish the task of integrating the two images.

Duplicating the Background Layer

Open PARKBLAH.PSD from the CHAP14 subdirectory (folder) of the Bonus CD that comes with this book	This is the target image for the SKYDARK.PSD image. You will work with this image through the remainder of the chapter.
Press F7 (Macintosh: F11) to display the Layers palette if it is not already open in your workspace. Click on the pop-up menu button to the right of the tabs (the black arrow)	Displays the Layers palette and the pop-up menu associated with this palette.
Choose Duplicate Layer from the pop-up menu; accept the default name for the layer and destination document; click on OK (see fig. 14.8)	Creates a new layer in the image that contains a copy of the background image.

The important difference between the new layer (background copy) and the background, is that when image areas are deleted on the Background Copy layer, the areas are filled with transparent pixels rather than opaque ones. If you have the Transparency Options (File, Preferences, Transparency) set at default values, transparent pixels are marked on a layer with gray and white checkerboard patterns. See Chapter 5, "It's All Done with Palettes," for more information on setting up transparency settings.

continues

continued

Click on the New Layer icon on the bottom left of the Layers Palette; click on OK	Creates a new layer with both a default name (Layer 1) and characteristics.
Click and drag the Layer 1 title on the Layers palette and drop it on top of the Background Layer title (see fig. 14.9)	Positions the layer between the Background layer and the Background Copy layer.

When you add the Background Copy layer, which contains a pixel-for-pixel copy of the Background layer, the amount of information Photoshop has to keep in memory doubles from 1.15 to 2.30 MB. Adding Layer 1 doesn't produce a similar effect because right now this layer is empty. This means that Photoshop doesn't have to store any additional information. The original Background layer is unneeded now and can be discarded. This reduces the amount of information Photoshop has to keep track of and makes your work go faster because memory resources are not unnecessarily tied up.

Click and drag the Background layer title into the Trash icon on the bottom right of the Layers palette	When the little hand is over the Trash can, the Trash can displays a dark outline border. Release the mouse button when this border appears, and the layer is deleted from the image.

If you change your mind about deleting a layer, you must press Ctrl(Cmd)+Z (**E**dit, Undo) immediately to restore the layer to the image.

You now have two layers in the image; the top layer is the Background Copy layer, and Layer 1 (which is currently empty) is on the bottom, as shown in figure 14.10. Deleting the Background layer reduces the amount of information Photoshop stores in memory back to the original 1.3 MB figure. Eliminating layers when they are no longer needed is an important practice to develop.

Choose **F**ile, Sa**v**e As and save the file to your hard disk, using the same file name and file format	You are offered Photoshop's PSD format for the file format because that is the only format that keeps layer information intact.

With the new layers in place, it's time to move on and use them!

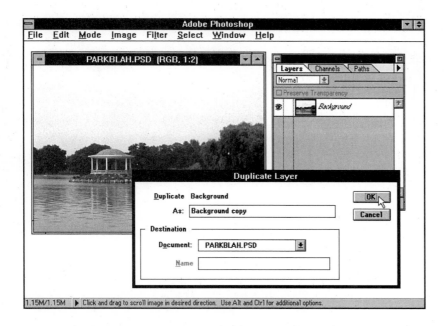

Figure 14.8

Create an identical copy of a layer with the Duplicate Layer command found on the Layers palette pop-up menu.

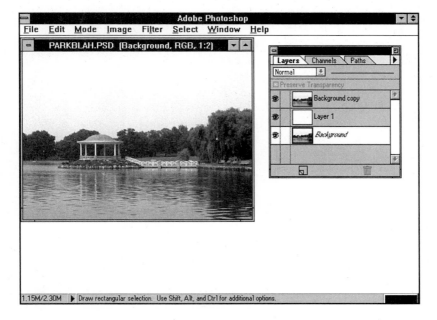

Figure 14.9

The new layer was dragged into a new position between the Background Copy layer and the Background layer.

Figure 14.10

The original Background layer has been deleted making the empty, transparent Layer 1 the bottom layer.

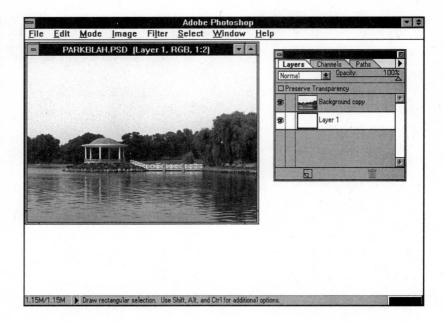

Using Color Range: First Step toward a Magical Sky

The number of unique colors in the PARKBLAH.PSD sky is minimal, which makes the Color Range command the ideal tool for selecting most of the sky in one fell swoop. To make this assignment work, the transition between new sky and the park must look seamless. Seamless integration of image elements hinges on the creation of precise selection borders. You can select into the nooks and crannies where sky meets tree much faster and with greater precision with the Color Range command than with selection tools such as the Magic Wand or the Lasso tool. As you saw in Chapter 12, "Correcting an Image," in which you faced a similar problem, the Color Range command's Fuzziness settings can be used to pick up not only the colors in the sky, but also the areas where the sky pokes through the trees.

Now put this powerful new Photoshop tool through its paces and gather up the sky.

Sampling the Sky with the Color Range Command

With the copy of PARKBLAH.PSD you saved to your hard disk open in the Photoshop workspace…

Click on the Background Copy layer title   Makes it the current and active layer.
on the Layers palette

New Riders Publishing
INSIDE
SERIES

Drag the image into the upper-left hand corner; it should be at a 1:2 viewing resolution	Positions the image so that you can see the image and dialog boxes at the same time.
Choose **S**elect, **C**olor Range; from the Sele**c**t drop-down list, choose Sampled Colors; click on the Selection radio button under the preview window in the dialog box; drag the **F**uzziness slider to about **50**	Your cursor turns into an Eyedropper used to select a color from the image.
Click on the sky in the image window in the workspace	The white areas that appear in the dialog box preview the selected pixels. These are the pixels in the image that match the one you clicked over in the image window.
Click on the Eyedropper+ button in the dialog box; click over several different sections of sky. Stop when the preview window looks similar to figure 14.11	Colors sampled with the Eyedropper+ are added to the selection.

Your preview window may look slightly different depending on where in the sky you clicked with the Eyedropper+. If you selected too much (too much white is displayed within the area occupied by the gazebo, and the lake), switch to the Eyedropper– tool and click over the area that made these areas go white in the preview window. A few white specks in the trees are desired.

Drag the **F**uzziness slider to the left to about **35**; stop when there is only a hint of the gazebo columns and railings to the right *and* the sky area remains quite white; a few scattered pixels in the sky or in the land are OK	Fine-tunes the area that will be included within the selection.
Press Ctrl(Cmd)+spacebar and click over the gazebo roof in the workspace image window until you are at an 8:1 viewing resolution; you can see the roof line clearly	Eyedropper toggles to the Zoom tool and moves you into a magnified view of the roof line.
Click on the Sele**c**tion Preview drop-down list on the dialog box and choose Quick Mask; make sure that the curve of the roof hasn't been eaten into by the selection	A Quick Mask overlay covers the non-selected areas of the image. This is not actually Quick Mask, it just looks like it (see fig. 14.12).
If the curve of the roof line looks intact, click on OK; if not, click the Eyedropper– tool over one of the pixels that is part of the roof; if all looks well, click on OK	The dialog box closes and Photoshop takes a moment to create the selection.

continues

continued

Choose **S**elect, **S**ave Selection; click on OK to accept the default name and location	Saves the selection to an Alpha channel so that it can be recalled if it is accidentally deselected in the next exercise.
Double-click on the Hand tool on the toolbox	Zooms the image out to a 1:2 viewing resolution.

Figure 14.11

The white areas in the proxy window in the Color Range dialog box display selected areas.

Notice little specks of marquee outlines running around on the gazebo and in the water. The Color Range command included these areas because they have the same brightness and color values as the sky. Many of these color values are in fact *reflections* of the sky. Don't worry about them now—when you use the Layer Mask in the next exercise, you can easily remove them from the selection.

Figure 14.12

The Quick Mask overlays the areas not selected.

Refining a Selection with the Layer Mask

Photoshop's Layer Mask is a great way to refine a complex selection. As you saw in previous chapters, when you create a Layer Mask and paint in the Layer Mask with black, image areas are hidden. Painting with white reveals the pixels on the layer associated with the Layer Mask. The Layer Mask can be modified as sort of a preview of editing work; you selectively hide layer image areas through the use of the Layer Mask, and then apply the Layer Mask, which discards the areas you've hidden. Changes you make to your view of a layer while in Layer Mask mode don't become permanent until you choose Remove Layer Mask from the Layers palette's pop-up menu.

In the following exercise, you create a Layer Mask for the Background Copy layer and refine the selection you created with the Color Range command.

Masking Your Way to a Perfect Selection

With the PARKBLAH.PSD image open, the Background Copy layer the active layer, and the selection marquee still in place from the last exercise...

Click on the pop-up menu button and choose Add Layer Mask	A blank icon window with a black border appears to the right of the Background Copy layer.
Press **D** (**d**efault colors), then press **X** (switch colors)	Sets background color to black, which when used in Layer Mask mode, hides image areas.
Press the Delete key (see fig. 14.13)	Transparent checkerboard pattern appears where the sky used to be. Pixels are not actually deleted, but are hidden by the Layer Mask.

Also note that the Layer Mask icon now displays black where pixels are hidden.

Press Ctrl(Cmd)+D (**S**elect, **N**one)	Deselects the selection.
Click on the Layer 1 title; press Ctrl(Cmd)+A (**S**elect, **A**ll)	Layer 1 becomes the active layer. And you've selected the entire transparent layer.

It may appear that you've selected the layer that contains the park, but you haven't. Layer 1 is the active layer, and any actions you perform affect only Layer 1.

Press F6 (Macintosh: F10); then click on the Swatches tab of the Picker/Swatches/Scratch palette group	Displays the Swatches palette.
Click on the first color swatch, the bright red one; press **K** (Paint Bucket); click the Paint Bucket over Layer 1	Sets red as the foreground color. Flood fills Layer 1 with red.

Filling Layer 1 with red makes it easy to see the areas in the water and on the land that should not be included in the selection that will hold the sky.

Press **D** (**d**efault colors); press **X** (switch colors)	Resets foreground color to black and background color to white. Switches the default colors so that white is the foreground color.
Double-click on the control menu button upper-left corner of the Swatches palette	Closes the Picker/Swatches/Scratch in the palette group; conserves screen real estate.
Click on the Layer Mask icon to the right of Background Copy layer icon on the Layers palette	Any editing you do now affects the Layer Mask.

New Riders Publishing
INSIDE
SERIES

Double-click the Paint Brush tool on the toolbox; click on the Brushes tab. Choose the 100 pixel soft-tipped brush	Chooses a large brush.
Click and drag over the water several times with the Paint Brush to hide any red pixels or partially red pixels that poke through	Hides (removes from the selection) unwanted areas in the water.
Click on the second brush tip from the left on the second row of the Brushes palette	Selects a smaller brush tip.
Press Ctrl(Cmd)+plus twice	Moves you in to a 2:1 viewing resolution.
Click and drag the Paint Brush over any areas of red on the gazebo, the lake walls, and the grassy areas; also hide the red on the lamp posts; stay away from the fringe area immediately adjacent to the skyline; choose a smaller brush tip if necessary (see fig. 14.14)	If you wander into the sky or the edge between the sky and the trees, switch your foreground color to black and paint over the area.

Toggle the Paint Brush to the Hand tool by pressing the spacebar, or use the scroll bars to move around the image. You're done with this phase when you have covered up all the red except along the skyline.

Press Ctrl(Cmd)+S (**F**ile, **S**ave)	Saves your work up to this point.

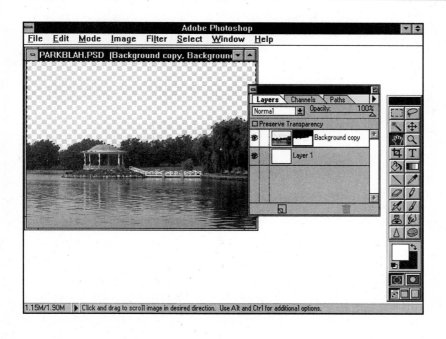

Figure 14.13

The selection created with the Color Range command is used to create a selection in a Layer Mask.

Figure 14.14

Use a small Paint Brush to paint white on the Layer Mask; white unhides areas, for further refining of the selection.

Figure 14.14

Use a small Paint Brush to paint white on the Layer Mask; white unhides areas, for further refining of the selection.

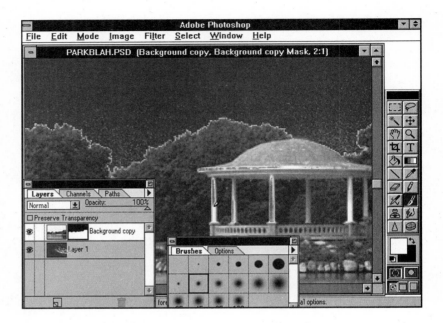

Layer 1 is where the SKYDARK.PSD sky will go. It will replace the red. Don't apply the Layer Mask at this point because you'll work with it again after the new sky is in place. All your work so far in hiding the red has continued to refine the selection that will create the hole in PARKBLAH.PSD that allows the new sky to be displayed. This could have been done with the sky on Layer 1 instead of the red, except that some of the colors in the sky would not contrast sufficiently against the park colors, thus making them harder to spot.

It's time to make a most dramatic change in the appearance of this image. It's time to bring the sky into the image.

Copying the Sky into the Target Image

To recap for a moment: the SKYDARK.PSD image is a 1.7 MB image. Its dimensions are larger but its resolution of 150 pixels per inch is the same as that of PARKBLAH.PSD. Ultimately, SKYDARK will fill Layer 1 in the PARKBLAH.PSD image so Photoshop's working memory requirements won't change much from what they are now because all of Layer 1's red pixels use the same amount of memory resources as will be used when the red pixels are replaced with the sky pixels. What *will* take system resources is having more than one image open at a time. These two images are fairly small in file size, so you probably won't feel the drain, but when working with larger images, see if you can optimize your memory resources before opening

another image. You can increase your memory resources by closing unnecessary images in the workspace or other programs that you have running at the same time Photoshop is running.

Additionally, before bringing in the SKYDARK image, it is a good idea to delete any unneeded layers, channels, layer masks, or saved selections. All these take up memory resources. Out of these four categories, PARKBLAH.PSD only has one thing that falls in the unnecessary category—the saved selection you created from the Color Range marquee. The Layer Mask you've been working on is a more refined version of that selection.

Another consideration you should be aware of before you bring in the SKYDARK.PSD image, is *image clipping*. The SKYDARK image's dimensions are larger than PARKBLAH's. This is good because it gives you the leeway to position the most interesting parts of the sky in a compositionally pleasing way within the image. Photoshop does not discard any of the portions of SKYDARK.PSD that hang outside the PARKBLAH's boundaries *if and only if* you choose the Move tool as the current tool for positioning the image on the layer. If you perform any editing with any other toolbox tool, if you change to Channels or change the active layer, or if you change the Opacity or mode on the Layers palette, Photoshop "sees" that you're continuing to edit the image and discards image areas that fall outside the image window! You can use the keyboard arrow keys while the Move tool is chosen to nudge the image on the layer, however, any actions other than the ones described here will send image areas outside the image window to Never-Never Land. This unusual set of conditions and circumstances for working with an image on a layer doesn't create an overriding concern in this assignment because it is relatively easy to bring in a new copy of the sky; but as you see in Chapter 15, "Special Effects with Ordinary Photographs," image window clipping can pose a significant hazard when working with selections.

The next set of exercises puts this information and the two images together.

Copying an Image to a Layer

Click on the Channels tab of the Layers/Channels/Paths palette group; scroll down the list of channels and then click and drag the #4 (Ctrl+4) channel into the Trash icon at the bottom of the palette (see fig. 14.15)	Deletes the saved selection #4. *Do not* drag the channel that says Backgro.. and Ctrl+~ on it. This is the Layer Mask!
Click on the Layers tab; then click on the Layer 1 title on the Layers palette	Makes Layer 1 the active image layer where editing can occur.
Press Ctrl(Cmd)+O (**F**ile, **O**pen) and open the color-corrected SKYDARK.PSD image you saved to your hard disk earlier in the chapter	SKYDARK.PSD opens and becomes the active image.

continues

continued

Press Ctrl(Cmd)+A (**S**elect, **A**ll); press Ctrl(Cmd)+C (**E**dit, **C**opy); press Ctrl(Cmd)+W (**F**ile, **C**lose)	Selects the entire image, copies it to the clipboard, and closes the file. PARKBLAH.PSD is the active image again.
Press Ctrl(Cmd)+V (**E**dit, **P**aste); press Ctrl(Cmd)+D (**S**elect, **N**one)	The copy of SKYDARK.PSD floats above Layer 1 as a floating selection and is then deselected, making it part of Layer 1 (see fig. 14.16).
Press **V** (Move tool); click and drag the sky into a position that pleases you	Moves the selection on the layer.

Areas outside the image window can be dragged back into the image as long as only the Move tool and the arrow keys are used and no editing takes place.

Most of the interesting parts of the sky are toward the bottom-left of the SKYDARK copy. Check figure 14.17 to see what the authors thought looked the best. If you position the opening in the clouds on the right of the SKYDARK image over the willow trees, you save yourself some work when it comes time to integrate the edges of the two images. When you have the image more or less in place, you can use the arrow keys to nudge the sky by one pixel per keystroke, or by ten pixels if you hold down the Shift key and press an arrow key.

When you're sure the sky is in the position you like…

Press Ctrl+S (**F**ile, **S**ave)	Saves your work up to this point.

Figure 14.15

Delete unnecessary selections to conserve system resources.

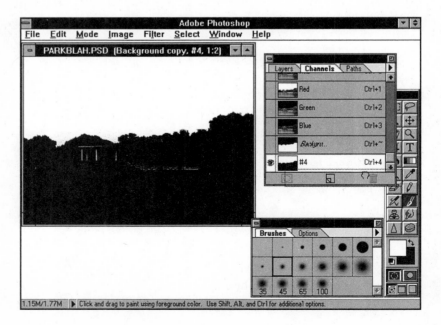

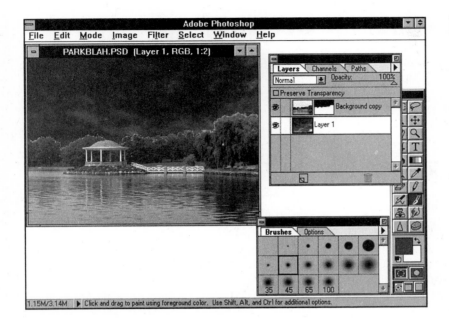

Figure 14.16

The sky is pasted on Layer 1. It can be repositioned with the Move tool.

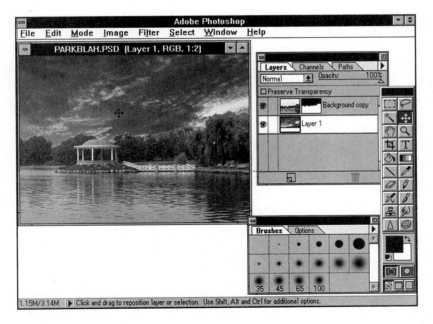

Figure 14.17

Drag the sky on Layer 1 until it makes a pleasing composition with the overlying park image.

Don't worry about the fringing you see along the skyline. You can take care of that with the Layer Mask that you have in place. You'll attend to the fringe after you color-correct the land (including the edge pixels) and water part of the image.

Harmonizing Colors Within an Image

This wonderfully warm sky has been transplanted into the park scene. But the recipient, PARKBLAH.PSD, still has a color scheme similar to that of frostbite. The color balance that warmed up SKYDARK .PSD can warm the land, too. As you saw when you worked with the SKYDARK.PSD image, a quick trip to Color Balance can make a cold world warm.

Warming Up the Colors in the Landscape

Color-correction of the land is performed at this point in the assignment because the main elements have been put together. With the sky in place, you can make a better judgment as to the amount and direction the colors in the land need to move on the Color Balance dialog box. The sky is so dramatic that the land now must hold its own. In real life, a sky like the one in the image now would throw much of its innate color onto the land. When you perform the color-correction for this image area, concentrate on how the land looks. The water gets a special lift of its own later in the assignment.

The following exercise returns you to the Color Balance command.

Warming Up a Cold Day

Click on the Background Copy layer title on the Layers Palette	Makes the layer that contains the land the active layer.
Press Ctrl(Cmd)+Y or Choose **I**mage, **A**djust, and then Color Balance; make sure that the **P**review and the Preserve **L**uminosity check check boxes are checked	Displays Color Balance dialog box.

Move the Color Balance dialog box, if necessary, so that you can see all the land in the image.

Click on the **M**idtones radio button; enter the following values in the Color Levels: input boxes, from left to right: **+52, –21, –3** (see fig. 14.18)	Skews the midtone pixels heavily toward red, a medium amount toward magenta, and a tinge toward yellow; cuts the overly green nature of the scene and warms it up.
Click on the **H**ighlights radio button. Enter the following values in the Color Levels: input boxes, from left to right: **+39, –13, –11**	Pushes the highlights toward red, magenta, and yellow. Beware of making the colors too brown; you don't want the foliage to look dry.
Click on the **S**hadows radio button; enter the following values in the Color Levels: input boxes, from left to right: **0, –8, –28**	The shadows move toward yellow and green; no red or cyan is added. Warms and lightens, keeping the dry brown away.

Click on OK	Image takes on the new color values for the land and water. The sky was not altered because it is on a different layer.
Press Ctrl(Cmd)+S (**F**ile, **S**ave)	Saves your work up to this point.

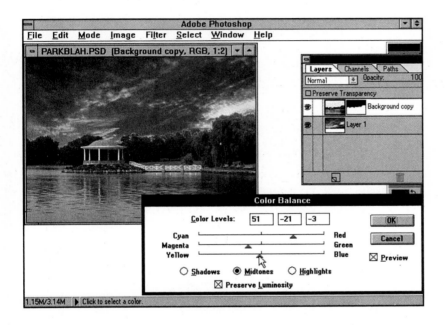

Figure 14.18

Image warmth is easy to achieve with the Color Balance command.

Tip   Again, the values used to warm up the scene were arrived at by personal aesthetics—the product of the author's eye—not secret formulas. Whenever you adjust for color or tonal balance, your *own* eye must guide you. Staring intently at the monitor for a while can make seeing subtle changes difficult.

In such cases, take a short break before you click on the OK button. Walk around the room, look out the window for a minute or two, or close your eyes for a while. When you return to the assignment, you can better evaluate the scene with an impartiality you can't aspire to with retinal fatigue!

Using One of Photoshop's Premade Selections

The image is shaping up pretty good now, but you still have that awful fringe separating the sky and the trees. It's time to take care of that. Photoshop 3 stores information about the contents of layers in channels. You saw in Chapter 5, "It's All Done with Palettes," that layers and channels are very close kin. Because Photoshop has the layer contents information on hand at all times, there are "saved" selections that you might not have stumbled across awaiting you on the Load Selection dialog box. The following section explores what selections are tucked away, how you can put one of them to good use, and how you can rid the image of the fringe.

The Background Copy Mask

Photoshop has stored a selection that will come in very handy in the next exercise. When a Layer Mask is in place and is selected, a premade selection called the Background Copy Mask is available for you to use, but you can't see this option from the list on the Layers palette. The Background Copy Mask is a selection that contains all the filled in areas—the white, unhidden areas contained within the Layer Mask. In the assignment, you've been working on this selection; it encompasses the park part of the image. The Load Selection dialog box sports a very useful check box option that enables you to invert any selection you are about to load. This check box, combined with the Background Copy Mask, gives easy access to the hidden, black areas of the Layer Mask because it is the inverse selection.

In the following exercise, it is the inverse selection of the Background Copy Mask that you're after. With this selection loaded, you can employ another new Photoshop feature–the Expand Selection command. Together, these features enable you to remove the fringe around the trees quickly, without ruining the natural undulation of the tree line.

Using the Background Copy Mask

Click on the Layer Mask icon on the Background copy layer	You need to use the Layer Mask to hide the edge pixels.
Choose **S**elect, **L**oad Selection, and choose Background Copy Mask from the **C**hannel drop-down list; click to put a check mark in the Invert check box below the Channel drop-down menu; leave the New radio button set in the Operation field; click on OK (see fig. 14.19)	Loads a selection of the transparent sky areas (areas that have been hidden by the Layer Mask).

New Riders Publishing
INSIDE
SERIES

Choose **S**elect, M**o**dify, and then choose **E**xpand (see fig. 14.20); in the Expand Selection dialog box, enter **1** in the **E**xpand text entry box; click on OK	Expands the selection by 1 pixel. This setting includes most of the fringe pixels.
Press Ctrl(Cmd)+H (**S**elect, Hide **E**dges)	Hides the marquee "marching ants" so that you can see what's going on.
Press **D** (**d**efault colors) and then press **X** (switch colors)	Ensures that black is the background color. Black hides pixels when applied to a Layer Mask.
Press the Delete key	Fills the area within the marquee selection with black, which hides the pixels.

Most of the fringing went away, and the tree line still has many natural-looking nooks and crannies!

Press Ctrl+D (**S**elect, **N**one)	Deselects the marquee selection.
Press Ctrl(Cmd)+S (**F**ile, **S**ave)	Saves your work up to this point.

Figure 14.19

Check the Invert check box to load the inverse of the selection you've chosen in the Channel drop-down list.

Figure 14.20

Use Expand to increase the size of a selection by the number of pixels you specify.

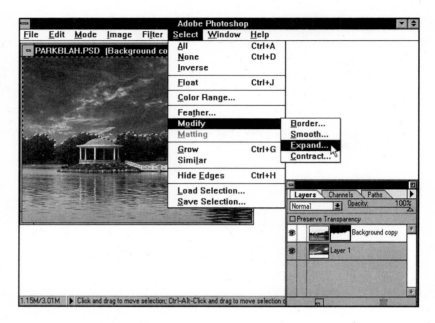

Painting on a Layer Mask

You've done almost all the editing and refining of the Layer Mask that you need to do before you actually have to decide if this is the selection you need to replace the original sky. Although the new sky seems like it's in place if you Discard (don't use) the Layer Mask, the lovely sky on Layer 1 will be covered by the original sky that still exists on the Background Copy layer. After the minor edits you perform in the following exercise, you remove the Layer Mask by Applying it to the image. Only then are the original sky pixels you've been so carefully hiding deleted from the image file.

Additionally, you remove the rest of the fringe in the next exercise. Concentrate on the fringe and don't go into the trees. Keep an eye on preserving as much of the original irregular outline the trees make against the sky. You don't want to make them look like they have a smooth, helmet hairdo.

Hiding the Remaining Fringe

Click on the Layer Mask on the Background copy, if it doesn't have a black border around it, to show that it is the active editing area

Ensures that you are editing the Background copy, Layer Mask.

Press **Z** (**Z**oom tool); marquee-zoom over the top of the willow trees on the right of the image; click on the Maximize/Minimize button in the upper right corner; click the Zoom tool or press Ctrl(Cmd)plus or Ctrl(Cmd)minus if necessary to move in over the top of the willows at a 2:1 viewing resolution	Sets up the workspace so that you can clearly see where the willow trees meet the sky. Use the scroll bars or the Hand tool to make sure that you are at the image's right-hand edge.
Double-click on the Paint Brush tool on the toolbox; choose Normal mode from the drop-down list on the Paintbrush Options Palette; set Opacity to **100%**; click on the Brushes tab and pick the first brush tip from the left on the second row	Selects a small soft-tipped brush with which to apply paint to the Layer Mask. Darken mode will only affect pixels that are lighter than the the color you paint with.
Press **D** (**d**efault colors)	Sets Paint Brush to apply black, which hides pixels on a Layer Mask.
Press the Caps Lock key	If you are using the Standard tool cursors (the one with the pictures) this turns you cursors into the Precision crosshairs cursor, which give a better view for this job.
Place the crosshair cursor in the sky above a fringe area on the willow trees so that the cross hairs almost touch the fringe you want to remove (see fig. 14.21); click. Move closer to the tree line and click again if necessary or press Ctrl(Cmd)+Z (**E**dit, **U**ndo) if you got too much	You want to gently remove these edge pixels; don't go into the tree itself. These areas are better corrected in the image instead of with the layer mask.

Press Ctrl(Cmd)plus and the Ctrl(Cmd)minus frequently to move in and out of the image. Zoom out to a 1:1 viewing resolution to check the appearance of the work. If it looks good at this resolution, it would print that way too.

Use the Hand tool or the scroll bars to scroll along the tree line. Almost all the work done using this technique is from the right edge of the image to the gazebo. When the image looks like figure 14.22, you're done. Notice that just edge areas were taken care of, not areas that lie within the trees.

Press Ctrl(Cmd)+S (**F**ile, **S**ave)	Saves your work up to this point.

Figure 14.21

Place the crosshair cursor in the sky so that it almost touches the fringe you want to remove.

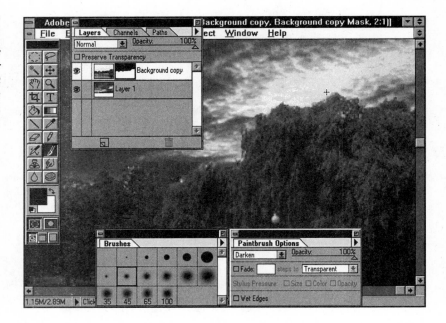

Figure 14.22

Your image should look like this now.

Applying the Layer Mask

The long-awaited moment is about to arrive; the removal of the Layer Mask. You won't notice any change in the image, but the Layer Mask icon disappears from the Layers palette, and Photoshop deletes the Ctrl+~ channel from the Channels palette. The Ctrl+~ channel is where Photoshop has been storing the Layer Mask information.

When you choose Apply from the Remove Layer Mask dialog box, the Layer Mask deletes pixels from the image. When the pixels are deleted, the only way to get them back is to immediately press Ctrl(Cmd)+Z (**E**dit, **U**ndo) after you've applied the Layer Mask. Your image is in perfect shape now, so it's okay to apply the Layer Mask. However, when you work on your own assignments, take a minute or two to look at the image and think it over before you click on Discard (throw away without using it, no hidden pixels are deleted) or Apply a Layer Mask.

Removing the Mask

With the Layer that contains the Layer Mask you want to remove (Background Copy layer) selected...

Click on the Layers palette pop-up menu. Choose Apply Layer Mask (see fig. 14.23)	The Layer Mask is applied and all hidden pixels are removed from the Background Copy layer.
Press Ctrl(Cmd)+S (**F**ile, **S**ave)	Saves your work up to this point.

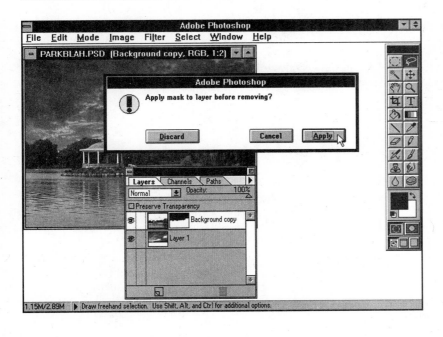

Figure 14.23

Apply deletes hidden pixels; Discard throws the Layer Mask away without altering any pixels.

Filling in the Trees

Although the overall image is a glorious attraction now, the *dis*traction—the original hazy sky areas between the leaves—is still painfully obvious. In this type of situation, you have an artistic call to make. Do you keep faith with reality and fill the holes with new sky? Or do you use artistic license to improve upon nature?

You try both techniques in the following exercises. This and other chapter assignments in this book demonstrate the problem-solution approach to using Photoshop. The type of image enhancement a client would pay good money for requires a working knowledge of a variety of image editing tools and techniques. The creative solution to the problem in this example is to restore some areas of the sky to the trees and, in other areas, replace original sky portions with tree samples.

Doing Mother Nature One Better

You should see fairly large holes in the center maple-tree section and in the gap in the trees to the left of the gazebo. An imaging person's natural instinct would be to fill these holes with new sky color because that is what nature filled them with. But the holes in the center section are caused because the trees didn't grow nice dense crowns. The tree tops to the right of the gazebo pull the viewer's eye away from the gazebo instead of receding into the background. There is no artistic reason not to correct Nature's flaws instead of accentuating the homeliness by adding a piece of new sky to these areas. You second-guess nature in the next exercise by filling the gaps with tree samples rather than sky. Painting samples into an image area always calls for the Rubber Stamp tool.

Fixing Background Areas within Trees

Here's the scoop on each approach to the areas in the trees in question and on the applicability of Photoshop's tools from an aesthetic point of view. The very small flecks of sky in the maple trees to the right of the gazebo add reality to the image— some bits of sky usually show through the treetops. Using the Paint Brush tool, you give these pixels a sky color. The large holes in the tree line are ideal candidates for the Rubber Stamp tool, which applies not only the colors of the sky or tree but also the visual detail (not easily accomplished with the Paint Brush tool). Because the holes in the maples to the right of the gazebo, when filled with sky, distract the eye from the gazebo—the focal point in the image—you will fill them with tree. The holes between the maples to the left of the gazebo look better filled with sky, to show the natural break in the trees.

A Soft Touch for Invisible Retouching

The Rubber Stamp tree repair method requires some care to avoid creating hard edges and repeating patterns. To make your retouching invisible, use Anti-alias, soft brush tips, and resample for color and pattern at points along the way. Don't be afraid to practice initiative in areas you feel need work beyond the basic steps we guide you through. Every artist sees things differently; developing your individual artistic sensibilities is as vital to an imaging career as a working knowledge of Photoshop.

In this next exercise, you may come across small bits and pieces that could use special attention. Fix them last, after you have tried different approaches to the larger areas.

Oh—and before you retouch an area, zoom out and make sure that you're looking at a hole, not one of the three lampposts in the image!

Tree Repair

Click on the Background Copy layer title

Selects this layer for editing.

Marquee-zoom into the area to the right of the gazebo

Area you work on in this exercise.

Double-click on the Rubber Stamp tool; make sure that the Rubber Stamp options are set to Clone (aligned), and that Sample Merged is checked; choose Darken from the drop-down list: slide the Opacity to **100%**

Now Rubber Stamp tool continuously samples from trailing cross hair. Only pixels that are lighter will be replaced.

Click on the Brushes tab and choose the third soft tip from the left, second row

Chooses a small soft-tipped brush tip.

Press Alt(Option) while you click the Rubber Stamp tool on the lighter green area under the lowest large hole

Sets initial point from which Rubber Stamp will clone.

Move the Rubber Stamp tool over the hole; click. Then move it slightly to get the rest of the hole; click again; do not drag the Rubber Stamp tool (see fig. 14.24)

"Bursts" some pattern in the area, replacing hole with sample of tree image.

Press Alt(Option) while you click the Rubber Stamp tool on the darker green area to the right of the highest large hole

Sets new sample point, with color values more in keeping with section of tree addressed next.

continues

continued

Move the Rubber Stamp over the right side of the highest large hole; click. Then move the tool over slightly and click again	Fills in the hole.
Press Alt(Option)while you click over the darker green area to the left of the hole. Move the cursor over the remaining portion of the hole; then click	Both large holes are filled.
Choose a smaller brush tip. Repeat this procedure of sampling and then clicking over the smaller holes in this area. Try not to go into the sky	Fills in the sky areas in this section only.

Use the Hand tool or the scroll bars to scout around other areas of the trees and fill them in. If you think sky would look better, set your sample point in the sky and then click the Rubber Stamp tool over the tree area to be filled with sky.

Double-click on the Hand tool on the toolbox	Displays full-frame view of PARKBLAH.PSD, to give you some perspective on your accomplishment (see fig. 14.25).
Press Ctrl(Cmd)+S (**F**ile, **S**ave)	Saves your work up to this point.

Picking a Few Pixels and Darkening Them

At this point, a single, oddball pixel or two from the original PARKBLAH sky is probably sticking through the dark maple trees to the right of the gazebo. Funny, isn't it, how zooming into an incongruous image area shows the cause of the damage to be much less severe than you estimate at a 1:1 view? This sort of situation calls for light artillery, not for something as heavy-handed as the Rubber Stamp tool. The appropriate strategy is to use the Eyedropper tool to pick up a color from the sky, and then paint the light areas with the Paint Brush tool set to Darken mode.

When you use Darken mode with the Paint Brush tool, only pixels lighter than the color you chose with the Eyedropper (the foreground color) are painted in. You need to select several colors and use as few brush strokes as possible to cover the offending pixels. The best view for this retouching work is at 1:1, actual size, because if you have

obliterated the pixels at a viewer's resolution, laboring in the area one nanosecond longer than necessary is pointless. Learn to spot and analyze a sore spot in a picture at a high resolution but (wherever possible) do the actual retouching work with as large a sense of the whole image as possible. In many instances, precision retouching in Photoshop requires a magnified view of the problem area; whereas other times, such as in the last exercise, it doesn't. If you can see what you're doing at 1:1, and can do the required image editing comfortably at this view, stick to it.

Figure 14.24

Use the Rubber Stamp tool to hide areas rather than re-create them.

Figure 14.25

Full, dense tree tops enhanced with the Rubber Stamp tool.

Lightly Painting

Press **Z** (**Z**oom tool); click once on the maple trees to the right of the gazebo, and then click on the Minimize/Maximize button; Macintosh users should use the resize box to enlarge the image window	Displays 1:1, full-screen view of PARKBLAH.PSD image.
Press **I** (Eyedropper tool); then click over the sky above the trees until you find a dark rich color	Sets foreground color you'll paint with.
Double-click on the Paint Brush tool on the toolbox	Displays the Paint Brush Options palette.
Choose Darken mode from the drop-down list; set the Opacity: slider to **71**%; then choose the second brush from the left in the top row	Sets characteristics for Paint Brush to apply color with partial transparency that colors only pixels lighter than specified foreground color.
Click and drag with short strokes over the light-colored dappled areas (see fig. 14.26)	Colors original sky pixels with darker foreground-color selection.

Go for effect, not precision with Paint Brush tool; leave large areas of original sky alone. They are covered (no pun intended) in next exercise.

Continue using small, short strokes to fill in areas of original sky	Retouches only "pinholes" between leaves in image. (Stop when all pinholes are filled.)
Press Ctrl(Cmd)+S (**F**ile, **S**ave)	Saves your work up to this point.

By applying the color at 71 percent opacity in the preceding exercise, you preserved some of the tonal values in the pixels you stroked. Gray, tonal information constitutes much of the visual detail in images. You do yourself (and the image) a service when you change only the color aspect of an image area.

Let your eye be your guide when you set opacity and select which pixels to color. Your intent should be to create the impression (for viewers) that the sky is filtering through the leaves of the tree.

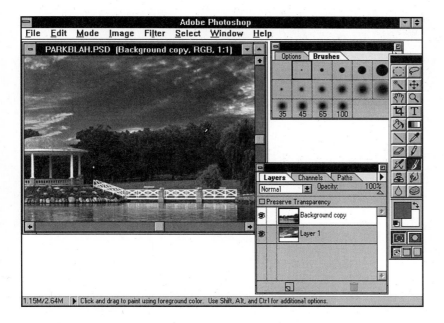

Figure 14.26
Painting in sky color, using the Brushes palette's Darken mode, affects the image's lighter pixels only.

Making a Beeline for the Tree Line

In the next exercise, you concentrate on the tree line. You use the Blur tool along the finished edge of the tree line. As it stands now, the tree line is a bit too sharp. Photographic image elements, especially when in the distance, rarely have sharp, totally focused edges. Instead, edges in these areas tend to ease their way into the adjacent image elements. The Blur tool reduces the contrast between adjacent pixels by averaging the *brightness value*, the neutral cast contained in color pixels. When used sparingly, the Blur tool creates a smooth visual transition. But when applied full-strength (large Brushes tip, 100 percent opacity), it noticeably fuzzes image details as the pixels lose more and more unique color value and become desaturated. Whenever you use the Blur tool, be sure to zoom out frequently to a 1:1 image view to see what the effect is accomplishing. Be prepared to use the **E**dit, **U**ndo command if your eye tells you that you've overdone it.

The next exercise is an example of using both tools sparingly to achieve a natural, gradual transition between sky and tree line. The prudent use of the Blur tool is a technique you might apply to a variety of situations in your own work. This set of steps for producing subtle transitions is essential, not just for sky-ectomies, but whenever you bring different elements together.

It's time to go where the trees meet the sky, to restore a sense of harmony to nature.

Taking the Edge off a Nature Scene

Double-click on the Blur/Sharpen tool on the toolbox; set mode to Darken and Pressure to **50%**; check the Sample Merged check box; click on the Brushes tab and choose the second tip from the left on the top row	Sets Blur tool to pixels you drag over (to shade closer to area first clicked on).
Press **Z** (**Z**oom tool); click twice just below the tree line at the extreme right of the image; then click on the Minimize/Maximize button	Zooms in to 2:1 view of tree line at right edge of image.

Use the Hand tool, if necessary, to bring the tree line into view.

With the Blur tool, click on the sky side of the tree/skyline and (without letting go of the mouse button) drag a single stroke to the left, following the tree/skyline edge (see fig. 14.27)	Darkens light edge pixels.

Zoom out to a 1:1 view after each stroke with the Blur tool to make sure that you haven't over-fuzzed the border. If it's too fuzzy, Press Ctrl(Cmd)+Z (**E**dit, **U**ndo). Go over the edge once more, if necessary, checking whether you have over-blurred.

With the Hand tool (press the spacebar to toggle to the Hand tool), reposition the image as necessary to keep moving along the edge with the Blur tool. Keep Zooming out to check across each section, until you reach the left border.

Double-click on the Hand tool on the toolbox to change to a 1:2 view of the full image	Completed image should look like figure 14.28.
Press Ctrl(Cmd)+S (**F**ile, **S**ave)	Saves your work up to this point.

Was the last exercise a test of your eye-hand coordination? Perhaps. When you make short, precise mouse movements, you can work faster and get immediate feedback on the effect. The blurring was done to the image while working at a 2:1 viewing resolution of PARKBLAH .PSD. We choose this view to work in because if you zoom into a view that's too close, what you see may not accurately reflect the impact of your editing work on the image. A pixel that may look dark enough is not dark enough, and vice versa. A view from different resolutions of an image enables you to assess your work at various stages of completion.

And this is why large monitors are vital to the imaging profession. You avoid eyestrain and mousing errors when your field of vision isn't constrained by small, physical boundaries.

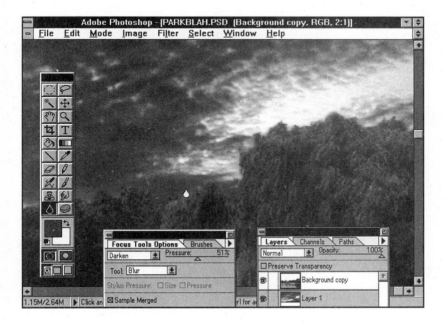

Figure 14.27

Use the Blur tool to softly blend the sky and tree line.

Figure 14.28

The Blur tool reduces contrast in neighboring pixels creating a more photogenic look.

Adding Reflections of New Sky in the Lake

One more area in this image—the water—needs a touch of Photoshop magic. Water, by its nature, is reflective. The current image has nice reflections of the land, but no reflection of the sky. The original sky had nothing to reflect into the water except a shade of humdrum! The new sky would look great in the water, though, and if you think about it, it's only natural!

In the next exercise, you use Photoshop's Layer Mask, Gradient tool, and Layer Opacity controls to precisely and realistically add the shimmer, the colors, and the pattern of the sky to the water's surface. And you do this without destroying the equally necessary and interesting reflections in the lake of the image's land areas.

 Tip When you create or modify scenes in Photoshop, you often will want to consider how image areas interact (or should interact) with other, pasted-in selections. The two features most often overlooked in image retouching and composition are shadows and reflections. Everything in the world has a shadow, a reflection, or both. If you add or change an element in an image without restoring or creating the shadows and reflections, your work will look unreal. Readers may respond directly or just have a subconscious feeling that something about the piece is hoked-up.

Selecting a Place for the Reflection

Before you can put the sky into the water, you need to create a selection border around the water. The easiest way to create the selection is with the Lasso tool. Because anything contained within this selection border gets the sky treatment, this border needs to be fairly accurate. The Lasso tool is the tool of choice for making this selection. And pay careful attention to the stone walls, which reflect rather heavily into the water. Zoom out to determine where the water line is, so that you can accurately select only the water, not part of the wet, mossy wall.

A good approach to this water-definition is to first use the Lasso tool to create a coarse outline of the area you want. Next, refine the selection area a little by using the Shift key with the Lasso tool to add to the first selection, including image areas of the lake you originally missed. Then press and hold down the Ctrl key while you lasso areas you want to subtract from the selection. Put on your imaginary wet suit for the next exercise!

Gathering the Water

Double-click on the Hand tool; then click on the Minimize/Maximize button	Displays image window in middle of screen at 1:2 viewing resolution to make clicking around the image easy.
Press **L** (for **L**asso tool)	Selection tool used for this exercise.
Press Alt(Option) and click at the waterline in the center of the gazebo; then (still pressing the Alt key) click completely around the water, back to your starting point; when you reach the edge of the image, click outside the image to select right up to the edge	Alt key constrains Lasso tool to create straight lines between successive click points. Clicking outside image window enables you to create a selection border edge flush with edge of the image window.
Marquee-zoom into the left edge of the gazebo's island	Area of imprecise selecting (with Lasso tool) that needs attention now.
Press Shift while you click and drag an image area not included in your present selection marquee	Adds to selection border (see fig. 14.29).
Press Ctrl(Cmd) while you click and drag an image area you don't want included in the selection marquee	Lets you subtract an area from the present selection when you click and drag with Lasso tool.
Reposition the image with the Hand tool or the scroll bars	Moves your view of PARKBLAH.PSD to different areas in image that must still be included in or excluded from active selection.
Continue pressing Ctrl(Cmd) (or Shift) while you click and drag near the selection border, as necessary	Creates refined selection border around water area in PARKBLAH.PSD (for editing you'll do shortly).
When all the water is selected, double-click on the Hand tool	Zooms to 1:2 viewing resolution.
Check the entire selection border for any missing or "wrong" areas in the selection	If border looks fine, continue with next step; otherwise, correct it by using Ctrl and Shift with the Lasso tool.

continues

continued

When your selection looks like
figure 14.30, choose **S**elect, **S**ave
and choose New

If the image looks fine, save
the Selection as #4.

Press Ctrl(Cmd)+D

Deselects the selection you saved.

Figure 14.29

*Adding to the
selection border
with the Lasso
tool.*

Using a New Layer for the Reflection

You need to create a new layer to hold the reflection of the sky. This new layer will be
above Background copy layer. The sky from Layer 1 will be copied into the new layer,
Layer 2. With the selection you've just created, you can quickly remove the portions
of the sky that overlap the land on Layer 2. Then by using the Opacity controls on
Layer 2, you can fade the sky back so that it appears to be a reflection on the sky.

This may sound like a great deal of work, but it really does go quickly.

Figure 14.30

Selecting just the water, so that you can paste the sky into it.

Making a Reflection Layer

Click on the New Layer icon on the bottom of the Layers palette; click on OK	Creates a new layer, Layer 2, above the Background Copy layer.
Click on the Layer 1 title; press Ctrl(Cmd)+A (**S**elect, **A**ll); press Ctrl(Cmd)+C (**E**dit, **C**opy)	Makes this the active layer and selects the entire image area and copies to the clipboard.
Click on the Layer 2 title; press Ctrl(Cmd)+V (**E**dit, **P**aste)	Makes Layer 2 the active layer, and the copy of the sky is a floating selection above the layer.
Choose **I**mage, **F**lip; then choose **V**ertical	Flips the sky so that the reflection will be accurately portrayed (see fig. 14.31).
Press Ctrl(Cmd)+D to defloat the selection; press **V** (Move tool) and drag the flipped sky image down so that the bottom of the flipped sky aligns with the bottom of the image window	The sky image becomes part of Layer 2. Moves it into place.
Choose **S**elect, **L**oad Selection; choose #4; check the **I**nvert check box and click on OK	Loads the inverse of the selection you saved of the water. It is used to "cut" away the sky that covers the land.
Press the Delete key	Deletes the sky covering the land. Your image should look like figure 14.32.

continues

continued

Press Ctrl(Cmd)+D (**S**elect, **N**one)	Deselects the selection.
Drag the Opacity slider on Layer 2 to about **50%**	Reduces the Opacity of the layer.
Things are looking great!	
Press Ctrl(Cmd)+S (**F**ile, **S**ave)	Saves your work up to this point.

Figure 14.31

Flip reflections so that they appear natural.

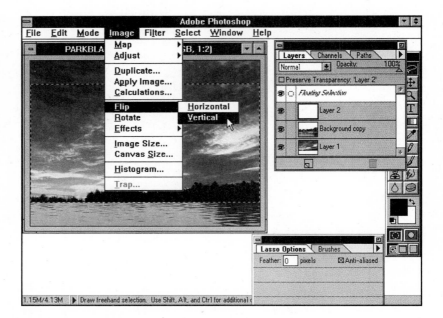

Using a Gradient Fill in a Layer Mask

The cloud forms on the right of the SKYDARK image are very strong, with some delicate wisps on the left side. Reducing the layer's opacity with the Opacity control affects the whole layer. To reduce the prominence of the white on the right of the image requires one last use of the Layer Mask feature. By applying a Gradient fill in the Layer Mask, the white areas are partially hidden. Black areas in Layer Masks are totally hidden, and white areas totally revealed, but gray areas are only partially hidden. You'll use the Gradient Fill tool to create a nice transition from black to white in the Layer Mask. In the next exercise, you create Gradient Fill in a Layer Mask that doesn't affect the wispy clouds on the left, but quite literally "tones down" the heavy clouds on the right.

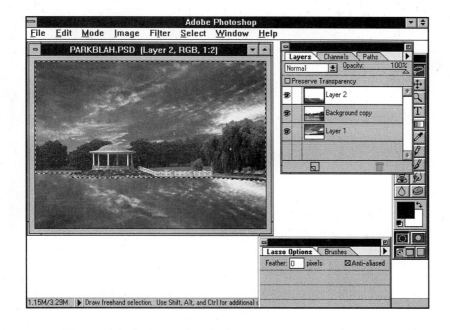

Figure 14.32

The water is filled with sky now.

Filling the Layer Mask

Click on the pop-up menu button on the Layers palette; choose Add Layer Mask	Creates a Layer Mask for Layer 2.
Hold down the Alt(Option) key and click on the layer mask icon	Takes you to a view of the actual mask. Image areas are not shown.
Click on the center window mode on the toolbox	Gives you a view of the layer surrounded by gray pasteboard.
Double-click on the Gradient Fill tool on the Gradient Fill Options palette; set Style to **N**ormal, set Type to **M**idpoint, Skew to **50**%, and Style to Linear if not already set that way	Sets the Gradient Fill tool to default characteristics.

The gradient fill produced by these settings will shade from the foreground color to the background color linearly, with the midpoint between the colors occurring at the 50 percent point of direction line you create with the Gradient Fill tool.

From about one screen inch from the right edge of the of the image window, click and drag the Gradient Fill tool straight across to the image; then release the mouse button	Graduated fill should resemble figure 14.33.

continues

continued

If it doesn't, double-click on the Eraser tool on the toolbox and click on the Erase button; answer Yes to the prompt and try the Gradient fill again	Erases only the gradient fill in the Layer Mask channel.
Hold down the Alt(Option) key and click on the Layer Mask icon	Takes you to a view of the image and not the mask.

The Gradient Fill in the Layer Mask is hiding the overly strong white clouds reflected in the lake.

Click and drag the Opacity slider if you want to further increase or decrease the Layers opacity if you feel too much or too little is obscured. When you like what you see…

Click on the pop-up menu button and choose Remove Layer Mask; choose Apply when prompted	The hidden sky reflection pixels are deleted from the image.
Choose **F**ile, **S**ave	Saves changed image to hard disk.

Figure 14.33

A gradient fill created in a Layer Mask can be used as a mask.

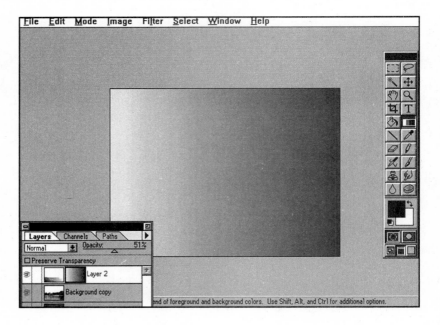

New Riders Publishing
INSIDE
SERIES

Cleaning Up

The image looks very different from when you started! You're to be congratulated. You're all done except for one small detail. The PSD format is great because it can handle layer and other Photoshop features, but it's not very portable. If you want to use this image in a desktop publishing program, you have to save it in a different file format that doesn't understand layers. The image needs to have all its layers combined into one. It only takes a minute, and you do it in the next exercise.

Cleaning Up

Click on the pop-up menu button on the Layers palette; choose Flatten Image (see fig. 14.34)	Blends the layers together into one background layer.
Select File, Save As. Name the file PARKWOW.TIF and choose the TIFF format from the Save File As Format Type list box	Saves the finished, layerless image to a different name.

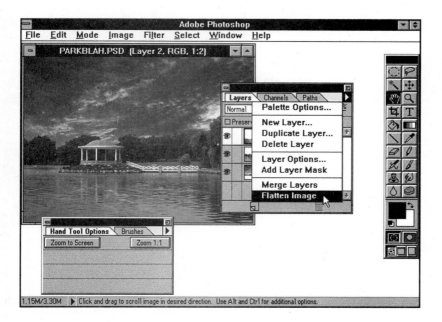

Figure 14.34

Flatten Image blends all the layers together.

You're done. Take a nice long look at your handiwork. As you can see from figure 14.35, you've come a long way with this image. It's a place you'd like to visit, a place to dream about. Creating idyllic situations, making the pedestrian seem special, and painting a dream with realistic strokes is what imaging with Photoshop can be all about.

Figure 14.35

The enchanted gazebo.

This chapter has shown you that a beautiful image of a photograph doesn't always just happen. Sometimes, creating a beautiful image takes a little pushing and prodding, a good selection of stock images you can choose from to augment the budding image, and a midwife as capable as Photoshop to assist in the creation.

But all the fancy moves and techniques you'll continue to pick up about computer imaging won't automatically generate a breathtaking landscape unless you tip your own vision into the recipe. You have to start with a dream, discover the possibilities in images you take (or have taken for you), and polish the rough edges to create the appearance of a calm, quiet beauty in the picture. To be able to convey this while frantically rushing to beat the deadline, the weather, or the time of day is the real magic Photoshop can help you with.

For the average viewer, the art of digital imaging is "magic." A well-executed magic trick always hides what the magician doesn't want the audience to see. But when you reach the point in your imaging career at which you have total control over what the viewing audience sees and takes away from one of your pieces, it's no longer magic—it's called Art.

Special Effects with Ordinary Photographs

If you remember the *Patty Duke Show* (before the actress was Patty Duke Astin and before the authors turned 30-something, okay?), you'll recall that the concept of the show was about a family who had identical cousins, the cousins being played by the same actress. There's a global fascination with identical twins, and real-life twin brothers and sisters are frequently used in advertising to convey a point. The media decided long ago that if actual twins can't be found, the next best thing is to manufacture the effect.

Technologically, we've come a long way from the 1960's situation comedies in which an actor had to stand on one side of the room and then run the same script from the other side of the room. An editor then had to splice the footage together to simulate the actuality of identical twins. In fact, in this chapter's assignment, you are the editor. Your tools are Photoshop's tools, and you learn how to take one actor, in two different poses, and make him look as chummy with his "twin" as if he had a twin brother in real life.

Creating the Source Images for an Identical Twin Picture

To create a natural-looking, finished photograph of two identical individuals interrelating and shaking hands, a photographic stand-in is required to take the place of the missing "twin" in the original images. The stand-in you use should be a person who is about the same height, weight, and body shape. The stand-in and the subject must be of similar height and build so that they occupy the same amount of physical area within the image. Matching the sex, race, age, and general level of physical fitness is also a good idea—for some obvious reasons and some subtle ones that you will learn—to help the image editing. In figure 15.1, you can see that two images were taken in front of the same background, to arrive at two poses for Dave, the fellow in the striped shirt who will become twins in this chapter's assignment.

Gary, the actor in the dark shirt in figure 15.1, was chosen to shake hands and get buddy-buddy with Dave, the future twin, because Gary is about the same height and weight as Dave. Therefore, the interaction in the two images puts Dave's hands, arms, and body stance into positions that will make the integration of the two images of Dave easier to accomplish.

Figure 15.1

To create photographic twins, use a stand-in to interact with the model, switch poses between the actors, and take two pictures.

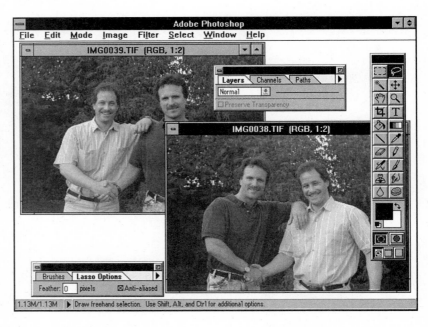

Image detail is a critical element when combining images of people—when performing the extensive retouching work you'll see in this chapter's assignment, you need to begin with high-quality digital samples that have good image resolution. To get the best photographic quality and detail from the two images, the film was transferred to a PhotoCD.

Chapter 3, "Color Theory and the PhotoCD," covers the finer points of Kodak's PhotoCD technology and gives working examples of the gamma adjustment often necessary when working with PhotoCD images. PhotoCD technology is wonderful and definitely the right choice of digital media when working with people pictures, but as you saw in the last figure, PhotoCD images in their native format display a high gamma, a quality that muddies image contrast. The next section takes you through a sort of "batch conversion" of PhotoCD images to get them into a beautiful and workable state for photographic retouching.

Creating a Perfect Tonal Landscape in an Image

The images you use in this chapter's assignment, IMG0038.TIF and IMG0039.TIF, were taken within moments of each other on a slightly overcast day. Both images, therefore, display almost identical lighting conditions. You can conclude, then, that whatever tonal corrections used on one image to bring out more detail and contrast should be applied in identical amounts to the other image. Photoshop's Levels command is used in the next exercise to compensate for the PhotoCD's lack of native gamma (the range of contrast in image midtones) correction for images used with personal computers. Although the Macintosh and IBM/PC computers use slightly different gamma settings, the changes you make to the images on the Bonus CD that came with this book are relative ones, and the Levels command enables you to save a setting you're happy with and apply the setting to other images.

Here's how to use the Auto option in the Levels command along with a little manual fine-tuning to create perfect tonal balance within the first of two images used to create the appearance of identical twins:

Working with the Levels Adjustment Command

Open the IMG0039.TIF image from the CHAP25 subdirectory (folder) on the Bonus CD

This is the first of two images you'll tonally correct in this assignment.

continues

continued

| Click and drag the IMG0039 image so that it's positioned in the upper left corner of Photoshop's workspace | Positions the image so that you can see both it and the Levels command dialog box in the next step. |

You might also want to open the IMG0038.TIF image at this time and keep it minimized. You'll be working with this image after you've adjusted '0039, and our figures show the image in the background, but if you don't have a great deal of RAM on your system, it's best to conserve resources and keep only the images you work on open. You are told when you need the IMG0038 image in a following step.

| Press Ctrl+L (**I**mage, **A**djust, **L**evels) | Displays the Level command dialog box. |
| Click on Auto | Automatically clips 5 percent off the high and low ends of the histogram of the image and redistributes the mapping of tones in the image without changing color qualities; improves contrast. |

Usually, you'll perk up the contrast in an image by clicking on Auto or using the **I**mage, **A**djust, **A**uto Levels command, which serves the same function as the button in the Levels dialog box. However, the Auto option is not intelligent, and your own eyes can tell you that further modification of the Auto option's proposed tonal changes (as reflected in the histogram in the middle of the dialog box) need to be made to create a better image. A black point and a white point can be found in the image and used to set a more accurate tonal "landscape" for the image *(see Chapter 7, "Restoring an Heirloom Photograph," for a comprehensive exploration of the Levels command)*.

Click on the left of the three Eyedroppers on the Levels dialog box	Chooses the Black Point Eyedropper; samples a point in an image to set as the darkest value for the Levels histogram.
Press Ctrl(Macintosh: Cmd) and the spacebar and hold the cursor over the image	Cursor turns into the Zoom (in) tool when it's over an active image window.
Click once over the shaded fern area of the IMG0039 image to the left of Dave; then click again over the darkest shaded area of fern	Zooms you in to a 2:1 viewing resolution of the darkest area of the IMG0039 image (see fig. 15.2).
Release the Ctrl key and spacebar	Returns the cursor to the Black Point tool.

Click over the darkest pixel you can see within the ferns (see fig. 15.3)	Establishes a new Black point for the image based on the darkest value you've found in the image.
Click on the far right Eyedropper icon on the Levels dialog box	Chooses the White Point Eyedropper.
Hold down the spacebar, then click and drag within the image until you see the white collar of Dave's shirt	Spacebar turns the cursor into the Hand tool, and you can scroll within the active image to display other areas within the image window.
Press Ctrl(Cmd) and spacebar, then click once over Dave's collar	Zooms you in to a 4:1 viewing resolution of Dave's collar, where you can see the brightest area in the IMG0039 image.
Release the Ctrl and spacebar keys, then click over the brightest area of Dave's collar	Sets the White point for the IMG0039 image, as shown in figure 15.4.
Click on Save in the Levels command dialog box	Displays the Save dialog box.
Type **DAVE39** in the File **N**ame field, then choose a drive and directory (folder) on your hard disk that's easy to locate later. Click on OK	Saves the settings you've made for the Levels command to an *.ALV file you can recall later (see fig. 15.5).
Click on OK in the Levels command dialog box	Applies the changes you've made to the tonal levels in image IMG0039.
Choose File, Sa**v**e As; then save the image as IMG0039.TIF (choose the *.TIF format from the Save File as Format **T**ype drop-down list) to your hard disk	Saves your work up to this point.

The Auto levels adjustment is a good beginning step when you want to correct the gamma and other contrast qualities in an image, but as you saw in the preceding exercise, the Auto setting can be improved upon by manually specifying white and black points for an image based on your own artistic evaluation.

New Riders Publishing
INSIDE
SERIES

Figure 15.2

Use the spacebar in combination with the Ctrl and Alt keys to reposition and zoom in and out of the active image window.

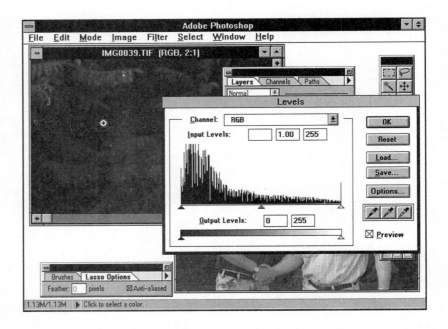

Figure 15.3

Click on the darkest pixel you see in an image using the Black Point Eyedropper to specify a new black point within an image.

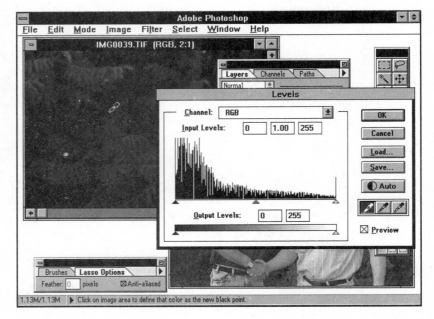

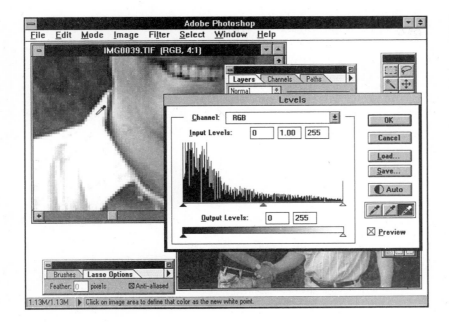

Figure 15.4

Click on the brightest point you see in an image with the White Point Eyedropper to set a new white point in an image.

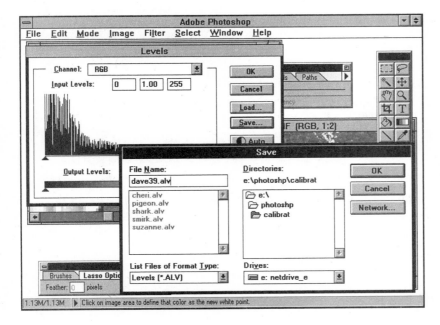

Figure 15.5

Save the changes you've created to the tonal map of an image to an ALV file Photoshop can read and apply to a different image.

Because you saved the Levels setting for the IMG0039 photo, the same settings can be retrieved and applied to the IMG0038 image. The two images display similar lighting conditions, so the changes you made to one image are good for the other. This is a handy facility in Photoshop and can be used to "batch correct" an entire roll of film that came back to you on PhotoCD displaying the same lack of contrast. Additionally, you can save the settings you make with other Adjust commands, such as Variations and Curves, by using the Save option in their respective dialog boxes. Using saved settings makes batch-correcting other flaws, such as color-casting, quicker when you have multiple images that display similar problems.

Naturally, if you save a Levels setting for an image and apply it to an image not photographed under the same lighting conditions as the first image, you won't get very good results. A saved Levels setting is only meaningful when you want to apply it to an image that was taken at a similar time, with a similar camera attitude, and that has similar lighting conditions to those found in the image used to create the setting. Additionally, images to which you apply saved settings must have the same image mode as the image from which the Levels setting was created. If you save a Levels setting for an RGB image and then apply the Levels tonal mapping to an image that's LAB mode, you'll be very disappointed with the results.

 Stop Photoshop version 3 arranges the file information within ALV settings differently from its predecessor, Photoshop 2.5. For this reason, you cannot load a setting saved in version 2.5 and apply it to an image when you are using Photoshop 3.

 Tip The Levels command may produce strange results when changing the tonal densities of an image that was not acquired, but instead was manufactured using illustration or modeling software. Pixels whose colors come from an application's color palette, rather than those acquired through a scanner or PhotoCD, contain evenly dispersed amounts of tonal information. In a way, computer-synthesized color can be thought of as being pure, and the neutral-density, grayscale components within computer-generated images are slight when compared to a digitized, real-life photograph.

For this reason, you usually see an atypical mapping histogram within the Levels command for a photorealistic bitmap computer image, and you should apply tonal adjustments *manually* using the Black and White Point Eyedroppers and the sliders beneath the histogram. Don't use the Auto option when optimizing the tonal distribution in a computer-created graphic.

Applying an Auto Level Setting to an Image

In the next exercise, you load and apply the saved ALV setting to the IMG0038 image. The two images should be identical in their need for gamma adjustment, but your eye must be the final judge when your goal is to bring images into the same tonal balance. You always have the option of loading an ALV setting as your starting point, and then using the Levels command sliders and Eyedroppers to make any minor adjustments necessary to give the images the same lighting conditions and contrast. For this reason, you should always arrange your workspace so that you can see both images and the Levels dialog box at the same time.

Here's how to apply a saved Levels setting to the second of the source images you'll use to create virtual twins:

Loading and Applying ALV Information

Open the IMG0038.TIF image from the CHAP15 subdirectory (folder) of the Bonus CD that came with this book	This is the image that needs tonal balancing next.
Press Ctrl+L (**I**mage, **A**djust, **L**evels)	Displays the Levels command dialog box.
Click on **L**oad (see fig. 15.6)	Displays the Load dialog box.

Photoshop "remembers" paths on your hard disk and CD-ROM drive that you've accessed last, so if you haven't roamed your hard disk between this exercise and the last, Photoshop offers you the last-accessed location on your hard disk in the Load dialog box, and the DAVE39.ALV file should be in clear sight.

Click on the DAVE39.ALV file; then click on OK	Loads the ALV setting you saved, and displays the tonal changes in the IMG0038 picture in preview on your workspace.
Click on OK in the Levels dialog box	Applies the changes, and you're returned to the workspace.
Choose File, Sa**v**e As; then save the image as IMG0038.TIF (choose the TIFF format from the Save File as Format **T**ype drop-down list) to your hard disk	Saves your work up to this point.

Don't close either image yet. You need to perform an image transplant in the next section.

Figure 15.6

Use the Load option in the Levels command dialog box to load a saved tonal map setting and apply it to an image.

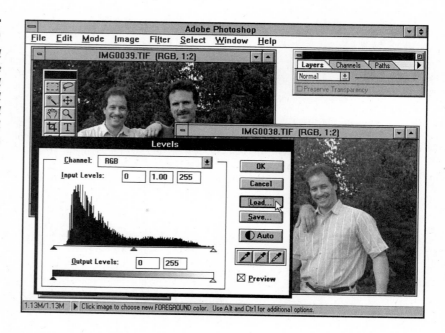

Two rolls of film were taken of Dave and Gary to arrive at the best two images for the compositing work you'll perform in this chapter. One usable picture per roll is the average for professional photographers, and the ideal image isn't usually evident through the lens at the time a picture is taken. The remaining images are generally evaluated as unacceptable, not because of exposure or other image quality conditions, but because image elements—a smile or a blink in this example—aren't quite perfect. As you can see in the selection of these two images for the twin-creation assignment, the attitude of both actors is good, and they relate in a way that will create a terrific "twin" image when Dave in IMG0039 is copied to meet himself in IMG0038.

However, because the two actors were asked to "mix it up" and get lively for the camera, they moved positions relative to camera distance, and the authors had to get out of the way on occasion during the photo session. This creates a problem you learn about next.

Resizing an Image Selection

Dave in IMG0038 takes up more image space than he does in IMG0039 because he's slightly closer to the camera. If these two guys had been bolted to the concrete, accurate relative sizes between the two images might have been achieved, but the activity going on between them would have been lost. And this would've been a shame, because people pictures always "say" more to the viewer when an activity is perceived in the image.

If you simply selected and copied the Dave in IMG0039 to IMG0038, the two Daves wouldn't be exactly the same size, and therefore the illusion of twins would become unconvincing. As discussed in earlier chapters, it's always better to *sample down* (create fewer pixels in an image, or shrink) a selection than to enlarge (*sample up*) or force Photoshop to interpolate new pixels for a selection. Therefore, because Dave in IMG0038 is slightly larger than Dave in IMG0039, the wise approach to this scaling problem is to decrease the image size for IMG0038.

It becomes a question, then, of how much IMG0038 needs to be reduced. The Info palette, used in combination with the Rectangular marquee tool, is the best approach to measuring the relative sizes of an area within both images. Another valuable instrument in determining the amount of size reduction for the IMG0038 picture is your own eye; statistics assisted by intuition and a little "guesstimating" can often provide the answer for resizing problems.

In the next exercise, you measure Dave's head in both images to come up with a fractional proportion you plug into Photoshop's Image Size command. Notice that there isn't a lot of similarity in Dave's two poses, and the angles of his torso and arms don't remain consistent. Even Dave's head is canted at a slightly different angle in the two images, so a precise measurement isn't possible, and this is where your artistic judgment can complete the equation you need.

Here's how to use the Info palette and the marquee tool to get a value for image size reduction:

Using the Image Size Command

Press **M** (for **M**arquee tool) until the Rectangular marquee tool is selected on the toolbox (or click on the tool while holding down Alt)	The Marquee tool toggles in function between the Elliptical and Rectangular marquee tool.
Press F8 (Macintosh F12), or choose **W**indow, **P**alettes, **S**how Info	Displays the Info palette.
Click on the IMG0039 image window; then click and drag a marquee from the top of Daves's head down to his chin	Displays the Width and Height of the marquee selection on the bottom field on the Info palette.

The authors' value for the height of Dave's head was 1.817. You'll probably get a different value, depending on where you start and end the marquee. You only need the height

continues

continued

measurement here for comparing to your next reading, so you should write this value down someplace, particularly if this was an assignment of your own!

Press Ctrl+D (<u>S</u>elect, <u>N</u>one)	Deselects the marquee.

Do *not* click within the image with the cursor to deselect the marquee! Many an image has been ruined through this practice. It is very easy to move the selection inside a marquee when you click on an image with a selection tool. You want to measure the height of Dave's head, not move it!

Double-click on the Hand tool, press **M** (**M**arquee tool), then click on the IMG0038 image window; then click and drag a marquee from the top of Dave's head down to his chin	Brings the viewing resolution to 1:2; displays the Width and Height of the marquee selection on the bottom field on the Info palette (see fig. 15.7).
Write down the value of the Height of the selection the Info palette now displays	This is the second piece of information you need for creating a percentage value to use in resizing IMG0038.
Get out a calculator and divide the smaller value (from IMG0039) by the larger value (from IMG0038)	Gives you the percentage that IMG0039 needs to be scaled by.

Because this is an exercise and not a test, we'll clue you into the best percentage value here: it's 92 percent. It's possible to get anywhere from 90 to 94 percent for the resulting amount, depending on exactly where in the two images you created the marquees. The authors tried three different percentages ranging from 90 to 94 percent before deciding that 92 percent is the best scaling factor to produce identical images of Dave in the two photos.

With the IMG0038 image window as the active document, choose **I**mage, **I**mage Size	Displays the Image Size dialog box.
Uncheck the Constrain **F**ile Size check box, choose Percent from the drop-down list at the right of the width field, and then type **92** in the Width field	Tells Photoshop to make the image 92 percent of its original dimensions (see fig. 15.8).

When the Constrain Proportions checkbox is checked (which it should *always* be), it's not necessary to enter a percentage in both Height and Width fields; Photoshop proportionately scales both dimensions when you fill in either field.

Click on OK	Photoshop scales the image to 92 percent of its original size.
Press Ctrl+S (<u>F</u>ile, <u>S</u>ave)	Saves your work up to this point.

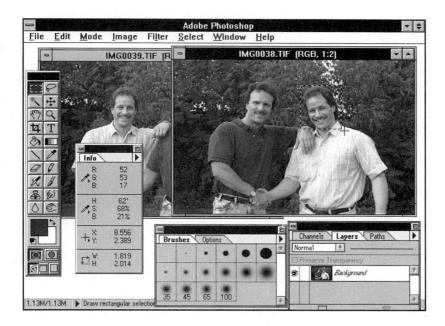

Figure 15.7

Use the Info palette to measure the relative sizes of an image area to create a fractional amount used as scaling information.

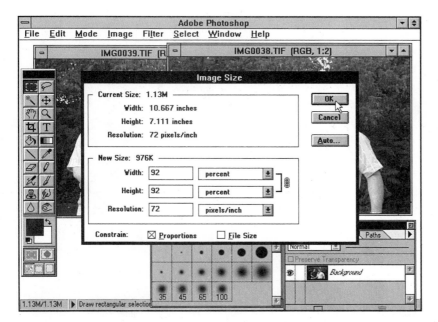

Figure 15.8

Use un-constrained File Size option in the Image Size command to scale an image to the correct dimensions.

By default, Photoshop's settings in the Image Size dialog box have both Proportion and File Size checkboxes checked, and this is because you distort (change) visual data when they're unchecked. You've actually created a change in the number of pixels in the IMG0038 file by assigning it a different percent of height and width. Keep a sharp eye on these settings before you use the Image Size command again with your own work to make certain that the Constrain field's checkboxes are returned to their default value of checked (on).

> **Tip**
>
> A calculator is a handy companion to Photoshop's tools, and you might already own one, right on your computer, without realizing it. Macintosh users have a desktop calculator found in the Apple menu as a Desk Accessory (DA), and Windows users have a Calculator in the Accessories Group in Program Manager (the file is CALC.EXE in the WINDOWS directory in case you removed the icon). With both operating platforms, it's a breeze to put Photoshop in the background for a moment while you pop up the digital calculator, plug in the readings you get from Photoshop's Info palette, and then use the data in the Image Size command (or on the Cropping tool Options palette) to resize an image.

Figure 15.9 is an example of how Dave looks in the resized IMG0038 when compared to Dave's "twin" in IMG0039. The scaling work you performed in the preceding exercise should provide the same results on your own screen, and if you now have this sort of dimensional relationship between the two images, you're all set to create a digital "family reunion" of sorts in the next section.

Figure 15.9

Compare the resized image to the IMG0039 image. Dave should appear to be the same size in both pictures.

Understanding the Secrets of Trick Photography

Before we even get to the refining of edges, cloning in areas using the Rubber Stamp tool, and the other enhancements you'll perform to the images to create a piece of trick photography, it's important that you learn a very important technique used by professional magicians:

Misdirection can help you accomplish an illusion.

For centuries, magicians have directed an audience's attention away from their left hand by doing something with their right, to hide a coin, scarf, or other artifact in their left hand. In terms of the illusion you're creating in this chapter's assignment, you need to perform a little misdirection, too, beginning with where you create the marquee selection in the IMG0039 picture to copy Dave. Your audience is going to scrutinize the finished image—they're going to look hard and close around the edges of both Daves to see where the border is, because at some level of perception, they'll suspect the finished image has been retouched.

So how do you misdirect the viewer's eye until the viewer gives up and accepts the image for the wonder that it is? Simple. You *don't crop tightly* around Dave to create a tight selection border, but instead copy Dave and about 1/4 inch of Dave's background into the IMG0038 file. The two backgrounds are almost identical in both images, and the visual content is of leaves—a visual element that can support some random cloning with the Rubber Stamp tool and still look like a natural clump of leaves. In the next exercise, you use the Lasso tool to make a freehand selection marquee around Dave and some of his surroundings, and then float the selection and use Photoshop's internal copying engine to drag and drop a copy of Dave into IMG0038.

Here's how to use the identical properties of the image backgrounds as a little camouflage in the finished design:

Creating a Loose Selection Marquee

Minimize the IMG0038 image. Windows users: click the minimize button on the upper left corner; Macintosh users: use the resize box to reduce the size of the image window

Makes IMG0039 the active image window and conserves system resources.

continues

continued

Double-click on the Zoom tool; then resize the image window so that you have a view of Dave's upper torso and head	This is the area where you'll begin creating the selection.
Press **L** (for **L**asso tool), then click and drag counterclockwise around Dave, leaving about 1/4 to 1/2 inch of background around his outline	Starts the freehand selection border (see fig. 15.10).

When you reach the bottom of the image window, you don't have far to go to reach the bottom of the image, but you can't use the window's scroll bars without releasing the Lasso tool, and thereby allowing Photoshop to auto-complete what would be an inaccurate selection marquee. Fortunately, Photoshop offers auto-panning within a window when you use a tool, and you access this feature in the next step. When you reach the bottom of the image window, perform these steps:

Drag down, and about a fraction of an inch to the left	Pans your view in the image window and continues with the Lasso tool to create a border line that extends to the bottom of the image.

You want to move in a direction away from the intended selection area when you use image window panning with a tool, to avoid accidentally trimming any portions of the actor out of the finished selection marquee. Doing this is very much like trimming a piece of paper with shears: you trim *away* from the area of the paper you want to remain.

Continue clicking and dragging against the bottom of the image window; when you're 1/4" to the right of Dave's left pant leg, click and drag upwards, and include Gary's (actor in dark shirt) arm inside the border	Creates a bottom to the selection border that's flush with the image edge; finishes most of the right side of the selection border.

It is critical to include the other actor's contribution to the handshake in the selection of Dave. You use part of Gary's arm in the finished image. Skip ahead to figure 15.11 to see what the finished selection marquee should look like if you're uncertain about this step.

Click and drag away from the right side of Dave; then *slowly* click and drag at the top edge of the image window	Forces the image window to pan upwards, so that you can see the beginning of the marquee.
When the Lasso tool is positioned close to the beginning of the selection, and is positioned outside areas of Dave, release the mouse button	Completes the selection border, and the outline becomes a marquee selection.

Double-click on the Hand tool

Zooms you out to a full frame view of the image (see fig. 15.11).

If you need to take a break at this point, save the selection by clicking on the (Save to) Selection icon on the lower left of the Channels palette. If you're game to continue, however, you don't have to save the marquee, but don't accidentally deselect it. The remaining steps for copying Dave to the IMG0038 are presented in the next section.

Figure 15.10

Include about 1/2" of background foliage in your selection of the foreground actor.

As an alternative method for selecting Dave and parts of the background in the preceding exercise, you could have first created a selection that only extended to the edge of the image window. You'd then release the mouse button to create a marquee, and then add to the marquee to make it include the areas you couldn't see by holding down the Shift key and click and dragging to add to the selection. Many ways to accomplish a specific task are available using Photoshop's tools, and the auto-panning feature for document windows offers a unique advantage when you can't view the area you want to select from the view a window affords.

Magic trick #2 in this chapter's assignment is making the twins in the image appear to be shaking hands, and this is why you were asked to include the other actor's arm in the selection marquee around Dave. People aren't going to look at the twins' hands in the finished image, and for this reason it's far easier to incorporate the entire handshake in the finished image than to try to trim and cut around Dave's fingers in both images. You'll blend areas of Dave's forearm with the other actor's hand to achieve a seamless blend that appears very natural in this assignment, and people absolutely will not look at the forearm area to see where you edited the two images together. This is why finding a stand-in of the same sex, race, and build as the actor is so important. Again, misdirection, by placing image areas together where the viewer won't notice them, will make the finished image stupendous and much easier to execute!

Figure 15.11

Releasing the mouse button automatically finishes (closes) the marquee selection. Make sure it includes all of the actor.

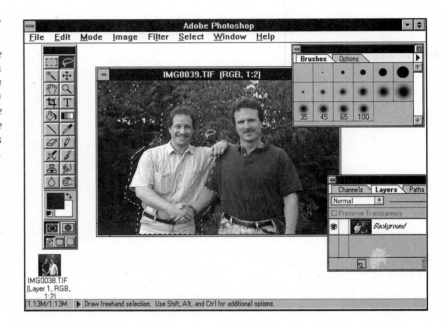

Copying and Positioning a Floating Selection

The next exercise teaches you a trick for positioning the copy of Dave in the IMG0038 image before you deselect it and it becomes a layer object. Floating selections and layers can both be assigned an opacity, and this is the key to accurately positioning the copy of Dave. First, you'll assign a 50-percent opacity to the floating copy to check out the relative position of the copied selection upon the layer; floating selections can have any mode or opacity assigned to them, and the effect is not permanent until you deselect the image into the layer. After you have the copy on the layer, you then assign a partial opacity to the layer, to see through the layer image, and line up the pasted copy so that the area of the layer that contains the other actor's hand lines up better with the image of Dave on the Background layer.

When positioning and repositioning the copy, whether it's a floating selection or actually part of the layer, a possible design hazard exists that the next exercise steers you clear of. Make certain that when part of a copied or floating selection falls outside the image window, you don't do any kind of editing, and this includes changing opacity. If you do, the area outside the image window will be discarded. Additionally, if the floating selection is deselected while part of the image is off the image window and any editing occurs (effects applied, painting, changes in opacity), Photoshop will clip the area that's outside the window. If a floating selection is deselected and no editing is performed, the Move tool can be used to bring the image areas outside the window back into the image window, and no image-clipping or loss will occur.

These are important points to remember because if image areas are clipped off, it can ruin the assignment. Very little image detail exists between the hands shaking and the bottom edge of the selection, and you need as much of the bottom of the copy as you can spare to make the composite, finished image look real. Additionally, if the floating selection is deselected while you've assigned it a partial opacity, the image will stay partially opaque on the layer, and no further adjustments can make it more opaque. Finally, if you change opacity for Layer 1 while part of the image is out of the image window, Photoshop considers this a Layer Option edit (change) and discards the image area outside the image window. This assignment has a few rules that seem tough, but the rewards are absolutely sterling image editing.

In the next exercise, you use varying layer and floating selection opacities to help you position the handshake part of the floating selection so that it's slightly to the right of the handshake in the background image (IMG0038). The handshakes in IMG0039 and IMG0039 have slightly different angles, and you use parts of both images in the finished right arm area in the picture. The blend of Dave's forearm and Gary's hand would produce a super-muscular, ridiculously wide forearm on the Dave in IMG0038 if you didn't "cheat" a little on positioning of the two elements.

Follow these steps to copy and position the contents of the selection marquee you created last to set up the scene of our twins:

Copying and Positioning a Twin Image

Restore the IMG0038 image	Makes IMG0038 the current image window.
Press F7 (Macintosh: F11) (**W**indow, **P**alettes, Show **L**ayers). Click on the New Layer icon on the bottom of the palette; then click on OK in the New Layer dialog box	Displays the Layers palette, creates new Layer 1, and it becomes the current editing layer.

Both image windows should be at 1:2 viewing resolution now, and you should reposition the images so that you have a clear view of both.

continues

continued

Click and drag the marquee selection in IMG0039 to IMG0038. Do *not* deselect it	Makes a copy of the marquee selection; the copy is now a floating selection above Layer 1 in the IMG0038 image (see fig. 15.12).
Press **5** on the keyboard	Photoshop makes a compositing change to the floating selection; it becomes 50 percent opaque.

Similarly, you can click and drag the Opacity slider to the 50 percent position on the Layers palette to make the floating selection 50 percent opaque. This is *not* recommended in this assignment, however. You should keep your cursor inside the floating selection, which means using keyboard shortcuts instead of the cursor, to prevent accidental deselection.

Now that you can see Gary (the actor in dark shirt) on the background and Dave as a floating selection, you now position the two images so that they line up for final compositing of the floating selection into Layer 1.

Click and drag the floating selection so that both actors' hands in the floating selection and in the Background image basically line up	This is the coarse positioning of the floating selection (see fig. 15.13).
Press Ctrl+plus, then click and drag on the image window to maximize the IMG0038 image	Provides a full-frame view of the image. Windows users can click on the maximize button on the upper right of the image window.
Press the arrow keys until the handshake area on the floating selection is on top of the handshake in the image background, and the bottom edge of the floating selection is inside the image window	Keyboard arrow keys nudge the floating selection 1 pixel in any of four directions for precision placement.
Press **0** on the keyboard, then press Ctrl+D (**S**elect, **N**one)	Returns the floating selection to full (100 percent) opacity and deselects the image.
Press **Z** (**Z**oom tool); then click and drag a marquee around the handshake area	Zooms you to a 2:1 viewing resolution of the handshake area.
Press **V** (layer **M**ove tool); then press **5**	Chooses the Layer Move tool, and decreases the opacity of Layer 1 to 50 percent.

The selection on Layer 1 appears as a 50-percent opaque image once again, so you can refine the position of its selection. You can assign an opacity to a layer (and its contents) with any

tool chosen, but you can only *move* layer contents, the image objects in the transparent layer, when the Move tool is chosen. You won't use the Move tool, per se, in the next step, but the arrow keys can only nudge layer contents when the Move tool is active.

Press the arrow keys until the top of Gary's arm (shaking Dave's hand in the selection) on Layer 1 is slightly to the right of Dave's arm on the background layer	Moves layer contents by one pixel per arrow keystroke. See figure 15.14 for an illustration of the final position for the selection on Layer 1.

Make certain now that the image areas on Layer 1 that you want included in the finished image are inside the image window before the next step. You're deciding on the final position of the layer's image contents now, not to be changed for the image again. When you change the opacity back to 100 percent for the Layer to complete this exercise, Photoshop considers this a change to the Layer Options, and any part of the layer's image content that's outside the image window will be clipped (discarded).

Press **0** on the keyboard (or click and drag the Opacity slider on the 100%)	Changes the Layer Options for degree of Opacity assigned to layer Layers palette to contents to 100 percent.
Choose **F**ile, Sa**v**e As; then save the image as DAVE2X.PSD to your hard disk	Saves your work up to this point.
Close the IMG0039 image	You're through with it.

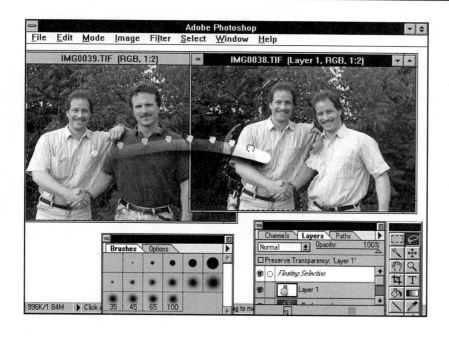

Figure 15.12

Click and drag the marquee selection into the IMG0038 window to copy the selected image areas.

Figure 15.13

Change the opacity of the floating selection so that you can see both images by pressing a keyboard number key.

Figure 15.14

Nudge the layer contents to exactly the right position on the layer by using the keyboard arrow keys.

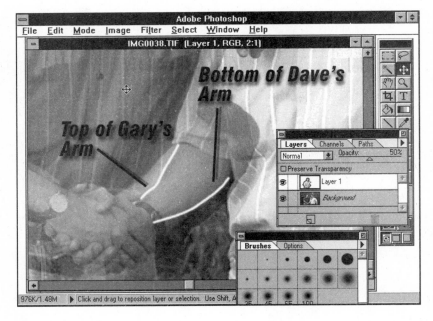

The position and opacity of the copy of Dave on Layer 1 results in the new DAVE2X image looking like the image in figure 15.15. You begin the editing process to seamlessly integrate the images on the two layers next, so do not reposition the copy of Dave on Layer 1 any further!

Both the Background and Layer 1 now contain unwanted image areas that will be removed using a number of different Photoshop techniques.

You have several technical advantages going for you in the retouching work in this assignment because the composite of the two images exists on separate layers. Begin the visual integration of the DAVE2X image by working on the edges where Gary, the other actor, still peeks through Layer 1.

Figure 15.15

The final positioning of Layer 1's contents should reflect a correct anatomical positioning of the copy and background image.

Blending Natural Texture Using the Rubber Stamp Tool

A quick glance at the DAVE2X image right now shows you that the edges of the image on Layer 1 do indeed integrate well into the corresponding areas on the Background layer. The natural patterns of the trees behind the actor display little evidence of photo-trickery because the eye doesn't spend much time examining every individual leaf. Instead, the human eye tends to accept masses of leaves as a texture, and the edges where Layer 1's leaves meet the Background layer's leaves are well-hidden by the irregular pattern found in the trees.

Still, Gary, the stand-in on the Background layer presently behind the copy of Dave, sticks out to the left of Dave's shoulder, because the copy of Dave isn't in exactly the same position as Gary, and their respective body positions aren't identical. In the next exercise, you use the Rubber Stamp tool in combination with the Sampled Merged painting option to sample from one layer and clone to the other, to blend the visible edges around the trees into a flawless landscape to support the image's composition.

Here's how to clone random texture into both layers and remove unwanted image details from the DAVE2X picture:

Cloning Between Layers

Press Ctrl+plus to view the image at 2:1 viewing resolution	This is a good resolution to accurately retouch the superfluous areas on both layers.
Double-click on the Rubber Stamp tool	Chooses the Rubber Stamp tool and displays the Options palette for the tool.
Choose Clone (aligned) from the Option drop-down list, set Mode to Normal, Opacity: **100%**; then check the Sample Merged checkbox	Sets the characteristics for the Rubber Stamp tool to sample from both image layers in opaque, normal style of cloning.
Click on the Brushes tab on the Brushes/Options palette; then click on the second from the left tip, second row	Defines the size and softness of the tip you use with the Rubber Stamp tool.
Click on the Background layer title on the Layers palette list	Makes the Background the current editing layer.
Scroll the image window so that you can see the upper left corner of DAVE2X	This is the area you'll edit with the Rubber Stamp tool.
Press Alt (Option) while clicking and click over an area of the background trees that is deeply shaded	Pressing Alt sets the travelling sample point for the Rubber Stamp tool.
Release the Alt key; then click and drag over the dark blue shirt area outside the borderline you see around the copy of Dave	Clones sampled Background image areas over the shirt on the Background layer (see fig. 15.16).

Because you're editing on the Background layer, the Rubber Stamp tool will apparently stop cloning when you reach the hard outline of the Dave copy, which is on Layer 1. That's okay; continue clicking and dragging to remove the dark blue shirt and other Background areas that don't consist of foliage. When you've cloned over the dark shirt areas on the Background, perform these steps:

Click on the Layer 1 title on the Layers palette's list	Makes Layer 1 the target (current editing) layer.
Press Alt and click over the light foliage between the two Daves and towards the top of his heads	Sets the sample point for the cursor.
Click and drag on the left edge of the copied layer image	Blends sample image from the Background layer into image areas and transparent areas on Layer 1 (see fig. 15.17).
Reset the sampling point for the Rubber Stamp to sample foliage of the corresponding colors you find on the edge of the image on Layer 1; then click and drag over the image edge	Continually resetting the Rubber Stamp tool's sampling point helps break up repeating patterns of foliage and keeps the texture and color of the foliage you're cloning consistent with Background image details.

You're done when you reach the edge on Layer 1 where the hand(s) are on Dave's right shoulder.

File, **S**ave (or press Ctrl+S)	Saves your work at this intermediate stage of completion.

You'll find that to blend the edge on Layer 1 in a convincing way so that the copy looks like part of the Background layer, the Sample Merged option for the Rubber Stamp tool needs to be in effect when you clone on both layers. The greatest challenge in blending the edgework into the background is the proper matching of the different kinds of foliage; choose a lighter sampling point when you want to clone over lighter colored edge details, and use a darker foliage sample for the edge areas that contain darker trees. And don't be afraid to clone in an extra pine cone or two to further distract the viewer from your handiwork around Layer 1's image edges!

Figure 15.16

Clone in background foliage to remove the dark shirt area that's exposed on the Background layer.

Figure 15.17

Use the Sample Merged option to sample from the Background layer and clone in image areas on Layer 1.

Using the Layer Mask To Remove Superfluous Areas

Because the other actor's hand is already on Dave's shoulder on the Background layer, any areas you may have copied to Layer 1 that included Dave's hand-on-shoulder from the IMG0039 image are now unwanted in the DAVE2X image. And as you've seen in the preceding figures, Gary's hand makes the hand presently on the Background image of Dave's shoulder appear to have a surplus of digits. The next area you work on in this image is where Layer 1 Dave's left shoulder meets the hand on Background Dave's left shoulder and the areas below the hands.

The best option Photoshop affords for accurately defining an image edge on a layer is the Layer Mask. The Layer Mask is invisible and can best be thought of as a special property a layer has; when you add foreground color to a layer that has a Layer Mask, the image areas you paint over with black foreground color are hidden. Similarly, areas you've hidden reappear when you paint over them with white foreground color.

Note The property that black foreground color indicates when working on a Layer Mask is, by default, set to indicate hidden areas—that is, you add black to a Layer Mask and it hides image areas on the corresponding layer.

Most of this book refers to an effect or an editing step with Photoshop's default settings to ensure consistent results among readers who perform the exercise steps. If you've changed the default setting for the Layer Mask, you should double-click on the Layer Mask icon after the Add Layer Mask step is performed, click on the Color Indicates: Hidden Areas radio button, and then click on OK. This restores the Layer Mask Options to their default settings, and you can successfully perform the exercise steps!

In the next exercise, you remove image areas on Layer 1 that shouldn't be in the final image by "painting" Layer Mask over the unwanted areas to hide them. Then you apply your editing and remove the hidden areas from the DAVE2X image. Some of the other actor's dark shirt will show through from the original image on the Background layer because of your editing, but that's perfectly fine, and this is addressed as a different part of the image editing process later.

The following exercise shows you how to use the Layer Mask option to refine the image area presently on the transparent background of Layer 1:

Using the Layer Mask To Remove Layer Areas

Click on the Layer 1 title on the Layers palette's list	Makes Layer 1 the target layer for editing.
Scroll the image window so that you can see the hand-on-shoulder area	This is the image area on Layer 1 you'll edit.
Click on the pop-up menu icon to the right of the Layers tab on the palette, and choose Add Layer Mask (see fig. 15.18)	Adds a Layer Mask to Layer 1, and you're now editing on a Layer Mask, not the Layer itself.

An icon appears to the right of the Layer icon with a thick black outline around it, indicating that the active element of Layer 1 is the Layer Mask, not Layer 1. By default, the image icon is white, but it reflects any changes you make to the mask by displaying black within the icon wherever you've hidden image areas on Layer 1.

Press **B** (Paint **B**rush tool), keep the tip the same (on the brushes palette), and set the Options to **100%** Opacity, Normal mode	Sets the characteristic of the Paint Brush to apply opaque foreground color to the Layer Mask.
Press **D** (**d**efault colors icon)	Sets the current painting color to black.
Click and drag over the hand area that's part of Layer 1 (the leftmost hand) (See fig 15.19)	Hides the hand; exposes more of the hand on the Background layer.
Continue clicking and dragging until the outstretched hand on the Background layer is completely exposed	You're hiding image areas on Layer 1 that should not appear in the finished image.

Because the Background and Layer 1 feature images are identical in content, it's easy to edit a little too far into Layer 1 and remove some of Dave's shirt. This is bad. You want the outstretched hand on the shoulder to be exposed up to the edge of the hand. If you've gone too far to the left with the Paint Brush in the image, follow these steps:

Press **X** (switch colors icon on the toolbox)	Changes the current foreground color to white. Painting on the Layer Mask with white restores image areas that are hidden.

Click and drag over areas you want to appear in the final image	Clicking and dragging restores your view of the hidden areas.
Press **D** (**d**efault colors icon)	Restores current foreground color to black.
Scroll the image window down so that you can see where the two Daves' shirts meet	This is the next area to be edited.
Press Ctrl+plus	Increases your viewing resolution to 4:1. Precision editing and an adequate view are required in the next steps.
Click and drag to the right of the blue shirt area; then work your strokes up and down from right to left	Removes the blue shirt from Layer 1, exposing Dave's shirt on the Background layer.

The shirt area will be hardest to edit without exposing Background layer detail of leaves and other areas. In other words, you will edit too far into Layer 1 because of the identical detail in the two Daves's shirts on different Layers, as shown in figure 15.20. No problem; when you do, follow these steps:

Press **X** (switch colors icon); then click and drag, starting from the left edge of the blue shirt, stroking up and down, moving from left to right	Restores hidden areas on Layer 1 to make Dave's shirt on Layer 1 and his shirt on the Background appear to meet (see fig. 15.21).
When you're done editing the hand and shirt areas, click on the pop-up menu button on the Layers palette and choose Remove Layer Mask	Displays a dialog box that offers options concerning removal of the Layer Mask.
Click on **A**pply	Permanently removes the hidden image areas from Layer 1.
Press Ctrl+S (**F**ile, **S**ave)	Saves your work up to this point.

Tip You can increase the size of the image icons on the Layers palette by clicking on the pop-up menu, and then choosing Palette Options. In the Palette Options dialog box, you can choose various sizes for the image icons, or choose to have no icon on a Layer title.

By choosing the largest image icon, you get a better icon view of the editing changes you make when in Layer Mask mode. Unfortunately, the larger the image icons, the more system resources are required to display and redraw them. You may experience system slowdowns when large image icons are on the palette.

Another factor to consider when choosing the size of palette icons is that the palette needs to be larger when large icons are used, which means that you have less screen real estate within which to do your work.

An alternative technique that gives you a better view of a Layer Mask is to press Shift and click on the Layer mask image icon. This displays the areas over which you've edited as Quick Mask tint overlay. This changes the display of the Layer Mask, but the way you edit, and results you achieve, are identical to those achieved when Photoshop hides the areas you cover with foreground color. To change the display back to default mode for Layer Mask editing, press Shift and click on the Layer Mask icon a second time.

Figure 15.18

Choose Add Layer Mask from the Layers palette's pop-up menu to create an editing layer upon Layer 1.

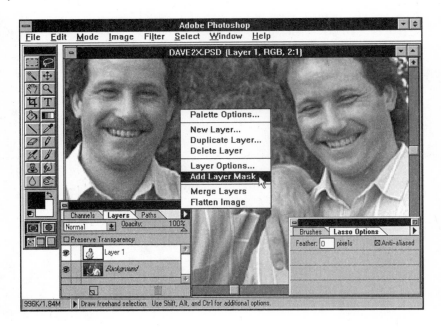

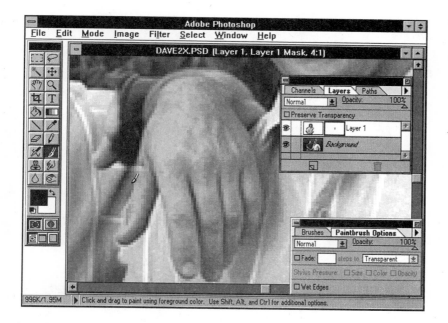

Figure 15.19

Hide the image areas you don't want on Layer 1 by painting over the areas with foreground color.

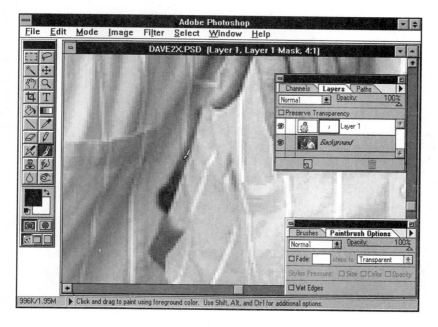

Figure 15.20

Foreground color hides the dark shirt area on Layer 1 that separates your view of the two actors.

Figure 15.21

Restore hidden image areas by painting with white foreground color.

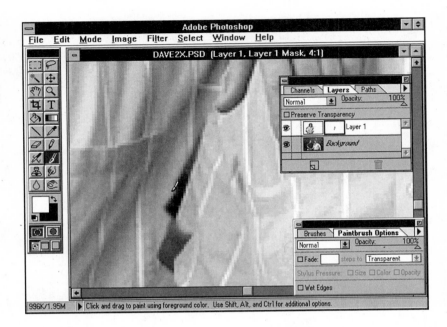

As you saw in the preceding exercise, changes you make to Layer 1 are actually a function of the Layer Mask you are painting on and aren't permanent until you choose Remove Layer Mask, then click on Apply. After you click on Apply, the hidden image areas are discarded from the file and can't be retrieved unless you immediately press Ctrl+Z (or choose **E**dit, **U**ndo) to negate the Apply command.

The area where Layer 1 Dave meets Background Dave around the shoulder area looks better now that the original hand area copied from IMG0039 is no longer there, but you're now left with a gap in the image. Because Dave's hand in the copy on Layer 1 covered part of his shirt, removing the area exposes background image where the viewer should see an extension of his shirt.

For every problem, multiple solutions are available when you work in Photoshop, and in the next section, you see how to use the first of two techniques for restoring a shoulder that in real life wasn't photographed!

Quick Masking an Area for Retouching

Like the Layer Mask, Photoshop's Quick Mask feature enables you to refine the definition of a masked or selected area before you commit to anything. Quick Mask is sort of a selection marquee that's in a "paint state." You can use the painting (and editing) tools to design a selection area and refine it, and when you're satisfied with it

you can convert it to a selection marquee. While in Quick Mask mode, you cannot harm or edit the underlying image; you're defining an image area with tinted overlay, and until you switch back to Standard editing mode, all the changes you make on an image or image Layer are made to the tint, not the image.

Using Quick Mask is a marvelous way to precisely define an area. You need the precision that the Quick Mask provides to restore the missing part of Dave's shirt on Layer 1 without altering original image areas. You also need a steady hand and critical eye if the areas you restore are to seamlessly blend into the rest of the image. In the next exercise, you set up the selection marquee for the missing shoulder area by using the Paint Brush tool to apply the Quick Mask overlay; then you perform a little Rubber Stamp tool magic to clone in areas that can be replaced with existing image details.

The following exercise shows you how to restore an area defined by a selection created with Photoshop's Quick Mask feature:

Defining and Editing a Quick Mask Area

Double-click on the Quick Mask button (the right bottom one) on the toolbox	Displays the Quick Mask Options dialog box.
Click on the Color Indicates: **S**elected Areas radio button; then click on OK	Defines areas covered with Quick Mask overlay as selected areas; image areas without the overlay tint are masked (protected) areas.
Press Ctrl+plus; then scroll to Dave's missing shoulder area on Layer 1	Moves you to a closer viewing resolution of the area that requires editing. Ultra-precision is required in defining the Quick Mask.
Press **B** (for Paint **B**rush tool), choose the first visible brush tip on the top row from the Brushes palette, then click and drag outside the edge of the hand	You're creating an edge to the Quick Mask that excludes the hand from the selection.
Continue downwards, clicking and dragging slightly into the shirt area; then paint slightly into Dave's shirt on Layer 1, going upward	You're defining the bottom left edge of the Quick Mask.

continues

continued

Complete the edge of the Quick Mask area with a stroke that connects the left side of the mask border to the point where you first started applying Quick Mask	You've defined the outskirts of the area you'll paint into with Quick Mask tint overlay. The dark shirt area above the missing area of Dave's shirt should be included in the Quick Masked areas.
Click and drag inside the border you've created (see fig. 15.22)	Begins to define the interior of the Quick Mask outline.

When you have a solid outline defined for the Quick Mask area, it's time to fill the interior because the inside areas need to be selected for painting, too.

Press Ctrl+minus, then fill the interior of the outline you created (see fig. 15.23)	Zooms out one field of resolution; defines everything covered with Quick Mask as image areas that can be edited; non-tinted image areas will be protected when you switch from Quick Mask to Standard Editing Mode.
Click on the Standard editing mode button (to the left of the Quick Mask button) on the toolbox	Changes the Quick Mask overlay to an active selection with a marquee border defining the boundary of the selection.

It's important not to accidentally deselect the marquee selection at this point. The selection marquee is not a saved selection, but fortunately, you can't deselect the selection by clicking on the image when a painting tool is active.

Press Ctrl+plus three times	Zooms you back into the area to be edited.
Press **S** (for Rubber **S**tamp tool), make sure that the Sample Merged checkbox is checked on the Options palette, and then press Alt and click on background foliage above the marquee selection	Sets the sampling point for the Rubber Stamp tool, and you can now sample from Background layer areas to cover the dark shirt above the missing area of Dave's shirt.
Choose the third tip, second row on the Brushes palette	Sets a very small size for the sampling point and the cloning tip for the Rubber Stamp tool.
Click and drag over the dark shirt area within the marquee border	Replaces transparent pixels on Layer 1 with foliage, hiding the blue shirt area (see fig. 15.24).

Press Alt and click outside the marquee, on Dave's shirt, directly to the left of the missing shirt area inside the marquee	Samples the shirt area.
Click and drag from left to right over the missing shirt area	Replaces the missing shirt with cloned image sample.

You're now at an editing impasse, as shown in figure 15.25. There simply aren't any more image areas you can sample from to replace the image areas that presently feature a thumb and the dark shirt on the Background layer. You need a new approach, you need to read about it in the next section, and you need to save the carefully defined marquee selection you've created.

Click on the Channels tab on the grouped palettes; then click on the (Save to) Selection icon on the lower left of the Channels palette	Saves the marquee selection to a new Alpha channel #4.
Press Ctrl+S (**F**ile, **S**ave)	Saves your work up to this point.

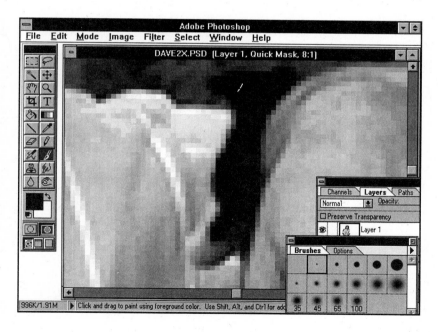

Figure 15.22

Use a very small Brushes tip to first create an outline of the area you want selected in the image.

Figure 15.23

Fill in the Quick Mask outline with a larger Brushes tip to make the interior of the Quick Mask border a selected area.

Figure 15.24

Use an image area from the Background layer to add to Layer 1's visual information and cover unwanted areas on the Background.

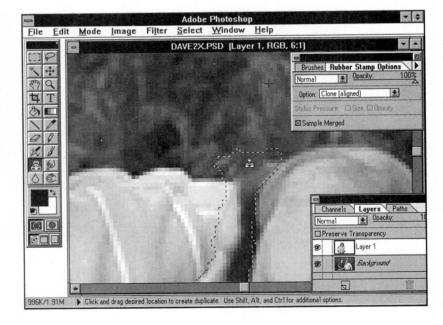

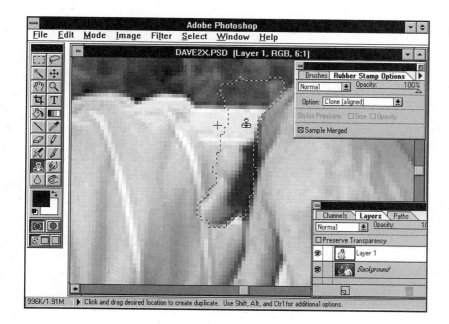

Figure 15.25

Cloning is not possible with the Rubber Stamp tool when no more sample information is in the image!

As mentioned at the beginning of this section, you need to adopt a two-part technique for restoring this particular area of the DAVE2X image. The first part, that which you've accomplished so far, can be called the "cloning as much as you can" technique, and it's a fair enough practice up to the point when you run out of image areas to sample!

The next steps get you into a different area of Photoshop, that of painting over a small image area. How does painting compare to copying and cloning to retouch an image? When done correctly, it produces the same, invisible results. Read on!

Retouching with the Paint Brush Tool

Many imaging professionals cringe when they don't have enough source material to cover damaged or missing areas in a photo they're trying to restore. The reason for the reaction is simple; if you don't fully understand Photoshop's marvelous set of tools and features, it's easy to get in a rut and depend on familiar tools and editing techniques to finish an assignment. The DAVE2X image is simply missing an area that would produce a glaring error in the finished image if left alone, and yet you don't have any available source image areas to patch the shoulder on Layer 1. Cloning from other areas of Dave's shirt to replace the missing area is out of the question: the missing area must be replaced with the correct striped pattern and shading found outside the edge of the missing area.

Instead of attempting to clone and reset the Rubber Stamp tool's sampling point a dozen times to produce an image area that looks phony and awkward at best, take a different approach. Foreground color samples of areas next to the missing area can be taken with the Eyedropper tool, and the Paint Brush tool can be used to paint in the missing shoulder area. This is a revolutionary concept, but the successful use of this technique has its roots in the principles of bitmap image types and resolution. Not as many pixels as you think are required to reconstruct this part of Dave's shirt (the image resolution is only 72 pixels/inch, like all PhotoCD format images), and the visual content of the area is slight when compared to the rest of the image. Additionally, the viewer's eye will be drawn to areas of more interest, such as the handshake and the "twins'" faces, if other areas don't call too much attention to themselves.

In the next exercise, you'll recall the saved selection to serve as your "virtual dropcloth" when you paint over transparent areas of Layer 1. You'll also hide the Background layer so that you can see the problem areas on Layer 1 against Photoshop's checkerboard layer background without the visual distraction of the Background image. Although the visual integration of the two image layers is critical to making the "identical twins" effect a convincing one, you have to separate the visual integration you see on-screen during this phase of the retouching so that you can adequately evaluate the areas that need editing.

The following exercise shows you how to paint the DAVE2X image to perfection using sampled foreground colors and the Quick Mask feature.

Painting Foreground Image Details

Press Alt and click on the Channel #4 title on the Channels palette's list	Loads the marquee selection you saved in the preceding exercise.
Press Ctrl+H (**S**elect, Hide **E**dges)	Hides the marquee selection so that you can see the area you need to paint into. The marquee is still active, however.
Press **B** (for Paint **B**rush tool); then click on the second row, second tip on the Brushes palette	Chooses the Paint Brush tool and sets the characteristics for the tip and the way foreground color is applied.
Press Alt(Option) and click on the shirt directly to the left of the image area that still displays the dark blue shirt	Alt key toggles the Paint Brush tool to the Eyedropper and samples a foreground color from the image.

Release the Alt key, click on the eye icon on the Background layer on the Layers palette, and then click and drag left to right beginning where the image ends, from the same horizontal point where you sampled the foreground color	Applies foreground color to the transparent areas within the selection on Layer 1.

When you get to a certain point toward the right of the transparent area you're painting over, the Paint Brush tool appears to stop working! This is where the hidden marquee selection ends, and you should, too. The area of Dave's shoulder in Layer 1 displays shading, top to bottom, light to dark. After you've made one or two horizontal passes with the Paint Brush tool and the first foreground color value you sampled, it's time to sample a darker shade.

Press Alt and click over a deeper shade of gray on Dave's shoulder area	Samples a deeper foreground color.
Release the Alt key; then click and drag horizontally, starting at the area where you sampled and travelling horizontally, left to right over the transparent area on Layer 1	Fills the transparent area with foreground color (see fig. 15.26).
Press Alt and click over a white stripe on Dave's shoulder; then click on the left tip, second row on the Brushes palette	Chooses a very small Paint Brush tip, with which you'll paint a white stripe.
Release the Alt key; then click and drag horizontally to paint a shirt stripe in the selection area	Completes the stripe of Dave's shirt.
Click to the left of the Background Layer title, directly beneath the eye icon next to the Layer 1 title	Restores your view of the Background layer so that you can see your progress.
Press Alt and click on a different shade of shirt sleeve in Layer 1	Chooses a different foreground color with which to paint.
Release the Alt key; then click and drag horizontally, from left to right	Covers more transparent image areas on Layer 1 (see fig. 15.27).

By now, most of the Background areas have been hidden by your painting on Layer 1. It's time to deselect the hidden marquee and get to one or two strokes of edgework around the selection marquee.

continues

Press Ctrl+D (**S**elect, **N**one) selection; you're free to paint anywhere on Layer 1 to better blend image tones together	Deselects the hidden marquee.
Click and drag a short stroke wherever a sharp edge appears to be between original image and your paint strokes on Layer 1	Hides the Background image areas and disguises obvious Paint Brush strokes.
Press Ctrl+S (**F**ile, **S**ave)	Saves your work up to this point.

Figure 15.26

Sample a foreground color from existing image areas, and then paint in the transparent pixels on Layer 1.

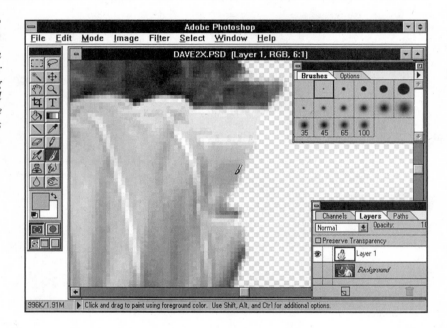

The marquee selection you used in the preceding exercise was created by using a soft-tip Paint Brush in Quick Mask mode, and because the resulting selection marquee has soft edges, soft areas of transition between painted areas and original image were blended together. However, the edge of the hand on Dave's shoulder should make a clean transition from hand color to Dave's shirt color. And it doesn't, because some dark blue shirt is still poking through transparent areas of Layer 1 right around the edge of the hand.

To correct this area requires no painting or cloning with the Rubber Stamp tool. Instead, use an editing tool, the Blur tool, to hide the tell-tale edge pixels in the next section.

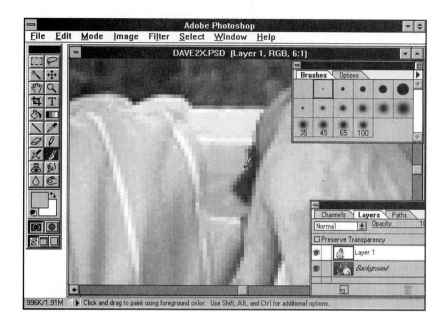

Figure 15.27

Hide and display Layer 1 so that you can see where the paint strokes are covering the Background layer.

Using the Blur Tool in Lighten Mode

A fascinating thing happens when use you the Toning, Smudge, or Focus tools on an image area that has both colored pixels and transparent Layer pixels on it. You can "push" the colored, opaque color values into the transparent areas to create a smooth transition between opaque and transparent pixels. With any of the image editing tools toward the bottom of Photoshop's toolbox, the technique to use with them is to blend *from* an area, *to* a different area. Unlike the painting tools (except for the Gradient Fill tool), these editing tools are directional in the sense that they produce different results based on the direction you in which you use them.

In the next exercise, you use one of the Focus tools—the Blur tool—to spread some of the color values in the painted areas of Dave's shirt on Layer 1 to the edge of the hand on the "other" Dave's shoulder. Take your time when using this tool and use precisely-positioned, short strokes. Using precise, short strokes will take some of the color values from the painted areas and spread them into the left edge of the hand without ruining the area that defines the edge of the hand. The objective here is not to remove the hard, dark edge of the hand, but instead to "bleach" it using semi-opaque pixels whose color comes from the area you first click over with the Blur tool.

You now use the Blur tool to create partially transparent pixels that partially cover the Background layer.

Using the Blur Tool for Image Editing

Press Ctrl+minus twice	Zooms the image window out to 4:1 viewing resolution so that you see a less pixellated view of DAVE2X.
Press **R** (for Blur tool), then set the Options palette to normal Mode, **50%** Pressure	Sets the characteristics of the Blur tool to work at half-strength.
Uncheck the Sample Merged checkbox on the Options palette if it's checked	You don't want to sample colors from the Background layer as part of the blur effect.
Choose the tip that is the second from the left, on the second row on the Brushes palette	Sets the size and softness of the Blur tool's tip.
Click and drag a short stroke from the painted area of Dave's shirt to the dark edge of the hand	Partially obscures the dark edge with semi-opaque pixels taken from Dave's shirt.
Click and drag another stroke from the painted area of Dave's shirt to the edge of the hand	Continues to obscure the dark edge (see fig. 15.28).

Four or five strokes with the Blur tool should do the trick. You're done when you see no clear distinction between the brightness value of Dave's painted shirt and the hand on his "twin's" shoulder.

You actually accomplished two things in the preceding exercise: you decreased the contrast in an image area that displayed a harsh outline, and you lightened the area by adding semi-transparent pixels of a lighter value to Layer 1. This covers the sliver of dark shirt that showed through the transparent pixels on Layer 1 from the Background layer. When used on totally opaque pixels on background images, the Blur tool decreases contrast between neighboring pixels, so you can think of the Blur tool in normal mode as a "pixel brightness averaging" tool. However, when you click and drag with the Blur tool from an area of opaque pixels to transparent ones, as you did last, the effect of the Blur tool is to average the *opacity* of neighboring pixels to achieve a blend. This is why it's important to always begin the Blur tool stroke in an opaque area, and then drag to a transparent one. If you go back and forth on a layer with the Blur tool, you'll subtract opacity from pixels that are at the end of your stroke!

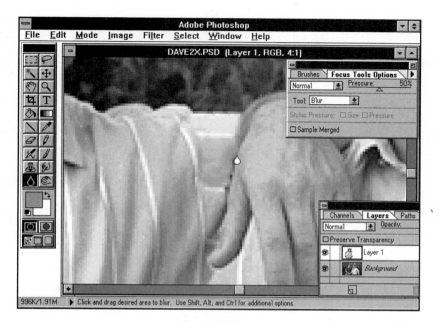

Figure 15.28

Use the Blur tool to create semi-opaque pixels in transparent areas bordering the opaque image areas.

Restoring and Editing Between Image Layers

You need to go back for a second helping of the Layer Mask feature next to create the most distracting, and most effective, illusion the finished image will present: Dave's going to shake hands with himself. You were asked to include part of the other actor's arm in the marquee selection of Dave in IMG0039 at the beginning of this chapter for an important reason; the area where Layer 1 and the Background layer will meet around the handshake area will be at a diagonal. Areas of Gary's *and* Dave's arm will both be included in the final composition—you're going to sculpt and blend the image layers together in an area that a viewer would never suspect because the area is so clearly out in the open!

To accomplish the blend between layers is easier than you might think. Many steps were taken at the beginning of the chapter to ensure that the handshake between layers line up in such a way that the Layer Mask can be used to selectively hide a portion of Layer 1 and let the angle of Dave's forearm on the Background naturally flow into the information on Layer 1.

The following exercise shows how to use the Layer Mask to visually integrate the handshake between image layers.

Revealing Background Image Layer Elements

Press **B** (Paint **B**rush tool); then choose the middle, second row tip from the Brushes palette	Sets the characteristics for the tool you'll use with the Layer Mask.
Press Ctrl+minus twice; then scroll to the handshake area in the DAVE2X image	Zooms your view out to 2:1 resolution and moves to where you'll add Layer Mask information.
Press **D** (**d**efault colors icon)	Sets the foreground color to black.
Click on the pop-up menu on the Layers palette, and choose Add Layer Mask	Adds an editing layer above Layer 1.
Beginning at the edge of background of Dave's shirt sleeve, click and drag (slowly)across the bottom edge of his forearm	Hides the area on Layer 1 (see fig. 15.29).

This will look quite weird on-screen, but please continue! What's happening is that you're hiding a part of Gary's (the other actor's) arm that was copied along with Dave from the IMG0039 image, to reveal Dave's forearm on the Background layer.

Continue clicking and dragging along the edge of the forearm until you see Dave's forearm on the background almost meet at Gary's wrist on Layer 1	You've completed the bottom edge for Background Dave's arm.

The arm is going to look a little bulged out because the positioning of Gary's right arm on Layer 1 and Dave's right arm on the Background layer aren't at the same angle. You'll fix this shortly; don't worry; you're doing great!

Press **7** on the keyboard, then click and drag over the middle of the forearm until it looks like it has one seamless skin tone	Reduces the Opacity of foreground color to 70 percent. You're only partially hiding areas on Layer 1 now.
Press **0** on the keyboard, then click and drag over the edge of Dave's shirt sleeve	Increase foreground color Opacity to 100 percent; hides areas on Layer 1 to display shirt sleeve areas on the Background layer.

Remember that when you're in Layer Mask mode, hidden areas can be revealed again by setting the foreground painting color to white. Spend a moment or two refining the area in the middle of the forearm where image areas meet. Although Gary and Dave clearly have two different color complexions, the transition between one skin color and the other at the forearm really won't be noticeable in the finished image. Use figure 15.30 as a guide to which image areas should be displayed on Layer 1.

When you're done editing the Layer Mask, click on the pop-up menu on the Layers palette and choose Remove Layer Mask	Displays a dialog box that decides the fate of the hidden areas on Layer 1.
Click on **A**pply	Deletes hidden image areas on Layer 1.
Press Ctrl+S (**F**ile, **S**ave)	Saves your work up to this point.

If you completed the preceding exercise, most of the image editing that needs to be performed in this assignment has been completed. The hardest part of integrating two different forearms to represent a single one is in the matching of the natural flow of the arm's pose.

Depending on exactly where you positioned the copied area from IMG0039 at the begining of the chapter, you might be "home free" with your twin image at this point. However, if you examine the image now, and Dave's forearm is posed correctly but he looks as though he's been eating a lot of spinach, we have the solution in the next exercise. His upper forearm needs trimming down to present a more natural muscu- lature. In the next exercise, you use the Paths palette's Pen tool to create a selection that encompasses the area of Dave's arm that bulges out too much. Then you'll use the Rubber Stamp tool to fill the selected area with foliage. Unlike the Quick Mask feature or the Lasso tool, a selection created from path information is smooth and relatively sharp, both necessary qualities if you're going to play plastic surgeon here with any degree of aesthetics!

Read Chapter 11, "Paths, Selections, and Layers," before using the Paths tool in the next exercise. Directions for shaping the path you need to create are given in the following exercise, but to fully understand the properties of the Path palette's tools, and how paths can save you substantial image editing time, check out Chapter 11.

Figure 15.29

Restore the view of some of Background Dave's forearm by hiding areas on Layer 1 with the Layer Mask mode.

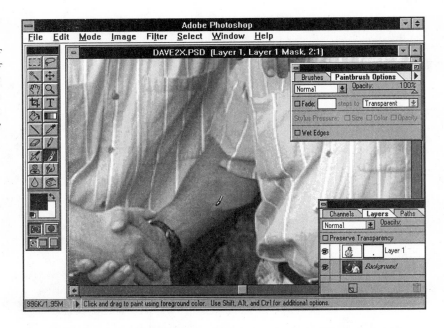

Figure 15.30

Disguise the transition between the arms on the two layers by blending the two in an unlikely place.

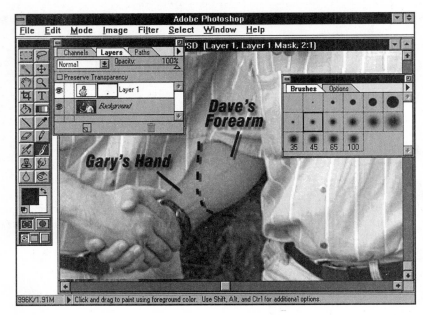

Here's how to create a path, define it as a selection, and make Dave's forearm look more natural:

Creating and Editing a Path Selection

Press **T** (or click on the Paths tab on the Paths palette; then select the Pen tool)	Chooses the Pen tool, used for creating paths.
Click a point at the edge of the watch's wristband, on the outside of the wrist on Layer 1	Creates an Anchor point.
Click and drag slightly inside the forearm, about halfway between the wristwatch band and the edge of Dave's sleeve	Clicking and dragging creates a second Anchor point, and by dragging, you're shaping the curve of the path segment between the first and second Anchor points.
Click at edge of Dave's forearm where his forearm touches the sleeve on the bottom edge of the arm; hold the mouse button, then drag away from the Anchor	Sets a third Anchor point, and you're steering the second path segment by dragging the cursor.
Click a fourth and fifth Anchor points below the first and second path segments, traveling clockwise toward the first Anchor point	Creates three sides of a completed path.
Click on the first Anchor point	Closes the path.

In figure 15.31, you can see an example of what the finished path should look like. It trims into the bottom of Dave's forearm, and when a selection marquee is created from the path, the selection area will be cloned with Background foliage, making Dave's arm appear less bulged. However, paths seldom come out perfect-looking on the first try, and this means that if the top side—the most important edge of the path in this exercise—doesn't have a smooth flow, it needs to be edited as follows:

Hold down the Ctrl (Command) key, place the cursor over an Anchor Point you want to adjust, and then click	Anchor Point is selected, and two direction points are produced (at the end of direction handles).
Keep holding down Ctrl, then click and drag on a direction point	Steers the path segment the direction point is associated with.

continues

continued

Click and drag on an Anchor Point you feel is misplaced	Repositions the Anchor point.
When you have the Path the way you want it, double-click on the Work Path icon, then click on OK	Saves the Path as Path 1 in the DAVE2X image.
Click on the Make Selection icon on the Paths Palette	Creates a selection marquee based on the Path 1 outline information.
Press **S** (for Rubber **S**tamp tool); press Alt and click on an area of background foliage. Then click and drag along the bottom edge of Dave's forearm	Clones in foliage, trimming Dave's forearm to look more natural (see fig. 15.32).
Press Ctrl+S (**F**ile, **S**ave)	Saves your work up to this point.

Figure 15.31

Create a path that describes how the bottom of Dave's forearm should appear.

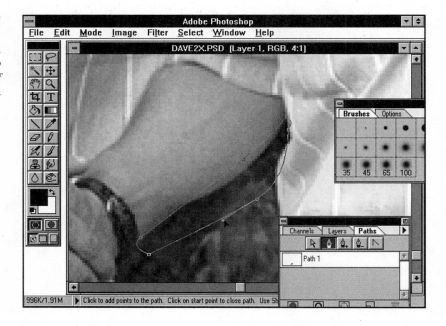

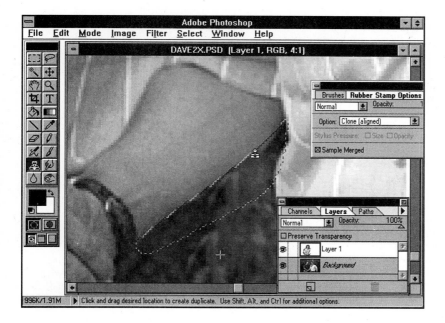

Figure 15.32

Clone background foliage into the selection area to make the forearm look posed and natural.

Paths are an important part of your image editing arsenal in Photoshop, and you only get better by practicing using them. Paths are vector shapes, similar to the lines and shapes you can draw in a design program such as Adobe Illustrator. Paths are used to quickly define an accurate, smooth shape that can be stroked, filled, or as in the last exercise, used as a source of information from which a selection border can be created. Paths can be easily disposed of when you no longer need them, and it would be a good idea to drag Path 1 into the Trash icon on the Paths palette if you intend to send the finished image file to a commercial printer or service bureau. Paths, like Layers and Channels, are proprietary Photoshop features. Layers cannot "leave" Photoshop; you can only save a file that contains a Layer in Photoshop's PSD file format. Channels and Paths can be saved to a TIFF and TGA format image, but they cause a world of headaches for co-workers, and service bureaus that use imaging programs other than Photoshop3.

A Potpourri of Detail Work

If you double-click on the Hand tool right now, you see that with one or two minor touches, the DAVE2X image is finished! Your miracle of image editing might not look as impressive as you'd like, though, because a few minor areas in the image mar its overall stupendous look.

The following exercise can be considered a little professional clean-up work on the DAVE2X image; you're already familiar with the techniques, but you've gained something through the course of this assignment in addition to a good working knowledge of the tools. It's called a *working methodology;* you evaluated the problem at hand in completing the assignment. You analyzed and chose the source images for the task, performed the rough retouching work, and left the minor details for last. You should approach every design project in this way:

1. Evaluate an assignment.

2. Pick your source materials for the assignment.

3. Work over the general composition.

4. Polish the smaller details.

This working methodology is as valuable in your imaging experiences with Photoshop as the techniques and knowledge of the tools' uses. You never go wrong when you plan ahead, and leaving the details for last ensures that your composition has a firm foundation and isn't composed of a neat visual trick scattered here and there.

Here's how to use the Rubber Stamp tool and the Blur tool to complete the illusion in DAVE2X.PSD:

Saving the Finishing Touches for Last

Press **R** (for Blur tool); then set the Pressure to **20%** on the Options palette and check the Sample Merged checkbox	Chooses the Blur tool and specifies a fairly weak setting.
Click on the second (from the left), second row tip on the Brushes palette	Specifies a small size for the tip of the Blur tool.
Click and drag across the bottom of Dave's forearm once (See fig. 15.33)	Blends the bottom of Dave's forearm into color sampled from the Background layer foliage.

You'll probably only need to click and drag once over the area. Remember that you're at an increased viewing resolution right now, and an inconsistent, sharp edge at this viewing resolution won't really show at 1:1 actual image size if you print the image.

Double-click on the Zoom tool	Restores the image to 1:1 viewing resolution.
Scout the image for any Background image areas of the other actor, then press **S** (for Rubber **S**tamp tool)	This is the tool for removing any unwanted image areas you might not have addressed yet.

When you work at a very high viewing resolution, areas outside the area that has your immediate attention can sometimes become overlooked. For example, in figure 15.34, the authors overlooked extraneous image "artifacts" way outside the immediate area of the two Daves. If you have original areas of Gary, the other actor, peeking though Layer 1 from the Background Layer, do the following:

Make sure that the Sample Merged checkbox is checked on the Rubber Stamp tool Options palette	Ensures that regardless of which Layer you're presently on, the Rubber Stamp tool will sample and clone opaque areas on any layer of the image.
Press Alt and click on an area of foliage that corresponds in color and detail of the image area you want to replace	Sets the sampling point for the Rubber Stamp tool.
Click and drag over the areas you want to replace	Clones sampled image areas onto Layer 1 taken from the Background layer (see fig. 15.35).
Scroll to the bottom of the image window	This is an area easily overlooked when an image more than fills the screen.

The very bottom edge of the image window for DAVE2X has one or two "artifacts" that still need to be removed.

Press **Z** (**Z**oom tool), then marquee-zoom to a 4:1 viewing resolution toward the bottom left of the image	This is the last area that needs to be retouched.
Press Alt and click on the road, to the left of Layer 1 Dave	Sets the sampling point for the Rubber Stamp tool.
Click and drag through the light blue area (see fig. 15.36)	This is the other actor's pant leg; you're adding a sample of the road area to Layer 1 to cover it.
Press Ctrl+S (**F**ile, **S**ave)	Saves your work up to this point.
Double-click on the Hand tool, leap out of your chair, and shout, "I've done it!"	Expresses sense of achievement and a personal triumph with Photoshop.

Figure 15.33

Use the Blur tool on Layer 1, in Sample Merged mode, to soften the contrast between Dave's lower forearm and the foliage.

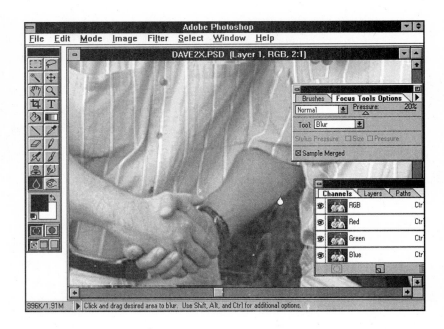

Figure 15.34

Be sure to check all areas of the image for artifacts you may have overlooked.

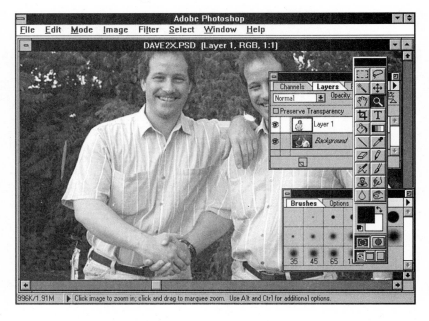

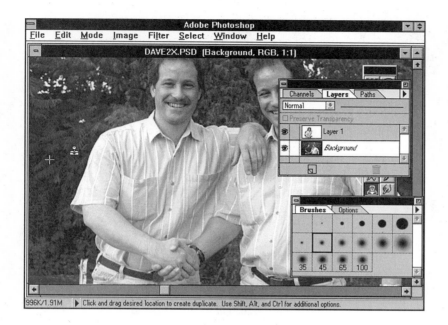

Figure 15.35

Use the Sample Merged setting for the Rubber Stamp tool to sample from one Layer and clone to another.

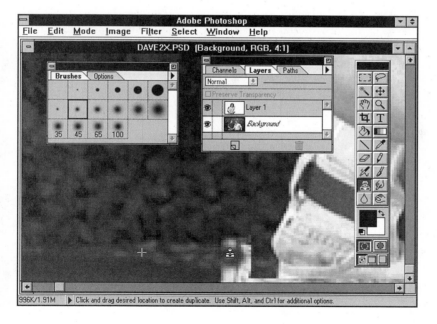

Figure 15.36

Scroll to every corner of the image to see whether areas hidden within the image window view need retouching.

Now would be a good time to choose File, Save a Copy. Save a Copy is a new command to Photoshop 3 and enables you to automatically strip a PSD image of Alpha Channels, flatten the image, and save this copy to a file format that can be exchanged with other operating systems and applications that can use bitmap files. The TIF format is pretty universal, so if you want to keep the DAVE2X image onscreen while Photoshop saves a "show 'em around" copy to your hard disk, choose File, Save a Copy now.

Using Creative Cropping as Another Magic Trick

If you followed the exercise in this chapter, you don't need the images on our Bonus CD to begin creating identical twins of your own now—any time you can find a couple of willing actors or actresses, you have the knowledge, techniques, and working methodology to create your own reality from source images.

In figure 15.37, you can see one finishing touch being put on the DAVE2X image, and that's a tighter cropping for the image than the image was originally captured. The original IMG0038 and IMG0039 images were photographed with a loose crop in anticipation of needing to clone similar image areas into the focal areas of the composition. The loose crop around our two actors provided enough background image area to clone in the extra leaves and road when these elements were needed. However, a professional photo, even a "special effects" photo, still needs to be aesthetically cropped, to convey the impression that these really are identical twins, and the person who photographed them knew how to frame them within the camera's viewfinder.

If you think about it for a moment, when you photograph two actors in different poses, you don't necessarily generate the source for creating a single set of twins. We've recycled the unused portions of IMG0038 and IMG0039 in figure 15.38 to show you another route you can take when you plan your photography carefully and see the creative potential in your digital images.

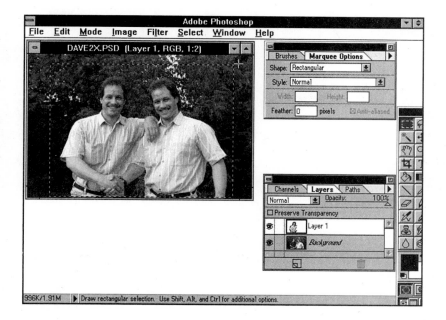

Figure 15.37

A good photographer doesn't leave excess background around the image's subject; a good retouched photograph demands similar cropping.

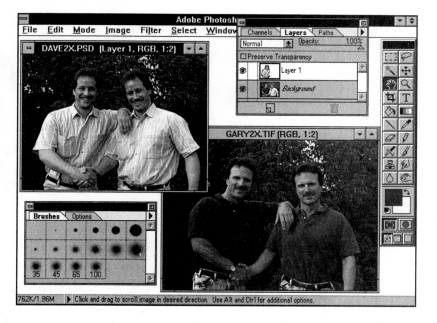

Figure 15.38

You can double your pleasure and double your fun, when you double-click on the Rubber Stamp and other Photoshop tools!

Creating a Digital Collage

As you've seen in other chapters, it's remarkably easy to copy and paste your way to stunning collages, Photoshop-style. *Collage*, loosely translated from the French, means "pasting stuff from different media onto a page." The photo collage, as redefined by Photoshop's remarkable features, can be used to create powerful, eye-catching artwork from a combination of digital images, synthetic software-based designs, and a Photoshop brush stroke or two.

Collage is an art form that lends itself equally well to both the fine and commercial arts. And Photoshop's capability to bring diverse materials together and seamlessly integrate them makes Photoshop the software tool of choice for doing great collage work. In this chapter, you create a poster by bringing together text, graphics, photographic images, and a corporate logo.

This Chapter's Assignment

You're going to create a poster for the fictitious MegaBurger chain of fast-food restaurants. MegaBurger is the home of the MegaCheese&Bacon burger, a 48 oz. (precooked weight) feast, and your charge is to illustrate this gastronomic preposterousness in a convincing, appetizing fashion.

But don't hop in the car with your camera gear to search for a larger-than-life prop for this assignment; the exercise that follows shows you the tricks you need to know in order to exaggerate real photographic images to portray the scene. With techniques described in earlier chapters, and quite a few new ones, you'll use Photoshop to create a collage that fits the bill (of fare) to photographic perfection.

Using the Color Range Command

For this assignment, an ordinary burger (with all the trimmings) was photographed at closer-than-average range, against a solid color backdrop. The close-up is to create the illusion that the person holding the burger is smaller than he really is. The solid white backdrop makes selecting the burger easier to do.

The photograph, BURGER.TIF, consists of well-defined geometry; the edges of the hamburger are sharp, and could be defined by a path to create a selection border. However, because the geometry is not only well-defined but also complex, a simpler method than basing a selection upon a path is used to isolate the burger. The Color Range command is the first step to create a selection of the white background, that can then be inverted to exclude the background image areas, then the burger can be copied to an image of the guy who's supposed to be eating it.

The following exercise demonstrates the use of the Color Range command to select the burger image so that you can add it to a different image.

Defining a Selection by Color Range

Open the BURGER.TIF image from the CHAP16 subdirectory of the Bonus CD. This image will appear in the foreground of the poster.

Choose **S**elect, then **C**olor Range   Displays Color Range dialog box.

Click on Selection radio button, then choose Quick Mask from **S**election Preview drop-down list	Displays masked areas as black in preview, and displays Quick Mask around chosen color ranges on image in workspace.
Click on white background in BURGER.TIF image	Quick Mask appears in white areas on BURGER.TIF image.
Click on the Eyedropper+ tool, then click on shadow area in image	Adds Quick Mask selection to color range of part of burger's BURGER shadow (see fig. 16.1).
Click and drag the Fuzziness slider to about the **88** position	Tightens selected color range and allows some areas inside the burger to be masked.

Your goal here is to define a good, tight selection border around the burger. It's okay if some of the Quick Mask overlay encroaches on the lettuce and onions inside the sandwich. You can remove these areas manually after the selection has been saved.

Click with the Eyedropper+ tool over any remaining shadow areas in the BURGER image or in the preview window	Photoshop offers both the preview and the image as targets for selecting color ranges.
Click on OK	Displays workspace, with a selection marquee defining the areas you selected.
Choose **S**elect, **I**nverse	Creates a marquee selection around the burger and masks areas you selected earlier.
Choose **S**elect, **S**ave Selection, then click on OK	Saves selection of the burger to new Channel #4.
Choose **F**ile, Sa**v**e As, then save the BURGER.TIF image to your hard disk	Saves image in TIFF format.

The selection of the burger in the image is good, but not yet perfect. Although the Color Range command is a good automatic tool for accurately describing outlines at which two colored image areas meet, it chooses all instances of the colors within a specified range, which usually includes areas that you *don't* want selected. In this example, the burger highlights and parts of the onions have the same range as the white background.

Figure 16.1

The Color Range command can create selection areas based on one or several color values.

Editing Alpha Channel Information

Because bitmap images create image areas with pixels (rather than with outlines as vector illustration programs do), areas perceived as objects often flow together and don't have distinct edges. For this reason, your prime concern as you define a selection is the edgework; pixels that fall outside a selection boundary you want selected can be manually edited to be included in the selection. This is why the Fuzziness slider was tuned a little too low in the last exercise to include all the contents of the burger's boundary. If you had specified a higher Fuzziness (broader tolerance) for the color range, the onion and hamburger highlights would have been selected, but so would pixels on the outside edge of the burger—not what you wanted.

Think of the Fuzziness slider as a brightness/contrast adjustment used to tune the color range you want to select; the higher the Fuzziness, the more highlight values are allowed to show through, but the more precise the selection edges become.

Information about the selection you saved is in Channel #4, represented by grayscale pixels. If you have the Channel options set up so that color indicates selected areas, you'll have a pretty decent, high-contrast image of the burger awaiting you in this channel. The trick in the next exercise is to transform "pretty good" selection information into *precise* selection information by filling in the areas that the Color Range command masked inside the burger.

New Riders Publishing
INSIDE
SERIES

To do this, you use the Pencil tool. Because the Pencil tool offers no anti-aliasing, you can be certain that the color you add to the Alpha channel is flat and solid. To Photoshop, solid colored areas indicate 100-percent selected areas in the RGB view, as well as in the view of any of the other channels.

The following exercise shows you how to complete the Alpha channel information you need to select the burger.

Adding Information to an Alpha Channel

Click on Channels tab on Layers palette, then click on #4 title (or press Ctrl+4)	Displays Alpha channel view of BURGER.TIF.
Press **D**, then click on Pencil tool (or press **P**) to activate it	Sets default colors (black foreground and white background), and chooses Pencil tool.
On Brushes palette, click on the far right top row tip, then click and drag over lighter areas within burger shape	Turns areas black, which means that Photoshop will include them when selection is loaded (see fig 16.2).

Alternatively, you can use the Lasso tool to quickly make the entire inside of the burger selection black, as follows.

Click on Lasso tool, click and drag around an area inside the burger shape, then press Alt (Option)+Delete	Fills selected area with foreground color (see fig. 16.3).
Continue with either the Pencil tool or the Lasso tool until inside of burger shape is entirely black	Don't fuss with areas around the edges; they are anti-aliased, and their soft edges will help create a smooth selection of the burger.
When you're done, choose **F**ile, **S**ave (or press Ctrl+S)	Saves your work up to this point.

You might also want to delete the sesame seed shape in the lower left of the Channel 4 view; it will look awkward hanging off the burger after you've pasted it into the actor's hands. To delete the seed, click and drag around the seed with the Lasso tool, then press Delete.

Learn to depend on Photoshop's features for work that would be frustrating or impossible to accomplish manually, but also understand the limitations of any tool. You've seen that the Color Range command is invaluable for *roughly* defining the area you want selected, but it wasn't designed for a specific purpose, such as the one you accomplished semiautomatically. When you understand the features, you can supplement their functionality with your own skills.

Figure 16.2

Adding black to the Alpha channel adds information Photoshop uses to create a selection area.

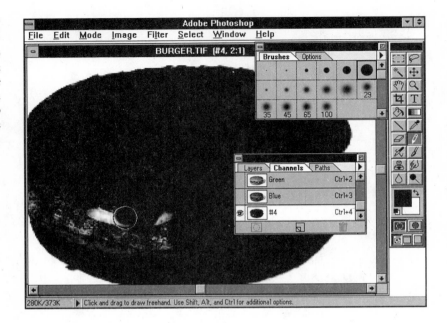

Figure 16.3

Pressing Alt(Option)+Delete is the shortcut for filling a marquee selection with foreground color.

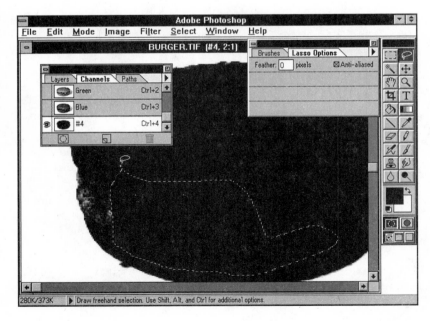

Using Layers to Create a Composite Image

The burger's ready to be copied to a second image, MEGA_GUY.PSD. MEGA_GUY.PSD is a picture of an actor who was asked to pose as though he's digging into a hamburger roughly the size of a watermelon. To create a *convincing* image, the burger must be positioned in front of the actor, but his fingers must be placed on top of the burger.

Here's a revolutionary way to accomplish this effect—one that takes full advantage of Photoshop's Layers feature. Copy the burger selection, place it on a new layer, then reposition the burger until the model looks as though he's holding it. Next, copy only the model's fingers to a different layer, one positioned above the layer that holds the burger. This is simpler than it sounds. (And if you've come from version 2.5 of Photoshop to version 3, surely you'll agree that this technique is much easier than manipulating multiple saved selection areas.)

In the next exercise, you learn how to get a show-stopper of a burger into the right hands.

Copying and Arranging Layer Selections

Press Ctrl+0, then press Ctrl+minus until BURGER image's viewing resolution is 1:2	Displays RGB composite view of image and reduces its size on the workspace so that you can open the next image and see both images.
Open MEGA_GUY.PSD image from CHAP16 subdirectory on Bonus CD	Target image for burger.
Click on New layer icon on Layers palette, accept the defaults, and click on OK	Adds Layer 1 to MEGA_GUY image.
Click on title bar of BURGER image, then choose **S**elect, **L**oad Selection, then click on OK	Loads selection area #4 that you defined earlier.

Alternatively, you can load a selection by pressing Alt and clicking on any Alpha channel icon on the Channels palette. But when you press Alt and click on a channel icon, you don't get the Invert option check box.

continues

continued

With any selection tool active, click and drag the selection into the MEGA_GUY image window	Copies selection to MEGA_GUY image (see fig. 16.4).

Tip Any tool except the Hand and Zoom tool can be used to click+drag a selection, by holding the Ctrl (Command) key as you do. The Ctrl key toggles the function of most toolbox tools to that of the Arrow pointer tool.

Time out for a second. Clearly, if you can't see the model's fingers, you can't position the burger so that it fits into his hands—so don't try. Instead, you need to deselect the floating selection, reduce the opacity for the layer, then get on with positioning the burger. See the next Warning for the scoop on opacity and floating selections.

Stop Floating selections, such as the burger in this exercise, can have an opacity assigned to them *before* being deselected and added to a layer. This is a permanent change you make to a floating selection; after the selection has been deselected, it cannot be reassigned a greater or lesser opacity.

For this reason, it's usually a better idea to paste a selection into a layer at 100% opacity, deselect it, then use the Layers Opacity settings to experiment with the opacity for objects contained on the layer.

Layer opacity can be set and reset until you merge the layer to the background. Floating selections, on the other hand, permanently retain the opacity you've specified for them at the time you deselect them and they are composited to a layer, or the background image.

Now that we understand the perils and preferences for floating selection versus Layer modes, let's serve up the main course in this exercise:

Choose **S**elect, **N**one (or press Ctrl+D), then close BURGER.TIF image	Deselects floating selection in MEGA_GUY.PSD image, closes BURGER image (no longer needed), and makes MEGA_GUY the active image window.
Click on Move tool (or press V), then press **4** (on keyboard or keypad) or click and drag on Opacity slider on Layers palette	Chooses Move tool, reduces opacity of Layer 1 to 40%.

Click and drag the semi-opaque burger until it fits beneath actor's middle fingers, *not* his index fingers	Positions burger so that actor appears to be holding it.

You'll notice that the actor's fingers are not in an optimal position to hold the burger; his index fingers curl inward—hey, he's an actor, not a mime. An exercise later in this chapter shows you how to correct this. First, however, you need to copy the original fingers areas from the background layer, and paste them on a layer on top of Layer 1.

Click on Background title on Layers palette	Makes background image available for editing/painting; Layer 1 is now protected.
Click on Lasso tool, then click and drag around fingers on actor's left hand	Try to make selection a precise one without missing any area where burger overlaps actor's fingers.
Press Shift while you click and drag with Lasso tool around fingers of actor's right hand	Adds selection containing fingers of right hand to preceding selection.
Choose **S**elect, **F**loat (or press Ctrl+J)	Makes floating copy of both selection areas, positioned directly above the original.
Click on Layers pop-up menu triangle (to the right of the tabs), then choose Make Layer. Click on OK (see fig. 16.5)	Creates a new layer (2) on top of background layer but beneath Layer 1.
Click on Layer 1 title, then press **0** (zero) on keyboard (or click and drag Layers palette's Opacity slider to **100%**)	Changes Layer 1 characteristic to full opacity.
Click and drag Layer 2 title on Layers palette above Layer 1 title, then release mouse button	Reorders layers so that Layer 2 is above Layer 1 (see fig. 16.6).
Choose **F**ile, Sa**v**e As, and save MEGA_GUY image to hard disk in PSD format	Saves your work up to this point.

Figure 16.4

Click and drag on the burger selection to copy it to the MEGA_GUY image.

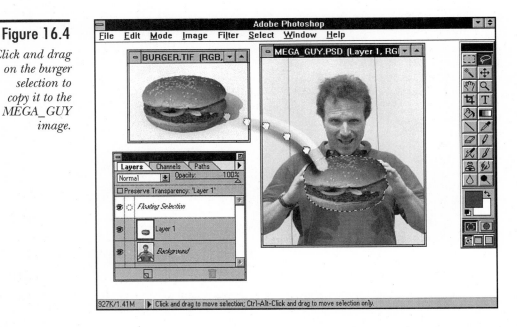

Figure 16.5

Use the Make Layer command to assign a floating selection its own layer.

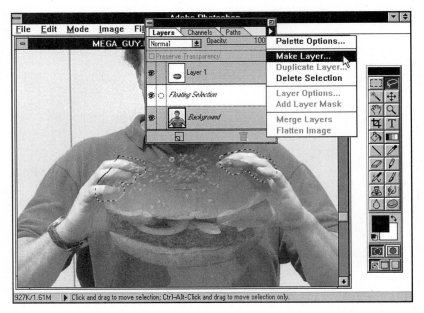

Figure 16.6

Click and drag on a Layer title to reorder the position of Layers on the Background image.

Masking Layers

Chapter 5, "It's All Done with Palettes," described the ways you can edit selection areas viewed in Quick Mask mode. Quick Mask gives you a view of a selection area as a color overlay that remains on top of an image and can be edited with selection and painting tools. A Quick Mask is temporary; the tinted overlay of a Quick Mask does not represent the current saved selection when you edit it. Additionally, you must save your Quick Mask editing work by switching back to Standard mode and choosing **S**elect, **S**ave Selection. Otherwise, the edited Quick Mask will disappear when you deselect the selection created by the Quick Mask.

The Layer Mask feature in Photoshop 3.0, however, is a whole new ball game—one that opens a new world of editing possibilities. Layer Masks begin as an invisible "layer on top of a layer." After you assign a Layer Mask to a target layer, you can paint on the Layer Mask, or marquee select and fill or delete areas on the mask. The purpose of the Layer Mask, unlike that of the Quick Mask feature, is to hide or expose the image areas on the layer with which the Layer Mask is associated. The Layer Mask icon next to the image icon on the Layer palette shows the areas being hidden (masked) by the Layer Mask.

The beauty of the Layer Mask is that you can edit layer image areas indefinitely, experimenting with different effects until you decide to apply the mask and make the changes permanent. The rules are very simple. By default, the Layer option is set so

754   Part III ◆ Gourmet Assignments

that Color Indicates is set to Hidden Areas. When you paint with black as the foreground color, you hide Layer image areas; conversely, by painting with white you reveal any hidden image areas. Filling areas of the Layer mask with gray creates partial selections; the darker the gray, the more completely hidden the image areas become. To make the masking edits permanent, you remove the mask and apply the changes.

As you saw in figure 16.6, the actor's fingers on Layer 2 partially obscure the edges of the burger on Layer 1. This is a perfect opportunity to test the Layer Mask feature and remove the areas on Layer 2 that inappropriately cover the burger.

Using the Layer Mask

Click on Zoom tool (or press **Z**), then click and diagonally drag (marquee zoom) over actor's left hand (right side of image)	Zooms to a higher viewing resolution of area to be edited. A 3:1 viewing resolution is good.
Click on the Layer 2 title on the Layers palette for editing	Chooses the target layer.
Click on pop-up menu button on Layers palette, then click on Add Layer Mask	Icon appears to right of Layer 2 icon. (Icon is empty because you haven't edited anything yet.)
Press **D** (or click on **d**efault colors icon on toolbox), click on Paint Brush tool, then click on tip on top row, second from left, on Brushes palette	Sets foreground color to black (hides areas you paint over in Layer Mask mode), and sets a small, hard-edge tip with which to apply mask to Layer 2.
Choose Normal mode and **100%** Opacity from Paint Brush Options palette	Sets Paint **B**rush tool to apply foreground color with total coverage.
Click and drag over an area where actor's blue shirt obscures burger	Masks area, hiding it from view (see fig. 16.7).
Continue clicking and dragging over areas of "missing burger" until edge of fingers on actor's left hand meet burger outline	Removes areas from Layer 2 to reveal burger on Layer 1.

A common mishap—removing more image area than you intend—certainly applies to working with Layer Masks. Fortunately, you haven't permanently altered the information on Layer 2. If you've painted into the fingers, perform the next step:

Press **X** (or click on Switch Colors icon on toolbox), then click and drag with the Paint Brush where you painted too far	Removes Layer Mask information from area.

Continue using the last two steps until the burger seems to be beneath the actor's hands, and the burger's edge is visible on the right side of the image. Also, paint over the small area where the actor's index finger is visible. Painting over this small area with black foreground color masks areas of the image, on Layer 2, that you don't intend to keep. Your edits are updated in the icon to the right of the Layer 2 icon on the Layers palette. The black color indicates where you've painted the mask.

Choose **F**ile, **S**ave (or press Ctrl+S)   Saves your work up to this point.

Figure 16.7

Use the Layer Mask mode to hide unwanted image areas on layers.

At this stage of the game, the changes you've made to Layer 2 by using Photoshop's Layer Mask feature on areas aren't permanent; the changes are simply displayed on the image so that you can preview your editing work to see what it looks like. You can continue to edit the layer mask until you get the results you want.

In the next section, you finalize the mask you've created. First, however, a few other features of layer masks merit a mention. Layer masks aren't identical to Quick Masks or marquee selections, but the options for displaying layer masks are quite rich.

Layer Mask Options

Photoshop provides you with an icon view of the way a layer mask is shaping up, but often you'll want to see the areas you've masked (hidden) as tangible, graphical data displayed upon the image, instead of having image areas that are masked hidden from view. The following list explains the set of commands that are at your disposal in Photoshop, but are *not* found on Photoshop's menu:

◆ Press Shift and click on the Layer Mask icon—displays masked areas on a layer as Quick Mask overlay. While in this viewing mode, you can use painting and selection tools on the Quick Mask areas to edit the layer mask. To remove the Quick Mask display, again press Shift and click on the Layer Mask icon.

◆ Click on the Layer icon, choose the Move tool, then click and drag on a layer— by default, the layer contents (the image area) and the layer mask move to- gether. This effect is visible when Quick Mask is displayed as a visual proxy for the layer mask. This is a good option when you want to reposition the contents of a Layer, but have a Layer Mask in place and don't want to quit your Layer Mask editing session.

◆ To display the Layer Mask Options dialog box, double-click on the Layer Mask icon. When you choose the Position Relative to: Image option (instead of the default option, Layer), and the Layer icon (not the Layer Mask icon) is high- lighted, you can move the Layer's contents (the image) and the Layer Mask independently of one another. This is handy for repositioning a Layer Mask.

◆ When you want to edit the image on a Layer without disturbing the Layer Mask, click on the Layer icon (to the left of the Layer Mask icon). With the icon highlighted (surrounded by an outline), you can edit the image.

When you want to edit the Layer Mask without altering the underlying image, click on the Layer Mask icon.

◆ When you want to view the Layer image without any areas being hidden from view, press Ctrl (Macintosh: Cmd) and click on the Layer Mask icon to turn off the Layer Mask. To display the image with the results of your Layer Mask editing, press Ctrl and click on the Layer Mask icon again.

◆ Press Alt and click on the Layer Mask icon—Displays the Layer Mask as a grayscale channel view, similar to viewing an Alpha channel saved selection. You can add text, or a gradient fill to the "channel view" of the Layer Mask in this way, and see the results more clearly. Click on the eye icon to the left of the Layer icon to restore your view of the Layer. The Layer Mask channel is not permanent; it automatically disappears when you remove the Layer Mask.

Applying a Layer Mask

After you've added a layer mask to a layer and performed all the editing work you need to, it's time to apply the layer mask. The Remove Layer Mask command on the Layer's palette pop-up menu is somewhat misleading; you remove a Layer Mask in one of two ways. First, you can choose to **D**iscard the Layer Mask, which means you're negating your editing work, and not one pixel of the Layer you've masked will be touched. The other command you are offered in the dialog box after you choose Remove Layer Mask is **A**pply. *Apply* means that areas you've painted over will be deleted from the Layer.

You want to edit the actor's right hand in the same way you edited his left hand, before you chose the Remove Layer Mask command. In figure 16.8, you can see the finishing touches being applied to areas in which the actor's shirt and fingers overlap the burger on Layer 2.

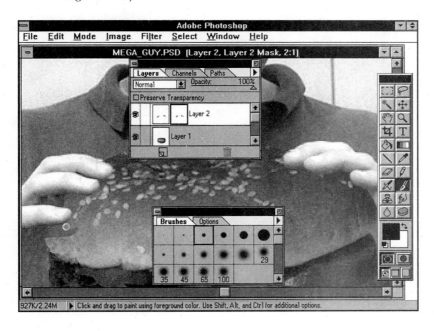

Figure 16.8

To edit the layer mask around overlapping image areas, use the techniques described earlier.

After you've edited the layer mask, excluding shirt and index finger details by hiding the areas on the left side of the MEGA_GUY image, you're ready for a two-stepper to finalize your edits.

Here's how to delete the areas, on Layer 2, to which you've added Layer Mask.

Removing the Layer Mask

Click on pop-up menu button to right of
tabs on Layers palette and choose Remove
Layer Mask (see fig. 16.9)

Displays exclamation dialog box for this
Remove command.

Click on Apply

Applies changes you've made to Layer 2 by
masking areas. Hidden areas are now
removed from image layer.

Figure 16.9

*The Remove
Layer Mask
command
discards your
mask editing
work or applies
the editing
changes you've
made on the
layer.*

You've performed some pretty high-order image editing up to this point, but the most
critical hurdle is yet to come. As mentioned earlier, the actor's index fingers weren't
posed at an attitude that suggested he's holding a huge burger. Your first step to
remedy this situation was to erase the index fingers. The next step is to *replace* what
you've erased with original image areas. And this technique, done correctly, leads you
from excellent imaging to the graduate level of *incredible* imaging.

Replacing Image Areas with Copies from the Original

Whether the images you work with are digital or chemical, working with a portrait of a person requires infinite finesse and sensitivity. Unlike images of trees, desks, or other inanimate objects, images of the human anatomy—the face, the torso, the hands—are viewed as having a flow and underlying structure that's visually reinforced every time you meet a person. Something strikes you immediately as being phony and artificial when a portion of human anatomy has been even slightly retouched in a way that disturbs the structure of the anatomy and flow of the image. This is why the cover "photographs" of the tabloids seen in supermarkets seem laughable and unnatural instead of convincing.

Adding index fingers to the actor's image is a real editing challenge. You need a source, and your replacement areas should exactly match original areas of the actor's. Unfortunately, the camera didn't capture a large enough area of the index fingers for you to simply copy it. So where can you get an image area that fits on top of the burger and looks exactly like the actor's index fingers?

Look at your own hands. Index fingers and ring fingers are nearly identical in width and length, and the actor's ring fingers are clearly visible in the background layer.

Here's how to count on someone else's fingers.

Rearranging Original Image Areas

Zoom in to a 4:1 viewing resolution of actor's left hand (stage left)	Provides a view suitable for performing intricate editing work.
Choose Lasso tool, then click and drag a selection around actor's ring finger (see fig. 16.10)	Selects this area; you'll use it to add an index finger to the actor.
Choose **E**dit, **C**opy (or press Ctrl+C), then press Ctrl+D (**S**elect, **N**one)	Copies ring finger to the clipboard, and deselects active marquee.

What you can't see *can* interfere with your image editing; Layer 2 needs to be cleaned up a little before you add the selection on the clipboard to the MEGA_GUY image. Specifically, the top of the actor's left hand on Layer 2 probably has blue shirt areas above it, which will prevent you from displaying the copy of his ring finger beneath the rest of his hand on a new layer.

continues

continued

Click on the eye icon on Background Layer title on Layers palette	Toggles view of background image to hidden, and displays only Layers 1, 2, and the checkered Transparent pattern. Click on Layer 2 title to make sure that Layer 2 is still the active layer.
Choose Eraser tool, click on a small Brushes tip on Brushes palette, then click and drag over blue shirt	Erases shirt area from Layer 2 (see fig. 16.11).
Carefully trace around edge of actor's left middle finger to remove any visible shirt area	Ensures that pasted copy of ring finger tucks neatly behind middle finger, when pasted (on its own layer) beneath Layer 2.
Choose **E**dit, Paste La**y**er, then click on OK	Selection appears on top of Layer 2, as Layer 3, and is active layer for editing.

If you want to reposition the ring finger on the layer so that it's closer to its final relative position, choose the Move tool and then click and drag the ring-finger area.

With Eraser tool, click and drag around ring finger on Layer 3, to remove blue shirt areas (see fig. 16.12). If you remove too much, choose **E**dit, **U**ndo (or press Ctrl+Z); then start over	Makes image area perfect for positioning behind Layer 2.
Click and drag Layer 3 title to Layer 2 title position	Reorders Layers so that Layer 3, with the ring finger, is behind actor's other fingers on Layer 2.
Click on Move tool, then click and drag on Layer 2	Repositions ring finger to match correct position and placement of actor's index finger (see fig. 16.13).
Select **F**ile, **S**ave (or press Ctrl+S)	Saves your work up to this point.

You performed an amazing feat in the last exercise. The ring finger is a perfect substitute for the index finger that was in the wrong position to hold the burger. With this kind of advanced imaging technique, you can solve design problems that seem impossible to solve.

Repositioning fingers, hands, and other image elements that belong to a person is *not* an escapade to be indulged in frivolously, however. The possibility always exists that you may do something gross and unflattering to pictures of people—and whimsical anatomical adjustments are a childish sport unworthy of the profession you aspire to.

Additionally, you always stand the chance of an "injured party" discovering your
unflattering work and deciding to rearrange *your* body parts.

Figure 16.10

*Create, around
the actor's ring
finger, a selection
area to copy and
use on a separate
Layer.*

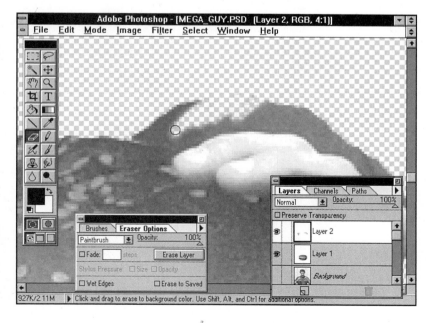

Figure 16.11

*By clicking off the
eye icon next to
the Background
Layer title, you
can see image
edges on other
layers.*

Figure 16.12

Erase image areas on Layers that will conflict with areas on the Background image.

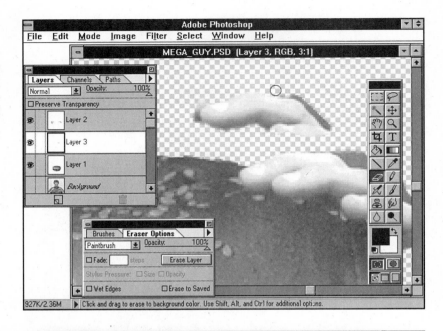

Figure 16.13

Use the Move tool to reposition an image area on a layer.

Reusing a Copied Selection

To accomplish the same effect with the actor's right index finger, you must copy the contents of Layer 3 and flip the pasted selection before you position it on the same layer. Floating selections on a layer can be positioned independently of the layer's contents because the selections are not actually part of the layer over which they are floating. Only when a floating selection is deselected does it become part of the layer.

The following exercise explains how to complete the arrangement of layers and image areas for the MEGA_GUY image.

Copying and Flipping an Image Area

Click on Layer 3 title on Layers palette	Makes Layer 3 the active Layer for editing.
Click on Lasso tool (or press **L**), then click and drag around ring ("index") finger area	Creates selection border around finger in Layer 3, the active layer.
Select **E**dit, **C**opy (or press Ctrl+C)	Copies lassoed area to clipboard.

Although the selection marquee might encompass a broader area than only the finger selection on Layer 3, other areas (those that don't contain the fingers) are transparent and don't copy to the clipboard. In effect, you copied a very tight selection area that you refined, in an earlier step, when you erased the blue shirt areas on Layer 3.

Click on the Layer 2 title on the Layers palette	Makes Layer 2 the target (current editing) layer.
Scroll to left side of MEGA_GUY image	The next area that needs work.
Choose Eraser tool, then click and drag over any image areas above actor's right, middle finger	Removes blue shirt area so that pasted selection will look natural beneath Layer 3.
Choose **S**elect, **N**one (or press Ctrl+D)	Deselects active marquee.

Pasted selections are "attracted" to marquee selections, and you don't want the copy of the index finger to land inside the marquee. You can't see the marquee now that you've scrolled to the left, so the last move (Ctrl+D) ensures that the pasted finger selection won't "land" out of view, but instead, will paste in the center of the image window.

Click on the Layer 3 title on the Layers palette	Makes Layer 3 the current (target) layer.
Select **E**dit, **P**aste (or press Ctrl+V), then choose **I**mage, **F**lip, **H**orizontal	Mirrors finger selection so that it looks like a right index finger.

continues

continued

Click and drag inside marquee selection and move finger behind actor's right, middle finger (see fig. 16.14)	Puts selection in position that looks natural for actor holding burger.
Choose **S**elect, **N**one (or press Ctrl+D)	Deselects floating selection, making it part of Layer 3.
Choose (**F**ile, **S**ave (or press Ctrl+S)	Saves your work up to this point.

Figure 16.14

Floating selections don't belong to a layer; you can freely reposition them, using any selection tool.

It's only fair to mention here that if you've completed the last two assignments successfully, both you and the actor should be complimented on having a fine pair of hands.

The image is figure 16.15 is "almost there," in terms of conveying an implausible idea photorealistically. The next section includes the details for blending the edgework and a few other tasks you need to do to completely integrate the four layers into one seamlessly retouched image.

Figure 16.15

At this stage, you cannot detect the edges where the image layers overlap.

Creating a Shadow

Because the burger wasn't originally photographed against the actor (and wasn't originally gigantic), it casts no shadow in the MEGA_GUY image. Although the lack of shadow on the actor's shirt is not a big detail, people consciously or subconsciously perceive such small factors as false.

If you glance back at figure 16.4, you'll notice two dinosaur-shaped shadows on the actor's shirt, cast by his hands. The sun was high when the photograph was taken; had the actor been holding the burger, it too would have cast a shadow—an ellipse shape—in the same area of the shirt.

Cloning in a Realistic Shadow

In the next exercise, you create a shadow for the burger on the actor's shirt. You don't try to make the new shadow (for the burger) match the shadows cast by the hands. Such an endeavor would be frustrating, because the edges simply wouldn't match perfectly. Instead, you first define the area for the burger shadow, then use the Rubber Stamp tool to sample original shadow areas and create a visual mixture of original and cloned shadow areas over the actor's shirt.

The following exercise shows you how to enhance the shadow areas and reinforce the visual reality of this fictitious scene.

Reshaping and Blending Shadows

Make certain the eye icon is displayed for the Background layer on the Layers palette	Makes the Background layer visible.
Click on Background Layer title on Layers palette	Displays layer on which you'll create burger's shadow.
Choose Elliptical marquee tool, then click and drag over burger an area that roughly defines burger	Serves as guideline for bottom edge of burger shadow.

Don't worry about the top edge of the burger. Had the scene been photographed as you choreographed it, the top edge of the burger shadow would not be visible; it would be hidden from view by the bottom of the burger.

Press Ctrl+Alt (Cmd+Option) while you click and drag inside the marquee selection. Stop when marquee is between the two hand shadows	Moves selection marquee only, not the underlying Background image area.
Press S (or click on Rubber Stamp tool), then click on Brushes tip, second from the right, middle row	Chooses Rubber stamp tool; sets medium-sized, soft-edged tip with which to clone.
Press Alt and click over an area of hand shadow on left	Sets traveling sample point for Rubber stamp tool.
Click and drag inside elliptical marquee (see fig. 16.16)	Paints samples of hand shadow into the ellipse.
Reset sampling point of Rubber stamp when obvious patterning begins to show in elliptical marquee selection (an unwanted effect)	Resampling every four or five strokes prevents area into which you're cloning from displaying repeating patterns.
Choose Select, None (or press Ctrl+D) when bottom lip of ellipse is covered with cloned image areas	Deselects ellipse. (You needed it only to define edge of burger's shadow.)
Continue click and draggging, and resampling with Rubber stamp tool, until interior of burger shadow is completely filled	Completes shadow design; original hand shadow areas are integrated with new, fake burger shadow.
Press Ctrl+D (Select, None), then Ctrl+S (File, Save)	Deselects the floating selection and saves your work up to this point.

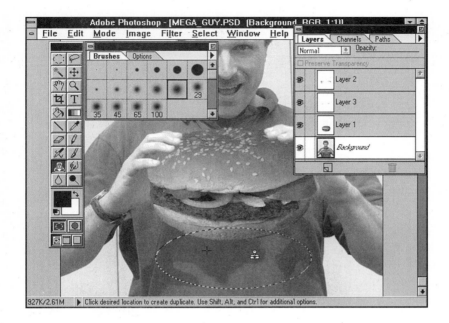

Figure 16.16

*Use the Rubber
stamp tool to
paint a burger
shadow into the
background
image.*

Fortunately, there is little distinctive design to the actor's shirt; when people look at
this image, they'll see only the correct texture and color value of your shadow
creation. By cloning into the original hand shadow areas, you achieved perfect
integration of the fake burger's shadow and the shadows of the hands. Because a
shadow with this shape would fall over the actor's shirt if this were a real image,
you've added another detail that contributes to the overall effect.

Creating Shadows with Multiply Painting Mode

Another visual detail that would be displayed in a real-life image of a guy holding a
big burger is the shadow(s) cast where his fingers meet the burger. Shadow areas are
created when you hold things; light is often kept from the spot where your fingers
meet an object, because either your finger or the object is obstructing light.

In the next exercise you use a special Paint Brush mode, the Multiply mode, to
progressively darken small image areas on the burger to suggest that the actor is
denting the bun slightly while holding it. Multiply mode, when set to partial Opacity,
is very effective for creating small, realistic shadow areas.

Here's how to make the burger look as though it actually meets the actor's hands:

Using the Multiply Mode in Painting

Press **B** (or click on Paint Brush tool)	Tool for applying foreground color to image.
Click on Layer 1 title on Layers Palette	Makes Layer 1 the active (or *target*) layer for your editing work.
Hold down the Alt key while you click over darkest area of burger within your view	Samples foreground color, which you'll apply to areas between actor's fingers.
Choose Multiply from Paint Brush Options drop-down list, then press **5** (or click and drag Opacity slider down to **50%**)	Chooses painting mode similar to using felt-tip pens; Multiply progressively soaks an area with color. With 50% Opacity, you can stroke an area quite a few times before it's totally covered.
Choose a small, soft-edged tip from Brushes palette, then click and drag where actor's fingertips meet	Darkens area with color you sampled (see fig. 16.17).
Repeat process along other fingertip areas where burger meets fingertips	Less is more here; for this subtle effect, don't make more than three strokes per area.
When you finish one hand, repeat the process with actor's other hand	Creates shadow areas that visually integrate burger and actor.
Choose File, Save (or press Ctrl+S)	Saves your work up to this point.

Unlike Photoshop 2.5, when you have different image elements on discrete layers, the need to mask areas before painting up to the edge of something is unnecessary. The finger areas of the actor's hands are untouched by the painting you did in the last exercise because the actor's hands are on an inactive layer. When the layers are merged, the shadows you painted in will be composited and integrated into the actor's hands.

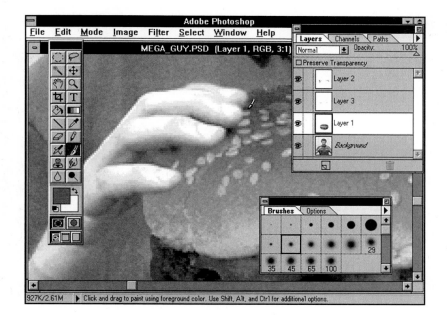

Figure 16.17

Multiply mode is excellent for "faking" small shadow areas.

Blurring Image Edges

As you work with larger files and high-resolution photographic images, you'll find that image focus in the digital image is represented by pixels of steep or gentle contrast. In the MEGA_GUY image, camera focus was good, but image areas (where the actor's hair meets the background wall, for example) are made up of color pixels that make the foreground-to-background color transition in three or four different shades.

At this stage, photofiction is still separated from photoreality by the quality of the edge where the burger meets the actor's shirt. Because the burger was pasted into a separate Layer as a selection, the burger's edge displays no transition pixels at all; this sudden contrast makes the burger look a tad unreal (its size notwithstanding!).

You can correct this by making a pass or two with the Blur tool, set at partial pressure. Wherever you paint with the Blur tool, it creates pixels of transitional color values. It lessens contrast and can make a sharp edge in an image seem a little more photographic.

Here's how to blend the burger into the actor's shirt, without leaving mustard stains:

Softening Focus between Image Layers

Make sure that Layer 1 is still the image layer	Always keep an eye on which layer is the active one.
Choose **S**elect, **M**atting, then **D**efringe	Displays Defringe dialog box.
Type **1** in **W**idth field, then click on OK	Removes edge pixels, copied along along with burger, that contained color values not found inside burger. Defringe helps Blur tool smooth transitions only between background and burger.
Press **R** until Blur tool is displayed on toolbox (or press Alt and click on the tool)	Selects tool used to locally decrease image contrast.
Keep same tip size on Brushes palette, but set Pressure on Focus Tools Options palette to **30%**, Normal mode	Now Blur tool will decrease contrast at about 1/3 its total intensity, (ideal for making multiple passes).
Check Sample Merged check box on Focus Tools Options palette	Blur tool will now use visual information from all visible layers to lessen contrast along the edge of the image on Layer 1.

The Blur tool can't function correctly on the edge between transparency and image area on a layer. It acts like a soft eraser tool unless you check the Sample Merged box.

Click and drag over an area where burger meets actor's shirt (see fig. 16.18)	Decreases contrast between neighboring pixels.
Repeat stroke in same area, then continue around border of burger	Blends areas from other layers into burger's edge on Layer 1.
Choose **F**ile, **S**ave (or press Ctrl+S)	Saves your work up to this point.

Photoshop's editing tools, Blur, Sharpen, Smudge, and Toning, do not add foreground or background color in the editing process. Rather, they work with existing values in the image, moving color and tonal values around.

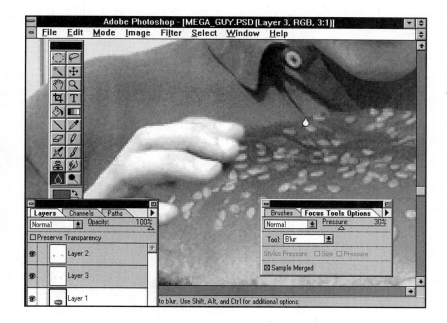

Figure 16.18

The Blur tool samples different pixels and decreases the difference in tonal value between them.

Shading an Area with a Sampled Value

The last step in creating this work of art is to examine the image for any other telltale areas where image detail, lighting, or focus is not quite authentic. Because the lighting in the MEGA_GUY image is from steep left, the burger should cast a slight shadow in the actor's left palm.

In the next exercise, using the same technique you used to create the "dents" in the burger, you'll conclude part one of the digi-collage experiment with a quick flick of the Paint Brush tool in Multiply mode.

Fine-tuning Shadows

Scroll to right of MEGA_GUY image	Provides view of actor's left hand and right edge of burger.
Click on Paint **B**rush tool (or press **B**)	Chooses Paint Brush tool.
Click on bottom, left tip on Brushes palette, then choose Multiply mode and about **40%** Opacity on Paint Brush Options palette	Creates a Paint Brush characteristic for making a faint shadow.

continues

continued

Press Alt and click on actor's palm	Toggles Paint Brush to Eyedropper, and samples a foreground color for the shadow you'll create.
Click and drag once over palm area	Adds a slight shadow (see fig. 16.19).
Choose **F**ile, **S**ave (or press Ctrl+S)	Saves your work up to this point.

Figure 16.19

Partial Opacity settings allow background detail to show through.

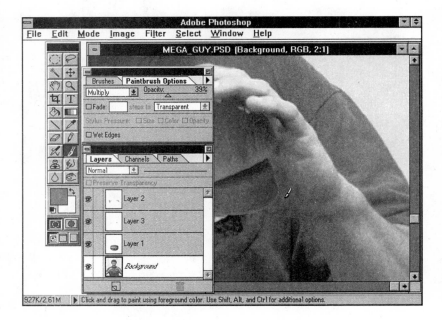

Never underestimate the power of the Eyedropper tool in photographic retouching assignments. By sampling a color found in an image, you guarantee that your editing work won't add "artificial" colors to the image. Because our eyes are naturally attracted to stimulating colors, we all are prone to picking a color that might be too intense to be blended into a digital image. Fortunately, the Eyedropper tool seems not to be subject to any human weaknesses.

Assembling the Collage Pieces

As promised at the beginning of the chapter, this assignment entails using several source materials to create a digital collage. After you temporarily tuck away the image you've been working on (to conserve system resources), you'll turn your attention to some graphic design. You'll discover the secrets of the Displace command, and create

"Aurene Splendour"

Ingredients: Photoshop, Renderize Live!, Gallery Effects, PhotoCD image, scanned images

"Restoring and Retouching an Heirloom Photograph"
(Chapters 7 and 8)

Ingredients: Photoshop, scanned image

"Enhancing Images"
(Chapter 15)

Ingredients: Photoshop, PhotoCD images, scanned images

"Nedrow Beach"
(Chapter 18)

Ingredients: Photoshop, MacroMedia MacroModel, Pixar RenderMan, Fractal Design Painter, CorelDRAW!

"Flavors"
(Chapter 11)

Ingredients: Photoshop, PhotoCD images,
KPT Glass Lens Bright

"Poster"

(Chapter 18)

Ingredients: Photoshop, PhotoCD images

"The Faces of Surfaces"

Ingredients: Photoshop, Andromeda 3D
filter, Pixar One Twenty-Eight

"Congratulations!"
(Chapter 20)

Ingredients: Photoshop, Flair pen, Pixar One Twenty-Eight, PhotoCD image, KPT Gradient on Paths filter

"Plunge!"
(Chapter 25)

Ingredients: Photoshop, Visual Software's Renderize Live!,
Biomechanics Corporation of America's Mannequin

"Creating Special Effects with Ordinary Photographs"
(Chapter 15)

Ingredients: Photoshop, PhotoCD images

"Correcting an Image"
(Chapter 12)

Ingredients: Photoshop, PhotoCD images

"Combining Photographs"
(Chapter 13)

Ingredients: Photoshop, PhotoCD images, Lifeguard, CMCD visual symbol, MacroMedia MacroModel, Pixar RenderMan

"Study"

Ingredients: Photoshop, MacroMedia MacroModel, Pixar RenderMan, CorelDRAW!, Bill's Tropical DECOrations Type 1 pi font

"Games"
(Chapter 6)

Ingredients: Photoshop, MacroMedia MacroModel, Pixar RenderMan, Bill's Tropical DECOrations Type 1 pi font, Andromeda 3-D filter

"Mr. Drippy"

Ingredients: Photoshop, MacroMedia MacroModel, Pixar
RenderMan, CorelDRAW!, flour, sugar, eggs

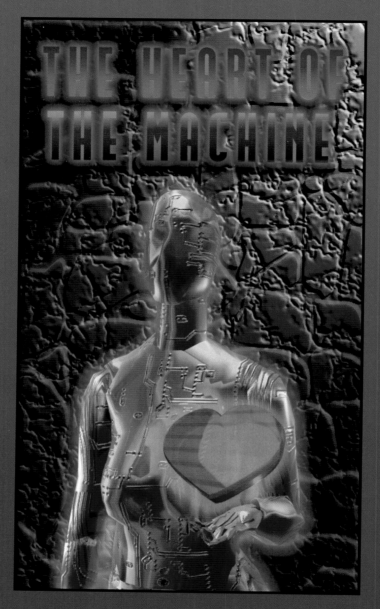

"The Heart of the Machine"
(Chapter 22)

Ingredients: Photoshop, Visual Software's Renderize Live!,
Biomechanics Corp. of America's Mannequin, CorelDRAW!,
KPT Gradient Designer 2.0

a pattern from a simple logo, adding a wallpaper effect to the background of the MEGA_GUY image.

Before closing the MEGA_GUY image, however, you need to define a selection area so that you can separate the actor from the original background.

The Magic Wand Versus the Color Range Command

Photoshop offers at least two ways to accomplish an effect; the tools you choose to create a specific effect may vary according to the image and problem you have to deal with. The MEGA_GUY image, for example, now contains a fascinating foreground element—but the background is Blah City. Before you can replace the background (with some splashy wallpaper, featuring the MegaBurger logo), the actor must be accurately selected. Which do you use: Photoshop's Color Range command or the Magic Wand tool?

The Color Range command is ineffective for isolating the actor from the background, because pixel values on the burger and actor are too similar in color to the background wall. When you try to pick the background by using the Color Range command with the Eyedropper tool, areas of foreground are included; you cannot totally correct this problem by adjusting the Fuzziness slider. The reason similar color values are scattered through the MEGA_GUY image and the burger area is that light reflects color; it physically bounces off objects and partially reflects inherent color values.

The better choice is to use the Magic Wand tool to separate the actor from the background. With the Magic Wand, you can select a tight or loose area that's based on color similarities in one *contiguous* image area. By using the Magic Wand in combination with the Similar command, you can achieve a very precise selection without picking up color values randomly scattered throughout the image. The Magic Wand operates according to a tolerance you specify. Finding the right tolerance level is a trial-and-error technique, depending on the image area you need to isolate and the color value of the pixels over which you click the Magic Wand.

This exercise shows you how to select the background of the MEGA_GUY image.

Using the Magic Wand tool

Click on Flatten Image command on Layers palette pop-up menu

Because you've finished editing the MEGA_GUY image, you no longer need separate layers.

The only way to retrieve the layered property of this image is to select **E**dit, **U**ndo (or press Ctrl+Z) now. If there's the *slightest possibility* that you'll need to reedit an image you are about

continues

continued

to flatten—choose File, Save As and save a copy of the image under a different name. Be sure to save it in Photoshop's PSD file format to preserve the image layers.

Double-click on Hand tool	Zooms out to full-frame viewing resolution of MEGA_GUY image.
Click on Magic **W**and tool (or press **W**)	Chooses Magic Wand tool.
Click in Tolerance field on Magic Wand Options palette, and type **40**	Specifies that pixels with same color value as (but a difference of no more than 40 brightness values from) the point you click over will be included in a selection marquee.

Photoshop evaluates brightness values on a scale of 0 to 255, so the value suggested here is a moderate tolerance.

On the Options palette, make sure the Anti-aliased check box is checked	Ensures that selection created with Magic Wand tool has smooth edges.
Click on far-right panel behind actor	Depending on the exact location you clicked over, entire top of the paneling might be selected now.

Don't fret over the grooves between the paneling. You don't need to select them with the Magic Wand tool—selecting them in a saved Alpha channel is easier.

Choose **S**elect, Simi**l**ar	Includes in selection other image areas not adjacent to point you clicked over with Magic Wand (see fig 16.20).

The Similar command, because it uses the same Threshold value as the Magic Wand, also includes color pixels that are about 40 brightness shades off from the original Magic Wand selection.

Choose **S**elect, **I**nverse	Masks background selection areas, and selects actor.
Click on (Save to) Selection icon (see fig. 16.20)	Adds current selection to an Alpha channel as grayscale information.

The function of the (Save to) Selection icon is equivalent to that of the **S**elect, **S**ave Selection command. The biggest difference between the two functions is that clicking on the (Save to) Selection icon automatically gives the new channel a default name, which in this case is Channel #4.

Press Ctrl+D (**S**elect, **N**one)	Deslects the marquee around the saved selection.
Click on #4 title on Channels palette	Displays view of Channel #4 in image window.

By default, Photoshop displays masked areas in black and selected areas in white. In earlier chapters, you learned how to reverse the default. If you currently don't have black areas as *selection* areas, follow the next two steps, which are optional:

Double-click on #4 icon	Displays Channel Options dialog box.
Click on Color Indicates: **S**elected Areas radio button, then click on OK	Inverts grayscale information in channel, so that working on channel view with editing tools is easier to do.
Click on **P**encil tool (or press **P**), then choose a medium tip from second row on Brushes palette	Pencil tool is good for editing Alpha channel areas that Magic Wand didn't select.
Click and drag inside the border of actor selection	Adds selection information to Alpha channel (see fig. 16.21).

While you're here, press **X** (switch colors) then click and drag over the lines that represent the grooves in the panelling on the RGB channel to erase them to white foreground color. Now, the grooves in the RGB channel won't be selected when you load this channel's information.

Choose **F**ile, **S**ave (or press Ctrl+S), then close MEGA_GUY image	Saves your work up to this point. You close the image because it's time to work on a different collage element, and closing MEGA_GUY conserves system resources.

Figure 16.20

Use the Magic Wand tool to select image areas that have similar color values.

Figure 16.21

Add black foreground color to the Alpha channel to add selection information.

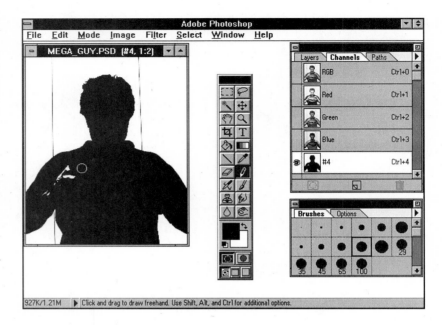

Creating a Color Logo Pattern

Some of this assignment's design work has already been completed for you; it's in the MEGALOGO.TIF image on the Bonus CD. The MegaBurger logo, which is used for a pattern design behind the actor, consists of two Alpha channels you can load and fill with the MegaBurger Corporation's corporate colors. These corporate colors have been saved as color areas in the RGB channel view of the file. Creating a color logo from black and white art is as simple as loading each saved selection and filling it with sampled color.

The logo was created with a vector drawing application (Adobe Illustrator and CorelDRAW! are vector programs) and exported to Photoshop as an EPS image. This EPS image was opened in Photoshop, which rasterized the vector image into a bitmap format. Then the logo was saved as a TIFF image. Don't overlook illustration software in your collection of graphics tools. Designing the logo in Photoshop would have been tedious, because Photoshop's strengths lie in photographic imaging, not drafting-table-type design work.

Here's how to create a color logo to use as the wallpaper pattern behind the actor in the MEGA_GUY image:

Coloring Saved Selections

Click on **d**efault colors icon on toolbox (or press **D**)	Sets foreground color to black, and background to white.
Open MEGALOGO.TIF image from CHAP16 subdirectory of Bonus CD	Image you'll add color to and create a pattern from.
Press **L**, then click and drag around black-and-white logo (see fig. 16.22)	Chooses Lasso tool and creates selection border around logo.
Press Delete key	Removes logo and replaces it with white background color.

The complete black-and-white logo doesn't play a part in the finished color art; it was placed here to give you an idea of what the two Alpha channel elements will look like when combined in color.

Choose **S**elect, **L**oad Selection, Channel #4 (or press Alt and click on Channel #4 icon on Channels palette)	Loads selection in Channel #4.
Click on Eyedropper tool (or press **I**), then click on turquoise part of swatch in RGB view of MEGALOGO	Samples color to use as foreground color.
Press Alt and click over pink part of swatch	Samples color to use as background color.
Press Alt(Option)+Delete. (see fig 16.23)	Fills loaded selection area with foreground color.
Press Alt and click on Channel #5 icon on Channels palette	Loads Channel #5 selection.
Press Delete	Fills selection area with background color.
Choose **S**elect, **N**one (or press Ctrl+D)	Deselects active marquee.
Click on **d**efault colors icon on toolbox (or press **D**)	Resets foreground and background colors to black-and-white.
Press **L**	Chooses Lasso tool.
Click and drag around swatch on MEGALOGO image, then press Delete	Removes swatch from RGB view of image.
Press Ctrl+D (**S**elect, **N**one)	Deselects the active marquee.

continues

continued

Press **M** until Rectangular **M**arquee tool is selected (or press Alt and click on Marquee tool until it appears). Press Shift while you click and drag diagonally, starting in upper left of image; release mouse button when you reach lower right of image

Shift constrains rectangular selection to a square, and creates a selection marquee.

Press Ctrl+Alt while you click and drag the marquee; center it around the color logo

Pressing Ctrl+Alt makes only the marquee moveable; the underlying image is not repositioned.

Choose **E**dit, **D**efine Pattern (see fig. 16.24)

Creates, from image selection, a pattern that can be applied to image areas.

Choose **F**ile, Sa**v**e As, then save MEGALOGO.TIF in TIFF format to your hard disk

Saves your editing work, in case you need it again.

Figure 16.22

Remove the black-and-white logo by deleting it to the background color (white).

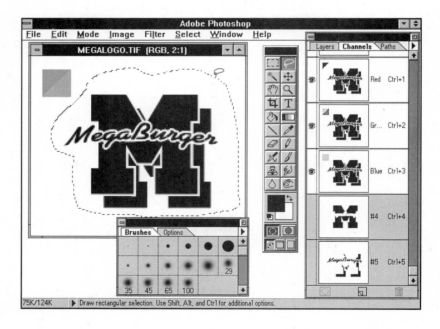

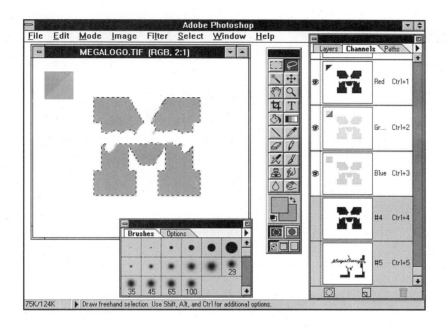

Figure 16.23

Load a selection, then press Alt (Option)+Delete to fill it with foreground color.

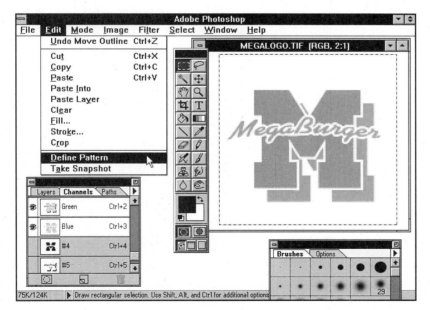

Figure 16.24

Use the Rectangular marquee tool to define a pattern from an image area.

You must use the Rectangular marquee tool to define the area you want as a pattern, whether the pattern you're working with is made up of 1-bit-per-pixel bitmapped images or 24-bit RGB images.

Creating a Splashy Poster Background

Now that the color logo has been defined, it can be applied to the MEGA_GUY image as a repeating, tiled pattern. Because the image of the actor in the MEGA_GUY file is part of a saved selection, you can copy that image to a new layer, and fill the original Background layer with the MegaBurger logo.

Here's how to make the background of the MEGA_GUY image as attention-getting as the foreground:

Filling a Background with Pattern

Open MEGA_GUY.PSD image from your hard disk	Loads image you edited earlier.
Press Alt and click on #4 title on Channels palette	Loads selection of the actor.
Choose **S**elect, **F**loat (or press Ctrl+J)	Creates copy of actor image area as a floating selection.
Choose **S**elect, **M**atting **D**efringe, type **1** in **W**idth field, then click on OK	Removes from floating selection the edge pixels that contain background color.
Click on Layers tab on Layers palette, then press New Layer icon, and click on OK	Displays Make Layer dialog box; you accept default name of Layer 1 for new Layer.

The selection marquee disappears from the MEGA_GUY image, because active floating selections are placed on a new layer when the Make Layer command is issued. The Make Layer option is only available from the pop-up menu on the Layers palette when an image already contains a Layer, and a floating selection is on the image.

Click on Background Layer title on Layers palette, then choose **S**elect, **A**ll (or press Ctrl+A)	Chooses entire background layer, making all of it available for editing.
Choose **E**dit, **F**ill	Displays Fill dialog box.
Choose Pattern from the **U**se: drop-down list, Opacity: **100%**, and Mode: Normal, then click on OK	Fills background layer with pattern, as shown in figure 16.25.

The wallpaper background presents viewers with a strong company identification, but because it was created using Photoshop's pattern-fill feature, it lacks depth. If the actor were really standing in front of a wall covered with MegaBurger wallpaper, he'd cast a shadow on it, right?

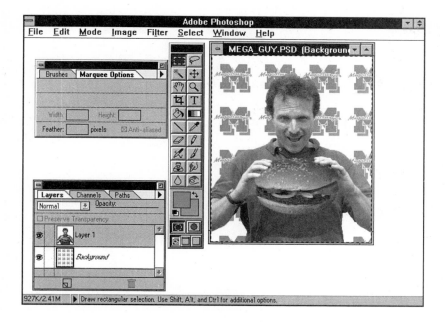

Figure 16.25

Fill the background layer with the pattern you defined.

Using a Saved Selection as a Shadow

You'll use the saved selection in Channel #4 to create a shadow on the wallpaper background. You no longer need the selection information of the actor because the actor is already saved to a layer, and selection information is black, similar in most respects to a real shadow.

However, one or two things are missing from the "photogenic" properties of the saved selection, used as the actor's shadow. First, the saved selection information is far too dense; some surface detail usually shows through shadows. Also, the selection information is too sharp around the edges to serve as a realistic shadow.

The following exercise addresses these problems and shows you how to use the saved selection information as the actor's shadow on the wallpaper.

Creating a Shadow from an Alpha Channel

Click on Channels tab on Layers palette	Displays individual channels for MEGA_GUY image.
Click on #4 title	Displays Alpha channel selection of actor.

continues

continued

Choose **I**mage, **A**djust, **B**rightness/Contrast (or press Ctrl+B)	Displays Brightness/Contrast dialog box.
Enter **25** in Brightness field, then click on OK	Lightens black areas of Alpha channel.

When you want to turn a solid black area into one more suitable for portraying a shadow, 25–35 is usually a good value range to use. Keep this value in mind in your own imaging adventures.

Choose **F**ilter, Blur, Gaussian Blur	Displays Gaussian Blur dialog box.

Gaussian is a sophisticated method of blurring that can create photorealistic shadows from grayscale information. Gaussian blur gives the selection area a dense center, and feathers off the edges. Its effect is frequently described as a bell-shaped curve—high in the center and steeply tapering off on the sides.

Click on minus sign below preview window in Gaussian Blur dialog box, place cursor inside preview window, then click and drag	Zooms preview window out, and scrolls your view so that you can see the Gaussian effect on the Alpha channel.
Click and drag **R**adius slider until it reaches about **4** pixels (see fig. 16.26)	Produces an adequate amount of blurring in Alpha channel.
Click on OK	Applies the filter.
Choose **S**elect, **A**ll (or press Ctrl+A), then choose **E**dit, **C**opy (or press Ctrl+C)	Selects entire Alpha channel and copies it to clipboard.
Click on RGB title (or press Ctrl+0) on Channels palette)	Moves view back to color composite of MEGA_GUY image.
Choose **E**dit, Paste La**y**er	Displays Make Layer dialog box.
Choose Opacity: **70**%, Mode: Multiply, then click on OK	Creates a New Layer 2, where white Alpha channel areas are transparent and the black, blurred areas are semiopaque.

Because you were working last on the background layer, Layer 2 is created on the layer on top of the background, which is perfect—it's beneath Layer 1 of the actor.

Click on Move tool (or press **V**), then click and drag the shadow below and to the right of the actor	Creates appearance that actor casts a shadow on wallpaper background (see fig. 16.27).
Choose **F**ile, **S**ave (or press Ctrl+S)	Saves your work up to this point.

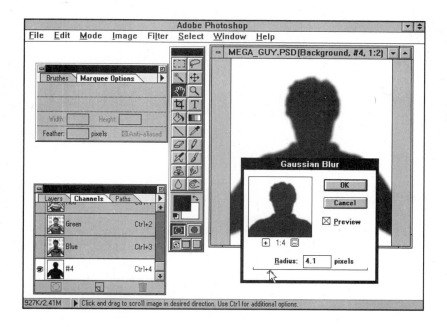

Figure 16.26

Increasing the Radius of the Gaussian Blur filter decreases the focus of the selection area.

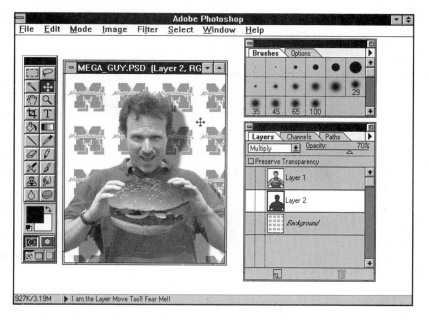

Figure 16.27

Use Multiply mode on the Layers palette to make Layer 2's white areas drop out.

As a mode for the shadow Layer 2, Multiply mode makes color areas beneath it (on the background layer) much darker, but has less of an effect on areas of white background. Neither the mode nor the opacity is carved in stone at this point—you can increase or decrease the opacity of Layer 2 by clicking on and dragging the Opacity slider on the Layers palette. The changes will become permanent when you merge the layers.

If you're happy with the composition now, you should click on the Layers palette's pop-up menu button and choose Flatten Image. Layers and channels add to the size of the image you're working with—and working in a large image can be a slow process. Save the file again and close it. (Closing inactive image windows conserves system resources.) Next, you're going to twist some text.

Displacing Text

In addition to the MEGA_GUY image, the digital collage has three other elements—a headline, a subheadline, and the poster background—all supplied on the Bonus CD.

Creating Special Effects with Type

In the next exercise, you'll be loading some lettering that was created in RGB mode. The lettering was created with the Lithos typeface—a nice display font, but one that lacks dimension (see fig. 16.28). This is a perfect opportunity for you to get acquainted with Photoshop's Displace filter, one of many filters that can be applied to text as well as to other image areas to create special effects.

Figure 16.28

The type is clean and to the point, but lacks dimension.

The Displace filter maps pixels in an image according to a *displacement map*, an image that contains dark and light areas that Photoshop reads much as it reads Alpha channel information. The big difference between displacement and Alpha channel information, however, is that Photoshop *moves* pixels in a target image according to the visual information in the displacement map image. If you use a grayscale image as a displacement map, Photoshop reads darker-pixels information as, "move pixels in the target image down," whereas brighter pixels indicate to Photoshop that pixels in the target image should be moved up. Photoshop ignores neutral grayscale pixels (128 brightness value out of a possible 255) in the displacement map image, and no corresponding pixel rearrangement is done to the target image.

You have the option to displace target-image pixels horizontally and vertically, or across only one plane. Additionally, a displacement map image containing two channels serves as both a horizontal and vertical displacement map. Photoshop uses Channel #1's information for horizontal displacement, and Channel #2 as the source of vertical displacement information.

Like all of the high-level calculations Photoshop is capable of, the effect of displacing pixels in the lettering image files is better seen than described here! In the next exercise, you'll create a displacement map that bends the lettering images, creating the sort of effect you expect from lettering on a poster with punch.

Building a Homemade Displacement Map

Open APPETITE.TIF and CHEESE&.TIF images from CHAP16 subdirectory of Bonus CD	Displays images you'll distort, using Displace filter.
Choose **S**elect, **A**ll (or press Ctrl+A), then choose **E**dit, **C**opy (or press Ctrl+C)	Copies active image to clipboard.

It doesn't matter which image is the active window; both images are the same size. You're only copying the image to the clipboard so that Photoshop will read the size and resolution of the image, and offer you the same size and resolution for a new image. This trick beats going to the Image Size command, remembering the data, and entering it correctly in the New Image dialog box.

Windows users: Click on the Maximize\Minimize button on both lettering images to free desktop space. Macintosh users: click on the image window Size box and drag it to make the lettering images smaller.

Choose **F**ile, **N**ew (or press Ctrl+N), then choose Grayscale from Mode drop-down list, and click on OK	Displacement map image is same dimension and resolution as the lettering images; mapping of displacement will be 1:1.

continues

continued

Why choose a Grayscale mode? Because the mapping effect is easier to see in a single channel. You may want to experiment with 2-channel displacement mappings in your own assignments. And, if you're interested, some premade Photoshop displacement maps are stored in the PHOTOSHP\PLUGINS\DISPMAPS subdirectory on your hard disk.

Click on **d**efault colors icon on toolbox (or press **D**), then choose **G**radient Fill tool (press **G**)	With Gradient tool, you'll create a tonal map on Untitled-1 image.
Press Shift while you click and drag cursor from left to right edge of Untitled-1	Creates smooth transition from black to white (see fig. 16.29). Shift constrains stroke to a straight line.

When creating a displacement map, even distribution of grayscale pixels is the first step. The Gradient tool covers the Untitled image nicely. Now you need to reassign the pixels' brightness values so that they map an upward arc for Photoshop to use as displacement information.

Choose **I**mage **A**djust, **C**urves (or press Ctrl+M)	Displays Curves dialog box.
Click on right triangle below Curve graph until gradient bar goes from black to white	Specifies that you want Curves map to go from dark to light values.
Click and drag right node on graph all the way to bottom	Specifies that all values in Untitled image are black (0 Output).
Click and drag middle node on graph upward until Output value reads about 190	You're reshaping distribution of tonal values in Untitled image (see fig. 16.30).
Click on OK, then choose **F**ile, Sa**v**e As. Save image to your hard disk as WARP.PSD (Photoshop 3 format)	Saves displacement map in an image format Photoshop can use.

WARP.PSD should look like an image of two mirrored gradient fills, butted together. What the curves command did was reassign the brightness values in the Gradient fill so that zero output was defined at either end of the image, and a value of about 25 percent gray was assigned to the middle. For all the complicated math involved in displacement maps, the one you've created is actually quite easy to "read" with your own eyes; when applied to the lettering (or any other image), the black pixels at each end of the image will displace corresponding image areas down, and the lighter middle will displace target image areas up, producing an arc.

After you choose the Displace command, your lettering will look very much like the curve on the grid in the Curves command.

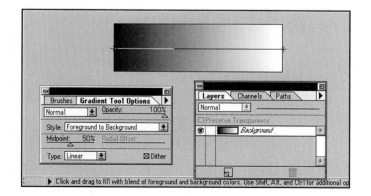

Figure 16.29

Use the Gradient tool to fill the Untitled image with pixels of different tonal values.

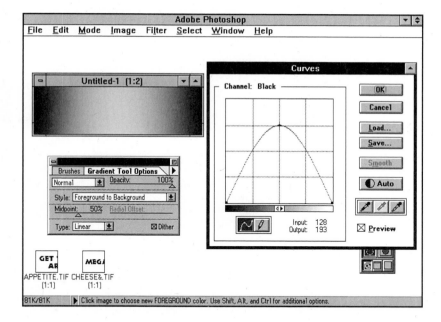

Figure 16.30

The Curves command reassigns brightness values for the different tonal ranges in an image.

Making an Arc out of Lettering

You're all set to twist some type, Photoshop-style. You don't need to close the WARP.PSD image to use it on the lettering images, but you probably should at least minimize WARP.PSD.

First, you'll work with the APPETITE.TIF image:

Distorting Lettering

Restore APPETITE.TIF image to 1:1 viewing resolution	Image you'll work with first.
Choose Filter, Distort, then Displace	Displays Displace dialog box.
Type **0** in Horizontal Scale: field, type **40** in Vertical Scale field, then click on OK (see fig. 16.31)	Specifies that displacement will be performed only across APPETITE.TIF image's Vertical axis.

The other options in the Displace dialog box aren't relevant to this assignment. They refer to undefined areas; areas in the displacement image that don't correspond to the APPETITE target image. The WARP.PSD image maps 1 to 1, however. Because it's the same size as the APPETITE image, you don't need to tile and repeat edge pixels.

Choose WARP.PSD from directories list in Load dialog box	Specifies that displacement map you created should be used as blueprint for distorting APPETITE image.
Click on OK	Applies Displace command (see fig. 16.32).

The Displace command has its limitations, and although the lettering arcs now, the "climb" of the curve it follows is a little too straight. You *could* spend more time and care creating a displacement image in the Curves command—but the job of adding more dimension to the lettering goes much faster when you use the Spherize command.

Choose Filter, Distort, Spherize	Displays Spherize dialog box.
Click on Mode: **H**orizontal only, type **50** in **A**mount field, then click on OK	Applies half-strength sphere distortion to image (see fig. 16.33).
Choose File, Save As, then save the image in TIFF format to your hard disk	Saves your work up to this point.

Stop   Don't choose **F**ilter, Last **F**ilter or press Ctrl+F if you want to change the parameters of the filter you last used. If you choose Last **F**ilter, Photoshop will apply the last filter you used without offering the dialog box where the settings are made.

Instead, Press Ctrl+Alt(Option), then press F. This tells Photoshop to display the last filter's dialog box, where you have the choice of defining different settings than you did last.

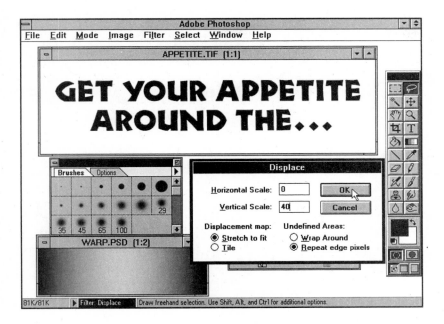

Figure 16.31

With the Displace command, you can set the plane of Displace mapping to horizontal, vertical, or both.

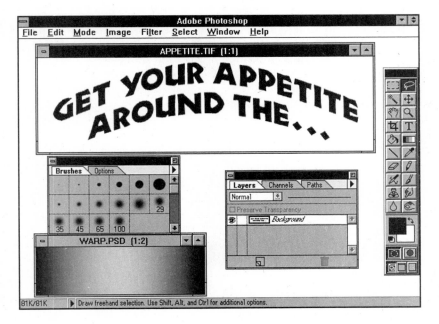

Figure 16.32

From left to right, dark pixels in the displacement map push image areas down, and light pixels push target-image pixels upward.

Figure 16.33

See the effect on the target image in the Spherize preview window before applying the effect.

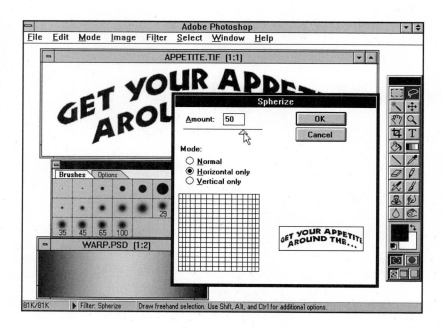

To fully appreciate the power of the Displace command—a Distort filter—you have to play with it independently. You can use photographic images as displacement maps for other images, and you can create repeating waves by tuning a displacement map with the Curves command. Photoshop users often create their own artist "hook" by experimenting with a feature such as the Displace command or Gaussian blur. It's important in your learning experience, however, not to overuse an effect, but instead to know how an effect can best serve a creative idea.

Displacing Text in a Negative Direction

Using the same steps you used on the APPETITE image, you need to bend the CHEESE& image—but let's make the CHEESE& lettering slope downward. You'll use the two lettering images as a frame, above and below the MEGA_GUY actor, in the finished poster.

Follow these steps to slope the cheese and bring home the bacon:

Negative Displacement Mapping

Click on CHEESE& image window title bar	Makes CHEESE&.TIF the active image.
Choose Filter, Distort, Displace	Displays Displace dialog box with the settings you used last.

Type **–40** in **V**ertical Scale click on OK	Changes the amount of upward field, then displacement; displays the Load dialog box.
Pick the WARP.PSD file from the list of File **N**ames from the Load dialog box, then click on OK	Photoshop reads displacement image information backward, moving pixels up when it reads darker tonal regions, and moving pixels down when it reads lighter tonal regions.
Choose Fi**l**ter, Distort, Spherize, then click on OK	Most commands in Photoshop retain their settings in a single session, so the 50% value is still set in this command.
Choose **F**ile Sa**v**e As, and save CHEESE& image to hard disk in TIFF format	Saves your work up to this point.

Your two lettering images should now look like figure 16.34.

Figure 16.34

The two lettering images are perfect for framing the MEGA_GUY image in the poster.

Next, you'll use Photoshop's Channels feature to "auto-mask" the lettering and apply striking colors that complement the MEGA_GUY image.

Using Text as Its Own Selection Mask

When you have black foreground colors on a white background (as you do with this lettering), Photoshop can use the visual information as selection information. It's as simple as moving the RGB composite image to a user-defined Alpha channel.

In the next set of steps, you'll move the lettering to Alpha channels; then color in the selection areas, using the same method you used with the MegaBurger logo.

This exercise shows you how to create an attention-getting element for the collage.

Coloring a Selection Area

Click on APPETITE.TIF image's title bar	Makes APPETITE.TIF the active image window.
Choose **S**elect, **A**ll (or press Ctrl+A), then **E**dit, Cu**t** (or press Ctrl+X)	Cuts lettering from APPETITE image and places it on clipboard.
Click on New channel icon on Channels palette, then click on OK	Adds Channel #4 to APPETITE.TIF image.
Choose **E**dit, **P**aste (or press Ctrl+V)	Pastes image on clipboard into Alpha channel.
Press Ctrl+0 (or click on RGB title on Channels palette)	Moves your view to color composite of image, which should be blank right now.
Click on foreground color on toolbox	Displays Photoshop's color picker.
Click and drag circle in spectrum box to red, then click on OK	Changes foreground color to red (shade of red is not critical).
Click on background color on toolbox	Displays Photoshop's color picker.
Click and drag the Hue slider to between yellow and orange, click and drag the circle in the spectrum box to get a gold color, then click on OK	Changes background color to gold (shade of gold is not critical).
Click on Gradient tool (or press **G**), then click and drag from top to bottom on APPETITE image	Creates a gradient fill in in selection area.
Repeat procedure for moving CHEESE& lettering to *new* Alpha channel in CHEESE&.TIF image, load selection, then	You now have two lettering images, with Gradient fills going in opposing directions (see fig. 16.35).

click and drag from top to
bottom, using Gradient tool

Save CHEESE& image as a TIFF file to
your hard disk

Saves your work up to this point.

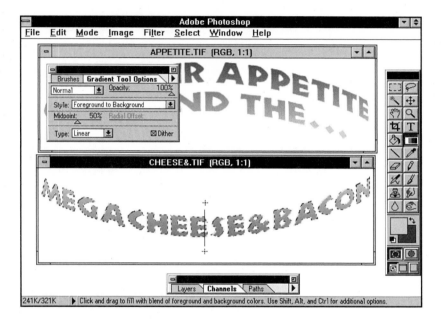

Figure 16.35

*Gradient fills
flood selection
area, with a
transition between
foreground and
background
colors.*

Assembling the Digital Collage

You've created all the elements necessary for creating the collage poster. The
POSTER.TIF file, a background with a line or two of text, created with the dimensions of the lettering and MEGA_GUY image in mind, is in the CHAP16 subdirectory
(folder) of the Bonus CD. You will have to make a few minor adjustments as you
assemble the collage, but you've already leapt across the big hurdles in this assignment.

Here's how to add the lettering elements to the POSTER image:

Copying Lettering to the Collage

Open POSTER.TIF image from CHAP16
subdirectory (folder) on Bonus CD

This is the background for all the other
image elements you've created.

continues

continued

Click on APPETITE.TIF image's title bar, then press Alt and click on #4 title on Channels palette	Makes APPETITE.TIF the active image, and loads Alpha Channel selection.
Choose Edit, Copy (or press Ctrl+C)	Copies selection to clipboard.
Click on title bar of POSTER.TIF image, then choose Edit, Paste Layer, and click on OK	Makes POSTER.TIF the active image window, and pastes lettering on a new Layer 1.
Click on Move tool on toolbox (or press **V**), then click and drag lettering to top of POSTER.TIF image	Repositions lettering, as shown in figure 16.36.
Click on CHEESE& title bar, then press Alt and click on #4 title on the Channels palette	Loads selection area.
Click and drag selection into POSTER.TIF image window, to an area just above text at bottom of poster	Copies selection to Layer 1 of POSTER image.

The CHEESE&BACON lettering might be a little too wide for the POSTER image—displacing and distorting text tends to have this effect. *Don't* deselect the floating cheese selection yet; because it's a floating selection, it's not part of the layer yet, and can be manipulated independently of the APPETITE lettering.

Choose Image, Effects, Scale	A Scale box appears around floating cheese selection.
Press and hold Shift key while you click on a corner box handle and drag it, ever so slightly, toward center of selection (see fig. 16.37)	By holding down the Shift key, you're scaling down the selection proportionately.
Click inside Scale box	Applies the effect; tiny hammer "nails" selection to degree of Scaling you performed.
Choose File, Save As, and save file to your hard disk as a *.PSD image	The PSD format is the only one that can retain Layers information.

After you deselect the floating cheese lettering, both the APPETITE and CHEESE&BACON areas on the layer necessarily move as one object. The reason for not choosing a new layer for the cheese lettering is to conserve overall file size. Photoshop displays a status line that tells you the current size of the active image. The POSTER image is more than 1 MB, both original lettering images are open, and soon

you'll open the MEGA_GUY image—all of which causes computers with less than 8–12 MB of RAM installed to teeter, crash, then burn to the ground.

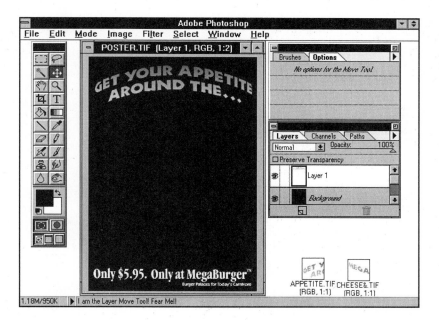

Figure 16.36

The lettering should have its own Layer, so that you can reposition the elements later.

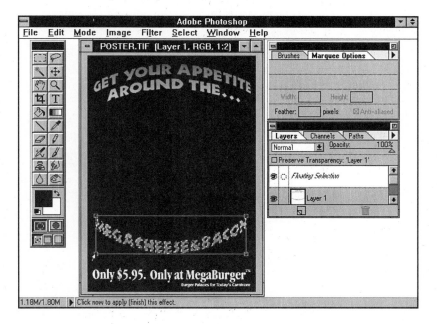

Figure 16.37

Use the Scale command to shrink or expand a floating selection.

To work around the "linked" property of the two lettering selections on Layer 1, select one area with the Lasso or Marquee tool. Then click on the selected text and drag it to reposition it in the layer. The areas outside the lettering are transparent and aren't included when you move a selection. Anything you select and drag in a layer becomes a floating selection that you can move.

Adding the Actor to the Poster

The much-awaited moment has arrived—it's time to add the actor and his overstuffed sandwich to the POSTER image. After copying the image to a new layer in the POSTER.PSD file, you'll be able to compose the elements for the final image.

Here's how to put the final touches on the POSTER.PSD image:

Adding and Modifying Elements on Layers

Close APPETITE and CHEESE& images	Conserves system resources.
Click on New Layer icon, then click on OK	Adds Layer 2 to POSTER image.
Click on Layer 2 icon and drag it below Layer 1 title	Reorders layers so that lettering is top layer.
Open MEGA_GUY.PSD image from hard disk	Windows users can use hot keys (Alt(Option)+F, then 1, for example) to access the four most recently opened images.
Choose a selection tool, then choose <u>S</u>elect, <u>A</u>ll (or press Ctrl+A), then click on MEGA_GUY image and drag it to POSTER.PSD image window	Copies MEGA_GUY image to Layer 2 (see fig. 16.38).
Choose <u>F</u>ile, <u>C</u>lose (or press Ctrl+W)	Closes MEGA_GUY image. (You're done with MEGA_GUY, and the fewer image windows you have open, the more system resources you have available).

The MEGA_GUY image is a little large for the Poster image, isn't it? You could use the Scale command to size it down. But you can make the composition more effective by cropping the image to exclude two elements that aren't essential in the burger message: a lot of the background logo, and the actor's elbows.

Chapter 16 ◆ Creating a Digital Collage   **797**

Here's how to crop an image on a Layer:

Choose **S**elect, **N**one (or press Ctrl+D), then click on Rectangular **M**arquee tool on toolbox (or press **M**)	Deselects image so that you can reselect a portion of it with the Rectangular marquee tool.
Click and diagonally drag a marquee around the important elements of MEGA_GUY image on Layer 2	In other words, crop about 1/4 screen inches (at 1:2 viewing resolution) off each side.
Choose **S**elect, **I**nverse	Selects cropped areas, and masks center image area.
Press Delete key	Removes cropped areas (see fig. 16.39).
Choose **F**ile, **S**ave (or press Ctrl+S)	Saves your work up to this point.

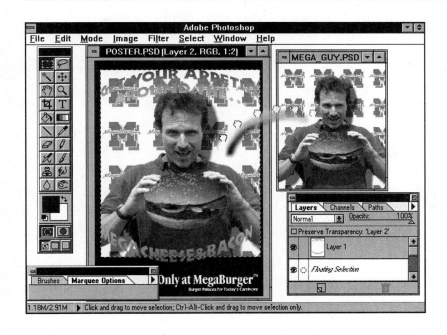

Figure 16.38

Click on the selected image and drag it to the POSTER.PSD image.

Figure 16.39

*Use the Select,
Inverse command
to crop the outside
of an image
you've defined
with a selection
tool.*

Advanced Type Enhancements

You don't need a book to tell you how to arrange the elements to complete this collage image. Trust your artist's eye, and use the arrow keys in combination with the Move tool to nudge image areas on the layers into precisely the right place.

Before you merge layers, however, there's one small but outstanding trick you might want to use on this digital collage to help separate the APPETITE and CHEESE&BACON lettering from the background. That trick is to create drop-shadow lettering.

The following exercise shows you how to make text stand off an image, regardless of the colors used in the text or in other image areas.

Creating Drop-Shadow Text

Click on Layer 1 title on Layers palette	Makes Layer 1, the layer with lettering, the active layer.
Choose Duplicate Layer from Layers palette pop-up menu, then click on OK	Creates copy of Layer 1 above Layer 1.

Click on Layer 1 title	Makes Layer 1 the active (target) layer, which you'll adjust.
Click on Preserve Transparency check box	Protects from change any transparent areas on Layer 1.
Click on eye icon on Layer 1 Copy title	Hides Layer 1 copy from view.
Choose 100-pixel-diameter tip from Brushes palette, choose the Paint Brush tool, (which should then click and drag	Covers only gold and red lettering with foreground color be default black).
Uncheck Preserve Transparency box	Now you can freely move the black drop shadow text around the transparent layer.
Press **V**, then click on lettering and drag it down slightly	Chooses Move tool, and repositions black lettering.
Click on eye icon on Layer 1 copy title on Layers palette	Toggles Layer 1 copy back to active view.

If the drop shadows aren't exactly where you want them, or if you'd like to move the top independently of the bottom, marquee select one of the shadows with a selection tool and click and drag to reposition it.

When you have completed the collage, you can choose to flatten the layers and save POSTER.PSD as a TIFF file, or keep it on your hard disk as a *.PSD image. Unlike physical collages, a multilayer Photoshop file can be reorganized ad infinitum.

Choose **F**ile, **S**ave (or press Ctrl+S)	Saves your work up to this point.

Now's a perfect time to take a break, put on some contemporary music, click on the full screen without menu bar button (the botton on the right at the bottom of the toolbox), press the Tab key to hide palettes and the toolbox, and take a good look at your handiwork. If it looks like figure 16.40, you deserve accolades on your collage. (Try saying that two times, fast.)

Photoshop's integrated feature set helps you integrate different types of image areas into powerful artistic compositions, as this chapter demonstrated. Whether for an ad, or for the pure love of working in the computer graphics medium, you'll always find more solutions than problems when you know what a tool does, and more important, *what it's good for.*

Figure 16.40

*The finished
digital collage.*

The Wonderful World of Black and White

Color imaging is emphasized in this book because color is the way people see the world. The capability of the personal computer to display 24-bit color, and the development of software such as Photoshop to work with these images are fairly recent events. But as exciting as color photography and imaging is, black-and-white photography still has a place in the world of media. You probably need to produce black-and-white work for a newsletter, flyer, or other promotion. There's both a photographic purism and an economy to be had with the black-and-white medium.

This chapter is a potpourri of techniques and special effects you'll want to adopt in your own work with monochrome, grayscale, black-and-white photographic images. An image created or photographed in color can be manipulated as a grayscale, and vice versa. In this chapter, you start with a color image and learn how to create the ultimate black-and-white masterpiece. And after a sidestep to Photoshop's Filter effects (and a couple of homemade ones), you find out how to add color to a grayscale photo! Photoshop handles image data adeptly, regardless of color mode. You soon see how to get the most out of any type of image you have to work with.

From 24-bit Color to 8-bit Grayscale

In Chapter 2, "Acquiring a Digital Image," you were advised not to acquire a color image with a grayscale scanner. Color reduction shouldn't be performed at the digital image acquisition phase, because scanners typically don't use a color model that can adequately handle conversion from RGB image information directly to grayscale. Grayscale is a single channel format, whose visual information is displayed as brightness.

If you simply remove the other characteristics of light from an RGB image to get grayscale samples, unequal components of hue and purity of hue (*saturation*) can make areas of an image darker or lighter than you expect or want. *Luminance* (also called *brightness*), the measurement of the brilliance an area displays, is actually measured by the weighted average of the combined brightness values of the R, G, and B component channels, to the tune of about 30-percent red, 60-percent green, and 10-percent blue. The reason each color channel's contribution to the brightness of an area is unequal is that wavelengths of light don't behave like the simple depictions of them we see in color models.

For example, the wavelengths of light we see as having unique color characteristics are not parceled out evenly across a color wheel; wheels and triangles that describe color components are merely color models humans have invented to explain a phenomenon we can't touch, and to provide an intuitive, familiar set of controls and labels for working with the phenomenon. Color models belong to color theory (covered in Chapter 3, "Color Theory and the PhotoCD"). In practice, color measurement gets a little tricky, especially when you want to separate the brightness values from a color image to arrive at an aesthetic-looking grayscale image.

You can avoid the headaches associated with color reduction by scanning a color image in an RGB mode, then working with the digital image using Photoshop's capability to display RGB values in *other* color modes.

Sampling Original Colors in an Image

Your introduction, then, to the wonderful world of black-and-white begins, paradoxically, with the color image LAURIE.TIF on the Bonus CD. You will work with this sample image as you explore the techniques and special effects in this chapter.

First, you'll sample and preserve some of the original colors from an image before it is converted to grayscale. The Scratch palette is the ideal storage place for these sample colors. When this chapter comes full circle, from RGB to grayscale to RGB, you will have custom-specified colors that you can use to hand-tint a black-and-white image.

The Scratch Palette

The Scratch palette is one of three palettes in the Picker/Swatches/Scratch group whose function is closest to that of a blank canvas. You can specify and save custom colors on the Scratch palette. You also can sample colors from an image, then use any Photoshop painting tool to apply the color (or image area) to the Scratch palette. You can clone into the palette, and zoom in and out of it. You can even create a marquee selection on the palette, and click and drag the marquee selection out of the Scratch palette and into an image window, where it can be used exactly like a selection made from an image.

In terms of this chapter's assignments, however, the most important feature is the capability to save your own custom-made Scratch palette. By sampling and saving a number of unique colors from an RGB image, you can apply the saved colors to an image that has only grayscale values, thereby performing the digital equivalent of hand-tinting an image.

Because you are going to remove the color qualities in the LAURIE.TIF image, the first exercise shows you how to save sample colors from an image, in case you want to use them later. Colors sampled and saved from an RGB image can also be applied to an entirely different image.

Here's how to set up the Scratch palette to make and save a custom collection of colors found in an RGB image.

Creating a Color Collection from an Image

Open LAURIE.TIF image from the Bonus CD	Target image from which you'll sample colors.
Press Ctrl+plus	Zooms to a 1:2 viewing resolution of image, so that you can see it better.
Press F6(Mac: press F10), then click Picker/Swatches/Scratch on Scratch palette tab	Displays palette group, and displays Photoshop's default sampling of colors in scratch area.
Press **D** (for **d**efault colors icon)	Makes current background color white.
Click on pop-up menu arrow to right of tabs, and choose Clear	Removes default color sampling on Scratch palette, replacing it with background white (see fig. 17.1).

continues

continued

Press **P** (for **P**encil tool), then choose a medium tip from second row on Brushes palette	Tool for sampling original image colors, and for rendering them on Scratch palette.

The Pencil tool is a poor choice for most image retouching because it has no Anti-alias, soft-edge characteristics. However, the Pencil tool excels at creating flat areas of color on an image or on the scratch pad area. This makes it the ideal tool for creating a color collection from the LAURIE.TIF image.

Press Alt(Option) while clicking on an area of Laurie's face and a foreground	Alt toggles Pencil to Eyedropper tool (see fig. 17.2), color sample is taken from area your cursor is over.

Release Alt key, then click in upper-left corner of Scratch palette	Places on scratch pad a flat dot of color you sampled with Eyedropper tool.

You want to place the first color you sample from the image in the upper-left of the Scratch palette, to leave room for other samples, and to create some organization as you proceed.

Press Alt while clicking on a different color area of Laurie's face, then release Alt key, and click to right of first dot on Scratch palette	Samples a second unique color, and adds another color dot to your collection.

As you can see in figure 17.3, I've copied five color areas from the image, all taken from Laurie's face. These are samples that will be used later, after the color has been removed from this image, as the tints for hand-coloring a copy of this image. Take about five samples, then move on and sample background colors, Laurie's hair color, and other unique colors you see in the image. Arrange the samples on the Scratch palette according to the image area from which you took them.

 Tip   When you want to create several variations in the *tint* (the amount of white mixed with a color) from a single sampled color, type a digit (use the number keys on keyboard or the numerical pad) before you apply the color by clicking on the Scratch palette. The numerical keypad changes the Opacity on the Brushes palette in increments of 10. For example, if you sample a color area and want to save a 40 percent tint of the sampled color, type **4** and then click on the Scratch palette. Photoshop's Brushes palette will automatically lower the percentage of the color sample's opacity to 40 percent.

New Riders Publishing
INSIDE
SERIES

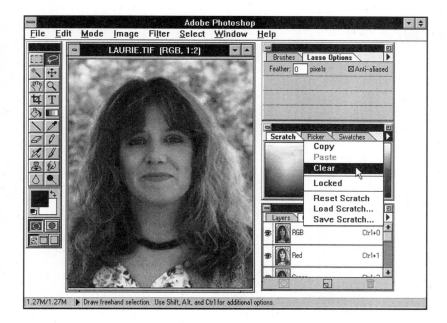

Figure 17.1

Choosing Clear from the Scratch palette's pop-up menu causes the live area to become solid background color.

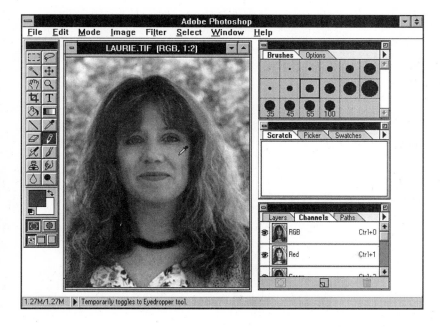

Figure 17.2

Pressing the Alt(Option) key toggles the Pencil tool to the Eyedropper tool, so you can sample a foreground color.

Figure 17.3

Organize a collection of color samples as you create them.

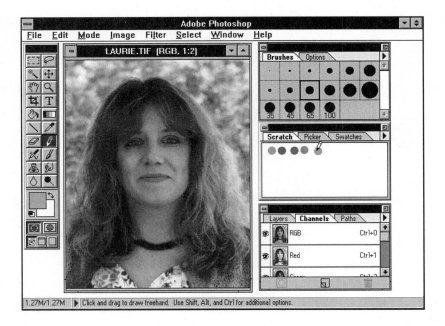

Because the Scratch palette behaves very much like a blank image canvas, you can also use any of the marquee tools to select a color dot and reposition it.

The collection of colors you've taken from LAURIE.TIF will serve as your virtual artist's palette. You'll use this palette as the source of the color you'll apply to a grayscale version of the LAURIE.TIF image (saved in RGB mode) in an exercise at the end of this chapter. Before you save the Scratch palette, however, it would be useful to label the areas from which you sampled colors. You could use the Pencil tool, but most people's penmanship with the mouse in an area this small generally produces illegible chicken scratches! In the next section, you'll refine the palette so that sampling colors from it for a future assignment will be easy.

The Type Tool and Scratch Palette Labels

In Photoshop, typography is a graphical element whose appearance is composed of foreground color, so in this respect the Type tool is a Photoshop painting tool. As you saw in the last exercise, paint can be applied to the Scratch palette—so it's not surprising to find that the Type tool also can be used on the Scratch palette. Use the Type tool to label the groups of sampled colors with a reference to the area from which they were taken; it will only take a moment, but will save you lots of time when you need to select appropriate colors for hand-tinting the image.

Because the Scratch palette is a Photoshop screen element, text created on the palette appears at your screen's resolution. Therefore, pick a typeface and size for the label text that is legible onscreen at a 100% view resolution; 12- or 14-point text is usually a good choice.

This exercise shows you how to use the Type tool to label color samples on the Scratch palette.

Typing on an Onscreen Element

If you need to organize your color dots before adding type to your custom palette, use the Lasso or Rectangular marquee tool to click and drag color samples to different positions.

Press **D** (or click on default colors icon on toolbox)	Sets foreground color (color of Type you'll apply) to black.
Press **Y** (for Type tool), then click an insertion point on Scratch palette	Displays Type tool dialog box.
Choose a bold sans serif, such as Arial or Geneva, from the font drop-down list	Both fonts offer ease of reading at small point sizes.

These are suggestions, but you can use any screen font, TrueType, or Type 1 font with Photoshop's Type tool. The authors chose a condensed, Futura font for the custom Scratch palette label text.

Type **14** in Size field, **15** in Leading field, and choose points from drop-down list of typeface measurements	Specifies point size of font. Chances are you won't need to use two lines of type, but 15-point leading keeps lines of type very close together.
Type **Face** in type field at bottom of Type tool dialog box, then click on Left horizontal alignment radio button (see fig. 17.4)	Label for skin tones sampled from Laurie's face Type will be aligned flush left, to right of your insertion point.
Click on OK	Displays image, with black type on Scratch palette as a floating selection.
Click and drag inside floating type selection until it's positioned next to color dots created from samples of Laurie's skin tones	Moves floating selection into positon.

continues

continued

Positioning 12-point type is not the easiest thing to do at 100-percent viewing resolution. If you like, you can click the Zoom tool cursor over the Scratch palette's live area to magnify your view. Your cursor must be inside the marquee outline to click and drag the floating selection. If it's not, the selection will become deselected and composited into the Scratch palette if you click outside the marquee border!

Click an insertion point on Scratch palette and repeat the last three steps, except type **HAIR** in Type tool dialog box. Click and drag floating selection next to hair color samples	Adds a label for color dots that are samples of Laurie's hair colors in the image.
Finish labeling each group of color dots (see fig. 17.5) from image.	Completes labeling of unique color values you've sampled
Choose Save Scratch from Scratch palette's pop-up menu	Displays Save dialog box.
Name your custom palette, and choose a drive and directory (folder) that's easy to locate later	Saves palette to hard disk.

Windows users must add the ASR suffix to the eight-character name for the palette file. Tip: Photoshop installs a CALIBRAT subdirectory, where test images for output and color modes are stored. This is also a good place to save custom palettes, brushes, and monitor and output specifications.

You can recall the ASR file at any time. It can be used as a color palette for the LAURIE.TIF image, or for one of your own images. Custom palettes are an invaluable addition to your other Photoshop tools, because colors sampled in RGB mode from real-world pictures display color characteristics that are more natural looking than a home brew specification. When attempting to color-match a digitized image, we have a very human tendency to pick colors that have too much pure hue. In nature, colors generally contain several different primary values, with one value a *little* more predominant than the others. We recognize the predominant hue in an amount of light that's composed of several hues as a shade of color.

You'll notice that the color samples you took earlier from the LAURIE.TIF image were extremely muted. Compositionally, they supported and contrasted each other within the context of the photo, but when isolated against the white background of the Scratch palette, they displayed very little individual predominant color value. This is why you can be assured of total accuracy in color replacement when you sample color values from an image instead of specifying them in the Color Picker or Picker palette. The human eye is drawn to the point of distraction by colors that are too

brilliant and vibrant to be natural. If you doubt it, think about all the detergent boxes and flashy sports cars sold in America!

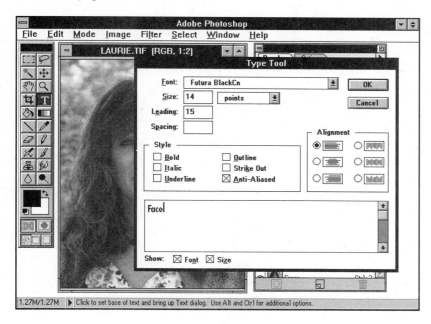

Figure 17.4

In the Type Tool dialog box, type the label for a group of color dots.

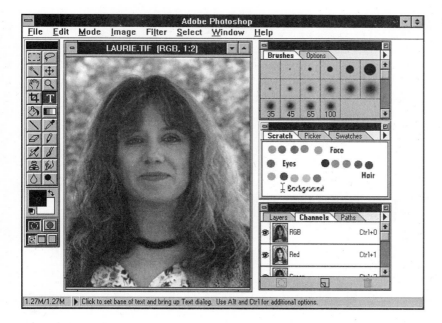

Figure 17.5

You can reposition type on the Scratch palette by clicking and dragging inside the marquee border.

Figure 17.6

Save your custom palette as a file with an ASR file extension—a proprietary Photoshop format.

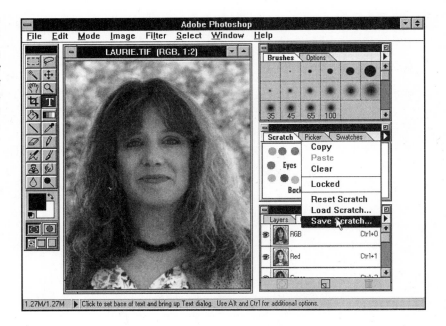

 Tip

The Scratch palette is 200 pixels wide by 89 pixels high. If you have a small image whose colors you'd like to sample and apply to a different image, select the entire area, choose **E**dit, **D**efine pattern, then use the Rubber stamp tool in Pattern (aligned) mode to paint the entire image onto the Scratch palette's painting area. The Scratch palette does not use inches as a measurement of live space you can clone or paint into, so the target image you want to use as a color sample can be of any resolution—it simply needs to be 200 by 89 pixels to fit in its entirety. You can also use the Crop tool to perform image resizing for the purpose of copying an image to the scratch palette.

Because the Scratch palette is a Photoshop element and not an image file, you do not use the Edit menu for Copy and Paste functions—instead, use the Copy and Paste commands in the Scratch palette's pop-up menu to transfer clipboard contents to and from the Scratch palette. You can select an area with any marquee tool, or choose to Copy the entire palette area. Additionally, you can click and drag a marquee selection's contents into an active image window from the Scratch palette.

Working with LAB Color

All the color arrangements you see under Photoshop's <u>M</u>odes menu are different *color spaces* (based on color *models*; see Chapter 3, "Color Theory and the PhotoCD") within which a digital design can be created or displayed. Each color space has a limitation; the color capability of a Mode falls inside of the range of human vision, and certain color modes are a subset of others. In reality, there is a limitation to the way you can look at images that have different color modes, because your monitor is modeled upon the RGB color gamut. Fortunately, most color models fall within RGB's capability to accurately represent them, and RGB monitor color was created to mimic the red, green, and blue cones found in the human eye.

Unfortunately, being able to accurately define and reproduce color that will be displayed or rendered to different output media (television, print, film) is extremely difficult. This is because no two computer monitors are exactly alike in their display. Color matching between electronic and physical media is no picnic either; the pigment in ink and the photoreactive chemicals in film respond to light differently than your monitor does, and our perception of color changes dramatically when an object is viewed under different lighting conditions.

A need was seen early in this century for a device-independent color description method—the color formula for a shade is the same for a monitor as for a printing press, as for a logo stenciled on a basketball, and so on. In 1931, CIE, the *Commission Internationale d'Eclairage* (the International Commission on Illumination) established a standard for describing primary colors. LAB color is a result of the CIE's original color model, and LAB color is based on the way the human eye perceives light. Today, when Photoshop converts a color image from one color mode to another, the program uses the LAB color model as an internal, intermediate color model.

In addition to LAB color's natural depiction of a color gamut, the most attractive quality of working in LAB color is that it is a superset of all other digital color models. All of the other color models Photoshop uses are subsets that fit within the gamut of color that can be defined with the LAB color model. Figure 17.7 is a chart of color gamuts imaging professionals frequently use. As you can see, the RGB gamut (the computer monitor gamut, which is based on the RGB color model) fits inside the LAB gamut. The gamut of CMYK colors (the color model for process color printing) is even narrower than RGB. Because LAB color encompasses (is the *superset* of) the RGB gamut, you can convert an RGB image, such as the LAURIE.TIF image, to LAB color without any translation or loss of image data.

Figure 17.7

*LAB color
describes the
visible range
(or gamut) of
color the human
eye can see—
LAB's gamut
encompasses RGB
color values.*

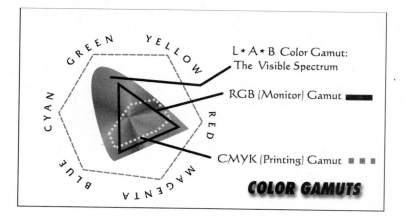

The tongue-shaped color space of the LAB gamut is based on the energy distributions of light wavelengths that make up our visible spectrum. The hexagonal color wheel superimposed on the LAB gamut in figure 17.7 is a more common color description convention, but it fails to depict the unique color strengths light waves have when describing a specific color value. A color wheel is useful for plotting complementary colors (color opposites), but lacks a color model characteristic that depicts the sums of color values.

As you've converted images to other models in previous chapters, you've seen the visible effects of going from a wider gamut to a narrower one. For example, an indexed color mode has fixed, limited color values, and when you limit the unique colors in an RGB mode image to indexed color, the color reduction displays dithering (the *simulation* of additional unique colors) and image content is compromised (lost). However, when you convert an RGB image to the LAB color model, no loss of image information occurs in the translation process, because RGB values comprise a smaller gamut than the LAB model; the RGB gamut is contained within—it is a subset of—the larger LAB gamut.

Translating RGB Values to LAB Values

The first step in creating a grayscale image from the RGB LAURIE.TIF file is to translate the RGB values to those of LAB. The RGB format has no facility for isolating the brightness aspect found in an image, because the model for RGB consists of red, green, and blue strengths. However, as you'll soon see, LAB color has a component that's ideal for use as a grayscale image.

Moving an Image to a Larger Color Space

Choose **M**ode from menu bar, then choose **L**AB color (see fig. 17.8)

Photoshop converts LAURIE.TIF image to LAB color model and color space.

Choose **F**ile, Sa**v**e As, then save image to your hard disk in PSD format (from Save File as Format **T**ype drop-down list)

Saves your work up to this point.

The TIFF file format also supports images arranged according to LAB color channels, as do the EPS and RAW image formats, but because Photoshop uses the LAB model in conversion processes, Photoshop's proprietary PSD format is a good file format in which to save the converted image.

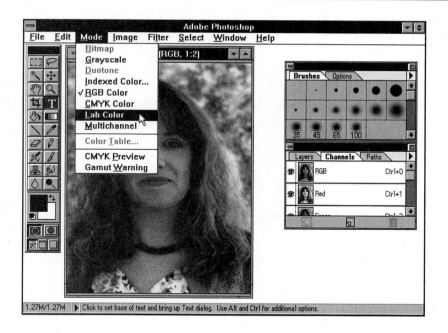

Figure 17.8

You are not transforming color information when you convert an RGB image to the LAB color model.

Now that the copy of the LAURIE image is arranged according to LAB's method of specifying color, you can isolate only the brightness characteristic in the image. Isolating the brightness characteristics (luminosity) of an image provides you with the image information you need to obtain a detailed, tonally balanced grayscale image.

Using a Single LAB Color Component

LAB color mode is a valuable intermediary step for images destined for color capabilities other than their original mode. The way in which color characteristics for light are organized and manipulated in the LAB color model makes LAB interesting to anyone who wants to create an eye-pleasing grayscale image from a color channel image.

The RGB color model describes a specific shade of color by using various intensities of red, green, and blue color components. However, the LAB color mode expresses a wider range of values (or gamut), by using one brightness (or luminance) channel, and two color channels that describe hue.

If you've experimented with Photoshop channels, and copied a single RGB channel to a new file, you've seen that the result is a grayscale image. Because a single RGB color channel contains information about the relative strength of one color component, no single grayscale representation in a channel contains accurate grayscale information about a photo. This is why LAB color can be a boon to anyone who regularly converts color images to grayscale in their work. Photoshop offers separate channel views of the L(Luminance), a (blue-to-yellow axis), and b (green-to-magenta) components. The a and b chromatic components are fairly meaningless as artistic, visual information in a Photoshop channel, because the a and b channels each represent proportions of primary and secondary colors to define a specific color value. But the L channel... now we're talking serious grayscale information! Figure 17.9 is a model of the LAB description of color.

Now that the LAURIE.TIF image has been saved in a mode that arranges color information according to LAB specifications, you can use a copy of the Luminance channel in the LAB image to create a new, grayscale mode image. The new grayscale image is as accurate a depiction of the light characteristics found in the original image as is possible to obtain, using Photoshop's color modes.

Here's how to perform an accurate and pleasing color-to-grayscale transformtion, using the LAURIE.TIF image.

Using Luminance as a Grayscale Image

Press F7 (or choose **W**indows, **P**alettes, Show **C**hannels)

Displays Channels/Layers/Paths group of palettes. If you used the menus to get to this command, click on Channels tab now.

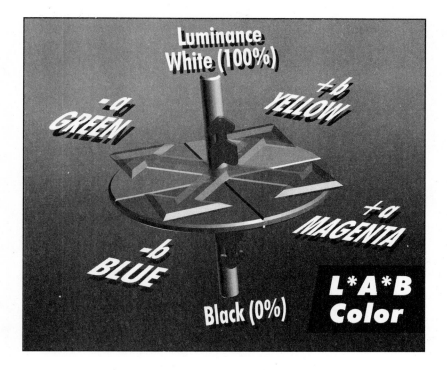

Figure 17.9

The components of LAB color consist of a brightness channel and two color channels.

Click on Lightness channel title on Channels palette (see fig. 17.10)	Displays a view of Lightness (Luminance) channel within the image window as 8-bits-per-pixel information.
Choose **M**odes, then choose **G**rayscale	Photoshop displays an attention box asking whether you want to discard other channels.
Click on OK Lightness channel becomes Black	Image converts to grayscale mode, and channel.
Choose File, Sa**v**e As, then save image to your hard disk in TIFF format (from Save File as Format **T**ype drop-down list), as LITENESS.TIF	Saves your work up to this point.

Figure 17.10

The Lightness channel in a LAB image consists only of brightness values. Chromaticity is not shown in the Lightness view.

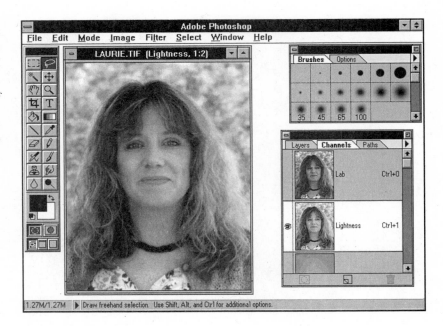

If you still have doubts as to whether the last exercise is the best method for extracting ideal grayscale information from a color image, check out figure 17.11. On the left is the LITENESS.TIF image you saved; on the right is the LAURIE.TIF RGB image, converted straight from RGB color to **G**rayscale mode through the **M**odes command.

LITENESS.TIF might not be an award-winning grayscale image right now, for reasons unrelated to the procedure you've learned. First, the image had good lighting, but LAURIE.TIF does not contain excellent separations of different tonal regions—English translation: the photograph was not taken on a brilliant day. Generally, it's really unflattering to photograph people with harsh lighting that produces a lot of contrast and clear tonal variation. Second, our eyes are influenced by color, and our perception of image quality revolves around information gleaned from both color and tone. Without the color, we see that something is missing from the image.

In either case, if you read Chapter 7, "Restoring an Heirloom Photograph," you saw how to redistribute the tonal values in an image by using the Levels command. With the Levels command (Ctrl+L) at your disposal, you've got the ticket for tweaking the LITENESS.TIF image or any other grayscale image you've created by copying the L channel in a LAB color image.

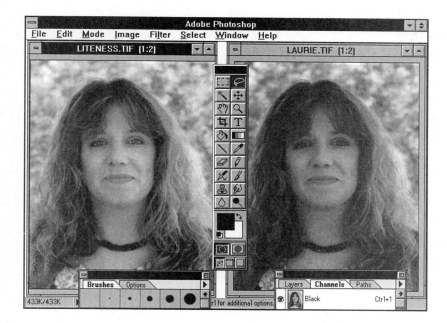

Figure 17.11

When grayscale values are averaged from the three brightnesses of the R, G, and B channels, the result is a duller picture.

With the LITENESS.TIF image the active window in your Photoshop workspace, Choose **I**mage, **A**djust, **L**evels (Ctrl+L is the shortcut), then experiment with the midrange control. Depending on your monitor calibration, you may want to decrease the *gamma* (the midrange contrast) to reveal more visual information in the photo. Read Chapters 2 and 3 ("Acquiring a Digital Image" and "Color Theory and the PhotoCD," respectively) to learn about system calibration and gamma adjustments, because these adjustments play a large role in the successful manipulation of grayscale, tonal values. When the image looks right to you, save it to your hard disk (press Ctrl+S or choose **F**ile, **S**ave). You'll use this image in the exercises that follow.

Creative Uses of Filters and Grayscale Images

As mentioned earlier, the human eye is attracted subliminally to a color image over a grayscale one, often for the wrong reasons. The eye is attracted to bright pastels and saturated colors, and often overlooks poor composition in a color image. When you look at a grayscale image, which contains no distracting color information, you are forced to analyze the image solely on its visual detail. The special effects you'll work with in this chapter are particularly effective when applied to an image that contains only visual detail (without the distracting element of color).

Photoshop's Filters work as artistic enhancements within grayscale images for the following reasons:

◆ Shifting the focal point in a color photo by adding a special effect is almost impossible. The eye is drawn primarily to an interesting color area and registers an effect as a secondary consideration.

◆ Blending a special effect into a grayscale image is much easier than blending it into a color image. You don't have to worry about matching saturation and hue values between special and not-so-special areas of the image, because there are no hues!

Think about the uses you have for black-and-white photography in everyday assignments. When the budget is tight for a flyer or newsletter, process color printing is out of the question. And that puts the brunt of the printed material's attraction on the composition of art and photographic images. So why not make them as eye-catching as possible with a few Photoshop effects?

The Filters menu in Photoshop comes packed with many dramatic, processor-intensive effects you can apply to selections or to entire images. Although these effects are useful for distorting and randomizing simple still life images, they are absolutely inappropriate to apply full-force to a portrait image. Later in this chapter we'll explore some creative uses of Photoshop's more powerful filters, which are more suitably applied to still life images.

Adding Noise to a Grayscale Image

Noise, in the context of digital imaging, is the random dispersal, within an image, of pixels that have different brightness levels. Because the connotation of noise is generally an unpleasant one (except when it's your stereo, and not your neighbor's), it seems on the surface as though one's ultimate goal in digital imaging is to remove noise from an image.

However, noise is neither good nor bad—it's a quality you can add to a grayscale image to create a stunning effect, if you treat video noise as a design element. When the Noise filter is applied, it removes some of the original image detail (as do all Photoshop filters). So the real trick to working successfully with the Noise filter is to strike a balance in the image between the effect and the way it interacts with the original image.

In the next exercise, you'll use the Noise filter to gently modify the visual information in the LITENESS.TIF image. Uniform Noise is the option you'll use in the Add Noise dialog box, because Uniform Noise can create an interesting texture in an image with many areas that gradually move into deeper and lighter brightness values. Digital grit is often an attention-getting enhancement to images that lack contrast. Noise is not a

substitute for improving contrast in an image, but it can add interest and complement original image detail.

In this exercise you create a look that's very popular in magazines—they use it to make portrait photography look more like a graphic design.

Creating a Granular Look in an Image

Double-click on Hand tool, then maximize LITENESS.TIF image window so that it fills the screen	Changes viewing resolution of image to 1:1.

Unlike most Photoshop filters, Noise requires at least a 1:1 view of the target image to accurately view and assess the effect. Noise randomly disperses single pixels throughout an image, and Photoshop cannot offer you exactly the same Noise preview effect at, say, 1:2 as at 1:1, because how do you display half a pixel?

Choose Filter, Noise, Add Noise…	Displays Add Noise dialog box.
Click on Uniform radio button	Chooses type of Noise to be blended into image. Uniform noise is softer in appearance than Gaussian noise.

The Monochromatic check box doesn't affect the outcome of the LITENESS.TIF image, because the LIGHTNESS image itself is monochromatic. If you're working with a color image and the Monochromatic check box is unchecked, the Noise filter disperses color pixels throughout the image. With the box checked, various amounts of gray component are randomly added to pixels. Adding gray component to the image pixels creates different shades of the original color and creates the appearance of noise.

Place cursor inside preview window, then click and drag until you've scrolled to an image area with visual detail	Lets you see a preview of the effect on image detail, and not the image background or a flatly shaded area.
Click on the plus button beneath the preview window	Zooms you into a better viewing resolution in the preview window.
Click and drag Amount slider to about **47** (or enter this value in Amount field)	Sets amount of Uniform noise to be added to image (see fig. 17.12).

The Amount slider offers a blend of Noise with original image information, in exponential (not linear) increments from 1 to 999. The halfway mark on the slider is 100. Amounts you specify in excess of 100 tend to ruin image detail.

continues

continued

Click on OK	Applies the effect.
Choose **F**ile, Sa**v**e As, then save image to your hard disk as DUSTY.TIF (choose TIFF format from Save File as Format **T**ype drop-down list)	Saves your work up to this point.

Figure 17.12

To simulate texture in an image that has too little overall contrast, add noise to the image.

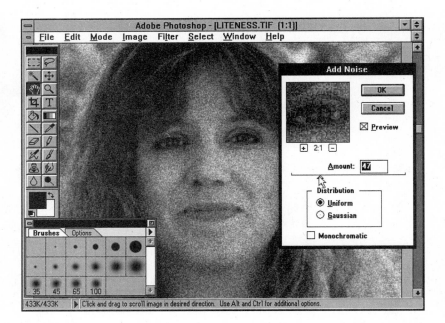

An extra perk that comes with noisy images is that they print well to low-resolution laser printers. The Noise filter breaks up continuous tone regions in an image, and 300–600 dpi printers don't have as hard a time plotting this information as they do reproducing smooth shades of gray.

Unlike Uniform noise, Gaussian noise tends to deposit a clump of random pixels in the target image. For this reason, Uniform noise is the best choice for creating an effect in an image whose subject is a person. However, you might want to experiment with images of landscapes and still life scenes and the Gaussian noise filter.

Creating a Crystallized Image

The more dramatic an effect you create in an image, the more original image detail you lose, but that shouldn't stop you from applying a fairly intense effect to *part* of an image.

The Crystallize filter—one of many Photoshop filters you may want to experiment with in your imaging work—creates a pebbled, almost painterly effect in an image. Although the Crystallize filter destroys much original composition detail, the effect can be worked into a portrait image in such a way that the Crystallize filter enhances, rather than disrupts, a pretty picture.

The next effect you'll create is a two-part assignment. In the next exercise, you apply the Crystallize filter. Then you'll use the Eraser tool in its Erase to Saved setting to gently restore image areas, thereby creating a smooth transition between crystallized areas and original image.

Creating a Painting from an Image

Open copy of LITENESS.TIF you saved on hard disk, and close DUSTY.TIF image	To experiment with Crystallize filter, you need a fresh copy of grayscale image.
Choose Filter, Pixelate, then Crystallize	Displays Crystallize dialog box.

By default, the Crystallize **C**ell Size is set to 10. The Cell Size value roughly corresponds to the average of the height and width of individual crystals produced in the image by averaging the color values found in the corresponding original image area. Figure 17.13 shows the preview of the Crystallize effect; a cell size of 10 looks pretty dramatic.

Set **C**ell Size to **10** (or leave it set at 10), then click on OK	Applies the effect.

Wait a little while. Crystallize, like most Photoshop filters, is extremely processor-intensive; even PowerMacs and Pentiums can take a while to execute a filter when it's applied to an image larger than 1 MB. Why not read ahead while you wait?

Although the Crystallize filter produces an interesting, abstract effect, you want to augment LITENESS.TIF with the Crystallize effect, not let the effect become the main visual attraction. By restoring some of the original image details with the Erased to Saved mode of the Eraser tool, you can restore some of the original LITENESS.TIF image in a very artistic fashion. Because you applied the Crystallized filter to an image that was saved before you applied the effect, Photoshop can read the saved version from your hard disk into memory. The Eraser tool looks at the before copy in memory, and changes the areas it passes over in the current image to their pre-Crystallized state.

Okay, your processor has probably finished processing the Crystallize effect by now, and if your screen looks like figure 17.14, you're ready to get on with image restoration.

Figure 17.13

The cell size of the Crystallize filter determines the size of the area to be averaged to create a corresponding, single tone.

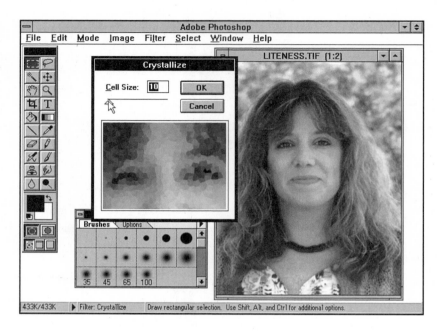

Figure 17.14

Some image areas look good with the Crystallize effect applied, but others need to be restored to original image information.

Erasing Back to Last-Saved Versions

Double-click on Eraser tool on the toolbox	Tool for restoring areas of LITENESS.TIF image; double-clicking displays Options palette for Eraser tool.
Choose Airbrush from drop-down list on Options palette, set Pressure to **50**%, and click on Erase to Saved check box in lower-right corner of Options palette	Sets characteristics for Eraser tool to partially restore image information from last saved version.
Click on Brushes tab on Brushes/Options grouped palette, then click on 65-pixel diameter tip	Sets size of Eraser tip.
Click (don't drag) on LITENESS.TIF image	Tells Photoshop you want to begin Erasing to Saved.

Whenever you Erase to a Saved version of an image, Photoshop must read a saved version into system memory. This takes a moment or two. Clicking and dragging with the Eraser tool set to Erase to Saved is a futile effort, because Photoshop needs to read that saved image copy first. You stand a chance of making a mistake on the image if you immediately click and drag, because Photoshop needs to catch up with your last input. Therefore, when working with the Erase to Saved option, it is best to click once, wait for Photoshop to load a copy of the original image, and then proceed with your work after the Photoshop cursor has returned from the Windows hourglass or the Macintosh stopwatch.

Click and drag over facial areas of LITENESS.TIF	Restores these areas to saved original version, but not completely, because Eraser tool is set to 50% Pressure (50% strength).
Continue clicking and dragging around edge of Laurie's face, until her Crystallized hair blends into original facial areas	Don't click and drag through background of image (see fig. 17.15).
When you have a masterpiece, choose File, S**a**ve As, then save image to your hard disk as CRYSTAL.TIF (choose TIFF format from Save File as Format **T**ype drop-down list)	Saves your work up to this point.

Figure 17.15

The Eraser tool restores original image areas, but only back to the last-saved version of an image.

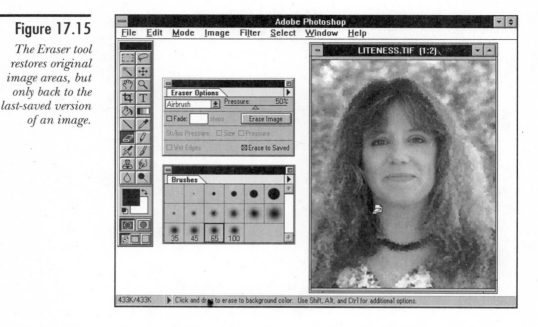

The Eraser tool's work would be obvious if you had chosen Block or Pencil from the drop-down list of options. But the Airbrush setting made the blending of original and crystallized areas perfect, because the Airbrush doesn't leave brush strokes, and 50-percent pressure gives you the option to use multiple strokes to vary the amount of coverage or, as in this case, of erasure.

It's been stressed at many points in this book that, when setting a percentage for a painting tool, partial opacity, pressure, and intensity really net out to the same thing. The Options slider controls how completely an effect or color is applied with a Photoshop tool, and you gain more overall artistic control when this slider is set to below 100 percent.

Tip

In figure 17.15, the Brushes and Options palettes have been separated so that you can see the settings on each palette in a particular step. To separate palettes, simply click and drag the tab on one palette away from the other palette.

To restore the palette, click and drag it on top of the group it belongs to. Do not choose Reset Tool or Reset all Tools from the pop-up menu on the Options palette, however. The Reset command resets the opacity and mode of palettes to Adobe's default, and does zilch for regrouping palettes.

If you've pulled apart all the palettes and want to restore them all at once to their original location, press Ctrl+K (or choose **F**ile, Pre**f**erences, **G**eneral), then click on

the **M**ore button on the General Preferences dialog box. After you make sure that the **R**estore Dialog and Palette Positions check box is unchecked, click on OK in Photoshop's query box regarding your decision. Be forwarned, however, that this resets *all* of Photoshop's defaults, and ruins any customizing work you may have done to palettes.

The Zoom Blur Effect

In other chapters, you've seen how to use the Gaussian blur effectively to create convincing shadows in images. Photoshop's other Blur filters also come in handy. Each can be applied in different ways to achieve a special look.

The Radial blur comes in two flavors—Spin and Zoom. The Zoom is particularly nice. It does a faithful reproduction of the rack/zoom effect photographers use to focus the center of attention on an area in an image. This effect is difficult to achieve in real time in the real world, because your subject doesn't always remain motionless while you simultaneously zoom the lens and squeeze off a relatively long exposure time.

Although you can pick the focal center of a Radial blur, the Radial Blur dialog box has no option for defining an area that remains in focus; only a small central area of the image is left intact. In the next exercise, you'll see how to manually adjust the image area where the Radial blur concentrates—it's as simple as creating a selection area with a feathered border.

Here's how to draw the viewer's eye into the LITENESS.TIF image in a very compelling way by using the Radial blur filter.

The Forced Focal Point of an Image

Press **L** (or click on **L**asso tool on toolbox)

Photoshop's tool for creating freehand selections.

Type **12** in Feather field on Options palette, and make sure **A**nti-Aliased box is checked

Immediately applies feathering to any selection you create.

Click and drag a very loose selection marquee around Laurie's face area, to include her neckline and part of her hair

Creates feathered selection (see fig. 17.16) that makes gradual transition between masked and selected area, beginning 6 pixels inside marquee and ending 6 pixels outside marquee.

continues

continued

Choose **S**elect, **I**nverse	*Very important step.* Inverts marquee border so that current selection excludes Laurie's face and includes rest of image and background.
Choose Fi**l**ter, Blur, then choose Radial blur	Displays the Radial Blur dialog box.
Click and drag Amount slider to **15** (or type **15** in field), then click on **Z**oom in Method field, and click on Best in Quality field	Sets amount, type, and quality of zoom blur effect.
Click and drag upward inside Blur Center window to set origin of zoom blur	Moves center of zoom blur so that effect will appear to be emanating from Laurie's face, not from center of image (see fig. 17.17).
Click on OK, then go do some yard work	Confirms your settings, and you amuse yourself while Photoshop processes this complicated command.
Press Ctrl+D (**S**elect, **N**one)	Deselects the selection marquee.
Choose **F**ile, Sa**v**e As, then save image to your hard disk as WINDY.TIF (choose TIFF format from Save File as Format **T**ype drop-down list)	Saves your work up to this point.
Press Ctrl+W (**F**ile, **C**lose)	Closes the image window. You're done with the image.

As you can see in figure 17.18, the selection area in the original image took most of the Radial zoom blur effect. The effect diminishes as it reaches the feathered masked area of Laurie's face.

Stop When you've finished an assignment that calls for the use of the Feather option with the Lasso tool, setting the Feather option back to **0** is a good idea. If you don't, and you don't have the Options palette displayed, you're going to surprise yourself (unpleasantly) when you use the Lasso tool for regular freehand selection work.

Figure 17.16

Create a selection marquee around the face area, then invert the selection to mask the face and select the rest of the image.

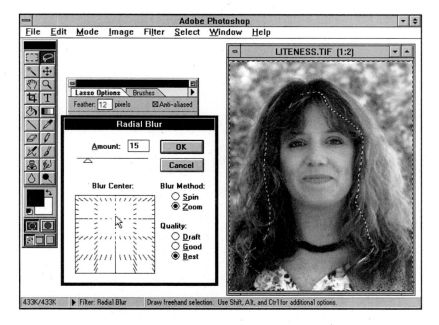

Figure 17.17

Set the center of the Motion Blur by click+dragging in the Blur Center window in the dialog box.

Figure 17.18

Point an audience's attention to a visual area through the selective use of the Radial blur effect in zoom mode.

To avoid a telltale selection border when you applied the powerful Radial blur effect to the image's background, the Feather command came to the rescue again. The option to Feather a selection is also available on the Options palette for the Elliptical and Rectangular marquee tools. If you've already created a selection, but didn't specify a Feather amount, you must use choose the Select, Feather command, pick Feather on the Commands palette, or press Shift+F6 (Windows version) or F7 (Macintosh version).

The Radial blur, like the Gaussian blur and Stylize filters, needs to use as much of your system's resources as possible to execute an effect. Some heavy-duty interpolation is going on behind the digital scenes—which is yet another reason grayscale images and special effects go hand in hand—executing this sort of filter on an RGB image would require much more processing power, and possibly swapping out to hard disk if you don't have a great deal of system RAM. Whenever you swap to hard disk, the time needed to accomplish the effect increases substantially.

Using Filters with Grayscale Still Life Images

Even Photoshop filters that only work with RGB image formats can be used to create a spectacular grayscale effect. For example, the Lighting Effects filter will produce an effect only when you begin with an RGB image. Therefore, you can begin an assignment destined for black-and-white publication by acquiring an RGB image, applying Lighting Effects, then converting the image to grayscale as a last step.

Setting Up Texture Channel Information

In the next exercise, you'll see how to create, in an Alpha channel, information that is used by the Lighting Effects filter to simulate a relief topology in an image. You can create wondrous images by adding texture without creative lighting to an image. First, you need to create an Alpha channel that is a grayscale, high-contrast copy of the original image. The Lighting Effects filter reads the lighter areas of the Alpha channel image as areas that protrude from the surface of the RGB composite of the image, whereas darker Alpha channel values make the RGB view of the image appear to recede. The result of copying a grayscale image to an Alpha channel for use as a texture channel is an image that appears to be embossed, but has much more detail and virtual topology than it would if you used the Emboss filter.

And because using the Lighting Effects filter in this slightly unorthodox but very creative way produces a noticeable distortion of original image information, it's not an ideal choice of image-enhancement tools to use with people pictures. So, you'll use a photograph of some autumn rushes in this example—beginning with defining the texture (Alpha) channel information—to make a grayscale fall image that no one has ever photographed!

Copying a Color Channel for Use as a Texture Channel

Open RUSHES.TIF image from CHAP17 subdirectory on Bonus CD	The RGB image you'll use to create a relief effect, shown in figure 17.19.
Click on Channels tab on Channels/Layers/Paths group, then click on each color channel title, and decide which channel displays the most tonal variation	Displays red, green, and blue component color channels for RUSHES.TIF image as brightness (grayscale) information.

continues

continued

You want to find the color channel that displays the most detail about the RUSHES image, so that you can use it as texture channel information for the Lighting Effects filter. Unlike the process described earlier for accurately converting an RGB image to Grayscale mode through the LAB mode, tonal balance is not critical in the selection of a color channel image. No photographic detail of the channel information will appear, per se, in the finished image—you are looking for good tonal separation that Photoshop can use for texture information. The Green channel looks the most promising for this exercise, but different images have different color characteristics, so always use your own judgment.

When you've decided on a color channel (hint: pick the Green channel), press Ctrl+A (or choose **S**elect, **A**ll), then press Ctrl+C (or choose **E**dit, **C**opy)	Copies grayscale information to clipboard.
Click on New channel icon on Channels palette, accept defaults in Channel Options dialog box by clicking on OK, then press Ctrl+V (or choose **E**dit, **P**aste)	Pastes copy of Green channel into new channel #4 (see fig. 17.20).
Press Ctrl+D (or choose **S**elect, **N**one)	Deselects floating selection.

Although the Green channel will serve nicely in its present state for texture channel information, it can be improved upon slightly by adjusting the tonal values. This will create a more pronounced texture effect in the finished image.

Press Ctrl+B (or choose **I**mage, **A**djust, **B**rightness/Contrast)	Displays Brightness/Contrast dialog box.
Click and drag **B**rightness slider to –4, then click and drag **C**ontrast slider to +4 (or enter values directly in each field), then click on OK	Makes grayscale copy a little darker and displays a little more contrast (see fig. 17.21).
Choose **F**ile, Sa**v**e As, then save image to your hard disk as RUSHES.TIF (choose TIFF format from Save File as Format **T**ype drop-down list)	Saves your work up to this point.
Click on RGB channel title on Channels palette	Restores view to color composite of RUSHES image.

New Riders Publishing
INSIDE
SERIES

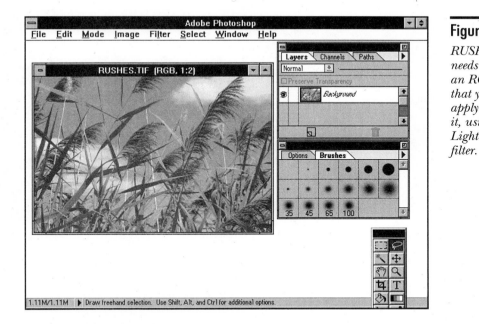

Figure 17.19

RUSHES.TIF needs to remain an RGB image so that you can apply a texture to it, using the Lighting Effects filter.

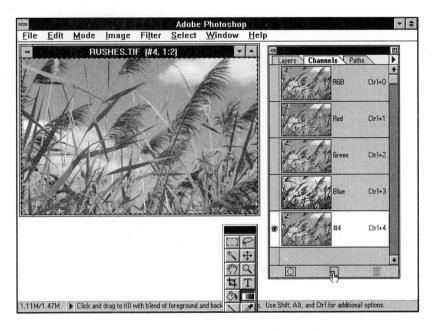

Figure 17.20

Copy a color component channel you feel best displays well-defined tonal information about the image.

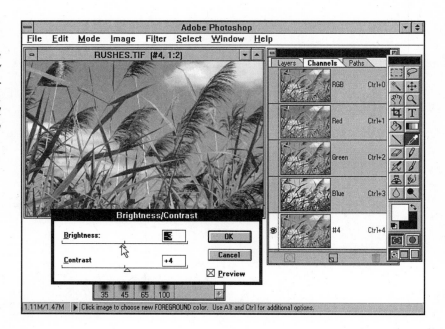

Ordinarily, when you create a new (Alpha) channel and add a photographic element
to the channel, the Channel Options dialog box gives you the option to specify
whether the bright areas in the channel are supposed to represent masked or selected
areas. In this instance, however, Photoshop won't base a selection on the channel
brightness information; rather, Photoshop uses the channel brightness data as
information about mapping the lighter and darker areas to create a 3D relief in the
image. Therefore, it didn't make any difference whether you chose Color Indicates
Selected or Masked Areas when you created the new channel.

Photoshop's Lighting Effects filter can use any color channel in an RGB image as
texture channel information. On occasion, you might find that a color channel in
one of your own images has exactly the right amount of tonal balance and detail to
forego the creation of a channel based on a copy, for specific use as texture information. By copying and tonally modifying the Green channel in the last exercise,
however, you also gave yourself more control over the channel to be used as texture
information. You cannot tonally adjust a color channel to make it better as texture
information without ruining the RGB composite image! It's usually better to work
with a copy of a color component channel when you plan to use it as selection or
texture information.

Creating a Relief Picture

Getting the RUSHES.TIF image to look as though it's pushing toward the viewer in some areas and receding in others is the easy part of this assignment: Photoshop does the calculations for you in the Lighting Effects filter. What is not so easy, however, is defining lighting characteristics that neither contribute nor steal from the RUSHES image itself. Lighting Effects is intended to provide both dramatic lighting and texture to an image, or selected image area, and there isn't a toggle switch in Photoshop to access one without the other. You can't add texture to an image without defining a lighting scheme (you can access lighting without texture, however).

The solution, then, is to create flat illumination that covers the RUSHES image, of an intensity that doesn't wash out or hide areas in the picture. The following exercise walks you through a series of settings you might want to save in the Lighting Effects filter's dialog box, for future use with your own images.

Creating a Relief Landscape

Choose Filter, Render, then Lighting Effects	Displays Lighting Effects dialog box.
Click on Light type drop-down list, and choose Directional	This light type displays no fall-off; unlike a spotlight, no visible boundary of Direction light casting is rendered to the image.
Click and drag dark dot at end of line in Preview window so that it touches edge of preview image edge at about 1 o'clock	This dark dot determines direction of light; line that connects this dot with center circle determines how far from image light appears.
Click and drag Intensity slider to about 45	Makes directional light bright enough to evenly illuminate image from distance you specified in last step.

You cannot change a directional light's focus; focus remains a constant. This area should appear dimmed when a directional light is the active light in the preview window.

It's time to move on to the Properties section of the dialog box. Properties defines how the light you've set up interacts with the virtual surface of the image and the texture channel options.

continues

continued

Click and drag sliders in Properties field so they read as follows: Gloss: **34**, Material: **0**, and Ambiance: **0**	Sets characteristics for interaction of light against a surface—the surface Exposure: **10**, reflects light with equal metallic and plastic characteristics, and overall image is slightly overexposed by directional light.
Click on Texture Channel drop-down list, and choose channel #4	Chooses copy of Green channel you placed in channel #4, to use as information for creating a relief on RUSHES image.
Click and drag Height slider until it reads about **150** (toward Mountainous)	Exaggerates difference in relief heights and depths, based on shades of gray in channel #4.

Because Photoshop has to make many calculations before displaying the effects of the texture on the image displayed in the preview window, the last two steps may take a few moments to redraw on-screen.

When you're happy with image in preview window, choose Save in Style field	Displays Save As dialog box.
Type a name for the settings you've made. Pick an evocative name you'll recognize in the future. Your screen should look like figure 17.22	Windows users can type an eight-character name here; spaces are legal (but you can't use reserved characters or a question mark). Macintosh users can choose a long file name for the custom Lighting Effect.
Click on OK	Applies Lighting filter.
On Channels palette, click and drag channel #4 into Trash icon	Deletes Alpha channel from image. You're done with it.
Press Ctrl+S (or choose **F**ile, **S**ave)	Saves your work up to this point.
Choose **G**rayscale from **M**ode menu, then click on OK in dialog box	Converts image to grayscale (see fig. 17.23).

Choose File, Save As, then save image to your hard disk as RELIEF.TIF (choose TIFF format from the Save File as Format Type drop-down list)	Saves a grayscale copy of image. You still have RUSHES.TIF as a color relief image on your hard disk.
Press Ctrl+W (File, Close)	Closes the image. You're finished with it.

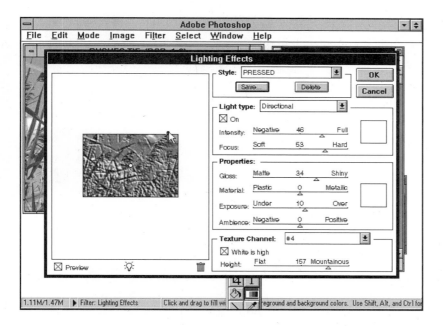

Figure 17.22

Use the Lighting Effects dialog box to save a unique lighting setup for future use with other images.

By using the Lighting Effects filter as you did in the last exercise, you can achieve a blend of original tonal qualities with a relief map of the same image—something you can't do with the Emboss filter. You might also try offsetting the Alpha channel information (the grayscale image) by one or two pixels to heighten the effect of the relief, or texture map. For a more detailed discussion of Photoshop's Lighting Effects filter, see Chapter 18, "Photoshop's Native Filters"—and we spend more time with this effect in an assignment in Chapter 22, "Virtual Reality: The Ingredients of Dreamwork."

 Tip   Photoshop's Lighting Effects filter can read Alpha channel information as *White is high* (white areas in the Alpha channel push corresponding areas in the RGB image toward the viewer). Conversely, when you leave this option unchecked in the Lighting Effects dialog box, white areas in the Alpha channel cause corresponding areas in the RGB image to recede.

Additionally, you can create an inverse texture map by inverting the grayscale information in an Alpha channel you specify as the Texture channel in the Lighting Effects dialog box. When the box titled "White as high" box is checked, a photographic positive of an image produces highlight areas in the finished image that bump outward in the direction of the light angle.

Figure 17.23

Grayscale images display textures particularly well because they don't include distracting colors.

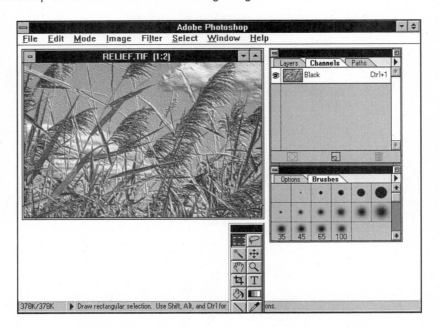

Using Black-and-White Imaging in Your Profession

This chapter's tightrope-walking between the worlds of color and grayscale imaging has given you some insights into their relationship to each other, as well as into the ways grayscale images can be edited to make them as beautiful and provoking as their 24-bit counterparts. If you keep in mind the conversion process and the techniques for manipulating grayscale images, you can put the tips to practical commercial use. Because very few run-of-the-mill photofinishing places do custom work on black-and-white images these days, clients are likely to hand you a color image for a newsletter or other in-house organ.

A black-and-white corporate annual report the authors worked on is a typical example of this situation. The photos submitted for the report were an odd assortment of black-and-white and color images. This was a desktop publishing document destined

for one-color printing. We could have used a quick, one-step solution, converting the color photos by scanning everything with a grayscale scanner, but the results of grayscale scanning would have made the report look amateurish. The board members' RGB portraits would have suffered a brute force conversion, benefiting not at all from an understanding of color theory and the creative control one has by using the LAB color model as an intermediate conversion phase. Straight sampling of a color image in Grayscale scanning mode would have produced portraits with skin blemishes emphasized, and muddiness in the highlights in the board members' eyes; and it would have made the printed product resemble a photocopy. Instead, we scanned the color photos in color, then converted the images, used the Levels and Curves commands to tonally correct the grayscale images (see Chapter 7, "Restoring an Heirloom Photograph"), and had time to spare for retouching and a special effect or two. Happy client, handsome report, professionally finished digital photographs.

Black-and-white printing is still a popular medium, for technological and monetary reasons. If you know how to make the most of the grayscale image, your talents will always be in demand in the business community.

Converting Grayscale to RGB

For video slide shows, avant garde presentations, and the simple pleasures of restoring a monochrome family photo, Photoshop offers you the capability of hand-tinting a grayscale image. At the beginning of the chapter, you sampled the predominant colors in the RGB version of LAURIE.TIF and learned how to save the collection as a custom Scratch palette. These digital tints are good for hand-coloring the grayscale version of the original, LITENESS.TIF, because the colors are the same as those in the original image.

In the next exercise, you need to convert the grayscale LITENESS.TIF image back to RGB mode. Although the LITENESS image won't spring back to its original color values when you switch modes here, you nevertheless need the color capability found in the RGB mode to add colors to the image. The Grayscale file format does not support unique color values.

The mode switch you'll make from Grayscale to RGB in the next exercise enables Photoshop to express up to 16.7 million possible shades of color, including the 256 grayscale tones already in the image. You'll also set the Brushes palette to use Color mode instead of Normal mode when you apply any of the colors from the collection you defined earlier. Painting in Color mode changes the hue and saturation of the pixels you paint over, but does not affect the *luminosity* (the measure of brilliance) in the pixels. In other words, the gray levels in the LAURIE.TIF image are preserved when you tint them. Additionally, in this mode, Photoshop ignores the neutral, grayscale content found in the samples you collected on the Scratch palette, and enables you to paint with the predominant color value the hue of each color sample.

In this exercise, your explorations into the wonderful world of black-and-white come full circle, and you hand-tint a grayscale image using the colors originally sampled from the RGB original.

Color-Enabling a Grayscale Image

Open LITENESS.TIF image from your hard disk	The image you converted to grayscale earlier in this chapter.
Press Ctrl(Cmd)+plus	Zooms you to a 1:2 viewing resolution for more precise editing work.
Choose **M**ode, **R**GB Color	Converts grayscale LAURIE.TIF image to an RGB image. Picker/Swatches/ Scratch palette group again displays color; Channels palette has three color channels (in addition to the color composite channel).
Press **B** (for Paint Brush tool), then choose **Color** mode from Options palette drop-down list; click and drag Opacity slider to about **30**%, then click on middle tip in second row of Brushes palette	Sets characteristics of Paint Brush tool to apply color broadly, with a very mild concentration.
Press Alt(Option) while clicking on a skin tone color you defined earlier on Scratch palette in Color mode with Paint	Paint brush toggles to Eyedropper tool, and you choose a skin tone to paint with brush tool.
Release Alt(Option) key, then click and drag over facial areas in LITENESS.TIF image until you have covered all the facial area	Applies skin tone tint to image. Do not release mouse button until entire area you intend to cover is covered.
Press Alt while clicking on a darker skin tone you defined earlier on Scratch palette	Samples color you will apply to shaded facial areas in image.
Reduce and/or increase Opacity value on Options palette	Reduces/increases amount of color you tint image areas with. Higher opacity percentages are best used on darker shaded image areas.

Continue applying tints to image, sampling different colors labeled on Scratch palette, then paint in corresponding image area

You are well on your way to creating a digital hand-tinted image (see fig. 17.24, which, unfortunately, isn't tinted).

Choose File, Save

Saves your work to your hard disk.

Figure 17.24

Color painting mode uses only the Hue and Brightness components of a color sample when the sample is applied to an image.

Users accustomed to using Color painting mode in Photoshop 2.5 will be happily surprised by the revisions made to this feature in version 3. In Photoshop 3, Color mode does not apply the neutral grayscale component (the brightness value) of a sampled color to the image area you paint over. In Photoshop 2.5's Color painting mode, you could theoretically reach black, or total saturation, by repeatedly stroking the same area. You can apply a more brilliant color to LITENESS.TIF, or to a grayscale image of your own that you've converted to RGB mode, but you'll never replace grayscale values with foreground color as long as you choose Color as the painting mode on the Options palette.

Additionally, areas of absolute white in an image cannot be covered with a color while your painting tool is in Color mode. Color mode needs a percentage of gray (neutral color) to work against. If you colored the entire image in the last exercise, you may have noticed that it's impossible to color the white areas of Laurie's blouse. When you want to tint a totally white area in a converted grayscale image, you can use the Brightness/Contrast command to slightly decrease the brightness in a selected area or an entire image, then use Color mode to tint the image.

Tip   To instantly turn a grayscale image to a digital sepiatone, define both the foreground and background colors in Photoshop as a medium, warm brown. Then choose the Gradient tool, and choose Color mode on the Options palette. Click and drag across a portion of the image (the Gradient tool fills an entire selection area, regardless of how far you click and drag).

Voilá! Instant sepiatone—or any other color you'd like to define as the foreground and background color. If you want to learn how to *restore* a sepiatone image to its original colors, however, check out Chapters 7, "Restoring an Heirloom Photograph," and 8, "Retouching an Heirloom Photograph," for more information on image restoration.

Working with grayscale images doesn't have to be an uninspired task, as this chapter has shown you. And if you have a laser printer capable of at least 600 dpi, the printed results of your labors can be immediately gratifying. When your client has a modest imaging need, you now have the tools, and some understanding of techniques, to far surpass this client's expectations. If you are a dyed-in-the-wool photographer just adopting some of the new computer-imaging powers, Photoshop might be your very last stop for digital equivalents of familiar real-world imaging tools. And the crossover between color and grayscale is effortless with Photoshop. Most of the tools and effects featured throughout this book can be applied identically to both grayscale and RGB images.

This chapter has been a small sampling of the things you can do with an image and the knowledge of how a Photoshop filter can best be used. We turn from a sampling to a banquet in Chapter 18, "Photoshop's Native Filters," where you'll discover some of the hidden powers and features the Filters menu holds for you and your design work.

Photoshop's Native Filters

If you've upgraded from Photoshop 2.5, you'll be immediately impressed with version 3's Filter menu, which practically extends to the bottom of the screen. New filters have been added, and the ones you've grown familiar with have been optimized for speed. In addition, many of Photoshop 3's filters now sport "proxy" boxes—an advancement over preview windows—that enable you to zoom, pan, and compare a proposed filter effect to the original image *before* you click on OK.

In this chapter, we provide documentation on some of the "classic" Photoshop effects possible using filters. We'll also show creative possibilities for filters users commonly overlook because the filter name or the dialog box looks too complicated.

Photoshop's native filters, the ones that shipped with the application, can provide the pizzazz that's lacking in an image, and they can be used as part of a procedure for manually accomplishing a special effect not offered in the Filter menu. This chapter will guide you through some of the outstanding and useful things you can add to your personal designer's toolkit by understanding digital filters.

A *filter*, when used by a computer application, translates data to a different format. You can also call this process distorting, modifying, or optimizing data; regardless, filters change the organization of data. In the case of Adobe Photoshop, *graphical* data is transformed when a filter is used.

Filters are arranged in categories within a menu command, but you might find filters that work together, or perform similar design functions in not-so-obvious places in Photoshop. Our first look at filters is in the **F**ile menu; import and export filters are listed here, not under Fi**l**ter.

Using Filters in the File Menu

In the **F**ile menu, **O**pen and **P**lace are honest-to-goodness Photoshop plug-in filters. They might not provide as dramatic effects as, for instance, the Lighting Effects Filter, but without them you may never get your work started! If you have a drawing program that can save designs in the AI or EPS vector formats, the **F**ile menu is where the import and export filters are accessed for bringing a design into Photoshop as a bitmap graphic, and for saving the image in formats other than Photoshop's own PSD format.

The next section's assignment uses the **P**lace command to open and rasterize an Adobe Illustrator file and then automatically place it on a layer in the active image window. Designs that have been saved to the AI format are actually Encapsulated PostScript printing instructions, but you can treat an AI file that Photoshop has opened exactly like any other image element after Photoshop has converted the information to bitmap format.

Using the Place Command

The **F**ile, **P**lace command places a low-resolution display of an AI file within an active image window. A high-resolution image is generated that replaces the low-resolution display after you've had a chance to position and size the low resolution copy of the imported graphic. In the next exercise, you'll add a layer to an image to give the AI image a place to "land" before using the **P**lace command.

Adding a new layer before you place an image is a wise step to follow in your own work because placed AI or EPS images need to be composed independently of the rest of an image in the same way any element on a layer does. If you export a design from a vector drawing program that's surrounded by empty space, Photoshop imports the design surrounded by transparent pixels, which are assigned as Layer 1, not the usual Photoshop Background layer. However, vector images that are converted by using the Place filter sometimes can have an unwanted opaque background that

surrounds the foreground image—this happens when your exported vector design has a solid background element. Although the opaque background of an imported AI design might not affect your overall image, you can't use Multiply or other Layers modes to make the background drop out of the picture before the rasterizing process is completed. This means that resizing and repositioning a placed AI graphic can obscure your view of underlying layer elements unless you know about one of the special features of Photoshop layers that provides a "clear" view of a placed graphic.

In the next exercise, you'll add a logo to a poster. The logo was created in CorelDRAW!, a Windows drawing program similar to Adobe Illustrator that can export a CorelDRAW! design to AI format. The logo was purposely designed to be much too large for the poster so that you have an opportunity to work with resizing a placed AI file. NED_LOGO.AI is a simple treatment of some graphics and text—a black circle with a clear interior design. Unfortunately, however, this design has an opaque background, with white letters on top of a black graphic—Photoshop "sees" this information as black and white, not black and clear when it imports the design, which causes a problem.

Here's how to use the **P**lace command and Multiply mode on a new image layer to make a black and white design appear to be black and clear as a bitmap image:

Using the Place Command as an Import Filter

Open the NEDBEACH.TIF image from the CHAP18 subdirectory (folder) on the *Inside Photoshop 3* Bonus CD	This is the image file you'll place converted vector information within.
On the Layers palette, click on the New layer icon (the left icon; looks like a turned-down page)	Displays the New Layer dialog box (see fig. 18.1).
Type **Beach Logo** in the **N**ame field, choose Multiply from the **M**ode drop-down list, then check the Fill With Multiply-Neutral Color (white) check box, and click on OK	Creates a new layer that has white pixels, and the layer is in Multiply mode.

The non-appearance of the "neutral white" pixels on the NEDBEACH.TIF image is misleading. In Multiply mode, lighter pixels on a layer give way to transparency, and display the Background layer detail. And so will the lighter areas of the AI image that's placed next.

Choose **F**ile, **P**lace, then choose NED_LOGO.AI from the CHAP18 subdirectory of the Bonus CD	The file that was exported from a drawing application.

continues

continued

Wait a moment or two while Photoshop "parses" (understands, translates) the AI file, and creates a low-resolution on-screen display for you to position and resize. The placed NED_LOGO.AI image first appears on Layer 1 as an empty wireframe, which then becomes filled with the design, as shown in figure 18.2.

Click and drag on the intersection of the two diagonal lines within the box, then move it so it's in the bottom, right of NEDBEACH.TIF	Repositions the AI low-res image. Do *not* click inside or outside the box.

Like the Effects boxes produced when you use the Distort, Scale, and other commands, the Place box will disappear if you click outside the box, and will (prematurely) finalize your placement edits if you click inside the box; only by click and dragging on the center can you reposition the box. The NED_LOGO.AI image is clearly too large for the NEDBEACH.TIF image.

Click and drag the upper left handle on the Place box toward the lower right of the NEDBEACH.TIF image until it overlaps the starfish's leg slightly	Proportionally resizes the placed NED_LOGO.AI file (see fig. 18.3).
When the placed AI file is the right size, click inside the box	Finalizes the placement of the file; Photoshop takes a moment to complete the actual rendering of the placed file.
Press Ctrl+D (Select, None), choose File, Save As, then save the image as NEDBEACH.PSD to your hard disk	Deselects the floating selection; Photoshop recognizes the image as having layers; PSD is the only format that can retain layers.

Although this exercise shows you how to place an AI design within an image window, you now need to remove the white areas from the image layer so the black logo can be treated as a normal layer element, not one that displays transparency through the use of Multiply mode. In the next section, you'll see how to refine an imported vector graphic.

Another way to "knock out" the white in an imported AI or EPS image is to use the Place command to import a design directly on top of the Background image. You would then use Multiply on the Layers palette as a *compositing* mode for the import after you've clicked inside the Place box and the finalized, placed image is a floating selection. However, during the process of resizing and positioning the low-res image, the background of the graphic is white, and you might find that you can't see the underlying image in your own design. Additionally, you cannot reposition a placed design after a floating selection has been deselected (composited) into the Background layer.

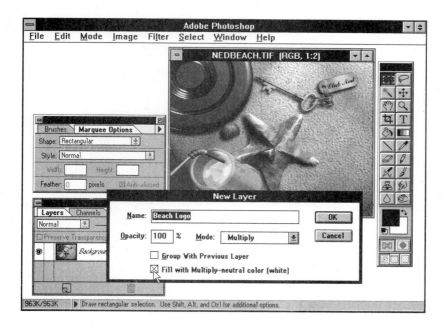

Figure 18.1

Add a new layer in Multiply mode and add neutral white pixels as a layer element.

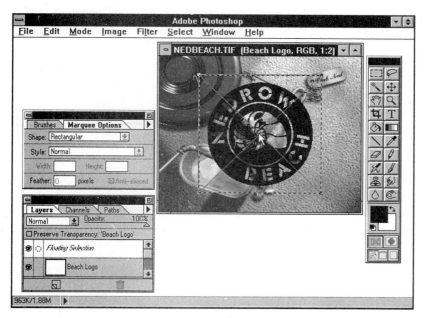

Figure 18.2

The background of the placed design is actually white; Multiply mode doesn't display colors lighter than the Background layer.

Figure 18.3

*Click and drag
on a corner
Place box to
proportionately
resize it.*

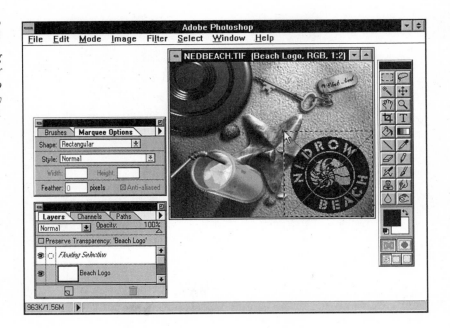

At this point, you have a nice, black logo seated on top of the NEDBEACH.TIF image.
However, you can't color it in a conventional fashion because the Beach Logo layer is
in Multiply mode. Anything you paint on the black logo that's lighter than black will
disappear. To edit the black logo, read on.

Anti-Aliasing and the Color Range Command

Photoshop's vector import filter (the Rasterize Adobe Illustrator Format) keeps
smooth Anti-aliased edges around vector designs as they are converted to bitmap
format. The next exercise shows you how to *keep* them smooth as you remove the
white areas from the layer.

Anti-aliasing disguises the jagged, stairsteppy edges of vectors converted to bitmap
images by placing semi-transparent pixels where a shape meets another shape of
contrasting color. This makes the Color Range command an ideal one for separating
the black from the white background now on the Beach Logo layer. With the Color
Range command, you can select every incident of a range of color; the Fuzziness
slider enables you to control how much of the Anti-aliased edge pixels are discarded
along with the white.

In the next exercise, you'll create a selection border that encompasses all the white
areas on the Beach Logo layer, then delete them to create a perfect logo element on
the transparent layer.

Editing a Placed Graphic on a Layer

Marquee zoom using the Zoom tool, to get a 1:1 viewing resolution of the Nedrow Beach logo on the Beach Logo layer	You need to see which edge pixels will be selected with the Color Range command.
Click on Normal mode from the drop-down list on the Layers palette	Makes the Beach Logo layer Normal. You can now see the opaque, white pixels surrounding the black logo on the Beach Logo layer.

The Background layer should now be completely obscured from view because you specified in the last exercise that neutral pixels should be the starting contents of the new layer. Now white foreground color fills all the Beach Logo layer areas except for the black logo.

Choose **S**elect, **C**olor Range	Displays the Color Range dialog box.
Choose Sampled Colors from the Sele**c**t drop-down list	Chooses the mode that provides the most control and accesses to the Fuzziness slider.
Click on the S**e**lection radio button, and choose Quick Mask from the Sele**c**tion Preview drop-down list	Displays the selections that Color Range creates in the preview window, and places Quick Mask over the NEDBEACH.TIF image where the selection will appear.
Click the Eyedropper cursor over any image except the black logo	Selects the white in the area on the image (see fig. 18.4).

Here's the kicker—you want no white displayed through the Quick Mask presently on the Beach Logo layer. This calls for an extraordinarily high Fuzziness amount, to include most of the semi-transparent Anti-aliased pixels around the edge of the logo. The Fuzziness option always creates an Anti-aliased edge around the selection borders it creates, so you're doing yourself a favor by setting a high Fuzziness in the next step. You should try this next step whenever you want to select an imported grayscale graphic accurately, *and* you want to retain the smooth edges that Photoshop's Anti-aliasing provides.

Click and drag the **F**uzziness slider up to **200** (the maximum)	Picks the broadest color range of whites possible in the image (see fig. 18.4).
Click on OK	Creates a marquee on the Beach Logo layer.

continues

continued

Press Delete	Deletes all white areas on the Beach Logo layer (see fig. 18.5).
Press Ctrl(Cmd)+D (**S**elect, **N**one), then Ctrl(Cmd)+S (**F**ile, **S**ave)	Deselects the floating selection and saves your work up to this point.

Figure 18.4

The highest Fuzziness value selects the greatest range of a single color value in an image.

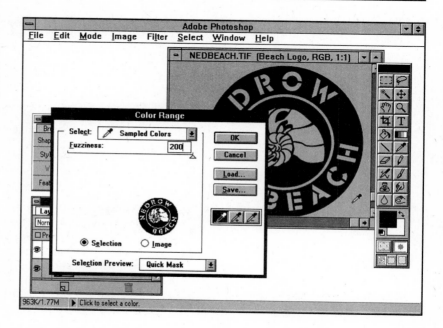

There are a multitude of things you can do with the modified layer now. You can take advantage of the Preserve Transparency option on the Layers palette and color the logo. You can also create a selection based on the logo and paste a texture into the marquee selection (**E**dit, Paste **I**nto command).

The next section shows you how to work with several filters to produce an eye-catching image that takes very little technical skill to create. The exercise shows you how filters can be used to generate the necessary source images for a completed design.

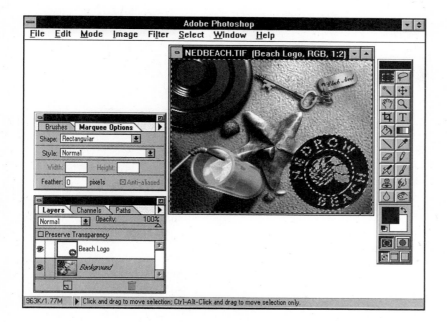

Figure 18.5

Delete all the white pixels on the Beach Logo layer, so only the black logo and trans- parent pixels remain.

Building a Bitmap from a Vector Design

In addition to the **P**lace command, Photoshop 3 can understand and convert (*parse* and *rasterize*) vector information, when the AI or EPS file is desired as a new image; no Placing required. In the next exercise, you'll use the **F**ile, **O**pen command to rasterize the NED_LOGO.AI design to bitmap format. Then you'll use the new file containing the NED_LOGO design as selection information in a second file that contains a texture. Because vector images are resolution-independent, they can be scaled prior to converting the information to bitmap format. This means in the next exercise that you can scale NED_LOGO.AI to any dimension you choose. Keep the image to a dimension that'll fit comfortably within the workspace though; image dimensions and resolution are directly proportional to file size, and the speed which you can work with images.

Here's how to use the <u>O</u>pen filter in the <u>F</u>ile menu to create a bitmap image:

Opening a Vector File as an Image Window

Choose <u>F</u>ile, <u>O</u>pen, then choose
NED_LOGO.AI from the CHAP18 subdirectory
(folder) of the *Inside Photoshop 3* Bonus CD

Displays the Rasterize Adobe Illustrator
Format dialog box.

A file exported from Adobe Illustrator or another drawing program has information stored in
the header of the file that indicates the dimensions of the image when it was originally created
in the vector drawing program. These dimensions are read by Photoshop and are offered by
default in the Width and Height fields of the Rasterize Adobe Illustrator Format dialog box.
You can, however, change the dimensions to something more suitable. Resolution-
independent graphics have no link to dimensions or resolution until they're rasterized to
bitmap format. In the steps that follow, set up the import to make the NED_LOGO image a
comfortable size and resolution for working with on-screen.

Enter **3.5** (inches) in the <u>W</u>idth field,
type **72** in the <u>R</u>esolution field, choose
Grayscale from the <u>M</u>ode drop-down list

Sets the dimensions and resolution
for the NED_LOGO import (see
fig. 18.6).

The <u>A</u>nti-alias and <u>C</u>onstrain Proportions boxes should always be checked. To make sure these
and other options are checked from session to session, check <u>R</u>estore Dialog Boxes and
Palettes option in More Preferences in the Pre<u>f</u>erences, <u>G</u>eneral dialog box.

Click on OK
then displays a grayscale image

Photoshop processes your command
based on the vector information in
NED_LOGO.AI.

The NED_LOGO image will serve as the template for a selection border you'll create in a new
image. Ideally, the new file and the converted NED_LOGO file should be different color
modes, but the same dimensions and resolution. Typically, a shortcut way to measure an image
is to copy it to the Clipboard. By doing this, Photoshop automatically sets up the New dialog
box with the dimension, resolution, and mode of the Clipboard's contents. However, this
NED_LOGO import was never on the clipboard, so here's an alternative method to make a
new image that's dimensionally identical to NED_LOGO.

Choose <u>F</u>ile, <u>N</u>ew

The New dialog box appears.

Click on <u>W</u>indow, then select
NED_LOGO.AI from the list
(see fig. 18.7)

Fills the New dialog box fields with the
dimensions, resolution, and color
mode of NED_LOGO.AI.

Choose RGB Color from the Mode
drop-down list, then click on OK

Creates a new document the same
size as NED_LOGO.AI.

Press Ctrl(Cmd)+S (File, Save), then save Untitled-1 as SANDLOGO.TIF	Saves your work at this intermediate stage of completion.
Click on the title bar to NED_LOGO.AI, then choose Flatten Image from the pop-up menu on the Layers palette	Flattens the image so it now has a background, and the NED_LOGO design can be saved in a conventional bitmap file format.
Press Ctrl(Cmd)+S (File, Save), and name the image NED_LOGO.TIF to your hard disk	Saves the image.

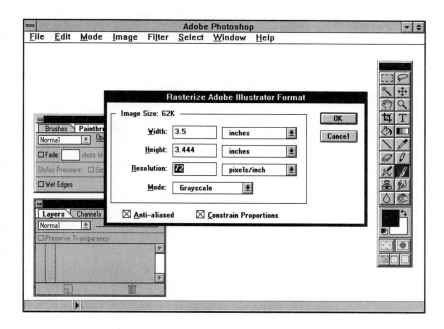

Figure 18.6

You can import AI or EPS files in any resolution, color mode, or image dimensions.

Now that you have a color canvas and the selection area of the logo set up, it's time to use the Emboss filter with a special painting mode to make a dynamic graphic.

Tip Hold the Alt (Option) key before you choose File, New to make Photoshop ignore Clipboard information. The Cancel button becomes a reset button, and the dimensions, color mode, and resolution of the Clipboard's contents aren't entered in the New image dialog box.

Figure 18.7

You can create a new image whose dimensions are identical to an image you have open, by using the Window menu.

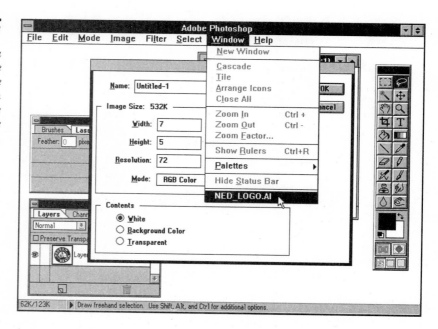

Embossing and Tinting Foreground Pixels

In this section we're getting a little sidetracked exploring the **F**ile menu's filters. We now need to rely on the Fi**l**ter menu. Filters are not an island in Photoshop. Sometimes you must use a combination of tools, effects, and filters from several different places to produce outstanding work.

Suppose you need to create a smart-looking graphic when your available source images are practically nil. The Dissolve mode of painting can "splatter" foreground color on a canvas, and the Emboss filter is particularly adept at converting your splatters to a texture that looks like sand. If your work calls for producing quick, simple, handsome graphics, you're in for a treat in this section. You're going to see how a handful of filters, and a little strolling through Photoshop for the right tools and dialog boxes can produce clever, fresh graphics.

Here's how to use an Effect on a Dissolve mode paint stroke or two to create the texture you need for this assignment.

Creating a Texture Source with Dissolve Mode

Double-click on the Paint Brush tool	Chooses the tool, and displays the Brushes/Options group.
Click on the 100 pixel tip on the Brushes palette, then click on the Options tab and choose Dissolve mode, and about **35%** Opacity	Sets the size and characteristics of the Paint Brush tool.
Press **D** (**d**efault colors icon), then make one or two strokes on SANDLOGO.TIF	Creates a diffuse pattern of black pixels (see fig. 18.8).
With the Rectangular marquee tool, click and drag an area of SANDLOGO about 1/4 the size of the window and in an area of you feel has the potential to look like sand	Selects this area for the Scale command.

Scale is not a filter; it's an effect, but it does remap pixels in a similar way to the Filters in Photoshop.

Choose **I**mage, **E**ffects, then choose Scale	A Scale box appears around your selection marquee.
Click+drag on the Scale box handles until the box covers the entire image window	Makes the small scattered pixels into larger, more sand-like foreground detail (see fig. 18.9).
Click inside the Scale box, then press Ctrl(Cmd)+D (**S**elect, **N**one)	Executes the Scale command and deselects the selected image area.
Choose Fi**l**ter, Stylize, then Emboss	Displays the Emboss dialog box.
Set the **A**ngle to 5**5**°, set the **H**eight to **2** pixels, and make the A**m**ount about **50%**	Specifies the angle of the emboss, the height, and how much of the original image is retained in the Emboss (see fig. 18.10).

The Amount slider in the Emboss dialog box ranges from 1 to 500%. At higher percentages, the Emboss filter retains a lot of original image information. However, you *don't* want the black and white pixels in the emboss; the effect is too harsh. By setting the Amount to about 1/10th "strength," you'll get more effect than original image detail; and a more of a sand appearance in your piece.

Click on OK	Applies the Emboss filter.
Press Ctrl(Cmd)+S (**F**ile, **S**ave)	Saves your work at this intermediate stage of completion.

Figure 18.8

Create an effect similar to grain, erosion, or a scattering of sand with the Paint Brush tool in Dissolve mode.

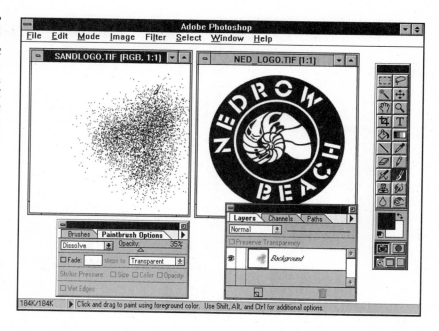

Figure 18.9

Increase the size of the random pixels by freehand scaling a selected area.

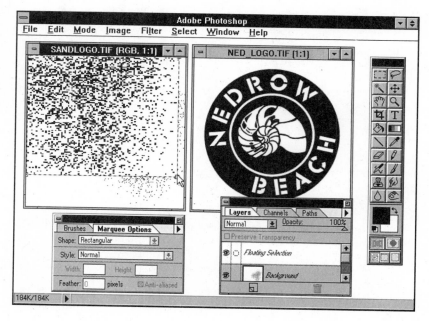

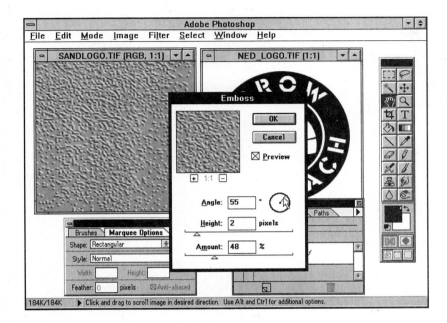

Figure 18.10

The Emboss filter can retain a lot, or a little of the original image detail.

In the next section, you'll see how to complete the SANDLOGO.TIF design by remote-control selection work!

Using Hue/Saturation on an Embossed Texture

The next exercise brings your examination of the **F**ile menu and the design full-circle to a finished piece. The only problem with using the Emboss filter on artwork is that the resulting background color is always gray. The Hue/Saturation command's Colorized option comes in handy in this case because you can use it to turn mono-chrome artwork into *tinted,* monochrome artwork. The beauty of this option in regard to the SANDLOGO image is that the subject matter, sand, generally is monochrome.

Here's how to use Hue/Saturation and a unique deployment of the Load Selection command to create an attractive color logo design.

Colorizing an Image and Copying a Selection

Press Ctrl(Cmd)+U (**I**mage, **A**djust,   Displays the Hue/Saturation dialog box.
Hue/Saturation)

continues

continued

Click on the C<u>o</u>lorize check box, then enter the following in the fields (or use the sliders): <u>H</u>ue: **40**, <u>S</u>aturation: **64**, and Lightness: **+7**	Colorizes the SANDLOGO image to a dull brownish-orange (see fig. 18.11).
Click on OK	Applies the Hue/Saturation Colorize option.
Click on the foreground color on the toolbox	Displays the Color Picker.
Enter H: **234**, S: **100**, and B: **72** in the HSB fields (or use the color field and color slider to pick deep blue)	Defines the foreground color for use in the image.
Click on OK, then press **B** (Paint **B**rush tool)	Returns you to the workspace, and chooses the Paint Brush tool.
Click and drag the Opacity slider to about **50%**	Applies foreground color with the Paint Brush at half-strength.

You last used the Paint Brush tool in Dissolve mode; it should still be set to Dissolve for the next steps.

Choose <u>S</u>elect, <u>L</u>oad Selection	Displays the Load Selection dialog box.
Choose NED_LOGO.TIF from the <u>D</u>ocument drop-down list, click on Background Black from the <u>C</u>hannel drop-down list, Click on the Invert box, then click on OK	Uses the Black Channel in NED_LOGO.TIF as selection information to be applied to the active window, SANDLOGO.TIF.

By default, when you use a "stand-in" for selection information, Photoshop considers the black areas of the image to be used as masking information. Black areas correspond to areas that cannot be painted or edited. Therefore, clicking on the Invert option in the Load Selection dialog box spared you the need to use the <u>S</u>elect, <u>I</u>nverse command after the selection loaded.

Click and drag through the selection marquee until you can read the logo	Applies foreground blue in dissolve mode; creates a logo on the sand. (see fig. 18.12).

You might want to press Ctrl(Cmd)+H (<u>S</u>elect, Hide <u>E</u>dges) to keep the selection marquee hidden while you paint.

Press Ctrl(Cmd)+D (<u>S</u>elect, <u>N</u>one), then Ctrl(Cmd)+S (<u>F</u>ile, <u>S</u>ave)	Deselects the floating selection and saves your work up to this point.

Press Ctrl(Cmd)+W (**E**dit, **C**lose)   Closes the SANDLOGO image.

Press Ctrl(Cmd)+W (**E**dit, **C**lose)   Closes the NED_LOGO image.

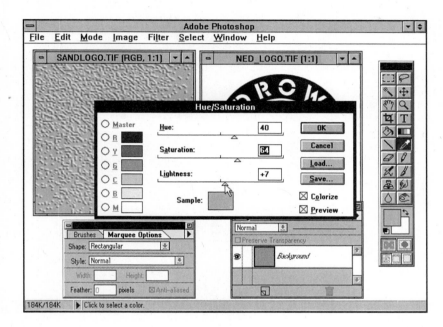

Figure 18.11

Use the Hue/ Saturation command to colorize a monochrome, RGB image.

As you've seen, Photoshop filters aren't always found under the Filter menu. As the sun sets on the shores of your Nedrow Beach adventure, keep the following concept in mind as you backtrack to the **F**ile menu for a few more filters:

◆ Filters are used to carry out a complex set of math equations that reshape original graphical data. They're only as effective as your understanding of the situations where they are appropriate. In other words, treat the more exotic filters covered in this chapter as the icing, not as a flashy substitute for the cake.

Figure 18.12

The logo appears to have taken some pounding on the shore!

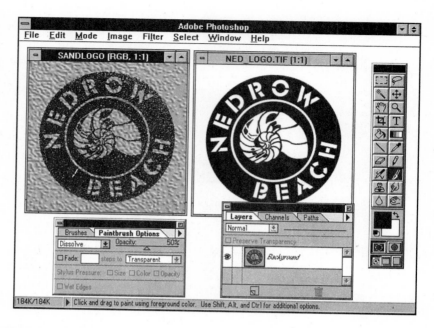

Using Other File Menu Filters

Some command names in the **F**ile menu become invaluable when you can't find a filter under the Filter menu. Like the **P**lace and **O**pen commands, it's not apparent that these are filters, but they *do* transform data in useful ways.

Open As

It is possible in the DOS/Windows world to strip a file of its three character extension. When and if this happens, an image file loses its association, and Windows-compliant programs (Photoshop for Windows is one) can't figure out how to open the file. PCX, Targa, and several other graphical bitmap formats are actually opened in Photoshop through the use of native plug-in filters. If the plug-in can't read the file's extension, or if in the unlikely event Photoshop can't find your plug-ins directory (see Chapter 4 on this), you're stuck. That is, unless you specifically point Photoshop to the type of image you want opened by using the Open **A**s command. **F**ile, Open **A**s has retrieved images with no extensions for the authors, and has enabled the authors to read a Macintosh TIF image after the Macintosh user who sent the image didn't type *.TIF as the file's extension.

Export Paths to Illustrator

Photoshop offers passage of vector information back to the AI format in the File, Export, Paths to Illustrator command. If you have saved a path in an image, and want to use the path as a guide for designing something else in an Adobe Illustrator-compatible program, select the path by clicking on its title on the Paths palette. Then choose File, Export, Paths to Illustrator to export the information.

Check the documentation for the drawing program you have to see whether it can import AI or EPS files.

Export Amiga HAM

If you need to get a PICT file to a Commodore Amiga system, choose to export your work as Amiga HAM (File, Export, Amiga Ham). The Amiga HAM file format is also a compression/encoding scheme, which is non-standard to Windows or the Macintosh, so don't save the only copy of a masterpiece you've created in the HAM format.

Acquire Quick Edit and Export Quick Edit Save

These two commands can be a life-saver if you need to edit the bottom corner of a 50 MB file. For instance. File, Acquire, Quick Edit enables you to open a portion of a huge image, which you can then edit. When the changes have been made, Photoshop can stitch the edited portion back into the original file when you choose File, Export, Quick Edit Save. Quick Edit works seamlessly, and you can save the hunk of edited image as a separate file by using the Save a Copy command under File. While working on a Quick Edit portion of an image, the File, Save command is dimmed. You can choose File, Save As if you only want a fraction of the original image, but you must choose a different file name, or you'll overwrite that 50 MB original with the saved portion.

In addition to the Acquire and Export filters that come with Photoshop, third party plug-in filters (covered in Chapter 19) may appear under these commands after you install them.

The Filter Menu

The kinds of filters that most imaging folks think of when they hear the term are the ones that do jazzy special effects, or help integrate images. These kinds of plug-in filters are found on Photoshop's Filter menu and are stored in Photoshop's PLUGINS directory (folder), as are the File menu filters. The following sections skip around the Filter menu because the exercises use a combination of filters. If we jump ahead, we'll come back to explain the rest of a Filter category.

Photoshop's Blur Filters

You've seen in several other chapters how the Gaussian Blur filter can be used to produce realistic shadows, and read in Chapter 17 how the Motion Blur filter can create a dramatic rack-focus lens effect even when the photograph's already been taken. In addition to these filters, you'll want to know what to expect from the other filters under the Filter, Blur submenu.

The Blur and Blur More Filters

Bitmap images obtain their visual detail and color from the same source: the pixel, the unit of light. When pixels are arranged with other pixels along a grid, they create an image a viewer can recognize. The Blur (Filter, Blur, Blur) and Blur More (Filter, Blur, Blur More) filters basically provide the same distortion of image detail by averaging the color values found in neighboring pixels. For example, the edge of a ball in a photo is represented by an arrangement of pixels whose color values are distinctly different from the interior and exterior of the ball. When you use the Blur filter on such a ball, the ball's "edge" of perhaps one or two pixels in breadth is given a color value more similar to the interior and exterior of the ball.

The Blur More filter performs its color averaging at about four times the strength of the Blur filter. You would use this filter as an alternative to Gaussian Blur when you want to soften an image area *without* destroying its visual content. For example, the background of SANDLOGO.TIF that you created in an earlier exercise can benefit from the use of Blur or Blur More to soften the focus of the dissolve mode pixels that were embossed. Sharp pixel color transitions are a peril to digital imagists' work because, in many cases, it makes the image look hard edged and phony. Blur and Blur More filters can take the "edge" off a sharply pixelated image.

Using the Motion Blur Filter

The use of the Motion Blur filter (Filter, Blur, Motion Blur) is usually best confined to an image layer; you can blur an image element without messing up the rest of an image if you first copy a selection to a layer. The Motion Blur effect can be used to create anything from a speeding bullet to a speeding super hero. The angle and distance of the Motion Blur filter are user-defined.

In the next exercise, you create the effect of a marble hurtling though the air, and learn the secret to conveying motion within a still image. Figure 18.13 shows the image of a marble placed on a layer on top of the Background of MARBLE.PSD. To convey the sense of motion while still retaining the figure of the marble, you'll need to first make a copy of the layer.

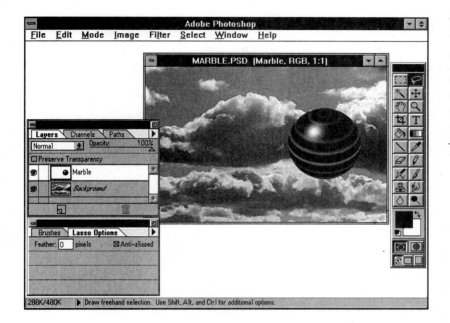

Figure 18.13

Keep image elements that you want to blur, distort, or otherwise filter, on layers separate from the Background layer.

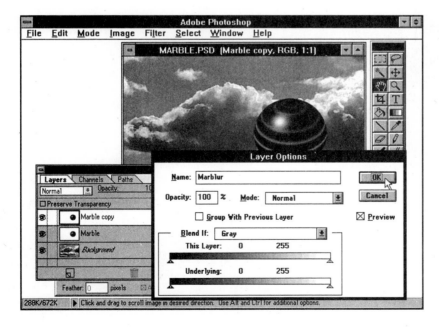

Figure 18.14

Create a copy of the element you intend to Motion Blur.

When you work without an active selection marquee in an image, Photoshop assumes that you want a filter to affect the entire image. When working with Filters, it's a good idea to create a separate backup copy of a layer, or the background, to ensure that if the filter doesn't produce the effect you want, you still have an intact copy.

Here's how to make a marble accelerate from 0 to 100 mph without leaving skid marks on the Background layer.

Using the Motion Blur Filter

Open the MARBLE.PSD image from the CHAP18 subdirectory (folder) of the *Inside Photoshop 3* Bonus CD	This is the image you'll apply to the Motion Blur.
Click and drag the Marble title on the Layers palette into the New Layer icon	Makes a copy of the layer; Marble copy is the current editing layer.
Double-click on the Marble copy title	Displays the Layer Options dialog box.
Type **Marblur** in the **N**ame field, then click on OK (see fig. 18.14)	Gives the copy a unique name (easier to locate later).
Choose Fi**l**ter, Blur, Motion Blur	Displays the Motion Blur dialog box.
Click and drag the **A**ngle pointer to the right of the **A**ngle field so that the **A**ngle box value is **0°**, then click and drag the **D**istance slider to **111** (pixels)	Creates a lateral Motion Blur that you can preview in the proxy (see fig. 18.15).
Click on OK	Applies the Motion Blur.
Press **V** (Move tool), then click and drag the blurred marble on the Marblur layer so it trails to the left of the marble on the Marble layer	Creates a Motion effect in the MARBLE.PSD image (see fig. 18.16).
Choose **F**ile, Sa**v**e As, then save the image as MARBLE.PSD to your hard disk.	Saves your work to disk.
Press Ctrl+W (**F**ile, **C**lose)	Closes the saved image.

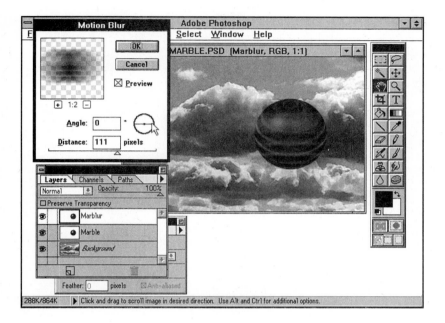

Figure 18.15

You can direct the angle and amount of Motion Blur in the dialog box.

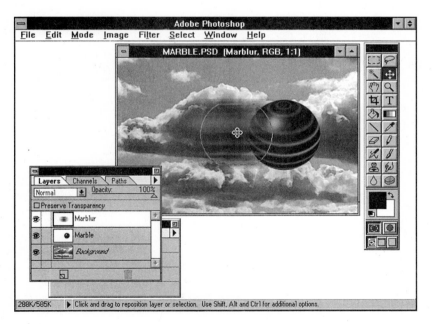

Figure 18.16

Reposition the blurred marble so it appears as a trail from the original marble on the layer beneath.

This is the most basic of motion blur effects. The biggest trick to getting impressive results with the filter is to always blur a copy of the original, and let the "effect" be on the top layer. In figure 18.17, we had some fun and pointed the Angle of the Motion Blur at 45°, then –45° for a second copy of the original marble. We then copied the layers, and assigned them a decreasing opacity as the layers went from top to bottom.

Figure 18.17

Change of direction can be suggested for a moving object by using multiple layers of Motion Blurred elements at different angles.

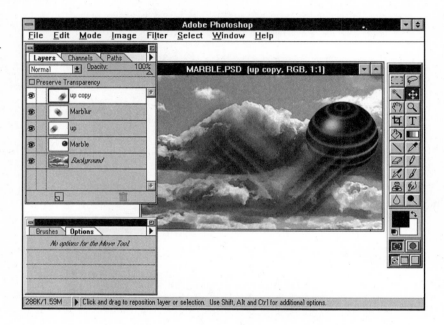

Try this technique with pool balls on a pool table, golf balls, or anything else you want to put in motion.

The Distort Filters

The Distort filters can be thought of as commands that map an image to a different set of coordinates than the typical planar grid. You can give the appearance that something's lifted off the image window, or that you're viewing into a pond by using a Distort filter, a combination of Distort filters, or by repeating an application of a filter over the same selection. The following section describes effects of the Distort filters, and provides hands-on examples of creative uses for them.

The Pinch Distort Filter

This filter's name is a straightforward description of the filter's effect—you can "pinch" part, or all of an image to make it appear as though someone dented an image in the direction of the back of your monitor. Because the Pinch filter has

settings from –100% to +100%, you can displace an image area in a negative direction to create a "punch from behind" effect. Negative displacement doesn't create a punch in an image as clearly defined or pronounced as the Spherize command, but if you want a "lump" in an image area, displace it using the Pinch filter (Filter, Distort, Pinch).

As with all the distort filters, you can use a creative technique to affect only part of an image. The secret? Use the Lasso tool to select part of an image, with a Feather setting of 4 or more pixels. You can set a Feather radius at the time you create a selection by setting the Feather option on the Options palette, or you can add a Feather to an existing selection by choosing the Select, Feather command. This creates a gradual transition between the distorted, selected area and the rest of the image.

Polar Coordinates

The Polar Coordinates filter (Filter, Distort, Polar Coordinates) gives you the option of mapping a rectangular image to spherical, using the center of the selection as the "pole." Polar Coordinates can create a stunning globe from a Mercator projection of the world, or it can take an image that's spherical and make it a flat projection.

You can create some interesting effects by deliberately mapping an inappropriate image—mapping an image of a sphere to Polar Coordinates. The center of the Polar Coordinates effect is always the center of the image, but by creating a selection marquee within an image, you can "direct" the filter.

The Ripple Distort Filter

You don't have many user-defined options in Ripple Filter's dialog box; it creates an 11 o'clock to 5 o'clock displacement in waves of Large, Medium, or Small undulations. You can control the intensity of the Ripple effect with the Amount slider. You access the Ripple filters dialog box by choosing Filter, Distort, Wave. This is a good filter to use to produce flame-stitching patterns, or to create a look like the wavy, marbleized patterns used as endpapers in fine hard-cover books.

If you're looking for a water reflection filter, this isn't it. The ZigZag and Wave filters (also Distort filters) provide nice water reflection simulations. See Chapter 13, "Combining Photographs," for a detailed explanation of the Wave Filter; the ZigZag filter is demonstrated later in this chapter.

The Shear Distort Filter

The Shear filter (Filter, Distort, Shear) creates a fun-house mirror effect. The dialog box displays a vertical line on a grid that you first click on to create an anchor, then click and drag to distort the line. The image you apply the Shear filter to will bend according to the anchors you place on the vertical line. You can add as many anchors to the control line as you like, and you can choose from two options for image areas that fall out of the display. The Wrap Around option begins the image at the image edge when the Shear displaces image pixels off the image window; Repeat edge pixels continues the pixel it finds at the edge of the distortion to the edge of the image window.

Unfortunately, you cannot perform a horizontal Shear with this command. If you turn the target image on its side (**I**mage, **R**otate, **9**0° CW, or 9**0**°CCW) prior to using the filter, you can achieve a horizontal shear.

The Twirl Filter

The Twirl filter creates the impression that you're standing directly over a drain, watching your target image being washed away. The Twirl filter can be used to produce effects on standard stock photography, but is not recommended for use with portrait images, unless you want to lose clients and friends.

If you're an illustrator at heart, the Twirl filter can be used to create a great simulation of the cosmos. In the next exercise, you'll see how to create a galactic cluster with only the Paint Brush tool and the Twirl filter.

Creating a Cosmic Background image

Press **D** (**d**efault colors icon), then **X** (switch colors icon)	Makes the current foreground color white, and background color black.
Choose **F**ile, **N**ew, then specify a **3** inch by **3** inch image, Grayscale **M**ode, at 72 pixel/inch **R**esolution, click on the **B**ackground Color radio button in the Contents field, then click on OK	Creates a black background image window you'll use in this exercise.
Click and drag a diagonal stroke across the Untitled-1 canvas, but don't begin or finish at either corner	Creates a random pattern of white pixels on the black background.
Choose Fi**l**ter, Distort, then Twirl	Displays the Twirl dialog box.
Enter **254** in the **A**mount field, then click on OK (see fig. 18.18)	Sets the Twirl filter to map the effect in a clockwise direction.
Choose Normal mode from the Paint Brush Options palette, then choose a small tip from the top row of the Brushes palette	Sets the characteristics of the Paint Brush tip to apply foreground color in its default mode.

Click once or twice on the Untitled-1 canvas, then press **7** on the keyboard and click a few more times (see fig. 18.19)	Creates planets among the galaxy you created, and the keyboard keys reduce or increase the present Opacity for the Paint Brush.
Press Ctrl+W (**F**ile, **C**lose), then either save the image, or click on **N**o in Photoshop's attention box	Saves the image and closes it, or simply cloes the image window.
Press **0** on the keyboard	Restores the Brushes palette Opacity to 100% (so you're not surprised the next time you use the Paint Brush tool).

A shortcut to creating various intensities of foreground color is to alternate the Opacity of foreground white. If you press 5 on the keyboard, you're painting white at 50% opacity, which, in effect, creates a medium gray on the black background.

The Twirl filter is excellent at twisting a pattern, but occasionally you'll find that this filter and others need a human touch after you've used them.

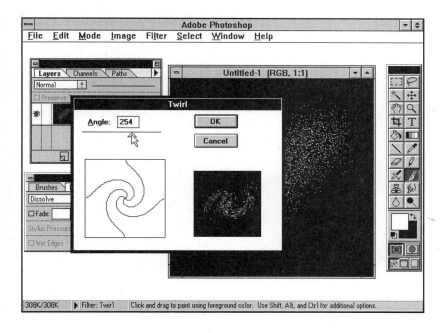

Figure 18.18

The Twirl filter can displace an image in either a clockwise or counterclockwise direction.

Figure 18.19

*Set different
Opacity levels for
the Paint Brush
tool to create
different shades of
the current
foreground color.*

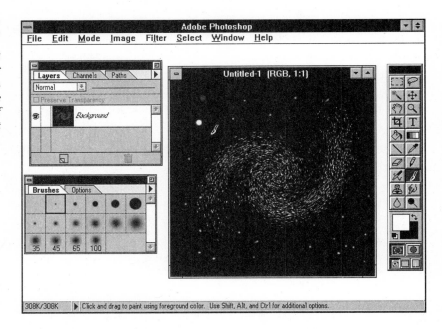

Using Displace and ZigZag Filters Together

We're going to leave the Spherize filter in the Distort group alone until the end of this chapter, where we have an exercise cooked up to use it in combination with Lighting Effects. Sometimes, you'll find that one filter can help enhance the product of another one. This is certainly the case with the Displace and ZigZag Distort filters.

If you read Chapter 16, "Creating a Digital Collage," you saw how the Displace filter could be used to bend type. The Displace filter can use any image except bitmap mode images as the source, or *map*, for displacing a selected image. PLUGINS\DISPMAPS is a collection of Adobe displacement maps that was installed when you ran Photoshop Setup. You can also create your own displacements maps, as long as they are saved in the PSD image format.

In the next exercise, you'll see how to create a displacement map by using the ZigZag filter, then apply it to a photo of a New York skyscraper. Most of Photoshop's Distort filters produce the most noticeable effects when sharp geometric angles are the predominant elements in a picture's composition. Images of soft landscapes and portraits tend to disintegrate visually when Distort filters are applied.

Working with the ZigZag and Displace Filters

Open the 53RD&LEX.TIF image from the CHAP18 subdirectory of the *Inside Photoshop 3* Bonus CD	The image for the effect .
Press Ctrl(Cmd)+N (**F**ile, **N**ew), then choose **W**indow, and click on 53RD&LEX.TIF at the bottom of the menu	Automatically creates the same dimensions for the new file as the 53RD&LEX image.
Type **Displace** in the **N**ame field, then click on OK	Creates new, blank canvas entitled Displace.
Press **D** (**D**efault colors icon)	Makes the current foreground color black, and background color white.
Minimize the 53&LEX.TIF image window	Leaves more room on your workspace You don't need the image displayed at the moment.
Press **G** (**G**radient tool), then on the Options palette, set Normal mode, **100%** Opacity, Foreground to Background Style, and Type: Linear	Sets the Gradient tool to sweep foreground to background color where you click and drag.
Press Shift while clicking and dragging from top edge to bottom edge within the displace image	Shift constrains the Gradient fill to a straight line; you have an image that blends from black to white.

The ZigZag filter produces the most pronounced effects when an image displays a lot of tonal variation; the Gradient tool provides a quick, easy way to flood an image window with as many different tones (shades of black) as is possible for a grayscale mode image to hold.

Choose Fi**l**ter, Distort, then ZigZag	Displays the ZigZag dialog box.
Click on the Around **c**enter radio button, set the **A**mount to **100**, set the **R**idges to **8**	Specifies a distortion that creates concentric circles of modified tones within the image (see fig. 18.20).
Click on OK	Applies the filter (see fig. 18.21).
Save the Displace image as POND.PSD to your hard drive	Saves the POND image in a format Photoshop can use as a Displace map.
Maximize 53RD&LEX.TIF, then choose Fi**l**ter, Distort, Displace	Makes 53RD&LEX the current image window; calls the Displace filter.

continues

Type **20** in the **H**orizontal Scale field, and **30** in the **V**ertical scale field	Specifies more displacement vertically than horizontally; helps widen a narrow map a little.

Make sure the **R**epeat edge pixels radio button is on. The choice of tiling or stretching Displacement maps does not produce different results, because the mapping on POND.PSD is 1:1 with 53RD&LEX.TIF. Neither tiling nor stretching the POND map are applicable to a map that is the same dimensions as the taget image.

Click on OK	Displays the Load dialog box.
Click on the POND.PSD image, then click on OK (see fig. 18.22)	Chooses the POND.PSD image for the displacement map for 53&LEX.TIF; applies the Displace effect.

It's okay to have a displacement map open while you create the effect in a different image. Photoshop simply reads the information. However, if you use an active image as a displacement map for itself, you'll get a subtle embossed result, and you won't see a dramatic effect.

Choose File, Sa**v**e As, then save the image as 53RD&LEX.TIF (choose the TIFF format from the Save File as Format **T**ype drop-down list)	Saves your work.

Figure 18.20

The ZigZag filter can be set to clockwise, or counterclockwise mapping of three different effects.

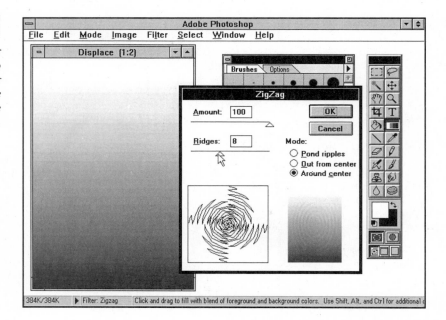

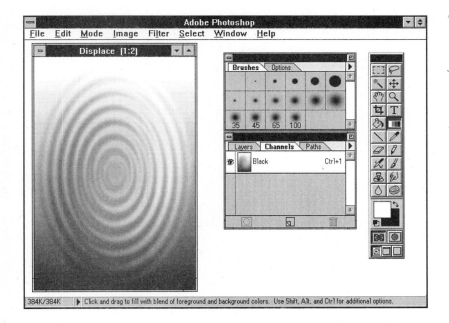

Figure 18.21

Use the ZigZag filter to create a complex displacement map that simulates a pond reflection.

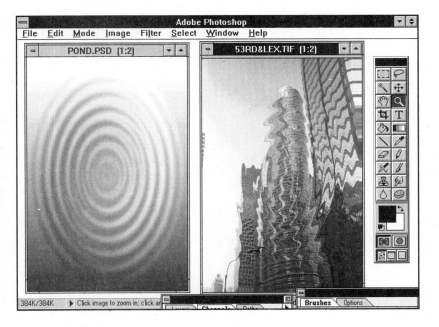

Figure 18.22

The Displace filter maps the brightness values of an image as distortion information for a second image.

If you used the ZigZag filter directly on the 53RD&LEX image, you'd see similar, but not identical results to the application of a Displace map of a ZigZagged image. The Displace filter can use *any* source image for the map. You might want to check out the KPT 2.0 Gradient Designer as a source for generating elegant displacement maps. A working sample copy of Kai's Gradient Designer is on the *Inside Photoshop 3* Bonus CD. This filter, which produces multicolor gradient fills, is covered in Chapter 19, "Third-Party Plug-In Filters."

Noise Filters

Photoshop's Noise filters (Filter, Noise) are capable of reducing and increasing image noise. Image noise is the 1990's euphemism for *static* when applied to the video medium. Random pixels of tone or color can appear at the scanning phase of imaging, or might result from using too much of a particular effect, such as the Sharpen Filter. The selective noise-reduction features found under the Noise filter command can rescue an image that is unusable in its present state. On the flip side, occasionally your work may have a "squeaky clean" image that needs a little grit. The following sections describe the Noise filters, what they do, and when you should use them.

Add Noise

The Add Noise filter can be set to Gaussian or Uniform. Another choice when using an RGB image is whether you want a Monochromatic distribution of random pixels in the image, or full-color noise. The Add Noise filter is best used to hide artificial elements you've added to an image. Paint strokes or images that have been modeled (see Chapter 22) are synthetic and as such, don't display film grain or random distributions of pixels. With the Add Noise command, you can create a subtle impression that the computer-generated color or image was scanned from a photograph. Each type of Add Noise filter can come in handy:

◆ **Uniform.** Creates a pleasing effect when applied to grayscale images. Uniform Noise provides a diffuse look to a portrait (see Chapter 17, "The Wonderful World of Black and White," for an example). Image quality naturally takes a nose-dive when you add noise to a picture. If you're looking for an effect, however, noise definitely can liven up a flat photo, and "noisy" images print well when they are output to lower resolution laser printers.

◆ **Gaussian.** Creates a hard-grain effect within the image. Don't confuse Gaussian noise with the Blur, Gaussian Blur filter; "Gaussian" is a mathematical description of a distribution curve for an effect, and doesn't relate to what an effect *does*. At a high **L**evel percentage, color images become unrecognizable with Gaussian Noise, but when applied to selection areas, you can simulate textures.

The Despeckle Noise Filter

The Despeckle Noise filter is similar to the Blur filters in that it removes harsh areas of contrast within an image. To do this, Despeckle averages tonal values within the image. Image detail is mostly preserved when the Despeckle filter is used to soften image contrast because the filter detects edges—areas of sharp tonal contrast within an image—and does not apply tonal averaging to these areas.

The Dust & Scratches Noise Filter

Do not expect miracles from this filter. As the name implies, the Dust & Scratches Noise filter helps reduce flaws that are part of an image acquired through the scanning process. Photoshop intelligently reads image areas, and when it detects areas that display an orderly absence of pixels, it fills in the gaps with tones and colors sampled from the edge of the missing areas.

If you need to restore a damaged photograph, we recommend that you create a selection marquee around the areas in the image to which you'll apply the Dust & Scratches Noise filter. Photographs lose visual detail when the filter is applied to the entire image. The **R**adius control specifies how many pixels from the defect you want the filter to search to correct the defect; the **T**hreshold is the amount of difference a pixel has to display from a neighboring pixel to be considered "wrong" and thus eliminated from the image.

Your best bet, however, when trying to restore an image, is to scan a clean photo-graph that's in good condition, so there's no *need* to compensate with a filter that removes dust, scratches, and other defects. We realize this isn't easy, but don't promise a client you can restore an image they've run a lawnmower over a few times simply because you have the Dust & Scratches Noise filter. See Chapter 7, "Restoring an Heirloom Photograph," and Chapter 8, "Retouching an Heirloom Photograph," for techniques you'll want to use in image restoration.

The Median Noise Filter

The Median Noise filter (Filter, Noise, Median) helps reduce the number of random pixels—the noise in an image. A random pixel displays a sharp difference in its brightness value compared to its neighboring pixels. The Median Noise filter reduces the number of random pixels by looking at each pixel and replacing that pixel's brightness value with the median brightness value of the pixels found within a user-defined area around the pixel being examined.

Because the radius from which the median brightness is determined is small (between 1 and 16), there is a high probability that many of the pixels share the same bright-ness values and that this common brightness value will be assigned to the pixel being evaluated. This will make a "sore thumb" pixel blend into the neighborhood. Because this process of examining adjacent pixels and assigning them median values happens over and over again, even small user-specified radiuses can produce dramatic results. Unfortunately, the cost of these results is a serious loss in image detail. It is not recommended that you use high radius settings over entire image areas, unless your goal is to produce abstract art.

Photoshop's Sharpen Filters

Sharpen filters (Filter, Sharpen) in Photoshop produce the opposite effect of some of the Noise and Blur filters covered earlier. Sharpen filters emphasize the original contrast in an image, and can sometimes provide more visual detail in an image that's out of focus. The Sharpen filters cannot replace lost image detail, but emphasized contrast in an image frequently convinces the viewer that the image detail is accurate and complete.

The Sharpen and Sharpen More Filters

These filters provide the most basic contrast enhancement functions: they do not provide a dialog box within which you can set the amount of sharpening effect. Sharpen More provides a more dramatic modification of an image, but both filters move the tones of similarly colored pixels toward areas of contrast in the image.

Sharpen is not a substitute for poor original photographic detail. You might find that a single application of the Sharpen filter produces *pixelation*, the unwanted occurrence of random pixels in an image. You might want to try the Median Noise filter after using the Sharpen or Sharpen More filter to reduce the noise that these filters create.

 Tip   If you're printing to a low-resolution laser printer, you can use the Sharpen filter once on an image to make it snappier.

The Sharpen Edges Filter

The Sharpen Edges filter basically is the inverse of the Despeckle Noise filter. It seeks the edges represented in image detail, and creates more contrast within them, while ignoring smooth areas of tonal transition. Like Sharpen, Sharpen Edges is helpful when printing an image that displays poor detail and a lack of focus.

The Unsharp Mask Filter

This is the filter you'll want to use to bring out edge details in an image in the most photogenic, subtle way. Unsharp Mask emphasizes the edges within an image by creating a slightly darker line on one side of an image edge, and a slightly lighter line

on the other. In the Unsharp Mask dialog box, you can set the Amount, or percentage of the effect. You also can specify the Radius, or number of pixels from any edge Photoshop detects in the image to be included as the target for edge emphasis. The Threshold control tells Photoshop how different in brightness value a pixel must be before Photoshop includes it in its view of an edge in the image.

Unsharp Mask is a remarkable feature that can add snap to a slightly blurry original image. The Unsharp mask can be of the great use in restoring out of focus portrait images. Before you apply this or any of the other Sharpen filters, experiment with copies of an image and compare versions to see which settings provide the most natural results.

The Other Photoshop Filters

The following section is *not* a lump-sum of the filters we've yet to mention! The Filter, Other submenu contains the Offset, Custom, Minimum, Maximum, and High Pass filters. A very user-friendly filter is contained in this submenu that you can use to make an image seamlessly tile when filling a selection or entire image window.

The High Pass Filter

This filter places the most emphasis on the sharp transitions found in an image, and portrays areas of little transitional colors and tones as a flat shade. Depending on the subject matter within an image, you can achieve an effect similar to that of photocopying a photograph. Use the High Pass filter (Filter, Other, High Pass) to "clean up" a poor scan of a line art image.

The Minimum and Maximum Other Filters

The Minimum filter spreads out the darkest values and shrinks the light values in an image or a selection. The Maximum filter produces the opposite effect. Both filters produce stylized, thickened images where detail is lost. These are not good filters to use on photorealistic images, although they do produce some interesting abstract color work. Their intended use is not artistic; they make masks that are used to produce trapping for four color printing separations.

The two filters look at each pixel in the image and then compare the pixel to pixels around it. The filter then reassigns the pixel a brightness value that is equal to the dimmest (Minimum filter) or the brightest (Maximum filter) pixel found within the area of pixels. The **R**adius setting determines the number of surrounding pixels Photoshop compares with the pixel currently being evaluated.

If the **P**review box in the dialog box is checked, the image in the workspace window and the proxy box in the dialog box show the results of the current value (from 1–10) of the filter.

The Custom Filter

This filter's dialog box lets you enter numerical amounts that specify how Photoshop should recalculate the brightness values of every pixel in an image. If you treat the center field as the brightness value of a selected pixel, subsequent values you enter are multiples of the brightness of the pixel directly adjacent to it in the image. In the Scale box, you can enter a value between 1 and 2 to divide the sum of the Brightness values of the Custom calculation, which in effect, reduces the overall brightness of the effect. The Offset box can be set to either a negative or positive value to add or subtract from the result of the Scale value. Whew!

Is the Custom filter intuitive? Not at all. You must spend a fair amount of time watching the preview window to see the results of the values you enter. People who work with color models to create filters, programmers, and designers who have a firm grasp on the relationship between mathematics and digital images will get the most from using the Custom filter.

The Offset Filter

If you've ever created a unique texture, and wanted a larger area to use as, say, a background, the Offset Filter is your answer. Many companies, including Pixar, Image Cels, and Wrapture use technologically-sophisticated methods for creating a photographic image that can be tiled as a pattern with no visible seams, but you can perform a similar effect by using the Offset filter.

In the next exercise, you'll use the Offset command to wrap a texture we've created around the top, left of itself; the "center" texture image then becomes the edge of the image, and therefore will seamlessly tile. The only problem with this plan of action is that the former edges of the texture picture then become the center, and you'll see some incongruous image areas. But enough problems! This is a solutions book, and we'll show you the workaround so that the image will never look like it repeats, and the method for making a seamless repeat pattern from a texture image.

Using the Offset Filter

Open the TEXTURE.TIF image from the CHAP18 subdirectory (folder) of the *Inside Photoshop 3* Bonus CD

This is a texture created as an example for this exercise.

TEXTURE.TIF, as shown in figure 18.23, was created in Fractal Design's Painter, an application that offers traditional painters a digital medium that closely resembles oil paint, charcoals, and canvas textures. You can substitute a texture of your own in this exercise, but make sure there is no distinctive image detail within the image. Textures of rocks, grass, oatmeal, or other organic materials are great for seamless tiling—a photo of a building, your family, and other recognizable images are not.

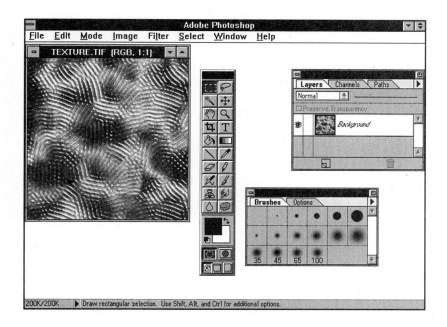

Figure 18.23

Create a texture that doesn't have distinguishing characteristics to use with the Offset filter.

Choose Filter, Other, then Offset	Displays the Offset dialog box.
Enter **30** in the **H**orizontal field, **40** in the Vertical field, then click on the **W**rap Around radio button	Moves the image relative to the image window 30 pixels down and 40 pixels to the right (see fig. 18.24).

By choosing the Wrap Around option, the positional displacement of TEXTURE.TIF's contents repeats, starting at the top left of the image window. Repeating edge pixels or exposing the image background color are not good options for creating a tiling pattern, because they would leave tell-tale edges wherever the texture begins a repeat pattern.

Click on OK	Applies the Offset filter.
Press **S** (Rubber Stamp tool), then pick the fourth (from the left) tip, middle row on the Brushes palette, and set the Options palette to **100%** Opacity, Normal mode, and Clone (aligned) Option	Sets the size and characteristics of the Rubber Stamp tip to default method of cloning.
Press Alt(Option)+click in the center of TEXTURE.TIF, then click and drag along a visible edge toward the top of the image	Samples an image area that doesn't have an edge ruining it, and clones this area into the area that has a visible edge (see fig. 18.25).

continues

Figure 18.24

Choose to wrap the image around the image window areas that are exposed by offsetting the picture.

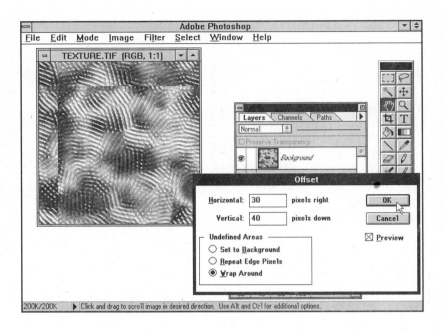

Figure 18.25

Use the Rubber Stamp tool to clone original image areas over the edge where the Offset filter displaced the image.

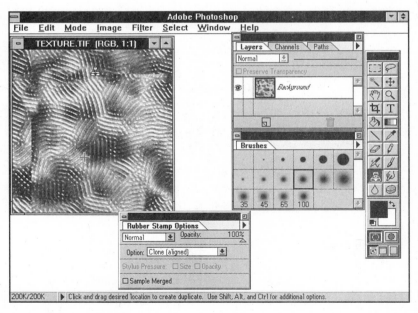

continued

Continue your cloning activity, and resample frequently from image areas that have no edge running through them. The idea here is to conceal the edges with a random pattern.

When you're done, press Ctrl(Cmd)+S (**F**ile, **S**ave), then name the image TEXTURE.TIF to your hard disk	You've created and saved a seamless texture pattern.

Here's the payoff. In the next step, you'll create a new image that's much larger than TEXTURE.TIF, then fill it with a pattern of TEXTURE.TIF. See if you can detect any edges or repeating patterns in the larger image.

Press Ctrl(Cmd)+A (**S**elect, **A**ll), then Choose **E**dit, **D**efine Pattern	Defines all the TEXTURE image as a pattern that can be used with the Edit, Fill command, the Rubber Stamp tool, or the Paintbucket tool for filling a selection with a repeating pattern of the TEXTURE image.
Press Ctrl(Cmd)+N (**F**ile, **N**ew), set the **W**idth and **H**eight units to inches, then enter **2.5** for each. Choose RGB Color **M**ode, **R**esolution **150** pixels/inch, and enter **FILL** in the **N**ame field, then click on OK	Creates a new file, FILL, that is about twice the size as the TEXTURE image.
Press Ctrl(Cmd)+A (**S**elect, **A**ll), choose **E**dit, **F**ill, choose Pattern from the **U**se field, then click on OK	Fills the Fill image window with a seamless, tiled pattern of the TEXTURE.TIF image (see fig. 18.26).
Press Ctrl+W (**F**ile, **C**lose), then either save the image, or click on **N**o in Photoshop's attention box	Saves the image and closes it, or simply closes the image window. You won't use the image in future exercises.

If for no other reason than to compensate for the way the Texture Fill filter works, this trick with the Offset filter is invaluable. The Texture Fill Filter (described later in this chapter) will tile a selected PSD image, but will not create a seamless transition at the image's edges. This creates a visible edge(s) running through an image.

By using seamless textures, either homemade or provided by third party manufacturers, you can create large instant backgrounds *and* conserve hard disk space. You only need to keep a small file that is used as the repeat pattern on your hard disk, and not the whole background created with a pattern fill.

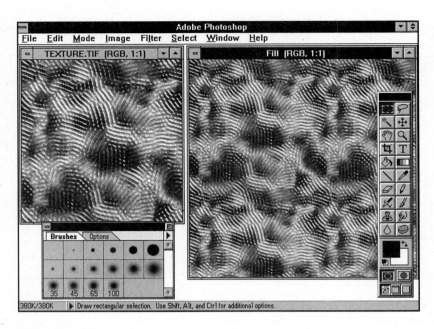

Figure 18.26

Fill any sized area with a seamless repeating pattern that was an image retouched with the Offset filter.

The Pixelate Filters

This group of filters takes original image information and creates fewer colors in the information's pixels. The difference between the Image Size command's method of reducing the number of pixels and the Pixelate filters is that the image retains its original dimensions, and the pixels that are created display a more artistic sense than your standard "rectangle in a grid" variety of pixel. An illustration at the end of this section shows the effect of some of the most dramatic filters.

Color Halftone filter

The Color Halftone filter is *not* the way to make camera ready separations from your original image. Color Halftone doesn't provide the accuracy, resolution, or other considerations you must use when converting a continuous tone image to halftone process screens (see Chapter 23 for the real McCoy). Instead, the Color Halftone filter provides an eye-pleasing, overstated reduction of color information to halftone dots. It produces an image reminiscent of the artists Roy Lichtenstein and Andy Warhol's work with silk screen blow-ups of a simple subject. For images of about 1 MB in size, try 8 pixels as the Max radius size for the color halftone dots, and you may want to leave the screen angles alone.

Color Halftone actually performs a color separation (not accurate enough for printing), and if you look at the color channel thumbnails on the Channels palette after you've used the filter, you'll notice that the halftone dots for each color channel are neatly separated and organized. You can also apply a Color Halftone to a Grayscale image.

Crystallize Filter

The Crystallize filter produces irregular polygons of solid color from an original image. This filter is processor-intensive, so take a good look at the preview window in the dialog box before clicking on OK. Cell size refers to the size of each color polygon; you can attain some interesting color field illustrations when you specify a high cell amount. Conversely, if you specify a small cell size, then use a color channel as the texture map channel in the lighting Effects filter, your image will look as though it was made from pebbled glass. See Chapter 17, "The Wonderful World of Black and White," for an exercise that uses the Crystallize filter.

The Facet Filter

This filter changes the color values of pixels to form clusters of similarly-colored pixels in an image that match the dominant color values in the overall image. The filter has no dialog box, and produces a very subtle effect on a photographic image. By repeat applications of the Filter (press Ctrl+F after you first choose it), you'll eventually create an image that looks like it was painted by a realist using a dry brush technique. This is how the background clouds were created in MARBLE.PSD, the image you used earlier with the motion blur filter.

The Fragment Filter

This filter can be used to induce headaches! Do not use this filter for any other purpose than to create an April Fool's Day eye exam. The Fragment filter creates four copies of the original image, then offsets them by a pixel or two at partial opacity. You can create this effect yourself, and take the blame instead of using the Fragment filter. Occasionally, a software developer will create a filter because it *can* be created, not for any particular artistic objective. This is one of those filters.

The Mezzotint Filter

In traditional printing, Mezzotint filters are screen laid on top of a continuous tone photograph to add a pattern to the image as it's being rendered to the page. Photoshop's Mezzotint filters replicate the look of a physical Mezzotint. You have the option to choose dots, lines, or strokes for the shape of the resulting pattern in your design. Although color images produce a more interesting Mezzotint effect than Grayscale images, the Mezzotint filter should not be thought of as a digital substitute for commercially printed Mezzotints. You can achieve the look, but not the precision of a genuine Mezzotint screen with Photoshop's Mezzotint filter.

Mosaic filter

The Mosaic filter *samples down* color information—creates one composite pixel to represent several original pixels—you can take a group of, say, 16 pixels in an image and instantly create one huge pixel that's composed of an average of the 16 pixels. The Mosaic filter can give you a "fly's eye" view of an image, and at coarser **C**ell Sizes, the resulting image cannot be recognized. Use this filter only with a *copy* of any image you really like. We've included 5CENTS.TIF, an example image in the CHAP28 subdirectory of the *Inside Photoshop 3* Bonus CD for you to use as a target image for the Photoshop filters. It's safe, it's not your own, and it can't be overwritten.

The Pointallize filter

The Pointallize filter creates the look of Pointallistic paintings from your image. You can specify the shape of the dots of color with the **C**ell size slider, and set the current background color, which is the color between the Pointallized dots. Whites and pastels generally work best as background colors to create a painterly effect.

Figure 18.27 shows the Facet, Pointallize, and Color Halftone filters compared to the original 5CENTS.TIF image.

Figure 18.27

Reduce the information in an image, in an artistic fashion, by using the Pixelate filters.

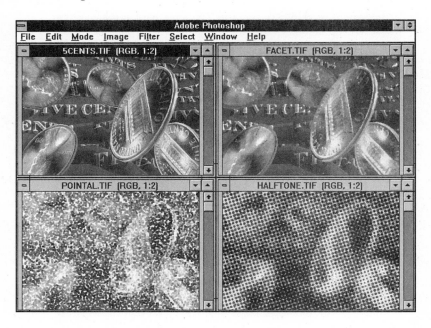

The Stylize Filters

You'll find that the effects produced by the Stylize filters resemble the Pixelate filters, with a hint of the Distort filters. Each Stylize filter is capable of producing a certain "look" for an image that is more pronounced with subjects containing softer elements.

The Diffuse Filter

This filter seems to corrode the content of an image. Diffuse displaces pixels toward the edge of image details. The only option you have is to displace Lighter or Darker pixels. There is no slider for this filter. You can achieve a more intense effect by multiple uses of the filter on the same image.

The Extrude Filter

The Extrude filter makes a honeycomb rendering from an image, that appears to be coming toward the viewer. This stylized effect can be used to simulate a sewing pattern, an aerial view of a congested city, or a collection of children's building blocks. In the Extrude dialog box, you have your choice of Random block or Pyramids, or Level-based. With Level-based, the height of the Extrude is evaluated by the relative brightness value of the pixel that's being stylized.

The Find Edges and Trace Contour Filters

Find Edges can come in handy when you have a poorly exposed image and want to display a sort of pencil-sketch representation. The Find Edges filter displays the sharp transition area in a color image most predominantly, and drops solid fields of color to a light pastel, using the color wheel opposite (example: magenta>green) of the original colors for the display of the edges. Trace Contour thickens the areas of sharp transition in an image by outlining each color channel. The background of a Trace Contour filtered image is white. You might want to try both of these effects by using the **I**mage, **M**ap, **I**nvert command prior to using the filter to create dramatic, abstract effects.

The Solarize Filter

The Solarize filter creates a composite of the image positive and the image negative. There is no dialog box for this filter, and you can get more artistic effects by using a Grayscale image.

The Tiles Filter

The Tiles filter literally dices your image into squares of equal size. You have the option of filling in the background of these tiled components of an image with foreground or background color, inverted, or unaltered original image. You can define how scattered the resulting tiles are with the Maximum offset option, and how many tiles will be created (minimum value) in the Number of Tiles field in the dialog box. No preview is available for this filter; experiment until you find parameters you like, then write them down.

The Wind Filter

This is a great "effects" filter for simulating a strong wind, or the appearance of wet paint. The Wind filter displaces the highlights in an image in a horizontal direction. You can specify the degree of strength for the wind, as well as a Left or Right displacement for the filter.

In figure 18.28 examples of the Wind, Extrude, Tiles, and Find Edge Filters have been applied to the 5CENTS.TIF image.

Figure 18.28

The Stylize filters displace pixels in an image, in artistic and creative ways.

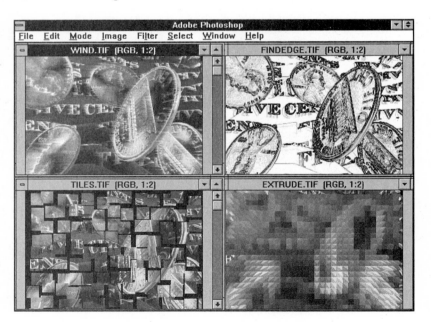

Additional Photoshop Filters

Three other filters deserve mention, and should be used under certain circumstances:

◆ **Render, Lens Flare.** This filter creates a simulation of a camera lens flare at different lengths and Brightness. You click on the proxy image in the dialog box to set the point for the lens flare, decide on a camera lens, adjust the amount of Brightness, then click on OK. This filter is useful for photorealistic images of rendered models; it suggests at a first glance that an image was photographed, not created inside a computer.

◆ **Video, De-Interlace.** This filter should be used on images that were captured using a video capture adapter card and a video source such as a camcorder or VCR. Video signals are sent in alternating lines of video pixels, or *interlaced*, as they are broadcast The De-Interlace filter valiantly and intelligently tries to stitch the video information back together to create a bitmap image.

Many users are intrigued by the possibility of using video captures as part of a Photoshop bitmap design, but in 1994, video capture utilities for PCs and the general quality of video recording for private use ranges from poor to unacceptable. The De-Interlace filter makes the best of a bad situation in image conversion techniques.

◆ **Video, NTSC Colors.** As with commercial process color printing, television has a *gamut*, a range of color expression, much narrower than the digitally-fed monitor hooked up to your computer. NTSC brings the range of colors in an RGB image back into broadcast television gamut, and reduces the streaking and color bleeding a digital image can display when broadcast on TV. If you're creating a title slide for TV broadcast, use this filter before you pack your image off to network.

The Filter Factory

Despite it's inviting name, Photoshop's Filter Factory is not a factory that creates instant, wondrous filters with the flick of a switch or the click of a button. On the contrary, the Filter Factory is a software developer's tool, meant to provide programmers and others who understand C programming language an interface for designing custom plug-in filters. If you've taken at least a semester of C language programming (and the prerequisite courses for a C class), you'll be able to pick up and master Photoshop's symbol programming language, and be able to design a custom plug-in filter that might address a special imaging need. You will also need to understand how Photoshop works with brightness values and other characteristics to create meaningful filters. The Synthetic menu item under Filters is *not* installed by default when you run Photoshop setup; this is where the Filter Factory is located only if you install it from the Adobe Deluxe CD-ROM.

If you don't know how to write code, you aren't necessarily excluded from using the Filter Factory, however. Sample code is on the Adobe Deluxe CD-ROM, and you can load it, generate a filter from it, and use the custom filter as easily as any other in the Filters menu. In the next section, we'll walk you through the steps required to install the Filter Factory and generate a filter that averages image colors and turns them into solid circles of light. The filter's name is "Light Pegs;" we'll show how to get the code for this filter from the CD and make a new filter entry in the Synthetic menu.

Removing the Attributes of the FFACTORY.8BF File

Before you can use the Filter Factory plug-in, you must remove the read-only attributes of the file. CD-ROMs are read-only, and the file you need to use must have its read only (Macintosh: locked) property removed before it can be used. You remove this after the file has been copied from the CD and added to Photoshop's plug-ins directory.

If you're using the Windows version, close Photoshop, then copy the FFACTORY.8BF file from the GOODIES\FFACTORY subdirectory on the Adobe Photoshop Deluxe CD-ROM to the PLUGINS subdirectory of Photoshop. Then, from Windows File Manager (or another Windows shell such as Norton Desktop), click on the FFACTORY.8BF file name, choose **F**ile, Proper**t**ies, and uncheck the **R**ead Only check box.

Macintosh users need to drag the Filter Factory file from the Filter Factory folder nested inside the Other Goodies folder to their Photoshop plug-ins folder on their hard disk. Then select the Filter Factory icon, choose Get Info from Finders File menu. To unlock the file, uncheck the Locked check box in the Filter Factory Get Info dialog box and then close the Get Info dialog box.

While Photoshop is closed, also copy the FFEXAMP.AFS and LIGHTS.AFS files from the GOODIES\FFACTORY subdirectory files to your hard disk. Macintosh users will find the Filter Factory Example.afs in the Other Goodies\Filter Factory folder and the Lights.afs in the Lite Pegs Example folder nested within Filter Factory folder.

These are sample code files you'll use in the upcoming exercise to generate the *.8BF plug-ins for use in Photoshop. You will also have to remove the write protection (locked) property from these files as you did with the FFACTORY.8BF (Filter Factory) filter.

 Tip
If you don't feel like loading, exploring, or using the Filter Factory, but still would like to use the pre-made filters on the CD, copy the FFEXAMP.8BF and LIGHTS.8BF files to your PLUGINS directory, remove the locked, read-only attributes, and use these plug-ins that Filter Factory created from sample code.

Making a Filter Factory Filter

In the next exercise, you'll restart Photoshop after the FFACTORY.8BF file has been copied and its attributes changed, and look at the options you can specify for running the sample code. You don't need to know how to write a line of code, but you'll see the parameters necessary for generating an Adobe-compliant plug-in filter.

The Adobe Deluxe CD-ROM also contains basic information about the structured language necessary to work in the Filter Factory's interface, and can be found as the FFACTORY.PDF file in the FFACTORY subdirectory under GOODIES. On the Macintosh version of the Adobe Deluxe CD-ROM, the Acrobat file (FFACTORY.PDF) is found in the Other Goodies\Filter Factory folder. To read the document, you must have Adobe Acrobat Reader installed on your hard disk (you can't run the executable file from the CD). Adobe Acrobat Reader is supplied on both the Windows and the Macintosh versions of the Adobe Photoshop 3 Deluxe CD-ROM.

Here's how to use the computer code from the LIGHTS.AFS file to generate a new entry in your Filter menu in Photoshop.

Running the Filter Factory

Restart Photoshop, then find an RGB color image you'd like to use as a target for a Filter Factory Filter	Choose any image. You won't apply a filter in this exercise; the image is simply to give you a visual example of what the filter does.
Choose Filter, Synthetic, then click on Filter Factory	This new menu entry was made when Photoshop read the FFACTORY.8BF addition to the PLUGINS directory when you restarted the application.
Click on Load, then choose LIGHTS.AFS	Displays the Load dialog box. This (see fig. 18.29) is where you choose the AFS file that contains the sample code language for building a filter.
Click on OK	Returns you to the Filter Factory, with sample code entered for mapping the red, green, and blue channels of an image.

As you can see in figure 18.30, the Filter Factory is not a picnic for those who have concentrated their efforts on design instead of programming! Don't alter the sliders or the code while you're in this dialog box, or you'll change the parameters for the filter. The Save button saves code you've written. You shouldn't choose this option unless you're writing something in here (and you understand what you're writing). Invalid parameters are signified by an exclamation triangle; by clicking on the triangle, the filter Factory highlights the invalid portion of the expression string.

continues

Figure 18.29

You can use sample code provided by Adobe to construct a special plug-in filter through the Filter Factory's dialog box.

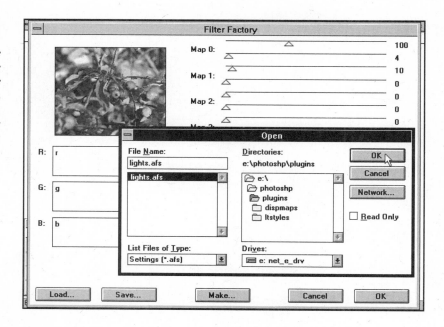

Figure 18.30

Choose Make to create a filter from the expression strings you loaded or created.

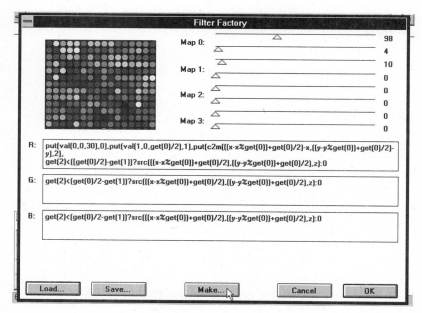

continued

Click on Make	Displays the Build Filter dialog box (see fig. 18.31).

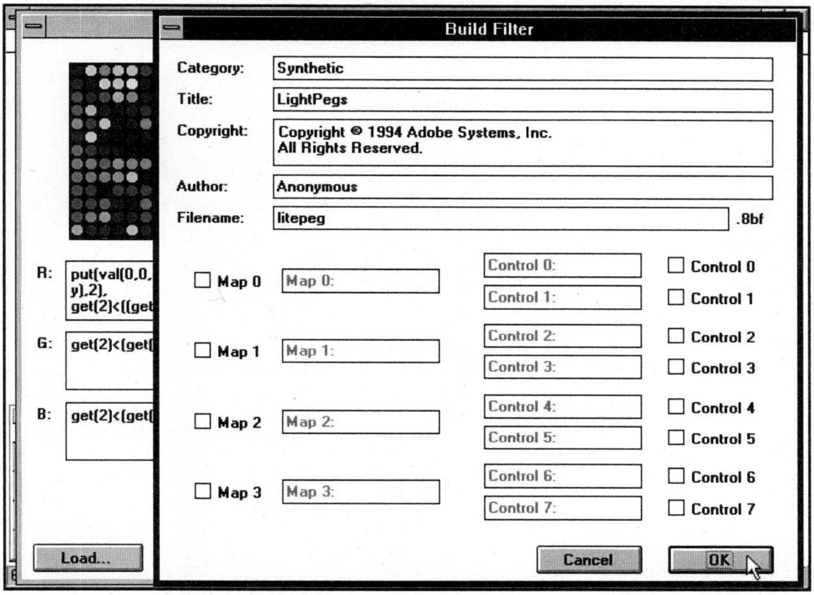

Figure 18.31

The Build Filter dialog box offers options for how the created filter's dialog box will appear; with or without option sliders.

Enter the name that you'd like to appear on the Filter menu in the Title field	LightPegs is a good choice.

Give the filter a DOS (eight character) name if you're using Photoshop for Windows. The Controls and the Maps refer to operations performed to the individual color channels of a target image you'd like to filter. If you want pairs of sliders to control a channel filter map, click on a Map check box. If you'd like individual control settings, click on a Control check box.

We realize that if you don't have a programming background, the expression strings for this filter are fairly meaningless, but *do* check a Map box or two here; the resulting sliders in the LightPeg dialog box for the filter offer some control over the size and color sampling that the filter produces.

Click on OK	Photoshop processes the filter, then displays a dialog box that tells you that the filter has been successfully built.
Close Photoshop, then restart it	Loads the LightPeg filter under the Synthetic menu. The filter is ready for use in Photoshop.

The Filter Factory is obviously not for every Photoshop user, and you shouldn't feel cheated or deprived because you don't have the background to create code. If you do understand code, the Filter Factory gives you the opportunity to expand Photoshop's standard plug-in offerings a hundredfold. It shouldn't be long before you see plug-ins offered commercially or as shareware on online services as a result of the Filter Factory.

In figure 18.32, you can see the filtered image, performed by choosing Filter, then LightPeg from the Synthetic submenu.

Figure 18.32

You can choose from a filter you created if you run or create code in the Filter Factory.

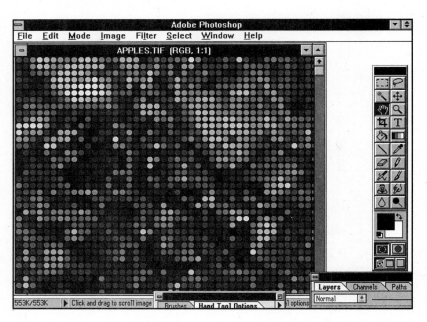

We have an epic exercise in the final section of this chapter that pretty well covers the rest of the Photoshop filters.

Using Filters, Tools, and Features Together

There are some Photoshop filters that seem to be created to work with one another. You've seen in this chapter that you need to add a little inspiration here and there to make a filter work best. If you simply click on an effect, so can someone else. The uniqueness of a design is knowing how to use a filter to accomplish a design element.

In the next assignment, our "Filter Medley" will take advantage of the Adobe Illustrator Rasterizer and the Spherize filter to create a dimensional representation of the Earth. You'll see how to texturize, light, and create an instant background for the Earth in the exercises to follow, but before you embellish the Earth, you have to create it.

Here's how to use the Spherize filter on an imported vector graphic.

World Imports

Choose **F**ile, **O**pen, then choose the EARTHMAP.AI image from the CHAP28 subdirectory (folder) on the *Inside Photoshop 3* Bonus CD	Displays the Rasterize Adobe Illustrator dialog box.

The dialog box should tell you that the image's Height is 4.708 inches, and Width is 3.347 inches. This is the native file format dimensions to which the image was originally designed. *Definitely* check your computer if you don't get these dimensions.

Type **100** in the **R**esolution field, choose Grayscale **M**ode, then click on OK	Determines the resolution of the imported vector design, and the color mode.

You can choose any color mode you like for importing an AI or EPS graphic, but increased color capability takes Photoshop longer to rasterize to bitmap format. The design is a black-and-white design, but you'll convert the resulting bitmap image file to RGB color after it imports to save time.

Press **M** until the Elliptical marquee tool displays on the tool box, then press shift while clicking and dragging from the tip of Alaska until the marquee reaches the bottom of South America	Creates a circular marquee selection that encompasses the continents you'll use as source images for this assignment.

If you're unhappy with the positioning of the marquee selection, press Ctrl+Alt (Mac: Cmd+Option) then click and drag only the selection marquee (not the image contents) to a new location.

Choose Fil**t**er, Distort, then Spherize	Displays the Spherize dialog box.
Click on OK	Applies the Spherize filter in its default settings of 100% horizontal and vertical distortion of the selected image area, at 100% intensity (**A**mount) (see fig. 18.33).

continues

continued

Click on the (Save to) Selection icon on the Channels palette	Saves the circular marquee selection. You'll need it later.
Choose Flatten Image from the pop-up menu on the Layers palette	AI and EPS imports are brought into Photoshop as Layer images without backgrounds. The Flatten image option enables you to save the EARTHMAP image in a variety of graphic file formats.
Choose **M**ode, **R**GB Color	Creates a color channel file from the imported graphic. You can use colors within the design next.
Choose File, Sa**v**e As, then save the image as EARTHMAP.TIF (choose the TIFF format from the Save File as Format **T**ype drop-down list) to your hard disk	Saves your work up to this point.

Figure 18.33

The Spherize filter can create cylinders and spheres by setting the plane of distortion.

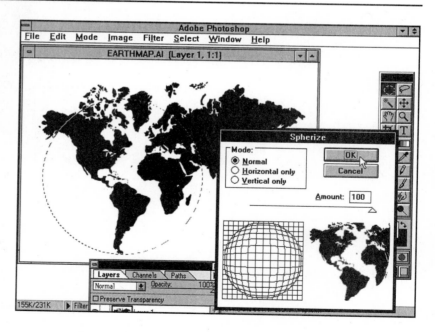

The reason why the EARTHMAP image was imported instead of created in Photoshop is that the Spherize command pushes information away from the selection center, and tends to bunch up pixels toward the edge of the selection marquee. For this reason, the EARTHMAP illustration itself needed to be a little distorted before exporting it in AI format. You'll notice that the continents are smooshed together;

you can practically swim to Europe on this map. A vector design program enabled the authors to rearrange continents easily because vector designs are object-oriented. You simply click and drag on a discrete shape to reposition it. To create this map, we scanned an atlas map, converted the information to vector format, then optimized the image in preparation for its use with the Spherize filter.

The Clouds Filter and Saving Selections from Channels

In the next set of steps, you'll add clouds behind the Earth. This is easily accomplished by inverting the selection area you saved in the last exercise, and defining color values for the Clouds filter to render. Both Clouds and Clouds Difference generate a random fractal design that looks quite a lot like natural texture. The Clouds and Clouds Difference filter use the current foreground and background colors to make a cloud-like pattern.

The difference between the two filters is that Clouds Difference inverts the current image color scheme, and uses image information in its creation of clouds. Repeated application of either filter produces different designs. With the clouds filter, you can press Ctrl+F (Last Filter used) after choosing the Filter to keep creating foreground/background color cloud patterns until you decide which one you like. If you repeatedly apply the Clouds Difference filter, the image colors will continue to invert, but the clouds will take on a harder appearance, like that of marble.

Here's how to get some clouds surrounding the Earth, and refine a selection border along the way to isolate the Earth's continents from the ocean regions.

Creating Clouds

Press Alt(Option)+click on the channel #4 title on the Channels palette
Loads the Earth selection you previously saved.

Choose **S**elect, **I**nverse
The Earth is masked now, and the background is available for editing.

Press **D** (default colors icon), press **X** (switch colors icon), then click on the background color icon
Creates white foreground, and displays the Color Picker to choose a new background color.

Choose a deep blue by using the color slider and the color field, then click on OK
Sets the background to blue, and white is the current foreground color.

Choose Fi**l**ter, Render, then Clouds
White clouds against a blue field appear in the selected area (see fig. 18.34).

continues

continued

If you don't like the arrangement of the clouds, press Ctrl+F	Clouds generate again, producing a different pattern.

The continents and oceans on the Earth deserve different color schemes, so you'll save a selection of the continents before saving the file.

Press Ctrl+D (**S**elect, **N**one), then Alt(Option)+click on the Blue channel on the Channels palette	Loads the Blue channel as selection information.

Pressing Alt+clicking on a color channel thumbnail on the Channels palette is a neat trick for selecting the continents in the image, but Photoshop always treats *color* channel information as white equals selection, and black equals masks. This is the inverse of what you want to save.

Choose **S**elect, **I**nverse, then click on the (Save to) Selection icon on the bottom left of the Channels palette	Selects the black area of the image and saves the selection to channel #5 (see fig. 18.35).

Press Ctrl+D (**S**elect, **N**one), then Ctrl+S (**F**ile, **S**ave)	Deselects the selection and saves your work up to this point.

Figure 18.34

Repeated application of the Clouds filter results in a new pattern every time.

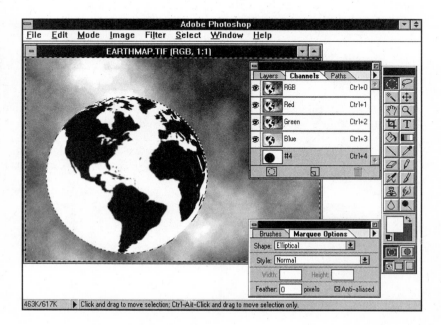

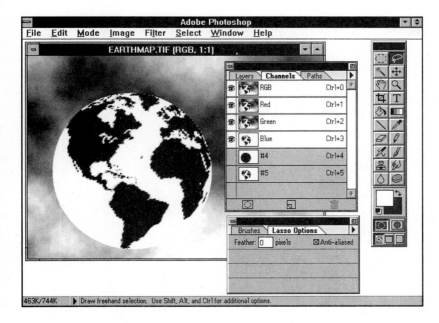

Figure 18.35

*Save a selection based on color channel information by choosing **S**elect, **I**nverse, then clicking on the (Save to) Selection icon.*

We've advised throughout this book that you specify Color Indicates: Selected areas in the Channel options dialog box to make it easier to discern what your selection area is, as represented in an Alpha channel view. However, Photoshop evaluates the whites in color channels as selection areas when you load a color channel in this slightly unorthodox method of auto-creating an accurate continental border. The reason why this trick worked is because you chose the inverse of the loaded selection before saving the selection, and because the Blue Channel of a black-and-white illustration contains the same values as the RGB composite channel.

Using the Subtract From Selection Shortcut

Because you now have a saved selection of the Earth and the continents, you can create a selection marquee that represents the oceans. In the exercise that follows, you learn a shortcut to subtracting a selection from a saved selection, then you see how to add a Gradient fill to the selection to represent highlighted water. It will add dimension to the piece, and support the visual elements you'll add later to represent the terrain on the continents.

Here's how to create a new selection based on two saved selections so that you can add oceans to the Earth.

Auto-Creating a Selection

Press Alt+click on the Channel #5 title on the Channels palette	Loads the selection of the continents.
Press Ctrl (Cmd) while clicking and dragging the (Save to Selection) icon into the Channel #4 thumbnail icon on the Channels palette	Subtracts the active selection from the selection of the Earth in Channel #4.

If you need the Earth as a whole again, it's easy; you copy Channel #4, load Channel #5, then Press Shift while clicking and dragging the (Save to) Selection icon into the copied channel. Ctrl(Cmd) subtracts an existing selection from a saved one, and Shift adds a current selection to a saved selection.

Press Alt(Option)+click on Channel #4	Loads the new saved selection of the Earth's oceans.
Press **G** (**G**radient tool), then set the Options palette to foreground to Background Style, 100% Opacity, and Radial Type	Sets the Gradient tool to use the current colors to create a transitional fill that emanates from a central point outwards.
Click and drag from Greenland to Brazil	Applies a gradient fill to only the ocean areas, creating a highlight effect beginning in the northern Atlantic ocean (see fig. 18.36).
Press Ctrl+D (**S**elect, **N**one), then Ctrl+S (**F**ile, **S**ave)	Deselects the selection and saves your work up to this point.

Adding a Texture Fill

Photoshop's Lighting Effects filter does amazing things to the surface of an image, but does even more amazing things when you have a texture channel defined within an image. The Texture Fill Render Filter is used in the next example for setting up the continent regions in EARTHMAP.TIF for some dimensional relief. The Adobe Photoshop Deluxe CD-ROM has a number of PSD images in the GOODIES\TEXTURES subdirectory; we'll use one of them to give the continents the bumpy sort of relief commonly found on grade school globes.

Before the next exercise, you need to remove the *Inside Photoshop 3* Bonus CD that came with this book, and load the Adobe Photoshop Deluxe CD-ROM in your CD-ROM drive. There are no more images on this book's CD that you'll need for the balance of this chapter.

All set? Here's how to create a texture channel out of the saved Channel #5.

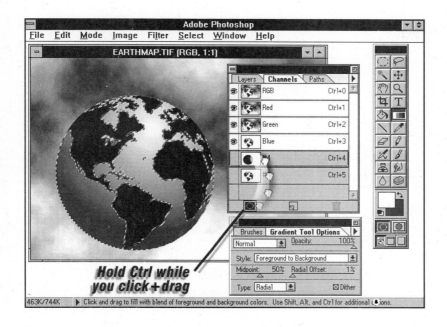

Figure 18.36

Subtract the continents from the Earth selection to select the oceans; fill them with a Gradient fill.

Using the Render, Texture Fill Filter

Press Alt(Option)+click on the Channel #5 title on the Channels palette	Loads the Channel #5 selection.
Click on the (Save to) Selection icon on the bottom of the palette	Saves a copy of the continents selection. You're going to edit Channel #5; you'll need a copy later.
Double-click on the Channel #6 title, type **Continents** in the **N**ame field, then click on OK	Renames the channel for easy identification.
Click on the Channel #5 title	Moves you to a view of Channel #5.
Choose Fi**l**ter, Render, then choose Texture Fill	Displays the Texture Fill dialog box.
Choose your CD-ROM drive location, then click on the CARPET.PSD file in the TEXTURES subdirectory of **GOODIES**	Selects a grayscale, seamlessly tiled pattern of carpeting (see fig. 18.37).
Click on OK	The Texture Fill filter floods the loaded selection area with texture of carpeting (see fig. 18.38).

continues

continued

Figure 18.37

Choose from the PSD images on the Deluxe CD-ROM for the Texture Fill filter.

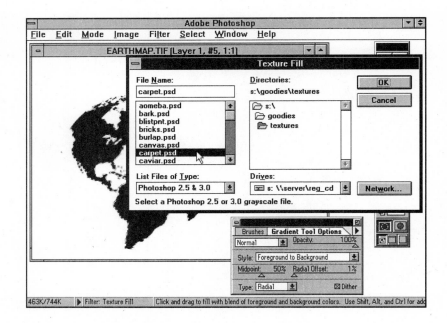

Figure 18.38

The Texture Fill only fills the marquee you loaded earlier.

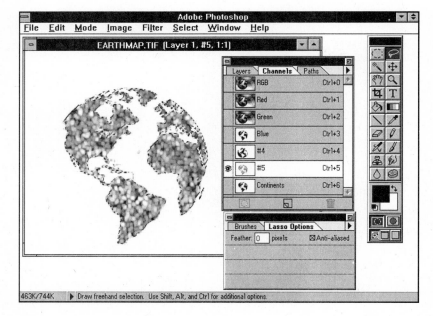

continued

At this point, you've obliterated the black selection information in Channel #5 with carpeting, and will be of no further use as selection information, per se. This is why it was important to save a copy of Channel #5 in its unedited state.

Click on the RGB title on the Channels palette, then click on the foreground color on the toolbox	Displays the Color Picker.
Create a warm earth brown by using the color slider and color field, then click on OK	Chooses a brown foreground that can be used with painting tools.
Press **B** (Paint **B**rush tool), then choose Normal Mode, 70% Opacity on the Options palette, and choose the 100-pixel tip on the Brushes palette	Sets the characteristics for the application of foreground color.
Click and drag a few times through the selection marquee areas	Creates a brown and black surface on the continents (see fig. 18.39).
Press Ctrl+D (**S**elect, **N**one), then Ctrl+S (**F**ile, **S**ave)	Deselects the floating selection and save your work up to this point.

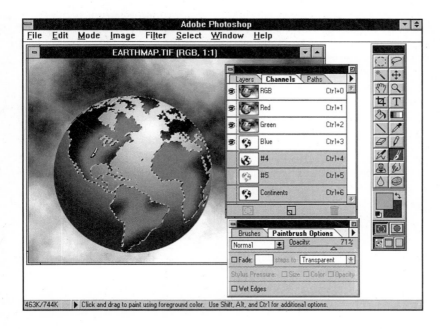

Figure 18.39

Add a splash of color to the selected area while it's still loaded.

The Channel #5 information now contains a grayscale texture that you'll use with the Lighting Effects filter. Because of this, the channel cannot be used again to select the continents from the EARTHMAP.TIF image. Fortunately, you now have the continents Channel to load, and Channel #5 now serves a different purpose than holding selection information: it contains texture mapping information the Lighting Effects filter can use.

The GOODIES Texture Maps are a "starter kit" for the Texture Fill Filter, and they were created exactly the way you'd create a tiling texture map. This means that as long as the image you want to use is Grayscale and saved as a PSD image, you can start your own collection of texture maps for use with the Lighting Effects filter.

The Physics of the Lighting Effects Filter

Photoshop's Lighting Effects filter can add a surface quality to an image, add dimensional relief to the target image by specifying a texture channel for the Lighting Effects, and shade an image to suggest it's hanging on a wall and being lit by a small lamp.

Before you create the textured surface of the continents, here's the rundown on the Lighting Effects dialog box. You might want to examine figure 18.40 as you read about the parameters you can set within this dialog box:

- ◆ **Style.** Photoshop ships with five different settings for a lighting arrangement, with three different types of lights. You can try these out by clicking on the Style drop-down list in the dialog box. Some are dramatic and some are splashy, and by loading some of them, you can take apart the arrangement to examine how an effect is accomplished. When you create your own lighting Style, you can Save it to hard disk by clicking on the Save button, and giving it a name. Windows users are limited to an eight character name; you can type your heart out in the Save field, but Photoshop will only save the first eight characters.

- ◆ **The Spotlight Light type.** Spotlight is one of three light types you can access by clicking on the Light type drop-down list. This light has an elliptical cast that can be modified by clicking and dragging the handles on the circumference of the lighting cast. The center of the ellipse in the proxy window is the extent of the Spotlight; the line represents the direction of the light. You can direct the Spotlight by clicking and dragging on the point where the direction line meets the ellipse.

- ◆ **The Omni Light.** This light has no direction line because it is intended to represent sunlight—light that appears to emanate from everywhere. Use this light when you want to create a texture effect, but don't want the shading that typically is a by-product of the Spotlight. Drag the center point in the proxy box to move the light, and drag any of the four points on the circle to increase/decrease its apparent distance from the image.

◆ **The Directional light.** This light provides an indication of lighting direction, but without the Spotlight effect of a concentrated ellipse of light on the image. The directional light is represented in the proxy box by a single line. Dragging on the white point in the middle of the proxy image moves the light; dragging on the outer point moves the direction of the light. The length of the line connecting the points determines the strength of the light.

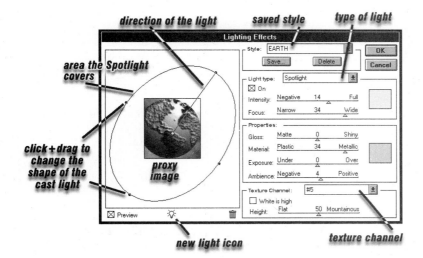

Figure 18.40

The Lighting Effects filter dialog box.

You can add up to 16 different lights to the proxy window, with each light having a different characteristic. To add a light, click and drag the new light icon on the bottom of the dialog box up and into the proxy window. To find your away around a multi-light configuration, press the Tab key. Only one light is displayed at a time in the Proxy window, although the effect of multiple lights is displayed on the background image. To shut off a light effect, choose the light by clicking on its source point in the proxy window, then uncheck the On check box in the light Type field.

The Light Type field also has sliders for controlling the Intensity (the strength of the light), and the Focus (the spread; this slider only works with the spotlight type of light). Because these aren't real lights, you can set a negative Intensity, which produces results similar to darkening an image.

If you want colored lights, click on the color swatch in the Light type field, and choose a color from the Color Picker.

◆ **Lighting Effects Properties.** You can choose how your lights react to the surface of the active image. The Gloss slider controls how much of a "hot spot" is added to the image. The Material slider sets a shiny highlight as the light color (Plastic) or the color in the image (Metallic). Exposure controls the intensity with which light strikes the image surface, and Ambience determines how contrasty the image will appear. Ambient light is light that comes from everywhere in a scene. It is reflected from other objects and has no apparent source.

You can also set the color of the ambient light by clicking on the color swatch to the right of this slider. You can actually mix colored lights from a specific, and a general source to illuminate the scene.

◆ **Texture Channel.** This field lets you pick the channel you want the lighting effects filter to read into the image to create relief. The Height slider controls how exaggerated the relief will be. You can see the effects of using the slider in the proxy window. Another feature is Photoshop can read the white areas in a texture channel as areas that should protrude or recede. By default, the White is High checkbox is checked in the Texture Channel field; if you uncheck it, black areas in the texture channel you've defined can create image areas that come toward the viewer.

You'll probably find that "less is more" when adding your own lights to a scene. Three or more lights can overpower and bleach an image to white. In the next exercise, you'll modify the Lighting Effects filter and only use one light to create mood and texture in the EARTHMAP.TIF image.

Adding Lighting and Texture to the Continents

You have a fine looking image on your desktop right now, and it's all because you understand the prudent use of Photoshop filters. The correct use of any effect should contribute to a scene, not steal from it. Many computer graphics you see in magazines and software packages are created with a flashy filter, but they fail to display content, composition, or an aesthetic that a good designer always keeps in mind before stroking a brush or clicking on an icon.

Creating Mountains with a Texture Fill

Click on the RGB title on the Channels palette	Returns you to the Composite view of EARTHMAP.TIF.
Press Alt(Option)+click on the Continents channel thumbnail on the Channels palette	Loads the selection of the continents.

Choose Filter, Render, then choose Lighting Effects	Displays the Lighting Effects dialog box.
Click and drag the point (where the direction point intersects the Spotlight) away from the proxy window so it points to 1 o'clock	Creates a highlight in an area on the image that is similar to the white point of the Gradient-filled oceans in the image.
Click and drag the 10 and 4 o'clock points on the ellipse so that the ellipse covers the entire proxy image	Covers the entire selected area.

A texture effect will not occur in the image unless the area is covered by the Spotlight ellipse. You aren't going to "wash out" the illustration because only the selection marquee area can be affected. In this respect, the proxy image is a little misleading.

Set Intensity to 14 and Focus to 34	Creates a moderately bright Spotlight with a wide coverage of the image.
In Properties, Set Material to 34, and Ambiance to 4	Creates a surface on the image that looks metallic, with a slight ambient light source smoothing out image details.
Choose Channel #5 from the Texture Channel drop-down list, leave the Height slider at 50, and uncheck the White is high check box	Sets the Channel #5 carpeting to be read as a relief; thedarker areas in the channel make the surface appear to protrude.

See figure 18.41 for a view of what the Lighting Effects setting should look like before clicking on OK.

Click on OK, then press Ctrl+D (**S**elect, **N**one)	Applies the Lighting Effects, and deselects the marquee selection.
Press Ctrl+S (**F**ile, **S**ave)	Saves your work to hard disk.

In figure 18.42, you can see the added highlight around the earth in EARTHMAP.TIF, and added lettering to show you how this image, or one you create using the techniques described earlier, can create a smart-looking backdrop for a slide presentation. It all started with a scan of a map; several filters later, you have a striking digital image.

Figure 18.41

Set lighting direction, color, surface characteristics for your image, and texture mapping in the Lighting Effects dialog box.

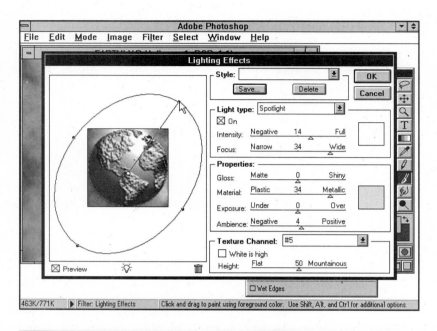

Figure 18.42

Create a slide background by starting with the right stock design, then use filters to flesh out the composition.

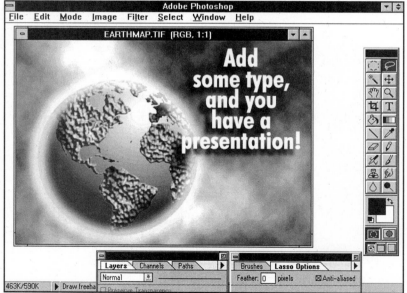

Because Adobe Systems created an open plug-in architecture, many third-party manufacturers have created plug-in filters for use with Photoshop. They're wild, they're exotic, and they're on the *Inside Photoshop 3* Bonus CD that came with this book! Why not drop by Chapter 19 to see what's in store after you *thought* you had every conceivable Photoshop plug-in Filter?

Part IV

Fantastic Assignments in Photoshop

19 3rd-Party Plug-In Filters 909

20 Mixed Media and Photoshop 957

21 Advanced Type Usage and Presentations 1025

22 Virtual Reality: The Ingredients of Dreamwork .. 1069

New Riders Publishing
INSIDE SERIES

3rd-Party Plug-In Filters

In the last chapter, you explored the sumptuous collection of filters that ship with Photoshop 3, and saw how the native filters address almost every conceivable design need. Adobe Systems looked ahead to the possibilities of enhancements to programs that have yet to be invented, and made the plug-in specification for filters an open-ended one. Several software engineers working independently of Adobe already have created exotic, fantastic filters that conform to the plug-ins architecture of Photoshop, and are accessed exactly the same way as native filters such as Gaussian Blur or Lighting Effects.

The independent development of plug-ins has added the creative talents of third-party manufacturers to the recipe of Photoshop's success as the leading imaging tool. As a special gift to Photoshop users and readers of this book, trial versions of plug-in filters from several manufacturers are included on the Bonus CD that comes with this book, and on the Adobe Photoshop Deluxe CD-ROM that ships with version 3. In this chapter, you see how to load and use these filters in order to produce results that you might not have thought possible.

Adding Only the Plug-Ins You Really Want

This chapter is organized by sections that correspond to the manufacturers of the plug-in filters you find on both CDs; instructions for loading and accessing each of the trial versions are at the beginning of each section. You need to swap CDs in your CD-ROM drive at a certain point in this chapter, because New Riders Publishing and Adobe Systems offer a different sampling of plug-ins. However, NRP and Adobe have arranged the CDs so that the Macintosh and Windows partitions on the CD basically are identical and similarly named; if this book tells you to look in the PIXAR128 subdirectory of the Bonus CD, for example, both Windows and Macintosh users should look on that CD for the PIXAR128 subdirectory or folder. Macintosh users have a long file name capability, and there will be instances where this book mentions the "short" or DOS/Windows file-name convention, but it will not be hard to figure out the Macintosh equivalent.

This chapter also is arranged by manufacturers so that you can decide whether you're really interested in adding a specific plug-in to your system. Of course, you could copy everything to your hard disk in one fell swoop, and this would save you from having to restart Photoshop after a chapter section. And after purchasing this book and Photoshop 3, this might have been your first step! But for those of you who want to conserve disk space, follow the sections of this chapter in sequence, read ahead at times, and you'll have only the filters you want as well as some valuable lessons on the filters' uses.

This chapter is task-oriented, and our approach sometimes will lead you to use a combination of filters from different manufacturers to accomplish an assignment. Some very talented individuals have gathered under one roof—that of Photoshop—to bring you the product of their best skills. Now see how you can turn out a work of art based on a little insight of a filter's capability and your *own* skills.

Kai's Power Tools

HSC Software's Executive Vice-President Kai Krause is fascinated with the properties of pixels. So much so, that he wrote Kai's Power Tools for the Mac and Windows, and today the suite of tools is used by graphics designers to bend or shape a digital design with tools that Photoshop's native features and tools don't provide. The commercial version of Kai's Power Tool's (KPT) is divided into KPT extensions and filters.

The trial version of KPT comes with a single extension, the Gradient Designer, and a collection of one-step filters. The KPT filters deserve some explanation, because

although they provide no dialog box, you do have some user options right on your keyboard.

Using the KPT Gradient Designer

You learned in many exercises in earlier chapters how to achieve an airbrush effect from Photoshop's Gradient tool, but you might need a more complex gradient for a specific design of your own than Photoshop's Option palette provides. Enter the KPT Gradient Designer. This Photoshop plug-in contains more ingredients and options than you possibly could ask for to make square gradients, repeating gradients, and even gradients that contain transparency mask information!

To get you up and running with the Gradient Design filter, you first need to install it from the Bonus CD, so you should close Photoshop for a moment. Filters that conform to the Adobe plug-in architecture need to be added to Photoshop's PLUGINS directory (folder) prior to launching a Photoshop session. In addition to the Gradient Designer, there are 11 KPT filters for Windows and five KPT filters for the Macintosh on the Bonus CD. Adding the filters is a matter of copying the filter file to the PLUGINS directory in Photoshop. If you want to skip ahead in this chapter to see what the filters do, you can add the filters later.

Here's how to set up the KPT Gradient Designer 2.0 from the Bonus CD for use in Photoshop:

◆ **Windows users:** Copy all the filters (the file extension is 8BF) from the KPT subdirectory on the Bonus CD into the Photoshop PLUGINS directory (C:\PHOTOSHP\PLUGINS, for example), and copy the KPT20HUB.DLL and KPTWIN20.HLP files into the Windows directory.

◆ **Macintosh users:** Click and drag all filters from the KPT folder on the Bonus CD's Macintosh partition (for non-Power PC Macintoshes, drag the 68 KB filters; for a Power Macintosh, drag the two PPC filters), along with the KPT Support Files folder, into the Adobe Photoshop plug-ins folder.

There are no setup programs for adding the plug-in filters on the Bonus CD to your PLUGINS directory, and this is about as hard an installation as you will see in this chapter! Your trial copy of Gradient Designer is all set to test drive in Photoshop. The next section familiarizes you with the options, conventions, and functions of the KPT user interface (called the *U-I* in its documentation).

Copying a Gradient Fill to the Gradient Designer

As mentioned earlier, the KPT Gradient Designer has the capability to blend a number of colors with different degrees of opacity into a complex pattern gradient fill that looks like a work of art all by itself. The Gradient Designer's Gradient bar is used primarily to define your own custom gradient fills. Before you learn how to do this, however, you see how a special capture function of the Gradient Designer plug-in can make quick work of starting your own collection of fills.

In the next exercise, you copy the patterns in the KPTFILL.PSD image into the Gradient Designer, and save the patterns as part of a category of filters you will define. You can build other categories to hold gradients you design if you want to organize your saved gradient patterns. By default, the Gradient Designer retains the last-used setting each time you open a new Photoshop session.

KPTFILLS.PSD is not intended to replace the *commercial* version's vast collection of preset fills; any graphics artist would be hard-pressed to match the stunning and complex presets you get when you buy the full program. In the next exercise, however, you see how to sample the colors in images and use them as presets that you can recall and use again later. Of particular importance is the layer in KPTFILL.PSD called "Successful Guy's Tie." You should follow the next exercise and copy and save this gradient design, because you use it in Chapter 20's, "Mixed Media and Photoshop," assignment.

Using an Image for a Gradient Design Source

Open KPTFILL.PSD from the CHAP19 subdirectory of the Bonus CD	This is a layered image that contains patterned gradients you will use with the Gradient Designer.

The KPTFILL.PSD image should open up to The Successful Guy's Tie layer, because Photoshop retains current target layer information as part of the PSD image file.

Press F7 (Macintosh: press F11) to display the Layers palette if it's not presently on the workspace	Shows the layers within the KPTFILLS.PSD image.
Click and drag the Layers palette's borders so you can see all the layer thumbnails on the list	Displays different layers with different titles (see fig. 19.1).

The Successful Guy's Tie layer should be highlighted and visible, because that's the way the PSD file was written to the CD. If, by chance, the layer is not visible, you need to make it visible. You should make Successful Guy's Tie the current editing layer by clicking on it and making sure that no Eye icon (indicating a visible layer) can be seen on other titles on the Layers palette. Here's where the fun starts.

Choose Filter, KPT 2.0 Extensions, then Gradient Designer 2.0	Opens the Gradient Designer interface.

Click and *hold* on the Option button, drag down the Option list, and then release when your cursor is on Preferences	Displays the startup preferences for the Gradient Designer.

The KPT plug-in options and controls operate in a slightly different fashion than Windows users are accustomed to. To expand menus, you click and hold, and then scroll (drag) to the next nest of options. This is the method of selecting interface options for the Macintosh OS and applications.

Click on the Load Normal Gradient from Image radio button in the On Startup field and click on OK (see fig 19.2)	Specifies that upon launching the filter in the future, an open image window is examined across a horizontal plane by the Gradient Designer, and the color sample is loaded for use in designing a new gradient preset.
Press Cancel	Leaves the plug-in and sets the startup preference for the Gradient Designer.

You can now open any image, and, by default, the Gradient Designer loads a color sample taken horizontally from the open image. At present, Successful Guy's Tie is the only visible layer on KPTFILLS.PSD, so you use it as a color sample next.

Click on Filter, KPT 2.0 Extensions, and then Gradient Designer 2.0	The fill on the Successful Guy's Tie layer of the KPTFILLS image is loaded on the *Gradient bar*—the wide strip that runs through the center of the interface.
Click and drag the handle in the Direction Control box until it reads about 65° at the bottom of the window	Sets the angle of the gradient fill and displays it in the composite preview window (see fig 19.3).
Click on the Add button. Then click and drag on the Category field and release the mouse button on Add New Category	Changes the dialog box to offer a new category in the Name field.
Type **Starter Kit** and click on OK (see fig. 19.4)	Changes the dialog box fields to offer a name for the custom gradient design in the Name field.
Type **Successful Guy's Tie** in the Name field and click on OK	Adds the gradient design to the Starter Kit category within the PLUGINS hub of the Gradient Designer.

continues

continued

Click on Cancel

Closes the Gradient Designer. You now have a new category of gradient designs and a new entry to this category.

Figure 19.1

Any open image in Photoshop can be sampled by KPT's Gradient Designer to use for color values in a gradient design.

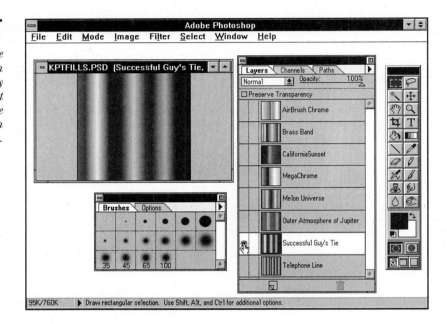

As long as you have the swing of it, you might as well spend a few moments and add the other seven designs in **KPTFILLS.PSD** to the Starter Kit category. Deselect the Eye icon next to the Thumbnail icon on the Layers palette and click in the Eye column by the next design you want to sample. By default, when you click on the Add button in the Gradient Designer, the category is Misc, but you change this to Starter Kit by clicking and dragging down on the Category field.

The Gradient Designer provides a large area in which to store a collection, and if the drop-down list grows too long, you can add up to five total hubs to the filter. Specify a new preset hub in the field above the Category field. After you stock up on sample designs, your last step should be to choose Preferences again from the Options drop-down list and click on the Return to Previous State radio button. Doing this ensures that if you design a gradient you really like, but don't save it immediately, you can save it in a subsequent session with the Gradient Designer.

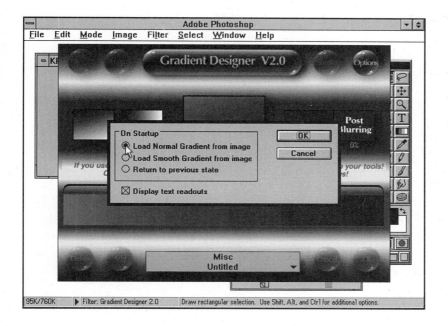

Figure 19.2

Set your startup preferences for the Gradient Designer by choosing Preference from the Options menu.

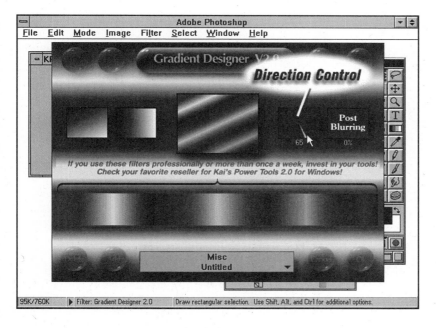

Figure 19.3

Set the angle at which a preset gradient design loads by clicking and dragging in the Direction Control box.

Figure 19.4

Create a category and specify a unique name for a gradient design in this dialog box.

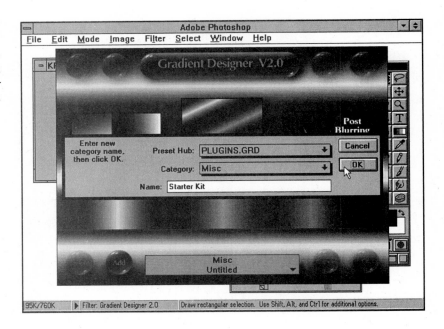

Tip

Unlike many other applications, it's almost impossible to accidentally delete a saved preset in the Gradient Designer. The filter does not enable you to duplicate a name for a preset, and you must load and then click on the Delete button to remove a preset.

On the other hand, it's really easy to *lose* a design you have happened into and failed to save. If you like what you see in the preview window in the Gradient Designer, you should save it immediately. The Gradient Designer uses algorithms that simulate random mutation characteristics found in nature, and a specific pattern is fairly impossible to backtrack and save later. The file in which the presets are stored is compact; the commercial version of the Gradient Designer comes with about 200 presets, and the PLUGIN.GRD file is about 500 KB.

Touring the Rest of the Gradient Designer Interface

Before you learn about the core of the Gradient Designer, the Gradient bar, there are some controls that don't look like controls within the interface that you should examine. The Gradient Designer interface is an absolutely stunning design; it is perhaps the most elegant design ever created for an application, but intuitive, it's not!

The samples in the KPTFILLS.PSD file are all vertical bands because the Gradient Designer samples image colors horizontally, but this does not mean that the gradient

designs you can create in the plug-in all have to be tube-like fills. In fact, the layer called Melon Universe was created in the Gradient Designer as a radial sweep (a cone-like gradient fill); its color scheme repeats several times as it fills a selection area. In the next exercise, you get some hands-on experience with the Algorithm Control and the Looping Control in the filter to see how to shape any selection of colors you want to add as a preset. If you didn't copy the Melon Universe layer in KPTFILLS.PSD, that's okay; you can use the Successful Guy's Tie preset in the following exercise.

Touring the Gradient Designer's Options

Close the KPTFILLS.PSD file when you're through sampling designs. Then press Ctrl(Cmd)+N, or choose **N**ew from the **F**ile menu	Closes the KPTFILLS image and displays Photoshop's New dialog box.

None of Photoshop's plug-in filters can be used unless there's an open image window.

Choose **W**idth: **3** inches, **H**eight: **3** inches, **R**esolution: 72 pixels/inch, RGB color **M**ode, and Contents: **W**hite. Then click on OK	Sets up a new document, Untitled-1, to experiment with.

If you applied one the KPT filters earlier, press Ctrl+Alt+F. If not, choose Fi**l**ter, KPT 2.0 Extensions, then Gradient Designer	Displays the Gradient Designer dialog box.

Although Ctrl(Cmd)+F is the shortcut key combination to the Last Filter Used command, pressing Alt(Option) along with these keys makes the last filter's dialog box appear.

At this point, anything could be displayed in the preview window—possibly the $1\frac{1}{2}$-by-1" rectangle in the center of the interface, depending on what design, if any, you created or sampled last. For this tour, you need to load a preset. We're rooting for Melon Universe here, but if you didn't copy this one, continue with the following steps.

Click and hold on the Preset menu box. Then scroll over to Starter Kit on the pop-up menu and release the mouse button when your cursor is over a saved preset	Loads the Preset. You can see the colors of the preset design in the Gradient bar.

Click and hold on the Algorithm Control menu. Then choose Radial Sweep and release the mouse button (see fig. 19.5)	Displays the preset gradient as a sweep of colors, emanating from a center point.

continues

continued

It is a good idea to reference the figures in this section before performing a move. All options aren't clearly labeled in the Gradient Designer interface, so the figures are annotated to show you exactly where elements are located. Moving horizontally on the controls, from left to right, continue with the exercise.

Click and hold on the Looping Control menu, choose the third row of dots, and release the mouse button	Makes the pattern repeat four times within the gradient design (see fig. 19.6).

Don't count the dots in the row in the Looping Control menu to decide how many times the gradient design repeats. The dots are graphical representations; they are a design element in the interface—each row represents one more loop for the gradient design, from two to eight times, with Repeat Once and Repeat Ten Times clearly marked on the top and bottom of the dot pyramid.

Click and drag in the preview window	Moves the center of the gradient design, as it will appear in the Untitled-1.
Click on Add, click+drag in the field to Starter Kit, then type a fanciful name in the Name field	Adds the fill, with Radial category and scroll sweep, looping repeat, and off-center orientation to your Start Up Category.
Click on OK	Applies the fill to Untitled-1.

Although you usually are instructed to save your file at the end of an exercise, you're under no obligation, artistic or educational, to do so here. In fact, you might want to keep Untitled-1 out on the workspace and use it in the next section, which continues with the Gradient Designer experiment.

The other options on the Looping Control menu are for controlling the appearance of the transitions between gradient colors. The first set of options chooses a waveform. You can have the gradient displayed on the Gradient bar make a left to right transition (Sawtooth: A to B), right to left (Sawtooth: B to A), or from one side of the Gradient bar to the other and then back again (the Triangle options). The Looping Control box shows a grayscale miniature of the option you have chosen when the menu is closed. Additionally, you can choose from four distortion options; this is the second area of the Looping Control menu. Although gradients typically make a linear progression from one color to another, if you want to feature more of one segment of blend than another, choose a method of distortion from the menu.

If you have restored the startup preferences from the "Touring the Gradient Designer's Options" exercise to Return to Previous State, KPT Gradient Designer retains your last-used gradient between Photoshop sessions. The preset menu at the

New Riders Publishing
INSIDE
SERIES

bottom of the interface, however, always starts up with the Misc category and an untitled fill; even though the fill *looks* like the one you used last, the gradient design in the preview window is an untitled, unsaved design that you can modify or use as is.

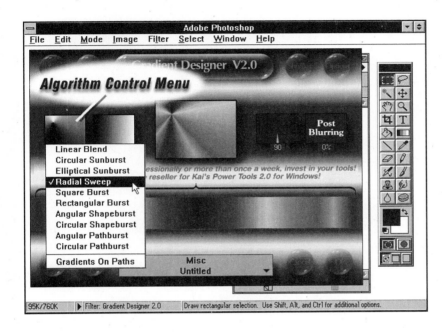

Figure 19.5

Choose from any of 10 configurations for a gradient design from the Algorithm Control menu.

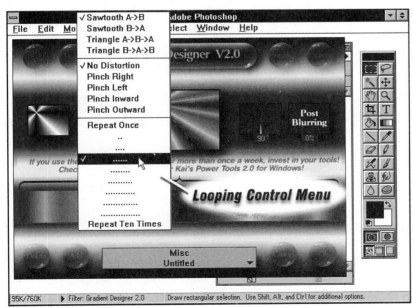

Figure 19.6

Choose a waveform for the gradient, a type of distortion, and the number of times the gradient repeats within a selection area.

So where are your saved preset designs? In figure 19.7, you can see the Starter Kit category and the fly-out presets that the authors created and use. To recall *your* saved preset designs, click and hold on the face of the preset menu, scroll to a category, and release the mouse button when you have chosen the preset you want to use.

Figure 19.7

Load a gradient design preset by clicking and holding on the preset menu, scrolling to the category, and moving the cursor to a preset.

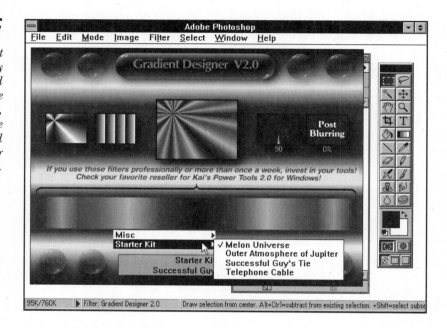

Using the Other Gradient Designer Buttons

The buttons on the Gradient Designer interface light up as you pass your cursor over them. This is not a significant occurrence and you should not attach a hidden meaning to it. Kai simply has designed an interface that's as fun to be in as it is to experiment with. The upper-left button—the calligraphic treatment of "Kai"—reveals the co-engineers of the program when you let your cursor linger over it. Additionally, if you double-click on the button, the interface collapses, and you can see Photoshop's workspace more clearly. Double-clicking on the interface background (not on a button or menu) restores the interface to full size.

The Help button calls the documentation for the trial version of the Gradient Designer (in Windows, the plug-in provides a standard Windows Help file). You can click and drag the title bar to move the interface partially off screen so that you can read the documentation.

The Delete button removes a chosen preset from the active category, and if you delete the only entry in a category, the category disappears from the preset menu. You are prompted after you click on Delete to confirm your decision.

The Shuffle button is turned off by default in the Gradient Designer. If you click and hold on the button for a moment, you see a drop-down menu that lists the parameters you want to Shuffle. If you choose All and then click on the Shuffle button, a random assortment of fills, algorithms, and other parameters for the gradient design are generated. Clicking on Shuffle with different parameters defined is a great way to start a collection of presets; stop at one you like, and then click Add and save it.

The Options drop-down menu has three option areas; you use the bottom set of options to set preferences. Real-time linking also is an option in the bottom Preference area, and you should leave this enabled. *Real-time linking* is a euphemism for the sort of lookup table animation Photoshop provides that makes it possible to see a dynamic preview of an effect or command.

The top area of the Options menu provides modes for the gradient fill, as applied to an image. Most of these modes will seem familiar; their equivalents can be found on the Options palette in Photoshop. Tie Me Up and Tie Me Down, however, have no Photoshop blend mode sound- or look-alike, and these affect the intensity with which gradient colors are applied.

The middle Options area is used to specify a visual proxy of an image to which you want to apply a gradient design, and the proxy image and gradient design both appear in the Composite preview window. You can choose to view the Gradient against a checkerboard, a sample image (the Detail option), or other color and tonal qualities. If you check any of these options, the preview window displays the current fill placed against your choice of background. The background is not added to your current Photoshop image, however. The option to preview a gradient fill against a background is a useful one, because you can define a segment of a gradient design to be transparent; the Gradient Designer uses transparency masks within fills in the same way that Photoshop offers them on image layers.

You can use all these options with others to produce fantastic and original gradient fills in an image. The best option has been saved for last, though; in the next section, you learn where the controls are for color specification. Color is defined in a unique way in the Gradient Designer. By now, why should this come as a surprise?

Using the KPT Gradient Bar

Up until now, your experimentation with KPT's Gradient Designer has been primarily with the shape of a gradient design; color specification has been left out of the discussion for a good reason. If you think that Photoshop's Color Picker is more robust than the Mac or Windows Color Picker, you will realize that the KPT Gradient Designer's control over color specification is a league apart from anything you have worked with. Like the rest of the interface, the Gradient bar and the color-specification bars that hide beneath it are a little mystical, and not at all standard issue. The idiosyncrasies of the interface can grow on you after experimenting for a while in it, however, and you will be able to blend both transparency and color information into a custom-designed fill to produce stunning results in your imaging assignments.

In the next exercise, you are presented with a mock problem—STILL10.PSD is an image with a background that lacks interest. As you can see in figure 19.8, the background is on a separate layer, which makes selecting it a breeze; the image file was created deliberately this way so that you could pay attention to the Gradient Designer and not worry about using Photoshop's tools at all in the exercise. Additionally, the title on the STILL10.PSD image is on a separate layer in case you want to trash it at a future point and experiment with only the photographic elements.

Figure 19.8

STILL10.PSD has good compositional elements, but lacks a sense of motion and lively colors.

Although you've seen several ways in this book to add a background element to an image, occasionally you'll find that something more abstract than a stock photo can direct a viewer's attention to a design in a more compelling way. This exercise is more of an exploration of Kai's color-specification controls than a goal-oriented task, and to succeed at the exercise, you *absolutely* have to take the steps at a leisurely pace. Hang a Do Not Disturb sign on a closed door and consider this assignment an excursion that has no pass or fail grade.

Using the Full Capabilities of the Gradient Designer

Open the STILL10.PSD image from the CHAP19 subdirectory of the Bonus CD

This is the sample image to which you'll add a gradient design.

Click on the Background title on the Layers palette	Ensures that the Background layer is the target layer for the assignment.
Press Ctrl+Alt+F (Macintosh: Cmd+Option+F)	Shortcut to display the dialog box of the last filter used.

This shortcut won't display the Gradient Designer if you haven't done the previous exercises, or if you chose a different filter between the last exercise and this one. To choose this filter, choose Filter, KPT 2.0 Extensions, and then Gradient Designer 2.0.

Click and drag the right side of the bracket above the Gradient bar all the way to the right	This is the Selection bar, and it determines how much of a total gradient design is assigned a particular color.
Click and drag the left side of the bracket all the way to the left of the Gradient bar	Specifies that the entire gradient design now is defined to receive color values.
Click and hold on the Gradient bar. Then press Alt(Option), drag the cursor down to the red part of the spectrum on the Color bar, and release the mouse button (see fig. 19.9)	Fills the area of the gradient marked by the Selection bar with flat color and no transitional colors.

As you experiment with the Gradient Designer, it's helpful to think of a gradient design as a number of foreground fills added to a background color. You usually would want to press and hold Alt while setting your first color, but after the background is set, don't use the Alt(Option) key combination; Alt(Option) prevents blending. The Gradient bar contains the background color red right now, and by moving and resizing the Selection bar, you specify a segment of the overall gradient background to which you add a foreground color, or colors. The Gradient Designer then makes a transitional fill based on the foreground and background values, with the center of the Selection bar indicating the location of the foreground color you added to the gradient. Although you will not use a transparent color in the fill for the STILL10 background, try this feature out next.

Click and drag the right side of the Selection bar so that it vertically aligns with the right side of the Direction Control menu	Specifies the limit for the right side of the new foreground color you'll select.
Click and drag the left side of the Selection bar so that it vertically aligns with the left side of the Looping Control menu	Specifies the left limit of a new foreground color you'll add to the current background color.

continues

continued

Choose Linear Blend from the Algorithm Control menu, and then choose Repeat once from the Looping Control menu	Sets default values for the gradient design; makes the colors you'll select next appear in a more straightforward way in the Preview window.
Click and hold on the Gradient bar, scroll down to the Alpha Bar, and release the mouse button when the Opacity (indicated above the Color bar) is reading about 60	The Gradient bar blends a transparency into the background red (see fig 19.10).
Click and hold on the Gradient bar, scroll down to the Color bar, and then release the mouse button when you're over a yellow-orange area	The Gradient bar blends this color into the background red. This is the design you'll modify further and use for the STILL10 background layer.
Choose Circular Sunburst from the Algorithm Control menu. Then choose the fourth menu item in the Number of Repeats field in the Looping Control menu	Creates a repeat pattern from the color arrangement presently displayed on the Gradient bar.

The Selection bar is for defining color segments within the Gradient bar. The entire length of the Gradient bar, however, is used as a fill for the current open image in Photoshop.

Click and drag inside the preview window	Moves the center of the Circular Starburst design (see fig. 19.11). For this assignment, you can position the center anywhere—this is an experiment. There's no right or wrong positioning.
Place your cursor within the segment of the Gradient bar marked by the Selection bar. Then press Alt (Option) and click and drag to the left	Moves the foreground center of the gradient within the Selection bar; creating a beautiful effect (see fig. 19.12).
Click on Add and name and save the design to your Starter Kit collection; choose OK	The Gradient Designer remembers the colors, number of repeats, and shape of the gradient design.
Click on OK	Applies the gradient design to the background of STILL10.PSD.

Choose Sa<u>v</u>e As from the <u>F</u>ile menu, and save the image to your hard disk	Saves your work in the PSD format.
Press Ctrl(Cmd)+W, or choose <u>C</u>lose from the <u>F</u>ile menu	Closes the active image window.

Tip

The Eyedropper cursor that you use in the Gradient Designer to select foreground colors can sample a color from anywhere on-screen; you're not limited to the Color bar. If you click and drag the title bar of the Gradient Designer so that you can see Photoshop's workspace and an active image, for example, you can release the mouse button over the image and add a color to a segment of the Gradient bar.

Although Macintosh users always have a clear view of the desktop, Windows users usually maximize an application window so that the desktop is hidden. If you do not maximize Photoshop's window upon startup, you also can sample wallpaper and icon colors when in the Gradient Designer.

In figure 19.13, you can see the finished design. The 10-cent dessert has more overall appeal and the viewer's eye is drawn to the center of the almost hypnotic gradient fill you've created. This is a splashy example of a possible fill. You can create muted tones and achieve geometrically complex fills with the Gradient Designer that would otherwise take an eternity with Photoshop's Gradient tool.

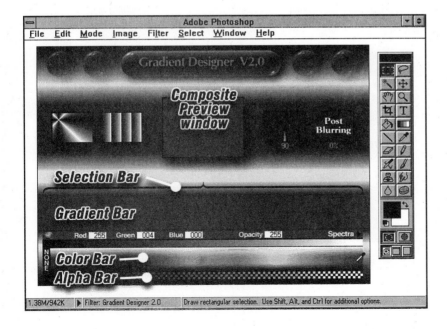

Figure 19.9

Choose a segment of the Gradient bar with the Selection bar and then scroll to a color you want to add.

Figure 19.10

You can make a partially transparent segment of the overall gradient design.

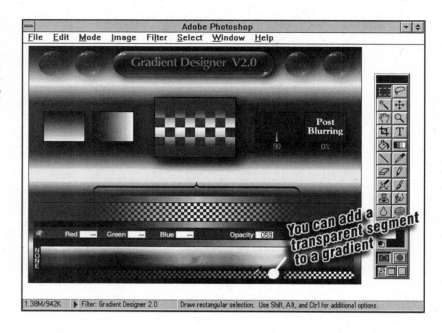

Figure 19.11

Clicking and dragging inside the preview window changes the center of Algorithm fills that have a center, like the Circular Sunburst.

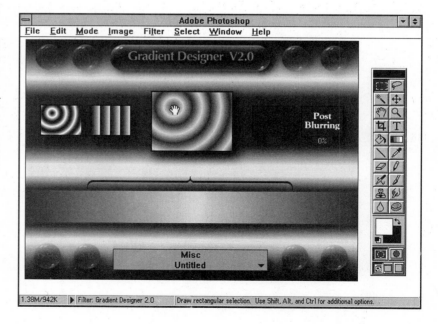

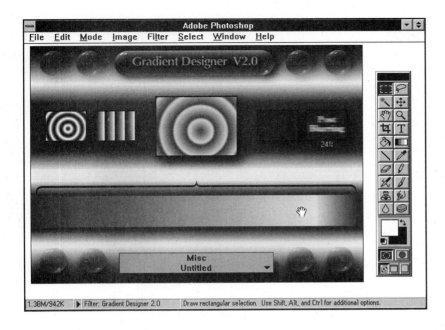

Figure 19.12

Pressing Alt (Option) while clicking and dragging within a segment defined by the Selection bar moves the center color within the design.

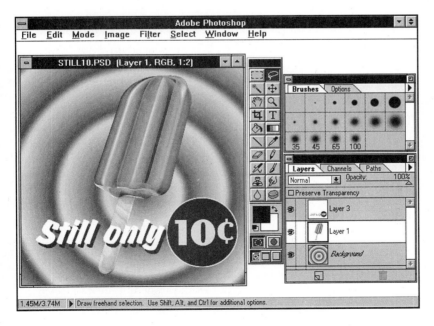

Figure 19.13

You can create sumptuous, wild, or subtle complex fills with the KPT Gradient Designer filter sampler version.

Accessing Extended Functions of the Gradient Designer

Have you fully explored the potential of the KPT Gradient Designer yet? Not quite, but due to the space limitations of this book, we must leave you to further independent experimentation. As you practice, keep these keyboard commands in mind to extend the functionality of the tools and commands you've learned so far:

◆ Press Ctrl(Cmd)+I to create the color opposite the gradient currently defined by the Selection bar.

◆ Press Ctrl(Cmd)+C to copy a segment of a current gradient design. This is an internal call, and you can't actually see a segment of gradient blend if you then go to the system clipboard, but you then can create or load another gradient preset and press Ctrl+V to paste the copied segment into another gradient.

◆ Press Ctrl(Cmd)+F to rotate the segment of gradient defined by the Selection bar by 180°.

◆ Clicking and dragging the top of the Selection bar moves the bar without resizing it.

◆ You can choose to use the system Color Picker instead of the Color bar by clicking on the spectrum circle to the left of the Color bar.

◆ You can choose a different color model for the Color bar. Click and hold on the spectrum title to the right of the Color bar to access a menu of eight color models, including a CMYK model.

◆ Press the spacebar before choosing KPT Gradient Designer to make the background workspace black. The current image window will be the only visual element behind the Gradient Designer interface when you do this.

◆ Scroll to None (on the left of the Color bar) if you want to define a completely transparent segment within your gradient design.

By purchasing the commercial version of Kai's Power Tools 2.0, you receive three other modules that are a tightly integrated set of interfaces for creating gradients along paths, textures, and fractal patterns. You can define a gradient fill and then use it to create a stroked path in an image, or you can sample the colors in a texture for use as a gradient design. Be sure to look at the KPT2READ.TXT file in the KPT subdirectory for a special offer for *Inside Adobe Photoshop 3* readers.

After reading this section, you've learned that your work can be unique and fresh when you use a combination of commands to create a gradient design. KPT is criticized unfairly sometimes for being an instant special-effects filter, but as you now can see, your individual taste and artistic talent always are necessary ingredients to produce the best work with a tool. You just need to understand how the tool works.

Using the KPT Filters

Unlike the Gradient Designer extension, there are also one-step KPT filters included on the Bonus CD that don't feature a user interface. The following sections describe what each filter does and why you might want to use it.

Glass Lens

The Glass Lens filter is used in Chapter 20, "Mixed Media and Photoshop," to produce a convex image area that looks like a wristwatch face. This filter comes in three types: Bright, Normal, and Soft. (The Macintosh sampler on the Bonus CD features the Normal filter.)

The Glass Lens filter makes a selection area appear to bump outward; detail within the selection is distorted to suggest a view through a fish-eye lens. A highlight appears within a selection that Glass Lens is applied to, and by default, this highlight is at 11 o'clock. You can specify the location of the highlight by pressing and holding a number key and choosing Glass Lens from the Filter menu. The most visually intuitive way to set the highlight position is to think of the keypad on your keyboard as compass directions. For example, pressing 1 before choosing the filter produces a highlight in the lower left of the Glass Lens sphere, and pressing 3 creates an eastern highlight.

By creating a partial selection area in an image, you can make multiple passes of the Glass Lens effect, each time positioning the highlight in a different area. To create a partial selection, save a selection to an Alpha channel, use the Channels palette to display the selection information, and use the Brightness/Contrast dialog box to lighten the channel (you access this dialog box by pressing Ctrl(Cmd)+B). Then move back to the RGB view of the image, load the selection by pressing Alt (or Option for the Macintosh) and clicking on the thumbnail icon for the saved selection. Then use the Glass Lens effect.

Like many third-party filters, a selection in an image must have some opaque pixels to work with. In other words, don't use the Gradient Designer or the Glass Lens filter on a section of a layer that is completely transparent.

Hue Protected Noise

Although the Hue Protected Noise filter can produce some artistically pleasing results, it also serves a valuable function in pre-press work. As explained in Chapter 23, "Personal Printing Basics," *PostScript* is a page descriptor language that laser printers and high-end imagesetters use to convert continuous tone information in an image into halftone cells on a printed page. Part of the PostScript language limits the number of unique colors in a gradient fill to 255 steps of solid colors. You almost never see the banding of a gradient on-screen, because your monitor is capable of a wider range of color expression than PostScript printing, but that's why you have a dithering option on the Gradient Options palette in Photoshop. *Dithering* is Photoshop's method for breaking up visible demarcations of solid color bands in a fill that exceeds 255 unique color steps.

The Hue Protected Noise filter, on the other hand, can break up any banding patterns in a gradient fill in a different way. Random pixels are dispersed throughout a selection area (or entire image) in which the color content—the noise's hue—is very similar to the color values found in the selected image: no more than about 40 color values off. Hue Protected Noise works well with CMYK mode images, and you can control the intensity of the Hue Protected Noise by using the keyboard number keys: 1 corresponds to 10 percent noise added to an image and 0 corresponds to 100 percent. By default, Hue Protected Noise operates at about 80 percent.

Pixel Storm, Breeze, and Wind

The "meteorological" filters featured on the Bonus CD disperse pixels in a selection area at random over the entire selection area. This process produces different effects according to what image content is selected when you apply any of this trio of KPT filters. You easily can achieve an effect that looks like pebbled glass by using the Pixel Storm's default setting, and you can vary the intensity of the effect by pressing number keys prior to choosing the effect: 0 represents the greatest amount of Pixel Storm, and 1 represents the mildest application.

Sharpen Intensity

The Sharpen Intensity filter brightens the colors in an image without driving the color values out of the printable gamut when working with a CMYK mode image. This filter is a terrific pre-press tool for adding a little life to the typically dull process printing colors an image becomes when rendered with a combination of opaque pigments. Use the number keys on the keyboard to increase or decrease the amount of Sharpen Intensity directly before choosing this filter: 0 equals the greatest amount and 1 represents the least amount of the effect.

You can create a highly posterized effect from an original image by repeatedly using the Sharpen Intensity filter on the same image.

Creating Effects Worthy of an Art Gallery

Aldus Corporation became a subsidiary of Adobe Systems in the fall of 1994, and brought with them *gallery effects*—plug-in filters that transform images (particularly photographic ones) into different types of paintings. Three working, fully functional Gallery Effects filters are on the Adobe Photoshop Deluxe CD-ROM. In this section, you'll want to close Photoshop, take the Inside Photoshop Bonus CD out of your CD-ROM drive for a moment, and load the Gallery Effects plug-ins into Photoshop's PLUGINS directory (folder). Be sure to put the Bonus CD back into the drive, because you'll use the Gallery Effects filters with exercise images contained on the Bonus CD.

To load the filters, follow these steps:

◆ **Windows users:** Close Photoshop and then load the Adobe Photoshop Deluxe CD-ROM. Then, from File Manager, go to GOODIES, 3RDPARTY, and choose GEFFECTS. Copy the GE1SAMPL.8BF, GE2SAMP1.8BF, and GE2SAMP3.8BF files to Photoshop's PLUGINS directory on your hard disk, and copy the files with the HLP extension to the PLUGINS directory, too. Some programs call Help files from the Windows subdirectory, but not the Gallery Effects filters.

Additionally, you might already have the MSVIDEO.DLL in WINDOWS\SYSTEM from another application. Check and see if it's there; if not, copy the MSVIDEO.DLL file in the GEFFECTS subdirectory to WINDOWS\SYSTEM on your hard disk.

◆ **Macintosh users:** Click and drag all filters from the Gallery Effects folder into the Adobe Photoshop plug-ins folder.

Insert the Bonus CD back into your CD-ROM drive and restart Photoshop; you're in business to explore gallery effects in the exercises that follow.

Using the Watercolor Filter

The Watercolor filter is best used with photographic images that do not contain many dark areas. Lightly colored portrait images and scenes of nature work quite well with the Watercolor gallery effect to produce a version of an original image that looks like dried watercolors. Edge detail in images is enhanced to give the appearance of concentrations of pigment surrounding image edges. Image detail is lost in the Watercolor effect, but you should think of the effects as a translation of image data, usually to a very eye-pleasing one. The Watercolor gallery effect can take a bland photograph (you use one in the next exercise) and add visual interest.

In the next exercise, you become familiar with the settings and the interface of the Watercolor gallery effect, and you see how images can be stylized in a painterly fashion. To create a watercolor even if you don't paint, work through this exercise.

Creating a Watercolor Painting

Open the BRANCHES.TIF image from the CHAP19 subdirectory (folder) of the Bonus CD	This is a boring image of fall that you'll enhance through the use of the Watercolor filter.
Choose Filter, Gallery Effects: Classic Art, and then GE Watercolor Sampler	Displays the Effect Settings dialog box.

Windows users will get the Help file for the Watercolor filter pop up every time the filter is chosen. It is not a user-defined option to hide the Help window on startup of the filter, so simply double-click on the Control menu button on the upper left of the window to close it.

Click and drag the floating frame in the preview window, and then click on the **P**review button	The preview area displays a Before and After image of the area the floating frame marks in the preview window.
Click and drag the Brush Detail slider to **9**	Increases the detail with which the Watercolor filter will convert the image: 1 produces blobs, while 14 is a Watercolor effect so faithful to the original image detail that it doesn't look like a watercolor.
Click and drag the Shadow Intensity slider to **0**	Turns off the option. The image displays enough shadow areas in its original state without additional shadows.
Click and drag the Texture slider to **1** (see fig. 19.14)	Specifies the roughness with which the filter renders a watercolor. 1 is the lowest setting, 3 is the highest. A setting of 1 creates a smooth painting.
Click on Sa**v**e As, type **BRANCHES** in the dialog box, and click on **A**pply	Saves the settings you've made in case you have an image with similar detail to which you want to apply similar Watercolor effects.
Click on OK, then wait a while	Applies the Watercolor effect (see fig. 19.15).
Choose Sa**v**e As from the **F**ile menu. Then save the image to your hard disk (choose the TIFF format from the Save File as Format **T**ype drop-down list)	Saves your work to the hard disk.

Press Ctrl(Cmd)+W. Or choose **C**lose from the **F**ile menu	Closes the active image window.

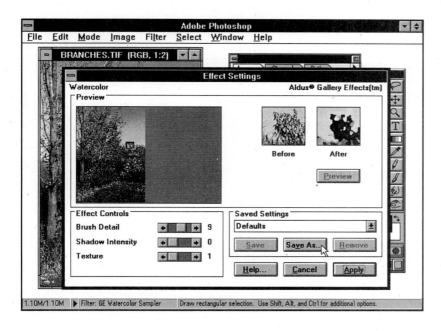

Figure 19.14

You can save settings you've defined in the Effect Settings dialog box for the Watercolor effect.

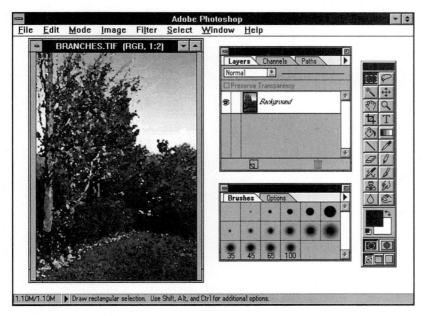

Figure 19.15

The Watercolor gallery effect creates concentrated areas of color and smooth washes from original image information.

The Watercolor gallery effect can get you out of a bind when the source images for a publication, for example, are unacceptable in their original state. Viewers don't question abstract representations of images nearly as much as a flawed photographic image. And if you convert a watercolor image to grayscale mode, you might be surprised at how well the image renders to a low-resolution laser printer. The Watercolor gallery effect does not add color to the image you apply it to; it samples and filters original image colors.

Using the Note Paper Filter

Unlike the Watercolor effect, the Note Paper effect uses the current foreground and background colors (as seen on the toolbox) in Photoshop to create a dimensional effect that simulates real, embossed note paper. Darker image areas become the "holes" in a top layer of note paper, while lighter image areas represent the top sheet.

The Note Paper effect is best used with simple black-and-white illustrations; you can quickly create dimensional, colored work from a grayscale AI or EPS imported image. In the next exercise, you use the CACTUS.PSD image—a flat, monochrome illustration—with the Note Paper plug-in to create a more lively logo for a fictitious chili parlor. PSD, Targa, TIFF, and other images that have RGB color capability and grayscale mode images can be used with the Note Paper filter, although you'll get dismal results with grayscale, because Note Paper depends on color. Here's how to make some sample stationery using the Gallery Effects, Volume 2 sampler.

Creating a Note Paper Effect

Open the CACTUS.PSD image from the CHAP19 subdirectory (folder) of the Bonus CD	This is a black-and-white illustration saved in RGB color mode that you'll use with the Note Paper filter.
Press F6 (Macintosh: press F10) if the Picker palette isn't already on-screen	Displays the Picker palette.
Click on the foreground, then click and drag in the Color bar to define a deep turquoise; choose OK	Sets the color for the darker color box areas of the CACTUS.PSD design. These areas will show through the holes in the textured color areas that represent the top page of note paper.
Click on the background color box on the Picker palette, then click on an orange-brown area of the Color bar; choose OK	Defines the color for the lighter image areas of CACTUS.PSD. (see fig. 19.16).

Although the Note Paper filter always embosses the darker areas of a design to make them appear as though they peek through holes in the top sheet of note paper, the current foreground color always is assigned to the darker areas. You, therefore, are about to produce a turquoise cactus and lettering; the background, or top sheet of note paper, will be desert colored.

Choose Filter, Gallery Effects: Volume 2, and then GE Note Paper Sampler	Displays the Effect Settings dialog box.
Click and drag the floating frame in the preview window to an area of the lettering in the image. Then click on **P**review	Displays the present and proposed changes to the image in the Before and After windows.
Click and drag the Image Balance slider to **31**; then click on **P**review (see fig. 19.17)	Makes more of the image detail appear through the "holes" in the desert-colored image areas. Clicking and dragging to a lower Image Balance value makes less of the image design appear through the top sheet of desert-colored paper.
Click and drag the Graininess slider to **10**	Adds dark pixels to the foreground and background colors in the image, simulating a paper texture.
Click and drag the Relief slider to **14**	Controls the amount of embossing of the image.

The Graininess controls are affected by the Relief controls. If you specify a great deal of grain, for example, the Relief controls emboss the grain, and you can achieve interesting and sometimes ugly results by specifying high values for both these options.

Click on Apply	Applies the effect.
Double-click on the Zoom tool	Gives you a close-up, 1:1 viewing resolution of CACTUS.PSD, so that you can better examine the Note Paper filter's effect (see fig. 19.18).
Choose Sa**v**e As from the **F**ile menu, then save the image to your hard disk	Saves your work to your hard disk.
Press Ctrl(Cmd)+W, or choose **C**lose from the **F**ile menu	Closes the active image window.

Figure 19.16

Choose a foreground and background color before you choose the Note Paper filter.

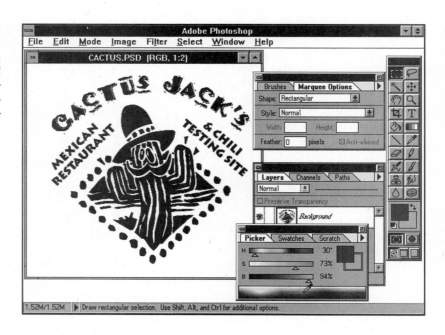

Figure 19.17

You control the amount of background paper showing through the foreground sheet, graininess, and emboss amount in the Effect Settings dialog box.

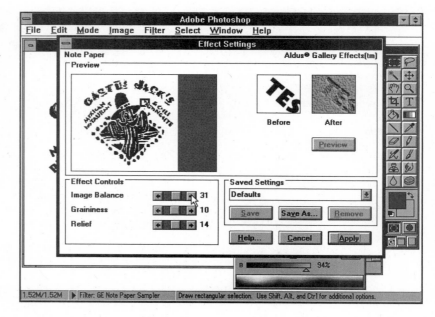

Figure 19.18

The Note Paper gallery effect makes quick work of dimension-alizing and coloring a black-and-white design.

Any RGB color or grayscale mode image is a candidate for the Note Paper filter, but original image information is modified severely with this filter, so don't expect a glorious sunset photo to contain much recognizable detail if this is your target image. You might want to try copying an image to a layer, changing the opacity of the layer to less than 50 percent, and then applying the Note Paper filter to the background image. This procedure enables you to blend original details with filtered information. Also, try using the filter more than once on the same image; you'll get a design that looks like it was created from barnacles.

Using the Plastic Wrap Filter

The Plastic Wrap filter creates highlights on an image's surface, much like those you see when a head of lettuce or other vegetable is tightly wrapped in clear plastic. The Plastic Wrap filter uses a combination of embossing and highlighting that can be used with a combination of other filters you have to produce effects ranging from a shiny stamped look to the hand-edited Polaroids that once served as the introduction to NBC's *Saturday Night Live.*

In the next exercise, you see how to use the Plastic Wrap effect with a graphic that was created in Fractal Design Painter with some lettering and a picture (or *pi*) font. You see how a dimensional graphic can be given a photographic feel by tweaking the controls in the Plastic Wrap's Effect Settings dialog box.

Using the Plastic Wrap Filter

Open the SEALED.PSD image from the CHAP19 subdirectory (folder) of the Bonus CD	You'll use this graphic in this exercise.
On the Channels palette, click and drag channel #4 into the Trash icon	This Alpha channel describes the black foreground areas. It's used in an exercise that follows, but you don't need it in this exercise.
Choose Filter, Gallery Effects: Volume 3, and then GE Plastic Wrap Sampler	Displays the Effect Settings dialog box.
Click and drag the floating frame in the preview window to an area of the lettering in the image. Then click on **P**review	Displays the present and proposed changes to the image in the Before and After windows.
Click and drag the Highlight Strength slider to **16**, and then click on the **P**review button	Increases the size and brightness of highlights in the image.
Click and drag the Detail slider to about **4**, and then click on the **P**review button	Higher Detail values result in more original image detail being used in the highlight areas.

Because the floating frame in the preview window is so small, you might want to reposition the frame after making a slider adjustment, and then click on Preview to see how various image areas are affected by the settings, as seen in figure 19.19. The small proxy view of the active image window is an inconvenience, but it means that the preview can redraw very quickly while in the Effect Settings dialog box.

Click and drag the Smoothness slider to **6**	Makes the surface of the plastic wrap above the image smoother, as opposed to wrinkled, suggesting that a fastidious grocer has performed the work on the image.
Click on Sa**v**e As and name the saved settings Freshness. Then click on **S**ave	This is actually a very good setting for graphics that have a great deal of contrast. Save this setting to recall for use with your own work.
Click on **A**pply	Applies the effect.
Choose Sa**v**e As from the **F**ile menu, and then save the image as ORANGES.PSD to your hard disk	Saves your work to hard disk.

Open the SEALED.PSD image from the Bonus CD again and compare the original to the Plastic Wrap image, as shown in figure 19.20.

Close both images and exit Photoshop   You'll need to load a new filter for the upcoming exercise.

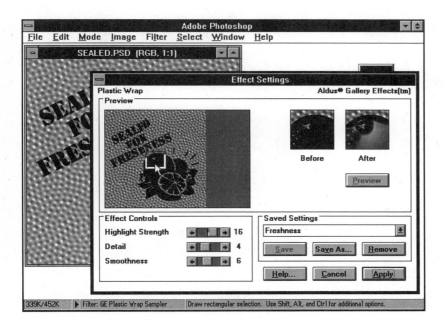

Figure 19.19

You can set the amount of Plastic Wrap effect and the amount of highlight in the image through the Effect Settings dialog box.

Exploring Alien Skin Software's Drop Shadow Filter

Like Kai's Power Tools, Alien Skin Software markets a commercial product known as *Black Box* that is a suite of filters you can use in Photoshop. A fully functional copy of the Drop Shadow filter is one of the six filters in the complete suite, and it's on the Bonus CD. To load the filter for the next exercise, follow these instructions:

◆ **Windows users:** Go to the BLAKBOX subdirectory of the Bonus CD, and copy the DROP.8BF file into Photoshop's PLUGINS directory on your hard disk. You also might want to check out the sample images in this directory, which illustrate some of the other Black Box filters. These images are marked with the JPG file extension, and you can view them in Photoshop by choosing **O**pen from the **F**ile menu.

◆ **Macintosh users:** Copy the Drop Shadow folder from the BLAKBOX folder on the Bonus CD that came with this book into Photoshop's PLUGINS folder. The sample images in this folder are of the effects you can create with the commercial version of Alien Skin's Black Box.

Restart Photoshop; next you see what type of enhancements you can make using a Drop Shadow filter.

Creating a "Punch Out" Graphic

Usually, you want to add a drop shadow to a foreground image area to make it stand off the page, as you learned in Chapter 21, "Advanced Type Usage and Presentations." However, Alien Skin Software's Drop Shadow filter produces such a convincingly realistic shadow effect on a selected image area that it can sometimes serve as the main element in a design. To give you a better idea of the creative potential of the Drop Shadow filter, you use the SEALED.PSD image from the Bonus CD again in the next exercise. A saved selection has been placed in an Alpha channel of this image, so you don't need to perform any selection work in the exercise that follows. Instead, you concentrate on using the Gradient fill tool with sampled colors from the SEALED image to make it blend into the orange-skin background. The graphic in the image will be impossible to see, then, right? Not when you apply a Drop Shadow effect to the loaded selection of the graphic; you'll see a suggestion of the foreground graphic "punched out" of the background image and, if done correctly, the graphic portion will be completely legible.

Using the Drop Shadow Filter

Open the SEALED.PSD image from the CHAP19 subdirectory of the Bonus CD

This is the image with an Alpha channel in it that describes the foreground black in the image.

Press Alt(Option) while clicking on the channel #4 thumbnail on the Channels palette

Loads the selection of the oranges and lettering.

Press **D** (**D**efault Colors icon), then press **X** (Switch Colors icon)

Makes your current foreground color white and your background color black.

Press **I** (Eyedropper tool). Then press Alt (Option) and click on an area of orange on the SEALED.PSD image

Samples a new background color: orange.

Double-click on the Gradient tool, and then set the Options palette to **100%** Opacity, Normal mode, Foreground to Background Style, and Radial Type

Specifies that you want to create a Radial type fill, in which the colors make a concentric transition from white to orange.

Click and drag from the word "for" in the SEALED.PSD image to the center of the half orange

Creates a gradient fill (see fig.19.21).

continues

Choose Filter, Alien Skin, then Drop Shadow	Displays a reminder of the filter's manufacturer, with instructions on ordering the retail version.
Wait about five seconds, and then click on the advertisement screen	Displays the Drop Shadow filter's interface (see fig. 19.22).

If you purchase the complete suite of Black Box filters from Alien Skin software, the advertisement screen doesn't appear each time you use the filter—which is pretty good incentive if you find that you have a need for this filter in your work. You have an attractive set of options in this dialog box, which are explained after the exercise. For now, accept the default settings and continue.

Click on OK	Applies the Drop Shadow effect and deselects the selection marquee you loaded earlier (see fig. 19.23).
Choose Save As from the File menu. Then save the image as SHADOW.PSD to your hard disk	Saves your work to the hard disk.

Figure 19.21

Create a gradient fill that removes the black foreground details from the SEALED.PSD image.

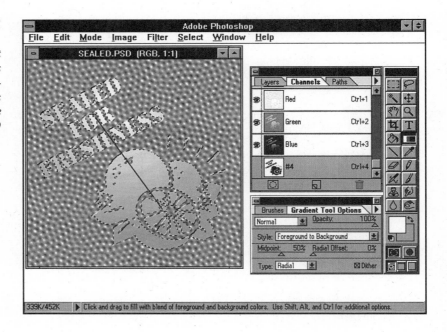

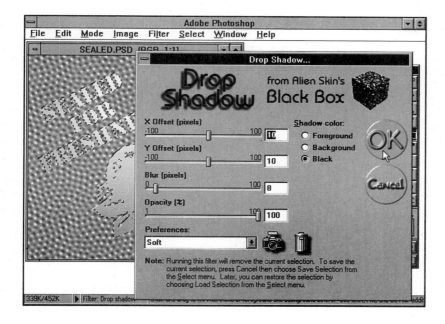

Figure 19.22

The Drop Shadow dialog box provides controls for creating a shadow, as well as some presets in the Preferences list.

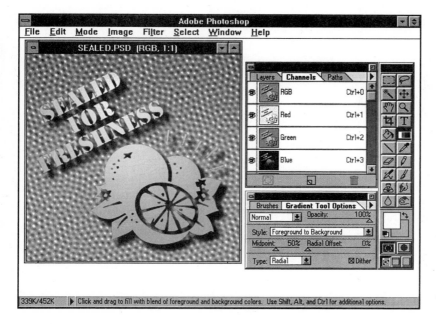

Figure 19.23

A design with visual detail consisting of a shadow, but no real foreground element.

Congratulations on your study in use of negative space! The Drop Shadow effect tends to "flatten" any perspective a selection has in relation to other image areas, but the effect is photorealistic and definitely can perk up a headline. If you want to imitate *PC Magazine*'s tradition of adding a Gaussian Blur drop shadow to headlines, Alien Skin Software's filter is your ticket to quick, effortless, elegant shadows.

You'll also note that part of the Drop Shadow effect's process deselects the selection marquee in the image, so only use this filter after you have saved a selection you've worked on.

You aren't obliged to always create black drop shadows; you also do not have to let the filter completely hide the areas of the image it covers. The following is a brief list of options you can set in the Drop Shadow interface:

◆ The X Offset slider controls the horizontal placement of the shadow. Positive values place the shadow to the right, and negative slider values place the shadow to the left.

◆ The Y Offset slider controls the vertical placement of the shadow. Positive values equal a downward direction, and negative values move the shadow upward.

◆ The Blur slider controls how much spread you want to add to the shadow, and the Opacity slider controls how much original image detail you can see in the shadow area after it's applied.

◆ The Camera icon saves a setting you originated; you're prompted to give the setting a unique name, and the custom shadow can be recalled for future use.

◆ The Drop Shadow filter comes with eight preset shadows, and you can load them by clicking on the Preferences drop-down list. Additionally, you can access any custom filters you saved by choosing them from the Preferences list.

◆ Click on the Trash icon when you want to delete a current preset shadow from the Preferences list.

◆ In the **S**hadow color field, you can pick from the current background or foreground colors in Photoshop as the color of the drop shadow effect. You can make some fascinating neon effects by choosing a color other than default black, but you must specify a color before calling the Drop Shadow filter.

Alien Skin Software's Drop Shadow filter is fun to use, and it automates a procedure described in Chapter 22, "Virtual Reality: The Ingredients of Dreamwork," for manually creating shadows. The authors use both the manual and the filter technique for creating shadows, and if you're in a rush with an assignment, the Drop Shadow filter can be invaluable.

New Riders Publishing
INSIDE SERIES

Using PIXAR's One Twenty-Eight Filter

The Pixar One Twenty-Eight filter is a tiling engine for creating repeating sampled images in a selection area in an image. The uniqueness of the One Twenty-Eight filter however, isn't that it can tile an image (Photoshop can do this), but that the filter comes with two free samples of Pixar photographic seamless tiling creations. Blue Lattice and Woven Flowers are TIF images that have been carefully edited so that traces of image edge are undetectable. Additionally, these images are on the Bonus CD in two resolutions, so you can create a background with One Twenty-Eight that will scale perfectly to any size image. Also, you can use your own TIF (or Windows BMP) image in the One Twenty-Eight interface to create a tiled pattern. For more information about creating a stock image that seamlessly tiles, see Chapter 18, "Photoshop's Native Filters."

Macintosh and Windows Photoshop users can install the Pixar One Twenty-Eight by following these directions:

◆ **Windows users:** Quit Photoshop and then copy the PIXAR128.8BF file into Photoshop's PLUGINS subdirectory from the PIXAR128 subdirectory on the Bonus CD. You'll see two subdirectories called HIRES and LOWRES in the PIXAR directory. Both these subdirectories contain the same file names for low- and high-resolution lattice and flowers patterns. If you want to avail yourself of both in your Photoshop work, create a subdirectory on your hard disk and copy the low-resolution files there. Then copy the high-resolution image files to the Photoshop PLUGINS directory.

◆ **Macintosh users:** Copy the Pixar One Twenty-Eight plug-in from the PIXAR128 directory on the Bonus CD into the Photoshop PLUGINS folder on your desktop, along with the image files. Your system supports long file names and can point out the difference between the low- and high-resolution images.

After you copy the image files and the filter program, you're ready to start the next exercise.

Creating an Instant Background

GORDGARD.PSD, an image on the Bonus CD, features a nice arrangement of flowers, and would in fact make a nice graphic for a nursery. The picture was taken in front of a public park, however, and most of the background detail in this image definitely detracts from its general appeal. Given a situation like this, you can select the foreground elements of interest and transplant them, or you can use the One Twenty-Eight filter to generate a pleasant supporting background as a replacement. In the next exercise, you follow the latter procedure, and in the process you see how to create a fresh image from only a fraction of the original image content. Again, this document has been set up so that you don't have to perform any selection work; instead, focus on the magic this filter can bring to your work.

Creating a Background Image

Open the GORDGARD.PSD image from the CHAP19 subdirectory (folder) Bonus CD	This is a multilayer image with a saved selection you use to complete this assignment.
Press Alt (Option) and click on the channel #4 thumbnail on the Channels palette (see fig. 19.24)	Places a selection marquee around the background. The flowers are masked.
Choose Filters, PIXAR128, then Textures	Displays the Pixar One Twenty-Eight dialog box.
In the **D**irectories field, choose the PLUGINS location where you placed the TIFF image files	The file names appear to the left of the **D**irectories box.

Because One Twenty-Eight is designed for both Mac and Windows, Windows users have a choice of the dialog box displaying DOS names for the files, or the long names encoded into the header of each of the two images. Clicking on Long Names sorts the two files out of your list of other filters very quickly.

Click on Blue Lattice, and check the **P**review check box	Selects the Blue Lattice image and displays a small sample image in the preview window.
Click on the Size-to drop-down list, and then choose 256×256	Chooses a resolution for the blue lattice pattern that will complement the flowers with an appropriate scale (see fig. 19.25, and see following tip).
Click on **O**pen	Applies the blue lattice design as a fill in the selected image area.
Press Ctrl (Cmd)+D, or choose **N**one from the **S**elect menu; then click on the column above the background Eye icon on the Layers palette	Deselects the current selection, and a logo appears on layer 1 to complete the design (see fig. 19.26).
Choose Flatten Image from the Layers palette drop-down list. Then click and drag the channel #4 title on the Channels palette into the Trash icon	Flattens the image and decreases the file size.
Choose Sa**v**e As from the **F**ile menu, and save the image as GORDGARD. TIF (choose the TIFF format from the Save File as For-mat **T**ype drop-down list) to your hard disk	Saves your work up to this point.

Figure 19.24

Press Alt (Option) while clicking on the Channel #4 icon on the Channels palette to load the selection of the background only.

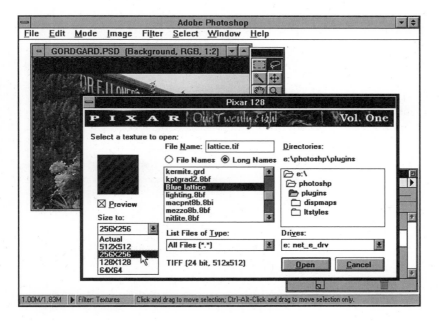

Figure 19.25

Choose the file you want to fill the selection area with, and choose a resolution that scales nicely with other image elements.

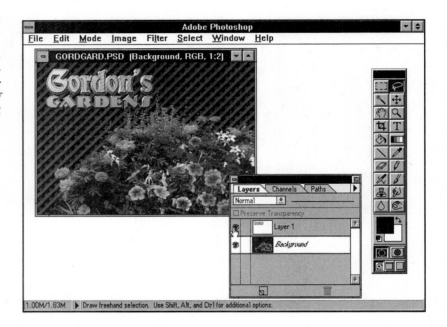

Figure 19.26

A finished design can look outstanding by using a combination of photographic and digital media.

Tip The resolution of a Pixar One Twenty-Eight image has a direct impact on how large it looks when filling a selected area. It is therefore a good idea to measure the size of the selection before entering the 128 dialog box. You can use the Info palette to measure the dimensions of a selection (choose pixels from the XY field by clicking and holding on the Plus icon), or you can press Alt(Option) and click on the Document size box to see the overall dimensions of an image window. In Photoshop for Windows, the Document size box is on the left of the status bar; on the Macintosh, it's on the bottom left of an image window.

By choosing a Size To option that's similar in size to a selection or an entire image, you can scale the visual content of a 128 to create backgrounds that appear quite realistic.

The commercial version of Pixar One Twenty-Eight contains 128 textures, from wood to stone, with many fascinating photographic patterns to suit most design needs. Later in this chapter, you see how an image was created entirely through the use of 128 and another filter.

The "surprise" logo that appeared at the end of the *Creating a Background Image* exercise is a product of another PIXAR imaging program: Pixar Typestry. This was created to show you how a finished design can be completed with a minimum of stock photography. A special edition of Typestry is on the Bonus CD, and you can see

examples of how the application can be used in Chapter 22, "Virtual Reality: The Ingredients of Dreamwork." Check out the back of this book to learn how to locate and install the limited version of Typestry on your hard disk.

Using the Andromeda Software Sampler

Andromeda Software has worked closely with Adobe Systems in the past to help design such programs as Adobe Streamline. Now, Andromeda Filters has three series of plug-in filters for Photoshop that address three areas of image enhancement. Series 1 consists of photographic filters that provide special effects that traditionally have been accomplished with the use of special camera lenses. Series 2 offers the 3D filter, which molds a flat image around a geometric surface. And, by the time you read this, Series 3 will be available for both Macintosh and Windows users; it contains pre-press special effects.

A fully working Series 1 filter—the Circular Multiple, or cMulti filter—and a preview-only version of the Series 2 filter—3D effects—are on the Adobe Photoshop Deluxe CD-ROM. You need to close Photoshop and then swap CDs if you currently have the Bonus CD in your CD-ROM drive. Although the Macintosh file names on the Deluxe CD use the long-name convention, the files and locations on the CDs for both platforms are identical. Here's how to load both Andromeda filters into Photoshop:

◆ Copy the CMDEMO.8BF file from the GOODIES\3RDPARTY\ANDRMEDA\SERIES1 directory to Photoshop's PLUGINS directory on your hard drive. Then copy the 3-DDEMO.8BF, 3-D.PRF, and 3-D.HLP files to the PHOTOSHP\PLUGINS directory on your hard drive from the GOODIES\3RDPARTY\ANDRMEDA\SERIES1 directory.

The READ.ME files and sample images of the Andromeda filters can be accessed directly from the CD, so copying these files is not necessary.

Using the cMulti Filter

Andromeda's cMulti filter creates patterns from an area you define in a proxy box of the current image in Photoshop. The overall appearance of the Circular Multi image filter is that of viewing an image through a kaleidoscope, but variations can be specified to create other special effects. Before going through the exercise in this section, look at the controls in the cMulti interface (shown in figure 19.27), and what each control modifies in the effect:

◆ The Radial and Square buttons in the Areas field control the shape of the multi images as they emanate from the source area you define by clicking and dragging the floating frame in the preview window.

◆ The Radius, Width, and # Areas sliders determine the size, shape, and number of multi-images within the current image.

◆ The Transition slider determines how much of a feather effect is generated between the multi-images and the target image.

◆ The Intensity slider provides control over how transparent the multi-images are on top of the target image.

For a test drive of the features in the cMulti plug-in, use the GORDGARD image you saved in the last exercise for the exercise that follows.

Using the cMulti Plug-In Filter

With the GORDGARD.TIF image open in Photoshop's workspace, choose Filter, Andromeda, and cMultiDemo	Displays the Splash screen for this special edition.
Click on the Splash screen	Displays the Circular Multiple Design dialog box.
Click and drag the x in the preview window so that it is directly on top of a geranium	Sets the sample point for the filter, and several smaller duplicates now surround the target area in the preview window.
Click on the Square radio button in the Areas field	Changes the shape of the multiple images to squares.
Click and drag the Radius slider to **15**	Moves the multiple images closer to the center, target image area.
Click and drag the Width slider to **55**	Increases the size of the sample area and the multiples, while maintaining the relative distance between them.
Click and drag the #Areas slider to **8**	Determines the number of multiples that surround the target image area.
Click and drag the Transition slider to **20**	Sets a fair amount of feathering between the multiples and the background image.

| Click and drag the Intensity slider to **100** | Makes the center of the multiple images 100-percent opaque. |
| If your screen now looks like figure 19.27, click on OK | Applies the effect. |

If you want to save this image, choose Sa_v_e As, and then save it to a different file name, so you still have a copy of the GORDGARD original file.

Figure 19.27

Click and drag on a palette tab to separate it from its group. Doing this can provide a simultaneous view of both palettes' settings.

In figure 19.28, you can see the effects of the Circular Multiple Design filter on the GORDGARD image. Although its primary effect is one of looking through a kaleidoscope, you can use the filter to quickly and seamlessly clone a target image area. The flowers now are a more predominant element in the GORGARD image, and look like they could use a little digital pruning!

Figure 19.28

Use the cMulti filter to replicate a target image area, and make the duplicate revolve around the source area.

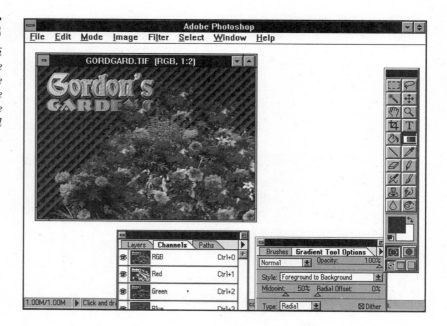

Using the Andromeda 3D Filter

The 3D filter is a read-only limited edition of the commercial filter, but you still can experiment with how a flat 2D surface would look mapped to a 3D cylinder, sphere, or cube. Figure 19.29 shows the 3D interface, and it's here that you can decide where the current image will be located on a 3D surface, how the surface reacts to lighting, the 3D model's position relative to the viewer, the dimensions and proportions of the model to which the target image is mapped, and a point of lighting for the 3D model.

You cannot choose OK from the menu, but you have the option to view a 3D creation in a good-sized preview window. You have four sets of parameters for the Model aspect of a 3D image:

◆ **Surface.** Defines the dimensions of the 3D model to which you map and image. Cylinder, cube, and sphere are your options, and you can elongate and move around the sides of the geometric primitives to create boxes and pie wedges.

◆ **Colors.** Controls the areas of the model not covered with the target image, as well as a background color for the model. You use Colors to separate the model from the image background in the commercial version, by choosing the Color Range command or by using Photoshop's Magic Wand tool.

◆ **Grids.** Can be displayed for the 3D surface or the image you map to the 3D model.

◆ **Photo.** Controls the size and attitude of the current image in relation to the 3D model. As you can see in figure 19.29, the Gordon's Gardens text appears to be spilling off the top of the cube onto the other exposed sides. You control the placement of the target image with the Photo options.

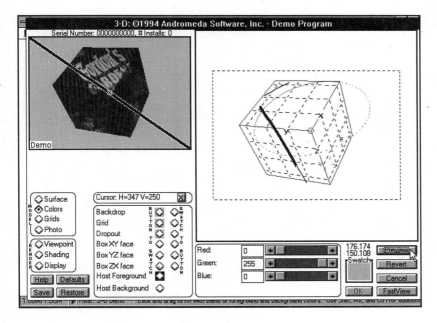

Figure 19.29

You can set the properties of light, the size, the shape, and the viewer's orientation of a 3D image in the 3D interface.

Three additional options appear after you choose a Render option. These relate to how you see this object in space (Viewpoint), how light strikes the surface of the Model (Shading), and the 3D object's altitude and position relative to the viewer (Display).

Because this is a limited version of the 3D filter, you only have options to Preview the image or FastView (a low-resolution image) the 3D creation in the preview window. In figure 19.30, the commercial version of Andromeda's 3D filter was used to render the GORDGARD.TIF image to a cube.

Because the 3D filter on the Adobe CD can't be used to render an image, but only to preview the effect, you can't get a feel for the power and potential use as part of your imaging tools. Make no mistake, though—this filter can accomplish some basic modeling effects without the assistance of a separate modeling or rendering application. If you come from a photographic rather than CAD/Design background, the appeal of the 3D filter can be a great one, and can help you create astonishing, dimensional images you can select and add to other images. Considering that you need less than $100 and the investment of a little time setting up the model for a target image, you would be hard pressed to find another plug-in that produces even remotely similar effects.

Figure 19.30

A two-dimensional image can take on a 3D appearance with the use of Andromeda's 3D plug-in filter.

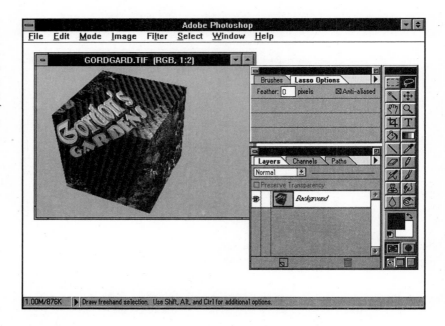

Figure 19.31 is an example of Photoshop, Pixar One Twenty-Eight, and Andromeda's 3D filter used together to create a design that looks quite photographic in content. Wooden photo samples were added to an image window using the One Twenty-Eight filter, the wood textures were mapped to different shapes that can be defined in the 3D filter, and the background is a scan of a crumpled sheet of paper that was texture mapped and lit using Photoshop's native Lighting Effects filter.

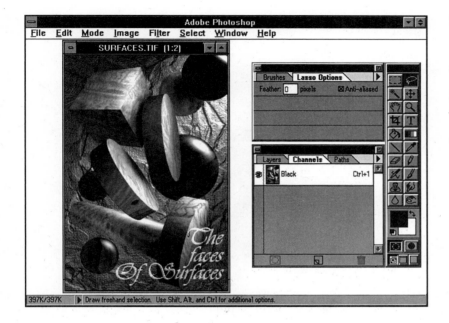

Figure 19.31

You can create your own reality by using third-party plug-in filters together to complete a graphical concept.

Looking At the Changing Shape of Photoshop Plug-Ins

You've seen the bounty that's waiting for the ambitious imagist on both Adobe's and NRP's CDs, but this is not the end of offerings from these third-party manufacturers, and you can expect further contributions from these and other firms as the demand for expanding on Photoshop's native filters increases.

John Knoll, the software engineer and Hollywood special effects artist who was a co-creator of Adobe Photoshop, recently went into the plug-ins business. Knoll Software now produces the CyberMesh plug-in for both the Macintosh and Windows. *CyberMesh* is a filter that converts image data into *polymesh* information—small planes in 3D space that are arranged together to form a complex, dimensional surface. The polymesh surface is created by taking readings of brightness values in the image then is exported from Photoshop into the Data Exchange (or DXF) format. DXF files made from bitmap images can be manipulated in a modeling or rendering program, and then imported into Photoshop as a rendered bitmap image.

If you see the CyberMesh filter in direct-mail publications, you'll find it to be a steal, but be aware that this is an *export* plug-in filter—you can't dimensionalize a bitmap image within Photoshop, and you must use a rendering program that can accept DXF information to create a finished piece. In figure 19.32, the author (a novice with the plug-in) anticipated the possible unflattering results of experimenting with the

CyberMesh filter, and used an image of himself as a target image for the filter. As you can see, it's a caricature of a human likeness, which captures the spirit, if not the likeness, of the author.

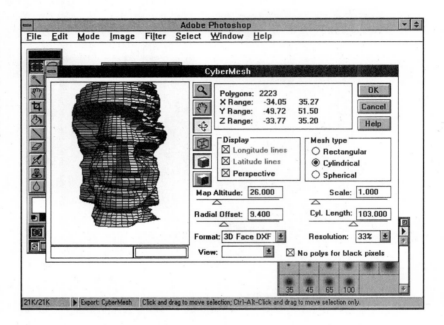

Every plug-in filter you learned about in this chapter has a unique niche in the pixel-based world of digital imaging, and thankfully, the creative minds of these software creators *don't* think alike. There are almost no overlapping areas of the third-party filters' functionality, and it seems like whatever you can imagine, you can image—all within the workspace of Adobe Photoshop.

Mixed Media and Photoshop

Digital art is a very broad, catch-all category for the graphics produced with the assistance of a computer and an integrating application as feature-rich as Photoshop. In this book, we've explored how photographs can be used as a starting point, a base layer, to launch a concept into a different medium and type of self-expression.

However, it would be a mistake to overlook Photoshop's capability to enhance drawings—physical, pen-and-ink sketches—that can be ported to an electronic format as easily as a color snapshot. This chapter, dedicated to the "cocktail napkin doodler" in all of us, shows how to add color, depth, and warmth to a simple line art cartoon and, in the process, transform an idea to a symbiosis of digital and traditional craftsmanship.

This Chapter's Assignment

The concept in this chapter's assignment is to color in a greeting card—specifically, a whimsical one whose message is "Congratulations." Although the task might sound simple, the "crayon box" for this assignment goes way beyond 64 colors—it includes textures, lighting effects, and swatches of photographic images! If you don't consider yourself a pen-and ink-type person, not to worry. You'll use SUCCESS.PSD, a file from the Bonus CD, and we'll show you a trick or two as to how it was created and cleaned up so that it could serve as the framework for the greeting card. If you learn this chapter's techniques for enhancing a line art drawing, you'll be able to use your physical drawings to create the same sort of hybrid illustration as the one covered here. And even if—as a very tired saying goes—you can't draw a straight line, there are plenty of sources for line art that you can use with the same procedures and techniques we use on the SUCCESS.PSD image.

Creating, Modifying, and Filtering Source Artwork

If you've ever wondered how those collections of digital clip art you see advertised in the magazines were created, it's simple; an artist sits at a drafting table, inks in a pencil sketch, cleans the pencil lines from the paper, then scans the image. In figure 20.1, you can see an original pen-and-ink sketch being scanned at half size, and at 150 *pixels per inch* (ppi). A sampling rate of 150 ppi is good for the example to follow, and not a bad one to choose when you want to enhance your own artwork. If you come from a background of traditional art, translating a physical image to a digital format is actually the easy part.

In Chapter 2, "Acquiring a Digital Image," you were advised that pen-and-ink drawings should be scanned at the appropriate scanner color depth to acquire all the information that's present in the source image. In this example, the line art drawing contains pencil and felt tip marker information. The scanner's Grayscale setting acquires both pencil and pen information. The Line Art, 1 bit per pixel sampling mode, on the other hand, would have lost the pencil information and made the felt tip lines a little harsh.

Removing Imperfections

The scanned image of the pen-and-ink drawing now contains all the original design information, as well as some unwanted information—the pencil marks that weren't completely erased. These residual pencil marks need to be cleaned away, and

Photoshop's Eraser tool (set to Paint Brush mode), does a good job of removing the pencil lines (see fig. 20.2).

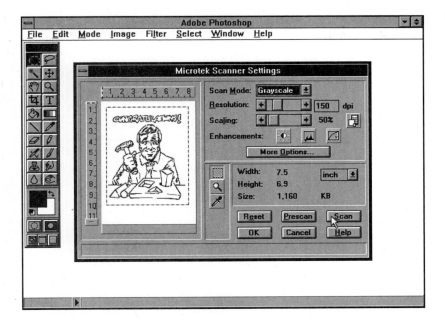

Figure 20.1

To acquire black-and-white line art, use Line Art or Grayscale scanner settings.

Figure 20.2

Use the Eraser tool, set to the same background color as the image's background, to remove unwanted image areas.

Enhancing the Image

In theory, you could begin enhancing the pen-and-ink drawing directly after doing minor clean-up work. Scanners are very precise in their acquisition of visual information, however, picking up every tiny imperfection in a hand-drawn brush stroke or pen line. For this reason, ACHIEVE.TIF, the scanned image used in this example, had to be converted from its bitmap format to a vector format so that it could be further modified.

Using Photoshop's brushes to try to clean up a scan of a drawing is usually not a good idea; the Brushes palette's tips can be modified and reshaped to accommodate practically every design need, *except* those needed to imitate the physical stroke of a pen on paper. The strokes produced with the Paint Brush tool look too "perfect," compared to the original design information—and even a digitizing tablet produces lines that don't hold the humanity of a hand-drawn pen stroke.

Figure 20.3 shows a view of the ACHIEVE.TIF image loaded in Adobe Streamline, a bitmap-to-vector conversion utility that creates an accurate vector-format copy of an original bitmap image. In Streamline, minor modifications can be made to the vector outline of the image; control points along the outlines of the vector objects can be smoothed. The vector version of the image is then saved in Adobe Illustrator (*.AI) format, which is a type of Encapsulated PostScript that many drawing and desktop publishing programs can import. Although Streamline offers a basic toolset for "tweaking" the vector copy of the image, the copy is now destined for an application with a more complete set of editing tools.

A vector format is appropriate for a scan of a line drawing, because traditional pen-and-ink designers conceptualize creations in an object-oriented way. For example, I saw the CONGRATULATIONS lettering in the ACHIEVE image as a separate object from the successful guy's hand, hammer, and aptitude test as I was designing the piece on paper. Similarly, Streamline auto-traced the outline shapes from the original TIFF image as discrete objects, and as such, the objects can be easily manipulated in a vector drawing program.

In figure 20.4, you can see that the file created by Streamline has been opened in CorelDRAW! 5, a vector drawing program similar to Adobe Illustrator. You can also see that the original hand-drawn CONGRATULATIONS! lettering has been deleted; in its place, Type 1 format text has been fitted along an arced path. When an image that contains text has been scanned, the text loses sharpness and may even break up. Replacing scanned hand-lettering with computer generated text is a great option computer graphics designers frequently choose.

Figure 20.3

Adobe Streamline creates a vector copy of a bitmap image.

Figure 20.4

You can modify a bitmap scan by converting it to vector information, then adding or deleting different objects.

Exporting an EPS Vector Image to Photoshop

Next stop, Photoshop! After the drawing has been refined, it's exported as an *Encapsulated PostScript* (EPS) file, which Photoshop can import as a bitmap image. Because EPS images are resolution-independent, they can be scaled before Photoshop rasterizes them to bitmap format. Both the AI and EPS file formats are accepted in Photoshop; the program sees them as the same type of vector information. One of the design payoffs to converting the original bitmap design to vector is that it can be rasterized to dimensions smaller or larger than the original scan without losing image quality. To rasterize SUCCESS.PSD, the bitmap image you'll work with in this chapter, we first used Photoshop's File, **O**pen command to open ACHIEVE.EPS. Then, in the Rasterize Adobe Illustrator Format dialog box, we specified a width of 3.7, height of 5.1, and resolution of 150 pixels/inch, and made sure that the **A**nti-Aliased box was checked.

When the image is rasterized, Photoshop's Anti-Aliasing feature places lighter-value pixels along the edges of foreground color in the image, thus ensuring smooth edges in the vector-to-bitmap conversion. Because pixels are rectangular, Anti-Aliasing helps most in image areas that display curves and diagonal lines, reducing the jaggy, stairsteppy appearance of design areas that aren't rectangular in design.

Grayscale mode also was chosen, because although this image will ultimately be a full-color design, Photoshop's EPS Rasterizer works more quickly when creating a Grayscale 8 bit per pixel image than it does in a higher color mode such as the 24 bit per pixel RGB mode.

Setting Up the Digital Design

Although the preceding steps are optional (for this chapter's assignment), they nevertheless can help traditional artists set up a scanned line-art image for editing in Photoshop. You always want to pick the best source image when you work with photographic media, and the same is true for illustration work. Figure 20.5 is a side-by-side close-up comparison of the original scanned image and the ACHIEVE.EPS image rasterized by Photoshop. You'll notice that the visual detail is almost identical, but the EPS import features smooth, Anti-Aliased lines. So in a way, the greeting card design has already been enhanced a little.

The name of the file in which the EPS file was opened is SUCCESS.PSD; you'll find it in the CHAP20 subdirectory of the Bonus CD. You need to set up this image to get it ready for coloring, the addition of textures, and the other enhancements you'll make in the image. You'll use Photoshop's Layers feature to copy only the black areas of the SUCCESS image to a transparent layer, so that you can fill the empty areas of the design without disrupting the black foreground design.

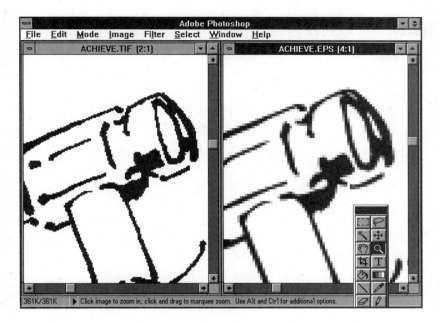

Figure 20.5

Anti-Aliasing is a digital enhancement that creates smooth edges in imported vector art designs.

Converting to CMYK Color

Additionally, you'll need to convert the mode of the SUCCESS image to CMYK color, the mode used for process color printing. In Photoshop's CMYK color mode, the colors displayed are a little duller than those displayed in RGB color mode, and the range (or *gamut*) of colors you have to work with is more limited than those available in RGB mode. The reason is that printing inks have a narrower range of color expression than the red, green, and blue primary colors that make up an RGB image.

When you do the exercises in this chapter, however, your monitor will display an accurate representation of the completed design when it's printed. Knowing what your final output will be is always important when you create a digital image—less so, perhaps, when you're handed an RGB or LAB image to retouch. When *creating* an image that will be printed commercially, using process color, choose CMYK mode for the best idea of what your printed work will look like.

The following exercise shows you how to modify the SUCCESS.PSD image so that it's ready for some color.

Setting Up a Process-Color-Ready "Canvas"

Open SUCCESS.PSD image from CHAP20 subdirectory on the Bonus CD	Grayscale image you'll work with in this chapter.
Choose **M**ode, then **C**MYK Color	Changes color mode of image to cyan, magenta, yellow, and black, each displayed as a color channel.
Press F7 (Macintosh: F11), then click on Channels tab (or choose **W**indow, **P**alettes, Show **C**hannels) if the Layers Palette isn't on your workspace.	Displays channel tab components for SUCCESS.PSD image.
Press Ctrl+A (or choose **S**elect, **A**ll), then press Ctrl+C (or choose **E**dit, **C**opy)	Copies CMYK view of design to Clipboard.
Click on New icon on Channels palette, then click on color Indicates: Selected Areas, then click on OK	Creates channel #5 in the image, whose white areas are masked; any black areas created in channel represent selection information.
Press Ctrl+V (or choose **E**dit, **P**aste), then press Ctrl+D (or choose **S**elect, **N**one)	Pastes copy of design in an Alpha channel (#5), and deselects it (see fig. 20.6).

Because the design was imported as a grayscale image, it contains no more visual information than eight bits per pixel, the same amount of information a color or Alpha channel can hold. And because the grayscale information can be fully expressed in the Alpha channel, a perfect copy of the design is created in the channel. This copy can be used as selection information.

Press Alt while clicking on Channel #5 icon (or choose **S**elect, **L**oad Selection, then choose Channel #4 from Channel drop-down list, then click on OK)	Loads selection information (the design) from channel #4. You see this as a marquee around image.
Click on CMYK channel title, then click on Layers tab on grouped palette	Displays color composite view of image.
Click on new layer icon on Layers palette, then click on OK in New Layer dialog box	Creates new Layer 1 in SUCCESS.PSD image; Layer 1 is now active (target) layer.

Click on new layer icon on Layers palette, then click on OK in the New Layer dialog box	Creates new Layer 2 in SUCCESS.PSD image; Layer 2 is now active (target) layer.

The Background layer is largely unused in this assignment. Layer 2 is for the black outline of the design, and Layer 1 is for adding color and textures.

Double-click on Paint bucket tool	Chooses tool, and displays Options palette for Paint bucket.
Enter **255** in Tolerance field of Options palette, choose Normal (paint) mode, make sure Anti-Aliased check box is checked, choose Foreground from drop-down list, then click and drag Opacity slider to 100%	Sets characteristics of Paint bucket to "flood" a selection (or an entire image) with foreground color.
Press **D** (or click on default colors icon on toolbox)	Sets current foreground (paint) color to black.
Click inside a marquee line on SUCCESS.PSD image (see fig. 20.7)	Floods selected areas on Layer 2 with black.

Because the design is mostly composed of thin lines, clicking inside of one at less than 1:1 viewing resolution might be difficult. Press Ctrl+plus once or twice to increase your viewing resolution without switching tools.

Press Ctrl+D	Deselects selection.
Click on Background title on Layers palette, then press E (for **E**raser tool)	Makes Background layer the active layer, and chooses Eraser tool.
Click on Erase Layer button on Options palette, then click on OK in dialog box	Erases entire Background layer to white.
Click on Channels tab, then click and drag channel #5 into trash icon at bottom of Channels palette	Displays Channels palette. You no longer need this selection; deleting channel from image conserves memory resources.
Click on Layers tab, then click on Layer 1 title on Layers palette	Displays layer on which you'll do most of the painting in this assignment.
Choose **F**ile, Sa**v**e As, then save image to your hard disk as SUCCESS.PSD	Saves your work up to this point. PSD format is the only file format that can save Photoshop Layer information.

Figure 20.6

Copy the CMYK image channel to an Alpha channel to make the visual information available as selection information.

Figure 20.7

Fill the selection marquee with foreground color to create a black-and-transparent layer image.

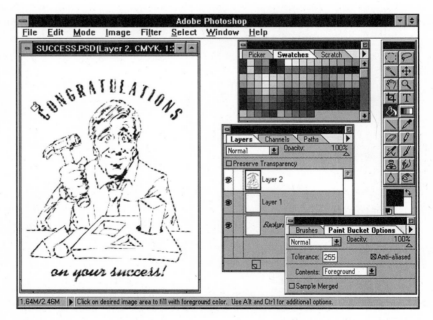

In a certain sense, by filling the active selection in Layer 2, then deleting the original design on the Background, you've moved the visual information to a transparency layer. The design will now be easier to modify, because everything you paint and add to Layer 1 and the clean Background layer will show through the transparent areas of Layer 2. Additionally, there's not much chance now of accidentally painting over the design elements on Layer 2.

Because the design in Channel #5 contains anti-aliased edges, the edges were represented in the selection you filled in by areas of partial opacity, or partial selection. Now all the original design detail is present on Layer 2; because the Paint Bucket tool was set to the maximum tolerance of 255, every area of the selection was filled with foreground color, with each area corresponding to the amount of black (Color Indicates: Selected Areas) in Channel #5.

Tip If you've created an image in a drawing program that supports AI or EPS exports, you can leave the interior of black objects empty, and Photoshop will import the graphic as a Layer with transparent pixels surrounding the object. This is great if you're *not* working with a vector design that was converted to vector format from a bitmap original. Vector conversion utilities such as Streamline and CorelTRACE! must create separate vector objects from converted bitmaps, and this means placing a white vector shape on top of a black one to represent, say, an empty circle. The white shape, in this example, will appear as white, not clear, when the AI or EPS file is rasterized in Photoshop.

Additionally, if you use CorelDRAW! to export an AI design, specify Adobe Illustration 3.0, not version 1.1 in the Export dialog box of CorelDRAW. Experienced designers will recognize that this is a change of rules; AI version 1.1 is a classic vector export format commonly used by many graphics programs as a medium of exchange—but not with Photoshop 3.0.

Creating an Airbrush Effect

The first area you'll work on in the SUCCESS.PSD image is the successful guy's face. You're not striving for ultrarealism in this assignment; let's face it, the guy's a cartoon! Nevertheless, you can create a very elegant cartoon—one that could easily command $3.50 at a card store—by keeping the color shading smooth and flowing, in contrast to the sketchy lines that make up the design.

Using the Picker Palettes

In the next exercise, you'll use the Picker group of palettes to specify colors for the design. You'll use the Swatches palette (which has many colorful samples, including six or seven flesh tones) in combination with the Gradient tool to give the successful guy's face some dimension and shading. With the exception of the first six colors on the Swatches palette, which are pure primary and complementary colors, all the samples on the Swatches palette are "legal" CMYK colors; these colors can be faithfully reproduced on paper, using cyan, magenta, yellow, and black inks.

You'll use the Lasso tool in the next exercise to define the fill area for the successful guy's face. But painstaking accuracy isn't necessary, for the following reasons:

- Because you'll be painting on Layer 1, you can erase any colored areas that might fall outside the guy's face, without messing up the design on Layer 2.

- You have a fairly broad margin of error in defining the area to be filled within the guy's face because the black areas on Layer 2 that comprise the design are relatively wide (compared to selection marquees produced by the Lasso tool).

By pressing Alt and clicking to define several straight line segments with the Lasso tool on the image, you'll define and then fill the guy's face, and be able to move on fairly quickly to different design areas.

Using Gradient Fills To Create Flesh Tones

Look on the Layers palette, and make sure you're still on Layer 1; if not, click on its title on the layers palette list	Layer 1 is the Layer you'll edit.
Double-click on Zoom tool on toolbox, then scroll and resize image window so that you have clear view of successful guy's face	Zooms view to 1:1 resolution, a a good view of area you'll select and fill.
Press **L** (for **L**asso tool), then press F6 (F10, for Macintosh users) if Picker group of palettes isn't already onscreen	Makes Lasso tool the current tool, and displays palettes for defining colors.
Make sure Feather option is set to **0** on Options palette	For these steps, you want an accurate selection border, not one with a soft, feathered edge.

Press and hold Alt key (Option key on Macintosh), then click a point on successful guy's hairline	Defines first point for Lasso tool's straight-line selection marquee.
Click a second point to right of first, making sure that second point is directly on a black area of design. Keep holding down Alt (Option) key	Creates straight line between first and second points.
Continue clicking points in a clockwise direction, to create straight-line selection outline that falls directly on black areas of design	Creates straight-line selection border (see fig. 20.8).

You need to make the distance between points you click short enough that the straight segments Photoshop creates between points fall on the black outline areas of the successful guy's face. This might seem hard at first, but you'll quickly develop a technique that you'll use for selecting other design areas. As you can see, areas are "missing" from the design (where the author didn't continue a well-defined outline that describes the guy's face). In instances like these, complete the design line with your Lasso marquee.

Release Alt key when you reach the first point you clicked	Outline becomes a marquee, and area that defines guy's face is selected on Layer 1.
Click on Swatches tab on Picker group of palettes, then click on third swatch (from left) on third row	Sets foreground color to light flesh color.
Press Alt (Option) while clicking on second swatch on third row	Sets background color to a deeper flesh color.

In a portrait, you'll usually see a highlight on the person's forehead, with a gradual transition to darker skin colors as you move down the face. This is the effect you create next, using the Gradient tool.

Press **G** (for **G**radient tool), then set Options palette to Normal mode, Opacity: **100%**, Foreground to Background Style, and Radial Type	Sets Gradient tool's characteristics to produce a smooth, concentric transition from foreground to background color.
Click and drag from successful guy's forehead to tip of his nose	Produces gradient fill that's light in the center and gradually falls off to darker background color (see fig. 20.9).

continued

continued

Press Ctrl+D (**S**elect, **N**one)	Deselects the selection marquee.
Press Ctrl+S (or choose **F**ile, **S**ave)	Saves your work up to this point.

Figure 20.8

Press Alt (Option) while clicking a straight-line selection marquee around the guy's face while Layer 1 is the active (target) layer.

Because the successful guy's eyes were included in the Lasso tool selection, they, too, have been filled. You could have removed these areas from the selection before using the Gradient tool. But because you give the eyes a unique color next, painting over the flesh tone area in the eyes is a workable, expedient alternative.

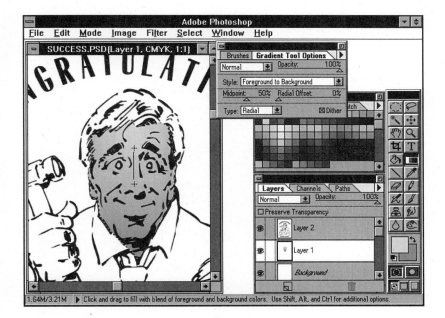

Figure 20.9

Use the Gradient tool to create a smooth blend of two colors in the selection area.

Using Gradient Fills

Because this greeting card is a caricature of a person, it stands to reason that the lighting, shading, and color you add to it can have the same qualities. In other words, shading you add to the design can help bring out dimension in the overall picture, but the shading doesn't have to be photo-realistic to be an effective design element!

When most people look into someone else's eyes, they find mystery and attraction—but as an artist, you'll find *shading*: one's eyebrows cast a slight shadow toward the top of the eye, and it gets brighter toward the pupil. To create this same sort of effect in the SUCCESS.PSD image, you'll use the Gradient tool once again. This time, however, you'll define a light gray and white as the foreground and background colors, and use a Linear fill to make the eye shading effect a little more pronounced than you'd find in real life. Which is okay—this is not a real life subject, and exaggeration sometimes compensates for lack of overall, realistic detail in a design.

This exercise shows you how to add an eye-catching element to the greeting card.

Gradient Filling a Noncontiguous Selection

Press Ctrl+plus, then scroll and resize SUCCESS.PSD image window so you can see successful guy's eyes	Zooms to a 2:1 viewing resolution, giving you better view of area to be filled.
With Lasso tool, click and drag a selection marquee around successful guy's right eye	Selects this area to be filled on Layer 1.

You can also use the "press Alt while clicking" technique to build a selection marquee made of straight lines between points if you don't think that you can accurately define the eye area by simply click and dragging.

Press Shift while clicking and dragging around successful guy's left eye	Holding down Shift key while you click and drag adds left eye to existing selection of right eye.
Click on second (from left) swatch at bottom of Swatches palette, then press Alt (Option) and click on white swatch (top row, seventh from left)	Sets foreground color to a light, warm gray, and background color to white.
With Gradient tool chosen, set Options palette to Linear	Defines a linear type fill for Gradient tool.
Click and drag between successful guy's eyes, beginning slightly above eyebrows, and ending about 3/4 screen inches straight down	Creates a sharp, linear fill inside both selection marquees (see fig. 20.10).
Press Ctrl+D (or choose Select, None), then press Ctrl+S (or choose File, Save)	Deselects marquee, and saves your work up to this point.

As you can see, when you use the Gradient tool it doesn't matter whether an active selection is composed of a single area, or several areas that don't touch. Gradient fills are created in available image space, with the Gradient's beginning and ending points defined by the initial and final points you define with the tool's cursor.

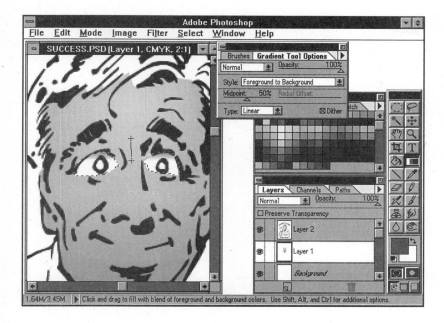

Figure 20.10

Create a Gradient of sharp transitional colors inside the selection marquee.

The shorter the distance you click and drag with the Gradient tool, the more quickly the fill makes a transition between foreground and background colors, or any style you set on the Options palette. As a result of the last exercise, the successful guy's eye area now has dimension. Now he could use some pupils...

Shading and Refining Your Coloring Work

In medium to large image areas, the Gradient tool is quite useful for providing movement and the smooth shading traditional designers used an airbrush to create. But smaller areas in the SUCCESS.PSD design call for the use of other painting tools.

In the next exercise, you'll finish coloring the successful guy's face. Using the Paint Brush tool, you'll not only give color to his eyes but also break up a little of the monotony of the gradient fill in his face. Screen mode, used with a painting tool, gives the appearance of bleaching an area toward a foreground color; and when the Paint Brush tool is set to low Opacity, the effect is one of lightening the color area you stroke over. By stroking one or two areas of the successful guy's face with the

Paint Brush tool in Screen mode, you can add highlights similar to those found on someone's face in real life. By adding a stroke or two of foreground white to the facial areas in the design, you make the bridge of the nose, the cheekbones, and the forehead areas more pronounced—and the overall image will look as though traditional painting media were used to color it.

Enhancing the Shading of the Gradient Fill

Click on light blue swatch on Swatches palette	Selects light blue as foreground color.
Press **B** (for Paint **b**rush), then choose Mode: Normal, and Opacity: **100%**. Click on Brushes tab on palette, then choose tip at far left on second row	Sets Paint brush characteristics for painting guy's eyes.
Click and drag inside guy's pupils	Fills pupil areas with foreground color.
Press **D** (for default colors icon), then press **X** (to Switch colors icon)	Sets colors on toolbox to foreground white and background black. You can do this also by clicking on icons that frame colors on toolbox.
Choose Screen mode; click and drag Opacity slider to about **55%** on Options palette	Sets characteristic of Paint brush tool to "bleach" image areas to foreground white.
Click on Brushes tab on palette, then click on third tip, second row	Defines larger tip for Paint brush, to better cover image areas.
Click and drag a long stroke down bridge of successful guy's nose	Lightens bridge of nose.
Click and drag along left side of guy's face	Creates a gentle highlight.

You'll notice that this design has some innate lighting to it. Shadows were drawn in the original in the neck area, and beneath and to the right of the tip of the guy's nose. For this reason, keep your coloring and shading the same: light is suggested from the upper left of the design, and shadows should fall to the lower right of image areas. In the last step, highlighting the left side of the guy's face is accurate and in keeping with the suggested lighting conditions in the drawing.

Click and drag a short stroke beneath each of the guy's eyes	Suggests cheekbones (see fig. 20.11).
Don't overdo it! When you've added four or five highlights, press Ctrl+S (or choose File, Save)	Saves your work up to this point.

Figure 20.11

To bleach image areas toward foreground color, use Screen mode when you paint.

Screen mode is ineffective when you paint over an image area whose color is lighter than the current foreground color. For this reason, white is usually a good, all-purpose foreground color to use in Screen painting mode (because no colors are lighter).

Using a Minimalist Approach To Suggest Lighting

Some areas in the drawing contain a great deal of design detail, and other areas need the help of gradient fills and textures. The successful guy's hair is composed of several strokes that suggest strands of hair; unlike the face, the hair requires a minimum of embellishment. As a rule, don't try to overwork an area that can stand on its own as a compositional element.

In the next exercise, by adding two shades of brown to the hair, you create hair that is strongly lit from the upper left, gently decreasing in brightness as it reaches the successful guy's hairline. Because you've already used two smooth gradient fills for the guy's face, the Gradient tool isn't a good one to use for coloring the guy's hair. The Paint Brush tool is the one to use for this task—you can choose a soft tip, use it to blend together the shades of brown, and keep the coloring work as interesting and diverse in application as the drawing itself.

Creating Blended Areas with the Paint Brush Tool

Choose Normal mode and about **70%** Opacity on Options palette	Sets Paint Brush tool characteristics for applying a gentle wash of foreground color.
Click on a light brown color on Swatches palette	Sets foreground color for Paint Brush tool.
Click and drag over successful guy's hair (see fig. 20.12)	Applies a partially opaque tint of brown to hair.
Click on a darker brown swatch on Swatches palette	Defines color for shaded areas of guy's hair.
Click and drag two or three long strokes through light brown areas in guy's hair	Adds shading to hair (see fig. 20.13).

You don't have to let your brush strokes cover the entire interior of the guy's hair area. It's okay if your strokes leave a little white showing through around the edge of the design. The important thing is not to color *outside* the lines. (If you color outside the lines, you'll have to use the Eraser tool in an additional, unnecessary step!)

Press Ctrl+S (or choose **F**ile, **S**ave)	Saves your work up to this point.

Partial Opacity for the Paint Brush didn't saturate the hair areas with one color or the other; instead, the two shades of brown blended together to make soft transitions where both colors were applied. The result of choosing a partial opacity setting and soft Brush tip characteristics is often similar to airbrush strokes.

Figure 20.12

Apply a light shade of brown to the hair area with the Paint Brush tool.

Figure 20.13

It's perfectly natural and socially acceptable for a cartoon of his age to have his hair colored.

Fleshing out the Design

Now that you've finished the successful guy's head, it's time to work on the other areas of the piece. The guy's shirt is not of paramount importance; you'll add a little color here and there to suggest lighting on the folds of the shirt, but it will remain white and is more of a background element than the other image areas.

The guy's hand needs shading, and the tools of choice for this task are the Paint bucket, the Paint Brush, and the Gradient tool. The Paint Bucket is good for quickly filling a selection area with flat color, the Paint Brush tool is ideal for adding uneven shading, and the Gradient tool creates smooth shading to color in the successful guy's thumb.

If you're ready to begin painting with a combination of Photoshop tools, here's how to add some dimension to the guy's hand area:

Coloring with a Combination of Tools

Scroll over to guy's hand, then press Ctrl+plus (zoom in one field)

Area you'll color in next. A 2:1 resolution provides good working view of area.

Choose Lasso tool, then press Alt (Option) and click around outline of hand, *excluding* the thumb, releasing Alt key when you reach first click point

Defines area to be filled. Always try to stay exactly in center of black outlines of design you see on Layer 2. (Makes fills you add to Layer 1 fit defined area edge-to-edge.)

Press **K** (for Paint Bucket tool), then click on a medium bright flesh tone color on Swatches palette

Chooses Paint Bucket, and defines color Paint Bucket applies.

Until you change them, Options palette settings remain as they were the last time you used a specific tool. The Paint Bucket should still be set to Foreground color, Normal mode, and 100% Opacity.

Click over selection marquee

Applies medium flesh color to selection area.

Press **B** (for Paint **B**rush tool), then click on third from last swatch on bottom row of Swatches palette	Defines a warm, light brown for foreground color you'll use with Paint Brush tool.
Set Opacity to about **40%**, and Mode: Normal on Options palette	Makes foreground color you'll apply semitransparent.
Click and drag over guy's knuckles	Adds shading to knuckles. Because his knuckles bend inward, adding shading is correct in terms of overall lighting presentation of this design.
Click and drag over bottom of guy's hand (see fig. 20.14)	Adds shading in another area that needs it to correctly display lighting and shading.
Press Alt and click on same medium flesh tone on Swatches palette that you chose for Paint Bucket tool	Sets background color.
Press **L** (for **L**asso tool), then press Alt while clicking around guy's thumb	Defines area you'll add color to next.
Press **G** (for **G**radient tool), then click and drag from left to right over thumb, matching angle on thumb	Creates a shaded thumb (see fig. 20.15).
Press Alt while clicking around guy's arm with Lasso tool, then use Gradient tool to shade selection from light flesh on left to medium brown on right	Fills in guy's exposed arm.
Press Ctrl+D (**S**elect, **N**one)	Deselects the selection marquee.
Click on a dark brown color on Swatches palette, choose Paint Brush tool, click on the second, middle row tip on the Brushes palette, click and drag over watch band	Fills in watch band. *Don't* color face of watch. (You'll fill this area in a later exercise.)
Press Ctrl+D (or choose **S**elect, **N**one)	Deselects selection marquee.
Press Ctrl+S (or choose **F**ile, **S**ave)	Saves your work to this point.

Figure 20.14

Use partial opacity with the Paint Brush tool to create shading in a flat image area.

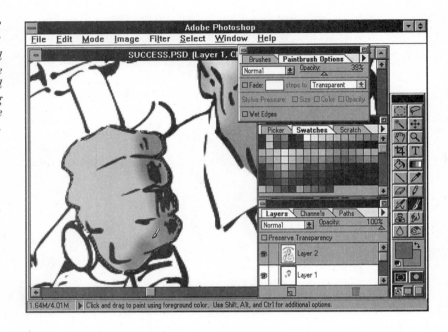

Figure 20.15

Make sure the direction you use with the Gradient tool creates shading that matches the rest of the image's lighting.

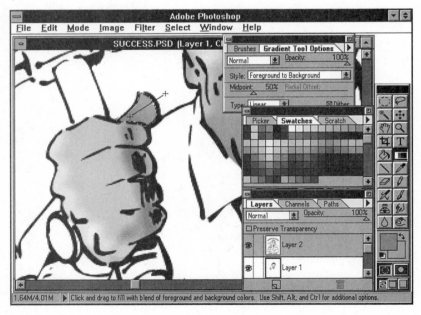

Now only the successful guy's shirt remains to be shaded. After the next section, you'll add texture and a special effect or two to the guy's hardware and his aptitude test.

The Suggestion of Color

Part of being a good designer is to know when to leave color *out* of certain image areas. This image contains several colors. The outline drawing on Layer 2 is alive with visual detail, and you've used bright colors to fill a number of areas in the image. Therefore, if you're going to dress up the image's background, as well as provide additional visual interest to the shapes in the aptitude test and the hammer, something in the design has to "give."

This is purely an aesthetics call, but perhaps the successful guy's shirt should be a plain white. This doesn't mean it doesn't need a little shading, but a pattern fill or bright color will surely distract from the rest of the composition. Again, turn to the natural shading you see in life for the color value of the shading in the guy's shirt. If you hold up a brilliant white sheet or other piece of clothing on a clear day, you'll see light blue near the creases of the fabric. This phenomenon is caused by the blue sky reflecting some tint into the white fabric—an occurrence frequently overlooked by designers. Many people, thinking that realistic color casting must be a neutral shade, use a neutral gray color to shade white.

This is a cartoon, however, and you can bring a phenomenon into the picture from wherever you like! Because this image is in CMYK mode, colors are, by their nature, a little duller than you'd usually see (or prefer), and shading the guy's shirt by adding gray to it would make it duller than it needs to be. Light blue will not only help attract the viewer, but also keep the image as light in color value as it is in theme.

In this exercise, you add some dimension by suggesting folds in the guy's shirt.

Folding the Laundry

Press **D** (for **d**efault colors)	Sets current foreground color to black, and background color to white.
Click on light blue (third row, middle) on Swatches palette	Sets foreground color to light blue.
Press **L** (for **L**asso tool), then click and drag a freeform shape around guy's upper-left shirt sleeve	Defines area to be shaded.

In this instance, it's okay if your freeform Lasso selection goes into the pegs of the aptitude test. You'll be adding a texture to the pegs that will cover any stray paint strokes. Make certain, however, that your marquee selection doesn't go outside the guy's shirt.

continues

continued

Press **G** (for **G**radient tool), then click and drag straight down in selection marquee; don't go outside selection area with either beginning or ending point with Gradient tool	Creates a soft, subtle shading on guy's upper-left shirt sleeve (see fig. 20.16).
Create a selection marquee around other areas in design where crease marks are drawn	These areas also need shading, as you'd see them in real life.
Click and drag in selection areas with Gradient tool	Adds shading to selection areas.

As mentioned earlier, the Gradient tool creates perfect transitions between foreground and background colors, but these transitions are a little too perfect to represent shading on the creases in clothing. The solution is to use the Smudge and Burn tools to mess up the gradient fills slightly.

Press Ctrl+D (or choose **S**elect, **N**one), then press **U** (for Smudge tool) on keyboard	Deselects current marquee selection, and chooses Smudge tool.
Choose Normal mode and **50%** Pressure from Options palette, and check Sample Merged option	Defines amount of smudging Smudge tool will do, and allows tool to sample white from Background layer.

The Sample Merged option allows the Smudge tool to use colors on all visible layers, which includes the drawing of the guy on Layer 1. Take a little care not to include the black outline areas while you use the Smudge tool.

Click and drag from an image area that has faint blue, into an area that appears white	Spreads faint blue color into white areas, as though you were drawing your finger through wet paint.
Repeat last step in other shirt areas that look a little too perfect	Gives a slightly unkempt, humorous look to shirt (see fig. 20.17).
Press **O** (for **T**oning tools) repeatedly until Burn tool (little hand) appears on toolbox	Chooses tool for burning (saturating and darkening) image areas.

Alternatively, you can select the Burn tool by pressing Alt (Option) while clicking on the Toning tool on the toolbox, or you can set this option on the Options palette from the drop-down list.

Set Exposure to **50%** and range to Highlights on Options palette and choose the third (from the left) middle row tip on the Brushes palette	Sets characteristics of Burn tool to most greatly affect lighter image areas.
Click and drag over light blue areas on guy's shirt, following direction of creases (the black outlines on Layer 2)	Makes blue areas darker, without affecting hue of color (see fig. 20.18).
Press Ctrl+S (or choose **F**ile, **S**ave)	Saves your work to this point.

If you haven't installed any of the goodies on the Bonus CD, close the image and Photoshop for the time being. You're going to get hands-on experience with a third-party Photoshop plug-in or two.

Figure 20.16

Click and drag inside the selection area to create a faint crease in the guy's white shirt.

The last exercise was a study in making gradient fill image areas seem a little more hand-painted. Part of the trick to successfully convey a "computer image" as simply "an image" is to add human expression to your shading work. There isn't an "auto-fill" button in any application that can match the sensitivity, and sometimes charming imperfection, of a paint stroke executed by a human hand.

The black image on Layer 2 displays many human touches, and the colorizing of the image should reflect the same quality.

Figure 20.17

Use the Smudge tool to make gradient filled areas look less perfect.

Figure 20.18

Use the Burn tool to make faint, light areas more concentrated with color.

Putting a Glass Lens on a Wristwatch

It's time to add an attention-getting, photo-realistic detail or two to the SUCCESS.PSD image. Special effects cannot truly "own" a composition, but the prudent use of a Photoshop Plug-In filter can add a touch of class and refinement to your work, and create an effect that would be too difficult to execute manually. We haven't touched the successful guy's wristwatch yet, and this is a perfect opportunity to test drive one of Kai's Power Tools. A limited version of KPT version 2.0's Filters and Extensions is on the Bonus CD, and you'll need to install the suite of tools to use them from within Photoshop. In the next section, you learn how to load the Gradient Designer 2.0 and the Glass Lens filter. You'll use both of them in this chapter's assignment.

Installing the Filters

For Macintosh Photoshop users: click and drag all filters from the KPT folder on the Bonus CD's Macintosh partition (for non-PowerPC Macintoshes, drag the 68K filters; for a Power Macintosh, drag the two PPC filters), along with the KPT Support Files folder, into the Adobe Photoshop Plug-ins folder.

For Windows users: copy all the filters (the file extension is .8BF) into the Photoshop PLUGINS directory (for example: C:\PHOTOSHP\PLUGINS), then copy the KPT20HUB.DLL and KPTWIN20.HLP files into the Windows directory.

If you've already installed KPT's sampler version from the Adobe Deluxe CD-ROM, you don't need to perform the installation a second time. But for both Macintosh and Windows users, if you haven't read Chapter 19, "Third-Party Plug-In Filters," you haven't created the flashy KPT Gradient fill for the Successful Guy's Tie yet. We'll recap the steps needed to copy and save a complex gradient fill in a separate section of this chapter. Although you don't need to reference Chapter 19 to perform the exercises in this chapter, it's a good idea to explore the possibilities of the KPT Gradient Designer 2.0 by making a stop at Chapter 19, if you haven't done so already.

Using the Glass Lens Filter

Restart Photoshop after you've loaded the KPT filters. When Photoshop restarts, it scans for the Plug-Ins files and adds them to the Filter menu. Reopen the SUCCESS1.PSD image from your hard disk, and we'll show you how to put a glass lens on the successful guy's watch!

Using the Glass Lens Filter

Press **Z** (for **Z**oom tool), then marquee zoom on guy's watch	Area that will receive Glass Lens effect.
Press **B** (for Paint **b**rush tool), then click on a light blue color on Swatches palette	Base color for watch face.
Press **L** (for **L**asso tool), then click and drag around watch face	Selects watch face.
Press Alt+Delete (Mac: Option+Return)	Fills selection area with foreground color.
Choose Fi**l**ter, KPT 2.0 Filters. Macintosh users should choose Glass Lens Normal, and Windows users should choose Glass Lens Bright from submenu	Applies Glass Lens filter to selection area, producing a shiny, convex watch lens (see fig. 20.19).
Press Ctrl+D (or choose **S**elect, **N**one), then press Ctrl+S (or choose **F**ile, **S**ave)	Deselects marquee selection, and saves your work to this point.

Figure 20.19

Kai's Glass Lens filter creates a highlight on a convex, round surface from information in a selection area.

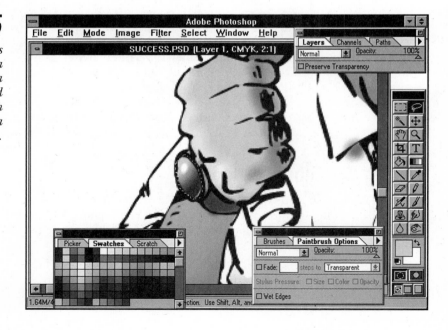

If you wanted to be extra ambitious and really "gild the lily," you could add numbers to the guy's watch before applying the Glass Lens filter. Glass Lens Soft, Normal, and Bright all distort the underlying selected image outward. To control shading and highlights produced by the effect, you hold down a number key before choosing the filter. Number 9 on the keypad corresponds to a 1 o'clock position for the Glass Lens' light source, 7 (the default) is an 11 o'clock light source, and so on. See Chapter 19, "Third-Party Plug-In Filters," for the run-down of KPT and other third-party Plug-In filters included on this book's Bonus CD.

It's worth mentioning here that the Kai's Power Tools sampler from HSC Software, Inc. includes only a fraction of the complete commercial version's capabilities. Due to a minor difference in the way the Kai's sampler was built for the Windows and Macintosh operating platforms, the Windows sampler includes three variations on Glass Lens and Hue Protected Noise, whereas the Macintosh sampler contains one variation of each effect. HSC has shown exceptional goodwill toward Photoshop users by providing these filters on the Bonus CD, with no limitations or restrictions other than your own conscience. If you find a regular, professional use for these filters, you definitely should purchase the whole set. You'll get more options, more filters, and tech support when you do.

As you can see from figure 20.20, the successful guy is looking pretty good. But now it's time to turn to his greatest accomplishment, the square peg hammered into the round hole, and use it as the target for a different sort of color fill.

Figure 20.20

Now, where is he going to put the round peg?

Patterned Textures and the Layered Cartoon

Perhaps you've seen photographic images combined with line drawings on greeting cards; this approach to creating a mixed-media composition produces attention-getting results and motivates people to pick up the card and, gasp, purchase it. There's no reason you can't use Photoshop to create this sort of effect in the SUCCESS.PSD image, and as long as the photographic element doesn't overwhelm the composition, the enhancement makes the piece more commercially salable.

Using PIXAR Filters

In the next exercise, you'll use three different images of olive wood, created by using PIXAR's One Twenty-Eight Plug-In filter, a filter that creates seamless, tiled photographic textures. See Chapter 19 for more information about the Bonus CD's two texture plug-ins from PIXAR.

Because these image files were carefully created to present the wood at different viewing perspectives, the areas you'll fill in the SUCCESS.PSD image will have different grain patterns. The square peg will look as though it could have been carved from a piece of wood. Almost.

Using Pattern Fills in a Selection

Open WOOD2.TIF image from CHAP20 subdirectory of Bonus CD	Wood image you'll use to fill part of square peg.
Size up how much of WOOD2.TIF image you'll need by zooming both windows to a 1:2 viewing resolution, then using Rectangular marquee tool to select an area of WOOD2 that's larger than right side of square peg	Selects an area that can be defined as a pattern. Only the Rectangular marquee tool can be used to define patterns.
Choose **E**dit, **D**efine Pattern (see fig. 20.21)	Photoshop loads selected image area in system RAM.
Press **L** (for **L**asso Tool), then press Alt while clicking around right side of square peg	Creates selection area around right side of peg.
Choose **E**dit, **F**ill, then choose Pattern from Contents, **U**se: drop-down list, and click on OK	Applies wood texture to selection area, as shown in figure 20.22.

Press Ctrl+B (or choose Image, Adjust, Brightness/Contrast)	Displays Brightness/Contrast dialog box.
Click and drag Brightness slider to about –25, then click on OK	Darkens selected wood noticeably. This suggests shading, because right side of peg faces away from light source in image.
With Lasso tool, press Alt while clicking around left side of square peg	Defines next area to be filled.
Choose Edit, Fill, then click on OK in dialog box	Fills left side of peg with wood pattern.
Open WOOD_END.TIF image from CHAP20 subdirectory on Bonus CD	Image (of same wood) has been filtered to look like end grain on piece of sawed wood.
Press Ctrl+A (or choose Select, All), then choose Edit, Define Pattern	Photoshop stores copy of WOOD_END image in system RAM.
With Lasso tool, press Alt while clicking around top of square peg	Defines selection marquee around top face of square peg.
Choose Edit, Fill, then click on OK in dialog box	Fills top of peg (see fig. 20.23).
Press Ctrl+D (or choose Select, None), then press Ctrl+S (or choose File, Save)	Deselects top of peg, and saves your work to this point.
Click and drag a tiny rectangle with Rectangular marquee tool, then choose Edit, Define Pattern	"Flushes" large WOOD_END image from system RAM, replacing it with a small selection.

The Define Pattern command can be used at any time to create repeating, tiled patterns, if the sample you define as a pattern is smaller than the target selection. In the last exercise, the pattern sample is larger than any face of the square peg, so you see no tiling effect. An another way to create the same effect is to use the Edit, Paste Into command after *copying* a selection of the wood to the Clipboard, but if you try both methods, they take an equivalent amount of time. The advantage to the Fill, Pattern scenario is that if your pattern is too small to fill a selection, it will repeat automatically. The disadvantage of using a Pattern fill, however, is that the pattern color mode must match the target selection. In this case, this is not a concern, because the wood TIFF images are CMYK mode, as is the SUCCESS.PSD image.

Figure 20.21

With the Rectangular Marquee tool, create a selection area to define a pattern.

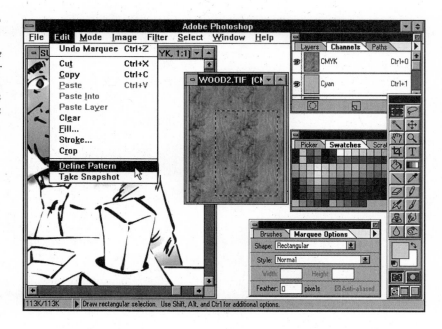

Figure 20.22

Fill the selection with the pattern of the wood you sampled.

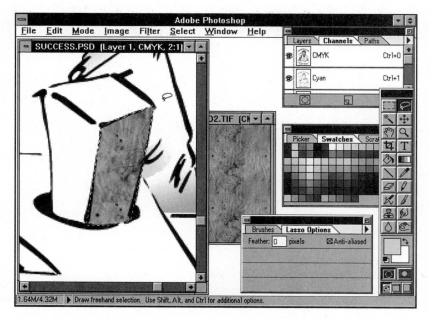

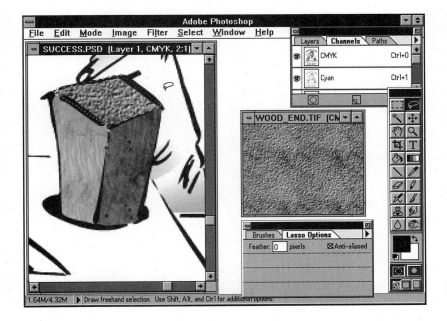

Figure 20.23

Edit the Brightness value of selections of the same wood image to create lighting and dimensional effects.

Tip   You can use the Paint Bucket tool as an alternative to the **E**dit, **F**ill command. Choose foreground color, Pattern, or another fill attribute from the Options palette for the Paint Bucket tool, set the Tolerance to 255, and click inside a selection marquee.

Using the Toning Tools on Texture Fills

The other two pegs in the greeting card also need filling, but now that you've accomplished the Pattern fill of the square peg, the other two pegs are easy to finish. You don't need a structured exercise to accomplish these fills, but you'll want to open WOOD1.TIF from the CHAP20 subdirectory on the Bonus CD and create a pattern from it, because this image has wood grain at a diagonal angle, perfect for use on the sides of the triangular and round pegs. In figure 20.24, you can see that the end caps have been filled, and the WOOD1 image has been sampled and used as a Pattern, filling the long dimension of the pegs.

After you've filled them, here's a trick for making these pegs appear as dimensional as the square peg. This trick is disguised as an exercise, which shows you how to add shading to the pattern-filled pegs.

Figure 20.24

Select the peg areas to be filled, then use the WOOD1.TIf image as a pattern sample for these areas.

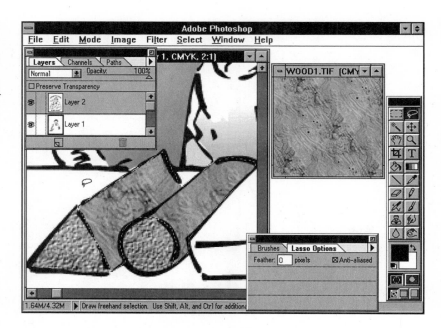

Using Toning Tools for Shading

Press **O** (for Toning tools), then choose Dodge from Tools options drop-down list on Options palette; then set Exposure to **50%**, and choose Highlights from drop-down list on Options palette

Sets characteristics of Dodge tool to decrease saturation and increase brightness, primarily in highlight areas of design.

Click on the Brushes tab, then choose the fourth (from the left), middle row tip

Sets the size of the tip of the Dodge tool.

Click and drag once across left side of cylinder peg

Adds a subtle highlight to left side of peg (see fig. 20.25).

Click and drag Exposure slider to about **70%**, click on Brushes tab on palette, then click on a smaller, soft tip

Decreases size of Dodge tool's tip, and increases intensity of effect you apply with it.

Click and drag over same area on cylinder

Creates a more brilliant highlight on cylinder.

In real life, highlights have a "spread" to them, and by varying the size and Exposure setting of the Dodge tool, you create this effect on the cylinder in two strokes.

Choose Burn from drop-down list on Options palette, then set Exposure to **50%**, and choose Shadows from drop-down list	Sets characteristics of toning tool used to decrease brightness in image areas; areas with least amount of brightness are the most affected.
Choose the second (from the left), middle row tip on the Brushes palette	Specifies the size of the Burn tool.
Click and drag across right side of cylinder	Decreases brightness, and creates a mild shadow area on right side of cylinder.

Because the triangular peg is angled in such a way that two of its three long sides are hidden from view, you don't need to shade it with the Toning tools. You might, however, make a quick stroke across its visible long side with the Burn tool to create a tonal contrast between this side and the texture on the end of the peg.

Press Ctrl+S (or choose **F**ile, **S**ave)	Saves your work to this point.

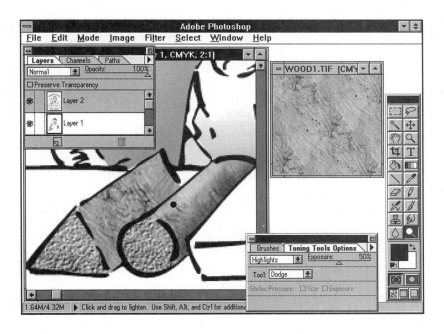

Figure 20.25

Use the Dodge and Burn tools to increase the tonal contrast in areas on the pegs.

Creating a Plausible Hammer

Let's face it—no one, not even a cartoon, can succeed at driving a wood-textured square peg into a round hole with a hammer as completely lacking in color and dimension as the one our friend presently holds. Giving the hammer shading and texture is a two-parter in the next exercise. First, you'll use the same techniques you used with the aptitude pegs to give the hammer's handle a wooden look. Then you'll use a flat, neutral color and a combination of opacity settings with the Paint Brush tool to create a metallic finish on the hammer's business end.

Adding Texture and Shading to the Hammer

Press **L** (for **L**asso tool), then press Alt while clicking around portion of hammer handle between hammer head and guy's hand	Selects top portion of hammer handle.
Press Shift+Alt while clicking points around hammer handle below guy's hand; *don't* include bottom face of handle	Pressing Shift key adds bottom hammer handle selection to top selection.
Open WOOD1.TIF and WOOD_END.TIF images from the CHAP20 subdirectory on Bonus CD	Images used earlier on pegs are used to fill hammer handle.

The Windows version of Photoshop supports a listing of the last four files accessed. You can quickly load these images from the **F**ile menu.

Click on title bar of WOOD1 image, then press Ctrl+A (or choose **S**elect, **A**ll)	Makes WOOD1 the active image window and selects entire image.
Choose **E**dit, **D**efine Pattern, then close WOOD1 image	Defines entire WOOD1 image as a pattern.
Click on SUCCESS.PSD image title bar, then choose **E**dit, **F**ill, choose Pattern, then click on OK	Makes SUCCESS image the active image window, and fills hammer's handle with wood texture.
Press Ctrl+D (or choose **S**elect, **N**one), click on WOOD_END.TIF title bar, then press Ctrl+A (or choose **S**elect, **A**ll)	Selects entire WOOD_END image.
Choose **E**dit, **D**efine Pattern, then close WOOD_END.TIF image	Defines WOOD_END image as a pattern.
With Lasso tool, click and drag around bottom of hammer handle	Selects bottom of hammer.

Choose **E**dit, **F**ill, then click on OK	Fills bottom of hammer handle with WOOD_END texture.
Press **O** (for T**o**ning tools), then choose Burn, set **50%** exposure on Options palette, then choose Midtones from drop-down box	Changes tool to Burn tool, with a setting that will most affect midtones of an image.
Click and drag once or twice over active selection of bottom of hammer handle	Burns in midtones of wood texture, creating shading (see fig. 20.26).
Press Ctrl+D (or choose **S**elect, **N**one), then press **Z** (for **Z**oom tool), and marquee zoom to a 2:1 viewing resolution of hammer head	Image area to be colored next.
Press **L** (for **L**asso tool), then press Alt while clicking around outline of hammer head	Defines area as a selection.
Press **B** (for Paint **B**rush), then click on a medium, neutral gray color in top row of Swatches palette	Chooses Paint brush tool, and sets a medium gray foreground color.
Click on Brushes tab on palette, and choose second tip (from left), in middle row	Sets size and characteristic (soft-edged) of Paint Brush tip.
Click on Options tab, then set Opacity to **100%**, and mode to Normal on Options palette	Sets opacity and characteristic of paint (the foreground color).
Click and drag a straight stroke across selection area, following angle of hammer head	Creates soft-edged stroke of gray on hammer head.
Press **5,** then click and drag above first stroke	Creates a 50% opaque gray stroke.
Click and drag single strokes, pressing different numbers on keyboard before clicking and dragging	Creates smooth shades of gray on hammer head, producing a nice imitation of shiny metal, as shown in figure 20.27.
Press Ctrl+S (or choose **F**ile, **S**ave)	Saves your work to this point.

Figure 20.26

Use the Burn tool to create shading on the wood texture, where the source of light in the image faces away from the area.

Figure 20.27

Use various opacities of foreground color to create a shiny metallic appearance.

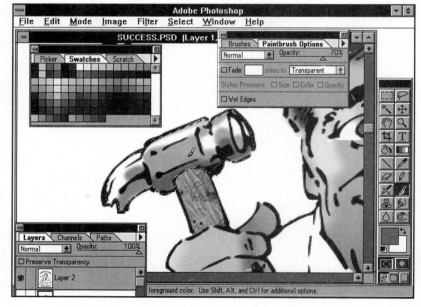

Tip The numeric keyboard keys are a shortcut for setting the opacity of foreground color; opacity increases in increments of ten, and the zero key changes the opacity value to 100%. By setting different opacity levels for the neutral gray in the last exercise, you needed only one foreground color to create complex shading. This is a technique you can use to quickly color any monochrome image.

Subtracting from a Selection, and the Picker Palette

The aptitude pegboard needs coloring and a little shading, to keep the large area from becoming static within the image. In the following exercise, you'll use the Gradient tool to fill the pegboard. But as you can see, the pegboard has holes that shouldn't be filled. The solution to defining the area, then, is to subtract the triangular and round areas from a selection of the pegboard. To do this, you'll first define the pegboard, save the selection, then use the Channels palette's shortcut features to remove the shapes from the overall selection.

Additionally, the Swatches palette can get a little tiring and confining when it's used as the sole source for color definition. To relieve the tedium, you'll set up the Picker palette for CMYK gamut colors in the next exercise, and choose unique foreground and background colors for the gradient fill.

Now to create and fill a compound selection.

Dimensionally Shading the Aptitude Pegboard

Press **L** (for Lasso tool), then press Alt while clicking on the four top corners of the pegboard	Creates a marquee selection that outlines the pegboard.

You'll need to guesstimate where the fourth corner is on the pegboard, because the square peg hides it in the design. Don't worry that the marquee includes part of the square peg; in this exercise you learn about a painting mode that automatically fills around the square peg where it intrudes on the pegboard.

Click on Channels tab on grouped palette, then click on new (save) selection icon	Saves selection to a new channel #5.

continues

continued

Click on Picker tab on grouped palette, click on pop-up menu button on palette's right, then choose HSB Sliders from menu	Specifies that sliders on Picker palette control amounts of hue, saturation, and brightness independently.
Click on pop-up menu button on Picker palette, then choose Color Bar (see fig. 20.28)	Displays Color Bar dialog box.
Choose CMYK Spectrum from **S**tyle drop-down list, then click on OK	Displays a spectrum of colors you can choose from on Picker palette; all are within CMYK gamut.

You now have (on the Picker palette) a complete range of color values from which to choose. These colors are totally "legal" values. Because this is a process-printing-ready image, it's important to use colors that can be faithfully reproduced with printing inks. If you add to this design colors that aren't CMYK, it won't print as you see it onscreen.

Press Ctrl+D (or choose **S**elect, **N**one)	Deselects active marquee.
Click on a warm gray tone on CMYK color spectrum on Picker palette.	Sets foreground color.
Press Alt (Option) while clicking on a darker, warm neutral color on CMYK color spectrum	Sets background color.
Press **L** (for **L**asso tool), then press Alt while clicking on corners of the bottom of the triangular hole	Creates a selection marquee around triangular hole.
Press Shift+Alt while clicking around the bottom of square peg's hole	Adds square peg's hole to selection of triangle.
Press Ctrl and click on new (Save to) Selection icon on Channels palette, then drag icon into channel #5 title	Removes active selection from saved selection (see fig. 20.29).

In figure 20.29, the icons on the Channels palette have been enlarged (by using Channel Options on the pop-up menu) so that you can clearly see what takes place here. You can't really remove the triangle and round shapes from an active marquee around the peg board in a simpler way than the one described in this exercise. Unfortunately, you *can't* subtract from the interior of an existing selection by using the Ctrl and Alt keys simultaneously; this key combination is for moving a selection, but not the image contents. So a straight line selection (created by pressing Alt and clicking), such as the triangular peg hole bottom, can only be accomplished by saving the pegboard selection, then using the "press Ctrl while clicking and dragging the icon" shortcut offered on the Channels palette.

With the Paint Brush tool, color the left interior sides of the square and triangle holes a medium shade of neutral gray	These areas should display a darker shade, because the light in the image is casting away from their faces.
Press Alt while clicking on Channel #5 icon on Channels palette	Loads selection you modified.
Press **G** (for **G**radient tool), then set Options palette to Behind mode, **100%** Opacity, and Foreground to Background Style	Sets painting mode for Gradient tool to cover only transparent areas of Layer 1.

Behind painting mode is sort of a misnomer; you can't really see colors you apply from behind the current image information on a layer. However, the power behind this euphemistic title is invaluable—it only works on Layers (not on the Background layer of an image). In this painting mode, you cannot paint over existing layer information. Therefore, the portion of the peg that covers the corner of your saved selection border cannot be ruined when you use the Gradient tool.

Click and drag from left to right across selection, at about a 4 o'clock angle	Adds gradient fill to pegboard (see fig. 20.30).
Press Ctrl+D (or choose **S**elect, **N**one), then Click+drag Alpha channel #5 into the trash icon on the Channels palette	Deselects marquee and deletes the Alpha channel from the file. You're done with it.
Press Ctrl+S (**F**ile, **S**ave)	Saves your work at this intermediate stage of completion.

Art imitates life, right? Your *own* aptitude test in the last exercise gave you an education in a new painting mode, more CMYK color options, and the easiest way to subtract a complex selection area from a saved one. In the next section you explore more of the potential of the Behind mode as you add a splash of color to the successful guy's desktop.

Tip The HSB sliders on the Picker palette are a more intuitive arrangement of color component specifications than RGB, or CMYK. In other words, you can more quickly define, say, a shade of green with the HSB sliders than with the other color models. However, you can indeed "push" a color out of CMYK "legal" colors by using these sliders, and the resulting color won't print as the same color you see on your monitor.

continues

As we play with color specifications in this chapter, you have the opportunity to define foreground and background colors by using the perfectly legal CMYK color spectrum, but you can also click and drag the HSB sliders to "tune" a color you want to use. If, by chance, the color you want falls out of the printable CMYK gamut, you'll see an exclamation icon near the foreground/background color swatches. The exclamation icon indicates that something's amiss—you're out of the CMYK gamut—and a small swatch next to the exclamation point is Photoshop's suggested alternative color, one that is CMYK-compliant. By clicking on the exclamation button, you accept Photoshop's recommended color, and can then use the CMYK "legal" color in your work.

Figure 20.28

To keep the spectrum of colors displayed on the Picker palette CMYK "legal," choose a CMYK Color Bar.

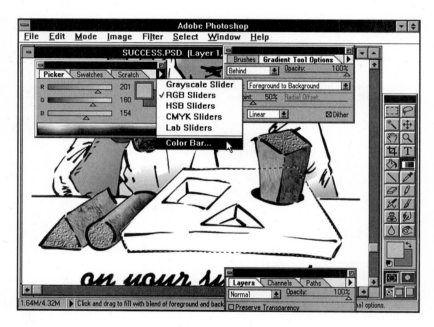

Figure 20.29

Subtract an existing selection from a saved selection by clicking and dragging the new (Save to) Selection icon into a channel.

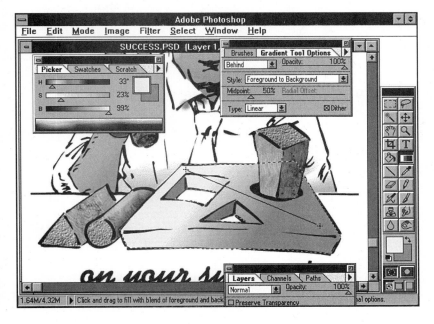

Figure 20.30

Paint Behind mode can only fill transparency areas on a layer; you can't paint over color areas.

The Behind Mode Color "Wash"

The pegs, the aptitude pegboard, the successful guy's instrument of success (the hammer, okay?), and the successful guy have a lot of detail and color now, which leaves the few areas you haven't covered looking a little sparse. In the cartoon world, when an illustrator doesn't have the time to create elegant backgrounds and props, the next best thing for fleshing out a composition is a color wash. A splash of color that gently fades to the edge of the composition is easy to accomplish by feathering a selection in Photoshop—and this is what you'll do in the next exercise.

The surface the pegboard sits on in this image is the target area for the color wash. You might be wondering why you've been asked to color different, seemingly unrelated areas in this greeting card. The reason becomes obvious from here on in. Now that the foreground elements have been colored in, you can use Behind mode extensively in this design to color in other areas without worrying about accidentally painting over an area you've completed. As you saw in the last exercise, Behind painting mode protects existing image detail in a manner that's exactly the inverse of the Preserve Transparency option on the Layers palette. In Behind mode, transparency pixels are selected, while image areas are masked.

In this exercise, you add the suggestion of a supporting surface for the successful guy's aptitude pegboard.

Creating a Freeform Color Wash

Press **L** (for **Lasso** Tool)	Chooses Lasso tool.
Enter **12** in Feather field on Options palette	Makes feathered selection areas wherever you click and drag Lasso tool.
Click and drag a freeform shape around pegboard in image (see fig. 20.31)	Shape of color wash you'll create.

Don't mistake the marquee border for the actual edge of the selection you've created. A feathered selection is a soft-edge selection, and although the marquee indicates the position of the selection, it fails to depict the soft-edge transition between selected and masked image areas.

Click on a mustard color in CMYK color spectrum on Picker palette	Defines foreground color you'll add to selection.

Press **K** (for Paint Bucket), then set Options palette for Behind painting mode, Tolerance **255**, **100%** Opacity, Contents: Foreground (color)	Chooses Paint Bucket tool and sets characteristics for tool.
Click inside marquee (see fig. 20.32)	Fills uncolored areas with foreground mustard color, which fades to transparent at edges.
Press Ctrl+D (**S**elect, **N**one), then Ctrl+S (**F**ile, **S**ave)	Deselects the selection and saves your work up to this point.

The Paint Bucket fill appears to have created a blend from foreground mustard color to background white, but because you're painting on a layer, the fill blends to transparent at the borders, and the white you see is actually the vacant Background layer.

Be sure to check the Lasso tool Options before using the tool again. Photoshop retains your last settings for a tool, and you don't want to accidentally create freehand selections with a huge feather value. Make a practice of resetting the Lasso and marquee tools to a 0 Feather value on the Options palette after you've finished using this option.

Figure 20.31

Use the feather option for the Lasso tool to automatically feather a selection after you define it.

Figure 20.32

The feathered selection fades the foreground color to transparent at the edges.

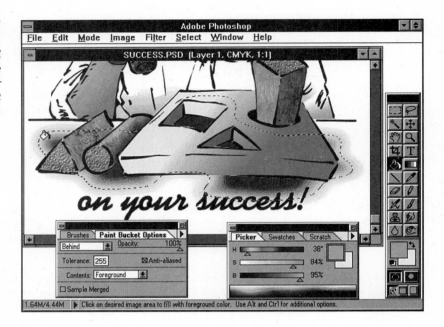

The KPT Gradient Designer "Jump Start" Instructions

To create the pattern for the successful guy's tie, you'll use Kai's Gradient Designer, because this Plug-In filter has the capability to create complex, multicolor gradient blends in selection areas. However, to apply even a simple gradient fill, you must either have a preset fill already defined, or have a basic working knowledge of how to create one. And this is why Chapter 19, "Third-Party Plug-In Filters," came before this chapter; it contains the how-tos for creating, saving, and editing a complex gradient fill created in the Gradient Designer.

But you don't have to learn all the ins and outs of the KPT Gradient Designer right now to take advantage of the filter's capabilities. In fact, part of the GradienDesigner's features is to take sample colors from a target image and create a complex gradient fill based on the color information. In essence, you can *copy* the gradient fill we've designed for use in the successful guy's tie and save the fill's settings for future use.

Following is the one way to create a Successful Guy's Tie setting in the Gradient Designer without extensively exploring the filter's interface:

Copying and Saving a KPT Gradient Designer Fill

Open the GUY_TIE.PSD image from the CHAP20 subdirectory on the Bonus CD	This is the gradient design you'll copy into the KPT filter.
Click on Filter, KPT 2.0 Extensions, then Gradient Designer 2.0	Opens the Gradient Designer interface.
Click and hold on the Option button, then while still holding, scroll down and then release when your cursor's on Preferences	Displays the startup preferences for the filter.

Click+holding and scrolling is not how a typical Windows menu operates, but this is the familiar way to "drill down" a menu for Macintosh users.

Click on the Load Normal Gradient from Image radio button, then click on OK	Specifies that upon starting the filter, image color information from an open document is read into the filter.
Press Cancel	Sets the startup preference for the Gradient Designer.

The Gradient Designer will now read the KPTFILL.PSD image as the source for a complex fill the next time you choose the filter.

Click on Filter, KPT 2.0 Extensions, then Gradient Designer 2.0	The design in the GUY_TIE.PSD image displays in the preview window.
Click on the Add button, then type **Successful Guy's Tie** in the Name field, and click on OK	Adds the gradient design to the Presets Grid (File) for the Miscellaneous category of fills.
Press Cancel, then close the GUY_TIE.PSD image	You've added the gradient design to the Gradient Designer for future use.

The preceding steps are illustrated in Chapter 19, where you'll find the steps for creating a gradient design using the KPT Gradient Designer's set of user controls. For now, however, you have one working preset for the filter, and can fill the successful guy's tie in the next section.

Kai's Ties

You'll use the sampler edition of KPT's Gradient Designer 2.0 in the next exercise to fill the successful guy's tie with a pleasant, conservative, striped pattern. If you experiment with the Gradient Designer on your own, you'll discover two things:

1. You should buy the commercial version, because the Gradient Designer integrates with the other KPT filters to produce extraordinary fill and stroke effects.

2. It's far easier to create an *outlandish* tie than a conservative one, using Kai's Power Tools!

Now to fill in the successful guy's tie with a complex gradient blend.

Picking Out a Successful Guy's Tie

Press **L** (for **L**asso tool), then press Alt (Option) while clicking around knot area only	Selection area for Gradient Designer fill (see fig. 20.33).
Press Alt(Option)+Delete	Fills the selection area with foreground color.

Because you're working on a transparent layer, the KPT Gradient Desiner needs opaque pixels to perform its magic. The current foreground color is of no matter here; you only need some opaque pixels within the selection that can be filled with the gradient.

Choose Filters, KPT 2.0 Extensions, then Gradient Designer 2.0	Displays Gradient Designer User Interface.
Click and hold on the Misc. category in the presets box at the bottom of the Gradient Designer; while holding, scroll to Successful Guy's Tie, then release the mouse button	Chooses the preset gradient design you copied earlier and displays it in the preview window.

This part of the assignment invites experimentation—there is no "wrong" design for the guy's tie. If you'd like to use your own creative imagination here, click and drag the selection bar, and choose different colors from the color bar (hidden until you click and hold on the gradient bar). Again, for a more complete understanding of the Gradient Designer, read Chapter 19.

Click and drag in Gradient Direction control window until you see 115 at bottom	Creates a gradient pattern that will run diagonally on tie (see fig. 20.34).

Click on OK	Confirms your selection, and applies effect.
With Lasso tool, press Alt while clicking around edges of front of tie, then press Shift+Alt while clicking around remaining neck portions of tie	Selects uncolored portions of tie.
Press Alt+Delete (Mac: Option+Return)	Fills these areas with the current foreground color.
Press Ctrl+Alt+F (Mac users: press Cmd+Option+F)	Recalls last-used filter's dialog box.
Click and drag Gradient Direction preview so that stripes point at 5 and 11 o'clock, then click on OK	Fills other parts of tie with gradient fill that goes in opposite direction to fill in knot (see fig 20.35).
Press Ctrl+D (or choose Select, None), then press Ctrl+S (or choose File, Save)	Deselects the selections, and saves your work to this point.

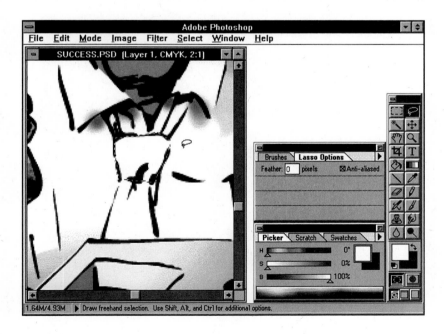

Figure 20.33

Create a selection marquee around the area you wantto fill with KPT'sGradient Designer 2.0.

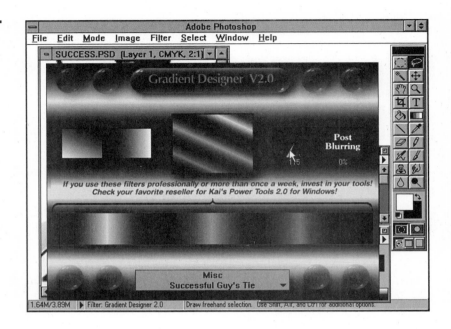

If you chose to create your own tie pattern in the last exercise, you might notice that it's a little duller than what's displayed by the preview in the Gradient Designer 2.0. This happens because, by default, you use the RGB color model in the Gradient Designer, and the SUCCESS.PSD image is based around CMYK colors. If you want to access CMYK values while you build a gradient design, you must click and hold on the Spectrum options in the Gradient Designer, then choose Spectrum, CMYK Modulated. Like Photoshop's Picker palette, Kai's Gradient Designer offers a spectrum based around the CMYK color model, which includes the values for printing inks, not the RGB monitor gamut you usually work in. The Spectrum options are located to the right of the color bar, which you access in the Gradient Designer by clicking and holding on the Gradient Bar.

Coloring and Drop-Shadowing the Lettering

The lettering in this greeting card is far superior to the hand-lettering scanned from the original graphic, but it doesn't stand a chance, colorwise, when competing with all the lush texture and color fills you've added. This lettering makes the card a little less than eye-catching. Fortunately, by adding some color and a drop-shadow, you can pump up the *CONGRATULATIONS* and *on your success!* text and make the sentiment fairly leap off the image.

In the next exercise, you'll use the Preserve Transparency option to select only the text, copy it, fill the original lettering, then paste the black copy behind the colored lettering to create a drop-shadow. The Preserve Transparency option makes it easy to precisely select only the image lettering you want and preserves your handiwork on the lettering when you paste the copy back into the image. Now—make the greeting card's lettering as dynamic as the rest of the piece.

Creating Hand-Painted Lettering

Scroll to top of SUCCESS.PSD image	First area you'll edit.
Click on Layer 2 title on Layers palette	Makes Layer 2 (where black lettering is) the target (current) layer.
Press **L** (for **L**asso tool), then click on Preserve Transparency check box on Layers palette	Masks transparent areas on Layer 2 (protects them from editing).
Click and drag around CONGRATULATIONS lettering, then press Ctrl+C (or choose **E**dit, **C**opy)	Copies lettering to Clipboard.

continues

continued

Click on an orange area of CMYK spectrum on Picker palette, then press Alt (Option) while clicking on a dark red on Picker palette	Sets foreground and background colors you'll use for coloring lettering.

Alternatively, you can pick values from the Swatches or Scratch palettes.

Press **G** (for **G**radient tool), set Options palette to Linear fill Type, **100%** Opacity, and Foreground to Background Style	Chooses Gradient tool, and sets characteristics of how gradient fill will be applied.
Click and drag from top to bottom over marquee selection	Fills only the CONGRATULATIONS lettering with orange-to-red fill (see fig. 20.36).
Click on Layer 1 title on Layers palette, then press Ctrl+V (or choose **E**dit, **P**aste)	Pastes copy of black lettering onto Layer 1.

While the lettering is still a floating selection above Layer 1, choose a selection tool (the Lasso tool is fine), then click and drag inside the marquee border to position the lettering about one-half screen inch below the gradient-filled lettering on Layer 2, as shown in figure 20.37.

Press Ctrl+D (or choose **S**elect, **N**one), then press Ctrl+S (or choose **F**ile, **S**ave)	Deselects floating selection and saves your work to this point.

The Preserve Transparency option is assigned to layers on a case-by-case basis. Layer 2 presently has the option turned on, but Layer 1 does not have the transparent pixels masked, which makes this a terrific time to perform a similar effect to the lettering at the bottom of the greeting card! You're going to make this guy's success an unqualified one.

Figure 20.36

Preserve Transparency protects the transparent pixels on a layer; only pixels with colors can be edited.

Figure 20.37

Pasting the copy of the lettering to Layer 1 places the element behind the colored lettering.

Creating Drop-Shadow Lettering

Scroll down to bottom of SUCCESS.PSD image	Location of second part of card's message, which needs to be edited.
Click on Layer 2 title on Layers palette	Makes Layer 2 (layer with original lettering) the target layer.
With Lasso tool, click and drag around the *on your success!* lettering	Selects lettering only; Preserve Transparency option should still be checked on Options palette.
Press Ctrl+C (or choose (<u>E</u>dit, <u>C</u>opy)	Copies lettering to Clipboard.
Press **X** (for switch-colors icon)	Makes current foreground color dark red.
Press Alt+Delete (Mac: Option+Delete)	Fills current selection with foreground color (see fig. 20.38).
Click on Layer 1 title on Layers palette, then press Ctrl+V (or choose <u>E</u>dit, <u>P</u>aste)	Pastes copy of lettering (as floating selection) on Layer 1.
Click and drag inside floating selection to position it below and to right of red lettering on Layer 2	Creates drop-shadow lettering that has same lighting source as rest of the drawing (see fig. 20.39).
Press Ctrl+D (or choose <u>S</u>elect, <u>N</u>one), then press Ctrl+S (or choose <u>F</u>ile, <u>S</u>ave)	Deselects floating selection and saves your work to this point.

Now for a little score-keeping: at this point, Layer 2 contains the black information about the design (with the exception of the lettering), and Layer 1 contains the shading and textures. We have some grand plans in store, shortly, for adding a photographic background to the design. And although the background layer is available, it presently fills in the uncolored areas on the two design Layers. In other words, the successful guy's white shirt and parts of the hammer head have no fill right now. By adding an image to the background layer, you can have a photo on the background peek through these "empty" areas.

No problems in this book, however. Only solutions. In the next section, you'll see how to use Behind painting mode to fill in areas in preparation for adding a background photograph.

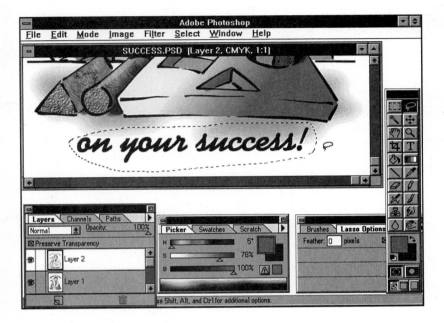

Figure 20.38

Use Alt+Delete (Options+Return) to fill a selection with the current foreground color.

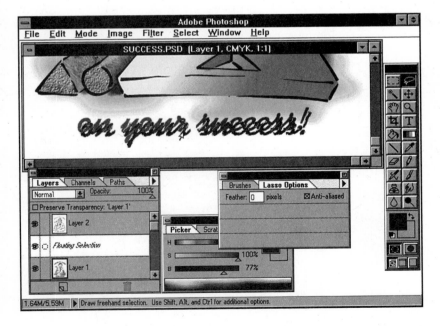

Figure 20.39

Cast the drop shadow in the same direction as the lighting source in the image.

Using Digital Correction Fluid on Digital Acetate

In this assignment, we've had the luxury of a supporting background layer to auto-matically fill in design areas where one would expect white, or "empty space." As we've stressed in this and other chapters, however, the concept of "empty" cannot truly be achieved (or even simulated) with a bitmap-type image. In reality, the transparent pixels on a layer are a transparency mask that you don't see. You can even use the **S**elect, **L**oad Selection command and choose Layer Transparency to mask the tranparent pixels and select the opaque ones on a layer, even when you haven't saved a selection in an Alpha channel. All pixels are held in position by an imaginary grid, and whether the pixels are assigned a color or a transparency, each of them must occupy a position within the grid—if even as a placeholder.

If you want to place an image on the background layer of SUCCESS.PSD, the next logical step is to replace some of the transparent pixels on Layer 1 with white, opaque pixels. You want to fill in any areas that are currently transparent and shouldn't be "filled" with the photographic background. In this way, the fancy fills you created on Layers 1 and 2 will display the same visual continuity they presently have with the white background layer peeking through, and the white areas will mask unwanted background detail in the finished image. In figure 20.40, the background layer is hidden, so that you can see Photoshop's checkerboard pattern (or *grid*)—a visual indicator of the transparent areas in a file when only the layers are viewed. Set up your SUCCESS.PSD image this way, by clicking on the eye icon next to the Back-ground Layer title, in preparation for the exercise.

Figure 20.40

Click on the eye icon next to the Background Layer to hide it, and to display transparent and colored areas on layers.

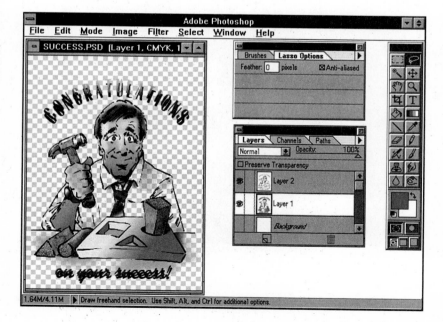

Now you'll use the Behind painting mode to create sort of an "inverted mask" for the design, so that a photographic background can be integrated into the image.

"Inking In" Transparent Image Areas

Double-click on Zoom tool	Moves viewing resolution of image to 1:1.
Press **D** (or click on default colors icon), then press **X** (or click on switch colors icon)	Changes foreground/background colors to black and white, then inverts colors, making white the current foreground color.
Press **P** (for **P**encil tool), then set Options palette to Behind mode, **100%** Opacity, and leave Auto-Erase option *un*checked	Sets characteristics for the way Pencil tool applies foreground color.

The Auto-Erase option, which automatically switches foreground color to background color (in this case, black) when you release the mouse button and stroke over an area you've previously covered, is *not* a good option for this part of the assignment!

Click on Brushes tab on palette, then choose fifth tip on second row	This 21-pixel-diameter tip is ideal for the sort of coverage needed in transparent image areas.
Click and drag Pencil tool over an area of shirt that displays checkerboard pattern (see fig. 20.41)	Fills in transparent pixels only; Behind painting mode protects colors and textures already occupying space on Layer 1.
Scout around for other areas that show checkerboard pattern, then click and drag in them	Because hammer head was filled with partially opaque gray, this area needs filling, too.

As you fill in transparent areas with white, make sure you don't go outside the edges of the black design you can see on Layer 2. The Pencil tool applies color with no bleed—no soft-edge, Anti-alias characteristics—so when you fill an area right to the border of a design element, you can be sure that nothing placed on the background layer will show through.

When the interior of the successful guy, his hammer, and other areas above the horizon of the desktop have been filled, as shown in figure 20.42...

Press Ctrl+S (or choose **F**ile, **S**ave)	Saves your work to this point.

Figure 20.41

Use the Behind painting mode in combination with the Pencil tool to fill in transparent areas on Layer 1.

Figure 20.42

None of the areas within the cartoon figure should show the checkboard grid, an indicator of transparent layer pixels.

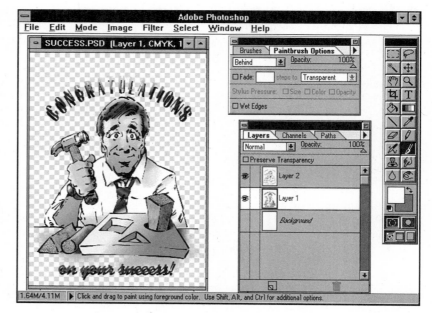

One of the great things about working with layers is that you don't have to duplicate your efforts; because Layer 1 now has the interior of the design completely filled with color, absolutely no further editing is required on Layer 2 before the image is flattened. Layer 1's information protects the detail on Layer 2.

Creating a Photographic Wash

It's always a good idea to choose the background to a graphic design with extra care, to ensure that the photographic realism of the background doesn't overpower the image you've worked so hard to create. In this chapter's assignment, the successful guy could use a background that's eye-pleasing but doesn't have too much innate visual interest. For this reason, we created REWARD.TIF from a PhotoCD image of a sky with clouds. Then we enhanced REWARD.TIF a little, using KPT's Gradients On Paths 2.0 filter to add a rainbow (a traditional icon of good fortune and optimism). Unfortunately, this filter is not on the Bonus CD.

Simply plopping the REWARD.TIF image into the Background layer would be a mistake. The black outline of the design on Layer 2 contains all the hard-edge compositional elements this greeting card needs, and a hard-edged rectangular border around the image of the clouds would conflict with all the softly colored organic shapes in the image. Therefore, in the next exercise you'll create a feathered selection on the Background Layer, and then use the Paste Into command to create a soft, framed effect for the photograph.

Here's how to integrate a digital image into a digital illustration:

Pasting a Photo into a Drawing

In the Layers Palette, click the Eye in the Background Layer, then click the Background Layer	Makes the Background layer visible and active.
Press Ctrl+minus to display SUCCESS.PSD image at 1:2 viewing resolution, then resize image window so that entire image is visible	You need a view of entire image to better create a selection marquee on Background layer.
Press **M** (for **M**arquee tool) until Elliptical marquee tool is selected	Tool used to create part of photo-framing area.
Enter **14** in Feather field on Options palette, then marquee-select (click and drag diagonally) an oval that encompasses most of background	Creates a feathered selection area on Background layer (see fig. 20.43).

continued

Press **M** (for **M**arquee tool) once	Toggles to Rectangular marquee tool.
Type **0** in Feather options field on Options palette	Sets no feathering for Rectangular marquee tool.
Press Ctrl while clicking and dragging (Mac: press Cmd⌘ while clicking and dragging) a Rectangular marquee whose top edge meets edge of successful guy's desktop (see fig. 20.44)	Removes bottom of feathered ellipse from selection. Selection marquee's top edges are feathered; its bottom side has a hard edge.
Open REWARD.TIF image from CHAP20 subdirectory on Bonus CD	The CMYK image prepared for greeting card. Resolution, color mode, and dimensions match those of SUCCESS.PSD image.
Press Ctrl+A (or choose **S**elect, **A**ll), then press Ctrl+C (or choose **E**dit, **C**opy), then close image by pressing Ctrl+W (or choose **F**ile, **C**lose) (see fig. 20.45)	Copies entire REWARD image to Clipboard. Closes REWARD; you don't need it any more.
Choose **E**dit, Paste **I**nto, then click and drag selection to position it (see fig. 20.46)	Pastes REWARD copy into partially feathered selection, creating a soft drop-off to white where selection area makes transition to masked areas on background.
Press Ctrl+D (or choose **S**elect, **N**one), then press Ctrl+S (or choose **F**ile, **S**ave)	Deselects floating selection and saves your work to this point.

If the image on your monitor looks like one of the figures in the last exercise, you might want to send this congratulations card to yourself! You've done the seemingly impossible—integrated many types of digital and acquired media into a file-format type that's ready to roll off the process color presses.

In the next section we've created a little goof in the image, to show you the procedures you should take if your image is less than perfect-looking. The procedures are in the form of an exercise—a little clean-up work you might want to do before merging the layers into an image format other applications can read.

Figure 20.43

Create a feathered selection on the background layer by entering a value in the Options palette field.

Figure 20.44

Subtract the bottom of the ellipse selection by marquee-selecting with the Rectangular Marquee tool.

Figure 20.45

Copy the REWARD.TIF image to the Clipboard.

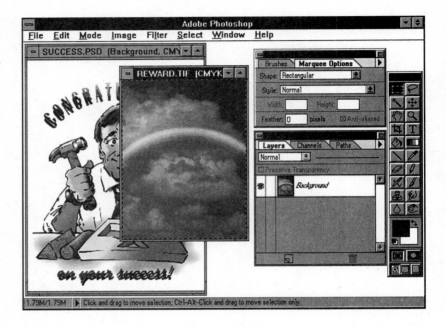

Figure 20.46

The Paste Into command eliminates pasted image areas outside of the selection marquee.

Addressing the "Colored Outside the Lines" Syndrome

It's not easy, even for an experienced imaging-type person, to see where white meets white across image Layers. Although the background layer was white (prepasted photograph), and the guy's shirt on Layer 1 was white, everything in this greeting card might have seemed quite in order. But if you look back at figure 20.46 and focus on the successful guy's shoulder, you'll notice a hunk of white pixels, just above the black line. The hunk of white pixels was caused by coloring outside the lines a little with the Pencil tool when filling in transparent areas on the layer. If this happened to you, the solution is a simple one, and we'll get this card sorted out, lightning-fast, in the next exercise.

In this exercise, you use the Layer Mask feature to remove color pixels from the outside edge of Layer 1.

Using the Layer Mask for Clean-Up Work

Click on Layer 1 title on Layers palette, click on pop-up menu button, then choose Add Layer Mask	Adds an invisible mask to Layer 1. Wherever you apply foreground color, Layer mask will hide image detail on Layer 1.
With Black as foreground color, choose Pencil tool, then click and drag over white area on Layer 1 fig (see 20.47)	Hides white on Layer 1.
When all traces of white outside successful guy's shirt (or anywhere else) have been hidden, choose Remove Layer Mask from pop-up menu on Layers palette	Displays exclamation dialog box, asking whether you want to Apply or Discard the Layer mask.
Click on Apply	Removes Layer 1 areas you hid by applying foreground color.
You're done! Ready for the big event?	
Choose **F**ile, **E**dit, Save a Cop**y**	Displays Save a Copy dialog box.
Check Don't Include **A**lpha Channels box, choose TIFF in Save File As Format **T**ype box, and save image as SUCCESS.TIF	Saves copy of image to your hard disk as a TIF image, without Alpha channels; copy has no layers.

continues

continued

You still have SUCCESS.PSD as the active image window, with all the Layers still intact, so you can perform any sort of tweaking on the image, while the copy you've tucked away can be read by other imaging and desktop publishing applications.

Press Ctrl+S (or choose File, Save)   Saves your work in Photoshop's proprietary PSD format.

Figure 20.47

Use Photoshop's Layer Mask option to remove any superfluous white paint strokes from Layer 1.

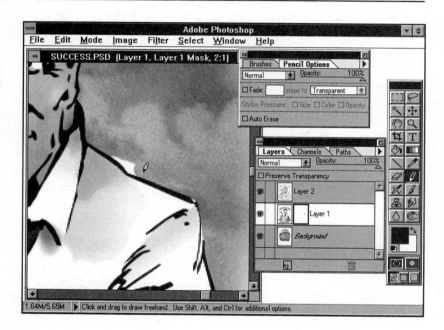

Here's a bonus section for all of us who have a hard time coping with the inherent inadequacies of the CMYK printing gamut.

The KPT Sharpen Intensity Filter

Kai's Power Tools transcends "artistic" filters—several of the filters can be used as production tools. One such filter, Sharpen Intensity, can be used very effectively to punch up CMYK images. Sharpen Intensity is on the Bonus CD (SHARPEN.8BF). You might want to use this filter as a final step in this assignment (or one of your own), before sending an image to a production house for color separations. See Chapter 24, "The Service Bureau," for more information about commercial printing.

Sharpen Intensity does two things to the pixels in a selection area, or an entire image: it improves contrast, and increases saturation. In the process, however, the Sharpen Intensity filter does not throw any colors out of the CMYK gamut. In most cases, what you wind up with is a clearer, more attractive image. If you'd like to try out the Sharpen Intensity filter on the SUCCESS image, simply choose Filter, KPT 2.0 Filters, then Sharpen Intensity. By default, KPT Sharpen Intensity will affect the image at 50 percent strength. By holding down a numerical keyboard key before choosing the filter, you can set the strength, with 0 producing 100% Sharpen Intensity, and the other numbers corresponding to percentages, in increments of 10.

Repeated application of the Sharpen Intensity filter on an image will posterize it. Although this creates an interesting effect, it's more of an artistic use than a pre-press one.

Mixing Other Media with Your New Skills

At the beginning of this chapter, we promised that the techniques you were to learn weren't just for people gifted at using pen and ink at a drafting table. If you come from a traditional art background, you now have a different approach for completing a pencil sketch, but those of us who earn a living designing don't necessarily have to be a Michelangelo (the painter, not the virus) to enhance black-and-white designs with the methods in this chapter.

Figure 20.48

A good design can be improved upon by applying shading, good color composition, and photographic sources.

Figure 20.49

Typographic design by Bruce Haber; embellishment, depth, and dimensionality by Photoshop and someone who read Chapter 20.

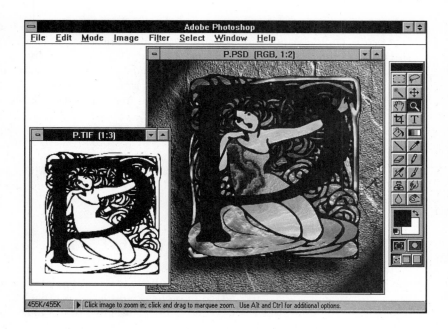

In figure 20.48, you can see a before-and-after of the SUCCESS.PSD image. What element is it that creates the most difference to a viewer?

The typographic character shown in figure 20.49 is from a Type 1 font designed by Bruce Haber (the font is on the Bonus CD). This character was filled in, using the same techniques you used with the SUCCESS image. As a professional, you're obliged to secure the rights to source images that you enhance. But as you can see, the complexity, style, and concept of your framework, the outline of an idea you embellish, can be just about anything you imagine when you have an understanding of Photoshop's tools and a good working knowledge of what image enhancement is all about.

CHAPTER

21

Advanced Type Usage and Presentations

Nothing is sadder today, during the renaissance of graphics through computer tools, than to sit in a boardroom and watch a slide show that consists of gradient-filled backgrounds and Arial Bold text. As a Photoshop user, you already know that digital source images can be acquired from all sorts of places and integrated into a wondrous, seamless finished composition.

Photoshop works very well with images from both photographic and digital, application-created sources. This chapter explores the use of a digital resource that speaks Photoshop's bitmap, Alpha-channel language.

Typestry, a Pixar program that can create dimensional, photorealistic typography using either Type 1 or TrueType fonts, is used along with Photoshop in this chapter to produce a slide presentation that will positively knock the socks off any board meeting in town (with the possible exception of Pixar's own board meetings).

This Chapter's Assignment

Perhaps the hardest part of any assignment is where to begin, and slide presentations often suffer from a lack of concept that precipitates occasional snoring from the back row. This chapter's assignment has been laid out for you, and this section explains why certain elements are used, and why you should consider using them in your own work.

Iron Sheep Industries, makers of fine steel wool products, wants a short presentation as a "pep talk" for their sales force. The elements of a bulleted list of sales points and a strong corporate image need to be included. Therefore, as the designer of this slide show, it's your responsibility to create slides that portray Iron Sheep's logo dynamically and to use an attention-getting graphical hook to make the sales force read the bulleted list within the slide show.

Acquiring the Image

Your first step is to acquire Iron Sheep's logo so that you can use it as a digital source element. The steps are outlined in the first part of this chapter in case you have the applications shown to produce the source material for this assignment by yourself. However, the images you actually use in Photoshop in this chapter's exercises are provided on the Bonus CD that comes with this book.

In figure 21.1, you can see Iron Sheep's logo as a scanned image in Adobe Streamline, a program imaging professionals frequently use as a file translator. The image was scanned from Iron Sheep's letterhead stationery in Grayscale mode at 150 pixels/inch sampling resolution. This creates enough information about the logo for Streamline to translate the graphical information to a format Typestry can use.

Typestry, version 2.0 can use information in both typeface and AI (Adobe Illustrator) file formats. To make the acquired image ISSY.TIF compatible with Typestry's import criteria, Streamline is used on the scanned image to produce an AI file. Streamline is a bitmap-to-vector conversion program that accurately traces the edges found in color areas of a bitmap image to produce outline paths, very similar to those produced with the Pen tool in Photoshop. In figure 21.2, you can see the result of Streamline's work, and the ISSY.AI file is ready for import into Typestry.

Chapter 20, "Mixed Media and Photoshop," shows how a vector file in either AI or EPS (Encapsulated PostScript) format can be "cleaned up" using a separate illustration package such as Illustrator or CorelDRAW!. The ISSY.AI image looks okay as is, and there's really no need to further modify the vector design.

Figure 21.1

Acquire a company logo with a scanner so that the logo can be manipulated as digital information.

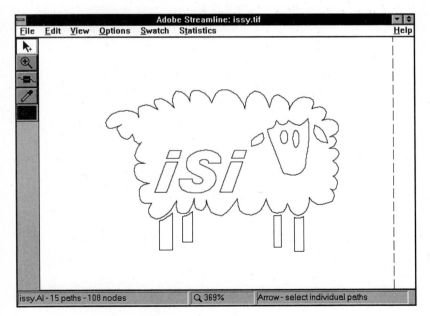

Figure 21.2

Adobe Streamline converts bitmap information to a vector format that can be used with modeling, CAD, and vector drawing programs.

Using an Exported Path as Vector Information

If you don't own a drawing program, you really should get one to complete your suite of computer graphics tools, but in a pinch, Photoshop's capability to export paths in the AI format for use in programs like Typestry can be used. Paths can be automatically created from selection marquee information by first loading (or creating) a selection and then clicking on the New Path icon at the bottom of the Paths palette. However, it is not a good idea to ask Photoshop to create paths from an extremely complex selection marquee because paths are created with path segments and anchor points at every point a selection displays a sharp turn in its path (called a *point of inflection* on a curve). The Iron Sheep logo, for instance, could be placed in the Alpha channel of a new image; the channel is loaded; and the New Path icon is clicked. In this case, Photoshop would grind away for moments on end, only to inform you that the selection is too complex (that is—you've wasted your time).

If you need a quick, simple AI file created, follow these steps:

Converting a Selection to a Path

Press Ctrl+N (<u>F</u>ile, <u>N</u>ew)	Opens the New Image dialog box.
Set the <u>W</u>idth and <u>H</u>eight to **200** pixels, choose Grayscale Mode, enter **72** in the <u>R</u>esolution field, then click on OK	Creates a new image file with the dimensions, color mode, and resolution you specify.
Choose the Elliptical marquee tool; then press **D** (default colors icon)	Chooses the tool for creating a very simple logo and sets foreground color to black.
Press Shift while clicking and dragging within the New-1 image window	Shift constrains the elliptical marquee selection to a perfect circle.
Press Alt (Option)+Delete	Alt key combination fills the selection marquee with foreground color.
Press **N** (for Line tool), then enter **8** in the Line Width field on the Options palette	Chooses the Line tool and specifies the width of lines you draw with it.

Press **X** (switch colors icon); then click and drag two or three lines through the black circle	This is the logo you'll convert to paths.
Press Ctrl+A (**S**elect, **A**ll); then Ctrl+C (**E**dit, **C**opy)	Copies the ball with the lines to the clipboard.
Click on the New Channel icon on the lower left of the Channels palette, then click on OK in the dialog box	Creates Alpha channel #2 within the New-1 image window. Channel #2 is your current view of the image.
Press Ctrl+V (**E**dit, **P**aste), then press Ctrl+D (**S**elect, **N**one)	Pastes the copy of the Black channel into Channel #2.
Click on the Black Channel title on the Channels Palette, press Ctrl+A (**S**elect, **A**ll), and then press Alt+Delete	Moves you to the view of the Black channel; selects the entire image and fills it with foreground white color.

You can't clearly see the effects of making a path from a selection with the logo design still on the black layer; you have a copy as selection information in Channel #2, so it's okay to delete the information on the Black channel.

Press Alt(Option) and click on the Channel #2 icon on the Channels palette	Loads the selection from Channel #2.
Click on the Paths tab on the grouped palettes, then click on the Make Selection icon on the bottom of the Paths palette	Makes a path based on the selection marquee (see fig. 21.3).
Double-click on the Work Path title on the Paths palette, name the path **Generic Logo** in the dialog box, and then click on OK	Saves the Path.
Choose **F**ile, **E**xport, and then Paths to Illustrator	Displays the Export Paths dialog box.
Give the file a name. With the AI extension, choose a directory (folder), then click on OK	You've exported a path as an Adobe Illustrator type file that can be read and used by Typestry and other programs that can read AI files.

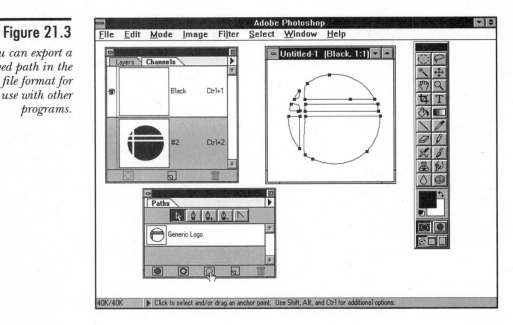

Figure 21.3

You can export a saved path in the AI file format for use with other programs.

Naturally, you can also design a path in Photoshop for exporting as an AI file by using the Paths palette's tool set, and you can modify an "auto-traced" path made from a selection with the same tools. Photoshop's Paths palette can be thought of as a mini-vector drawing program within a bitmap application. The tool features of the Paths palette aren't nearly as robust as a package such as Illustrator, but if you're in a jam to get a vector design out of Photoshop and into another application, the Paths palette can be your ticket.

Using Typestry to Create Presentation Elements

PIXAR, a firm founded by Drs. Ed Catmull and Alvy Smith, has dedicated its research in computer graphics to give businesses visualization solutions in the form of hardware and software that produce photorealistic images. Pixar is responsible for many special effects you see in motion pictures. You'd have to ignore every third computer publication not to know that it was Pixar's pioneer work in computer animation and rendering (the other half of computer modeling; see Chapter 22, "Virtual Reality: The Ingredients of Dreamwork") that brought us the "polymetal alloy" creation in *Terminator II.*

Pixar builds dedicated graphics workstations that run proprietary software, and Photoshop 3 can read and write to the Pixar (*.PXR) format of bitmapped images. The good news for IBM/PC and Macintosh users, however, is that you don't have to own a large, expensive, RISC-based workstation to take advantage of Pixar's digital alchemy.

If you look ahead to Chapter 25, "The Film Recorder," you see that the aspect ratio of 35mm slides is 2:3. This is the proportion you should always use when sending digital images to be made into 35mm slides at places that offer the service. The next stop after procuring, creating, or otherwise glomming the necessary AI vector design of the Iron Sheep logo, is Typestry.

 Stop Although a demonstration version of Typestry 1.1 is on the Bonus CD that comes with this book in both Windows and Macintosh format, you can't perform the steps you see next with the special version of Typestry. In this trial version, AI files and user-defined text can't be imported, but you *can* (and should) experiment with the photorealistic materials and lighting within the special version. And you can produce a TIFF image with an Alpha channel, which you learn how to use in this chapter.

Defining the Dimension and Resolution of An Image

After you start Typestry, you must define the dimensions and resolution of the images you want to create. In figure 21.4 the Image Format dialog box shows a 2:3 aspect ratio for a new image, which is required to produce an edge-to-edge image from a film recorder. A setting of 600×400 pixels, by 96 pixel/inch resolution produces a file that's a little too small in file size to produce a high-quality, film-recorded 35mm slide, but you can work with the exercise images easily in Photoshop because they aren't large.

Note in figure 21.4 that the image File Type specified for final output from Typestry is TIFF RGBA. Different applications use different terms for Alpha channels, and Typestry gives the user an option whether a rendered design should include three channels (RGB color), or four—Red, Green, Blue, and *Alpha*. The fourth channel Typestry creates in files is a mask containing selection information about any foreground object you create within the program. Because Photoshop uses Alpha channels, Typestry's file format feature enables the designer to easily select the Typestry images and place them in a new background.

Figure 21.4

When setting up an image size to use as a 35mm presentation slide, specify a 2:3 aspect ratio.

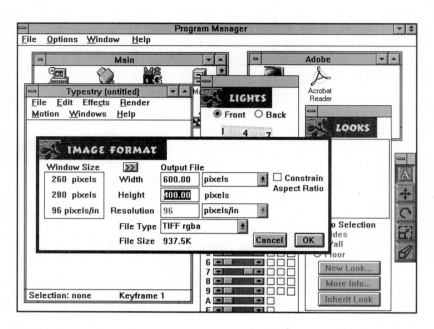

Creating Realistic Text

Typestry's toolbox consists of four basic features for creating dimensional text and AI graphics, and has separate palettes for defining lighting and materials. After the Iron Sheep AI file is imported into the 600×400 pixel new image file, Typestry's Text tool is then used to enter the name of the company, as shown in figure 21.5. Typestry offers four different types of bevels for Text Objects (the 3D objects made from anything typed in the text entry field).

Choosing a Typestyle

Helvetica Black (Italic) was not chosen for its innate charm, or intricate detail, but for its plainness. Typestry embellishes plain text through extrusion and rotational effect, as well as through the materials and lighting the user defines for the final rendered image. The less ornamental the font that you choose for a Text Object, the more the Text Object's dimensionality will captivate the audience and steal the (slide) show.

Rendering to Screen

In figure 21.6, you can see the wireframe view of the elements used in Photoshop for creating the slide show. Both objects are assigned the brushed chrome Look (the teapot on the right is a preview of the surface property for the objects), lights with color gels are pointed at the objects, and the Rotate tool was used to spin the bottom of the Iron Sheep Helvetica Text Object toward the viewer.

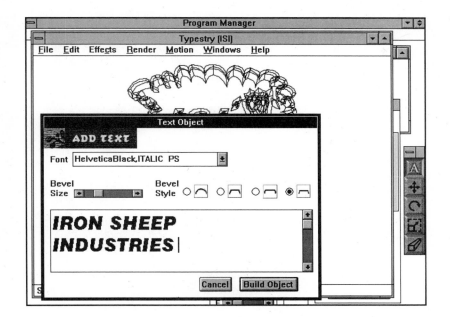

Figure 21.5

Choose from an installed font in Type 1 or TrueType format to create a Text Object in Typestry.

Typestry is a special-purpose *modeling* program; there is a limitation to the complexity of the typographic or AI design you can build as a 3D object in Typestry. The rendering—the other half of the modeling graphics process—however, is handled by Pixar's RenderMan engine within Typestry. RenderMan is an ultra-high caliber program whose final output is seen on television and in movie theaters on a daily basis.

A test render to screen at a low image resolution is usually a good idea before having Typestry render the image file to the final TIFF image that contains an Alpha channel. Rendering is a time-intensive process; many designers who use a modeling program set up a computer to render complex models overnight. The final rendering of the Iron Sheep logo, however, only took about five minutes on a fast 486 class machine. By rendering to screen, the authors could quickly see that the slide looks fine (nothing falls outside the image window; lights are casting where they should), as shown in figure 21.7, so a final render to TIFF format is made.

Adding Bullets

Earlier it was mentioned that Typestry would serve as the resource for a slide show, and so far you've seen how a single slide is made. Because Typestry can render an Alpha channel along with the RGB TIFF file information, the Iron Sheep text object can be reused for a slide other than the one you saw last.

Figure 21.6

Wireframe models are the underlying structure of the finished rendered image in Typestry.

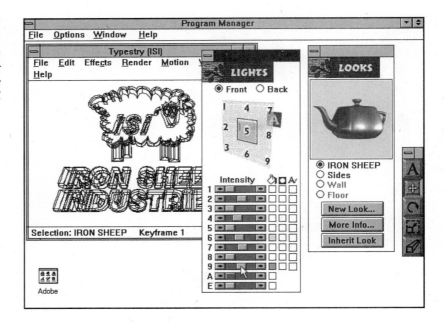

Figure 21.7

Test renders made to screen at low resolution help ensure accurate final renders to file.

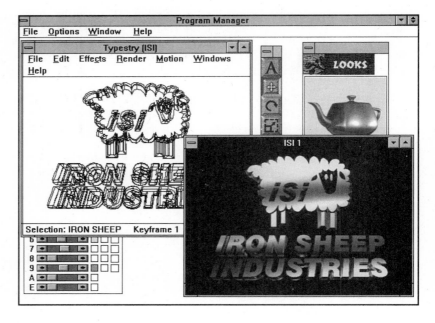

Additionally, your shopping list for the slide show should include 3D bullets to call attention to the sales points you create using Photoshop's Type tool. Although Typestry can really perk up a sales presentation, two or three lines of Typestry 3D type would overwhelm the audience and make the sales points a little hard to read. Typestry is best used to embellish a slide or other graphic; as a designer, it's your duty to scout for the best source materials for a composition from a number of different places.

Zapf Dingbats was chosen in figure 21.8 to serve as the wireframe outline for a new Typestry image. Zapf Dingbats is a graphic designer's staple; they're clean, elegant symbols that communicate a bulleted list with impact.

 Note   There are many *pi* symbol sets (or *picture fonts*) available in both Type 1 and TrueType from various manufacturers, and they too can be used with the commercial release of Typestry.

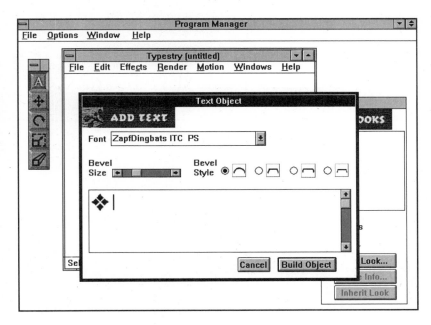

Figure 21.8

Symbol, or Pi, fonts can be used in Typestry in the same way as any digital font.

We conclude the image resource shopping in figure 21.9 with two renders of a character from Zapf Dingbats that looks quite like a four-pack of steel wool pads, perfect for Iron Sheep's presentation. The less empty space you tell Typestry to render to finished TIFF format, the quicker the render goes. In figure 21.9, you also can see crop marks around the wireframe bullet; Typestry created an RGBA type file in a matter of minutes with only the image area inside the crop box included. Figure 21.9 is not in color, but BULLET1.TIF and BULLET2.TIF are the images in the

CHAP21 subdirectory of the Bonus CD that accompanies this book. If you open the image files in Photoshop, you'll see in the following sections that the bullets are dark blue and brilliant red. Why the bullets need to be different is explained shortly.

Figure 21.9

An image element can be cropped from Typestry's background to only render the area you need.

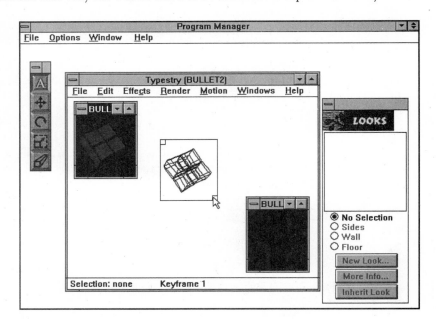

Organizing the Presentation Elements

Pretend that you performed all the steps up to this point and now have a healthy collection of Typestry designs rendered to TIFF format, with selection information already defined in an Alpha channel. Your next step is to make a background for the slides. Typestry surrounds the foreground images with a solid color (by default black), and as a designer, you can come up with something a little livelier than a solid color background. In the next exercise, you load the SHEEPBAK.TIF image from the CHAP21 subdirectory. This image was chosen to serve as the background for the four slides.

Typestry has built the Alpha channel that contains outline information about the sheep logo and dimensional text. In figure 21.10, ISI.TIF (the splashy opening slide) is opened; the channels tab on the Channels palette is clicked; and Channel #4 is clicked. As you can see, Typestry defines the colored areas in an Alpha channel to be masked, whereas the white areas are selection information. Throughout this book, you've been asked to set up saved selections in Photoshop the other way around. It's a little more intuitive to see areas filled with black as selection areas, however; you have your choice how selections are viewed, and you can set this option by double-clicking on an Alpha channel title on the Channels palette list.

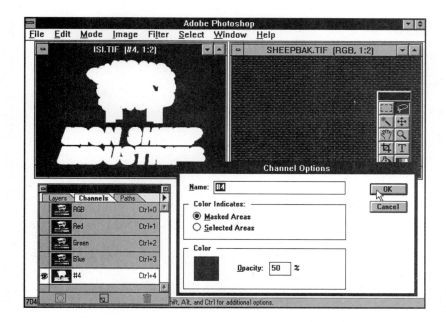

Figure 21.10

Typestry and many "Alpha-aware" programs define masked areas as black, and white areas correspond to selected areas.

Tip

The view of an Alpha channel is a convenience provided by Photoshop, and although you can edit, erase, or otherwise modify the Alpha channel information from a channel view, the information is primarily used by Photoshop in the creation of a marquee selection. Because the colors used to present selected and masked (protected) image areas are user-definable in Photoshop, it can get quite confusing when you want to load a selection. "Is the area inside or outside the marquee the selected area?" is a common concern.

Besides changing the Color Indicates' attributes of an Alpha channel, you can also use the **S**elect, **I**nverse command to turn a loaded selection marquee "inside out" when you've loaded the inverse of what you need selected. This command is on the default configuration of the Windows Command palette, and the shortcut key combination is Shift+F7. Photoshop for Macintosh doesn't come with Shift+F7 preinstalled on the Commands palette, but both Mac and Windows users can configure the Commands palette and create any key combination from the function keys to produce easy-to-reach commands.

Additionally, selection information is defined as colored and uncolored areas on a channel-to-channel basis. You can indeed have selected areas represented as color in, say, Channel #4, whereas Channel #5's *masked* areas are represented by foreground color.

Fortunately, Photoshop and Typestry work well together in terms of synchronous Alpha channel information, and if you're ready to begin creating the slide show, Photoshop will load Typestry's Alpha channel to make selecting the 3D objects a breeze.

The exercise that follows is not demanding of your design skills, but it shows you a wonderful way to take advantage of the Duplicate Layer command in Photoshop 3. With one background image, you create multiple background copies using this command, and because Duplicate Layer is an internal Photoshop command, no strain is placed on system resources by using the external (system) clipboard.

Creating a Title Slide

Open the ISI.TIF image from the CHAP21 subdirectory (folder) on the Bonus CD that comes with this book

This is the image created in Typestry that you use as a title slide for the show.

Click on the Channels tab on the Channels palette, then press Alt (Option) and click on the Channel #4 title

Loads the selection marquee you saw in figure 21.10.

Open the SHEEPBAK.TIF image from the CHAP21 subdirectory of the Bonus CD that comes with this book

This is the background you use to create all four slides in the presentation.

Click on the Layers tab on the Layers/Channels/Paths grouped palette. Click on the New Layer icon; click on OK in the New Layer dialog box

Creates a new Layer 1 on the SHEEPBAK.TIF image.

Click on a selection tool, click on the title bar on the ISI.TIF image window, then click and drag the selection into the SHEEPBAK.TIF image

Copies the foreground selection in ISI.TIF to SHEEPBAK's Layer 1 (see fig. 21.11).

Press Ctrl+D (**S**elect, **N**one)

Deselects the floating selection and the copy becomes part of Layer 1.

Click on the Background layer title on the Layers palette

Makes the background of SHEEPBAK the current editing layer.

Now you begin copying the SHEEPBAK image without using the clipboard.

Close the ISI.TIF image, then click on the Layers palette's pop-up menu and choose Duplicate Layer

Displays the Duplicate Layer dialog box.

In the Destination field, click on the New Document, then type **SLIDE2&3** in the Name field (see fig. 21.12)

Because the destination is a new document, you don't have an option for the title of the layer you're duplicating; you start the new image with the Background layer.

Click on OK

A new image window appears, entitled SLIDE2&3 (no file extension), with a copy of the wire screen as its Background layer.

You're now free to edit on the Background layer of SHEEPBAK.TIF without having to open another copy of the image from the Bonus CD. CD images can't be altered, but if this was your only copy of the SHEEPBAK image, using the Duplicate Layer command would be one way to ensure against accidentally altering your only copy.

Save both the SHEEPBAK and SLIDE 2&3 images in the PSD format to your hard disk

Both images will be further edited using layers, and the PSD format is the only Photoshop format that can support layers.

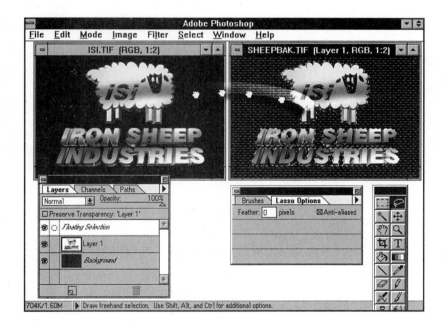

Figure 21.11

Drag and drop a copy of the selected image area onto SHEEPBAK's Layer 1.

Figure 21.12

You can copy an entire image layer and create a new document at the same time by using the Duplicate Layer command.

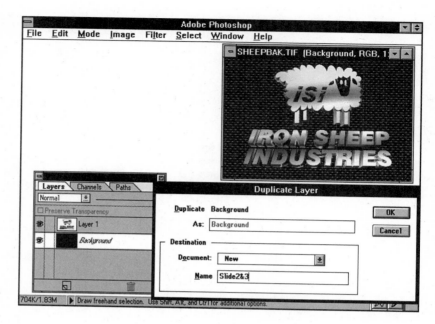

You have a splashy title slide for Iron Sheep now, saved as SHEEPBAK.PSD because you're not finished dressing it up.

The *Inside Photoshop 3* Bonus CD contains several trial and working versions of programs and Photoshop plug-in filters. You use one of the filters, Alien Skin's Drop Shadow plug-in, in the next exercise. If you're like most of us, you immediately installed every goodie from the CD onto your hard disk before reading this book, but on the outside chance that you haven't, close Photoshop and install Alien Skin's Drop Shadow before reading the next section!

Tip

For Windows users, Alien Skin's Drop Shadow plug-in can be loaded into Photoshop by copying the DRP.8BF file from the ALIENS subdirectory on the Bonus CD that comes with this book into Photoshop's PLUGINS directory on your hard disk. When you restart Photoshop, Alien Skin appears in your Filter menu.

Macintosh users should drag the DROP SHADOW folder into Photoshop's plug-in folder, and upon restarting Photoshop, the plug-in appears on the Filter menu.

Read the accompanying documentation in the same subdirectory where the plug-in filter is located on the Bonus CD for further information about this and other great filters made by Alien Skin Software, a name you can trust for out-of-this-world imaging effects.

Giving a 3D Image a 3D Background

Shadow-making in Photoshop was covered in Chapter 11, "Using Paths, Selections, and Layers," and it's important to know how to add a shadow to an image when you need to bring a background element out of the background or make an image area appear to hover above a landscape. Alien Skin Software's Drop Shadow plug-in filter can turn shadow-making into easy work; in fact, it automates the complicated procedure for designing a drop shadow.

In the next exercise, you finish the title slide for Iron Sheep by using the Drop Shadow filter on the Background layer of SHEEPBAK.TIF. The shape of the shadow will be that of the image elements on Layer 1, but you can't apply Drop Shadow, (or many other Photoshop plug-ins), to transparency layers, because *opaque* pixels are required for the plug-in to work. Therefore, you must create a selection marquee around the logo and lettering on Layer 1, but make the Background layer the target for the Drop Shadow filter. Alien Skin's Drop Shadow will only place a drop shadow effect outside a selection marquee, so it makes no difference whether the shadow is created on a layer or the background for our design purposes—the shadow effect will look as though the images on Layer 1 are producing the shadow.

One word of caution when you use Drop Shadow in your own assignments and before you begin the following exercise: the Drop Shadow filter uses selection marquee information to create the effect, but also deselects the marquee in the process. Therefore, you should save unsaved marquees (**S**elect, **S**ave Selection, or use the Save Selection icon on the Channels palette) if you want to use the same selection marquee in further editing work, or if the shadow produced is not what you expected, and you want to try again.

Here's how to make Iron Sheep leap off the presentation screen:

Using the Drop Shadow Filter

After the Drop Shadow plug-in filter has been added to Photoshop's PLUGINS directory…

Open the SHEEPBAK.PSD image you saved to your hard disk	This is the image you saved from the last exercise.
Click on the Layer 1 title on the Layers palette's list	Makes Layer 1 the current editing layer.
Press **M** until the Rectangular Marquee tool is displayed on the toolbox, then click and drag to marquee select the entire Layer 1 contents	Choose the Rectangular marquee tool and select Layer 1's contents.

continues

continued

Because transparent areas of Layer 1 are, well, transparent, your marquee border might appear to encompass all of Layer 1. But in fact, only the opaque areas—those of the lettering and logo—will be affected in the next step. Ever try to swat air? Same principle.

Press the up arrow key once, then press the down arrow key once	Moves only the opaque contents on Layer 1—that of the lettering and logo.

This last step deserves a tiny explanation, so please check out the note that follows this exercise.

Click on the Background title on the Layers palette list	Makes the Background layer the current layer for editing.
Choose Filter, Alien Skin, then Drop shadow	Displays an advertisement for Alien Skin's Black Box suite of other filters for Photoshop.

The ad screen must be displayed for five seconds before you can click on the screen to display the Drop Shadow dialog box. If you're impatient, clicking before five seconds is up produces nothing. The information on this screen is also in the Resource Guide in the back of the book, and registered users don't get the ad screen.

In the Drop shadow dialog box, enter X Offset: **0**; Y Offset: **−20**; Blur: **8**; and Opacity: **90** (or click and drag on the sliders) extends pixels	Creates a custom drop shadow for the selection that is horizontally (x offset) centered beneath Layer 1's contents, but 20 below the selection (−20 y offset).
Click on the Camera icon	Displays the Save Settings dialog box.
Type **Sheep Shadow** in the name field; then click on OK	Saves the settings to Drop Shadow's Preference list. You can call the same settings back at any future time (see fig. 21.13).
Click on OK	Applies the effect to the selection (see fig. 21.14).
Choose Flatten Image from the pop-up the Layers palette	Merges Layer 1 to the Background menu on layer.
Choose File, Save As, then save the image as SLIDE1.TIF (choose the TIFF format from the Save File as Format Type drop-down list) to your hard disk	Saves the first of four slides to a format that can be imaged to a film recorder or used in other applications or presentation software, such as Microsoft PowerPoint.
Press Ctrl+W (or choose File, Close)	Closes the SLIDE1.TIF image.

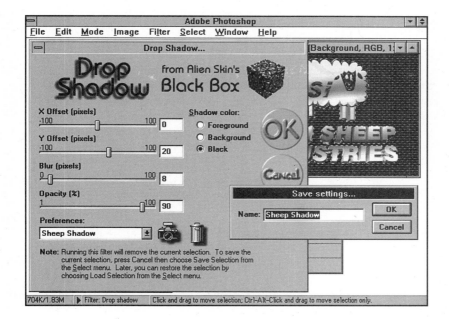

Figure 21.13

Define the distance (offset) from the selection area, the opacity, and blur value of the Drop Shadow in the number fields.

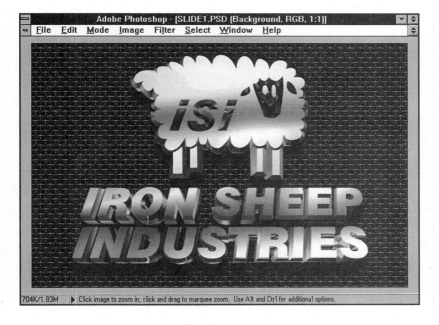

Figure 21.14

Add a drop shadow to any selected image area around opaque pixels with the Drop Shadow filter.

Note   In the preceding exercise, you selected the entire contents of a layer that contained an image element surrounded by areas of transparency. When you pressed the up arrow, you moved the opaque pixels on Layer 1 by one pixel upward. If you looked carefully, you noticed that the selection marquee "shrank" to exactly fit around the opaque pixels. Pressing the down arrow then moved the opaque foreground pixels downward by 1 pixel, so no overall repositioning of the images on Layer 1 occurred. The Rectangular marquee you originally created became a custom selection marquee because Photoshop "realized" that the editing you were performing with the Rectangular marquee tool was that of movement. Consequently, Photoshop responded to the movement command (nudging the opaque selected pixels by pressing the keyboard arrow keys) by displaying an accurate marquee of the pixels that were moving.

The technique of moving a selection on a layer and then moving it back into position is a handy one for making deselected image areas become floating selections once again on a layer. On the other hand, if instead of *moving* the layer you had pressed Alt(Option)+Delete, the marquee would have remained rectangular shaped. This is because Alt+Delete is the Fill command (a *painting* command, that would've ruined Layer 1—so don't do it).

It's worthwhile to point out that a *drop shadow* is one of two kinds of shadow effects you can add to images using Photoshop. A drop shadow is one that is cast on a surface the viewer perceives is directly beneath the subject in an image. A drop shadow's light source comes from the viewer's point of view. A *cast shadow* is produced *below* the subject in an image, as though the light source is above the subject, not the viewer. You use both drop and cast shadows to enhance realism in images, and Alien Skin's Drop Shadow filter takes the labor out of creating the kind most commonly used in presentations containing text.

Moving From Slide 1 to Slides 2 and 3

Because slide presentations are presented over a duration of time in a sequence that creates transitions, slide shows can be thought of as slow-motion animation. A good way to approach the creation of an effective slide show is to choreograph the appearance of image elements as they move or disappear from slide to slide. In the next exercise, you move on to making slides 2 and 3 of the presentation. However, you want to keep a thread of continuity going between slides 1 and 2, so a smaller sheep logo was created using Typestry (BAA_ICON.TIF) to serve as a common element in the presentation. Keeping an identifying element onscreen throughout a presentation is a good way to remind the viewer who's giving the presentation!

ote Jerry Della Femina, one of the advertising world's founding fathers, once proposed at a sales group meeting that a good slogan for Ford's Lincoln Continentals would be "The Rolls Royce of Automobiles."

This is why you need to reinforce corporate identity in a slide presentation.

Because slides 2 and 3 in this show will contain common elements and only the bulleted list will change, this is a perfect opportunity to design a Background layer that contains image elements the two slides can share. Doing this eliminates inconsistency between slides, allows the viewer to concentrate on the elements that do change from slide to slide, and saves you some serious design work!

Here's how to drag and drop your way to beautiful, eye-catching presentations:

Composing a Common Background Layer

Open SLIDE2&3.PSD from your hard disk	This is the duplicate image you created earlier of the SHEEPBAK.TIF image.
Click on the New Layer icon on the Layers palette and type **Slide2** in the **N**ame field of the dialog box; click on OK	Adds a layer to SLIDE2&3.PSD and clearly labels the layer for future identification.

In most of the exercises in this book, you've worked with dissimilar elements on layers, and we've usually recommended that you click on OK to accept the default name for a layer (for example, Layer 1). However, this assignment calls for nearly identical images on different layers, so labeling the layer that holds slide 2's contents is a prudent move, and this way you won't lose your sheep.

Open the following images from the CHAP21 subdirectory on the Bonus CD that comes with this book: BAA_ICON.TIF, BULLET1.TIF, and BULLET2.TIF	These are Typestry images rendered to RGB color with an additional Alpha channel for selecting the foreground elements from the background.
Click on the BAA_ICON.TIF title bar, then press Alt and click on the Channel #4 icon on the Channels palette	Loads the selection information and a marquee appears around the Iron Sheep logo.
Click and drag the Selection in BAA_ICON to the SLIDE2&3.PSD image window	Copies the selection to the Slide2 layer on Slide2&3.PSD (see fig. 12.15).

continues

continued

When the logo is positioned in the upper left of the Background image, press Ctrl+D (**S**elect, **N**one)	The logo becomes part of the Slide2 layer.

The tiny sheep serves nicely as a decoration for the bulleted list slides 2 and 3, but you need some sort of graphical separator between the fields of the logo and the bulleted list to compartmentalize each element. Create a horizontal line across the Slide2 layer, using a shade that's sampled from the image. Keep your color scheme simple in slide presentations, and you can have more fun with the graphic composition!

With the Rectangular marquee tool, click and drag a 1/8-inch deep horizontal line-shaped rectangle about 1/2" below the sheep logo's legs	Creates a wide line, making a top and bottom field to the slide (see fig. 21.16).
Press **I** (for Eyedropper tool; a phonetic mnemonic), then click over a darker portion of the sheep logo	Samples a dark steel color for the current foreground color.
Press Alt(Macintosh:Option)+Delete	Fills the Rectangular selection with foreground color (see fig. 21.17).
Click on the BULLET2.TIF title bar, press Alt and click on the Channel #4 title on the Channels palette, and then press Ctrl while clicking and dragging the selection into the SLIDE2&3.PSD image window	Copies the BULLET2.TIF image to the Slide2 Layer on SLIDE2&3.PSD.

Holding down the Ctrl(Command) key when the Eyedropper tool is chosen turns the Eyedropper cursor into an Arrow cursor that can be used as a selection tool. Doing this saves you from having to change tools in the middle of an editing step.

Press Ctrl while clicking and dragging the blue bullet so that it lines up vertically with the sheep logo and is positioned toward the bottom of the image window; then press Ctrl+D (**S**elect, **N**one)	Copies the blue bullet to Slide2 layer and deselects it.
Click on the BULLET1.TIF title bar, press Alt and click on the Channel #4 title on the Channels palette, and then press Ctrl while clicking and dragging the selection into the SLIDE2&3.PSD image window	Copies the BULLET1.TIF image to the Slide2 Layer on SLIDE2&3.PSD.

Press Ctrl while clicking and dragging the bullet to line up vertically with the sheep logo and directly above the dark blue bullet; then press Ctrl+D (**S**elect, **N**one)

Copies the bullet to Slide2 layer and deselects it (see fig. 21.18).

Press Ctrl+S (**F**ile, **S**ave)

Saves your work at this intermediate stage of completion.

Close the BULLET1, BULLET2, and BAA_ICON images

You're finished copying from them.

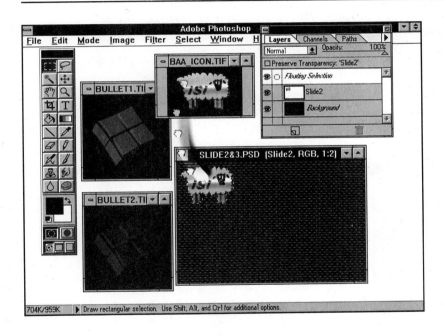

Figure 21.15

Drag and drop the selection from the BAA_ICON image to the image window that contains the presentation background.

Figure 21.16

Sample a foreground color with the Eyedropper tool to define a color for the selection you want to fill.

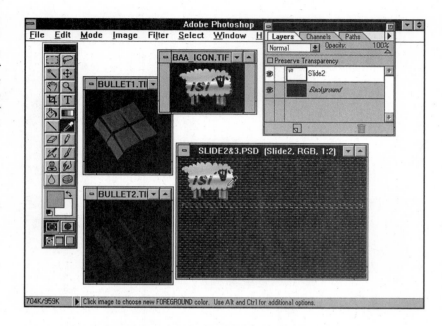

Figure 21.17

On a layer, you can fill a selection marquee with foreground color by holding down the Alt(Option) key and then pressing the Delete key.

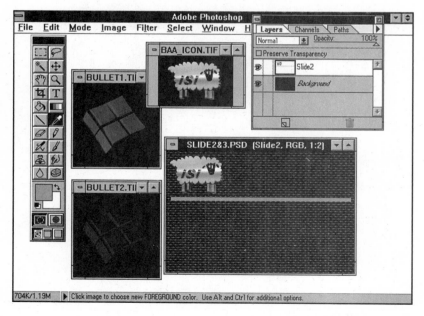

New Riders Publishing
INSIDE SERIES

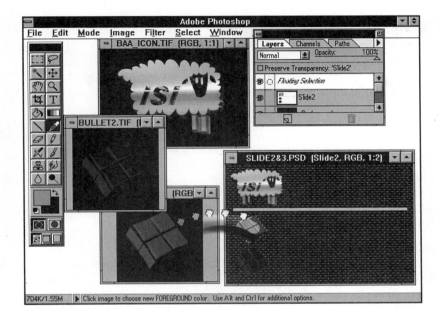

Figure 21.18

Press the Ctrl(Command) key to toggle the Eyedropper tool's function to that of the Arrow pointer tool.

Unfortunately, you cannot use the Delete key to fill a marquee selection on a layer with the current background color; you simply can't delete from an area that's transparent. But as the preceding exercise demonstrated, you can use key combinations in Photoshop to extend the functionality of the tools and options while you work. Photoshop's toolbox is arranged, from top to bottom, with selection tools, painting tools, and editing tools. Every tool that isn't a selection tool can be toggled to an Arrow pointer cursor by holding down the Ctrl key.

As mentioned earlier, you use the SLIDE2&3.PSD images as the creation site for both slides 2 and 3 in the presentation. A logical question at this point would be, "Why not use the Background layer as the common ground for visual elements that appear in both slides?" Fair enough. The answer is because you still need a pristine background of the wire screen in the creation of slide 4. In the next section, you use the Duplicate Layer command in a few new ways to make copies of the slide layers and to reinforce the idea that using the clipboard and images on disk aren't necessarily quicker ways to make duplicates of the compositional elements you need for an assignment.

Measuring Type with the Info Palette

Chapter 9, "Using Type in Photoshop," briefly discussed Photoshop's Units Preferences (under File) and how (by pressing Ctrl+R) you can spec type by using the Ruler Options' points unit of measurement. Using rulers is great when you estimate how much space several lines of type will take within a given area, but this section shows you how to precisely spec a single line of type.

Now that the bullets are positioned on the Slide2 layer, they're the typographic cheerleaders for the words of sage advice that have yet to come. In the next exercise, you use the Info palette to see what the best height, measured in *points*, the text should be for a line of type. A well-presented slide show doesn't linger or faun over any one slide, so messages have to be succinct; a bulleted phrase longer than five words can't be clearly read or understood in a fast-paced presentation.

In the next exercise, you see that the authors have chosen Gill Sans Extra Condensed Bold as the font for the slide. You might not own this typeface, so you can substitute a different font. Just try to use a typeface that is condensed. Condensed type is terrific for presentations (as long as it isn't overly ornamental) because you can use a large point size without much concern that a line of type is too long for the image's width.

Here's how to spec and apply the first bulleted item to the second slide:

Specifying and Adding Type to a Slide

Double-click on the Zoom tool; then resize the image window so SLIDE2&3.PSD fills the screen	Provides a good viewing resolution (1:1) for measuring the image for type.
Press F8 (Macintosh:F12) or choose **W**indow, **P**alettes, Show **I**nfo	Displays the Info palette.
Click on the crosshair icon on the bottom of the palette; then choose Points from the pop-up menu (see fig. 21.19)	This is a shortcut to set a specific reading on the Info palette. The Mouse Coordinates field takes readings from your cursor's position onscreen and also measures the dimensions of a selection marquee.
Press **M** (for **M**arquee tool), then click and drag a rectangle that's a little shorter than the height of the top bullet in SLIDE2&3.PSD	Defines the optimal height of type for the image, and the Info palette reports the marquee's height in points (see fig. 21.20).

The Width and Height fields on the Info palette only extend when you have an active selection marquee. You can see in figure 21.20, that 56.3 is a good measurement, in points for the first bulleted list item. Let's call it 55 points even and add the first line of type.

Press **D** (default colors icon) and then **X** (switch colors icon); then press **Y** (for **Type** tool)	Chooses white for the current foreground color; you must define a color for type before clicking on the image to create an insertion point.
Click an insertion point with the Type tool cursor to the right of the top bullet	Sets the point at which your type begins, and displays the Type tool dialog box.
Choose a condensed font from the **F**ont drop-down list, type **55** in the **S**ize field, click on the top, left Alignment radio button, then type **Fine Steel Wool Pads** in the type entry box	Sets the font and size you'll use for the bulleted list item; enters a hokey slogan in the type entry field (see fig. 21.21).
Click on OK	Returns you to the image with the type on the Slide2 layer as a floating selection.
Click and drag inside the floating selection marquee until the type is aligned with the middle of the bullet's height, then click outside the selection	Positions the type and makes the floating selection part of the Slide2 layer (see fig. 21.22).
Click an insertion point to the right of the blue bullet, then type **Half a Decade in Business** and click on OK	Adds a slogan to the second bullet.
Click and drag inside the floating selection marquee until the type is aligned with the middle of the blue bullet, then click outside the selection	Positions the type and makes the floating selection part of the Slide2 layer.
Press Ctrl+S (**F**ile, **S**ave)	Saves your work up to this point.

Figure 21.19

Set the units the Info palette uses to report a selection's dimensions by clicking on the cross-hair icon.

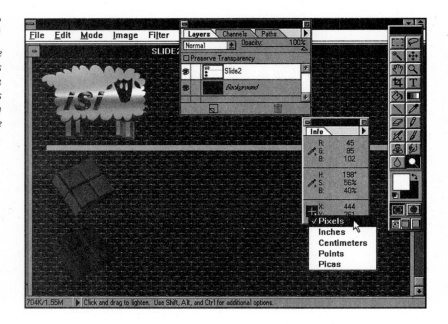

Figure 21.20

The Info palette takes screen and image readings and reports them in the units of measurement of your choice.

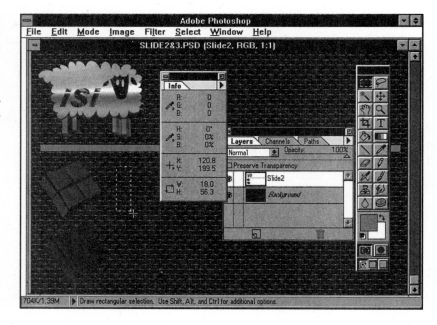

Figure 21.21

Use a condensed font for headlines to get more words per line, or fewer words in a larger point size.

Figure 21.22

Align the type with the middle of the bullet to create a graphic relationship between the two elements.

You also can customize all the parameters of the Info palette at once, by clicking on the pop-up menu button; then choosing Palette Options.

In the next section, you get into an area of slide presentations that captivates the viewer; you build animation into the presentation by duplicating slide 2 and modifying the new slide 3, so when they're presented back to back, the audience will believe that the bullets are behaving like staged light bulbs.

Duplicating Layers and Switching Layer Contents

When each successive slide in a presentation contains an element from the slide that precedes it and presents an additional element, the technique is called a *build*. Much of the success of presentation builds relies upon keeping the common elements in absolutely the same position from slide to slide. In this section, you learn how to perform a variation on the traditional slide build, by copying the Slide2 layer to a new layer and switching the position of the bullets. The red bullet represents the active line in the presentation, whereas the dark blue button is sort of a "coming attractions" bullet. By alternating the position of the bullets between the two slides, when the slides are shown in sequence, the only element that changes is the bullets. The viewer's eye sends the message that one bullet "light" has dimmed, and the other has now flashed on, effectively drawing the viewer's attention to a different onscreen element.

In the next exercise, you duplicate the Slide2 layer and use the Marquee tool to float the opaque bullet areas and reposition them so that they're exactly on top of the corresponding bullets on the Slide2 layer. If you've come to Photoshop 3 from version 2.5, you'll appreciate how easy image layers make it now to precisely position floating selections!

Here's how to animate a bulleted list:

Building a Presentation "Build"

Click on the pop-up menu on the Layers palette, and choose Duplicate Layer (see fig. 21.23)	Displays the Layer Options dialog box.
In the As: field, type **Slide3**. Make sure that the Document field says *not* New; click on OK	Creates a copy of the Slide2 layer's contents, in exactly the same SLIDE2&3.PSD, position as Slide2 layer's contents, one layer on top of the Slide2 layer.

Click on the Rectangular marquee tool; then click and drag around the red bullet on Slide3 layer; take care not to include any other image element in the selection	Selects the area containing the red bullet.
Place the cursor inside the selection, then click and drag the bullet to a transparent area of the Slide3 layer	The bullet becomes a floating selection, and you've moved it so that the blue bullet can be placed in its former position (see fig. 21.24).
Press Ctrl+D (**S**elect, **N**one), then click and drag around the blue bullet	Deselects the red bullet; selects the blue bullet.
Place your cursor inside the marquee, then click and drag the blue bullet so that it's positioned directly on top of the red bullet on the Slide2 layer	The blue bullet now occupies the same spatial position as the red bullet on the Slide2 layer. (see fig. 21.25).

When you've selected and moved a layer object, it becomes a floating selection above the layer; the Layers palette displays the object as a floating selection title. As a floating selection, you can use the keyboard arrow keys to nudge the selection into precise position. Press Ctrl+H (**S**elect, Hide **E**dges) to hide the marquee lines around the floating selection if they hinder your view of the correct positioning.

Press Ctrl+D (**S**elect, **N**one); then click and drag around the red bullet you relocated	Deselects the blue bullet; selects the red bullet. Make sure that the bullet is the *only* opaque image area you've marquee selected!
Click and drag the red bullet so that it's positioned directly over the blue bullet on the Slide2 layer	You've exchanged bullets and aren't even at war (see fig. 21.26).
Press Ctrl+D (**S**elect, **N**one), then press Ctrl+S (**F**ile, **S**ave)	Deselects the floating selection and saves your work up to this point.

Figure 21.23

Use the Duplicate Layer command to copy the image elements to a new layer in the exact position they appear on the Slide2 Layer.

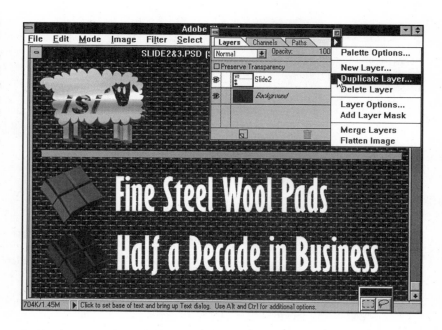

Figure 21.24

Select the image area on the layer with the Marquee tool; move it, and it becomes a floating selection.

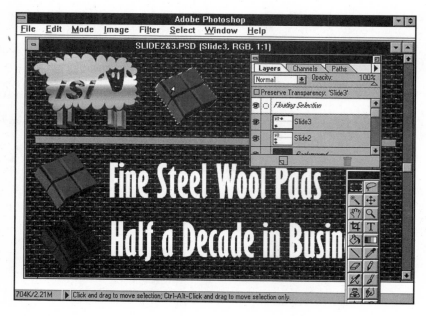

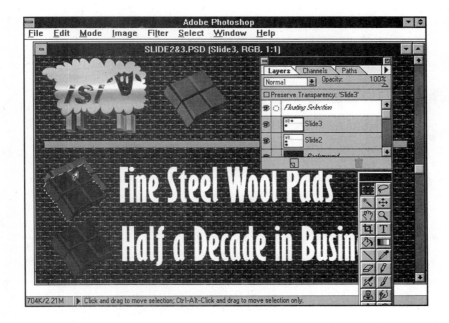

Figure 21.25

Use the arrow keyboard keys to precisely position the blue bullet on top of the red bullet visible on the Slide2 layer.

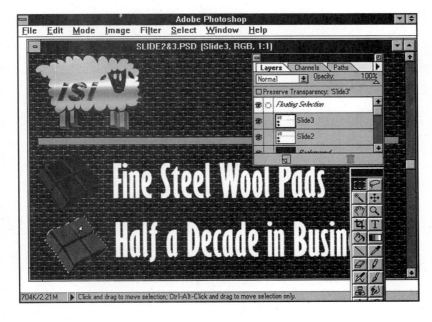

Figure 21.26

By switching the position of the bullets on Slide2 and Slide3 layers, the slide show appears to animate between slides.

Having created two layers with near-identical composition, the next section shows you how to create two separate image files for the slide show.

Creating Multiple Slides from a Layered Image

As you saw in the preceding exercise, it's easy to rearrange elements on different layers, yet be completely assured that they'll line up when the layers are broken down to individual images that can then be rendered to film. As with the bullets, different lines of type can be added to the Slide3 layer, and a Slide4 layer, and so on, to create a larger presentation; but alas, Iron Sheep Industries is bleating at the door for its slide show, and you must shepherd this assignment to its conclusion.

In the next exercise, you create two different image files from the Slide2&3.PSD image, create the Background layer for the fourth slide, and perform a trick that makes the transition between slides 2 and 3 more dramatic. In the same way that the blue bullet appears to be dimmed, you'll darken the line of type to the right of each blue bullet. By doing this, the viewer's eye cannot help but follow the bulleted epithets highlighted in white onscreen.

Here's how to double your returns on a small investment of time in Photoshop:

Creating Separate Image Files from Layers

Click on the Background title on the Layers palette	This is the target layer for duplication.
Click on the pop-up menu button on the Layers palette, then choose Duplicate Layer	Displays the Duplicate Layer dialog box.
Choose New from the Document drop-down list, type **Slide3** in the **N**ame field, and then click on OK	Creates a new image window in Photoshop's workspace, with the wire screen image as the Background image layer (see fig. 21.27).
Click on the title bar of SLIDE2&3.PSD, then click on the Slide3 title on the Layers palette	Makes the Slide3 Layer the current editing (target) layer.
Choose Duplicate Layer from the pop-up menu on the Layers palette, then choose	Copies the Slide3 layer from SLIDE2&3.PSD to the Slide3

Slide3 from the Document drop-down list and click on OK	image (see fig. 21.28).
Click on the Slide2&3.PSD image, then click and drag the Slide3 title on the Layers palette into the Trash icon	Removes Slide3 layer from the image, and the image windows clearly display a visible difference in image information!
Click on the Eyedropper tool; then click over a dark area of the sheep logo in SLIDE2&3.PSD	Samples a dark foreground color.
With the Rectangular marquee tool, click and drag around the "Half a Decade in Business" type on the Slide2 layer of SLIDE2&3.PSD	Selects the type area.
Click on the Preserve Transparency check box on the Layers palette	Protects all transparent areas on the Slide2 layer from editing.
Press Alt(Option)+Delete	Fills only the type area within the marquee selection with dark foreground color (see fig. 21.29).
Click on the Slide3 title bar; then repeat the last steps, but make the marquee selection around the "Fine Steel Wool Pads" type	Dims the lettering in the Slide3 image (see fig. 21.30).

As you can see in figure 21.30, the proper screen elements are now dimmed on the respective slides. The audience will be directed to the first bullet, and then move on to Iron Sheep's long track record in the business in the third slide. (I have some CDs that'll mature before this company does.)

Choose Flatten Image from the pop-up menu on the Layers palette	Collapses SLIDE3 image to a single background RGB image.
Choose File, Save As; then save the image as SLIDE3.TIF (choose the TIFF format from the Save File as Format Type drop-down list) to your hard disk	Saves your work up to this point.
Click on the SLIDE2&3.PSD title bar; then press Ctrl+S (File, Save)	Saves SLIDE3 as a TIF image and saves the editing you've performed on SLIDE2&3.PSD.

You weren't asked to flatten the SLIDE2&3.PSD image yet because you need to copy the Background for the fourth and final slide in this presentation.

Figure 21.27

Quickly generate an identical Background layer in a new image file with the Duplicate Layer command.

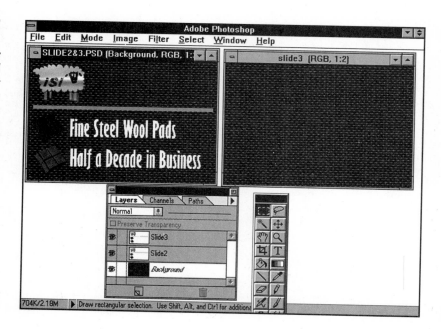

Figure 21.28

Copy the current editing (target) layer to the new SLIDE3 image using the Duplicate Layer command.

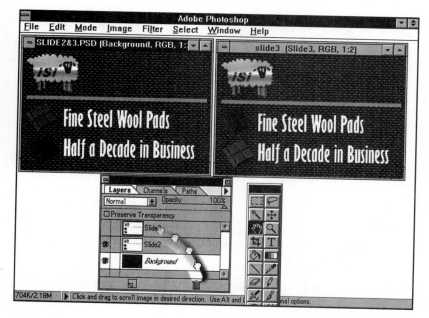

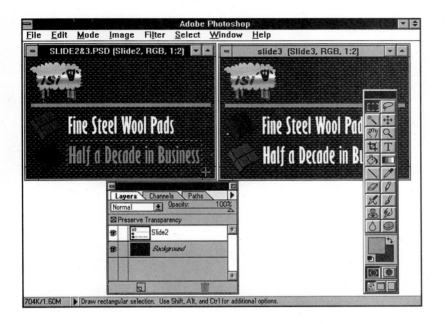

Figure 21.29

Use the Preserve Transparency option on the Layers palette to protect transparent pixels on a layer.

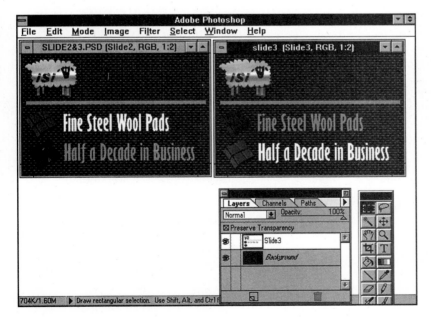

Figure 21.30

The transition between the slides directs the viewer's attention to the appropriate sales point.

Again, you've seen how to create a transition between two slides in a presentation, but you can trump this number up to 10, 20, or however many slides it takes to communicate a sales message. Keep common elements between slides in alignment by first creating them on image layers, and then duplicate the information to a new image background.

Pixar is also responsible for the background you're using for the Iron Sheep presentation. Pixar One-Twenty-Eight is a Photoshop plug-in filter that fills a selected area or entire image background with seamless textures or natural and man-made materials. Two fully-working seamless textures from the Pixar One-Twenty-Eight collection and the plug-in filter that makes them work are on the Bonus CD that accompanies this book. Check out Chapter 19, "3rd-Party Plug-In Filters," for how to use this remarkable technology.

Creating the Splashy Exit Slide

To create slide number four in this presentation, you beg and borrow a little from the preceding slides you already finished. Iron Sheep Industries wants a catchy tag line at the conclusion of the sales meeting and a graphic that's every ounce as powerful and silly as the opening slide.

Use the tiny sheep logo and the Background layer from the SLIDE2&3.PSD image, the Iron Sheep Typestry rendering from the ISI.TIF image, and a little colored text to cap off the presentation in slide 4.

Here's how to work with partial selections from different sources to create slide 4 in the presentation:

Reusing Image Selections

Click on the Background title on the Layers palette, then choose Duplicate Layer from the layers palette pop-up menu	Displays the Duplicate Layer options dialog box.
Choose New from the D<u>o</u>cument drop-down list, then enter **Slide4** in the <u>N</u>ame text box and click on OK	Creates a new image, Slide4, with the wire screen background.
Open the ISI.TIF image from the CHAP21 subdirectory (folder) of the *Bonus CD* that comes with this book	This is the image you used to complete SLIDE1.TIF earlier.

On the Channels palette, press Alt (Option) and click on the Channel #4 icon	Loads the selection of Channel #4.
With the Rectangular marquee tool, press Ctrl while clicking and dragging around the large sheep logo (see fig. 21.31)	Ctrl(Command) subtracts the Sheep logo from the marquee selection, leaving the "Iron Sheep Industries" type selected.
Place your cursor inside the marquee selection; then click and drag the selection into the Slide4 image window	Copies the Iron Sheep type onto the Background layer of the Slide4 image (see fig.21.32).

You're working "live" in this exercise; the floating selection is *not* on a Layer, and if you accidentally deselect the selection before you position it, you can't make it float again without carving a hunk out of the Background image. If you do this with care, a layer isn't necessary, and you'll have one less Flatten image command to perform to save this slide to a TIFF format.

The tag line and tiny sheep logo will be brought into the top 2/3 of the image soon, so make sure that the lettering is comfortably toward the bottom of the Slide4 file, but not touching the bottom edge.

Click and drag to position the lettering close to the bottom center of the image	This is the final position for the selection.
Press Ctrl+D (**S**elect, **N**one)	Deselects the floating selection.
Close the ISI.TIF image	You no longer need it.
Click on the SLIDE2&3.PSD title bar, then click on the Slide2 layer title on the Layers palette	Makes SLIDE2&3.PSD the active image, and Slide2 layer is the target layer.
With the Rectangular marquee tool, click and drag around the small sheep logo, then click within the selection marquee and drag the sheep into the Slide4 image (see fig. 21.33)	Copies the small sheep logo into the Slide4 image.

The copy of the sheep logo almost magically migrates to the upper left of the Slide4 image because Photoshop enables you to precisely position partial selections of layers when the background layer is a duplicate of the source image file. However, you occasionally (like now) *don't want* the selection positioned relative to its original position on the source image.

Click and drag the sheep icon to the top center of the Slide4 image; then press Ctrl+D (**S**elect, **N**one)	Centers the logo, leaving space for a tag line on Slide4, and deselects the sheep so that it won't run back to the upper left corner again.

Click on the foreground color on the toolbox	Displays the Color Picker.
Click and drag the Hue slider to orange, move the spectrum circle to create a bright gold-orange, and then click on OK	Defines the foreground color for the type you'll add.
Press **Y** (for T**y**pe tool); then click an insertion point on the far left, center of the image	Defines where the type will begin and displays the Type tool dialog box.
Enter **Americans Count on Sheep!** in the type entry field, then click on OK	Photoshop remembers your last Type specs, so 55 point type appears flush left as a floating selection on the Slide4 image (see fig. 21.34).
Center the type; then press Ctrl+D (**S**elect, **N**one)	Deselects the type.
Choose File, Sa**v**e As; then save the image as SLIDE4.TIF (choose the TIFF format from the Save File as Format **T**ype drop-down list) to your hard disk	Saves the slide to TIFF format.

When saving files as TIFF images that might be used by other programs, don't check the **LZW** check box. Many programs have difficulty reading compressed images.

Click on the SLIDE2&3.PSD title bar, choose Flatten Image from the pop-up menu on the Layers palette, and then Choose File, Sa**v**e As. Save the image as SLIDE1.TIFF to your hard disk	Saves the image to the same format as the other three slides.

It's show time!

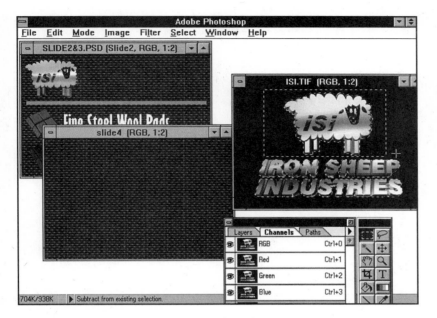

Figure 21.31

Use the Ctrl(Command) key to subtract the logo from the loaded selection of the lettering in ISI.TIF.

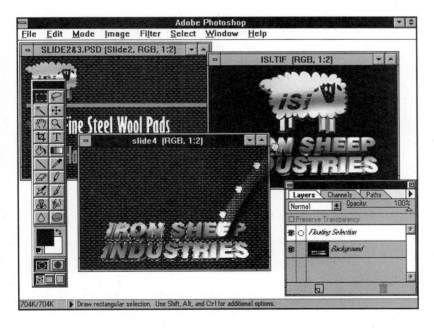

Figure 21.32

Copy the lettering to the Slide4 image and position it to leave room for a tag line and the smaller logo.

Figure 21.33

Copy a selection from the Slide2 layer of SLIDE2&3.PSD by dragging and dropping between image windows.

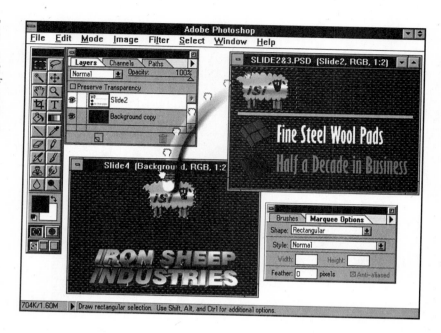

Figure 21.34

Add Photoshop type to the slide to complete the image.

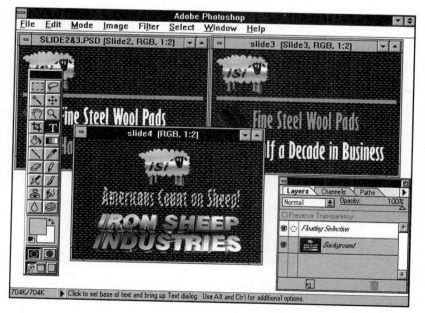

This assigning didn't use cloning, painting in exotic modes, or extraordinary, nerve-shattering colors, but then again, most of the visual interest in this slide presentation was supplied by another program. When you explore the capabilities of software applications other than Photoshop, ironically, you're lead back to Photoshop to complete your composition. This is because Photoshop's greatest strength is its capability to integrate digital images, regardless of their origin. Photoshop is an image-editing application, and through practice, your knowledge of how the tools and features work can lead you to accomplishing the impossible on occasion.

Curtain Call for Slide Presentations

In figure 21.35, the cast is reassembled for a final call so that you can see what this slide presentation looks like as a finished product. The figure was captured at an 800×600 monitor resolution because the four images wouldn't fit running a 640×480 video driver!

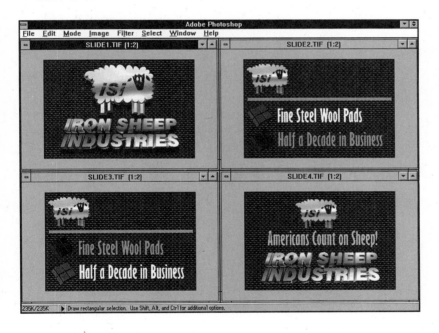

Figure 21.35

Photoshop can be used to integrate images from both real-world and computer-generated sources.

As mentioned earlier, the finished files you now have on your hard disk are a little lean in the file size department to send to a service bureau and expect flawless images. However, at the images' present resolution and dimensions, they will play well onscreen in a number of presentation software applications, manufactured by such companies as Lotus, Microsoft, MacroMedia, and Corel. To learn how to convert a slide show of your own to physical, 35mm slide format, read Chapter 25, "The Film Recorder."

If you have an appetite to further explore the possibilities of rendering and modeling programs to complement and supplement your Photoshop work, turn the page and take a look into virtual reality.

Virtual Reality: The Ingredient of Dreamwork

A great deal of space in this book has been devoted to redefining the art of retouching real-world photographs. The time has come to work on *non*-real-world images. Photo-realistic, virtual-reality images can be created inside the computer when modeling and rendering software are used. This new kind of software has given the entertainment industry the tools to create all sorts of science fiction creatures, flying saucers, and other special effects. Modeling and rendering programs used to be found only on high-performance, *Reduced Instruction Set Command* (RISC)-based graphics workstations (such as those produced by Pixar, Silicon Graphics, and Sun Microsystems), but times have changed. In the past three years, manufacturers have ported capable modeling and rendering programs to the personal computer.

In this chapter's assignment, you'll see how a modeling program uses digital images as surfaces for three-dimensional wireframes, and how a model is then rendered to a format that can be used in Photoshop. Like photographic images, photo-realistic, computer-generated images often need a trip through Photoshop's features to be to be retouched and integrated with other design elements.

This Chapter's Assignment

Suppose you're given an assignment to illustrate the cover story for a magazine whose feature article is on industrial robots, entitled "The Heart of the Machine." For the composition, you need to generate the following elements:

◆ The components of a robot

◆ A heart

◆ Some sort of background

◆ The title

For the assignment in this chapter, you'll use a rendered model along with other image files that are enhanced using some of Photoshop's special effects.

The components are all on the Inside *Adobe Photoshop 3* Bonus CD. You'll build a "virtual reality" scene in Photoshop, and in the process you'll learn how other, high-end computer graphics programs work together. Check out the Adobe Photoshop 3 Deluxe CD-ROM and this book's Bonus CD for special edition versions of the other kinds of graphic software you'll see used in this chapter.

Creating a Texture Map

Its important to learn how to create a surface texture, and to integrate different computer graphics applications to create a texture. You might be interested in adding a modeling/rendering program to your own suite of design tools, if you haven't already. With an understanding of how to create 2D surfaces, you can make original texture and image maps for wireframe models.

If this assignment was a paying, real job, the first place you'd want to look for raw materials would be a modeling application so that you could build the robot. To begin the assignment, an image of a circuit board needs to be created, so that it can be mapped to the wireframe of a robot model.

Understanding Mapping

A rendering program can use one of two basic methods to map 2D images to a 3D model's wireframe. *Color-* or *image-mapping* wraps a repeating 2D image, such as those you'll create in Photoshop, to a 3D model to add surface properties to the wireframe. *Bump-* or *texture-mapping* creates a relief pattern on the surface of the wireframe when it is rendered to 2D format. Bump-mapping usually gets its information from a grayscale image of a design; the darker areas of the design correspond to areas on the surface of a model that recede. Conversely, lighter areas of the grayscale image indicate that the surface of the target image (the model surface) should bump outward. The degree to which surface areas elevate and recede depend on how bright or dark the corresponding pixels on the bump-map appear. The bump-mapping process that modeling programs use is similar to the results achieved with Photoshop's Emboss filter.

Creating an EPS Design for an Image Map

On the
CD

A demonstration version of *RenderCAD-Pro* for the Macintosh and a special edition of Caligari's *TrueSpace* for Windows are on the *Inside Adobe Photoshop 3* Bonus CD. Both of these modeling/rendering programs can use images you design in Photoshop as information for bump and image mapping.

You won't actually use the image of the circuit board as a texture for the wireframe robot model for the following reasons:

◆ HARTPOSE.TGA, a finished, rendered image is already supplied on the *Inside Adobe Photoshop 3* Bonus CD.

◆ The modeling and rendering process is time-consuming, and doesn't directly contribute to your Photoshop education, which is the purpose of this chapter.

◆ You might not own *Mannequin* or *Renderize Live for Windows*, the applications used to generate the Targa format image of the robot used in this assignment.

The starting place for this assignment is a drawing program (such as Adobe Illustrator or CorelDRAW!), where a circuit board "blueprint" is designed and then exported as an *Encapsulated PostScript* (EPS) image. Photoshop converts this image to a bitmap format. In figure 22.1, you can see the finishing touches being put on the circuit design in the vector-drawing application CorelDRAW!. Photoshop's strengths are photographic-quality imaging, and vector-drawing programs offer better features for designing crisp, complex geometric shapes.

Figure 22.1

Vector designs can be imported as EPS information into Photoshop for use in bitmap format.

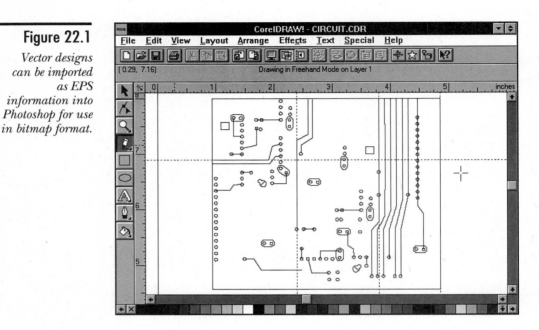

You'll be using the CorelDRAW!-exported EPS design as the foundation for a dimensional, color-circuit image you'll create in Photoshop. (F.Y.I.—I have no idea what this circuit board does; I looked inside my Sony Walkman, found some good-looking parts, and drew them!)

EPS images are actually a complex set of PostScript printer instructions about a graphical image that are "encapsulated," as the name implies, in a file format that can be placed within a document, usually a desktop publishing application's document. However, the EPS standard was written as an open specification that many software manufacturers saw as more than simple printer code. Today, there are variations within the EPS format to accommodate both printing instruction and graphical design needs (placeable EPS files, for instance, cannot be edited or rasterized to bitmap format).

EPS images can be imported by design applications that understand the vector-based information in an EPS file, and bitmap imaging program can decode EPS information to rasterize a bitmap version of the printing instructions for use as a graphic. The EPS format today creates a bridge between vector-drawing programs on both the Macintosh and Windows platforms as a description of vector graphics that is almost a universally understood and accepted file format.

EPS images are resolution-independent; they have no fixed size until you convert them to bitmap format. Usually, EPS images are created in a specific image dimension. Photoshop reads an EPS file's header to see what the dimensions are and offers the same dimensions in the **H**eight and **W**idth boxes. In the following exercise, you convert the CIRCUIT.EPS image into a bitmap format.

Rasterizing an Image

Open the CIRCUIT.EPS image from the CHAP22 subdirectory on the *Inside Adobe Photoshop 3* Bonus CD	Displays the Rasterizer dialog box.
Enter **72** in the **R**esolution field, choose RGB Color from the **M**ode drop-down list, make sure **A**nti-Aliased and Constrain Proportions check boxes are checked, then click on OK	Creates a bitmap format image from the EPS file information, with a specific resolution and color mode.

You left the **H**eight and **W**idth fields alone in the last step because they are not critical to this exercise. However, you always have the option of specifying the Rasterize image dimensions when importing EPS or AI (Adobe Illustrator) images. Anti-aliasing helps keep the edges in the image smooth, and Constrain Proportions adjusts the image's Width relative to any changes you make to the image's Height.

Adding Dimension to a Texture

In keeping with the mapping theme of this chapter, the first step after Photoshop rasterizes the EPS image of the circuit board is to give the flat, black-and-white graphic some depth and color. Photoshop's Emboss filter is a handy way to suggest a source of lighting and create a relief pattern from a piece of flat, two-dimensional art.

Photoshop's Emboss filter simulates hard light falling at an angle on the visual content of an image by replacing foreground color information with a lighter and a darker copy of the information. The Emboss command offsets the copies from the original foreground detail at a diagonal angle, and replaces the background area with a neutral gray.

The Angle control specifies where the highlight of the Emboss filter occurs—click and drag on it to point the line in the wheel at the light source for the emboss. The Height slider controls how far apart the two image copies are displaced, which simulates shallow or steep areas of embossing.

The Amount control only creates a change in an original image that has color areas. Amount controls how much original color information is included in the final Embossed image. A value of 0 retains no color information; a value of 500% places the most original colors and chromatic opposites inside the highlight and shadow areas of the Emboss effect. The circuit image you're working with doesn't contain any colored image areas, so you won't use the Amount control in the next exercise.

That's the technical explanation—the Emboss capability provides the designer with instant image enhancement, and is ideally suited to make the flat, black-and-white circuit design appear three-dimensional!

Using the Emboss Filter

Choose Filter, Stylize, then Emboss	Displays the Emboss dialog box.
Enter **45** in the **A**ngle field, **3** in the **H**eight field, and **100**% in the A**m**ount field (see fig. 22.2)	Sets the characteristics for the Emboss filter.
Alternatively, you can click and drag on the Angle wheel and the sliders to set the characteristics.	
Click on OK	Applies the effect.
Choose **F**ile, Sa**v**e As; in the File **N**ame text field enter **CIRCUIT.TGA**, and choose the TGA format (from Save File as Format **T**ype drop-down list)	Saves your work up to this point.
Using the Dri**v**es and **D**irectories fields, choose a location on your hard disk for the file, then click on OK	

You chose Targa (*.TGA) as the file format for the rasterized CIRCUIT.EPS image because it's a format commonly used by modeling/rendering programs. Targa and TIFF images share the capability to store color information in channels, and both formats can handle transparency mask (Alpha channel) information. The rendering program used to create the robot in this chapter is Visual Software's *Renderize Live for Windows*. Just as most applications "prefer" to work with a specific file format, *Renderize Live* likes Targa images. You may need to save texture maps you create for modeling work in different formats, depending on the rendering program's specifications.

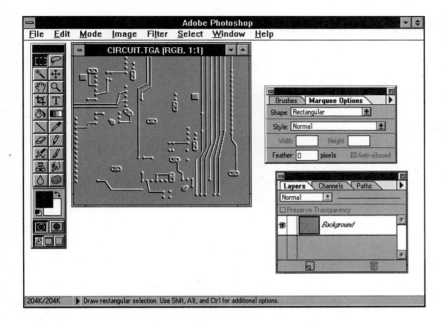

Figure 22.2

Use the Emboss Filter to create a "stamped metal" effect from flat monochrome or color illustrations.

Selective Color Adjustment

Photoshop 3 sports many color correction filters that assist in pre-press refining of an image destined for four-color, CMYK process printing. Selective color can become an indispensable Photoshop feature if you have a 32-bit CMYK scanner that's miscalibrated; you can correct deficiencies in a scanned 32-bit CMYK image without rescanning the source image. However, the Selective Color command can be used with images that are in RGB or CMYK mode, for an entirely different reason—to move a specific range of color in an image to a different value. For more information about CMYK mode, see Chapter 2, "Acquiring a Digital Image," and Chapter 20, "Mixed Media and Photoshop."

The CIRCUIT.TGA image needs a splash of color or two, and the Selective Color command is the best way to add these colors because, unlike the Color Range command, it can select neutral tones. The embossed circuit board is made up of only gray, white, and black. The Replace Color command is ineffective for changing the gray to gold, for example, because there are no prominent color values in CIRCUIT.TGA to replace!

Selective color operates on the CMYK color model, with options for Relative or Absolute changes to the four printing inks used to create color, hard-copy work from digital images. You can choose from the primary and secondary additive colors, or whites, neutrals, and blacks as the target areas in the image you want to modify. The *Relative* method increases the presence of a C, M, Y, or K color by the percent of color found in the image (example: adding 10% black to a 50% gray area produces 55% black). The *Absolute* method doesn't make relative adjustments to colors found in the image, but instead gives you control over how much of each CMYK value appears in the target image. In a way, the Relative method is best used for color *correction*; the Absolute Selective Color method is simply good for coloring an image.

CMYK is a subtractive color model, which means that adding all four color components produces black, not white as the RGB color model does. Chapter 23 goes into more detail about process color printing. Table 22.1 is an equivalency table that shows you what to expect when you add and subtract CMYK values from a target image that's composed of neutral (grayscale) colors using the Selective Color command.

TABLE 22.1
Subtractive Color Combinations

Color 1	Color 2	New Color
+Cyan	+Magenta	Blue
+Magenta	+Yellow	Red
+Cyan	+Yellow	Green

Values of Cyan, Magenta, and Yellow can replace neutral tones by moving individual CMYK sliders, and these color values can be further enhanced by reducing the other CMYK color components. CMYK color correction is a science when applied to process color printing, but it can be used as a creative tool and an alternative to the Colorize option in the Hue/Saturation command when you want to tint an image that's only composed of neutral, grayscale shades.

In the next exercise, you use Photoshop's Selective Color command to change the CMYK color values of the circuit board you embossed earlier. You create the golden circuit board that was used as an image map for the wireframe of the robot in this assignment.

Selective Color Modifications

Choose **I**mage, **A**djust, then **S**elective Color	Displays the Selective Color dialog box.
Choose Neutrals from the **C**olors drop-down list	Picks the color range you want to adjust.
Click on the **A**bsolute Method radio button	Changes the color *content* of the image.
Enter **100**% the **Y**ellow field	Adds the maximum amount of Yellow to the CIRCUIT image.
Click and drag the Cyan slider to about **-40**%, then click and drag the Magenta slider to about **-20**% (see fig. 22.3)	Specifies that these respective values should be removed from the neutral shades found in CIRCUIT.TGA.
Click on OK	Applies the changes to the image.
Press Ctrl+S (**F**ile, **S**ave)	Saves your work up to this point.

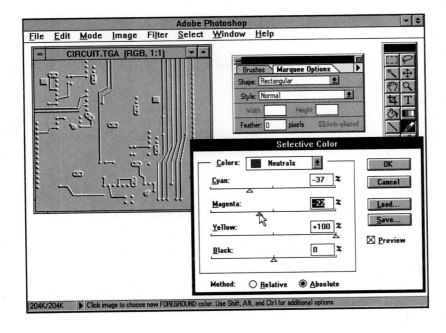

Figure 22.3

Neutral colors in an image can be shifted to display distinct hues through the Selective Color command.

You're playing a "what if" scenario when you choose the Selective Color command to tint an image having no intrinsic color values: in effect, what if the RGB color components were printing inks, and you have the option to respecify the recipe for printing an image. In addition to modifying neutral tones, you can colorize blacks in an image using the Selective Color command. Blacks in an image can't be colorized using the Hue/Saturation command because colors based upon RGB values represent a black pixel as having *no* color. Therefore, you can't move the absence of color to a different color value.

Whenever you run into a stumbling block in achieving an effect, try using different color specifications or the different models of color (RGB, CMYK, HSB, LAB) Photoshop offers for defining and changing a color value. You'll find that the **I**mage menu offers adjustments for the tonal qualities in an image, and the Picker palette can be set up through its Options command to represent the different models for color.

Filtering and Editing Details in An Image

You can perform a number of maneuvers on the CIRCUIT.TGA image to enhance it in ways the vector design program that was used to create it can't offer. As a bitmap image, CIRCUIT.TGA can be thrown out of focus slightly, and image areas can be burned and dodged to create surface imperfections. Small details often contribute a lot to the believability of a computer graphic, and this is particularly true when a bitmap image is used as a tiling, or repeat pattern for the surface of a computer model.

A glowing pilot light would be a nice detail to add to the surface of the image, and you have exactly the right tool to accomplish this. A sample version of *Kai's Power Tools, v2.0* from HSC software, which includes the KPT Glass Lens plug-in filter is found on the Bonus CD. You might already have this filter at your disposal if you installed this set of filters when they were first used in Chapter 19, "Third-Party Plug-In Filters." If not, close Photoshop now and install the filters as follows:

1. For Macintosh Photoshop users, close Photoshop and click and drag all filters from the KPT folder on the Bonus CD's Macintosh partition (the 68 KB filters for non-Power PC Macintoshes; for a Power Macintosh drag the two PPC filters), along with the KPT Support Files folder, into the Adobe Photoshop Plug-ins folder.

For Windows users, close Photoshop and copy all the filters (they end in the file extension .8bf) into the Photoshop PLUGINS directory (example: C:\PHOTOSHP\PLUGINS), then copy the KPT20HUB.DLL and KPTWIN20.HLP into the Windows directory.

2. Restart Photoshop.

Macintosh users will find the Glass Lens filter under the Filter, Distort menu in Photoshop.

Windows users will find the Glass Lens under the Filter, KPT 2.0 Filters menu.

If you have the Glass Lens plug-in filter installed, the next steps will help embellish the CIRCUIT image. If you haven't installed the program yet, no need to worry; the steps aren't critical to the final image. The Glass Lens filter can be used in many design situations to create a unique special effect. Other third-party filters also create unique effects; they are described in detail in Chapter 19.

Here's how to use the Glass Lens plug-in filter to create a pilot light on the circuit board image.

Distorting an Image Area with Glass Lens Normal

Press Ctrl+ plus keys until you're at a 4:1 viewing resolution of CIRCUIT.TGA	Zooms you into a good viewing resolution for creating an effect that's small in scale.
Press **M** until the Elliptical marquee tool is selected	Keyboard shortcut for choosing the mode for the marquee tool. Alternatively, you can Alt+click on the tool on the toolbox.
Shift+click and drag a small marquee in an area on the circuit where there's no embossed design work	Selects the area you'll use to create the pilot light.
Click on the Foreground color on the toolbox	Displays the Color Picker for setting foreground color.
Click and drag the hue slider until it's in the blue range, then click and drag the circle in the spectrum box toward medium blue, then click on OK	Sets the foreground color. You can also enter R: **75**, G: **71**, B: **255** in the RGB fields to get a nice, medium blue.

continues

continued

Press Alt+Delete	Fills the marquee selection with foreground color.
Choose Fi<u>l</u>ter, <u>D</u>istort, KPT Glass Lens Normal 2.0	Creates a "fisheye" lens effect in the selection area (see fig. 22.4).
Press Ctrl+D (<u>S</u>elect, <u>N</u>one), then Ctrl+S (<u>F</u>ile, <u>S</u>ave)	Deselects the marquee and saves your work up to this point.

Figure 22.4

KPT Glass Lens Normal filter distorts and creates highlighting in a selection area.

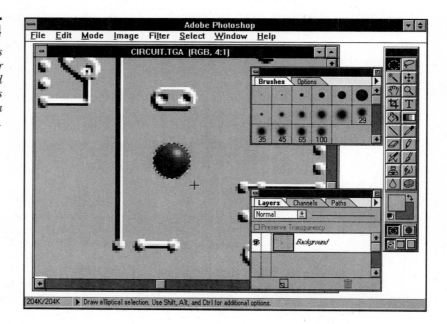

 Tip

Because the area you selected in the last exercise was a flat color, you only saw the lighting effect the Glass Lens Normal filter created in the selection area. Glass Lens can also be used to produce special effects in image areas, such as transparent bubbles distorting and catching reflections of the image area that is beneath a selection.

Part of the Glass Lens Normal's effect is to make the affected area round-shaped, so it's usually best to apply the effect to an elliptical selection. Rectangular selections tend to have missing corner areas when the Glass Lens Normal filter is applied.

To specify where the highlight will be in the Glass Lens effect, press the keypad number keys 1–9 before clicking on the command. These set the direction of the highlight. Compass directions correspond to the keypad number positions. For example, pressing 7 produces a highlight in the upper-left of the selection, and pressing 2 creates a southern highlight. By default, the Glass Lens Normal plug-in creates a highlight in the upper-right of the selection.

Try using Glass Lens several times on the same selection to create multiple light source highlights in a selected area.

Because this image will serve as a repeating pattern over the surface of the robot wireframe, it's usually not a good idea to create more than one or two areas of visual interest, such as the Glass Lens effect. The single pilot light will be repeated many times, and three or four pilot lights would make the CIRCUIT image call more attention to its design than the underlying geometry of the wireframe robot. Texture images should be interesting, but should lack distinctive elements so that the viewer isn't distracted by a pattern when the image is tiled across the surface of an object.

Blurring an Image Channel

Everything in the CIRCUIT image is perfectly in focus now, and this is perhaps why the image doesn't look as photographic as it should. Drawing programs create perfect vector geometry, but viewers have a hard time relating to this perfection because nothing in real life is in perfect focus. Certainly photographed images, which viewers frequently can relate to as being "real," contain minute flaws that make the image warmer, more fragile, and a little more human.

Photoshop's Blur Filters don't have to be applied to an entire image, or even to a selection, to soften the appearance of a digital image. Filters can be applied to a single channel of any image format that supports channels, and this leads to some interesting possibilities.

In the next exercise, you'll blur a color channel of the CIRCUIT.TGA image. When viewed from the RGB composite view, the effect causes some slight color shifting because the color channels become slightly out of sync in terms of their visual information. The CIRCUIT image will retain reasonable focus, but by blurring a single channel, you'll add a quality most commonly recognized by viewers as being photographic in nature.

Modifying a Color Channel

Press Ctrl+ minus key twice	Zooms out to a looser viewing resolution, so that you can see the effects of your editing.
Click on the Green channel title on the Channels palette	Displays the green component of the RGB image.
Choose Filters, Blur, Gaussian Blur	Displays the Gaussian Blur dialog box.
Enter **1** in the **R**adius field, then click on OK	Applies a small amount of blur to the Green channel, as shown in figure 22.5.
Click on the RGB title on the Channels palette	Returns you to the color composite view of the CIRCUIT image.

The slight overlapping areas of Red in the image are due to the Green channel's misalignment with the other channel's visual detail, which suggests shiny metal.

Press Ctrl+S (**F**ile, **S**ave)	Saves your work up to this point.

The Green channel was chosen for the blur instead of the Red or Blue channel because the Green channel contains a medium amount of visual information. If you look at the thumbnail icons on the Channels palette, you'll see that Blue contributes the least to the overall image (low brightness values), and Red contributes the most. The Green channel is the best channel to blur to produce an effect without totally fuzzing the RGB view.

Channels can be great fun to play with when you want to stylize an image. If you ever want to create a "Sunday Comics" effect with a color channel image, try selecting entire color channels (**S**elect, **A**ll), then nudge them over by one or two pixels with the keyboard arrow keys.

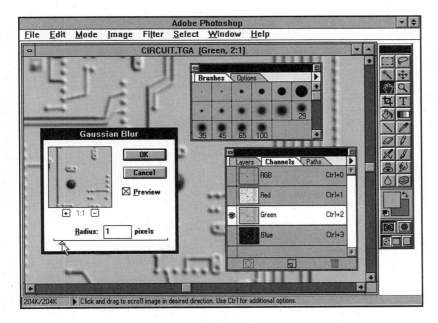

Figure 22.5

Use a Blur filter to change a single color channel in an image to create a soft focus effect.

Using the Dodge Tool

Photoshop's Toning tools can adjust areas of an image to increase or decrease brightness of pixels, without disturbing the original Hue. The Dodge tool will be used in the next exercise to create an effect in parts of the CIRCUIT image that suggest metallic highlights scattered around the surface.

When Highlights is selected from the drop-down box on the Options palette, the Dodge tool will increase the brightness and reduce the Saturation most visibly in the lighter image areas. At a low Exposure setting, the Dodge tool can be used several times on a single image area to create uneven highlights, like those you'd see on a brass banister that's a little dulled by fingerprints.

This is the final phase of transforming the EPS blueprint of a circuit into an image that will serve as the image and bump map of the wireframe robot.

Painting Highlights with the Dodge Tool

Press **O** (not zero) until the Dodge tool is displayed on the toolbox	Chooses the Dodge Tool. Alternatively, you can Alt+click on the tool on the toolbox to choose it.
Press Enter	Displays the Options palette for the currently selected tool.
Click and drag the Exposure slider to about **40%**, and choose Highlights from the drop-down list	Sets the strength the Dodge tool uses to lighten areas to less than half; areas of brighter values will be affected most.
Click on the Brushes tab on the Brushes palette, then choose the middle row, third from the left tip	Sets the characteristics with which the Dodge tool lightens areas.
Click and drag over a wire area of the CIRCUIT image	Brings out the highlights in the area you chose.
Click and drag over the same image area (see fig 22.6)	Turns light area almost to white, and reveals pure color in midtone and darker areas.
Click and drag over other areas	Applies the highlight effect to other image areas.
Press Ctrl+S (**F**ile, **S**ave)	Saves your work up to this point.

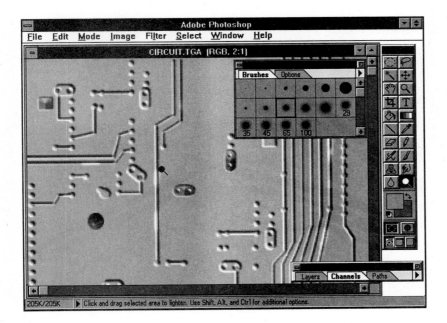

Figure 22.6

The Dodge tool selectively increases brightness and reduces saturation in areas over which you click and drag.

Instant Robots: Rendering a 3D Image

Although this next section is not "hands-on," you'll learn about the process of rendering a 3D image, and learn how to apply your CIRCUIT image to your own 3D models . Youll also learn the process of mapping the CIRCUIT.TGA image to the DXF (Data Exchange Format) file of a 3D robot.

The goal of this section's assignment is to generate a photo-realistic bitmap image of the robot, which is used as one of several compositional elements you manipulate in Photoshop to create the finished image.

The second part of creating a virtual subject for the illustration is to make a model to which a rendering program can map the CIRCUIT.TGA image. Biomechanics Corp. of America makes a splendid program, *Mannequin*, a CAD (Computer-Assisted Design) program that automatically creates a model according to gender, weight, height, and even nationality! Mannequin's ability to almost instantly create human 3D shapes takes days, if not weeks, away from the process of designing the human figure used for the robot. And no CAD experience is necessary. In minutes, with a pull and tug here and there, the model is posed and ready to be exported to the rendering application. Figure 22.7 shows the Mannequin interface, and the robot-to-be.

Figure 22.7

A DXF file can contain 3D information about an object or several objects grouped together.

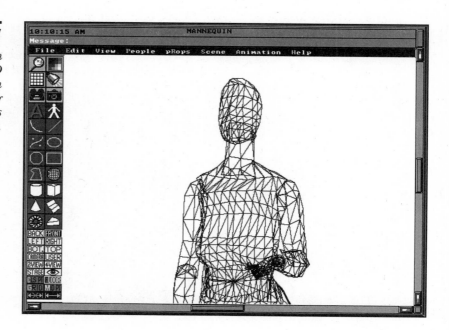

Note Although many 3D-graphics packages offer both modeling and rendering capabilities, many times the process is broken into two phases, each handled by a separate application. Mannequin's strong point is that it creates a pre-made human topology that can then be posed. Image-mapping features, however, are not offered. For this reason, Mannequin can be thought of as a *modeling* program that generates a file ready for rendering.

A separate rendering program is used to apply information to the DXF file of the robot, as you'll see in the next section.

Putting the Pieces Together

Renderize Live for Windows uses bitmap images (such as CIRCUIT.TGA) to create surfaces on vector information (like DFX files) to produce a rendered image whose file format can be edited in Photoshop. After loading the CIRCUIT.TGA image, along with HARTPOSE.DXF (the Mannequin creation), into the Renderize program, lighting is defined, surface reflection properties are set, and the CIRCUIT.TGA image is used as both an image map (a repeating design) and a bump map (a repeating relief) for the surface of the HARTPOSE.DXF file.

Properties are set for how the "material" is mapped to the HARTPOSE data. The CIRCUIT image is mixed with information about the nature of the light that is

bounced off of the image map when it's mapped to the DXF wireframe, how much of the surface is shiny, and what component colors are used when a highlight occurs on the surface. The CIRCUIT.TGA image is also bump-mapped to the wireframe's surface to create "texture" out of the pseudo-technical doodads and pilot light.

As an extra enhancement, an environment map is specified for the model, which is a special feature Renderize Live offers. *Environment mapping* is a reflection of a back-ground scene on a surface to make shiny surface properties look more realistic. The "environment" in this case is a hastily-painted bitmap image of the tropics. Environment mapping produces an effect similar to that of looking into a chrome hubcap—you see the detail of the hubcap, but you also see yourself and visual elements in the background. In figure 22.8, you can see *Renderize Live*'s workspace.

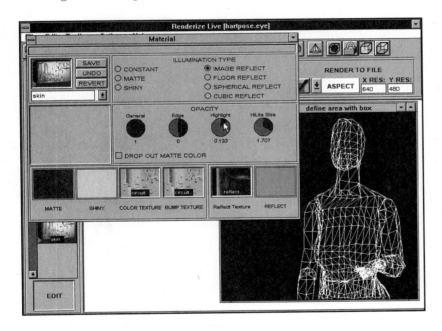

Figure 22.8

The CIRCUIT.TGA image is used in Renderize Live *as the main component of the "material" used as the robot's surface.*

Rendering a model is simpler than it sounds. Renderize Live offers drag and drop support for virtual spotlights, the ability to define materials for objects, and also reposition objects, all in a 3D workspace. Except for using a cursor instead of your own hands, the *Renderize Live* workspace "feels" very much like a large movie stage, where you can move actors and props, and even have a virtual makeup call!

Take a good look at figure 22.8. The controls for defining materials will seem familiar when you create a background for the robot in Photoshop. Photoshop's Lighting Effects Filter offers controls for material properties and mapping textures to an image.

A low-resolution preview can be executed in most rendering programs to ensure proper lighting and positioning of all the elements; afterward, the final render is made. In figure 22.9, the rendering process is about half complete. *Renderize Live* can render an image based on wireframe and image mapping information to any image dimension, and an Alpha channel is specified for the finished file to isolate rendered objects from the background.

Figure 22.9

Rendering programs create image files based on dimensional data, surface properties, and lighting.

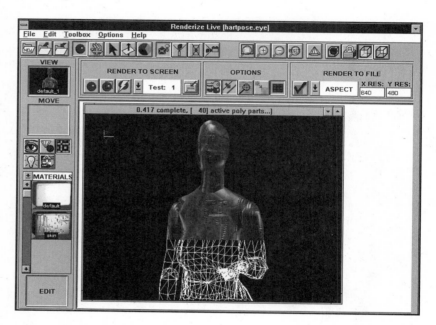

The finished, rendered file, HARTPOSE.TGA, is on the *Inside Adobe Photoshop 3* Bonus CD, ready to be copied to a background image that's yet to be created.

Creating A Surrealistic Background

Photoshop 3 has a number of texture and lighting features that can be used to create a photo-realistic background scene. The finished image in this assignment should be fantastic, yet incorporate familiar real-world shapes and design elements so that the viewer has a familiar point of reference.

The STONES.EPS image on the *Inside Adobe Photoshop 3* Bonus CD is a black-and-white graphic image with shapes that suggest a stone wall. In the next series of exercises, you'll use techniques you've already learned, and a few new ones, to transform the black-and-white image into a wall that has depth, mood, and a source of light similar to that found in the HARTPOSE.TGA image.

First, you use the same steps used earlier on the CIRCUIT image to create an embossed background—one that displays depth for the stone wall. Here's how to "tweak" the Emboss options to produce deep, dimensional recesses in the STONES image.

Creating Stones from a 2D Image

Open the STONES.EPS image from the CHAP22 subdirectory of the *Inside Adobe Photoshop 3* Bonus CD

Displays the Rasterize dialog box.

Enter **150** in the **R**esolution field, choose RGB Color from the **M**ode drop-down list, leave the **A**nti-Aliased and **C**onstrain Proportions boxes checked, then click on OK

The **H**eight and **W**idth were measured when the EPS files was created. STONES.EPS is larger than the HARTPOSE.TGA image, so accept the defaults.

Choose **F**ilter, Stylize, then Emboss

Displays the Emboss dialog box.

Enter **47** in the **A**ngle field, **7** in the**H**eight field, and leave the **A**mount at **100**% (see fig. 22.10)

Specifies a relatively "deep" emboss effect for the STONES image.

The angle used for the emboss effect creates highlights in a direction similar to the light source in HARTPOSE.TGA.

If you look back at figure 22.9, you'll see that the final render of the robot has lighting coming from about 1 o'clock. By setting the angle at 47°, you'll make the "lighting" in the Emboss effect cast at the same angle. The background and foreground in this composition should display identical lighting conditions.

Also, 45° is not the best angle to produce embossed stones because some of the angles of the STONES' design fall at 45°. An Emboss at the same angle would result in image areas with missing sides on some stones. Always set an embossing Angle that is not the same as any geometric angle found in a design, such as 47°.

Click on OK

Applies the Emboss filter.

Choose **F**ile, Sa**v**e As, then save the image in the TIFF format as STONES.TIF (from Save File as Format **T**ype drop-down list) to your hard disk

Saves your work up to this point.

Figure 22.10

You can set the angle of the Emboss effect to indicate the direction of a light source on the embossed graphic.

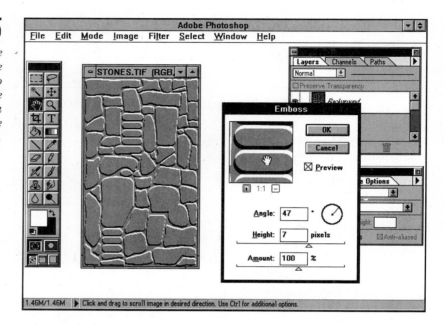

Like most of the preview windows in Photoshop's Filters, you can scroll your view of the target image within the preview window by click and dragging the cursor inside of it. This is a great feature when you apply the Emboss filter because you can check specific areas of the target image to see whether the filter is applying the effect you intend before clicking on OK.

Colorizing the Stones

The Selective Color command is a useful feature for both pre-press color-correction and creative tinting of an image with only neutral color values, as you learned earlier with the CIRCUIT image. The STONES image now needs a little color enhancement. The Colorize option in the Hue/Saturation dialog box will be used as an alternative method of adding a distinctive hue to an image whose RGB color components are all equal (producing shades of neutral gray).

Colorize, like the Selective color command, doesn't use the RGB color model for reassigning colors in an image. Instead, Colorize uses the HSB, or Hue, Saturation, Brightness model, which makes it easier for the Photoshop user to define and preview changes in color properties. Colorize only works on image areas that have some inherent color values, such as the gray areas of the embossed STONES image. STONES.TIF has no prominent Red, Green, or Blue component, but has a definite

hue that the Colorize command can change. Areas of pure black and white are unaffected by the Colorize option because you can't change the hue of an area that either has no light or is completely brilliant.

Saving the Highlight Areas Before Colorizing

The highlight (white) areas in the STONES image is a nice touch, and these areas should be saved as a selection in an Alpha channel before commencing with the filtering, lighting, and colorizing of the image. Later, you'll be able to recall the highlight areas and make them stand out from the rest of the STONES image. Saving areas described by a selection in a channel is an alternative to placing the areas on a separate Layer. You may often find that saving selections instead of the underlying image provides you with a clearer view of how an image is shaping up.

Before using the Colorize option on the STONES image, here's how to set up the highlight areas of the stones image so you can edit them later:

Saving a Color Range Selection

Choose **S**elect, **C**olor Range	Displays the Color Range dialog box.
Choose Sampled Colors from the drop-down box	Specifies that you'll use the Eyedropper tools on the dialog box to choose color ranges you want marquee selections around.
Click on the Selection radio button, then choose quick Mask from the **S**election Preview drop-down list	Displays selected areas in white in the Preview window, and selected areas as Quick Mask overlay in the active image.
Press Ctrl+spacebar, then click over the STONES image	Changes the cursor into the Zoom tool.

When you click outside the Color Range dialog box with Ctrl and spacebar held, you zoom into the STONES image, which helps you select an image area more precisely.

If you've over-zoomed, press Alt+Spacebar and click on the image. This zooms you out. While you're in a dialog box, this is how you adjust the viewing resolution of an image. (*Tip:* Shift+spacebar toggles to the Hand tool.)

continues

continued

Release the keyboard keys, then click over a white area in the STONES image	The cursor reverts to an Eyedropper and selects all the highlights in the image (see fig. 22.11).
Set the Fuzziness value to about **100**	Includes the Anti-alias fringe pixels around the white highlight areas you've selected.
Click on OK	

You now return to the STONES image, with marquee selections surrounding areas displayed as Quick Mask in the color Range dialog box.

Press Ctrl+S (**F**ile, **S**ave)	Saves your work up to this point.

Colorizing a Monochrome Image

Generally, you don't have to define a high Fuzziness value to select color ranges in an image such as STONES, where there is a definite color contrast between the highlights and midtones, and a limited number of unique colors in the image. However, the STONES image began its career as a rasterized EPS file.

If Anti-aliasing is enabled when you rasterize an EPS image, semitransparent edge pixels are rendered to smooth the image edges. These semitransparent pixels should be included in your selection of the highlights to keep the selection smooth; a higher-than-expected Fuzziness setting is necessary to include these pixels.

Here's how to use the Colorize option to turn the embossed stones into *slate-colored* embossed stones:

Colorizing a Monochrome Image

Click on the (convert to) Selection icon on the bottom left of the Channels palette	Turns marquee selection into saved selection information in a new image channel.
Press **F7** to access the Layers/Channels/Paths palette if it isn't already on the workspace	Displays the group of palettes.

Press Ctrl+D, then Ctrl+U (**I**mage, **A**djust, Hue/Saturation)	Deselects the active marquee and displays the Hue/Saturation dialog box.
Click on the C**o**lorize box, then enter **-175** in the **H**ue field, **100** in the S**a**turation field, and **-58** in the L**i**ghtness field	Turns the STONES image to a dark, monochrome slate blue (see fig. 22.12).
Click on OK	Applies the effect and returns you to the workspace.
Press Ctrl+S (**F**ile, **S**ave)	Saves your work up to this point.

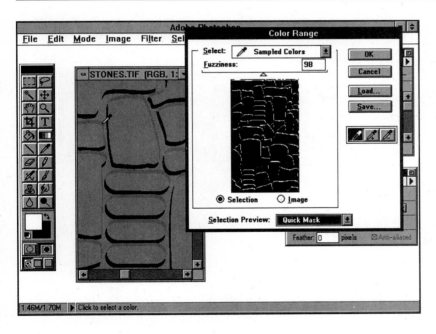

Figure 22.11

Chose a highlight area to select its color range, then save the selection areas to an Alpha channel.

By decreasing the Lightness value, the highlight (white) areas in the STONE image take on some shading, which is then affected by the Colorize option. Pure white is not colorized in images, so your option is to add some grayscale component to the pixels (decreasing lightness) so that the areas can be tinted with Hue.

Figure 22.12

*Colorizing an
image removes
color values, and
replaces them
with one shade of
Hue.*

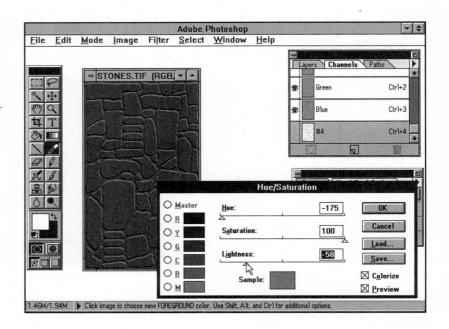

Texture Fills and the Lighting Effects

Photoshop ships with sample image files on the Adobe Photoshop 3 Deluxe CD-ROM
that can be used as texture, or bump maps in the creation of lighting effects in a
target image. Like the image map you created as an exercise earlier for the surface of
a wireframe, Photoshop uses image information to map relief, recesses, and protru-
sions in areas illuminated by the Lighting Effects filter. For more details on the
Lighting Effects, see Chapter 18, "Photoshop's Native Filters."

The ground rules for texture map images are as follows:

◆ They must be Grayscale mode images.

◆ They must be saved in Photoshop 2.5 or 3 as PSD images.

◆ They can't have Alpha channels. Texture fills used by Photoshop in the Lighting Effects filter are *themselves* placed in channels, so an Alpha-capable grayscale
within an Alpha channel is redundant, and also impossible.

Right now's a good time to scout the Adobe Photoshop 3 Deluxe CD for the
BLISTPNT.PSD image. It's in the Textures (for Lighting Effects) subdirectory (File)
of the GOODIES subdirectory (Folder). You'll need this image to set up the next
exercise. If you're like most of us and don't have two CD-ROM drives, you should

copy this image to your hard disk, then put the *Inside Adobe Photoshop 3* Bonus CD back in because you'll need more image files from this book's CD to complete the chapter's assignment.

Here's how to add a texture to the STONES image that will be used as bump map information when the Lighting Effects filter is used.

Defining a Texture Map

Click on the New channel icon on the bottom of the Channels palette	Displays the Channel Options dialog box.
Accept the default name of Channel #5, and click on the Color Indicates: **S**elected Areas radio button, then click on OK	Creates a new channel in the STONES image, and channel #5 becomes your active view.
Choose Fi**l**ter, Render, then Texture Fill	Displays the Texture Fill dialog box. You need to specify the texture image's location.
Choose the directory where BLISTER.PSD is located, click on the file name, then click on OK	Applies the texture map image to the Alpha Channel #5 in the STONES image.

As you can see in figure 22.13, the Alpha channel is filled with the image information from the BLISTER.PSD file. It's okay to have the texture image open when you use the command.

Click on the RGB title on the Channels palette	Returns you to the composite color view of the STONES image.
Press Ctrl+S (**F**ile, **S**ave)	Saves your work up to this point.

Apparently, you've poured grayscale garbage into a user-defined channel, then saved your work in the last exercise. Fortunately, Photoshop doesn't evaluate this channel information the way our own eyes do, and the following section is a little explanation about the phenomenon that's about to happen.

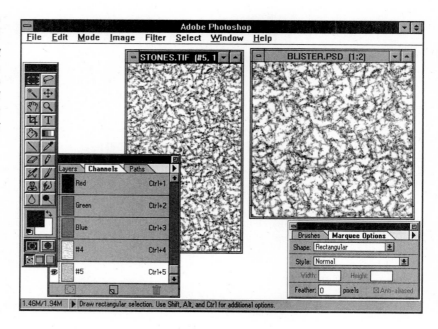

Figure 22.13

*The Texture Fill
command tiles a
PSD image into
an Alpha channel
to be used as
mapping
information.*

Texture Mapping, Photoshop-Style

As described in previous chapters, Photoshop reads image information differently
from the way users do. As humans, we see Alpha channel information as having visual
content; the BLISTER.PSD image looks like the mating of barbed wire and seaweed.
But to Photoshop, the bright and white areas have a correlation to the pixels in the
RGB image—pixel #49 in the Alpha channel corresponds to pixel #49 in the RGB
composite view of the image, and so on.

If the Alpha channel information was loaded as a *selection* area, Photoshop would
create marquee selections based on the black areas of the Alpha channel, and protect
the lighter areas from editing. However, the Alpha channel information won't be
used by Photoshop as selection information in the next exercise; instead, it will be
used to create *texture* in the RGB view of STONES.TIF.

The texture effect happens only when you apply Lighting Effects to the image. Darker
areas in the Alpha channel will correspond to areas in the RGB image that recede,
and areas will appear to rise off the surface where Photoshop reads lighter areas in
the Alpha channel. Only areas that are covered by a virtual light will receive the
texture treatment, so assigning the right lighting to the image is important.

Here's how to add texture mapping and a lighting effect at the same time with Photoshop's Lighting Effects filter:

Adding Lighting to the Stones

Choose File, Render, Lighting Effects	Displays the Lighting Effects dialog box.

By default, you always start a "session" in the Lighting Effects filter with one light source. You'll set the specifications of this light to suggest a little more drama and add mood to the scene, which is fantastical in nature.

Choose spotlight from the Light Type drop-down list	Creates a spotlight effect.

The spotlight's edges are shown as an elliptical outline in the Preview window. The light source (the center dot) and the point at which the light is aimed are connected by a line within the ellipse.

Click and drag the Intensity slider to **83**, then click and drag the Focus slider to **62**	Makes the spotlight fairly strong, with a hard concentration of light.
Click on the sample color icon for the light, choose light gray from the color Picker, then click on OK	Gives some neutral cast to the spotlight, preventing it from "burning in" bright areas on the STONES image.
In the Properties field, click and drag the sliders to read: Gloss: **0**, Surface Material: **53**, Exposure: **0**, and Ambiance **14**	These are properties for the STONES image, not properties of the spotlight.

You've defined the way light strikes the STONES image if the light and the stones were viewed in real life. Basically, the stones are now slightly metallic, with a little Ambient light property. Ambient light is indirectly reflected light; white walls in a room that has indirect lighting display their color from ambient lighting.

Click on the Properties sample color, choose light gray from the Color Picker, then click on OK	The STONES image will display no color characteristics other than those you defined when you Colorized it earlier.

continues

continued

Click and drag on each of the four boxes on the corners of the light ellipse in the Preview window	These boxes define the edges of the light. Shape the light to create a narrow ellipse.
Click and drag the center circle in the light ellipse outline to a position slightly lower and to the left of the center of the Preview window	Moves the source of the light.
Choose #5 from the Texture Channel drop-down list, click on the White is high check box, then click and drag the slider to **41**	Tells Photoshop to use Alpha channel #5 as the source for texture mapping, that white in the channel should produce protruding (not receding) areas, and the degree of bumpiness should be moderate.

Your Preview window sort of came alive at this point, didn't it? This is the texture mapping effect working in combination with the lighting you're defining. Displaying the proposed changes in the Preview window requires a *lot* of Photoshop calculations; depending on your processor, you may have a moment to spare to visit the water cooler.

Click and drag the edge box connected to the center circle of the ellipse to a 1 o'clock position	This is the target box for the light. You direct the target for the light to fall outside of the image, at an angle similar to that of Emboss Effect on the STONES. See figure 22.14.
Hang tight for a moment, and don't click on OK yet	This is the end of the exercise, but *not* the end of the options you need to set in the Lighting Effects dialog box. Read on!

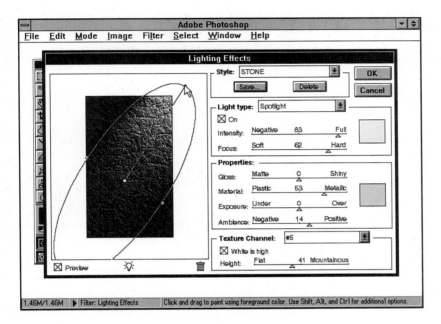

Figure 22.14

*Set the
characteristics of
the light you add
to a scene in the
Lighting Effects
dialog box.*

The Omni Light and Texture Mapping

If you look closely at the Preview window right now, you'll see that the areas *not*
covered by the outline of the light in the Preview window don't display any of the
glorious texture you've defined for the STONES image. The reason for this anomaly
is that the texture fill information is read only into areas in the image that have direct
light shining on it. The ambient setting for the light you've just modified won't
produce texture in the darker areas of the STONES image because it's indirect
lighting.

In the next exercise, you'll add a universal source of light to the image—the Omni
light. The Omni light simulates light coming from nowhere, which creates an even
illumination everywhere on an image, sort of like the light on an overcast day. You
won't have to tune the Omni light to create textures in the shaded areas of the
image—an Omni light simply has to be present to add texture mapping throughout
the image. As a result, the elegant spotlight effect you've created won't be changed.

Here's how to complete the lighting and texturizing of the STONES image.

Adding an Omni Light to the Image

Click and drag the New light icon (the lightbulb on the bottom left of the dialog box) into the center of the Preview window	Adds a light to the scene. Its center should be slightly above and to the right of the Spotlight.
Choose Omni from the Light type drop-down list	Turns the outline of the light into a circle. There is no direction line for an Omni light—Omni light direction is from everywhere to everywhere. Spiritual, huh?
Click and drag one of the edge boxes toward the border of the Preview window	Stop when you've covered most of the Preview window with the circle. This covers the image with Omni light.
Click and drag the Intensity slider to **+4**	Adds a barely detectable amount of Omni light to the image.
Click and drag all the Properties sliders to **0** except the Ambiance slider; set Ambiance to **5** (see fig. 22.15)	Adds very slight amount of indirect lighting to the image.
Click on OK	Applies the effect and returns you to the workspace.
Press Ctrl+S (<u>F</u>ile, <u>S</u>ave)	Saves your work up to this point.

In figure 22.16, you can see the product of your labors with the Lighting Effects filter. The blistered paint image map, BLISTER.PSD, creates a mottling effect on the surface of the STONES image that suggests an age-old background, which contrasts nicely with the state-of-the-art robot image. This creates a dynamic tension between foreground and background elements, inviting the viewer to take a second look at this graphic image. And a third, and a fourth!

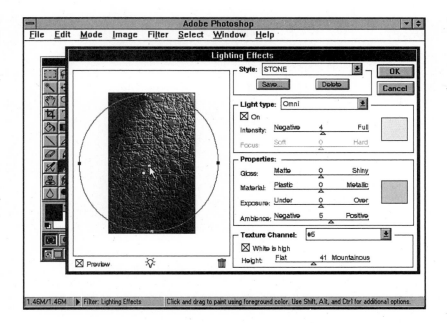

Figure 22.15

Choose Omni lighting to add flat, even illumination to an image.

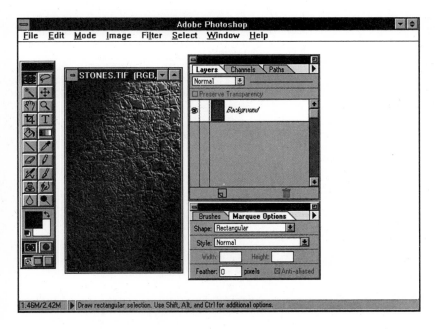

Figure 22.16

You can add a mood to an image by suggesting a source of lighting on the Background layer.

Reinforcing Original Design Elements

Between the dramatic lighting and texture effects, it's easy for the compositional elements of the stones in the STONES.TIF image to get lost. In the next exercise, you'll load the selection channel containing the highlight areas of the embossed stones, and use the Brightness/Contrast adjustment to make these areas speak a little more clearly within the total design.

Here's how to increase the emboss effect long after extensive image editing has been performed:

Increasing Brightness in a Selection Area

Click on the Channel #4 title on the Channels palette	Displays the view of the saved selection in Alpha channel #4.
Choose Filter, Blur, then Blur	Slightly blurs the Alpha channel information, creating a soft selection.
Alt and click on the Channel #4	Loads the selection as a icon marquee.
Click on the RGB title on the Channels palette (see fig. 22.17)	Displays the RGB color composite view of the STONES image.
Press Ctrl+H (Image, Hide Edges)	Hides the marquee border. The selection area is still in place, but the "marching ants" aren't displayed.
Press Ctrl+B (Image, Adjust, Brightness/Contrast)	Displays the Brightness/Contrast dialog box.
Click and drag the Brightness slider to +57, then click and drag the Contrast slider to –7	Gives the original highlight areas a little "glow" (see fig. 22.18).
Click on OK	Applies the effect.
Click on the New Layer icon on the Layers palette, then click on OK	Accepts the defaults for the new Layer 1 on the STONES image. Layer 1 is now the target (active) layer.
Click on the Channels tab on the palette, then click and drag the channel #5 title into the Trash icon	You no longer need the channel, and by deleting the BLISTER texture map, the saved file size is smaller.

Click and drag the Channel #4 title Trash icon

You have cleared the Alpha channels into the from the document.

Choose **F**ile, Sa**v**e As, then save the image in the PSD format (from Save File as Format **T**ype drop-down list) as HARTMACH.PSD to your hard disk

Saves your work in the Photoshop format that will retain layer information. This will be the background for the finished image.

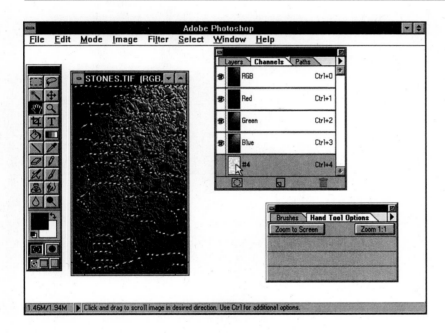

Figure 22.17

Press Alt (Option) and click on an Alpha channel image icon on the Channels palette to load the selection information.

The Blur filter helps take the "edge" off the original selection areas in the Alpha channel. Whenever you're trying to transform pure, digital graphics into something a little more photogenic, it's best to introduce some imperfection and softness, as a camera would capture in real life.

 Tip

When performing precise alignment of a floating selection, it's often helpful to hide the marquee border surrounding an active selection. To do this, press Ctrl+H (**S**elect, Hide **E**dges).

Ctrl+H does not deselect the floating selection, but instead removes the marquee from view. Press Ctrl+H to turn on the marquee again.

Figure 22.18

*Use Brightness/
Contrast controls
to lighten selected
areas in an
image.*

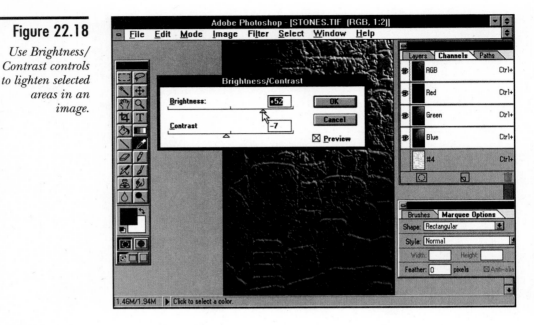

Defining a Glowing Area

Now that the stone wall background image has been handsomely enhanced and edited, it's time to add the HARTMACH.TGA image. Copying the robot image is performed the same way you'd click and drag a marquee selection from an image created in Photoshop—many rendering programs, including Renderize Live, create and save Alpha channel information to isolate foreground objects.

Copying the robot to the stone wall is the easy part of this next assignment; you simply press Alt and click on the HARTPOSE.TGA's Alpha channel icon on the Channels palette, and the perfect selection border around the robot becomes active. Because this image is to be a fantastic creation, now's a good time to explore some of the ways you can create a "neon glow" effect around an image area. Stroking a path is one way, but defining a path around the robot is the long way around creating the same effect when you have a selection border already defined (see the following warning). In the next exercise, you'll use the Border command to create a soft-edged selection based on a selection marquee, then save the information in an Alpha channel as a template for the glow.

Stop It's not such a good idea to convert a complex selection marquee into a path, although it's possible. Users of Photoshop 2.5 are already familiar with using the Stroke Subpath command to produce a neon outline, but complex selection marquees generally produce even more complex paths.

Depending on how close a **T**olerance value you choose for the Make Path command, even simple selection shapes can become paths with hundreds of Anchor points. The processing necessary for Photoshop to accurately place all the Anchor points will slow your computer down, and in some cases, Photoshop will crash because the calculations are too extensive.

The best selection marquees for converting to paths are simple geometric shapes without a lot of curves.

Here's how to define a soft-edged border using the selection marquee:

Augmenting a Selection with the Border Command

Open the HARTPOSE.TGA image from the CHAP22 subdirectory of the *Inside Adobe Photoshop 3* Bonus CD

This is the image created using the modeling and rendering programs.

Reposition the two image windows so you have a good view of both images

You need to see both the source (HARTPOSE.TGA) and target (HARTMACH.PSD) images for drag-and-drop copying.

Click on the title bar of the HARTPOSE.TGA image, then Alt+click on the Channel #4 icon on the Channels palette

Loads the selection border Renderize Live created in the image.

With a selection tool active, click and drag the selection into the image

Copies the selection of the robot to Layer 1 in the HARTMACH.PSD image window (see fig. 22.19).

Click and drag the selection so its bottom edge is flush with the bottom of the image window

Positions the selection on the layer. *Don't* deselect the robot yet!

When the selection of the robot is aligned, choose **S**elect, **M**odify, then **B**order

Displays the Border dialog box.

continues

continued

Enter **20** in the **W**idth field, then click on OK	Creates a selection border around the selection marquee whose edges are 10 pixels inside and 10 pixels outside the marquee.
Click on the Selection icon on the Channels palette	Saves the Border selection to a new channel #4 (see fig. 22.20).
Press Ctrl+D (**S**elect, **N**one)	Deselects the marquee.
Press Ctrl+S (**F**ile, **S**ave)	Saves your work up to this point.

Figure 22.19

Drag and drop the selection of the robot into the HARTMACH.PSD image after you've created a new layer in the document.

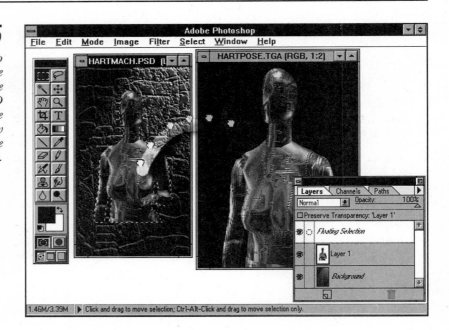

Creating the "Neon Glow" Effect

Neon trim is used in advertisements for everything from motorcycles to floor wax, and much use has been made of Photoshop 2.5 ability to create a neon glow enhancement. With version 3, creating a glow around something, such as the robot, is much simpler. In addition, you don't have to make the neon effect a permanent addition to the finished image when it's created on a layer other than the robot's. You can refine, modify, and even delete the neon glow at any time before the different image layers are merged into the Background.

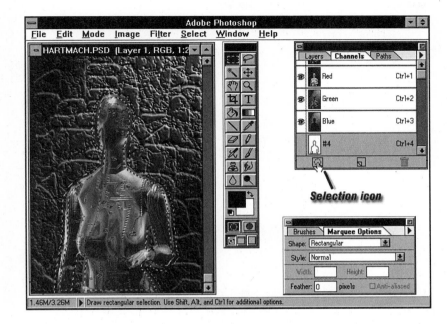

Figure 22.20

Save the modified selection to an Alpha channel for future use.

Because the Border command redefined the selection of the robot, you now have a saved selection that's 20 pixels around the *edge* of the original selection. The Border command produces an anti-aliased selection, which makes it a near-perfect selection to load onto a new layer and then paint within the resulting selection marquee on a new layer to create the effect. If you further soften the selection with the Gaussian Blur filter before painting, you'll achieve a more diffuse, subtle, photo-realistic effect that'll make the robot positively electric.

All charged up? Here's one method for creating the "Neon Look" in Photoshop.

Creating a Glowing Border

Click on the New layer icon on the Layers palette, then click on OK	Adds Layer 2 to the HARTMACH image; Layer 2 becomes the active Layer.
Click on the Channels tab on the Channelspalette, then click on the Channel #4 title	Displays the view of the border selection you saved.
Choose Filter, Blur, then Gaussian Blur	Displays the Gaussian Blur dialog box.

continues

continued

Enter **4** in the Radius field, then click on OK	Softens the border selection information (see fig. 22.21).
Alt+click on the Channel #4 icon, then click on the RGB title on the Channels palette	Loads the border selection and returns you to the color composite view of the image.
Click on the Layers tab	Displays the view of the Layers for HARTMACH.PSD.

You're on the right Layer (Layer 2) for creating the neon effect without destroying the robot on the other Layer. It's a really good idea to keep the Layers palette displayed when working on multilayer images because this book can't remind you when you're working on your own assignments!

Click on the Foreground color on the toolbox	Displays the Color Picker.
Define a bright purple color, then click on OK	Sets the foreground color in Photoshop to the color you'll use for the neon glow.

Actually, you can choose any foreground color you like. Purple seems to fit in nicely with the gold and slate blue of the image.

Press **B** on the keyboard (or click on the Paint **B**rush tool), then press Enter	Chooses the Paint Brush tool and displays the Options palette for the Paint Brush.
Click and drag the Opacity slider to about **80%**, click on the Brushes tab, then click on the 100-pixel diameter tip	Sets the characteristics of the Paint Brush tool.

Partial opacity gives you the option to repeat strokes in one area without totally covering the area with foreground color. Neon is supposed to be a soft, semitransparent lighting effect.

Click and drag in the marquee selection area	Applies foreground color to Layer 2 (see fig. 22.22).
Press Ctrl+H (**S**elect, Hide **E**dges) if the marquee is hindering your view	Toggles the marquee edges off. You still have a selection active, however.
Continue clicking and dragging around the edge of the robot, but don't paint around the bottom edge of the image window	The border extends all the way around the robot, and you don't want neon around the bottom edge of the image window. It would look stupid.
When the image looks like figure 22.23, press Ctrl+S (**F**ile, **S**ave)	Saves the image up to this point.

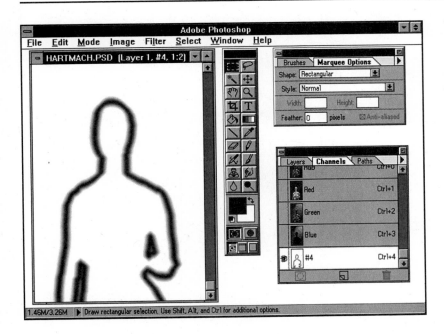

Figure 22.21

Use the Gaussian blur filter to further soften the saved Border selection.

Figure 22.22

Use the saved Border selection as a guide to applying foreground color around the edge of the robot.

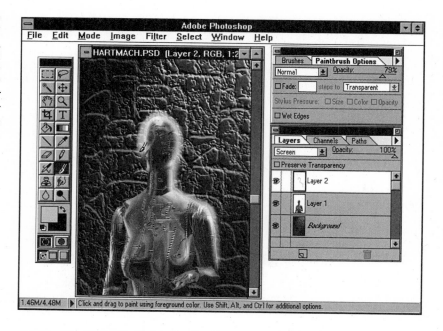

Figure 22.23

The finished Neon glow effect.

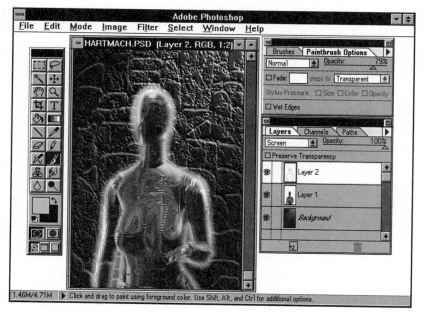

Adding a Second Virtual Reality Element

In the next set of steps, you'll add a heart to the image that appears to float above the robot's outstretched hand ("The Heart of the Machine," right?). The HEART.TIF image was also created in a modeling/rendering program, and it, too, has a built-in Alpha channel to make selection work effortless.

Here's how to add a heart to the composition. Put on the soundtrack to *The Wizard of Oz* to accompany this exercise right now.

Copying a Photorealistic Element to a Layer

Click on the New Layer icon on the Layers palette, then click on OK	Adds Layer 3 to the image.
Open the HEART.TIF image from the CHAP22 subdirectory of the *Inside Adobe Photoshop 3* Bonus CD	This is the image you'll add to the HARTMACH.PSD image.
Click on the Channels tab, then Alt+click on the Channel #4 icon	Loads the selection for the heart image.

An alternative to Alt+clicking on an Alpha channel icon is to choose **S**elect, **L**oad Selection, then fill out the quiz in the Load Selection dialog box. This is not the quickest way to load a saved selection, but most experienced Photoshop 2.5 users know this command as second nature.

With any selection tool chosen, click and drag the selection into the HARTMACH.PSD image window	Copies the heart selection onto Layer 3 (see fig. 22.24).
Position the heart as shown in figure 22.25, then click and drag the Selection icon on the Channels layer into the Channel #4 title	Overwrites (replaces) the border selection in channel #4. You don't need the border any more, and this action conserves file size.
Click outside the selection border	Deselects the floating heart, and it becomes part of Layer 3.

You can click anywhere on an image to deselect a floating selection when a selection tool is active, but it's a good practice to click outside of a selection border. If you click inside a floating selection, you always run the risk of moving it while you deselect it.

continues

continued

Click and drag the Opacity slider on the Layers palette to about **90%** (or press **9** on the keyboard)	Reduces the opacity of the contents on Layer 3.

When the image layers are finally merged to create a single image, the heart will allow a little of the robot and areas of the background to show through. You can change modes for a layer, and alter the Opacity (as you just did) at any time until the layers are merged into the background.

See Chapter 5 for more information about the various Photoshop modes and the effects they produce.

Press Ctrl+S (**F**ile, **S**ave)	Saves your work up to this point.

Figure 22.24

Load a saved selection by Alt and clicking on the Alpha channel title on the Channels palette.

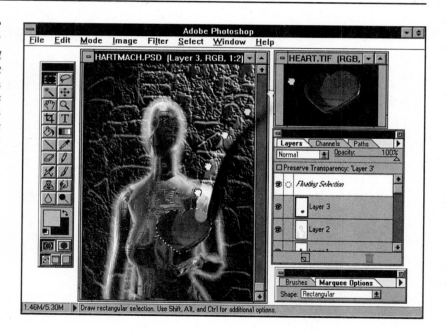

You can't achieve a mode effect when placing a floating selection on a layer that contains no pixels—floating selections can only have compositing modes when they have background pixels to composite *against*. Assigning the layer a mode is like giving the layer a "preview" capability—you can see the effect of merging layers with different modes before you merge them, and you can reassign layers different modes any time before you merge the layers in an image.

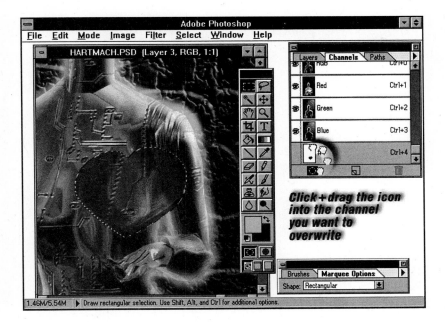

Figure 22.25

Overwrite a saved selection by clicking and dragging the Selection icon into a Channel title while a marquee selection is active.

The "From Behind" Neon Glow Effect

Understanding how light operates in the real world can be a great help in creating artificial light sources in Photoshop images. The neon effect around the robot now suggests that there's an electric charge emanating around the edge of the figure, and this glow partially obscures the area where the robot meets the background image.

The heart should have a glow, also, but it shouldn't compete with the fine neon work you've added to the image so far. The best way to create a glow and still retain edge detail around the heart is to blur the saved selection in channel #4, then assign it its own layer in Screen mode. Screen mode drops out darker tones, and emphasizes lighter ones—it's the inverse function of Multiply mode. When the screened layer is placed behind the heart, a glow will emanate from *behind* the heart, and the edges of the heart image will retain all their detail.

Here's how add a "from behind" glow to the heart.

Using Screen Mode To Create a Glow

Click on the Channel #4 title on the Channels palette, then Alt+click on the Channel #4 icon	Moves you to a view of the saved heart selection, and loads the selection.
Choose **S**elect, M**o**dify, **E**xpand	Displays the Expand Selection dialog box.

When you use Gaussian Blur on a selection the blur tends to move the selection border inward. In this case, it would make the glow effect too small to show behind the heart selection. The solution is to expand the selection border before blurring it.

Enter **4** in the **E**xpand by: field (see fig. 22.26), then click on OK	Enlarges the marquee selection by 4 pixels.
Click and drag the Selection icon into the Channel #4 title	Saves the Expanded selection by overwriting the original saved selection information.
Press Ctrl+D (**S**elect, **N**one)	Deselects the expanded marquee selection around the heart.
Press Ctrl+I (**I**mage, **M**ap, **I**nvert)	Creates a black background and a white heart in the channel.
Choose the Rectangular marquee then click and drag a loose tool, rectanglearound the heart	Creates a marquee selection around the heart.
Press Ctrl+F (Fi**l**ter, Last **F**ilter)	Blurs the selection area, as shown in figure 22.27.

The reason why you defined a marquee around the heart is that you only need this area to copy to a Layer for the glow effect. If you had allowed the Gaussian blur filter to blur the entire channel, it would take more time for your computer to process the command.

Press Ctrl+C (**E**dit, **C**opy)	Copies the selection area to the Clipboard.
Click on the RGB channel title, click on the Layers tab on the palette, then click on the Layer 2 title	You'll add a new Layer next that you want to add on top of Layer 2, but beneath Layer 3.

Click on the new Layer icon on the Layers palette, then press Ctrl+V (**E**dit, **P**aste)	Pastes the selection onto Layer 4.
Click and drag the selection to center it beneath the heart image, press Ctrl+D (**S**elect, **N**one), then choose Screen mode from the Layers drop-down mode list	Screen mode drops out the black areas of the image on Layer 4, and allows the white, blurred shape to show behind the heart on Layer 3.
Press Ctrl+U (**I**mage, **A**djust, **H**ue/Saturation), click on the Colorize check box, enter **–50** in the **L**ightness field, then click on OK	Colorizes the white areas of Layer 3, darkening them slightly.

By default, Photoshop offers red as the hue for Colorizing an image. On a color wheel that represents the hues of the visible spectrum, Red is at 0°, so this default value is an appropriate color for the glow around the red heart.

Press Ctrl+S (**F**ile, **S**ave)	Saves your work up to this point.

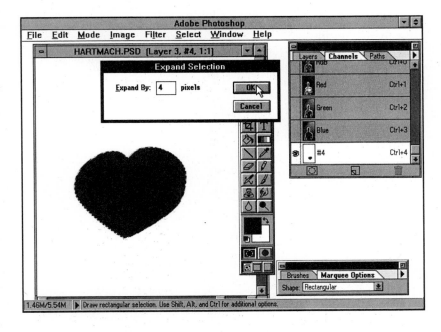

Figure 22.26

Use the Expand command to increase the size of an active marquee selection area.

Figure 22.27

Copy only the area you need from channel #4 to create the glow.

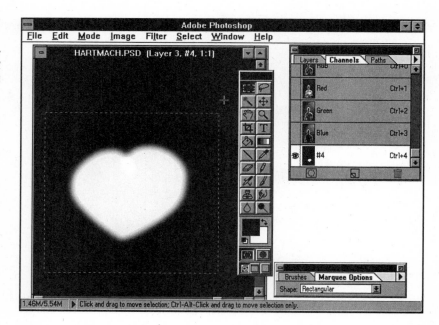

Although we've been practicing pretty shrewd file conservation throughout this chapter, you'll notice that this file has grown a great deal from its original size. The left figure of the Document Sizes field (on the status line for Windows users, on the image window for Macintosh users) tells you that if you saved the image to disk right now, the HARTMACH image would take up 1.5 MB, but the right number says more than 6 MB is being tapped from system resources right now to hold the image in RAM.

If you have less than 12 MB of RAM installed on your computer, you may experience some slow-downs in processing the steps in this assignment. If this is the case, follow these steps.

1. Click on the eye icons on Layers 2, 3, and 4 to hide the layers. When a layer is hidden, it can't be merged.

2. Click on the Background title on the Layers palette to select it as the active layer.

3. Choose Merge Layers from the pop-up menu to the right of the tabs on the palette.

4. Click on the eye icons again to make the layers visible again.

These steps will merge the robot on Layer 1 to the Background layer, freeing up some system resources. You won't be able to edit the background and the robot as separate objects any longer, so be sure everything is as you want it to be in the final image before you merge these layers together.

If you're stocked up on RAM, and you're game to continue piling two more layers on the image before you finish, you can skip the steps mentioned previously.

Completing the Detail Work on the Image

When the last elements of the image—the "Heart of the Machine" title and an effect to surround it—have been added to the HARTMACH image, you'll be able to evaluate the modes assigned to the layers, make last-minute adjustments, and decide on the final order in which the layers are merged to the Background image. For instance, now that the heart on Layer 3 has an opaque, white area behind it (on Layer 4), perhaps you'd like to try out the Hard Light mode for Layer 3; you can change compositing modes before merging Layer 3 by clicking on it on the Layers palette, and specifying a different mode from the drop-down list.

For the moment, let's put a little paint on the Background layer to help integrate the elements you already have in the composition. Overlay mode, one of the new painting and editing modes in Photoshop 3, acts as both Multiply and Screen mode; it accentuates the shadow and highlight areas, while combining foreground color with color that exists in the image area you paint over.

When you set a foreground color in the next exercise that is sampled from the gold on the robot, applying the gold color in Overlay mode will saturate the midtones with pure hue, and increase the contrast in shadow and highlight areas. In effect, you'll be painting a highlight on the robot's palm to suggest that the heart above the hand is casting light on the hand.

Here's how to use the Airbrush tool to cast some light on the subject.

Using the Overlay Mode in Painting

Press **A** on the keyboard (or click on the Airbrush tool), then press Enter	Chooses the Airbrush tool, and displays the Options palette for the tool.

continues

continued

Chose Overlay from the modes drop-down list, then click and drag the Pressure slider to about **30%**	Sets the characteristics of the Airbrush tool to apply foreground color with a fairly weak intensity (Pressure).
Click on the Brushes tab on the Brushes palette, then click on the 35 pixel diameter tip	Defines the size you use for the tip of the Airbrush.
Click on the Layer 1 title on the Layers palette	Makes Layer 1, the Layer containing the robot, the target Layer.
Alt+click over the palm of the robot	Toggles the Airbrush to the Eyedropper tool, and samples the color you click over.
Release the Alt key, then click over the robot's palm—don't drag	Applies foreground color in Overlay mode to the robot's palm.
Click 2 or 3 more times without dragging (see fig. 22.28)	Saturates the gold color, and creates a brilliant highlight effect on the robot's palm.
Press Ctrl+S (**F**ile, **S**ave)	Saves your work up to this point.

The Airbrush tool is a good choice when you want a painting tool that doesn't leave brushstrokes. As you saw in the last exercise, clicking on a painting tool without dragging it can add color to an image. Because the tip you chose has a soft edge, most of the Overlay painting mode was concentrated in the center of where you clicked, and the soft-edge characteristic of the tip faded the application of color to nothingness toward the outside of the tip's diameter.

The piece is coming together beautifully, and if you're still zoomed in on the robot's palm, double-click on the Hand tool right now to see your handiwork full-frame. Figure 22.29 is a view of the results of all the steps so far—the only thing missing is a snappy title at the top of the image.

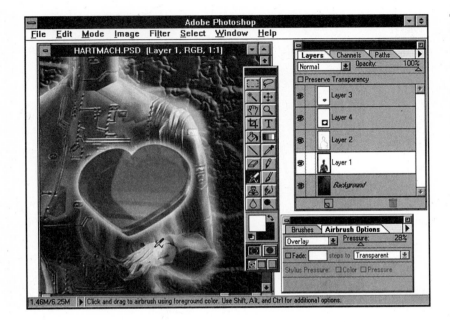

Figure 22.28

Overlay mode blends foreground color values with image colors, and intensifies highlight and shadow areas.

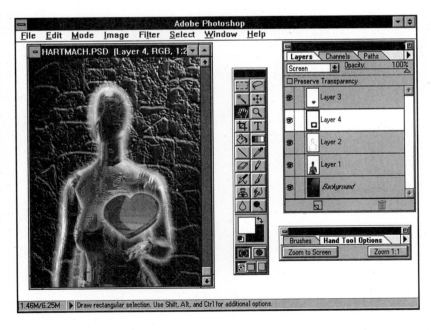

Figure 22.29

Because the image elements are on separate layers, you can still rearrange their order.

Tip   Whether the slider reads Opacity, Pressure, or Exposure for editing or painting tools, low percentages on the slider mean you can repeatedly stroke an area without applying the full effect or color. This gives you the opportunity to vary the amount of effect (or color) within a selected area, adding detail and interest to an image.

Adding Some Text Appeal

To complete the illustration for the hypothetical magazine article, the composition needs some text. Photoshop was used to create the HARTLOGO.TIF image on the *Inside Adobe Photoshop 3* Bonus CD. This grayscale lettering will be added to an Alpha channel to create a selection border. You'll paint within the selection border, then the selection will be edited to create a drop-shadow for the lettering. Drop-shadowing is often used to make lettering stand out from a background.

The HARTLOGO lettering was created using the font ITC Industria Heavy. This typeface was chosen because it is a condensed typeface, which allows the title to fit in a small width at a large point size, and because Industria Heavy has a distinctive, futuristic flavor. Inter-character spacing was accomplished using the S**p**acing option in the Type Tool dialog box, and inter-word spacing was fine-tuned with techniques described in Chapter 9.

Here's how to add the HARTLOGO lettering to the Alpha channel you already have defined in the HARTMACH image.

Importing Text

Open the HARTLOGO.TIF image from the CHAP22 subdirectory of the *Inside Adobe Photoshop 3* Bonus CD	This is the grayscale lettering you'll use as selection information.
Press Ctrl+A (**S**elect, **A**ll)	Selects the entire HARTLOGO image.
Click on the title bar to the HARTMACH.PSD image, then click on the Channel #4 title on the Channels palette	Makes HARTMACH the active image window, and displays a view of channel #4's contents.

Press **E** (for **E**raser tool), then press Enter	Chooses the Eraser tool, and displays the Options for the tool on the Brushes palette.
Press **D** for **d**efault colors (or click on the default colors icon on the toolbox)	Sets the foreground color to black, and the background color to white.
Click on the Erase Channel button on the Options palette	Displays the exclamation dialog box asking you to confirm or cancel this action.
Click on OK	Removes the blurry heart information in Channel #4, and makes the entire channel background white.
Click on the title bar on the HARTLOGO.TIF image, with any selection tool active, then click and drag the selection into the channel #4 view of HARTMACH.PSD, and position it toward the top of the image window	Allows Photoshop to use the black lettering as selection information (see fig. 22.30).
Press Ctrl+D (**S**elect, **N**one), then press Ctrl+S (**F**ile, **S**ave)	Deselects the lettering, and saves your work up to this point.

Tip   The Windows version of Photoshop supports "cool switching" between image windows on the workspace. Pressing Ctrl+Tab to move from one image window to another to select the active image is an alternative to clicking on an image's title bar.

Macintosh Photoshop users should *not* press Ctrl+Tab, because this produces the same effect as pressing Tab—it hides the toolbox and palettes.

Adding Some Drama to Text

As you've seen several times in this assignment, the "Neon Glow" effect adds an element of interest to the composition, but it also helps define image elements, such as the robot and the heart.

Figure 22.30

The visual information in a grayscale image is used as selection information when placed in an Alpha channel.

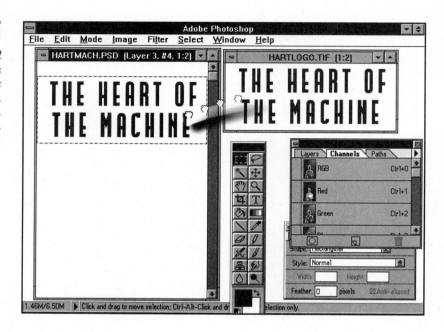

You'll create an effect with the lettering selection in the next exercise that's more of a design element than a special effect. You'll paint the lettering a similar shade as the background stones, then outline the lettering with the **E**dit, Stro**k**e command using a contrasting foreground color to create a separation between the lettering and the stones.

Here's how to add the title to the composition:

Using Contrasting Colors To Separate Elements

Alt+click on the Channel #4 icon on the Channels palette	Loads the letter selection.
Click on the RGB title, click on the Layers tab, click on the Layer 3 title, click on the New Layer icon, then click on OK	Moves you to the color composite view of the image and creates a new Layer 5 on top of the HARTMACH image, where you'll paint the title for the composition.

Press **M** (**M**arquee tool), then Ctrl+Alt+click and drag the marquee selection so that it's centered above the robot

The Ctrl+Alt combination moves only the marquee without moving the underlying image. This only works when a selection tool (such as the marquee) is active.

Press **B** (Paint **B**rush) (or click on the Paint Brush tool), then Alt+click over an area of the stones in the image

Samples a slate color for Photoshop's foreground color and the Paint Brush.

Choose Multiply from the modes drop-down list on the Brushes palette, and keep the Brushes tip set at 35 pixels

Chooses a painting mode that will darken and saturate areas you paint over.

Release the Alt key, then click and drag over the entire marquee area *without* releasing the mouse button

Covers the area with the foreground slate color.

Release the mouse button, then click and drag short strokes through the selection

Creates darker areas within the selection, making areas you haven't stroked twice look like highlights on the lettering (see fig. 22.31).

Don't worry that you can't read the lettering at this point; the foreground color you're applying is basically the same color as the background stones!

Press **D** (**d**efault colors), then press **X** (**s**witch colors) (or click on the default colors icon, then the switch colors icon on the toolbox)

Makes the current foreground color white.

Choose **E**dit, Stro**k**e, enter **2** in the **W**idth field, click on the O**u**tside radio button in the location field, then click on OK

Strokes the outside of the marquee selection with foreground white (see fig. 22.32).

Press Ctrl+D (**S**elect, **N**one)

Deselects the current selection.

Press Ctrl+S (**F**ile, **S**ave)

Saves your work up to this point.

Figure 22.31

Fill and darken selection areas in a layer with the Paint Brush tool in Multiply mode.

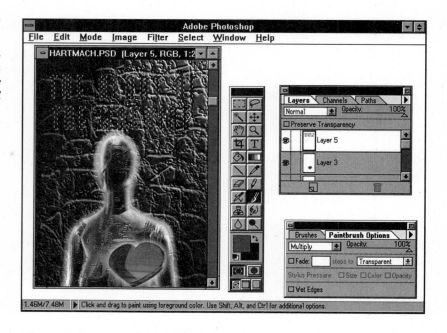

Figure 22.32

Use a color that contrasts with the selection's contents to separate the selection from the background.

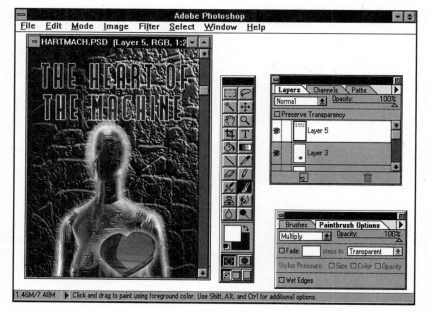

Tip

When using a painting or editing tool, Photoshop considers a click and drag action to be a single stroke—when you release the mouse button, the action is finished, and your next click and drag is a second application of color or an effect.

However, if you click and *hold* the mouse button without releasing, you can increase the area you cover with color or an effect, and this counts as a single "session" with the tool. By clicking and dragging, plus holding with a tool that darkens image areas in successive applications (like Multiply mode with the Paint Brush), you have more control over which image areas get one, two, or more applications of an effect or color.

The trick is usually to cover a selection area in one click and drag, then use small, individual stroke "sessions" to increase an effect in a particular area.

The Stroke command doesn't use a painting tool tip to apply foreground color, although you can set the Opacity and mode with which the command outlines a selection. In addition, if you want to Feather a selection before you use **E**dit, St**r**oke, you can achieve a "Neon Glow" effect. The only limitation of stroking a selection to create a glow is that you have no control over the edge of the stroke beyond how much a selection is Feathered.

Embellishing the Text

Everything in the composition has a 3D look, except the lettering. There's really no tool or effect in Photoshop to extrude the lettering—it will always remain flat because it was not created in a 3D rendering program.

However, you can lift the lettering off the background by creating a drop-shadow. You already have the lettering saved as a selection in an Alpha channel; by using the Feather command after loading the selection, you can fill it in using another Painting mode that's new to this version of Photoshop.

Here's how to paint a drop-shadow without messing up the lettering work you've done so far.

Using the Behind Painting Mode

Choose **S**elect, **L**oad Selection, then click on OK	Loads the Alpha channel #4 selection.

When you have only one Alpha channel defined for an image, and you're in the Layers view on the Layers palette, using the menu command is sometimes quicker than Alt+clicking on a Channel icon.

continues

Part IV ◆ Fantastic Assignments in Photoshop

continued

Choose **S**elect, M**o**dify, then **E**xpand	Displays the Expand Selection dialog box.
Enter **8** in the **E**xpand by: field, then click on OK	Makes the selection grow outward from the lettering.
Choose **S**elect, Fea**t**her, enter **20** in the Feather **R**adius field, then click on OK	Softens the border of the marquee selection.

The Feather command creates a transition between selected areas and protected ones, as a *partial* selection, beginning 10 pixels inside the selection edge, and ending 10 pixels outside the selection edge.

Press Ctrl+Alt+Shift, then press the keyboard down arrow once	Moves the selection marquee only (not the underlying image) down ten pixels.
Press **D** (**d**efault colors) (or click on the default colors icon on the toolbox), then choose Behind as the Paint Brush mode	Sets the Paint Brush to apply black to the selection, but only to selection areas that are clear.

The Behind painting mode protects opaque pixels already on a layer. Each stroke you make can only be applied "behind" the pixels that already exist. It's like painting on the backside of a traditional animation cel, and each paint stroke becomes a collection of pixels that you paint behind with the *next* stroke.

Choose the 100-pixel diameter tip from the Brushes palette, then click and drag over the selection area	Covers areas with black that don't have any color pixels on Layer 5.
Continue click and dragging until you have an image like the one in figure 22.33	The Behind painting mode filled in selection areas that didn't contain the lettering.
Press Ctrl+S (**F**ile, **S**ave)	Saves your work up to this point.

You have all the elements needed to complete the composition now, and it looks like a winner. However, there's the layer issue you need to address, and if you look closely at the next figure (fig. 22.33), you'll notice an element that's compositionally wrong that needs correcting.

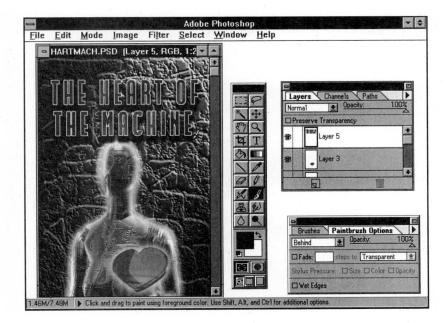

Figure 22.33

Use the Behind mode for painting "behind" pixels already on a layer.

Shifting Compositional Elements

There is a reason why we asked you to keep a number of separate layers in this design until the very end of the assignment. Part of the power of layers is their ability to be rearranged; to shift compositional elements to the back and to the front of the "stack" of elements.

Before you reduce the size of this image by about seven-fold (and substantially reduce the stress on your system RAM!), take a look at the neon glow around the robot. The top of the glow is eclipsed by the drop-shadow you've set on Layer 5. In real life, sources of light *remove* shadows, and so must our virtual lighting in this image if it's to maintain a quality of photo-realism.

The next exercise is a two-stepper; it's simple, but makes a world of difference when you need to assign a layer a dominant position to make its contents the foreground element in a design.

Here's how to finish your illustration for the fictitious magazine cover story, "The Heart of the Machine."

Reordering and Merging Layers

Click and drag on the bottom of the Layers palette	Displays all the Layers titles in one, non-scrolling view.
Click and drag on the Layer 5 icon, then drop it on the Layer 2 icon	Moves the lettering layer to beneath Layer 2, the layer containing the glow for the robot (see fig. 22.34).

If you've designed this piece so that the lettering actually touches the robot on Layer 1, or overlaps its head, click and drag the Layer 5 title to meet the Layer 1 title instead of the Layer 2 title. This will put the lettering behind the robot, but in front of the Background layer.

Click on the triangle to the right of the tabs on the Layers palette, then choose Flatten Image	Displays the pop-up menu, and creates a single Background layer out of your collection of layers.
Click on the Channels tab, then click and drag the Channel #4 title into the trash icon on the palette	Deletes the channel from the image. You no longer need it.
Choose File, Save As, then save the image in the TIFF format (from Save File as Format Type drop-down list) to your hard disk	Saves your work up to this point.

You now have a rather large PSD image, with all the layers in place, and the same image, with layers merged, in the TIFF format, which can now be read by many different applications on several operating platforms.

Press **F** on the keyboard twice now for a good view of your finished piece, as shown in figure 22.35. Press Tab to hide the palettes and toolbox, and invite anyone within 50 feet of your computer to come over and stare in awe.

This chapter has shown you some of the techniques for piecing together pixels and making an image appear very real, but you still need some information about how to make all the assignments in this book (and those of your own) real in the tangible, *physical* sense.

Great imaging has a significant life outside your computer, as real world hard copy and 35 mm slides. In the next part of your Photoshop adventures, you explore the world of printing, and pay a virtual trip to the service bureau—a strange and wonderful place that will turn your Photoshop files into something you can hold up, tack on a wall, or even find framed in a museum.

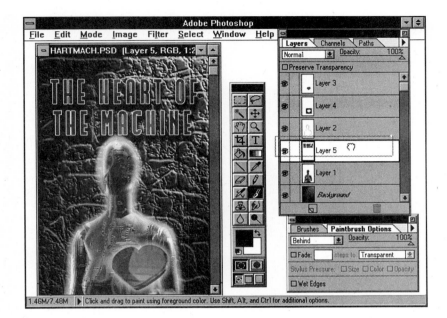

Figure 22.34

Click and drag a Layer title to a new position in the stack of layers.

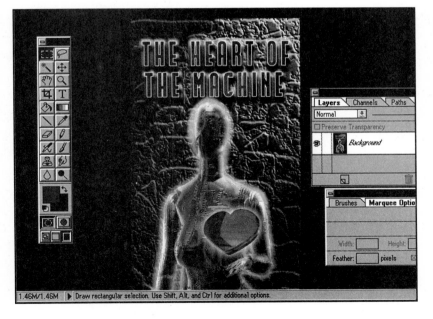

Figure 22.35

The finished piece. What a shame this illustration won't actually accompany any writing!

Part V

Inking Up and Doing Yourself a Service

23 Personal Printing Basics 1133

24 The Service Bureau 1173

25 The Film Recorder 1221

26 How Good is Good? 1247

C H A P T E R

23

Personal Printing Basics

As an imager, photographer, artist, or retoucher, much of the satisfaction (and certainly the paychecks) comes from sharing your finished work with others. Paper and film are still the most practical method of distributing your work. Converting your creations from colored light generated by digital ones and zeros to physical media is the subject of this section, which is Part Five: Inking Up and Doing Yourself a Service.

The need to free the digital image from the confines of the monitor has spawned several industries: the digital output hardware industries (printers, film recorders, video output devices), and electronic pre-press and print service providers. Digital imagery also has radically changed the equipment, methods, and practices of the most ancient and established communication medium: the commercial printing industry. As a Photoshop designer or artist, you should become familiar with the many kinds of output for digital work.

Every output device uses mathematical formulas in the rendering and printing process to make your graphical work speak as elegantly on paper as it does onscreen. Fortunately, computers handle complicated math excellently, and also assist in artistic creations. With this book as a resources most of the calculations you need to know for optimal printing are plug-and-play. You also have the skilled professionals at service bureaus and commercial printers to turn to for advice.

From the Source to the Sample to the Printer

Computer and printing technologies have advanced in recent years to the point at which a black-and-white laser proof can also serve as a camera-ready piece of artwork. The physical line screens and halftone dots used in traditional printing can now be simulated with laser printers and digital imagesetters to provide quality printed copies of your work to suit design, publication, presentation, and "send one to your mom" needs.

All digital imaging hardware must convert color information to whole, quantized amounts of pigment (called *dots*). Different kinds of dots are used; the two primary types are halftone and non-halftone dots. The type of dot used can significantly impact whether you can have your work commercially printed. This chapter helps you become more familiar with the physiology of electronic dot-making, and provides you with the knowledge to make every rendered electronic image look as faithful to your on-screen display as possible.

Personal Color Printers

Personal color printing is a relatively recent offering by computer hardware manufacturers; we need to go a little off-course in our discussion of personal imaging to pay a passing nod to the medium. Much talk has been made in trade magazines and computer publications about "affordable" color printing from the desktop. Personal color printing is an exciting concept, but affordable shouldn't become synonymous with "professional" if you're serious about your craft. Personal color printing is still in its infancy, and at best, 1995's personal color printer offers output that pales in comparison to the product of a color printing press or a photographic print.

Advantages and Disadvantages of Personal Color Printers

If you compare color output to the same image on-screen, high-quality printing or film-recorded slides, the magnitude of difference in image quality and accurate color reproduction is similar to the comparing a Polaroid snapshot to an 8×10" transparency. Personal color printers have much smaller color *gamuts* (the range of colors they can reproduce) than a monitor, film, or printing press. To make matters more

troublesome, every kind of printer has a different gamut because of the different physical methods and materials used to produce desktop color. Colors on one kind of personal color printer may be impossible to create on another kind of printer. Trying to design within the color gamut of a particular personal color printer is difficult and limiting.

For general business applications, the personal color printer is a boon to anyone who wants to splash a report cover with a color logo, make charts readable from across the room, or add color clip art to a proposal. Because of the color inaccuracy and low-resolution of personal printers costing under $7,000, however, a personal color printer is not a good output choice for professional quality images you create in Photoshop.

Significant advances in the quality of personal color printers are being made daily; all the harsh truths about the current state of personal color printing will undoubtedly change. But for now, personal color printing can't be considered the final output medium for professional imaging work.

This doesn't mean that professional-quality personal output can't be generated. Professional quality *black-and-white* desktop output is within the reach of almost everyone. Black-and-white output is a stable, mature medium in the computer graphics community. This chapter focuses on the paths you can take with Photoshop to produce high-quality professional black-and-white output from your desktop.

Converting a Color Image for Grayscale Printing

Photoshop is capable of printing a color image to a black-and-white printer, and it even offers you three different options. As you can see in figure 23.1, the bottom of the print options dialog box contains three radio buttons: Grayscale, RGB, and CMYK. These appear in the Print dialog box for all kinds of printers when the image you're printing is in color. They don't appear if the image you are printing is already a Grayscale image. Although these options are convenient for default printing to a personal printer, they aren't really acceptable if you want to get the best possible black-and-white print from an image.

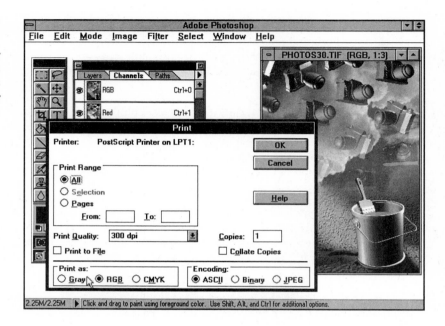

Choosing RGB or CMYK

A black-and-white (grayscale) printer doesn't understand color information; instead, it only wants and needs to know where black toner should go. When the RGB or CMYK radio button is chosen in the print dialog box, Photoshop sends all color information in the file to the printer. The printer discards most of the information and only processes what it thinks is pertinent to printing the image as black dots of toner on the page. Exactly how the printer goes about sifting through the information varies from manufacturer to manufacturer. Printing a color image to a grayscale printer rarely yields optimal results, and takes much longer to print because the printer must figure out what information to discard and what to keep based on an unvarying set of rules. A similar printer "bottleneck" is trying to print an image with a resolution higher than the printer resolution (covered later in this chapter).

Choosing Grayscale

If you choose the Grayscale radio button, Photoshop (instead of the printer driver) decides what information is used to produce the print. Photoshop makes an internal copy of your color image and converts it to Grayscale using its normal method for converting color images to Grayscale mode. Although this is a better course of action than clicking on the RGB or CMYK radio buttons, Photoshop's Grayscale mode

conversion methods are not the best way to produce a grayscale image. But as discussed in Chapter 17, "The Wonderful World of Black and White," Photoshop's Grayscale mode conversion methods are not the very best way to produce a grayscale image.

Saving as Grayscale

The "default" method of printing (choosing the <u>G</u>ray radio button) might be force of habit from working with other programs that feature automated printing controls, but as you've come to learn in this book, Photoshop automates calculations, not artistic sensibilities. The best quality laser prints are produced from images that start with good tonal separation of image areas, have been manually converted to the appropriate grayscale image type, *and* the grayscale image has been adjusted to bring it in line with the capability of the printer. These adjustments are not and cannot be made when you print a color image directly to a grayscale printer by choosing Gray, RGB, or CMYK from the bottom of the Print dialog box.

If you're as serious about your output as you are with your craft, you need to make a copy of your work and save it in Grayscale. The use of the Photoshop Mode menu to convert RGB or CMYK images to Grayscale doesn't always produce the best results. You should treat Chapter 17 as a companion to this chapter when the image you want a hard copy of is an RGB or CMYK image. Converting an image to LAB color and then using the Lightness channel as the source for your output is a necessary first step to creating an acceptable black-and-white laser copy.

Deciding on Your Final Output

The output of your grayscale image can travel two roads, with a few paths that crisscross in between. Figure 23.2 illustrates your options. You can use a laser printer for a quick copy of an image, or use an imagesetter for high-resolution, PostScript output that can then travel to a commercial press for printing.

The laser printer and the imagesetter are the key devices used to make a physical copy of the images displayed on your monitor. Laser printer and imagesetting technology and prices differ tremendously.

Imagesetters and laser printers have one thing in common—they create dots on a surface that represent the pixels in your digital artwork. However, there are many types of dots: The quality, frequency, and shape of dots make the difference between a decent hard copy print, and a halftone rendering that's ready to go to a commercial printer's copy camera.

Figure 23.2

The hardware you choose for output has a bearing on the quality and purpose of a digital print.

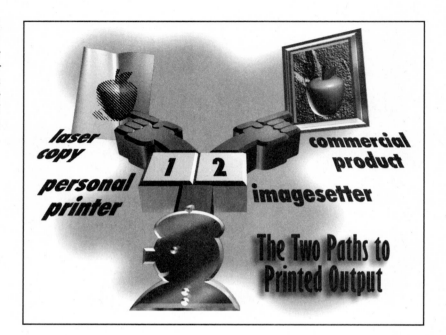

Using a Printer Command Language (PCL) Printer

Hewlett-Packard, one of the grandfathers of laser printing hardware, wanted to provide the general business community with a way to print high-quality text and line art. The introduction of HP's LaserJets fulfilled this need and took the business community by storm. The technology that drove the LaserJets, HP's *Printer Command Language* (PCL), became an industry standard that other manufacturers emulated. PCL-based printers are noted for their speed and the rich blacks they produce. They have become the workhorses of today's business correspondence.

Grayscale and color digital images have a gamut much wider than a laser printer can express with its limited palette of available colors. Laser printers can place a dot of colored toner (usually black) on a surface (usually white paper). The gamut of color for laser printer output is exactly 2—black-and-white, with no shades of gray in between. PCL-based printers simulate the appearance of gray using a technique similar to what commercial printing presses use to create shades of gray. Both use dots arranged on a page in such a way that your eye integrates the dots and your brain "sees" them as different shades of gray. Collectively the shades of gray are interpreted as a tonal image. In figure 23.3, NUT&BOLT.TIF is a grayscale image in Photoshop, and PCL.TIF is a file that was created by scanning a laser copy of the same image.

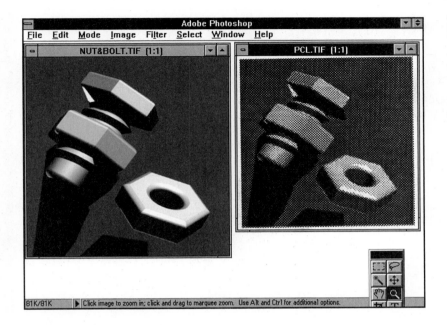

Figure 23.3

A grayscale image rendered as a collection of dots simulates grayscale values.

Because *Inside Adobe Photoshop 3* is itself printed, we've exaggerated the examples in the figures in this chapter. The scans of the printed artwork were acquired at 35 pixels/inch, about 1/4 the sampling rate required to produce a medium-quality print.

How faithfully a laser copy represents its original grayscale image depends on three factors:

◆ How accurately the printer places dots on a page

◆ The organization or pattern of the dots on the page

◆ The resolution of the printer (size of the dots as expressed in dots per inch)

Laser printers that use the PCL technology have a resolution of either 300 dpi or 600 dpi. Although 300–600 dpi is an adequate resolution for producing a business letter or a chart, you may be disappointed by the limitations of these resolutions when trying to reproduce a Photoshop masterpiece. The human eye easily perceives the dot patterns in a grayscale image that has been printed at 300 dpi or at 600 dpi. A laser printed continuous-tone image must meet or exceed 1200 dots per inch before a viewer's eye focuses on its composition and tonality, and not the toner dots that make up the image.

Resolution Enhancement

Another technology Hewlett-Packard built into its PCL printers and that others have emulated is *Resolution Enhancement*. With this technology the laser printer varies the size of the dots the printer creates and places the dots in a tighter pattern. This technology makes it easier for the viewer to read a print as a grayscale image. Figure 23.4 is a close-up of the NUT&BOLT image on a monitor, and the same image printed using resolution enhancement. As you can see, the dots that correspond to grayscale information are square, have different sizes that correspond to the densities on the grayscale image, and are fitted together into a weave to assist in visual integration.

Figure 23.4

Resolution enhancement creates combinations of toner dot sizes to simulate shades of gray when seen at a distance.

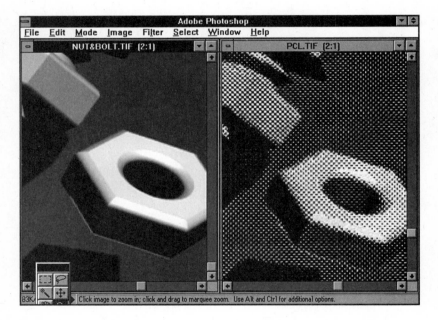

Disadvantages of PCL Printers

PCL printers are almost a necessity if you're printing correspondence, an invoice, or a simple graphic to show to a client. The drawback to PCL printers is that they fail to interpret grayscale information accurately because they cannot organize and place their dots in a pattern that directly corresponds to the pattern of a printing press. Faithful copying of the way a printing press places dots of ink requires more information, more processing power, and more precision than the PCL technology and the printer's controller circuitry were designed to handle.

If you have a 300–600 dpi PCL printer hooked up to your machine, and you want to print a grayscale picture from Photoshop, there aren't any options you can choose to increase the quality and accuracy of the printed piece. Because a PCL printer cannot accurately arrange dots into traditional line patterns, Photoshop's Screen options in the Page Setup dialog box are, by default, dimmed. You can uncheck the Use **P**rinter Defaults box and enter a (line) **F**requency and **A**ngle of your choice, but this will not improve the quality of a PCL print. A stylized version of your grayscale work will appear, but your work cannot print more accurately than the printer's language can understand.

Error Diffusion Printing

Error diffusion printing is an alternative to the harsh, pixelated prints of PCL printers. Error diffusion, as the name implies, uses a mathematical formula similar to Photoshop's diffusion Dither option to soften the harsh areas of contrast when an image goes from a high color capability (such as the 256 brightness value grayscale image), to a much lower color capability (such as black toner on white paper). Unfortunately, error diffusion is not a Photoshop option; Adobe Systems is trying to encourage users to follow the professional route with imaging, and error diffusion printing is often met with gentle smiles and occasional laughter when mentioned in publication circles.

Nevertheless, error diffusion printing is alive and well in the PC world, and you can find this feature in such programs as WordPerfect for Windows (versions 6.0*a* and 6.1) and Logitech's FotoTouch software that comes with their grayscale scanners. You can even add the capability to use error diffusion printing by using a program called SuperPrint, a custom printer driver manufactured by Zenographics, Inc.

Error diffusion printing using a PCL-based printer requires a proprietary *printer driver*. A printer driver is a software program on your computer that takes information from an application and converts the information to machine code that a printer can understand. If you have Photoshop and a 300 dpi PCL printer, think about investing in an error diffusion printer driver. The error diffusion printer driver intercepts the information an application sends to your system, and instructs the printer to follow its own instructions rather than the instructions in the default printer drivers that were installed when you installed your printer. Figure 23.5 is of an error diffusion print placed next to the PCL image you saw in figure 23.4.

The most notable disadvantage to error diffusion printing is its inherent imprecision. Error diffusion takes into account the inability of the printer to represent original

image areas as grayscale values. As a result, dots of toner are spread in a random
fashion on the page; denser areas receive more toner, and lighter areas receive less.
There is no organization of dots in an error diffusion print, which makes it unsuitable
for commercial camera-ready artwork. If you are not concerned with producing
camera-ready artwork, error diffusion printing creates a smooth, eye-pleasing image
from a printer that has limited resolution.

Figure 23.5

*Error diffusion
printing creates
an imprecise, yet
wonderfully
diffuse rendition
of a grayscale
image.*

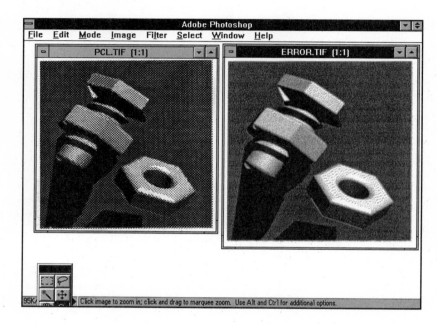

Figure 23.6 is a close-up of an error diffusion print and a print made using Windows'
standard printer driver for a PCL printer. The shades represented by the "stippling"
of toner dots is not as accurate as PCL's resolution enhancement technology, but the
error diffusion print is easier to view.

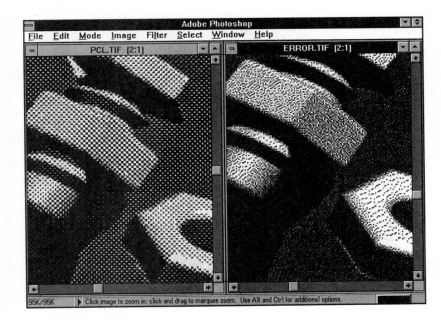

Using an Effects Screen with Your Images

In the quest to wring more beautiful prints from the limited language of a PCL laser printer, you might try a different approach: use Photoshop's Modes command to change a copy of your work from Grayscale to Bitmap. As discussed in Chapter 1, "Understanding Image Types, Formats, and Resolutions," Bitmap type images contain 1 bit/pixel of image information, which is precisely the amount of tonal values a laser printer can produce. When you convert a grayscale image to Bitmap mode, Photoshop discards a lot of image information about relative shades of brightness and substitutes dots, lines, and shapes that correspond in size to the original areas of density found within the grayscale image.

In figure 23.7 the image on the left, LINESCRN.TIF, is an example of a grayscale image that was converted to Bitmap mode in Photoshop. A setting of 35 pixel/inch was chosen for Output in the Bitmap dialog box (which is a low resolution for a

300dpi printer); Halftone Screen was also chosen, which in turn displays a second dialog box where settings for Frequency, Angle, and Shape of the dots can be specified. The image on the right, PCL.TIF is a grayscale image that was printed from Photoshop using standard settings.

Photoshop is not the only program that can produce "line screen" effects. Some desktop publishing programs such as PageMaker offer a "line screen" effect that can be used effectively to stylize a grayscale image. When a PCL printer is used, this effect produces a print that is stylized but has greater clarity than if you used the "normal" default settings.

Figure 23.7

Photoshop discards grayscale information, and averages all shades to black or white patterns when converting to Bitmap.

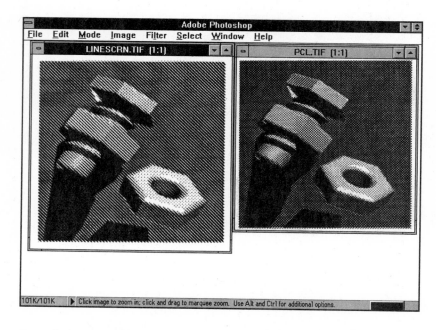

Converting a grayscale image to bitmap and applying an effect screen during the mode conversion process does *not* produce the same effect as using a line screen setting for producing a grayscale image. Information is lost in the original image when you convert from 256 possible shades to two. This is one reason why it's always best to convert *copies* of your work. The use of line screens is part of the halftone printing process, which is covered a little later in the section "Understanding the Halftone Cell, Resolution, and Other Factors." You'll see that there is a difference in image quality between a rendered grayscale image and an image that was "prearranged" for bitmap output.

In figure 23.8, you can see a close-up of the bitmap image with the line screen pattern applied to it. The image will print as displayed to a PCL printer, but large amounts of original detail have been sacrificed. If you want to create a special effect through printing, however, adding a screen effect might be your ticket.

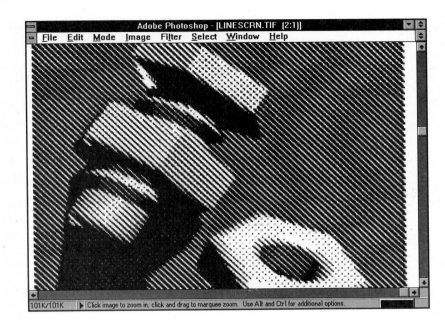

Neither Bitmap mode nor any fancy deployment of screening effects in another application can create a true "line screened" image. Mezzotints, pattern dithering, and other effects have a legitimate use in printed media when the paper is too coarse to hold a finer screen, and artists can make beautiful abstract creations from this limited amount of digital information. However, a "line screen," halftone dots, and the accurate representation of the grayscale image as a printed art requires that we head for higher ground, search for more exotic equipment, and explore Adobe's world of PostScript technology.

PostScript Printers

PostScript personal printers aren't news to Macintosh users; one of the first high-quality printing specifications for the personal computer came along with the Macintosh operating system years ago. When compared to a PCL laser printer, PostScript printers are very slow, but their results are astoundingly faithful to original imagery. The method PostScript printers use to organize and place toner dots is almost identical to output of physical screens used by commercial printers.

Unlike Hewlett-Packard's Printer Command Language, Adobe System's PostScript descriptor language is a complete, complex programming language that was designed to be used and understood by a wide range of devices. Imagesetters, laser printers, film recorders, fax machines, and equipment that hasn't even been invented yet can all "read" a PostScript-standard file or image if their manufacturers outfitted them with PostScript interpreters. Therefore, one of the benefits of PostScript printing is a consistent standard of quality. You can rest assured that your image will reproduce as accurately as possible when it's translated from pixels to dots, regardless of whether your image is printed at home or to a film recorder at a service bureau (see Chapter 25, "The Film Recorder").

The underlying concept behind PostScript technology is to duplicate the screen patterns of traditional printing presses, so that hard copy can serve as camera-ready artwork. If you think about this, how would any of the images you've created in the assignments in this book be reproduced? As recently as ten years ago, a digital image would have to be rasterized by a film recorder, the resulting photographic negative was then printed, a physical line screen was dropped over it, and finally the image was copied again to a photographic press plate. Generations of image quality are recaptured with the advent of the digital halftone, and Adobe's PostScript technology provides the means to create dots from printers and imagesetters that can faithfully hold up to traditional methods of imaging.

Examining a Digital Halftone Image

Unlike PCL-based printers, PostScript printers can simulate the effect commercial printers use to produce black-and-white images from grayscale, continuous images. Continuous-tone images have a gamut (a range of color) so close to that of the human eye's perception, that banding (the demarcation of solid color values between transitional shades) is not seen. In other words, the tones in an image are continuous, without a beginning or end to a shade's component colors. A Photoshop gradient fill is a good visual example of a design element that displays continuous tone characteristics. In contrast, you can clearly see where the chocolate ends and the strawberry begins in Neapolitan ice cream; as long as the ice cream is kept frozen, it does not display continuous tone characteristics.

As described earlier in this chapter, the color gamut of printed material is limited to foreground color and background color; to express the brightness values in a grayscale image, dots of different sizes are arranged in a precise pattern to correspond exactly to the values they represent in the original image. Figure 23.9 shows a PostScript printed image with the PCL print next to it. As you can see, the dots in the PostScript copy are of different sizes and are consistent in their shape. The quality is good enough to give to coworkers or clients, but also is invaluable in commercial printing.

To give you a better idea of how the PostScript dots correspond to their grayscale equivalents in a digital image, look at figure 23.10. As you can see, areas that are roughly 50 percent black in the original are represented halftone cells in the PostScript print that occupy half the "white space." Each dot you see is a *digital halftone cell* with a boundary created by an invisible grid that contains all the halftone dots.

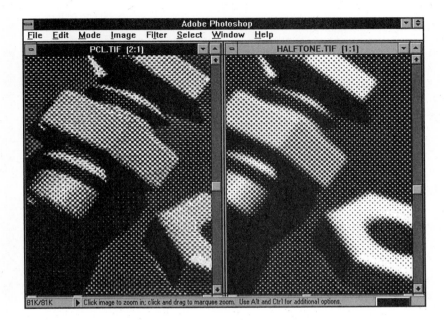

Figure 23.9

PostScript printing creates accurate dot shape and placement to represent a continuous tone original image.

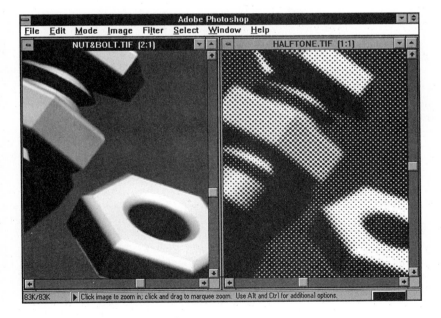

Figure 23.10

The amount of area covered by ink or toner within a halftone cell determines the shade of gray.

Try a little experiment: Make sure no one's standing behind you, then hold this book about four feet in front of you and look at the halftone example in the last figure. Try the same thing with the PCL and error diffusion figures. You'll see that the consistency of the dot shapes, size, and organization (called line screens) enables you to assemble in your mind the nut and bolt as a whole image very quickly. This is the primary difference between halftone screening and other technologies. In the next section, you read about the organization of dots that compose a halftone image, and what you can do to optimize your images for this sort of printing.

Understanding the Halftone Cell, Resolution, and Other Factors

Printer resolution and on-screen resolution are measured differently and have different color capabilities. Resolution plays an important role in printed image quality; you define resolution in PostScript printing not in dots per inch, but in lines (or halftone dots) per inch. Halftone frequency and resolution are used to evaluate a printed image for aesthetic reasons, and for commercial printing possibilities.

To get a better idea of halftone printing, imagine a grid that covers the area on the printed page where you want an image. This grid, or *line screen*, is composed of *cells*. Each cell in the line screen itself is composed of a small grid of toner dots that collectively make up the larger dot that you see. How many slots within the halftone cell's grid are filled with toner determines the density of the individual halftone cell. The more grids within the halftone cell that are filled, the darker the cell, and the larger the digital halftone dot. The size of a single PostScript halftone dot has a direct relation to the shade, or degree of density, in the original image. Figure 23.11 is a representation of this halftone screen with halftone dots placed inside. The percentages of coverage at the bottom of the figure correspond to the size of the halftone dot in the cell. You can see the relationship in this figure between the traditional, physical halftone screen, the digital halftone, and a continuous tone source image that has the same halftone values. When arranged in a line and viewed from a distance, halftone dots convey the feeling of continuous tones in a grayscale image.

Traditional pre-press screening conversions offered on personal printers is a marvelous capability. Nevertheless, halftone dots on an invisible grid are not the only factor that determines good printed output. Other important factors are line angles and how many places on a line are available for the halftone dots.

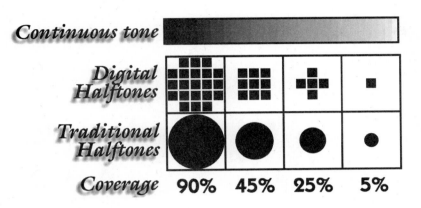

Figure 23.11

Different densities in a grayscale image are expressed by different-sized halftone dots.

Line Angles

The halftone dots themselves need to be arranged on the page in lines that collectively form the *line screen*. The angle at which the lines are positioned is called the *line angle*.

In nature, continuous-tone images contain many right angles, such as the sides of buildings and the stripes in someone's shirt. For this reason, setting a halftone line angle at zero or 90 degrees is not a good idea. You should specify a halftone line-screen angle that's *oblique* to the elements in a digital image—45 degrees works in most cases. Line-screen patterns that closely resemble the patterns in images visually *resonate*, creating unwanted, unappealing *moiré* patterns. Figure 23.12 illustrates the way different-sized halftone dots are arranged in a 45-degree-angle screen.

Most applications, including Photoshop, offer a default line angle of 45 degrees for halftone dots. In Photoshop, you have the option of adjusting this angle, but you'd only really need to do this if you'd photographed an image containing strong diagonal stripes.

To define specific halftone screens for printing, you use Photoshop's File, Page Setup, Screen command. Although the same Screen options appear when a PostScript printer or a PCL printer is defined as the Specific Printer, the shape and frequency of dots are not rendered as true halftones with a non-Postscript (PCL) printer. To achieve a true digital halftone effect, you *must* use a PostScript-capable output device.

The options in Photoshop's Halftone Screen dialog box include Frequency and (dot) Shape, in addition to halftone Angle (see fig. 23.13).

Figure 23.12

Lines of halftone dots are arranged at an angle to create a line screen.

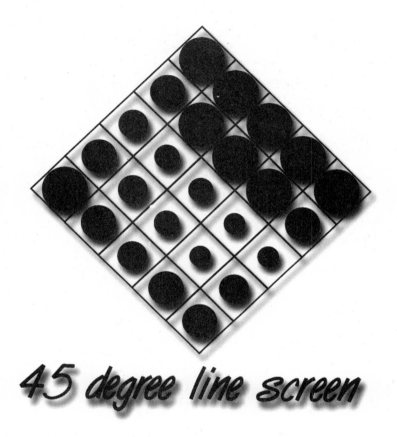

Note The A<u>c</u>curate Screens option in the Halftone Screens dialog box refers to an Adobe technology designed for high-end PostScript Level 2 printers and printers with Emerald controllers. PostScript Level 2 interpreters are installed in some of the newer PostScript printers, and they produce better and faster halftone prints than the older PostScript standard.

Accurate Screen technology is usually found on imagesetters and not personal laser printers, but it's worth checking the documentation for your printer to see if it supports PostScript Level 2 and Accurate Screens. If it does, be sure to check this box so that you can benefit from this feature. If you're not sure your printer supports Accurate Screens, check the box anyway. If your printer doesn't support Accurate Screens the information will be ignored.

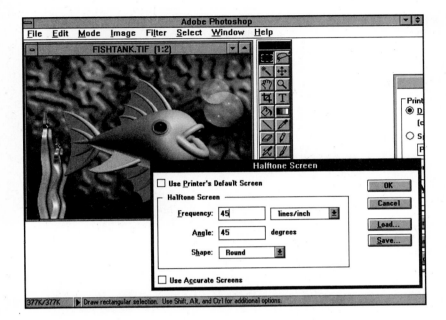

Figure 23.13

You can set a custom angle for halftone dots from the Photoshop Halftone Screens dialog box.

Halftone screen *frequency* is another option to specify when you print from Photoshop. The frequency of lines per inch used when printing halftone dots has a direct correlation with *the number of shades of gray* you can simulate in a print. There's a simple way, using your eyes and a little math, to achieve the best line frequency for a grayscale image.

Line Frequency

Usually, the lines that make up an image printed from a 300 dpi printer are visible to the naked eye. When you specify the *lines per inch*–the line frequency of halftone dots–you need to strike a compromise. The default setting for a 300 dpi laser printer is usually about 45 to 60 lines per inch; this number varies among manufacturers. The basic truth about medium- to low-resolution laser printer output is that to *increase* lines per inch, you *decrease* the number of grayscale values you're simulating on the printed page. There is a direct correlation here.

Two factors govern the maximum number of tonal values that laser printing can simulate: the resolution of the *digital* image, expressed in pixels per inch, and the number of densities that can portray the gray shades in the printed image.

The Times Two Rule

An accurate halftone print of a grayscale image should have a lines-per-inch value no less than half the pixels-per-inch value of the original file. For example, the FISHTANK.TIF image (in the CHAP23 subdirectory on the *Inside Photoshop 3* Bonus CD and in these figures) has a resolution of 150 pixels per inch. To portray this image with any sense of aesthetic value, the halftone screen should be no less (or more) than 75 lpi.

Tip Keep this rule in mind when you specify image dimensions and resolution for a *copy* of an image you want printed. When you create an image, "shooting for the stars" is good practice. If you're particularly proud of some work you've done in Photoshop at 300 pixels/inch, save it this way. You might get to print it at a high resolution some day. But then make a *copy* of it, keeping in mind the resolution of your *present* target printer. You can use Photoshop's **I**mage, Image **S**ize command to specify a lower resolution for an image.

Math for Determining Lines per Inch

To calculate the optimal resolution for printing a digital image, use this mathematical formula:

Printer Line Frequency (in lpi) × 2 = Image Resolution (in pixels/inch)

Photoshop displays a warning when you try to print an image with a resolution of more than 2.5 times the line frequency specified for laser printing (see fig. 23.14). You can continue with the operation, but it's useless to try to squeeze more visual detail out of an image than the printer is capable of producing.

Note If you're printing with a PCL printer from Photoshop, you will *not* receive the warning illustrated in figure 23.14. This is because Photoshop cannot send true halftone screen information to a PCL printer. Regardless of whether you specify Use **P**rinter's Default Screen or uncheck the box and specify your own screen settings, the information sent to a non-Postscript printer does not create accurate halftone dots.

It doesn't hurt an image, or printed image quality, to click on the **P**roceed button in Photoshop's warning box. What can hurt, however, is a production schedule! Excess image information is spooled to the printer, then discarded at printing time, creating an unnecessary waste of time for you to receive your hard copy. You have two alternatives if you press Cancel when Photoshop informs you that a file is too large to be handled at its present resolution:

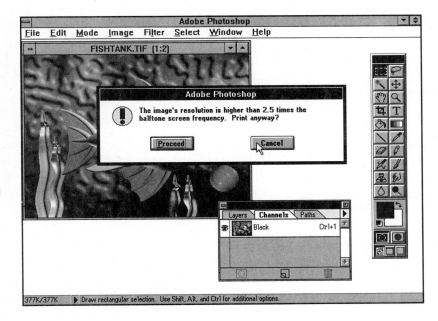

Figure 23.14

Photoshop warns you if you're trying to print an image whose resolution is more than 2.5 times the line frequency of the printer.

◆ You can click on Cancel, then choose Image, Image Size, uncheck the File Size check box in the Constrain: field, then enter a Resolution for the New size image. The resolution you enter must be less than 2.5 times the Frequency of the Halftone Screen in the Halftone Screen dialog box within the Page Setup command.

Because image resolution is inversely proportional to image dimensions, you are physically changing the arrangement of pixels to create a new resolution. If you choose this option for printing, remember to save the resulting image file to a different file name, and remember to check the File Size box again before you use the Image size command in a subsequent Photoshop session (Photoshop retains previously saved option settings). The File Size check box usually should remain checked to prevent inadvertent distortion of images you work with in the future.

◆ If you have no particular image dimensions in mind for your laser copy, you can also choose Image, Image Size, then reduce the Resolution to less than 2.5 times the Halftone Screen Frequency value with the File Size box checked. In figure 23.15 you can see that a value of 90 pixels/inch has been entered in the resolution field, and this increases the image's dimensions by nearly 50 percent. Unlike most Windows and Macintosh applications, Photoshop does not offer sizing options from the Print command dialog box; image dimensions should be considered before you print. Because the File Size check box is checked, you don't actually create a change in the data within the file, and you can change the image resolution for the file back to its original state after printing.

Figure 23.15

When proportions and File Size are constrained for an image, lower resolution increases the image's dimensions.

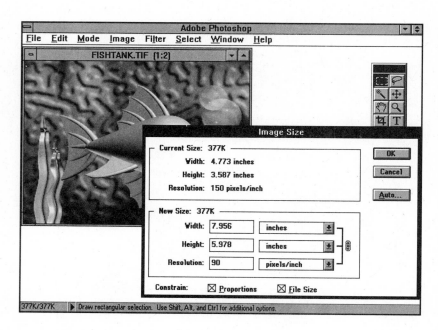

When you print from Photoshop, the active document is printed in the center of the page. A useful feature in Photoshop is the image preview box, which is displayed before you print by clicking on the Document Sizes box. This is found on the left side of the Photoshop for Windows status line, and it's located on the bottom left of the image window in the Macintosh Photoshop version. As you can see in figure 23.16, the active image of FISHTANK.TIF barely misses the border of the printable page at its new image dimensions. The white area of the page preview box is the live area of the printed page, and the box with the "x" inside it is your document.

The 50 percent black area outside the white page border is actually a black-and-white checkerboard of pixels that clearly display the image border if it runs outside the printable page. FISHTANK.TIF is a little less than 8" on its widest side, but if its new increased dimensions (decreased resolution) had been over 8", Photoshop would flash a warning before it would print the file. If this happens to you, you have three alternatives (besides letting the printer crop your work!):

◆ Rotate the page using the **F**ile, Pa**g**e Setup command, so that the widest side for a letter-sized sheet is 11".

◆ Go to **I**mage, **I**mage Size and *uncheck* the **F**ile Size check box in the Image Size dialog box, and enter smaller values in the Height and Width boxes to create a smaller image. Click on OK and print your image. This is not a recommended course of action because it changes image qualities, as described earlier.

◆ Go to **I**mage, **I**mage Size and with **F**ile Size check box *checked*, increase the resolution. This will decrease the physical dimensions of the image. Click on OK. Choose **F**ile, **P**rint and ignore Photoshop's warning that the file resolution is more than 2.5 times the Halftone Screen Frequency. This process wastes a little time while the printer driver discards superfluous image information as it sends the information to the printer.

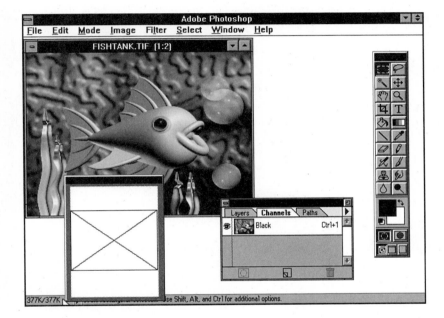

Figure 23.16

Click over the document size area within Photoshop to see the positioning of your image on the page before your print.

Note Even though no physical change to the file is made when you increase image resolution in the Image Size dialog box while the Constrain **F**ile Size check box is checked, Photoshop sees this as a change in the file. Photoshop will flag you if you've respecified an image's dimensions/resolution before you close the image.

Because the resolution of a bitmap image affects image output, many applications that can accept TIFF images handle image resolution differently. For example, PageMaker places an image by its dimensions, with no regard as to whether image resolution is a good one for the printer you have defined for the active document. If you use PageMaker for producing publications, it is your responsibility to "do the math," and figure out what the optimal image resolution should be for your work.

continues

Microsoft Publisher, on the other hand, scales an imported TIFF image to correspond to the printer settings you have defined. Automated resizing is nice if you don't know how to size a file, but it can mess up your dimension measurements. Always choose the correct resolution for your printer's output capability to ensure the least amount of wait, and the best image quality.

You're not quite ready to print from Photoshop yet. You hold some of the keys to printing the correct image resolution, but you still don't know how to achieve a balance between Halftone Screen Frequency and the number of gray shades your printer can handle. The Times Two Rule is only half the equation for printing a grayscale image from a laser printer.

As mentioned earlier, you have some flexibility in determining the lines-per-inch value when you use a PostScript printer. You can adjust the coarseness of the lines (the space between them) by specifying a lower line frequency, but depending on your printer's resolution (measured in dpi), you may not get a very good-looking print. The print may look blocked in or muddy and lack refinement. This is why you need to determine *how many grays* in a grayscale image can be represented by halftone lines.

The Number of Grays in a Grayscale Image

An 8-bit grayscale image can contain up to 256 unique tones. Your laser printer has a definite threshold for expressing all the grayscale information; this may become particularly obvious when you print to a low-resolution, 300 dpi printer.

You need to strike a balance between line frequency and the number of gray shades the halftone dots can represent. The balance is expressed as this mathematical equation:

$$\frac{\text{Printer Resolution (in dpi)}}{\text{Printer Line Frequency (in lpi)}} = n \text{ (squared)} = \text{shades of gray}$$

You'll "plug and play" with this equation next to see how faithfully a 300 dpi printer can represent the tonal values in a grayscale image.

Using Calculations To Determine Image Quality

Suppose that you have an image with a resolution of 150 pixels/inch like the one used earlier as an example. You know from the first equation that the setting for the halftone screen's lines-per-inch frequency should be half the image's pixel-per-inch resolution, or 75 lines per inch. The following calculation is for a 300 dpi printer:

300 (dpi) / **75** (lpi) = **4**, then

4^2 = **16** shades of gray

Pretty pathetic, right? When a 256-shades-of-gray image is reproduced at 75 lpi on a 300 dpi printer, all the tonal information is arbitrarily lost and squashed into 16 shades! This is unacceptable for the serious imaging-type person.

To be fair, a 75 lpi halftone screen is way too high a value for a 300 dpi printer. Most manufacturers recommend a value between 45 and 60. The line screen frequency you should use with a printer, then, is really a question of aesthetics. The fewer lines per inch used to express the halftone patterns, the more shades of gray they simulate, but the more visible the lines are in the image. A line screen frequency of *less* than 45 per inch becomes *painfully* obvious on the printed page, to the extent that the line pattern overwhelms *the composition* of the printed image!

Higher-Resolution Printers

To get a reasonable facsimile of your digital image, a printer capable of 600 to 1,200 dpi is more in keeping with hard-copy proofing needs. 600 dpi laser printers are as affordable as 300 dpi printers were a few years ago. In addition, several add-in cards are available that can step a 600 dpi printer's resolution up to 1,200 dpi PostScript output. The following equation shows the gamut of grayscale a 600 dpi PostScript printer can simulate with a halftone line screen of 45 lpi:

600 (dpi) / **45** (lpi) = **13.3**

13.3^2 = **176.89**

Not bad! 177 of the 256 possible gray shades in a grayscale image can be represented at 600 dpi with a line screen.

Setting Up Images for Commercial Printing

You've come a long way down the path of creating good printouts on a personal laser printer. Now it's time to backtrack to explore how you create an accurate halftone image on a high-resolution output device.

As we mentioned earlier, halftone images are a re-creation of physical commercial printing screens. They are used as a camera-ready source for making production plates for printing presses. Chapter 24, "The Service Bureau," has the details you need for setting up an image to be rendered to super-high resolution output devices. In this chapter, you learn about the possibilities for your work on toner-on-paper and ink-on-paper mediums.

In the last section you learned how to calculate the shades of gray your printer can simulate through halftone dots. Now it's time to apply the theory to practical, real world use, as you see how to set up an image as camera-ready artwork for commercial printing.

Optimizing the Quality of Home-Brew Camera-Ready Imaging

Camera-ready halftoned images from a laser printer can produce images suitable for a medium-quality publication. We're not talking fashion-magazine or coffee-table book quality; *medium-quality* publications are the backbone of hard-copy communications in America today. Today's laser printers are capable of generating up to 1,800 dpi resolution prints; it's anyone's guess how much this resolution can or will increase in future years. Chemists have been able to formulate finer toner particles, but the real hurdle to desktop imagesetting for now is the limitation of the lens system inside a laser printer. This is why *film*-based *imagesetters* play an important role in high-quality reproductions that can be used for mass-quantity printing.

Regardless of laser printer limitations, something irresistible in the budding imaging person's soul craves the instant gratification of high-resolution laser copies of his or her work. With the help of some special tricks that can be performed using Photoshop, and a shareware utility that's included on the *Inside Photoshop 3* Bonus CD, creating a camera-ready image can be a gratifying experience.

To make the experience *rewarding* as well as gratifying, the next section is devoted to the steps you need to take to optimize a copy of your grayscale image file before you click on <u>F</u>ile, <u>P</u>rint.

How Many Shades of Gray Should You Render?

A fairly common screen used for printing a medium-quality publication at 1,200 dpi is 85 lines per inch at a 45-degree angle. Many commercial printers use this screen to *physically* process the continuous-tone, physical photos they get. If you plug these numbers into the mathematical formula listed earlier:

$$1200 \div 85 = 14.12$$

$$14.12 \times 14.12 = 199.34$$

This formula tells you that the printer (your laser printer or the print press) will be able to represent a maximum of 199 shades of gray.

What happens when you use these settings for a grayscale image that contains *more* than 200 shades of gray? Although a "personal" high-resolution copy of your work won't display much error, you do lose some control over the finer visual details in the image. You leave the extra shades to chance, and if your print is to serve as camera-ready art for commercial printing, you run the risk of a final, ink-on-paper print that has harsh, contrasty areas where you least expect them because you gave the machine more visual information than it could handle.

Rather than permitting the print presses to arbitrarily mess up your image, consider an alternative. Although you can't change the screen, you *can reduce* the number of grays in a *copy* of the image with such subtlety and finesse that viewers will never notice that anything's missing. To reduce the number of grays in your image to match the printer-imposed limit, you first must determine how many grays are in your image and then use Photoshop's Levels feature to eliminate as many shades of gray as necessary.

Paint Shop Pro: A Utility with an Angle

Despite Photoshop's imaging prowess, it can't easily tell you how many unique colors are in a digital image. But JASC's *Paint Shop Pro,* a Windows shareware program, can. Paint Shop Pro is used in the next exercise to determine how many shades of gray the image has, so that you can make intelligent decisions about how to reduce the number of grayscale shades, instead of "guesstimating." If you use the Macintosh version of Photoshop, the section that follows this one describes an alternative method for counting grayscale shades in an image with Photoshop.

 Note JASC distributes a shareware version of *Paint Shop Pro* through computer user-group meetings, bulletin boards, and nationwide on-line services. The shareware version is also included on the *Inside Photoshop 3* Bonus CD.

Shareware is distributed with the expectation that folks who evaluate the program and find it useful will register (buy) it by paying a small fee to the software author. Shareware is *not* freeware. It's marketed unique software—you can evaluate its worth before you buy it.

For the next exercise, which is optional, you need to install the Paint Shop Pro program found in the SHARWARE subdirectory (or Folder) of the *Inside Photoshop 3* Bonus CD that came with this book. If you didn't install it when it was first mentioned in Chapter 1, now's the time. But even if you want to sit out this exercise as a specta-tor, you'll see how Paint Shop Pro can help you in the early stages of preparing a digital image.

Counting the Shades in a Grayscale Image

Double-click on the Paint Shop Pro icon in Windows Program Manager	Launches Paint Shop Pro application.
Choose File, Open (or press Ctrl+O)	Opens a drive directory structure.
Open FISHTANK.TIF from the CHAP23 subdirectory on the Bonus CD	This is the image you'll use to count colors.
Choose Colors, Count Colors Used	Paint Shop Pro counts unique color values in FISHTANK image and finds 227 colors in this image (see fig. 23.17).
Click on OK, then select File, Exit (or press Alt+F)	Exits program and redisplays Windows Program Manager.

Figure 23.17

Paint Shop Pro counts the unique color values in a digital image.

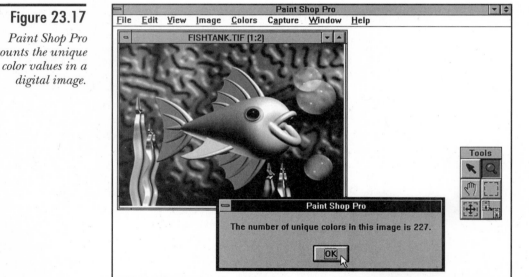

The Photoshop Method of Counting Colors

Photoshop can be used to determine the number of unique shades in a grayscale image. However, the approach you must take is not straightforward, and you should definitely have a spare copy of the image saved under a different name before you try this. You may have noticed that when you convert an RGB image to Indexed mode,

the Indexed Color dialog box's **O**ther field sometimes reports the number of colors in an image (see fig. 23.18). If Photoshop does not offer this option, it means that the image contains more than 256 colors.

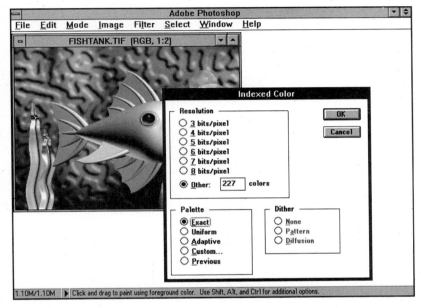

Figure 23.18

The Indexed Color dialog box displays the number of colors in an image when there are fewer than 256 in the image.

The Indexed Color dialog box, where the numbers of colors information is reported, only appears when you convert an RGB image to Indexed. So if the image you wish to examine is already in a Grayscale mode, you will have to convert it to RGB and then choose Indexed from the Mode menu to determine the number of colors. You don't want to convert the image to Indexed mode, however; you simply want to see how large a lookup table would be created for the image if you were to convert it to Indexed mode. Photoshop has the capability to create custom lookup tables for Indexed mode images. If, for example, you have an image that only has 100 unique colors, it would be a waste of image file header information to create 256 lookup table registers, and then leave 156 of them blank. So in a sense, you're telling Photoshop to calculate the minimum number of registers that need to be created to accommodate the unique shades in your image, which provides the answer you need, for an entirely different purpose.

Be sure to choose Cancel after you've made a note of the number of colors. Your image will still be in RGB mode and will need to be converted back to Grayscale before you print.

Paint Shop Pro and the Indexed Color dialog box both will tell you that the FISHTANK image contains 227 unique shades of gray. To print this image successfully with a halftone line screen at a frequency of 85 lpi from a 1,200 dpi printer, 27 of these unique shades in the image must go!

But which ones? The range of grays in an image that you ask Photoshop to produce, versus how many your laser printer can reproduce, is best decided after a talk with your commercial printer. Your printer knows the capability and limitations of printing from a plate made from your camera-ready image, on their presses. In fact, as you'll see in the next section, you may have to reduce the tonal information in an image to something less than what your laser printer can handle in order to create an image that can be successfully transferred to the ink-on-paper medium.

Ink Is Different from Toner

A print press and a laser printer are two different *physical* ways of rendering a halftone image. Halftone dots of ink on paper soak in, whereas laser toner dots sit on top of the paper. Experienced commercial printers will tell you to avoid shades that approach absolute white and absolute black in the halftone you give them. The reason for this is that although a halftone screen printed from a laser is capable of fusing a 100 percent dense, black area *onto* a page, print press inks soak *into* a page and spread. Depending on the paper, the ink, the presses, and the line screen used, a digital halftone that contains halftones that represent the extreme ends of possible brightness values won't "hold." For example, an area that screens at, say, a 90 percent or 95 percent density might completely saturate the corresponding printed area with ink. When a screen doesn't "hold" on the press, the dark grays become black and bleed together into a muddy area.

The converse is true with white areas. A no-coverage area on a laser copy sent to a commercial press sometimes results in an image area that contains a "hot spot," a glaring reflection caused by an absence of halftone ink dots in the image. Zero percent and 1 percent densities in an image expressed as ink halftone dots create an unwanted border within the image. Think about this one for a moment. The 1 percent dots have to *start* someplace, don't they? The idea is to cover even totally white areas in the original image with at least a 1 percent density of halftone dots.

Decreasing Contrast in the Laser Copy

To handle these extremes, go back to your original digital image and make a *copy* of it for modification. Then, in the copy, reduce the contrast of the image so that there are no "black" blacks or "white" whites. Although the modified image will look flat and dull on the monitor, the image will snap up when printed from a plate made from your laser hard copy. When you know that an image file contains an excess of grayscale information, and where that information lies, the areas of extreme contrast are the ones that usually need to be modified.

For instance, if the press operator tells you that the press doesn't handle halftone percentages of less than 12 percent density, the solution is to change the distribution of values in your image so that the first 12 percent (the very light grays) are reassigned to darker values. This shifts the tonal range of the image into a printable range of tonality. Don't think of it as degrading your work, but rather as optimizing the image for display in a different medium. And now for an example of how you optimize the image...

The Math Behind Optimizing an Image for Press

The first thing you need to do is figure out which levels of gray occupy the upper 12 percent of the image's tonal range. A brightness gamut that ranges from 0 to 255 doesn't correspond directly to a density percentage that ranges from 0 percent to 100 percent. You use the following equation:

$$256 - [\text{Halftone Density (in percent)} \times 2.56] = \text{Brightness Value}$$

Now to plug the 12 percent minimum density value for the print press into the equation:

$12 \times 2.56 = 30.72$

$256 - 30.72 = 225.28$

The solution, then, is to bring the output level for an image's upper range down to 225.

Similarly, if your printing person tells you that 90 percent black is *the densest* halftone dot the press can render, you should apply the same rule, as follows:

$90 (\text{ percent}) \times 2.56 = 230.40$

$256 - 230.40 = 25.60$

In this case, you'd enter a **26** in the left Output Level box in the Levels command dialog box.

You actually experiment with the FISHTANK image in this exercise, gaining some hands-on experience with the grayscale reduction process that's usually necessary to create accurate camera-ready art.

Decreasing Image Contrast for the Print Presses

Open the FISHTANK file from the CHAP23 subdirectory of the Bonus CD

This is the image that needs adjusting to produce good laser-printed, camera-ready copy for a commercial printer.

continues

continued

Choose **I**mage, **A**djust, Levels (or press Ctrl+L)	Displays Levels command dialog box.
Enter **225** in the right Output Levels box (or use the white Output Levels slider)	Reassigns pixels above 225 brightness point in tonal range to darker ranges.
Enter **26** in the left Output Levels box (or use the black Output Levels slider)	Reassigns pixels below 26 brightness point in tonal range to lighter ranges (see fig. 23.19).
Click on OK, Choose **F**ile, Sa**v**e As, then save the image as DULLFISH.TIF (choose the TIFF format from the Save File as Format **T**ype drop-down list) to your hard disk	Saves your work in a format most applications can read.

The DULLFISH.TIF image can now be printed from a 1,200 dpi laser printer, and can be optimally used by a commercial press with requirements outlined earlier.

Figure 23.19

Reduce the output level in an image to match the print press's halftone capability.

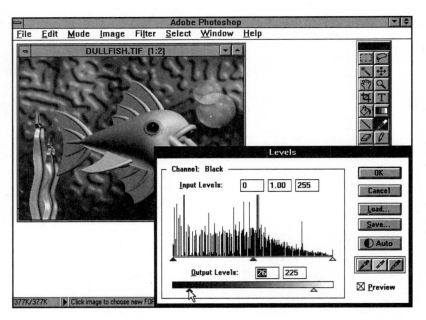

Stop If your commercial printer specifies only a top *or* a bottom density threshold, don't use Levels to readjust both the bottom *and* top ranges. Photoshop recalculates and redistributes all the pixels in an image when you make a change in a particular area of brightness. Photoshop's ability to reproportion the scheme of tonal values so that they look smooth can wreck your chances of an optimal print if you specify an Output Level that the commercial printer has not specified!

Generally, when you follow the specifications a commercial printer gives you for maximum or minimum halftone densities or both, the number of unique colors in the image file falls below the maximum capability of a 1,200 dpi laser printer to render halftones at a medium-quality, 85 lpi screen frequency. If, after doing the *last* exercise, you were to repeat the Paint Shop Pro exercise outlined earlier, you'd find that the unique number of colors in your saved copy of the DULLFISH image is now 187. With this amount, a 1,200 dpi laser printer has more than sufficient resolution to render a halftone dot to represent each of the grayscales found in the new image. And the commercial printer can faithfully copy the image, because the halftone values in the laser copy fall within the capability of the screens for the press.

 Tip After you finish printing, you can free up hard drive space by deleting the copy of the image. It's served its purpose. By specifying a lower resolution for the copy, you *degrade* the image quality by substituting larger, fewer pixels/inches that a laser printer with limited resolution can translate to toner dots more easily. After you degrade an image in this way, you can never retrieve the pixel information that's now been simplified for printing purposes. That's why you should always specify digital image dimensions and resolutions for printing from a *copy* of your work .

Adding a Style to Your Camera-Ready Print

You've seen the advantages of high-resolution personal printing. Whether the final print is for personal use, or for a printing press, high-resolution and halftoning are the ingredients of successfully conveying a grayscale image as a collection of dots. However, there's one last stop in Photoshop we need to visit to learn about *stylizing* the PostScript information to enhance the printed image.

You can define the *dots* in "dots per inch" by using Photoshop's Halftone Screen dialog box's Shape option. Although round dots are the convention you might choose when you create a halftone image for personal use, *other* shapes of dots can add detail, as a refinement to the image rendered from a laser printer.

Shaping the Dots in a Laser Copy

In a newspaper, have you ever come across a photographic print that seems to have been printed through a special-effects screen? The image might look diffuse, or stylized, and may have been unusually printed for a number of reasons. Newspaper is highly absorbent. When a dot of ink is applied to it, the dot spreads out and, if not controlled, bleeds into its nearest neighbor. Many presses use line screens with specially shaped halftone dots that help control this problem.

Newsletters printed on "copy paper" use the same frequency of line screen (85 lpi) that newspapers do, but because "copy paper" is less porous than newsprint, publishers usually don't have to resort to using custom-patterned halftone dots. Newsletters and other medium-quality business materials are printed on different kinds of presses from newspapers, which also affects the way the ink reacts with the paper.

For practicality's sake or purely for effect, a special line screen composed of irregularly shaped halftone dots can be specified straight out of Photoshop to your laser printer or a high-end imagesetter.

How a Squashed Dot Fits in a Screen

In figure 23.20, you can see the Halftone Screen Shape option's drop-down list of shapes in which Photoshop can render the halftone dots. If you intend to take a laser copy to a commercial printer, ask whether they prefer a specific dot shape, angle, and frequency of halftones for reproducing work. Print presses have many variables, such as the speed of the press and ink formulation, and the dot shape of halftones has a bearing on how effectively a grayscale image is expressed as a halftone.

Figure 23.20

Digital halftone cells can be arranged to accommodate dots of different shapes.

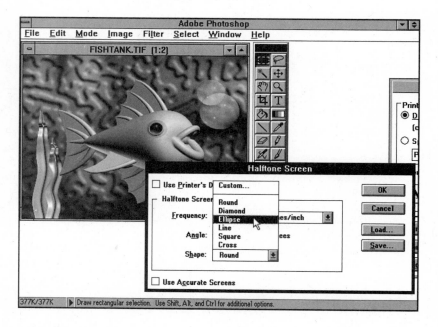

Specifying a halftone dot shape is not the same as converting a Grayscale image to Bitmap type and assigning the resulting pattern a dot shape, however. You physically alter your image when you create a bitmap pattern of dot shapes; PostScript printing and Photoshop offer you a selection of dots that go on a printed page while retaining the characteristics of your original image.

The folks who run the local commercial presses would know what shape halftone dot will reproduce the best on their printing presses. It can't be stressed enough—a conversation with the specialists who render your work to ink on paper is the most important step you can take when creating a camera-ready print. If you want a stylized halftone print for the sake of Art, however, and a laser copy of your masterpiece is considered *finished*, you can create several special effects by using different-shaped dots. The relationship between a digital halftone cell and a single line of a line screen is a fixed one; a dot representing 50 percent black (a medium gray) occupies half a cell's dimensions, regardless of line frequency. But the *shape* of this dot influences the overall design of the print. Figure 23.21 is a representation of Photoshop's Ellipse dot shape; the halftone dots sit in a line screen set at a 45-degree angle.

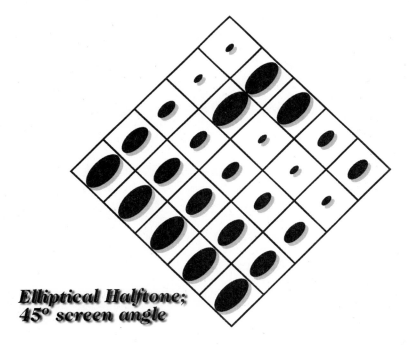

Figure 23.21

Changing the halftone dot shape stylizes the printed grayscale image.

Figure 23.22 is an enlarged scan of the FISHTANK image printed at 85 lines per inch, 45° screen angle, with Ellipse chosen as the dot shape. It's a particularly striking effect you may have seen in publications. Owners of lower-resolution printers can achieve pleasant results with this halftone dot shape. Keep in mind, though, that altering halftone dots to more exotic shapes detracts from the composition of the original image. Sometimes an irregular dot shape even becomes *part* of the image's composition. You should experiment and evaluate, on an image-to-image basis, which "effects screen," if any, produces the most eye-pleasing results.

Figure 23.22

An Ellipse dot shape can add another dimension to the printed grayscale image.

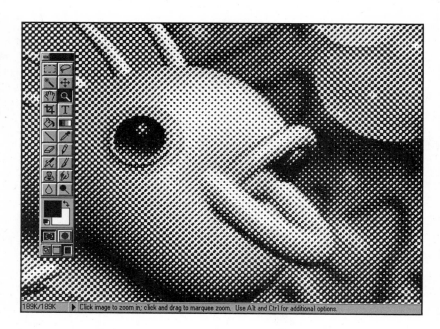

 Tip
Different-shaped dots in a halftone line screen can add excitement and drama to the printed image. But you may need to prepare your work on a copy of the original image before you print it. The higher the *contrast* in an original image's composition, the better that image lends itself to special dot shapes. When tonal densities in the original display only mild variation, the effect of the irregularly shaped dots in the screen pattern is not visually pronounced. An image with higher than average contrast will produce halftone dots that vary widely from one neighboring dot to another—you can see the *effect* of the distorted dots more clearly.

A Word on Corruption

The Tagged Image File format is the *lingua franca* of computer images; practically every professional-level application on both the Windows and Macintosh platforms supports and imports this graphical file format. In this chapter, you've read about many different elements of personal printing, from modifying images within

Photoshop, to placing an image in a desktop publishing application for rendering along with text. You can print a finished image from almost any application on any platform as long as:

◆ You give the finished image a file format another application or another computer can read, and...

◆ You don't have any Photoshop-proprietary "elements" within the finished image.

If you happen to leave an Alpha Channel or path in your TIF image, a file can appear corrupted. The appearance of corruption in a bitmap image is hard to tell sometimes, and that's why we need to mention it in this chapter. TIF images corrupt more easily than other types of files, such as databases and spreadsheets. File corruption can happen when your system crashes and you have an image open. An image can even get banged around too often and become corrupted when it resides on a hard disk partition that is subject to a crash.

The point here is to determine whether a Photoshop Alpha channel is to blame for a file's lack of readability at the commercial printer, or whether your image file has indeed become corrupted. Fortunately, Photoshop won't let an image with Layers be saved to any other format than Photoshop's own PSD format, but increasingly, other applications read and write Alpha channel information (sometimes called *Transparency masks*). Their documentation might not include whether the application will read an Alpha channel, ignore Alpha channel information, or display something that looks like a corrupt file on-screen.

Figure 23.23 is a copy of the FISHTANK image after it went through the wringer on the author's hard disk during one of Windows' "unexpected enhancements." You can see horizontal areas of "noise" that streak the image. This file is corrupted. The image can't be restored by any of the software "recovery" schemes you may have purchased as utilities. It's a goner and should be deleted. Hopefully, the author has a spare copy of the image.

On the other hand, a file that can't be understood by an imaging application because it contains a proprietary Photoshop doodad, such as an Alpha channel, looks quite different from a corrupt file. Different programs respond in different ways to this weird stimulus. Figure 23.24 shows what an image with an Alpha channel looks like when Logitech's PhotoTouch software tries to load it.

The point here is not to confuse a corrupt file with one that contains additional information you set up using Photoshop. Always save copies of your images and archive them to a location that's not on your machine, and bring *copies* of your images to a commercial printer, as we advise in the next chapter.

Figure 23.23

Video "noise" running across an image file is the most common sign of file corruption.

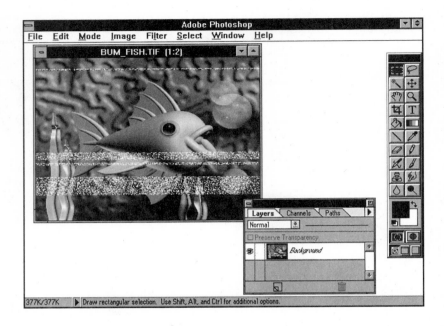

Figure 23.24

An imaging program that doesn't have the same features as Photoshop won't be able to understand Alpha channels or paths.

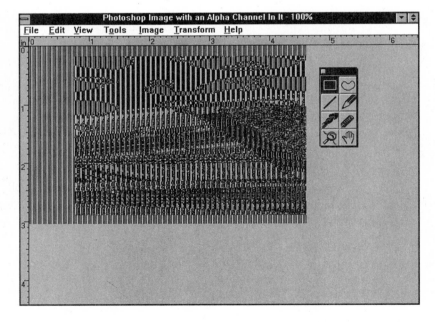

Increasing Print Quality, Decreasing Artist Involvement

You've seen what you can do by yourself with a high-resolution laser printer and Photoshop methods that optimize your grayscale image for the best reproduction. As you gain experience with imaging, you'll find that you are spending equal amounts of time at your PC and at the commercial printer. You'll become familiar with the special requirements of a specific print press and learn to trust the people who render your work as ink on the printed page.

This is also the time when you might consider abandoning the "home brew" halftone from your laser printer and letting the commercial printer render your computer file directly to an *imagesetting* device. Imagesetters don't depend on toner dots to render halftones. Imagesetters produce film positives and negatives from digital files. The film produced by an imagesetter can be made into printing press plates. Some imagesetters skip the film step altogether and instead create a printing plate directly from your digital file.

Many of the formulas and techniques you've learned in this chapter also apply to work that is sent to an imagesetter. If you are producing images that will be part of a color printing run, there are additional Photoshop features you can take advantage of to ensure great work. If you are ready to take the plunge into color printing, the next chapter is for you.

24

The Service Bureau

The laser printer is not intended to mass produce documents, particularly not a halftone copy of a digital image. Laser printers are slower than most other reproduction methods and limited as to the size and kind of paper on which they can print. And a PC has to be dedicated (tied up!) while a massive quantity of copies is printing. Only in the most lavish office environments are laser documents distributed to more than 50 people at a time, for example. The prudent, pragmatic approaches to mass distribution of computer documents are by electronic mail (e-mail), by printing photocopies of a laser copy, or by using the printing press.

The first two options are not suitable for getting the world to appreciate your digital masterpiece. You have to use the third option: commercial printing presses. And to get an image "prepped" for commercial printing, you'll want to engage the talents of the experts at a service bureau. This chapter describes the Dos, the Don'ts, and a few tricks you'll want to be aware of before your work is printed commercially.

From Source, to Sample, to the Printed Page

Throughout this book, you learned how to take images from the real world and im-ages that exist in your imagination, and create glorious compositions on your moni-tor's screen. In the last chapter, "Personal Printing Basics," you explored one avenue—the personal laser printer—as a route to transferring grayscale images to paper. To share your imaging work with the world at large, however, you need the specialized equipment, the skills, and the expertise of a service bureau and a commercial printer.

Most people don't have a commercial printing press hooked directly into their computer, however, and a necessary link needs to be established between the ethereal nature of digital images and physical, tangible things like press plates and ink on paper. Your allies in bridging the gap between your artistic input and physical output are the pre-press service bureau and the commercial printer.

In this chapter, you explore how the specialized equipment and the skills and expertise of many people—you, a service bureau, and a commercial printer—can bring your images to life.

What Is a Service Bureau?

A service bureau prepares and transforms your file into a form and a format that can be used to produce physical output. Service bureaus use very expensive and complex equipment; imagesetters, film recorders, high-resolution color printers, and proofing devices are all the tools of high-quality output trade. The output from these devices might be all you need, as in the case of color laser prints or slides, to make your image come alive. On the other hand, to bring your images to the world, you might need film separations made that any commercial printer then can use to make printing plates. If color printing from a commercial press is your goal, you'll need the services of a pre-press service bureau's imagesetter as the intermediate step to the printing press.

Service bureaus and commercial printers are not always two different business; sometimes you find them under one roof. And even when they are separate businesses, the services they offer might overlap. Both a commercial printer and a service bureau might own imagesetters, digital color printers, and proofing devices. The difference between service bureaus and commercial printers is that the commercial printer makes printing plates from negatives and mass produces your work on high-speed presses that apply ink to paper. Regardless of whether your service bureau and commercial printer are at the same location, the roles that both firms play, and their

New Riders Publishing
INSIDE
SERIES

knowledge of a specialized craft, are vital to successfully producing beautiful printed copies of your work.

Why Do You Need Service Bureaus?

Service bureaus and commercial printers enable you to produce copies of your work that are of a higher level of quality and in greater quantity than you could possibly produce on your desktop. Service bureaus and commercial printers are essentially in the business of "renting" you time on equipment that you couldn't afford realistically.

Printing, like photography and design, is an *art*. Commercial printers and pre-press service bureaus typically are staffed by capable, diligent folks who have spent many years mastering and perfecting their craft—which is more time than you can spend while still developing your *own* craft.

How Pre-Press Savvy Do You Need to Be?

As a computer imagist, your first responsibility is to devote your skills, talents, and time toward producing outstanding work. Like artists who seek mentors to assist in refining their skills, you need to send your creations off to people who are experts in their line of work. Although your level of involvement in producing a finished, printed copy of your imaging work is a limited one in some respects, you should understand a *few* things about the printing process. There are things you can do with a digital file before sending it to the service bureau or commercial printer that will make your business partner's work go more smoothly, and you'll be happier with the completed image.

Although you certainly don't need to acquire all the skills and knowledge that these folks have, you *do* need to know how to deliver digital copies of your color and grayscale work to them so that they can be successful in transforming your digital image into a physical image. You also need to know what kinds of services they provide, what to expect when you engage their services, and how their equipment affects many of your most basic design decisions.

If you're reading this book in sequence, you already have begun the process of learning what you need to know to be able to make the service bureau and the commercial printers your partners. In the last chapter, "Personal Printing Basics," you learned about some of the fundamentals of the printing process—the importance of PostScript technology, how halftone cells and screening work, how large your files should be, and what you can do to prepare images for grayscale printing. These concepts and concerns are as important to the production of commercially printed output as they are to personal printed output. Much of the discussion in this chapter is based on the presumption that you are familiar with these concepts.

Two Ways To Get Your Image to Press

To get the digital image to press, you can print a grayscale laser copy of your work and have the printer make the press plates from the laser copy. This commonly is referred to as *camera-ready art*. Even if you own a high-resolution laser printer, one that is capable of more than 1000 dpi output (they start at more than $4,000), you'll eventually outgrow the desire to make camera-ready art an in-house process. Why? Because as you refine your craft of digital imaging, you'll expect more refined hard copy of your work. This means trusting a firm with the responsibility of rendering your digital images, and this means taking image files to an outside resource.

To increase the distribution of your work in a high-quality medium, you need to give a commercial printer a copy of your digital image file, so you obviously have to use a printing firm that's computer-enabled. Because not all printers are computer savvy and partly because properly preparing photographic images for reproduction on a printing press always has been highly specialized work, the service bureau was born. The job or service the staff at a pre-press service bureau performs is to take your files and prep them for printing. Preparing your files for printing, at the very least, entails the use of an imagesetter or film recorder that renders digital files to film. After your image is on film, any printer can make the printing plates for the press.

Most of the time you will not be printing just an image; instead, your imaging work will be part of a document of some kind. A service bureau's staff has developed the expertise to determine what is the best way to incorporate images into documents that have been generated by desktop publishing programs like PageMaker, by proprietary publishing systems such as Scitex systems, or even by traditional physical paste-up methods.

If you take the personal route to camera-ready or finished art, or choose to deliver a design to a service bureau in electronic format, you need to understand a little about the color printing process. Depending on how you want color output, your finished piece can be a result of color separations or passes of color halftone inks made directly inside a color printer. The next sections describe how color prints are made from Photoshop, how the color-separation process works, and the options you have for color output of your images.

Glorious Color from Digital Printers

A few years ago, a personal color printer was out of the budget and out of the question for most imaging-type individuals, and for many it still is. But the demand for presentations and color proofing has driven prices down to a point that makes it fairly

affordable to print small runs of your work with a color digital printer. Personal color printers don't generate an image nearly as refined as offset or lithographic commercial printing, but they do provide a reasonable way to get a sample of your work across town. Service bureaus usually have a wide range of personal color digital printers available, and if you're thinking about buying a color printer, you should try out several printers at your service bureau to see whether a particular make and model of printer produces the results you want.

Printer manufacturers have come up with several ways to get color images onto paper. The technologies deployed, and what the color printers use for pigment follow: color ink ribbon (dot-matrix printers); sprayed ink on paper (inkjet); heated, colored wax (thermal wax transfer); superheated dyes that are absorbed by special papers (dye sublimation); and the color laser printer. Color printers range in price from $500 for a dot-matrix printer to $20,000 for a color laser printer.

The range in price is significant, and so is the quality of the work these printers can produce. If you are looking for something that approaches photographic quality, expect to pay at least $8,000 for a good dye-sublimation printer. What you get for less money produces anything from an approximation to a parody of your original digital image.

Don't rely on personal color printers to provide *proof* colors for images destined for slide or printing-press reproduction. Each type of color printer mentioned earlier uses different kinds of pigments and papers that don't correspond to your monitor, to photographic film, or to print press ink. And each technology produces a different range, or *gamut*, of color. Blue easily can shift to purple, and yellow to orange, when you're using personal color printers.

At the current time and level of color technology, *personal* color printers cannot be recommended as faithful reproducers of photorealistic work. At best, they give you a general overview and feeling for your image if you remember that what you're looking at is rendered with only a fair degree of faithfulness to your digital file.

High-end versions of some these technologies (in the $20,000 to $250,000 price range), however, can produce images that range from splendid to final-proof quality. These machines typically are found at your printer or service bureau.

If you want to see what your work really looks like, have a slide made of it. The cost is between $10 and $15. If you need an idea of what your work will look like when it's process-color printed to a press, take your file to your printer or service bureau and have them make a proof for you. The cost usually ranges from $15 to $50 per page, depending on the capability of the printer used to make the proof.

Tip

Not everything you do is color critical, nor does it have to be serious and all business.

Most service bureaus can print an image file to T-shirt transfer paper, for example. This stuff is great. You iron the transfer onto a T-shirt and presto—you have an instant, custom promotional or gift item.

Keep your design simple because the colors available aren't very subtle, and intricate detail can get lost. But hey, T-shirts aren't *supposed* to be subtle, and it's just plain fun to wear your own designer T-shirt.

Printing a Color Image from Photoshop

If you have a color digital printer or are preparing an image for digital printing at a service bureau, you will find this section helpful when optimizing your file and printing it from Photoshop.

Remember that many of Photoshop's color options and features refer to color *separations*—four black-and-white halftones from which plates are made to print process color using a commercial press. These options *don't* apply to producing a finished image on a personal color printer.

Most personal color printers that cost less than $2,000 do not have PostScript capability. This makes faithfully reproducing photographic images a difficult matter because you can't take advantage of the PostScript digital halftoning technology, as discussed in Chapter 23, "Personal Printing Basics." Although a non-PostScript color printer can't access some of Photoshop's imaging features, color printing to a personal printer is basically the same as printing from any other Windows or Macintosh application.

Many printer manufacturers—the most prominent being Hewlett-Packard and Epson—have developed quite sophisticated printer drivers that push the limits of non-PostScript printing to a point where the results are quite pleasing, although they fail to produce work as accurately as PostScript output. Like the black-and-white, PCL-based laser printer, non-PostScript color printer drivers use proprietary halftones and screens to enhance output. Many of these printers offer a choice of dithering patterns such as diffusion (also called *scatter*), clustered (a dithering pattern optimized for photocopy reproduction), and pattern. If your printer driver offers these options, be sure to choose diffusion (scatter) when printing your Photoshop work. See Chapter 23 for more information on diffusion dithering.

Common Considerations When Printing

The first step when printing an image to a digital color printer is to open the file you want to print. Photoshop does not enable you to change any settings for color or black-and-white printing unless an active image window is in the workspace. Not all color printers support the same features, and unavailable features are usually dimmed or do not appear in Photoshop's Page Setup and Print dialog boxes. Therefore, the examples in the next section are general in nature rather than constructed as an exercise. They apply to both PostScript and non-PostScript color printers unless otherwise noted. The STATUE.PSD image, shown in figure 24.1, is used as an example in this section.

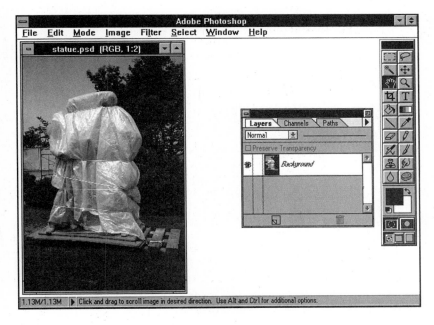

Figure 24.1

An RGB image can be sent directly from Photoshop to a color printer.

The first step is to make sure that your image is in RGB color mode. Photoshop displays this information on the image window title bar, or you can go to the **M**ode menu and make sure that **R**GB is selected. You don't want to have CMYK, LAB, or Indexed as the color mode for the image you want to print. The CMYK color mode is not wanted because you need a complete image, not separations. You don't want your image in LAB color mode because very few printers (except Level 2 PostScript printers) understand the LAB format. Indexed is a poor choice of color modes because it limits the color capability of an image to a maximum of 256 colors. As a rule, your color image will be going from a display gamut that is wider than your printing gamut; that is, there are more colors in an RGB image than can be accurately expressed as pigment on paper. Indexed color images, however, have substantially fewer colors than can be rendered by a color printer, so you're limiting the amount of color information for the printer to use by specifying Indexed color as the mode of the image you want to output. With personal color printing, you want to give the printer driver all the color information you can, and then let the printer perform color reduction as part of the process of printing your image. RGB gives the printer driver plenty of elbow room to discern how to dither the colors that it can't reproduce accurately.

The second step is to make sure that all of the image layers you want to print are visible. If your image has been flattened so that it only has a background, all is well. If your image has layers, make sure that you want them all in the finished image. If you have a layer in the image that you don't want to print, you don't have to delete it. Instead, click on the eye icon next to the layer and it will be hidden from your view and the printer driver's view. Photoshop only prints visible layers.

Check the dimensions and resolution of your file. For most color printers (most of which are 300 dpi) an image resolution of about 150 dpi is best. Make sure that the dimensions of your image will fit on the paper size you're using, and use the **I**mage, **I**mage Size command on a *copy* of your image if the picture is too large. Non-PostScript printers usually don't offer the option to enlarge or reduce the printed image size, and even when they do, the printer must *interpolate* (add or throw out information), which degrades image quality. Photoshop will do a better job of adjusting image size than the printer.

Always print in Portrait orientation, because doing so speeds up printing. If your image has a *Landscape* orientation (the image is printed wider than it is high), use the Rotate command to rotate the image instead of making the printer do this. To rotate the image, press Ctrl+D (Macintosh: Cmd+D). Or, choose **N**one from the **S**elect menu. Then choose Rotate from the **I**mage menu, and choose **9**0° CW or 9**0**° CCW.

After you address the issues of dimension, resolution, and color capability of the image you want to print, it's time to move on to Photoshop's Page Setup dialog box. This is where many of the Photoshop print options are set.

Using the Page Setup Dialog Box

When you choose Pa**g**e Setup from the **F**ile menu, the Page Setup dialog box appears (see fig. 24.2). The Page Setup screen always looks the same, regardless of which printer driver you have loaded on your system. In this dialog box, you have the option to print from the default printer (the one currently defined for your system), or you can choose another printer from the Specific **P**rinter drop-down list. This is a list of all printer drivers currently installed on your system. Although there are many buttons and check boxes within this dialog box, most of them usually can be left at

their default settings. The next few sections explain these settings so that you'll know what settings to change if you have a special application or printing need.

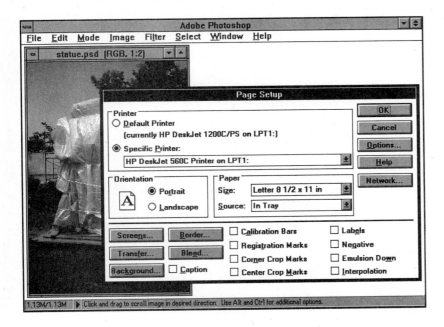

Figure 24.2

Photoshop's Page Setup dialog box.

Screens

Like commercial printing presses, personal color printers use three colors (cyan, magenta, and yellow) or four colors (cyan, magenta, yellow, and black) to produce the colors in your image. These pigments can be in the form of wax, ink, toner, or dye. Printers that use four colors produce better results than three-color printers, because pigments contain many impurities, and blacks in an image need a reinforcing pass of black pigment from the printer so that darker areas in the printed image will not display a greenish color cast.

The screen angles for each color the printer uses are set at angles that are oblique (non-resonating angles) to each other. Using different screen angles greatly reduces the chance that the cyan, magenta, yellow, and black pigments will build a moiré pattern into your printed image when they are printed, one on top of the other. A *moiré* pattern is the result of screen lines (lines composed of halftone cells) overlapping at regular intervals within the image.

Clicking on the Screens button in the Page Setup dialog box displays the Halftone Screens dialog box shown in figure 24.3. Notice that the Use Printer's Default Screens check box is selected. Unless you're attempting to achieve a special effect with your color print, or are very familiar with the specifications for your machine, this is a good option to leave checked. Personal color printer manufacturers have built the optimal screen angles right into the machine—there's really no need to change them. When you enable this option, all other options are dimmed, and you can't change the Halftone Screen settings.

Figure 24.3

The Use Printer's Default Screen option tells your color printer to use factory-set angles and frequencies.

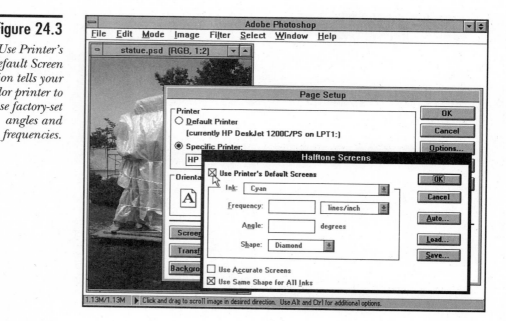

Border

Clicking on this button accesses a dialog box that enables you to place a black border around the edges of your image. You can specify the width of the border, but you can't choose a color other than black.

Bleed

If you intend to physically crop the printed image, you can have Photoshop insert crop marks within the image to guide the person who runs the paper cutter. You can specify how far into the image the crop marks appear.

Background

If your image doesn't fill the page, and you want color around your image, you can choose a color here. Choosing this option really eats up the costly ink/wax/toner the printer uses and increases print time dramatically. You should not choose this option frivolously.

Transfer

Transfer functions are designed to compensate for a miscalibrated imagesetter. These functions are not used with the typical color digital printer. Clicking the Transfer button displays the Transfer Functions dialog box, where you can adjust the values used to compensate for dot gain. *Dot gain* is the growth in the size of halftone dots that occurs when the ink used to print an image on a printing press expands as it's absorbed into the paper. Imagesetters compensate for dot gain by reducing the size of the halftone dots they put on the film from which the press plates are made. Exactly how much imagesetters reduce the size of the dots is determined by the settings you determine in the Printing Inks Setup dialog box (which you access by choosing Preferences from the File menu). The information needed to determine the values you enter in the Printing Inks Setup dialog box *must* come from the commercial printer. Only the commercial printer knows what the appropriate value is for the paper, ink, and press your image will be printed on. If all this sounds complicated, it is. It is far better to calibrate the imagesetter instead of trying to guess and correct on the image side of the equation.

Caption and Labels Check Boxes

Put an X in the Caption check box if you want the caption text that might have been entered in the Caption field of the File Info feature printed in nine-point Helvetica in the margin of your printout. File Info is a new feature in Photoshop 3 found on the File menu. It is used to insert descriptive text into the header of the file. This feature is commonly used by newspaper wire services to identify images they send. Put a check in the Labels check box if you want the file name and channel name printed on the image in nine-point Helvetica. The size and typeface for these options can't be changed.

Registration Marks

When printing color separations for spot color, process color, or duotones, checking this box places bullseyes in the margin around the image, which enable the commercial printer to align the printing plates. Registration marks are not used when printing a composite image to a digital color printer.

Calibration Bars

Enabling this feature causes a gradient-filled rectangle to be printed in the margin of the page. This is used by commercial printers to check that their press or printer is producing the proper density of color. The 10 percent part of the gradient, for example, actually should be 10 percent when the commercial printer measures it with a device called a densitometer. *Densitometers* are precision instruments designed to measure the tonal values in printed material. If you are printing CMYK separations, the Calibration Bar feature adds a progressive color bar. Progressive proofs are used at commercial printers to check the alignment and density values of the C, M, Y, and K values of pigments as they are applied in combination on the printed page. To see an example of what a calibration bar looks like in action, take apart a cereal box or other printed package. You usually find calibration bars printed on the inside flaps as a method for proofing a production run as it comes off the presses.

Corner and Center Crop Marks Check Boxes

If your image does not fill the page and will be trimmed physically to the edges of the image, you can specify that Corner or Center crop marks be printed. Checking both boxes prints both kinds of crop marks.

Negative and Emulsion Down Check Boxes

You use these options when printing film to make printing plates. Check with your printer to determine how these options should be set for the printing press that will be used. *Don't* guess or make an assumption based on a hard-and-fast rule you might have heard or read, or you might go to the expense of producing film that is unusable. When printing a complete, finished image on paper, these check boxes always should be left *unchecked*.

Interpolation Check Box

This option only applies to some PostScript Level 2 printers. If you are printing a low-resolution image, checking this check box instructs the printer to increase (sample up) the resolution of the image. The advantage to using this option is that interpolating reduces a low-resolution image's tendency to produce jagged edges. The disadvantage is that overall image quality is reduced, and the focus of the image will not be as clear as you see it on the monitor. If you feel that interpolation of the image is necessary for final output, choose **I**mage, **I**mage Size on Photoshop's menu bar instead of checking this option at printing time. In Photoshop, you have the opportunity to see what the *effect* of the interpolation will be; when the printer does it, you pay for a print that you might be dissatisfied with.

Using Printer Specific Options

The options you have to choose from on the Page Setup dialog box are standard options that always appear and are not specific to any one printer. However, clicking on the **O**ptions button of the Page Setup dialog box displays options and controls that are specific to the printer chosen in the Printer field of the Page Setup dialog box. The dialog box that appears is not supplied by Photoshop; it is supplied by the printer driver, so its appearance will vary. In the next section, you see the options you can specify for a popular, non-PostScript inkjet printer: the Hewlett-Packard 560C. This is a low-end color printer with a list price of about $700.

Printing Options for a Non-PostScript Color Printer

Clicking on the **O**ptions button on the Page Setup dialog box produces the dialog box shown in figure 24.4 when the HP 560C is the printer specified. The settings you can make vary with the printer you have chosen; the settings in the figure are given only as an example of what non-PostScript printing options are in Photoshop.

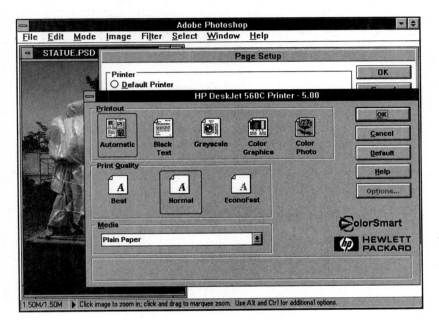

Figure 24.4

These options are specific to the chosen printer and are supplied by the printer driver.

The HP 560C uses a technology called *Color Smart,* which analyzes a document and uses the settings that will produce the best color print. When printing photorealistic images, you should click on the Color Photo icon in the **P**rintout field, choose Best in the Print **Q**uality, and then choose the media on which you will print the image. This printer will print to plain paper, but all color printers produce better results when special, glossy papers specifically designed for a make and model of printer are used. Choosing a media type and then using a different kind of paper produces unacceptable to ghastly results, because the printer uses different methods for applying the ink, based on the paper type chosen here.

If you click on the Op**t**ions button, the Color Photo Options dialog box appears. Here you can see what the default settings are for printing color photos (see fig. 24.5). Scatter (diffusion dithering) is the Half**t**oning method, **I**ntensity is set to a middle value, and Co**l**or Control is set to match your screen. These settings produce the most realistic printouts for photorealistic color images. Leave the settings as they are shown on-screen.

Figure 24.5

Choose a Scatter (diffusion) halftoning method when printing images to a non-PostScript printer.

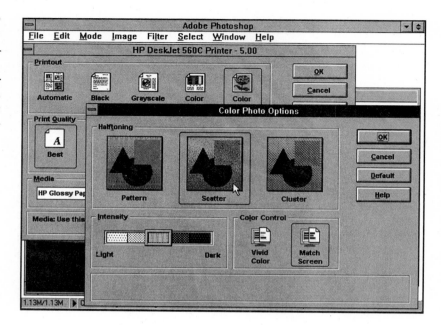

When all settings are made in the respective dialog boxes, click **O**K to return to your document. When you choose **P**rint from the **F**ile menu, these settings are used.

Printing Options for a PostScript Color Printer

The printing options that appear after **O**ptions is chosen from the Page Setup dialog box are quite different for PostScript color printers. In this section, you see what kinds of options might be available. The printer chosen for this example is the Hewlett-Packard 1200C/PS printer. This is a medium-quality PostScript Level 2 inkjet printer, with a list price of about $2,400.

Click on the **O**ptions button in the Page Setup dialog box, and the Setup dialog box for the HP 1200C/PS printer appears. As you can see in figure 24.6, the options are different than those in the preceding section. This section takes a quick look at the options you use when printing a final, composite color image to this printer.

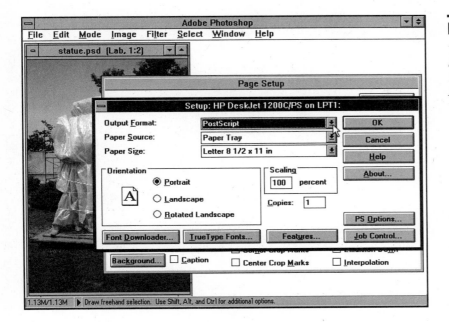

Figure 24.6

The Setup dialog box for the HP 1200C/PS PostScript printer.

The most important choice on this opening screen is Output **F**ormat. It always should be set to PostScript when printing directly to a printer. The other setting that is available in this drop-down list is Encapsulated PostScript. This option is used only if you want to insert your image into another document as a graphic with all the printing instructions for the graphic predetermined. This is usually not a good idea, because the settings that are in effect when you create the Encapsulated PostScript file override those set in the document in which the file is placed. This option locks you into settings that might not be optimal for the image when it actually is printed.

Clicking on the Feat**u**res button displays the Features dialog box, as seen in figure 24.7. These settings tell the printer to use its halftone screens or to take instruction from Photoshop, specify whether the image is printed in color, determine the kind of paper used, and specify the level of printing quality. You should set these options to enable the application to determine the halftone screens, to print in color, to use the paper you will use, and to use high-quality printing.

Figure 24.7

The Features dialog box for a color PostScript inkjet printer.

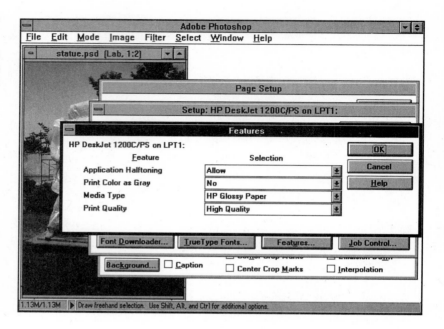

Clicking on the PS **O**ptions button in the Setup dialog box displays the PostScript Options dialog box seen in figure 24.8. Almost all the default settings are ones that you normally should use with this printer. You should uncheck the Send Data in **B**inary check box if your network print spooler is unable to handle binary information. Check with your systems administrator. You also should enable **M**atch Color Across Printers if your image is in the LAB color mode. Because this printer is a Level 2 PostScript printer, you would want your image to be in LAB mode and not RGB. Level 2 PostScript printers understand the LAB color mode and will be able to better match the colors in your image. To change an image's color mode from RGB to LAB, go to Photoshop's **M**ode menu and choose **LA**B.

The Font **D**ownloader, **T**rueType Fonts, and the **J**ob Control buttons display dialog boxes that concern how fonts are handled. When printing images from Photoshop, you *don't have any* fonts even if text is included in your image. This is because the stuff that looks like text in your image isn't text. The Type tool produced text as a bitmap, just like the areas of your image that comprise a tree, or a person's face. Text produced with the Type tool is not editable text like the kind a word processor produces. Leave the settings in the dialog boxes associated with these buttons set to their defaults.

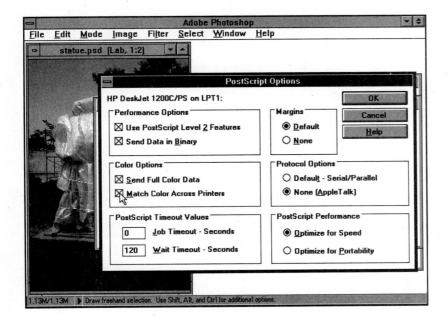

Figure 24.8

PostScript options are set here for the HP 1200 C/PS inkjet printer.

You'll notice that screens and halftones were not mentioned anywhere in these dialog boxes. This particular printer driver does not give you a choice of screens. If you have a special need for different screens, you must have set the Application Halftoning to Allow in the Features dialog box and specified custom screens in Photoshop's Page Setup dialog box. As with the non-PostScript digital printer discussed earlier, you are more likely to get better results if you use the default printer screens that the printer manufacturer has optimized for that particular printer.

After you make all your settings, click on OK in all the dialog boxes until you are back to Photoshop's workspace.

Using the Print Command from the File Menu

After you have set all the Page Setup options, it time to actually print the image using Photoshop's File, Print (Ctrl (Cmd)+P) command. As you can see in figure 24.9, there isn't much to this dialog box. This dialog box usually looks the same, no matter what kind of printer you are printing to. The important settings are Print Quality, Print as, and Encoding. Print Quality should be set to the highest level your printer is capable of producing. The radio button selected in the Print as field should match the color mode of your image.

An additonal field—Encoding—sometimes appears on the bottom right of the Print dialog box. Whether it appears or not depends on the printer driver you are using. When Encoding is an option, it should be set to ASCII for greatest compatibility when printing over a network and to Binary if your printer supports binary mode and your printer is attached to your computer. Binary prints about twice as fast as ASCII. JPEG is when you want to print very fast and you are willing to put up with the information loss associated with JPEG compression. See Chapter 2, "Acquiring A Digital Image," for more information about this lossy compression scheme.

Figure 24.9

The Print dialog box appears after you press Ctrl+P.

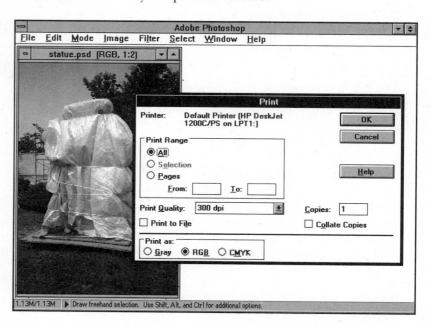

The Print to File check box should be *unchecked.* You check this option only when you do not want the file to print to the printer, but instead you want the printer driver to create a file that contains the information that *would have* gone to the printer. This is a useful option if you are creating Adobe Acrobat files using Acrobat Distiller. The Print to File option also is used when you don't have the printer you specified, and you want to take the file to be printed by a service bureau or a colleague who has the printer and doesn't have Photoshop. This choice is very limiting because if any of the settings are incorrect, the print file will not print as you expected and it can't be altered to correct the problem.

After you determine all the settings on this dialog box, click on OK and wait for your image to come out of the printer. You might have to be patient; large, photorealistic images, when printed at high-quality settings, can take five minutes or more per copy.

Tip   If you want to print only part of an image, use the Rectangular Marquee tool to select the area you want to print. All the pixels within the marquee must be opaque. Press Ctrl (Cmd)+P (or choose **P**rint from the **F**ile menu). In the Print dialog box, choose Sel**e**ction, and then click on OK.

Creating Duotones

Duotones are a convention adopted many years ago to compensate for the reality that the printing inks used commercially don't express the range of grayscale in an original halftone image. Duotones, tritones, and quadtones are grayscale images printed using different colored inks, with each ink covering and reinforcing a particular density range in the representation of the original grayscale image. If you were to see a well-done black and medium-gray duotone print in a book, you might not even realize that different inks were used. The gray, in the case of the duotone in such a book, was added by the commercial printer from a second screen of the grayscale, in which the image displayed more or less contrast than the screen for the black plate.

When inks other than black and gray are used, duotones create wonderfully evocative images. *Steeltone* images (black and cold blue inks) and sepia tones created by using duotones have become an art form. Although Photoshop can build the color separations that a commercial printer would need to print a duotone, personal color printers can achieve the same effect if you know how to navigate the Photoshop controls for this feature.

Creating Duotones from Grayscale Images

Whether your color printer is PostScript determines whether you can faithfully render a duotone image. Photoshop saves a duotone image only as a proprietary PSD format, EPS, or RAW image file. To create a duotone, you first must be working with a grayscale image. Then when you print, the Encapsulated PostScript language interprets the duotone qualities of the image, which is the graphical information that is saved in a single, special duotone channel. This EPS information about the duotone image then is passed along to a PostScript printer as specific, color-coded parameters that affect only part of the grayscale image.

Specifying a Type of Duotone

Creating a good-looking duotone from a grayscale image takes a great deal of trial, error, and practice. For this reason, Photoshop includes many sample schemes to apply to a grayscale image. You learn how to access this Photoshop sample library in the next exercise. Even if you don't own a color printer, duotones simply are nice for creating something special out of a grayscale image. Imaging work shouldn't be limited to only the tools you own. If you like your duotone image enough, you might want to have it printed commercially!

Creating a Duotone Image

Open the VANILLA.TIF image from the CHAP24 subdirectory (folder) on the Bonus CD	Image you use to create a duotone image.
Choose **M**ode, **G**rayscale and click on OK when asked if it is all right to discard color information	Converts VANILLA RGB image to grayscale.

You might want to use the method of converting images to grayscale that is featured in Chapter 17, "The Wonderful World of Black and White." This method uses the Lightness values found in a LAB color mode version of the file as the basis of the grayscale image.

Choose **M**ode, Duotone box	Displays the Duotone Options dialog box.
Choose Duotone from the Type drop-down list on the Duotone Options dialog box	Chooses the number of inks that are used.
Click on **L**oad	Displays directory (folder) structure of your hard disk.
Find the DUOTONES subdirectory (folder) under your Photoshop directory	Duotone sample files were installed here when you installed Photoshop.
Double-click on the DUOTONES subdirectory (folder) beneath the duotones subdirectory you clicked on in the last step	Chooses the DUOTONES subdirectory under the DUOTONES directory.
Double-click on the PMS subdirectory	Contains presets that specify PANTONE color inks used to create duotone.
Scroll down to the 349-1.ADO file in the files list, click on it, and then click on OK	Selects PANTONE Process Black P and PANTONE process color 349 P as the colors used to make the duotone (see fig. 24.10).

Click on OK in the Duotone Options dialog box	Accepts defaults for this duotone color scheme, and displays Photoshop's workspace.
Choose Save As from the File menu. Save the file as VANILLA.PSD to a directory on your hard disk	Saves file in Photoshop's format (one of three formats in which a duotone can be saved).

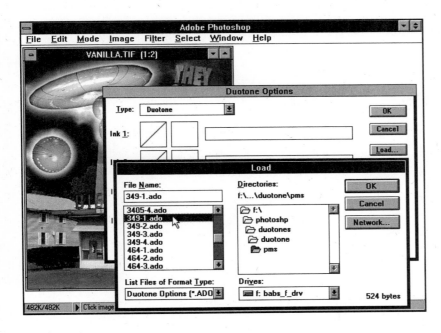

Figure 24.10

Photoshop installs with many selections of premade duotone schemes.

If you followed the last exercise, you now should have an emerald-shaded duotone on your screen. It's striking, eye-pleasing, and is *not* the same as colorizing an image in Photoshop. In fact, a great deal of thought went into building the curves that distribute each color of ink across the tonal range of the grayscale image. These are tried-and-true formulas, but if you want to tinker with duotone color distributions of your own, click on the curve box to the left of the color names before you click on OK. You clicked on the curve next to PANTONE 349 P and, as you can see in figure 24.11, the curve for distributing this ink heightens the percentages so that the middle densities of green ink are more pronounced.

Figure 24.11

The PANTONE color is most visible in the medium tonal range of the printed image.

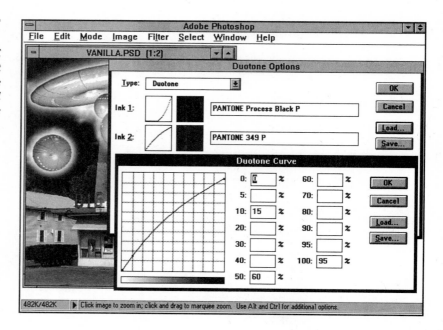

You can "tune" a duotone curve to produce different effects. But *don't* confuse the duotone curve with Photoshop's Curves command. When you adjust an ink-distribution curve in a duotone, you change the densities of ink across a percentage scale. The Curves command is used to redistribute tonal values in pixels across a brightness scale of 0 to 255. Ink and pixels aren't the same thing. If you're really interested in creating duotone prints, try experimenting with some of Photoshop's sample files of duotone curves before creating your own.

 Tip

The names for the beautifully designed duotone samples that ship with Photoshop are logically opaque; the names in the duotones subdirectory for duotone, tritone, and quadtone samples are *numbers* that relate to the type color you should see when printing to exacting ink and paper specifications.

If you come across a duotone combination you like, write down the number and the effect, because you'll never remember the file name alone!

PANTONE colors are numbered and coded for specific color values as ink is reproduced on coated, varnished stock paper and uncoated paper. Process colors (CMYK) also are combined to produce other color values. If your assignment calls for precise color matching, you should invest in a PANTONE color swatch book, available for about $80 at commercial art supply stores.

Taking a Duotone to Another Application

As mentioned earlier, Photoshop images can be imported to other applications, such as desktop publishing programs. If you own a PostScript color printer, you also can print a duotone image from another application that "speaks" the PANTONE color-naming system.

PageMaker is used in the next exercise, which explains how to save and export a duotone. Although you might not own PageMaker, if you have another application that uses the PANTONE naming convention, you would use the same techniques.

Exporting a Duotone

Open the VANILLA.PSD file from your hard drive	Image Saved As a duotone in the last exercise. (Skip this step if image still is open in Photoshop's workspace.)
Press Ctrl (Cmd)+S or choose Save As from the File menu	Displays Photoshop's Save As dialog box.
Choose EPS (*.EPS) as Save File as Format Type, and name the file VANILLA.EPS	Displays EPS Format dialog box.
Choose TIFF (8 bits/pixel) from the Preview drop-down list, choose ASCII from the Encoding drop-down list, then click on OK	Tells Photoshop to give you an 8-bit, 256-color "thumbnail" image that you can use to place the image in another application for position only.

ASCII is chosen instead of binary or the JPEG options because PageMaker can understand only the EPS file if it is in ASCII format. This also eliminates problems with some network print spoolers.

Leave the Include Halftone Screen and Include Transfer Function check boxes *unchecked* (see fig. 24.12), then click on OK	Saves a copy of VANILLA.PSD as VANILLA.EPS, which can be used in PageMaker and other programs.

Figure 24.12

Choose ASCII Encoding when exporting EPS files to PageMaker.

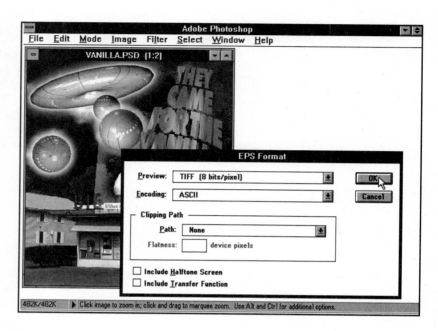

An *Encapsulated PostScript* file is a description for the printer as to how an image should be rendered, or *rasterized.* Unlike other image file formats, EPS images aren't viewable—they are printer instructions. For this reason, a low-resolution bitmap of the duotone file travels along with the EPS printer information file so that users can position the image in a different application. At print time, the low-resolution thumbnail image is replaced automatically by the high-quality image that is rasterized from the EPS PostScript code.

An Encapsulated PostScript image can be rasterized through the printer to get hard copy, or to a screen and image file by opening an EPS or AI image in Photoshop. See Chapter 20, "Mixed Media and Photoshop," for more information on working with the EPS file format. The EPS format for images is an instruction set—the architecture for building an image—and for this reason, it is called a *device-independent* image format. EPS files are good for physical output, and you can work with them in both vector and bitmap imaging programs, across both the Macintosh and PC platforms.

Placing a Duotone in a Desktop Publishing Document

PageMaker was chosen as the application that receives the exported VANILLA.EPS image file because PageMaker understands the short PANTONE names contained in the EPS image information. You need to specify short PANTONE names before exporting an image that uses a PANTONE color as a part of the image. If you look back to Chapter 4, "Photoshop Defaults and Options," you'll see that using Short

PANTONE Names is an option set in General Preferences (press Ctrl (Cmd)+K to get there) in the More Preferences dialog box. This is the only way to ensure that an application that speaks PANTONE can read the correct color.

Tip

If you want to use an application that can't understand the PANTONE naming system as the host for a duotone, you must choose (in the Duotone options box) a name the other application can understand and send to the printer as PostScript information for the color.

This PANTONE 349 P color, for example, is a shade of green. If you typed **Green** as the name for this color in the Duotones Options box, most other applications would recognize the information in the EPS file and send their interpretation of what green looks like when the application sends your file to the color printer.

You won't get *exactly* the same PANTONE color you specified when you created the duotone in Photoshop, but the duotone *will* print from another, PANTONE short-name-"unaware" application.

For figure 24.13, we created a PageMaker document that calls for the sort of subject matter VANILLA.EPS suggests. PageMaker will print to a color printer, as well as perform color separations from which a commercial printer can run the press. You lose control over further refinements to an image when you export it to an application that features no image-editing tools, but the printed color image will look just the way it did when you saved it—all within the context of another document. As you can see, PageMaker's color palette, generally used for specifying its own native text and borders, registers the short PANTONE names as the same ones you specified in Photoshop.

Printing Duotone Separations

If you have a color PostScript printer that provides PANTONE capabilities, you can print separations of a duotone image directly from Photoshop. The complete image can be printed only on a printing press. You don't need to (and shouldn't) convert the Duotone image to CMYK to print the separations. Converting to CMYK would convert the PANTONE custom colors to their CMYK equivalents, which are never as good as the original PANTONE color. Instead, choose **P**rint from the **F**ile menu, and a Print Sepa_r_ations check box appears on the Print dialog box. Leave the box checked and click on OK to print the separations.

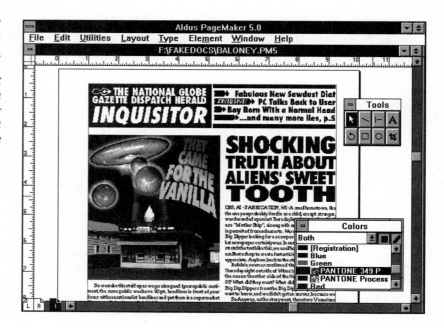

Producing Spot Color

Except for duotones, Photoshop does not support the printing of spot-color separations. When you specify a PANTONE, TRUEMATCH, or other custom color, Photoshop translates the spot-color specifications into CMYK or RGB equivalent component color values. This is not accurate enough for corporate logo work or other color-critical work; however, you can work around this problem.

You can use Photoshop's rule that only visible layers or channels will print (what you see onscreen when you issue the Print command) to your advantage.

1. Put the elements that contain a specific spot color on their own layer. When you've finished, your design and all the layers should be in the proper order.

2. Select all the elements on a layer where you've put spot color elements. Save the selection. Click on the Alpha channel that contains the selection. Make sure that the areas that represent the areas that are selected are in Black; if they are not, choose **M**ap from the **I**mage menu, and then choose **I**nvert (Ctrl(Cmd)+I).

3. Choose **P**rint from the **F**ile menu, and print the image as grayscale. This is your separation for that spot color.

4. Go back to the image and load the selection that contains the spot color information and delete the contents of the selected area to either transparent (on a layer), or white on the Background layer, on all the layers that are beneath the spot color layer. This process *knocks out* the area that will be filled with the custom spot color in the finished design.

5. Deselect all selections (press Ctrl (Cmd)+D), make sure the color composite channel is the selected one and that you've hidden or deleted the spot color layers, and then print your CMYK separations. The four CMYK separations along with the spot-color separations you printed earlier make up the complete image.

The disadvantage of "tricking" Photoshop into producing spot-color separations is that it does not give you precise control over trapping. *Trapping* is when you slightly overlap different colored elements to prevent a white gap when the registration of the press is not perfect. These measurements usually are specified in thousandths of an inch. The best you can do is use the Expand or Contract feature to enlarge (*spread*) or reduce (*choke*) the areas that you knock out by a pixel or two. Pixel sizes change depending on your resolution, so making the calculations isn't easy. You will have to talk to your printer to find out by how much you should enlarge or reduce. You might be better off having your service bureau trap the image for you using special software or traditional methods. Talk to them and see what services they can offer in this area. Also, producing separations with this method means that your job is less portable, because the printing of the spot-color separations must be done in Photoshop.

Working with CMYK images

If the intended output for your Photoshop work is a four-color printing press, you'll need to work with images that use the CMYK (Cyan, Magenta, Yellow, Black) color mode. This color model uses four color channels to produce the colors that can be printed on a printing press. The gamut of colors is much more limited than that available when working in the RGB mode. This is because the RGB color model works with light, which has additive color properties. When different wavelengths of light are mixed, they form a color that is perceived as being a new color of light. CMYK, which is a subtractive color model, is based on the nature of pigments, which display their color by *reflecting* specific wavelengths of light. Red paint looks red, for example, because white light (which is made of a combination of all wavelengths or colors) shines on the paint, and all the wavelengths of light *except* red are absorbed by the pigments in the paint. The red wavelengths of light are reflected. We see the red reflected light and perceive the object that reflects the light as being red. The capability of substances that can be used as inks to selectively absorb and reflect specific wavelengths of light is limited, which in turn produces a smaller range of colors that can be expressed in the RGB color model.

When the three process colors—cyan, magenta, and yellow—are mixed, they produce other colors. When the colors are mixed in equal proportions, black should be produced; however, because of the impurities in ink pigments, perfect black (absorption of all light) is not achieved. An additional black color plate is used to apply black ink in order to circumvent this problem. A black separation plate usually is made from the weighted average of the three other color plates used to produce CMYK process color images.

Because the monitor you use to display your work uses a different color model, you can never truly see what a CMYK color image looks like on-screen. What you see is a *translation* of CMYK values to RGB. Cyan, for example, has color wavelength characteristics that cannot be displayed accurately on an RGB monitor. Because of this, and because the extra channel that the CMYK model uses creates much larger files, most image editing is done using the RGB color model. When editing is completed, the image then is converted to the CMYK model. When color separations for printing are made, all the information in each of the four color channels is printed as a separate grayscale image. These four grayscale images then are used to produce the four printing plates used on the printing press.

Using the Gamut Warning Feature

It is very easy to specify colors when working in RGB that can't be faithfully reproduced in the CMYK model. These colors are said to be *out of gamut*. Happily, Photoshop provides you with several ways to identify and correct out-of-gamut colors. In Chapter 20, "Mixed Media and Photoshop," you saw how to specify colors that were CMYK "legal." You also saw how you can use the Color Picker, the Picker palette, and the Info palette to identify a color that is out of gamut. But what if the image you are using already contains many out-of-gamut colors? How do you find and correct each pixel? You use Photoshop's new Gamut **W**arning feature found on the **M**ode menu.

In the following exercise, you use Photoshop Gamut Warning to identify any colors in the STATUE.PSD image that can't be converted faithfully to a CMYK color formulation.

Displaying Out-of-Gamut Colors

Open the STATUE.PSD image from the CHAP24 subdirectory (folder) on the Bonus CD

This is the image you'll work with.

Press Ctrl (Cmd)+ + and click on the bottom of the image window while dragging it to display the entire image on-screen

Sets the viewing resolution and window size so that you can see the entire image as large as possible.

Choose **M**ode, Gamut **W**arning

Suddenly the trees and part of the grass have spots of flat color all over them (see fig. 24.14). These specks mark the colors that are out of gamut.

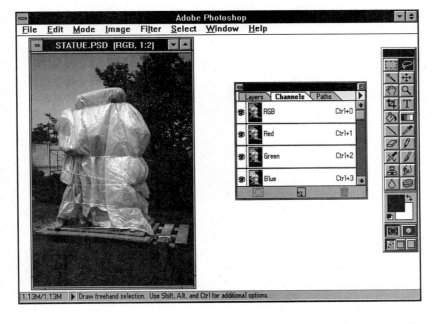

Figure 24.14

The specks of light, flat color in the trees and in the grass mark out-of-gamut colors.

You set the color used to mark out-of-gamut colors by choosing Pre**f**erences from the **F**ile menu, and then choosing Gamut **W**arning. If you haven't changed this color from its default of gray, do so now because the gray doesn't show well and can be confused with the specks of sky that are visible in the trees. When the Gamut Warning Preference dialog box is displayed, click on the color swatch to the left. Choose a new color (bright purple or yellow is good; so is pure white) with the Color Picker and click on OK until you are returned to the image. (See Chapter 4, "Photoshop Defaults and Options," for more information on setting preferences.)

You'll notice that most of these specks cover green colors. To correct this problem, you need to change these colors to similar colors that are CMYK-legal. That job is most easily and precisely accomplished by using the new Selective Color command. This is the same command you used in Chapter 22, "Virtual Reality: The Ingredients of Dreamwork," when you made color enhancements to the circuit board. That time, you used the Selective Color command in an unusual way. In the next exercise, you use the command in a more conventional way—to bring colors back into gamut.

Bringing Colors Back into Gamut

With the STATUE.PSD image the active image, and with the Gamut Warning Preferences dialog box still displayed, follow these steps:

Choose **I**mage, **A**djust, **S**elective Color	Displays the Selective Color dialog box.
Choose Greens from the Colors drop-down list; make sure that the Preview box is checked	Changes made by adjusting CMYK values will affect only the Green pixels in the image and changes will appear in the image window.
Click on the **A**bsolute radio button	Instructs Photoshop to add or subtract the percentage of each CMYK color you specify with the sliders from the percentage of the CMYK colors that make up the green pixels.

Move the sliders around. Notice how the gamut warning in the image window changes when you add or subtract color from the green pixels. Also notice that all the greens in the image do change color. Keep moving the sliders around until all the out-of-gamut warning specks go away *and* you still have a pleasing amount of green color onscreen. The authors found that values of **–31%** for **C**yan, **+17%** for **M**agenta, **–14%** for **Y**ellow, and **–34%** for **B**lack gave good results (see fig. 24.15). When you have found a workable and pleasing set of entries, continue with the following steps:

Click on OK	Photoshop applies the changes, and all your colors are now in gamut for printing CMYK color separations.
Choose Sa**v**e As from the **F**ile menu and save the image to your hard disk using the same name and file type (PSD)	Saves your work up to this point.

Many times, when colors are brought back into gamut, the image becomes dull looking. If you've installed the Kai's Power Tools sampler from the Bonus CD, you have a powerful CMYK pre-press filter at your disposal. The Sharpen Intensity filter will remove what appears to be a dull film covering the image *without* moving any colors out of gamut. And that's a pretty neat trick!

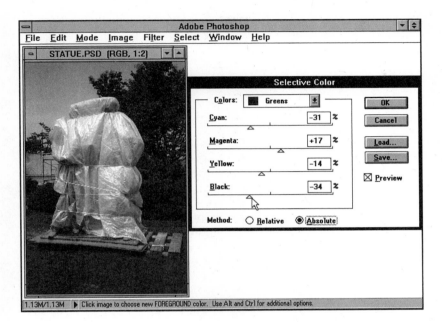

Figure 24.15

Use the Gamut Warning and the Selective Color command to bring colors back into gamut for CMYK color separations.

Install KPT's Sharpen Intensity filter if you haven't done so already (see Chapter 20, "Mixed Media and Photoshop," for directions). You see in the following exercise how a filter can improve this image dramatically and still keep all the colors within the CMYK gamut.

Removing the Dullness from an Image

With the Sharpen Intensity filter installed, and with the STATUE.PSD image you saved in the last exercise open, follow these steps:

Press and continue to hold the 2 key on the keypad while you choose Filter, KPT 2.0 Filters, and Sharpen Intensity from the menu

Holding down the 2 key applies a small amount of the effect, but enough to produce a dramatic improvement.

As with most of the KPT filters, holding down a number on the keypad controls the strength at which a filter is applied. Holding down any key from 1 to 9 produces increasingly strong effects. The zero key applies the greatest effect.

If you were too busy holding keys and mousing your way through menus to see the effect, press Ctrl (Cmd)+Z

Undoes and reapplies the effect. Undo is a toggling function.

continues

continued

(or choose Undo from the <u>E</u>dit menu). Press Ctrl (Cmd)+Z again to see the effect the filter made	
Press Ctrl (Cmd)+S or choose <u>S</u>ave from the <u>F</u>ile menu	Saves your work up to this point.

Converting RGB Images to CMYK

Converting an RGB image to CMYK is simple to do; choose <u>C</u>MYK Color from the <u>M</u>ode menu. But if that was all there was to it, it wouldn't deserve its own section. As you might remember from Chapter 4, "Photoshop Defaults and Options," you learned about the importance of calibrating your monitor. This process is important because Photoshop uses the RGB values it finds in your image and builds equivalency tables that convert RGB colors to the appropriate CMYK formulations. If your monitor is not calibrated properly, you won't get what you expect when your image rolls off the presses.

But monitor calibration is not the only factor that goes into the calculations that are used to accurately convert RGB values into CMYK values. Photoshop also considers the settings you made in the Printing <u>I</u>nks Setup and the <u>S</u>eparation Setup dialog boxes found on the <u>F</u>ile, Pre<u>f</u>erences menu (see figs. 24.16 and 24.17).

We won't tell you what you should set the values to in these dialog boxes. It's not that we're holding out on you, but rather that the only person who can tell you what they should be is the commercial printer on whose presses this particular image will be printed. All these values depend on the kinds of paper, ink, and printing press that are used. The choices you make in the Separation Setup dialog box require you to know which method—GCR or UCR—the printer plans to use, and what the settings for each should be. *GCR (Gray Component Removal)* and *UCR (Undercolor Removal)* are strategies that printers use to reduce the amount of process colors used in areas that are neutral or black, and replace them with black ink. This is done to prevent muddiness and prevents more ink from being applied in one area than can be absorbed by the paper. In the Printing Inks Setup dialog box, there is a huge laundry list of different kinds of paper and printers. Additionally, Photoshop compensates for the percentage of *expected dot gain*—the amount of spread a dot of ink will take on when applied and absorbed into the paper fibers.

Never guess about these settings, and don't waste your time and money converting RGB images to CMYK and then printing separations unless you have thoroughly discussed these settings with the commercial printer.

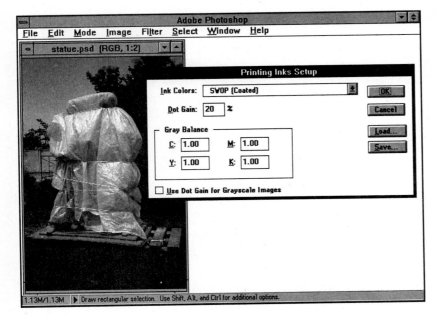

Figure 24.16

The Printing Inks Setup dialog box. Never, never guess at what these values should be.

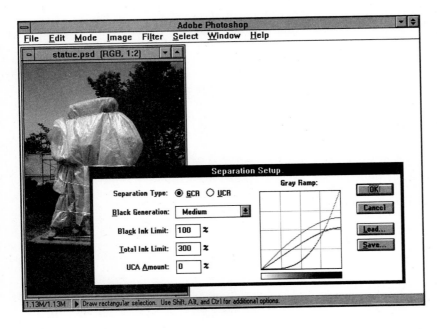

Figure 24.17

The Separation Setup dialog box. Don't guess with these values either!

Stop   If you change any of these pre-press settings, *including* Monitor Calibration settings after you've converted an image to CMYK, you will have to throw out the image and create a new one from a saved RGB copy of the image. You should *never* convert a RGB image to CMYK and then convert it back. You will lose a great deal of color information, because the CMYK color gamut is smaller than the RGB color gamut. Once the color information has been converted to CMYK, it can't be returned to its original RGB values, and you are stuck with CMYK colors.

Always make a copy of an RGB image and convert the copy to CMYK. Then, if you have to make adjustments you still have the original RGB image from which a new CMYK file can be created.

Now we come back to the subject of this section: how to convert an RGB image into a CMYK image if you have all the Preference settings correctly made. It involves only two steps: Choose Sa**v**e As from the **F**ile menu and save your image to your hard disk under a new name. Then choose **C**MYK Color from the **M**ode menu.

Printing Color Separations

When you have a properly-made CMYK image before you, you can print color separations if you know exactly what printer settings to make. These settings were described in the personal color printing section "Using the Page Setup Dialog Box" earlier in this chapter. To make a perfect CMYK file, you need to have long conversations with your commercial printer. To print color separations, you need to know everything there is to know about the printer that will be used to create the separations. Most likely, if you are going to the expense of printing the image to a commercial color printing press, you will need better resolution than any printer you own. You need the services of an imagesetter. Imagesetters have resolutions that span the range from 1200 dpi to more than 3000 dpi, and can cost up to $500,000.

If you are having a service bureau print the separations to paper or film, just give them the CMYK file and let them set it up for their imagesetter. Make sure that they know who the commercial printer for this project is and encourage them to discuss the job with the commercial printer if they have any questions. You are expected to supply at least the following amount of standard information about the commercial printer's requirements:

◆ Whether the image should be negative or positive

◆ Whether the image should be imaged emulsion up or down

◆ The optimal screen frequency for the printing press, the paper, and the inks that will be used

◆ The shape of halftone dots that should be used, and the screen angles for the plates that the commercial printer finds works best with the printing press

◆ The expected dot gain on the press

If, by chance, you have a PostScript printer that you want to use to create the color separations, you would make these settings—along with settings for crop marks, registration marks, and calibration bars—for your printer in the Page Setup dialog box as discussed earlier in this chapter. Because you probably will be printing to paper and not photographic film, you leave the Negative and Emulsion Down option unchecked. Then you choose Print from the File menu and enter the necessary print quality value. Click on the Print Separations check box (see fig. 24.18). Click on OK, and four grayscale prints come tumbling out of your printer. These paper print separations can be used as camera-ready separations by the printer from which to make the printing plates.

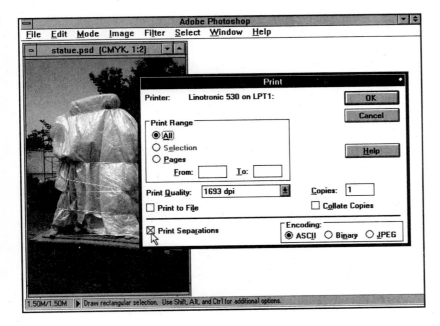

Figure 24.18

The Print dialog box provides a Print Separations check box when an image is in the CMYK color mode.

Deciding Whether To Do Your Own Color Separations

You now know that Photoshop has the *capability* to generate color separations from an image. This means that the cyan, magenta, yellow, and black plates a commercial printer runs on a press can be made from laser camera-ready art you can provide. But just because Photoshop gives you the tools to generate the separations *doesn't* mean that you necessarily want to do this, or should do this.

Besides being the application of choice for artists on both the Mac and PC platforms, Photoshop is a magnificent tool for commercial printing houses to use in their work. Many copies of this program are used in production departments, service bureaus, and advertising agencies because the *other* half of creating an image is *printing* an image. And Photoshop has features to do both.

But color printing is a science, and as such, it is best left to professionals. For this reason, we recommend that artists and designers do *not* use the bulk of Photoshop's color pre-press features. Let the people who know best about the medium of *publishing* handle your work. You might go through two or three commercial printers or service bureaus before you settle on one that you can work with who understands the style or look you want to convey in an image. You will learn much working with a good pre-press service bureau or printer, but making a career of printing dots of ink precisely on a page easily could take you as long as it's already taken these professionals.

A good commercial printer or service bureau wise in the ways of Adobe Photoshop can guide you and your work through the world of process printing. They can show you how to make duotones out of grayscale mode images. And only they know the best line screens, ink coverage, dot-gain settings, and emulsion placement needed to yield optimal results with the presses and the papers used to bring your work to life.

Knowing When Not To Create Color Separations

It might seem strange to encounter the following thought in a "computer" book, but using digital files from start to finish is not always the best way to ensure a cost-effective, quality product. Rendering many high-quality photographic images within a multipage document layout takes a long time; more specifically, it takes an *expensive* long time. A desktop publishing document file with even a half-dozen, high-quality RGB images placed within it gets very large and becomes a pain to transport—and even harder for an imagesetter to print! Some files, particularly if they contain large bitmaps or complex, vector graphic files, might fail to print to the imagesetter. So, your quest for hard copy from digital images still requires the assistance from some outside, physical traditional methods on occasion, and common sense and alternative routes to a goal should also be part of your imaging expertise.

Many magazines prevent production bottlenecks due to enormous digital image sizes by adopting the following procedure:

◆ Use Photoshop to create and/or edit an image digitally.

◆ Send the digital image to an imaging center's film recorder to be made into a traditional photographic negative (35mm, 4×5, or 8×10). See Chapter 25, "The Film Recorder," for more information on this fascinating aspect of imaging.

◆ Send the text and layout of the document to a pre-press service bureau's imagesetter to have film made.

◆ Take all the film to any printer and have the job processed using traditional separating, screening, and stripping methods.

Although the above process sounds costly, it actually can be less expensive and quicker than tying up the services of an imagesetter for hours on end. A good technician can *hand-strip* (piece together several negatives that are used as one) many images in an hour, and can see immediately whether there is a problem with an image.

This doesn't mean that you should never produce an assignment from beginning to end using digital tools. On the contrary; the *bulk* of designers' and photographers' work these days exists from start to finish within the digital medium. So how do you know when to choose one approach over another? Before you start an assignment, talk to your service bureau. Then talk to your printer. Have your service bureau and your printer talk to each other. Ask them to help you evaluate the components of an assignment and develop the output strategy that will produce the best results for your time frame, your budget, and the intended use of the finished piece. And let this talking occur *before* you modify one pixel of a design's elements.

When you know how the assignment will be completed after it leaves your hands, you can plan your work (file size, color capability, resolution, and so on) in a way that ensures the best possible finished output.

Schemes for Getting an Image out the Door

Most of the image files on the Bonus CD are "lightweights" in terms of file size. A grayscale image with a 300-dpi resolution will print beautifully from a 2540-dpi imagesetter, using a line-screen value of 133 lpi to 150 lpi. This is magazine quality. But an 8 1/2-by-11-inch grayscale image, which is not an uncommon size for magazines, takes up more than 8 MB of file space!

As you gain experience with Photoshop, you will become more ambitious—which means higher-resolution images, RGB images, and files that can't possibly fit on a floppy disk!

So how do you get your images out the door and down the street to the commercial printer? There are several ways, as you discover in the next few sections.

JPEG Compression

You learned in Chapter 2, "Acquiring a Digital Image," that JPEG is a lossy compression scheme, and that this compression affects color work. A quick refresher: Photoshop gives you the option to save RGB, CMYK, and Grayscale images in the JPEG format. JPEG can compress the file size of an image from anywhere from 5:1 to 100:1, depending on the composition in the image and how much compression you specify in Photoshop. JPEG technology compresses the file by averaging almost imperceptible neighboring pixel-color differences in a color image.

Although the purist in most artists shuns the idea of removing information from a piece of work, JPEG is becoming a preferred file format for many service bureaus and commercial printers. JPEG files are easier for printers and service bureaus to handle; their small file sizes fit comfortably on a floppy disk, they transfer quickly from your media (floppy, tape, removable drive) to a network's hard disk, and they don't take up much space on the commercial printer's hard disk.

Most graphic software today directly supports JPEG files. Because JPEG images decompress when loaded into system RAM, you (or your commercial printer) don't have to own or run a separate decompression utility. Saving files and transporting them as JPEG images cannot only relieve an overcrowded hard drive, but also can give you a chance to place large, high-resolution images onto a floppy disk!

The next exercise shows you how to use JPEG on an oversized file, but don't think that you're missing out on a Photoshop feature if you don't participate. In its present state, HUGEFILE, a 3.25 MB RGB image on the Bonus CD obviously won't fit on a 3 1/2-inch, high-density disk. And if this were an image *you* created, you would need at least 10 MB (15 MB recommended) of free system RAM and an equally healthy amount of *virtual* memory space on your hard drive to work quickly and comfortably with this file. This requirement is necessary because Photoshop needs multiple copies of the same image loaded into memory to calculate effects you might apply to it.

For this reason, some of you might decide to sit out this next exercise. But if you're up to the challenge, here's one way to make a large image file portable.

JPEG Squeezing Your Image

Open the HUGEFILE.TIF image from the CHAP24 subdirectory (folder) on the Bonus CD

Produces the 3.25 MB image you'll work with.

New Riders Publishing
INSIDE
SERIES

Press Ctrl (Cmd)+S or choose Sa**v**e As from the **F**ile menu	Displays Photoshop's Save As dialog box.
Choose JPEG (*.JPG) as Save File As Format **T**ype from the drop-down list, select a Dri**v**e and **D**irectory that has some room on your hard drive, keep the File **N**ame as HUGEFILE.JPG, and click on OK	Displays the JPEG Options dialog box.
Click on the Maximum radio button in the Image Quality field of the JPEG Options dialog box	Saves HUGEFILE image as a JPEG with the least amount of image loss, and therefore the least amount of compression (see fig. 24.19).
Click on OK	Saves HUGEFILE.JPG to the directory you specified.

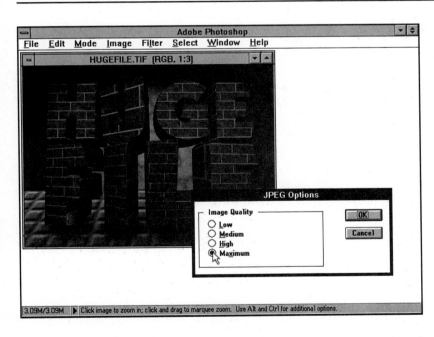

Figure 24.19

*JPEG quality ranges from **L**ow (best compression) to Ma**x**imum (least amount of compression).*

If you followed the preceding exercise, you should close Photoshop for the moment and check the file size of HUGEFILE.JPG from Windows Program Manager or the Macintosh List View using Finder. You'll see that using the Maximum Image Quality setting for the on-disk file size reduced the size from 3.2 MB to only 295 KB. If you had picked **H**igh, the file would be 173 KB; **M**edium (which is Photoshop's default setting) would yield a 97 KB image. The JPEG file size you get from different images with the same initial file size varies according to differences in the visual complexity of the images. The more detail and the more abrupt the changes of color in an image, the less compression and the larger the on-disk file size for an image that's been JPEGged.

Because you picked the JPEG format for HUGEFILE in the last exercise, the high-quality image now fits on a floppy disk and is transported easily. Commercial printers, service bureaus, clients, friends who own Photoshop, or any number of other software applications that understand the JPEG compression scheme can open the file and use it.

Note   The image-mode formats that support color channels, RGB, CMYK, and the Grayscale mode can be compressed and saved as JPEG files. Indexed images, Bitmap, MultiChannel, and LAB modes can't be compressed and saved as JPEG files, due to their unique organization of color within a file format.

If you have an indexed image with a file size larger than will fit on a floppy, you might try converting the indexed image to RGB mode in Photoshop, and then saving it as a JPEG. The converted image scales down in file size exactly like a native RGB image. When the JPEG image then is read into memory on a commercial printer's system, the image will take longer to print than you might expect because the printer will have to read and process a much larger file. The RGB image format has a higher color capability than indexed color, and the structure of the image type is necessarily larger than an image saved in an indexed color file format. For this reason, you might decide to convert the image back to indexed once again when your image file on floppy has reached its destination.

However, you usually will be able to reduce the amount of disk space that an indexed image occupies more if you use one of the popular archiving and compression programs like PKZIP (for DOS/Windows), or StuffIt or Compact Pro (both for Macintosh). Before using one of these compression programs, make sure that whoever you give the file to also has the program you used to compress the file so that they can decompress it. See the next section for more information on how these archiving/compression programs work.

Because results vary from image to image, try both methods and see which one reduces the on-disk file size the most.

Trying both methods takes some time and effort on your part, but an image can't be printed at all if you can't get it out the door to the presses!

If lossy compression simply isn't your style, you always can use loss*less* compression to make a large file portable. PKZIP and CompactPro are shareware programs found on the Bonus CD that can be used to losslessly compress your image files. The following

section explains how a somewhat more complicated compression scheme can ensure that every pixel in your image is in place when you arrive at the commercial printer.

File-Compression Programs

The one thing that practically everybody needs is more hard disk space. Hard disks are like closets—no one has an empty one. To maximize the use of hard disk space, a number of programs have been written that compress files. A compressed file can't be used in its compressed state, but it is easy to restore it to its original size when you need it. The most widely used compression programs are marketed as shareware, which is the "try it before you buy it" philosophy. PKZIP, developed by Phil Katz, is the most widely used compression program among PC users. DropStuff (compressor) and StuffIt (decompressor) by Aladdin Systems, and CompactPro by Bill Goodman at Cyclos, are the compression programs most favored by Macintosh users. PKZIP and CompactPro are found on the Bonus CD.

If you've used online services or BBSs where file compression is necessary to reduce modem transmission time, you might be familiar with these compression programs. Unlike the JPEG image format, PKZIP, StuffIt, and CompactPro don't perform their compression on-the-fly. A compressed file can't be read until it's decompressed. None of these compression programs offer as dramatic a reduction in file size as JPEG does, but you don't lose any image information by using them. Your file has complete integrity when you "ZIP" it, "StuffIt," or "Compact" it.

Traditionally, when short file names (DOS names such as FILENAME.DOS) are used to name a file that has been compressed with PKZIP, the file name has a ZIP file extension. StuffIt files have the SIT extension and Compact Pro files have the CPT extension. Use these extensions when you share your work with others so they will know what file-compression program to use to *de*compress the files.

Macintosh users can create ZIP files with a program written by Tommy Brown called *ZIPIT*. This comes in very handy when a Macintosh user needs to give a compressed file to a PC user. ZIPIT also can be used on a Macintosh to unzip (decompress) a file that a PC user has compressed using PKZIP. You don't have to scour the BBSs and online services to find a copy of this gem, because ZIPIT can be found in the ZIPIT folder on the Bonus CD that came with this book.

Unfortunately, PC users don't have any way to create or decompress StuffIt or CompactPro files. So if Macintosh and PC-based folks are going to exchange compressed files, the files must be in the ZIP format.

Perhaps the nicest thing about PKZIP and CompactPro is their capability to *span* disks. A single file that is larger than the capacity of a 1.44 MB floppy disk safely can be broken into pieces onto separate floppies and transported. When you take an image that has been spanned to a commercial printer or service bureau, they use

PKUNZIP or CompactPro to read the disks and to restore the information back into a single image file on hard disk. This is a great way to get a file onto disks, but make sure that you check with the printer or service bureau to see whether they have the appropriate software (PKUNZIP for PC files and CompactPro for Macintosh files) *and* if they are willing to take the time to restore the file. ZipIt can't create or restore spanned ZIPped files, so you have to be sure that the printer or service bureau can handle the file you give them.

Because PKZIP is a program that still runs in DOS, it uses a command-line interface—you type commands to make it work. It's a great and powerful program, but it lacks a graphical interface that provides the convenience of drag-and-drop, toolbars, menus, and icons that Windows users are accustomed to using. Most find the command-line interface rather intimidating and just plain difficult to use. But another shareware program found in the Bonus CD's SHAREWARE subdirectory makes the process of working with PKZIP as graphical and as hassle-free as one could imagine. WinZip, by Niko-Mak, is a ZIP "shell" that makes program calls to PKZIP directly from the Windows environment. PKZIP is a DOS-based utility, and WinZip addresses the Windows-oriented user's need to work completely within the Windows environment. WinZip is particularly invaluable when it comes to using PKZIP to span a large file across several floppy disks.

In the next exercise, you see how to use WinZip and PKZIP together to span the HUGEFILE image across several floppies. Although HUGEFILE is used here as the example, feel free to experiment with an oversized image of your own. PKZIP is risk-free. It uses a *copy* of your original for the compressed version of your image. Before you begin, the PKZIP and WinZip programs must be installed on your hard disk. To do this, look at the documentation that accompanies each program in its own subdirectory.

Spanning and Zipping a Large Image File

Have two formatted 1.44 MB disks handy	The floppies needed to hold the HUGEFILE.TIF image you ZIP in this exercise. Have more handy if you decide to experiment with a file larger than HUGEFILE.
From Windows Program Manager, double-click on the WinZip icon	Launches WinZip. (WinZip creates an icon in a program group of your choice when you install it.)

Insert a 1.44 MB disk into your floppy drive

This exercise assumes that drive B is your 3 1/2-inch drive; if not, substitute A for B throughout the exercise.

Click on the New button

Displays the New Archive dialog box.

Choose your drive B from the **D**irectories list

Specifies 3 1/2-inch floppy drive as target for the zipped, spanned file you create.

Type **HUGEFILE.ZIP** in the Archive **N**ame text box, and check the **A**dd Dialog check box

Name for file PKZIP copies from original (see fig. 24.20).

Click on OK

Displays the **A**dd Dialog box.

Choose **C**ompression: Fast, **M**ultiple Disk Spanning: No format, and then select the HUGEFILE image from the Sel**e**ct Files list box (see fig. 24.21)

Sets compression with speed more important than compression rate; no format because floppies already are formatted.

Click on OK

PKZIP compresses the HUGEFILE image to the floppy disk.

When a DOS window pops up over WinZip, remove the first disk, place the second one in your hard drive, and press Enter

You instruct PKZIP (from a DOS window) that the second disk is ready to be written to.

Choose **E**xit from the **F**ile menu (or press Alt+F4) when a screen similar to that in figure 24.22 is displayed

After WinZip finishes using PKZIP, the file is compressed and spanned to floppy disks; WinZip displays specifics on how compression went.

Figure 24.20

A file with a ZIP extension is a compressed copy of the original. (It can have the same eight-character name as the original.)

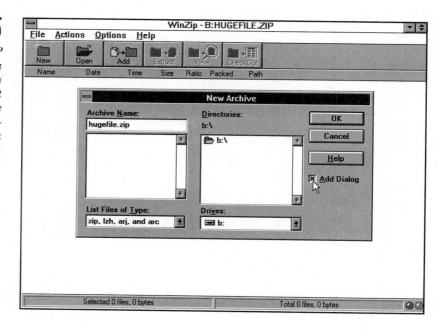

Figure 24.21

ZIP-type compression can be done on a single file over multiple floppy disks.

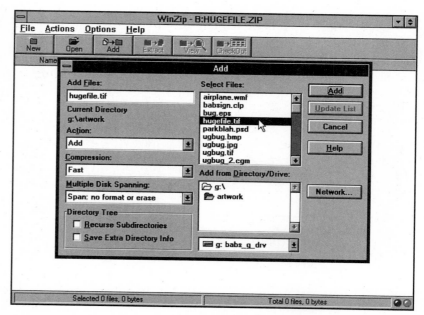

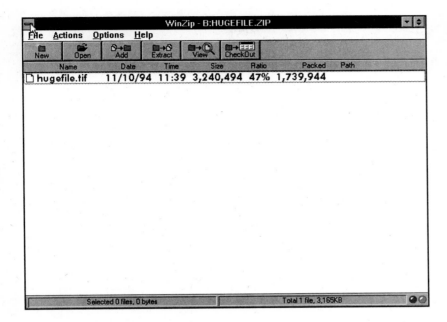

Figure 24.22

WinZip gives a report of each compressing session.

Before taking the spanned disks to your printer, double-check to make sure that they have PKZIP (version 204g or later), or they won't be able to put the image back together.

The capability of PKZIP to span floppy disks means that compression is not of tantamount concern. You can get away with a minimum of compression which, in fact, makes the process of creating and restoring the image, or images, much faster.

Note Some file types, like Kodak's PCD PhotoCD image, already are compressed in their native format. Don't use compression when you ZIP (or Compact) these types of files; they simply won't squish more than the way they're already written. In fact, because file archiving and compression software creates a header that tells how to decompress the file created, a file that already is compressed (a PCD file or a JPEG format file, for example) actually becomes *larger* than the original because this header information is added to it.

In such a case, you want to set the Spanning option for your file(s) and specify None as the compression type when using WinZip or CompactPro.

Large-Format Removable Media

You can use more exotic forms of transporting your digital images to a commercial printer. Large-format, removable media comes in a wide range of formats from a variety of manufacturers. SyQuest, Bernoulli, and MO (magneto-optical) cartridges; floptical disks; and DAT and QIC 40 or 80 tapes can hold anywhere from 21 MB to more than a gigabyte of image data, depending on which media you use. They are ideal for moving large amounts of data.

The catch with these drives is that each kind of removable media drive usually reads only media produced on a similar or identical drive. If you have a large-format, removable media drive, check with your printer or service bureau before making your copies to see whether they have a compatible model. If you are *thinking* of buying one of these devices, find out what kind of removable media your favorite printer or service bureau uses, and get one like theirs. It makes life much simpler.

 Note   What can you do when you or your printer or service bureau don't have a high-capacity, removable media drive; or theirs doesn't match yours; and floppies just aren't practical?

Send your hard drive to the printer. It's a pretty drastic move, and not one to be done on a whim. But if it's the only way to move tens of megabytes of image files, and your service bureau or commercial printer is capable (and willing to share some of the responsibility/liability), you can do it.

But before you pack up the hard drive, be sure you have a backup of the entire disk. You should never allow your only copy of anything to leave the premises.

Questions (and Answers) for the Commercial Printer

It's a foregone conclusion that if you want your commercial printer to image Photoshop files, the printer must have a computer. But does it have a PC or a Macintosh? Computer graphics began on the Macintosh four years before the Windows graphical interface and identical graphics applications were offered for IBM/PCs, and most commercial printers and service bureaus have Macintoshes. Many service bureaus, however, have since purchased PCs so they can work with both Macintosh and PC customers.

Photoshop's files and graphic files like TIF, EPS, and Targa are platform-independent, so it doesn't matter what kind of computer is used to create or read one of these file formats. What *is* a concern is the *media* the file is stored on. Macintoshes

and PCs write information to physical media (floppy disks, SyQuest cartridges, tape, and so on) differently. If the printer or service bureau can't read the disk or other media you've placed your images on, your files won't get processed.

Do They Have the Right Drive?

The IBM/Mac issue is not a problem if you are transporting your image on a PC formatted, single (non-spanned) 3 1/2-inch floppy disk. Macintoshes don't have 5 1/4-inch drives, and older Macs only read low-density, 3 1/2-inch disks. Any Macintosh with a SuperDrive can read 3 1/2-inch disks that are written to with an IBM/PC. If you are going the other way, for a Macintosh-formatted disk to be read by a PC, the PC will need special software to read the disk, such as Pacific Micro's Mac-In-DOS. Mac-In-DOS only works with high-density, 3 1/2-inch disks.

If you are using some of the other removable-media, mass-storage devices, such as SyQuest or Bernoulli cartridges, you might run into a stone wall. Unless the printer or service bureau has purchased additional software that enables them to mount (recognize) and read this kind of media, when it comes from an operating system other than the one the printer owns, you're stuck. Always check to see whether the printer or service bureau has the appropriate software and hardware to read your media if they use a different kind of computer than you do.

Does Your Printer Own Photoshop?

Even though TIF images are platform-independent, as you've seen throughout this book, Photoshop can do some pretty special things with them. Alpha channels and paths in a TIF image are *not* understood by some other imaging software applications. And no hard-and-fast rule exists as to which applications don't understand Alpha channels and paths because more and more software manufacturers are adopting the Alpha channel feature every day.

If your commercial printer owns Adobe Photoshop 3, either the Macintosh or the Windows version, you'll have no problem getting it to print an image file, regardless of what you've stuck in an Alpha channel. The reason is that Adobe has written Photoshop to both platforms with identical features and file compatibility in mind. If your printer has Photoshop 2.5, remember to check the 2.5 Compatibility check box in Photoshop's General Preferences settings before you save the copy of your file that you'll give to the printer. (See Chapter 4, "Photoshop Defaults and Options.")

You might have some problems if you take a TIF file you've enhanced using Photoshop to a printer that uses an imaging software application *other* than Photoshop. The printer's application might not be able to read Alpha channels—and your file won't make it to press. That's if you're *fortunate*. This other-than-Photoshop application *might crash* trying to read an Alpha channel, and your printer or service bureau is not likely to thank you for the experience. See Chapter 23, "Personal Printing Basics," for more information on the problems associated with other applications and Alpha channels.

As someone interested in creating computer graphics, you owe it to yourself to learn about every means available to make virtual images into real, physical images. There's a world outside the computer, filled with people who might not *use* computers. And printing is one way to bring your art to them.

25

The Film Recorder

A s you've discovered throughout this book, there is a close, strong relationship between bitmap graphics and traditional photographic images. *Bitmapped images* portray graphical information as light and dark areas of continuous tones that our eyes recognize as a picture. The photosensitive grain of film and photographic paper also portrays images as a wash of continuous tones. Many of the images you've worked with in this book, and many of the elements that comprise your own assignments, are traditional, photo-chemically-based photographs that have been digitized.

Remarkable news for the digital imagist—and the subject of this chapter—is that the conversion of photographic information to digital information is a two-way street. A device called a *film recorder* can take any image you've created or enhanced in Photoshop and faithfully render it to the familiar, aesthetically pleasing, and eminently practical medium of color film, as a film negative or transparency. No other rendering, or *rasterizing*, process can reproduce what you see on your screen more faithfully than film.

Unlike the scanner that brings images into Photoshop, you probably won't find this pixel-to-film wonder film recorder on your desktop; you will, however, find high-resolution film recorders at a special kind of service bureau, commonly called a *slide imaging service bureau,* or *imaging center.* Learning how to work with this type of service bureau should be high on your list of priorities, because there is no greater satisfaction for the professional designer or hobbyist than to hold in your hands a photograph of your Photoshop work.

In this chapter we'll look at the different kinds of output you can get from a film recorder, as well as how a film recorder operates. By understanding the principles behind a film recorder, you'll be able to prepare a digital image in Photoshop to produce the best results on photographic film.

What Film Recorder Output Is Used For

The most common film recorder found at an imaging center is one that renders digital images to 35mm film. Both the business user and the professional photographer take advantage of the film recorder's flexibility. Slides are the mainstay of business presentations today, whereas a photographer gets more mileage from a 35mm negative. Each of these needs is accommodated through the use of the same film recorder.

Larger-format output film recorders are also found in specialty imaging centers that handle 4×5-inch film, or 8×10-inch film. The 4×5-inch formats can be used to produce high-quality, poster-sized prints for high-quality color publishing and for the television industry. The 8×10 format is most commonly used to produce high-quality overhead transparencies for corporate and educational presentations. This format is also used to produce wall-size enlargements for trade shows, for motion picture industry special effects work, and to meet the demanding requirements of very high-end, color-critical publishing.

Examining the Components of a Film Recorder

A film recorder has three basic components: a *raster image processor* (RIP), a *cathode ray tube* (CRT), and a camera that is mounted in a special vibration-resistant housing. The RIP is the hardware (or software) component of the film recorder that interprets the image file and directs a light source that exposes the film in the camera. The light source, a CRT, is a small picture tube that looks a lot like a television set. The camera in a film recorder usually holds 35mm film, but some film recorders are designed for the larger formats of 4×5-inch film or 8×10-inch film.

The Purpose of a RIP

Your image file (usually in a TIF or TGA format), is sent to a film recorder for processing by the film recorder's RIP. RIPs can be hardware based, software based, or a combination of the two. The RIP is the "brains" of a film recorder, and can be thought of as a supersophisticated combination of a conversion program and a printer driver.

The RIP's job is to convert the information that describes your image into machine-specific instructions a particular make and model of film recorder can understand. These instructions are used to direct the display of light, emanating from the CRT tube, that exposes the film. The RIP processes your image file in two steps: first, the RIP converts the image file to a PostScript language file, then the language file is converted into the machine instruction language. Additionally, the RIP is in charge of resizing an image, as well as other tasks such as rotating an image to ensure quality film rendering.

The Light Source—a CRT

The CRT in a film recorder is black and white. To produce a color image on the film, the CRT must expose the film loaded in the camera in three separate passes, each time with a different color filter in front of the CRT. The CRT filters are red, green, and blue, and their use corresponds directly to the red, green, and blue color channel information in your image file. Like Photoshop, the film recorder uses the RGB color model to create color. The information displayed on the CRT when the red filter is in place, for instance, is the information that comes from an image file's red channel.

You might expect that the CRT would display the entire image at once, as your monitor does when you click on a channel view of an image. This is not the case, however; the CRT flashes each pixel on its screen in succession, line by line, moving from left to right. If you were to watch a film recorder CRT in action, you'd never see your image drawn on-screen. What you *would* see is analogous to thousands of flash bulbs going off in an orderly, choreographed succession.

Developing the Film

After the film has been exposed, it is removed from the film recorder and developed using the same chemicals and steps required to finish film that is exposed through the lens system of a conventional camera. Many centers offer 24-hour turnaround times for slide imaging (other formats may take longer), so it doesn't take long until you see the fruits of your work.

Transferring a Photoshop Image to Film

Before you start packing up images to take advantage of the digital-to-film experience, you need to explore some of the finer points of working with film and the imaging center. To ensure that your Photoshop-to-film work looks every byte as good as it does on your monitor, you need to understand the special requirements a film recorder has for the data it rasterizes—preferred file formats, data types, aspect ratios, monitor settings, and the size of your file. These are universal considerations, regardless of the type of film recorder output you need. This chapter shows you how each of these digital issues can affect your work, pleasantly or otherwise, by focusing on the most popular product of a slide imaging center: the 35mm slide.

Your Monitor's Setup

Both your monitor and a film recorder use an RGB color model. When you save a Photoshop file in a 24-bit RGB file format, such as TIFF or Targa, every color used in the file has been described in terms of its red, green, and blue values. The film recorder reads these values to determine how to expose the film. If your monitor is properly calibrated, the colors you see on-screen will be represented accurately on the slide. If your monitor is *not* properly calibrated, you might get orange instead of gold, and purple where you wanted blue, in the finished piece of film.

The best insurance against this potential problem is to calibrate your monitor as described in Chapter 4, "Photoshop Defaults and Options." An additional measure you can take to ensure consistency between a monitor and the colors you see in the slide is to use a PANTONE or other color-matching swatch book. Pick the Custom option on Photoshop's Color Picker dialog box, choose the PANTONE color you want to compare to the physical swatch, then fill an area on your screen with the color. Hold the physical PANTONE swatch (with the same number as the on-screen PANTONE color) up to the monitor to see how well they match. The match will not be perfect—colored light can never perfectly represent opaque ink on paper. But if the colors are way off, you need to recalibrate your monitor to match the swatch book.

Color-matching is a sport to be engaged in by every individual who cares about accurate output, but it's also a game you can never declare a decisive "win" by playing. Every output medium varies in its color-display capability, and how closely colors match between different media depends as much on viewer aesthetics as technology. A monitor, a television set, film, press ink on paper, the *same* ink on *different* paper, and different printing technologies—inkjet, thermal wax, dye sublimation—all display color differently, because they use different physical materials and different technologies to express color. One technology might not be able to express a color that another technology can express. Fortunately, *film* can express a wide range of

colors. If you used a properly calibrated monitor to edit your image, the colors you see on-screen can be accurately rendered to film.

Consistency of gamma between your screen and a film recorder's CRT is also an important consideration. As we explained in Chapter 3, "Color Theory and the PhotoCD," when the gamma of your monitor doesn't match that of another device, images can look overly brilliant (too high a gamma) or dull (too low a gamma). Your goal, *before* you send your work to the service bureau, is to match your monitor's gamma to that of the film recorder's CRT. This is the only difficult part you have to deal with when you choose to have your work imaged with a film recorder. Precisely matching the gamma between two RGB devices is difficult, even when both machines have been individually calibrated.

Matching your monitor's gamma to an individual film recorder's CRT involves an element of trial and error. Ask your service bureau what the gamma of their film recorder is, and set your monitor to match their figure. The gamma of a film recorder's CRT will most likely fall somewhere between 1.7 and 2.1. After calibrating your monitor to match the imaging center's gamma, send them an image to process as a test image. If the slide comes back too brilliant or too dull, reduce or increase your gamma by a couple tenths of a point and try again. When you find the magic gamma figure, save the setting so that you can reuse it when you create images that will be rendered to film by the *same* film recorder at the *same* service bureau. See Chapter 4, "Photoshop Defaults and Options," for information about calibrating your monitor, setting monitor gamma, and saving custom settings.

The gamma setting that produces the best results with the imaging center's film recorder may change over time. Gamma is a somewhat elusive factor—as monitors and CRTs age, their light-producing phosphors dim and gamma values change. The changes in gamma caused by aging phosphors happen gradually, and you may not notice that changes are occurring. It's a good idea to take a critical look at your output for signs that you and the service bureau are drifting out of synchrony. If you find that your images are coming out a tad brighter or duller than they used to, it's time to make adjustments to your gamma settings.

Using the Proper Aspect Ratio?

Creating and saving your images with the proper aspect ratio is another practice you'll need to adopt for images that will be sent to a film recorder for imaging. *Aspect ratio* is the height-to-width proportion of an image. If you want your image to fill the entire frame of the film to which it's rendered, your image must have the same aspect ratio as that of the film. The aspect ratio of 35mm film is 2:3; 4 × 5 and 8 × 10-inch film share the same 4:5 aspect ratio. If you anticipate sending an image to a film recorder, you should plan your composition so that the ratio of the image's height to width will match that of the film format to which you'll render the image.

One of the things that sends technicians at a service bureau up the wall is a file that doesn't have the proper aspect ratio. Regardless of how artistically inclined the bureau's staff is, you probably won't be happy if the bureau adjusts your image to fit the aspect ratio. When your image doesn't fill the frame, the service bureau has a decision to make—to crop or not to crop. If they crop the image, they are forced to make an artistic decision that was *your* responsibility to make as a designer.

Cropping an image is never a service bureau's responsibility, and most *won't* crop an image unless they've been instructed in writing to do so. If they don't crop the image, it will not fill the frame, and you will be left with unattractive borders on two sides of your image. This can be particularly irritating if you are having slides made. Unfilled areas on slides are clear, and tend to blind audiences when the slides are projected. A good service bureau will add a dark background to fill in around your image. A still *better* bureau will call you and ask what you want to do.

All of this means extra work and headaches for the bureau—and you'll most likely be charged for their consultation time. More important than the extra money you might be charged (and the deadlines you might miss), when you fail to prep an image properly, you relinquish artistic control and responsibility for producing finished artwork that meets your design criteria. It's a shame to use your creative talents to produce good work, only to have it ruined by a bad crop or an unaesthetic border.

Achieving the Proper Aspect Ratio

All of this trouble can be avoided. You don't have to be a math wizard, or even own a pocket calculator, to ensure that your work has the proper aspect ratio. Let Photoshop do the math for you, then use your eye to decide whether to crop or to place a background around the image to make the overall image dimensions correspond to the aspect ratio of the film.

The next exercise shows you how to "trick" Photoshop into figuring out the dimensions your image has to have to achieve the proper aspect ratio for imaging to 35mm film.

Determining an Image's Aspect Ratio

Choose <u>F</u>ile, <u>N</u>ew (or press Ctrl(Cmd)+N)	Displays New dialog box.
Click on each of the drop-down boxes and click to set units to inches and pixels/inches	Sets units of measurement.

Click on Mode drop-down box and set to **G**rayscale	Sets Image Mode for new window. Any mode is OK, but Grayscale uses fewer resources.
In **W**idth text box, enter **3**; in H**ei**ght box, enter **2**; enter **72** in **R**esolution box; any current entry in Contents field is all right (see fig. 25.1); then click on OK	Opens new file, with aspect ratio of 2:3, in workspace. This aspect ratio is appropriate for 35mm images.

If you will be sending your work for large-format output (4 × 5 or 8 × 10-inch), put **5** in the Height box and **4** in the Width box (for 4 × 5-inch output). These two formats share the same 4:5 aspect ratio. Traditionally, 35mm work is imaged in landscape mode and larger formats are imaged in portrait mode.

Choose **F**ile, **O**pen OCT_FEST.TIF from CHAP25 subdirectory (folder) on Bonus CD	OCT_FEST.TIF is active window in workspace.
Choose **I**mage, **I**mage Size; change settings to inches (if not already set that way)	Opens Image Size dialog box. Establishes units of measurement.
With **P**roportion box *checked* and **F**ile Size box *unchecked*, enter a value of **3** in **W**idth text box (see fig. 25.2)	**H**eight value automatically changes to 1.808.

The Height value of 1.808 means that the OCT_FEST.TIF image has an aspect ratio of 1.808 to 3, which is not the desired 2:3 aspect ratio for full-frame rendering to a 35mm film recorder.

Write (on paper) the Current Width and Height values shown in upper part of dialog box (4.967, 2.993), and then click on Cancel	Image size remains unchanged.

You pressed Cancel because you *do not* want to change the image size of OCT_FEST.TIF yet.

Figure 25.1

Use these settings when you create a file to use as an aspect ratio "calculator."

Figure 25.2

The Image Size dialog box, showing OCT_FEST.TIF image's current dimensions.

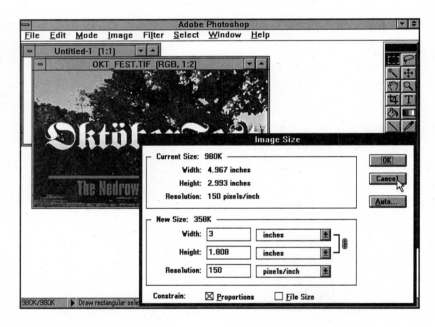

When the Proportion box is checked, changing one dimension changes the other automatically to a value that retains the image's *current* aspect ratio (proportions). By setting the value to 3 in the width box, you can quickly determine whether the image can be scaled to a 2:3 proportion. In this example, the height came up short of 2, which indicates that it is not a 2:3 proportioned image.

If you remove the check from the Proportion box and increase the height to bring it into a 2:3 ratio, you *distort* the image. To bring this image into a 2:3 ratio without altering the design, you have to crop the image or add to it. But you might not want to crop one of your finished images *or* build more image information around one aspect of the image's borders. A good alternative, which is also image-enhancing, is to increase the size of the background canvas to create a border around the image, bringing the overall image into the proper aspect ratio.

When you do this yourself, you decide what the background color should be and how large the border should be to add artistic value to the slide. You please the service bureau folks, too! No one likes to play art critic, especially when they're not getting paid to do it. In the next exercise, you use your new file—the one you just created with a current aspect ratio of 2:3—to figure out how large to make the new canvas for OCT_FEST.TIF.

Calculating an Aspect Ratio

Click on Untitled-1's title bar	Makes Untitled-1 the active image.
Choose **I**mage, **I**mage Size	Displays Image Size dialog box for Untitled-1.
Enter a value of **5.25** in **W**idth box; H**ei**ght value changes to 3.5, the dimension that maintains current 2:3 aspect ratio (see fig. 25.3); write these numbers down, then click on Cancel	These dimensions will bring OCT_FEST.TIF into a 2:3 ratio and provide a good-sized border around image.
Press Ctrl(Cmd)+W (or choose **F**ile, **C**lose)	You don't need your "calculator" image any more. OCT_FEST.TIF is the active image.
Press **I** or click on Eyedropper tool in toolbox, then click Eyedropper over a dark green color on one of the trees to the left	Sets new color for foreground (see fig. 25.4).
Press **X** (or click on switch colors icon on toolbox)	Changes foreground to white and background color to green sampled with Eyedropper.
Choose **I**mage, Canvas **S**ize, set measurements to inches, if necessary, then click on center square in Placement field	Displays Canvas Size dialog box; sets image for placement in center of a new canvas.

continues

continued

By default, the canvas color is the current background color displayed by the Background color box on the toolbox.

Enter **5.25** in **W**idth box and **3.5** in H**ei**ght box (see fig. 25.5)	Numbers calculated for you by Untitled-1's Image Size box.
Click on OK	Nicely centered image with attractive color border is in proper ratio for slides (see fig. 25.6).
Choose **F**ile, Sa**v**e As, and give file a new name	Saves altered version of your file to hard disk.

Stop   Changing the canvas size of the image changes the image. Be sure to save the bordered image under a different file name, so that you still have a copy of the unbordered image.

Figure 25.3

When you change the value in the width box, the value for height changes to maintain the current image proportions.

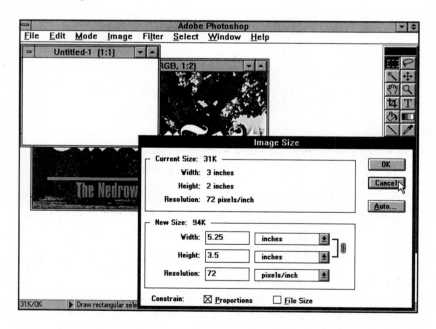

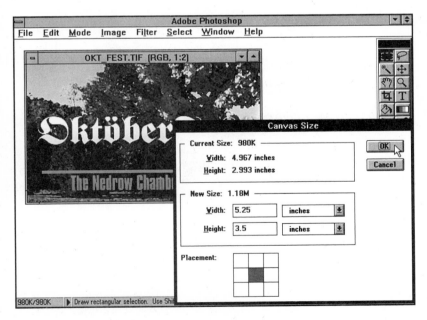

Figure 25.6

OCT_FEST.TIF now has the proper aspect ratio for a slide— and also looks good.

If you want to make this image span the width of the slide, you enter its length (4.967) in Untitled-1's Image Size Width box. This will produce a calculated value of 3.311 for the Height. Setting the OCT_FEST.TIF Canvas size to these measurements puts a border at the top and bottom only (see fig. 25.7). An image's size and the way it's positioned on the canvas are design decisions you make for each image—but the math for obtaining the proper aspect ratio is always the same. When preparing a file destined to be rendered on a large-format film recorder, you use the same procedures you followed to bring OCT_FEST.TIF into a 2:3 aspect ratio, but substitute the numbers 4 and 5 for 2 and 3.

Figure 25.7

OCT_FEST.TIF with only a top and bottom border produces a larger image.

Note If you have a film recorder attached to your machine, and you're imaging your file from Photoshop, you could have Photoshop insert a background color for you. This option is available by choosing **F**ile, Pa**g**e Setup and then clicking on the Bac**k**ground button in the lower-left corner of the Page Setup dialog box. Choose a color for the background in the Color Picker and click on OK. This doesn't change the image—just the way it prints. If you use this option, you can't preview the image to see how it looks before you image the file—this method leaves more to chance than adjusting the canvas size.

When Photoshop inserts a background as a printing option from Page Setup, it adds background only to the sides where you are "short." The printed image would look like figure 25.7. Don't give up your artistic control to save a few steps. Use the Canvas Size command instead.

File Formats and Data Types

Most imaging centers want to work with files saved to either the TIF or Targa format. These are two technologically sophisticated 24-bit, RGB file formats. Because a bureau might prefer one to the other, you should ask which format they prefer before you take them your file. What they definitely *don't* want are image files that contain Alpha channels or paths, which not only bloat a file unnecessarily but also might cause some software to crash. Time is money to a service bureau, and the operators don't need the headache of files containing unnecessary Alpha channels and paths. Save a file with paths and Alpha channels for your own use, but when you make a copy for the bureau, delete them.

When you save a file to take to the service bureau, try to choose a file format that will preserve the color structure you used when you designed the image.

If you created a grayscale image to be finished at the service bureau, definitely save the image as a Grayscale Mode image in Photoshop and give the bureau a grayscale image. Grayscale image files are inherently smaller than those (for the same image) saved as RGB TrueColor. Whether you send the image to the bureau by modem, by tape, or by disk, an 8-bit image in an 8-bit file format is always easier to transport and takes less time to image after it arrives at the service bureau than does a larger image in another format.

If your image is color, send it as RGB—all the glorious colors are available when you print to film, so use them. Send an indexed color, 8-bit file only if your image can be faithfully expressed within the limited color range this indexed format can accommodate. If you send a 24-bit TrueColor image to a bureau as an indexed 8-bit file, your colors will be rendered to film as *dithered* colors. You end up with only 256 (or fewer) colors to represent your once glorious 16.7 million color image—the print or slide will look awful. Let your monitor be your guide. See Chapter 1, "Understanding Image Types, Formats, and Resolutions," for more information about determining the proper data type for an image; and for a look at images that have been color dithered, check out Chapter 2, "Acquiring a Digital Image."

Converting a Portrait Design to a Landscape Slide

Most slides used in business presentations are *landscape* (wider than they are tall) views, in which the 3 aspect represents the design's horizontal dimensions and the 2 aspect represents its vertical dimensions. A landscape presentation that includes *portrait* slides (which are taller than they are wide) can be disorientating to the audience (and drive a projectionist nuts). When you sit down to design images for slide presentations, stick to the landscape view of your 2:3 aspect ratio.

If you are having your work made into slides or film from which you'll print photos, you don't have to limit your designs to landscape proportions. But you still want to have the image in a 2:3 aspect ratio so that it fills the film frame. Instead of assigning the 2:3 proportion to the height and width, let it represent the height and width of the image.

Most film recorders are set up for landscape imaging, which satisfies most users' needs. Before you save your file to disk to send to the service bureau, you might want to turn your image on its side, to get the whole image in frame and avoid excessive cropping.

Photoshop makes this easy for you to do, although the process is not so easy on your system's resources. Rotating images is processor-intensive. It's a Photoshop effect, similar to the Perspective or Distort command, in that Rotate tells Photoshop to recalculate the color values for every selected pixel in the image. Before you use the Rotate command, be sure that you've flattened the image and eliminated any unnecessary channels and paths. You should also close any other images you have open and make sure that you aren't running any other applications, such as word processors or screen blankers, in the background. To rotate the image from portrait to landscape, click on the **I**mage menu, choose **R**otate, and then click on **9**0° CW or 90° **C**CW.

Rotating Extremely Large Images

After you've closed down everything except Photoshop and eliminated the unnecessary paths, channels, and layers in a file, you might find that you *still* don't have enough memory to rotate the file. If you don't have enough resources to perform the rotation, Photoshop very politely tells you that it can't perform the requested action. Don't despair; there are ways to accomplish the same effect (short of buying more memory). The easiest way to solve this problem is to ask the service bureau to rotate the file before they image it. They can do this for you, but only if they are made aware of the need before they fire up the film recorder. The downside to this approach (and any that involves delegating extra responsibility to a business partner) is that you have to remember to tell them, and they have to remember to do it. Also, they might charge you a preparation fee because your file is not ready for imaging.

Alternatively, you may have enough resources to rotate the file if you rotate *each individual channel, one at a time*. Rotating a single channel requires only a third of the memory resources necessary for rotating the entire RGB image in one fell swoop. This trick works with many of Photoshop's processor-intensive commands, but you

must make sure that you use exactly the same settings for each channel, or you'll get some very strange results. The next exercise shows you how to rotate channels independently of each other. You'll be using a small file for the exercise, but keep this trick in mind and use it when working with large files.

Tip It's not a mandate that you *discard* Alpha channels and layers in an image when performing intensive effects such as rotation or distortion. If you've worked long and hard on a saved selection, and will continue to work on the file after applying the effect, you can save your selections and layers in another image file.

To copy Alpha channels to a new file, click on the title of the channel you want to copy. Then click on the pop-up menu button on the Channels palette and choose Duplicate Channel. From the Document drop-down list in the Destination field of the Duplicate Channel dialog box, choose New. In the **N**ame field, enter a name for the new file that will hold the copies of your channels or layers, and click on OK. Photoshop creates a new file that contains a copy of the Alpha channel. Now click on the title bar of your original image and drag the channel you copied into the trash icon. To copy additional Alpha channels, repeat the procedure you used for the first one, but instead of choosing New from the Document drop-down list, choose the name of the new file you created.

Layers can also be saved to a separate file. The procedures are the same as for saving Alpha channels, except that you click on the layer you want to save and choose Duplicate Layer from the pop-up menu. Layers and Alpha channels can be saved to the same file, but only if the file matches the color mode of the original—so save layers first, and Photoshop will automatically match the color modes.

To restore the layers and channels to the original image, you do the process in reverse: click on the layer or channel in the storage file, choose Duplicate Layer (or Duplicate Channel), and choose the original image as the destination file.

As long as you don't change the resolution or the dimensions of either file, the Alpha channel or layer information that is saved to a separate file can be perfectly reunited with the original image. If you change resolutions and sizes, you can copy back the layers and Alpha channels, but they won't match their former sizes or the locations they originally occupied in the original file.

Here's how to rotate a file, channel by channel...

Rotating One Channel at a Time

Open APLETRE.TIF from CHAP25 subdirectory (folder) on Bonus CD	Opens file you'll rotate.
Choose File, Save As, rename the file APLETRER.TIF, and click on OK to save hard disk	Makes copy of file. Now you'll have the original, and a rotated file to your copy to send to the service bureau.
Click on center screen mode button, or press F until you have chosen Full screen without menu bar display mode. Press Z and click Zoom tool once over image	Sets up workspace so that you can see entire image.
Press D or click on default colors on toolbar	Sets Foreground color to black and Background color to white.
Choose Image, Canvas Size from menu	Displays Canvas Size dialog box.
In Width field, enter value (**5.12**) found in Height field; Leave Placement field grid at its default setting, where center box is gray, then click on OK	These settings produce a square canvas, which keeps image from truncating when it is rotated. New canvas areas are white (the current Background color).
If Layers/Channels/Paths palette is *not* open, press F7 (Macintosh: F11); click on Channels tab, then click on Red channel title	Displays Channels palette and Red channel, making channel available for editing, independent of other channels.
Press Ctrl(Cmd)+A (or choose Select, All)	Selects entire Red channel.
Choose Image, Rotate, then choose **9**0° CW (see fig. 25.8)	Rotates Red channel 90° in a clockwise direction. Icon for Red channel changes to display new landscape orientation of channel.
Click on Green channel title on Channels palette, then repeat the last step	Displays Green channel. Selection marquee is still active, except the rotation will now occur in Green channel.

Click on Blue channel title on Channels palette and rotate channel 90° clockwise, as you did the other two channels	Rotates last image channel.
Now your image should look like figure 25.9.	
Press Ctrl(Cmd)+D (or choose **S**elect, **N**one), then press Ctrl(Cmd)+S (or choose **F**ile, **S**ave)	Deselects image and saves your work to hard disk.

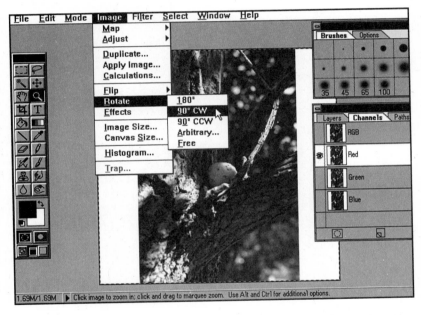

Figure 25.8

*With only the Red channel selected, rotate the image **9**0° CW.*

The image has been rotated successfully, but you now have an unwanted white border across the top and bottom of the image. There are two different tools you can use to select just the image area *and* be assured that your selection has the proper 3:2 aspect ratio. The Crop tool can be set to crop an image to specific dimensions, enabling you to accurately select the image and return the file to its proper 2:3 aspect ratio. But this works properly only when you know what the image dimensions should be to achieve the 2:3 ratio.

To accomplish the same results, you might find it simpler to use a feature that is new to both the Rectangular and the Elliptical marquee tools in Photoshop 3. Marquee tools in version 3 have style properties—Normal, Constrained Aspect Ratio, and Fixed Size—in addition to shape properties—Rectangular, Elliptical, Single Row, and Single

Column. The Constrained Aspect Ratio style is just what you need for the task of accurately picking an image out of the canvas—you don't need to know image dimensions, but only what you want the ratio between them to be. When the Rectangular marquee tool is set to Constrained Aspect Ratio style, any selection marquee you draw, large or small, is automatically confined to the aspect ratio you specified.

Figure 25.9

Images can be rotated one channel at a time.

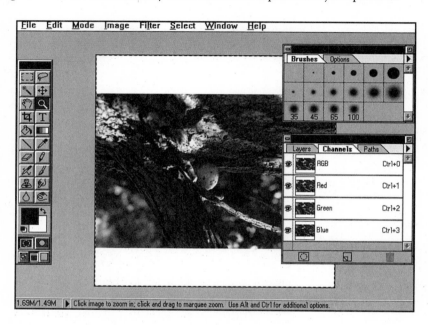

Although Photoshop does have a shortcut key combination for constraining the dimension of a selection made with the Marquee tool, holding down Ctrl(Cmd)key while you marquee-select only constrains a selection border to a dimension of 1:1. The Constrained Aspect Ratio Style on the Options palette offers greater flexibility in proportioning selections. You'll find this to be a handy, useful feature in cropping work to slide dimensions, or any other dimensions a specific piece of work requires.

In the next exercise, you'll check out the Rectangular marquee tool's new feature and get the image back to its proper shape.

Using the Constrained Aspect Ratio Style

Double-click on Marquee tool on toolbox	Chooses Marquee tool and displays Marquee Options palette.

Choose Rectangular from Shape drop-down box on Marquee Options palette, then choose Constrained Aspect Ratio from Style drop-down box; enter **3** in Width box, and enter **2** in Height box; make sure Feather is set to **0** pixels	Selects Rectangular marquee tool and constrains its action to creating selections that have a 3:2 aspect ratio and will have precise edges without Feathering.
Place cursor just outside upper-left corner of image, so that right spoke of crosshair touches (and seemingly disappears into) top row of image pixels (see fig. 25.10); click and drag down and to the right, stopping at a point below image and outside image window	Selects image area you want, excluding white canvas areas.

Starting with the cursor outside the image window and dragging to a point outside the image window on the right ensures that the selection will include the entire width of the image. After one dimension is precisely determined, the other is automatically ensured because you are using the Constrained Aspect Ratio style.

Choose **E**dit, **C**rop	Crops image, leaving only the area inside the marquee.

If you ended up with a row of white pixels along the top of the image, press Ctrl(Cmd)+Z (or choose **E**dit, **U**ndo) and redo the last two steps. Your image should look like figure 25.11.

Press Ctrl(Cmd)+S (or choose **F**ile, **S**ave), then press Ctrl(Cmd)+W (or choose **F**ile, **C**lose)	Saves rotated, cropped image to your hard disk and closes file.

This chapter has dwelt, for a very good reason, on techniques for manipulating larger-than-life file sizes. Sometimes, getting a decent image from a film recorder means having to create a large file. Unlike the ink-on-paper print process, film recorders don't care a whit about a file's resolution, as measured in dots per inch. Film recorders measure resolution in terms of how many pixels an image contains, not how many pixels will fit in an inch. Although a large number of pixels in an image means larger, more unwieldy file sizes, it also means better results when imaging to photographic film. The next sections guide you through the process of establishing a happy medium between file size and the quality of your output; you'll see what ingredients need to be in a digital file to produce a good 35mm slide.

Figure 25.10

Position the cursor so that the right spoke blends in with the top row of pixels.

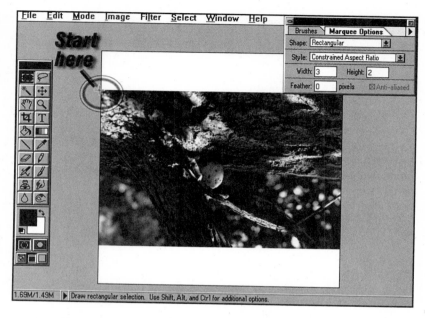

Figure 25.11

The image after it was cropped by using the Rectangular marquee tool and the Edit, Crop command.

Sending the Right Size File

Determining the proper file size to send to a service bureau for slide-making is not as straightforward a process as determining resolution for print presses. Printing to paper and film imaging are different processes and different media. Measurements for image files rendered by film recorders are expressed in storage units (kilobytes/megabytes), not in pixels per inch. The ultimate quality of a film recorder's output is based on *how much* information the film recorder can handle *and* how much information you've given it to work with.

When service bureaus describe their services, they'll sometimes say that they do 2-KB (2,000-line), 4-KB (4,000-line), or 8-KB (8,000-line) imaging. These terms refer to the size of the *pixel grid* the film recorder can render. When a file is imaged at 2 KB, the "2 KB" describes a pixel grid 2,048 pixels wide by 2,048 pixels high. A 4 KB image is a pixel grid of 4,096 by 4,096.

A 24-bit RGB file that is 2,048 pixels wide by 1,365 pixels high (2:3 ratio) produces an 8 MB file. A grayscale image of the same size is only 2.67 MB. A 24-bit RGB file imaged to 4 KB and in a 2:3 ratio would be 4,086 pixels wide by 2,731 pixels high and would occupy 32 MB, whereas its grayscale counterpart would occupy only 10.7 MB.

This doesn't mean that creating a 32 MB image for a service bureau to image is necessarily a good idea, or even *feasible!* To manipulate a file in Photoshop with any degree of ease, your computer must have memory resources that are three to five times the size of the file. To produce a 32 MB file, your PC and the PC at the service bureau would have to have a minimum 96 MB of memory, and you'd need 160 MB to operate with any degree of ease. Many motherboards can't *hold* more than 128 MB of memory. Even if they did, at current RAM prices you'd have to invest nearly $8,000 to accommodate this image. At which point, most imaging-type people would start counting up how many boxes of charcoals or Nikons they could buy with this much cash.

Service bureaus usually base a large portion of their imaging fees on the size of the file you bring to them, because the larger the file, the harder it is to handle. Large files also take up large amounts of the bureau's hard disk space and take longer to image than smaller files. Files under 5 MB are fairly inexpensive to image (usually under $20), but you should expect substantially higher imaging costs for 20–30 MB files.

How Large Is Large Enough?

So how large *should* your file be? There *is* no hard and fast rule. It depends on what you want to do with the slide, how detailed the slide is, and how critical an eye your viewing audience has. Slides have nice juicy colors; when slides are projected, the difference between a "low resolution" slide and a "high resolution" slide is often difficult to see because of the typically low quality of the projection equipment on the screen. If you look at both slides, side-by-side, through a loupe, on a good day, in a good mood...you might see a significant difference.

Most service bureaus are willing to run a test slide or two for you or provide you with samples of slides imaged from different size files. Experiment with different sizes of files to find the size that suits your needs, your patience, and your pocketbook. Files that are too large to fit on a floppy disk are unwieldy to transport. Time is money to a service bureau. Large files take longer to process—and you are charged for that time.

The fundamental question of how large your image should be boils down to your definition of *acceptable*—a relative term, but we place it at somewhere between 1.13 MB and 4.5 MB.

If your job absolutely depends on a fantastic, "no one could ever criticize you" slide, design your piece for 4.5 MB. If the slide is for you to keep, for in-house use, or even to be used as part of an information package you send clients, create a copy of your image to a smaller file size. Our personal experience has been that slides created from 1.13 MB files produce quite acceptable film copies. (This is the default size of Kodak PhotoCD [*.PCD] images.) Start at the low end of the file size range and work your way up to the point that gives you the results you need for your situation. Ask your service bureau to show you slides they've made from files of different sizes so that you get the scope of the meaning of "acceptable."

Misjudging the file size can get you caught between a rock and a hard place. If you start with an image design that's too small, you can't increase the information without interpolating the data and losing some file integrity and quality. On the other hand, if you design to create a large file, say of a house, at a 1:1 scale, you tax your system, your patience, and your wallet. Remember also that moving large files from place to place is not simple. Moving large files to the service bureau involves the same potential problems as moving them to a commercial printer. Chapter 24, "The Service Bureau," has a section that's an "idea resource" for handling large image file transportation.

 Stop   If you think a design you've created has too small a file size to be successfully made into a slide, *don't* consider increasing it with Photoshop's Image Size commands. When a film recorder gets an image, it does interpolation of its own; the interpolating you did to increase the file size would be subject to interpolation a second time. One interpolation is more than enough averaging of original image data—let the film recorder handle the size increase when it images your file.

What To Do if Your File Is Too Small

If you already have a piece designed, and it's smaller than you think it should be—image it anyway. You might be pleasantly surprised. Figure 25.12, MAKEWAVE.TIF, is "small"—only 924 KB. It's in the CHAP25 subdirectory on the companion CD, if you'd like to look at it in color. The center image was created in a computer modeling and rendering program; the background was created in Photoshop with a Kai's Power Tools texture, and the two elements were brought together and then retouched a little in Photoshop. MAKEWAVE.TIF was sent to a service bureau as an RGB TIF and made into a slide. The slide impressed a conference room full of people—and not one stood up and criticized the resolution.

Figure 25.12

MAKEWAVE.TIF produced a good quality slide from a file that is only 924 KB.

After the meeting, we decided to have some inexpensive 4 × 6 color prints made for the sort of handouts one never expects to get back. We could have taken the file back to the service bureau and had a film negative made, thereby avoiding one generation of processing and the resulting loss of some image quality. Instead, we checked the slides into the local one-hour photo place, had a negative made from the slide, and ordered regular, batch-mode color prints made from the new negative.

The *prints* looked fine, too! If MAKEWAVE.TIF were destined for a museum, or if it were going to be the source material for producing a magazine cover by traditional means, we probably wouldn't have been so cavalier with this image. But if we'd been more careful with the image, we would never have discovered what the *perceived* quality was for a third generation, 924-KB digital image. Although the prints did not match the original on-screen colors exactly, they were close enough to convey the image accurately and were suitable for their intended purpose.

Having a Negative Made

You might want to have your service bureau image your file to 35mm negative film, instead of slide film. With a negative, you can have photographic prints made of your image. Or you can give the negative to a printer who is not computer savvy and uses traditional photographic production methods.

The process of making a 35mm negative is almost identical to that of making a 35mm slide. The following sections detail a few differences that you'll want to keep in mind. If you are imaging to formats larger than 35 mm, the same basic concerns apply—only the file sizes and aspect ratios will be different.

File Sizes for Making 35mm Negatives

If you plan to have a large, high-quality photographic print made from the negative, the first consideration you need to address is file size. You'll want to send a larger file than you normally send for a slide. Just as you need a large-format negative to make a really large print in traditional photography, with digital photography, larger files go hand-in-hand with larger prints because they contain more information.

As with a slide, there is no hard and fast rule for what size file makes an "acceptable" print. Kodak states that photofinishers should not make prints larger than 8 inches by 10 inches from the standard version of a Kodak PhotoCD file, a special digital format whose multiple resolutions include an 18 MB BASE file. We believe that Kodak's definition of what an acceptable print looks like is a little overestimated and that you will find a print made with a much smaller file to be "acceptable." Again, as with the slides, file size is a matter in which you have to find your own level of comfort, as you find the balance between file size and quality of the output.

If your commercial printer is not a computer "guru," and you plan to give them the negative for traditional prepress production and placement into a printed document, produce your negative from a larger file size.

Whether it's for the printing press or for yourself, tell the service bureau *why* you want a negative made. If the service bureau is aware of the specific purpose for the negative, they can make tiny adjustments to the film recorder's settings and "tweak" the negative so that it is optimized for photographic printing, or print press printing.

Aspect Ratios for 35mm Negatives

The aspect ratio for 35mm *negative* film is the same as for 35mm slide film—a 2:3 ratio. All the techniques and considerations that go into getting a file into the proper aspect ratio for slide-making apply, except one: what you do if your image is not full-frame.

In the exercise on slide preparation earlier in this chapter, you increased the canvas size of an image to a 2:3 proportion, and made that additional canvas a dark color. Dark borders on slides are good because they keep the audience's attention on the image information, and spare viewers from the brilliant light of the projector as it passes through clear areas in the slide. But on prints and negatives, the tradition is to use *white* borders instead of dark ones. White is the border color most people expect on a print. And if the image is to be cropped, white usually makes the "live area"—the image area—easier to crop.

Choosing a Service Bureau

When you choose a service bureau, you are choosing a design partner. These are the people who take your design and move it from the digital world to the physical world. When you choose an imaging center, you need to look for the same kind of qualities you look for in any other partner you choose. You need to be able to trust them, you need to be able to talk to them, and you need to be able to work together to achieve a common goal—producing great output.

Shop Around for the Best Capabilities

It is worth your while to talk to *several* service bureaus. Ask them to send you samples of their work. Send them samples of your work. Then make an appointment to call or visit them so that you can talk to them about the following things:

- ◆ Your work.

- ◆ The applications you use.

- ◆ What you do with the images you produce.

- ◆ What services you think you'll need from them.

- ◆ What *other* services they have that they think might be useful to you. Some service bureaus offer typesetting, desktop publishing, and basic design capabilities that might make it easier for you to integrate your images into your portfolio or use them for promotional purposes.

- ◆ Whether they have a preferred file format, what file size they recommend for each service they offer, and what gamma setting they recommend for each kind or size of output.

- ◆ Turnaround time (rush service is always more costly).

◆ Whether they require advance notice if you send them large amounts of work at one time, if you send unusually large files, or if you need to have your job imaged to special film.

◆ Find out who you should talk to at the service bureau if you have technical questions and who you should talk to when you have business or customer service questions.

◆ Last but definitely not least, ask how they prefer to receive large files. A good service bureau has several methods for receiving large files and will advise you what works best for them. Then, together, you can work out what's most convenient for both of you.

The key to good relations and good results with your service bureau is to ask ahead of time. Never leave anything to chance. If you need images rotated, or other special services, make sure those instructions are clearly written on your order form. No one likes last minute surprises—they can cause you a world of grief and make you miss your deadlines.

The *rewards* are great when you invest the time to prepare your files properly and when you develop a good working relationship with the folks at the slide service bureau who give your digital image a physical form. There is no way to show readers just how excellent a well-done 35mm slide looks after a film recorder renders your file to this format. But when you slip one of your images into a ho-hum presentation, the looks of wonder and appreciation your work receives are a reward in and of themselves. Simply put, slides of your Photoshop work will blow the audience away!

This book has taken you from the source to the sample, to finally getting your Photoshop work to media that your clients, your boss, your friends, and family can hold in their hands. The next—and final—chapter has nothing to with these other people, file formats, pixels, or even very much to do with Photoshop. Having read the chapters and followed the exercises, you—the artist—have a very natural need to reflect on your knowledge and skills and discover what you've earned by learning. Naturally, we want to give you the next stepping stone.

How Good Is Good?

People from all corners of the business world are attracted by the promise that a personal computer can help them improve their craft. And all sorts of people whose professions and interests involve conveying a message graphically are discovering Adobe Photoshop. But no matter how much you integrate computers in your work, or what level of skill you achieve with Photoshop, every once in a while, you'll wonder how far you've actually come. You'll question whether the images you produce—the images that have been digitized, modified, sliced, diced, blended, and otherwise tinkered with as computer information—are conveying their intended message as powerfully as they could.

This chapter is intended as a guide you can turn to for a little "reality check" every once in a while. It's also a combination checklist/point-of-reflection for you to glance back to as you evaluate how working with Photoshop and computer imaging in general has altered your perspective. Instead of using formal exercises, this chapter asks you to think about how the various topics covered in this book relate to you and the goals you set for your work. If you followed this book's exercises, you've probably acquired new skills and techniques that you might be unaware of yet. In fact, you're probably better at this computer graphics stuff than you imagine! But how good *is* good?

The Uniqueness of the Photoshop Professional

Although this book covers some of the ways graphic designers and photographers can use Photoshop, *Inside Adobe Photoshop 3* is not complete coverage of the program. Photoshop is so feature-rich that a complete documentation would fill a library shelf. And the uses for Photoshop go beyond art and photography. Commercial printers use the program to do color separations, and the motion picture industry uses it to create special effects in movies. Wherever a concept needs graphic expression, Photoshop can plug in.

You may never use Photoshop for anything more than retouching part of an image. But even the simplest task, accomplished through Photoshop, adds uniqueness to both your assignment and your craft.

Color-Correcting Is a Breeze

The authors own several computer-graphics applications, each of which has unique strengths. But Adobe Photoshop addresses the task of color-correcting a photographic image more directly and simply than any of the other programs.

If you work for an ad agency, newspaper, or any other place where tons of photos come in every day, the folks you work for will definitely appreciate your ability to "crank out" color-corrected images. Custom-developed and printed photos are rare. About 99 percent of the images that come your way usually come via the local Fotomat or other bulk-processing place. Bulk-processed prints can't do justice to what the photographer saw because they were not given the individual attention an image needs to make it shine.

Consider how effortlessly you can adjust most of these photos with an **I**mage, **A**djust, **A**uto Levels command. The Auto Levels command dramatically restores a muddy picture to readability. In many cases, the only step you need to take to create a presentable image from an unpresentable one may be to use the Auto Levels command.

Variations and Color Balance are two other **I**mage, **A**djust commands that make simple work of removing color casting from a photo. Many people still use indoor film outdoors, and vice versa. This mismatching of the film's color temperature to the photographed environment produces an orange or blue cast to the print. *If you skipped over Chapter 7, "Restoring an Heirloom Photograph," invest the time to learn how about 30 seconds of work with these two commands can correct an image.*

Not all of Photoshop's tools are automatic, as you'll realize after you spend more time with this program. Although Photoshop can be used very effectively in an "assembly line" environment at work, the program's main virtue lies in its features that enable you to refine individual images according to their needs. The point to reflect on here is that in time, as you gain experience with Photoshop, you'll be able to mass-produce acceptable images quickly—and have more time to concentrate on images that need extra work and attention.

I can't think of another software program that you can work with in this way. When you are familiar enough with Photoshop to be able to work on assignments in a seemingly effortless way, other professionals will come to you for answers. They'll be amazed, but you'll know that the appearance of effortlessness is achieved through the combination of Photoshop's adaptability to different situations and your ability to put it to use. Color-correcting a ton of pictures is only one area where you can excel, and your excellence will stand out because you've invested some "front end" time exploring the features in Photoshop.

Treating Visual Information as Data

Throughout this book, you've been asked to accept many conventions for working in Photoshop as though the tools and effects had some roots in reality. Photoshop's capability to save a selection in an additional channel within an image is nothing short of wondrous. If you come from a traditional chemical photography background, you're probably considering tossing all the custom masks you've created for images right out the darkroom window, followed by the traditional dodge and burn tools! We hope you're "buying into" the digital method of imaging after spending some time with the program and this book because this *is* the visual communication wave of the future.

Photoshop displays visual data in a remarkably user-friendly way that can be easily accessed by users of all skill levels. By displaying pixels as transparent on layers, you can get an immediate grasp of what steps need to be taken to complete, or compose, an image's elements. But are pixels actually capable of being transparent? Of course not because pixels *themselves* aren't real. They're as intangible as an inch or a quart. You have to fill the unit of measurement with something. Photoshop provides the graphical interface to work with the implausible by proxy, and color models and graphs become more than a representation of data—they become the tools for reshaping data. And it's all because Photoshop can display visual data in a way the user feels at home with. The Rubber Stamp tool acts like a physical rubber stamp; image layers have the feel of real-world acetate; and other tools and features have characteristics people can relate to from their familiarity with physical equivalents.

The Infinite Malleability of a Digital Image

Before discovering Photoshop, the authors were firmly convinced that computer graphics had matured more on the vector side of graphical formats than bitmap images and that serious, professional work could not be accomplished with bitmap editing programs. This was before RGB images, displays, and Photoshop disproved the belief that photographic images couldn't be twirled, retouched, and modified, and still display the clarity and realism of the photographic original. Indeed, bitmap imaging is coming closer in capability to vector design and will always exceed vectors at portraying the realistic qualities such as focus, warmth, contrast, and feeling in a finished picture.

By the time you finish this book, you'll have the tools and techniques to become a professional image retoucher—a profession that was thought to be dying in the 1970s, but has shown a dramatic resurgence and revitalization due to the personal computer's power. The effects that you used to perform with a utility blade and adhesive can now be accomplished without a trace of editing. In fact, many people believe that legislature should be enacted to require a digitally edited image to be labeled. This is overreaction from an undereducated few individuals, and we'll see an act passed the day we see "This is a Special Effect" flashed along the bottom of a science fiction movie in theaters. Photoshop makes it easy to reshape reality, but you alone hold the skills to create the reality.

Photoshop's layers, saved selections, and cloning powers present you with a completely different way of retouching an image. The image detail becomes plastic, but with the right approach, a photo can be reshaped, recolored, and bent around the surface of another object yet still retain its photographic properties. Interpolation and anti-aliasing are two of Photoshop's greatest features, and through the deployment of them in rendered type, resizing, and filter effects, you have more tools awaiting your skills than you can imagine. They say every image is unique, and with Photoshop's capabilities to accurately define and retouch isolated areas, you can take a unique *approach* to every one of these unique images.

Photoshop also offers the user simple ways to do complex things. Although it's not a simple program to master, the work you can do in it is heads above average imaging. Don't ever get the idea that the exercises in this book can be accomplished as simply, or even at all, with a different application. Yes, you are doing the fantastic with Photoshop! Take a look at what you can accomplish through this book's exercises. Could you do these sorts of things before you got Photoshop?

An Integrated Workspace

If Photoshop is the only program you own for designing, you already own a wealth of tools in one application. Consider the effects and filters by themselves. Photoshop handles the creation of special-effects imaging masterfully because of its capability to

interpolate information. Whenever you stretch, bend, warp, spherize, or otherwise change the dimensional aspect of an image, Photoshop compensates for the gaps between pixels by mathematically averaging what color and type of pixel, or pixels, should fill the gap. *Interpolation* of image data is a science, and Adobe's contribution to refining this aspect of imaging is nothing short of remarkable.

In addition to special effects, Photoshop gives you smooth type-handling capability. Putting type in a digital photo is usually accomplished by exporting the image to a desktop publishing or other program that specializes in handling text. *Text as art* is becoming more and more popular in graphic design work. With Photoshop, you can treat type as a graphic and use all of Photoshop's features and filters to distort, emboss, or gradient-fill text—in short, to do anything with lettering that you can do to a photo. Because the Type feature is built into Photoshop, all the special treatments you may have for graphics can be placed on a layer, or on the photographic image itself without a trace of cutting or pasting.

The effects that Photoshop's patterns and custom brushes create can go head-to-head with artwork produced by vector-based design programs. Until I started using Photoshop, I used to labor for hours on end creating a repeat pattern for an illustration background. Then I got wise to the fact that you can marquee-select an image area with the Rectangular marquee tool, define the image area as a pattern, and then use the Paint Bucket tool to flood-fill any given amount of selected image area. And being able to define an image area as a custom Brushes tip enables the Photoshop user to "paint" with strokes that resemble anything from texture to a design.

Photoshop has enough spectacular features all under one roof to keep an ambitious individual learning for months on end. You will continue to expand your talents in handling the computer graphic, and adopt plenty of other tools to further your art—but you'll probably never find a program that steers your artistic sensibilities as firmly and convincingly into computer graphics as Photoshop.

Putting Your Skills to Work

You begin your career as an imaging person using Adobe Photoshop with an advantage. You have an understanding of how to work with features not found in many other imaging programs—and you should keep this in mind. By understanding and refining your skills through practice, you can offer a client a product that your competitors can't offer. But you should also keep in touch with reality and real-world needs because getting caught up in the fantastic Photoshop effects and features is easy to do—and sometimes that's not part of your assignment. Keep an eye on what your work really calls for as you keep a perspective on what your talent can produce.

The exercises in Parts Two and Three of this book are designed to give you experience in fixing the most common problems found in images. Although you don't learn to create incredible, surrealistic Photoshop masterpieces with these exercises, they are stepping stones to higher plateaus of computer graphics. Chapter 15, "Special Effects with Ordinary Photographs" and Chapter 16, "Creating a Digital Collage" are good examples of creating high-tech imagery using a few images you might even find commonplace.

The point to remember is that Photoshop is a very "concentrated" application; a little bit of it goes a long way toward completing a paying assignment. Use what you need of the tools and features, and trust your own judgment as to when you've completed a task. Don't embellish just because you can. If you use the features in Photoshop in combination with your artistic sensibilities, you're farther ahead of your competition than you think. Photoshop's edge is the speed and refinement it lends to an image. Your own advantage is your good taste. This is always true, regardless of whether the artist uses a computer.

Can I Make a Career out of Photoshop?

Many people come to Photoshop from a classical art background and are presently getting to know their computer's operating environment in addition to computer graphics programs. The capability to do high-quality computer graphics on a personal computer is fairly new. Prior to the introduction of the Macintosh personal computer, computer graphics required the use of proprietary software and a workstation or mini-computer. The release of Windows 3.0 in 1991 and the subsequent release of graphics software titles gave IBM-compatible PC users the interface and tools they needed to get up to speed with their Macintosh cousins in the production of high-quality graphics work on desktop personal computers. When Photoshop for Windows shipped in January 1993, a common standard for imaging excellence was finally reached for the personal computer. Today, digital artists and designers can create whatever they imagine, and the machine they use as a tool has become largely irrelevant.

If your threshold of interest in Photoshop is that of "hobbyist," you have some fine, exciting experiences in store for many years to come. But if you want to make a career of computer graphics, buying Photoshop was your very best first step. And following the exercises in this book (in addition to a lot of "woodshedding") should be your second. Definite career possibilities exist for an artist with experience in computer graphics. And it doesn't matter if you run Windows or Macintosh System 7.*x*; as long as you know your tools, both platforms are capable springboards for the creation of wonderful, professional images.

The Private Road to an Imaging Career

When you reach a level of proficiency with the program, you'll travel one—or possibly two—roads in your Photoshop career. You can work in a production department in a firm that does a great deal of photography and publishing. Or if you have the budget, you may decide to hang out your own shingle in the marketplace.

Building a computer graphic design business by yourself requires building a network of "support services" around it. Unless your last name is Getty, color printers, film recorders, proofing devices, and storage for megabytes of image files can put a serious dent in your wallet. Service bureaus and commercial printers are discussed in Chapter 24, "The Service Bureau," and Chapter 25, "The Film Recorder." Get to know the people who run these businesses. You'll need to depend on their expertise to produce a finished piece from your work. Spend your time concentrating on your craft with Photoshop and understanding your customers' needs to communicate ideas visually. Learn to make the folks at the service bureau and the commercial printer your partners in the production of fine work.

The Picture of Your Profession

Corporate annual reports, in-house business newsletters, flyers, slides, presentations, and product brochures are all business staples, whether the business is large or small. You can add your artistic flair to them with Photoshop, and people do pay good money for a handsome product. But they usually don't want to engage you, and then a service bureau, and then a proofing house, and then a commercial printer to get their printed piece done. As a computer graphic designer, you need to develop relationships with other professionals—photographers, service bureaus, copywriters, mailing houses, and other business links—who support your contribution and help bring an assignment to completion.

Private Partnerships

People communicate with pictures and words. And as an imaging-type person, you may want to strike up a relationship with a wordsmith to create a desktop publishing firm. It's not as involved or as difficult as it may sound. This kind of business also requires having good relationships with production-end contacts.

PageMaker, QuarkXpress, and several other desktop publishing applications are as feature-rich as Photoshop in their own milieu. They make it easy to place your imaging work in a publication. Like any software application, desktop publishing is complex, has its own rules, and people devote their careers to it. If you can find an experienced PC user or a Macintosh user who is proficient in desktop publishing, a partnership between you two could blossom into a wide range of work opportunities.

Like Photoshop, QuarkXpress and PageMaker are available for both the PC and the Macintosh, and their files are compatible with each other. Any individual who has skills in these programs is likely to contribute a wealth of experience in desktop publishing to your imaging experience.

Small partnerships and self-employment are steps you can take to making a living from your Photoshop skills. But as more and more businesses decide to do in-house publishing, opportunities also exist in production departments.

Taking Your Skills to a Business

Businesses whose products are based on publishing, communications, and art can definitely benefit from a person with a well-rounded art and computer background. Photoshop skills can give you a critical advantage over another person seeking employment at one of these places. The business you go to may be Macintosh-based, PC-based, or may not even have a copy of Photoshop, but the techniques you learn with Photoshop are portable. As you've seen in this book, the Macintosh and PC features of Photoshop are identical, and aside from a few different conventions that each operating system has, you can get up to speed quickly using Photoshop on any operating system.

Even if a business doesn't own Photoshop, your experience and understanding of this program can be put to good, productive use at a company. Artists find that when they have a firm grasp of the concept of bitmap imaging, the skills and approaches developed with Photoshop can be modified to accommodate other software packages. At this point, you become an accomplished designer, with your design tools in the background and your talents up front. This is the key to finding rewarding, satisfying employment as an imaging professional at a business. Then, when you're comfortable after a few months employment there, you can suggest that the company purchase Photoshop!

Careers and Applications Are Personal Decisions

How far you take your adventures with Photoshop on a professional level is largely up to your own ambition and the perspective you have on your own life. Photoshop can take you up to the Hollywood stars; many motion picture artists use Photoshop to enhance their artwork. John Knoll, one of several software developers who designed Adobe Photoshop, won an Oscar for LucasFilms, for Best Special Effects in a motion picture.

And technicians at department stores, who help prepare camera-ready art for newspaper advertisements, also find Photoshop rewarding in their careers. Regardless of the profession you decide on, whether it's for yourself or for a company, a direct correlation exists between the hours you invest in mastering Photoshop and the success with which you earn money from your talents. Which is true of any profession.

New Riders Publishing
INSIDE
SERIES

Expanding Your Artist's Toolbox beyond Photoshop's

It would be naive to suggest that Photoshop is an end unto itself in your computer graphics experiences. A mountain of software programs is available for creating computer graphics. Adobe Photoshop is simply one that's at the top of them.

Getting "lost" in a program as fascinating as Photoshop is an incredibly easy thing to do. That's why you should do a reality check regularly and look at the task you have at hand. We've stressed throughout this book that computer graphics are best produced with the right tool for the proper purpose. That's why artists own a collection of tools—to help them express themselves more completely.

The Bonus CD that comes with this book includes a wealth of utilities and image sources to augment your creative process with Photoshop. But these are only the tip of the iceberg, and you owe it to your craft to always be on the lookout for utilities and tools that can be used to enhance your images and make your work more productive. Certainly, you will find some programs you want that are very expensive, but many times you'll find invaluable stuff as freeware and inexpensive shareware. The Resource section in the back of this book lists names and numbers to contact about other applications that can round out your virtual toolbox, but every once in a while you should check the BBSes, online services, and talk with other imaging people about what is available. The graphics world is more exploding than expanding, and new programs, utilities, and source materials that can be used with Photoshop are entering the market daily .

Plug-Ins

Photoshop doesn't excite just graphically minded people. Computer programmers find Photoshop an exciting and hospitable program for which to write utilities and filters, and many examples of plug-in filters for use with Photoshop 3 can be found on the Adobe Deluxe CD, and the Bonus CD that accompanies this book. With Photoshop's capability to integrate, or to "plug in" third-party programs, you can continue to add effects and supplemental features to Photoshop long after you've purchased Photoshop.

Because Photoshop has had less years on the PC platform and because PCs handle memory usage differently from the Macintosh, many of the plug-ins you see advertised may have been designed as Macintosh-only. If Windows is the operating platform you use, be sure to check if a plug-in you might purchase is for the Windows version of Photoshop. Andromeda filters, Alien Skin, Kai's, Gallery Effects, and Pixar plug-in filters are all available in either Mac or PC versions. As time passes, more and more plug-ins will be available for Windows, particularly after the new version of Windows (Windows 95) is released, which handles memory more efficiently.

Similarly, if you work with a PowerMac, you will find that most of the available plug-ins are written for the older, 68 KB Macintoshes. You can still use these with Photoshop on your PowerMac, but they won't perform as quickly as a plug-in that is PowerMac-specific. But if you have a 68 KB Macintosh, make sure that the filter you want to buy will work with your equipment because if it's PowerMac-only plug-in, you won't be able to use it. Always ask before you buy to ensure compatibility.

The Drawing Application

Drawing programs, such as Adobe Illustrator, CorelDRAW!, Freehand, and Micrografx Designer are vector-based graphics programs that should be part of your arsenal of computer graphics tools to use with Photoshop. As discussed in Chapter 1, "Understanding Image Types, Formats, and Resolutions," a vector graphic is resolution-independent. It is composed of mathematical equations that describe the independent objects you draw. Vector drawing programs operate with the precision of a mechanical pencil.

By contrast, a bitmapped or *raster* graphic, which is the kind Photoshop produces, can only be thought of as object-oriented in the sense that you can move selections of opaque pixels around on layers. If a Photoshop image is to be shared with other applications and other users who don't have Photoshop, the image must be flattened and saved in a more conventional file format, such as TIF. And as a saved TIF image, the bitmap graphic obeys the same graphical conventions as every bitmapped image. Image detail is displayed as an arrangement of pixels that contain color information in an imaginary grid. The size of that grid determines how much resolution the image has. The way Photoshop treats images more closely resembles using a brush. The program excels at pouring soft, warm, naturalistic colors into an image window.

But sometimes your work on the computer calls for using both kinds of graphical images, just as in the world of traditional art, you might use both a pencil and a brush on a single piece. Photoshop understands vector-based information and how to convert (*rasterize*, or *map*) this information to bitmapped information. You can work in a drawing program; then export a vector drawing for use in your Photoshop creations by using Photoshop's Rasterize Adobe Illustrator Format command from **F**ile, **O**pen, or **P**lace.

CorelDRAW! has been the most successfully marketed vector-type drawing program on the PC platform, and for good reason. CorelDRAW!'s interface (shown in Chapter 22, "Virtual Reality: The Ingredients of Dreamwork") is designed with the physical-drafting-table sort of professional in mind. Within days of picking up the program,

people who are new to computers can create simple, salable artwork with CorelDRAW!. Adobe Illustrator, Micrografx Designer, and Freehand are also very capable vector drawing programs, each with their own unique interfaces, strengths, and features.

If you want to use a logo, some twisted or extruded type, or if you need to edit lines and curves with an *n*th degree of precision for use in Photoshop, you would want to use a vector drawing program. Again, it's a matter of using the right tool for the right job. Photoshop can import a wide variety of bitmapped file formats but is capable of importing only two vector file formats: EPS and Adobe's own AI (Adobe Illustrator). When you select a vector drawing program, be sure that it can export files to a bitmapped file format or as EPS and AI files. CorelDRAW!, Micrografx Designer, and Freehand all have good Import/Export features that transfer vector art successfully into Photoshop.

Utilities

Programs that simplify your work in other programs are called *utilities*. Regular use of Photoshop will produce hundreds of megabytes of image files on your hard drive, floppy disk, and backup tapes for years to come. You'll want to be able to view, index, compress, collate, and standardize not one, but hundreds of Photoshop images at a time! This is where file-management utilities come into your imaging life.

You will need to share your images with others, so invest in file archiving and compression software as well as software that makes disks and large format media readable on both Macintosh and PC computers. *These programs are described in Chapter 24, "The Service Bureau," and listed in the Resource Guide.*

Image Cataloguing

Fetch, CorelMOSAIC!, and U-Lead's Image Pals all offer cataloguing features for image files. You can print collections of "thumbnails" of images stored on your hard drive. The file formats each product supports vary, but all will view TIF image formats. For all the organizational power the computer has brought to your life, a printout or two of image files goes a long way in helping you retrieve files you want to edit out of the sea of image files you'll soon own.

An onscreen slide show of your work can provide immediate gratification after long weeks of building a collection of images for a corporate presentation. Chapter 25, "The Film Recorder," discussed the value of a slide imaging service bureau, but more and more companies are putting together a presentation that's run directly from a monitor or projected onto a wall by using an LCD panel hooked up to a computer. *See Chapter 21, "Advanced Type Usage and Presentations," for the steps you need to create an all-electronic slide show with Photoshop.*

The Shareware Video Slide Show Utilities

The most basic way to show your "slides" in sequence is to save them as GIF files. GIF files are CompuServe's contribution to the computer graphics image format. A GIF file is highly-compressed until it's read into your system RAM. CompuServe developed the GIF format so that it could offer subscribers high-quality, indexed, 256-color images to download without the users having to spend a fortune in connect time.

If you use online services or local BBSes, you'll find many shareware GIF-file "players." If you want to try out one of these inexpensive shareware programs, use Photoshop's Sa**v**e As command to save copies of your images as GIF files. For PCX shows, first use the **M**odes command to change your RGB image to an 8- or 4-bit indexed data type. Then use the Sa**v**e As command to save your image in the PCX file format.

The "try it before you buy it" policy of shareware designers is a great gift to artists. Shareware authors are often prompted to write a utility because they can't find a feature they want in an existing commercial application. These unexpected gems pop up in the least likely places—keep an eye on what's happening in this alternative method of software distribution.

Commercial Slide Show and MultiMedia Programs

You may already own a slide show program and be unaware of it. Many companies include a slide show feature as a sidekick to their main program. But whether it's a part of a program or a stand-alone, showing a collection of bitmapped slides at a reasonable pace on your computer requires a great deal of system "umph." You can address this problem by packing a fast computer with at least 20 MB of RAM, and you can use Photoshop's dithering options to convert a copy of an RGB image to Indexed color, which shrinks the image file size and demands less of your computer's re-sources.

If you want to include your images in a super slide show, complete with sound, video clips, and fancy dissolves, you'll want to get a full-featured presentation graphics package such as Microsoft PowerPoint, Persuasion, Lotus Freelance Graphics, or WordPerfect Presentations. All are mainstream, commercial presentation packages that support at 256-color, indexed images. These packages are more complex and more capable than the shareware programs and take longer to learn than their simpler siblings.

Full-fledged multimedia software, the top tier of show-type products, can be used to produce slide shows, video tapes, and CD-ROM-based shows. Mastering a multimedia application takes as much time and effort as mastering Photoshop, and authoring programs are not inexpensive. If you want to use your Photoshop imaging work as parts of high-quality animation sequences, moving slide shows, self-running demo

New Riders Publishing
INSIDE
SERIES

disks, and sight-sound-motion presentations, you might want to take a look at Adobe Premiere, which shares a similar interface and plug-in filters with Photoshop, MacroMedia Director, or HSC's InterActive.

Full-Featured MultiMedia Applications as "Utilities"

At some point, you cross a line where a utility becomes another application. Photoshop can be used to create a graphic whose purpose is to play a minor role in a desktop publishing document. In this sense, Photoshop has "played utility" to a program that doesn't have a rich set of graphics tools. Then again, in a rendering and modeling program (discussed in Chapter 22) that lacks sophisticated photofinishing tools, a design exists as several images until those images come to Photoshop for compositing. Sometimes it's difficult to tell which image "belongs" to a specific application. If the application in which you finish a design counts as "owner," you'll find that you own only one application—the rest are Photoshop utilities!

Manufacturers have their own definition of what a utility is. Some state that a utility is a program that depends on the finished product of another program, such as a word processing macro. Utilities have to be defined by the individual artist because the artist alone has to evaluate what a program is good for as it relates to his or her work. Sometimes a full-featured application has a minor feature you'd like to use as a utility. Buying an entire application to own a single feature is an expensive solution to whatever you're trying to accomplish—but sometimes a necessary one, and definitely worth it.

PIXAR Typestry was used throughout this book to create simple, graphical examples, and yet perhaps only a tenth of the program's feature set was used. Typestry was used because it is adept at creating dimensional text and graphics that could then be refined and fine-tuned in Photoshop faster than if the same image had been built entirely within Photoshop. *Chapter 21, "Advanced Type Usage and Presentations," shows how Pixar Typestry is used to produce the elements of a slide show, and you can try out the Pixar Typestry demo version on the Bonus CD that comes with this book.*

Define a utility, which helps your Photoshop work in your own mind. Don't depend on a label on a box.

The Fully Equipped Windows Shell

For Windows users, a good Windows "shell" is a must for making life with Photoshop a breeze. To use Photoshop on the PC platform, you need Microsoft Windows. But Windows Program Manager, the place where you copy and view programs, directories, and files, leaves much to be desired in ease of use and functionality.

Symantec's Norton Desktop for Windows is a replacement for Windows Program Manager and File Manager; several third-party manufacturers have products out to compensate for Windows' workplace, but Norton Desktop stands above the crowd for a user-friendly, graphical approach to managing your programs and files. Norton Desktop offers a collection of much-needed utilities that can assist you in everyday computer "housekeeping" so that you can spend more time on your imaging profession. Symantec's product features "must have" utilities such as virus-scanning, a simplified way of looking at directories and files, viewers for both images and text, file searchers (when you've forgotten what you named your image!), and many other items from a computer user's wish list.

How Good Can You Get?

We hope you're not disappointed that this chapter doesn't have an exercise on every page! This chapter discussed things that connect with Photoshop, such as other programs, and especially the artist, with the intention of providing you with a little scope and perspective on the rich, satisfying, complex aspects of computer imaging and graphics.

A creative person learns and does so much along the path to achieving a real, true masterpiece, that he or she can lose direction easily. Pinching yourself at regular intervals, as you pore over pages and pages of how-tos, helps to restore both your circulation and the humanity you bond to a software application in creating art. Technical skill alone isn't going to make you a great Photoshop designer. If getting great at image editing and design work is your heart's desire, you now have the learning tools and the software program on your side. But education and Photoshop alone won't make you as good at computer art as you'd like to be.

Patience, desire, perspective, and open-mindedness are other ingredients that complete the recipe for turning a good imaging-type person into a great one. Talent can be a big contributor to achieving Photoshop greatness. Let's get real; having artistic flair when you sit before a monitor for the first time can give you an edge. But I've seen many determined individuals with mediocre skills, or talent (whatever you want to call trained, reflexive inspiration), succeed in business and their personal lives because they had a perspective on the right methods at the right time to accomplish what they want. And I've seen people with phenomenal, innate artistic abilities fall by the wayside because they had no sense of humility or perspective about a craft they believe they mastered shortly after birth.

You must take responsibility for maintaining your own personal perspective as you determine the right blend of Photoshop, practice, and ingenuity for successfully communicating a thought—yours or someone else's—in a digital, visual fashion.

So how good is good? Here are some guidelines:

◆ If you practice diligently with Photoshop and can recognize elements in your work that are eye-pleasing and inspire you to keep on trying, then you are already "good."

◆ If you can share images you created using Photoshop— images that you're proud of—and still hang on to the "failures" and not feel embarrassed about them, then you are "great."

◆ If you can balance the yearning to learn more with a continuous sense of achievement, and allow an image to speak for itself with an eloquence you've freely given to it, then you are a "success".

Part VI

Back O' the Book

Appendix A: What's On the Bonus CD? *1265*

Appendix B: How to Install the Online Glossary:
PC and Macintosh Versions *1275*

Index *1281*

APPENDIX

A

What's on the Bonus CD?

Unlike a lot of other books, when you've reached the end of *Inside Adobe Photoshop 3* the fun is actually only beginning! The Bonus CD that comes with this book contains the exercise images and a whole lot of other great, carefully selected items for your continuing exploration of Photoshop 3. Helpful utilities, demonstration versions of commercial software, tons of freeware images, and fully working versions of plug-in filters for Photoshop are all included.

Bonus CD Operating Requirements and Directories

Like Photoshop itself, it's helpful to have a guide to the *Inside Adobe Photoshop 3* Bonus CD. Because you might not want to copy all the contents of the CD onto your hard disk in one fell swoop, the contents of the CD are listed in the following sections, with descriptions of what's in specific directories or folders. By reading through this list, you'll have a more rewarding experience with the rest of the book!

To open any of the images or programs on the Bonus CD, you must have a CD-ROM drive *and* drivers that are capable of reading ISO9660 standard disks. If you're unsure of your CD-ROM drive specifications, check the documentation that came with the drive. As a rule, if you purchased your CD-ROM drive after 1992, you have an ISO-standard CD-ROM drive and the appropriate drivers. Macintosh users might have a problem reading the CD if the appropriate ISO9660 driver is not installed.

Also be on the lookout for README text files and Adobe Acrobat (PDF) documents in the directories and folders. These file and documents provide information on how to reach the companies involved, licensing, and how to install or use the software.

The EXERCISE Directory

In the root of the Bonus CD, you'll find the EXERCISE directory (folder). Contained in this directory are all the images referenced in the chapter exercises. Because the images are in TIF, PSD, JPG, and AI file formats—formats common to both operating systems—Windows and Macintosh users can access and use the same exercise image files. Adobe Photoshop for Windows and Adobe Photoshop for the Macintosh reads image information about files in these formats the same way, so you shouldn't look for separate partitions on the CD meant for a specific operating platform.

When you're asked in an exercise step to open an image from the Bonus CD, a chapter reference is also made. For example, let's say an exercise step said the following:

Open TEST.TIF from the CHAP08 subdirectory(folder)

You should go to the EXERCISE subdirectory (folder), find the CHAP08 subdirectory (folder) within the EXERCISE subdirectory (folder), then open the TEST.TIF image you'll find within the CHAP08 subdirectory (folder). Exercise image files are almost always found within a subdirectory (folder) that is named to match the chapter in which you are working. Additionally, if you'd like to see what a completed

exercise image looks like you should look in the Gallery subdirectory (folder) for the chapter that contains the exercise.

The ARIS Directory

Aris Entertainment, Inc. has given us permission to include several high-quality images from their collections on our Bonus CD. These images include fantastic sunsets and moody beaches, incredible mountains and other types of terrain from all over the world. Read the documentation in the Resource Guide and on the CD in the ARIS subdirectory for more information about the usage of these image files, and how to get commercial versions of Aris' collection.

The GLOSSARY Directory

In the GLOSSARY directory, you'll find our super-duper illustrated *Inside Adobe Photoshop 3* Online Glossary. This Glossary is in Adobe Acrobat format, which makes it easy to access by both Windows and Macintosh users. Check out Appendix B, "How To Install the Online Glossary: PC and Macintosh Versions," for further details on how to use it, and how to install the Acrobat Reader.

The MATERIAL Directory

New Riders Publishing and the authors have created a collection of high-quality, original images not available elsewhere, and they are located in the MATERIAL subdirectory of the Bonus CD that comes with this book. These images are a combination of photographic and computer-created scenes that you can use for backgrounds in your own imaging adventures. These are freeware images and should not be mistaken for the *sampler* images from various manufacturers located in other CD subdirectories. Under the MATERIAL directory, you'll find the following categories of images:

- ◆ **BACKDROP**—These are images created with modeling and painting programs such as Fractal Design Painter. The Background images can be used to replace photographic image backgrounds—useful when you've taken a wonderful portrait picture, only to find later that a lamp or steam pipe is sticking through Uncle Bob's head!

- ◆ **ACTUAL**—The Actual images are PhotoCD images of nature and texture scenes that you can use with Photoshop's Lighting Effects Filter or other effects to enhance other image areas. The images are typically 1.3 MB, and offer ample coverage for most designs that are 3"×5" at 150 ppi resolution or less. The Actual images therefore print well to a high-resolution laser printer (600 to 1200 dpi) or an imagesetter.

- **HAUSHOLD**—The Haushold images are direct scans of cloth napkins, crumpled paper, and we also have some unusual synthetic textures in this directory that look like bubble gum and oatmeal.

- **ORGANIC**—These are synthetic images created with Fractal Design Painter, CorelDRAW!, and Photoshop that are abstract, yet eye-pleasing color files you can use for textures or background to photographic elements in your work.

- **TERRAIN**—Terrain images were created using a landscape modeling program, and the pictures in this directory can be used in photo realistic compositions. Images of tropical islands and densely wooded land masses (some images suggesting aerial views) can be found here.

- **GLASS**—Photoshop and Fractal Design Painter were used to create stained glass textures. You can create a photo-realistic stained glass piece by using these images with a "template" that can be a decorative or picture font.

- **ESOTERIC**—This is the catch-all category for the MATERIAL collection—we couldn't think of a more appropriate title for the textures and reliefs you'll find in this directory! Try using the Esoteric images as texture channels when you run the Lighting Effects filter on an image in Photoshop.

The images in the MATERIAL directory are in the TIF format, which can be opened and used in Photoshop for Windows or for the Macintosh.

The IMAGECEL Directory

This directory contains a collection of textures that can be used to create seamless tiled image areas. ImageCels has carefully altered actual photographic images so that you can choose the Define Pattern command in Photoshop, then use the Edit, Fill command to make a photographic texture of almost any size, without telltale edges. For further information on the ImageCels product line (collections available on CD), see our Resource section in this book, and check the README file in the IMAGECEL directory.

The ZECH Directory

Richard Zech is a talented professional photographer who has lent us a unique collection of digital macro-photography for the Bonus CD. These images are copyrighted works and are not for commercial use; but feel free to use the images in your personal digital imaging experiments as you explore the features of Photoshop. Richard has taken some stunning close-up pictures, and his work is available commercially. See the Resource Guide in this book for more information on how to contact him for commercial usage rights. Also see the ZECH.PDF file in the ZECH directory for information about the images.

Identical Programs for Different Operating Systems

While reading this book, you'll probably notice that there are few differences between the way Photoshop works on the Windows and Macintosh operating systems. The differences can be attributed to the fact that different processors are used in the Macintosh and IBM/PC personal computers, and because the conventions associated with Windows and the Macintosh systems have evolved independently from one another. For these reasons, the other contents of the Bonus CD are broken into a WIN subdirectory, and a MAC folder. Some of the shareware products are different between operating systems, because software authors sometimes write for a specific platform.

Some good news is that Pixar, HSC Software, and typeface creators have provided identical Macintosh and Windows versions of their product for your evaluation. The next section describes what Windows and Macintosh users will find in the WIN and MAC partitions of the Bonus CD that comes with this book.

The PIXAR128 Directory/Folder

The PIXAR128 directory on the Bonus CD in both the WIN and MAC partitions is a sampler of Pixar's seamless tiling engine. It's a Photoshop plug-in filter that can be used to create photographic backgrounds in images of just about any dimension or resolution. This is a limited version plug-in that comes with two photographic pattern styles: Blue Lattice and Woven Flower.

An example of how PIXAR128 works is shown in Chapter 19, in which an exercise shows the use of the filter, and instructions for installing it.

The TYPESTRY Directory/Folder

The TYPESTRY directory on both the WIN and MAC partitions is a demonstration version of Typestry, a modeling and rendering program that produces photo-realistic typeface characters. You can't spell anything except PIXAR with this demonstration version (which is only fair), but you can see how lights can be assigned to a text image, how different realistic textures such as metal, glass, plastic, and wood can be assigned to lettering, and how these 3D letters can be rotated in space. Best of all, anything you create in the demonstration version can be exported with an Alpha channel in it to a number of file formats that Photoshop can read. You can then separate the letter images from the background.

To install the Typestry demonstrations see the README text files in the TYPESTRY subirectory/folder on the Bonus CD.

The ALIENS Directory/Folder

Alien Skin Software has both a Macintosh and Windows version of Drop Shadow, one of the six plug-in filters that comes in their commercial version of The Black Box. The Drop Shadow plug-in for Photoshop can make quick work of creating realistic shadows from a selection marquee. Chapter 19, "3rd-Party Plug-in Filters" explains how to use this filter, shows examples of how to use it in a design, and provides installation instructions for the Macintosh and Windows.

The KPT Directory/Folder

A fully working version of Kai's Power Tools Gradient Designer is included on the Bonus CD in the MAC and WIN KPT subdirectory. In addition, KPT plug-in filters for Glass Lens, Sharpen Intensity, Pixel Storm, and Hue Protected Noise are located in the KPT subdirectory.

The Gradient Design 2.0 filter is covered in Chapter 19, "3rd-Party Plug-in Filters," which discusses how to access the menus and options, how to create your own presets with this working version, and how to install these filters. See the README file in the KPT directory for information on how to order the commercial version of KPT and how to take advantage of the special discount offered to *Inside Adobe Photoshop 3* readers.

Modeling and Rendering Programs

We have different modeling and rendering demonstration programs for our Macintosh and Windows readers to evaluate, and they are located in their respective partitions. To learn more about how modeling and rendering applications can help create a photo-realistic image, see Chapter 22, "Virtual Reality: The Ingredients of Dreamwork."

The 3DPRO Folder (Macintosh)

In the MAC partition is a 3DPRO folder with a README document that describes the installation procedure and instructions for using the shareware version of CADPRO 3D. Modeling and rendering programs are a natural companion for Photoshop imaging work, and you get a free sample experience of modeling possibilities with CADPRO 3D, an excellent, full-featured combination modeling and rendering program.

The TRUSPACE Directory (Windows)

In the WIN partition is the TRUSPACE subdirectory which contains all the files needed to run a read-only version of Caligari's trueSpace for Windows. Copy these files to a subdirectory you create on your hard disk, then use Program Manager to create the icon in a Program Manager group. You can't save a creation made in this read only version of TrueSpace, but you'll definitely get some hands-on experience with manipulating and texture-mapping surfaces to 3D wireframe objects. You can assign lights to a scene, rotate objects, and distort them. A handy palette of geometric primitives (sphere, cylinder, cube) is also included in this version. TrueSpace was the winner of *PC Magazine*'s 11th Annual Technical Excellence Award for Graphics Software.

The Shareware on the Bonus CD

The *Inside Adobe Photoshop 3* Bonus CD contains shareware fonts and utilities from talented software authors, and we've chosen some of the very best ones for both the MAC and WIN partitions of the Bonus CD. They are not identical versions of the same programs, because the operating systems have different requirements, and shareware authors tend to write for the platform with which they are most comfortable.

Shareware is an alternative distribution method that software authors often choose when traditional retail methods of distribution are unfeasible. Many shareware authors prefer to spend their time writing great software instead of trying to find distributors and other sales outlets. Shareware is *not* freeware—the term instead describes fully copyrighted works whose *distribution methods* are different. The incentive to register (buy) a shareware program comes from the user's conscience, but the obligation is a legal one. Shareware is distributed via online services and on CDs like ours as working, fully functional versions of programs so that the user (you) can "try before you buy." When you purchased this book and the enclosed CD, you didn't buy the software enclosed. If you try the shareware and like it, please buy and register it with the respective authors of the programs. You'll find information on how to register the software within each programs subdirectory.

The following sections list the platforms the shareware is written for, and what the file(s) on our Bonus CD provide.

The BOOLEANS Directory (Windows)

Don Leclair is a man of vision. He has seen the need for a Desktop Coffee Mug and written one! Toggle-Booleans' "Non-Productivity Tools" are located in the

BOOLEANS subdirectory of the Bonus CD, and contain working versions of such "must have" applets as the Desktop Elvis Detector and the Bit Recycler, a program that "realigns all the renegade, subversive ones and zeros that might be lurking on your hard drive."

Is it all silliness? Not quite. The Booleans RESMON.EXE file can sit on your Program Manager desktop and provide instant information about how Windows resources are doing at any time. Memory, graphical handles, and user handles are all metered out in percentages, and if you see these numbers slip dangerously low, it's time to restart Windows, before Windows does this *for* you in an unexpected way.

The COMPACT Folder (Macintosh)

Compact Pro by Bill Goodman at Cyclos software is a file-archiving and compression/decompression program for the Macintosh. This program not only compresses files, it can also span large compressed files across a number of floppy disks. It's a real lifesaver when you need to transport a large file on floppy disks.

The FONTS Directory/Folder (PC and Macintosh)

To add a textual element to a Photoshop design, you need typefaces that have an elegant, sometimes ornamental look. We've assembled some attractive shareware TrueType and Type 1 typefaces that can be found in the FONTS subdirectory (folder) of both the MAC and WIN partitions of the Bonus CD. Do yourself a favor, though, and only copy the fonts specific to your operating platform to your hard disk. The font collections are identical, but although TrueType and Type 1 fonts are used by both operating systems, you can't use a Mac Type1 font on an IBM/PC, and vice versa.

Also, most of the typefaces come in both Type 1 and TrueType formats. It is not a good idea to install the same typeface in both formats, so be sure you install *either* the Type 1 *or* the TrueType version of any particular typeface.

Windows users should install TrueType typefaces using the Windows Fonts utility found in the Windows Control Panel group. Type 1 typefaces are installed using the ATM Control Panel. If you can't find the icon for the ATM Control Panel, use Windows' File Manager to locate the file ATMCNTRL.EXE, found in the Windows subdirectory. When you find ATMCNTRL.EXE, double-click on the file name to launch the ATM Control Panel.

Macintosh users can install fonts by dragging the typeface files onto the System folder icon, and answering Yes when the System asks if it should put the files in the appropriate folder (Fonts Folder).

New Riders Publishing
INSIDE
SERIES

Have fun with these fonts, and don't forget to register them with their authors if you decide to use the typefaces.

The Bouton's Directory/Folder (PC and Macintosh)

The authors of *Inside Adobe Photoshop 3* would like to share their collection of Type 1 typefaces with you. These typefaces are mostly picture (pi) fonts, but a display face or two is included among them. In the Fonts subdirectory, you will find FONTS.PDF, an Adobe Acrobat document that displays the typefaces so you can see what they look like before you load them. The Bouton collection of typefaces are not shareware—they are charityware. If you enjoy these typefaces and use them, we ask that you make a tax-deductible donation (the size of the donation is up to you) to your local chapter of The American Arthritis Foundation or The Salvation Army. These organizations need the money for research, money to help people, and they are personal causes we hope you never have to personally relate to.

The Haber Directory/Folder (PC and Macintosh)

Blake Haber's, Dixie Delights Font Foundry has provided a splendid assortment of shareware display and picture (pi) typefaces. This font sampler collection includes Chiseled Open, Dixon's Vixens, Harlequin, Mayan Dingbats, Pre-Columbian Ornaments One, Tango!, and Taco Modern.

The Sansone Directory/Folder (PC and Macintosh)

Shareware author Ronald Sansone has provided Savannah and Spund from his collection of typefaces for your appraisal. Savannah is a 3D, block letter typeface and Spund is a bold, backward slanting san serif typeface.

The PAINTSHP Directory (Windows)

Paint Shop Pro is located in the WIN partition of the CD in the PSP2 subdirectory. This program offers basic image editing functions and can convert a bitmap image file to 17 of the most widely used image formats. Paint Shop Pro is TWAIN-compliant for scanning and can open a PhotoCD image. These are invaluable qualities in a program that can load in about two seconds. It's great for cropping and previewing images, and the retail version of the program comes with thorough, informative documentation. See the Resource Guide in this book for information about contacting JASC, the makers of Paint Shop Pro, and read the Help file for additional information.

To install Paint Shop Pro, copy all the files in the PSP2 subdirectory to a directory you have set up for the application on your hard disk. Then, go to Program Manager and create an icon for the program group where you want PaintShop Pro to reside.

The PKZIP Directory (Windows/DOS)

PKWARE's owner, Phil Katz, has created a compression program that is almost universally accepted in the Intel-based community for freeing up precious hard drive space and archiving files that can't fit on a diskette. PKZIP, the unregistered version, is available in this directory, and you can't span disks with WinZip if you don't have PKZ204G.EXE on your hard disk. Version 204G is faster and a more capable compression utility than previous versions, and you'll receive documentation and a special way to brand your compressed files when you register PKZIP.

The WINZIP Directory (Windows)

Nico Mak Computing, Inc. provides a convenient Windows shell for any of the popular archiving formats. WinZip archives and decompresses files to and from the ZIP, LZH, ARJ, ARC, and other popular formats. You don't have to exit Windows to unzip a file anymore, but you must already have the various compression utilities that create these kinds of archives on your hard disk to use this program. Additional features are the capability to span multiple disks (if you have the complete version of PKZIP installed on your hard disk), and to rename, edit, and view selected contents of a compressed file without "popping" an entire compressed volume.

To take full advantage of WinZip's features, you must already have PKZIP.EXE somewhere on your hard disk before you install WinZip. A copy of PKZIP is in the PKZIP directory on the Bonus CD, and you might have a copy already if you've purchased a program that uses PKWARE's compression on its setup disks. Create a directory on your hard disk, then copy the files in the WINZIP subdirectory to the new directory. Then go to Program Manager and create an icon for WinZip in the Program Manager group of your choosing. The first time you launch WinZip, the program will ask you to help it find your compression utilities, so you might want to write down where PKZIP or ARJ is located on your hard disk before installing WinZip.

The ZIPIT Folder (Macintosh)

ZipIt, a handy shareware utility by Tommy Brown, enables Mac users to create PKZIP files and decompress PKZIPPED files. ZipIt is a compression and archiving utility that spans computer platforms; it gives Macintosh users a convenient and efficient way to share files with PC-based clients and coworkers. Using ZipIt to transport files to a printer or service bureau is covered in Chapter 24, "The Service Bureau." You'll find ZipIt, installation instructions, and operating instructions in the ZIPIT subdirectory on the Bonus CD.

APPENDIX

B

How To Install the Online Glossary: PC and Macintosh Versions

The *Inside Adobe Photoshop 3* Online Glossary is an illustrated collection of terms, definitions, and cross-references that come in handy as you explore Photoshop. And it's in Adobe Acrobat format, which means it's an electronic document that can be read online, or printed in parts or total from a laser printer. Let's say you want to save an RGB masterpiece and want to know if the TIFF format is cool. The NRP *Inside Adobe Photoshop 3* Online Glossary tells you the color-capability of the TIFF format (24-bit), your alternatives, and whether or not you can save Alpha channels (yes) and Layers (no) along with it. You haven't even used the Online Glossary, and see how useful it is already?

Because the Online Glossary is in Adobe Acrobat format, you can easily find an entry you're looking for. Our Acrobat document has links within the text, so you can leap and bound around the virtual pages to gather as much information as you need about a topic in which you're interested. But before you can use this valuable Photoshop assistant, you need to install the Adobe Acrobat reader on your computer if you haven't done so already. The next section shows you where to find and install both the Acrobat Reader and the *Inside Adobe Photoshop 3* Online Glossary.

Installing the Acrobat Reader for Windows

You find the Acrobat Reader version 2 on the Adobe Photoshop 3 Deluxe CD-ROM in the ACROREAD subdirectory. You need about 2 MB of free hard disk space and have ATM 3.01 or later installed on your computer. Acrobat Reader cannot work if Adobe Type Manager 3.01 (ATM 3.01) or later isn't installed. If you already have installed Photoshop, the proper version of ATM has been installed. If you haven't installed Photoshop yet, you should do this as a first step, because you find this book's exercises to be exceptionally challenging otherwise.

To install the Acrobat Reader, you need to exit any DOS windows you may have open and close any applications you have running. Windows Program Manager (or a third party Windows shell, such as Norton Desktop) should be the only thing on your screen right now. The Acrobat Reader installation program needs to restart Windows after setup for the installation to be complete.

Open Windows File Manager, and choose **R**un from the **F**ile menu. In the Command Line text entry box, enter the following path to the Acrobat Reader installation program. Be sure to substitute the drive letter that corresponds to your CD for the X: in the example.

`X:\ACROREAD\ACROREAD.EXE`

When you have entered the path, click on the OK button. The installation program loads. It may take a minute or two to load from the CD.

Read the License agreement and then click on **A**ccept. The Acrobat Installer dialog box appears. If the default of C:\ACROREAD is not acceptable to you, enter the drive and directory where you want the reader to install for Acrobat Reader files in the Target directory field. Click on Install. Then click on OK to clear the reminder to register the product. Enter your Name and Organization in the appropriate fields in the next dialog box that appears, then click on OK. The program installs and then warns you to close any applications you have open so that the Acrobat Installer can restart Windows. Do this if anything, like a modem or Print Manager, is running (it shouldn't be). Windows restarts and you find a new program group, Acrobat Reader, with the Acrobat Reader icon inside.

Installing the Acrobat Reader for Macintosh

Acrobat Reader 2.0 wasn't ready in time for Adobe to include it in the initial release of the Adobe Photoshop 3 Deluxe CD-ROM, so you may find that you have version 1 instead. Version 2.0 of the Acrobat Reader is available direct from Adobe, or can be downloaded from the Adobe forum on CompuServe or Adobe's BBS. Additionally, version 2.0 of Acrobat Reader for Windows and for the Macintosh can be freely distributed, so if a friend or co-worker has the newer version, it's legal to share it.

The Acrobat Reader Installer is found on the Adobe Photoshop 3 Deluxe CD-ROM in the Acrobat Reader Installer folder. Click on the application icon to launch the installer. Be sure to choose the Custom Install option, then click on the Customize button and choose to install the Adobe Acrobat Reader 1.0, the ATM Mini Font Database, and pick one of the font options for installation. Do not choose to install ATM. Follow the instructions that appear on screen. It may seem strange not to install ATM, but there is a good reason. When you installed Photoshop, Adobe Type Manager (ATM) version 3.8.1 was installed. This is a newer version than the Acrobat Reader Installer uses (3.6.1). In order to work properly Photoshop 3 needs the newer version (3.8.1), and version 1 of the Acrobat Reader works just fine with the newer version of ATM that Photoshop also uses.

Using the *Inside Adobe Photoshop 3* Online Glossary

Once you have the Acrobat Reader installed, using the Online Glossary is as easy as pie. Double-click on the Acrobat Reader icon that the Acrobat Reader Installer program created in Program Manager (Macintosh: in the folder you specified) to launch the Reader. In the Open dialog box, use the Drives and Directories fields to go to the GLOSSARY subdirectory (folder) on the *Inside Adobe Photoshop 3* Bonus CD. Double-click on INSIDEPS.PDF in the box under the File Name text entry box, and the Online Glossary will open.

Navigating Within the Document

On the first page of the document, you see what appears to be a keyboard (see fig. B.1). Click on any of the letters to jump to the glossary section that contains the topics that begin with that letter. For example, if you wanted to look up the glossary definition for the Burn Tool, you would click on the B key. Clicking on the B key immediately takes you to the B Section page, as seen in figure B.2. Click over the words **Burn Tool** and you jump to the page that contains information about the Burn Tool.

Figure B.1

Click on any of the letter buttons to jump to the entries that begin with that letter.

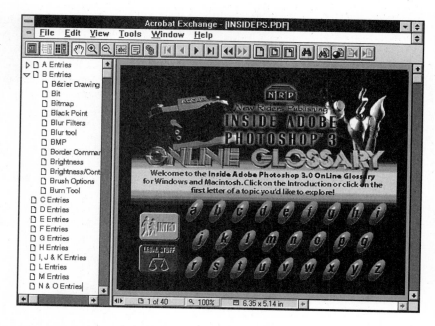

As you can see in figure B.3, within the text there are some words and phrases that have dashed outline boxes around them. If you want to look up the word or phrase that is within one of these boxes, click on the word and you are whisked away to that topic. For example, in figure B.3, if you click over the words **Dodge tool** or **Brushes palette**, you jump to that topic. If you want to return to the original topic, click on the Go Back button, (the arrow button pointing left) on the tool bar. The Reader controls for moving through Acrobat document pages are similar to those found on a VCR.

Other hot spots that jump you to another location are the *more* and *con't* arrows you see when a topic doesn't fit on one screen page. More takes you to the next page where the topic continues and con't turns the page back to the start of the topic. Also, on page 1, clicking on the Intro button takes you to the Introduction and Thanks sections, while the Legal Stuff button takes you to, well, the legal stuff—copyright information, disclaimers and so on.

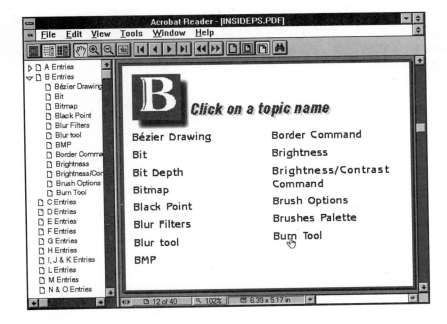

Figure B.2

Click on an entries title to move to that topic.

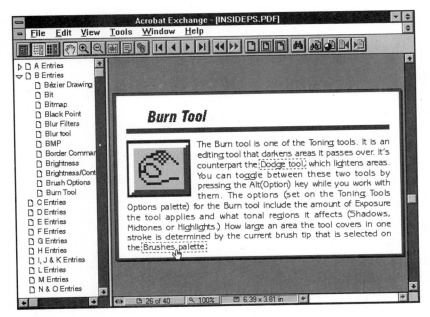

Figure B.3

Clicking on text that has an outline box around it will take you to that topic.

Note If you have never used Acrobat Reader before, be sure to spend some time reading the HELP_R.PDF document that the Acrobat Reader installer put in the ACROREAD\HELP subdirectory (folder). It can be opened using **F**ile, **O**pen from Acrobat Reader's menu bar or by choosing **H**elp, **A**crobat Reader Help from the menu bar. HELP_R.PDF discusses a number of methods you can use to navigate around any Acrobat document.

To exit the Acrobat Reader and the *Inside Adobe Photoshop 3* Online Glossary, choose **F**ile, E**x**it from the menu bar. That's all there is to it! Have fun exploring with Adobe Photoshop for Windows and New Riders Publishing's *Inside Adobe Photoshop 3*. That's what imaging is all about!

Index

Symbols

16.7 million colors, 38
256
    brightness values (grayscale
      mode), 36-37
    grayscale scanners, 74
3-Dimensional
    backgrounds, 1041-1044
    text, 1125-1126
    wireframe models, 1071
3D filter (Andromeda), 952-954
3DPRO folder, 1270

A

**Acquire command (File menu), 74,
76**
Acrobat Reader
    Macintosh installation, 1277
    Windows installation, 1276

Adaptive palette
    color reduction, 48-49
    indexed colors, 44
Add Noise dialog box, 818
adding
    anchor points to paths, 626
    borders, 357-360
    color to Gradient bar (KPT),
      925
    dimensions to color, 981-983
    layers, 796-797
    lettering to collage, 793-796
    Plug-ins, 910
    selections, 246-248
**Adjust command (Image menu),
86, 453, 1248**
adjusting
    cropped images, 596
    monitors, 150-158

Adobe Streamline utility (scanning), 385
AI (Adobe Illustrator), 1026
Airbrush tool, 1117-1120
airbrushing drawings, 967-970
Algorithm Control menu, 917
Alien Skin Software, 940
ALIENS directory, 1270
aligning type (vertical), 377
All command (Select menu), 233, 555
Alpha channel
    contents (loading), 187
    copying, 1235
    editing, 746-747
    grayscale mode, 829-832
    lettering, 792-796
    saved selections, 477-479
    selection (Channels palette), 205-206
    service bureaus, 1219
      film recorders, 1233
    shadows, 781-784
    Typestry program, 1037-1038
Alt (Option) key
    enhancing selection tools, 248-250
    Variations command, 302
ALV (Auto Level) settings, 695-696
ambient lighting, 1097
Anchor points (images), 616
    moving, 624
    paths, 468-469
      adding to, 626
      selections, 733
Andromeda filters, 949-956
    3D, 952-954
    cMulti, 949-951, 954
angled scans
    interpolation, 84-85
    moiré patterns, 84
    rotating, 84-85

animation cels, 30
Anti-alias PostScript, 166-167
Anti-aliasing
    Color Range command (Select menu), 846-848
    interpolation, 397
    sizing images, 397-398
    type, 364
    vector import filters, 846
Append command, 192
Apply command (Layer Masks), 718
Aris directory, 1267
Arrow tool (Paths palette), 470
aspect ratio
    constraining, 1238
    film recorders, 1226-1228
      calculating, 1229-1233
    negatives, 1244-1245
Assorted palette, 183
Attention dialog box, 526
Auto Level settings, *see* ALV
Auto Range Options dialog box, 88
automatically measuring images, 461-464
automating (Levels command), 689-691

B

BACKDROP images, 1267
Background Copy Mask, 664-666
background layers
    duplicating, 649-650
    Layer Mask, 655-658
backgrounds
    3-Dimensional, 1041-1044
    cloning, 711
    color printers, 1182
    cropped images (separating), 598

digital images (separating), 532-547

drawings (photographic washes), 1017-1018

environment mapping, 1087-1088

highlighting (Emboss filter), 1088-1093

image layers, 730-731

images, 946

Layer Masks, 520

patterns (filling), 780

Rubber Stamp tool, 341-344

slides, 1044-1049

surrealistic, 1088-1093

transparent
pixels, 229-231
selecting digital image elements,
547-553

balancing
color, 639-641
monitors, 157-158
digital image color, 308-321

banding (dithering), 391

Beep When Tasks Finish option, 170-172

Behind mode, 273

Behind mode (Options palette), 1002-1003, 1015

Behind mode (Rubber Stamp), 432-435

Behind painting mode, 1126

Bézier curves (Pen tool), 470

Bicubic interpolation, 594
pixels, 159

Bilinear interpolation (pixels), 159

bitmap clipart, see clipart

Bitmap dialog box, 1143

bitmapped images, 29-30
Anti-aliasing, 846-848
grayscale mode, 41-42

indexed color, 41-42

PCL (Printer Command Language), 1143-1145

pixels, 31-33

vectors, building from, 849-851

bits, 33

Black Box filters, 940

Black channel (grayscale mode), 36-37

bleeding (color printers), 1182

blending
Blur tool, 675-677
Fuzziness slider, 746
shades, 370
shadows, 765-767
textures
images, 709-711
weathering, 405-407

Block mode (Eraser tool), 556

Blur command (Filters menu), 1082

Blur filters, 629
color channels, 1081-1082

Blur tool, 328-331, 563, 675-677, 769-770
images, 727-728
retouching images, 736-737

blurring, 769-770
color channels, 1081-1082
Gaussian shadows, 782
Radial blur
Spin, 825-828
Zoom, 825-828

BMP file format, 59

Bonus CD, 1266-1268
shareware, 1271-1274

BOOLEANS directory, 1271-1272

Border dialog box, 1105

borders
anti-aliased, 599-600
color printers, 1182
digital images (hiding), 312

glow, 1104-1106
neon glow, 1106-1109
from behind, 1113-1117
retouching photographs,
357-360
sharpening, 370-373
straight-line, 969
see also paths
Bouton directory, 1273
**branding images (File Info
command), 283**
brightness (color), 109
HSB color model, 114
Luminance (color), 802
mapping, 115-118
gamma, 118
histogram, 87-88, 116-117
midpoints, 117-118
midtones, 117-118
PhotoCDs, 129-130
histograms, 125-127
Kodak Precision CMS, 130
pixels, 115, 129-130
texture mapping, 1102-1103
brightness curves
digital image color, 303-306
S curves, 307
brightness values
Blur tool, 675-677
selecting digital image ranges,
533-535
**brightness/contrast controls
(scanners), 83**
**Brightness/Contrast dialog box,
562, 782, 1102**
**browsing software (viewing
PhotoCDs), 143-145**
brush sizes
cursors (tools), 165-166
Rubber Stamp tools (increasing), 419-421

Brushes palette
brush tips, 183-188
customizing, 192
loading, 190-193
Modes, 272-275
options, 182-183
resetting, 190-193
builds (slides), 1054-1058
**bullets (Typestry program),
1033-1036**
bump mapping, *see* **texture
mapping**
Burn tool, 627

C

**CAD (Computer Assisted Design),
1085**
**calculations for commercial
printers, 1163-1165**
Calculator, 700
Calibrate dialog box, 156
calibrating monitors, 150-158
**calibration bars (color printers),
1183-1184**
camera-ready
commercial printers
(halftones), 1158
service bureaus, 1176
cameras (digital), 73, 101-105
downloading images, 101-103
hot spots, 102
**Canvas Size command (Image
menu), 1236**
Canvas Size dialog box, 1229, 1236
captions (color printers), 1183
capturing, *see* **scanning**
careers, 1252-1254
cataloging images, 1257
CD-ROMs (PhotoCDs), 140-141
CDs (Bonus), 126, 1266-1268
shareware, 1271-1274

cells (halftones), 1148

cels (animation), 30

Channel Options command, 318

Channel Options dialog box, 775, 832

channels

Alpha

copying, 1235

editing, 746-747

lettering, 792-796

service bureaus, 1219

shadows, 781-784

Typestry program, 1037-1038

Black (grayscale mode), 36-37

color (Blur filters), 1081-1082

Green, 830-832

blurring, 1082

images, 162

monochrome, 36

RGB, 51-52

rotating images (film recorders), 1234-1240

texture (grayscale mode), 829-832

viewing (Channels palette), 203-204

Channels palette, 203-204, 998

selection areas

Alpha channel, 205-206

marquees, 205

Quick Mask mode, 206

saved, 205

viewing color channels, 203-204

choking spot-color separations, **1199**

chromacity (color), 110

chromatic inversion (colors), 210

CIELAB color, 811-812

see also LAB color model, 111-112

circles (Elliptical marquee tool), 249

Circular Multifilter, *see* **cMulti**

cleaning drawings, 958-959

Clear mode, 273

clicking mouse (tools), 1125

clipart, 547

customizing, 958-962

Clipboard, 461, 535

Export preferences, 167-168

flushing, 464

clipping, 643, 659

picks, 301

video, over-saturation (color), 113

clips (digital image color), 302-303

cloning

backgrounds, 711

between layers, 573

Color mode, 421-422

digital image elements, 564-566, 572-574

foreground color samples, 724-726

images, 688-689

layers, 710-711

New Window command, 445-447

pattern sampling, 338-341

patterns, 416

Rubber Stamp tool, 250-252, 412-415

direction, 416-418

increasing brush sizes, 419-421

Lighten mode, 418-419

sample point, 250

selection marquees, 250-252

shadows, 765-767

transparency layers, 430-432

Close command (File menu), **796**

Clouds filter, 459, 464-468

Cmd+Option (Macintosh), 248-250
**cMulti filters (Andromeda),
949-951, 954**
**CMYK (Cyan, Magenta, Yellow,
Black)**
   color separations, 1206-1208
   correction filters, 1075-1078
   drawings, 963-967
   GCR (Gray Component
     Removal), 1204
   gradients, 1009
   grayscale mode (printing), 1136
   Kai's Power Tools, 1202
   model, 160-161
     gamut, 178
   out-of-gamut colors
     removing dullness, 1203-1204
     viewing, 1200-1204
   printing, 1199-1208
     grayscale, 1136
     spot-color separations,
      1198-1199
   RGB converting, 1204-1206
   screen, 1200
   UCR (Undercolor Removal),
     1204
**CMYK Color command (Mode
menu), 1204**
collage (lettering), 793-796
color
   adding to Gradient bar (KPT),
     925
   balancing, 639-641
   brightness, 109, 129-130
     HSB color model, 114
     mapping, 115-118
   channels, 162
   Channels palette, 203-204
   chromacity, 110
   chromatic inversion, 210

CMYK (Cyan, Magenta, Yellow,
   Black), 1199-1208
   converting to RGB, 1204-1206
   correction filters, 1075-1078
   drawings, 963-967
   GCR (Gray Component
     Removal), 1204
   Kai's Power Tools, 1202
   out-of-gamut colors, 1200-1204
   removing dullness, 1203-1204
   separations, 1206-1208
   UCR (Undercolor Removal),
     1204
   combining tools, 978-979
   complementary, 639
   darkening, 982
   defaults, 981
   digital images
     balancing, 308-321
     brightness curves, 303-306
     clips, 302-303
     contrast, 296-302
     evaluating, 293
     fuzziness values, 312
     global adjustments, 295
     isolated balancing, 311-315
     manual editing, 315-318
     previewing changes, 300
     ranges, 318
     restoring, 319
     tone redistribution, 294-296
   dimensions, 981-983
   drawings, 968-973, 978-983
     contrast/saturation, 1022
     gradients, 1004-1005
     lettering, 1009-1010
     shading, 973-975
     smudging, 982
   foregrounds, 1002
     cloning, 724-726
     opacity, 997

fuzziness, 536-541
gamut, 150, 178-179
gradient fills, 973-975
gradients, 922-925
hues, 109, 292-299
images
    diffusion dither preferences, 163
    printing, 1178
LAB, 811
    grayscale, 814-817
    translating from RGB, 812-813
lightness, 109-110
Luminance, 802
manipulating, 114-115
monitors
    ambient light settings, 153
    balancing, 157-158
    calibrating, 150-158
    parameters, 152-153
    room parameters, 153
    target gamma, 153-154
neutral density (gray), 113
PANTONE, 168-172
patterns (adding), 453-455
reduction, 802
RGB, translating to LAB,
  812-813
sampling, 802-810
    Scratch palette, 803-806
saturation, 109, 646, 982
    over-saturation, 113
saved selections, 776-779
selective adjustment, 1075-1078
shades, 110
shading, 978-979
shadows, 570
Swatches palette, 387-389, 968
text (contrasting), 1121-1125
tints, 110, 804
Tolerance, 536

tones, 110, 292-299
    Auto distribution, 297-298
    midranges, 297
transparent pixels, 229-231
type, 375
    adding, 387-389
Variations command (Image
  menu), 642-644
warming up, 662-663
**Color Balance command, 309-321,
318-319**
**Color Balance dialog box, 309,
312, 640, 662**
Color Bar dialog box, 998
**Color Bar tool (Picker palette),
998**
**color channels (Blur filters),
1081-1082**
color gamut, 110
color images
  16.7 million colors, 38
  channels (interpolation), 40-41
  counting colors, 49
  dithering
    diffusion, 45
    pattern, 45-46
  indexed, 39
    bitmapped images, 41-42
    *converting from RGB image,
      46-48*
    lookup tables, 43-44
    palettes, 44
    RGB images, 49-50
  RGB (red, green, blue), 38
    channels, 51-52
    converting to indexed, 46-48
    filters, 52-53
    indexing, 49-50
    tools, 52-53
    TrueColor, 50-51

scanning, hardware recommendations, 74-75
TrueColor (RGB), 50-51
video drivers, 68-70
Color mode
cloning, 421-422
painting, 275-276
color models
comparisons, 112-113
HSB (Hue/Saturation/Brightness), 110
brightness (color), 114
LAB, 111-112
PhotoCDs, 122
modes, 110
RGB, 110-111
Color Picker (general preferences), 158-159
Color Picker dialog box, 158
color printers
backgrounds, 1182
bleeding, 1182
borders, 1182
calibration bars, 1183-1184
captions, 1183
crop marks, 1184
emulsion down, 1184
interpolation, 1184
labels, 1183
layers, 1180
negatives, 1184
non-PostScript, 1185-1186
personal, 1134-1135, 1176-1220
Portrait orientation, 1180
Postscript, 1186-1189
registration marks, 1183
resolution, 1180
RGB, 1179-1180
screens, 1181-1182, 1183

Color Range command (Select menu), 311, 318-319, 441-445, 460, 652, 744, 1091
Anti-aliasing, 846-848
digital image element Fuzziness, 536-541
sampling, 652-654
selecting images, 459-461
separating digital image elements, 533-535
Color Range dialog box, 442, 460, 847
color separations
alternatives, 1208-1209
CMYK, 1206-1208
color tables, 39
color washes (drawings), 1002-1003
color wheel, 293
color-casting digital images, 293, 297
removing, 300-301
color-correcting, 1248
colorizing, 1090-1093
monochrome images, 1092-1093
saving highlights, 1091-1092
combining
photographs, 590
selection functions, 603
tools for color effects, 978-979
commands
Append, 192
Apply (Layer Masks), 718
Channel Options, 318
Color Balance, 309-321
Color Range, 311, 318-319, 533-535, 536-541, 846-848
Curves, 303-308
Defringe, 550
Duplicate Layer, 608-609

Edit menu
  Crop, 91, 1239
  Define Pattern, 339, 778-779, 989
  Fill, 235, 273, 431, 448, 780
  Paste Into, 349-350, 989
  Paste Layer, 782
  Stroke, 273, 1122
  Undo, 231, 519
Feather, 307
File menu
  Acquire, 74, 76
  Close, 796
  Exit, 1215
  Export, 1029
  Get Info, 284
  New, 33
  Open, 849-851
  Page Setup, 1149, 1180
  Place, 842-846
  Print, 1155, 1189-1191
  Revert, 302
  Save, 47
  Save As, 208, 319
  Units Preferences, 373
Filter menu
  Blur, 1082
  Distort, 788, 1080
  Last Filter, 1114
  Noise, 819
  Render, 466, 833
  Stylize, 1074
Flatten Image, 631
Image menu
  Adjust, 86, 453, 1248
  Canvas Size, 1236
  Effects, 349
  Flip, 648, 681
  Histogram, 125
  Image Size, 55, 131, 559, 638, 1153

  Map, 393, 1198
  Rotate, 261, 554, 1180, 1234
Image Size, 697-698
Layer Mask, 756
Layers palette (Merge Layers), 530
Levels, 292-293, 689-691
Merge Layers, 631
Mode menu
  CMYK Color, 1204
  Gamut Warning, 1200
  Indexed Color, 43
  RGB Color, 838
Monitor Setup, 151-158
Perspective, 559-560
Save a Copy, 319
Scale, 550-551
Select menu
  All, 233, 555
  Color Range, 441-445, 460, 652, 744, 846-848, 1091
  Feather, 337, 828
  Float, 264, 325, 780
  Hide Edges, 244, 437, 665
  Inverse, 221, 251, 745
  Load, 1111
  Load Selection, 251, 279, 664
  Matting, 770
  Matting Defringe, 780
  Modify, 253, 665
  None, 233
  Save Selection, 478
  Similar, 774
Variations, 300-302
Window menu
  New Window, 445-447
  Palettes, 196
Windows menu (Show Rulers), 374

Commands palette, 196-198
  customizing, 198-203
  hot keys, 198-203
  maximum, 202-203
  pattern filling, 233-235
commercial printers
  Alpha channels (Photoshop),
    1219
  calculations, 1163-1165
  camera-ready halftones, 1158
  contrasts, decreasing, 1162-1163
  grayscale, 1158
    Paint Shop Pro utility,
    1159-1160
    shades, 1160-1162
  ink, 1162-1163
  printing, 1157-1165
  toner, 1162-1163
  see also service bureaus
common backgrounds (slides),
  1044-1049
COMPACT folder, 1272
CompactPro (compression
  program), 1213
complementary color, 639
composite images, 749-758
compositing modes, 272-275
compressing files, 91-100
  comparing lossy to lossless, 101
  JPEG compression, 94-100
    service bureaus, 1210-1213
  lossless
    LZW (Lempel, Ziv, and Welch),
    92-94
    TIFF (Tagged Image File
    Format), 92-94
  lossy, 90
    JPEG, 94-100
  programs
    spanning, 1213-1217
    zipping, 1214-1217
  Stacker, 100-105

condensing type, 379-380
connecting TWAIN standard
  scanners, 75-76
constraining aspect ratio, 1238
content layers (slides), 1054-1058
continuous-tone images
  (halftones), 35-36
contrast
  Blur tool, 675-677
  digital image color, 296-302
  drawings, 1022
  Fuzziness slider, 746
  histograms (PhotoCDs), 127-136
  printing
    decreasing, 1163-1165
    commercial printers, 1162-1163
convert direction point tool (Paths
  palette), 471-477
converting
  CMYK to RGB, 1204-1206
  digital image elements to layer
    objects, 576
  drawings to CMYK color,
    963-967
  grayscale to RGB, 837-840
  paths to selections, 603-608
  RGB to indexed color, 46-48
copying
  Alpha channels, 1235
  digital image elements, 564-566
  floating selections, 704-709
  gradient fills, 928
    to KPT Gradient Designer,
    911-916
  hot keys, 201
  images, 399-400
    correcting, 325-327
    from original, 759-761
    reusing, 763-764
    to layers, 659-661
  KPT Gradient Designer fills,
    1005

layers, 608-609, 749
photo-realistic images (layers), 1111-1112
selections to images, 603-604
Corel CD-ROM Utilities (PhotoCDs), 143-145
correcting images
Blur tool, 328-331
copying, 325-327
pasting, 325-327
Rubber Stamp tool, 331-333
Smudge tool, 328-331
corruption (TIFF), 1168-1169
counting colors (PaintShop Pro), 49
Crop command (Edit menu), 91, 1239
crop marks (color printers), 1184
Crop tool, 135, 594-598
cropping
film recorders, 1225-1233
images, 594-598, 740
resolution (PhotoCDs), 132-136
Cropping tool, 398
CRT (Cathode Ray Tube), 1223
Crystallize dialog box, 821
Crystallize filter, 820-825
Ctrl (Command) key, 248-250
Ctrl+Alt, 248-250
Ctrl+Shift+Alt keys, 249
Current Pick thumbnail, 300
cursors
tool activation points, 545
tools, 163-166
Curves command, 303-308
Curves dialog box, 304
Custom Colors dialog box, 168
Custom palette (indexed colors), 44
customizing
Brushes palette, 192
clipart, 958-962

commands palette, 198-203
palettes, 226-228
cutting (hot keys), 201
Cyan, Magenta, Yellow, and Black color model, *see* **CMYK**
CyberMesh filter, 955

D

Darken mode, 274
Paint Brush tool, 672-675
darkening
color, 982
pixels (Paint Brush tool), 672-675
data type (service bureaus), 1233
decreasing contrasts
commercial printers, 1162-1163
printers, 1163-1165
defaults (color), 981-983
Define Pattern command (Edit menu), 339, 778-779, 989
Defringe command (retouching pixels), 550
deleting
digital images, elements, 541-546
paths, 602
selections from image layers, 714-715
densitometers, 1183
Desaturation tool (Sponge tool), 407
desktop publishing, importing duotones, 1196-1197
developing film (film recorders), 1223
dialog boxes
Add Noise, 818
Attention, 526
Auto Range Options, 88
Bitmap, 1143

Border, 1105
Brightness/Contrast, 562, 782, 1102
Calibrate, 156
Canvas Size, 1229, 1236
Channel Options, 775, 832
Color Balance, 309, 312, 640, 662
Color Bar, 998
Color Picker, 158
Color Range, 442, 460, 847
Crystallize, 821
Curves, 304
Custom Colors, 168
Duotones Options, 1192
Duplicate Layer, 608, 1038
Edit Commands, 199
Emboss, 1074, 1089
EPS Format, 1195
Expand Selection, 1114
Export Paths, 1029
Features, 1187
Fill, 780
filters, recalling, 1007
Gamut Warning, 178
Gamut Warning Preference, 1201
Gaussian Blur, 580, 782, 1082
Halftone Screen, 1149
Hue/Saturation, 646
Illustrator Format, 850
Image Format, 1031
Image Size, 131, 136, 698, 1154, 1228
Indexed Color, 43, 1161
Kodak Precision CMS PhotoCD, 120
Layers Palette Options, 224
Levels, 117, 295
Levels command, 87

Load, 695
Load Selection, 279, 1111
Make Layer, 264, 782
Memory Preferences, 172
Monitor Settings, 155
Monitor Setup, 152
More Preferences, 166
New Image, 1028
New Layer, 413
Page Setup, 1141, 1180-1184
Plug-ins, 180
PostScript Options, 1188
Printing Inks Setup, 1183, 1204
Radial Blur, 825
Rasterize, 1089
Rasterize Adobe Illustrator Format, 850
Rasterizer dialog, 1073
Remove Layer Mask, 669
Save Path, 367
Selective Color, 1077
Separation Setup, 1204
Texture Fill, 1095
Transfer Functions, 1183
Transparency Options, 229
Type tool, 375-410, 807
Unit Preferences, 176, 373
Variations, 642
Wave, 612
Difference mode, 274
diffusion dither preferences, 163
diffusion dithering, 45
scanning, 65
digital images
scanning, 84-85
digital cameras, 73, 101-105
downloading images, 101-103
hot spots, 102
digital halftone cells (PostScript printers), 1146-1148

digital illustrations *see also*
 drawings
digital images
 backgrounds, separating from
  other elements, 532-547
 bitmapped, 29-33
 borders (hiding), 312
 channels
  Black, 36
  monochrome, 36
 color, 38
  balancing, 308-321
  brightness curves, 303-306
  clips, 302-303
  contrast, 296-302
  *converting RGB image to indexed
   color, 46-48*
  counting colors, 49
  dithering, 45-46
  evaluating, 293
  Fuzziness values, 312
  global adjustments, 295
  indexed, 39
  isolated balancing, 311-315
  lookup tables, 43-44
  manual editing, 315-318
  previewing changes, 300
  ranges, 318
  RGB, 50-51
  tone redistribution, 294-296
  tones, 292
  TrueColor, 50-51
  video drivers, 68-70
 color-casting, 293, 297
  removing, 300-301
 digital cameras, 101-105
 editing with Layer Masks,
  519-527
 elements
  cloning, 572-574
  copying, 564-566
  deleting, 541-546
  disproportionate scaling, 552
  dragging to other windows, 550
  editing with Lasso tool, 544-545
  floating, 550, 554
  focusing, 562-563
  Fuzziness, 536
  integration, 575-577
  opaque, 583-584
  perspectives, 559-560
  resolution, 558-572
  retouching, 545-546
  rotating, 555
  scaling, 550-551
  *selecting from transparent
   backgrounds, 547-553*
  selecting with Lasso tool, 542
  shadows, 553-574
  skewing/scaling, 555-556
  windows, 534
 feathered marquee selection,
  303
 file formats, 57-62
  BMP, 59
  IFF (Amiga), 60
  JPEG, 60
  PCX Images, 59-60
  PICT, 59-60
  RAW, 61
  RGB, 58-59
 file sizes (white space), 81-83
 floating, 517
  converting to layer objects, 576
 gamma adjustment, 297
 grayscale, 36-37
  pixels, 41-42
  video drivers, 68-70
 halftones, 35-36
 hiding, 520-521

histograms, 87-91, 296
interpolation, 40-41
Layer Masks, 516-527
   applying changes, 525-527
   merging, 530
layers
   cloning between, 573
   linking, 566
   merging, 586
   RAM, 532
   saving, 530
masks, 519
noise, 818-820
pasting into drawings, 1017-1018
phases, 29
PhotoCDs, 118-119
   adding photographs, 140
   adjusting tonal levels, 119-130
   brightness, 125-130
   CD-ROMs, 140-141
   drives, 146-147
   histograms, 125-127
   Kodak Pro PhotoCD Master, 141-142
   LAB color model, 122
   multisession, 140
   opening file, 120
   PCD file format, 140
   Photographic Quality Kodak PhotoCD Master, 141-142
   previewing changes, 122-131
   resolutions, 131-132
   saving images, 123
   viewing, 142-145
photography, 28
   restoration, 291-292
pixels, 54-56, 114-115
   brightness (color), 115
   gamma, 115
Quick masks, 316

ranges
   hiding/revealing, 523-524
   selecting by brightness values, 533-535
reducing, 559
resolution, 44
scanning, 33, 85-86
   angled, 84-85
   dithering, 64
   saving, 90-101
   VGA video drivers, 64-66
targets, viewing, 517
textures, 528-532
tonal densities, 86-90
   Auto Range option, 88
transfers, 515-527, 547-553, 575-586
undoing Variations command changes, 302
vector, 30
vector-based, 29-30
White Point, 296
White Points, 294
WYSIWYG, 28-30
see also images; photographs
digitizing drawings, 960-967
dimensional shadows, 578-586
dimensions
   color, 981-983
   scan images, 78-81
      file sizes, 81-83
      sampling rates, 80-81
   texture mapping, 1073-1074
   Typestry program, 1031
direction of cloning (Rubber Stamp tool), 416-418
direction points (paths), 468-469
directions (paths), 472
directories
   ALIENS, 1270
   Aris, 1267

BOOLEANS, 1271-1272
Bouton, 1273
EXERCISE, 1266-1267
FONTS, 1272-1273
GLOSSARY, 1267
Haber, 1273
IMAGECEL, 1268
KPT (Kai's Power Tools), 1270
MATERIAL, 1267-1268
PAINTSHP, 1273-1274
PIXAR128, 1269
PKZIP, 1274
Sansone, 1273
TRUSPACE, 1271
TYPESTRY, 1269
WINZIP, 1274
ZECH, 1268
see also folders
disks, spanning (compression programs), 1213-1217
Displace filter, 785
displacement maps
negative, 791
text, 784-786
Display mode, 273
displays
General Preferences, 159-162
LUT (Look Up Table) Animation, 163
disproportionate scaling
digital images, 552
Distort command (Filter menu), 788, 1080
distorting
gradient fills, 918
images, 401-402, 611-615
editing with Layer Masks, 615-617
Glass Lens filter, 1078-1081
lettering, 787-791
negatively, 790-791
type, 379-380

dithering
banding, 391
diffusion, 45
pattern, 45-46
scanning, 64-65
Dodge tool, 606-607
highlighting, 1083-1084
retouching images, 423-425
DOS (palette files), 183
dots, 1134
non-halftone, 1134
pixels, 54-55
screens, 1166-1168
shaping, 1165-1166
downloading images (digital cameras), 101-103
dragging
digital image elements to other windows, 550
selections to image windows, 603
drawing programs, 1256-1257
AI (Adobe Illustrator), 1026
drawings
airbrushing, 967-970
cleaning, 958-959
CMYK color, 963-967
color, 968-973, 978-983
contrast/saturation, 1022
gradients, 1004-1005
lettering, 1009-1010
smudging, 982
color washes, 1002-1003
digital images, integrating, 1017-1018
digitizing, 962-967
dimensions, 981-983
shading, 997
editing, 997-1000
fills, 968-973, 1015
folds, 981-983

Glass Lens filter, 986
gradient fills, 971-975
layers (editing), 1021-1022
lettering (drop-shadows), 1012
lighting, 975-976
pattern fills, 988-989, 1006-1024
photographic washes, 1017-1018
scanning, 960
shading, 972, 976, 992-995
straight-line borders, 969
textures, 991-997
tiled patterns, 989
Toning tools, 991-997
viewing, 965
drivers
printers, 1141-1142
video
color images, 68-70
grayscale mode, 68-70
installing, 66-68
VGA, 64-66
drives
PhotoCDs, 146-147
removable media (service bureaus), 1218
service bureaus, 1219
Drop Shadow filter, 941-944, 1041-1044
drop-shadows
lettering, 1125-1126
drawings, 1012
text, 798-799
DropStuff (compression program), 1213
dullness (CMYK), removing, 1203-1204
Duotone Options dialog box, 1192
duotones, 1191-1197
creating, 1191-1194
exporting, 1195-1197
grayscale, 1191

printing separations, 1197
sepia, 1191
steeltone images, 1191
Duplicate Layer command, 608-609
Duplicate Layer dialog box, 608, 1038
duplicating
background layers, 649-650
layers (slides), 1054-1058
dynamic sliders (Picker palette), 171-172

E

edges
Blur tool, 675-677, 769-770
sharpening, 370-373
Edit Commands dialog box, 199
Edit menu commands
Crop, 91, 1239
Define Pattern, 339, 778-779, 989
Fill, 235, 273, 431, 448, 780
Paste Into, 349-350, 989
Paste Layer, 782
Stroke, 273, 1122
Undo, 231, 519
editing
Alpha channel, 746-747
digital images
elements, 541-546
manually, 315-318
with Layer Masks, 519-527
distorted images with Layer Masks, 615-617
drawings, 997-1000
layers, 1021-1022
images
layers, 729-735
with Blur tool, 727-728

layers, 570, 713-718
path selections, 733-734
paths, 476-477
Quick Mask mode, 206, 212-214, 392-394, 719-721
see also retouching
editing functions, 238-239
Effects command (Image menu), 349
electronic format (service bureaus), 1176
Elliptical Marquee tool, 46, 242-246
circles, 249
Emboss dialog box, 1074, 1089
Emboss filter, 1073-1074
backgrounds, 1089
texture mapping (brightness), 1102-1103
emulsion
color printers, 1184
Rubber Stamp, fixing chipped, 331-333
environment mapping, 1087-1088
EPS (Encapsulated PostScript), 166-167, 962
mapping images, 1071-1073
rasterizing images, 1073
EPS Format dialog box, 1195
Eraser tool, 823
Block mode, 556
Paintbrush mode, 545-546
patterns, 432-435
error diffusion printing, 1141-1142
ESOTERIC images, 1268
EXERCISE directory, 1266-1267
Exit command (File menu), 1215
exit slides, 1062-1068
Expand Selection dialog box, 1114
expanding KPT menus, 913
Export command (File menu), 1029

Export Paths dialog box, 1029
Export preferences (Clipboard), 167-168
exporting
duotones, 1195-1197
EPS files to Photoshop, 962
paths, 1028-1030
extending shadows, 579-581
Eyedropper tool, 243

F

Feather command, 307
Feather command (Select menu), 337, 828
feathering
images, 604-605
marquee selection, 304
Features dialog box, 1187
file formats
digital images, 57-62
BMP, 59
GIF (Graphics Interchange Format), 60
IFF (Amiga), 60
JPEG, 60
PCX Images, 59
PICT, 59-60
RAW, 61
film recorders (service bureaus), 1233
JPEG (service bureaus), 1210-1213
PCD (PhotoCDs), 119
Image Pacs, 140
RGB
PSD (PhotoShop default file), 58-59
Targa file (TGA), 58-59
TIF (Tagged Image File), 58-59
Targa, 1074

TIFF (Tagged Information File Formats)
  corruption, 1168-1169
  opening sections of files, 133
File menu commands
  Acquire, 74, 76
  Close, 796
  Exit, 1215
  Export, 1029
  Get Info, 284
  New, 33
  Open, 849-851
  Page Setup, 1149, 1180
  Place, 842-846
  Print, 1155, 1189-1191
  Revert, 302
  Save, 47
  Save As, 208, 319
  Units Preferences, 373
files
  compressing, 91-100
    comparing lossy to lossless, 101
    JPEG, 90
    lossless, 92-94
    lossy, 94-100
    programs, 1213-1217
    Stacker, 100
  EPS (Encapsulated PostScript), 962
  headers, 132
  layers, merging to conserve space, 269-272
  opening
    sections, 133
    shortcuts, 534
  PhotoCDs (sizes), 139
  service bureaus
    sizes, 1241-1243
  sizes, 81-83
    conserving, 1116-1117
    negatives, 1244

    service bureaus, 1242-1243
    white space, 81-83
  swap files, 173
Fill command (Edit menu), 235, 273, 431, 448, 780
Fill dialog box, 780
Fill Path tool (Paths palette), 601
fills
  background patterns, 780
  drawings, 968-973, 1015
  foregrounds, 601
  gradient fills, 968-975, 1004-1005
    copying to KPT Gradient Designer, 911-916
  patterns, 516
    drawings, 1006-1024
    fills, 988-989
  shadows, 570
film recorders, 1222
  aspect ratio, 1225-1233
    calculating, 1229-1233
    constraining, 1238
  aspect ratios (negatives), 1244-1245
  cropping images, 1225-1233
  CRT (Cathode Ray Tube), 1223
  developing film, 1223
  monitors
    calibrating, 1224-1225
    gamma, 1225
  orientations
    landscape, 1233-1234
    portrait, 1233-1234
  RIP (Raster Image Processor), 1223
  rotating images, channel by channel, 1234-1240
  service bureaus
    data types, 1233

file formats, 1233
file sizes, 1241-1243
negatives, 1244-1245
Filter menu commands
Blur, 1082
Distort, 788, 1080
Last Filter, 1114
Noise, 819
Render, 466, 833
Stylize, 1074
filters, 817-828, 858-905
3D (Andromeda), 952-954
Andromeda, 949-956
Black Box, 940
Blur, 629
color channels, 1081-1082
Clouds, 459, 464-468
cMulti (Andromeda), 949-951
CMYK color, 1075-1078
Crystallize, 820-825
CyberMesh, 955
Displace, 785
Drop Shadow, 941-944,
1041-1044
Emboss, 1071-1074
backgrounds, 1089
texture mapping, 1102-1103
Gallery Effects, 930-949
Glass Lens, 986-987, 1079
distorting images, 1078-1081
KPT, 929
Gradient Designer (KPT), 911
Hue Protected Noise (KPT),
929-930
import
Place command (File menu), 842
vector, 846
installation, 985
KPT, 910-930, 985-991
Glass Lens, 929

Gradient Designer, 1004-1005
Sharpen Intensity, 1022-1023
Lighting Effects, 833-836
grayscale mode, 829-832
texture mapping, 1096-1098
Motion Blur, 530
native, 842
noise, 818-820
non-Adobe filters, 181
Note Paper (Gallery Effects),
934-937
Open (File menu), 849
PIXAR, 988-991
Pixar One Twenty-Eight,
945-949
Pixel Storm (KPT), 930
Place command (File menu),
842-846
Plastic Wrap (Gallery Effects),
937-939
plug-ins, 1255-1256
preferences, 179-181
preset filters, 917
proxy boxes, 611
recalling, 917
dialog boxes, 1007
relief images, 833-836
RGB, 52-53
Sharpen Intensity (KPT), 930
third-party filters, 910-911
Watercolor (Gallery Effects),
931-934
Wave filter, 611-615
see also Plug-ins
finalizing effects, 381-382
finding shadow origins, 599
flatbed scanners, 71-72
Flatten Image command, 631
flattening images (patterns),
451-452

Flip command (Image menu), 648, 681

flipping images, 647-649, 763-764

Float command (Select menu), 264, 325, 780

floating

digital images, 517

elements, 550, 554

selections, 257-260

copying/positioning, 704-709

opacity, 750

flood-fill patterns, 441

flushing Clipboard, 464

focal point (Zoom blur), 825-828

Focus Tool Options palette, 562

Focus tool

Blur, 727-728

oversaturated pixels, 336-338

focusing

digital images, 562-563

softening, 769-770

folders

3DPRO, 1270

COMPACT, 1272

ZIPIT, 1274

see also directories

folds (drawings), 981-983

fonts

size

PostScript, 373

Traditional, 373

slides, 1049-1054

specifications, 375-378

Type 1, 364-365

Typestry program, 1032-1036

FONTS directory, 1272-1273

foregrounds

color, 1002

color samples (cloning), 724-726

fills, 601

Layer Masks, 520

opacity, 997

punch-out graphics, 941

formats

drawings, 960

JPEG (images), 591-605

Photoshop 2.5 compatibility, 171

vector formats, 960

Freehand selection mode (Lasso tool), 207

from behind neon glow, 1113-1117

function sets

editing functions, 238-239

paint application functions, 238-239

selection tools, 238-239

tools, enhancing, 248-250

Fuzziness

digital images, 312

elements, 536

slider, 538, 746

G

Gallery Effects filters, 930-949

Note Paper, 934-937

Plastic Wrap, 937-939

Watercolors, 931-934

gamma

adjusting, 297

brightness (color), 118

film recorders, 1225

monitor color setup, 153-154

pixels, 115

gamut (color), 150, 178-179

Gamut Warning command (Mode menu), 1200

Gamut Warning dialog box, 178

Gamut Warning Preference dialog box, 1201

Gaussian Blur dialog box, 580, 782, 1082

Gaussian noise, 820
Gaussian shadows, 782
GCR (Gray Component Removal), 1204
General Preferences (screens), 158-171
Get Info command (File menu), 284
GIF (Graphics Interchange Format), 60
GLASS images, 1268
Glass Lens filter, 929, 986-987, 1079
    distorting images, 1078-1081
global adjustments, 295
GLOSSARY directory, 1267
glossary, *see* **OnLine Glossary**
glow
    from behind, 1113-1117
    neon text, 1121-1125
    texture mapping, 1104-1106
        neon, 1106-1109
Goodman, Bill, 1272
Gradient bar (KPT), 921-925
Gradient Designer (KPT), 911, 1004-1005
    interface, 916-925
    key commands, 928
    preset filters, 917
gradient fills, 968-975
    color, 973-975
    copying, 928
        to KPT Gradient Designer, 911-916
    distortion, 918
    drawings, 971-975
    reflections, 682-684
    rotating, 928
    saving, 916
Gradient tool, 389-391, 969

gradients
    CMYK color, 1009
    drawings, 1004-1005
granularity (images), 819-820
graphics
    color, 38
    grayscale, 36-37
    halftones, 35-36
    line art, 33-34
Graphics Interchange Format (GIF), 60
gray (color), 113
grayscale mode, 36-37, 817-828
    Black channel, 36-37
    channels (texture), 829-832
    CMYK color, 963-967
    commercial printers, 1158-1162
        Paint Shop Pro utility, 1159-1160
        shades, 1160-1162
    converting to RGB, 837-840
    duotones, 1191-1197
        creating, 1191-1194
        exporting, 1195-1197
        printing separations, 1197
    LAB color, 814-817
    Lighting Effects filter, 829-832
    pixels (color components), 41-42
    printer resolution, 1156
    printing, 1135-1137
        converting to bitmap, 1143-1145
        CMYK, 1136
        RGB, 1136
        saving, 1137
    redistibution, 294-296
    relief images, 833-836
    sepia tones, 840
    Sponge tool, 407-409
    video drivers, 68-70
Green channel, 830-832
    blurring, 1082

H

Haber, Blake, 1273
Haber, Bruce, 1024
Haber directory, 1273
Halftone Screen dialog box, 1149
halftones, 35-36
camera-ready commercial
printers, 1158
dots, 1134
screens, 1166-1168
printer resolution
cells, 1148
line angles, 1149-1151
line frequency, 1151-1152
line screen, 1148
moiré patterns, 1149-1152
Hand tool
toggling to, 546
viewing images, 239-285
hand-held scanners, 71
Hard Light mode, 274
hardware
digital cameras, 101-105
scanners
256 grayscale, 74
brightness/contrast controls, 83
color recommendations, 74-75
digital cameras, 73, 101-105
flatbed, 71-72
hand-held, 71
preview, 76
sheet-fed, 71
TWAIN standard, 73-76,
virtual densitometer, 83
HAUSHOLD images, 1268
headers (files), 132
Help (Gradient Designer), 920
**Hide Edges command (Select
menu), 244, 437, 665**

hiding
borders (digital images), 312
digital images, 520-521
ranges, 523-524
palettes, 542
pixels, 521
toolboxes, 542
**high resolution printers (600-
1200), 1157**
highlighting
backgrounds (Emboss filter),
1088-1093
color-balancing, 310
colorizing (saving highlights),
1091-1092
Dodge tool, 423-425, 1083-1084
images, 606-607
**Histogram command (Image
menu), 125**
histograms, 87-91
brightness (color)
mapping, 116-117
PhotoCDs, 125-127
remapping, 117
contrasts (PhotoCDs), 127
digital images, 296
midtones (PhotoCDs), 127
home plans, 514-515
hot keys
commands palette, 198-203
Copy, 201
Cut, 201
Paste, 201
Undo, 201
hot spots (digital cameras), 102
HSB color model, 94
brightness, 114
comparing to other models,
112-113
**HSB color model (Hue/Satura-
tion/Brightness), 110, 292**

Hue Mode, 274
Hue Protected Noise filter, 929-930
Hue/Saturation dialog box, 646
hues (color), 109, 292-299

I

icons
    images, 715
    Layer Mask, 527
    thumbnail preview (palettes), 224-226
IFF file format (Amiga), 60
illustrations, *see* **drawings**
Illustrator Format dialog box, 850
image dimensions
    scanning, 78-81
        file sizes, 81-83
        sampling rates, 80-81
image files
    Beep When Tasks Finish option, 170-172
    RAM (random access memory), 173
    saving, 189
Image Format dialog box, 1031
image mapping (EPS), 1071-1073
Image menu commands
    Adjust, 86, 453, 1248
    cancelling, 555
    Canvas Size, 1236
    Effects, 349
    Flip, 648, 681
    Histogram, 125
    Image Size, 55, 131, 559, 638, 1153
    Map, 393, 1198
    Rotate, 261, 554, 1180, 1234
Image Pacs
    PCD file format (PhotoCDs), 140

    PhotoCDs, 118-119
image quality calculations (resolution), 1156-1157
Image Size command (Image menu), 55, 131, 638, 1153
Image Size dialog box, 131, 136, 698, 1154, 1228
IMAGECEL directory, 1268
images
    3D effects, 952-954
    ACTUAL, 1267
    ALV (Auto Level) settings, 695-696
    Anchor points, 616
    Anti-alias PostScript, 166-167
    anti-aliased borders, 599-600, 604-605
    BACKDROP, 1267
    backgrounds, 946
        surrealistic, 1088-1093
    Bicubic interpolation, 594
    bitmapped (vector), 849-851
    blurring, 769-770
    borders, 370-373
    cataloging, 1257
    changing visual content (Rubber Stamp tool), 255-257
    channels, 162
    clipping, 643, 659
    cloning, 688-689
        Rubber Stamp tool, 250-252
        sample point, 250
    color
        balancing, 639-641
        diffusion dither preferences, 163
        printing, 1178
        sampling, 802-810
        Variations command (Image menu), 642-644
    colorizing, 1090
        monochrome images, 1092-1093
        saving highlights, 1091-1092

copying, 399-400, 603-604
 from original, 759-761
 reusing, 763-764
correcting
 Blur tool, 328-331
 copying, 325-327
 pasting, 325-327
 Smudge tool, 328-331
cropping, 594-598, 740
displays (General Preferences), 159-162
distorting, 401-402, 611-615
 Glass Lens filter, 1078-1081
 editing, 615-617
 retouching, 617-623
edges, sharpening, 370-373
editing with Blur tool, 727-728
EPS, 962
ESOTERIC, 1268
feathering, 604-605
filtered images (previewing), 932
finalizing effects, 381-382
flattening, 451-452
flipping, 647-649, 763-764
focal point (Zoom blur), 825-828
foregrounds (cloning samples), 724-726
GLASS, 1268
gradient fills, copying to KPT Gradient Designer, 912-913
granularity, 819-820
grayscale, 817-828
HAUSHOLD, 1268
highlighting, 606-607
icons, 715
interpolation, 159
JPEG format
 scaling, 591-605
kaleidoscope filters, 949

layers
 adding, 649-650
 composite images, 749-758
 copying, 608-609
 copying to, 659-661
 editing, 729-735
 increasing resolution, 715
 integrating, 730-731
 merging, 269-272
 merging to final image, 1117-1120
 reordering, 1127-1128
 restoring, 714, 729-735
lettering
 removing, 368-370
lighting, 605-627
lossless compression, 597
mapping
 EPS (Encapsulated Postscript), 1071-1073
measuring, 395-396, 592-593
 automatically, 461-464
meaurements, 176-177
noise, 818-820
ORGANIC, 1268
orientation, flipping, 647-649
paintings, 821
PANTONE colors, 168-172
paths, 366-367
 converting to selections, 603-608
 deleting, 602
 outlining, 472-476
photorealistic (Typestry program), 1030-1044
printing part of (Rectangular Marquee tool), 1191
protecting, 283-285
ranges (tinting), 621
rasterizing, 962, 1073
rearranging original image areas, 759-761

reducing, 595-596
reflections, 623-626
relief, 833-836
rendering (environment mapping), 1086-1088
repeating, 945
retouching, 252-254, 628-629
  background patterns, 341-344
  borders, 357-360, 370-373
  changing content, 255-257
  cloning, 338-341
  Dodge tool, 423-425
  editing layers as one image, 355-357
  lens flare, 333-335
  New Window command, 445-447
  oversaturated pixels, 336-338
  pattern sampling, 338-341
  Rubber Stamp tool, 331-333, 671-672
  source material from other images, 344-355
  with Blur tool, 736-737
  with Paint Brush tool, 723-726
  with Quick Mask, 718-723
  with Rubber Stamp tool, 736-737
rotating, 260-262
  channel by channel, 1234-1240
sampling down, 598-601
scanning, 383-385
scratch disks, 173-174
selecting, 260-285
  by color range, 459-461
  Magic Wand tool, 773-775
selectings, 744-745
selections
  loading, 279-280
  resizing, 696-700
setting resolution/size for cropping, 592-594
shades, blending, 370

shading, 626-627
shadows, fine tuning, 771-772
sizing, 395-396
  Anti-aliasing, 397-398
slides
  creating multiple, 1058-1062
  reusing, 1062-1068
softening, 628-629
Sponge tool, 407-409
stock images, 637-639
TERRAIN, 1268
text
  contrasting colors, 1121-1125
  drop-shadows, 1125-1126
  importing, 1120-1121
texture mapping
  brightening, 1102-1103
  defining, 1094-1095
  glow, 1104-1106
  Lighting Effects filter, 1096-1098
  neon glow, 1106-1109
  Omni light, 1099-1100
textures
  blending, 709-711
tiling, 945
tonal landscapes, 689-694
transparency layer
  adding color, 453-455
  color range, 441-445
  Eraser tool, 432-435
  flattening images, 451-452
  Layer Mask mode, 447-451
  masking, 435-439
  New Window command, 445-447
  Paint Bucket tool, 439-441
  Rubber Stamp tool, 432-435
transparency layers, 426-428
  cloning, 430-432
truncated, 615
type
  measuring, 373-375
  measuring target, 402-404

viewing, 283, 410
  Hand tool, 239-285
  marquee selection tools, 242-246
  resolution, 241-242
  Zoom tool, 239-285
weathering, 405-407
White points, 691
windows, setting up, 463
see also digital images;
  photographs
imagesetters, 1137
import filters
  Place command (File menu),
  842
  vector (Anti-aliasing), 846
importing text, 1120-1121
**index sheets, viewing PhotoCDs,
142**
**Indexed Color command (Mode
menu), 43**
**Indexed Color dialog box, 43,
1161**
indexed colors, 39
  bitmapped images, 41-42
  converting from RGB image,
  46-48
  dithering
    diffusion, 45
    pattern, 45-46
  lookup tables, 43-44
  palettes
    Adaptive, 44, 48-49
    Custom, 44
    Uniform, 44, 49
  RGB images, 49-50
Info palette, 293
  slides, measuring type,
  1049-1054
**ink (commercial printers),
1162-1163**

installing
  Acrobat Reader
    Macintosh, 1277
    Windows, 1276
  Andromeda filters, 949
  Drop Shadow filter, 940
  fonts (Type 1), 364-365
  Gallery Effects filters, 931
  KPT filters, 985
  Pixar One Twenty-Eight filter,
  945
  video drivers, 66-68
**integrating images (layers),
730-731**
interfaces
  cMulti filter, 949
  Drop Shadow filter, 942
  Gradient Designer (KPT),
  916-925
interpolation
  angled scans, 84-85
  Anti-aliasing, 397
  color printers, 1184
  pixels, 40-41, 241
    rotating, 262
  resolution (PhotoCDs), 137-139
interpolation (images), 159
**Inverse command (Select menu),
221, 251, 745**
inverting
  colors, 210
  selection marquees, 221
isolated color-balancing, 311-315

J

JPEG file format, 60
  compressing files, 90
    comparing to lossless, 101
    Stacker, 100-105
  lossy compression, 94-99

scaling images, 591-605
service bureaus, 1210-1213

K

Kai's Power Tools, *see* **KPT**
kaleidoscopic images, 949
Katz, Phil, 1274
key commands
  Alt, Variations command, 302
  Gradient Designer (KPT), 928
  Option, editing digital images,
    521
  Tab, 542
keyboard, 248-250
Kodak Precision CMS (PhotoCDs),
  130
Kodak Precision CMS PhotoCD
  dialog box, 120
Kodak Pro PhotoCD Master,
  141-142
KPT (Kai's Power Tools), 910-930
  CMYK, 1202
  directory, 1270
  Glass Lens filter, 929
  Gradient bar, 921-925
  Gradient Designer, 1004-1005
  Hue Protected Noise filter,
    929-930
  menus, expanding, 913
  Pixel Storm filter, 930
  Sharpen Intensity filter, 930,
    1022-1023

L

LAB color, 811-812
  grayscale, 814-817
  RGB, translating from, 812-813
  models, 111-112
    comparing to other models,
      112-113
    PhotoCDs, 122

labels (color printers), 1183
Landscape orientation, 1180-1220
landscape orientation (film record-
  ers), 1233-1234
laser printers, 1137
  PCL (Printer Command
    Language), 1138-1141
    disadvantages, 1140-1146
    resolution enhancement, 1140
Lasso tool
  editing digital image elements,
    544-545
  Freehand selection mode, 207
  sampling, 652-654
  saving selections, 207-209
  selecting digital image elements,
    542
  selections, repositioning, 258
  shadows, 569
  Straight line mode, 207
Last Filter command (Filter
  menu), 1114
Layer Mask, 753-755
  Background Copy Mask, 664-666
  background layers, 655-658
  editing layers, 713-718
  integrating image layers,
    729-731
  options, 756
  pixels, removing, 666-668
  removing, 668-669, 757-758
Layer Mask option, 351-355
Layer Masks, 516
  Apply command, 718
  applying, 525-527
  backgrounds/foregrounds, 520
  digital images
    editing, 519-527
    opaque elements, 581-584
  distorted images 615-617
  drawings, cleaning, 1021-1022

opacity levels, 520
patterns, 447-451
pixels, hiding, 521
retouching, 525
layers
adding, 796-797
background
duplicating, 649-650
Layer Mask, 655-658
cloning between, 710-711
color printers, 1180
composite images, 749-758
copying, 608-609, 749
digital images
cloning between, 573
linking, 566
merging, 530, 570, 586
RAM, 532
saving, 530
drawings, editing, 1021-1022
duplicating, 1038-1040
edges, softening, 769-770
editing, 570, 713-718
images
cloning, 705-707
copying, 659-661
editing, 729-735
increasing resolution, 715
integrating, 730-731
restoring, 714, 729-735
merging, 355-357, 626-627, 631-632
saving, 269-272
Sponge tool, 408-409
merging to final image, 1117-1120
modes, 276-278
Move tool, 260
linking, 267-269
merging, 267-269

moving, 707
naming, 266
navigating, 609
opacity, 750
painting (Behind mode), 1126
photo-realistic images, copying, 1111-1112
reflections, 683-684
Gradient fill, 682-684
merging, 685-686
opacity, 682-684
reordering, 1127-1128
retouching photographs, 355-357
slides
common backgrounds, 1044-1049
duplicating, 1054-1058
multiple images, 1058-1062
switching contents, 1054-1058
transparency layers, 426-428
adding color, 453-455
cloning, 430-432
color range, 441-445
Eraser tool, 432-435
flattening images, 451-452
Layer Mask mode, 447-451
masking, 435-439
New Window command, 445-447
Paint Bucket tool, 439-441
patterns, 432-435
Rubber Stamp tool, 432-435
Layers palette, 520
image icons, 715
Merge Layers, 530
Modes, 272-275
Multiply mode, 553
pattern filling, 233-235
pixels, repositioning, 257-260
Preserve Transparency option, 614-615

saved selections, 257-260
transparent pixels, 228
colors behind, 229-231
Layers Palette Options dialog box, 224
Leclair, Don, 1271
lens flare (Toning tool), 333-335
lettering
Alpha channels, 792-796
collage, 793-796
color, 1009-1010
distorting, 787-791
negatively, 790-791
drop-shadows, 798-799, 1012, 1125-1126
removing (Paint Brush tool), 368-370
Levels command, 292-293, 689-691
Levels command dialog box, 87
Levels dialog box, 117, 295
Lighten mode, 274
Rubber Stamp tool, 418-419
lighting, 109-110
ambient, 1097
backgrounds (Emboss filter), 1088-1093
drawings, 975-976
glow from behind, 1113-1117
images, 605-627
Omni, 1099-1100
saturation, 646
texture mapping, 1094-1095
brightening, 1102-1103
dimensions, 1073-1074
glow, 1104-1106
Lighting Effects filter, 1096-1098
neon glow, 1106-1109
Omni light, 1099-1100
Lighting Effects filter, 833-836
grayscale mode, 829-832

texture mapping, 1096-1098
line angles (halftones), 1149-1151
line art, 33-34
line frequency (halftones), 1151-1152
line screen (halftones), 1148
lines per inch (printer resolution), 1152-1156
linking layers, 566
Move tool, 267-269
Load command (Select menu), 1111
Load dialog box, 695
Load Selection command (Select menu), 251, 279, 664
Load Selection dialog box, 279, 1111
loading
Alpha channel contents, 187
ALV settings, 695
Brushes palette, 190-193
selection marquees, 186
selections from different images, 279-280
Look Up Table, *see* **LUT**
Looping Control menu, 918
loose selection marquees, 701-703
lossless compression
comparing to lossy, 101
cropped images, 597
LZW (Lempel, Ziv, and Welch), 92-94
TIFF (Tagged Image File Format), 92-94
lossy compression, 90
comparing to lossless, 101
JPEG compression
future image deterioration, 94-100
service bureaus, 1210-1213
Luminance (color), 802

Luminosity mode, 275
LUT (Look Up Table) Animation
displays, 163
Gradient Designer (KPT), 921
indexed colors, 43-44
LZW lossless compression, 92-94

M

Macintosh
Acrobat Reader (installation),
1277
memory, 175-176
Magic Wand tool
pixels, 262-267
Quick Mask mode, 262-267
sampling, 652-654
selecting images, 773-775
Make Layer dialog box, 264, 782
Make Selection tool
(Paths palette), 602
manipulating color, 114-115
Mannequin (CAD program), 1085
Map command (Image menu),
393, 1198
mapped color, *see* indexed color
mapping
brightness, 115
gamma, 118
histograms, 116-117
midpoints, 117-118
midtones, 117-118
environment, 1087-1088
images (EPS), 1071-1073
texture
ambient lighting, 1097
brightening, 1102-1103
defining, 1094-1095
dimension, 1073-1074
glow, 1104-1106
Light Effects filter, 1096-1098

neon glow, 1106-1109
Omni light, 1099-1100
photo-realistic images,
1070-1074
marquee selection
Channels palette, 205
feathering, 304
paths, 220-224
Quick Mask mode, 214-217
tools
Elliptical marquee tool, 242-246
Rectangular marquee tool,
242-246
viewing images, 242-246
Marquee tool
constraining aspect ratio, 1238
toggles, 697
masking, 205-206
patterns, 435-439
Quick Mask mode, 206, 210-212
editing, 212-214
selection marquee, 214-217
selection marquees, 250-252
masks
layers, 519
type, 385-387
MATERIAL directory, 1267-1268
Matting command (Select menu),
770
Matting Defringe command (Select
menu), 780
maximizing memory, 174-175
measuring
images, 176-177, 395-396,
592-593
automatically, 461-464
for type, 373-375, 402-404
selections, 948
type (Info palette), 1049-1054
memory
Macintosh, 175-176
maximizing, 174-175

Photoshop preferences, 172-176
scratch disks, 173-174
**Memory Preferences dialog box,
172**
menus
Algorithm Control, 917
KPT, expanding, 913
Looping Control, 918
**Merge Layers command (Layers
palette), 530, 631**
merging
digital images, 530
layers, 355-357, 570, 586,
626-627, 631-632
Move tool, 267-269
reflections, 685-686
reordering, 1127-1128
saving, 269-272
Sponge tool, 408-409
to final image, 1117-1120
midpoints (brightness), 117-118
midtones
brightness (color), 117-118
color-balancing, 310
contrast, 297
histograms (PhotoCDs), 127
monitor color setup, 153-154
Mode menu commands
CMYK Color, 1204
Gamut Warning, 1200
Indexed Color, 43
RGB Color, 838
modeling programs, 1270-1271
models
3-D wireframe, 1071
CMYK color correction,
1075-1078
Modes
Behind, 273
Brushes palette, 272-275
Clear, 273

Color, 275
models, 110
painting, 275-276
Darken, 274
Difference, 274
Display, 273
Dissolve, 852-855
Hard Light mode, 274
Hue, 274
layers, 276-278
Layers palette, 272-275
Lighten, 274
Luminosity, 275
Multiply, 273
Normal, 273
Overlay, 274
Saturation, 274
Screen, 273
Soft Light, 274
**Modify command (Select menu),
253, 665**
moiré patterns, 84
halftones, 1149-1152
Monitor Settings dialog box, 155
Monitor Setup command, 151-158
Monitor Setup dialog box, 152
monitors
calibration, 150-158
saving, 154-155
color
ambient light settings, 153
balancing, 157-158
parameters, 152-153
room parameters, 153
target gamma, 153-154
film recorders, 1224-1225
gamma balance
film recorders, 1225
previewing, 156
resolution (pixels), 55-56
setup, 151-158

monochrome
  channels, 36
  images, colorizing, 1092-1093
More Preferences dialog box, 166
Motion Blur filters, 530
mouse (tools), 1125
Move tool, 257, 566
  layers
    linking, 267-269
    merging, 267-269
moving
  Anchor points, 624
  layers, 707
  lettering (Alpha channels),
    792-796
  selections, 246-248
multimedia programs, slides, 1259
multiple images, slides, 1058-1062
Multiply mode, 273
  Paint Brush tool, 568
    shadows, 767-768
multisession (PhotoCDs), 140

N

naming layers, 266
native filters, 842
navigating
  layers, 609
  OnLine Glossary, 1277-1280
**Nearest Neighbor interpolation
  (pixels), 159**
negative displacement maps, 791
negatives
  aspect ratios, 1244-1245
  color printers, 1184
  file sizes, 1244
  film recorders (service bureaus),
    1244-1245
neon glow
  borders, 1106-1109
    from behind, 1113-1117
  text, 1121-1125

neutral density (gray), 113
New command (File menu), 33
New Image dialog box, 1028
New Layer dialog box, 413
New Path tool (Paths palette), 602
**New Window command (Window
  menu), 445-447**
noise (pixels), 818-820
  Gaussian, 820
  printing, 820
  Uniform, 818-820
Noise command (Filter menu), 819
non-Adobe filters, 181
non-halftone dots, 1134
**non-PostScript color printers,
  1185-1186**
**None command (Select menu),
  233**
Normal mode, 273
**Note Paper filters (Gallery
  Effects), 934-937**

O

**object-oriented images (vector
  images), 30**
**Omni light (texture mapping),
  1099-1100**
OnLine Glossary, 1277-1280
opacity
  floating selections, 750
  layers, 750
    reflections, 682-684
opaque attributes, 583-584
  pixels, 1041
**Open command (File menu),
  849-851**
opening
  files
    sections, 133
    shortcuts, 534
  PhotoCDs, 120

Option key command, 521
Options palette, 188
    Behind mode, 1002-1003, 1015
ORGANIC images, 1268
orientation
    film recorders, 1233-1234
    images, flipping, 647-649
    Portrait (color printers), 1180
original images, rearranging,
    759-761
out-of-gamut colors (CMYK),
    1200-1204
    Kai's Power Tools, 1202
    removing dullness, 1203-1204
outlining images (paths), 472-476
over-saturation (color), 113
Overlay mode, 274
oversaturated pixels (Focus tool),
    336-338

P

Page Setup command (File menu),
    1149, 1180
Page Setup dialog box, 1141,
    1180-1184
PageMaker, importing duotones,
    1196-1197
paint application functions,
    238-239
Paint Brush tool
    Darken mode, 672-675
    editing in Quick Mask mode,
      213-214
    images (retouching), 723-726
    lettering, removing, 368-370
    Multiply mode, 568
    Screen mode, 584
    shadows (Multiply mode),
      767-768
Paint Bucket tool, 439-441
Paint Shop Pro utility, 1159-1160

painting
    Airbrush tool, 1117-1120
    Behind mode, 1126
    Modes, 272-275
      Behind, 273
      Clear, 273
      Color, 275-276
      Darken, 274
      Difference, 274
      Display, 273
      Hard Light mode, 274
      Hue, 274
      Lighten, 274
      Luminosity, 275
      Multiply, 273
      Normal, 273
      Overlay, 274
      Saturation, 274
      Screen, 273
      Soft Light, 274
    mouse, 1125
    shadows, 570
paintings (images), 821
PaintShop Pro, counting colors, 49
PAINTSHP directory, 1273-1274
Palette command (Window menu),
    196
palettes, 196-235
    Assorted, 183
    Brushes, 188
      brush tips, 183-188
      customizing, 192
      loading, 190-193
      Modes, 272-275
      options, 182-183
      resetting, 190-193
    Channels, 203-204, 998
      selection areas, 205-206
      viewing color channels, 203-204
    Commands, 196-198
      customizing, 198-203
      hot keys, 198-203

maximum, 202-203
pattern filling, 233-235
customizing, 226-228
displaying, 196
Focus Tool Options, 562
hiding, 542
indexed colors, 43
   Adaptive, 44, 48-49
   Custom, 44
   Uniform, 44, 49
Info, 1049-1054
Info palette, 293
Layers, 520
   Modes, 272-275
   Multiply mode, 553
   pattern filling, 233-235
   saved selections, 257-260
   transparent pixels, 228
masking (Quick Mask mode),
   210-212
Options, 188
Paths, 217-220, 366-367, 469,
   481, 598-601, 616-617
   Arrow tool, 470
   *convert direction point tool,
      471-472*
   directions, 472
   Pen tool, 470
   Pen–tool, 471
   Pen+ tool, 470-471
Picker, 168, 968-973, 997-1000
recalling, 171-172
restoring, 824-825
Rubber Stamp Options, 573
Scratch
   sampling color, 803-806
   size, 810-812
   Type tool, 806-812
separating, 226-228
Shadows, 183

Smudge Tool Options, 577
Square, 183
Swatches, 968
   color, 387-389
system, 162
thumbnail preview icons,
   224-226
unweighed, 49
PANTONE colors, 168-172
**Paste Into command (Edit menu),
349, 350, 989**
**Paste Layer command (Edit
menu), 782**
pasting
   digital images into drawings,
      1017-1018
   hot keys, 201
   images, correcting, 325-327
paths, 468-469, 481
   anchor points, 468-469
   converting to selections, 603-608
   deleting, 602
   direction points, 468-469
   directions, 472
   exporting, 1028-1030
   outlining images, 472-476
   points of inflection, 474
   refining (convert direction
      point tool), 476-477
   saved selections, 477-479
   selection marquees (viewing
      simultaneously), 220-224
   selections, 733-734
   see also borders
**Paths palette, 217-220, 366-367,
469, 481, 598-601, 616-617**
   Arrow tool, 470
   convert direction point tool,
      471-472
      editing paths, 476-477

directions, 472
Pen tool, 470
Pen–tool, 471
Pen+ tool, 470-471
pattern dithering, 45-46
pattern fills
   drawings, 988-989
   Layer palette, 233-235
pattern sampling
   cloning, 338-341
   Rubber Stamp tool, 338-341
patterns
   backgrounds, 780
   cloning (Rubber Stamp tool),
    416
   fills, 516
   flood-fills, 441
PCD file format, 119
PCL (Printer Command Language)
   bitmapped, 1143-1145
   laser printers, 1138-1141
    disadvantages, 1140-1146
    resolution enhancement, 1140
PCX Images file format, 59
Pen tool (Paths palette)
   Bézier curves, 470
   paths, 366
Pen–tool (Paths palette), 471
Pen+ tool (Paths palette), 470-471
pen-and-ink drawing, 33-34
Pencil tool, 392
personal color printers, 1134-1135,
   1176-1220
Perspective boundary box, 565
Perspective command, 559-560
perspectives, 559-560
phases (digital images), 29
photo-realistic images
   layers (copying), 1111-1112
   rendering (environment
    mapping), 1086-1088

texture mapping, 1070-1074
   wireframes, 1071
Typestry program, 1030-1044
   Alpha channel, 1037-1038
   bullets, 1033-1036
   dimensions, 1031
   rendering, 1032-1036
   resolution, 1031
   text, 1032-1036
   title slides, 1036-1040
   typestyles, 1032-1036
PhotoCD Access (software),
143-145
PhotoCDs, 118-119, 131
   adjusting tonal levels, 119-130
   brightness, 129-130
    histograms, 125-127
   CD-ROMs, 140-141
   drives, 146-147
   file sizes, 139
   histograms, 125-126
    contrasts, 127
    midtones, 127
   Image Pacs, 118-119
   Kodak Pro PhotoCD Master,
    141-142
   LAB color model, 122
   multisession, 140
   opening file, 120
   PCD file format, 119
    Image Pacs, 140
   Photographic Quality Kodak
    PhotoCD Master, 141-142
   photographs, adding, 139-140
   previewing changes, 122-131
   resolution, 131
    cropping images, 132-136
    interpolation, 137-139
    pixellating, 137
    proportions, 136-139
    resizing, 136-139

saving images, 123
viewing, 142
browsing software, 143-145
index sheets, 142
Photographic Quality Kodak PhotoCD Master 141-142
photographic washes, 1017-1018
photographs
adding to PhotoCDs, 139-140
combining, 590
digital images
color contrast, 299
restoring, 291-292
retouching
background patterns, 341-344
Blur tool, 328-331
borders, 357-360, 370-373
cloning, 338-341
copying, 325-327
Dodge tool, 423-425
editing layers as one image, 355-357
lens flare, 333-335
New Window command, 445-447
oversaturated pixels, 336-338
pasting, 325-327
pattern sampling, 338-341
Rubber Stamp tool, 331-333, 671-672
Smudge tool, 328-331
source material from other images, 344-355
stains, removing, 324-327
stock, 590
trick photography, 701-704
virtual twins (cloning), 688-689
see also digital images; images
photography, 28
Photoshop
advantages, 1248-1252
memory preferences, 172-176

version 2.5 format compatibility, 171
Windows, 1259
pica (measurement), 177
Picker palette, 168, 968-973, 997-1000
picks
clipping, 301
windows, 300
see also thumbnails
PICT file format, 59-60
PIXAR, 1030-1031
PIXAR filters, 988-991
Pixar One Twenty-Eight filter, 945, 945-949
PIXAR128 directory, 1269
pixel sampling rate (Info palette), 293
Pixel Storm filter, 930
pixellation, 242
resolution (PhotoCDs), 137
pixels, 54-56, 114-115, 1249
bitmapped images, 31-33
Blur tool, 769-770
brightness, 115
color, 129-130
darkening (Paint Brush tool), 672-675
dots, 54-55
gamma, 115
grayscale mode, color components, 41-42
hiding, 521
interpolation, 40-41, 241
rotating, 262
Layer Mask, removing, 666-668
layers, repositioning, 257-260
Magic Wand tool, 262-267
noise, 818-820
opaque, 1041
over-saturation (Focus tool), 336-338

resolution, 44, 55-56
    pixellating, 137
    scanning, 78-81
samples, 54-55
transparent
    colors behind, 229-231
    Layers palette, 228
    options, 229
PKZIP (compression program), 1213
PKZIP directory, 1274
Place command (File menu), 842-846
import filter, 842
Plastic Wrap filters (Gallery Effects), 937-939
plug-ins, 1255-1256
adding, 910
preferences
see also filters
Plug-ins dialog box, 180
points (measurement), 177
PostScript, 373
Traditional, 373
points of inflection (paths), 474
Portrait orientation
film recorders, 1233-1234
printers, 1180
positioning floating selections, 704-709
PostScript
printers, 1145-1148
    color printers, 1186-1189
    digital halftone cells, 1146-1148
    non-PostScript options, 1185-1186
sizes
    picas, 373
    points, 373
PostScript Options dialog box, 1188
precise cursors (tools), 164-165

Preserve Transparency option (Layers palette), 614-615
preset filters (Gradient Designer), 917
previewing
digital images (color changes), 300
filtered images, 932
monitors (gamma balance), 156
PhotoCDs, 122-131
scan images, 76
Print command (File menu), 1155, 1189-1191
printers
color
    backgrounds, 1182
    bleeding, 1182
    borders, 1182
    calibration bars, 1183-1184
    captions, 1183
    crop marks, 1184
    emulsion down, 1184
    interpolation, 1184
    labels, 1183
    layers, 1180
    negatives, 1184
    non-PostScript, 1185-1186
    personal, 1134-1135, 1176-1178
    Portrait orientation, 1180
    Postscript, 1186-1189
    printing, 1178
    registration marks, 1183
    resolution, 1180
    RGB, 1179-1180
    screens, 1181-1182, 1183
commercial
    calculations, 1163-1165
    camera-ready halftones, 1158
    decreasing contrasts, 1162-1163
    grayscale, 1158-1162
    ink, 1162-1163
    toner, 1162-1163

dots, 1134
    screens, 1166-1168
    shaping, 1165-1166
drivers, 1141-1142
duotones, 1191-1197
    exporting, 1195-1197
    grayscale, 1191-1194
    printing separations, 1197
laser, 1137
    PCL (Printer Command
      Language), 1138-1141
PCL (Printer Command
  Language), 1143-1145
PostScript, 1145-1148
    color, 1186-1189
    digital halftone cells, 1146-1148
resolution
    grayscale, 1156
    halftones, 1148
    high (600-1200), 1157
    image quality calculations,
      1156-1157
    line frequency, 1151-1152
    lines per inch, 1152-1156
service bureaus, 1174-1175
    camera-ready, 1176
    electronic format, 1176
TIFF (Tagged Information File
  Formats), 1168-1169
printing
  CMYK (Cyan, Magenta, Yellow,
    Black), 1199-1208
  color images, 1178
  color separations
    alternatives, 1208-1209
    CMYK, 1206-1208
  commercial, 1157-1165
  contrasts, decreasing, 1163-1165
  densitometers, 1183
  duotones (separations),
    1197-1200

error diffusion, 1141-1142
grayscale mode, 1135-1137
    commercial printers, 1158-1162
    converting to bitmap, 1143-1145
    CMYK, 1136
    Paint Shop Pro utility,
      1159-1160
    RGB, 1136
    saving, 1137-1139
    shades, 1160-1162
noise (pixels), 820
part of an image (Rectangular
  Marquee tool), 1191
separations (spot-color),
  1198-1199
**Printing Inks Setup dialog box,
1183, 1204**
process color, *see* **CMYK**
**professional imaging careers,
1252-1254**
programs
  AI (Adobe Illustrator), 1026
  CAD (Computer Assisted
    Design), 1085
  compressing files
    spanning, 1213-1217
    zipping, 1214-1217
  drawing, 1256-1257
  multimedia slides, 1259
  rendering/modeling, 1270-1271
  Renderize Live for Windows,
    1086
  slides, 1258-1259
  Typestry, 1025, 1026
**proportions (PhotoCDs resolu-
tion), 136-139**
protecting images, 283-285
proxy boxes (filters), 611
**PSD (PhotoShop default file),
58-59**
punch-out graphics, 941

Q

quartertones, 303
Quick Mask mode, 210-212, 355,
  718-723
  editing, 212-214, 932-394,
    719-721
    color, 316
    Paint Brush tool, 213-214
  Magic Wand tool, 262-267
  patterns, 435-439
  selection (Channels palette),
    206-235
  selection marquee, 214-217

R

Radial blur
  Spin, 825-828
  Zoom, 825-828
Radial Blur dialog box, 825
RAM (Random Access Memory)
  digital image layers, 532
  image files, 173
ranges (digital images)
  hiding/revealing, 523-524
  selecting by brightness values,
    533-535
  tinting, 621
Rasterize Adobe Illustrator Format
  dialog box, 850
Rasterize dialog box, 1089
Rasterizer dialog box, 1073
rasterizing images, 962, 1073
  Targa (file format), 1074
RAW file format, 61
real-estate brochures, 514-515
rearranging original image areas,
  759-761
recalling
  customized palettes, 171-172
  filter dialog boxes, 923
  filters, 917

Rectangular Marquee tool, 46,
  242-246
  printing part of an image, 1191
  squares, 249
reducing
  color, 802
  digital images, 559
  images, 595-596
refining
  paths (convert direction point
    tool), 476-477
  scanned images, 383-385
reflections
  Gradient fill, 682-684
  layers
    merging, 685-686
    opacity, 682-684
  retouching, 623-626
  water, 678-680
registration marks (color printers),
  1183
relief images, 833-836
remapping histograms (brightness), 117
removable media (service
  bureaus), 1218
Remove Layer Mask dialog box,
  669
removing
  color-casting from digital
    images, 300-301
  Layer Mask, 668-669, 757-758
  lettering (Paint Brush tool),
    368-370
  pixels (Layer Mask), 666-668
  stains from photographs,
    324-327
Render command (Filter menu),
  466, 833

rendering
images (environment mapping), 1086-1088
programs, 1270-1271
texture mapping, 1071
Typestry program, 1032-1036
Renderize Live for Windows (program), 1086
reordering layers, 1127-1128
repeating images, 945
repositioning
Lasso tool, 258
layers, synchronous, 269
pixels in layers, 257-260
resetting Brushes palette, 190-193
resizing
images (Anti-aliasing), 397-398
PhotoCD resolution, 136-139
selections, 696-700
resolution, 44
color printers, 1180
cropped images, 595
digital images, 558-572
images
layers, 715
viewing, 241-242
independence (vector images), 30
PhotoCDs, 131-132
cropping images, 132-136
interpolation, 137-139
proportions, 136-139
resizing, 136-139
pixels
dots, 54-55
pixellating, 137
samples, 54-55
printers
grayscale, 1156
halftones, 1148
high (600-1200), 1157

image quallity calculations, 1156-1157
line frequency, 1151-1152
lines per inch, 1152-1156
scanning, 78-81
file sizes, 81-83
sampling rates, 80-81
Typestry program, 1031
resolution enhancement (PCL printers), 1140
Restore Dialog and Palette Positions, 171-172
restoring
color in digital images, 319
digital images, 291-292
images (layers), 714, 729-735
palettes, 824-825
retouching
digital images, 545-546, 550
distorted images, 617-623
images, 252-254, 628-629
changing content, 255-257
reflections, 623-626
with Blur tool, 736-737
with Paint Brush tool, 723-726
with Quick Mask, 718-723
with Rubber Stamp tool, 736-737
photographs, 525
background patterns (Rubber Stamp tool), 341-344
borders, 357-360, 370-373
cloning, 338-341
copying, 325-327
Dodge tool, 423-425
editing layers as one image, 355-357
lens flare (Toning tool), 333-335
New Window command, 445-447
oversaturated pixels (Focus tool), 336-338
pasting, 325-327

pattern sampling, 338-341
Rubber Stamp tool, 331-333,
671-672
source material from other
images, 344-355
see also editing
reusing
copied images, 763-764
slide images, 1062-1068
Revert command (File menu), 302
RGB color (red, green, blue), 38
channels, 51-52
color model, 110-111
comparing to other models,
112-113
converting to indexed color,
46-48
CMYK converting, 1204-1206
file formats
PSD (PhotoShop default file),
58-59
Targa file (TGA), 58-59
TIF (Tagged Image File), 58-59
filters, 52-53
grayscale mode
converting, 837-840
printing, 1136
indexed color, 39
indexing, 49-50
LAB converting, 812-813
printing
color, 1179-1180
spot-color separations,
1198-1199
tools, 52-53
translating
CMYK, 1204-1206
LAB, 812-813
TrueColor images, 50-51
**RGB Color command (Mode
menu), 838**

**RIP (Raster Image Processor),
1223**
**RISC (Reduced Instruction Set
Command), 1069**
**Rotate command (Image menu),
261, 554, 1180, 1234**
rotating
angled scans, 84-85
digital images, 555
film recorders, channel by
channel, 1234-1240
gradient fills, 928
images, 260-285
interpolation (pixels), 262
**Rubber Stamp Options palette,
573**
Rubber Stamp tool, 710-711
background patterns, 341-344
Behind mode, 432-435
Clone Aligned mode, 516
cloning, 250-252, 412-415,
572-574
Color mode, 421-422
direction, 416-418
New Window command, 445-447
patterns, 416
From Pattern mode, 516
images, changing visual content,
255-257
increasing brush sizes, 419-421
Lighten mode, 418-419
pattern sampling, 338-341
retouching images, 252-254,
671-672, 736-737
shadows, 765-767

S

S curves (brightness curves), 307
sample point (cloning), 250
sampled down images, 598-601
samples (pixels), 54-55

sampling
  color, 802-810
  Color Range command
    (Select menu), 652-654
  Lasso tool, 652-654
  Magic Wand tool, 652-654
  rates (scanning), 80-81
  retouching images, 252-254
  scanned images, 33
Sansone directory, 1273
Sansone, Ronald, 1273
saturation, 109, 982
  adjusting, 646
  drawings, 113, 1022
  over-saturation (Focus tool),
    336-338
Saturation mode, 274
Save a Copy command, 319
Save As command (File menu),
  208, 319
Save command (File menu), 47
Save Path dialog box, 367
Save Selection command
  (Select menu), 478
saved selections
  Channels palette, 205
  color, 776-779
  Eraser tool, 823
  Layers palette, 257-260
  paths, 477-479
  shadows, 781-784
saving
  ALV settings, 695
  Brushes palette options, 184
  gradient fills, 916
  grayscale mode, 1137
  image files, 189
  KPT Gradient Designer fills,
    1005
  layers, 269-272, 530

  monitor calibration settings,
    154-155
  PhotoCD images, 123
  scanned images, 90-105
  selection marquees, 721
  selections
    converting to paths, 217-220
    Lasso tool, 207-209
  system resources, 1116-1117
Scale command, 550-551
scaling
  digital images, 550-551, 555-556
  images, 591-605
  source material from other
    images, 348-351
scanners, 70-73
  256 grayscale, 74
  brightness/contrast controls, 83
  color recommendations, 74-75
  digital cameras, 73, 101-105
  flatbed, 71-72
  hand-held, 71
  preview, 76
  sheet-fed, 71
  TWAIN standard, 73-76
  virtual densitometers, 83
scanning, 85-86
  Adobe Streamline utility, 385
  angled
    interpolation, 84-85
    moiré patterns, 84
    rotating, 84-85
  color, 38
  color reduction, 802
  drawings, 960
  grayscale, 36-37
  halftones, 35-36
  histograms, 87-91
  image dimensions, 78-79
    file sizes, 81-83
    sampling rates, 80-81

images, 33
line art, 33-34
refining, 383-385
resolution, 78-81
  file sizes, 81-83
  sampling rates, 80-81
saving (compression), 90-101
tonal densities, 86-90
VGA video drivers, 64-66
scratch disks, 173-174
  secondary locations, 174
Scratch palette
  sampling color, 803-806
  size, 810-812
  Type tool, 806-812
Screen mode, 273, 584
screens
  CMYK, 1200
  color printers, 1181-1183
  dots, 1166-1168
  General Preferences, 158-171
  scanning
    dithering, 64
    VGA video drivers, 64-66
  workspace, optimizing, 541
Select menu commands
  All, 233, 555
  Color Range, 441-445, 460, 652,
    744, 846-848, 1091
  Feather, 337, 828
  Float, 264, 325, 780
  Hide Edges, 244, 437, 665
  Inverse, 221, 251, 745
  Load, 1111
  Load Selection, 251, 279, 664
  Matting, 770
  Matting Defringe, 780
  Modify, 253, 665
  None, 233
  Save Selection, 478
  Similar, 774

selecting
  images, 260-285, 744-745
    by brightness values, 533-535
    by color range, 459-461
    Magic Wand tool, 773-775
  service bureaus, 1245-1246
  resolution (PhotoCDs), 131-132
selection marquees
  cloning, 250-252
  inverting, 221
  Magic Wand tool, 262-267
  masking, 250-252
  paths, viewing simultaneously,
    220-224
  Quick Mask mode, 214-217
selection masks, 385-387
selection tools, 238-239
selections, 182
  adding to, 246-248
  Channels palette
    Alpha channel, 205-206
    marquees, 205
    Quick Mask mode, 206-235
    saved, 205
  copying to images, 603-604
  deleting from image layers,
    714-715
  dragging to image windows, 603
  floating, 257-260
    copying, 704-709
    positioning, 704-709
  functions, 603
  images (loading), 279-280
  loose marquees, 701-703
  marquees, 183
    saving, 721
    shading, 188-190
    viewing, 702
  measuring, 948
  moving, 246-248
  path conversion, 603-608

paths, 733-734
Quick Mask mode (Magic Wand tool), 262-267
Quick Masks, 392-394
resizing, 696-700
saved, converting to paths, 217-220
saving (Lasso tool), 207-209
tools (enhanced functions), 248-250
selective color adjustment, 1075-1078
Selective Color dialog box, 1077
separating
cropped images from backgrounds, 598
digital image elements from backgrounds, 532-547
palettes, 226-228, 824-825
Separation Setup dialog boxes, 1204
separations
color, alternatives, 1208-1209
CMYK, 1206-1208
duotones, 1197
spot-color printing, 1198-1199
sepia tones
converting from grayscale, 840
duotones, 1191
service bureaus, 1174-1175
Alpha channels (Photoshop), 1219
camera-ready, 1176
disks, 1219
drives, 1219
electronic format, 1176
film recorders, 1222
data types, 1233
file formats, 1233
file sizes, 1241-1243
negatives, 1244-1245

JPEG compression, 1210-1213
personal color printers, 1176-1178
removable media, 1218
selecting, 1245-1246
see also commercial printers
setting up image windows, 463
setup
KPT Gradient Designer, 911
monitors, 151-158
shades
blending, 370
color, 110
grayscale mode, 1160-1162
shading, 771-772
color, 978-979
dimensions, 997
drawings, 972, 976, 992-995
images, 626-627
selection marquees, 188-190
see also gradient fills
shadows
3-Dimensional, 1041-1044
Alpha channels, 781-784
blending, 765-767
clonings, 765-767
color-balancing, 310
digital images, 553-574, 568-572
dimensions, 578
drop-shadows
lettering, 1125-1126
text, 798-799
extending, 579-581
finding origins, 599
fine tuning, 771-772
Gaussian, 782
Paint Brush tool (Multiply mode), 767-768
painting, 570
Rubber Stamp tool, 765-767
saved selections, 781-784

softening, 577
texture mapping (dimensions),
  1073-1074
Shadows palette, 183
shaping dots, 1165-1166
shareware
  Bonus CD, 1271-1274
  slides, 1258
**Sharpen Intensity filter, 930,
  1022-1023**
sharpening borders, 370-373
sheet-fed scanners, 71
shell (Windows), 1259
Shift key, 248-250
**Show Rulers command (Windows
  menu), 374**
**Similar commands (Select menu),
  774**
sine waves (image distortion), 614
sizes (files), 1116-1117
sizing
  images, 395-396
    Anti-aliasing, 397-398
  selections, 696-700
skewing digital images, 555-556
sliders
  dynamic sliders (Picker palette),
    171-172
  Fuzziness, 538
slides
  builds, 1054-1058
  bullets, 1033
  common background layers,
    1044-1049
  dimensions, 1031
  exit slide, 1062-1068
  Info palette (measuring type),
    1049-1054
  layers
    duplicating, 1054-1058
    multiple images, 1058-1062
    switching contents, 1054-1058

multimedia programs, 1259
programs, 1258-1259
resolution, 1031
reusing images, 1062-1068
shareware, 1258
text, 1032-1036
type, 1049-1054
Typestry program
  rendering, 1032-1036
  title, 1036-1040
Smudge tool, 328-331
Smudge Tool Options palette, 577
smudging color, 982
Soft Light mode, 274
softening
  focus, 769-770
  images, 628-629
  shadows, 577
software (PhotoCDs)
  Corel CD-ROM Utilities,
    143-145
  PhotoCD Access, 143-145
source material from other images
  Layer Mask option, 351-355
  retouching photographs,
    344-355
  scaling, 348-351
**spanning disks (compression
  programs), 1213-1217**
specifications (typefaces), 375-378
Spin blur (Radial), 825-828
Sponge tool (grayscale), 407-409
spot-color separations
  choking, 1199
  printing, 1198-1199
  spreading, 1199
  trapping, 1199
**spreading spot-color separations,
  1199**
Square palette, 183
**squares (Rectangular marquee
  tool), 249**

Stacker (compressing files), 100-105

stains,removing from photographs, 324-327

standard cursors (tools), 163-164

steeltone images (duotones), 1191

stock

    images, 637-639

    photographs, 590

storing

    digital images, 57-62

        BMP, 59

        GIF (Graphics Interchange Format), 60

        IFF (Amiga), 60

        JPEG, 60

        PCX Images, 59

        PICT, 59-60

        RAW, 61

        RGB, 58-59

Straight line mode (Lasso tool), 207

straight-line borders, 969

Streamline utility, 960

Stroke command (Edit menu), 273, 1122

Stroke Path tool (Paths palette), 602

StuffIt (compression program), 1213

Stylize command (Filter menu), 1074

surrealistic backgrounds, 1088-1093

swap files, 173

Swatches palette, 968

    colors, 387-389

system palette, 162

system resources, freeing, 1116-1117

T

Tab key command, hiding palettes/toolboxes, 542

Tagged Image File Format (TIFF)

    lossless compression, 92-94

    RGB file format, 58-59

Targa (file format), 1074

    RGB file format, 58-59

target images, 517

TERRAIN images, 1268

text

    Alpha channels, 792-796

    collage, 793-796

    contrasting colors, 1121-1125

    displacement maps, 784-786

        negative, 791

    drop-shadows, 798-799, 1125-1126

    importing, 1120-1121

    lettering (distorting), 787-790

    type, 364-365

        Anti-aliasing, 364

        condensing, 379-380

        distorting, 379-380

        finalizing effects, 381-382

    Typestry program, 1032-1036

texture channel (grayscale mode), 829-832

Texture Fill dialog box, 1095

texture mapping

    ambient lighting, 1097

    brightening (Emboss filter), 1102-1103

    defining, 1094-1095

    dimension, 1073-1074

    EPS (Encapsulated Postscript), 1071-1073

    glow, 1104-1106

    Lighting Effects filter, 1096-1098

    neon glow, 1106-1109

        from behind, 1113-1117

Omni light, 1099-1100
photo-realistic images,
1070-1074
textures
digital images, 528-532
drawings, 988-997
images, blending, 709-711
TGA (Targa file), 1074
RGB file format, 58-59
third-party filters, 181, 910-911
thumbnails, 300
Current Pick, 300
preview icons, 224-226
see also picks
TIFF (Tagged Image File Format)
corruption, 1168-1169
lossless compression, 92-94
opening sections of files, 133
RGB file format, 58-59
tiled patterns, 989
tiling images, 945
tint (color), 804
tinting images, 621
color, 110
title slide (Typestry program),
1036-1040
toggles
Hand tool access, 546
marquee tools, 697
Paint Brush/Eyedropper tools,
724
tool cursors, 164
Tolerance (color), 536
tonal densities
Auto Range option, 88
digital images, 86-90
tonal landscapes, 689-694
tone (color), 110, 292-299
Auto distribution, 297-298
brightness curves, 303-306
midranges, 297
quartertones, 303

toner (commercial printers),
1162-1163
Toning tools, 991-997
Dodge (highlighting),
1083-1084
lens flare, 333-335
toolboxes
hiding, 542
tools
Airbrush, 1117-1120
Arrow, 470
Blur, 328-331, 563, 675-677,
769-770
editing images, 727-728
retouching images, 736-737
brush size cursors, 165-166
Burn, 627
Color Bar (Picker palette), 998
combining for color effects,
978-979
convert direction point tool,
471-472
editing paths, 476-477
Crop, 135, 594-598
Cropping, 398
cursor activation points, 545
cursors, 163-166
Dodge, 606-607
highlighting, 1083-1084
retouching images, 423-425
Elliptical Marquee, 46
Elliptical marquee tool, 242-246
Eraser, 823
patterns, 432-435
Eyedropper, 243
Fill Path (Paths palette), 601
Focus (oversaturated pixels),
336-338
function sets
editing functions, 238-239
paint application functions,
238-239
selection tools, 238-239

Gradient, 389-391, 969
Hand, viewing images, 239-285
Lasso, 569
   Freehand selection mode, 207
   repositioning selections, 258
   sampling, 652-654
   saving selections, 207-209
   Straight line mode, 207
Magic Wand
   pixels, 262-267
   Quick Mask mode, 262-267
   sampling, 652-654
   selecting images, 773-775
Make Selection (Paths palette), 602
Marquee, constraining aspect ratio, 1238
marquee selection (viewing images), 242-246
mouse clicks, 1125
Move, 257, 566
   layers, 260
New Path (Paths palette), 602
Paint Brush
   Darken mode, 672-675
   editing in Quick Mask mode, 213-214
   removing lettering, 368-370
   retouching images, 723-726
   shadows, 767-768
Paint Bucket, 439-441
Pen, 470
   paths, 366
Pen–, 471
Pen+, 470-471
Pencil, 392
precise cursors, 164-165
Rectangular Marquee, 46, 242-246
   printing part of an image, 1191
RGB, 52-53

Rubber Stamp, 572-574, 710-711
   background patterns, 341-344
   Behind mode, 432-435
   changing content of images, 255-257
   cloning, 250-252, 412-415
   fixing chipped emulsion, 331-333
   increasing brush sizes, 419-421
   Lighten mode, 418-419
   pattern sampling, 338-341
   retouching images, 252-254, 671-672, 736-737
   shadows, 765-767
selection (enhanced functions), 248-250
Smudge, 328-331
Sponge (grayscales), 407-409
standard cursors, 163-164
Stroke Path (Paths palette), 602
Toning, 991-997
   lens flare, 333-335
Trash (Paths palette), 602
Type
   measuring target image, 403
   Scratch palette, 806-812
Zoom (viewing images), 239-285
Traditional size (fonts), 373
Transfer Functions dialog box, 1183
transfers (images), 515-527, 547-553, 575-586
translating
  LAB color from RGB, 812-813
  RGB to LAB color, 812-813
  CMYK to RGB, 1204-1206
transparency layers, 426-428
  patterns (color), 453-455
  cloning, 430-432
    color range, 441-445
    Eraser tool, 432-435
    flattening images, 451-452

Layer Mask mode, 447-451
masking, 435-439
New Window command, 445-447
Paint Bucket tool, 439-441
Rubber Stamp tool, 432-435
Transparency Options dialog box, 229
transparent backgrounds, 547-553
transparent pixels
    colors behind, 229-231
    Layers palette, 228
    options, 229
trapping spot-color separations, 1199
Trash tool (Paths palette), 602
trick photography, 701-704
TrueColor images (RGB), 50-51
truncating images, 615
TRUSPACE directory, 1271
TWAIN standard scanners, 73-76
type, 364-365
    Alpha channels, 792-796
    Anti-aliasing, 364
    collage, 793-796
    color, 375, 387-389
    condensing, 379-380
    displacement maps, 784-786
    distorting, 379-380, 787-791
    drop-shadow, 798-799
    finalizing effects, 381-382
    fonts, installing Type 1, 364-365
    images, measuring for, 373-375
    lettering, removing, 368-370
    measuring target image, 402-404
    scanning, refining image, 383-385
    selection masks, 385-387
    slides (Info palette), 1049-1054
    specifications, 375-378
    vertical alignment, 377
    weathering, 405-407

Type 1 fonts (installing), 364-365
Type tool
    measuring target image, 403
    Scratch palette, 806-812
Type tool dialog box, 375-410, 807
TYPESTRY directory, 1269
Typestry program, 1025-1026, 1030-1044
    Alpha channel, 1037-1038
    bullets, 1033-1036
    dimensions, 1031
    rendering, 1032-1036
    resolution of images, 1031
    text, 1032-1036
    title slides, 1036-1040
    typestyles, 1032-1036
typestyles (Typestry program), 1032-1036

U

UCR (Undercolor Removal), 1204
Undo command (Edit menu), 231, 519
undoing hot keys, 201
Uniform noise (pixels), 818-820
Uniform palette
    indexed colors, 44
    unweighed, 49
Units Preferences command (File menu), 373
Units Preferences dialog box, 176, 373
unweighed palettes, 49
utilities, 1257
    Adobe Streamline, 385
    Paint Shop Pro, 1159-1160
        counting colors, 49
    slides, 1258
    Streamline, 960

V

**Variations command
(Image menu), 300-302**
  color, 642-644
  undoing changes, 302
Variations dialog box, 642
vector formats (drawings), 960
vector images
  object-oriented images, 30
  resolution-independent, 30
**vector import filters (Anti-
aliasing), 846**
vector-based images, 29-30
vectors
  bitmapped images, 849-851
  paths, exporting, 1028-1030
vertical alignment (type), 377
**VGA video drivers (scanning),
64-66**
**video clipping (over-saturation),
113**
video drivers
  color images, 68-70
  grayscale mode, 68-70
  installing, 66-68
  VGA (scanning), 64-66
viewing
  Channels palette, 203-204
  CMYK out-of-gamut colors,
    1200-1204
  digital images ranges, 523-524
  digitized drawings, 965
  Gradient Designer (KPT), 921
  images, 283, 410
    3D effects, 952-954
    Hand tool, 239-285
    layers, 715
    marquee selection tools, 242-246
    resolution, 241-242
    Zoom tool, 239-285

  paths, 220-224
  PhotoCDs, 142-145
    browsing software, 143-145
    index sheets, 142
  selection marquees, 220-224,
    702
  target images, 517
**virtual densitometers (scanners),
83**
virtual memory, 174
  see also scratch disks

W

warming up colors, 662-663
water reflection, 680
  Gradient fill, 682-684
  layers, 683-684
**Watercolor filters (Gallery
Effects), 931-934**
Wave dialog box, 612
Wave filter, 611-615
weathering images, 405-407
White Point, 691
  digital images, 294-296
  setting, 297-298
white space (file sizes), 81-83
Window menu commands
  New Window, 445-447
  Palette, 196
  Show Rulers, 374
Windows
  Acrobat Reader (installation),
    1276
  shells, 1259
windows
  digital image elements, 534
  images, setting up, 463
  picks, 300
WINZIP directory, 1274
wireframe (3-D models), 1071

workspace
  optimizing, 541
  options, 182-193
WYSIWYG, 28-30

X-Y-Z

ZECH directory, 1268
Zech, Richard, 1268
ZIPIT (compression program),
  1213
ZIPIT folder, 1274
**zipping files (compression pro-
  grams), 1214-1217**
Zoom blur (Radial), 825-828
**Zoom tool, viewing images,
  239-285**

Inside Adobe Photoshop 3, Second Edition

REGISTRATION CARD

Fill out this card to receive information about future Photoshop books and other New Riders titles!

Name _____ **Title** _____

Company _____

Address _____

City/State/ZIP _____

I bought this book because: _____

_____

I purchased this book from:

☐ A bookstore (Name _____)

☐ A software or electronics store (Name _____)

☐ A mail order (Name of Catalog _____)

I purchase this many computer books each year:

☐ 1–5   ☐ 6 or more

I currently use these applications: _____

_____

_____

_____

I found these chapters to be the most informative: _____

_____

I found these chapters to be the least informative: _____

_____

Additional comments: _____

_____

☐ I would like to see my name in print! You may use my name and quote me in future New Riders products and promotions. My daytime phone number is: _____

New Riders Publishing 201 West 103rd Street • Indianapolis, Indiana 46290 USA

Fold Here

PLACE
STAMP
HERE

New Riders Publishing
201 West 103rd Street
Indianapolis, Indiana 46290
USA

WANT MORE INFORMATION?

CHECK OUT THESE RELATED TITLES:

	QTY	PRICE	TOTAL

Inside Adobe Photoshop for Windows. Users uncover the secrets of Adobe Photoshop with this illuminating tutorial and reference written by award-winning artist Gary Bouton—plus a bonus CD-ROM with images, exercise art, and shareware—this book is everything Photoshop users need. ISBN: 1-56205-259-4   ____ $42.00   _____

Adobe Photoshop NOW! Master the complexities of Adobe Photoshop—fast! Realistic 4-color images, complete with expert tips and techniques—plus a bonus CD-ROM that is loaded with images, textures, and fonts—this book is the end-all book for easily mastering high-end Photoshop imaging tricks now! ISBN: 1-56205-200-4.   ____ $35.00   _____

CorelDRAW! Special Effects. Learn award-winning techniques from professional CorelDRAW! designers with this comprehensive collection of the hottest tips and techniques! This full-color book provides step-by-step instructions for creating over 30 stunning special effects. An excellent book for those who want to take their CorelDRAW! documents a couple of notches higher. ISBN: 1-56205-123-7.   ____ $39.95   _____

CorelDRAW! Now! Users who want fast access to thorough information, people upgrading to CorelDRAW! 4.0 from a previous edition, new CorelDRAW! users—all of these groups will want to tap into this guide to great graphics—now! Developed by CorelDRAW! experts, this book provides answers on everything from common questions to advanced inquiries. ISBN: 1-56205-131-8.   ____ $21.95   _____

Name _____

Company _____

Address _____

City _____ State ____ ZIP _____

Phone _____ Fax _____

☐ Check Enclosed   ☐ VISA   ☐ MasterCard

Card #_____Exp. Date _____

Signature _____

Prices are subject to change. Call for availability and pricing information on latest editions.

Subtotal   _____

Shipping   _____

$4.00 for the first book and $1.75 for each additional book.

Total   _____

Indiana residents add 5% sales tax.

New Riders Publishing 201 West 103rd Street • Indianapolis, Indiana 46290 USA

Orders/Customer Service: 1-800-428-5331
Fax: 1-800-448-3804

- Fold Here -

New Riders Publishing
201 West 103rd Street
Indianapolis, Indiana 46290
USA

GRAPHICS TITLES

INSIDE CORELDRAW! 4.0, SPECIAL EDITION

DANIEL GRAY

An updated version of the #1 best-selling tutorial on CorelDRAW!

CorelDRAW! 4.0
ISBN: 1-56205-164-4
$34.95 USA

CORELDRAW! SPECIAL EFFECTS

NEW RIDERS PUBLISHING

An inside look at award-winning techniques from professional CorelDRAW! designers!

CorelDRAW! 4.0
ISBN: 1-56205-123-7
$39.95 USA

CORELDRAW! NOW!

RICHARD FELDMAN

The hands-on tutorial for users who want practical information now!

CorelDRAW! 4.0
ISBN: 1-56205-131-8
$21.95 USA

INSIDE CORELDRAW! FOURTH EDITION

DANIEL GRAY

The popular tutorial approach to learning CorelDRAW!...with complete coverage of version 3.0!

CorelDRAW! 3.0
ISBN: 1-56205-106-7
$24.95 USA

To Order, Call 1-800-428-5331

Special Pixar Pricing for
Inside Adobe Photoshop 3

Pixar Typestry

Pixar Typestry is exciting software which invokes RenderMan magic to turn your Type 1, TrueType, Postscript and GX fonts and Adobe Illustrator files into extraordinary three-dimensional images. Pixar Typestry is ideal software for those who are creating logos, brochures, newsletters, ads, and slide or multimedia presentations.

System Requirements:
Macintosh - Any MacII family computer with a math coprocessor or Power Macintosh, 8 MB of RAM minimum, System 7.0 or higher (7.5 is required for QuickDraw GX features), a color display and 10 MB of free disk space.
Windows - Windows 3.1 or higher, or Windows Intel NT, at least a 386 PC. A math coprocessor is recommended for 386 machines or 486 SX models. 8 MB of RAM minimum, a color display and 7 MB of free disk space.

Pixar Classic Textures

Pixar One Twenty Eight CD and Pixar Classic Textures Vol. 2 are Pixar's custom collections of high-quality, photographic textures. The high-quality techniques used to create the textures has earned these CDs the reputation for being the best collections of photographic textures available. The unique 512x512x24 bit images in TIFF format can be easily accessed through plug-ins for Photoshop. The CDs can be read by any application that can read TIFF files on Windows, Macintosh and UNIX.

System Requirements:
Macintosh, Windows, Unix - A compatible CD-ROM drive.

Pixar Typestry   ☐ Mac   ☐ Windows $145. $~~299.~~ _____

Pixar One Twenty Eight CD   Mac, Win, UNIX $99. $~~299.~~ _____

Pixar Classic Textures CD   Mac, Win, UNIX $99. $~~299.~~ _____

Both Pixar Classic Textures CDs $175. _____

CA, FL, & WA residents add applicable sales tax _____

Shipping: US ground $5, US 2-Day $10, Int'l Fed Ex $50 _____

ORDER TOTAL _____

Payment:

☐ Visa ☐ Master Card ☐ American Express ☐ Check/Money Order (drawn on US banks only)

Credit Card Number: _____ Expiration Date: _____

Card Holder Signature: _____

ShipTo:

Name: _____

Company: _____

Address: _____

City, ST, Zip: _____

Telephone: _____

1001 WEST CUTTING BOULEVARD ◆ RICHMOND, CA 94804
TEL (510) 236-4000, (800) 888-9856 ◆ FAX (510) 236-0388

PLUG YOURSELF INTO...

The MCP Internet Site

Free information and vast computer resources from the world's leading computer book publisher—online!

Find the books that are right for you!
A complete online catalog, plus sample chapters and tables of contents give you an in-depth look at *all* our books. The best way to shop or browse!

- ✦ **Stay informed** with the latest computer industry news through discussion groups, an online newsletter, and customized subscription news.

- ✦ **Get fast answers** to your questions about MCP books and software.

- ✦ **Visit** our online bookstore for the latest information and editions!

- ✦ **Communicate** with our expert authors through e-mail and conferences.

- ✦ **Play** in the BradyGame Room with info, demos, shareware, and more!

- ✦ **Download software** from the immense MCP library:
    - Source code and files from MCP books
    - The best shareware, freeware, and demos

- ✦ **Discover hot spots** on other parts of the Internet.

- ✦ **Win books** in ongoing contests and giveaways!

Drop by the new Internet site of Macmillan Computer Publishing!

To plug into MCP:

World Wide Web: http://www.mcp.com/
Gopher: gopher.mcp.com **FTP:** ftp.mcp.com

GOING ONLINE DECEMBER 1994!